THE BUILDINGS OF ENGLAND

FOUNDING EDITOR: NIKOLAUS PEVSNER

BIRMINGHAM AND THE BLACK COUNTRY

ANDY FOSTER
NIKOLAUS PEVSNER
AND
ALEXANDRA WEDGWOOD

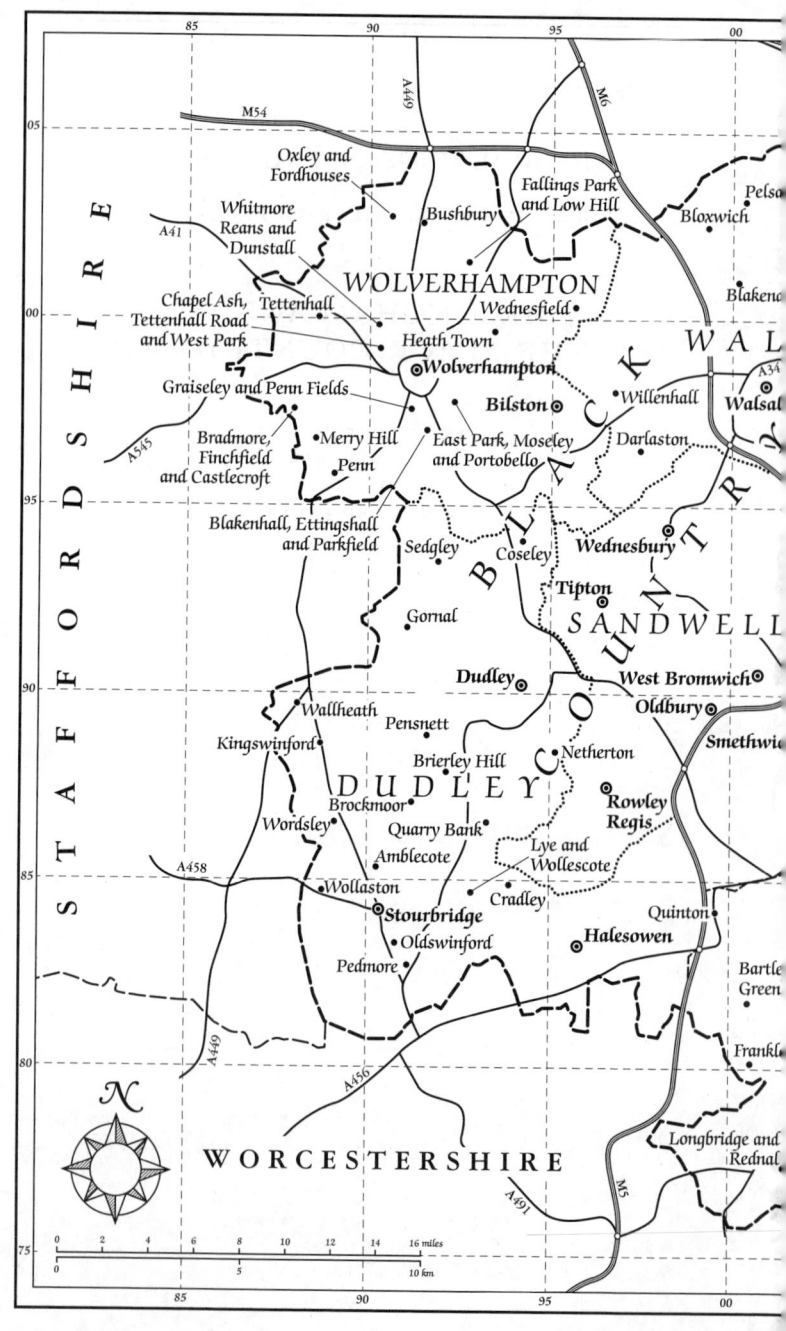

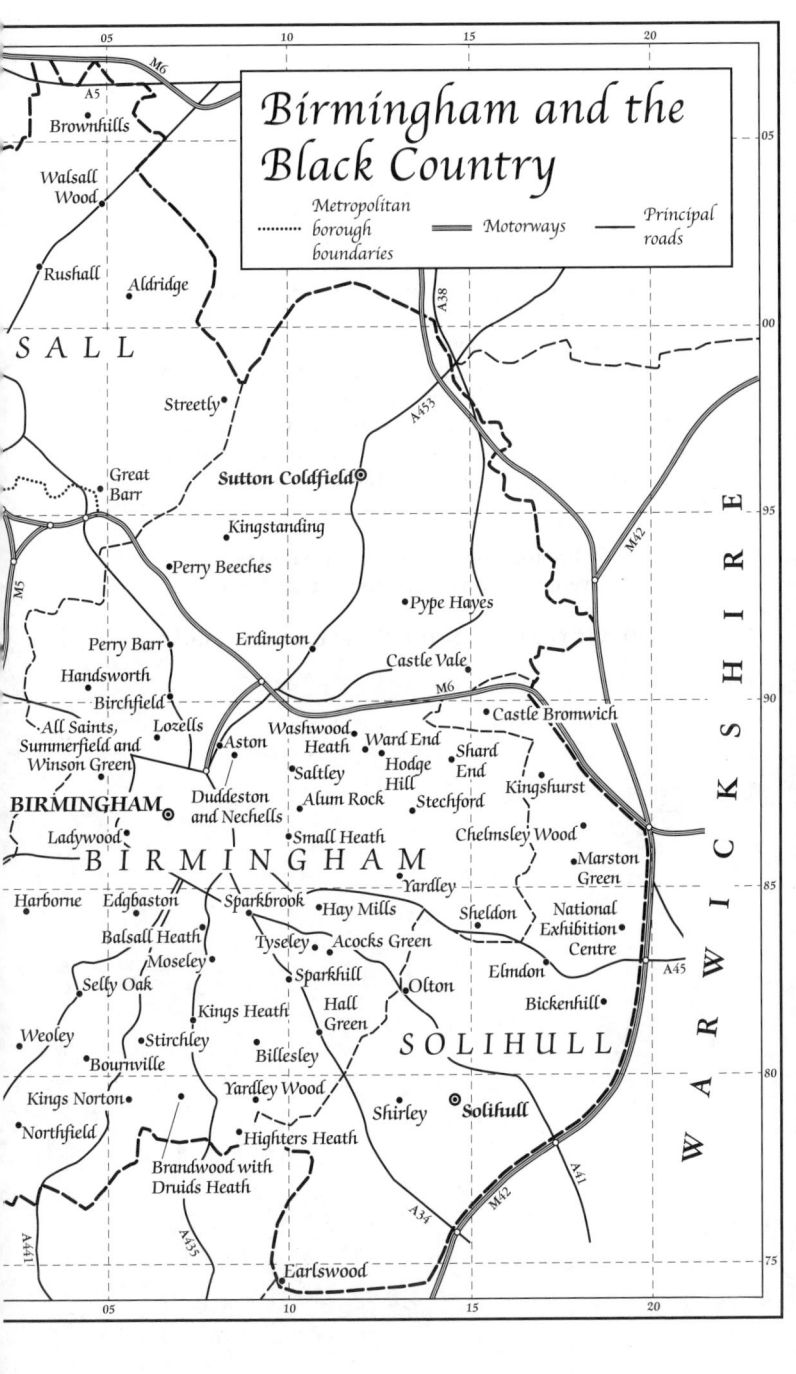

PEVSNER ARCHITECTURAL GUIDES

The *Buildings of England* series was created and largely written by Sir Nikolaus Pevsner (1902–83). First editions of the county volumes were published by Penguin Books between 1951 and 1974. The continuing programme of revisions and new volumes was supported between 1994 and 2011 by research financed through the Pevsner Books Trust. That responsibility has now been assumed by the Paul Mellon Centre for Studies in British Art.

Photography costs for this volume
were generously met by a grant from

THE VICTORIAN SOCIETY MARY HEATH TRUST

Birmingham and the Black Country

BY

ANDY FOSTER

NIKOLAUS PEVSNER

AND

ALEXANDRA WEDGWOOD

THE BUILDINGS OF ENGLAND

YALE UNIVERSITY PRESS
NEW HAVEN AND LONDON

YALE UNIVERSITY PRESS
NEW HAVEN AND LONDON

302 Temple Street, New Haven CT 06511
47 Bedford Square, London WC1B 3DP
www.pevsner.co.uk
www.lookingatbuildings.org.uk
www.yalebooks.co.uk
www.yalebooks.com

Published by Yale University Press 2022
2 4 6 8 10 9 7 5 3 1

ISBN 978 0 300 22391 0

Originally published in 1966, 1968 and 1974
© Nikolaus Pevsner and Alexandra Wedgwood
This edition 2022, new material © Andy Foster

Printed in China
through World Print
Set in Monotype Plantin

All rights reserved.
This book may not be reproduced
in whole or in part, in any form (beyond that
copying permitted by Sections 107 and 108 of the
U.S. Copyright Law and except by reviewers
for the public press), without written
permission from the publishers

Dedicated to the memory of
BIRMINGHAM CENTRAL LIBRARY
built 1969 to 1974
destroyed 2016

*and of its architects, the John Madin Design Group
including John Madin, Michael Holt, John Ericsson,
Brian Thompson, Len Vanes, and Ted Harris*

*also to those who tried to save it,
especially the late Alan Clawley*

CONTENTS

LIST OF TEXT FIGURES AND MAPS	x
PHOTOGRAPHIC ACKNOWLEDGEMENTS	xiv
MAP AND ILLUSTRATION REFERENCES	xv
FOREWORD AND ACKNOWLEDGEMENTS	xvi

INTRODUCTION — 1

GEOLOGY AND BUILDING MATERIALS, BY KEITH HODGKINS	2
ARCHAEOLOGY, BY MIKE HODDER	6
MEDIEVAL ARCHITECTURE	10
TIMBER-FRAMED BUILDINGS, BY NICHOLAS MOLYNEUX	13
LATER C16 TO LATE C17 ARCHITECTURE	15
FROM THE LATE C17 TO c. 1830	18
CANALS AND CANAL BUILDINGS, BY PAUL COLLINS AND ANDY FOSTER	27
THE INDUSTRIAL DEVELOPMENT OF THE BLACK COUNTRY, BY PAUL COLLINS	30
VICTORIAN AND EDWARDIAN, c. 1830 TO 1914	34
FROM 1914 TO 1939	73
FROM 1945 TO THE PRESENT	82
FURTHER READING	96

BIRMINGHAM	103
THE BLACK COUNTRY	469
SOLIHULL	753
GLOSSARY	787
INDEX OF ARCHITECTS, ARTISTS, PATRONS AND RESIDENTS	813
INDEX TO BIRMINGHAM	846
INDEX TO THE BLACK COUNTRY AND SOLIHULL	870

LIST OF TEXT FIGURES AND MAPS

Every effort has been made to trace or contact all copyright holders. The publishers will be glad to make good any errors or omissions brought to our attention in future editions.

Introduction

Sandwell, Tipton, showing St John the Evangelist, watercolour by Thomas Peploe Wood, 1837. Reproduced courtesy of the William Salt Library, Staffordshire Record Office	17
Walsall, Great Barr Hall, engraving by Thomas Radclyffe after Frederick Calvert (*Picturesque Views in Staffordshire*, 1830)	23
Birmingham, Handsworth, Soho Manufactory, engraving by Francis Eginton after Stebbing Shaw (*The History and Antiquities of Staffordshire*, vol. 2, 1801)	27
Sandwell, Tipton, Birmingham Canal Navigation, c.1769–72, engraving, c19. Courtesy of Paul Collins	29
Birmingham, Colmore Row, Town and District Bank, engraving by W. E. Hodgkin (*The Builder*, 10 July 1869)	50
Birmingham, Erdington, Lyndhurst Estate, shaded block plan, c.1958 (Anthony Sutcliffe and Roger Smith, *Birmingham 1939–1970*, 1974)	83
Birmingham, Central Library, section drawing, 1969–74. Birmingham City Archive	89

Birmingham

Birmingham, city and borough expansion, map (*Victoria County History: A History of the County of Warwick*, vol. 7, 1964)	109
Birmingham, St Philip's Cathedral, plan (Colen Campbell, *Vitruvius Britannicus*, vol. 1, 1715)	114
Birmingham, St Chad's Cathedral (R.C.), drawing (*The Builder*, 27 November 1897)	118
Birmingham, Council House, first-floor plan	127
Birmingham, Colmore Row, Scottish Union and National Insurance, lithograph and plan (*Building News*, 3 July 1903)	142
Birmingham, Corporation Street, Coleridge Chambers, lithograph and plan by John W. Allen (*Building News*, 12 August 1898)	149
Birmingham, Curzon Street Station, lithograph by J. C. Bourne (*A Series of Lithographic Drawings on the London and Birmingham Railway*, 1838)	192

LIST OF TEXT FIGURES AND MAPS

Birmingham, Aston Hall, ground- and first-floor plans	222
Birmingham, Aston Hall, staircase, engraving, C19	225
Birmingham, Erdington, Witton Cemetery, chapels, engraving (*The Builder*, 4 January 1862)	238
Birmingham, Handsworth, St Mary, engraving by T. Donaldson after Stebbing Shaw (*The History and Antiquities of Staffordshire*, vol. 2, 1801)	243
Birmingham, Handsworth Methodist College, elevation engraving (*Building News*, 25 July 1879)	250–1
Birmingham, Pype Hayes, St Mary, plan	270
Birmingham, Small Heath, St Oswald, drawing (*The Builder*, 27 November 1897)	287
Birmingham, Moseley Hall, engraving by W. Radclyffe after J. P. Neale (*Views of the Seats of Noblemen and Gentlemen...*, vol. 2, 1823)	323
Birmingham, Moseley, Chantry Road, Court Hey, drawing and plan by James Akerman (*Building News*, 8 April 1898)	327
Birmingham, Edgbaston, University of Birmingham, block plan	368
Birmingham, Edgbaston, The Homestead, perspective drawing by C. E. Bateman (*The Builder*, 2 March 1901)	392
Birmingham, Selly Oak, St Mary, brass to George Richards Elkington †1865 (David Meara, *Victorian Memorial Brasses*, 1983)	425
Sutton Coldfield, cemetery lodge, perspective drawing and plans (*Building News*, 10 September 1880)	448
Sutton Coldfield, Technical School, elevation drawing (*Building News*, 23 October 1903)	453
Sutton Coldfield, Four Oaks, Hindecliffe, perspective drawing (*Academy Architecture*, 1906)	459
Sutton Coldfield, New Hall, engraving by T. Radclyffe, 1830 (W. Smith, *History of the County of Warwick*, 1830)	464

Black Country

Dudley Castle, plan	476
Dudley Priory, engraving by Samuel and Nathaniel Buck, 1731	481
Dudley, Market Place, fountain, engraving (*The Builder*, 7 March 1868)	485
Dudley, Gornal, St Peter, watercolour by Thomas Peploe Wood, 1841. Reproduced courtesy of the William Salt Library, Staffordshire Record Office	509
Dudley, Halesowen Abbey, engraving by Samuel and Nathaniel Buck, 1731	515
Dudley, Halesowen, The Leasowes, engraving by James Mason after Thomas Smith, 1748. Reproduced courtesy of Shropshire Archives	518
Dudley, Pensnett, St Mark, engraving by James K. Colling, 1840s	539

Sandwell, Smethwick, Lloyds Bank, drawing
(*Smethwick Telephone*, 10 March 1906)   583

Sandwell, Wednesbury, St Bartholomew, engraving by
R.W. Basire after Stebbing Shaw (*The History and
Antiquities of Staffordshire*, vol. 2, 1801)   595

Sandwell, West Bromwich Institute, engraving and plan
(*Building News*, 1 August 1884)   607

Walsall, engraving by T. Donaldson after Stebbing Shaw
(*The History and Antiquities of Staffordshire*, vol. 2, 1801)   618

Walsall, Council House and Town Hall, elevation drawing
by Sprague & Co. (*The Builder*, 13 October 1900)   626

Walsall, Science and Art Institute, perspective engraving
(W. Henry Robinson, *Guide to Walsall*, 1889)   629

Walsall, Aldridge, St Mary, watercolour by J.C. Buckler,
1847. Reproduced courtesy of the William Salt
Library, Staffordshire Record Office   641

Walsall, Great Barr, Old Hall, engraving by R.W. Basire
after Stebbing Shaw (*The History and Antiquities of
Staffordshire*, vol. 2, 1801)   656

Walsall, Rushall Hall, engraving by R.W. Basire after
Stebbing Shaw (*The History and Antiquities of
Staffordshire*, vol. 2, 1801)   660

Wolverhampton, St Peter, engraving by Thomas Jefferys
after Isaac Taylor, 1751   673

Wolverhampton, Town Hall, engraving by H. Abbott
(*Building News*, 2 July 1869)   681

Wolverhampton, Bushbury, St Mary, engraving by
R.W. Basire after Stebbing Shaw (*The History and
Antiquities of Staffordshire*, vol. 2, 1801)   709

Wolverhampton, Chapel Ash, Parkdale, Montford
House, drawing, *c.* 1878, Staffordshire Archive
D1317/1/12/10/1. Reproduced courtesy of Stafford-
shire Record Office   716

Wolverhampton, Fallings Park, Victoria Road,
Nos. 34–46, drawing by Randall Wells (*Catalogue of
the Built Housing Exhibition at Fallings Park*, 1908).
Reproduced with permission of Wolverhampton
Archives   723

Solihull

Solihull, St Alphege, plan, 1882 (*Birmingham
Archaeological Society Transactions*, vol. 11, 1882–3)   754

Solihull, Bickenhill, St Peter, plan (*Victoria County
History: A History of the County of Warwick*, vol. 4, 1947)   767

Solihull, Castle Bromwich, St Mary and St Margaret,
reconstruction drawing by C.E. Bateman (*Birmingham
Archaeological Society Transactions*, vol. 19, 1893)   769

Solihull, Castle Bromwich Hall and church, engraving
by E. Kirkall after Henry Beighton (W. Dugdale,
The Antiquities of Warwickshire Illustrated, 1726)   771

MAPS

Birmingham and the Black Country	ii–iii
Birmingham City Centre	112–13
Birmingham Suburbs	212–13
Bournville	349
Dudley	471
Stourbridge	546
Wednesbury	594
West Bromwich	601
Walsall	619
Wolverhampton	671

PHOTOGRAPHIC ACKNOWLEDGEMENTS

The majority of photographs were specially taken for this book by James O. Davies. We are also grateful for permission to reproduce the remaining photographs from the sources as shown below.

Photo by Birmingham Museums Trust, licensed under CC0: 30
© Birmingham Museums Trust (James O. Davies): 51
© Historic England Archive: 61, 73
© Alamy: 79
© Michael Slaughter LRPS: 111
© National Trust: 97

MAP AND ILLUSTRATION REFERENCES

The numbers printed in italic type in the margin against the place names in the gazetteer of the book indicate the position of the place in question on the INDEX MAP (pp. ii–iii), which is divided into sections by the 5-kilometre reference lines of the National Grid. The reference given here omits the two initial letters which in a full grid reference refer to the 100-kilometre squares into which the county is divided. The first two numbers indicate the *western* boundary, and the last two the *southern* boundary, of the 5-kilometre square in which the place in question is situated. For example, Aston (reference 0585) will be found in the 5-kilometre square bounded by grid lines 05 (on the *west*) and 10, and 85 (on the *south*) and 90; Wednesfield (reference 9500) in the square bounded by the grid lines 95 (on the *west*) and 00, and 00 (on the *south*) and 05.

The map contains all those places, whether towns, villages or isolated buildings, which are the subject of separate entries in the text.

ILLUSTRATION REFERENCES are given as marginal numbers for photographs, and as marginal *italic* cross-references for images on other pages of the text.

FOREWORD AND ACKNOWLEDGEMENTS

This book has taken a very long time to write: over sixteen years since the Birmingham City Guide appeared in 2005. It owes a great deal therefore to the patience of Simon Bradley, my editor at Yale University Press; as it does to his skills in reducing the text to the necessary length with a minimum of loss and authorial anguish. I am deeply grateful to Gavin Watson, administrator of the former Pevsner Books Trust, who helped this book in many ways, far beyond the terms of his post; and to Sally Salvesen at Yale for her patience and her support in difficult moments. Karen Evans helped greatly with research in London archives. Of other members of the Pevsner team at Yale, Charles O'Brien was always supportive and helpful with information, and Alice Blows was resourceful in locating text figures during the pandemic. Linda McQueen was immensely professional and helpful as production editor, also far beyond the terms of her job, and always cheerful during a process which was fraught with troubles due to Covid. The book was copy-edited by Hester Higton, proofread by Charlotte Chapman, and indexed by Judith Wardman. Among other Pevsner authors, Clare Hartwell, Julian Orbach, Chris Pickford and Chris Wakeling provided solidarity, and useful nuggets of information.

This book, though greatly expanded, rests on the original *Buildings of England* guides to Staffordshire, Warwickshire and Worcestershire. My principal debt therefore is to Sir Nikolaus Pevsner, and for Birmingham buildings, to Alexandra Wedgwood. I am very grateful to the other contributors to this book: Mike Hodder on archaeology, Paul Collins on industrial buildings, Keith Hodgkins on building materials, and Nicholas Molyneux on timber-framed buildings. Also to those whose work has been brought forward from the City Guide: Ian Dungavell (Birmingham Law Courts, Aston Webb buildings at Birmingham University); Oliver Fairclough (Aston Hall); Elain Harwood (Birmingham University, post-war buildings and Barber Institute); and George Demidowicz (Soho House and Soho Foundry). Keith Hodgkins also helped greatly with Tipton buildings, and George Demidowicz with Sutton Coldfield.

A number of people deserve special thanks for significant help with this book. Stephen Price read the text for Kings Norton and made valuable suggestions. He also visited Moat House, Earlswood, with me, and returned to analyse it skilfully. I was also very grateful to use his work on Yardley and Sutton Coldfield and discuss it with him, and for his arranging access to the Birmingham Museum and Art Gallery local studies research collection.

FOREWORD AND ACKNOWLEDGEMENTS   xvii

Alan Brooks was an endless source of information on Victorian stained glass, as well as generously copying me his information on other church fittings. The entry on St Peter, Wolverhampton is the better for a discussion with the late Richard Morris ('Mouldings' Morris), although his untimely death prevented him from walking the draft round. The late Stanley Jones visited West Bromwich Manor House with me, his memory still perfect fifty years after he discovered and described the building. Frank Sharman helped with Wolverhampton entries and allowed me to use his collection of local architectural cuttings. Nicholas Riall spent a long afternoon at Holy Trinity, Sutton Coldfield, taking me round the C16 woodwork. Angus Kaye walked several of the Black Country drafts round and made many helpful suggestions. Roger Millward gave me a roof above my head, and space to write, for a month when I had no home to live in.

The greatest debt I have from writing this book is to archivists and local studies librarians. The following list is certainly not complete, but it is heartfelt. Birmingham: Lucy Angus, Geoff Burns, Rachel Clare, Nicola Crews, Peter Doré, Stephen Hodson, Mike Hunkin, Nicholas Kingsley, Rachel McGregor, Liz Palmer, Caroline Patel, Corinna Rayner, Sian Roberts, Alison Smith, Paul Taylor, Neil Treby and Eleanor Woodward. Also at Sutton Coldfield, Marian Baxter and Ariadne Plant. Dudley: Paul Bowen, Andy Bytheway, Ann Chandler, Jane Humphrey, Diane Matthews, Gillian Roberts; also Marilyn Ferris at Stourbridge. Sandwell: Sarah Chubb, Matt Skidmore, Richard Slaughter, Maureen Waldron and the late Chris O'Connor. Walsall: Paul Ford and Ruth Vyse. Wolverhampton: David Bishop, Chris Brown, Lisa Hale, Alf Russell and Guy Williams. Solihull: Elizabeth Jankowska and Tracey Williams. Also to members of staff at the County Record Offices for Staffordshire, Warwickshire, and Worcestershire.

Local authority conservation officers have been helpful on many occasions. I would particularly like to thank Sue Whitehouse and Jon Beesley, formerly at Wolverhampton; Peter Boland, John Hemingway and Jeni Foster, formerly at Dudley, and Jayne Pilkington still there; Martin Saunders at Solihull; Mark Stretton at Sandwell; and many people at Birmingham including, formerly, Julie Taylor, Stephen King, Toni Demidowicz (particularly for her knowledge of Georgian Birmingham), and at present, Chris Patrick.

I am grateful to many people for help on specific buildings or topics. The start is those who helped with the Birmingham city guide, and in several cases, this book: Laura Alden, the Rev. Jenny Arnold, Philip Aubury (Birmingham Botanical Gardens), the late Peter Baird, Phillada Ballard, Jim Berrow, David Blissett (Charles Barry), Anthony Collins (especially for John Bowen, builder), Chris Cronin, Jo-Ann Curtis (Birmingham Museum and Art Gallery), Michael Delaney, the late Fr Brian Doolan (Catholic churches), Chris Eckersley, Edward Fellows (St Alban, Highgate), Alan Flight (St Agatha, Sparkbrook), Richard Gale, the late Andor Gomme, Stephen Grainger, Roger Hancox (Birmingham Gun Barrel Proof House), Bill Harding, Stephen Hartland,

James Haworth, Nigel Haynes, Peter Heath, Michael Hodgetts, Julian Holder, Joe Holyoak, Peter Howell, Michael Huxley-Evans, the late John Kirwan, Martin Lawton, Eva Ling, the late Arthur Lockwood, David Low, Grace McCombie, George McHardy, Bernadette, Thomas, and the late Patrick Mellett, Ruth Mosley, Martin Mullaney, John Mullen, Fr Guy Nicholls, Dr and Mrs O'Neill (No. 12 Ampton Road, Edgbaston), Steve Parsons, Elizabeth Perkins, Alan Powers, Audrey Price, the Rev. Tom Pyke (St Paul, Birmingham), Alex Read, Michael Reardon, the late Colin Rodgers, the Rev. David Senior, Barbara Shackley, Fr John Sharp, the late Ron Singer, Paul Spencer-Longhurst, the late Canon Ralph Stevens, the late John Surman, Jean Templeton, Canon Nicholas Thistlethwaite, the late Tony Trott, the late Dame Rachel Waterhouse (St Alban, Highgate), Glennys Wild, Stephen Wildman, David and Fiona Williams, Bill Wood, Stephen Wycherley, John Yates and Andy Yeo.

In addition, for the current volume, I want to thank Philip Adams, Peter Allen (Great Barr), Kate Andrew, Peter Arnold (Walsall), Neil Avery (Dippons, Tettenhall), Nick Baker (Amblecote), the late Steve Beauchampé (Moseley Road baths, William Hale, and the architecture of recreation elsewhere), Jim Beeston (Heartlands, Birmingham), the late Geoff Brandwood, Tim Bridges (Victorian buildings, and churches generally), Darran Brookes and David Bursey of Kings Heath Computers, Charles Brown (Brown Matthews), Peter Brownhill (Brownhill Hayward Brown), Mark Bryant, Christine Buckley (Sedgley), Nigel Cameron (Solihull, especially Ashleigh Road), Ian Cawood, Peter Chandler (Kingswinford), Martin Cherry (Ewan Christian), John Claughton (King Edward's School Birmingham), the late Alan Clawley (John Madin, also Birmingham Airport), the late Vernon Crofts (J. Seymour Harris & Partners), Bill Dargue (especially for St Mary and St Margaret, Castle Bromwich), Paul Davis (University of Wolverhampton), Annie Creswick Dawson (Benjamin Creswick), Jean Diver (Newman University), David Eades (Halesowen), Fr Simon Ellis (St Margaret Mary, Perry Common), the late John Ericsson (Birmingham Central Library), Geoffrey Fisher (C17 monuments), Geraint Franklin (Howell Killick Partridge & Amis), Claire Gapper (plasterwork at the Talbot Hotel, Stourbridge, and Greyhound and Punchbowl, Bilston), Bob Ghosh (K4), Tony Green (Hortons Estates), Sidney Grey (Frankley), the Rev. Brian Hall (St Mary, Handsworth), Fr Rob Hall (Halesowen and Hasbury), Stuart Hancox (Dickens Heath), Harry Harper (his own buildings, and Clifford Tee & Gale), Sandy Haynes (Grey papers), David Hemsoll, Barry Henley, Richard Hewlings and Gordon Higgott (Castle Bromwich Hall), Julian Hunt (Halesowen), Jasna Jaksic, the late Pete James (Birmingham photograph collections), Mary Keating (post-war buildings), Chris Kennedy (Richard Twentyman), Julia Larden, Peter Larkham, Mark Lawson (Sir Sidney Stott), Ann Levitt (Birmingham City Architect's Department), Paul Lister (Associated Architects), Hilary Mander (Dippons, Tettenhall), Sir Nicholas Mander (The Mount), Andrew Maxam (particularly for Mitchells & Butlers pubs), Kieron MacMahon ('Midlands pubs' website, and

FOREWORD AND ACKNOWLEDGEMENTS

Oldswinford Castle), Jennie McGregor-Smith (John Cotton), Bob Meeson, the late John Madin, Ron Moss, Fr John Nankivell, Richard Newman (Bryant Priest Newman), Stephen Oliver, David Patterson (Solihull), Wendy Pearson, Alex Read, Gillian Roberts (W.J.H. Weller), former Councillor Lou Robson, Peter Scott (Wightwick Manor), Ray Shill (industrial history), the late Gavin Stamp (especially about Richard Gilbert Scott), Ian Standing (Associated Architects), Lynn Stead (Witton cemetery), Fiona Tait, Alan Taylor, Stella Thebridge (Holy Trinity, Sutton Coldfield), Walter Thomson (Associated Architects), the late Alan Trevis-Smith, Stuart Tullah (Four Oaks Estate), Geoffrey Tyack (Castle Bromwich), Robert Tolley (S.T. Walker & Partners), the late Chris Upton, Jean Weston (Lye, Stourbridge), Alison Wheatley (King Edward's School Birmingham), John Wilkes (Coseley), Anna Willetts (Stourbridge), Ned Williams (Black Country chapels and more), Graham Winteringham (S.T. Walker & Partners), and Mary Worsfold.

I was a Sutton Coldfield child, and the delight of writing a Pevsner to my old home town was slightly spoilt by the difficulty of access to several of its important buildings: a problem elsewhere as well. I do wish to thank the many people who kindly let me see their homes, churches, and schools, particularly Ram Aithal (Shri Venkateswara Balaji Temple), Jonathan Bostock (Edgbaston grotto), Deb Brownlee (St John, Dudley) the late Bill Colman (Carhampton House, Four Oaks), Christopher Firmstone (Wordsley Manor), Mike Fisher (Ravenshaw Hall), Fr Francis Gavin (Birmingham Oratory, and a journey to the Little Oratory), Barry Henley (Singers Hill synagogue), Amy Hickman (Dudley Castle), Bishop Anne Hollinghurst (No. 16 Coleshill Street, Sutton Coldfield), Naomi Johnson (Oscott College), David Large (St Margaret, Great Barr), Tony Lynch (Moat House, Earlswood), Michael Leek (who told me the history of Shirley Golf Club), the staff at New Hall (Sutton Coldfield), John Pryce-Jones (who searched for an hour and a half with me in the crypts of St Matthew, Walsall, for the Norman fabric mentioned in Pevsner's Staffordshire), Fr Barrie Scott (St John, Perry Barr), Keith Watkins (Christ Church, Tettenhall Wood), Mr and Mrs Williams (Redlands, Four Oaks), and John Wood (Wightwick Manor). There will be people who helped whose names I have missed out, and I do apologise to them and thank them. I owe it to everyone who allowed me into their houses to state firmly that descriptions of interiors here do not imply any right of access.

The superb photographs are almost all by James O. Davies. They make many points better than any text, and I am immensely grateful to him. I am also grateful to Michael Slaughter for one of the exceptions, No. 111.

Despite all this help, there will still be mistakes in this book. They are entirely my responsibility. I will be very grateful to readers who point them out, by contacting me via Yale University Press.

Andy Foster
November 2021

INTRODUCTION

This volume of the *Buildings of England* covers not a historic county but the West Midlands conurbation: the city of Birmingham, including Sutton Coldfield; the city of Wolverhampton and the metropolitan boroughs of Dudley, Sandwell and Walsall; and the urban part of the borough of Solihull, N and W of the M42. This is the greater part of the present county of West Midlands, except for Coventry and the rural E part of Solihull, which are dealt with in the Warwickshire volume.

The historical geography of the area is exceptionally complicated. Birmingham and Sutton Coldfield were originally Warwickshire towns, Wolverhampton and Walsall were in Staffordshire, Stourbridge (D)* in Worcestershire. Dudley town was until 1966 an island of Worcestershire surrounded by Staffordshire, but Dudley Castle was an outlier of Staffordshire until 1928. Halesowen (D) was a detached part of Shropshire until 1844. The manor of Warley, in Oldbury (Sa), was divided in a patchwork between Shropshire and Worcestershire, hence Warley Wigorn and Warley Salop. So a single revised volume for the conurbation is sensible.

The metropolitan county boundary is drawn tightly round urban areas, unlike, for example, those in west and south Yorkshire. The only rural settlements covered in this volume are Bickenhill and Earlswood, in Solihull. A finger of open land also runs S from the edge of the conurbation, between Aldridge (Wa) and Walsall, across Barr Beacon, and forms the Sandwell valley, between West Bromwich (Sa) and Handsworth Wood (B). What may appear a single urban area is profoundly divided into two parts. Birmingham is a great provincial city, to which the historic settlements of Solihull and Sutton Coldfield have become commuter towns. The boroughs to the NW form the Black Country.† Wolverhampton is now a city in its own right, and Walsall a substantial town, but the heart of the Black Country is a group of small, historically separate industrial towns and villages. It grew up away from great rivers or major highways, and was until very recently culturally distinctive, with a dialect of Anglo-Saxon origin and a fierce local patriotism.

---

*Abbreviations used in this Introduction are as follows: (B) Birmingham, (D) Dudley, (Sa) Sandwell, (So) Solihull, (Wa) Walsall, (Wo) Wolverhampton.
†For the purposes of this book. The precise boundaries of the Black Country have been a subject of endless debate.

This division is mirrored in the area's topography. Birmingham and Solihull are low-lying (though the city centre is on a noticeable hill), in the valleys of the Tame, the Cole and the Blythe, which drain into the Trent. The Black Country is hilly. A ridge, with a steep escarpment falling to the SW, runs NW–SE from Sedgley (D) to Halesowen (D), crowned with the town and castle of Dudley. At its highest, Turners Hill at Rowley (Sa), it reaches 891 ft (271 metres). This is the watershed between the Severn and the Trent. The land to the SW drains into the Stour, which runs to the Severn. The land to the NE drains into the Tame. Here are other towns built on hills: Walsall, Wednesbury (Sa), Sutton. In medieval times much of the area was wooded, with two substantial deer parks or chases. Of these, Sutton Park (Sutton Coldfield) survives as open space. The woods and industrial settlement of Pensnett Chase (D) can still be appreciated from the low hill E of St Mark's church.

GEOLOGY AND BUILDING MATERIALS
BY KEITH HODGKINS

The GEOLOGY of Birmingham and the Black Country conveniently divides and defines the two areas in quite a precise way. Birmingham straddles a wide outcrop of Bunter and Keuper sandstones, which facilitated an excellent water supply, advantageous to the town's early development. By contrast, the Black Country sits on the adjacent South Staffordshire coalfield, which produced all the mineral resources necessary for the industrial growth that conferred its name. The Coal Measures also yielded ironstone and fireclay, and the older underlying strata of Wenlock limestone in Dudley and Walsall provided the other vital ingredient for the iron-making process. In addition, the volcanic intrusions at Rowley Regis (Sa) and Pouk Hill, Walsall were extensively quarried for dolerite, widely used as a paving material. The extraordinary geological make-up of the Black Country warranted UNESCO conferring World Geopark status on the area in 2020, one of just eight such designations in the UK.

Much of the geology of Birmingham and the Black Country is overlaid with good-quality CLAYS, which resulted in BRICK-BUILDING becoming the norm by the late C17, albeit much later than in the eastern and south-eastern counties of England. Clay tiles were being made in north Worcestershire and east Warwickshire in the C15, the earliest record of established brick manufacture being in Yardley parish (B) in 1554. The earliest surviving uses are the fireplaces of the mid-C16 Renaissance range of Dudley Castle and the mid-C16 diaper-patterned refacing of Hay Hall, Tyseley (B). There is archaeological evidence of brick being used in Digbeth (B) in the same period, but the timber-framed Blakesley Hall, Yardley shows that brick was still not dominant by the close of the C16. However, from the start of the C17 brick began to supersede timber for high-status houses, notably at Castle Bromwich Hall (So) and Aston Hall (B). Other survivors include Haden Hall, Old Hill, Rowley Regis (Sa) (late C16 and C17) and Old Swinford Hospital (D) (1669). By the second half of the C17, brick was in widespread use in vernacular buildings, as exemplified by the cottage dated 1679 in Charlemont Road, West Bromwich (Sa). C18 brick can be seen in many fine town houses and churches across the area, such as Finch House, Dudley (1707) and St Thomas, Stourbridge (D) (1728–36).

Up to the C18 bricks were made on or near their site of use. For example, the building of two brick kilns is recorded in 1709–15 for the construction of St Philip, Birmingham. But following the first wave of canal-building in the late C18, permanent brickyards, as opposed to the itinerant type, saw massive growth. By 1849 there were over 100 brickmakers across the region, two-thirds of them in the Black Country, where the Amblecote and Brierley Hill areas (both D) specialized in firebricks and refractories. From the 1840s Staffordshire blue bricks, made from the Etruria marl which covers a large part of the northern Black Country, were produced in increasing quantities to suit the demands of the railway age.

Despite the predominance of brick, the Black Country's indigenous STONES were used locally to varying degrees in building construction. The oldest geologically, and most familiar by reason of its use in the area's most prominent ancient building, Dudley Castle, is the WENLOCK LIMESTONE of the Silurian period. Deposited around 428 million years ago, it was forced by subsequent earth movement up through the later Middle Coal Measures of the South Staffordshire coalfield to form Castle Hill, Wren's Nest Hill, Hurst Hill and Sedgley Beacon, where it has been quarried and mined for hundreds of years, most prolifically in the C19 for use as flux in iron-making.* Wenlock stone can also be seen at Dudley Priory, of the later C12 and C13, and in Dudley town, where walling survives in Green Man Entry and Rutland Passage. The only other complete structures all date from the C19 and have the Earl of Dudley as builder or benefactor: the churches of St John and St James (both 1838–40) with their respective schools; St Edmund's church school of 1848–9 (now the Dudley mosque); and the earl's lime kilns of 1842. The boundary wall of Dudley Castle with its one surviving lodge of *c.*1820 provides another highly visible use.

The same beds of limestone were also mined and quarried in great quantities in the Walsall area, again mainly for the iron industry, but with some use in building. Isolated fragments of walling survive around Walsall town centre, but the C14 or C15 Rushall Hall gatehouse and the adjacent St Michael's church of

---

*Some of the best-preserved Silurian fossils in the world have been found in the Wenlock limestone, and with the beginnings of the science of geology in the early C19 Dudley gained an international reputation. Such was the interest that in the 1840s there were three fossil dealers in the town. In recognition of this importance, the Wren's Nest was declared Britain's first geological nature reserve in 1956.

1854–6, plus several other churches N and E of the town, show that the stone also proved its worth in construction.

The Wenlock limestone is very hard and durable, but is too coarsely textured to be shaped or worked to any degree of accuracy. The earlier medieval work in the Priory and Castle is roughly coursed rubble. Only in the later phases of the Castle and in the C19 buildings is the stone worked into squared blocks and laid in level but random courses. In the medieval structures, the openings and angles were executed in Devonian sandstone imported from the SW peripheries of the Black Country, probably from numerous sources as there are wide colour variations, seen most prominently in the Triple Gatehouse of Dudley Castle.

For the dressings of the C19 buildings GORNAL STONE is used, from the Gornals, around two miles NW of Dudley. Here the village of Ruiton (D) sits on a 35-ft (11-metre)-thick outcrop belonging to the Downton Castle Group of Lower Old Red Sandstone, which is older than the surrounding Coal Measures. Its earliest identifiable use is in the quoins and string courses of Dudley Castle's C17 stable block. Thomas Baker's *Survey* of the geology of Dudley (1848) noted its use 'chiefly for works of more than common order, such as bridges and foundations of more than ordinary weight and strength, but in particular for the hearths of blast furnaces'. The low lime and high silica content which rendered the stone suitable for furnace bottoms was also exploited in ground form, as an ingredient of firebricks.

In the C18 and C19 Gornal stone was used in preference to brick in its district, where about thirty-five buildings constructed wholly or substantially of the stone still exist. These range from quite humble dwellings through to parish churches, the grandest of which is All Saints, Sedgley (D) of 1826–9. Others include Priory Hall, Dudley; Ruiton Chapel, Gornal (D); St Andrew, Netherton (D) and Christ Church, Coseley (D) (all of the 1820s–30s); also Sedgley Beacon Tower (D) (1846), St Mark, Pensnett (D) (1846–9), and St Mary, Hurst Hill, Coseley (D) (1872 and 1882). The Dudley churches of St John and St James plus their schools, referred to earlier, use Gornal stone as a base. Blocks may be up to 49 by 15 in. (125 by 38 cm.) in size, as on the best work such as All Saints, Sedgley, often with a diagonally tooled face and drafted margins. Although some uncoursed rubble walling survives, Gornal work is typically of squared blocks, usually laid in random courses varying between as much as 6 and 16 in. (15–40 cm.), and topped with triangular-section copings known locally as 'donkey's yeds'. The most striking impression of Gornal stone now comes from these boundary walls, many miles of which still exist e.g. along the main roads radiating from Sedgley. No building of Gornal stone is located more than four miles or so from Ruiton, and the boundary walls do not extend more than about six or seven miles from the source.

In and around Bilston (Wo), Darlaston (Wa) and Wednesbury (Sa), another type of sandstone also saw use as a building material, known locally as PELDON STONE. This fine-grained Carboniferous sandstone is similar in appearance to the buff-coloured

Gornal stone, but has patches of darker yellows and browns indicating the presence of iron. Extant examples are far fewer than those of Gornal and are insufficient to create any cohesive local identity. Some sections of walling survive in Bilston and Wednesbury, notably in Wood Green Road, Wednesbury, but only four buildings still exist in part or whole. The best known, by reason of its relocation to the Black Country Living Museum at Dudley, is the mid-C19 stone-cutter's hovel from Bilston, which illustrates the vernacular use of large, roughly squared but randomly sized blocks. The other Peldon survivors are the tower of St John, Tipton (Sa) (1683), St James, Wednesbury (1847–8) and the Wednesbury Masonic Hall, originally a Congregational church (1850). The most prestigious, St John's church, Wednesbury (1846), was demolished in 1985.

A fourth Black Country building stone is DOLERITE, a hard igneous rock known locally as ROWLEY RAG, which in molten form pushed up through the Coal Measures to form intrusions at Rowley Regis (Sa), Wednesfield (Wo), Barrow Hill near Pensnett (D) and Pouk Hill near Walsall. The largest of these intrusions, at Rowley Regis, covers an area of one square mile on the top of the Rowley hills, and at Turner's Hill reaches the highest point in the Black Country at 876 ft (267 metres). By the late C18 Rowley Rag was being quarried on a considerable scale. Its hardness made it eminently suitable for use as a road metal, and by the 1850s some 60,000 tons were produced annually from Rowley, with a further 19,000 tons from Pouk Hill. The stone also found widespread use as setts and kerbstones, examples of which can still be seen around the area. When polished through wear the stone takes on a blue-black sheen, similar to but shinier and smoother than Staffordshire blue brick, which was also used as a paving material. Rowley Rag was also used for dry-stone field walls on the Rowley hills, some of which survive on Dudley Golf Course. The boundary wall of St Giles, Rowley is a rare example of its use in carefully dressed courses, with angles and corners of shaped blocks.

The oldest recorded building using the stone was a house in Rowley dated 1663, which survived until the 1950s. In *c.*1935 Rowley quarrymen were described as living in 200-year-old cottages of 'great slabs...thrown together in a careless architecture which at once arrests the attention of the townsman'. A barn formerly at Old Portway Farm, Rowley was constructed of uncoursed rubble dolerite with brickwork corners, openings and gable apex. St Anne, Willenhall (Wa) (1858–61) is built uniquely of small squared and evenly coursed blocks of dolerite, presumably from the nearby Pouk Hill quarry, with sandstone dressings. The form and pattern of construction is similar to that of the Dudley churches of St John and St James.

In the mid C19 the civil engineer *Henry Adcock* conceived the bold idea of melting the dolerite and casting it in moulds. He experimented successfully with the help of the glass-makers *Chance Bros* of Smethwick, and in 1851 commenced the manufacture of pipes, chimney pots and architectural details, but the business failed after three years. A rare surviving example of the work is the Junction Inn, Oldbury (Sa), where quoins, string courses, window heads, sills and console brackets are made of the cast dolerite.

Another material used extensively for building in the Black Country is blast-furnace SLAG, a waste product which until the mid C20 littered the landscape, often in mountainous clusters. A rare surviving deposit can be seen in Moorcroft Wood nature reserve, Moxley, Darlaston (Wa). Slag was typically used in foundations, retaining walls and boundary walls as uncoursed random rubble, many examples of which remain. Complete slag buildings using brick for dressings are known to have existed into the 1970s, and were probably once common.

Examples of all these materials can be seen relocated at the Black Country Living Museum. A few other INDIGENOUS STONES saw use on a smaller scale, both in the Black Country and in Birmingham. Local sandstone was used in Sutton Coldfield for the Vesey cottages of 1527–c.1543, and in the C17 for houses in the High Street. Old quarries, for sand but also perhaps for stone, can be seen in several places nearby, e.g. Reddicap Hill. Hasbury sandstone, quarried just S of Halesowen (D), was used in the town's parish church and at Halesowen Abbey, but vernacular examples have all but disappeared. IMPORTED STONES from further afield include grey-buff Keuper sandstone from Tixall in Staffordshire, used at St Thomas, Dudley and St Paul, Birmingham, and Bromsgrove sandstone from the Sherwood Group of the Triassic, quarried at Ombersley and elsewhere, at e.g. All Saints, Kings Heath (B) of 1858–60. A distant exotic is the Roche Abbey magnesian limestone from the Cadeby formation of the Permian, used to face the interior of the Watt Chapel at St Mary, Handsworth (B) of 1825–6.

ARCHAEOLOGY
BY MIKE HODDER

Few remains of the earliest period of human occupation in Britain, the PALAEOLITHIC (c. 950,000–9500 B.C.), have yet been found in Birmingham and the Black Country. The most striking discoveries, quartzite handaxes from Saltley (B) and Erdington (B), lay in material probably deposited during the Anglian glaciation, around 450,000 years ago. The forested, postglacial landscapes of the following MESOLITHIC (c.9500–4000 B.C.) were exploited by hunter-gatherer communities using distinctively shaped flint tools and weapons. A peaty soil layer dated to c.8300 B.C., discovered under more recent structures near Curzon Street in Birmingham city centre, contained worked flints, and pollen of birch and pine from the trees surrounding it. Large numbers of flint tools of Late Mesolithic (c.6500–4000 B.C.) type and the debris from their manufacture have been found near springs and streams at Foxcote (Wollescote (D)), Bourne Pool (Aldridge (Wa)) and Sandwell Priory (West Bromwich (Sa)). Stakeholes and gullies excavated at Bourne Pool and Sandwell Priory may be the remains of dwellings or shelters.

Flint tools and polished stone axes of the NEOLITHIC (*c.* 4000–2400 B.C.), the period of the first farmers in Britain, have been found throughout the area. An apparently isolated pit at Bournville (B) which dated to around 2700 B.C. contained pieces of 'Grooved Ware' pottery vessels characteristic of the Later Neolithic. Pollen preserved in peat at Perry Barr (B) shows that the first significant clearance of woodland for agriculture here took place around 2100 B.C., in the earlier part of the BRONZE AGE (*c.* 2400–700 B.C.). King's Standing mound (B) and mounds at Rushall (Wa) and Aldridge (Wa) are probably ROUND BARROWS (Later Neolithic and Early Bronze Age burial mounds). Some other mounds in the area were destroyed in recent times, and ring ditches which may have surrounded now-flattened barrows have been noted on aerial photographs. Over fifty BURNT MOUNDS, dating from between 1700 and 900 B.C., have been found in open spaces within and around the conurbation. These mounds of heat-shattered stones and charcoal, in wet locations next to streams or springs, have been interpreted as the debris from cooking in water heated with hot stones, or from the production of steam for bathing by pouring water on to hot stones within a tent-like structure. Excavations at some sites have revealed burnt areas, pits and stake-holes. Isolated Bronze Age pits have been found at Northfield (B) and Perry Barr.

The majority of the area's IRON AGE (*c.* 700 B.C.–A.D. 43) population probably lived in farmsteads like the two excavated on the line of the M6 Toll motorway near Langley Mill Farm (Sutton Coldfield), dated to around 300 B.C., which consisted of circular houses within ditched enclosures. Cropmarks visible on aerial photographs suggest similar enclosures elsewhere in the area. Scantier remains of this period have been found at Tidbury Green, Damson Parkway (Elmdon (So)) and Walkers Heath (B). The only definite HILL-FORT (fortified hilltop settlement characteristic of the Late Bronze Age and Iron Age) wholly within the area is Castle Old Fort (Walsall Wood (Wa)). The larger Wychbury (Pedmore (D)) straddles the border with Worcestershire. Excavation of its inturned NW entrance suggested that the rampart was revetted with dry-stone walling. There may also have been hill-forts at other locations such as Wednesbury (Sa), Oldbury (Sa) and Castle Hill in Dudley, but none has yet been proven. Loaches Banks (Aldridge (Wa)), a triple-banked and ditched enclosure in a low-lying location near a stream, is likely to be of Iron Age date, like similar sites in the Welsh Marches.

Just as it now straddles three historic counties, Birmingham and the Black Country probably included parts of three Iron Age tribal territories that later became *civitates* (administrative units) of Roman Britain: the *Cornovii* in the NW, the *Dobunni* in the S and the *Corieltauvi* in the NE. A few coins of the latter two tribes have been found in the area. The ROMAN FORT at Metchley

(Edgbaston (B)) may have been deliberately located at the junction of these territories. The first fort here, built between the late A.D. 40s and late 50s, had defended annexes on all sides and a short-lived *vicus* (civilian settlement) of timber buildings outside its W gate. The fort subsequently became a supply depot containing buildings of irregular plan and fenced enclosures, with further enclosures and funnelling ditches to its W, probably for livestock management. In the A.D. 70s this was replaced by a smaller fort with granaries inside and enclosures outside. The site was occupied until the end of the C2, but its later phases were probably civilian rather than military, and included iron-working.

A network of ROMAN ROADS linked Metchley with other forts. A well-preserved stretch of the Ryknield Street in Sutton Park (Sutton Coldfield) consists of the *agger* (raised road surface), intermittent side ditches and even the quarry pits from which the gravel for the *agger* was dug. Some existing SETTLEMENTS continued in use after the Roman Conquest, and new settlements were established along Roman roads. A concentration on stock-rearing, possibly to supply animal products to military garrisons in north and west Britain, may have replaced mixed farming practised before the Conquest.

At least five large ENCLOSURES accompanied by droveways, suggesting livestock management, were constructed in the C2 and C3 next to the Iron Age enclosure at Langley Mill Farm (Sutton Coldfield). Charred grain found here was not accompanied by processing waste, indicating that cereals consumed on the site had been grown and processed elsewhere. At Longdales Road (Kings Norton (B)), regularly sized ditched plots alongside Ryknield Street and timber buildings in an enclosure and large compound dating from the C2 to C3 may have been a collecting point for stock prior to distribution of animals or their products to market at Alcester (Warwicks.). Rectangular buildings at Damson Parkway (Elmdon (So)) were stone-built, or had stone footings, in contrast to the wholly timber buildings at Langley Mill Farm and Longdales Road. Concentrations of pottery on field surfaces near Sutton Coldfield and Halesowen (D) indicate several Roman FARMSTEADS, but none of these includes flue tiles (from a heated room) or *tesserae* (from a mosaic floor) that might suggest a villa. The extent of Roman settlement is demonstrated by discoveries of pottery in excavations at the Bull Ring (Birmingham), Kings Norton (B), Castle Bromwich (So) and Sandwell Priory (West Bromwich (Sa)), and many Roman coins and pieces of metalwork have been found throughout the area. POTTERY KILNS in Mere Green (Sutton Coldfield) and Perry Barr (B) produced jars, bowls and tankards in the C2, serving mainly local consumers; the form of the Mere Green kiln suggests that the potter had moved here from south-east England. Other local mineral resources were exploited: coal used at Metchley fort was probably dug in the Black Country, and fossils in the mortar of Roman buildings at Wall (Staffordshire) show that the lime was produced from Rushall limestone.

Few ANGLO-SAXON remains have yet been found in the area. An Anglo-Saxon burial may have been inserted into a prehistoric barrow at Rushall (Wa), and a radiocarbon date of *c.* A.D. 700, a C10 pewter brooch and a possible Anglo-Saxon strap end from Dudley Castle suggest that the hilltop here was occupied before the motte-and-bailey was constructed. Place names and features mentioned as boundary points in C8–C10 charters provide glimpses of the Anglo-Saxon landscape. The only visible structure of this period is the decorated pillar or cross-shaft at Wolverhampton (*see* below), although some details in churches which have been identified as Norman work may be pre-Conquest in date.

Excavations in historic town centres, in former villages which are now suburbs, and in surrounding open land have considerably enhanced our knowledge of the MEDIEVAL period in the region. For example, they have shown that Birmingham originated as a planned town of the C12, and that its medieval industries included pottery manufacture, leather tanning, and horn- and bone-working, in addition to the better-known metalworking. Coal and iron, probably from the Black Country, were used in Birmingham by the C13. In Kings Norton (B), remains of C13 timber buildings have been found under the Saracen's Head (*see also* Timber-framed buildings, pp. 13–16). Earthworks of a former MEDIEVAL SETTLEMENT at Coopers Bank, Gornal, in Dudley are a rare survival in a mainly urban area.

All of the area's three CASTLES were originally of motte-and-bailey type, constructed in the C11 and C12. Excavations at Castle Bromwich (So) revealed a possible tower on the motte mound, timber defences on the earthen bailey bank, including a possible bridge over its entrance, and a timber building containing ovens in the bailey. Any such structures at Dudley Castle were later replaced in stone (*see* below), and the bailey at Kingshurst (So) was later occupied by Kingshurst Hall. Birmingham's medieval manor house, Birmingham Moat, may have originated as a RINGWORK (a circular or oval banked and ditched enclosure of C11 or C12 date). Licences to crenellate in the C13 and C14 respectively made Weoley Castle (B) and Langley Hall (Sutton Coldfield) FORTIFIED MANOR HOUSES (*see* below).

MOATED SITES were numerous in the area, especially in Solihull and S and E Birmingham. Several are still visible even where their buildings have disappeared, and a few have been excavated, showing that most were constructed in the C13 and C14 and surrounded timber buildings. Moats kept out unwanted visitors and animals, but most were not primarily defensive and served as status symbols. Excavation of the small moated site at Sydenhams in Monkspath (So) showed that it was constructed *c.*1240 and abandoned by *c.*1400. The main building was a hall, interpreted as having a central base cruck, with arcade posts defining a solar at one end and a spere-truss defining a cross-passage and service wing at the other.

Medieval water management also included the construction of dams for FISHPONDS such as those in Sutton Park and at Gannow Green (Frankley, B). Sutton Park was a DEER PARK, enclosed with a ditch, bank and fence in the C12 and subsequently subdivided, and parts of C13 deer-park boundaries survive at New Park (Dudley) and Great Barr (Wa). Some of the many WATER MILLS in the area originated in the medieval period, but all their surviving structures are later. The extensive water engineering works for mills include pools held back by dams, and head- and tail-races (feeder channels to and from the mill). At New Hall Mill (Sutton Coldfield), a diminutive mill pool is fed by an impressive 750-yd-long head-race on an embankment, the C18 head- and tail-races for Sarehole Mill (Hall Green, B) and Trittiford Mill (Yardley Wood, B) run parallel to the River Cole for one-and-a-half miles, and other pools and races are visible even where there are no other surviving mill structures.

MEDIEVAL ARCHITECTURE

The ANGLO-SAXON contribution is just one significant monument: the tremendous shaft of the C9 or C10 Wolverhampton cross, with high-quality carved beasts, foliage and acanthus leaves. The CHURCHES include a scatter of NORMAN work. St Peter, Wolverhampton retained much of its W front, with broad buttresses, until C19 restoration. Small survivals at St Alphege, Solihull show that a substantial Norman church existed there. The arcade at St Peter, Bickenhill (So) is a blunt but impressive early C12 piece, with unmoulded arches and massive abaci. Tympanums survive at Pedmore (D) and Kingswinford (D), minor outliers of the Herefordshire school of sculpture, with a Christ in Majesty and a St Michael and the Dragon respectively. The lower part of the tower at Kingswinford is also C12. Of the late C12 are the E parts of Dudley Priory, with broad buttresses and half-round shaft mouldings. The finest architecture of this moment, however, is at St John the Baptist, Halesowen (D), related to Pershore Abbey (Worcs.), including the E end with intersecting arcading in the gable and a hint of a barrel-vault in the chancel, W and S doorways with chevron ornament, and the W end of the aisled nave with composite piers. The N doorway at Northfield (B) also has chevron and (very worn) beakhead ornament. The TRANSITIONAL period around 1200 is marked by an unusual group of S transept towers. That at Handsworth (B) has clasping buttresses and slim lancets; that at Sedgley (D) has been refaced but is probably slightly earlier, with round-headed windows. In both cases only the lower parts survive. Could their upper parts have been timber? (The third of the group is at Claverley in Shropshire.)

The E end of Dudley Priory is EARLY ENGLISH GOTHIC work, with typical flat buttresses and string course. Sandwell Priory (West Bromwich (Sa)) was C13, with five E apses like Worcester Cathedral, and vaulting probably by masons from Buildwas or Wenlock. The most important building of this period of which something survives is Halesowen Abbey (D), founded in 1215. The fragmentary remains – just enough to appreciate its plan and scale – are severe but of fine quality. The chancel almost certainly had a quadripartite vault, on corbels. The finest intact E.E. work in the area is the chancel of Northfield church (B). The interior is richly treated, with triplet lancets with shafted jambs, set in outer arches again shafted, and even with slim end shafts for the hoodmoulds. Kingswinford (D) has the remains of an aisled C13 church: the jambs of the W doorway with shafts and bell capitals, circular piers of the N arcade, and one lancet in the chancel. The E window at Kings Norton (B) has stepped lancets. Later C13 is the crossing of St Peter, Wolverhampton, with more complex mouldings including filleted shafts, and the S porch with a rib-vault. The GEOMETRICAL style, with the appearance of bar tracery, is found in the fine chancel and N chapel of St Alphege, Solihull of after 1277, with intersecting tracery which has little doubled cusps, and by the chancel at Bushbury (Wo), also with cusped intersecting tracery. There is plain Y-tracery of c. 1300 in the S aisle at Northfield and in one window of the chancel at Kingswinford. A surviving monastic building at Halesowen Abbey, late C13 or early C14, has a fine crown-post roof, the earliest in the area.

The mature DECORATED style has not left much. There is minor work in the Warwickshire village churches now absorbed by Birmingham. What starts to appear here is what Pevsner called the 'relentless stolidity' of a standard arcade, with octagonal piers and double-chamfered arches. Kings Norton is like this except for some quatrefoil piers towards the E, those in the S arcade with fillets. The chancel arch here has ballflower ornament. The nave at Sheldon (B) is of c. 1330, with a row of standard S windows and a contemporary roof. The N arcade looks slightly later, with a continuous quarter-round moulding. The inventive window tracery is C19 (by *Slater & Carpenter*) but may follow C14 originals. The S transept at Yardley (B) has a window with elongated cusped shapes. *Salvin's* E window of 1852 at Aldridge (Wa) with petal tracery partly reproduces a fine predecessor. The architectural influence of the Edwardian castles, noticeable in Shropshire, reaches to St John the Baptist, Halesowen (D), then in that county, where the base of the tower has characteristic sunk-chamfer mouldings. Also Dec, with lancets having ogee tops, is the W crypt at Walsall. Later Dec, moving towards Perp, is the cusped reticulated tracery in the S aisles at Yardley and Kings Norton.

The wool trade grew in the C15, coal and iron mining had started, and metal working also. Unsurprisingly, therefore, the PERPENDICULAR style has left a larger mark. The nave of St Peter, Wolverhampton was rebuilt in a long campaign from 1439. The grid of windows in the clerestory looks particularly like Cheshire work, and so does the tower of after 1475, here attributed to *John Worseley*. St Matthew, Walsall was rebuilt between 1462 and 1474, but only the chancel survived recasting in the early C19. Its window detail, where this survives, is fairly conventional. The wide E part of the crypt underneath has a finely constructed four-centred tunnel vault. The C15 is the period of towers and spires in the village churches now in Birmingham. The finest is Kings Norton, one of a group which includes Coleshill in Warwickshire and Bromsgrove in Worcestershire, rising sheer to a belfry with multiple windows and blank ogee arcading. Yardley is plainer, with single belfry windows. It may be by *Henry Ulm*, who built the similar tower at Sheldon in 1461. Aston (B) has an unusual belfry stage with close-set ogee-headed lancets, the central pair each side open, the rest blank. Bickenhill (So) has a tower with unconventional Perp tracery. The N chapel here introduces a distinctive manner with exaggerated details, found in late medieval West Midlands work, e.g. the big headstops of the arch to the chancel. The roof survives, with arch-braced collars and wind-braces. The C15 N aisle at Yardley has an arcade of standard elements but a roof with moulded ribs and one remaining boss. The N transept at Wolverhampton, perhaps of c. 1510, is on a grand scale; the roof has moulded ribs and square panels.

There is an unexpected amount of work from just before the Reformation. The nave and aisles at Solihull were being roofed in 1533–5. Halesowen (D) has the chancel S aisle, probably of 1531, with simplified standard elements (single-chamfered arches), the small clerestory probably of 1533–4, and the N transept probably built in 1544 to house images from Halesowen Abbey, still in the West Midlands manner with exaggerated details, but here with late, uncusped window tracery. The most unusual work, however, is at Sutton Coldfield: Bishop Vesey's chancel aisles of 1533–4. The arcades have standard Perp four-shafts-and-hollows piers but round arches, just starting to move from Gothic to Renaissance in style, and apparently unique. They are still pre-Reformation work, built to create side chapels.

Medieval CHURCH FITTINGS start with FONTS. Halesowen's is Norman, with the bowl supported on corner columns, a South-West type unusual in the Midlands. Bushbury's (Wo) is a puzzling piece, of Norman shape, perhaps late C12 or early C13 but radically re-cut. There are C13 ones at Rushall (Wa), with vertical bands of dogtooth on the bowl, and at Solihull. There are several Perp ones, mostly modest. Bickenhill (So) is notable for its Art Deco-looking angels; Walsall, with shields held by angels, because we know carver and date (*William Masyn*, 1473). Wolverhampton has a superb C15 stone PULPIT with panelling and staircase, with at its foot a lion. Bickenhill has a remarkable survival in the N chapel: a stone REREDOS or altar screen, C15 or early C16, dividing off a small room behind, and carved with huge crocketed finials and headstops in the characteristic local manner. Solihull has a simpler Perp arcaded reredos in the S aisle.

Medieval church WOODWORK starts with the planked S aisle door at Northfield (B), probably of c. 1300. Wolverhampton and Solihull have modest late medieval screens. Walsall has C15 or early C16 stall work from Halesowen Abbey, with a set of eighteen misericords. Wolverhampton's simpler ones, of the same period, are probably from Lilleshall Abbey, Shropshire. Wednesbury (Sa) has a C14 or C15 wooden lectern shaped like a gamecock. The chancel fittings at Sutton Coldfield (now partly elsewhere in the church) are confidently classical Marian work of 1556–7, brought from Worcester Cathedral. This was a model restoration of a cathedral for Catholic worship, in which Queen Mary I was involved. The iconography includes e.g. the Five Wounds of Christ, and the quality, especially of details, is extremely high. The chancel side windows at St Peter, Wolverhampton have introduced C16 Flemish STAINED GLASS. Medieval MONU-MENTS include a succession of C14 knights at St Martin in the Bull Ring, Birmingham.

Most surviving MEDIEVAL SECULAR BUILDINGS are timber-framed (*see* below). Of STONE BUILDINGS the finest is Dudley Castle, the one substantial CASTLE in the area (for motte-and-bailey castles *see* Archaeology, p. 9). Minor survivals show the existence of domestic buildings here in the C12. The side walls of the Triple Gatehouse are of the same date. The keep, where recent analysis suggests a start in the 1260s, is a major work in the sequence of medieval great towers. Built on the existing motte, like the C13 Clifford's Tower in York, it had four circular corner towers and may in turn have influenced the gatehouse towers at Harlech and Caerphilly. The rest of the Triple Gatehouse is also C13, with convex quadrant mouldings and lancet windows. The early C14 chapel adds to the examples of the Decorated style locally with a W window formerly with flowing tracery, and a big ogee-headed S window. After Dudley come the remains of two FORTIFIED MANOR HOUSES of the type well known from Stokesay Castle in Shropshire. The start of Weoley Castle (B) is contemporary with the Dudley keep, and for the same family, the Somerys, but there are C14 rebuildings. The plan is preserved from just above ground level. What impresses now is the fine stonework of the revetted base of the walls, with some simple but well-made details. Rushall Hall (Wa) retains an almost complete circuit of late C13 or C14 limestone walls, and much of a C15 gatehouse with segmental archways. One later group of houses must be mentioned: the VESEY COTTAGES in Sutton Coldfield, built by Bishop Vesey between 1527 and c. 1543 for his 'pore kynesmen', of local sandstone. The availability of stone partly accounts for other survivals of this period in Sutton: the S range of New Hall, later medieval or C16, with remains of mullioned windows; the rear parts of Ashfurlong Hall, probably C16; and the early work in Nos. 1–5 Coleshill Street, perhaps of Vesey's time. Difficult to date, of Vesey's time or later, are minor stone buildings in the town, such as No. 59 Reddicap Hill.

TIMBER-FRAMED BUILDINGS
BY NICHOLAS MOLYNEUX

TIMBER-FRAMED BUILDINGS are unusual survivals, in an area of constant growth and rebuilding. There are a few manor houses, a notable timber church (at Castle Bromwich (So), re-cased in brick), some gentry houses, commercial premises, a number of lesser houses and some farm buildings. Many have been absorbed into the urban landscape as the industrializing towns expanded. Dendrochronology provides firm dates for about a dozen houses and a handful of barns.

The most impressive MEDIEVAL HOUSE is West Bromwich Manor House (Sa), formerly moated. The hall, dated to the 1270s or 1280s, has a base cruck surmounted by a crown-post roof to the open hall, and a characteristic spere-truss to the cross-passage. The gatehouse dates from 1590. There is no other house of such an early date, but there are other medieval survivals. The former guildhall at Deritend (B), now the Old Crown Inn, is of particular interest. It also includes a schoolroom, and a residence for the master which had a small Wealden-type hall familiar from nearby Coventry but otherwise unknown in the urban area, with a characteristic recessed bay for the open hall. When the hall was modernized by the introduction of a first floor, this bay was disguised by the insertion of close studding and a jetty, perhaps in the earlier C16.

At the heart of former villages and towns are a number of medieval structures. There is relatively simple late medieval framing contained within brickwork at the Great Stone Inn, Northfield (B), which has a C15 roof with trenched purlins and curved wind-braces. A more decorative roof survives at the Old Moat House, Earlswood (So) with a cusped truss. The Saracen's Head, Kings Norton (B), much of which became a pub, is an unusual domestic and commercial building, notable for its continuous jetty facing the churchyard and impressive coved gable end. The main entrance was through a (lost) two-storey porch into a cross-passage. The hall had a floor from the outset. A brick range attached at right angles contains much timber framing, with evidence for a cart entrance. This was the business premises of a substantial wool merchant. The whole structure of the frame is dated to 1492. The nearby Old Grammar School is from the 1660s, although it incorporates reused late medieval framing. Primrose Hill Farm in Kings Norton is another former open-hall house, of 1440, with a barn with large square framing and curved braces, dated to 1457. At Minworth Greaves, Sutton Coldfield is a barn dated to the 1460s.

A well-represented medieval form is the CRUCK TRUSS. At first sight, cruck-framed buildings may seem modest, their characteristic construction having mostly been hidden by later walls. When newly built, they were often of relatively high status. At least nine domestic examples survive in the area, including The Grove (C14) and the Old Smithy, Maney (1442–4), both in Sutton Coldfield, and the Lad in the Lane Inn, Erdington (B) (dated to 1400).

POST-MEDIEVAL TIMBER FRAMING sits at the junction of the decorative traditions of Shropshire and the North-West, where surface carving was more common, and the type we find more often: the plainer but heavily timbered Worcestershire/Warwickshire style. An impressive 1590s house built for an upwardly mobile family is Blakesley Hall, Yardley (B). Stylistically similar is Stratford House (built by a brother-in-law), dated to 1601, at Camp Hill s of Deritend (B). Both exhibit a wealth of herringbone framing. Bells Farm, Brandwood (B) is a complex C17 house exhibiting heavy close studding with some surviving panelling. It also had decorative plasterwork, a feature which rarely survives. There is more early plasterwork in the Old Crown, Deritend, and C16 wall painting at Graiseley Old Hall, Graiseley (Wo) and at Blakesley Hall, Yardley (B). At the Oak House, West Bromwich (Sa) we encounter a large house dated to 1604–29, built with money derived from industry. It is a U-plan, with close studding, and a belvedere added in 1647–73. Sheldon Hall (B), a moated site, is an H-plan early C17 house combining brick with stone dressings for the hall and timber-framed cross-wings, all of one date. Unusually for this region, the framing was rendered from the outset.

A small but interesting category is the buildings which were moved in the C20. The Golden Lion in Cannon Hill Park, Moseley (B) (moved due to early C20 road widening) has decorative framing characteristic of the late C16 or early C17. A small group in Bournville (B), at Selly Manor, was collected by the Cadbury family, including a cruck-framed building from Minworth (Sutton Coldfield).

LATER C16 TO LATE C17 ARCHITECTURE

Major POST-MEDIEVAL BUILDINGS in the area begin with the E range of Dudley Castle, work of the early 1550s for John Dudley, Duke of Northumberland and Protector of England. His circle, which included Sir William Sharington of Lacock in Wiltshire, shared an early interest in England in the Italian Renaissance. The symmetry and surviving classical detail of the range are progressive for their date. Of other HOUSES, the Sacheverell work at New Hall (Sutton Coldfield) starts in 1590. The major works here, the staircase and Great Chamber, are probably early C17, perhaps as late as the 1630s. They are richly treated, with full-height panelling articulated by pilasters and an ornate stair rail with beasts as finials. Vesey Manor in Sutton, a dignified farmhouse, has window details which link it to New Hall, so is also probably early C17. Castle Bromwich Hall (So), built between 1599 and 1622, is grander than New Hall. The exterior of a complete courtyard house survives, with impressively large mullion-and-transom windows, somewhat disguised by later C17 alterations. The central, brick block of Sheldon Hall (B) (see also above), of 1617–19, contemporary with the timber-framed work, has cyma and ovolo mouldings.

Slightly later than these, at least when it was started, is Aston Hall, a major country house now within Birmingham. The most important Jacobean work in the area, it was built between 1618 and 1635 from designs supplied by *John Thorpe*. Its height and its wonderful skyline of turrets and shaped gables link it to great Jacobean houses such as Hatfield or Blickling, or locally to Westwood House near Droitwich. It is conservative in its U-shaped plan but progressive in its external symmetry (helped by mid-C17 alterations). Among smaller gentry houses, two stand out with relatively progressive, formal H-plans: Holbeche House at Wallheath (D), probably of after 1618 for the Lyddyatt family, and Pype Hayes Hall (B). Both were much altered in the C19. More modest houses begin with Peddimore Hall, Sutton Coldfield, of between 1659 and 1671, originally with a three-gabled front. It has a direct-entry plan common to many smaller gentry or middle-class houses in the region. More vernacular still are smaller houses like Wollescote Hall (D), Wightwick Manor, Tettenhall (Wo), and Haden Hall, Old Hill, Rowley Regis (Sa). There is a local group, probably mid- to late C17, with distinctive large semicircular gables: the former White Hart at Caldmore, Walsall; Nickolls and Perks's shop in Stourbridge (D); and Wiggins Hill Farm, Sutton Coldfield. The demolished Old Still in High Street, Walsall, had a similar gable. Oldswinford Castle (D), certainly of before 1699, is one of a group of C17 West Midlands houses which combine stone and timber framing. The best surviving C17 TOWN HOUSES are in High Street, Sutton Coldfield, though all have been refronted. The earliest is probably No. 1, the former White Hart inn, 1619; the grandest is certainly Vesey House, the 'Brick House' of 1634, with, originally, a complete courtyard plan. Cull's House, No. 36, has both C17 stonework and timber work, a reminder that many smaller houses were still timber-framed into the C17: e.g. the Talbot Hotel in Stourbridge, a complete courtyard house, and the Greyhound and Punchbowl, perhaps originally a manor house, in Bilston (Wo). The C17 and C18 saw many such houses at least partly encased in brick: Ravenshaw Hall, Solihull; Castle Hills, Bickenhill (So); and Dovehouse Farm, Olton (So).

More DECORATION AND FITTINGS of the period survive than might be expected. Graiseley Old Hall has fragments of C16 WALL PAINTINGS, as noted above. The opulent STAIRCASE at Aston Hall has richly carved newels, pierced strapwork panels instead of balusters, and animals in the string. The almost contemporary staircase at New Hall, Sutton Coldfield (*see also* above) is very confined, but has standing beasts on the newels, and openwork panels. Peddimore Hall, Sutton Coldfield has a rustic example with shallow carving and odd fluting, and diagonal bracing rather than balusters. Full-height PANELLING survives in the gallery at Aston Hall and at Castle Bromwich Hall, and more modestly but still impressively in the Windsor Room at the Talbot Hotel, Stourbridge, and at Vesey House, Sutton Coldfield. No. 16 Coleshill Street, Sutton, has splendid imported panelling with portrait heads, geometric shapes and fruit. PLASTERWORK also starts with Aston Hall, where the Great Dining Room ceiling has intricate patterns centred on masks, and standing figures in arches in the frieze. The gallery ceiling also has patterning. The Windsor Room at the Talbot Hotel has boldly intersecting curved ribs above strapwork, and a remarkable overmantel with a central relief and curious buildings in a landscape. There is a simpler ribbed plaster ceiling at the Greyhound and Punchbowl, Bilston.

There is little C17 CHURCH WORK. The N transept of St Peter, Wolverhampton has unusual large windows with broad central mullions, probably restoration after Civil War damage. The upper part of the tower at Edgbaston Old Church (B) was rebuilt for the same reason. The gabled S aisle at St Nicolas, Kings Norton (B), is a heightening to accommodate a (lost) gallery. St John, Tipton (Sa) has a complete W tower, still in a basic Gothic, dated 1683. FURNISHINGS include communion tables at St Peter, Wolverhampton and (probably) Pelsall (Wa), and alterations to the screens at St Alphege, Solihull.

There is one significant C17 NONCONFORMIST building, the characteristically simple Friends' Meeting House of 1688–9 at Stourbridge (D), with original (or early) gallery, elders' seat and benches.

Late C16 CHURCH MONUMENTS reflect the nearness of the workshops of Burton-on-Trent. They include two alabaster tombs at St Peter, Wolverhampton: John Leveson †1575, and Thomas Lane †1585, with some Renaissance motifs, the latter perhaps by *Robert Royley*. C17 monuments are mostly minor, but also at Wolverhampton is *Hubert le Sueur*'s impressive bronze figure of Admiral Leveson of 1633–4.

Sandwell, Tipton, showing St John the Evangelist.
Watercolour by Thomas Peploe Wood, 1837

There are a few C17 INDUSTRIAL survivals. The best is probably Lifford Hall, Kings Norton (B), in origin a smart mill and house of the 1670s. New Hall Mill in Sutton Coldfield retains some impressive C17 or earlier stone walling. In Spring Head, Wednesbury (Sa) is a range which certainly contains some C17 brickwork and has a former malthouse at the rear.

FROM THE LATE C17 TO c. 1830

In this conservative area the English CLASSICAL TRADITION of Inigo Jones, Roger Pratt and Sir Christopher Wren was slow to arrive. Founder's Building at Old Swinford Hospital (D), being built in 1669, has a doorcase with enormous side volutes, still in the mid-C17 style sometimes called Artisan Mannerism. The lower part of the full-height porch at Castle Bromwich Hall (So), with its rather French doorcase and channelled rustication, is probably also of the 1660s. This 'frontispiece' was extended upwards, and a storey added to the whole front, after 1685 by *William Winde*, the one appearance of a C17 London architect in the area. Metropolitan sophistication is even more noticeable inside, in the grand staircase of 1688, and fine plaster ceilings by *Edward Goudge*. There is a group of houses of the late C17 and early C18 with a vernacular classical treatment in red brick, sometimes with one or more platbands, and parallel rear wings, still with quite steep roof pitches: Pipe Hall at Bilston (Wo); Nos. 47–49 Coleshill Street, Sutton Coldfield; and Nos. 153–157 Lichfield Road at Rushall (Wa). The brick treatment with platbands, and the roof pitches, continue through the early to mid C18, e.g. at No. 1 The Square, Solihull, at Cole Hall Farm, Stechford (B), and at Netherton House, Wightwick, Tettenhall (Wo), dated 1747.

Mainstream CLASSICISM develops with a group of houses with hipped roofs, deep, often dentilled eaves, and prominent chimneys. The simplest, and probably the earliest, is Oldswinford rectory (D), of 1700, with fine rubbed-brick lintels. A substantial house of this type which has disappeared is Sutton Coldfield rectory, of 1701 by *William Smith the elder*. The Grange, Halesowen (D), probably of after 1709, combines a steeply pitched roof with giant corner pilasters and a hefty segmental-pedimented doorcase, moving towards the Baroque. The Bradford Arms, Castle Bromwich (So), probably a small gentry house, traditionally dated 1723, also with a steeply pitched roof, has slightly projecting wings and a recessed centre. Inside is a grand but small-scale imperial staircase.

The change to a BAROQUE manner is first seen at the remarkable Moat House, Sutton Coldfield, by *Sir William Wilson*, probably of shortly after 1697. It is unsophisticated, a little gauche, but very progressive for the area, with its balustraded parapet and giant order. Moseley Hall, Bushbury (Wo) is simpler, still of the C17 type, with rubbed brick lintels and a doorcase with the cornice on consoles, but the alternating quoins suggest a date as late as the 1720s. Also in north Wolverhampton, Old Fallings Hall, Fallings Park, attributed to *Francis Smith*, is similar in details but has the doorcase extended up as a window surround, and giant corner pilasters. Swinford Old Hall, Oldswinford, 1720s or later, looks like a local designer's attempt at a house of the Francis Smith type: giant pilasters, swan's-neck window heads, but an incoherent central window.

A few TOWN HOUSES of around 1700 survive: No. 20 High Street, Sutton Coldfield, with its narrow bays, giant end pilasters and steep roof with dormers, is similar to the houses of the only planned urban development of the period, Old Square, Birmingham, begun in 1697 (demolished). In Dudley are No. 7 Priory Street of 1703 and Finch House, formally composed with pediments; Finch House an unusual double (semi-detached) pair. The Big House, Oldbury (Sa), supposedly of 1705 but more likely of the 1720s, has an odd swan's-neck doorcase with added timber pieces, either from ignorance or alteration. Cull's House, No. 36 High Street, Sutton Coldfield, is fully Baroque, with giant pilasters and a swan's-neck doorcase, close in manner to *William Westley*'s demolished houses in Temple Row, Birmingham. This type runs on, probably into the 1740s–50s: Nos. 31–33 Market Place, Wednesbury (Sa); Nos. 45–46 Market Place, Willenhall (Wa); and in a small country house, Light Hall, Shirley (So). The last datable example is at Nos. 1–5 Coleshill Street, Sutton Coldfield, *c.* 1748. Rock House, Tettenhall (Wo), with very basic pilasters and a rare (for this area) doorcase with Gibbs surround, must be of *c.* 1750. Well into the C18, less polite houses were still built in a traditional way, as the steeply roofed Fox and Grapes, Park Street, Birmingham, of 1728–31 (demolished 2018) showed.

C18 CHURCHES also begin with *Wilson* and his charming little chapel at Hall Green (B) of 1703, a very early case of a giant Doric order. St Philip, Birmingham, now the cathedral, of 1709–25, is in a different class completely: a major work of the English Baroque by *Thomas Archer*, the only one of the style's chief proponents who had seen the Italian Baroque at first hand. The tower, with its dramatic contrast of convex and concave, shows Archer's knowledge of the work of Bernini and especially Borromini. There is a giant Doric order with a full entablature and proper triglyphs, set against rusticated masonry. St Philip's was built under an Act obtained because of the increasing size of the town, the first sign of industrial growth resulting in significant architecture. It was followed by smaller, simpler churches. St Thomas, Stourbridge (D), probably by *William Westley*, 1728–36, also a result of urban growth, has an interior deriving from Wren's St James, Piccadilly. St Mary and St Margaret, Castle Bromwich (So), 1724–31, where *Thomas White* of Worcester was involved, is heavy provincial Baroque, with many features – for example, the Tuscan arcade columns with segmental arches – dictated by the medieval timber frame which it encloses. Smethwick Old Church (Sa) of 1729–32 is a good simple Baroque design, almost certainly by *Francis Smith*. St Edmund, Dudley, begun

1724, is clearly by someone who knew the work of Archer but was a little clumsy in replicating it.

CHURCH MONUMENTS after the Restoration start with Col. John Lane at St Peter, Wolverhampton, by *Thomas Cartwright I*, probably mid-1670s, with a finely carved panel including a crowned oak tree. Henry Pudsey †1677 at Sutton Coldfield, probably by *(Sir) William Wilson*, has angled busts. Dr Greswold †1700 at Yardley (B), attributed to *Richard Crutcher*, probably using a design by *Francis Bird*, shows him and his wife praying in a curtained recess. The tablet to Sir George Sacheverell †1715 at Sutton Coldfield, by *William Woodman the elder*, has a rich segmental-pedimented aedicule. Other tablets include three at Aston (B) by or attributed to *Edward Stanton* (†1712, *c.*1715 and the more Baroque Sir Charles Holte †1722, attributed jointly to *Christopher Horsnaile*), and a good architectural design in the same church to Sir John Bridgeman, 1726, designed by *James Gibbs*. One secular monument must be mentioned: the equestrian statue of George I, of 1717–22, attributed to *John van Nost the elder*, now at Birmingham University.

The most significant PUBLIC BUILDINGS of the first half of the C18 are three parish WORKHOUSES: Sedgley (D) of 1734, Sutton Coldfield of 1739, and Solihull of 1740–2 by *Thomas Sandal*. The first two are so reconstructed that little original work is easily visible; Solihull is a long, domestic-looking range (mostly refaced).

PALLADIANISM also appears in the area late. The grandest Palladian house in the area was the 1750s transformation of Sandwell Park, West Bromwich (Sa) with three-storey pyramid-roofed corner towers, where *Sanderson Miller* was almost certainly involved. It went in 1928, but its probably contemporary home farm survives, with similar corner towers. Smaller gentry houses and farms in the new, simpler manner include the work at Penn Hall (Wo) of 1748–54, by *William Baker*: alternating quoins, no pilasters, plain sash windows and a pedimented doorcase. Some original plasterwork survives here. Lloyd House (Farm), Sparkbrook (B), has an even simpler front of 1758. More obviously Palladian are two chaster, pedimented Black Country houses which share some details, such as their unusual segment-headed windows: Wordsley Manor (D) of 1757 and Dennis Hall, Amblecote (D), 1760s. Even in this period there are conservative smaller houses with quite steep roofs and end gables, such as the Manor House at Kingswinford (D). Other houses show change over the century, e.g. Shutt Cross House, Aldridge (Wa), where a vernacular classical block has detail added later in the C18.

From the mid C18, TOWN HOUSES survive in considerable number. The grandest are in Lower High Street, Stourbridge (D): Stourhurst of *c.*1750–60, and the Gothick Nos. 6–7, called 'new built' in 1767. These are a Worcestershire type (the bays of Stourhurst are very similar to those at Perrott House, Pershore), and have possible links to the work of *William & David Hiorne*. Wolverhampton Street in Dudley has several houses of the period, the finest so like Penn Hall in details that it is tempting to suggest that *Baker* had a hand in it. At King Street, Wolverhampton, cut c. 1751, almost all the N side houses survive, very simple, with sashes and moulded lintels, but also one or two old-fashioned basic giant pilasters. High Street, Sutton Coldfield has the Royal Hotel of c. 1751, with an equally old-fashioned gabled centre, and simpler designs like No. 2, and the refacing of No. 1, which continue the vernacular classical manner of the first half of the century.

GARDENS of the period begin with the rare surviving formal layout at Castle Bromwich Hall (So). Designs by *William Winde* show that the Best Garden and the North Garden here date from between 1685 and 1703, when he was also working on the house. The approach retains its forecourt, early C18 gatepiers and a fine quarter-mile-long avenue. A walled garden built by the horticulturalist Sir Samuel Clarke in the 1720s survives at West Bromwich Manor House (Sa). A large walled kitchen garden, now ruined, of 1744 is at Great Barr Hall (Wa), and another, probably late C18, at Elmdon Hall (So). There is more C18 LANDSCAPE GARDENING in the area than might be expected. *William Shenstone*'s romantic, associative work at The Leasowes, Halesowen (D) of 1743–63, influenced by Alexander Pope and William Kent, created twisting paths and vistas on a modest budget, always with water. *Humphry Repton* made three garden designs. At Great Barr, the Upper Pool and drives survive from 1797–1801 etc., when he was in partnership with *John Nash*. At Moseley (B), now divided by a road and houses, Repton's Red Book is dated 1792, but work took many years, the pool probably of after 1840. Warley Woods, Oldbury (D) (Red Book of 1795) retains a wonderful sweep of meadow rising to trees. There is one C18 FOLLY, best mentioned here: the Monument, Edgbaston (B), a Gothick tower of 1758.

From the 1780s DOMESTIC ARCHITECTURE becomes more austere, with the growth of NEOCLASSICISM. Sir *John Soane* altered Malvern Hall, Solihull in 1783, stuccoing it and removing details to make the design purer. His exterior has gone but a good, Adamish staircase hall remains. In 1798 Soane built a 'barn à la Paestum', now No. 936 Warwick Road, Solihull; not really like Paestum (it has paired, unfluted columns) but in the most progressive Parisian style of the late C18. Selly Hall, Selly Oak (B) of c. 1780, probably by *Samuel Wyatt*, has plain relieving arches over the windows and stone bands articulating the front, the first appearance in the area of a feature which becomes common. At Lightwoods House, Smethwick (Sa) of 1785, even more radical before its Victorian recasting, only the ruthlessly simple side blocks survive. Lea Hall, Handsworth (B), 'lately built' in 1798, is equally radical, and survives complete: a three-storey, three-bay cube with absolutely plain sashes and stone bands. Moseley Hall (B), mainly of 1792–6 by *John Standbridge*, has a plain central block flanked by pedimented wings: the emphasis on the ends rather than the centre is a typical Neoclassical trait. Soho House, Handsworth (B), recast in 1796–9 mostly by *James* and/or *Samuel Wyatt*, fits into this group, with its plain windows and central lunette. Its giant panelled Ionic order reinterprets an early C18 motif in Neoclassical terms. Ashfurlong Hall, Sutton Coldfield, of c.1800, perhaps also by *Standbridge*, has a pedimented centre with delicate pilasters to the first floor: so the central emphasis is reduced. Like Moseley it stands directly on the ground without a basement storey, another Neoclassical habit. The Lightwoods or Lea type runs on into the C19, e.g. Broadfield House, Kingswinford (D), probably of shortly after 1822.

Among slightly smaller houses the most sophisticated is the smoothly astylar Dormston House, Sedgley (D), c.1815. Oxley House (Wo), of c.1830, stuccoed, with a stone porch, is a good example of John Nash's style, almost certainly by his assistant *James Morgan*. *Rickman & Hutchinson*'s Harborne Lodge (St Mary's Retreat), Harborne (B) is both Neoclassical and picturesque, stuccoed, with pedimented end bays and deep eaves. The Manor House, Aldridge (Wa), was refronted in stucco, probably by *John Webb*, c.1813–16. The former parsonage, Bilston (Wo) by *Richard Tutin*, 1822, is an unusual Greek Revival design. Park Grove, Edgbaston (B) is a rustic villa, stuccoed, with a veranda. Fox Hill House, Sutton Coldfield, is an original stuccoed villa of c.1830 by a local builder, *Solomon Smith*. Near Birmingham city centre are early C19 houses swallowed up by industrial development: No. 3 Summer Hill Terrace, and Heaton House, Camden Street.

Stourbridge excepted, the earliest GOTHICK designs are mostly simple, a matter of crenellations and pointed windows. Great Barr Hall (Wa), as first altered from 1777, and the front of Greenhill House, Halesowen (D), of c.1780 are like this. Fairyfield House, Great Barr, is a little more sophisticated, with a doorcase derived from Batty Langley. Wheatmoor Farm, Sutton Coldfield, has a castellated Gothick front of c.1800 designed as an eyecatcher. A heavier but still pre-Puginian Gothic was employed to remodel Great Barr Hall in the 1830s. The remodelling of Holbeche House, Wallheath (D) in 1819–23, with shaped gables, Tudor-style hoodmoulds and lancets, should also be mentioned here. Much more sophisticated Tudor Revival is the picturesquely composed Priory Hall, Dudley, of 1825 by *Thomas Lee*, the agent's house for the Dudley estate. Metchley Abbey, Harborne (B), c.1827, is already Gothic for an industrial age, with large iron-framed windows. The Brewmaster's House, off Broad Street, Birmingham, of 1816, is a different type, the smart manufacturer's house next to his works (now demolished). It introduces a characteristic local window design of the earlier C19, with a cornice-like lintel supported on consoles.

Later Georgian STREET ARCHITECTURE survives in Birmingham around St Paul's Square, where the church of 1777–9 started development: three-storey terraces with standard doorcases with open pediments and often Doric half-columns. There are survivors in Bromsgrove Street of c.1792–3. Hagley Road began to develop in the 1790s; the one early survivor, No. 64, has Wyatt windows. Significant development of the Inge estate, Waterloo

Walsall, Great Barr Hall.
Engraving by Thomas Radclyffe after Frederick Calvert, 1830

Street and Bennetts Hill, started in 1818, and there are many stucco Regency survivors, with *Charles Edge* and *John Fallows* involved. The Soanian No. 36 Waterloo Street, *c.* 1828, is perhaps by *Thomas Stedman Whitwell*. A fine survivor nearby is Nos. 39–40 Temple Street, *c.* 1824, with Greek-key frieze. In Wolverhampton the late C18 is represented by George Street and neighbouring houses in Snow Hill.

Late Georgian Birmingham is notable for the SEMI-DETACHED and DETACHED HOUSES developed on the edge of the town. A lovely surviving group of houses on Moseley Road runs from *c.* 1813 to the 1850s. Most important of all, the development of Edgbaston started in 1810, with typical Late Georgian designs in Hagley Road and George Road. *George Jones*'s own house of 1814–15 facing Five Ways starts Calthorpe Road, with Soanian designs by *Fallows* of *c.* 1830 at the far end. In Wolverhampton, the s side of Queen Street was developed from 1812 with three-storey houses and standard doorcases. Some have a characteristic local fanlight with 'spider's web' and central panel. Great Cornbow in Halesowen (D) has houses of 1815–30. Development also happened in villages, with much of Yardley (B) rebuilt from the 1820s.

The development of FORMAL TERRACES of houses is characteristic of the Late Georgian period, but there are few of the period here. The Crescent project in Birmingham of 1790–5 by *John Rawstorne* and *Charles Norton* failed (dem. *c.* 1960). Nos. 97–109 Hagley Road, the centre and right-hand part of an incomplete formal terrace of 1819–20 by *Thomas* and *Joseph Bateman*, is a rare example. The terrace of after 1809 in Hamstead Road is another. The mangled Heath Terrace in West Bromwich (Sa) was there by 1819.

There are a few precious survivals of urban WORKING-CLASS HOUSING. Most famous are the back-to-backs in Inge Street, Birmingham, developed from 1809. The passage-entry houses in Lee Crescent, Edgbaston (B), probably of the 1820s, are a step up the scale from this. A small rural dwelling probably of the late C18 survives in Jerry's Lane, Erdington (B).

The two later C18 CHURCHES in the area are conservative in design, influenced by James Gibbs and his *Book of Architecture* (1728): St John, Wolverhampton of 1756–60, by *William Baker* (perhaps assisted by *Thomas Farnolls Pritchard*), and, especially so, St Paul, Birmingham, 1777–9 by *Roger Eykyn*. Both have an array of windows with blocked 'Gibbs' surrounds, a feature otherwise rare in the area. Other church work of the period includes the substantial internal rebuilding of Holy Trinity, Sutton Coldfield by *William Hiorn* in 1759–60, with convincingly Perp piers, but round arches. St Michael, Brierley Hill (D), begun in 1765, was much enlarged in the 1820s, a period when industrial expansion led to much church building. St Lawrence, Darlaston (Wa) was rebuilt as a big classical box with large galleries in 1806–7 by *Thomas Jackson*. The finest EARLY C19 CHURCH is St Thomas, Dudley, of 1815–19 by *William Brooks*. Its elongated octagonal exterior, tower and spire, and fine vaulted interior bear comparison with any church in England of the period. *Francis Goodwin* recast St Matthew, Walsall in 1820–1, with a pretty fan-vault with pendants in the nave.

The 1820s were the early years of the Church Building Commission, with the relatively generous government First Grant. *Goodwin* made great efforts to get the resulting church work, some of them successful. His Holy Trinity, Bordesley (B) of 1820–2 is a fine example of the then much-favoured King's College Chapel type, with corner turrets. His Bilston (Wo) churches are an attractive pair: St Leonard, as rebuilt in classical style in 1825–6, and St Mary of 1829–30, Gothic, with octagonal tower and rare surviving pinnacled reredos. The sad loss is his Christ Church, West Bromwich (Sa) of 1821–9, in Perp style, built on an ample budget. *Thomas Rickman*'s church work in Birmingham has been almost totally obliterated. His St George, Birmingham, of 1819–22, in convincing Perp, a landmark in the early Gothic Revival, was a major loss. Survivors are the Gothic tower and shell of the nave of St Barnabas, Erdington (B), 1822–3, and the fine classical tower and quadrant porticoes of St Thomas, Bath Row, Smallbrook (B), 1826–9. The short-lived *Thomas Lee* left his mark in the Black Country, rebuilding All Saints, Sedgley (D) in 1826–9, and building Christ Church, Coseley (D) and St Andrew, Netherton (D), both of 1827–30. All are of stone, solidly designed and detailed, in a mostly Perp style. *Lewis Vulliamy* designed the majestic Perp-style Holy Trinity, Wordsley (D), of 1829–31, with a tall pinnacled tower. In contrast, St Bartholomew, Wednesbury (Sa) was ignorantly and damagingly recast in 1827–8 by *Edward Ingle* and *George Dickinson*. The memorial chapel to James Watt at St Mary, Handsworth (B), by *Richard Bridgens*, *Rickman & Hutchinson* and others, 1825–6, is a beautiful setting for *Chantrey*'s statue of the engineer.

Staffordshire and Birmingham were centres of CATHOLICISM in the Georgian period. Buildings start with Giffard House, Wolverhampton, of 1728–33, built – to a high standard, with a splendid staircase – as a mass house as well as a dwelling for priests. Maryvale, Kingstanding (B), hidden from main roads and settlements, began with a house of 1753, extended as a seminary in 1800. The chapel was built in 1778 and extended by *Bishop John Milner* in 1809 and again (the Sacred Heart Chapel) in 1820. After the Catholic Relief Act of 1791 allowed the building of CATHOLIC CHURCHES, *Joseph Ireland* designed two beautiful classical examples: St Mary the Mount, Walsall, 1825–7, an economical but effective Greek temple design with a splendid interior with coffered ceiling and arcaded reredos; and St Peter and St Paul, Wolverhampton, built in 1826–8 behind Giffard House as the replacement for the C18 mass house. St Chad and All Saints, Sedgley (D), 1821–3, is lancet Gothic, probably designed by a builder and the local priest, but with a delicate plaster vault in the chancel obviously inspired by St Thomas, Dudley.

Georgian STAINED GLASS is always pictorial. Two works are particularly important: *Francis Eginton*'s E window of 1791, to a design by *Benjamin West*, at St Paul, Birmingham; and the Transfiguration window at St Thomas, Dudley, by *Joseph Backler*, 1819, with a Raphael-inspired Christ. Only the top lights, with armorial bearings, survive of *J. Helmle*'s E window at All Saints, Sedgley (D), of 1831.

Later Georgian CHURCH MONUMENTS include work by significant national sculptors. There is a tablet with exquisite angels' heads at Aston (B) (†1751) by *Michael Rysbrack*. Most of the major Late Georgian figures are represented. *Thomas Banks*'s John Halliday of 1797 at Halesowen (D) is a grand composition of obelisk, urn and mourning figures. *John Flaxman* has a tablet with mourning woman of 1802 at Penn (Wo) and a bust of Matthew Boulton (†1809) at Handsworth (B). *John Bacon the younger* has a tablet with a relief of 1816 at St Lawrence, Darlaston (Wa) and a simpler tomb-chest at Harborne (B) (†1831). *Sir Francis Chantrey*, already mentioned for his moving seated figure of James Watt of 1825 at Handsworth (B), also did a late bust of William Murdoch (†1839) there, and a tablet with zigzag sides and flowers of 1820 at the Presbyterian (Unitarian) chapel, Stourbridge (D). *Sir Richard Westmacott* did simple tablets at Birmingham Cathedral and at St Peter and St Paul, Aston (B)). Of the generation moving towards the Victorians, *E. H. Baily* did a mourning woman and urn (†1821) at Moseley (B). The early C19 saw the appearance of identifiable local mason-sculptors. Birmingham has many tablets by *William Hollins* (often with drooping laurels) and *Matthew Seaborne*, who did a respectable tomb-chest (†1828) at Yardley (B). *William Weale*, working in Bilston (Wo), is a good example of a small community's sculptor. There is one major PUBLIC SCULPTURE: *Westmacott*'s naturalistic Lord Nelson of 1807–9 in the Bull Ring, Birmingham.

The finest Georgian NONCONFORMIST CHAPEL is the Presbyterian, now Unitarian, one in Lower High Street, Stourbridge, of 1788 by *Thomas Johnson*, a dignified pedimented classical 'Templum' (so inscribed) with a pedimented porch. Original pews and gallery survive. Unitarians were active in the C18. Their earliest building is the Old Meeting House, Dudley, a much-altered stone-built box of 1717. Park Lane Chapel, Netherend, Cradley (D), is of 1795–6, but altered in the C19. Coppice Strict Baptist Chapel, Coseley (D), 1804, has a simple version of the conventional pedimented front with two rows of round-headed windows. One non-Christian building must be mentioned: the SYNAGOGUE of 1827 in Severn Street, Birmingham by *Richard Tutin* (now a Masonic hall), modestly classical but with a fine Greek Revival niche for the scrolls.

The best ensemble of Georgian CHURCH FITTINGS is at Castle Bromwich (So): almost complete, with a splendid pulpit and tester, pews, reredos, font and (probably) W gallery. St Paul, Birmingham retains its galleries and most of its pews, as does St Thomas, Stourbridge (cut down). Other interiors, such as St Bartholomew, Wednesbury (Sa), dominated until 1885 by a tremendous central three-decker pulpit, survive only in photographs.

LATE GEORGIAN PUBLIC BUILDINGS are nearly all by local surveyor-architects or the like. The best group is in Queen Street, Wolverhampton: the County Court, an unexpectedly successful combination of Greek Revival ground floor of 1814–15, architect unknown, and Roman Ionic upper floor of 1829 by *Lewis Vulliamy* (the one exception, a London architect); the Dispensary of 1825, *William Hollins*'s only surviving public building; and *William Walford*'s Mechanics Institute of 1835–6. The Market Hall in Stourbridge (D), of 1827 by *John White*, is small but grand, with a giant Doric order. The Court House in Oldbury (Sa), of 1816 by *William Harris* and *Thomas Whitehouse*, is modest. The Gun Barrel Proof House, Digbeth, Birmingham, a statutory institution for testing guns, occupies a lovely vernacular classical range of 1813–14 by *John Horton*, with a splendid trophy of arms over the entrance. The one significant SCHOOL is at Mere Green, Sutton Coldfield, of 1826 by *Thomas Bateman*.

A few Georgian PUBLIC HOUSES survive. The Masons Arms, Solihull is probably mid-C18, as is the Britannia, Rowley (Sa), though terribly mangled. The Dragon (now the Black Country Arms), Walsall, was rebuilt from 1769. The Three Tuns, Sutton Coldfield has a plain rendered front probably of the 1820s, hiding older fabric. The Bottle and Glass, re-erected in the Black Country Museum, Dudley, is also 1820s.

Of INDUSTRIAL BUILDINGS of the period, the most important, the Soho Manufactory, Handsworth (B) of 1765–7 by *William Wyatt*, exists only as archaeology. Of the many WATER MILLS which powered C18 local industry, New Hall Mill at Sutton Coldfield, Sarehole at Hall Green (B) (1764 etc.) and Henwood Mill, Solihull survive. Park House, Sutton Coldfield, is an C18 mill converted into a house. The glass industry in the Stourbridge and Wordsley area used bottle-shaped kilns of brick,

Birmingham, Handsworth, Soho Manufactory.
Engraving by Francis Eginton after Stebbing Shaw, 1801

similar to the more famous kilns in the Potteries. Two remain: a complete kiln at Red House, Wordsley (D), of 1794, now the centre of a museum, and the bottom of a kiln dated 1778 at Plowden & Thompson's nearby. A similar-shaped kiln of *c.* 1830 survives near Fox Hill House, Sutton Coldfield. In Gas Street, Birmingham are a gas retort house and contemporary coal store of 1822. A scatter of early C19 FACTORIES survive in the Jewellery Quarter, e.g. a japanning factory of 1822 in Constitution Hill with a splendid royal arms. In a special class is the former Foster, Rastrick & Co. foundry at Wollaston (D) of 1820–1, a massive brick arched building with a complex cast- and wrought-iron roof and remains of hearths.

CANALS AND CANAL BUILDINGS
BY PAUL COLLINS AND ANDY FOSTER

Transport for the Industrial Revolution which began in the later C18 was by a network of CANALS. They largely remained in commercial use until the later C20, and this account runs through until then.

Well before the first true canals, Andrew Yarranton (1619–84) sought a series of RIVER IMPROVEMENTS in Worcestershire. From 1664 to 1666 he spent £1,255 on making the Stour navigable between Stourbridge and Kidderminster (Worcs.), including work on locks, artificial channels, widening, sluices, weirs etc. His improvements required constant maintenance for breaches, floods and damage, until some time in 1680, when all of his works were destroyed by 'a sudden and violent flood'.

Yarranton's scheme included 'trenches' (artificial cuts), which a century later would be better known as CANALS. These began in the region with the Birmingham Canal, one of the first in the country that did not seek to extend or connect natural rivers. By 1838 a network of nearly 200 route miles was developed within Birmingham and the Black Country, off which many more miles of wharfs, arms and branches were built. The principal lines were as follows:

- Birmingham Canal Navigation (Old Line and branches) (26¾ m.), engineer *James Brindley*. Opened in stages from its Birmingham end, 1769–72. The first section, from Paradise Street Wharf to Wednesbury (1769), immediately reduced coal prices from 11d. to 6d. per hundredweight. Continued to Wolverhampton in 1771. The canal reached the Staffordshire and Worcestershire Canal (*see* below) at Aldersley, just s of Autherley (Wo), via a flight of twenty-one locks, opened 1772.
- Staffordshire and Worcestershire Canal (46½ m.), opened 1771–2. The Digbeth branch (1 m.) around the centre of Birmingham was opened in 1799.
- Stourbridge Canal (5⅝ m.), completed 1779. Proposed and built at the same time as the Dudley Canal (*see* below) to connect Lord Dudley's mines and works to the Staffordshire and Worcestershire at Stourton (Staffs.).
- Dudley No. 1 Canal (2⅛ m.), completed 1779; Dudley to Tipton (Sa) (2½ m.), completed 1792. The first stage (cost £9,700) ran from a junction with the Stourbridge line at Black Delph, with a close flight of nine locks, to the Park Head area of Woodside, where a reservoir was built. The extension (cost £50,000) linked with the Birmingham line at Tipton Green, and included a 3,172-yd (2,900-metre) tunnel beneath Dudley, the fifth-longest canal tunnel in England at that time.
- Birmingham and Fazeley Canal (20¾ m.), engineer *Robert Whitworth*, opened 1789.
- Wyrley and Essington Canal (10⅝ m.), opened 1794 to the Birmingham Canal Navigation near Wolverhampton, with an extension to the Birmingham and Fazeley Canal via Bloxwich, Pelsall and Brownhills (all Wa), opened 1797.
- Dudley No. 2 Canal (11⅝ m.), opened 1798. From the Dudley Canal to Halesowen, Lapal (D) and on to Selly Oak (B), with a 3,795-yd (3,470-metre) tunnel at Lapal.
- Walsall Canal (6¾ m.), opened 1799 from Broadwater in Wednesbury to Walsall, with three branches.
- Birmingham Canal Navigation New Line (4¾ m.), 1826–38. Surveyed by *Thomas Telford*. Opened between Birmingham and Smethwick (Sa) 1827, through Smethwick Cutting 1829, between Bloomfield and Deepfields (including a tunnel at Coseley) 1837, completed with the 'Island Line' 1838. The work included a reservoir at Rotton Park, Edgbaston (B).
- Worcester and Birmingham Canal (30 m.), original surveyor *Josiah Clowes*. Opened from Birmingham (Gas Street Basin)

to Selly Oak 1795, Kings Norton 1796, Hopwood 1802, and Worcester 1815.
- Stratford-upon-Avon Canal (25½ m.), opened from Kings Norton through Earlswood to Hockley Heath 1796, to Kingswood (Warwick and Birmingham Canal, *see* below) 1802, and Stratford 1816.
- Warwick and Birmingham Canal (22½ m.), opened from Digbeth 1800.
- Stourbridge Extension Canal (2 m., plus branches), opened 1840–1. Promoted by the Stourbridge Canal Co. Intended to go to Gornal, it reached only as far as Oak Farm in Kingswinford, with branches to the Shutt (or Shut) End and Corbyns Hall ironworks, to Ketley Colliery (the Sandhills Branch), and to collieries in Bromley.
- Bentley Canal (3⅜ m.), opened 1843. Linking the Birmingham Canal Navigation and the Wyrley and Essington Canal.
- Tame Valley Canal (8⅜ m.), opened 1844. A link between the Walsall Canal at Ocker Hill and the Birmingham and Fazeley Canal at Salford (B).
- Birmingham and Warwick Junction Canal (2¾ m.), from Salford to the Warwick and Birmingham at Bordesley, opened 1844.

Early survivals of CANAL STRUCTURES are mostly earthworks, locks (mostly rebuilt), tunnels and some brick bridges. The Fazeley line has several of the last: Berwood Bridge, Pype

Sandwell, Tipton, Birmingham Canal Navigation, *c.* 1769–72.
Engraving, C19

Hayes (B); Cottage Lane, Minworth, Sutton Coldfield; Wiggins Hill, Sutton. Little's Lane Bridge in Wolverhampton on the Birmingham Canal is another. Improvements to the Stratford Canal between 1813 and 1823, engineer *William Whitmore*, produced the Earlswood Lakes reservoirs (So) and the rare guillotine lock at Kings Norton. *Thomas Telford*'s New Line of the Birmingham Canal (1825–9) has left many remains: the beautiful cast-iron Galton Bridge at Smethwick (Sa) and the Engine Arm Aqueduct nearby; the tremendously deep Smethwick cutting; Edgbaston Reservoir; and aqueducts at e.g. Puppy Green, Tipton (Sa). The Tame Valley Canal has deep cuttings, high bridges and the Hamstead Aqueduct. In 1855–8 *Walker, Burges & Cooper* built the Netherton Tunnel, 3,027 yds (2,768 metres) long, and reconstructed the locks at Delph, Brierley Hill (D). From 1846 the Birmingham Canal fell under the influence of the London & North Western Railway, which encouraged its use for local traffic and built transfer basins for longer-distance cargoes. One late transfer basin, Chillington, of 1902, survives off Bilston Road, Wolverhampton.

CANAL BUILDINGS include two sets of headquarters offices: the Warwick and Birmingham Canal's at Warwick Bar, Fazeley Street, Birmingham, 1843–50 by *Edward John Lloyd*, blue brick classical, and the Stourbridge Canal's *Rundbogenstil* offices and – in its present form – Bonded Warehouse of 1849, at the terminal basin in Amblecote (D), by *Robert Robinson*. Modest canal settlements include the cottages and shop at Dock, Wordsley (D), of 1825, and the *Telford* toll house and stables (and elliptical-arched skew bridge) of the Birmingham and Liverpool Junction at Autherley, Oxley (Wo). Surviving toll houses are otherwise rare, but another of 1841 is at Birchills, Walsall. Much later is the big pumping station at Smethwick of 1892–3, by the canal engineer *G. R. Jebb*. Later C19 concern about the welfare of boatmen produced mission chapels, of which one of 1892–3 survives at Tipton; and the Incorporated Seamen and Boatmen's Friend Society built boatmen's rest rooms, one of which survives at Birchills.

THE INDUSTRIAL DEVELOPMENT OF THE BLACK COUNTRY
BY PAUL COLLINS

In many ways the Black Country is the expression on the surface of the area's 10-yd (9-metre)-thick seam of coal, upon which much of its wealth was founded. The first use of the term is often attributed to Elihu Burritt, the American Consul to Birmingham, whose *Walks in the Black Country and Its Green Border-Land* (1868) described the area as 'black by day and red by night, [which] cannot be matched, for vast and varied production, by any other space of equal radius on the surface of the globe'. The area had been heavily industrialized from after 1760, and by 1820 the die was cast as to what constituted the original Black Country. Three innovations in particular brought it into existence: the artificial cut (canal; see above), the mineral blast furnace and the puddling furnace. However, this pre-eminence was built upon a much longer history of industrial activity. There is evidence of COAL MINING from the late C12. In 1720 production was c. 100,000 tons, by 1805 1 million tons, by 1864 7 million tons. The ready availability of coal helps explain the large numbers of SMITHS recorded in the area by the C16. The Birmingham poet and historian William Hutton, visiting the area in 1741, was 'surprized at the prodigious number of blacksmiths' shops upon the road; and could not conceive how a country, though populous, could support so many people of the same occupation' (*An History of Birmingham*, 1781). NAIL MAKING, which also had its origins in the Middle Ages, was notable by that time in Sedgley (D), the Gornals (D) and elsewhere. GLASS was manufactured in the Stourbridge (D) area from the C17 by itinerant French glassmakers from the Lorraine region, attracted both by the resources of coal and by the fireclay in the Amblecote and Brettell Lane districts, which has the highest silica content of any in the country. IRON SMELTING was well established by the C17. Another key natural resource for this industry was water, to power forges. Indeed, a survey in the 1990s found evidence of forty-two such sites between Halesowen and Wordsley (both D) alone. One of the first of these works was leased in 1627 by Richard Foley of Stourbridge, who reputedly introduced the slitting mill to England. Dud Dudley, who managed his father's furnaces on Pensnett Chase (D), claimed to have made good iron with 'pit-cole' and produced good merchantable bar in 1619, ninety years before Abraham Darby's achievement at Coalbrookdale in Shropshire.

The Black Country lacked major navigable waterways, so the movement of goods before the arrival of canals was confined to local roads, whose condition was less than ideal. In 1781 Hutton called the road to Dudley 'despicable beyond description', and described that to Halesowen as 'like the life of man, chequered with good and evil, chiefly the latter'. A partial solution came in the form of TURNPIKE ROADS, the tolls on which were weighted against traffic which did the most damage. They were administered by trusts, with the toll money used for the upkeep and repair of the roads. Eleven turnpike trusts were established in the area, beginning in 1727 with the roads from Birmingham to Wednesbury (Sa), Bilston (Wo), Dudley and Kingswinford (D), and concluding in 1816 with the road between Stourbridge and Bridgnorth (Shropshire).

Individual Black Country TOWNS came to be known for particular industries or products, e.g. Cradley Heath (D) (anchors and chains), Darlaston (Wa) (bolts), Lye (D) (nails), Stourbridge (glass), Walsall (saddlery) and Willenhall (Wa) (locks).* Specialization came about for a variety of reasons. Black Country people worked hard, but were often poorly paid and treated. Their main 'currency' was their skills, which were transferrable to other firms in the same or related industries. A skilled lock-maker in Willenhall could find similar work more easily within that town than elsewhere. Firms in the same trade also proliferated through family disagreement, leading to new businesses being established in the same town, drawing upon the same pool of skilled workers. Traditionally, women, too, played a greater role in industry than elsewhere. The strike of the 'white slave' women chain-makers in Cradley Heath in 1910 is well known; less well appreciated are those women who ran their own businesses, or the widows and daughters who continued to run those of deceased husbands or fathers. However, simple town–trade pairings may overlook the fact that, for instance, Stourbridge had more curriers (where the noxious processes required to turn animal skins into leather began) than Walsall ever did. Similarly, the more than thirty works which comprised the Stourbridge glass industry were not in that town at all, but clustered around Amblecote and Wordsley (D).

The Black Country came to be served by a vast network of RAILWAYS, and also played an important role in railway history. Between 1819 and 1831 it was home to the pioneering engineer *John Urpeth Rastrick*. With *James Foster* of Stourbridge, he built the Shutt End Railway in 1826–9 to link Lord Dudley's collieries at Pensnett with Ashwood on the Staffordshire and Worcestershire Canal. The line had an inclined plane at each end, but its central section was level enough to permit the use of a steam locomotive, Rastrick's *Agenoria*. Eight years passed before the next lines opened in or near the Black Country, beginning in 1837 with the Grand Junction Railway from Birmingham to Wolverhampton and northwards, and the greater part of the London & Birmingham Railway, amalgamated in 1846 as the London &

---

*The following, more detailed digest is derived mostly from William White's *Directory of Staffordshire* (1851). Amblecote, glass manufacture, fireclay and ironworks. Audnam (Stourbridge), bottle- and flint-glassworks. Bilston, japanned goods, enamelled ware, iron. Bloxwich, mining, and manufacturing of locks, buckles, bits and stirrups, needles. Bradley, coal and ironworks. Brettell Lane (Amblecote), coarse pottery, flint glass, iron and fireclay. Brierley Hill, glass, chains, boilers, spades and fireclay products. Coseley, coal and nail making. Cradley Heath, chain making. Darlaston, bolts, nuts, screws, gun locks, railway ironwork, bridges and girders etc. Delph, nail making and firebricks. Dudley, bedsteads, fenders and fire-irons. Ettingshall, iron and coal. Great Bridge, engineering. Halesowen, weldless tubes, steel forgings, buttons, gun barrels. Heath Town, iron goods, coal and ironstone. Kingswinford, coal, ironstone, ironworks and brickworks. Rowley Regis, quarrying, nail, anchor, chain and rivet making. Sedgley with Upper and Lower Gornal, fireclay and coal mining. Shutt End, coal and ironworks. Stourbridge, ironworks, curriers and saddlers. Tipton, heavy articles such as forgings, boilers, anchors and railway goods. Wallheath, spades and shovels. Walsall, harness, saddlery and saddlers' ironmongery. Wednesbury, iron works, coal and clay. Wednesfield, locks and keys. West Bromwich, small metal goods, foundries and forges. Willenhall, locks, bolts, latches, keys, gridirons, hinges, ferrules and other small metal goods. Wolverhampton, ironmongery, hardware, locks and keys, safes, iron and tin japanned goods, *papier mâché* articles, tea trays and shoe-tips. Wordsley, glassworks.

North Western Railway. Within the wider region, further lines connected Birmingham with Gloucester (1840) and with Derby (1842), both later merged within the Midland Railway. Other early main lines include the Shrewsbury & Birmingham (1849) and the Oxford, Worcester & Wolverhampton (1852–4), which were taken over by the Great Western Railway, chief rival to the LNWR. The South Staffordshire Railway (1847–50) and Stourbridge Railway (1863–7) were among the more significant local companies.

As with canals, branch lines were built to serve large industrial concerns, such as the New British Iron Company's works at Corngreaves in Cradley (D). Of private industrial railways, the Shutt End became part of the Earl of Dudley's Pensnett Railway system, begun in 1846. This developed into one of the largest private mineral railways in the UK, an almost 40-mile system centred upon the Round Oak Iron & Steel Works, with its own locomotive and wagon shops. In total, 331 firms within the Black Country had internal railway systems, of which 28 per cent served collieries and 27 per cent iron/steel works.

Canals and railways coexisted well in the Black Country. Many of the former came under railway control when the LNWR acquired the Birmingham Canal Navigations company, largely because its canals penetrated deep into areas whose railways were dominated by the Great Western. Both companies, plus the Midland Railway, also invested in large transhipment sheds, where goods could be transferred between canal, rail and road, each served by their own branch rail line.

Black Country industry declined through the C20, and has continued to do so. Coal mining was one of the first to go, hampered by the effects of piecemeal digging, a dearth of surveys, and the lack of an overall drainage system. Many mines were abandoned to flooding, and by the 1930s the region's coal came mainly from Cannock in Staffordshire. Baggeridge Colliery, sunk in 1912 just outside the area covered by this book, maintained Black Country mining until its closure in 1968. The iron industry ended with the closure of steelworks at Bilston (1980), Patent Shaft in Wednesbury (1980) and Round Oak in Brierley Hill (1982). The 1980s also saw the closure of large industrial employers such as F.H. Lloyd in Wednesbury, and Chance's glassworks and the Birmid foundries in Smethwick. Despite these closures, in the 2011 census nearly 70,000 residents declared their occupation as manufacturing, more than in Birmingham and Coventry combined, and a greater proportion than in any other English Metropolitan County area. The census also showed that more than a third of this employment is still in metal products, machinery, electrical and electronic equipment, vehicles etc.

PHYSICAL REMAINS of the Black Country's historic industries, especially of its heavier branches such as mining and iron- and steel-making, are few and far between. Yet much does survive. Many company offices, having road frontages and architectural presence, have outlived the factories they served. Here and there, remnants of smaller trades and industries that exploited outworking – such as chain and nail making, hollowware and saddlery – stand forlorn in back gardens. In contrast, the infrastructure that knitted the Black Country's communities together has fared much better, with an abundance of churches, Nonconformist chapels and schools. Traces of past civic pride and munificence are also to be found everywhere, in the form of hospitals, dispensaries, Board Schools, civic and town halls, Urban District Council offices, swimming baths and public parks. Canals have similarly fared well, largely thanks to the actions of preservationists from the late 1950s onwards; but while the main lines survive in leisure use, many arms and basins are now features that only a knowledgeable eye can discern. Some disused railways, such as the Pensnett Railway, survive as landscape features, walks and cycle ways, but much of the system has succumbed to 'reshaping'. Electric traction, by trams and trolleybuses, came and went too, but each has left some traces.

VICTORIAN AND EDWARDIAN, c.1830 TO 1914

In these years Birmingham grew from a sprawling town to a great metropolis. Industrial buildings evolved from houses-cum-factories to the large enterprises of the late C19 such as Belliss & Morcom and Heath's. In government the period begins with the creation of the Borough Council in 1838 and ends with the grant of city status in 1889, reflected in buildings from the Town Hall to the Law Courts. In 1890 Birmingham was called 'the best governed city in the world' by *Harper's Monthly Magazine* of New York.

In the Black Country the period to 1860 marked the end of the enormous expansion of industry, based on coal and iron, and centred in the W on the Dudley estate. There are a few industrial survivors (*see* above), but the most obvious sign of this prosperity is in some of the smaller towns – Bilston, Oldbury, Willenhall – which retain a Late Georgian or Early Victorian look.

Anglican and Roman Catholic churches, to c.1890

The 1830s saw many new CHURCHES, most more modest than those of the 1820s, partly reflecting the smaller grants available by then from the Church Building Commission. The typical 1830s church has a wide, unaisled nave and short chancel (almost always rebuilt since), and rather basic Gothic trimmings: regular buttresses, lancet windows. Examples include St John the Evangelist, Perry Barr (B) (*Robert Studholme*), St Margaret, Ward End (B) (*John Frith*), and St James the Great, Shirley (So) (*Robert Ebbels*). Later examples include a group by *Ebbels*: St Paul, Tipton (Sa) (1837–9), St James, Handsworth (B) (1838–40), and St Peter, Upper Gornal (D) (1840–2), with a reduced King's College

Chapel-type front. Others include St Matthew, Duddeston (B) (*William Thomas*, 1839–40), St Peter, Walsall (*Thomas Smith* with *Isaac Highway*, 1839–41), Holy Trinity, West Bromwich (Sa) (*S.W. Daukes*, 1840–1), and St Michael and All Angels, Pelsall (Wa) (*George E. Hamilton*, 1843). Even *Rickman & Hussey* used a regular buttresses-and-lancets elevation at Christ Church, Quinton (B) (1839–40), though this does have a three-sided apse. Black Country conservatism, a recurring feature, continued the type to the mid C19: St James, Wednesbury (Sa) (*William Horton*, 1847–8) and, with more historically accurate massing, St James, Brownhills (Wa) (*G.T. Robinson*, 1850–1) and All Saints, Moxley, Darlaston (Wa) (*William Horton*, 1850–1). The major accent in many of these buildings was the w tower. *William Bourne*'s churches of 1838–40 in Dudley, St James and St John, are of this type, and particularly grand. The chief alternative to Gothic was Neo-Norman. Both surviving examples use Staffordshire blue brick: *Thomas Smith*'s St John, Brockmoor (D) (1844–5), with a delightful contrast of yellow firebrick details, and *H.J. Whitling* and *D.R. Hill*'s St John the Evangelist, Walmley, Sutton Coldfield (1843–5). The only classical scheme of the period is at St Thomas, Wednesfield (Wo), where *Wyatt & Brandon* in 1842–3 followed the style of the previous church and retained tower.

For the arrival of archaeologically correct and convincing Gothic we must look to Catholic churches and *A.W.N. Pugin*. The change of approach is visible in his St Chad's Cathedral, Birmingham, 1839–41, with its reduction of window area compared to wall, and irregular and picturesque but functional grouping. St Chad's is early Pugin, with Continental sources, not quite the perfect evocation of C14 English work which he achieved later. Its impact, both as a major Gothic building and as a sign of the new status of Catholicism, was great. The Birmingham Church Building Society (the 'Ten Churches Fund'), an Anglican and Tory project to build churches in poor areas near the centre, commissioned two churches by *R.C. Carpenter*, the 'Anglican Pugin': St Stephen, New Town Row (1842–3) and St Andrew, Bordesley (1844–6), both now demolished. The Ecclesiological Society, the Anglican group dedicated to creating fully neo-medieval churches, shared Pugin's ideal of the early C14 Decorated style, though one of the two best early Ecclesiological examples in the area is in C13 (Early English) style: St Mark, Pensnett (D), by *J.M. Derick*, 1846–9.

The finest church of these decades by a local architect, however, is Holy Trinity, Heath Town (Wo), of 1850–2 by *Edward Banks* of Wolverhampton. Banks was a new phenomenon, at least outside Birmingham: a highly competent local architect who was also a leading figure in his community, who would have become mayor but for his untimely death. Holy Trinity follows Ecclesiological ideas in both its Decorated style and its medieval plan, with a confidence which goes beyond imitation. Other examples by local architects are *Thomas Smith*'s E parts of Christ Church, Lye (D) (1846–7), *Hamilton & Saunders*'s St Mark, Ocker Hill, Tipton (Sa) (1848–9) in blue brick, and *F.W. Fiddian*'s St Silas,

Lozells (B) (1854). *William Bourne*'s St Michael, Handsworth of 1854–5 shows his acceptance of the new ideas, as does *Joseph James*'s contemporary St Matthew, Windmill Lane, Smethwick (Sa). *Thomas Johnson* of Lichfield, the architect of the remarkable All Saints, Leigh, Staffordshire of 1846, did St Peter, Greets Green, West Bromwich in 1857–8, with consistent features of *c.* 1300 and the feel of a medieval country church. St Philip, Penn Fields (Wo), by *Griffin & Weller*, 1858–9, is a competent Dec job.

The 1850s and 1860s were the heyday of a group of Gothic architects who used a picturesque and fanciful style with much originality of detail, the people whom H. S. Goodhart Rendel called 'rogue' architects. *S. S. Teulon* designed St James, Edgbaston (B) (1850–2) – for the 3rd Lord Calthorpe, a Low Church Evangelical, like many of Teulon's patrons – and St John the Evangelist, Ladywood (B) (1852–4), although neither is among his most extraordinary designs. Among local architects, *James Cranston* used this manner at St Michael the Archangel, Rushall (Wa) of 1854–68, where the tower has buttresses running straight into the spire broaches. The young *George Bidlake*'s St James, Wollaston (D), 1859–60, is another example. The most extraordinary practitioner was *G.T. Robinson*, for his cross-gabled w tower added to St Patrick, Earlswood (So) in 1860–1, and the contemporary St Luke, Blakenhall (Wo), an ebullient fantasy of multicoloured brick (in this respect influenced by William Butterfield).

From about 1860 a different generation of architects took over. *J.A. Chatwin* of Birmingham, the most significant and prolific, started in a 'rogue' manner, as at St Clement, Nechells (B) of 1859 (mostly demolished) and Holy Trinity, Birchfield (B) of 1863–4. His later output was more conventional, but is distinguished by his mastery of proportion, as might be expected from someone trained as a classicist by Charles Barry. His best work is the rebuilding of Aston parish church (B) from 1879. His rebuildings of St Martin in the Bull Ring, Birmingham (1872–5) and St Mary, Handsworth (1876–8) are also solid and confident, respecting existing fabric where he could. He also designed good cheap brick churches, such as the Catholic Apostolic Church in Summer Hill Terrace, Birmingham of 1873 (with notable polychromy in the Butterfield manner) and St Mary, Bearwood Road, Smethwick of 1887–8. The chancel he added to St Philip, Birmingham (now the Cathedral) in 1883–4 is a splendid essay in classicism, with Corinthian columns set forward under extensions of the internal entablature. He also added many new E ends to earlier churches, such as St John, Ladywood (1881) and St Barnabas, Erdington (B) (1883). In the 1880s he started to use the Perpendicular style, at e.g. Christ Church, Summerfield Crescent, Birmingham. Other competent Gothic Revivalists include *W.D. Griffin* (St Margaret, Great Barr (Wa), 1862, and the rebuilding of St Giles, Willenhall (Wa), 1866–7), *Edward Holmes* (St Mary, Selly Oak (B), 1860–1), *J.T. Meredith* (Holy Trinity, Old Hill, Rowley Regis (Sa), 1875–7), and *George Bidlake* in his later work (e.g. St Jude, Wolverhampton, 1867–9).

VICTORIAN AND EDWARDIAN, c.1830 TO 1914   37

Of London architects, only two great national figures are represented by churches in the area. *G.E. Street*'s St John the Evangelist, Stourbridge (D) of 1860–1 is a good, economical example of his Continental-influenced High Victorian manner; his All Saints, Darlaston of 1871–2 was destroyed in the Second World War. St Alban, Highgate (B) is a major work of *J.L. Pearson*'s late style, with austerity of detail, mastery of proportion, and stone vaulting throughout. Other Londoners include *Somers Clarke Jun.*, who rebuilt All Saints, West Bromwich, in 1871–2; *E.F. C. Clarke* for St Paul, Wood Green Road, Wednesbury, 1872–4; *T. Tayler Smith* and *G.F. Roper*, for the tough All Saints, Wolverhampton, 1877–9; and *Frederick Preedy* (originally of Worcestershire) at St Anne, Moseley (B), confident High Victorian of 1873–4, and the gentler St Peter, Pedmore (D), as rebuilt in 1869–71. The s part of the area is in Worcester diocese (as was Birmingham until 1905), and the Worcester architect *W.J. Hopkins* designed the economical but effective St Paul, Blackheath, Halesowen (D), 1868–9.

65

Street's influence can be seen in churches such as *F.B. Osborn*'s St Cyprian, Hay Mills (B), 1873–4. *Bateman & Corser* designed a number of churches with prominently gabled aisles and apses, influenced by Street and Butterfield but also the 'rogues'. The best survivor is Christ Church, Tettenhall Wood (Wo), 1865–6. *J.H. Chamberlain*'s one Anglican church, St Stephen, Selly Oak (B) of 1870–1, is also in a High Victorian manner with Street and Butterfield among its sources. St John the Evangelist, Sparkhill (B), by *Martin & Chamberlain* of 1888–95, after J.H. Chamberlain's death, is also in a tough Gothic style, in brick, but with a short, wide cruciform plan, a Low Church preaching place.

Victorian CHURCH RESTORATIONS begin with St Mary, Aldridge (Wa), where the young *George Gilbert Scott* added an aisle in 1841, and a full restoration was undertaken by *Anthony Salvin* in 1851–3, including French Flamboyant window tracery. *Ewan Christian*'s work at St Peter, Wolverhampton, mostly of 1852–7, includes an impressive new E arm, replacing a rebuilding of 1682–4, and a w front which destroyed surviving Norman work. He also restored the chancels at Kings Norton (B) and Walsall. At St Leonard, Bilston (Wo), in 1882–3, he altered and refitted the Late Georgian church. *Edward Banks* rebuilt the much-altered nave and aisles of Bushbury church (Wo) in 1851–3, leaving the medieval tower and chancel. *William Bourne* was active in Dudley, altering St Mary, Kingswinford and updating St James's church with an extended chancel, inserted arcades and clerestory. His successors, *Davies & Middleton*, did the same to St John's church, Dudley in 1872–3. *Joseph Nevill* rebuilt the s side of Bickenhill church (So) in 1855–6. At Halesowen the undistinguished *Henry Curzon* was replaced by *Scott* in 1873–5. Two Georgian parish churches were completely recast round the earlier structure: All Saints, Bloxwich (Wa) (*Davies & Middleton*, 1875–7), and St Lawrence, Darlaston (*A.P. Brevitt*, 1871–2, in an extraordinary S.S. Teulon manner). *W.J. Hopkins*'s restoration of Kings Norton church in 1870–2 marks the start of a new approach, because a protest by historians stopped him removing the gabled C17 roofs of the S aisle.

Reordering has removed many Victorian church FITTINGS in recent years, but a few substantial Anglican ensembles remain, and one or two almost complete original interiors. *Lewis Stride*'s screens, stalls and pulpit of 1849 at St Mark, Pensnett, are early survivals. *Edward Banks*'s Holy Trinity, Heath Town (Wo) of 1850–2 still has its nave fittings. *J.A. Chatwin*'s fittings of 1863–4 at Holy Trinity, Birchfield are a precious survival. Several Chatwin churches retain his characteristic choir stalls with scrolled tops to the ends, including St Mary, Handsworth (with other chancel fittings) and St Mary, Moseley. St Peter and St Paul, Aston (B), has his richest set, of 1883, with other surviving fittings, despite the sad loss of the dado screen. St Martin in the Bull Ring retains chancel fittings of 1875–6. St Augustine and St Bartholomew in Edgbaston both have nearly complete Chatwin ensembles; St Mary and St Ambrose, Edgbaston has very late fittings of 1897–1901. Other remarkably complete interiors are at *F.B. Osborn*'s St Cyprian, Hay Mills, *Edward Holmes*'s St Mary, Selly Oak (for the font *see* below), and *Preedy*'s St Peter, Pedmore. Christ Church, Blakenall (Wa), has most of its *Thomas Naden* fittings of 1868–70. St James, Dudley retains *William Bourne*'s fittings of 1869. Many of *George Bidlake*'s fittings survive at St Jude, Wolverhampton. Halesowen still has *Scott*'s nave fittings of 1875. St John, Sparkhill has some *Martin & Chamberlain* fittings of 1888. Significant C19 fonts include three by *Peter Hollins*: at Darlaston (1848), St Silas, Lozells (1854) and St Paul, Birmingham (1883), a late classical design. *Butterfield*'s font of 1861 at St Mary, Selly Oak is equally sculptural. St Thomas, Dudley has an elaborate medieval re-creation by *Edward Blore*, 1867, carved by *James Forsyth*. *Pearson*'s font at St Alban, Highgate, 1881, is of bright red veined stone. There are many good fonts by local architects, such as *J. Drayton Wyatt*'s at St John, Wolverhampton, 1866, and *W.D. Griffin*'s eight-sided wineglass at St Margaret, Great Barr, 1863. Among pulpits there are other good *Chatwin* examples at Aston (his finest) and St George, Edgbaston, both of 1885, at All Saints, Stechford (B) and St Mary, Moseley, both of 1898, and at Oldswinford (D), as late as 1903. Others worth mention are at All Saints, Bloxwich, by *Davies & Middleton*, 1875–7, with portrait heads carved by *John Roddis*; at St Lawrence, Darlaston, 1872 by *A.P. Brevitt*, alas painted; and at St Margaret, Great Barr, by *Walter Tapper*, of alabaster, 1895. St Mary, Bushbury has an exceptionally conservative twin pulpit and reading desk of 1878: a fashion of the 1830s and 1840s.

Of ROMAN CATHOLIC churches apart from St Chad's, *A.W.N. Pugin*'s only commissions in the area were Our Lady, Dudley of 1839–40, damagingly altered, and the mortuary chapel at Nechells of 1850, in his mature Decorated style. *Charles Hansom* imitated his style for clients who found Pugin difficult to deal with. Good examples are St Thomas and St Edmund (Erdington Abbey) (B), 1848–50, and St Mary and St John, Wolverhampton, 1852–5, completed as late as 1880. *E.W. Pugin* succeeded to his father's practice and developed his own, immediately recognizable style, using brick, combining English and German C13 and C14 elements, with very tall, attenuated proportions, exaggerated decoration and complex timber roofs. His most important church in the area is Our Lady and All Saints, Stourbridge, 1863–4. More modest are St Mary, Brierley Hill (D) of 1872–3, and the extension of his father's mortuary chapel as St Joseph, Nechells, 1872. *Gilbert Blount* at St Mary, Wednesbury, 1873–4, and *Dunn & Hansom* at St Mary, Harborne (B), 1875–7, followed the Pugins' manner. The tradition carries on at *Albert Vicars*'s St Anne, Deritend (B), 1883–4. The exception is the Oratorians, because of John Henry Newman's dislike of Gothic. They used *John Hungerford Pollen* for the Oratory's St Philip's Chapel, Italian Romanesque of 1858, and the chapel of 1856–7 at the Oratory House at Rednal (B).

CATHOLIC CHURCH FITTINGS of the period begin with two exceptional ensembles by *Pugin*, Gothic incorporating imported Continental furnishings. Oscott College Chapel (Sutton Coldfield) of 1838 includes stalls with Flemish C17 or early C18 rear seats, and a reredos with C15 and C16 panels and paintings by *J.R. Herbert*. St Chad's Cathedral, despite a famously damaging 1960s reordering, retains a C16 Flemish pulpit and stalls, and an important Pugin high altar. E end fittings elsewhere include Fr *John Ullathorne*'s Gothic high altar and reredos of 1880 at St Mary and St John, Wolverhampton, and the side altars in *Vicars*'s St Anne, Deritend. *Pugin* also revived the art of memorial brasses. His first, of 1841 to Bishop Milner, based on a C14 prototype, is at Oscott College. Another is at St Peter and St Paul, Wolverhampton. *Hardmans* made these, and several other later C19 examples.

CATHOLIC RELIGIOUS INSTITUTIONS of the period start with *A.W.N. Pugin*'s Convent of the Sisters of Mercy in Hunters Road, Handsworth, 1840–1, extended in 1850, in a simple brick domestic Gothic style which was extraordinarily radical at that date. The best later building is *Dunn & Hansom*'s tough and vigorous Gothic range at Olton Friary (So) of 1873.

Chapels and other places of worship, to c.1890

When looking at Nonconformist chapels one must first realize how many have gone, especially the grand Victorian chapels: in Birmingham including the Church of the Messiah of 1860–1 by *J.J. Bateman*, and the Church of the Redeemer of 1881–2 by *James Cubitt*; and in Wolverhampton the Queen Street Congregational Church, Italianate of 1863–6 by *George Bidlake*. Very few large Victorian or Edwardian chapels survive in their original use. Many small chapels in Black Country villages have also disappeared.

Late Georgian and Early Victorian chapels show the persistence of classicism. Ruiton chapel, Gornal (D), of 1830 by *Edward Marsh*, is a severe classical box with pediment and corner pilasters. Marsh, who called himself a 'surveyor', was one of the earliest Black Country architects. The standard Georgian design of three-bay front, basic pediment, central entrance and round-headed windows appears frequently: Five Ways Methodist, Lower Gornal (1841); Zion Methodist, Halesowen (1842); Upper Ettingshall Methodist, Coseley (D) (1850). Froysell Street Methodist, Willenhall (*c.* 1856) and Ebenezer Baptist, Coseley (1857–8) are dignified with pilasters. At Tipton Street Primitive Methodist, Sedgley (D) (*Hamlet Durose*, 1857–8), the basic scheme has acquired Jacobean trim, including a big shaped gable. The Wesleyan chapel, Oldbury (Sa), of 1853, is expanded to four bays and two doorways, a very Nonconformist denial of central emphasis. The standard design continues through the 1860s, sometimes with full-height windows. Hurst Hill Methodist, Coseley, 1864–5, is a reduced temple with pilasters all round. Ebenezer Baptist, Netherton (D), 1864 by *H. Grosvenor*, is similar. Ebenezer Primitive Methodist, Halesowen, 1868, has some brick polychromy. Strict Baptists remained faithful to the standard classical front. Providence Chapel, Bell End, Rowley, by a mining engineer, *William Keen*, 1875, is a good example, but with polychromy and a 'Baalbek' arch in the cornice. Until its mutilation in 2018, the most charming late example was Upper Lichfield Street Baptist, Willenhall, by *Charles Manton*, 1862, with its rustic Doric temple front. Even the grander Highbury Independent (Congregational) Chapel, Graham Street, Birmingham, 1844, now a Sikh temple, is an expansion of the basic type, with five bays and a slightly projecting centre. Mount Tabor Methodist New Connexion, Woodsetton, Coseley, 1859, is a smaller, single-storey version. The only notable SYNAGOGUE of the period, *Yeoville Thomason*'s Singers Hill, Birmingham, of 1855–6, is also classical: grand Italianate but with hints of Wren inside.

Occasionally different classical designs were used. The Wesleyan chapel, Bath Street, Birmingham, of 1839, has a severe trabeated front with basic pilasters. The former Little London Baptist Chapel, Willenhall of 1851, probably by *Henry Hall*, is a grander but incoherent version of this type, with a central attic. *J.R. Botham*'s Presbyterian chapel, Broad Street, Birmingham, 1849, has a (ritual) W tower in the Late Georgian church tradition, and a massive doorcase, though the body of the chapel is conventional enough. Equally grand, and unusual, is *Edward Banks*'s twin-towered Baroque refronting and recasting of Trinity Methodist, Willenhall, 1864.

Gothic chapels start with the still Georgian lancet design of Erdington Congregational, 1839. Full Victorian Gothic arrives with Sedgley Congregational, 1856–7 by (*George*) *Bidlake & Lovatt*, in a confident and correct Decorated style. The Unitarian chapel at Lye by *Francis Smalman Smith*, 1857–61, is a more larky High Victorian design, alas missing its spire. Christ Church Baptist, Aston, by *James Cranston*, 1864–5, now flats, is a vigorous and convincing design with much polychromy and a pinnacled spire. Coseley Old Meeting House, 1874–5 by *T.H. Fleeming*, is much smaller but prestigious, in an equally convincing early C14 Geometrical style. Other Gothic chapels in Black Country villages include Primrose Hill Congregational at Netherton of 1887 by *Alfred E. Hill*, and the Methodist church at Short Heath, Willenhall by *Benjamin Baker*, 1881–2. *George Ingall* was a significant figure in Birmingham. Much of his work has gone, and his finest chapel, Umberslade Baptist, is in nearby Warwickshire, but the city still has a much-altered Unitarian chapel in Fazeley Street of 1876–7, and the former Congregational church in Sutton Coldfield of 1879–80. The finest Birmingham architect of Nonconformist chapels, however, was *J.H. Chamberlain (Martin & Chamberlain)*. The Methodist church in Harborne of 1868 is a fine example of his early style, contrasting plain brick with pieces of rich detailing. His Selly Park Baptist Church of 1876–7 also survives. In West Bromwich, *Edward Pincher* designed Beeches Road Methodist of 1871–2 in Italian Renaissance style, and Ryders Green Methodist, 1873–4, in a dour round-arched brick style, its interior remarkably intact. *Thomas Flewett*'s Smethwick Baptist Church of 1877 is the very end of classical chapel design, with rich detail and a giant Corinthian order.

The 1880s produced larger Gothic chapels: Hatherton Presbyterian, Walsall, 1881–2 by *John Cotton* and *H.H. McConnal*, and two fine Baptist survivors in Birmingham suburbs by the young *J.P. Osborne*, at Hamstead Road, Handsworth and Moseley. *Thomas Robinson*'s big gabled Congregational chapel in Brierley Hill, 1882, shares in this new civic confidence in the context of a small Black Country town. Two Gothic chapels of the 1880s by younger architects who became figures in the Arts and Crafts Movement are *J.L. Ball*'s Asbury Memorial Methodist Church, Handsworth, with its Butterfieldian saddleback tower, and *Crouch & Butler*'s Presbyterian chapel, Long Acre, Nechells.

Many CEMETERY CHAPELS have been demolished, the finest being *Charles Edge*'s Greek temple in Key Hill cemetery, Birmingham, 1836, and *Hamilton & Medland*'s Gothic chapel, with tower and spire, at Warstone Lane cemetery nearby, 1847–8. The Nonconformist chapel at Halesowen, by *Francis Smalman Smith*, 1858–9, is steeply gabled 'rogue' Gothic; the Anglican chapel at Witton Cemetery, Erdington, by *Richard Clarke*, 1863, is like a full-sized Gothic church. The normal later pattern is paired Anglican and Nonconformist chapels with a central porch. The finest is Lye and Wollescote, by *Thomas Robinson*, 1877–9, with a central spire. *Smalman Smith*'s contemporary Stourbridge is a tougher design in rock-faced sandstone. This type carried on to the end of the C19, at e.g. Brandwood End (B) by *J. Brewin Holmes*, 1897–9, with a spire precariously perched over a high arched opening, and *Benjamin Baker*'s modest chapels at Willenhall Cemetery (Bentley) of 1898.

Stained glass, to c.1890

Victorian STAINED GLASS began with the rediscovery by *A.W.N. Pugin* of the medieval principle of two-dimensionality, with leading which defines the design. His first in a fully medieval style is the E window at Oscott College of 1838. The maker was *William Warrington*, who also made Pugin's windows in the apse of St Chad's Cathedral of 1841. Pugin later used *William Wailes*, as in the former baptistery at St Chad's, 1843. In 1845 he persuaded his friend and fellow Catholic *John Hardman*, already making metalwork for him, to open a stained-glass studio, and the most important firm in the area was born. The greatest Pugin and Hardman windows here are at St Chad's and Erdington Abbey, of 1849–54. Of later *Hardmans* windows, the best High Victorian sets are at St Laurence, Northfield (B); St Mary, Selly Oak; Holy Trinity, Birchfield; and St Cyprian, Hay Mills. Single windows worth mentioning are at St John, Ladywood, 1866, and St Silas, Lozells, 1868.

An interesting figure in the revival is *Charles Winston*, who achieved the re-creation of glass of medieval quality. At Bushbury he provided designs and advice. The windows were made in 1853 by *Ward & Hughes*, who are best represented at St Giles, Sheldon (B), of 1867. Other national figures include *Lavers & Barraud* at St Luke, Blakenhall (Wo), 1861; *Clayton & Bell* at St Giles, Willenhall, 1867, and St Alban, Highgate, 1883–96; and *O'Connor*, at St Peter, Wolverhampton, 1865.

Later Victorian glass moved towards three-dimensional pictorial compositions. An early and important example is *N.H.J. Westlake*'s windows of 1867 (*Lavers, Barraud & Westlake*) at Christ Church, Coseley. The Aesthetic Movement-influenced windows at All Saints, West Bromwich of 1871–3 were designed by *H.E. Wooldridge* and made by *James Powell & Sons*. Windows worth mentioning by national firms are *Burlison & Grylls*'s at St Matthew, Walsall, 1880–1904, and St George, Edgbaston, 1888; and the important series designed by *H.W. Lonsdale* and made by *Heaton, Butler & Bayne* at the Birmingham Law Courts of 1891. Local firms grew in importance at this time. In the 1850s–60s *Chance*'s of Smethwick made stained glass. Examples are at St Thomas, Stourbridge, designed by *Sebastian Evans*; and Trinity Methodist Church, Willenhall, 1864. When Chance Bros closed, some of their workers set up independently. *Thomas William Camm*, who designed the Willenhall window, worked for many years for the firm of *R.W. Winfield*, as at Christ Church, Lye, 1885; and St Margaret, Olton, 1886/8. Later he set up on his own, from which a fine example is at St John, Brockmoor (D), 1897. *Samuel Evans* was prolific; two of his best commissions are in Smethwick, at Holy Trinity, 1892–3, and St Matthew, 1895. Later, more pictorial sets of *Hardmans* glass, with a tendency to blues and clear lights, are at Our Lady and All Saints (R.C.), Stourbridge, 1875 and 1893 etc.; and St Mary and St John (R.C.), Wolverhampton, 1880–94; also a good E window at St Mary and St Ambrose, Edgbaston, 1898.

Public buildings, to c.1890

One Late Georgian public building stands out: Birmingham Town Hall of 1832–4 and later, by *Hansom & Welch*. Its design,

VICTORIAN AND EDWARDIAN, c.1830 TO 1914

based on the Temple of Castor and Pollux in the Roman Forum, marks the beginning of a Roman Revival in English architecture, here related also to the admiration of Roman republican ideals by the radicals of the Birmingham Political Union, especially Thomas Attwood.

The Town Hall is exceptional as a public building of the 1830s. St Matthew's Hall, Walsall of 1830–1, a small but powerful Greek Revival design probably by *John Fallows*, was built for a subscription library which could not keep it up. Workhouses were created under the Poor Law Act of 1834, though no early buildings survive. Improvement Commissioners had existed in some towns since the C18. However, the Municipal Corporations Act of 1835 allowed the establishment of borough councils in the larger towns: Walsall 1835, Birmingham 1838, Wolverhampton 1848, Dudley 1865. Local Boards of Health in smaller communities were created from 1848. The 1840s saw the growth of police forces: Bilston (Wo) has a modest police station of 1846 by *Joseph Potter Jun.*, and Dudley retains the impressive castle-like gateway of a police complex of 1847 by *Harvey Eginton*. One of the largest public schemes of the time is Birmingham gaol at Winson Green, by *D.R. Hill*, 1845–9, though it has lost its tremendous fortified gateway. Its neighbour is the former Birmingham Asylum, an ample Jacobean Revival design also by *Hill*, 1847–50. The Public Libraries Act of 1850 empowered local councils to provide LIBRARIES. The earliest in the area, and the second oldest surviving purpose-built example in England, is in Goodall Street, Walsall, by *Nichols & Morgan*, 1859. Others are in a scholarly Gothic style: Deritend in Birmingham, by *Bateman & Corser*, 1866, and the first library at West Bromwich (Sa), by *Weller & Proud*, 1874–5.

Victorian TOWN HALLS begin with Sutton Coldfield, now the Masonic Hall, a good Italian Gothic design by *George Bidlake*, 1858–9. The Town Hall at Wolverhampton is thoroughgoing French classical of 1869–71 by *Ernest Bates* of Manchester, where public provision was more advanced. The Guildhall at Walsall was rebuilt as a small but impressive palazzo by *G.B. Nichols*, 1865–7. Equally Italian are the Local Board offices, now library, at Smethwick (Sa), by *Yeoville Thomason*, 1867.

Birmingham, run by 'economists' committed to keeping the rates down, lagged behind in public provision. Between about 1865 and 1890, however, it was consciously made into a great city: the work of the Liberal Party under Joseph Chamberlain, elected to the Town Council in 1869. This was the period of the 'Civic Gospel', the belief that, in the words of the Nonconformist preacher George Dawson, 'A town is a solemn organism through which shall flow, and in which shall be shaped, all the highest and loftiest ends of man's moral nature.' The architectural style of Italian city states was used to dignify growing municipal power and status. The Council House of 1874–9 was the subject of a competition, but councillors chose a local man, *Yeoville Thomason*, rather than the architects recommended by Alfred Waterhouse, the assessor. The result is suitably grand but uninspired French and Italian classical. The extension of 1881–5 for the Art

Gallery, with its portico, and the clock tower, also by *Thomason*, is unexpectedly much better.

An enormous number of public buildings followed after c.1870. Town halls in the Black Country include Bilston, mixed classical of 1872–3 by *Bidlake & Fleeming*, and West Bromwich, 1874–5 by *Alexander & Henman*, with a splendid Gothic clock tower. In the 1880s a progressive Queen Anne style was used at Stourbridge (D), by *Thomas Robinson*, 1887–8, and Darlaston (Wa), properly the Local Board offices, by *Jethro Cossins*, 1887–8. In the districts surrounding Birmingham are a series of municipal buildings designed to be local landmarks, *William Henman*'s Handsworth (B) of 1877–9 and Aston (B) of 1880–1, and *Arthur Harrison*'s economical but impressive building for Yardley, now Sparkhill Library (B), 1900–2. Even small Black Country communities needed municipal offices, as at Sedgley (D), of 1882–3 by *A.P. Brevitt*, and Brownhills (Wa), by the Local Board Surveyor *John Siddalls*, 1882. Solihull, then an expanding village, has a handsome Gothic public hall, a private venture of 1876 designed by *J.A. Chatwin*.

Of MUNICIPAL ART GALLERIES, Birmingham's has already been mentioned. Others are at Dudley, 1883 by *Bateman & Corser* in progressive but uncertain Queen Anne style; Wednesbury (Sa), similar stylistically, by *Wood & Kendrick*, 1890–1; and Wolverhampton, 1883–5, one of *J.A. Chatwin*'s finest designs, using the language of Barry and Cockerell to dignify a relatively modest building. An allied building is the Science and Art Institute at Walsall, Ruskinian Gothic of 1887–8 by *J.G. Dunn & F.W. Hipkiss*.

POLICE STATIONS became more substantial. Those in Birmingham are by *Martin & Chamberlain*; two survive, a gabled block in Moseley Street of 1877 and a modest one at Summerfield of 1878–9. The only survivor in the Black Country of *Robert Griffiths*'s Staffordshire police stations is the modest but cleverly composed Old Hill, Rowley Regis (Sa), 1878–80.

The area also needed COURT HOUSES. County courts, for civil cases, were built from the mid century, to handsome classical designs by the official architect *Charles Reeves*: Dudley 1857–8, Stourbridge 1863–4. His successor, *James Williams*, designed Birmingham's, in Corporation Street, old-fashioned but impressive Italianate of 1882. Criminal cases were tried at assize courts in the surrounding county towns, until Birmingham, as part of its drive towards city status, gained assize courts in 1884. For its Victoria Law Courts of 1887–91, *Aston Webb & Ingress Bell* produced the greatest building of the city's 'terracotta style', in an eclectic French Renaissance manner. It gave Birmingham architecture a national profile: in 1897 *The Builder* called it 'one of the best planned modern buildings in England', and noticed that Birmingham was becoming 'a city of terra-cotta architecture'.

Surviving WORKHOUSES are mostly of this period. Kings Norton Union (later Selly Oak Hospital (B)) by *Edward Holmes*, 1869–72, is basic Gothic. The overpowering main range and entrance block at Aston Union (later Highcroft Hospital,

Erdington (B)) are by *Yeoville Thomason*, 1886–9. *Arthur Marshall* of Nottingham, a workhouse specialist, did New Cross Hospital in Wolverhampton of 1900–3, nearly all demolished, and Wordsley Hospital (D) (Stourbridge Union workhouse) of 1903–7, plain except for a Baroque clock tower. The Boards of Guardians who ran workhouses also built offices for themselves, of which several survive. Birmingham's, by *W.H. Ward*, 1882–5, are grand French classical (façaded); Wolverhampton's, by *William Doubleday*, 1879–80, are picturesque Gothic. Wordsley has Gothic offices by *Francis Smalman Smith*, 1874–5. West Bromwich's offices are by *Henman & Timmins*, 1887; Dudley's, severe Queen Anne, by *Wood & Kendrick*, 1888; and later Walsall, Tudor with an ogee-roof tower, by *H.E. Lavender*, 1898.

The growth of HOSPITALS started with workhouse infirmaries. At Birmingham City Hospital, Dudley Road, the infirmary of Birmingham workhouse, of 1887–9 by *W.H. Ward*, survives almost intact, with a pavilion plan and a very long corridor. West Bromwich Union (Sandwell General Hospital) has infirmary blocks with diagonally set projecting towers with Rhenish-helm roofs, by *William Henman*, 1884. The administration block survives at Selly Oak Hospital, by *Daniel Arkell*, 1895–7. Birmingham has a group of specialist hospitals, all in the Queen Anne style: *Payne & Talbot*'s Eye Hospital, Church Street, 1883–4; *James & Lister Lea*'s Skin Hospital, John Bright Street, 1887; and the finest, *Jethro Cossins*'s beautifully balanced Ear and Throat Hospital, Edmund Street, 1890–1, now façaded. The Eye Hospital in Wolverhampton, by *T.H. Fleeming*, 1886–8, is economical Gothic.

Hospital-building continued into the Late Victorian and Edwardian period, best treated here. *Henman & Cooper*'s General Hospital, Steelhouse Lane, Birmingham of 1894–7, now the Children's Hospital, is influenced by Alfred Waterhouse, for whom Cooper had worked, in its clear planning and its tough Romanesque terracotta style. Sutton Coldfield has a cottage hospital of 1897 etc. by *E.F. Titley*, with later work by *Buckland & Haywood-Farmer*, 1907–8. The only survivor of the Sister Dora Hospital at Walsall is *Bailey & McConnal*'s Scottish-looking nurses' home of 1902. Of other early C20 hospitals, the Royal Orthopaedic, Northfield (B) has work by *Batemans*, including towers for washrooms and lavatories (as at Sandwell) of 1908. The surviving buildings of Hayley Green Isolation Hospital, by *Henry T. Hare*, 1900–2, are Arts and Crafts vernacular. The former isolation hospital at Catherine-de-Barnes, Solihull, is by *W.H. Ward*, 1909.

Educational buildings, to c.1890

C19 SCHOOLS were developed partly for religious instruction: National Schools were Anglican, British Schools non-denominational. The earliest survivors in the area are mostly Anglican. The best are in Dudley, and by *William Bourne*: St Edmund's of 1848–9, Tudor Revival in local stone, is fairly conventional; St James's school, of 1842, has lancets (now re-erected at the Black

Country Museum, Dudley); St Thomas's school of 1847 is an urban three-storey block with a tower. A Tudor-style school of 1836 with stepped gables survives at Wordsley (D) by *Lewis Vulliamy*, architect of the church there. A Gothic school at Bloxwich (Wa), 1861–2, and the master's house from another at Walsall Wood, 1859, are both by *James Cranston*. George Bidlake's schools begin with the part-surviving school and master's house at Wollaston (D), 1858–9. *Francis Smalman Smith*'s school at Cradley (D) of 1855–6 survives almost entire, with two masters' houses. *Thomas Smith* did the picturesque tower and apsed hall of Stourbridge Grammar School (now King Edward VI College) of 1860–2. A pair of blue-brick Gothic teachers' houses survives from his contemporary National School at Oldswinford (D). A stylistic exception is *John Weller II*'s quite large *Rundbogenstil* schools at Tipton (Sa) of 1861.

The only surviving BRITISH SCHOOLS are Severn Street, Birmingham, extended and recast in 1851–2, and an attractive late one of 1871, now Cradley Baptist Church. Also in Cradley are two rare remaining RAGGED SCHOOLS, from the movement led by the Earl of Shaftesbury. Both developed into independent Methodist chapels: High Town of 1863 and Twogates of 1867.

Denominational schooling was largely replaced by the School Boards created by the Elementary Education Act, 1870. Campaigning by Birmingham figures such as George Dixon and Joseph Chamberlain was partly responsible for the Act, and unsurprisingly Birmingham has the finest BOARD SCHOOLS in the area. *Martin & Chamberlain* were appointed architects by the new School Board in 1871, and remained until it was abolished in 1902. Up to his untimely death in 1883, the designer was the most important local Gothic Revivalist, *John Henry Chamberlain*. Chamberlain – no relation of Joseph, but a close friend – was a devoted Ruskinian and a trustee of Ruskin's St George's Guild. Study of nature lies behind his mastery of naturalistic ornament, always growing out of the construction of his buildings. For his early Gothic domestic work, *see* below, p. 55. His career developed partly through his partnership from 1864 with William Martin, successor to D.R. Hill as the public works architect. He was also an early conservationist, helping to save the Old Crown Inn at Deritend (B) (above, p. 14).

Chamberlain designed his Board Schools to be the best-looking buildings in their neighbourhoods: gabled brick blocks with tall airy rooms and big windows grouped round boldly composed but functional ventilation towers, with as much decorative ironwork and terracotta detail as he could afford. The finest survivors include Oozells Street, now the Ikon Gallery (1877), Dixon Road, Small Heath, and Eliot Street, Nechells (both 1879), and Icknield Street (1883). His masterpiece is the Birmingham School of Art of 1884–5 (run by the council, not the School Board). Here his Ruskinian love of Gothic, his flair for naturalistic ornament and his functionalism – the asymmetrical wings arranged for north light to studios – reached their climax.

VICTORIAN AND EDWARDIAN, c.1830 TO 1914

The firm's later work remained of high quality, increasingly under the hand of William Martin's son *Frederick Martin*, as at schools such as Ladypool, Sparkbrook (1884–6). There was criticism of the firm's monopoly, and a few schools were designed by others, of which the finest is *Jethro Cossins*'s Cromwell, Duddeston, 1888–90.

In the outer communities of Birmingham and Black Country towns and villages, surviving Board Schools are still some of the best buildings. The Harborne and Smethwick board used *J.P. Sharp & Co.*, who designed in a cruder version of Chamberlain's manner, e.g. Harborne (B), 1880–1, and Crocketts Lane infants', Smethwick (Sa), 1884–5. Walsall used *George Bidlake*, who had established himself with robust Gothic designs for schools outside the board system: Handsworth Grammar School (B) of 1861–2, Tettenhall College (Wo) of 1865–7. He and the successor partnership *Bidlake & Fleeming* did e.g. the partly surviving Tantarra Street school of 1872 and Butts School of 1879. Sedgley School Board used *A.P. Brevitt*, whose strong designs can be seen at Daisy Bank (now Bilston (Wa)), 1878, and Red Hall Schools, Gornal (D), 1878–80 and 1891. Willenhall and Bentley Board (Wa) used *Benjamin Baker*, who tried Queen Anne style at the Central Schools of 1883. Other boards chose between different architects, sometimes holding competitions. Rowley School Board (Sa) used *Edward Holmes* at Old Hill schools of 1876–7, *J.T. Meredith* at the Corngreaves schools in Cradley Heath of 1890–1. Kings Norton Board (B) built a complex of infants' and junior schools in Clifton Road, Balsall, by *George Ingall* and his partnership *Ingall & Hughes*, 1878–85, but used *William Hale* at Kings Norton and Stirchley schools, and later *Edward Holmes* at Cotteridge, 1899–1900. Aston Board (B) used *Holmes* for Prince Albert School, Aston (1880–1), but chose *William Henman* for Osborne Primary School, Erdington (1884–5). *G.H. Cox* designed two impressive schools in Queen Anne style, Cape Schools in Smethwick of 1887–8 and the Norton Canes Board's Brownhills Central Schools (Wa) of 1892–3. There have been many losses: hardly any Wolverhampton Board Schools remain, and of *Edward Pincher*'s fine Kings Hill schools, Darlaston, all that survives is the caretaker's house.

School boards built themselves OFFICES, and several survive, most by the same architects as the schools: Birmingham, in Edmund Street, Gothic by *Martin & Chamberlain*, 1881–2; Smethwick, blunt Gothic by *Sharp & Co.*, 1883–4; and Wolverhampton, by *T.H. Fleeming*, 1885. A much smaller one is Kings Norton's in Balsall Heath, by *Ingall & Hughes*, 1884.

Early HIGHER EDUCATION INSTITUTIONS were mostly theological. Oscott College is educational Tudor by *Joseph Potter*, 1835–8 (for its Pugin fittings see p. 39). St Peter's College at Saltley (B) of 1850–2 by *Benjamin Ferrey* is, not surprisingly, Puginian Gothic. The greatest secular example before the 1890s, *Jethro Cossins*'s Mason College of 1875–80, was demolished in the 1960s.

Civic improvements, parks and public sculpture

CIVIC IMPROVEMENTS were the municipal projects which had the largest physical impact on their communities. The only Early Victorian one is in Wolverhampton: the enlargement of High Green, now Queen Square, after 1841 by *Edward Banks*, who probably designed the classical blocks on the s side. The Artisans' Dwellings Act of 1875 enabled local authorities to replace unsatisfactory houses with commercial development. Birmingham used these powers vigorously. Corporation Street was planned from 1875 and largely completed in 1882, when John Bright Street was also cut. Wolverhampton was close behind, with Lichfield Street and Prince's Square created from 1877. Even small Black Country towns tried to improve their centres, as at Brierley Hill (D), where the Local Board Surveyor *Josiah Beckley* created the Church Hill 'promenade' in 1883–4.

This is also the great period of the development of PUBLIC PARKS. The first in the area was Calthorpe Park, Birmingham, opened in 1855 on land given by the 4th Lord Calthorpe. The grounds of Aston Hall, opened as a private venture in 1858, became a public park in 1864. Highgate Park opened in 1876, and Summerfield Park was laid out in 1877–8 by the Birmingham Borough Surveyor, *W.S. Till*. Two large Birmingham parks were given or part-funded by one benefactor, Louisa Anne Ryland: Cannon Hill Park, 1873, and Small Heath Park, opened 1879. Wolverhampton has West Park, laid out from 1881, and East Park, designed by *T.H. Mawson*, 1893–6. Walsall's Arboretum, opened by a private company in 1874 with buildings by *Robert Griffiths*, was municipalized in 1884. Smaller Black Country towns followed suit towards the end of the period, e.g. Brunswick Park, Wednesbury (Sa), laid out in 1886–7, and Victoria Park, Tipton (Sa), 1899–1901.

There is surprisingly little Victorian PUBLIC SCULPTURE. Early examples are *Peter Hollins*'s fine Robert Peel statue of 1855, now in Pershore Road, Birmingham, caught as if speaking; *John Thomas*'s rather stiff Joseph Sturge of 1862 at Five Ways, Edgbaston (B), with subsidiary figures; and two in Wolverhampton by *Thomas Thornycroft*: Mayor Thorneycroft, in the Town Hall, of 1856, and Prince Albert of 1866, on a splendid horse. Birmingham also produced *J.H. Foley*'s Prince Albert of 1866 and *Thomas Woolner*'s attractive Queen Victoria of 1884, both now in the Council House, and *Alexander Munro*'s James Watt of 1868 and *Francis Williamson*'s Joseph Priestley of 1874, in Chamberlain Square (both currently in store). Its architectural commemorations include the fine Chamberlain Memorial Fountain, Gothic of 1880 by *J.H. Chamberlain* with portrait relief by *Woolner*, and the Burnaby obelisk in St Philip's churchyard.* Later Black

---

*Birmingham's current attitude to Victorian sculpture is as bad as that to Victorian buildings. Other statues in store are *John Thomas*'s Thomas Attwood of 1859, *Peter Hollins*'s Rowland Hill of 1868, *Woolner*'s George Dawson of 1881, and *Albert Bruce-Joy*'s John Bright of 1887. *Williamson*'s John Skirrow Wright of 1883 and George Dawson of 1885 were destroyed in Sir Herbert Manzoni's time.

VICTORIAN AND EDWARDIAN, c.1830 TO 1914

Country examples are *William Theed*'s C.P. Villiers of 1879, now in West Park, Wolverhampton, and terribly damaged; *Williamson*'s Sister Dora in Walsall of 1886 (recast in bronze in 1956), with particularly fine relief panels; and *C.B. Birch*'s Earl of Dudley of 1888 in Dudley. Among ARCHITECTURAL SCULPTURE the finest is on the Victoria Law Courts, Birmingham of 1887–91, by *Harry Bates*, *Walter Crane*, *W.S. Frith* and *William Aumonier*; the pediment group on the Art Gallery extension to the Council House, Birmingham of 1884–5 is by *Williamson*. In the Black Country, one can mention the figure panels on Chatwin's Wolverhampton Art Gallery, made by *R.L. Boulton & Sons*, 1887.

Commercial architecture, to c.1890

The growth of industry required capital, and Birmingham in particular became a considerable financial centre. Two modern clearing banks, Lloyds and Midland (now HSBC), originated there. As is usual, BANK BUILDINGS are mostly classical. The earliest survivor is *Rickman & Hutchinson*'s temple-like Birmingham Bank in Waterloo Street of 1830–1. The Dudley and West Bromwich Bank in West Bromwich (Sa) by *Bateman & Drury*, 1839, not quite so grand, was altered in the late C19. The 1860s saw a rush in Birmingham. *J.A. Chatwin*'s Birmingham Joint Stock Bank of 1864 in Temple Row West is a handsome and subtle Italianate design; *Edward Holmes*'s Midland Bank of 1867–9 in New Street is grander and more eclectic. The National Provincial Bank in Waterloo Street, 1869, is in the usual Renaissance style of the bank's architect *John Gibson*. The rebuilt N side of Colmore Row starts with *Yeoville Thomason*'s Birmingham Town and District Bank of 1869–75, with a large and decorative banking hall. In the 1870s bank building spread to the Black Country. The Staffordshire Bank in Walsall is a rare classical design by *George Bidlake*. Gothic designs appear now. *Yeoville Thomason*'s arcaded United Counties Bank in Cradley Heath (Sa) of 1873 sets the style. His bank in Tipton (Sa) of 1876–7 has alas been altered. Only when he added a banking hall to an existing building in Bilston (Wo) in 1881 did he design in eclectic classical. *Martin & Chamberlain*'s Lloyds Bank in Dudley of 1875 is in their usual brick Gothic with naturalistic foliage decoration. *T.H. Fleeming*'s Barclays Bank in Lich Gates, Wolverhampton, 1875–6, is intensely Gothic in the Alfred Waterhouse way. Lloyds Bank of 1878 in Wolverhampton is by *Chatwin*, who became their regular architect: an intelligent design using smoothly rusticated pilasters. Chatwin also designed smaller Lloyds branches in the 1870s, using a tough Gothic-inspired domestic style, at Deritend (B), Halesowen (D) and Solihull.

The only substantial INSURANCE COMPANY BUILDING to survive from the period is *Samuel Hemming*'s Unity Fire and General Insurance in Temple Street, Birmingham, Italianate of 1854. Its neighbour (now the Trocadero pub) is the former fire engine house for the Norwich Union, by *Edge & Avery*, 1846.

p. 50

Birmingham, Colmore Row, Town and District Bank.
Engraving by W.E. Hodgkin, 1869

Early Victorian SHOPS could be quite grand: Warwick House, New Street, Birmingham (demolished), by *William Thomas*, 1838, had a giant Corinthian order. Two severe stucco buildings probably intended for shops are on the corner of High Street and Stone Street, Dudley, 1841 by *George Hilton*, and on the corner of New Street and Temple Street, Birmingham, *c.* 1842, probably by *Charles Edge*. The Gothic Revival arrives with Powell's Gun Shop, Carrs Lane, Birmingham, a late work by Edge, 1860–1.

Birmingham was the main centre of mid-Victorian development, the opening of New Street station encouraging COMMERCIAL BUILDINGS to its N, with blocks of shops with offices etc. above, such as *Thomson Plevins*'s Burlington Hotel block of 1867–75 and *Yeoville Thomason*'s richer Birmingham Daily Post buildings of 1864–71 etc. *J.A. Chatwin* used Italianate at Nos. 79–83 Colmore Row, 1871–2. Corporation Street started with this style, mostly by *W.H.Ward*, 1879–81, but quickly became more eclectic and French, especially in Ward's Central Arcade of 1881. *Ward*'s greatest work of this kind is the Great Western Arcade of 1874–6. The type went on, in *Newton & Cheatle*'s terracotta-style Midland & City Arcades, 1900–1, and in the only Black Country survivor, in Walsall by *Jonathan Ellis*, 1896–7. Another fashionable French classical building is *J.J. Bateman*'s No. 55 Colmore Row of 1878. Corporation Street quickly becomes a stylistic mixture, very different from the earlier Colmore Row, with varied materials and a picturesque gabled skyline. Nos. 19–21 of 1880–1, *Martin & Chamberlain*'s only building on the street they planned, announces the arrival of 'terracotta style' in flaming Flemish Renaissance. Blocks by *Dempster & Heaton* (1884–5 and 1887–8) and *J.P. Sharp & Co.* (1887) are lively commercial Gothic; *A.B. Phipson*'s former Midland Educational shop of 1883–4 is classical. The influence of Ruskin can be seen in the Gothic shops by *J.S. Davis* in Constitution Hill (1881–2) and Summer Lane (1883). This style spread to the suburbs, e.g. at Nos. 141–143 High Street, Kings Heath, by *Sam Owen*, 1882. Nos. 189–195 Hagley Road, Edgbaston, of 1882 by *Bland & Cossins*, i.e. the young *Jethro Cossins*, has an austere simplicity which looks forward to the Arts and Crafts of *c.* 1900. Nos. 13–14 Cannon Street, Birmingham, by *J.L. Ball*, 1881–2, is in a delicate, rather Dutch, Queen Anne style.

It is remarkable how little impressive commercial architecture of these years survives in the Black Country. The Ruskinian Gothic of the John Taylor Duce building, Wednesbury (Sa), by *A.P. Brevitt*, 1879–80, is exceptional. Rhodes Buildings in Lye (D) of 1881–2, probably by *Owen Freeman*, is grandiose, unforgettable with its biblical inscriptions, but unsophisticated. The increased scale of later Victorian Wolverhampton really begins with the brick and terracotta shops in Lichfield Street by *George Willoughby*, 1884. Their Queen Anne style is paralleled by *Joseph Lavender* in Berry Street, 1889. There is a scatter of good 1880s commercial work elsewhere: *Wood & Kendrick*'s former Free Press offices at West Bromwich, 1883, and *Thomas Robinson*'s Church Street Chambers, Stourbridge (D), 1885. Bridge Street, Walsall has *F.E.F. Bailey*'s corner block with its iron crown, his Imperial Buildings of 1891–2, and *Samuel Loxton*'s music shop of 1891 with its carvings. An unusual survival is a Co-op shop of 1871 in Willenhall (Wa) by *George Bidlake*.

The Beerhouse Act of 1830 allowed the sale of beer (not spirits) without a licence. The result was a huge increase in PUBLIC HOUSES. At the Shakespeare, Dudley, built before 1835, most of the plan and some fittings are original. It typifies the humble

Black Country 'two-room drinker' of the C19, with a central entrance between a pair of rooms, one basic, one smarter. Other 1830s beerhouses include the Sir Robert Peel, Rowley (Sa), and, in an older building, the Sow and Pigs, West Bromwich. In Birmingham the Gunmakers Arms, Bath Street, is probably of c. 1835–40, the Jewellers Arms, Spencer Street, slightly later. The Combermere Arms in Wolverhampton and the Duke of Cambridge at Short Heath (Wa), both probably C18, perhaps opened as beerhouses after 1830. Grander pubs of the period, in a stucco classical style, are the former Angel Hotel, Sparkbrook (B) of c. 1834, perhaps by *Joseph Bateman*, and the Bournbrook Hotel, Selly Oak (B), of c. 1839, with a pilastered centrepiece. The Saracen's Head and Freemason's Arms, Dudley, has a show front of c. 1830 with giant end pilasters, probably by *Edward Marsh*. The Castle, Willenhall, probably 1840s, also has end pilasters. Slightly less grand, but more than beerhouses, are classical street-corner pubs such as the Moseley Arms, Highgate, Birmingham of c. 1840, the Eagle and Ball of c. 1850 by Birmingham City University, and the Great Western, Daisy Bank, Bilston (Wo), turned into a pub c. 1854. The Junction Inn, Oldbury (Sa), 1851–4, has classical detail in cast dolerite (*see* p. 6). The former White Horse, Amblecote (D), 1840s, is, unusually, stucco Tudor. The Beacon Hotel, Sedgley (D) and the Round of Beef, Cradley (D) have the 1860s fashion of sash windows with the upper lights ending in round corners or a semicircle. At the Albion Vaults, Nechells (B), c. 1865–6, the classical detail is heavier, in the manner once called 'debased'. The Bell, Rood End, Oldbury, 1859, is polychromatic brick Gothic with few pointed arches but many bays and bargeboarded gables, almost as if S.S. Teulon had designed a pub. Gothic with polychromatic brickwork appears in force at The Gothic, Great Hampton Street, Birmingham, 1867–8. The Old Contemptibles, Edmund Street, Birmingham of 1880–1 by *William Hale*, is more eclectic Italian. Hale's Big Bulls Head, Digbeth, 1885, uses the heavy gabled Gothic without pointed arches of much terraced housing. Two Wolverhampton pubs by *A.P. Brevitt*, the Sir Tatton Sykes of 1888 and the Vine of 1891, move towards Queen Anne and eclectic Late Victorian.

Of early PUB FITTINGS, The Bell at Rood End retains some seating, the Albion Vaults an original bar front and back. A bar back of c. 1878 survives at the New Inn, Harborne (B). Some late C19 pilastered fronts survive in Birmingham pubs, as at the Observatory, Handsworth, 1891. The Wheatsheaf, West Bromwich, of c. 1840, retains a decorative front of 1876 by *Elliott J. Ettwell*.

In a special class, and built for the Calthorpe estate, is the Plough and Harrow, Edgbaston, a hotel of 1832 by *John Fallows*, in sharply gabled Tudor style. Later HOTELS include the Burlington in Birmingham (*see* above), and the Victoria (now Britannia) in Wolverhampton by *Brevitt*, 1890–2. The two grandest were in Colmore Row, Birmingham: the splendidly classical Great Western of 1875 by *J.A. Chatwin* (demolished), and the Grand by *Thomson Plevins*, 1876–8, with magnificent *Martin & Chamberlain* interiors of 1893–5.

Domestic architecture, to c. 1890

In Birmingham, the 1830s marked the start of a major expansion of EDGBASTON: Hagley Road and the roads to the S, and Calthorpe and Highfield roads. The houses here are conservative: classical, almost always stuccoed, detached and less often semi-detached villas, in a style we would call Regency. *John Fallows*'s group of c. 1830 at the SW end of Calthorpe Road have already been mentioned. Then come the villas of e.g. Highfield Road of c. 1840 and the E side of Vicarage Road of 1838–40, with smooth rustication and Doric doorcases. A grander detached design with a single-bay pedimented centre is associated with *Charles Edge*: the villa of 1829 now the Priory School, No. 15 Chad Road, 1838, and (probably) Apsley House, Wellington Road, 1836. Nos. 4–5 Carpenter Road of after 1834 have lovely wrought-iron porches, but are so severe as to be almost styleless. The Neoclassical habit of not stressing the centre of a composition lent itself to semi-detached designs like the pedimented-ends pairs in Highfield Road and Wellington Road. *Bateman & Drury*'s pairs of 1836 and 1841 in Yew Tree Road, with their characteristic round-arched doorcases, are, unusually, not stuccoed. No. 43 Wellington Road, by *F. W. Fiddian*, 1840, has a doorcase characteristic of this architect, with a very deep frieze. A step beyond the pedimented-ends type is to split the design into a mirror pair, as at *J. J. Bateman*'s Nos. 13–14 Charlotte Road, red brick Italian villas of 1851. In the late 1840s and 1850s a heavily picturesque classicism appears, e.g. *Fiddian*'s Nos. 223–231 Bristol Road, where the mixture includes a bit of Tudor, and Nos. 11 and 12 Sir Harry's Road. *Samuel Hemming*'s No. 9 Sir Harry's Road of 1854–5 is similar. Nos. 16–17 Chad Road, of 1853 by *Deakin & Phipson*, are notable as the first appearance in Edgbaston of yellow London brick. Many larger mid-Victorian houses here were demolished in the later C20; notable survivors, all still classical, are The Corinthians, Bristol Road, 1850–1, No. 6 Norfolk Road, 1870–1, and the large but sympathetic extension to the Priory School villa by *T. Chatfeild Clarke*, 1878–9.

A scatter of classical Early Victorian houses survives in the Birmingham suburbs, some larger than Edgbaston villas but similar in style, e.g. Kings Heath House and Cannon Hill House, both 1830s. The grandest is Woodbrooke, Selly Oak, c. 1840–50. Red House, Great Barr, just over the Walsall boundary, is a fine Italianate villa of 1841 with a long service wing, earlier by several years than houses of this type in Edgbaston. Ward End House of c. 1850 is rich, deliberately asymmetrical Italianate.

TERRACES, characteristic of Late Georgian and Early Victorian architecture elsewhere, are rare in Birmingham. The town where they are commonest, unexpectedly, is Walsall. The grandest is

Nos. 24–30 Bradford Street, by *John Eglington*, of 1832 onwards. A contemporary but more modest terrace is in George Street; Grove Terrace off Birmingham Road, a formal pedimented composition, was there by 1832. Lichfield Street, developed from 1831, has detached villas and short terraces. Pairs, close-built to resemble a terrace, comprise the handsome Victoria Terrace by *Henry Farrington*, of before 1856. Wolverhampton has terraces on Tettenhall Road, 1830s to 1850s, the style becoming heavier and the details fancier. Poplar Terrace (Deansgate) is Italianate of *c.* 1860, perhaps by *Edward Banks*, with fussy detail.

Of Wolverhampton's detached houses of the period, the finest are the severe Ely House of 1841–2 and Bredon House further NW, clearly by the same unknown architect. Waterloo Road, developed from *c.* 1845, has a similar mix of terraces and villas. Substantial classical houses of this period elsewhere in Wolverhampton include Crescent House, Newbridge Crescent of the 1830s, Claremont House, Penn Road, *c.* 1845–50, and Compton Hall of *c.* 1840, the last two perhaps by *Edward Banks*. Hagley Road in Stourbridge (D) has Late Georgian and Early Victorian terraces. An example of the plain, almost styleless manner is Holy Trinity vicarage, West Bromwich (Sa), 1843 by *Thomas Cox*. The development of larger houses in Tettenhall for Wolverhampton manufacturers and merchants starts with Bromley House of 1850. Avenue House, 1860–1 by *J.J. Bateman*, is a simpler example of the asymmetrical classical manner.

CLASSICISM continued into the 1860s and 1870s for many houses. Those of Braithwaite Road, Sparkbrook (B), have paired porches with full entablatures and decorative eared architraves. The handsome houses of 1860–3 at Alcester Lanes End (Kings Heath (B)) are by *Edward Holmes*. The Uplands, Selly Park (B), has one survivor of a pair of Italianate villas of *c.* 1862–4 raised on terracing. The Rotton Park estate, Edgbaston, has richly detailed villas in Portland Road (1858–63) and Clarendon Road (*c.* 1873–4). Black Country houses are more modest but include pairs and terraces in South Road, Smethwick (Sa), by *John Harley*, 1876–7, and the enormously long Bristnall Terrace, Oldbury (Sa), 1879. The very rich No. 138 Hamstead Road, Handsworth (B), is as late as 1883, by *J.G. Dunn*.

OTHER STYLES for houses are quite uncommon. Birmingham's minimal Tudor 1830s terraces have gone. Picturesque cottages include a pair by *Bateman & Drury* in Yew Tree Road, Edgbaston (1834), and Pardoe's Cottage, Darlaston (Wo) and The Cottage, Wednesbury (Sa), both *c.* 1840. *Thomas Smith*'s own much-altered house in Oldswinford of *c.* 1845–50 is asymmetrical and picturesque, with an inset tower. Tudor or Jacobean was normal for ALMSHOUSES, e.g. Hornblower & Haylock's at Highgate, 1848–9, and Ladywood Middleway, 1858, and *Edward Banks*'s picturesque row at Heath Town (Wo), 1850. Jacobean enters house architecture in the 1860s at e.g. *J.A. Chatwin*'s No. 25 Somerset Road, Edgbaston and the extensions to New Hall, Sutton Coldfield by *Yeoville Thomason*. A later example is Tudor Grange, Solihull, by *T.H. Mansell*, 1887.

A crucial building type in the evolution of the Victorian detached house is the PARSONAGE. The succession begins here with two of 1847, both in that brick, steeply gabled, picturesque Tudor-cum-Gothic which has few pointed arches: Great Barr (Wa), probably by *Ewan Christian*, and Brockmoor (D), by *Thomas Smith*. Brownhills, 1855–8, attributed to *G.T. Robinson* shows his Late Georgian background in its lower proportions. More forward-looking, influenced by Pugin and Butterfield, are St Paul, West Smethwick (Sa) (*J.J. Bateman*, 1857–8), and Pensnett (*William Bourne*, 1858–60).

HIGH VICTORIAN GOTHIC arrives in domestic architecture with *J.H. Chamberlain*. His No. 12 Ampton Road, Edgbaston, of 1855, combines the picturesque composition of Pugin and the polychromy of Butterfield. Its tough manner shocked conservative Birmingham taste, and a decade passed before Chamberlain designed others: No. 50 Carpenter Road, Edgbaston, with its charming motif of the porch continuing as a blind arcade; and Ferndale, Harborne Road. By then *George Bidlake* was active in Wolverhampton, as at the very impressive No. 64 Waterloo Road (the Leaping Wolf), 1864 and Berrington Lodge, Tettenhall Road, 1866. The pedimented-ends Late Georgian pair evolved into the common gabled-ends Victorian type, of which one of the earliest and loveliest is Nos. 79–81 Greenfield Road, Harborne (B), of 1864 by *George Ingall*. Others are Nos. 114–116 Oakfield Road, Selly Park, of *c.* 1871, probably from a design by *Martin & Chamberlain*. *J.H. Chamberlain*'s Nos. 109–111 Greenfield Road, Harborne, 1870, are a plain gabled block with sparing detail and heavy, impressive porch hoods. His great houses, for his Liberal friends, come at the end of the 1870s, and are much richer. The grandest is Highbury, Moseley (B), for Joseph Chamberlain, of 1878–80. Its apparently casual exterior and characteristic three-gabled garden front faithfully express its planning, and it has much naturalistic decoration. Its main hall with staircase and hammerbeam and clerestory roof is J.H. Chamberlain's most sumptuous. The other survivor, Berrow Court, Edgbaston (B), for William Kenrick, 1879, is smaller but equally rich, with a vertiginous staircase hall.

From the 1870s Gothic was taken up by a large number of Birmingham architects, among them *T.H. Mansell* in Westfield Road, Edgbaston, 1875–6, *Henry Naden* in his own No. 20 Clarendon Road of *c.* 1874, and *J.P. Sharp & Co.* in Oxford Road, Moseley, 1875–82. Two Black Country examples, both former vicarages of 1874, are No. 2 Franchise Street, Darlaston by *A.P. Brevitt*, and Highfield House at Stourbridge by *Thomas Smith*. A smaller example is *Joynson Bros*' Nos. 6–10 Wharfedale Street, Wednesbury (Sa), 1886–7. The best development in Wolverhampton of this period, Parkdale off Tettenhall Road, by *John Weller II*, 1878–84, starts with Gothic houses and goes on to eclectic designs with steep gables, big dormers and some timbering.

The reaction against domestic Gothic in the area started about 1880. One alternative was the Free Renaissance manner in finely laid, sometimes moulded brick, with casement windows and sometimes terracotta reliefs of flowers and 'pies', which we call the QUEEN ANNE style, associated nationally with W. E. Nesfield and Basil Champneys. *J.A. Chatwin* pioneered it locally in his Lench's Trust almshouses in Conybere Street, Highgate (B), 1878–80. Elsewhere in the Birmingham suburbs there is No. 8 Wake Green Road, Moseley, of 1885 by *D. Henry Ward*, and Nos. 32–34 of 1889 by *Oliver Essex*. Osborn & Reading used the style often, e.g. in Westfield Road, Edgbaston. It was young architects' architecture, as at *Ewen Harper*'s Nos. 3–11 Somerset Road, Handsworth, where it purifies the standard gabled terrace. At its best it is austere and progressive, looking forward to Arts and Crafts simplicity, as in *Osborn & Reading*'s No. 17 Westfield Road, 1890. Its finest exponent was *Jethro Cossins*. His Nos. 8A–10 Bordesley Street, Digbeth (B), 1882–4, are clearly influenced by Philip Webb in their simplicity and free design. His shops and houses at Nos. 189–195 Hagley Road (with *J. G. Bland*) are hardly less radical. His finest house of this type, No. 15 Westbourne Road, Edgbaston, of 1887, relies on materials and craftsmanlike detail rather than 'style'. In the Black Country, Queen Anne is less sophisticated, sometimes more intention than achievement, as at No. 12 Spring Head, Wednesbury, by *Horton & Scott*, 1882, or *Henry Naden*'s reservoir house of 1881–2 in Park Lane West, Tipton (Sa). A Wolverhampton example as severe as Cossins's is Abbeyfield (a former vicarage), Church Hill Road, Tettenhall, by *T. H. Fleeming*, 1888–9.

Another alternative to Gothic was 'OLD ENGLISH', the consciously traditional half-timbered style pioneered by Nesfield and Norman Shaw, which developed in the 1880s into the gentler Domestic Revival manner. Ednam House, Dudley, by *Davies & Middleton*, 1877–8, is brick but already has a pretty timber porch and star-shaped C17-style chimneys. The change from Old English to Domestic Revival can be seen in its greatest building here, Wightwick Manor, Tettenhall, by *Edward Ould* for Theodore Mander. In its first part, of 1887, timber is mixed with tile-hanging, and red Ruabon brick: quaint, but bright and hard. The second part, of 1893, has more and richer half-timbering including a gabled bay, the fruit of Ould's study of ancient buildings. Wightwick set a fashion in Wolverhampton, noticeable in the huge timber-gabled terraces in Tettenhall Road of 1892 by *F.T. Beck*. Tyninghame, Tettenhall, probably by *John Weller II*, 1893–4, is a monstrous relative of these. A grander and more robust alternative to Domestic Revival was the brick C16 and C17 manner we call Jacobethan, of which The Mount, Tettenhall, also by *Edward Ould*, of 1891 and later, for Charles Tertius Mander, Theodore's cousin, is a fine example.

In Birmingham, the home of Old English above all is Moseley, where it starts with No. 38 Wake Green Road, of 1883 by *Osborn & Reading*. The finest stretch is on the S side of Chantry Road, large houses all of 1891–3 with a profusion of timbering and jettied gables. If the best examples are relatively restrained – *Arthur Harrison*'s No. 32 and *Ewen Harper*'s No. 22 – that does not stop us enjoying the spectacle of *Alfred Reading*'s No. 30 or *G. R. Faulkner*'s

No. 26. Elsewhere, *Essex & Nicol* and others stirred in French and Flemish to produce a rich and sometimes indigestible mix, as at Nos. 10–12 Wake Green Road of 1889, and there are the eccentricities of *Stephen Holliday* around Grove Avenue of 1894 etc. Other Birmingham examples include *William Doubleday*'s No. 21 Serpentine Road, Selly Park, 1884. *J.H. Chamberlain*'s delightful lodge to Oakmount, Westbourne Road, Edgbaston, 1879, shows elements of Old English and Queen Anne. Also in Edgbaston, *Alfred Reading*'s Oak Grange, Hermitage Road, 1894, combines half-timbering and C17-style shell porches.

Industrial buildings, to c. 1890

More C19 INDUSTRIAL BUILDINGS have been lost than any other type, and what we now see is not a typical sample. The best area, but a specialized one, is the BIRMINGHAM JEWELLERY QUARTER. Industrial development here started with domestic conversions and with combined houses and workshops, present by the 1820s. Later, rear 'shopping' wings covered the houses' gardens, producing a tightly packed but small-scale industrial townscape. They are brick structures with large iron-framed windows, which changed little throughout the C19. Surviving purpose-built factories begin with Elliott's button works of *c.* 1837–8 in Vittoria Street and Joseph Gillott's Victoria Works of 1839–40, the latter perhaps by *Charles Edge*. New Hall Works in George Street, a pin factory of 1847, is grander still. By the 1860s factory designs were of increasing architectural effect, e.g. *J.G. Bland*'s Argent Centre (Wiley's pen works) of 1862–3, and his multicoloured brick Gothic goldsmith's factory of 1865 (now the Institute of Jewellery, Fashion and Textiles). The 1870s saw more Gothic designs, such as Nos. 83–84 and Nos. 80–82 Great Hampton Street, the latter by *Yeoville Thomason*. Combined houses and workshops were still being built at this period, but often to architects' designs, such as No. 46 Frederick Street, by *Ewen Harper*, 1881. Later factories include *Thomas Frederick Proud*'s Aquinas House, Warstone Lane, Italian Romanesque of 1882, and *William Doubleday & James R. Shaw*'s spectacular Gothic-cum-Moorish H.B. Sale factory, Constitution Hill, of 1895–6.

91

Of other remaining Birmingham industrial areas, the Gun Quarter has plain workshop ranges of the 1820s–30s in Price Street and Loveday Street; a classical factory at No. 3 Princip Street, probably 1840s; and later C19 factory conversions including a Catholic school and a Wesleyan chapel. Digbeth and Deritend have early C19 houses converted to industry, and a converted Unitarian chapel and Sunday School in Fazeley Street. Purpose-built examples include the so-called Banana Warehouse on the canal of *c.* 1850, *J.R. Botham*'s Lion Warehouse of 1860, and the first part of Samuel Heath's factory, by *D. Henry Ward*, 1888–9. Heath's is a once-common type, the larger Birmingham factory expanding through the C19 and C20. Another is Belliss &

Morcom's in Ledsam Street, with much by *William Hale*, 1885–7, and later work by *W.T. Orton*, 1914–15, and *Buckland & Haywood*, 1953. Newey Bros in Summer Lane has a classical block of 1850, extended in 1916 and 1937. Notable industrial survivals elsewhere in Birmingham include the plain but historically important mill of 1864 at Webster & Horsfall, Hay Mills, where the first Atlantic cable was made; Armourer Mills in Sparkbrook, a huge Government-sponsored munitions factory of 1872; and the John Bowen builder's yard in Balsall Heath, of 1882 etc. Among larger engineering firms, the survivals at the Soho Foundry, Smethwick (Sa), especially the erecting shop of 1847, are noteworthy.

In the Black Country, COAL MINING has left Cobb's Engine at Rowley (Sa), part of a scheme of 1831 to drain mines in the area, and a full set of buildings at New Hawne Colliery, Halesowen (D), opened 1865. LIME-BURNING has left the Earl of Dudley's splendid set of kilns of 1842 by the Dudley canal basin (now inside the Black Country Museum). Industrial premises follow the same pattern of development as Birmingham but on a more modest scale. Early small-scale WORKSHOPS are now rare. The Black Country Museum has an oliver shop (forge); a chain shop survived in Cradley Heath, Rowley (Sa) until the early C21, and some buildings of the kind may survive in Quarry Bank (D). The functional tradition is represented by a group of Late Georgian and Early Victorian FLOUR MILLS and associated buildings: the Albion Flour Mill, Wolverhampton; the similarly named mill in Walsall; and the buildings round the former Union Mill, Wolverhampton. The GLASS industry has left Chance's impressive blocks of 1847 onwards at Smethwick, and the Stevens & Williams (Royal Brierley) works at Brierley Hill (D) of 1870. The finest survival of the HARDWARE industry is the Kenrick offices and warehouse at West Bromwich (Sa), of 1875–8 by *Martin & Chamberlain*. From the BREWING industry there are Showells Brewery at Langley, Oldbury (Sa) of 1870 and the much grander Springfield Brewery at Wolverhampton, 1873 and later. Showells also built the maltings at Langley, of 1898 by *Arthur Kinder & Sons*, still in the Victorian tradition. Another architecturally ambitious later Victorian factory is *Oliver Essex*'s Forder Carriage Works in Wolverhampton of 1886–7. In the area around Crabbe Street and Balds Lane, Wollescote (D), factories still sit among terraced housing, in a Black Country townscape otherwise almost lost.

Several Victorian WATERWORKS survive. In the Black Country they start with the Wolverhampton Waterworks Co.'s impressive pumping stations at Tettenhall of 1845 and Goldthorn Hill of c. 1851, by *Henry J. Marten*. Larger still is the South Staffordshire Water Co.'s pumping station at Wednesbury, of 1879 by *Henry Naden*. In Birmingham, where the municipalization of water was a centrepiece of the civic renaissance, pumping stations in *J.H. Chamberlain*'s fine brick Gothic style survive at Edgbaston (1862) and Selly Oak (1878–9).

Many RAILWAY STRUCTURES survive, though few stations. The finest and most important of these is also the earliest: the

Curzon Street terminus of the London & Birmingham Railway, of 1838 by *Philip Hardwick*, built as offices and as a splendid advertisement for the new method of travel. Near it are remains of the Grand Junction Railway: the station screen wall of 1838 by *Joseph Franklin*, and going E, a rusticated stone bridge by *Joseph Locke*, the Lawley Street viaduct and, at Duddeston, a wagon repair shop of the 1840s. Remains of the London & Birmingham elsewhere include the high three-arched bridge at Hill House Lane, Stechford. The other surviving early station is Wolverhampton Low Level by *William Wilson* and *John Fowler*, classical of 1854–5, as much an advertisement as Curzon Street. Of bridges and viaducts elsewhere, the most architectural is the Birmingham & Gloucester Railway's of 1840 in Highgate Place, with Egyptian pylons for side piers; the grandest is *Robert Stephenson*'s twelve-arch skew viaduct at Oxley (Wo), 1847–9. Later examples worth mention are the Harborne Railway's bridge at Park Hill Road (B) of 1869–74; the decorative Wednesfield Road railway bridge, Wolverhampton, by *Henry Woodhouse*, 1880; and the Stourbridge viaduct (D) of 1881–2, by the Great Western Railway engineer *W.D. Rowbotham*.

p. 192

The Arts and Crafts Movement and domestic architecture c.1890–c.1914

At the end of the C19 a distinctive school of ARTS AND CRAFTS MOVEMENT architects grew up in Birmingham. Its leaders were part of a network which included national figures: J.L. Ball was a friend of W.R. Lethaby, A.S. Dixon of C.R. Ashbee. It had a profile wider than just England: the work of W.H. Bidlake, C.E. Bateman, and W. Alexander Harvey at Bournville was included in Hermann Muthesius's influential *Das englische Haus* (1904). Its ideals spread through education: Bidlake taught at the School of Art from 1893, Lethaby lectured there twice in 1901. In 1909 the Birmingham School of Architecture was formed from the School of Art, with Ball as director. Its teaching emphasized materials, craftsmanship and functional composition, in contrast to the formal, Beaux Arts values taught at Liverpool under Charles Reilly.

Birmingham work is deliberately unassuming and reticent, using local materials – mostly brick – and emphasizing craft skills such as pointing and bonding. Its predecessors are the simplified versions of Queen Anne and Domestic Revival pioneered by architects from the offices of Norman Shaw and J.D. Sedding, of which an excellent example is *Ernest Newton*'s The Leasowes, Sutton Coldfield, 1893. There was an awareness in the city of the work of Philip Webb: *Ball* paraphrased the s aisle of St Martin, Brampton (Cumbria) at his Handsworth Methodist College (B) of 1880–1 (with *Goddard*), and at No. 54 Newhall Street and No. 87 Cornwall Street, Birmingham, *Henman & Cooper* used the bay windows sunk into the wall of Webb's Bell Bros offices in Middlesbrough. But the seminal domestic building was *Lethaby*'s

pp. 250–1

The Hurst, Sutton Coldfield of 1893–4, now demolished. Lethaby had strong links to Birmingham – half his executed works were either in the city or for Birmingham clients – and The Hurst exemplified his deceptively simple mature manner. The move towards this radical simplicity in Birmingham can be seen in buildings such as *Arthur Harrison*'s remarkable office and works in Albert Street of 1888, and especially in the early career of *J.L. Ball*, whose Methodist church in Sandon Road, Edgbaston (B), of 1889–90 (with *Ernest Barnsley*) also shows the progressive influence of G.G. Scott Jun. Buildings such as Ball's Nos. 17–19 Rotton Park Road, Edgbaston (including his own house) of 1895–6 and *A.S. Dixon*'s domestically inspired Guild of Handicraft building, Birmingham, of 1896 are so plain and unpretentious, though carefully detailed, that we may now miss their radicalism. The texture is important. Dixon disliked English and Flemish bonds, instead using brickwork of one header to three or four stretchers, or 'one course of alternate headers and stretchers...with two or three courses of stretchers'.

Of Arts and Crafts HOUSES, *Ball*'s in Barnsley Road, Edgbaston, 1898–1900, retain a little Queen Anne detail, but he continued his simplest manner in two Edgbaston houses of 1902: No. 415 Hagley Road, and the much grander Winterbourne in Edgbaston Park Road. The finest houses of Birmingham's greatest Arts and Crafts architect, *W.H. Bidlake,* include his own Woodgate, Ladywood Road, Sutton Coldfield, 1897, of special two-inch bricks, with dramatic contrasts of long horizontal sections and powerful gables. Garth House, Edgbaston Park Road, 1901, uses render as well as brick, with large areas of blank wall to balance the fenestration. No. 22 Ladywood Road, Four Oaks (Sutton Coldfield), of 1902, now ruined, contrasts a blank brick gable with a long, low main block. *C.E. Bateman*, the next major figure (working with *Bateman & Bateman*), moved from refined Shaw-style designs, e.g. in Stanley Road, Kings Heath (B), 1892, to more severity, in Vicarage Road nearby and in Castle Bromwich (So), of 1895–6. Also of 1896 is his original and picturesque Gable House in Vicarage Road. His simplest and most progressive houses are The Homestead, Woodbourne Road, Edgbaston of 1898–1900, and Redlands, Four Oaks, 1903–4.

W. Alexander Harvey was appointed architect of the BOURNVILLE VILLAGE TRUST (B) in 1896, at the age of twenty. The village, developed by George Cadbury from 1894, marks an advance beyond the company village of Port Sunlight (1888 etc.) towards the Garden City movement. Harvey designed delicately varied cottage-style houses in pairs and rows, in substantial gardens, and simple and handsome public buildings, clustered round a green. Housing of after 1908 is by *H. Bedford Tylor*. Cottage terraces by other Arts and Crafts architects include one by *Bidlake* in Handsworth New Road, Birmingham, of 1906. *Harvey*'s houses outside Bournville include Nos. 25–27 St Agnes Road, Moseley (B), 1904, with eyebrow dormers, and the miniature, Lutyens-like No. 48 Selly Wick Road, Selly Oak (B), 1913, now sadly mutilated. *Herbert Tudor Buckland & Edward*

Haywood-Farmer are seen at their best in Yateley Road, Edgbaston, where Buckland's own No. 21, of 1899, is more than an essay in vernacular revival, with an air of up-to-date Continental radicalism. Haywood-Farmer's own house, No. 12 Bracebridge Road, Four Oaks, 1902–3, has the same planar qualities in a more traditional design.

Of architects working in the Arts and Crafts manner who emerged in the early C20, the most important is *Edwin F. Reynolds*, who trained at the Birmingham School of Art. His early houses have Ball's simple austerity and Lethaby's feeling for mass, e.g. Low Wood, St Mary's Road, Harborne (B), and Nos. 94–96 Solihull Road, Shirley (So), both of 1910. *Holland W. Hobbiss*'s long career started with houses such as Nos. 33–35 Greenhill Road, Kings Heath of 1908, with Ball-style brickwork but almost organic curved porch roofs, and the cottage terrace in St Margaret's Road, Ward End (B), of 1907.

Among other architects, *Joseph Crouch & Edmund Butler* had a more associative and indulgent manner. Their early work is Domestic Revival – No. 75 Shirley Road, Acocks Green (B), 1888 – or Queen Anne – No. 133 Showell Green Lane, Sparkhill (B), 1892–3. Their Arts and Crafts work, starting with No. 59 Salisbury Road, Moseley, 1897–8, and The Anchorage, Handsworth Wood Road, 1899, is self-consciously picturesque, with timber gables and towers with fancy parapets. Crouch's own Seven Gables, Driffold, Sutton Coldfield, and Butler's No. 14 nearby, are similar. Perhaps their best house is the tightly composed, roughcast Avoncroft, No. 21 Four Oaks Road, 1900. *Owen Parsons* is easily underrated, but his best work – Hindecliffe, Bracebridge Road, Four Oaks, of 1905–6, and the Tudor-influenced No. 4 Amesbury Road, Moseley, of 1909 – combines simple treatment and considerable originality. *Cossins, Peacock & Bewlay* at their best – No. 20 Hermitage Road, Edgbaston, of 1899 (*F. Barry Peacock*'s own house), and No. 9 Pritchatts Road, Edgbaston of 1905–6 – approach Ball's or Bidlake's simplicity. Of other architects, *J. P. Osborne*'s No. 84 Handsworth Wood Road of 1906 could pass for Bidlake, and *Frederick Martin* (*Martin & Chamberlain*) houses such as No. 86 Westfield Road, Edgbaston, 1907, are nearly of Bidlake or Bateman quality. It would be good to know more about *Herbert R. Lloyd*, whose Nos. 174–176 Hamstead Road, Handsworth of 1894 is almost as simple as Ball's houses. The Sutton Coldfield architects *Marston & Healey*'s remarkable Nos. 22 and 24 Anchorage Road of 1901–3 show the influence of Mackintosh as well as Continental houses. The Birmingham school resisted Mackintosh influence, though *Bateman* designed a distinctly Scottish-looking lodge in Thimblemill Road, Smethwick (Sa), in 1912. *George E. Pepper* designed instantly recognizable small houses in a loud version of Bidlake's and Crouch & Butler's language, e.g. No. 16 Salisbury Road, 1905, and No. 44 St Agnes Road, 1906, both in Moseley. *W. de Lacy Aherne*, also very active in Moseley, designed in a basic, easily reproducible manner influenced both by Birmingham architects and also by C. F. A. Voysey. His best are Nos. 110–112 Oxford Road of 1906–7.

In the early C20 there was a turn to classicism, often inspired by vernacular Georgian. *C.E. Bateman* had a particular love for this manner, and great skill in reviving it, starting with two houses in Four Oaks of 1902: No. 14 Bracebridge Road, for his father and himself, and Carhampton House, Luttrell Road, with a particularly lovely garden front. His Nos. 89–91 Cornwall Street, Birmingham, of 1905 is one of a group of grand urban houses, a type only found in the city as doctors' houses and consulting rooms. Bateman also designed many vicarages in Birmingham, of which St Wulstan's, Bournbrook Road, Selly Oak, of 1914–15 is the finest, with its Burlington or Kent chimneys. *Ernest C. Bewlay*'s No. 68 Wellington Road, Edgbaston, 1913, is also notable.

Wolverhampton was also a significant Arts and Crafts centre. *W.J.H. Weller* was the most important figure here. His work is distinctively different from the Birmingham school, with greater use of half-timbering, influenced by Ould's work at Wightwick and The Mount, but in a craftsmanlike and honest way. Good examples are Longfield, Penn Road, 1903–5, and The Spinney, off Finchfield Hill, 1908. He contrasted big timber gabled blocks with finely made brick volumes at Leylands, Penn Road, 1905–6, and The Grove, Pedmore (D), 1908, where the double-height stair hall is the most spectacular Arts and Crafts interior in the area. His side gate and loggia at Longfield is radical, organic Free Style of the Harrison Townsend kind. Newbridge Avenue, Wolverhampton has his Voysey-ish The Cottage of 1911, and fine houses by *Owen Parsons* and *F.T. Beck*.

Other significant Wolverhampton Arts and Crafts works came from the *T.H. Fleeming* office at the turn of the C20. They are quite different from the firm's earlier work and perhaps by Fleeming's son, *W.H. Fleeming*. The former Pupil Teachers' Centre in Old Hall Street of 1899–1901 is a simple, radical brick statement, surely influenced by A.S. Dixon's Guild of Handicraft building. The Girls' High School of 1910–11 is less challenging but still shows Lethaby or Ball influence. Also in Wolverhampton is the Fallings Park Garden Suburb, Fallings Park, where the built housing exhibition of 1908 brought together Morris-inspired socialists who worked on site on their own schemes – *Detmar Blow*, *Randall Wells* and *Basil Stallybrass** – with Garden City specialists such as *C.M. Crickmer* of Letchworth and *Speir & Beavan* of Cardiff, and local men, particularly *W.J. Oliver* and *A.W. Worrall*. A small housing scheme worth mention is the cottage terraces of the Stourbridge Workmen's Dwellings Syndicate in Wollaston (D), of 1905–7 by *Tom Grazebrook*. Two significant Edwardian London architects represented in Wolverhampton are *Henry T. Hare*, with his inventively classical extensions to Penn Hall of 1902 etc., and *W. Curtis Green*, with a cool rendered house in Church Hill Road, Tettenhall, 1910.

---

*The group, associated with the Society for the Protection of Ancient Buildings, is described in Michael Drury's *Wandering Architects* (2000, 2nd edn 2016).

Religious architecture, c.1890–c.1914

Arts and Crafts CHURCHES in Birmingham are dominated by *W.H. Bidlake*. His first, St Oswald, Small Heath, of 1892, is indebted to Bodley and Pearson, but its splendid W front of 1899 brings us to his mature style. This starts with St Patrick, Salter Street, Earlswood (So), 1897–9. The interior has massive triangular wall piers and windows behind relieving arches, an arrangement of planes which is hardly a wall surface as such. His masterpiece, St Agatha, Sparkbrook of 1899–1901, continues this wiry, tense manner. Its landmark tower is a wonderful free interpretation of East Anglian Gothic. Bishop Latimer Church, Winson Green, of 1903–4, is more conventional inside but has an equally splendid tower, well grouped with a tall apse. His later churches are notable for their soaring proportions and spatial complexity: St Andrew, Handsworth, 1907–8, with low passage aisles opening into complex transepts and chapels; Emmanuel, Wylde Green (Sutton Coldfield), 1909, completed 1925–7; and Handsworth Cemetery Chapel of 1909–10, with unexpected narrow aisles and tall arcades. *C.E. Bateman*'s only pre-1914 church work is the E parts of St James, Hill, Sutton Coldfield, 1907–9.

The Arts and Crafts radicals sought to move away from conventional Gothic Revival to a round-arched Early Christian style, inspired by Lethaby and by J.F. Bentley's Westminster Cathedral of 1896–1902. They were encouraged by Birmingham's first bishop, Charles Gore, a cultured man with a love of the Mediterranean. *A.S. Dixon*'s St Basil, Deritend, of 1910–11, and *J.L. Ball*'s grander St Gregory, Small Heath, begun in 1911–12, both for strongly Anglo-Catholic clients, are intense designs, using brick, stone and tile in a complex, almost *cloisonné*-like texture evoking late Byzantine building. The latter also had a progressive liturgical arrangement, with the congregation near the altar. *Nicol & Nicol*'s St Benedict, Hob Moor Road, Small Heath, of 1908–9 is more conventional. *E.F. Reynolds*'s crustily textured St Germain, Edgbaston, 1915–17, is another Early Christian basilica. *C.R. Ashbee*'s free Romanesque scheme for St Stephen, Wolverhampton remained unbuilt.

Among other churches, St Aidan (now All Saints), Small Heath, by *Thomas Frederick Proud*, 1894–8, is a Perp design in the Birmingham terracotta style. Some Gothic Revival churches appeared with Free Style touches. *Philip B. Chatwin* took over his father's practice as *J.A. Chatwin & Son*, and his All Souls, Witton, Aston, and St Peter, Handsworth, both of 1906–7, are powerful designs with towers over the chancel in the Norman Shaw way. *Arthur Harrison*'s St Christopher, Sparkhill, also of 1906–7, has some larky detail (and sculpture by *Benjamin Creswick*). In Wolverhampton, *F.T. Beck*'s church hall at St Chad, Graiseley, 1898, is an original Free Style design, and his St Stephen, 1907–8, has good detailing. *J. Percy Clark*'s enlarged chancel at St Mark, Ocker Hill Road, Tipton (Sa), of 1909–10, is free Perp. Among national architects, *Basil Champneys* rebuilt the E end of St

Bartholomew, Wednesbury (Sa) from 1890, keeping to the Perp style of its predecessor. Bodley's successor *Cecil G. Hare* designed a convent chapel at Alum Rock (B) in 1911, and *Sir Charles Nicholson* a mission church at Minworth (Sutton Coldfield) in 1909. Two examples of classicism, conditioned by existing buildings, are St Michael, Brierley Hill (D), a Georgian church largely rebuilt by *Cossins & Peacock* in 1899–1900, and St Thomas, Wednesfield (Wo), where *Beck* rebuilt the interior in 1903 after a fire.

CHURCH FITTINGS of the period reflect both the Arts and Crafts Movement and Anglo-Catholic trends. The best sets of *Bidlake* furnishings are at St Patrick, Earlswood; Bishop Latimer Church, Winson Green, and particularly St Andrew, Handsworth, where the reredos has paintings by *Fred Davis*. *Bateman's* fittings at St James, Hill, Sutton Coldfield, climax in a reredos taking up the whole E wall. His fine screen at St Matthew, Walsall, 1914–15, has a cresting like crowns of thorns. He did splendid schemes of wall and ceiling paintings at St Bartholomew, Wednesbury (with *C.G. Gray*) from 1912 and Holy Trinity, Sutton Coldfield from 1914. Other significant wall paintings are at St Michael the Archangel, Rushall (Wa), by *E.R. Frampton*, 1906, and the Lady Chapel at Christ Church, Coseley (D), by *Florence Camm* of *T.W. Camm*, 1910. The chancel at *A.S. Dixon's* St Basil, Deritend is still complete, with chunky rood screen (figures by *George Jack*), apse mosaic, altar and tiled floor: an ensemble of quiet intensity. An altar by *Dixon* of 1913–14 survives at St Augustine, Holly Hall, Dudley. St Aidan, Small Heath, had fine 'English Use' fittings by *Frederick Bligh Bond* and *W.E. Ellery Anderson*, mostly of 1911–12; what is left after reordering includes a rood beam and figures, and the S chapel screen and loft of 1914 by *Bond* and *Thomas Falconer*. *Beck's* classical fittings at St Thomas, Wednesfield survive complete. The Late Victorian fashion for wrought-iron screens appears at St Andrew, Netherton (D) (*J.B. Davies*, 1892), St Alban, Highgate (B) (*J.L. Pearson*, 1897) and St Mary, Handsworth (*J.A. Chatwin*, 1898). *C.E. Bateman* transformed the type at All Saints, Kings Heath, 1893, with scrolls and flowerheads.

Of STAINED GLASS of the Birmingham Arts and Crafts school, *Henry Payne's* great E window at St Agatha, Sparkbrook, was destroyed in the Second World War. His work survives at St Alban, Highgate (1904), an angel with memorable wings, and St Agnes, Moseley (1908). *Mary Newill* did a small window of 1906 at St Mary and St Ambrose, Edgbaston, with Burne-Jones-style figures and landscape background; *Bertram Lamplugh* a small window in St Aidan, Small Heath, 1907, and the fine E window of 1908–9 in the St Alphege chapel at Solihull. The *T.W. Camm* firm, run by *Florence, Robert* and *Walter Camm*, can be seen at its best in the Halesowen (D) window of the Dignity of Labour of 1911. Among national figures, there are large schemes of *C.E. Kempe* glass at St Bartholomew, Wednesbury (1898–1912) and the chapel at the Royal School, Wolverhampton (1903–25). *Mary Lowndes's* richly coloured work can be seen at St Peter, Summerfield (B) (1906), Holy Trinity, Sutton Coldfield (1907), and St Saviour, Saltley (B) (1910). One of the finest windows by *J.H.*

Dearle of *William Morris & Co.* is at Oldswinford (D) (1915–16). The little-known *G.H. & W. Randle* of Kings Norton did a haunting window at St Augustine, Holly Hall (D) (1914).

ROMAN CATHOLIC CHURCHES remained conservative in this period. St Patrick, Dudley Road, Birmingham, of 1894–5 by *Dempster & Heaton*, is still in the E.W. Pugin tradition. Perhaps the best are by *H.T. Sandy*: the nave of St Edward, Selly Park (B), 1901–2, and his nearby convent chapel of 1914. The Oratory Church, Birmingham by *Doran Webb*, 1903–9, a memorial to Newman, is magniloquent Baroque-cum-Jacobean, with a wealth of furnishings. *Edward Goldie* designed a fine domed classical chapel at St Peter and St Paul, Wolverhampton, 1901. The most complete ensemble of fittings is at St Patrick, Dudley Road, which still has the feel of a pre-Vatican II church. *Frederick Bligh Bond* produced a spiky Gothic reredos at St Mary, Wednesbury, of 1904. The Oratory Church is exceptional, with rich fittings, some imported from Sant'Andrea della Valle in Rome, others including a spectacular oval font and cover by *Dunstan Powell* of 1912.

67

This is the last great period of NONCONFORMIST CHAPELS. The Arts and Crafts Movement is represented by *W.A. Harvey*'s Friends' Meeting House in Bournville of 1905, its composition with splayed wings deriving from Edgar Wood, and by *Crouch & Butler*'s majestic Four Oaks Methodist Church (Sutton Coldfield) of 1902 etc. A chapel by them of 1906–7 survives, much extended, at Stockland Green, Erdington (B). Of other chapels, the two finest are also Methodist. Darlington Street Methodist Church in Wolverhampton, of 1899–1901 by *Arthur Marshall*, marks the arrival of Nonconformity as a rival power to the Established Church, with its three domes and magnificent, almost unaltered interior. The Methodist Central Hall in Birmingham, by *Ewen & J.A. Harper*, 1900–3, has a scale and urban presence of the very finest kind. Demolitions elsewhere have left little. Two Free Style, Primitive Methodist chapels recently lost were High Street, Blackheath, by *Gerald McMichael*, 1902, and Graingers Lane, Cradley Heath (Sa) by the *Harpers*, 1906. Of the Harpers' many other chapels, only the Methodist New Connexion, Blackheath (Sa) and the Park Congregational Church in Dudley, both of 1906, and the former Long Lane Methodist Church, Blackheath (intended as the school for an unbuilt chapel) of 1909 survive. The grandest surviving village chapel is Zoar, Gornal Wood (D), by *P.H. Ashby Bailey*, 1906. The best Free Style survivors are *Scott & Clark*'s Primitive Methodist church, Wednesbury (now Baptist) of 1912, and the Baptist church in Acocks Green, by *F.B. Andrews*, 1913–14. Apart from Bournville, the only Friends' Meeting House of the period is Edgbaston, 1895, an unusual *Rundbogenstil* design by *William Henman*.

73
71

Public buildings, c.1890–c.1914

PUBLIC BUILDINGS include the area's finest example of Edwardian Baroque. Walsall Council made the inspired choice of *J.G.S.*

Gibson, the runner-up to Lanchester & Rickards in the Cardiff City Hall competition. His Council House of 1902–5, inspired by Wren and Vanbrugh, integrates sculpture (by *H.C. Fehr*) into the design, and its tower 'crown' climaxes in the Free Style. The staircase is a delight of flowing, intriguing spaces. The Council House Extension in Birmingham by *Ashley & Newman*, 1908–17, also influenced by Wren, with St Mary-le-Bow-style doorcases, is calmer, showing its later date. More modest Neo-Wren is Sutton Coldfield Town Hall, by *Arthur R. Mayston*, 1905–6. Smethwick Council House (Sa), by the local architect *Fred J. Gill*, 1905–7, is solidly impressive.

PUBLIC LIBRARIES in this period include a series in the Birmingham suburbs. *William Martin*'s Spring Hill of 1891 is still in J.H. Chamberlain's tough Gothic style; *Henry Martin*'s Small Heath of 1893 is terracotta-style, with a tapering circular tower. *Cossins & Peacock*'s Bloomsbury Library, Nechells, of 1891–2 is Queen Anne, but with much terracotta. Their Balsall Heath Library of 1895 is progressive Free Jacobean. Kings Norton and Northfield Council built several small but good libraries: Free Tudor buildings at Selly Oak and Stirchley, of 1905 by *J.P. Osborne*; Kings Norton of 1905–6, charming Tudor-cum-Baroque by *Benjamin Bower*; and Rednal of 1909, Arts and Crafts domestic with a touch of Lutyens, also by Bower. Erdington's library, by *Osborne*, 1906–7, was intended as the start of a municipal building, with a central tower. *C.E. Bateman*'s modest Neo-Georgian building at Northfield is of 1914.

Libraries of the period in the Black Country begin with *Tom Grazebrook*'s lively and robust designs at Netherton (D) and Woodside (D), 1893–4. Wolverhampton's, of 1900–2 by *Henry T. Hare*, architect of Oxford Town Hall and Bangor University, is still refined Free Jacobean outside, but Neo-Wren inside. The major local figure is *George Wenyon* of Tipton (Sa). His Tipton library of 1905–6 is Free Style. Dudley library, 1908–9, uses the manner of Michelangelo with almost the confidence of Beresford Pite. A very fine Free Style building using classical detail is *Crouch, Butler & Savage*'s Wednesbury library (Sa), 1907–8. *J.G.S. Gibson*'s library at Walsall of 1906 is Baroque, but deliberately modest next to his Council House. *Wills & Anderson*, indefatigable entrants of architectural competitions, designed libraries for Rowley Regis Council (Sa) at Cradley Heath, 1908, and Blackheath, 1909, modestly scaled and friendly English Baroque with suggestions of French and American Beaux Arts.

PUBLIC BATHS are dominated by the wonderful survival of Moseley Road Baths, Balsall Heath (B), by *William Hale*, 1906–7, not top-flight architecture, but the only Edwardian double swimming bath still in use in England. Also in Birmingham, Woodcock Street Baths, by *Frederick W. Lloyd*, 1902, are still in use; Nechells, Free Style by *Arthur Harrison*, 1910, and Tiverton Road, Selly Oak, classical by *E. Harding Payne*, 1905, survive in other uses. The splendid terracotta baths at Green Lane, Small Heath, by *Henry Martin*, 1902, were recast as a mosque by *Akram Bonham*, 2012–13. Of non-municipal places of assembly, DRILL HALLS

VICTORIAN AND EDWARDIAN, c.1830 TO 1914

include the larky Bilston building (Wo) of 1901 by *Henry T. Hare*. Others are by the Staffordshire architect *C. G. Cowlishaw*, both of 1910, in Wolverhampton and Tipton. Two municipal POWER STATIONS survive, the massive Summer Lane building in Birmingham by *Ewen & J. A. Harper*, 1902 etc., and Coleshill Road, Sutton Coldfield, by *W. C. C. Hawtayne*, 1901.

SCHOOLS continued under local School Boards until 1904, when they were superseded by borough and county councils. The Birmingham board in the 1890s still used *Martin & Chamberlain*, whose larger schools of the period frankly express their structure in an almost engineering way, e.g. Floodgate Street, Deritend, 1890–1, and also the extension to the School of Art of 1892–3. Others, all with characterful ventilation towers, include Anderton Park, Balsall Heath, and Marlborough Infants', Small Heath. Opposition to their monopoly led to the employment of other architects, including *Buckland & Haywood-Farmer*, and in 1904 *H. T. Buckland* became the city's Education Architect. His Arts and Crafts schools include the radically simple Handsworth New Road, Winson Green, of 1901 and the neo-Byzantine Oldknow Road, Small Heath, of 1905. Buckland's later schools are plainer, e.g. St Benedict's, Small Heath, 1912–13. *Crouch & Butler* designed the wonderful Baroque fantasy of the Aston Higher Grade Board Schools of 1898–1900, and the simpler schools at Bartley Green, 1914, and (outside Birmingham) Town Junior School, Sutton Coldfield, 1907. Their teacher training college of 1909 at Dudley, demolished 2003, was a great loss.

Black Country schools of the period were more conservative. *Alfred Long*'s unsophisticated but exuberant terracotta Board Schools include King George V, Beeches Road of 1892, and Lodge Primary, his most spectacular, of 1902–4, both in West Bromwich (Sa); and in Oldbury (Sa), Rood End, 1905, and Rounds Green, 1910. Wolverhampton used *T. H. Fleeming*, as at the Higher Grade School, Newhampton Road East, 1894. Dudley went to outside architects for the Grammar School of 1898, by *Woodhouse & Willoughby*, the Manchester school specialists, and the Upper Standard School (Claughton Centre) of 1903–4, by *Barrowcliff & Allcock* of Loughborough. Small School Boards engaged local men: Cradley (D) used *Meredith & Pritchard*, 1902, as did Rowley Regis (Sa), at Temple Meadow, Old Hill, 1898–1900. The Lea Marston board used *Arthur S. Clarson* at Minworth (Sutton Coldfield), 1900–2. The new county education authorities had their own architects: in Staffordshire, *John Hutchings* and later *G. C. Lowbridge*, e.g. at Salisbury School, Darlaston (Wa), 1910; in Worcestershire, *A. V. Rowe*, at e.g. Longlands School, Stourbridge (D), 1911–12 (demolished). Of *C. Whitwell & Son*'s Industrial School for 'epileptics and feeble-minded' children at Monyhull, Brandwood (B), blocks of 1913–14 and a chapel of 1917 remain. A pioneer open-air school survives at Uffculme, Moseley (B) by *Cossins, Peacock & Bewlay*, 1911.

HIGHER EDUCATION means one building, of great importance: Birmingham University, begun by *Aston Webb & Ingress Bell* in 1900, with tough but romantic buildings in an eclectic manner including Jacobean and Byzantine, and using Beaux Arts formal planning.

Of national bodies, the POST OFFICE carried out its largest building programme in this period. From 1884 to 1913 its Chief Architect was (*Sir*) *Henry Tanner*. His Birmingham office in Victoria Square, of 1890–1, is French Renaissance, enlivened by steep roofs and cupolas. Wolverhampton, of 1895, is in his favourite Northern Renaissance style; Tipton, 1896, combines terracotta and timbered gables. Of finer quality are two early C20 offices by architects working under Tanner: *John Rutherford*'s Dudley, French C18 style of 1909–11, and *H.A. Collins*'s West Bromwich of 1916–18, in revived Early Victorian classical style.

Among Late Victorian and Edwardian PUBLIC SCULPTURE only *Albert Toft*'s work in Birmingham needs mentioning: the disquieting Boer War memorial in Cannon Hill Park of 1906, and the stiff King Edward VII in Centenary Square of 1912–13. This is however the great age of ARCHITECTURAL SCULPTURE, Edwardian Baroque especially: *H.C. Fehr*'s lively figures on Walsall Council House of 1902–5; and *H.H. Martyn*'s Michelangelesque figures on Dudley Library of 1909. In Birmingham on the commercial side (*see* below) there are *Robert Bridgeman & Sons*' figures on the London & Lancashire Insurance building in New Street of 1906–8; but the great figure is Ruskin's discovery *Benjamin Creswick*, notably the feast of his work on *Crouch & Butler*'s Nos. 153–161 Corporation Street of 1896–9 (*see* below). His liking for sinuous lines can be seen on Bloomsbury Library, Nechells of 1891–2 and the baths in Nechells Park Road of 1910. *W.J. Neatby* is the other important figure, with two works of 1900–1: the St George and the Dragon panels on Nos. 56–60 Newhall Street, and the sea monsters and Atlantes on the Midland & City Arcades, Union Street.

Commercial and industrial architecture, c.1890–c.1914

The best COMMERCIAL ARCHITECTURE of the start of the C20 uses the Arts and Crafts-influenced Free Style. The greatest example by far is *W.R. Lethaby & J.L. Ball*'s Eagle Insurance, Colmore Row, Birmingham, of 1900, one of the most original buildings of its date in England. Here, in an office building in a street context, the ideal of honest building leads to simple, direct structural expression, combined with a complex personal symbolism in such motifs as the moulded bronze doors and crowning eagle. A few local buildings emulate its austere functionalism. *Wood & Kendrick*'s Gem Buildings, Hockley Hill, of 1913, is one, especially its plain rear elevation, but it sits alone in the firm's output. *Harry Campbell Hawkes*'s No. 53 Regent Place of 1906 is almost as simple.* More influential was Lethaby's innovative use

---

* *G.F. Hawkes* designed a functional factory at Nos. 50–54 St Paul's Square for the jeweller E.L. Gyde, but also Gyde's almost contemporary, huge Old English house at No. 129 Lichfield Road, Sutton Coldfield.

of historic precedent, in what is called the Free Style. The Birmingham firm who best rose to its challenge, in a short but brilliant career, were *Newton & Cheatle*. Their progress can be followed from No. 134 Edmund Street, luscious terracotta of 1897, through the domestic-looking Nos. 121–123 Edmund Street and the refined Shavianism and complex balance of Nos. 125–131 Edmund Street, to the extraordinary fantasy of Nos. 41–43 Church Street of 1900–1. Its immediate successor, Nos. 37–39 Church Street of 1901–2, heralds the renewed interest in classicism. The Scottish Union and National Insurance, Colmore Row, by *Henman & Cooper*, 1904, is a Free Style composition to match Newton & Cheatle's, with a big semicircular bow clamped between tapering towers. *J. G. Dunn*'s No. 16 (1910) and Squirrel Works (1912–13) in Regent Place bring this Free Style to industrial buildings. Wolverhampton has less to show. *Thomas Hind*'s simple Co-op building in Stafford Street of 1891 is remarkably progressive for its date, and *F. T. Beck*'s Gresham Chambers, Lichfield Street, 1896–7, stands out as a good Shaw-influenced Free Tudor block. The row in Broad Street by *William Edwards*, 1904–5, shows the new simplicity. *W. J. H. Weller*'s one commercial building, Nos. 85–86 Darlington Street of 1912, is Free Tudor. Minor architects can surprise: *G. Vernon Cale* of Birmingham designed a good Free Style warehouse in Green Lane, Walsall, in 1902. *A. T. Butler* of Cradley Heath and Dudley is dealt with below, pp. 72–3.

Mainstream commercial architecture of the period moved from the 'terracotta style' already mentioned to an equally eclectic Edwardian Baroque and Neo-Wren. The finest terracotta-style building is the former Telephone Exchange in Newhall Street, Birmingham, by *Frederick Martin* of *Martin & Chamberlain*, 1896. *Essex, Nicol & Goodman*, the most prolific firm, are at their liveliest and most attractive in the pair of buildings, with balancing corner turrets, where Newhall Street crosses Cornwall Street, of 1896–1900, and the block in New Street and Cannon Street of 1898. The one substantial terracotta building in Birmingham by an outside architect, the Futurist Cinema of 1914 etc. by *Arthur Stockwell* of Newcastle upon Tyne, is essentially classical. *Essex, Nicol & Goodman*'s grandest contribution is the former Royal London Insurance in Prince's Square, Wolverhampton, 1902–3, of stone, not terracotta, and with Baroque taking over from Jacobean. Also in Wolverhampton is *T. H. Fleeming*'s row of shops with its corner spire in Broad Street of 1897–1904. *Thomas Robinson*'s Bordeaux House, Stourbridge (D), 1892–4, would rank with these if it had not been cut down. A few Birmingham terracotta-style buildings express the structural grid behind: *F. B. Osborn*'s No. 29 Newhall Street and Nos. 106–110 Edmund Street of 1895, and *Mansell & Mansell*'s former Ocean Insurance of 1900–2 in Temple Row West. Nos. 18–22 Queen Street, Wolverhampton, by *Fred Hunter Lynes*, 1900, is similar. The stretch of Corporation Street, Birmingham, by the Law Courts has a fine commercial townscape, including *Crouch & Butler*'s Nos. 153–161, 1896–9, with Shavian gables and sculpture by *Creswick*, and buildings by *Ewen & J.A. Harper*, 1900–1. *Mansell & Mansell*'s No. 133 Edmund Street of 1895–6 also reworks Shaw's City of London office manner.

Birmingham shied away from full-blown Baroque; of the best surviving examples, the London & Lancashire Insurance offices in New Street are by *Riley & Smith*, 1906–8; the Atlas Insurance, Colmore Row, 1912, is by a London architect, *Paul Waterhouse*. Neo-Wren Baroque classicism is more frequent, as at the Alliance Assurance, Colmore Row, by *Goddard & Co.*, 1903. Marcus O. Type used Italian Mannerist devices, in the manner of J.J. Joass, to express the disjuncture between façade and structure, as at No. 55 Newhall Street. An unusual design is *A.E. Dempster*'s Nos. 29–31 Queen Street, Wolverhampton, 1907, with Neo-Georgian details but still in red terracotta. The Phoenix Assurance, Colmore Row, Birmingham, 1915–17 by *Ewen Harper, Bro. & Co.*, is 'Monumental classic', in Albert Richardson's phrase. Quite on its own is *George E. Pepper*'s Ye Olde Toll Gate House shops, Handsworth (B), 1904, with its combination of Old English with a dash of Mackintosh and Art Nouveau.

The return of classicism was natural for BANKS, for which it symbolized permanence. *T.B. Whinney*'s Midland Bank at Sutton Coldfield of 1902 is an attractive mélange of Tudor and Baroque. The former commercial centre of Smethwick (Sa) is marked by two banks, *A.E. Lloyd Oswell*'s Lloyds of 1905–6, mixing Jacobean and Baroque, and *Whinney*'s Midland of 1911, in his more mature Baroque style. *Whinney*'s Old Bank in Stourbridge, of 1916–20, is similar, with a hint of French influence. *Oswell*'s former Lloyds at Cape Hill, Smethwick of 1908–9 is Jacobean and Baroque. The calmer Baroque classical or Neo-Wren manner was used by *F. Barry Peacock* in his Metropolitan Bank in Lichfield Street, Wolverhampton, 1912–13. His smaller Midland Bank at Cradley Heath (Sa) of 1910 is gentler Neo-Georgian. The National Provincial Bank in Queen Square, Wolverhampton, 1913, is Baroque classical (with Michelangelesque figures over the doorway), by *Bromley & Watkins*. The development of *J.A. Chatwin & Son*'s style can be seen in the Lloyds banks at Walsall of 1901–3, still partly Italianate but also using Wren motifs, and Five Ways, Edgbaston (B) of 1908–9 (*P.B. Chatwin*), reflecting c18 Palladian villas.

There are two surviving Late Victorian and Edwardian THEATRES of interest. The Grand, in Wolverhampton, 1894, is a good example of the work of *C.J. Phipps*, with his usual rich classical interior. The Repertory Theatre in Birmingham (now Old Rep) is by *S.N. Cooke*, 1912–13, classical in the early Albert Richardson manner.

The building boom of *c.* 1900 is also the great period of exuberant PUBS. The most important Birmingham specialists were *James & Lister Lea*. Their grandest pub is the Bartons Arms, Newtown, 1901; their most sumptuous and eclectic the Red Lion, Soho Road, Handsworth, 1901–2. Others include The Swan and Mitre, Aston and their subtlest design, the Woodman, Curzon Street. An unusual job is their convincing Regency remodelling of the Wellington Hotel, Bristol Street, of 1890–1. Below them, 'the trade' was served by jobbing architects such as *Joseph Wood*, who cut a picturesque dash at the Crown, Dudley, 1897–8, and the be-medalled Queens Arms, Newhall Street, Birmingham, 1901; and *William Jenkins*, whose bargeboards and imitation-J.H. Chamberlain exposed roof trusses can be seen at the former Rose & Crown, Bromsgrove Street, Birmingham, 1900, and the Seven Stars, Oldswinford (D), 1904–5 (with excellent *Maws* tiling). *Wood & Kendrick* were more sophisticated. Their richly fitted Waggon and Horses, Oldbury (Sa), 1899, might almost be a Lea pub. At the Junction, Harborne (B), 1903–4, and the Waterloo, Smethwick, 1907–8 (with a basement grill room superbly tiled by *Carters* of Poole), they are quieter and more refined.

Wolverhampton has the rare survival of a smart city centre bar, the Posada, of 1900–1 by *F.T. Beck*. The city's best pub of this period is the Prince Albert, by *George Wormal*, 1900–1. Walsall's best is the Borough Arms by *Hickton & Farmer*, of 1905, exuberant Jacobean with lots of terracotta. The Chequers, Stourbridge, by *Fred Hunter Lynes*, 1906, successfully uses Voysey's roughcast manner in an urban context. The traditional Black Country 'tworoom drinker' continues into this period, as at the Waggon and Horses at Old Hill (Sa), of 1907 by *Frank C. Lewis*. Suburban pubs were more genteel; *Robert F. Matthews*'s Cup Inn, Sutton Coldfield, 1894, and *Arthur Edwards*'s Selly Park Tavern, 1901, herald the 'reformed' pub movement (*see* p. 80). A crucial early building of this type, on a different architectural level from other contemporary pubs, is *C.E. Bateman*'s Red Lion, Kings Heath (B) of 1903–4, a loving re-creation of a late medieval inn.

INDUSTRIAL ARCHITECTURE of the period includes some fine examples of the Birmingham Arts and Crafts school. The impressive round arches of *E.C. Bewlay*'s cold store of 1899 in Digbeth (B) owe something to A.S. Dixon. There is a consciously simple factory by *C.E. Bateman* of 1901–2 in Adderley Road, Saltley (B) (his even finer Westley Richards factory of 1898–9 in Selly Oak was demolished in 2009), and *Bateman & Bateman* designed much of Samuel Heath's brass foundry in Leopold Street, Highgate (B) from 1891. *Buckland & Haywood-Farmer*'s No. 58 Oxford Street, Digbeth, 1911–12, is as plain and well crafted as their houses. The Birmingham Jewellery Quarter has most survivals of mainstream industrial buildings, including *Newton & Cheatle*'s huge Barker electroplating works in Constitution Hill of 1901–3, *Crouch & Butler*'s No. 32 Frederick Street, 1914, in fashionable cream faience, and *Ewen & J.A. Harper*'s work for Taylor & Challen around Livery Street of 1904–5 and 1910–16. *Arthur McKewan* did a fine Free Style factory in Great Hampton Street, 1912, and *George E. Pepper* several in the 1911–13 period.

Early CAR AND CYCLE FACTORIES are particularly important in the area. Survivals include the Sunbeam buildings in Wolverhampton, of 1896 to after 1914, and the company's Motor Works in Upper Villiers Street, mostly of 1903–8 by *Joseph Lavender*; *A.T. Butler*'s Bean factory in Dudley, 1916; and Marcus O. *Type*'s Heron factory and showroom of 1902–3 in John Bright

Street, Birmingham. *J. L. Ball*'s factory extension of 1911 etc. for the pioneer car maker Frederick Lanchester in Sparkbrook (B) – another Arts and Crafts work – is also important. Recent demolitions include the West Works, the last part of the original Austin factory at Longbridge, and *J.J. Hackett*'s Wolseley factory in Drews Lane, Ward End, both in Birmingham. Surviving RAILWAY STATIONS include Stourbridge Junction, Oldswinford, 1901, Tyseley (B), 1906, and Birmingham Moor Street, 1911, all for the Great Western.

Local architects of the Black Country

Even more than the mid-Victorian period, this is the time of the LOCAL ARCHITECT in the smaller Black Country communities. The Arts and Crafts Movement hardly appears, but the Free Style enlivens many places. Walsall had *Bailey & McConnal*, and especially *Hickton & Farmer*; Smethwick, *Fred Gill*; West Bromwich, *Wood & Kendrick* and *J.W. Allen*; Tipton, *George Wenyon*, already mentioned; Wednesbury and Darlaston, *C.W.D. Joynson* and later *Scott & Clark*; Stourbridge, *Thomas Robinson*; Willenhall, *Benjamin Baker*. Several were leading figures in their communities: *Gill* was a borough councillor; *Joynson* was the youngest-ever mayor of Wednesbury, and a county councillor for forty years. Their best work is genuinely memorable: *Bailey & McConnal*'s Brookes leather factory of 1890 etc.; *Hickton & Farmer*'s Hatherton Works of 1901 and Imperial Cinema of 1914; *Gill*'s Smethwick Council House of 1905–7; *Wood & Kendrick*'s public buildings in West Bromwich, especially their School of Art of 1903; and *Allen*'s Nos. 113–123 Bratt Street in the same town of 1907. *Joynson* was responsible for every worthwhile building in central Darlaston except the church and the earlier Town Hall. Even villages had their architects: *Owen Freeman* of Lye also managed a firebrick works, and its distinctive yellow products appear in much of his work. Chapels were still designed by local surveyors or architects, e.g. *William Bloomer*'s Macefield's Mission and *Clarence A. Bloomer*'s Ebenezer Strict Baptist, both at Old Hill (Sa). The Strict Baptists' wonderfully preserved Cave Adullam chapel, Blackheath (Sa), of 1897–8, by a local builder, *William Willett*, is a conservative updating of a Georgian galleried type. The best survivor of *W.F. Edwards*'s Methodist chapels (he also specialized in bakeries) is Cocksheds, Halesowen (D), 1907, now flats.

Last but not least, in the southern Black Country is the early and original Free Style work of *A.T. Butler*. His Rose and Crown, Cradley, transforms the 'two-room drinker' with free detailing. The Workers' Institute, Cradley Heath (Sa), 1911–12, re-erected at the Black Country Museum, has his trademarks of wings pushing out behind the front, and round windows. Survivors *in situ* include some lively houses in Sydney Road, Cradley Heath; his own offices in Priory Street, Dudley, of 1911; Blackheath Congregational Church of 1908; the Lady Chapel at Christ

Church, Coseley (D), 1909–10; and his Voyseyesque houses in Pear Tree Lane of 1908–9.* Just before the First World War, the young *G.F. Webb*, then Butler's assistant, designed a few modest Bournville-like houses, e.g. No. 11 Bromley Lane, Kingswinford (D).

FROM 1914 TO 1939

The most obvious results of the First World War are WAR MEMORIALS. Birmingham has a whole building, the Hall of Memory by *S.N. Cooke & W.N. Twist*, 1922–4, with good seated figures by *Albert Toft* and exceptional relief panels by *William Bloye*. Bloye (1890–1975) is the great figure of Birmingham sculpture from the 1920s to the 1960s, prolific but of high and consistent quality. He was trained partly by Eric Gill, which explains his excellent low-relief work, but also produced fully modelled figures. Architectural memorials elsewhere include two by *Batemans*, a memorial garden at Wednesbury (Sa), 1926, and a Doric temple on Barr Beacon (Great Barr, Wa), 1933. *A.T. Butler* designed a cenotaph at Wordsley (D); *William Haywood*'s Scouts' war memorial at Edgbaston (B) and *G.F. Webb*'s at Pensnett (D) are both tapering triangular pillars. Late but good examples of the 'New Sculpture' are at Stourbridge (D), 1923, with a figure and reliefs by *John Cassidy*, and Heath Town (Wo), *A.G. Walker*'s standing soldier of 1920. Anti-war feeling produced the unusual Peace Memorial at Quarry Bank (D) (*George Edward Wade* with *Alfred Long*, 1931).

Birmingham saw a new interest in CIVIC IMPROVEMENTS in the period. In 1917 the city laid down improvement lines for major roads. The architect *William Haywood*'s book *The Development of Birmingham* (1918) took a formal Beaux Arts approach, with American influence.† Haywood set out much of the development agenda of C20 Birmingham: a Civic Centre at the E end of Broad Street, separated from Victoria Square by an extended Central Library; the remodelling of New Street Station; and a ring of boulevards surrounding the centre. The Civic Centre produced many schemes; a competition in 1926–7 was won by *Maximilian Romanoff* of Paris, but his scheme was judged too expensive. A plan made by *S.N. Cooke*, *A.J. Swann* and the City Engineer established the idea of an E–W space aligned along Broad Street, with a three-sided court of council offices to its N. In 1940 *Haywood* produced another Beaux Arts design, with a 140-ft (42.7-metre)-high column topped by a male nude statue representing 'The Spirit of Birmingham': again abandoned. The two survivors of these schemes are by *T. Cecil Howitt*: the confidently classical former Municipal Bank of 1931–3, and

---

* *Voysey*'s lodge in Bury Hill Park, Oldbury (Sa), was demolished in the 1970s.
† Haywood was the successor to his relative Edward Haywood-Farmer, †1917, as partner to *H.T. Buckland*.

Baskerville House, the E wing of the council offices court, of 1939–41. *Haywood* planned many other Beaux Arts schemes; survivors include the lodges at Kynochs, Perry Barr (B), of 1915; the avenue to the Scouts' memorial in Edgbaston, later joined by the museum of 1930 by *A.L. Snow* and *A.E. Leeson*; and the Birmingham University lodges of 1930 in Pritchatts Road.

The most complete set of interwar PUBLIC BUILDINGS is *Harvey & Wicks*'s Dudley Town Hall of 1926–8 and adjoining Municipal Buildings of 1934–5, a seminal example of Scandinavian influence in Britain. The turn from this progressive manner towards Modernism is splendidly seen at Wolverhampton Civic Hall of 1936–8 by the London architects *Lyons & Israel*, where the influence of Tengbom is combined with clear, simple massing and planning. A step further is the same firm's health centre at Bilston (Wo) of 1938–9 (as *Lyons, Israel & Elsom*), with its Dudok-style flat roofs and bands of windows. Of the Black Country's own municipal architects, Smethwick (Sa) had *Chester Button*, who moved from austere Neoclassical at e.g. his Magistrates' Courts of 1931, to Modernism in the interior of the swimming baths of 1933 and the library of 1936 in Thimblemill Road. *Wallace Wood* of Wolverhampton is at his best in the Heath Town baths of 1931–2. The unusual octagonal Low Hill (Wo) library of 1930 is probably also his.

In Birmingham, municipal design and planning were dominated by strong City Engineers: *Sir Herbert H. Humphries*, 1919–35, and *Sir Herbert Manzoni*, 1935–63. Architects occupied a low place, and designs were attributed to the Engineer. The results are solid but dull: police stations – Steelhouse Lane (1930), Handsworth (1938), Summer Lane (1939) – and fire stations – Ettington Road, Aston (1923–4; the best), Cotteridge (1930) and the Central Fire Station (1935). Some departments used outside architects, with better results, especially Health and Welfare: see *J.L. Ball*'s Carnegie Infant Welfare Institute in Handsworth, late Arts and Crafts of 1922; *J.P. Osborne & Son*'s Chest Clinic in Great Charles Street, Neoclassical of 1930–2; and *Ewen Harper, Brother & Co.*'s infant welfare centre in Lancaster Street of 1935. A fine sequence of BRANCH LIBRARIES by *J.P. Osborne & Son* moves from Neo-Georgian – Acocks Green (1926), Ward End (1927–8) – to more severe Neoclassical – Perry Common, Kingstanding (1934), and South Yardley, Soanian (1938).

Interwar COUNCIL SCHOOLS were mostly by the local authorities' own architects. Birmingham used *H.T. Buckland*, whose designs move from Neo-Georgian (Kingsbury School, Erdington, 1923; Starbank Junior, Small Heath, 1926–8) to flat-roofed near-Modernism (Twickenham Primary, Kingstanding, 1930–2). Staffordshire had *G.C. Lowbridge*, at his grandest at Bilston Girls' High of 1929–30. Warwickshire's county architect *A.C. Bunch* was solid but not inspired: Sutton Coldfield Girls' Grammar, 1929, and extensions to Bishop Vesey's Grammar, 1938–9. *A.V. Rowe* of Worcestershire was at his best at Oldbury County High (Sa), 1926 (demolished). His Technical School at Halesowen (D), 1937–9, combines Neo-Georgian and near-Modern. In small Black Country towns *C.W.D. Joynson* and *Scott & Clark* did much. More interesting in Birmingham are private architects' work, from *Harvey & Wicks*'s splendid Bierton School, Yardley of 1926–8, with its triumphal-arch entrance, to *S.N. Cooke*'s Great Barr schools (Perry Beeches (B)) of 1938–9. Modernism was pioneered at *J.B. Surman*'s flat-roofed Ward End school of 1930–1, with its wide V-plan. *W.T. Benslyn*'s Paganel Primary School, Harborne (1938), also flat-roofed, is steel-framed and faced in brick. Benslyn's Brearley Street nursery school (B) (1938–9), with its cantilevered side blocks and flying staircases, is a radical statement not paralleled in the area until the 1960s. *Wallace Wood*'s schools in Wolverhampton include Elston Hall (1938), with a central tower, and Warstones (1939–40), flat-roofed and more informal. An exceptional building is the new King Edward's School, Birmingham by *Holland W. Hobbiss*, 1937–47, moving from Tudor Revival to straightforward, large-windowed classroom ranges, but with steep Lutyens-pitch roofs.

The best interwar UNIVERSITY BUILDINGS at Birmingham are not for teaching: *Hobbiss*'s rich evocation of a Tudor manor house for the Guild of Students, 1928–30, and *Robert Atkinson*'s sophisticated and eclectic Barber Institute, 1936–9. The most important FURTHER EDUCATION BUILDING elsewhere is *Beresford Pite* and *Arnold Silcock*'s powerful Asbury Overseas House at Selly Oak (B), 1926. Black Country colleges (Wolverhampton Technical, *John Hutchings* and others, 1926 etc.; Dudley College, *G.C. Lowbridge* with *A.T. & Bertram Butler*, 1933–6) are not impressive. Smaller, and better, college buildings are Hobbiss's Neo-Georgian blocks and Romanesque chapel at Queen's College, Edgbaston; *Christopher Wright*'s College of the Ascension, Selly Oak; and *J.R. Armstrong*'s Day Continuation School of 1925 at Bournville (B) and the Rendel Harris Library of 1931 at Selly Oak.

Interwar Birmingham was the largest authority for MUNICIPAL HOUSING in England after the London County Council, but its City Engineer's designs were unremarkable. Early developments such as Vimy Road, Billesley are modest. Later estates were larger, Kingstanding (1928–37) and Weoley Castle (1931–7). Less conventional designs include the mansard-roofed flats on Garrison Lane, Small Heath; the U-shaped roughcast pairs of The Worthings and Barn Close, Stirchley, by an outside architect, *Arthur McKewan*; and the linked Barrack Street flats, Nechells. Kingstanding has the streamlined stuccoed houses of Hurlingham Road, and Weoley Castle the Bournville-like half-timbered houses on Shenley Fields Road. In the Black Country things were better. Some councils used their own architects for housing. *Wallace Wood* designed the Low Hill estate at Wolverhampton, 1925–9, and used a distinctive deep-roofed design in Old Fallings Lane and elsewhere. *Chester Button* of Smethwick's best are the Thimblemill Road flats of 1938–9. Smaller authorities used local architects, e.g. *A.T. Butler* for Kingswinford R.D.C. (D); *Tom Grazebrook* for Amblecote U.D.C. (D); *A.W. Worrall*, a housing specialist, for Heath Town U.D.C. (Wo); and *J. Homery Folkes* for Lye and Wollescote U.D.C. (D). Of nationally known housing architects, *T. Alwyn Lloyd* worked for Sedgley U.D.C. (D) at Greenway (1920–3), and *E.P. Mawson* for Dudley at the Priory Estate (1928–32, mostly demolished). The Bournville Village Trust under *S. Alex Wilmot* continued to build cottage terraces and pairs, e.g. at Selly Oak.

There is an enormous amount of 'Dunroamin': modest inter-war detached and semi-detached PRIVATE HOUSING. A good place to appreciate it is School Road, Hall Green, Birmingham, by the builders *H. Dare & Son*, 1933–6. Architecturally more significant houses in the Arts and Crafts tradition continued, but were smaller, for an age with fewer servants. The move to cool, rendered exteriors is represented by *Benjamin Bower*'s The White House, Erdington (1919) and *E.F. Reynolds*'s No.9 Hartopp Road (1920) and *Holland W. Hobbiss*'s No.9 Luttrell Road (1923) in Four Oaks (Sutton Coldfield). A deep love of traditional England, born in the horrors of war, is expressed at *David Gray* of *Webb & Gray*'s own house, No.6 Moss Grove, Kingswinford (D) of 1924, and in the developments of *Kenneth Hutchinson Smith*, using reclaimed timber and bricks from old houses, especially Castlecroft Gardens, Wolverhampton. Related is the extraordinary work of Gerald Mander and his architect *James A. Swan* at The Dippons, Tettenhall (Wo), where the house of 1914–15 was followed by garden towers and arches of 1922 etc. *Harry Weedon*'s Tudor revival houses are a sophisticated version, e.g. No.81 Farquhar Road, Edgbaston, and Kenwood, Four Oaks. An equally English alternative in the 1920s was Neo-Georgian, as at *Gerald McMichael*'s No.33 Grove Avenue, Moseley (B); *A.T. Butler*'s Trebant, Dudley; and – finest of all – *Harvey & Wicks*'s No.12 Fox Hill, Selly Oak. *J.B. Surman* excelled at austere Tudor revival or classical designs: No.37 Ashleigh Road, Solihull (1928) and the Charles Lane Trust almshouses, Hall Green (B) (1937).

1930s houses stuck to traditional styles. *Owen Parsons*'s No.6 Woodbourne Road, Edgbaston (1936) is a beautiful and nostalgic Tudor design. *G.F. Webb* designed a thatched house on Oakham Road, Dudley (*c.*1931). A 'Spanish' fashion is represented by *J.W. Wilson*'s own No.17 Beech Hill Road, Sutton Coldfield (1933–4) and *Francis Bromilow*'s No.2 Grange Hill Road, Kings Norton (B) (1939–40); something Expressionist by *Wilson*'s Oaklands Road, Four Oaks (1931 etc.) and *Bromilow*'s No.45 Moss Grove, Kingswinford (1939). Early Modernist houses are mostly by outsiders or fringe figures. The first flat-roofed houses, now mangled, were by the tragically short-lived partnership of *Tanner & Horsburgh* (†1932 and †1934): Nos.79 and 87 Westfield Road, Edgbaston. Others are *C. Edmund Wilford*'s Dudok-style No.9 Hillwood Common Road, Sutton Coldfield, 1936; the builder *C.K. Shepherd*'s Nos.38–48 Kensington Road, Selly Park (B), 1930; and *T. Dunkley Hogg*'s No.53 Beaks Hill Road, Kings Norton, 1935. Flats on Stratford Road, Hall Green of 1934 (*Jennens*, builder, with *F.W.B. Yorke*) and 1936 (*H. Peter Hing*) are similar. Wolverhampton houses of the 1930s had better architects but were not as advanced, still with pitched roofs: *S.D.W.*

Timmins's flats on Tettenhall and Compton roads, and *Richard Twentyman*'s early houses, of which the best survivor is Halfacre, 1938. The best Modern houses are No. 10 Beech Hill Road, Sutton Coldfield, early *Jackson & Edmonds*, 1936–7, rendered, with a curved corner; and No. 135 Skip Lane, Walsall, by *Lavender, Son & Close*, 1936.

Interwar ANGLICAN CHURCHES start with *A. S. Dixon*'s blunt but impressive rebuilding of St Giles, Rowley (Sa), 1922–3, and his chapel at Bishop's Croft, Harborne (B), refined Arts and Crafts Jacobean of 1923. For later churches the most important figures are *Edwin F. Reynolds* and *Holland W. Hobbiss*. *Reynolds* made his reputation with St Germain, City Road, Edgbaston, 1915–17, a rough-textured apsed basilica. His finest church, St Mary, Pype Hayes (B) of 1929–30, is a masterpiece of architectural logic, a complex plan marrying basilica and Latin cross, with spare details that seem to grow naturally from the brick structure. St Hilda, Warley Woods, Oldbury (Sa), 1938–40, has a central plan and groin-vaulted crossing. In contrast, *Hobbiss*'s churches are exquisitely made, eclectic, with spreading compositions and the deliberate disjunctions of the Webb tradition. They have the feel of holiday postcards: from Germany at Christ Church, Burney Lane, Alum Rock (B), 1934–5, with its *Westwerk* tower; from rural France at Holy Cross, Billesley Common (B), 1935–7, with its belfry clambering up the aisle roof; from Romanesque Italy at Queen's College chapel, 1939–47; and from the Welsh borders at St Francis' Hall (University of Birmingham chaplaincy), 1936. *C. E. Bateman*'s St Chad, Sutton Coldfield, 1925–7, is a spectacular one-off: a big Cotswold stone barn outside, but with arcades of rubble-faced piers. *H. G. Wicks* of *Harvey & Wicks* designed two massive churches of 1938–40: St Francis, West Bromwich (Sa), eclectic Romanesque, and the unfinished Immanuel, Highters Heath (B), Early Christian. *Percival J. Hunt* designed St Luke, Kingstanding, 1936–7, now sadly mangled, in a cool planar manner. *P. B. Chatwin*'s refined St Faith and St Laurence, Harborne, 1936–7 (completed 1958–60) combines plastered arcades with cross-arches. Bishop Barnes's extension campaigns in Birmingham produced many 1930s mission churches, the best survivors *Hunt*'s St Andrew, Stechford, and *J. A. Swan*'s Archbishop Benson Hall, Handsworth. In the Black Country the other significant new churches are *Sir Charles Nicholson*'s St John, Dudley Wood (D), 1931, and *Webb & Gray*'s mission buildings, St Michael, Stourbridge of 1929–30 and St Francis, Dudley of 1931–2. At the end of the 1930s come *Richard Twentyman* of *Lavender & Twentyman*'s early churches, again Early Christian looking towards Modernism: St Martin, Wolverhampton, and St Gabriel, Fulbrook, Walsall.

Most CHURCH FITTINGS of the period are modest, though *Reynolds*'s and *Hobbiss*'s are always good. *Bateman*'s work in Sutton Coldfield includes his reredos at St Chad and that at the Lady Chapel at St Peter, Maney, with paintings by *Sidney Meteyard*. STAINED GLASS by national figures includes work by *Ninian Comper* (St Mary, Kingswinford) and *Geoffrey Webb* (St Andrew,

Handsworth; St Edmund, Dudley). The Birmingham Arts and Crafts school is represented by *Richard Stubington* (Hall of Memory; St Mary and St Ambrose, Edgbaston), *Henry Payne* (All Saints, Kings Heath (B)), *Sidney Meteyard* (St Alban, Highgate (B); Emmanuel, Wylde Green (Sutton Coldfield)), and the prolific *Archibald John Davies* (e.g. at St Paul, Hamstead (B), and Moseley Baptist Church), and by two gloriously coloured windows by *A.E. Lemmon* at St Peter, Greets Green (Sa), and All Souls, Witton (B).

Among CATHOLIC CHURCHES this is the Early Christian Revival period, with its basilican planning. They were also the great years of *George Bernard Cox*, as at the Sacred Heart and St Margaret Mary, Aston (1920–2) and the progressive St Augustine, Handsworth (1938–9); and of *E. Bower Norris* of Stafford, whose best in the area are the English Martyrs, Sparkhill (B) (1922–3) and Our Lady of Perpetual Succour, Wolverhampton (1933–4). Perhaps best of all are the churches of *George Drysdale*, the former partner of Leonard Stokes, and Director of the Birmingham School of Architecture in 1924–47: Our Lady and St Thérèse, Saltley (1932–4), and the massive and spatially complex Our Lady and St Hubert, Warley (Sa) (1934). *McCarthy & Collings*'s St Margaret Mary, Erdington (B) is remarkably near Modernism for Birmingham in 1936. Among CATHOLIC CHURCH FITTINGS, *Benjamin Creswick*'s Stations of the Cross at Our Lady and St Brigid, Northfield (B), are exceptional.

NONCONFORMIST BUILDING between the wars is mostly modest and suburban. Pride of place must go to *W.H. Bidlake*'s last church, Sparkhill Congregational (1932–3, now a restaurant). *J.R. Armstrong* of Bournville Village Trust built a series of simple but satisfying brick chapels in the Arts and Crafts tradition: Selly Oak Friends' Meeting House; Trinity Congregational, Hall Green; Pype Hayes Congregational; and Weoley Hill Presbyterian, Selly Oak. The best Arts and Crafts chapel in the Black Country is *Harry Campbell Hawkes*'s Noah's Ark, Netherton (D), of 1925 (now flats). *W. Cyril Moss* of *Crouch, Butler & Savage* did the countrified Hall Green Methodist Church, and more massive 1920s Methodist chapels at Beckminster (Wo), and Stourbridge. *F.B. Andrews* did updated round-arched Baptist chapels at e.g. Cannon Street Memorial, Handsworth, 1930, and Hall Green, 1935. *F.W.B. Yorke*'s only chapel is the delicate and eclectic Warley Institutional Church, 1924–5. *Stanley Griffiths*'s self-conscious originality can be seen at Gigmill Methodist, Stourbridge, 1932–3. *George While*'s designs of the later 1930s are traditional, but look towards Modernism: Sutton Coldfield Methodist (with *Crouch, Butler & Savage*), and the Helier Chapel, Northfield.

Interwar BANKS are mostly suburban and small town branches, their classicism always making a positive contribution to the townscape. The most significant company was Barclays, using *Peacock & Bewlay*. Their grandest is Dudley (1930–1); others are at Cotteridge, Moseley (with a portico) and Great Bridge (Sa). The Birmingham Municipal Bank's headquarters is dealt with above; its branches are mostly Neo-Georgian, as at Bristol Street by *W.N. Twist*, 1929, and Halesowen, by *E.C. Bewlay*, 1939–40. The grandest BUILDING SOCIETY in the area is the Wolverhampton Freeholders', Queen Square, by *Cleland & Hayward*, 1932–3. The West Bromwich Building Society's old headquarters by *J.B. Surman* and *W.T. Benslyn* is subtle Neo-Georgian, by architects who later embraced Modernism. Its branches are by *Cecil E.M. Fillmore*: Oldbury (Sa), 1933, Neo-Georgian; Great Bridge, 1935, inventive Soanian. The Rowley Regis (Sa) society's headquarters at Old Hill are Neo-Georgian going modern by *Albert Bye, Simms & Gifford*, 1933–5. The Ideal Benefit Society of Birmingham's headquarters at Pitmaston, Moseley, 1930–1, is *Hobbiss*'s finest commercial building.

General COMMERCIAL ARCHITECTURE of the period is also emphatically classical. The most noticeable firm is *S.N. Cooke & Partners*, working mostly in Birmingham: the stripped classical No. 126 Colmore Row; Sun Building, Bennetts Hill; Stock Exchange, Margaret Street, all 1920s. Their Smart Bros' store, Temple Street, 1931, combines streamlined *Moderne* and classicism. Leicester Buildings, Walsall, 1932–3, has Neo-Georgian and Scandinavian motifs. Their Legal and General Assurance, Waterloo Street, Birmingham, 1931–2 (probably by *Edward Holman*) is exceptional, showing classicism influenced by the emerging Modern Movement. Stripped classical was also well done by *W.N. Twist* at Neville House, Waterloo Street, and in Wolverhampton at the *Express and Star* offices by *H. Marcus Brown*, both 1934. The decline of *Essex & Goodman* can be seen at Wellington House, Colmore Row, Birmingham, 1928, and King Edward House, New Street, 1936–7. Much in Bridge Street, Walsall is by *Jeffries & Shipley*, stripped Tudor or classical. *Farmer & Farmer*'s *Walsall Observer* offices of 1931–2 are also worth mention. *Cherrington & Stainton* of Dudley's intelligent, unobtrusive classicism has been much reduced by demolition. The best survivor, Nos. 42–44 Bristol Street, Birmingham, 1929, integrates showrooms, offices and workshops in a well-composed elevation. Full Modernism arrives at *Richard Twentyman*'s Clock Chambers, Wolverhampton, well-grouped flat-roofed blocks of 1939.

RETAIL ARCHITECTURE follows a similar pattern but with a little Art Deco and rather more *Moderne*. Stripped classicism is exemplified by *Gerald de Courcy Fraser*'s Lewis's store, Birmingham, of 1924–5, and Beattie's, Wolverhampton, 1929. Brierley Hill's Neo-Georgian market is by *Jennings & Homer*, 1930. Lee Longlands, Broad Street, Birmingham is in *Hurley Robinson*'s squared-up Art Deco (1931). Henn's in Princess Street, Wolverhampton, has a complete *Moderne* front of 1935 by *Frank Birch*. There are 'Metroland' shops at School Road, Hall Green (*Dare's*, 1935) and Poplar Road, Solihull (*W.T. Orton*, 1931). *H.W. Simister* designed shops for the Ten Acres and Stirchley Co-operative Society in streamlined classical or Dudok-style Modern (Kings Norton and Longbridge (B), both 1936). Full Modernism appears in *Richard Twentyman*'s extension to Beattie's, Wolverhampton, 1939. A rare survival is the Modernist motor garage in Bridge Street, Walsall, by *Lavender, Son & Close*, 1936.

Late C20 decline has left relatively few INDUSTRIAL BUILD-INGS. The E side of Birmingham Jewellery Quarter is a good place to see the interwar progression. *E.F. Reynolds*'s Taylor & Challen in Constitution Hill (1915–21) shows the later Arts and Crafts approach. *George E. Pepper*'s three factories in Great Hampton Street, also of 1919, show his versatility. *Hobbiss*'s Supreme Works, further out in Soho Hill (1922), is industrial Neo-Georgian at its best. Approaches to Modernism can be seen in the Cannings factory by *Peacock & Bewlay*, 1936, and *Watson & Johnson*'s factory in Constitution Hill, 1938. Elsewhere, the post-1918 boom left its mark with *Arnold Crush*'s British Cyanides in Oldbury and *C.W.D. Joynson*'s Atlas Works extensions in Darlaston (Wa); also *Wallis, Gilbert & Partners*' A.E.I. Witton (B) offices of 1920–2, already moving towards Art Deco, and the huge, mill-like Fort Dunlop, Erdington (B) of 1920 by *Sir Sidney Stott* and *W.W. Gibbings*. *William Haywood*'s front range of 1925 at the Soho Foundry, Smethwick is massive Beaux Arts classicism. Smaller Black Country factories include *H.E. Folkes*'s extension at the Monarch Works, Lye (D) (1919) and *G.F. Webb*'s Sutton's Holloware, Amblecote (1922). *Harry Weedon*'s big Ty-Phoo tea factory, Birmingham, started in 1929 with hints of Art Deco, ending with functional and near-Modernist ranges of 1937–8. Impressive 1930s functionalism can also be seen in Birmingham at *C.F. Lawley Harrod*'s factory in Hurst Street, and at *John Christie*'s Fisher & Ludlow factory in Bradford Street. The best Black Country 1930s factories are *Cecil E.M. Fillmore*'s J.B. & S. Lees, West Bromwich, and *G.F. Webb*'s front range for the Cookley works at Brockmoor (D).

Birmingham – with Smethwick, the home of Mitchells & Butlers brewery – was in the forefront of the REFORMED PUBLIC HOUSES movement. Mostly in the new suburbs, these were idealized village inns, in traditional English styles. The best local architects were employed, especially later Arts and Crafts figures. The most spectacular is the Black Horse, Northfield (1929), by *Batemans*' pub specialist, *Francis Goldsbrough*: a huge Tudor range with timber gables and exquisite stonework on the garden front. The firm's later pubs are gentle brick Tudor, e.g. the King's Arms, Sutton Coldfield, with a half-butterfly plan, and the Olton Hall, Solihull. *E.F. Reynolds* used massive Neo-Georgian – the Shaftmoor, Hall Green; the Abbey, Bearwood, Smethwick; the Grant Arms, Cotteridge; and the Blue Gates, Smethwick, all early 1930s. In 1935–6 he used slightly Spanish classical at The Towers, Walsall Road, Birmingham, and *Moderne* for the Three Magpies and the Baldwin, both in Hall Green. His partner *Spencer Wood* produced the dramatic quadrant of the Barleycorn, Smethwick (1939). *Hobbiss* ranged from grand but loose Baroque at the former College Arms, College Road, Kingstanding (1930), to Neo-Georgian at the Brookvale, Slade Road, Erdington (1934), and timber-gabled Tudor at the Navigation, Erdington (1926). *J.P. Osborne & Son* used restrained Neo-Georgian and Tudor, e.g.

the Dog and Partridge, Yardley Wood (1929 etc.). *J.B. Surman*'s beautifully austere manner can be seen at the King George V, Longbridge and the Beeches, Perry Beeches (B) (both 1935). *F.W.B.Yorke* wrote a standard guide for architects, *Public Houses* (1949); his best is the Journey's End, Yardley (1939). A good surviving interior is at *James & Lister Lea*'s British Oak, Stirchley (B) (1923–4).

Elsewhere in the Black Country the most important figure is *A.T. Butler* (*A.T. & Bertram Butler* from c.1932), architect to Wolverhampton & Dudley Breweries (Banks's). Butler's bold curving corners can be seen at the Hatherton Arms, Wolverhampton (1927) and the Four Horse Shoes, Pleck (Wa) (1928). The firm later did good Neo-Georgian, e.g. the Vine, Blackheath (Sa) (1935–6). Their finest, with Butler's complex rhythms of bays and dormers, is the Fairfield, Halesowen (1937). *W.A. Hutchings*'s personal Neo-Georgian appears at the County, Willenhall (Wa) (1924) and the Villiers Arms, Bilston (Wo) (1925–6). *James A. Swan* did the Giffard Arms, Wolverhampton (Tudor; 1929) and the deceptive recasting of the Greyhound and Punchbowl, Bilston (1936). *J. Percy Clark* of *Scott & Clark*'s personal Tudor revival with corbelled chimneys and wonky timbering can be seen at the Navigation, Oldbury (1931) and the Mitre, Stourbridge (1932). His other style is brick with shaped gables, e.g. the Four Ways, Portway, Rowley (1936). *F. Morrell Maddox* of *Watkin & Maddox* is best seen at the Vine, Wednesfield (Wo) (1937) with its conceit of an octagonal shape. *Twentyman*'s early pubs have fared badly; the best Wolverhampton survivors are the Golden Lion, Cannock Road, and the Red Lion, Amos Lane, Wednesfield.

Birmingham is important for interwar CINEMAS because Oscar Deutsch's Odeon chain was based in the city. His architects were *Harry Weedon & Partners*. The finest survivors are both by *J. Cecil Clavering*: Kingstanding (1934–5), with its tapering faience fins and surviving interior, and Sutton Coldfield (1935–6), with its slab tower contrasted with a rounded staircase. *Budge Reid*'s Dudley Odeon (1937) is also worth mention. Other cinemas are in a blocky, sometimes curvaceous, *Moderne* style. The best is *W.T. Benslyn*'s Rink, Smethwick (1930), with its bowed front enlivened by peacocks, and an Art Deco interior. *Roland Satchwell*'s Clifton, Lye; Clifton, Sedgley; and Grove, Smethwick, are all of 1936–7; *Ernest Roberts*'s Clifton, Perry Barr; and Danilo, Longbridge, are both of 1937–8. *Cecil E.M. Fillmore* rebuilt the Electric Cinema, Station Street, Birmingham, in 1936–7, recently well restored. *Webb & Gray* did Art Deco at the Majestic, Cradley Heath (Sa) (1930). Among THEATRES there are *Burdwood & Mitchell*'s classical Birmingham Hippodrome interior of 1924–5, and *Satchwell*'s Alexandra, Birmingham, of 1935. The finest exterior is *Hurley Robinson*'s massive Hippodrome, Dudley, 1937–8 (currently under threat).

Lastly there is the architecture of RECREATION, and a major early Modernist monument: Dudley Zoo, by *Berthold Lubetkin* and *Tecton*, 1935–7. Their free and original structures, disciplined by Lubetkin's classical training, informed by his social commitment, and placed among trees on the steep hillsides, are unforgettable. The only other building worth mentioning is *Webb & Gray*'s thatched lido, the Kingfisher, at Wallheath (D) (1937).

FROM 1945 TO THE PRESENT

The SECOND WORLD WAR has left a few structures in the area, the most interesting in Birmingham: the anti-aircraft battery on the Handsworth side of Sandwell valley, and the unusual pillbox in Stirchley shaped like a chimney.

After the war the Attlee government's building priorities were public housing and industry. A temporary housing solution was PREFABS: a group of *c.*1945–6 survives in Wake Green Road, Birmingham. The most interesting post-war HOUSING ESTATE, also in Birmingham, is Shard End of 1947–55, designed by the local *Shard End Panel* group on a formal Beaux Arts plan, with dramatic corner towers and blocks of flats articulating stretches of cottage-type houses. Two other places stand out. Bilston (Wo) called in outside housing and planning experts: *Otto Neurath* and *Sir Charles Reilly*. The best survivor of their time is *Ella Briggs*'s Lawnside Green of 1946. Sedgley (D) used *Richard Twentyman* for its housing of 1949–52. Elsewhere the planning can be formal, as at Bentley (Wa) for Darlaston U.D.C., by *Thomas Galbraith*, 1948–56; or more informal, as at Falcon Lodge, Sutton Coldfield, by the Borough Surveyor *Tom Porter*, 1947–59, with a network of cul-de-sacs linked by footpaths. The post-war Birmingham housing executed under the Public Works Department architect *D.H. Davies* is seen at its best in the Heathy Farm estate, Bartley Green of 1949–53.

The Conservative government from 1951 increased housing densities, resulting in more flats and the first tower blocks. Birmingham appointed a City Architect, *A.G. Sheppard Fidler*, a distinguished pupil of Reilly in Liverpool, in 1952. The best survivors of his schemes are Hawkesley Farm Moat (1957–8), Curtis Gardens in Acocks Green (1959–60) and the remaining part of Chamberlain Gardens, Ladywood (1961–6), the last two with landscaping by *Mary Mitchell*. The biggest, Lyndhurst, Erdington (1958–60), is much altered. The equivalent in Wolverhampton is the Dale Street estate by *Albert Chapman*, Deputy Borough Architect, 1956–60. Elsewhere in the Black Country are the Wolverhampton Road flats, Bloxwich (Wa), by *Austin Parrott*, Walsall's Borough Architect, 1962 etc., and the Bundle Hill estate, Halesowen (D), by *Remo & Mary Granelli* and *Miall Rhys-Davies*, 1962–4. The 1960s were a time of big estates and fast housing production. Birmingham, under the City Architects *J.R. Sheridan-Shedden* and *J. Alan Maudsley*, built Druids Heath (1963–6), Castle Vale (1964–9) and the biggest estate, Chelmsley Wood (So) (1966–73), with much system-built housing from local builders. Wolverhampton, under *Albert Chapman*, produced

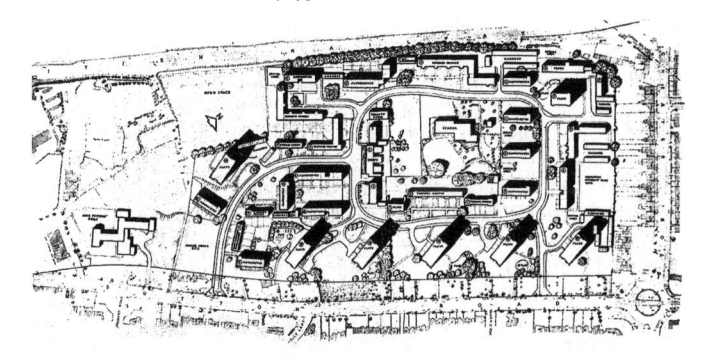

Birmingham, Erdington, Lyndhurst Estate.
Shaded block plan, c. 1958

impressive Brutalist estates at Heath Town, 1967–70, and New Park Village, 1969–72.

The last municipal schemes, from the mid 1970s, were smaller, gentler and more tactful. Birmingham, under *W.G. (Bill) Reed*, took the lead with the last major estate, Frankley, 1975–82 (*Will Howland*), and small developments such as the flats on Bristol Road, Edgbaston, of 1980–2 (*Nigel Davies*). Horseshoe Walk, Tipton (Sa), by *Diamond, Redfern & Partners*, 1978 etc., is also good. Late C20 and early C21 housing associations did much, the most interesting schemes including Leofric Court, Edgbaston, by *Hickton Madeley*, 1982–3, and the eccentric flats in Wordsley (D) by *Coventry Churches Housing Association*'s architects, 1985. *Ian Simpson Architects*' Focus Foyer, Snow Hill, Birmingham, of 1997–8, shows the revival of Modernism. *Howl Associates*' recent work in Wolverhampton stands out: the Foyer building, St George's Road, of 2001–3, and the Tempest Street flats of 2008.

PRIVATE HOUSING resumed in the mid 1950s, when building restrictions were lifted. The finest houses of this period have a common ancestry in Frank Lloyd Wright: *Robert Townsend*'s No. 23 Hintlesham Avenue, Harborne (B), 1955, and *Ross Harper*'s No. 79 Lovelace Avenue, Solihull, 1955–9. *John Madin* started with still traditional houses such as No. 21 Grassmoor Road, Kings Norton (B) of 1953–5, but his Edgbaston work is fully Modernist, starting with Nos. 4–5 Chad Road of 1958 and West Point flats, Hermitage Road of 1959. The finest of his groups of towers and lower blocks is High Point, Richmond Hill Road, of 1961. The low-rise Cala Drive and Estria Road, 1962–3, are particularly good. Madin also designed elsewhere, e.g. the Endwood Court tower, Handsworth (B), 1960–1. In the Black Country from this period are the houses in Vale Street, Gornal (D) of 1965 by *Douglas Billingsley* of *Mason, Richards & Partners*. Others by the same firm are No. 21 Perton Road, Wightwick, Tettenhall (Wo) of 1967 (*Charles Mason*'s own house) and a line in Woodcote Road, Tettenhall, of 1973. *Desmond T. Crews & Partners* designed the start of Buckingham Grove, Kingswinford (D), in 1962. Slightly later is No. 38 St Mary's Road, Harborne, 1976–7, *Fred Mark* of the *John Madin Design Group*'s own house. Another by the firm is a bungalow by Edgbaston Old Church (*Douglas Hickman*) of 1980. Of more recent houses, the classical revival is represented by Boundary Drive, Moseley (B) by the *Malcolm Payne Design Group*, 2000, and the revival of Modernism by No. 93 Oakfield Road, Selly Park (B), by *Sjölander da Cruz*, 2008–9. *John Christophers*' Zero Carbon House in Tindal Street, Balsall Heath (B), of 2009, is an intriguingly designed experiment in exactly that.

Late C20 and early C21 city living has produced many blocks of PRIVATE FLATS. A good early example is Stevens Terrace, St Paul's Square, Birmingham, by *Associated Architects*, 1980–2. The block in Albion Street in the Jewellery Quarter, by *Bryant Priest Newman*, 2003, is subtle and good. The overweening flats in Shadwell Street, Birmingham, by *GRID*, 2019–20, indicate things to come. STUDENT HOUSING is now common, but rarely good. Victoria Hall, by *oconnell east*, 2009, is Wolverhampton's only recent high building. In Selly Oak (B) the best block is Jarratt Hall, by *Associated Architects*, 2013. The rush to high-rise has produced the huge block in Bristol Road by *Glenn Howells*, 2018.

Surviving INDUSTRIAL ARCHITECTURE of the period starts with the *émigré* Modernist *Rudolf Frankel*'s Miesian repair shop in Wrentham Street, Birmingham, of 1944–5. *Ernö Goldfinger*'s concrete-framed Carr Bros' factory in Shirley (So) of 1955–6 is of exceptional quality. Local firms used the older brick Dudok-influenced manner into the 1950s: *S.N. Cooke & Partners* at BIP, Oldbury (Sa) of 1946 etc.; *Batemans* for Samuel Heath & Sons in Leopold Street, Birmingham, 1946; and *Buckland & Haywood* for Bellis & Morcom, Ladywood (B), 1953. *Seymour Harris*'s furniture warehouse in Blucher Street, Birmingham of 1954–5 is a progressive statement. The largest factory, Austin Motors at Longbridge (B), has mostly gone, but its big assembly hall by *C. Howard Crane* (1952) and *Harry Weedon & Partners*' larky circular showroom (1955) both survive. *Richard Twentyman*'s Mander Kidd offices and warehouse in Old Heath Road, Wolverhampton, 1962, are modest but a crisp design. *John Madin*'s Henry Hope & Co. offices at Smethwick (Sa) of 1963–4 show his early 1960s New York style moving towards Brutalism in the tough staircase tower. Also Brutalist, though not of Madin quality, is *Dron & Wright*'s Vittoria Street jewellery factory, Birmingham, of 1965.

SCHOOLS were a fertile ground for Modernism. In early postwar Birmingham, the best are by private firms: *Jackson & Edmonds*'s big curving block at Timberley Primary, Shard End, 1949–50, and *J.B. Surman & Partner*'s nicely grouped Four Dwellings, Quinton, 1949–53 etc. *T.M.Ashford*'s Hillcrest, Bartley Green, 1954, is an individual design with a long Y-plan and cranked, all-glass S front (alas renewed). *Norrish & Stainton* did Wychall Primary School, Kings Norton, 1957. The Black Country has a sequence of up-to-date designs by well-known London practices: *Yorke, Rosenberg & Mardall* (Causeway Green Primary, Oldbury, 1951–3; Crestwood, Kingswinford, 1956–9; Ridgewood, Wollaston (D), 1957–8); and *Richard Sheppard, Robson & Partners* (Howley Grange Primary, Halesowen, 1956–7; Menzies High, West Bromwich, 1960–4). Slightly later are *H.T. Cadbury-Brown*'s Grove Vale, Great Barr (Wa) of 1961–4, with its ingenious chain of octagons, and *Robert Matthew, Johnson-Marshall & Partners'* Queen Mary's Grammar, Walsall of 1962–6, with jazzy post-Festival of Britain detail. From 1952, the Birmingham City Architect *A.G. Sheppard Fidler* produced many simple, good designs; the best of the survivors is Selly Oak Trust School of 1962–3.

From the later 1960s, school designs became tougher. *Albert Chapman*'s Uplands Junior, Wolverhampton of 1969–70 is a good example. In Birmingham, this happened in *W.G. Reed*'s time as City Architect, particularly in the concrete language of designs by *Stephen Mitchell*: Small Heath School (1975–7) and the Design Centre at Bartley Green School (1978). Then came a move to friendlier, low-roofed assemblies: Kings Heath Primary (project architects *Gunars Zimbachs* and *Rod Hatton*), 1984, and Nelson Mandela, Balsall Heath (*Will Howland*), 1987, with much-praised flexible planning. From the turn of the century, by then under the name *Birmingham Urban Design*, there are angular, freely composed designs reflecting the work of international figures such as Frank Gehry: *Malcolm Leech*'s Adderley Primary extension, 2000, and Perry Beeches, 1998–2000. Recent Wolverhampton primary schools by *Architype* follow this approach: St Luke's, Blakenhall (2007–9), Bushbury Hill (2011–12), Wilkinson (2014). But most C21 schools are very different, particularly the fast-multiplying academies. They are concerned to make a statement, but the lack of an attractive formal architectural language to do this is desperately obvious. Many are by *Ellis Williams Partnership*, e.g. Summerhill, Kingswinford, 2001, and Q3, Great Barr (Wa), 2008–10; others are by *BHM*: Walsall Academy, Bloxwich, 2003; and Sandwell Academy, 2003–6. The best are Joseph Chamberlain College, Birmingham, by *Nicholas Hare* and *BDP*, 2008; the deceptively simple concrete-framed RSA Academy, Tipton, by *John McAslan & Partners*, 2010, and *Haworth Tompkins*'s angular but fanciful work at Rockwood, Saltley, 2012.

UNIVERSITIES AND COLLEGES, by contrast, began in a heavy, mid-C20 stripped classical manner: the old buildings of Aston University by *H. Fitzroy Robinson* and *Hubert Bull*, 1949–62, amended from a pre-war design by *Ashley & Newman*; and at Birmingham University, *Verner Rees, Laurence & Mitchell*'s Watson Building, 1958–61, and *Peacock & Bewlay*'s Mechanical and Civil Engineering building, 1951–7. Modernist buildings of this kind appeared first in the Black Country: Stourbridge College (D) by *Sir Frederick Gibberd*, 1956–7; the City of Wolverhampton College by *Albert Chapman*, 1959–62. In Birmingham the first equivalent is South and City College, Hall Green, by *S.T. Walker & Partners*, 1958. Birmingham University adopted Modernism with *Casson & Conder*'s plan of 1957, and its best 1960s buildings can equal any in the country: Casson & Conder's own Staff House of

1958–62 and Education Department of 1966–7; Ashley and Strathcona buildings by *Howell, Killick, Partridge & Amis*, 1961–4; and *Philip Dowson* of *Arup Associates'* Metallurgy and Materials building, 1964, and Muirhead Tower, 1968–9. Aston University went to *Sir Basil Spence, Glover & Ferguson* for its library of 1975, alas now mangled. The former Selly Oak Colleges have work by *Clifford Tee & Gale* (Barrow Cadbury House, 1961), and the Aalto-esque Prospect Hall by *C. Wycliffe Noble*, 1970. The best building of this period outside Birmingham is the School of Art at Wolverhampton of 1968–9 by *Diamond, Redfern & Partners*.

The late C20 was a fallow period for university architecture in the area – the Lakeside flats of 1999 at Aston University by *Feilden Clegg Bradley* an exception – but the C21 has made up for that. The self-consciously impressive and unfriendly manner of contemporary schools prevails here too. The finest building by far is *Glenn Howells Architects'* elegant reception and library block at Newman University, Bartley Green (B), 2011. Their Bramall Music Building of 2013 at Birmingham University, completing Webb's hemicycle, is also good, though with niggling details. The biggest group is at Eastside. *Feilden Clegg Bradley*'s textured brick Royal Birmingham Conservatoire of 2015–17 stands out, but the rest, including *Associated Architects'* work for Birmingham City University, 2013–17, are pedestrian. The University of Wolverhampton has a better if slightly heavy-handed recent work by the same firm, the transformation of the Springfield Brewery for the School of Architecture and the Built Environment, 2018–20. Among college buildings, the Erdington Skills Centre (Birmingham Metropolitan College) by *BPN*, 2014–15, uses fashionable motifs – repeated gables, asymmetrical oriels – with intimacy and freshness.

Post-war COMMERCIAL ARCHITECTURE is concentrated in Birmingham, where the major figure is *John Madin* (*John H.D. Madin & Partners* from 1962). His simple Modernist No. 16 Frederick Road, Edgbaston, 1957, was followed by his first major work, the Birmingham Chamber of Commerce building of 1959–60, well composed and beautifully detailed, with carefully chosen materials. His finest early work, the Post and Mail building of 1963–6, a sophisticated Miesian podium-and-slab design, was demolished in 2005. The offices at No. 12 Calthorpe Road, Edgbaston, of 1961–2 survive, as do altered towers on Hagley Road of 1962–5, and in Broad Street, and his branches for Barclays Bank at Shirley (1965–6) and Snow Hill, Wolverhampton (1969). The later work of the firm (as *John Madin Design Group* from 1967) includes the complex shape of Metropolitan House, 1972–4, and *Douglas Hickman*'s Neville House of 1975–6, both in Edgbaston. *J. Seymour Harris* started with an impressive furniture warehouse in Blucher Street of 1954–5; his Commercial Union development in New Street of 1959–65 retains its Gio Ponti-style tower but the podium has been flashily rebuilt. *James A. Roberts*'s record is more uneven. His long E range of 1958–62 on Smallbrook Queensway is fine townscape, but his other buildings here are ordinary. The Rotunda of 1964–5 is an icon of its time, for more than just its circular shape (see the contrasting, concave s side), but later work (the Sentinels, 1968–71; TSB, Temple Row, 1980) is uninspiring. Among other architects, *Hurley Robinson & Partners* produced the good Norfolk House, Smallbrook, 1958–60. *Sir Frederick Gibberd*, Birmingham-trained, did the cool and sophisticated Corporation Square development of 1963–6, finer than anything except Madin's best. *T.M. Ashford*, as original as ever, did the curving and zigzag-walled Britannic Assurance, Moseley, of 1960–3. The only work outside Birmingham needing mention is *Richard Twentyman*'s offices of 1959–66 in Waterloo Road, Wolverhampton.

The move to a tougher style in the late 1960s can be seen in *Fitzroy Robinson & Partners*' Bank of England, Temple Row, 1969–72, and *Richard Seifert & Partners*' Centre City, Smallbrook Queensway, 1972–5. The rear tower of the Bank of England scheme is the successor of an unbuilt 1960s proposal, consultant architect *Walter Gropius*.* The biggest project of this period is the hugely disappointing National Exhibition Centre (So), mostly by *Edward Mills & Partners*, 1973 etc.; the Arena there (1980), with its roof supported from pylons, nods to High Tech. Then there is a long gap, due to the oil crisis and the early 1980s recession. The start of the recovery was the International Convention Centre and Hyatt Hotel, by the *Percy Thomas Partnership* with *Renton Howard Wood Levin*, 1987–91. It has not worn well, but it ushered in Birmingham's finest post-war commercial architecture, centred on Brindleyplace, off Broad Street, planned from 1991 by the *Terry Farrell Partnership*, succeeded by *John Chatwin*. The buildings, which share a common height and a division into base, main storeys and top, run through traditional revival (No. 3 by *Porphyrios Associates*, 1997–8; No. 5 by *Sidell Gibson*, 1996), humanized Modernism (*Allies & Morrison*'s No. 2, 1996–7, and No. 6, 1998–9) and eclectic complexity (*Anthony Peake Associates*' No. 1, 1994–5). The planning reflects traditional city streets; the main square has a café by *Piers Gough*. Elsewhere, buildings start with 1980s London styles, the best the Neo-vernacular Cornwall Court by the *Seymour Harris Partnership*, 1989–92, then develop into revived traditional (Sovereign Court, Graham Street, by *Sinclair Architects*, 1990), and, curiously rarely, Postmodern (offices in Gas Street by *Peter Hing & Jones*, 1995–7). *Seymour Harris Partnership*'s Colmore Gate of 1990–2, with its revived New York Art Deco tower, is painfully near the Cathedral. *Stanley Sellers* in Solihull followed an instantly recognizable path of his own, with massive designs in brick and, mostly, Portland roach: No. 31 Homer Road, 1990, and No. 51, 1991. In Wolverhampton the traditional revival produced *Nicol Thomas*'s New Market Square block of 2001–4. Just worth a mention elsewhere in the Black Country is the Tipton and Coseley Building Society's headquarters of 1991 by *Building Design Practice*.

---

*Gropius had a Birmingham friend in the economist Professor Philip Sargant Florence, for whom he designed flats, also never built. He lectured in the city in 1934.

No. 4 Brindleyplace, by *Stanton Williams*, 1997–9, shows the move away from this stylistic plurality to a revived Modernism. *Associated Architects* also did this, starting with their offices of 1993 in St Paul's Square. No. 35 Homer Road, Solihull, by *Foggo Associates*, 2003, is a fine example of the same. *Glenn Howells*'s early block in Gibb Street, Deritend of 1997–8 has the delightful fantasy of a network of metal balconies. *Ian Simpson Architects*' Beetham Tower on Smallbrook Queensway of 2003–6 brings the return of the high building. In Birmingham there has been an aggressive fight to be 'original', especially at *Make*'s deconstructed Cube in Commercial Street, 2008–10. The 2010s' desire for height at all costs appears at *Doone Silver Kerr*'s No. 103 Colmore Row of 2018–21 and *Glancy Nicholls*'s Left Bank development off Broad Street, in painful proximity to Brindleyplace. The new Paradise buildings (No. 1 by *Eric Parry*, No. 2 by *Glenn Howells*, both 2019) are an improvement, but high blocks will rise behind. Things are better elsewhere. *webbgray*'s BT building of 2011 in West Bromwich is cleanly designed, and the new development by the railway station in Wolverhampton, starting with the i10 Building by *Austin-Smith:Lord*, 2014–15, retains the civic virtues Birmingham has lost.

Among RETAIL ARCHITECTURE, Birmingham's Bull Ring Centre by *Sydney Greenwood & T. J. Hirst*, 1961–7 (demolished 1998) was rightly reviled as an inhuman mess. The best is elsewhere. The low-cost Kingswinford scheme by *Jennings Homer & Lynch*, 1962–4, is still attractive. *Madin*'s shopping and community centre at Kingshurst (So) (1958–65) is intact but under threat. Other 1960s centres were good before recent recasting: *Madin*'s in West Bromwich, and *Sellers*' (*James A. Roberts & Partners*') Mander Centre in Wolverhampton. *Seymour Harris & Partners*' Ryemarket, Stourbridge, of 1972–4, tightly fitted into the urban fabric and lovably detailed, is very special; their Asda, Sedgley, of 1986, buttressed over the pavement, has some of the same charm. *McAlster, Jones & Associates*' Avion Centre, Whitmore Reans, Wolverhampton, of 1972, combines domesticity with a touch of Brutalism. After these comes a deeply unimpressive sequence starting with the huge out-of-town Merry Hill, Brierley Hill (D) (*Building Design Partners/Leslie Jones Architects*, 1984–9), and continuing in Birmingham with the Arcadian (*FaulknerBrowns*, 1990–2), the rebuilt Bull Ring (*Benoy*, 2000–3), and the free-form fantasies of *Future Systems*' Selfridges of 2001–3 and *3DReid*'s Primark of 2019. About the best recent centre is the tightly planned Touchwood, Solihull, by *Eric R. Kuhne & Associates*, 2001.

There are several post-war CIVIC CENTRES, none of them good. Brierley Hill (D) (1952–62) and the courts complex at Sutton Coldfield (1958–60) are of pedestrian quality. Walsall (1973–6) is fully Modernist, but not much better. Wolverhampton (*Clifford Culpin & Partners*, 1974–9) is about the best, though its fortress-like exterior is off-putting. Sandwell (in Oldbury, 1989–92) is a terrible warning of the dangers of bad Postmodern. The best COURTS building is at Dudley (*John T. Lewis* and *Philip Whittle*, Borough Architects, 1976). The Queen Elizabeth II Law Courts,

Birmingham, by the *PSA Midland Region*, 1981–7, are large but unremarkable; the Wolverhampton Combined Courts (*Norman & Dawbarn* with *PSA Projects*, 1990) have urban presence but are poorly handled. The prison gatehouse at Winson Green (B) by *HKPA*, 1983–7, is the best Postmodern work in the area.

GALLERIES AND MUSEUMS, a prestigious type, start with the modest but good E.M. Flint Gallery in Walsall (*Julie Lindon-Morris*, under *Austin Parrott*, Borough Architect, 1965). *Nicholas Grimshaw & Partners*' multi-use Millennium Point, Birmingham (1997–2001) is not as focused as this firm's best designs. The fashionable white aesthetic of the late c20 and early c21 can be seen in *Stanton Williams*'s recasting of the Gas Hall for Birmingham Museum, 1992–3, and *Niall Phillips*'s extension at Wolverhampton, 2004–7. Recent galleries have been conceived as anchors for regeneration, not to their benefit. Walsall's New Art Gallery of 1998–2000, in the windy spaces of the restored canal basin, made *Caruso St John*'s name, but is (for this writer) a bleak and distancing monument. *Will Alsop*'s self-consciously original The Public, West Bromwich, 2003–8, offered metropolitan cultural values to a sturdy Black Country town, and failed.

LIBRARIES are equally cultural monuments. The greatest architectural loss of recent years was the *John Madin Design Group*'s Central Library, Birmingham, of 1969–74, which combined Brutalist gestures with formal planning, and wonderful flowing spaces inside. *Stanley Sellers*'s library complex in Solihull (1976), in his trademark dark brick and concrete manner, also has good spatial treatment inside. *W.G. Reed*'s time as Birmingham City Architect produced the small but excellent library extension at Kings Heath (*Philip Howl*, 1983). Jack Judge House, Oldbury (*Sandwell M.B.C. Urban Design*, 2011) tries too hard to create a presence. The Village Centre (library and medical centre)

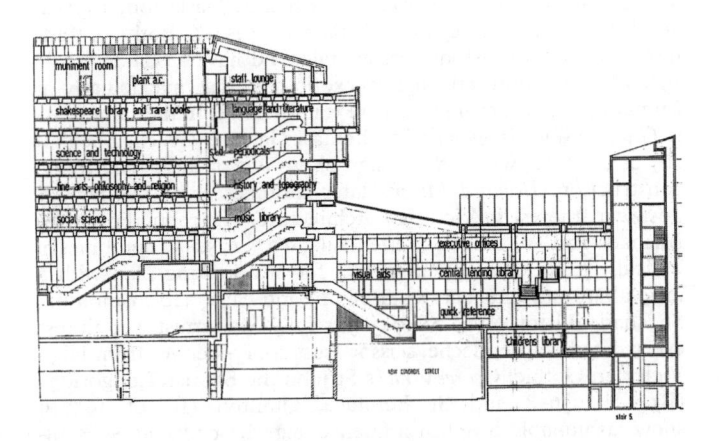

Birmingham, Central Library.
Section drawing, 1969–74

at Pelsall (Wa) (*Baart Harries Newall*, 2013) is better. The replacement for Madin's library, *Mecanoo*'s Library of Birmingham, 2010–13, is another cultural focus for regeneration, but its strong statement and good internal spaces were compromised by the commissioning and building process. Of many recent HEALTH CENTRES, the only one needing mention is *Penoyre & Prasad*'s Neptune, Tipton (Sa), 1998.

The architecture of RECREATION is disappointing. Every major football ground has been rebuilt, but not well. The County Cricket Ground in Edgbaston has the prominent but cheap-looking entrance block by *Broadway Malyan*, 2011. The only post-war swimming pools to mention are Walsall's Gala Baths, by *Austin T. Parrott*, 1961 and the new Sport and Fitness building at Birmingham University by *Lifschutz Davidson*, 2017. The best THEATRES were in Birmingham, the work of *Graham Winteringham*; but his Crescent Theatre of 1962 has been demolished, and his intriguingly assembled Repertory Theatre of 1969–71 has been mangled.

TRANSPORT ARCHITECTURE in the area includes the notorious New Street Station, as rebuilt in 1964–7 by *British Railways, London Midland Region*. The impressive new concourse is by *Foreign Office Architects* etc., 2009–15, the exterior (bolted on to its predecessor) another free-form fantasy. Impressive in a different way is *Bicknell & Hamilton*'s corrugated concrete signal box of 1964–5 at New Street. The best station from the 1964–7 electrification, Wolverhampton (*Peter Dunster* and *J.M. Collins*), has been demolished. Centro, the local transport authority, has built a number of interesting bus stations: Bilston (Wo) (*DGI International*, 1990–1), fashionable but crude High Tech; Walsall (*Allford Hall Monaghan Morris*, 2000), with oval canopy; Stourbridge (*Jefferson Sheard*, 2009–12); and Wolverhampton (*Austin-Smith: Lord*, 2009–11).

Post-war CHURCHES begin with two of the finest of the 1950s in England, *Richard Twentyman*'s All Saints, Darlaston, 1951–2, and Emmanuel, Bentley (also Darlaston), 1954–6. Both are traditional in plan but Modernist in style, and have a characteristic 1950s feel for unusual, slightly exotic materials, particularly at Emmanuel. The airy interior here is impressive. In the same class is *Graham Winteringham*'s St Thomas, Garretts Green, Sheldon (B) of 1958–60, where the design grows out of the portal-frame construction. *Bernard Miller*'s later churches show the revived post-war interest in Victorian architecture. His rebuilding of St Michael and All Angels, Tettenhall (Wo), 1952–5, combines a basically traditional appearance, a forward-looking plan with a nave altar, and unusual detail of C19 and early C20 inspiration. St Chad, Bilston (Wo) of 1953–5 is fully Modernist, yet almost every detail – apse, flèche, scissor-truss roof – derives from High Victorian Gothic. *George While*'s St John the Baptist, Longbridge (B) of 1956–8 and St Boniface, Quinton (B) of 1957–9 show fashionable Swedish influence, e.g. the belfry at St Boniface, but also historical awareness, e.g. the Fingest-type double-saddleback tower at Longbridge.

Churches of the period were increasingly influenced by the LITURGICAL MOVEMENT, with altars brought near the congregation, and centralized planning. *N.F. Cachemaille-Day*'s late St Columba, Banners Gate, Sutton Coldfield of 1957–60 moves towards this, and has concrete framing and a shell vault, while also being historically aware, here of the work of Soane. *Maguire & Murray*'s St Matthew, Perry Beeches (B) of 1959–63 is a major progressive church design, with a centralized plan based on ingenious rising spirals. *Richard Twentyman*'s last church, St Andrew, Whitmore Reans, Wolverhampton of 1965–7, has pews around the altar, numinous rendered walls and Ronchamp-like concealed lighting. Brutalism arrived with St David, Shenley Green, Northfield (B) by *Peter Carrick*, 1969–70, and *George While*'s last church, the rebuilding after a fire of St Michael, Boldmere (Sutton Coldfield) in 1966–7. These are the last single-use Anglican churches. Birmingham was a centre of radical liturgical ideas in the 1960s, centred on the Institute for the Study of Worship and Religious Architecture at the University of Birmingham. St Philip and St James, Hodge Hill, 1963–8, designed by students at the Institute with *Martin Purdy* (dem. *c.*2010), was their pioneer 'church centre', a completely multi-purpose religious and community space. Later Anglican places of worship have also been like this, e.g. *Charles Brown*'s at Balsall Heath (B), 1980, and *S.T. Walker & Partners*' at Lozells (B), 1985–6.

Equally significant have been church extensions, for kitchens, WCs and community rooms, and reorderings, to accommodate the modern liturgy. Many EXTENSIONS have been tactfully done: *P.B. Chatwin*'s work at St Martin in the Bull Ring, 1954–7 etc.; *Anthony Chatwin*'s porch room at St Augustine, Edgbaston, 1968; *Michael Reardon*'s underground rooms at St Philip's Cathedral, 1989. Others, particularly in the north Black Country, are much more uncomfortable: *Duval Brownhill*'s at Pelsall, 1983, and Walsall Wood, 1986–7; *Wood, Goldstraw & Yorath*'s at Brownhills (Wa), 1991. George While was uncompromising yet tactful in his work at Emmanuel, Wylde Green (Sutton Coldfield) (1967). The finest recent extension is that by *Arrol & Snell* at Penn (Wo), 2000. REORDERINGS, especially in Birmingham, have followed the work of the Institute there. *Maguire & Murray* turned the interior of St Mark, Londonderry, Smethwick (Sa) through ninety degrees in 1962. A later series of aggressive and destructive reorderings includes the breaking-up of an important set of early C20 fittings at St Aidan, Small Heath (B) in 1999, and – even worse – of the unique mid-C16 fittings at Holy Trinity, Sutton Coldfield in 2015–18. Elsewhere there is the empty modern Evangelical interior of St Mary, Aldridge (Wa) (1991 etc.). The finest recent reordering, with beautifully detailed altar and rails, is at Holy Trinity, West Bromwich, by *John Greaves Smith*, 1996–7. Among earlier post-war CHURCH FURNISHINGS one should mention *Matvyn Wright*'s moving wall painting at St Thomas, Garretts Green (1960), *George While*'s exquisite choir stalls at St Paul, Blackheath (D) (1961–3), and *George Pace*'s carefully wrought baptistery at St Augustine, Edgbaston (1964).

Post-war CATHOLIC CHURCHES begin conservatively, with the end of the Early Christian Revival. The best in the area are the work of *G.B. Cox* (Our Lady, Old Oscott, Kingstanding (B), 1956–7; Our Lady, Yardley Wood (B), 1964–6) and *E. Bower Norris* (Our Lady, Rednal, 1960; St John Fisher, West Heath, Kings Norton (B), 1962–4). *Eric Farmer*'s St Mary of the Angels, Aldridge, 1961–4, is similar. *Adrian Gilbert Scott*'s Our Lady and St Rose, Weoley Castle (B), 1959–61, is a good late work, with his trademark elliptical arches. The change then is sudden. The Second Vatican Council of 1962–5 approved the work of the Liturgical Movement, and opened the door to Modernism and centralized planning. The finest examples are *Richard Gilbert Scott*'s Our Lady Help of Christians, Tile Cross, Sheldon (B), 1966–7, with its unforgettable concrete 'crown', and St Thomas More, Sheldon, 1968–70. *Desmond Williams & Associates* come next, with St Michael, Merry Hill, Wolverhampton, 1966–8, and the spiral-planned St Dunstan, Kings Heath (B), 1968. *Louis Hayes* of *S.N. Cooke & Partners* moves from the interesting geometry of St Wilfrid, Hodge Hill, 1965, to the fully centralized St Vincent, Duddeston (B), 1967–8. *Harry Harper*'s quiet churches are easy to underrate: St Peter and St Paul, Pype Hayes (B), 1968–71, and his most dramatic, St Peter and the English Martyrs, Gornal (D), 1966–7, with a cross rising through the cantilevered porch. Later churches, including those by *Cyril Horsley*, are more modest. Post-Vatican Council reorderings include the drastic treatment of Our Lady, Dudley, and *Weightman & Bullen*'s notorious work at St Chad's Cathedral, where Pugin's screen was thrown out. A beautiful recent reordering is the altar area at St Peter and St Paul, Wolverhampton, by *Stephen Oliver*, 2009. One ancillary building to mention is *Charles Brown*'s hall front of 2003–4 at Maryvale, Kingstanding, a rare local example of Quinlan Terry-style classical.

There are few post-war CHAPELS of great architectural significance. Modernism arrived with *Jackson & Edmonds*'s angular and jazzy Digbeth-in-the-Field Congregational, Yardley (B) and Lyndon Methodist, Solihull, both 1958–9; and more soberly at *Bromilow, While & Smeeton*'s Sparkhill Methodist, 1959–60. Liturgical change, hinted at in *Desmond T. Crews & Partners*' Kingswinford Methodist (1965–6), was achieved impressively at *Charles Brown*'s Carrs Lane United Reformed, Birmingham (1968–71), with its plum-coloured Staffordshire brick, an industrial aesthetic. *Hulme Upright*'s Methodist work is in the same vein. *Harry Harper*'s understated manner is particularly appropriate at Cotteridge Friends' Meeting House, Kings Norton (B), 1962. The 1970s produced a few wilder designs, such as *Building & Urban Design Associates*' Church of God of Prophecy, Aberdeen Street, Birmingham, 1979. Some recent work has been in a chunky, Neo-traditional manner: Cranmer Methodist Church, Whitmore Reans (Wo) (*Ronald Baker, Humphreys & Goodchild*, 1991–2); Lea Road United Reformed, Graiseley (Wo) (*Brian Jeffries*, 2006).

STAINED GLASS includes the continuing work of *Hardmans*, especially by *Patrick Feeney*, and the last works of the *T.W. Camm* firm. The end of the Arts and Crafts tradition produced the fine work of *A.E. & P.E. Lemmon* at Hurst Hill, Coseley (D), and Lye (D). *Claude Price* at his best made beautiful use of colour (St Margaret, Ward End (B); All Saints, Stechford (B)). *Brian Thomas*'s dense, not-quite-abstract work is at St Mark, Pensnett (D); *Alan Younger*'s more angular windows at Walsall Wood and Sedgley. *Lawrence Lee*'s work is at Saltley (B) (with *Younger*) and St Mary, Moseley (B). *L.C. Evetts*'s largest piece in the area is the E window at St Agatha, Sparkbrook (B). *Yoxall & Whitford* can be seen at Holy Trinity, Sutton Coldfield.

PUBLIC ART begins after 1945 with *Hans Feibusch*'s mural of 1948 in Dudley Town Hall. The greatest amount is in Birmingham, of which the best is of the 1960s: the mural in the Chamber of Commerce building, Edgbaston, by *John Piper*, and *Kenneth Budd*'s murals in Holloway Circus, in Old Square and (re-created) in Digbeth. SCULPTURE includes *William Bloye*'s traditional figure frieze on the Engineering departments' building at Birmingham University (1954), and his Boulton, Watt and Murdoch statues in Centenary Square (1956). Modernism arrives with *John Bridgeman*'s play sculpture at Curtis Gardens, Acocks Green (*c.* 1960) and *William Mitchell*'s concrete murals at Hockley flyover (1968). The Postmodern re-planning of Victoria Square (1991–3), with sculpture by *Dhruva Mistry* and *Antony Gormley* (awaiting reinstatement 2021) is excellent. *Bruce Williams*'s Tony Hancock in Old Square (1996) is also worth mentioning. Black Country work includes the amusing clock tower at Stourbridge Junction Station, Oldswinford (D) by *Anuradha Patel* (1996), and *Tom Lomax*'s fountain sculpture in The Bridge, Walsall (2000–1). *Steve Field*'s work includes the Joe Darby obelisk, Netherton (D) (1991), and Beacon of Light, West Bromwich (Sa) (2002). The fashion for huge work has produced *Andrew Logan*'s Pegasus, Dudley (2001) and *John McKenna*'s miner at Brownhills (Wa) (2006).

Since the Second World War, architecture has been created in the context of REDEVELOPMENT and its C21 successor, REGENERATION. *Patrick Abercrombie* and *Herbert Jackson*'s *West Midlands Plan* of 1948 – the equivalent of Abercrombie's for London or Sharp's for Newcastle – was largely ignored. The West Midlands Group's *Conurbation* (1948) was a wider regional study. But Birmingham has national importance because of *Sir Herbert Manzoni* (1899–1972), City Engineer and Surveyor from 1935 until 1963. He was in charge of all its municipal works, from road building to new houses, and also helped frame the Town and Country Planning Act of 1944 which enabled comprehensive redevelopment.* He advocated 'proper zoning...the whole area must be new and it must look completely different'. His pioneering Emily Street housing scheme of 1939, designed by *Grey Wornum* and

---

*As City Architect from 1952, *A.G. Sheppard Fidler* had housing as his major responsibility, and only advised on planning decisions. After losing planning battles with Manzoni – a notable one was over the inflated Neo-Georgian Tube Investments headquarters (now Marriott Hotel) at Five Ways – he left in 1964.

A.C. Tripe, a parallel to e.g. St Andrew's Gardens in Liverpool, was demolished *c.* 1972. Birmingham's first high-rise blocks, by *S.N. Cooke & Partners*, went up in Great Francis Street in 1954. Its first Redevelopment Area, Nechells Green (Duddeston and Nechells), was approved in 1950 but not completed until 1972. Manzoni had stark views on architecture, saying in 1957, 'As to Birmingham's buildings, there is little of real worth in our architecture. Its replacement should be an improvement, provided we keep a few monuments as museum pieces to past ages.' Conservationists such as Tudor Edwards, who pleaded for the city's C19 heritage in *A Birmingham Treasure Chest* (1953), were ignored, and large-scale demolitions started with *Charles Edge*'s Market Hall of 1831–5, agreed in 1958. Other major losses were *Martin & Chamberlain*'s Central Library, Mason College by *Jethro Cossins*, 1875–80, the Liberal Club by *Cossins*, 1885, and the Central Technical College by *Essex, Nicol & Goodman*, 1895.

Manzoni inherited much of William Haywood's development agenda (*see* p. 73). The inner ring road was planned from 1943 and obtained its Act of Parliament in 1946. The first section was built in 1957–60 as Smallbrook Ringway (now Queensway), a wide boulevard lined with shops. A Public Works Committee visit to America in 1956, changes in government road policy and a strong attack on Smallbrook in 1959 by Leslie Ginsburg, professor at the Birmingham School of Planning, as mere road building, not town planning, helped change the remainder to the partly surviving urban motorway, opened in 1971.

Redevelopment in the Black Country has also been a catalogue of disruption and loss. Ring roads were built tightly round the centres of Wolverhampton (1960–86) and Stourbridge (1964–9), but these areas have otherwise survived quite well, except for the clearances for Wolverhampton's Mander and Wulfrun centres. Sutton Coldfield's ring road follows *Max Lock & Partners*' plan of 1962. Like Wednesbury's northern relief road of 1969, it splits the historic church area from the town centre. Walsall was redeveloped around St Matthew's church, with *Geoffrey Jellicoe*'s Memorial Gardens and flats, the finest landscape architecture here of the later C20; also the Digbeth development with *Jellicoe* as consultant, mostly demolished from 2010. Halesowen's Development Plan of 1948 was the prelude to almost total piecemeal historic loss. Dudley was redeveloped SE of the Market Place (itself mostly rebuilt) but survives to the NW. Bilston lost the S side of the town.

CONSERVATION was slow to develop. Significant early schemes were *James A. Roberts*'s rescue of West Bromwich Manor House (1957–60), and *F.W.B. Charles*'s of Sarehole Mill, Hall Green (B) (1964–9). Conservation areas began in the late 1960s (Birmingham's first in 1969). The reaction against large-scale development was fuelled by the conviction in 1974 of Birmingham's City Architect, *J.A. Maudsley*, for corruption; and encouraged by the Victorian Society's long campaign to save the Post Office in Victoria Square. Dudley designated Mushroom Green as a conservation area in 1970, restored the canals in the 1980s, and undertook the exemplary repair of the Bonded Warehouse and canal offices at Amblecote by *John Greaves Smith*, 1989–92. Birmingham finally acquired a Chief Planning Officer in 1974 – *Graham Shaylor*, a distinguished figure – but the West Midlands industrial recession of 1980–1 meant that he focused on development to retain jobs. The reaction against Manzoni really started in 1988 with the Highbury Initiative, a symposium which brought together local interests and international expertise, the work of a remarkable council leader, Dick (Sir Richard) Knowles. It continued with the publication of *Tibbalds Colbourne Karski Williams*'s City Centre Study of 1990, which stressed traditional streets, attractive vistas and human scale, and the arrival of *Les Sparks* as Director of Planning and Architecture in 1991. Conservation areas were expanded, national architects encouraged. The greatest achievements were the Brindleyplace development, from 1991, and the replanning of Victoria Square in 1991–3, as already mentioned. In the commercial centre, Lewis's store was tactfully redeveloped behind the façades in 1993. The back-to-back houses in Inge Street were repaired in 2002–4 (*S.T. Walker & Duckham*). In Wolverhampton a similar process took place under a conservation-minded Chief Planner, *Costas Georghiou*. The Chubb factory became an arts centre in 1990 (*Robert Seager Design*), but the most important project was the repair of Molineux House by *Donald Insall & Partners* in 2004–9. Walsall and Sandwell boroughs are a sad contrast. In Walsall, the Guildhall was rescued in 1985, but *Jellicoe*'s Digbeth scheme went in the early C21 without opposition. In 2011 a local election was fought partly on the fate of the town's finest Arts and Crafts building, *Hickton & Farmer*'s Mellish Road Methodist Church of 1910: the demolishers won. Three major historic buildings have succumbed to fires in the last decade, and road-focused development has started again on the N side of the centre. In Sandwell, astonishingly, comprehensive redevelopment has continued unabated. The loss of Wednesbury's historic Bridge Street in the late C20 was followed by the destruction of Cradley Heath from 2006.

In Birmingham, the reaction from the humane approach of Knowles and Sparks has been rapid and total, driven again by political leaders, Sir Albert Bore and Mike (Lord) Whitby, and a succession of chief officers, including Clive Dutton and especially, from 2011, Waheed Nazir. There have been some good historic building schemes: the repair of the Grand Hotel (*BGS*, 2010–19), and the conversion of the Central Fire Station (*K4*, 2015). But they are the exceptions. New buildings are bigger and, increasingly, taller. Current architectural design is largely in the hands of a small group of local practices. In 2010 the City Council produced an impressive Big City Plan, but its development policies have largely been ignored. In 2021, proposals include the 'Beorma' tower next to St Martin's; fifty storeys approved near the Law Courts; twenty-five storeys approved next to the conservation area in Digbeth; and a comprehensive demolition application approved for the whole area. Conservation areas have been de-designated, and a new one refused despite local support. Good buildings have also been demolished in conservation areas, such as *Hobbiss*'s No. 7 Luttrell Road, Four Oaks (Sutton Coldfield); as well as the finest interwar factory in the city, *Stockdale Harrison & Sons'* Tucker Fasteners, Perry Barr, of 1939. In 2021 the City Council launched a new Future City Plan, with images of tower blocks surrounded by the green spaces of urban clearance: in the words of the local architect and critic Joe Holyoak, 'reminiscent of the worst of 1960s planning'. There has been a precipitous decline in architectural quality: astonishingly, the practice which designed the Newman University reception building also did the recent flats in Selly Oak. In contrast, Wolverhampton's new central development near the railway station is well proportioned and carefully detailed, creating a real urban fabric. The lesson of Brindleyplace has been learned here. But Birmingham has gone back to Manzoni: 'there is little of real worth in our architecture...the whole area must be new and it must look completely different'.

FURTHER READING

All the old COUNTY HISTORIES cover buildings to some extent. Sir William Dugdale's *The Antiquities of Warwickshire Illustrated* of 1656 was the first. The revised and augmented edition of 1730 by the Rev. William Thomas includes splendid maps and plans drawn by Henry Beighton. For Staffordshire there are Robert Plot's *Natural History of Staffordshire* of 1686, and the two volumes of Stebbing Shaw's unfinished *History and Antiquities of Staffordshire* (1799 and 1801), the second of which includes much of the Black Country. Worcestershire has Thomas Habington's early C17 *History of Worcestershire*, published in 1717 and 1723, and the Rev. Treadway Russell Nash's *Collections for the History of Worcestershire* of 1781–2. The *Victoria County History* covers much of the area, and also includes older buildings. The Worcestershire volumes are early, so less good. Halesowen Abbey is in vol. 2 (*Religious Houses*, 1906). The remainder of the Black Country parts, in Halfshire hundred, are in vol. 3 (1913). In Warwickshire, the parts outside Birmingham, including Sutton Coldfield and Solihull, are in vol. 4 (Hemlingford hundred, 1947). Birmingham is the subject of the large vol. 7 (1964), with full and accurate lists of churches, chapels and schools. Two Staffordshire books cover parts of the Black Country: vol. 17 (part of Offlow hundred, 1976) describes Walsall, West Bromwich and Smethwick; vol. 20 (part of Seisdon hundred, 1984) includes Amblecote and Tettenhall. The Royal Commission on Historical Monuments did not venture into the area.

GENERAL HISTORIES must start, from sheer numbers, with BIRMINGHAM. The pioneer is William Hutton's *An History of Birmingham* of 1781 (6th edn by James Guest, 1835). Later C19 studies include R.K. Dent's *Old and New Birmingham*, 1880, and *The Making of Birmingham*, 1894. J.A. Langford's chronologies, *A Century of Birmingham Life* (2 vols), 1868, and *Modern Birmingham and Its Institutions* (2 vols), 1873 and 1877, are still valuable. The official *History of Birmingham* of 1952 is good: vol. 1 to 1865 by Conrad Gill, and vol. 2, 1865–1939, by Asa Briggs. The continuation to 1970 is by Anthony Sutcliffe and Roger Smith, 1974. The best short account of the Chamberlain period is in Asa Briggs, *Victorian Cities*, 1963, supplemented by P.T. Marsh, *Joseph Chamberlain: Entrepreneur in Politics*, 1994. Victor Skipp's *A History of Greater Birmingham down to 1830* (1980) and *Victorian Birmingham* (1983) have many insights. The best modern history is Chris Upton, *A History of Birmingham*, 1993. Roger Ward's *City-State and Nation* (2005) provides essential background for the city's late c19 architectural revival.

BLACK COUNTRY HISTORIES are fewer. Wolverhampton has Gerald Mander's posthumous *A History of Wolverhampton to the Early Nineteenth Century* (ed. Norman Tildesley), 1960: scholarly and very readable. Chris Upton's *History of Wolverhampton* (1998) is a fine if brief successor. G. Chandler and I.C. Hannah's *Dudley as It Was and as It Is Today*, 1949, is still the standard work. John Hemingway's books on Dudley Priory, Dudley Castle and Dudley town and manor (2005, 2006 and 2009) contain information on the buildings. Walsall has F.W. Willmore, *A History of Walsall and Its Neighbourhood*, 1887. Among smaller town histories are Mary Willett's old-fashioned *History of West Bromwich*, 1883; G.T. Lawley, *A History of Bilston*, 1893; and Norman Tildesley, *A History of Willenhall*, 1951. John S. Roper's *History of Coseley*, 1952, is very good.

For Sutton Coldfield there are W.K. Riland Bedford, *History of Sutton Coldfield*, 1891; Roger Lea (ed.), *The Story of Sutton Coldfield*, 2003; and one of the best of recent 'old photographs' books, Marian Baxter, *Sutton Coldfield*, 2001 (combined edn). F.W. Hackwood was a prolific author of Black Country local histories in the late c19. Good modern histories include Nigel Perry, *Stourbridge*, 2001, and Julian Hunt, *Halesowen*, 2004. At county level there are M.W. Greenslade and D.G. Stuart, *A History of Staffordshire*, 1984, and David Lloyd, *A History of Worcestershire*, 1993. Michael Greenslade's *Catholic Staffordshire*, 2006, covers a county second only to Lancashire in its historic attachment to the old faith. The *Shell Guides* to the area are readable and very informative: James Lees-Milne, *Worcestershire*, 1964; Henry Thorold, *Staffordshire*, 1978; and Douglas Hickman, *Warwickshire*, 1979. Ned Williams's many books on the Black Country wear their good scholarship lightly, especially his three volumes on *Black Country Chapels* (2004–8). Elihu Burritt's *Walks in the Black Country and Its Green Border-Land*, 1868, which first used the phrase, is still worth reading. Tim Cockin, *The Staffordshire Encyclopedia*, 2000, is a mine of information but should be used carefully. Two very good websites are the Wolverhampton History and Heritage Society (*www.historywebsite.co.uk*), which also covers Walsall, and the Sutton Coldfield Local History Research

Group (*https://sclhrg.org.uk*). Historic Environment Records for Dudley, Walsall and Wolverhampton are at Heritage Gateway, *https://www.heritagegateway.org.uk/Gateway/chr*.

GEOLOGY is described in J.H. Powell *et al.*, *Geology of the Birmingham Area*, 2000, and for the wider region in B. Hains, *British Regional Geology: Central England*, 1987. William Dargue's History of Birmingham website, *https://billdargue.jimdofree.com/*, and the Black Country Geological Society (*https://bcgs.info/pub/*) also cover the subject. Sir Roderick Murchison, *The Silurian System*, 1839, Thomas Baker, *Baker's Practical Survey of the Geology, Minerology and Historical Events of the District of Dudley*, 1848, and J.B. Jukes, *Memoirs of the Geological Survey of Great Britain: The South Staffordshire Coalfield*, 1859, are early studies of the Black Country's extraordinary geological structure. More recent examinations of the area's economic geology are H.E. Green, *The Limestone Mines of Walsall*, 1977; S. Powell, *The Dudley Limestone Mines*, 1999; A. Cutler, P.G. Oliver and C.G. Reid, *Wren's Nest National Nature Reserve Geological Handbook and Field Guide* (2nd edn), 2009; and N.A. Chapman, *The South Staffordshire Coalfield*, 2005. In anticipation of the UNESCO designation of the Global Geopark, the Black Country Geological Society, in conjunction with the local authorities, produced a series of pamphlets from 2008 on areas of interest, including all twenty-seven Geosites within the Geopark. On BUILDING MATERIALS, a chapter is included in *An Architectural Survey of Urban Development Corporation Areas: The Black Country* (RCHME), 1991. Alec Clifton-Taylor's chapter in *Timber Iron Clay* (West Midlands Arts), 1975, gives a useful regional overview. Richard Harris, *Discovering Timber-Framed Buildings* (3rd edn 1993) is a good introduction to that subject.

Overviews of Prehistoric and Roman ARCHAEOLOGY are in Paul Garwood (ed.), *The Undiscovered Country: The Earlier Prehistory of the West Midlands*, 2007; Derek Hurst (ed.), *Westward on the High-Hilled Plains: The Later Prehistory of the West Midlands*, 2017; Roger White and Mike Hodder (eds), *Clash of Cultures? The Romano-British Period in the West Midlands*, 2018; and Carl Chinn and Malcolm Dick (eds), *Birmingham: The Workshop of the World*, 2016. Mike Hodder, *Birmingham: The Hidden History*, 2004 (2nd edn 2011), covers the archaeology of the city from prehistoric to medieval, including investigations of buildings. Sarah Watt (ed.), *The Archaeology of the West Midlands: A Framework for Research*, 2008, includes an overview of the region's medieval archaeology. There are reports on specific sites and buildings in the *Transactions of the Birmingham and Warwickshire Archaeological Society*, the *Transactions of the [Lichfield and South] Staffordshire Archaeological Society*, the *Transactions of the Worcestershire Archaeological Society* and *West Midlands Archaeology* (formerly *West Midlands Archaeological News Sheet*).

INDUSTRIAL HISTORIES include Eric Hopkins's celebrated works on Birmingham: *The Rise of the Manufacturing Town* (1989, 2nd edn 1998), and *Birmingham: The Making of the Second City 1850–1939* (2001). Two useful collections of essays are Barbara

Tilson (ed.), *Made in Birmingham: Design and Industry 1889–1989* (1989), which includes Peter Atkins's chapter on the work of W. Alexander Harvey, and Carl Chinn and Malcolm Dick, *Birmingham: The Workshop of the World* (2016), already noted above. Trevor Raybould, *The Economic Emergence of the Black Country* (1973) is still the classic account of the factors behind the area's late c18 and early c19 development. Ray Shill's books are also valuable, e.g. *Birmingham's Industrial Heritage 1900–2000* (2002) and *South Staffordshire Ironmasters* (2008). The Association for Industrial Archaeology's *Guide to the Industrial Archaeology of the West Midland Iron District* (1991) is a useful overview.

The standard histories of the area's CANALS are Charles Hadfield, *Canals of the West Midlands* (1966, 2nd edn 1969), and (for the Warwick and Birmingham and the Birmingham and Fazeley canals) *Canals of the East Midlands* (1966, 2nd edn 1970). S. R. Broadbridge's *The Birmingham Canal Navigations vol. 1: 1768–1846* (1974) is a substantial history, but was never continued. Also useful is J. Ian Langford's *Staffordshire and Worcestershire Canal (Towpath Guide No. 1)*, 1974. More recent studies are Paul Collins, *Black Country Canals*, 2001 (several later editions), and Ray Shill, *The Birmingham Canal Navigations*, 2002.

The standard work on the area's RAILWAYS is Rex Christiansen, *A Regional History of the Railways of Great Britain, vol. 7: The West Midlands*, 1973 (3rd edn 1991). Paul Collins's *Rail Centres: Wolverhampton*, 1990, and *Britain's Rail Super Centres: Birmingham*, 1992, have much information, as does the Industrial Railway Society's *Industrial Locomotives of West Midlands*, 1992, about industrial lines. The Pensnett Railway is covered by W. K. V. Gale, *History of the Pensnett Railway*, 1974, and Ned Williams, *The Earl of Dudley's Railway*, 2014.

The small number of books on the area's ARCHITECTURE are nearly all about Birmingham. Douglas Hickman was the city's leading architectural historian until his untimely death in 1990, but his *Birmingham (City Buildings Series)*, 1970, and Warwickshire *Shell Guide* (*see* above) are constrained by format. Brian Little, *Birmingham Buildings*, 1971, is a general study. Peter Leather, *A Guide to the Buildings of Birmingham*, 2002, is strong on rural pre-1800 buildings. Tudor Edwards, *A Birmingham Treasure Chest*, 1955, is poignant in its pleas for buildings since demolished. In the 1990s the city's Department of Planning and Architecture published a series of pamphlets on c20 architecture; the most substantial is *Architecture and Austerity: Birmingham 1940–1950* (1995). Liam Kennedy (ed.), *Remaking Birmingham*, 2004, prefigures rather different c21 development attitudes. Andy Foster, *Birmingham (Pevsner Architectural Guides)*, 2005, covers the centre and selected outer buildings. Among picture books, Stephen J. Price, *Birmingham Old and New*, 1976, stands out.

Victorian and Edwardian buildings and architects have their own literature. Phillada Ballard (ed.), *Birmingham's Victorian and Edwardian Architects*, 2010, contains chapters on twenty-six architects from Thomas Rickman to the Arts and Crafts Movement, with lists of works: splendid evidence of the range and quality of the period. The same period is well illustrated in John Whybrow (ed.), *How Does Your Birmingham Grow?* (1972), with descriptions by Douglas Hickman, and in John Whybrow and Rachel Waterhouse, *How Birmingham became a Great City* (1976). Remo Granelli's chapter in Alan Crawford (ed.), *By Hammer and Hand: The Arts and Crafts Movement in Birmingham*, 1984, was the pioneering account of Bidlake, Ball and other local architects, in an equally pioneering book. Roy Hartnell, *Pre-Raphaelite Birmingham*, 1996, has much information. Michael W. Brooks, *John Ruskin and Victorian Architecture*, 1989, has a perceptive account of J. H. Chamberlain. Two useful studies on individual architects are Jennie McGregor-Smith, *John Cotton: The Life of a Midlands Architect 1844–1934* (2002), and (for the C20) Alan Clawley, *John Madin* (2011).

In contrast there is hardly anything specifically about Black Country architecture. John S. Roper was a scholarly building historian but published only a modest *Historic Buildings of Wolverhampton*, 1957. Peter Arnold, *A Guide to the Buildings of Walsall*, 2003, is a useful survey. Tim Bridges, *Churches of the Black Country*, 2008, is comprehensive and very readable.

Because of the city's size and national importance, Birmingham PLANNING is well covered. The best history is Gordon Cherry, *Birmingham: A Study in Geography, History and Planning*, 1994. D. Chapman *et al.* (eds), *Region and Renaissance*, 2000, updates the story. Official in character but full of helpful information are J.L. Macmorran, *Municipal Public Works and Planning in Birmingham 1852–1972* (1973), and Ian Heard, *Developing Birmingham 1889–1989: 100 Years of City Planning* (1989). Peter Larkham, *Replanning Birmingham: Process and Product in Post-War Reconstruction*, 2007, has many insights. Sir Frank Price, *Being There*, 2002, is a remarkable autobiography, badly edited.

Regarding specific BUILDING TYPES, the early *Transactions of the Birmingham and Warwickshire Archaeological Society* (1870 onwards) have very useful articles on the historic parish churches, mostly by A.E. Everitt. Entertainment is covered by Chris and Rosemary Clegg, *The Dream Palaces of Birmingham*, 1983, and impressively by Ned Williams, *Black Country Cinemas* and *Black Country Theatres*, both 2011. The most important cinema chain based in Birmingham, in its architecturally important early period, is covered in Allen Eyles, *Odeon Cinemas 1* (2002). Sports buildings are included in Steve Beauchampé and Simon Inglis's *Played in Birmingham*, 2006. Alan Crawford, Mike Dunn and Robert Thorne, *Birmingham Pubs 1890–1939* (2nd edn 1986), is excellent. Geoff Brandwood, *Britain's Best Real Heritage Pubs* (2016), includes unspoilt Victorian and early C20 pub interiors in the area. Paul Collins and Michael Stratton, *British Car Factories from 1896* (1993), covers Birmingham's most important C20 industry. Ned Williams, *The Co-op in Birmingham and the Black Country* (1993), includes accounts of buildings.

The earliest book on specific AREAS AND BUILDINGS is Dr George Oliver's *An Historical and Descriptive Account of the*

Collegiate Church of Wolverhampton, 1836, of which Gerald Mander said 'its illustrations by Robert Noyes must always be valued and redeem his faulty text'. More recent books are confined to Birmingham. Joe Holyoak, *All About Victoria Square*, 1989, and Ian Latham and Mark Swenarton, *Brindleyplace: A Model for Urban Regeneration*, 1999, are self-explanatory. Frank Salmon, *Building on Ruins: The Rediscovery of Rome and English Architecture*, 2000, covers the Town Hall. Anthony Peers, *Birmingham Town Hall: An Architectural History*, 2012, and George Demidowicz, *The Soho Manufactory, Mint and Foundry*, 2022, are standard works. Stuart Davies, *By the Gains of Industry: Birmingham Museums and Art Gallery 1885–1985* (1985) is a good short account. The Jewellery Quarter is superbly surveyed in John Cattell, Sheila Ely and Barry Jones, *The Birmingham Jewellery Quarter*, 2002, and in John Cattell and Bob Hawkins's shorter guide of 2000, both for English Heritage. On Edgbaston see Philip B. Chatwin, *A History of Edgbaston*, 1914, and Terry Slater, *Edgbaston: A History*, 2002. The classic account of the Calthorpe estate is in David Cannadine, *Lords and Landlords: The Aristocracy and the Towns 1774–1967* (1980). The Botanical Gardens have Phillada Ballard's excellent history, *An Oasis of Delight*, 1983 (2nd edn 2003). On Bournville, Martin Harrison, *Bournville: Model Village to Garden Suburb*, 1999, is the standard work. P.B. Chatwin and E.G. Harcourt, *The Bishop Vesey Houses and Other Old Buildings in Sutton Coldfield*, c.1947, is still significant. Oliver Fairclough, *The Grand Old Mansion*, 1984, is the recent account of Aston Hall. Chris Upton, *Living Back to Back*, 2005, is both a history of the surviving court in Inge Street and a wider study. Carl Chinn's many works on social history include architectural and landscape accounts in e.g. *Homes for People*, 1999, and *Free Parks for the People*, 2012.

For SCULPTURE, the important works are the directories published by the Public Monuments and Sculpture Association: George Noszlopy and Fiona Waterhouse, *Public Sculpture of Birmingham*, 1998, and *Public Sculpture of Staffordshire and the Black Country*, 2005; and George Noszlopy, *Public Sculpture of Warwickshire, Coventry and Solihull*, 2003. STAINED GLASS has an extensive literature. Michael Harrison, *Victorian Stained Glass*, 1980, is the standard work. Roy Albutt's *Stained Glass Windows of A.J. Davies*, 2005, and *A.E. Lemmon (1889–1963), Artist and Craftsman*, 2008, are very helpful. Michael Fisher, *Hardman of Birmingham*, 2008, is the best study of that firm.

Finally there are national works, and books on relevant NATIONAL ARCHITECTS AND ARTISTS. Howard Colvin, *A Biographical Dictionary of British Architects 1660–1840* (4th edn 2008), and Ingrid Roscoe *et al.*, *A Biographical Dictionary of Sculptors in Britain 1660–1851* (2009), are essential. Andor Gomme, *Smith of Warwick*, 2000, has much about the area in the early C18. There is an extensive literature on A.W.N. Pugin: Phoebe Stanton, *Pugin*, 1971, is a short general study; Paul Atterbury and Clive Wainwright (eds), *Pugin: A Gothic Passion*, 1994, is essential for more recent scholarship; Rosemary Hill, *God's Architect*, 2007, is a stimulating biography; Roderick O'Donnell, *The Pugins and the*

Catholic Midlands, 2002, covers both A.W.N. and E.W. Pugin. Godfrey Rubens, *William Richard Lethaby*, 1986, is a standard work. Michael Drury, *Wandering Architects*, 2000 (2nd edn 2016), is an account of the group of radical William Morris followers involved at Fallings Park. Stephen Wildman and John Christian, *Edward Burne-Jones: Victorian Artist-Dreamer*, 1998, is the best recent account of the artist.

The lack of published work on buildings in the area has meant that this book involved much research in ARCHIVES. From the mid-Victorian period onward, local authority building control plans are the most important record. There are substantial survivals for Birmingham, Wolverhampton, Walsall, West Bromwich, Sutton Coldfield and Solihull. Many Smethwick and Oldbury plans survive on microfiche in the Sandwell planning department. For the smaller Black Country towns, many records were destroyed in the 1960s–70s amalgamations; in Dudley M.B.C., all old building plans were destroyed after 1974. The next best source, from the late 1850s onwards, is local newspapers. Birmingham papers tend to operate at a national level with less local coverage, but in the Black Country there were the *Wolverhampton Chronicle*, *Walsall Observer*, *Smethwick Telephone*, *Dudley Herald*, *Brierley Hill Advertiser* and others. The best was the *County Express* of Stourbridge (1867–1980). There are several architects' collections, some very large, like the Bateman papers in Birmingham archives and the Folkes archive at Worcester. Others are occasional survivals, such as the single, precious Martin & Chamberlain cash book at Birmingham. Every parish except Great Barr has significant records at the local archives, or at the former County Record Office. Commercial holdings include the T.W. Camm archive at Sandwell, useful also for their simple painted glass used by Black Country architects whose works are recorded there. Also at Sandwell is a single Mitchells & Butlers pubs ledger. Family papers include the Dartmouth archive at Stafford, the Calthorpe estate papers at Birmingham, and the Grey papers still at Enville Hall. The Dudley estate papers at Dudley archives are mostly C20 but include accounts from 1798 to the 1820s.

BIRMINGHAM

Introduction	104
City centre	111
Churches	111
Public buildings	125
The commercial centre: streets	137
The Newhall Estate	159
Inner areas	164
Broad Street and Brindleyplace	165
The Jewellery Quarter and Summer Lane	174
The Gun Quarter	187
Eastside	188
Digbeth, Deritend, Bordesley and Highgate	193
Smallbrook and the Gough Estate	203
Suburbs: north and north-west	211
All Saints, Summerfield and Winson Green	211
Aston	218
Birchfield	230
Castle Vale	231
Duddeston and Nechells	232
Erdington	235
Handsworth	242
Kingstanding	261
Lozells	264
Perry Barr	265
Perry Beeches	268
Pype Hayes	269
Suburbs: east	271
Alum Rock	272
Hay Mills	273
Hodge Hill	275
Saltley	275
Shard End	278
Sheldon	280
Small Heath	284
Stechford	291
Ward End	292
Washwood Heath	294
Yardley	295
Suburbs: south and south-east	300
Acocks Green	300
Balsall Heath	303

Billesley	307
Brandwood with Druids Heath	307
Hall Green	309
Highters Heath	314
Kings Heath	314
Moseley	320
Sparkbrook	335
Sparkhill	338
Tyseley	343
Yardley Wood	345
Suburbs: west and south-west	346
Bartley Green	347
Bournville	348
Edgbaston	357
Frankley	394
Harborne	395
Kings Norton	406
Ladywood	413
Longbridge and Rednal	415
Northfield	418
Quinton	422
Selly Oak	423
Stirchley	433
Weoley	435
Sutton Coldfield	437

INTRODUCTION

Birmingham is the largest city in Britain outside London (population 1,145,000 in 2020). Between the C16 and the C19 it grew from a modest Midlands town into one of the greatest manufacturing centres in the world: the 'city of a thousand trades'. It has no advantage of geography: it is on neither the sea nor a navigable river. The old town lies on the w bank of the little River Rea, on a slope leading to a modest ridge along the present Colmore Row. It gained a market charter in 1166 but was not incorporated as a borough. This made it open to immigrant craftsmen and labourers, without the restraints that a system of burgesses put upon trade. The cutting of New Street in the C14 suggests that it was already a thriving market centre. Its advantage was its location, immediately SE – on the side nearer London – of the scatter of villages which became the Black Country, then already a centre of iron- and coal-working. Birmingham used these resources to make metal goods. In 1538 Leland saw 'a good market town...one street going...up a meane hill, by the length of a quarter of a mile. There be many smiths in the towne that use to make knives and all mannour of cutting tooles, and many lorimers that make bits, and a great many naylors.' Birmingham entered national history in 1643, when Prince Rupert sacked the unfortified town because its gunmakers were supplying Parliament's armies.

The late medieval town was overwhelmingly composed of timber-framed buildings. Early depictions show St Martin's churchyard surrounded by tall, multi-gabled jettied houses of the C15 to C17, with framing in distinctive West Midlands patterns: close studding, herringbone work, square panels with quadrant braces. Examples included Lamb House, High Street (dem.) and the Golden Lion, Deritend, partly re-erected in Cannon Hill Park (Moseley). The town had a small Augustinian priory (its name survives in the Minories, by Old Square) and two guilds: the Guild of the Holy Cross, re-founded at the Reformation as King Edward's School, and the Guild of St John the Baptist of Deritend, whose guildhall is now the Old Crown Inn. Aston Hall is a major Jacobean country house now within the city.

The engine of Birmingham's continuing transformation was the metal trades, mostly small workshops, producing the small items known as 'toys'. But the architecture of the period up to c.1830 is mostly lost. It included the first planned development, Old Square, begun in 1698; Temple Street, laid out from 1709, with Temple Row, from 1715, and centred on *Thomas Archer*'s Baroque St Philip's church, now the Cathedral; Cherry Street and Cannon Street, from 1732; and the Bristol Street area to the SW, from c.1778. The Newhall estate, NW of Colmore Row, was started in 1747. St Paul, the only later Georgian church surviving in use, was built in 1777–9 as a focus for development at the estate's NW end. The surviving shell of *Francis Goodwin*'s Holy Trinity, Bordesley of 1820–2, and the surviving W end of *Thomas Rickman*'s St Thomas, Bath Row of 1826–9, show the early C19 spread of the town. *Rickman* designed five other churches here, of which only part of St Barnabas, Erdington of 1822 survives.*
Georgian public buildings, such as *William Hollins*'s Old Library of 1798 and his Public Offices of 1805–7, have all gone. Industry has survived slightly better, including the Brasshouse, Broad Street, and the Gun Barrel Proof House of 1813–14, an early public institution for manufacture; also a few Late Georgian factories such as the Union Mill in Grosvenor Street West. Matthew Boulton's Soho Manufactory, by *William Wyatt*, 1765–7, perhaps the first modern factory in Britain, was demolished in the 1860s.

p. 27

Town houses survive around St Paul's Square, and occasionally elsewhere: one in Horse Fair, and Nos. 99–100 Bromsgrove Street of c.1792–3. In Broad Street are two manufacturers' houses: the Brewmaster's House of 1816 by the Convention Centre, and the Islington Glassworks house of 1815. The back-to-back houses of 1809 etc. in Inge Street remain from hundreds of similar

---

* The others were St George, 1819–22, a landmark of the early Gothic Revival; St Peter, Dale End, 1825–7, classical; All Saints, 1832–3, Gothic, and octagonal; and Bishop Ryder Church, Gem Street, 1834, with a tall Gothic tower with octagonal belfry. C18 churches now demolished include St Mary, Whittall Street, by *Joseph Pickford* of Derby, 1773–4, with an octagonal nave, and St Bartholomew, Jennens Row, probably by *William & David Hiorne*, 1749–50.

courts which surrounded the centre. The Inge estate, between St Philip's church and the present Victoria Square, was developed mostly from 1823, and original houses remain in Waterloo Street and Bennetts Hill. Further out, a few villas survive among later industry: No. 3 Summer Hill Terrace; Heaton House, Camden Street. The development of Edgbaston began c. 1810.

In the years around 1830, Birmingham was at the forefront of national politics. The Birmingham Political Union, founded by Thomas Attwood, held huge rallies which helped secure the Reform Act of 1832. A further campaign and petition gained the town a borough charter in 1838. This new self-confidence was reflected in a series of large-scale public buildings: *Charles Edge*'s Market Hall of 1831–5 (dem.), *Hansom & Welch*'s Town Hall, begun in 1832, and King Edward's School of 1833 (dem.) by *Charles Barry*, with *A.W.N. Pugin*. Pugin's St Chad's, begun in 1839, was the first English Catholic cathedral built since the Reformation. His influence can be seen in the work of the Birmingham Church Building Society (the 'Ten Churches Fund'), which moved from the Georgian box with lancets of St Matthew, Duddeston, through St Mark, Ladywood, an early design by *George Gilbert Scott*, 1841 (dem.), to two churches by the 'Anglican Pugin', *R.C. Carpenter*: St Stephen, New Town Row of 1843–4 and St Andrew, Bordesley of 1844–6 (both dem.). *S.S. Teulon*'s 'rogue' Gothic works, especially St James, Edgbaston of 1850–2, were done for an Evangelical patron, Lord Calthorpe.

The town grew, with new suburbs such as Small Heath, developed from the 1860s, and outside its boundaries in Aston and Handsworth, starting with the Soho Hill and Lozells areas from the 1830s. Much of its C19 industry remained small-scale, nowhere more so than in specialist areas such as the Jewellery Quarter and Gun Quarter. But some firms in the metal trades grew large, including brass works, of which Samuel Heath & Sons survives, and wire drawers such as the surviving Webster & Horsfall.

In 1851 the Borough Council absorbed the Street Commissioners and gained their vigorous Surveyor, *John Pigott Smith*. But the Council was increasingly controlled by 'economist' Liberals averse to public spending, who frustrated Pigott Smith's highway and sewerage schemes, and in 1857 dismissed him. Between 1865 and 1890 Birmingham went through profound political and physical changes, so that it came to be seen by historians such as G.M. Young as symbolizing Late Victorian England, as Manchester symbolized the earlier years of Victoria's reign. Nonconformist preachers such as George Dawson, H.W. Crosskey and R.W. Dale taught the 'civic gospel' of practical idealism: 'A town is a solemn organism through which shall flow, and in which shall be shaped, all the highest, loftiest and truest ends of man's moral nature' (Dawson). Crosskey was probably the 'adventurous orator' recalled by Dale as 'dwelling on the glories of Florence, and of the other cities of Italy in the Middle Ages, and suggest[ing] that Birmingham too might become the home of a noble literature and art'. The Italian ideal was replaced, particularly after 1880, by an admiration for Paris as replanned by Haussmann for Napoleon III, and also for America. The political leader who put these principles into action was a member of Crosskey's congregation: Joseph Chamberlain, a Unitarian screw-maker who was a councillor from 1869, mayor between 1873 and 1876, and leader of the city's Liberal caucus (arguably the first modern organized political party).

If the Birmingham Liberals followed an artistic thinker, it was Ruskin. *J. H. Chamberlain*, a devoted Ruskinian, was also a trusted member of Joseph Chamberlain's inner circle, a unique position for an architect in Birmingham history. The Pre-Raphaelites were exhibited at the Birmingham Society of Artists from the early 1850s. Ruskin visited Birmingham in 1877. *Benjamin Creswick*, the Sheffield knife-grinder discovered as a sculptor by Ruskin, came to Birmingham in 1889 as Master of Modelling at the School of Art. But attitudes were slightly ambivalent. The town's industry was centred on craft trades of a type that Ruskin admired, but those trades used metal, a material Ruskin rejected from 'true architecture'; Chamberlain's Ruskinism was modified by ideas of evolution drawn from Darwin.

The new role of the Council meant many new public buildings. The best architectural expression of those years are the Board Schools designed in Ruskinian Gothic by *J. H. Chamberlain* from 1871 (thirty of them by 1883), and his School of Art of 1883–5. The Council House, including offices for the newly municipalized gas and water services, was begun in 1874. The Library, opened in 1866, was rebuilt after a fire in 1879. The Art Gallery was built in 1881–5 above new offices for the gas service, which paid for it. The status of architects in the town rose, and a local professional body, the Birmingham Architectural Association, was founded in 1868. However, the Council House also shows the weaknesses of the Liberal period: it was designed by a local architect, *Yeoville Thomason*, who was chosen after the selection process was derailed by lobbying.

The new idea of the city also meant development. Corporation Street (begun 1878) was the first scheme in England to use the Artisans' Dwellings Act of 1875, which Chamberlain had discussed with the Home Secretary, R. A. Cross, during its drafting. A further section to Aston Road was started in 1902, when the *Birmingham Daily Post* reported that Corporation Street had 'quite eclipsed New Street as the premier street of the city'. John Bright Street was cut in 1882, Martineau Street (off Corporation Street) in 1887. Even after he had become a national politician, Chamberlain still pursued his programme for Birmingham: he was the main proponent of the University, begun in 1900, and helped obtain an Anglican bishop and diocese for the city in 1905.

Birmingham architects' work is covered in the general Introduction, but the profession in the city has interesting features that are worth mention here. Mid-C19 Birmingham taste remained conservative and classical, as the shock at the young *J. H. Chamberlain*'s Gothic No. 12 Ampton Road (Edgbaston) of 1855 showed. From that time onwards, stylistic preferences tended to divide along political lines, but not according to those exemplified by the Foreign Office competition of 1856–7. Birmingham classicists such as *J.J. Bateman*, *W.H. Ward* and (usually) *Benjamin Corser* were Tories; Goths, like *J.H. Chamberlain* and *Jethro Cossins*, were passionate Liberals. Chamberlain, as Surveyor for the new Corporation Street, clearly saw it as a challenge to classical orthodoxy. Cossins, like London Goths such as Basil Champneys, moved later to the Queen Anne style. Other architects, such as *Yeoville Thomason* and *F.B. Osborn*, used classical or Gothic as required. *J. A. Chatwin*, a fine classicist, was also the most prolific Anglican church architect of the area, using Gothic distinguished by its fine proportions. *Edward Holmes* did classical villas in Kings Heath and the classical Midland Bank in New Street, but used perfectly competent Gothic at St Mary, Selly Oak.

By the early C20 Birmingham had far outgrown the boundaries of 1838. Large parts of Aston, Erdington, Handsworth, Sparkhill and Selly Oak, all outside the city, were covered in streets of terraced houses. Some of the finest are those by *Grants Estates* in south Bournville and Selly Park. George Cadbury developed Bournville village itself, from 1894. And so in 1911 the city boundaries were greatly enlarged to include nearly all the present city, except for Sutton Coldfield.

These were the great years of the Arts and Crafts Movement in Birmingham architecture (*see* Introduction, pp. 59–62). Birmingham is not a stronghold of Edwardian Baroque; the classicism which developed after 1900 in the city was mostly of a more Neo-Wren kind, less offensive to Arts and Crafts sensibilities. Up to the Second World War and even beyond, a small number of prestigious Arts and Crafts figures were responsible for most churches, many public buildings and schools, and the finest houses: *Ball*, *Bidlake*, *Bateman*, *P.B. Chatwin*, and later *E.F. Reynolds*, *Holland W. Hobbiss* and *Harvey & Wicks*. Below them were the best commercial firms, including *Newton & Cheatle* (the finest), *Henman & Cooper*, *Ewen & J.A. Harper*, *Mansell & Mansell*, *Arthur Harrison* (later *Harrison & Cox*), *Cossins, Peacock & Bewlay* and *Marcus O. Type*. Further down were a host of mainstream commercial architects, and below them the doubtful world of architect-surveyors.

The new industry which symbolized the city for much of the C20 was motor-car manufacture. A very early factory of 1902, Heron, survives in John Bright Street. Austin Motors at Longbridge, the largest factory in the city, started in 1905. Car parts makers grew as well – Serck radiators, Girling brakes, Hardy Spicer transmissions – as did older firms such as the electrical manufacturers Lucas. Dunlop tyres came in 1917. The city escaped the worst of the Depression following 1929, and attracted people from the depressed areas to find work. Partly as a result, Birmingham has extensive interwar suburbs. These include some of the largest municipal estates in England, such

BOROUGH & CITY BOUNDARIES 1838-1931

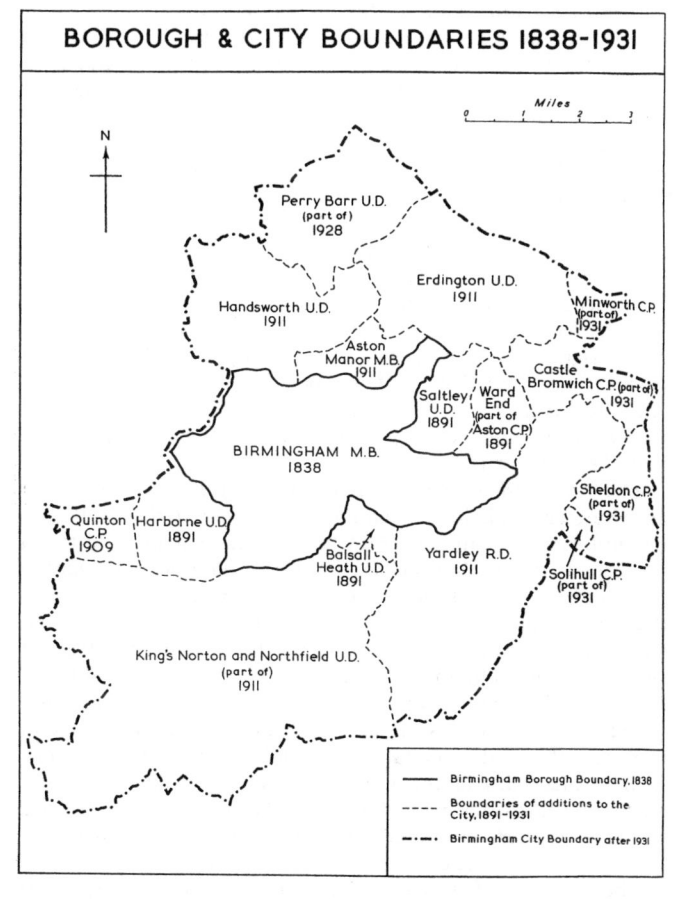

Birmingham, city and borough expansion.
Map, 1964

as Kingstanding and Weoley Castle, and private developments in areas like Handsworth Wood and Hall Green: the most extensive 'Metroland' outside London.

The city centre and inner areas suffered badly from air raids in 1940–1. The last and worst raid destroyed much of lower New Street and the E side of the Bull Ring. The damage enabled *Sir Herbert Manzoni*'s post-war redevelopment schemes (*see* Introduction, pp. 93–4). But Birmingham industry prospered after the war – by the 1960s Austin at Longbridge employed *c.* 25,000 – and people still came to the city to find work. The influence of America also returned. A council deputation of 1955 visited Chicago, Pittsburgh and New York, and a policy change in 1957 favoured more road building and car parks. The inner ring road was built between 1957 and 1970. The Sixties boom produced much commercial architecture, large municipal estates at Castle Vale and Chelmsley Wood (So), and New Towns outside, at Redditch (Worcs.) and Daventry (Warwicks.). Edgbaston was replanned by *John Madin* from 1957 with smaller-scale housing, but other private post-war housing has tended to develop over the boundaries, in Warwickshire and Worcestershire. Sutton Coldfield, already a dormitory town, was absorbed into the city in 1974.

Birmingham's School of Architecture has remained important. *George Drysdale*, Director from 1923 to 1947, introduced the procedures and formal values of the Beaux Arts tradition. His successor, A. Douglas Jones (1947–63), turned studies towards Modernism, and introduced 'live' projects: real buildings designed as teaching exercises, partly by students. Influential teachers after the Second World War included *Arthur Ledoyen* and *Oscar Naddermier*. Under *Jim Howrie* and (from 1982) *Tony Collier*, the School became part of the Polytechnic, now Birmingham City University.

The recession of 1980–2 hit the West Midlands worse than anywhere else in Britain. Manufacturing contracted sharply, and unemployment in the city rose from 7 per cent in 1979 to 20 per cent in 1982. Birmingham industries disappeared: Dunlop in 1980; Lucas's old headquarters at Great King Street by 1988; the Longbridge works finally in 2005. Planning in this period was mainly concerned to broaden the city's economic base and create new jobs. The International Convention Centre and Hyatt hotel were the largest projects of this kind. To expand the centre, the inner ring road was bridged at Centenary Way in 1989, and broken with the demolition of Masshouse Circus in 2002. The Brindleyplace development (masterplan 1991, built from 1995) was followed by the new Bull Ring, the much less impressive Eastside (masterplan 2002, major buildings 2006–17), schemes in Digbeth and Deritend, and proposals for Ladywood.

The failures of post-war Modernism made conservation popular in the late C20, but the C21 saw a reversion to development at all costs. The change in local government structure in 1999 concentrated power in officers and political leaders. That marks the resumption of intrusive high-rise development, with suggestions that Birmingham could become another Chicago. The 'High Places' policy of 2002, which enabled tall buildings in a greater area, especially along the Colmore Row ridge, was soon abandoned for a free-for-all, often accompanied by hostility to the city's architectural heritage. The digital age has shrunk local newspapers and, with them, debate on the future of the city. Birmingham is now a proudly multi-cultural city, but an unexpected result of this has been to reduce debate on development and architecture. Taken together, these trends increasingly mean that a small number of planning officers, architects, commercial surveyors and developers can control the city's built form without reference to a wider audience. Not since the 1960s has Birmingham's architectural future seemed so bleak.

CITY CENTRE

Churches ... 111
   Cathedral of St Philip ... 111
   Cathedral of St Chad (R.C.) ... 117
   Other churches ... 122
Public buildings ... 125
The commercial centre: streets ... 137
The Newhall Estate ... 159

CHURCHES

CATHEDRAL OF ST PHILIP
Temple Row and Colmore Row

By *Thomas Archer*, 1709–25. A building of national importance, and a most subtle example of the elusive English Baroque, exceptional in what was a modest C18 town. It is small for a cathedral – only some 160 ft (49 metres) long, even with its 1880s extension – and was a parish church until the Diocese was created in 1905. Archer was a local man, whose brother Andrew owned Umberslade Hall in Warwickshire. But he was also the only English architect of the generation after Wren who knew Italian Baroque at first hand. He had visited Padua and almost certainly Rome, where he would have seen at first hand the work of Francesco Borromini. It is the Borromini-like treatment of details, and use of dramatically contrasted convex and concave shapes, which make St Philip's so remarkable.

The church was built by a Commission set up under an Act of 1708, obtained because St Martin's church (*see* p.122) was inadequate for the growing town. The Commissioners were mostly local landowners, including Andrew Archer. As a gentleman, holding the lucrative Court position of Groom Porter, Thomas Archer must have given his design free. The site was sold at favourable terms by William Inge and Elizabeth Phillips, who were developing Temple Street and Temple Row (Phillips is remembered by the dedication). The body of the church was completed in 1715. It cost £5,073 13s. 10d., nearly all raised by small local subscriptions. The tower was completed between 1722 and 1725, when George I gave £600. The craftsmen included *Joseph Pedley*, stonemason, *William Davis*, who carved 'ye 4 Pediments and Windows over ye Doors', *Richard Pimley*, brickmaker, *Richard Huss*, plasterer, and carpenters and joiners *William Westley*, *Thomas Lane*, *Richard Perks*, *John Blun* and *William Ashes* (or *Ashcroft*). The stone was from Andrew Archer's quarry at Umberslade, and nearby Rowington. It did not last, and the body of the church was refaced starting in 1859, supervised by *Peter Hollins*, and completed in 1871, when *Yeoville Thomason* redecorated the interior. In 1883–4 *J.A. Chatwin* extended the church E with a full chancel, replacing the original small apse and E nave bay, created NE and SE vestries, and opened out the ground floor

Birmingham City Centre

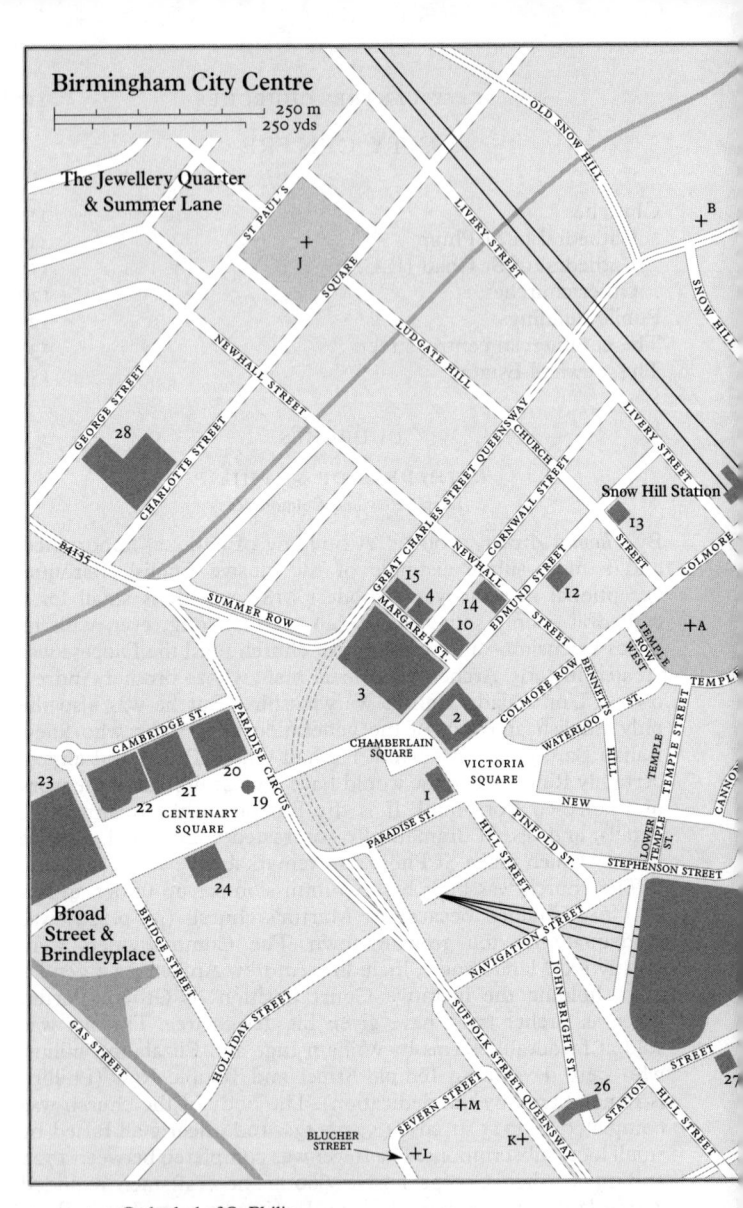

|—————| 250 m
|—————| 250 yds

The Jewellery Quarter & Summer Lane

Snow Hill Station

Broad Street & Brindleyplace

- A Cathedral of St Philip
- B Cathedral of St Chad (R.C.)
- C St Martin in the Bull Ring
- D St Michael (R.C.)
- E Methodist Central Hall (former)
- F Carrs Lane United Reformed Church
- G Friends' Meeting House
- H Salvation Army Citadel (former)
- J St Paul
- K Christadelphian chapel (former)
- L Singers Hill Synagogue (Birmingham Hebrew Congregation)
- M Athol Masonic Hall

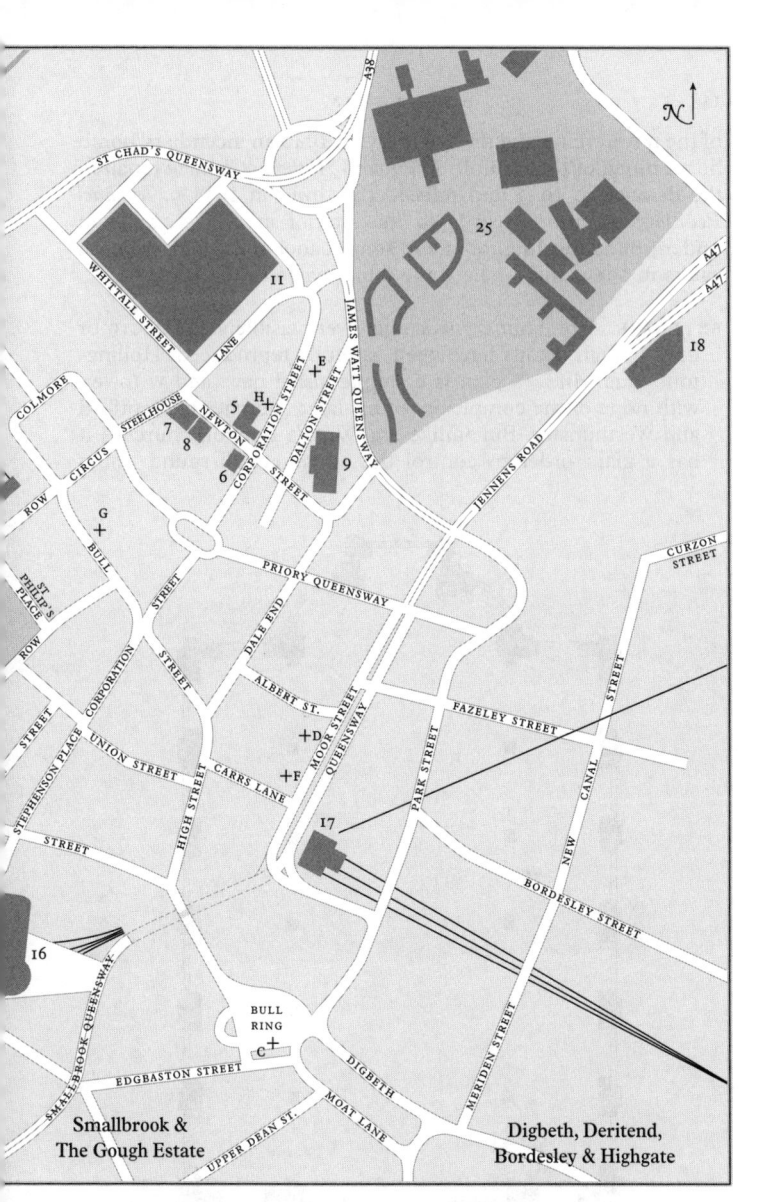

1. Town Hall
2. Council House, Museum and Art Gallery
3. Council House Extension
4. Birmingham and Midland Institute
5. Victoria Law Courts
6. County Court (former)
7. Juvenile Court (former)
8. Coroner's Court
9. Queen Elizabeth II Law Courts
10. School of Art
11. Birmingham Children's Hospital
12. Ear and Throat Hospital (former)
13. Birmingham and Midland Eye Hospital (former)
14. Louisa Ryland House
15. Stock Exchange (former)
16. New Street Station
17. Moor Street Station
18. Royal Birmingham Conservatoire
19. Hall of Memory
20. Baskerville House
21. Library of Birmingham
22. Birmingham Repertory Theatre
23. International Convention Centre
24. Birmingham Municipal Bank (former)
25. Aston University
26. Alexandra Theatre
27. Old Rep Theatre
28. University College Birmingham

of the tower, removing the w gallery. In 1940 an incendiary bomb burnt much of the roof off. *Philip* and *Anthony Chatwin* repaired the damage in 1947 and refaced the tower in 1958–9. *Michael Reardon & Partners* reordered the interior in 1980–2, built an underground meeting room and song school in the former burial vaults in 1989, and repaired the fabric again in the 1990s.

EXTERIOR. A preliminary warning: every visible stone is C19 or C20, though details have been carefully reproduced. Hollington stone. *Archer*'s plan is a simple aisled nave and w tower, with none of the complexity of his later churches at Deptford and Westminster. But unlike e.g. Wren's London churches it has a giant order to control the elevations all round: sober

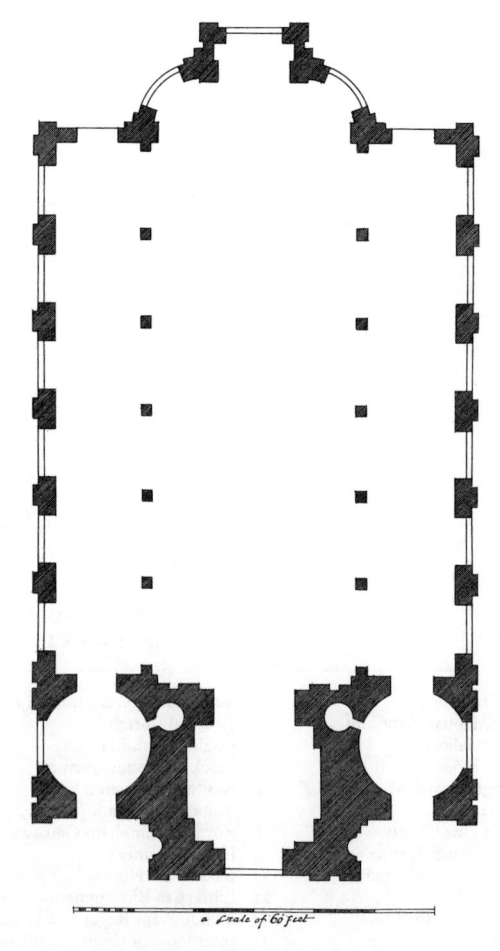

Birmingham, St Philip's Cathedral.
Plan, 1715

Doric pilasters, coupled on the w bay, and with a full entablature throughout. A controlling giant order appears only once before on an English church, at Dean Aldrich's All Saints, Oxford (1706–10), though Sir William Wilson's Hall Green church (p. 309) has a naïve treatment without a proper base. Archer would have known both. The walls have channelled rustication, highlighting the plain pilasters and bases, and above the windows are raised blocks – a three-dimensional, plastic treatment. The doorways are particularly Borrominesque: the w ones have incised pilasters tilted outwards, enclosing a fluted architrave tilted inwards, and hugely extended triglyphs supporting a pediment broken forward in the middle and with its ends tilted backwards to mirror the pilasters. The E ones have plain panelled pilasters but extraordinary bulbous shapes above, like table legs supporting big segmental pediments. The 'windows over ye doors' are oval, with scrolly surrounds growing into goggling masks at the tops. The urns were originally over alternate pilasters, though the full set was present by 1756. *Chatwin*'s E end follows Archer's elevation closely, even to the quarter-rounds flanking the E window repeated from the C18 apse. Only the windows are taller, so the raised blocks are omitted.

The w end projects with a big segmental pediment; its sides have deep round-headed and circular niches. The tower is where the Roman Baroque character is strongest. Above the convex shape of the pediment is a tremendous bell-stage with four deep concave sides running to paired Corinthian piers set at the diagonals; then the clock stage with big paired volutes to the diagonal faces, and an elongated octagonal dome. The clock faces incorporated into the design are also a step beyond London churches of the period. Above, an open colonnaded lantern, encircled by an ironwork balcony made by *Robert Bakewell* of Derby, is topped by a boar's-head weathervane. All the way up, convex and concave shapes succeed each other in dramatic contrast, but the result is perfectly unified.

INTERIOR. Entrance is by the D-shaped sw porch, its gallery stair retaining the original rail by *Bakewell*. The nave has five-bay arcades of square fluted Doric piers, the lower parts reeded. Arches with plain soffits, perhaps a C19 alteration, as early illustrations show panelling and rosettes. Stepped keystones with big attached consoles. Deep entablature with four-part architrave, plain frieze, and cornice with alternating leaf consoles and rosettes; coved ceiling. The galleries are flush with the piers. Their fronts have fielded panels of Norway oak. The original giant Corinthian order survives in the pilasters at the w end, their unusual low capitals with one big tier of leaves and flying volutes. The E vestries were extended into the aisles in 1905. *Chatwin*'s tower arch tactfully follows the design of the arcades. Looking E, the view is dominated by his magnificent CHANCEL, enriching the Baroque character of the interior. Its three bays are divided by giant Corinthian columns and sections of entablature coming forward on each side, with answering pilasters behind. The inspiration must be Cockerell, who gave the young Chatwin a reference with Charles Barry. Capitals more conventional than Archer's; shafts marbled by *Michael Reardon*, 1979–80. The narrow set-backs of the coved ceiling between each bay follow the original E end treatment. The dramatic stroke is the omission of a chancel arch. The ceiling runs straight through, in the chancel coffered with rosettes. Floor by *Reardon*, 1980, Hopton Wood stone, with black-and-white paving for the chancel.

FURNISHINGS. Former ALTAR RAIL, E end. A beautiful wrought-iron piece by *Bakewell*, 1715, with rosettes, sprays of leaves and religious symbols: flaming urns and St James's cockleshells. – STALLS by *Chatwin*, 1884, rich Renaissance designs with his typical scrolled tops to the ends. – BISHOP'S THRONE and CANONS' STALLS by *P.B. Chatwin*, 1905. – ORGAN CASE. Early C18; probably by *Thomas Swarbrick*, who repaired it in 1748. Big putto heads, and towers with traditional crown and mitre finials. Facing the N gallery, a second ORGAN CASE with beautiful carved trophies of instruments. Made by *Dr Justinian Morse* for Barnet church, Herts. before 1749; installed here *c.* 1980. – Forward ALTAR RAIL by *Michael Reardon*, 1980–2. – PULPIT. A simple C20 wooden drum. – ALTAR, heavy, with blind arcading, probably by *A.S. Dixon*, 1908. – SCULPTURE. N aisle. A crucified Christ carved from railway sleepers, and two standing figures, by *Peter Ball*, 1984. – BOX PEWS. Two survivors probably from re-pewing in 1814 (altered 1850), W end. More in the galleries. – Bronze DOOR HANDLES, S aisle, E end door, finely fashioned as three-winged heads of a lion and bull, symbols of the Evangelists (the other two on the inner face). By *David Wynne*, part of the Bishop Barnes memorial (*see* below). – DADO (aisles and pier bases) made from C18/C19 pews. – FONT by *John Poole*, 1982. A lettered bronze-gilt bowl. – STAINED GLASS. Chatwin acted as the intermediary between Emma Villiers-Wilkes, who met most of the bills for three new E windows, and the greatest stained-glass designer of the day, *Edward Burne-Jones*. Burne-Jones was born close at hand in Bennetts Hill in 1833, and had – like Chatwin – been baptized in the church. By the mid 1880s he was at the height of his powers, and his long-time collaborators *William Morris & Co.* knew exactly how to translate his designs into the bolder outlines and simpler colours the medium required. The subjects are the Ascension (centre, E), 1885, and Nativity and Annunciation to the Shepherds (NE) and Crucifixion (SE), both 1887–8. Colours are vibrant and exciting, with reds and blues predominant; designs are simple and dramatic, with a strong division between upper and lower zones, and with figures of an exceptional scale. – W window of 1897–8, also by *Burne-Jones*. The Last Judgment, glowing from within the tower. Christ and angels above, the resurrected below, shattered and tumbling buildings between.

MONUMENTS. Many tablets, with much contrast of limestone and grey marble and many urns. Particularly appealing the ones with obelisk tops on the nave piers. These include: N side, Chief Justice Oliver of Massachusetts †1791; Girton Peake †1770, with soul rising above; s side, William Higgs †1733, the first rector; William Vyse †1770; Rev. Charles Newling †1787; also Edward Villiers Wilkes †1835 by *Hollins*, urn and mourning woman. – Entrance to chancel, s side, Bishop Barnes †1953, small bronze portrait relief by *David Wynne*, 1954. – N aisle: N wall, Rebecca and William Grice †1781 and †1790, by *William Thompson*. – Henry Perkins †1817, by *William Hollins* with his typical drooping foliage. – Rear of nave pier, Francis Rogers M.D. †1804, by *P. Rouw*, oval tablet, snakes coiling round a club in the pediment. – w wall, Sobieski Brookshaw †1811, by *Thompson*, with scrolls and urn. – Moses Haughton, 'eminent artist', †1804, by *Rouw*. Good portrait medallion, books and palette below. – Sir Edward Thomason †1849. Small tomb-chest, and a bird holding a twig, symbolizing hope. – Royal Worcestershire Regiment war memorial, 1920 by *A.S. Dixon*. An original arrangement of five tablets, central rectangle with triangular projections surrounded by four diamonds. – s aisle, s wall. James Bayley †1834, William Taylor †1825, and Edward and Hannah Wilkes †1787 and †1820, all *W. Hollins*. – w wall, Beatrix Outram †1810, by *Sir Richard Westmacott*. A rose in bud above, a rose broken off below. – Edward Outram, Archdeacon of Derby, †1821, by *W. Hollins*. Draped tomb-chest. – William Westley Richards †1865 by *J. Gow*, still in the C18 tradition. – Tower, s side, G. Yeoville Thomason †1896, by *Roddis & Nourse*, alabaster. – Rev. John George Breay †1839, with portrait medallion; Rev. Albert Workman †1881, by *T. Chaplin*; John Bennett †1856; all from Christ Church, Colmore Row (dem. 1899). – Edward Palmer †1818, by *W. Hollins*, with draped urn. – sw lobby, David Owen †1823, by *W. Hollins*. Draped urn and more droopy foliage.

CHURCHYARD. Originally laid out with lime avenues for promenading. Landscaped as a garden by the *City Council* in 1912, refurbished in 1970 and again in the 1980s. A Lottery-funded scheme of 1998–2003 included gross railings with gilded arrowheads and ironwork piers, and paths of mechanical York stone. – MONUMENTS. w of the church, Bishop Gore, statue by *Stirling Lee*, 1914. – s side, obelisk to Col. Burnaby, killed in Sudan, by *Robert Bridgeman*, 1885; smaller obelisk to Lt-Col. Unett, killed at Sebastopol, by *P. Hollins*, 1857. – Further E, John Heap and William Badger †1833, killed building the Town Hall. The base and lower part of a fluted column, in Anglesey marble. – E again, an iron former DRINKING FOUNTAIN of 1859. Brooding angel by *E.J. Payne* and shell-shaped bowl.

CATHEDRAL OF ST CHAD (R.C.)
St Chad's Queensway

A major work by *A.W.N. Pugin*, 1839–41, and a landmark in the Gothic Revival. It was built for Bishop Thomas Walsh, whom Pugin had met when working at Oscott College (*see* p. 445).

Birmingham, St Chad's Cathedral (R.C.).
Drawing, 1897

Significantly in the revival of Gothic, Pugin replaced *Thomas Rickman*, who had produced designs in 1834. His builder was *George Myers*, an early collaboration. The first Catholic cathedral built in England since the Reformation, in a town with a long Catholic tradition. The site is that of St Austin, by *William Hollins*, 1808–9.*

St Chad's is early Pugin. It follows the programme suggested by his *Contrasts* (1836), creating a Catholic Gothic church in a heathenish industrial town whose medieval originals have been defaced, rather than recovering the logical structural tradition defined in his *True Principles of Pointed or Christian Architecture* (1841). When built it was tightly surrounded by the factories and workshops of the Gun Quarter. The ritual w front, now diminished by the dual carriageway of the inner ring road, originally faced the narrow Bath Street. The style is north German C13,

---

*The town's first Catholic church was St Peter, off Broad Street, 1786 (dem. 1969). Also demolished in the 1960s was *Pugin's* BISHOP'S HOUSE of 1840–1 opposite the Cathedral, a major loss.

which Pugin, describing his first design of 1837, defended as 'cheap and effective and...totally different from any *protestant* errection [*sic*]'. In plan and elevation it is like a reduced version of St Elizabeth, Marburg: a tall church with aisles but no clerestory, and a centralizing E end of transepts and sanctuary. The tracery is influenced by English Geometrical and Decorated, but also has German parallels. Also German is the use of brick, but laid in English bond, with dressings of Bath stone. Pugin had to create a convincing cathedral, not just a parish church, on a relatively small budget; Bishop Walsh contributed nearly £14,000 of the total cost of just under £20,000.

EXTERIOR. The W front immediately announces a cathedral, with its symmetrical pair of towers with spires flanking the gable of the nave. SW tower completed only in 1856 by *E.W. Pugin*. Central doorway divided by a stone pier. Tympanum with relief of the Virgin and Child with censing angels. Majestic six-light W window with spectacular Geometrical tracery: three large circles each containing seven small quatrefoiled ones. In the gable, a small spherical-triangle window containing three small foiled ones. The towers are carefully designed to stress the height: very tall two-light windows with statue niches treated integrally below them, very tall and thin paired lancets above. The spires have their main faces dying into very flattened broaches. More statues in niches flanking the doorway. Those on the W front are all English saints. To the NW, St Edward's Chapel by *Sebastian Pugin Powell*, 1933, with a three-sided apse. Beyond, the nave has two-light windows with sexfoiled circles (cf. the Liebfrauenkirche at Trier). Then a well-grouped, rather domestic extension, planned as a school, including the entrance to the crypt, and the former baptistery. The transept has a tall six-light window. The altar end groups most impressively above Shadwell Street, with the three-sided apse rising sheer out offices to the l. and the Lady Chapel to the r. The chapel was redesigned by Pugin during building, in English C14 style comparable to his church at Cheadle, Staffs. Its three-light E window has a spherical triangle with split cusping in the head, remarkable for 1841. Modern extensions for offices: CATHEDRAL HOUSE, NE, brick with steep gables by *Gordon H. Foster*, 1992, and behind at a lower level, a six-storey block of 1963 by *Harrison & Cox*.

INTERIOR. The great surprise of the building is the nave. This appears from outside as a single volume, but has five-bay arcades, exceptionally tall and delicate. They define a space which is at once complex but more unified than the additive plans of later Pugin, e.g. Ramsgate. They have circular columns with four attached three-quarter-rounds, a similar section to Marburg, and foliage capitals. The arches have a quite different, rather English, section with keeled rolls and hollows. The crossing has similar piers and arches. The Lady aisle (ritual N) is wider than the S aisle. Roofs of daringly thin timbers delineate the different parts, as Pugin thought essential. The nave has high queenpost trusses with arched braces to an upper collar, supported by curved braces to wall-posts on stone shafts rising from the springing of the arcades. The aisles have plain purlin and rafter roofs supported by diagonal struts. The crossing roof is flat, in nine panels; the chancel's moulded rafters and ridge purlin are supported by curved brackets.

CRYPT. For Pugin, 'the first fully Catholic place of sepulture to be revived', with private chapels for donors. Staircase from the N aisle with a big moulded stone handrail. Plain whitewashed brickwork and round arches. St Peter's Chapel at the E end has an impressive Neo-Norman arch of two orders with massive roll mouldings, chunky columns and scalloped capitals. Imaginary history: but Pugin may be stressing the continuity of Catholic England.

FURNISHINGS. Significant original items include important C15 and C16 German and Netherlandish work, and a major collection of *Pugin*-designed stained glass. The sanctuary was rearranged by *E.W. Pugin*, 1854. Otherwise the cathedral remained largely unaltered until *Weightman & Bullen*'s drastic reordering of 1966–8, making it a single space.* Some of its original character has been regained in alterations since 1992 by *Duval Brownhill* (now *Brownhill Hayward Brown*). – Nave. PULPIT. Moved from the S side in 1968, when it lost its sounding board. Given by the 16th Earl of Shrewsbury; probably early C16, and from the Abbey of St Gertrude, Leuven. Transitional in style between Gothic and Renaissance. Hexagonal, of oak. Elaborately carved columns with small figures divide concave panels with seated figures, probably the four Latin Doctors, under rich layered canopy-work. Plain moulded and panelled pendant vault. Entrance stairs and door by *Pugin*. – ORGAN CASE. Spectacular but slightly thin Gothic of 1992 by *David Graebe*. – Encaustic TILE FLOORS of 1992 by *H. & R. Johnson*, in C19 style. – PEWS of Japanese oak by *G.B. Cox*, 1940. – Wooden STATUE of St Chad, S side, C19. He holds a model of Lichfield Cathedral before Scott's restoration. Expressive face in German late medieval style. – N aisle. FONT. By *Pugin*, 1846. Octagonal, with the symbols of the Evangelists on the cardinal faces. – N transept. Elaborate MONUMENT to Bishop Walsh by *Pugin*, made in 1850 by *George Myers* and shown at the Great Exhibition. Bath stone. English C14 style. Ogee arch with big cusps containing angels. Reclining effigy with mitre and crozier. Back patterned in squares containing four-petalled flowers. – Ledger BRASS to John Bernard Hardman †1903, surrounded by small tablets. – S aisle. War memorial of 1921 by *Gerald J. Hardman* with relief of the Deposition. – STATIONS OF THE CROSS by *Albrecht Franz Lieven de Vriendt* of Antwerp, 1875. – ALTAR, St Edward's Chapel. By *Gerald J. Hardman*, 1933.

Chancel. HIGH ALTAR by *Pugin*, 1841. An important, early, medieval re-creation, comparable with Pugin's thrones in the

---

*Pugin's ROOD SCREEN is now in Holy Trinity, Reading.

House of Lords. The ciborium has a canopy with a large gable enclosing a cusped and sub-cusped pointed arch with foliage and angel-stops. The original altar now has a tabernacle of 1878 by *J.H. Powell* with enamels on the doors depicting the Agony in the Garden. – REREDOS with seven two-light bays. Above it, a relic chest by *Pugin* with crowning spire, supported by angels, by *Gerald Hardman*, 1933. – Oak CHOIR STALLS of *c.*1520. Five seats on the s, six on the N; detached seat, now the Provost's chair, to their E. Said to be from St Maria-im-Kapitol, Cologne, but probably Netherlandish. Substantially restored, but with original linenfold on the backs and beasts on the arms. C19 desks with fine C15 or C16 ends with tracery and carvings. N side, a Pietà on the W end, one of the Magi presenting a chalice to the infant Christ on the E. s side, monks preparing food, and two laymen, one with clawed feet holding a shield with the Imperial eagle. The Provost's chair has a backboard, probably re-assembled, with a Virgin and Child, angels, praying monks, two saints and panels of vines. – Lady Chapel. ALTAR by *Pugin*, 1841 with carvings of the Presentation in the Temple, the Nativity and the Adoration of the Magi. Circular tower tabernacle. – Contemporary REREDOS, Virgin and Child flanked by Annunciation and Visitation. – Also by *Pugin* the WEST SCREEN and PARCLOSE SCREEN. – C15 German STATUE of the Virgin and Child, given by Pugin. Heavily modelled faces; the Virgin memorably enduring and serene. – STATUE of St Joseph by *Michael Clarke*, 1969; fibreglass. – Crypt. Painted geometrical PATTERNS of *c.*1883. The Hardman Chantry has remains of painted decoration of 1877 (restored 1998). – MONUMENT to Archbishop Ullathorne †1888, by *Peter Paul Pugin*, 1890. Four-centred-arched canopy, reclining effigy in vestments. Relief on the back wall with monk, pointing angel and Virgin and Child.

STAINED GLASS. An important C19 collection, mostly by *Hardmans* (the family were prominent members of the church). Their early windows have bright reds and blues contrasted with quieter greens and browns, and grisaille. Nave, aisles and chancel are treated clockwise from the W end. N aisle. Second from W, the glassworkers' window, 1865, given by Hardman employees. Under St Luke and St Andrew of Crete are scenes of glass-making. Then a window of 1851 with St Francis and St Thomas the Apostle. Above, St Cecilia playing a portative organ, given in 1850. – Former baptistery. Three windows of 1843 designed by *Pugin* and made by *William Wailes*. Characteristic dense colouring; small figure scenes strongly contrasted with the dark backgrounds. – N transept. Immaculate Conception window, 1868 by *John Hardman Powell*. Six large scenes in ovals, many smaller panels. In memory of John Hardman, who kneels at the bottom l. in his choir cope; lines of Gregorian chant run along the bottom. – Lady Chapel. N, Annunciation with small scenes of children by *Warrington*, 1844; E, Our Lady, St Cuthbert and St Chad. – Chancel. Apse windows, saints designed by *Pugin* and made by *Warrington*. Paid for by

Lord Shrewsbury. Canopy-work with heavily stressed verticals to add to the sense of height. s side, two four-light windows, 1928. – s transept. Scenes from the life of St Thomas of Canterbury, 1865. – s aisle. War memorial, 1921, with darker, muted colours showing Kempe's influence. Our Lady and St George, 1850. – St Edward's Chapel. The story of the relics of St Chad, all of 1928, by *Donald Taunton* of Hardmans.

OTHER CHURCHES

St Martin in the Bull Ring. The ancient parish church of Birmingham, now dramatically placed in an amphitheatre created by the shopping centre of 2000–3. The development has swallowed its churchyard, and the church now rises directly from the space to its N, with the slight feeling of a big ornament or artwork.

A church probably existed by the C12 and is documented in 1263. The late medieval building had an aisled nave, chancel and NW tower. Walls and tower were encased in brick in 1690, a brick clerestory was added in 1733, and *William Hiorne* added a SE vestry in 1760. In 1853–5 *P.C. Hardwick* restored and re-cased the tower and rebuilt the spire. Then in 1872–5 the rest was rebuilt by *J.A. Chatwin*, slightly larger, with transepts and chancel aisles. In 1941 a bomb seriously damaged the W end and destroyed nearly all the glass. *Philip* and *Anthony Chatwin* repaired the church in 1950–3, and added the parish rooms, s, in 1954–7 and the SW octagon in 1960–1. In 2000–1 *APEC* reordered the interior, and in 2002–3 they extended the parish rooms and octagon to form a café and meeting spaces.

Looking from the new Bull Ring, the NW tower dominates. Grey-brown sandstone, rough-faced, with smooth quoins and details. The Dec style follows evidence discovered during the restoration: reticulated W window, petal forms in the belfry. On the N side two arched tomb-recesses, restored from medieval remains, and the external Miller Pulpit, under a little hood. *Chatwin*'s rebuilding was typical in being guided by existing work. Grinshill stone, again rough-faced. Dec windows, Geometrical (E) or reticulated (transepts). Wavy parapet on the nave, quatrefoiled on the chancel. Impressive gabled and pinnacled E end. The s side has exquisite *Anthony Chatwin* detail: rubble base merging into smooth stone above, well-placed beasties on the cornice. His octagon now has a cantilevered upper floor by *APEC*, with a similar gabled s porch to its E.

Inside, medieval stonework survives in the lowest stage of the tower. C14 tower s arch into the nave, with heavy plain chamfers. A narrow passage runs above. The rest of the interior is Codsall sandstone, deep rose-pink with some grey. Arcade piers with four attached half-columns, arches with two chamfers, the outer with a wave moulding. N arcade spandrels with a diaper pattern of flowers. Crossing piers more complex, with attached shafts. Rich roof: alternating hammerbeams and big arch-braced trusses, both with angels. Of 2000–1 the glass porch and limestone floor. w doorway arch with two big chamfers, much restored. Typical *Chatwin* chancel arch with shafts on corbels. Chancel arcades with boldly ogee-cusped arches. Boarded chancel roof with decorative trusses on paired angel corbels. Quarter-round linking passages between chancel and aisles. The 1954–7 link from the s aisle to the café modified by *APEC* for a disabled lift, a nice spatial effect.

Chatwin's FITTINGS include characteristic CHOIR STALLS; REREDOS, made by *Farmer & Brindley*, 1876, Scottish red sandstone, with serpentine shafts and alabaster reliefs of scenes from the Passion of Christ; PULPIT carved by *John Roddis* with seated figures under canopies; and PEWS (nave), restained. – Minton TILES in the chancel. – N transept ORGAN SCREEN by *George Pace*, 1954. – N chapel REREDOS by *Pace*, 1956, with very attenuated gilded columns; also the ALTAR and RAIL. – FONT, by *Jacqueline Gruber Stieger*, 2002. Three shallow bowls in bronze with water flowing between them and into a shallow pool. – NAVE ALTAR and READING DESK by *Toby Winteringham*, 2000–1. – STAINED GLASS. s transept, a major work of *Burne-Jones*, made by *Morris & Co.*, 1876–7. Three tiers. Top, Our Lord (the Salvator Mundi first designed by *Burne-Jones* in 1864) flanked by the Evangelists; middle, Prophets; bottom, small scenes in panels, of which the Flagellation and Entombment were new designs for this window. In the tracery, angels playing instruments. Autumnal colours, browns, greens, dark reds, blues. Graceful, slightly serpentine figures, the aged Moses (middle l.) particularly effective. Other glass post-war: E and W windows by *Hardmans*, 1952–4, the latter partly following their original of 1875; N chapel E by *H.W. Harvey*, 1956, very like his master, Harry Stammers; s aisle westernmost by *Lawrence Lee*, 1980. – MONUMENTS. Four medieval effigies, traditionally of the de Birmingham family. Between chancel and N chapel, going E, Sir William c. 1325, cross-legged knight, soft red sandstone; Sir Fulk c. 1370, grey sandstone. N chapel, Sir John c. 1390, alabaster effigy in armour, his feet on a lion, on a panelled Gothic tomb-chest designed by *M.H. Bloxam*, 1846, when all the effigies were 'restored'. Between chancel and s chapel, alabaster effigy of a priest in choir robes, C15. Original tomb-chest with angels holding shields.

ST MICHAEL (R.C.), Moor Street Queensway. The shell of the Unitarians' New Meeting House of 1802, the replacement for Joseph Priestley's chapel burnt down by rioters in 1791. Temple front with segmental ground-floor arches, paired Ionic pilasters and pediment. Two tiers of windows. In 1975 *Cyril Horsley* of *Horsley, Currall & Associates* roughcast the exterior, infilled the arcade, built the side porch with hanging arches, fitted new windows, and gutted the interior. Small presbytery of 1933–4 by *Victor S. Peel*, behind.

METHODIST CENTRAL HALL (former), Corporation Street. 1900–3 by *Ewen & J. Alfred Harper*. The town's first Wesleyan chapel opened in Cherry Street, 1782 (rebuilt 1822). In 1887 it was replaced by a Central Hall by *Osborn & Reading*, seating

1,100, in Corporation Street near Old Square. By 1899 this was already inadequate. The Harpers' successor has a main hall to seat 2,000 and over thirty other rooms including three school halls: 'clearly the local men's answer to the Victoria Law Courts opposite, to which it does indeed form the perfect complement' (Alexandra Wedgwood, 1966). It cost £96,165. Faced entirely in terracotta like the Courts, it is otherwise a deliberate contrast. The Courts are angled to the street, the Hall follows its alignment. The Courts are picturesquely informal, the Hall's three very tall storeys are powerfully defined by vertical piers, cornices and a parapet. The tower marks a step down, following the fall of the street. It rises sheer to a complex and strongly modelled belfry, partly enclosing an octagon, and a spirelet. Five bays of schoolrooms and offices to its l., with canted bays and arcading including paired windows above; seven bays with the main hall to the r., lit by big three-light free Perpendicular windows above gently curving bays. Remarkably eclectic detail, e.g. corner turrets resembling Indian chattris. The ground floor retains several original shopfronts. Very Baroque porch, with swinging voussoirs and paired stubby blocked Ionic pilasters. Much sculpture, modelled by *Gibbs & Canning*. On either side of the pediment, allegories of Methodist Teaching: large draped figures instruct cherubs holding discreetly placed books. Inside the porch, panels of scenes from the life of Wesley. The charming triangular lamp over the r. door is by *Ewen Harper, Brother & Co.*, 1928. The main staircase rises on the l. of the entrance hall to a seven-bay aisled and clerestoried hall with SE apse, which rises to the roof. Iron arcades. The gallery has a good iron balustrade of Art Nouveau flourishes. Narrow corridors between hall and outside walls, largely glazed. Disused and decaying (2021).

CARRS LANE UNITED REFORMED CHURCH. Founded 1748, rebuilt 1802, and again in 1820 by *Thomas Stedman Whitwell* in Greek Revival style, to seat 1,800; refronted by *Yeoville Thomason*, 1876. Again rebuilt 1968–71 by *Charles Brown (Denys Hinton & Partners)*. A tough piece, typical of its date, with echoes of Aalto and Butterfield. Red and plum Staffordshire brick, laid in Sussex bond. Four blocks linked by a glass foyer. At the S the octagonal chapel, to E and W hexagonal meeting-room blocks, at the N flats. The chapel has blank gables split by V-shaped window recesses, the meeting rooms have horizontal windows. Tall dark steel cross at the Moor Street entrance. In the foyer, seated STATUE of R.W. Dale by *E. Onslow Ford*, and MURAL by *Edward Bawden*, 1971: relief panels of the former chapels and a list of ministers, surrounded by circular patterns of nailheads, 20,000 in all. The chapel has rendered walls and quite a low ceiling, with light entering side alcoves.

FRIENDS' MEETING HOUSE, Bull Street. By *Hubert Lidbetter*, 1931. Cubic Neo-Georgian. The first meeting here began in 1703.

SALVATION ARMY CITADEL (former), Corporation Street. *See* p. 148.

PUBLIC BUILDINGS

Civic and cultural

TOWN HALL, Victoria Square and Paradise Street. Birmingham's first large-scale civic building: a Roman temple on a high podium, begun in 1832 and designed by *Joseph Hansom & Edward Welch*. As the first substantial C19 Roman Revival building in England, it is also a work of European importance. The choice reflected an interest in Roman learning and government among leading citizens. Thomas Attwood, former chairman of the Street Commissioners and active in commissioning the building, also led the Birmingham Political Union in support of the Great Reform Bill in 1832. When new, the building dominated by sheer size, like 'an ocean liner anchored in a fishing village' (Joe Holyoak). It was the venue of the Birmingham Triennial Musical Festival, and saw the premieres of Mendelssohn's *Elijah* and Elgar's *Dream of Gerontius*; Dickens gave readings here; political rallies included a near-riot in 1900 when Lloyd George spoke against the Boer War. The decline of big meetings reduced the need for the hall, and in 1996 it closed, after the City of Birmingham Symphony Orchestra moved to Symphony Hall (p. 168). Restored and the interior reconstructed in 2004–7 by *Birmingham City Council Urban Design Department*, with *Rodney Melville & Partners*.

In 1828 the Street Commissioners obtained an Act to erect a Town Hall to accommodate 3,000. A competition for the present site advertised in *The Times* in 1830 attracted seventy entrants, including *Charles Barry* (a Greek Revival design) and *Thomas Rickman* (*Rickman & Hutchinson*). The finalists were *Rickman & Hutchinson*, *John Fallows* and *Joseph Hansom & Edward Welch*. On 6 June 1831 Hansom & Welch were selected. Their radical politics may have helped. The Commissioners accepted a tender from *Thomas & Kendall* of £16,648, the architects to stand surety for major excess. Costs escalated, and Hansom was declared bankrupt in May 1834 and removed from the work, which was supervised to completion that December by *John Foster* of Liverpool. The actual cost was c. £25,000.

Hansom & Welch designed a free-standing temple, fourteen bays by eight (as it now exists). This proved too large for the site, and had to be cut down. The 1832–4 building was only twelve bays long, with a plain podium on the w where houses stood close, and a blank N end. To make space for an orchestra, in 1837 *Charles Edge* extended the N end with a large rectangular internal recess, and moved the organ into it. Then in 1849–51, when a new street was opened on the N and W sides, Edge completed the W podium to match, extended the building, and built the N front with a pediment to match that on the S. He also excavated the basement room below the Great Hall, and completed carving the columns. The new N front had two internal columns flanking the organ recess, removed in 1889–91 for staircases designed by *Cossins & Peacock* to give access to the roof-space. In 1995 the arcade at the S end of the podium, with its wonderful vistas through the arches, was infilled by the City Council's *Department of Planning & Architecture*, to enlarge the foyer.

The 'simple Corinthian temple' (Welch) is closely modelled on the Temple of Castor and Pollux (then called Jupiter Stator) in the Roman Forum, as reconstructed in Taylor and Cresy's *Architectural Antiquities of Rome* (1821–2). It stands perfect and aloof, as a temple should. The stone is 'Anglesey marble', a white Carboniferous limestone from Penmon. The proportions are almost exactly those of the temple in Rome, scaled down to about three-quarters. The temple's very tall podium with rough rustication is repeated, but with the round arches of the original transferred to the window openings above. The result was a completely new concept in England. The Corinthian order also follows closely, but the entablature is simplified, with a plain architrave and dentil cornice. The capitals, restored in 2004–7, have rich acanthus leaves and distinctive interlocking spirals. The cella is lit by large windows with eared architraves. At the N end it is set back, and the stair-towers of 1889–91 can be seen, flanking the organ recess of 1837. At the S end was an open entrance arcade two bays deep.

The INTERIOR has a complex history. Originally, there was a single gallery with side balconies, a rich ceiling of three large roses with border panels, and deep-coffered coving. *Martin & Chamberlain*'s proposed improvements produced only the staircases to the cloakrooms and gallery at the S end, 1875–6. In 1891 *Cossins & Peacock* constructed the present S entrance hall, shortening the Great Hall by 7 ft (2.1 metres), and created a crush hall on a mezzanine above. C19 redecorations were succeeded in 1927 by Sir Charles Allom of *White, Allom & Co.*, decorators of London and New York, best known for their work on ocean liners. He replaced the single gallery with separate upper and lower ones to increase capacity, removed the paintings of scenes from Birmingham's history of 1893 by *Henry Payne*, *Charles Gere* and others, and replaced the ceiling and nearly all the internal decoration. Finally in 2004–7 Allom's balconies were replaced by a single gallery as originally envisaged.

The entrance is still at the S end through the glazed-in arcade, painful in this emphatically classical context. *Cossins & Peacock*'s ENTRANCE HALL has opulent brown marble pilasters and a high dado. Square coffered ceiling. N and S lobbies lead to SIDE PASSAGES with original plain pilasters supporting cross-beams, serving rooms in the podium. The hall itself is a surprise: the exterior suggests a hall raised above subsidiary rooms, but a single GREAT HALL rises the whole height of the building. This places the windows high up, impressive visually and useful for noise insulation. The fluted Corinthian pilasters, cornice, and shape of the cove of the ceiling are of 1834, the N organ recess of 1837. The band of leaf decoration below the pilasters seems later C19. *Allom*'s ceiling has a restrained

Baroque starburst, and richly modelled city arms with trophies in the corners of the coving. The little window balustrades and not-quite-Greek-key ornament below are also his. Metal and glass galleries of 2004–7, creating a chillier interior than before. The ORGAN, built in 1834 by *William Hill* and moved in 1837, has a spectacular case designed by Mr *Mackenzie* of London. Five crowned towers of large-diameter pipes, linked by arrays of smaller ones. Large acanthus patterns of 1890. *Allom* could not resist altering the tower tops, and adding garlands and a portrait medallion of Queen Victoria.

COUNCIL HOUSE, Victoria Square. A richly detailed classical composition by *Yeoville Thomason*, 1874–9, extended 1881–5. The city's principal municipal building, and a major monument of the reinvigoration led by Joseph Chamberlain.

The site was bought in 1853, but early proposals were frustrated. In 1870 a competition was held for council buildings and assize courts, with Alfred Waterhouse as assessor. Designs were supposed to be anonymous, but competitors' names were well known. Waterhouse recommended two in turn by outside architects, but the council substituted local ones, with *Thomason*'s placed first. His scheme placed the council buildings on the S half of the site and the courts on the N. The elevations were in an expanded version of his Italianate commercial manner, with round-headed windows separated by paired

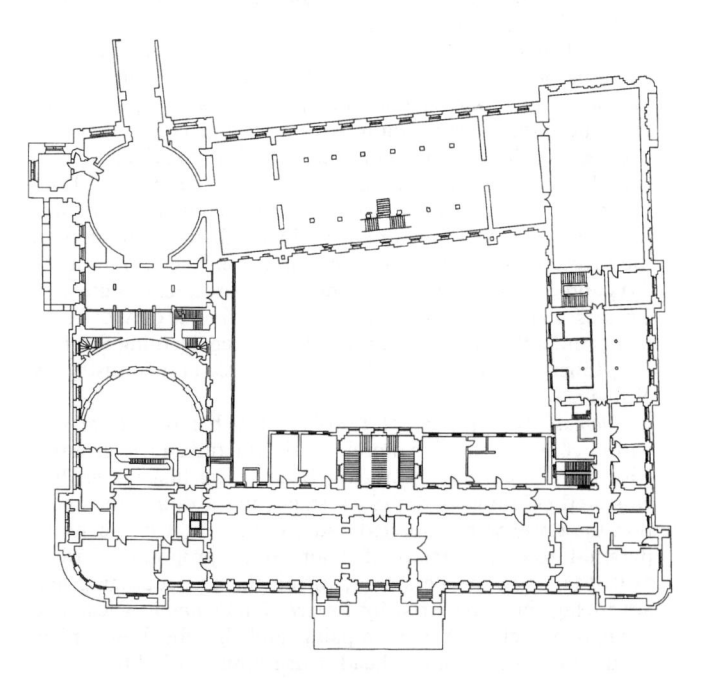

Birmingham, Council House.
First-floor plan

Corinthian columns (cf. his Birmingham Daily Post building, New Street, p. 151). Square turrets hinted at George Gilbert Scott's Foreign Office, and in the centre was a huge tower with a concave truncated pyramid top. *The Builder* praised the planning, but compared the elevations to 'a monster railway hotel'. In 1873 the Estates Committee persuaded Thomason to introduce a giant order, in sympathy with the Town Hall. The foundation stone was laid by Joseph Chamberlain on 17 June 1874, the Council first met in its new chamber in 1878, and formal opening followed in 1879. The courts were not built. In 1880 the Tangye brothers offered £10,000 to buy works of art, on condition that the Council built a dedicated art gallery. A deal was struck by which the gallery was built on the empty N part of the site, above accommodation for the gas department. The foundation stone of *Thomason*'s new design was laid in 1881 and the gallery opened in 1885. The whole building remains in use essentially for its original purposes.

Thomason's opulent Renaissance façade to Victoria Square has a giant Corinthian order and central dome. Mainly Wrexham and Coxbench stone. Battered rusticated ground floor with a heavy projecting portico on columns and square piers. Above, the centrepiece has a deep round-headed niche breaking up into a pedimented attic. The source seems to be French C16: Bullant's Petit Chantilly. Deep cornice of Denby Dale stone, with luscious foliage decoration carved by *John Roddis*. The dome seems small because of the fall of the square. The order is packed close along the sides, but the fluted columns of the centrepiece are far apart, so the superstructure looks like a heavy body on spindly legs. Big projections near the corners with columns *in antis* and large segmental pediments. The columns continue round a typical Thomason rounded SW corner, marking the Council Chamber and Lord Mayor's Parlour. SCULPTURE: central pediment, Britannia rewarding the Manufacturers of Birmingham; pediments of the projections, from W to E, Manufacture, The Union of the Arts and Sciences, Literature and Commerce, all designed by *Thomason* and carved by *R. L. Boulton & Sons*. MOSAIC: in the niche under the central pediment, figures representing Science, Art, Liberty, Municipality, Law, Commerce and Industry, by *Salviati*.

Thomason's W façade of 1881–5 is much more successful, with a confident double-storey portico picturesquely grouped with the NW corner tower, 'Big Brum'. The first design had clustered columns at the clock stage, and a dome; in execution the tower was simplified and given its truncated concave pyramid roof, a version of Thomason's proposal of 1870. SCULPTURE in the pediment, Birmingham encouraging and advancing the Fine Arts, by *Francis J. Williamson*. Clear and strongly modelled. A woman paints and cherubs draw a plan, l.; more cherubs sculpt a head, r. Birmingham holds a laurel wreath to crown the artists' efforts. Simpler N elevation with two tiers of round-arched windows.

CITY CENTRE: PUBLIC BUILDINGS   129

INTERIOR. The main elements are laid out clearly and logically. The style is Thomason's normal Italianate, with much use of coloured marbles. The main STAIRCASE rises inside the entrance to a landing. On the r. the decorative grilles of the King's Lift, made by *Waygood* in 1909 for a visit by Edward VII, who was unable to climb the stairs. COMMITTEE ROOMS along the main S front, with big doorcases and dark wood dadoes. The staircase returns in two flights to the upper corridor and the principal rooms. Above, the inner shell of the dome, on spectacular squinches with three set-backs. Statues on the half-landings: Prince Albert by *J.H. Foley*, 1866; Queen Victoria by *Thomas Woolner*, 1884, portrayed as a young woman.

The grandest interiors are the BANQUETING ROOMS. They have pilasters and round-headed niches, and depressed barrel-vaults with decorative ribs. The W room is separated from the central ante-room by paired columns supporting a cornice and an open arcade. Painting in the E tympanum, Peace, by *Joseph Southall*, 1937–40. Only the top part of his design. Central seated figure, in an aedicule sculpted by *Bloye*, flanked by a boy and girl in contemporary dress, in twining stylized foliage. At the W end a glass-domed lobby, and to its N the semicircular COUNCIL CHAMBER, lit by lunette windows in each bay. Altered in 1911 to accommodate the enlarged Council by *Cossins, Peacock & Bewlay*. They removed Thomason's paired Doric columns, leaving piers with paired pilasters in each third bay, and installed the handsome benches with segmental ends. Survivors of 1878–9 the dais and the screen of Riga oak behind it, richly carved by *Collier & Plucknett* of Warwick. In the central bay a panel with a reminder to politicians, an hourglass inscribed Tempus Fugit. Cornice with a central wreath of Italian walnut. In the coving painted panels of Truth and Justice, survivors of a larger C19 scheme. In the E wing the square former RATING HALL. Ceiling supported by four decorative iron columns.

The MUSEUM AND ART GALLERY is entered through the W portico. Also Italianate inside, but with delicate strapwork ceilings. Its location above the Gas Department left limited space on the ground floor behind the portico. Thomason's solution has a richly detailed ENTRANCE HALL and a STAIRCASE rising effectively behind a screen of columns. Plaque to George and Sir Richard Tangye, 1908, by *W.R. Colton*. Painting on the E wall at the top, 'Corporation Street in 1914', *Southall*'s most important *buon fresco* panel, painted 1915–16. The title refers to Southall's horror at the outbreak of war; the figures are portraits of friends, evoking a lost peaceful world. The upper landing, with coved ceiling and square roof-light, leads to the ROUND ROOM, with a low conical glass roof above a strapwork band. To the E the INDUSTRIAL GALLERY, all exposed ironwork: six aisled bays with columns in two tiers, semicircular arcades and cross-arches in the aisles, larger semicircular trusses supporting the roof, all of exposed I-beams with the rivets prominent. T-plan staircase of 1893. Further E the present TEA ROOM has a cantilevered iron gallery. N of the Round Room is the Council House Extension (*see* below). The WATERHALL (former Gas Department) below the Industrial Gallery is similarly impressive: four fluted iron Corinthian columns support I-beams with brick vaults between, the construction again completely exposed. Refurbished by *Associated Architects*, 2000.

COUNCIL HOUSE EXTENSION, Chamberlain Square and Margaret Street. By *Ashley & Newman*, 1908–17. In 1905 John Feeney, proprietor of the *Birmingham Post*, left £50,000 to build an additional art gallery N of the Council House. Following the earlier building, the new galleries are on the first and second floors, with council offices below. W, S and E ranges built 1908–12; N range to Great Charles Street 1912–17. The S side, damaged by bombing in 1941, was reconstructed in 1955–8 by the *Birmingham City Architect's Department*. The Extension is linked to the Council House by a chunky bridge. The W front has a low central dome, now seen in steep foreshortening. Impressive Baroque classicism, more learned than Thomason, but linked visually by its rusticated ground floor and Aberdeen granite basement. The main material is Denby Dale limestone. The *piano nobile* plays variations on the Ionic order: paired pilasters on the W, single columns on the corner pavilions, framed by corner piers with plain pilasters, paired columns free-standing against the blank wall of the galleries on the S. The entrances derive from Wren's St Mary-le-Bow: Doric doorcases, in round-headed niches articulated by rusticated voussoirs. Over the N entrance a rusticated arched staircase window with the city arms flanked by seated figures of Art and Industry above.

INTERIORS. The BRIDGE to the Extension starts with a grand arch with Doric columns. The bridge itself and the galleries at the far end were rebuilt plainly in 1955–8. The best remaining early C20 interiors are up the staircase at the far end, part-hidden behind display fittings. The DOME ROOM has a circle of eight Ionic columns set in a square, and consoles between the entablature and the dome, a typical Edwardian touch. GALLERIES to either side with shallow barrel-vaults and a wide W aisle separated by panelled piers. The main NORTH STAIRCASE rises in a hall with a pronounced Byzantine flavour to its split marble panels and niches with arches checked in at the springing. Stained glass by *Harvey & Ashby*. The GAS HALL, accessed from the N side of Chamberlain Square, was the Gas Payment Office of 1910, with barrel-vault and pilasters. In 1992–3 *StantonWilliams* reconstructed its entrance hall, which had been altered after bombing, in a white planar style, and converted the main hall for an exhibition gallery.

BIRMINGHAM AND MIDLAND INSTITUTE, Margaret Street. Built 1899 as the Birmingham Library (a private members' library), by *F. Barry Peacock* of *Peacock & Bewlay*. Loose but friendly Jacobean, brick with big stone windows, many divided by banded columns or pilasters. Composition with two end gables, a simplification of its neighbour to the S, the School of Art (p.133). Slightly fussy entrance with banded columns, rusticated arch, and side panels with semicircular pediments, the l. one containing a clock. The handsome entrance hall and staircase survive. The Institute moved here when its building in Paradise Street was demolished. To accommodate it, in 1972–3 *Associated Architects* extended the building via a glazed link into No. 95 Cornwall Street (*see* p. 164).

Court houses

VICTORIA LAW COURTS, Corporation Street.* Until the granting of an Assize in 1884, major civil and criminal cases were heard at Warwick. Having inspected the courts in several other assize towns, the Council committee was in no doubt that it wanted as architect *Alfred Waterhouse*, the designer of the Manchester Assize Courts (1859–65) – 'The best courts of law in the world', according to *The Times*. But Birmingham architects agitated for an open competition, and Waterhouse instead became the assessor, his sketch plans being offered as a guide. Of the top five entries only one came from a local firm, *Bateman & Hunt*, and the winners in 1886 were *Aston Webb & Ingress Bell* of London. Foundation stone laid by Queen Victoria, 23 March 1887; opened in 1891, having cost about £113,000.

The winners' pseudonym was 'Terracotta', and the whole building is faced in it, a hard red shade from *J.C. Edwards* of Ruabon: decorative, with shafts and mouldings dying back into the wall surfaces. It draws from both Gothic and classical, predominantly French Renaissance, but combining Flemish, Plateresque and Tudorbethan elements. Webb & Bell departed from Waterhouse's plan by stepping the front back from the street, creating a picturesque oblique arrangement of gables and towers, while keeping the plan regular and basically symmetrical. The principal entrance is at the centre of the long side of the Great Hall, which screens the courts behind from the noise of the street. Two courts open directly off the Great Hall. A central corridor leads to a smaller square hall for the Civil and Criminal Courts, and through to the barristers' library at the rear. Secondary corridors at each end of the Great Hall give access to two further courts near the front of the building, and to offices behind.

The Great Hall has a steep slate roof, against which is a large gable and clock above the central bay. Five large segmental-headed first-floor windows. Round-arched entrance porch, inspired by the C16 s transept of the cathedral at Senlis, France. The figure of Queen Victoria enthroned beneath the gable is by *Harry Bates*, one of several features by leading workers in the Arts and Crafts movement. Other figures representing the attributes of Justice, designed by *Walter Crane* and modelled

*Entry by Ian Dungavell.

by *W.S. Frith*, who also modelled the figure of Justice crowning the clock gable. Much ornament elsewhere – putti supporting the brackets of the cornice, dolphins, and classical mouldings – all by *William Aumonier*. This block is flanked by octagonal tourelles which articulate the former refreshment rooms, projecting on the l., and the offices, receding on the r., both at a lower level. At the corner with Newton Street, far l., the projecting bay with its bow window and the recessed bay five windows wide is an extension of 1891–4 by *Webb & Bell* for police offices, now incorporated. Further extensions along Newton Street by *Henry E. Stilgoe*, City Engineer and Surveyor, submitted to Aston Webb for approval in 1914.

Inside is one of the most striking interiors of any C19 court building in England. Instead of red terracotta, the GREAT HALL and public corridors are faced in a sandy-yellow shade by *Gibbs & Canning* of Tamworth, and judicial gravitas takes second place to the golden glow of civic pride. The decoration is lavish and intricate. Great pseudo-hammerbeam roof of dark-stained softwood, no doubt intended to recall Westminster Hall, the traditional hub of English justice. The archways with the royal arms derive from the main gate at Christ's College, Cambridge. The first-floor corridors across each end, with their curved central balconies on profusely ornamented corbels, look like minstrels' galleries. Pairs of exceedingly pretty putti support the empty niches between the windows. Only the inscriptions from Chaucer and Magna Carta remind the visitor of the seriousness of the business at hand. The five great ELECTROLIERS are by *Starkie Gardiner*. The STAINED-GLASS WINDOWS, designed by *H.W. Lonsdale* and executed by *Heaton, Butler & Bayne*, are Birmingham's Golden Jubilee memorial. Along the street front, scenes that show the contribution of the Queen or Prince Consort: Labour and Recreation bring Health (the Queen opening Aston Hall and Park, 1858); Theory and Practice combine in Technical Education (the Consort laying the first stone of the Midland Institute, 1855); Justice and Mercy in Law (the Queen laying the first stone of the Law Courts, 1887, a scene in which Webb and Bell themselves appear); Love and Discipline in Elementary Education (the Queen inspecting schoolchildren in 1887). Victoria also appears in the glass above the great terracotta royal arms on both long sides, as in 1837 and 1887, with other personifications. End windows with figures representing Birmingham manufacturing trades and Warwickshire worthies.

The COURTS themselves are more sombre. The most impressive is Court 5, panelled in dark oak linenfold with an elaborate canopy over the bench carved by *H.H. Martyn* of Cheltenham. Elaborate plasterwork throughout by *George Jackson & Sons*.

COUNTY COURT (former), Corporation Street. 1882 by *James Williams*, the first building on this part of the street. A conservative but beautiful Italianate palazzo. Ground floor with channelled rustication and Doric porch, *piano nobile* with pedimented windows, like a Charles Barry club of 1835.

CITY CENTRE: PUBLIC BUILDINGS 133

JUVENILE COURT (former), Newton Street. 1937 by *Peacock & Bewlay*. Brick with stone dressings, the corner to Steeelhouse Lane nicely turned by Ionic pilasters.

CORONER'S COURT, Newton Street, immediately S. Also of 1937 by *Peacock & Bewlay*. Early C18 style with rusticated ground floor, swept-up parapet, and curly broken pediment over the central first-floor window.

QUEEN ELIZABETH II LAW COURTS, Dalton Street. 1981–7 by the *Property Services Agency, Midland Region Design Unit Architects*. Three storeys. Long, low-pitched intimidating roofs, glazed entrance. – SCULPTURE in front by *Vincent Woropay*, 1988. The 'Wattilisk', five surmounted heads based on Chantrey's head of James Watt in the City Art Gallery, becoming smaller and more defined as they go up.

Educational buildings

SCHOOL OF ART (BIRMINGHAM CITY UNIVERSITY DEPARTMENT OF FINE ART), Margaret Street. The Municipal School of Art is *J.H. Chamberlain*'s last work, and his finest. His devotion to Ruskin and his belief in the 'Civic Gospel' are powerfully expressed in its use of brick Gothic and naturalistic ornament. Appointed in 1882, he completed the drawings just before his sudden death in October 1883. His partner *William Martin* executed the designs in 1884–5, with *Sapcote & Sons* as contractors. The building owes its existence to Edward R. Taylor, appointed as head of Birmingham's Government school of design in 1877, who then persuaded the Council to take it over. An early Arts and Crafts man, he changed teaching methods to emphasize craft skills, with 'art laboratories' for e.g. metalwork. The building cost £21,254, of which the Tangye brothers gave £10,937 and Louisa Ryland £10,000. An extension to the N range, along Cornwall Street, was added by *Martin & Chamberlain* in 1891–3. The exterior was cleaned in 1990–2, and in 1993–6 *Associated Architects* refurbished and renovated the major interiors and cleverly adapted other interior spaces.

The original building is U-shaped, with the three-storey W front to Margaret Street, with its two-storey central porch, between slightly projecting four-storey wings. The basic material is orange-red brick from Adderley Park, a flaming challenge to the stone classicism of the Council House opposite. Grey Derbyshire stone dressings, with a small amount of pink. The W front balances plain areas with rich decoration. The blank top storey, hiding studios, is treated with a terracotta arcade and discs. Tall gabled centrepiece, the porch with some richly decorated stonework, mostly with leaf patterns in small squares, also the buttresses. The top gable has a tympanum and circles with leaf decoration on a brilliant gold mosaic background. The S wing is taller, so that its upper studio can get north light. Its large canted mullion-and-transom bay window

85

is supported by a richly decorated bracket on a chunky three-lobed wall-shaft. Flanking it, big buttresses cut back from broad flat fronts and enriched by panels of terracotta tracery. The s elevation to Edmund Street, visible from Colmore Row, has three bays with paired stone windows, rising from lintelled to cusped and plain pointed, and exuberant gables enclosing complex little kingpost trusses with blue tiling in their braces. Between the windows, buttresses which sprout typical little Chamberlain canopies. The vertical force is balanced by the long balcony with its wrought-iron balustrade below the gables.

The N wing is simpler, with three large plain lancets and a deep terracotta foliage band at arch level, to set off the glorious circular stone window in its gable, carved by *Samuel Barfield* of Leicester: huge curving lilies with trumpeting flowers, set against a square trellis. Impressively functional N side: five bays of big pointed brick arches with flower and leaf tympana, enclosing windows with massive shouldered lintels, a motif which repeats on the ground floor. Above the cornice a long range of wooden-framed studio windows. The 1891–3 extension continues this for another eleven bays, identical except for simpler metal studio glazing, typical of the firm's engineering approach after Chamberlain's death. The whole exterior is tied together by a continuous band of *Doulton* tilework containing lozenges of lilies and sunflowers on blue backgrounds, and by a repeating motif of a square enclosing a quatrefoil, in turn enclosing a circular disc, mostly containing a flower or leaf pattern, seen on e.g. stone panels breaking the tile frieze, and more simply on the area railings made by *Hart & Co.* Crowning the roofs two ventilation towers, chunky chamfered squares with projections rising to little gablets. A charming wooden bridge carrying a duct, best seen from inside, links the s studio roof to the adjacent tower.

The entrance has arcading with oak, apple and strawberry designs in the tympana, naturally proportioned. A lobby opens into the central corridor. Immediately in front is a two-bay arcade, the column capital decorated with sunflowers. Beyond is the MUSEUM, the show interior, beautifully restored in 1993–6. A tough, rich aisled Gothic hall, not large: three-bay arcades with columns of pink granite with grey bases, and complex moulded arches. Their capitals have all kinds of leaves and flowers: oak, lilies, crocus, poppies, anemones. Brick walls, tuck-pointed in white mortar. Steep roof trusses with tie-beams and upper collars, linked by kingposts. No clerestory, but roof-lights. Pitch-pine dado; mosaic floor by *Craven Dunnill*, in curving patterns. Imaginative use of space, e.g. where the upper corridor opens into the museum through a triple arcade, and where the main corridor opens into the flanking staircases on two levels (now glazed in). STUDIOS at the top of the main block and N wing, and on two levels on the S, treated as great halls; the consummation of Chamberlain's Board School halls. Lines of huge pointed iron trusses, each unit with the disc-in-quatrefoil motif, here with a central ivy leaf. The N extension has the trusses boarded in. *Associated Architects* inserted an ingenious mezzanine here, with a cunningly sited glass access lift. The courtyard exteriors are plain, with a glass staircase of 1993–6 at the NE end.

Hospitals

BIRMINGHAM CHILDREN'S HOSPITAL, Steelhouse Lane. The former General Hospital of 1894–7 by *Henman & Cooper*. The original E-shaped plan altered but still recognizable. Thomas Cooper had worked for Waterhouse and uses here the Romanesque style of the Natural History Museum in Kensington, but in rich red brick and terracotta. The wings end in pairs of spires with (infilled) triplet arcades between. In the rear corners huge octagonal ventilation towers with spires cut off for tapering open caps. Central entrance and porch from alterations of 1995–8 by *Powell Moya Partnership*, also the operating theatre wing at the rear.

EAR AND THROAT HOSPITAL (former), Edmund Street. 1890–1 by *Jethro A. Cossins (Cossins & Peacock)*. Severe but elegant Queen Anne. Three storeys, brick. Dutch-gabled ends, central entrance with a double-height canted bay, under an elliptical arch. The window lit the staircase. Extended along Barwick Street, 1902–3. Reduced to façades and one side gable for a bulky office scheme by *Glazzard Associates*, 2002–3.

BIRMINGHAM AND MIDLAND EYE HOSPITAL (former), Church Street and Edmund Street. 1883–4 by *Payne & Talbot*. Queen Anne style in red brick, progressive for Birmingham at this date. Tall windows with moulded brick surrounds and glazing bars in the upper lights only. Dormers with fluted pilasters and a variety of pediments. Corner oriels on impressive leaf corbels, old-fashioned heavy entrance with banded columns. Hotel refurbishment 2000–1 by *Michael Phillips Associates.*

Other institutions

LOUISA RYLAND HOUSE, Edmund Street and Newhall Street. Three former public buildings, combined as retained façades by *PCPT*, 1984–6. The PARISH OFFICES and BOARD OF GUARDIANS of 1882–5 by *W.H. Ward* face Newhall Street. Very large, cleanly articulated French Renaissance, in cream stone with banded Cornish granite columns to the centrepiece and ends, rusticated lower floors, and panelled pilasters flanking the second-floor windows. (Extra floor and new entrance to Newhall Street by *Hickman & Smith* approved 2019.) A dome on the Edmund Street front was lost in the Second World War. The SCHOOL BOARD OFFICES, adjoining on that street, are of 1881–2 by *Martin & Chamberlain*. Brick Ruskinian Gothic like the firm's schools, here with more extensive stone dressings. Sashes under Gothic architraves or cusped relieving arches. Vigorous central entrance with canted bay window above. Beautiful low-relief flower decoration, e.g. above the second-floor windows. The MEDICAL INSTITUTE, l., next to the School of Art, is of 1879 by *Osborn & Reading*. Victorian classical turning Queen Anne. Porch with paired Corinthian columns, tall windows with Venetian tracery, relief panels of flowers and a pretty little pediment. Good original railings.

STOCK EXCHANGE, Margaret Street and Great Charles Street. 1928 by *S. N. Cooke*. A seven-bay Portland stone block, the tall ground floor with smooth rustication. Small recessed windows, pulled together by a well-proportioned cornice. Closed 1987 and converted to offices.

Railway stations

NEW STREET STATION. Built in 1849–54 by the London & North Western Railway, replacing termini on the edge of the town: Curzon Street (*see* p. 192), Vauxhall and Lawley Street. It had handsome Italianate buildings by *John Livock*, facing Stephenson Street, and a single-span iron sickle-truss roof with a maximum width of 212 ft (64.6 metres), the largest in the UK when built, designed by *E.A. Cowper* of *Fox, Henderson & Co.*, the builders of Paxton's Crystal Palace. Removed after bomb damage in 1940. Extended s in 1881–5, with Station Street along its far side. All rebuilt in the 1960s: dark and claustrophobic station with platforms below a concrete raft, by *British Railways, London Midland Region*, planner in charge *Kenneth J. Davies*, 1964–7; bland shopping centre (now PALASADES SHOPPING CENTRE) and nine-storey office block above by *Cotton, Ballard & Blow*, 1968–70. Completely recast above the raft in 2009–15, concept design by *Alejandro Zaera-Polo* of *Foreign Office Architects*, later *AZMPL*, executive architect *Atkins*, interior architect *Haskoll*. AZMPL left the project acrimoniously in 2014. The concrete structure above the raft has been clad in curving, free-form stainless-steel panels, with three 'media eyes' over the entrances, large screens showing endless videos: an uncompromising approach, and for one critic 'a silvery slug'. The best thing is the huge concourse, with big curving roof ribs clad in tensioned ETFE fabric. Low entrance ways with ceilings of wavy baffles, partly to hide service ducts. It is difficult to find your way around, and the platforms, though refurbished, are still low and just as claustrophobic. The shopping centre survives on an upper floor, with a balcony. (For the signal box *see* p. 206.)

MOOR STREET STATION. By *W.Y. Armstrong*, Great Western Railway Superintendent Engineer, 1911. A twin-gabled brick block, a standard GWR design, with open canopies to the platforms. Restored by *Simons Design*, 2002–3, with a new N porch.

THE COMMERCIAL CENTRE: STREETS

A network of streets, alleys and precincts, sloping up NW from the Bull Ring to the ridge of Colmore Row and beyond. Streets are listed alphabetically, followed by the Newhall estate as a perambulation. Late Georgian survivors in the Waterloo Street area; otherwise the character is late C19 onwards, with much late C20–early C21 rebuilding in High Street, lower New Street and the middle part of Corporation Street.

ALBERT STREET runs E off Dale End. On the S side Nos. 20–26, 1898 by *J.A. Chatwin*. Entrance with a big broken pediment biting a two-light window. Nos. 28–34 of 1888 by *Arthur Harrison*, pinky-red brick with a rusticated stone ground floor. This and the segmental windows look almost Neo-Georgian of 1930. The dormers give the date away.

BENNETTS HILL. Part of the early C19 Inge estate development (*see* Waterloo Street, p. 156). Starting from New Street at the S end, on the W side No. 13, a stucco survivor of 1823. Windows in panels cut back from the façade, which forms fluted pilasters at the sides. Nos. 11–12, the former SCOTTISH WIDOWS, 1930–1 by *Peacock & Bewlay*, minimal classical over a steel frame. The SUN BUILDING is by *S.N. Cooke*, 1927–8, stripped classical. On the E side, No. 21 by *W.S. Clements*, 1933–4, *Moderne* with prominent central fins. Nos. 23–24, very late Neo-Georgian of 1961 by *E. Bower Norris*. No. 25 is by *Riley & Smith*, 1926–7, for the COMMERCIAL UNION ASSURANCE. Handsome but slightly coarse, with giant fluted Ionic pilasters and a bowed central bay. Then Waterloo Street. Beyond, W side, early C19 fronts: one of five bays, then two-bay shops stepping uphill. Windows in recessed panels, typical of *Charles Edge*. Façaded in 1976 as part of Waterloo Court (p. 157). Opposite, three-storey Italianate office buildings of *c.*1860. No. 37 has first-floor windows with decorative spandrels, below alternating pediments, suggesting *Edward Holmes* (cf. the former Masonic Hall, New Street, p. 150). No. 38, plainer, with a rich cornice. Late C19 rusticated ground floor.

BULL RING. The historic town centre. Peter de Bermingham, the lord of the manor, obtained a market charter in 1166, though the name Bull Ring is only C18. Originally the market place fell sharply S from the junction of High Street and New Street, widened out in front of St Martin's church and forked into Digbeth, E, and Spiceal Street and Jamaica Row, W. The island site between Digbeth and Moat Lane probably represents late medieval encroachments. The medieval manor house survived until 1822, SW of Moat Lane. In the early C19 the space was dignified by the statue of Nelson, and by the large classical Market Hall by *Charles Edge*, 1831–5, on the W side. Later piecemeal rebuilding was of poor quality. Bombing in 1940 gutted the Market Hall. Completely rebuilt as the BULL RING CENTRE in 1961–7 by *Sydney Greenwood* and *T.J. Hirst*.

Pedestrians were funnelled under elevated roads, a classic case of subjugating people to traffic. Replaced again in 2000–3 by *Benoy*.

At the junction of New Street and High Street, the sole survivor (due to listing) of the 1960s rebuilding, the ROTUNDA, by *James A. Roberts*, 1964–5. A twenty-four-storey concrete-framed circular tower, a simple and dramatic shape well suited to its commanding site. Original appearance lost in re-cladding by *Glenn Howells*, 2008. SCULPTURE, *ciment fondu* relief by *John Poole*, 1965, richly textured abstract patterning, now in a shop. Beyond, a pedestrian street runs s, rises slightly to cross an underground bus route, then falls steeply to St Martin's church (p. 122). Covered malls of 2000–3 on either side, their lower parts on three levels with balconies and bridges. Architecturally depressing: crude Postmodern, abstract relief panels, conventional entrances with full-height glazing, a trite circular tower at the W. SCULPTURE by the top of the walkway, a slightly over-life-size bronze bull by *Laurence Broderick*, 2002. A dramatic stroke at the end, a curving balcony above the open space in front of the church. Here is the bronze STATUE of Nelson by *Sir Richard Westmacott*, 1807–9.* Deliberate simplicity, a contrast to his idealized Nelson at Liverpool of 1808–13. The admiral, in modern dress, his missing arm apparent, stands so easily that the anchor he leans on, and the model of HMS *Victory*, do not appear incongruous. 12-ft (3.7-metre)-high drum pedestal, originally with a relief of Birmingham mourning her dead hero, and four surrounding lamps with columns shaped as piled muskets, on bases of real naval cannon. Railings shaped as boarding pikes and linked by twisted rope.

Attached to the development, SELFRIDGES store 2001–3 by *Future Systems*. An organic, waveform shape, as instantly recognizable an icon as the Rotunda was for the Sixties. Nicknamed the Blob, the Digbeth Dalek. Nostalgia for adolescent science fiction thrills lurks behind the silver anodized aluminium discs bolted to the skin. The architects suggested Paco Rabanne. The outside wall tapers in like a fortification, then sweeps out and up, and rounds back at the top. The shape goes all round. Glass entrances like mouths. A vertiginous glazed steel-box footbridge shoots out over Park Street to the car park, E. The rejection of traditional scale, massing and relationships is a hallmark of its designers, the sources of whose 'plastic freedom' lie more in design than in architecture, though there is influence from Archigram (a Sixties group of course), as well as Mendelsohn's Einstein Tower. But the organic concept is only skin deep – blown concrete on steel mesh, covered in fibre insulation and blue render – on conventional steel post-and-beam construction. It looms over St Martin's from the s, with the vehicle entrance close to the church's E end. Two

---

*Nelson, with Sir William and Lady Hamilton, visited Birmingham in 1802, when he was 'repeatedly greeted with the applauding shouts of the surrounding multitude'.

light-wells, the larger E one curved and raked upwards. Escalators and balconies in shiny plastic resembling vitreous enamel. Poor detail, e.g. where escalators join balconies.

The open-air market, N of St Martin's from the C12 until 1999, has been banished to the S. Simple COVERED MARKET of 2000 by the city's *Urban Design* team. To the NE, Moor Street Station (p. 136).

BULL STREET. SE of Corporation Street, the Martineau Place and Corporation Square shopping precincts (p. 146). NW of Corporation Street, House of Fraser l. and the former Lewis's r. (*see* Corporation Street). N of Temple Row, l., PEARL ASSURANCE HOUSE of 1958–60 by *S. N. Cooke & Partners*. Opposite, the Friends' Meeting House (set back; *see* p. 124), No. 41 by *Gerald de Courcy Fraser*, 1936–7, and Nos. 42–43 by *S. N. Cooke*, 1934.

CANNON STREET runs NE from New Street, parallel to Corporation Street. Cut in 1732; the best buildings now Late Victorian. Globe LAMPS on brackets, 1980s copies from a surviving C19 example in Needless Alley, W. From New Street, on the W side first Newton Chambers (p. 151), then a block of 1906 by *Frederick W. Lloyd*. Big canted terracotta bays, doorway with huge masks and a pediment perched on the architrave. The WINDSOR pub was rebuilt in 1990 by *PCPT*, the Jacobean façade a near-replica of that of 1888 by *William Wykes*. The CITY PLAZA development is by *Halpern Partnership*, 1987–9. Beyond, the former Bank of England development (*see* Temple Row, p. 153). Returning down the E side, Nos. 13–14 on the corner of Cherry Street, by *J. L. Ball*, 1881–2, a massive brick block, but with delicate detail, e.g. the steep triangular quasi-pediments to the second-floor windows, echoed by the dormers. Casement windows and shallow bays, painted white. A Dutch flavour, suggesting a Protestant city (Ball was a Methodist). Then the rear of *A. B. Phipson*'s Midland Educational Co. of 1883–4 in Corporation Street (p. 146). Nos. 10–11, 1887 by *J. P. Sharp & Co.*, stone lintels and lots of terracotta rosettes. Tactful 1987 top floor to No. 10, r. Beyond Fore Street the rear of *Martin & Chamberlain*'s Corporation Street building of 1880–1 (p. 146). Then parts of the Post and Mail site scheme (cf. Colmore Circus), 1996–7 by *Seymour Harris Partnership*: a nice replica of *W. H. Ward*'s 1881 Central Arcade (*see* Corporation Street), and some mildly Postmodern infill. Plaques of Shakespeare and Walter Scott, 1923, from the former W. H. Smith's in Corporation Street.

CARRS LANE. On the N side the former POWELL'S GUN SHOP of 1860–1, a late work of *Charles Edge*. Italian Gothic. Four storeys and gables, red brick with blue-brick patterns (now part-rendered), stone dressings. The window arrangement narrows on each succeeding floor. Many sculpted heads. The first-floor projections are recent. Narrow five-storey workshop wing behind.

CHAMBERLAIN SQUARE. NW of Victoria Square, between the Town Hall and the Central Library. Remodelled to *Madin*'s designs as part of the library scheme (*see* p. 166) in 1978, and again in 2016–21 by *Grant Associates*. In the centre, the CHAMBERLAIN MEMORIAL FOUNTAIN of 1880 by *J. H. Chamberlain*, commemorating Joseph Chamberlain's mayoralty. A High Victorian combination of strong masses, influenced by medieval reliquaries. Belfry-like main storey with steep gables on a tall base with massive clasping buttresses. Set in its arches, mosaics of aquatic plants, and a portrait medallion of Chamberlain by *Thomas Woolner*. Above, a pierced octagon and a spire with lucarnes and bristling crockets. Carving by *Barfield* of Leicester. Below, an installation sculpture of Thomas Attwood M.P. by *Siobhan Coppinger & Fiona Peever*, 1993, reclining on the steps.* To the W the first two buildings of the new PARADISE DEVELOPMENT on the site of the 1970s Central Library, both completed 2019. No. 2 is by *Glenn Howells*, nine storeys with a tall portico-like front canopy. No. 1 is by *Eric Parry*, a long curving front with fins of white terracotta.

COLMORE CIRCUS. A depressing area at the E end of Colmore Row, replanned in 2002. Prominent but poor Postmodern offices for the WESLEYAN AND GENERAL ASSURANCE by *Peter Hing & Jones*, 1988–92. Central core with a pyramid roof, four radiating wings. Pink granite facings, angled between floors. On the S side a bulky piece by *Level Seven Architects*, 2002–4. On the N, a block by *Aedas*, 2008.† On the W, LLOYD HOUSE, *Kelly & Surman*, 1962–4, refaced by *Associated Architects*, 2016. Down SNOW HILL, N, blocks by *Sidell Gibson*, 2013–18, making a dark canyon.

COLMORE ROW was rural New Hall Lane, linking the Lichfield and Dudley roads out of Birmingham. St Philip's church (p. 111) was built on the S side from 1709. General development began only after the Colmore Act of 1746 (*see* Newhall estate, p. 159). The S side W of St Philip's was developed by the Inge estate (*see* p. 156) from 1823.

Starting from the W end, the whole street is now dominated by the new tower at No. 103. At Victoria Square there is a sharp contrast between C19 and early C20 buildings on the S side and more recent redevelopment on the N. The S SIDE first. No. 130 is by *Goddard & Co.* of Leicester, 1903, for the ALLIANCE INSURANCE. Two ample storeys in Wrenaissance style. Good domed corner turret, and a canted bay to Waterloo Street. Juicy garlands. No. 126 (NORTH BRITISH & MERCANTILE INSURANCE), 1926 by *S. N. Cooke*, starts a line of four- and five-storey fronts. Cleanly articulated, with giant quasi-Composite pilasters.

Nos. 122–124 are the former EAGLE INSURANCE offices, by *W. R. Lethaby & J. L. Ball*, 1900. One of the most important

---

*STATUES of James Watt by *Alexander Munro*, 1868, and Joseph Priestley by *Francis Williamson*, 1874, are due to be replaced W of the Town Hall (2021).
†It replaced *John H. D. Madin & Partners*' POST AND MAIL BUILDING of 1963–6, the finest commercial building of its time in the city. An early British example of a podium-and-slab block, inspired by Skidmore, Owings & Merrill's Lever House, New York.

monuments of the Arts and Crafts Free Style in the country. The design is essentially Lethaby's; Ball was the executant. Pevsner saw it as an early example of functionalism, but Lethaby's interest in symbolism and primitive forms, described in his *Architecture, Mysticism and Myth* (1892), is also obvious here, in the ancient use of the eagle to symbolize the sun god. The structure of load-bearing walls, concrete floors and steel joists is expressed directly and simply in the façade. Banking hall lit by a large mullion-and-transom window carried down to the ground. The doorways have segmental hoods and three-part mouldings deriving from Buddhist temples. Glowing bronze doors with moulded discs representing the sun. Above, three floors of offices with a grid of chamfered pilasters between chunky cornices, again with three-part mouldings. Over the top floor a dramatic motif of alternating round and triangular heads. Godfrey Rubens suggested a reworking of the basic round and pointed architectural shapes that Ruskin identified in 'The Nature of Gothic'; Alexandra Wedgwood noticed the primitive, Anglo-Saxon appearance of the triangular heads. Finally a parapet with a chequer design of alternating wide and narrow brick and stone panels, with more sun discs and an eagle relief in the centre. The interior is confused by alterations of 1982 by *Nicol Thomas Viner Barnwell*. Ground-floor banking hall (now café), not large, but tall and full of light from the big window. Sharply rectilinear, mirroring the façade grid. Curves are treated as something precious: the circle in the centre of the beamed ceiling, and the elliptical relieving arches to the doorways. Deep frieze with framed panels of green marble, cut and laid outwards from single stones to give a symmetrical effect, like the Byzantine pavements which for Lethaby symbolized the sea. The octagonal Director's Room behind has been knocked through into the banking hall, and its skylight filled in. It has the best surviving fireplace, again stressing right angles, without decoration. The l. corridor has a typical Lethaby plain groin-vault. The staircase retains the original balustrade with knot patterns, squares with the lines projecting as loops, and a cusp pattern symbolizing the heavens.

Nos. 118–120 are entertaining mongrel stucco Italianate of *c*. 1875. Nos. 114–116 is a Baroque wedding cake of 1912 by *Paul Waterhouse*, for the Atlas Assurance. A big portico is hoist aloft above much rustication, circular windows, garlands and all the panoply of commerce. An extreme contrast to Lethaby, but very effective. Mannerist detail: the large lunette window on the ground floor, and the two heavily blocked windows immediately under the pilasters. No. 112 of *c*. 1823, stucco with delicate detail: pediments with anthemion decoration, garlands and oval discs. No. 110 is an original, rather Art Nouveau, piece of 1904 by *Henman & Cooper* for the SCOTTISH UNION AND NATIONAL INSURANCE, hence the Aberdeen granite. Narrow brick bands. Big semicircular oriel with original railing, between tapering three-storey towers. The design had a big Parisian dome, probably not built. Nos. 104–106, *c*. 1827

Birmingham, Colmore Row, Scottish Union and National Insurance.
Lithograph and plan, 1903

(altered), the doorway with Tuscan pilasters. Paired pilasters to the first floor. No. 102 is of *c.* 1829, when the plot was leased to Thomas Edge. His son *Charles Edge* was probably the architect. Now façaded as part of the Waterloo Court development (*see* Waterloo Street, p. 157).

Now the N SIDE. No. 125, offices by *Sidell Gibson*, 1999–2001. Tactful but less adventurous than their work in Brindleyplace (p. 170). The frame is heavily expressed in reconstituted stone, enclosing grey anodized metal windows, and a corner turret reflects a traditional Birmingham form. Then a ten-storey block, stepping back, by *Seymour Harris*, 1996–7, on part of the site of the *John Madin Design Group*'s National Westminster Bank development of 1973–4.* On the rest of the site, No. 103, a twenty-six-storey tower by *Doone Silver Kerr*, 2019–21. Utterly dominating from both Victoria Square and St Philip's churchyard. Stepped-up glass blocks; street front aggressively cut back to increase impact. The Brutalist NatWest tower was far less disruptive.

At the SE corner with Bennetts Hill, WELLINGTON HOUSE by *Essex & Goodman*, 1928, uninspired but contextual Portland stone with a big mansard. Down an alley here, the surviving rear elevation of *Thomas Stedman Whitwell*'s New Library of 1820–1, with smooth rustication and a big pedimented doorcase. Nos. 84–90 was the PHOENIX ASSURANCE CO., 1915–17 by *Ewen Harper, Bro. & Co*. Monumental classic, in Albert Richardson's phrase. Giant fluted Doric half-columns, end bays with slightly stepped-back tops, concave corners with inset porches, channelled rustication.

The N side beyond Newhall Street was redeveloped from 1869, as leases fell in. A fine mid-Victorian commercial line, nearly all Italian Renaissance, with a common cornice height, a requirement of the Colmore estate. No. 85 is the former UNION CLUB. By *Yeoville Thomason*, 1869, but altered and the façades rebuilt in 1885, to match the new street line. Two ample storeys faced in Derbyshire limestone. Rusticated ground floor. Typical Thomason rounded corner and rich detailing, with big bearded-head keystones and juicy foliage frieze. Slightly projecting r. end with a big canted bay. Porch with coupled columns; tactful flanking shopfronts by *S. T. Walker & Partners* c. 1968. Carefully detailed mansard added in 1988 by *ISH Partnership*, consultant *Douglas Hickman* of the *John Madin Design Group*. Thomason's cornice with its line of urns still registers on the skyline. Nos. 79–83 are by *J. A. Chatwin*, 1871–3, for William Spurrier. He sold silver and plated goods, hence the busts of Renaissance goldsmiths, Ghiberti and Cellini, in roundels on the top floor. A rich, original and functional three-storey front. Five bays: the three wide central ones project and have an ornate bracket cornice. Rich porch with coupled Corinthian columns, arched showroom windows with vermiculated rustication, side entrances with segmental pediments on odd consoles like headless birds. First-floor offices with rich aedicules and pediments with foliage and vases, second-floor workrooms lit by a row of round-headed windows. Nos. 75–77 of 1872–3 are by *Thomason* for Sanders & Co., metal brokers. Arched windows throughout, ornate three-storey

---

*It was the most important Brutalist commercial building in the city, disastrous in context but with its own integrity: low banking hall, tower behind, stepping up to twenty-one storeys. Rough concrete aggregate and plum-coloured Staffordshire bricks.

central feature. The rest are of four storeys, but little more than façades and one banking hall survive. Nos. 71–73, 1873–4, with engaged columns, Corinthian over Doric. Cast-iron columns to the ground floor, probably part of the original shopfront. Then three more by *Thomason* (Nos. 61–67), all for the Birmingham Town and District Banking Co. Five-bay blocks flank a six-bay centre. All originally faced in Bath stone. The centre is the earliest, designed 1867, built 1870. Its rich cornice survives, and the composition with porches in the end bays is original. In 1937 *Peacock & Bewlay* put Corinthian pilasters on the central four bays, creating the awkward effect of a pilaster in the middle, and altered the ground floors of the side buildings to match. The rest of *Thomason*'s elevations here remain. Plain rustication and simple architraves; l. block designed 1872, built 1875, with a little more decoration, r. block 1873–4. No. 55 runs round into Church Street. A very different flavour, the best piece of Second Empire French in the city. 1878 by *J.J. Bateman* for the Midland Land and Investment Corporation. Rich yet with classical discipline. First and second floors articulated by pink and dark grey granite columns, Corinthian over Doric. Rounded corner with oriel and Venetian window above. Nearly everything behind rebuilt twice, by the *Seymour Harris Partnership*, 1991–2, and again by *Aedas*, 2014–17, with a bigger, dominating mansard. *Thomason*'s grand classical banking hall of 1869 remains. Nine bays by five, articulated by round-headed arches and Corinthian pilasters. Former entrances (r.) with huge head keystones. Rich coved ceiling with dome and panels of leaf decoration. Main ribs with plaster roses and foliage, supported by columns on foliage corbels.

Beyond Church Street the GRAND HOTEL, built in 1876–8 for Horton's Estate and designed by *Thomson Plevins*. Excellently repaired and refurbished by *BGS*, 2010–19. The front is a little flat, though repairs have revealed its contrasting sandstone and limestone features. Supremely important as townscape, its French pavilion roofs a picturesque sight from the Cathedral churchyard. Porch with paired granite Corinthian columns on elegant tall elongated bases, probably of 1890 when *Martin & Chamberlain* extended the building to the rear in Barwick Street. Another extension by them here, of 1893–5, brick and terracotta with canted bays running right up. This includes the finest interior, the GROSVENOR ROOM, with rich French C18-style plasterwork and swinging balconies enclosed in an arcade on the N side. Art Deco hanging electroliers of the early 1930s. More impressive plasterwork in the withdrawing room, and a grand open-well staircase. Extra bedrooms by *Henman & Cooper*, 1900. On the corner of Livery Street, r., a block faced in creamy-brown stone, of 1986–7 by the *Weedon Partnership*. Large round-headed dormers which stare alarmingly.

Beyond the churchyard, s side, the Colmore Row entrance to the GREAT WESTERN ARCADE, a replacement of 1989 by *Douglas Hickman (John Madin Design Group)*. A late work, moving towards Postmodernism. Polished blue pearl granite. Central round-headed niche with top pediment and round window inspired by San Miniato al Monte, Florence. (For the arcade *see* Temple Row, p. 153.) On the corner of Bull Street, COLMORE GATE, shops and offices of 1990–2 by the *Seymour Harris Partnership*, with a sixteen-storey tower. Silver reflective glass and more blue pearl granite. The mullions defining the centre of each side end at the top in Art Deco-y half-rounds. Opposite, Nos. 1–9 Colmore Row, six- and ten-storey purple brick and glass blocks of 1983–6. Thin green canopies mark the Snow Hill Station entrance.* Multi-storey car park over the platforms with blue-brick facings. All by the *Seymour Harris Partnership*.

CORPORATION STREET, with OLD SQUARE and PRIORY QUEENSWAY. The largest of the municipal improvements of the 1870s (*see* Birmingham Introduction, p. 107). Work began at New Street in 1878 and reached Steelhouse Lane by 1882. The surveyors were *Martin & Chamberlain*. It is 66 ft (20 metres) wide, influenced by Haussmann's boulevards in Paris. In 1902 the *Birmingham Daily Post* reported that Corporation Street had 'quite eclipsed New Street as the premier street of the city'. The buildings are very different from earlier C19 developments such as the N side of Colmore Row: gables and turrets instead of regular cornices, the styles French Renaissance, Gothic, Flemish and Jacobean. In 1908 W.H. Bidlake described them as 'what a seedsman would call "Selected varieties of sorts"'.

The original NW side survives from New Street as far as Cherry Street, and fortunately also the corner building on the SE side, PRINCE'S CORNER by *Dempster & Heaton*, 1890. On the NW side good commercial façades, mostly four storeys. QUEEN'S CORNER, 1879–80 by *W.H.Ward*, continues the elevation of Yeoville Thomason's Birmingham Daily Post building in New Street (p. 151), but with slightly more licence in the rich triplet corner windows and the sandstone pilasters with sunk panels. VICTORIA BUILDINGS is also by *Ward*, of 1879–80, handsome French Renaissance. Two-storey rounded bays, and a great variety of pediments. The doorway has Michelangelesque broken pediments. Nos. 9–13 by *Thomason*, of 1879, built for John Feeney of the Daily Post, are linked to his New Street offices, but are quite different in style. Two-storey canted bays, a plain storey with paired round-headed windows, shaped gables with small, almost semicircular broken pediments (restored 1996–7). Then the former CENTRAL ARCADE by *Ward*, 1881, again French Renaissance, but very tightly composed. The r. entrance bay has a lunette in a giant arch, an oriel above, and a complex Chambord gable with Corinthian

---

*First built by the Great Western Railway in 1852. *J.A. Chatwin*'s GREAT WESTERN HOTEL of 1875 on Colmore Row, the finest C19 hotel in the city, was demolished in 1971. The STATION BUILDING itself, rebuilt in 1911–12 to designs by the GWR's engineer *Walter Y. Armstrong*, came down in 1976–7. An archway survives in Livery Street.

columns. Finally in this row Nos. 19–21 by *Martin & Chamberlain*, 1880–1; their only surviving building on the street they planned. Flemish style in red terracotta, with some brick above. Five bays to Corporation Street with a big gable, the symmetry broken by the off-centre entrance and first-floor display windows. Octagonal corner turret with a short spirelet. Iron-framed structure concealed inside. In 1996–7 all the buildings between New Street to Fore Street were façaded, except for this iron frame, by the *Seymour Harris Partnership* (*see also* Cannon Street, p. 139).

Beyond Fore Street, Nos. 25–39, 1884–5, l., and 1887–8, r. by *Dempster & Heaton*. Builder's Gothic turning Queen Anne, in attractive orange brick. The octagonal corner turret has windows under triangular hoodmoulds, but has lost its spire. Nos. 41–43 were the MIDLAND EDUCATIONAL CO., 1883–4 by *A.B. Phipson*. Five storeys, French Renaissance. Pilasters with decorated panels. A big gable, built up in tiers of arcading; typical of Phipson, who always liked something impressive on the mantelpiece (cf. No. 10 Church Street, p. 161). Finally Nos. 45–49 of 1887 by *J.P. Sharp & Co.* A commercial version of Ruskinian Gothic, with a lively rhythm of windows and a rounded corner to Cherry Street. Two-storey aedicules with big architraves.

On the SE SIDE after Prince's Corner, a six-storey block of 1949 by *North & Partners*, linked with their work on New Street (p. 151). Glass top storey and canopy of 2000. VICTORIA HOUSE is of 1996 by *Robert Seager Design*, modified by *Peter Hing & Jones*: revived late C19 in terracotta and brick, not well done. Next, the COMMERCIAL UNION development of 1959–65 by *J. Seymour Harris & Partners*. Bold fourteen-storey tower with tapered ends, like Gio Ponti's Pirelli tower in Milan. Shops around it replaced 1999–2001 by *Leslie Jones Architects*. Gimmicky. Blue mullions topped with gold saucers. The 1960s development replaced Martineau Street, cut in 1887 as part of the Improvement Scheme. Opposite, the very big HOUSE OF FRASER (formerly Rackhams), by *T.P. Bennett & Son*, 1957–61, eight storeys rising higher to Bull Street. Rebuilding and heightening proposed (2020).

Beyond Bull Street, SE side, the CORPORATION SQUARE shopping precinct, by *Sir Frederick Gibberd*, 1963–6, job architect *Gerald Goalen*. Gibberd's only building in the city where he trained, and Birmingham's best Sixties shopping development. A cool Portland stone podium with carefully placed slit windows, over a recessed ground floor. Plant rooms treated as rectangular sculptural masses, with vertical slits linking visually to the podium. The plan is defined by walkways from Bull Street (Dalton Way) to a central square and through to the Priory. Mangled in 1990 by *Bob Bowyer Associates*, with heavy glazed canopies, and Gibberd's minimalist advertising tower recast as a lumpy Toytown clock tower. (Threatened by residential redevelopment 2020.)

Opposite (NW side), the former LEWIS'S store of 1924–5, by the firm's architect *Gerald de Courcy Fraser* of Liverpool. A huge but carefully proportioned block, the SW and NE entrances articulated by fluted Doric columns (restored 1993). These entrance sections originally comprised bridges built in 1928 across the narrow street of Minories behind, joining an older block, itself rebuilt in 1931–2. The Minories is an impressive canyon, reopened and glazed in by *Peter Hing & Jones*'s conversion to offices and courts, 1993. Tactful extra storey all round.

OLD SQUARE, beyond, was developed from 1697. Some original houses, with giant corner pilasters, lasted until the early C20. Corporation Street cut through it, and Upper and Lower Priory, running NW–SE, were reconstructed in the 1960s as PRIORY QUEENSWAY, part of the inner ring road. Central paved space of 1998, when subways were filled in. 'Festival' column LAMP STANDARDS, moved from Colmore Row. SCULPTURES. Tony Hancock, the comedian, a looming presence, by *Bruce Williams*, 1996. A 10-ft (3-metre)-high sheet of bronze with Hancock, in Homburg hat, with cup of tea, made of inset glass rods, symbolizing the dots of an analogue television screen. To the N, *Kenneth Budd*'s relief panel of scenes from the history of Old Square, in brass, iron and fibreglass. Made 1967, repositioned and restored 1998. On the N side of the square, Cannon House, a long block with sweeping curves of 1961–4 by *Essex, Goodman & Suggitt* with *J. Alfred Harper & Son*, refaced by *Seymour Harris*, 2007–8. On the E, MAPLE HOUSE, a recasting of 1996–7 by *Level Seven Architects* of a 1966 block by *Cotton, Ballard & Blow*. Adjoining to the S, the former THOMAS WOOLF'S furniture store, 1972 by *Paul Bonham & Associates*. Elegant Travertine façade, its slit windows taking their cue from the Gibberd opposite (*see* above). Dramatic interior with a two-level showroom on ground floor and basement. The MCLAREN TOWER beyond is also of 1972 by *Bonham*.

Beyond Old Square the finest remaining stretch of the street. On the SE SIDE GAZETTE BUILDINGS, built as lawyers' chambers in 1885–6, by *W.H. Ward*. Ground floor altered 1928 by *W.H. Martin*; mutilated top. What remains is Ward's finest surviving commercial design. Venetian arrangement of two-light windows with relieving arches. The first-floor niches placed illogically above the ground-floor piers derive ultimately from Raphael's Palazzo dell'Aquila. Beyond, on the corner, the CROWN INN of 1888 by *Charles J. Hodson*. Very French, with tall canted bays and panelled pilasters. On the NW side, Nos. 153–161 of 1896–9 by *Crouch & Butler*. An exuberant design in red brick and buff terracotta. Giant arches cut by swinging balconies above the shopfronts. Built for A.R. Dean, house furnisher, and Pitman's vegetarian restaurant, so we have *Benjamin Creswick*'s frieze of carpenters at work and diners at table above the shops, coats of arms above the arches, and first-floor cornice with its amusing cable moulding pulled by putti at either end.* Picturesque skyline: a small oriel, l., with octagonal dome, a huge Flemish gable, and a smaller gable, r., flanked by small turrets. Figures on the large gable, an allegory of Birmingham and Industry, also by *Creswick*. Then the County Court (p. 132) and, beyond, the Victoria Law Courts (p. 131). On the SE side the former Court Restaurant, 1882 by *George Henry Rayner*. Then the former SALVATION ARMY CITADEL of 1891 by *W.H. Ward*. Cleanly articulated, with much rustication; a pair of domed turrets. Rebuilt behind. No. 190 was built for Coopers, bookbinders, in 1890 by *W. Hawley Lloyd*. Red brick and terracotta. The ogee mouldings to the second-floor windows give a Gothic feel. Entrance with a little flying arch. The first design was revised to include the tall gable, evidence for the picturesque approach to design in the new street. Then the former Methodist Central Hall (p. 123). Opposite, i.e. beyond the Law Courts, COLERIDGE CHAMBERS, 1898 by *John W. Allen* of West Bromwich. Red brick and cream terracotta. Flemish gables, piers topped by heraldic beasts, and a little ogee dome. RUSKIN CHAMBERS is a much grander thirteen-bay block of 1900 by *Ewen & J.A. Harper*, for themselves as developers. Carefully articulated, with a very big Flemish gable, projecting ends, two-storey canted bays, and a recessed top floor behind stubby attached columns. Many original shopfronts, divided by terracotta columns with reversed volutes supporting shields. Turning the corner to Steelhouse Lane, the KING EDWARD BUILDING of 1900–1, also by *E. & J.A. Harper*. Plainer, with Doric columns on the ground floor, plain giant pilasters above, and clock under a pediment.

HIGH STREET. Probably the oldest street in the city. C16 timber-framed buildings survived until the late C19. Victorian rebuilding, including the spectacular Louvre department store of 1896 by *Essex, Nicol & Goodman*, was replaced after the war to depressingly poor standards. On the E side, S end, WATERSTONES bookshop was Times Furnishing, by *C.J. Eprile* of *Burnett & Eprile*, 1936–8. A seven-storey *Moderne* tower, its height emphasized by windows vertically linked by lead panels and central fins with a kind of cubic billet moulding. Side piers with curved tops, and roof canopy floating free. The sophisticated Pavilions shopping centre, Postmodern by *Chapman Taylor*, 1986–8, was recast for PRIMARK by *3DReid*, 2019. Enormous faceted aluminium mesh panels: anti-architecture in the Selfridges way. MARKS & SPENCER'S front is by *James M. Munro & Son*, 1956–7. A big old-fashioned classical job with *Moderne* details – but a welcome relief here. Opposite, the altered Big Top, 1956–61 by *Cotton, Ballard & Blow*, with a thirteen-storey tower behind. Nos. 54–58, E side, are by the

---

*The joke is a clever one. Creswick was a Sheffield knife grinder discovered as a sculptor by Ruskin. At the start of *The Seven Lamps of Architecture* Ruskin makes a distinction between architecture and building, using as his example the addition of a cable moulding. Here it is pulled by classical putti, symbols of a style Ruskin despised.

Birmingham, Corporation Street, Coleridge Chambers.
Lithograph and plan by John W. Allen, 1898

Seymour Harris Partnership, 1980. Also by them, immediately beyond in DALE END, a Postmodern block of 1988–90. Opposite, the Corporation Square development (*see* p. 146).

LOWER TEMPLE STREET. On the w the SHAKESPEARE pub, Neo-Georgian by *Arthur Edwards*, 1911, the successor to the Pit Bar of the demolished Theatre Royal.

NEW STREET. First mentioned in 1397, probably cut in the C14 as a better-graded and more direct route from the Halesowen and Dudley roads to the top of the Bull Ring. Mid-C19 Birmingham's most fashionable shopping street, until supplanted by Corporation Street. Always the link between the Bull Ring and the Victoria Square and Broad Street area.

Starting from Victoria Square, on the s side Nos. 79–83, 1870, on the corner of Pinfold Street. Enjoyable but ignorant Gothic, e.g. the second-floor clutter of pilasters. Suspiciously classical cornice and keystones. Top storey on the corner rebuilt in 1912 by *Nicol & Nicol*. Nos. 84–86 for the stationer E. C. Osborne, also of 1870, must be by *W.H. Ward* (cf. his Gazette Buildings, Corporation Street, p. 147). Giant arches, pairs of round-headed windows, plain triplets above. Nos. 88–91, TOWN HALL CHAMBERS, is of 1867, probably by *Thomson Plevins*. Mongrel classical, but with giant pilasters banded with rows of nailhead and cogging. Pairs of round-headed windows above. On the corner of Ethel Street the former MASONIC HALL of 1865–9 by *Edward Holmes*. Classical, stuccoed. Ornate first-floor windows with decorative panels and spandrels. The corner oriel lit clubrooms and allowed a view down New Street. Converted to a cinema by *Bertie Crewe*, 1910; cinema reconstructed by *William Glen* in 1930, with a steep-pitched attic.

On the N side, WATERLOO HOUSE of 1926–7 by *Essex & Goodman*, a weak faience design with old-fashioned details. Then the former ROYAL BIRMINGHAM SOCIETY OF ARTISTS building by *Crouch & Butler*, 1912, on the site of *Rickman & Hutchinson*'s 1829 gallery. A good faience design, influenced by London fashion: canted inset bay windows, end bays rising into built-up dormers. The former gallery is a top-lit room in a two-storey rear block. Next, a former Lyons Corner House by *F.C. Baker* of their architects' department, 1926–7. On the corner of Bennetts Hill, GROSVENOR HOUSE by *Cotton, Ballard & Blow*, 1951–3. The City Surveyor Herbert Manzoni asked for 'some improvement in the architectural treatment', and the result has rows of sawtooth projections, little pointed iron balustrades on the corner, and a brise-soleil. Flashy but undeniably effective. Opposite is New Street's architectural disaster, the WOOLWORTH BUILDING by *Cotton, Ballard & Blow*, 1958–61 (E part) and 1962–4 (w).* A shapeless mass of Portland stone, mosaic cladding and green slate. The clunky glass lift tower added by *Temple Cox Nicholls*, 1990, is now the principal accent in the street from Victoria Square.

Now the best surviving part. On the N side the former LONDON & LANCASHIRE INSURANCE CO. of 1906–8 by *Riley & Smith* (*Eric Browett*). Edwardian Baroque, rare in Birmingham. Its big pediment and low dome are excellent street scenery. Cherubs, garlands, and the company's arms with fearsome gryphons (sculpture by *Robert Bridgeman & Sons*). Partly original shopfronts. Opposite, the PICCADILLY ARCADE was built as a cinema in 1910 by *Nicol & Nicol*. White and green

---

*It replaced both the THEATRE ROYAL by *Runtz & Ford*, 1904, and *W.H. Ward*'s masterpiece, the COLONNADE BUILDING of 1881.

faience. Giant arch entrance, open colonnade above, Free Baroque turrets. Conversion with bronze fascia and shopfronts of 1928 by *J. R. Shaw*. The slope inside reflects the original rake of the seating. Refurbished in 1989 by *Douglas Hickman* of the *John Madin Design Group*, with *trompe l'œil* ceiling paintings by *Paul Maxfield*. No. 111 THE WHITE HOUSE, by *Thomson Plevins*, 1874–5, was reconstructed 1911–12 by *Nicol & Nicol*. Fine concrete render, scored to imitate faience – a touch of New York – and another open top colonnade. Attic with Greek altars and pediments.

On the N side again, the W corner of Temple Street is a modest three-storey block of 1842, probably by *Charles Edge*. Cornice with paired brackets. Windows in panels cut back from the wall-plane. Beyond, over-scaled shops and flats by *GMW*, 2003–4. Opposite, the BURLINGTON HOTEL, formerly the Midland, of 1867 and 1875 for Isaac Horton by *Plevins*. Italianate white brick, now rendered; good street architecture. Burlington Passage, between the two parts, was made the hotel entrance *c.* 1994. For the S extensions *see* Stephenson Street, p. 152. On the N side opposite, Nos. 41–42, exuberant Free Jacobean offices and shops of 1898 by *Essex, Nicol & Goodman*. Pale orange terracotta with red bands. Giant three-centred arches with soffit scrolls enclose the shopfronts. Canted bay windows above. Domed corner turrets, and a wide Flemish gable with a little serpentine balcony. The Cannon Street elevation, r., has the entrance to the upper offices. Next the former BIRMINGHAM DAILY POST offices and printing works, by *Yeoville Thomason* for its proprietor John Feeney. Four storeys. Six-bay middle section 1864–5, flanking blocks 1871. Rich Italianate, with rows of round-headed windows set in double arches and strong cornices. Plainer extension up Cannon Street, 1882. For the NE corner *see* Corporation Street, p. 145.* The whole block bounded by New Street, Cannon Street, Corporation Street and Fore Street was redeveloped behind retained façades in 1996–7 by the *Seymour Harris Partnership*, with an extra floor behind a mansard roof (*see also* Cannon Street).

Opposite, the former MIDLAND BANK, rich classical of 1867–9 by *Edward Holmes*, on the SW corner to Stephenson Place. Grand Ionic porch with paired columns of Cornish granite. The ground floor has wide rusticated pilasters and big arched openings with decorated transoms; the first floor, window aedicules separated by Corinthian half-columns, paired on the New Street front. Pilasters at the corners. Acroteria break the top balustrade. The corner turrets are chimneys. Original railings by *Hart & Son*. The banking hall has giant Corinthian pilasters and a heavily coffered ceiling. Five-storey office extension of 1875 behind.

Beyond Corporation Street there is less interest and too much Portland stone. On the N side the former MARSHALL

---

* In 1959–62 the developer Jack Cotton proposed a huge development stretching from here to the Cathedral churchyard, with *Walter Gropius* as consultant.

AND SNELGROVE store, by *North, Robin & Wilsdon* of London, started in 1938 but not completed until 1956. Former entrance with the upper floors in a curved recess, with projecting balconies and curly ironwork. Hotel conversion by 1970 by *Ted Levy, Benjamin & Partners*. Opposite, the bland classical KING EDWARD HOUSE of 1936–7 by *Essex & Goodman*, replacing Charles Barry and A.W.N. Pugin's King Edward's School of 1833 (*see also* p. 374). The ODEON CINEMA, by *Frank Verity & Samuel Beverley*, 1936–7, retains a tall roof feature on its single-storey front. Central fin altered.

PARADISE STREET runs W from Victoria Square. On the N side the Town Hall. On the S, offices by *Watkins Gray Woodgate International*, 1985, incorporating the cream terracotta façade of QUEEN'S COLLEGE CHAMBERS, by *Mansell & Mansell*, 1904. French Renaissance. No. 36 is a single-gabled Postmodern front of 1991 by *David Delaney-Hall (Sinclair Architects)*, refacing a block of 1959. No. 35 is latest classical by *H.W. Way Lovegrove*, 1955. No. 34, DAIMLER HOUSE, originally a showroom and repair shop. By *A. Gilbey Latham*, 1911. Doric porch with big broken pediment; giant Ionic order above. TRAFALGAR HOUSE on the W corner, originally *J. Seymour Harris & Partners*, 1960, badly re-clad.

ST PHILIP'S PLACE. The E side of the Cathedral churchyard, originally with the Blue Coat School of 1722–4 by *Samuel Avery* (rebuilt 1792–4 by *John Rawstorne*) at the N end, and the rectory at the S, with its garden between. At the N end now a Beaux Arts block of 1935 in Portland stone by the *Prudential Assurance Architects' Department*, but *P.B. Chatwin*'s papers suggest he was involved. Recast with extra storey and irritating canopy by *Temple Cox Nicholls*, 2002. The former Provost's House has a Cotswold stone front. Ground floor with three-centred arches, first floor with canted bay and broken pediment, from the replacement rectory of 1885 by *Osborn & Reading*. The rest of 1950 by *Caröe & Partners*. Reconstructed behind as offices by *Temple Cox Nicholls*, 1981–2. At the S end a tactful office building by *Level Seven Architects*, 2001–2. Cream stone with silver-grey anodized bay windows.

STEELHOUSE LANE. The E continuation of Colmore Row, originally the medieval Priors Conygree Lane. The N side has FOUNTAIN COURT, barristers' chambers by *Holland W. Hobbiss & Partners*, 1963–4. Conservative red brick, but well proportioned, with a majestic Bath stone cornice. In the courtyard a BRONZE, Fountain (Nude Girl), by *Bloye*, 1964. The NURSES' HOME by *Martin & Martin & W.H. Ward*, 1947, a late example of their cubic Neo-Georgian, heralds the Birmingham Children's Hospital beyond (p. 135). The S side has the Juvenile Court (p. 133), the rear of the Victoria Law Courts (p. 131), including a small POLICE STATION of 1897, and its ponderous Neo-Georgian successor of 1930 by the *Birmingham City Engineer and Surveyor*.

STEPHENSON PLACE and STEPHENSON STREET. Stephenson Place runs S from New Street opposite Corporation Street,

CITY CENTRE: STREETS 153

turning w into Stephenson Street. On the E side the uninspired ten-storey replacement for *Holmes*'s Exchange Building, Gothic, of 1865; by *Cotton, Ballard & Blow*, 1965–7. In front, a ramp leads to the same architects' shopping centre and office block over New Street Station (*see* p. 136). On the N side, *Henman & Cooper*'s additions of 1900 to the BURLINGTON HOTEL (*see* New Street, p. 151). Brick with stone dressings, Jacobean. The central gable especially shows Cooper's Waterhouse ancestry. Further w, on the corner with Lower Temple Street, a shop of 1914 by *Essex & Goodman*, cream terracotta with inset canted bays and two floors of display windows (the first floor was a car showroom, originally with a 'motor lift' at the rear). In the triangle with Navigation Street and Pinfold Street, s side, GUILDHALL BUILDINGS by *Frederick W. Lloyd*, 1899. A plain brick and terracotta job, but well proportioned.

TEMPLE ROW. The s side of the Cathedral churchyard, developed by William Inge in the early C18, it continues E to Bull Street. Its last original terraced houses, in a provincial Baroque style, were demolished in the late 1950s. Starting at the E end, on the s side the rear of House of Fraser (*see* Corporation Street, p. 146). On the N, the GREAT WESTERN ARCADE of 1874–6 by *W.H. Ward*. The best survivor of the city's many C19 arcades, supported on iron arches which span the railway line into Snow Hill. Builder *Henry Lovett* of Wolverhampton. Rich Renaissance façade: paired columns with much banding and decoration, and heavy cornices. Giant arch with figures of Art and Industry in the spandrels. Top floor lost in the Second World War. Inside, shops divided by plain pilasters lead to a central space with side apses. Upper storey with rows of round-arched windows recessed behind a balcony with original ironwork. Simple steel post-war roof. Refurbished in 1984–5 by *Douglas Hickman* of the *John Madin Design Group* with decorative transverse plaster arches which deliberately do not touch the roof ribs. Electroliers to the original 1874 design by *Best & Lloyd*, and a chiming clock at the N end. (For the Colmore Row front *see* p. 144.)

Continuing w, on the s side the former TSB bank, by *James A. Roberts Associates*, 1980, a heavy design in Travertine and dark pink-grey granite. Then the former BANK OF ENGLAND (now CBRE) of 1969–72 by *Fitzroy Robinson & Partners*. It covers a whole street block back to Cannon Street. Heavy podium block set back up steps. Dark granite facings below, copper-clad cantilevered beams and bronzed window surrounds, and tall pierced rectangles of Portland Roach, like huge architraves, above. Blocky recessed attic. Twenty-storey office tower faced in grey granite behind, the successor to *Walter Gropius*'s proposal of 1962 (*see* New Street, p. 151). A dominating, authoritarian design, very damaging in context. Just into Needless Alley, a blunt, fat glass turret of City Plaza (*see* Cannon Street, p. 139). UNION CHAMBERS by *Ewan Harper, Bro. & Co.*, 1936, is a plain nine-storey block of Portland stone with concave corner. Then a tactful building faced in cream and brown reconstituted stone by *Robert Turley & Associates*, 2001, defined by square turrets of differing heights. Across Temple Street, a big range in two parts, of 1963 by *Tripe & Wakeham*.

TEMPLE ROW WEST. The W side of the Cathedral churchyard, developed from c. 1820 by the Inge estate (*see* Waterloo Street). At the S end the former OCEAN INSURANCE CORPORATION, 1900–2 by *Mansell & Mansell*. A fine office block in brick and cream terracotta, the steel structure firmly expressed in the grid of the façade. Bands of roses and thistles, and waves and fishes, on the corner oriel. Finely moulded entrance. Shallow canted end bays. Delightful fantasy at the top: ogee windows, parapet with heart-shaped piercings, corner turret, end gables with diapering. Waterloo Street extension of 1983–4 by *Peter Hing & Jones*: narrow fins of tinted glass, brick piers. Nos. 5–7, 1876–7, probably by *George Ingall*. Stucco. End pilasters topped by consoles, emphatic cornice. Terrible 1970s ground floor. The OLD JOINT STOCK pub was built as the Birmingham Joint Stock Bank in 1864 by *J.A. Chatwin*. His first bank building, which made his reputation. A subtle, scholarly and beautiful palazzo, its façade a study in interpenetrating orders. Doric lower order on panelled bases. Its cornice has a feeling of weight produced by compressing the frieze. The band above can be read as the attic of the lower order – lunette windows with head keystones – or the base of the upper order – rustication and panelled column bases. Corinthian upper order, with round-headed windows in aedicules. These have Corinthian pilasters, and their cornices, repeated between the columns, read almost as part of the upper entablature. The balustrade has unfortunately lost its urns. Banking hall with deep coved ceiling on decorated ribs, taller than the lower external order, so that the lunettes outside light the cove. Converted 1997 by *Langford & Williams*. No. 3 has a stucco front of five low storeys and attic, and a complex history. An older building was leased to the artist Samuel Lines in 1820, a good date for the two-storey pavilion shown on mid-C19 drawings. The ground floor has an Early Victorian shopfront with Corinthian columns. In 1877 two storeys were added, the first floor refronted, and the narrow entrance bay built over a former passage. Almost certainly by *George Ingall*, who occupied the ground-floor office. Reconstructed with extra storey and attic by *Edwin Hill & Partners*, surveyors, 1972.

TEMPLE STREET. Cut in the early C18 to link New Street to St Philip's churchyard, as part of the development by William Inge and Elizabeth Phillips. The plots on the W side were leased again in 1842–53. Now a mixture of C20 office buildings, especially on the W side, its intimacy damaged by demolitions at the New Street end. Starting from here, on the W side Nos. 19–20 by *Newton & Cheatle* in 1900 for Ludlow and Briscoe, surveyors. Red brick with delicate Jacobean windows. The outer bays have wavy parapets and little domes with finials. No. 17 was the Norwich Union's Fire Engine House, 1846 by *Edge &*

CITY CENTRE: STREETS 155

Avery. Four bays, recessed centre, still stucco. Small sashes and heavily rusticated quoins. The present sumptuous tiled front with Corinthian pilasters and mosaic frieze is probably by *Maw* of 1902, when it became the TROCADERO. Part of a contemporary smoke room survives at the rear. Nos. 14–17 is a grand four-storey Italianate palazzo of 1854 by *Samuel Hemming* for the Unity Fire and General Insurance Associations. Very Baroque two-storey centrepiece. Beautiful, world-weary lion's head over the former fire-engine-house entrance. Nos. 11–13 are *Moderne* of 1931 by *S.N. Cooke* for Smart Bros, house furnishers. Offices expressed as a bronze fascia decorated with rosettes, set in a Portland stone surround. Giant pilasters play hide-and-seek at the corners. Nos. 9–11 is an intrusive eight-storey tower of 1962 by *Essex, Goodman & Suggitt*, refaced in 2016. No. 8, the BIRMINGHAM LAW SOCIETY, hides a complex history behind *C.E. Bateman*'s Neo-Georgian, Portland stone façade. Cornice with the date, 1933. In the l. bay, door with bronze relief of the society's seal. The building started in 1858 as a Temperance hall by *Yeoville Thomason*. His painted brick side elevation to Temple Passage is still recognizable: two storeys of windows in shallow giant arches. The rear of the hall is a semi-ellipse, disguised by additions from *E. & J.A. Harper*'s alterations of 1900–1, which also included a terracotta façade. *Bateman* replaced this, and filled the shell of the hall with three floors of offices and a library. His is the dignified oak staircase with square newels and hanging arches leading to the double-height library, which has square giant Doric columns faced with single pieces of oak. Original bookcases and pedimented doorcases. No. 4, a classical office building of 1862, was crassly refaced in black granite in 1964 by *Thurlow, Lucas & James*. The side elevation in white brick with red detail is still there.

Returning down the E side, Nos. 39–40, a delightful survivor of *c.*1824. Pedimented first-floor windows, Greek-key frieze. Tuscan pilasters on the ground floor. Then big, streamlined SOMERSET HOUSE of 1936 by *Essex & Goodman*, with window bands between tower-like end bays. Over the entrance, relief of a sailing ship. IMPERIAL HOUSE has the retained façade of the NEW IMPERIAL HOTEL of 1905–7 by *Wood & Kendrick*. Mildly Baroque, with blocked segmental arches, stubby stone columns, and a centrepiece with a big broken pediment. Bulky upper storeys by *Temple Cox Nicholls*, 1996–7, red brick and reconstituted stone. Finally ESSEX HOUSE of 1924–5 by *Essex & Goodman*, who were also the developers. Their usual watered-down classical faience.

UNION STREET. On the S side, the surviving part of the MIDLAND & CITY ARCADES, of 1900–1 by *Newton & Cheatle*. Pink terracotta and brick, with cream terracotta dressings. The entrance has a giant arch and a big shaped gable. Flanking canted bays rising into domed turrets with bold curving buttresses. Jacobean details but a Baroque feeling of movement. Enjoyable sculpture by *W.J. Neatby*: heads, a frieze of sea monsters and tridents, and on the towers Atlantes playing wind instruments. Green faience interior. Shopfronts divided by pilasters with niches and domed tops, balcony with more sea monsters. Iron roof with swirling supports to the top rib.

VICTORIA SQUARE. The premier civic space of the city began as a rural road junction, reached by late C18 development. It was originally smaller, roughly the W half of the present space. The E part was occupied by Christ Church, built in the angle of New Street and Ann Street (Colmore Row) in 1805, replaced in 1901 with picturesque domed offices, 'Galloway's Corner', by *Essex, Nicol & Goodman*, demolished 1970. Civic identity grew with the Town Hall (p.125), built on the W side in 1832–4, the Council House (p.127) on the N in 1870–4, the General Post Office on the S in 1891. The successful campaign of 1973–8 to save the Post Office marked the temporary end of the post-war comprehensive development philosophy in the city.

The square gained its name when *Thomas Brock*'s STATUE of Queen Victoria was unveiled in 1901. A copy – at the insistence of the patron, W.H. Barber, a Birmingham solicitor – of Brock's statue at the Shire Hall, Worcester. Originally white marble, recast in bronze in 1951 by *William Bloye*, who made the pedestal. To its E, LANDSCAPING of 1991–3 by the sculptor *Dhruva Mistry*, working with *Rory Coonan*. Dramatic in conception, exotic in detail, and triumphantly successful as urban planning, creating a N–S axis of steps to either side of upper and lower pools, it aligns the expanded square on the Council House portico. Sandstone walls. STATUE in the top pool, a large reclining nude called The River. She holds a vase which acts as a fountain. In the floor of this pool, six bas reliefs of salmon. In the lower, two smaller figures, a boy and girl representing Youth, face a fountain of three vertical bowls. In the early C21 the pools were, alas, drained and filled with planting. To either side here, the two sphinx-like GUARDIANS (Mistry suggests a source in C1 figures at the Great Stupa at Sanchi, India). To each side at the top, an OBJECT/VARIATION, a tapering pillar suggesting lighthouses or pyramids. The quotation from T.S. Eliot's 'Burnt Norton' round the rim of the top pool was carved by *Bettina Furnée*. In 2017–19 the square in front was altered for the Metro tram line.*

GENERAL POST OFFICE. By *Sir Henry Tanner* of the Office of Works, 1890–1. *The Builder* called it 'coarse and commonplace... Pots and tea urns of abnormal dimensions are perched about on ledges and on cornices; the whole of it is fussy, pretentious and totally lacking in dignity.' Its simple French Renaissance style has worn quite well, and the pots and urns, actually pediment and cupolas and a dome on the l., make their mark against C20 neighbours.

WATERLOO STREET. The principal street of the Inge estate, the area between St Philip's (E), Colmore Row (N), Victoria Square

---

*Antony Gormley's SCULPTURE, Iron:Man, of 1992, is in store (2020). Instantly recognizable: a 12-ft (3.7-metre)-high torso, enclosed by beams, in rusted iron, leaning slightly backwards and to the l.; uncomfortable in front of the Town Hall, intended to refer to the industrial tradition of the area.

CITY CENTRE: STREETS 157

(W) and New Street (S). Development started in 1818 on New Street. Plots on Waterloo Street and Bennetts Hill were leased between 1823 and 1838, mainly working W. The most active architect was *Charles Edge*, but nothing surviving here is definitely his. By the late C19 commercial uses had taken over, and many houses were rebuilt in the 1930s when the leases ran out. Most of the early C19 survivors were façaded in the 1970s for the Waterloo Square development (*see* below), an early development of this kind in the city. Several banks and offices have been converted into wine bars.

Where Waterloo Street runs E from Victoria Square, the N SIDE has an unbroken three-storey stucco row, mostly with rusticated ground floors. The first are all of *c*. 1835. Nos. 27–30, curving round the bend, are almost certainly by *John Fallows*, as they have his favourite tapering architraves. Dentil cornice. Nos. 31–32 look like *Edge*: four bays with the centre projecting, channelled rustication. Nos. 33–34, like Nos. 27–30 but without the cornice. No. 35, APSLEY HOUSE, is *c*. 1831. Six bays: a 1–3–1 composition, with the extra bay recessed at the r. Central first-floor window with pediment on consoles; porch with Ionic columns. Pilasters with incised decoration, and a blocking course hinting at a pediment. No. 36 is *c*. 1828, in Soane's Bank of England version of Greek Revival. Four bays, severely plain. Ground floor behind a Corinthian colonnade, with Tower of the Winds capitals. Heavy attic with paired pilasters. Perhaps by *Thomas Stedman Whitwell*, whose Carrs Lane chapel of 1820 used similar motifs. In 1976 all these and the upper W side of Bennetts Hill were façaded as WATERLOO COURT by *James A. Roberts Associates*. The attics on e.g. Nos. 33–34 are theirs. A hole punched through the ground floor of No. 36 leads to a courtyard. Brick-and-render elevations and imitation sashes.

The S SIDE was largely rebuilt between the wars. The scale was set by WATERLOO HOUSE of 1926–7 by *Essex & Goodman*, which extends down the steps of Christ Church Passage to New Street. NEW OXFORD HOUSE is a poor stripped classical job of 1934–5 by *S.N. Cooke*. A single swan's-neck pediment with a putto by *William Bloye*, also the stylized heads emerging from the stonework of the porch. NEVILLE HOUSE, 1934 by *W. Norman Twist*, is a good seven-storey *Moderne* block, with window bands cutting fluted pilasters, a big frame with channelled rustication, and an Art Deco cornice. Then two surviving bays of a front of *c*. 1834.

The cross-roads with Bennetts Hill has fine Victorian and Edwardian buildings on each corner, a unique survival in central Birmingham. On the SW, the former NATIONAL PROVINCIAL BANK of 1869 by *John Gibson*, replacing a building of 1833 by *C.R. Cockerell*. In the opulent Renaissance style Gibson used for many of the bank's buildings. Warm pink-grey Wrexham sandstone. Two tall storeys articulated by giant Corinthian pilasters. Round-headed windows to the banking hall, simple paired lights above. Rich cornice, the frieze with a long date inscription, and foliage band between the storeys with the bank's initials. Entrance in the rounded corner, where the giant pilasters become fluted half-columns. On the cornice the Birmingham coat of arms crowned by a helmet and veil, and seated figures of Art and Industry, by *S. F. Lynn*. The porch has a rich coffered half-dome, and fine relief panels of Birmingham industries by *Lynn*: metalworking, glass-blowing, electroplating, gun-making. They are composed like classical friezes but the figures are modelled realistically, and almost in the round. Gibson's building had six bays to Waterloo Street, r., and three to Bennetts Hill, l. In 1890 *Charles Risdon Gribble*, the bank's architect, added two bays on Waterloo Street. In 1927 *C. E. Bateman* added two in Bennetts Hill. Walking in is a shock, as Bateman recast the whole banking hall (now a wine bar) in a grand but sophisticated Neo-Grec. Huge Doric columns with correctly profiled capitals but leaf decoration hinting at Art Deco. Theatrical cornice with mutules set at a proper angle.

On the SE corner the former BIRMINGHAM BANKING CO., 1830–1 by *Rickman & Hutchinson*. The best survivor of their work in Birmingham. Five bays by seven, articulated by plain pilasters, a grand four-bay Corinthian portico to Waterloo Street, and six bays of columns without a pediment to Bennetts Hill. Its isolated, formal quality is unusual in a commercial building. The corners were originally exposed, as still at the l. end of the Waterloo Street front. A single tall window in each bay lights the banking hall. In 1870 *Yeoville Thomason* added the rounded extension between Rickman's porticoes. It continues Rickman's cornice but adds a blank attic. Typical doorway with Aberdeen granite pilasters and luscious foliage frieze. Also Thomason's the Vanbrughian paired arched chimneys over the N pediment. He remodelled the interior with paired Corinthian columns running down the banking hall, which survive behind shop fittings. Addition in Bennetts Hill, s, by *Harris & Martin*, 1881–4.

The NW corner is a heavy three-storey French Renaissance block, built *c.* 1872 for the Inland Revenue. Thumping dentil cornice. The NE corner is the former PARR'S BANK of 1904 by *Cossins, Peacock & Bewlay*. Originally three storeys, the upper ones unfortunate additions. Grey sandstone. An elegant design with a French C18 air to its rusticated pilasters and end bays. Restrained decoration of garlands, and a fine cornice. Ground floor with segment-headed windows and cartouches, a 1990s reinstatement. Next door to the E, CAVENDISH HOUSE of 1937–9 by *W. T. Orton*, consultant *T. Cecil Howitt*. A thirteen-bay *Moderne* block, the seven-bay centre projecting in a frame, with reeded pilasters. On the S side the former LEGAL AND GENERAL ASSURANCE of 1931–2 by *S. N. Cooke*. A distinguished piece of stripped classicism moving towards Modernism, quite unlike his other contemporary work, and probably by his assistant *Edward Holman*. A square block, five bays by five. Five storeys. Portland stone with bands of green instead of a cornice. Recessed lantern-like attic. Windows set between piers with very slightly concave faces, between almost sheer square corner piers. Near the tops of these, reliefs by *Bloye*:

CITY CENTRE: NEWHALL ESTATE 159

simplified, hieratic figures of Wisdom, Fortitude, Charity and Faith, their tight frames emphasizing the geometric quality of the building. Plain ground floor; doorcase with a roundel of Temple Bar, the Legal and General emblem, also by *Bloye*. Entrance to the upper storeys in a six-storey SW tower. Original cylindrical lanterns.

THE NEWHALL ESTATE

The area NW of Colmore Row, developed by the Colmore family following an Act of 1746. Helped by the cutting of the Digbeth Branch Canal in 1786–7, the whole estate was built up by 1810. From 1870, when leases fell in, William Barwick Cregoe Colmore and his surveyor *Thomson Plevins* replanned this area, cutting new streets and realigning others. Rebuilding was almost complete by 1900, with commercial premises and warehouses, but also hospitals, which attracted many doctors' houses and consulting rooms. The city's best architects were employed, producing a fine and consistent townscape, almost unbroken until the 1960s. In 1984 it was designated as the city's Primary Office Area, and in the C21 it is still being damaged by unsympathetic development. The estate continued beyond Great Charles Street to include St Paul's Square. For this area, *see* the Jewellery Quarter, pp. 174–83.

Perambulation

The start is the W end of EDMUND STREET, by the School of Art (p. 133). Next to it the former Medical Institute, School Board Offices, and Parish Offices and Board of Guardians (p. 135). On the SE side, first the rear of No. 125 Colmore Row (p. 142), then offices of 1962–3 by *Fitzroy Robinson & Partners*. Eleven storeys, Portland stone facing, pale grey infill.

Across Newhall Street, on the E corner, Nos. 17–19 of 1896 by *Frederick Martin* of *Martin & Chamberlain*, built as the National Telephone Co.'s offices and exchange. The finest commercial building of Birmingham's brick and terracotta period. Ten years after the School of Art, Chamberlain's successors are more eclectic, less Ruskinian, but still enormously original. Massively articulated by three-storey brick piers with panels of pierced terracotta high up, linked by arches with fierce beast-head keystones and lots of foliage. On the Edmund Street front the piers run up through two big Dutch gables to form tall chimneys. There is a Baroque sense of movement in the three-quarter-round corner oriel and two-storey canted bays. They dance in and out between the piers and leave dark spaces above, with deeply recessed lunette windows. Fantastic animals, like gryphons with fish tails, recline against the balustrade ends. The gables have roundels with tracery, like the School of Art. Fine entrance gates with writhing poppies. The corridors are spanned by tiled three-centred arches. Staircase with paired cast-iron balusters with tiny square tapering Ionic

93

pillars. The top floor was the equipment room, articulated by full-height pointed trusses like those of the architects' school halls. Internal alterations of 1994 by *Mark Humphries*.

On the N corner, No. 29 Newhall Street and Nos. 106–110 Edmund Street, by *F.B. Osborn*, 1895. Solicitors' offices with doctors' consulting rooms on either side. A subtle design in red brick and dark grey stone. The canted bays rising to shaped gables and the continuous balconies with iron railings impose a grid which expresses the offices behind. Osborn's typical elongated consoles to the doorways. Blunt, unmoulded windows, corner turret with charming ogee cap. SE up Newhall Street, Nos. 7–15 of 1962 by *Essex, Goodman & Suggitt*, Portland stone with fins, and Nos. 1–3 of 1967–9 by *Fitzroy Robinson & Partners*, re-clad.

Continuing down Edmund Street, on the SE side the former Ear and Throat Hospital (p. 135). Opposite, No. 120 by *Watson, Johnson & Stokes*, 1956–7, with new porch and forecourt wall by *GMW Architects*, 1994–5. Then No. 134, 1897 by *Newton & Cheatle*. Brick and terracotta, with double-height sunk canted bays. Typical slightly projecting centre and semi-octagonal dormer. Lots of jolly moulded ornament on swinging balcony-like bands between floors. Nos. 136–138, Venetian Gothic of *c.* 1875, must be by *J.H. Chamberlain*. Arcaded ground floor with a gabled doorway breaking the cornice, double-height brick arches enclosing the office floors, and an unusual attic, probably built as a workshop: twelve tightly packed lancets with round lights, rich cornice above. Both now little more than a porch for a block by *Associated Architects*, 2004. Nos. 140–146 is by *Jonathan Wingfield* of *WSM Architects*, 2000. Minimalist blue-tinted glass, dominating top canopy. No. 148 on the corner of Church Street by *Trehearne & Norman, Preston & Partners*, 1959–60. Back on the SE side, the former WHITE SWAN pub, plain with brick pilasters, mostly of 1890 by *J.S. Davis*; façaded in the early 1990s. Then a very fine late C19 row, showing Norman Shaw influence, and the approaching Free Style. Nos. 121–123, 1898–9 by *Newton & Cheatle*, have a simple brick front given character by the giant relieving arch. Swept-up parapet, dormer window with shouldered gable. Typical Newton & Cheatle doorways with round arches breaking across little pilasters. Nos. 125–131, also *Newton & Cheatle*, 1898–1900, were their own offices. One of their finest designs. The ground floor is a four-bay stone arcade. Powerful short columns, arches with big keystones. Four two-storey wooden canted bays (largely renewed 2000–2), linked in pairs by perky top arches and a deep cornice. Their upward movement is stopped by a pair of seven-bay mullion-and-transom windows. Plain severe gables, rising to little swan's-neck pediments. All through, horizontals and verticals are held in perfect balance. No. 133, CHAMBERLAIN HOUSE is of 1895–6 by *Mansell & Mansell*, for Thomas Savage, surgeon. Brick, with stone bands linking the cross-windows. Cornice with Savage's initials and the date, tall hipped roof with finials. The doorcase is a combination of two demolished Norman Shaw designs in the City of London, New Zealand Chambers and Barings Bank: a large segmental pediment on long consoles and short pilasters, broken by a tiny window, itself pedimented and with a big keystone. No. 135 on the corner is well proportioned but basic Gothic of 1877–8 by *J.A. Chatwin*, for the merchants Scholefield Goodman. Up Church Street, s, No. 10, 1885 by *A.B. Phipson & Son*. Terracotta relief panels, and a built-up gable with shell niche and pediment. No. 16 next door, a former hotel of 1876–7 by *Yeoville Thomason*. Broad brick pilasters separating pairs of windows with delicate shouldered lintels. The whole block from No. 121 Edmund Street to here was savagely restored, with much demolition behind, by *Glazzard Associates*, 2000–2. Opposite, NE, the former Eye Hospital (p. 135).

Back in Edmund Street, NW side, No. 158 of 1891 by *J.W. Allen* of West Bromwich. Giant Ionic pilasters, ornate swan's-neck window pediments, corner doorway. Chimneys also with pedimented tops, rebuilt to the original design 1986. Then infill of 1986, from a scheme by *Bonham Seager Associates*, consultant *Douglas Hickman* of the *John Madin Design Group*. It retained the façade of Nos. 168–170, simple brick of 1873 with moulded window reveals. No. 172, 1874–5, slightly richer, with paired brackets to the cornice. No. 174, with windows linked vertically, was built with the OLD CONTEMPTIBLES pub, on the corner with Livery Street. Originally the Albion, 1880–1 by *William Hale*. A rare survival for Birmingham of a Victorian commercial hotel. 'Mixed Italian', with e.g. first-floor pediments poking up into Gothic windows. Surviving ground floor, the corner with Corinthian pilasters and big, mostly original, windows with delicate colonnettes. Plain high former public bar, with shouldered relieving arches as the bar back. Lounge bar, the rear part a former billiard room, with skylight. Opposite, large new offices by *Associated Architects*, 2003–4.

Back SE, and NW down Church Street. On the NE, Nos. 37–39 and 41–43, both by *Newton & Cheatle*, 1900–1 and 1901–2. The first simple brick with stone bands and ground floor. Typical doorways with semicircular hoods breaking across a three-light window. Dormers arranged 2–1–2–1–2, in counterpoint. Nos. 41–43 are a beautiful and original Free Style composition, like a fantastic castle in low relief. Wide shallow bays, with windows separated by lead panels, rise to concave caps, set against segmental brick gables. Entrance bay with a stone canted turret-like top. Semicircular doorhead on stubby half-columns, linked to the shallow bay above. The grossly overscaled No. 45 by *Corstorphine & Wright*, 2007–8, is on the site of *Newton & Cheatle*'s superb Buckler & Webb printing works of 1898.

On the N corner with Cornwall Street, the jolly OLD ROYAL pub, originally the Red Lion, 1899–1900 by *Arthur Hamblin*. Pinky-red brick and cream terracotta. Concave gables rise to little pediments. Lots of Jacobean decoration. Corner turret with lion weathervane. Big canted bays on the first floor mark the assembly room. NE down Cornwall Street No. 2, CORNWALL COURT, 1989–92 by the *Seymour Harris Partnership*. Orange brick with insistent blue bands. Bulky, but redeemed by lively Neo-vernacular gables and semicircular projections responding to its neighbours. Continuing down Church Street, on the SW side, stretching through to Great Charles Street, EMBASSY HOUSE, 1982–3 by the *Hitchman Stone Partnership*, retaining the façades of a corner building of 1899 by *Owen & Ward*. Opposite, Nos. 57–59, 1909 by *G.A. Cox*. Heavy cornices and a grid of big mullion-and-transom windows separated by brick piers. Tower-like end bays, off-centre doorway with big keystone. No. 63 is Postmodern imitation by the *Seymour Harris Partnership*, 1990. Finally, No. 65, the former Diocesan Lodge of the Girls' Friendly Society, i.e. a women's hostel, 1908 by *Osborn, Pemberton & White*. Warm orange-red brick with giant Ionic pilasters, appropriately feminine and domestic. Oval windows under the parapet.

Now SW up GREAT CHARLES STREET, with the A38 road running into the Queensway tunnels of 1967–71. On the SE side a nine-storey block by *Hurley Robinson & Son*, 1955–7. On the corner of New Market Street the former GUILD OF HANDICRAFT, 1897–8 by *Arthur S. Dixon*. The pioneer building of Arts and Crafts radicalism in Birmingham, and a perfect example of the quiet understatement which Dixon and others cultivated around 1900. Facing New Market Street, two three-storey gabled blocks separated by a two-storey range with a deep swept roof and big dormers. The ends differ slightly, the l. one with windows linked vertically by shallow recessions. The Great Charles Street front is a compressed version, stepped uphill, so the corner block is cross-gabled. Rough-textured brick, probably local seconds, with wide mortar joints. Casement windows. Typical Dixon round-headed relieving arches. The roots of his style lie in the Gothic Revival, but he never pointed an arch unless absolutely necessary. Inside, the attic is supported by a complex timber structure, a tie- and collar-beam roof on posts rising from the first floor. Originally there was a rear workshop wing with a fully glazed upper floor. Alterations in 1988–90 by the *ISH Partnership* replaced the windows and destroyed the original interior. ISH also designed the five-storey block further up Great Charles Street. Then No. 40, 1954 by *Essex, Goodman & Suggitt*. Portland stone, fins, but still very basic classical columns on the ground floor.

At the Newhall Street cross-roads, Great Charles Street regains urban character as a wide boulevard, with mostly anodyne Portland stone blocks. N corner, LANCASTER HOUSE of 1932–3 by *Essex & Goodman*, minimal classical. SE side: YORK HOUSE by *Crouch, Butler & Savage*, 1930, red brick, with Portland stone dressings. No. 36 alongside, 1973 by *S. Elden Minns & Partners*, has Inca-like abstract reliefs. It replaced *W.H. Bidlake*'s offices of 1902 for Keep Brothers, his only commercial building. Adjacent, the former Stock Exchange (p. 136). Finally the NW side: GALBRAITH HOUSE,

CITY CENTRE: NEWHALL ESTATE

by *Surman, Kelly & Surman*, 1960; LOMBARD HOUSE by *S.N. Cooke*, 1933; and CML HOUSE, a nine-storey stepped tower of 1938 for Colonial Mutual Life Assurance by *Hennessy, Hennessy & Co.* of Sydney, with *Stanley Hall & Easton & Robertson* of London. The best building is Nos. 150–152 next door, the former BIRMINGHAM CHEST CLINIC. By *John P. Osborne & Son*, 1930–2; part of the national effort to eradicate tuberculosis. Elegant and subtle Neo-Georgian. Nine bays. The central seven project slightly and have a cornice. Careful use of smooth rustication and raised panels. Entrance with Doric columns *in antis* and relief of Aesculapius by *Bloye*. Nos. 154–155 is by *Surman, Kelly & Surman*, 1958–60; CIVIC HOUSE, 1981 by *Scott, Brownrigg & Turner*.

Back down Great Charles Street and SE down NEWHALL STREET. On the NE side, No. 61 by *Newton & Cheatle*, 1904–5. Round-headed relieving arches with herringbone work. Carefully casual side elevation to Great Charles Street, with a hint of Mackintosh in the small, perfectly placed bay window. No. 55, AVEBURY HOUSE, is of 1905–6 by *Marcus O. Type*. The keystone of the central relieving arch pushes up into the pediment, a touch of the London Neo-Mannerism of e.g. J.J. Joass. Ground floor with paired Doric columns. On the SW side, Nos. 56–60 by *Newton & Cheatle*, 1900–1: the l. part for Rheece W. Palk, their client in Church Street, the rest for the Birmingham Office Co. Flemish and Jacobean Renaissance, with elements of Arts and Crafts Free Style. Pink brick – which must have looked shocking when new – and terracotta. Seven bays, divided 3–1–3, with big shaped gables separated by a central bay. The chequering in the gables suggests Lethaby. Two-storey porches with tent roofs, their height important in the composition. Sinuous cartouches, with little columns and plaques with the numbers above the doorways. On the top floor, centre and ends, reliefs of St George and the Dragon modelled by *W.J. Neatby*. No. 54 is of 1897 by *Henman & Cooper* for F.W. Richards, dentist. Brick with dark stone dressings. Porch with banded columns and Cape-style pediment. Ground and first floors with canted bays recessed between brick pilasters, deriving from Philip Webb (Bell Brothers' offices, Middlesbrough) and almost the architects' signature. The top-floor windows sit behind Doric columns. Then the corners of Cornwall Street, guarded by a pair of balancing brick and terracotta corner turrets with domed tops: delightful townscape. Both are by *Essex, Nicol & Goodman*, in Flemish-cum-Jacobean Renaissance style. On the W corner Nos. 50–52, doctors' consulting rooms of 1896–7. Wide bays with large windows lighting the consulting rooms. Shaped gables, as also at the larger Nos. 43–51 of 1898–1900 opposite. Built for the Birmingham Hospital Saturday Fund, a low-cost medical insurance society. Two-storey canted bays. Big portal with a shaped parapet and canted corners, and stylized flower sculpture. The far end down Cornwall Street was largely rebuilt after the Second World War. Across the street, Nos. 33–41, good Postmodern of 1986–7 by the *Percy Thomas Partnership*, was vacuously refronted and heightened by *Aedas*, 2006. Opposite, the Parish Offices (p. 135).

Now sw up Cornwall Street. On the l. the studio block of the School of Art. Opposite, doctors' houses and consulting rooms, rare in the city as high-quality houses in a tight urban street, the equivalent of e.g. parts of Chelsea. No. 87 is by *Henman & Cooper* for Dr Parrott, 1899. Three storeys and a big gable. Subtly asymmetrical windows with the firm's characteristic deep-set canted bays, behind piers and Tuscan columns (cf. No. 54 Newhall Street, above). Nos. 89–91 by *C. E. Bateman*, 1904, for J. Mountford, 'surgeon-dentist'. Arts and Crafts Neo-Georgian, showing the contemporary interest in local early C18 buildings. Four storeys, with three-storey canted bays ending in cornices with a gadrooned frieze. Tall attic showing Lethaby influence in the segmental pediments and diapering. The doorcases have pilasters and scrolly broken pediments, that to No. 91 with a little window with a shell-hood above. No. 93, *Newton & Cheatle*, 1902, for Sir James Sawyer. Sash windows linked by blocked surrounds extended as stone bands. Doorway canopy hanging from iron brackets. Dramatic curved parapet with swept-up ends. Finally No. 95, 1901 for Dr Smith Priestley, also *Newton & Cheatle*, and also with good railings. Stone ground floor with heavy porch; giant brick pilasters above; heavy cornice. Now part of the Birmingham and Midland Institute, l. (*see* p. 130). Beyond, the Council House Extension (p. 130).

INNER AREAS
Described clockwise, from w to s

Broad Street and Brindleyplace	165
Places of worship	165
Major buildings	165
Perambulation	168
The Jewellery Quarter and Summer Lane	174
Places of worship	175
Public buildings	176
Perambulations	177
The Gun Quarter	187
Eastside	188
Aston University	188
Perambulation	188
Digbeth, Deritend, Bordesley and Highgate	193
Places of worship	193
Perambulations	195
Other buildings	203
Smallbrook and the Gough Estate	203
Places of worship	203
Theatres	205
Perambulations	206

BROAD STREET AND BRINDLEYPLACE
w of the centre

Broad Street was a medieval lane linking New Hall Lane (now Colmore Row) with the Hagley Road. Development started with the Birmingham Canal, cut in 1768–72, with its terminal basin s of the street at its E end. Iron and brass manufacturing grew up around it. In the early C19 a separate development, Islington, began at the w end, and by the 1840s the area was almost completely built up. The street was a fashionable shopping area until the mid C20. Regeneration started in 1988–91 with the creation of Centenary Square, and the Convention Centre and Hyatt hotel complex at the E end, followed by Brindleyplace on the N. In the 2010s the high-rise fashion produced the badly sited and grouped 'Left Bank' towers.

PLACES OF WORSHIP

ST LUKE, Gas Street. *See* p. 173.

PRESBYTERIAN CHURCH OF ENGLAND (former), Broad Street. 1848–9 by *J.R. Botham*. Blue Staffordshire brick, locally fashionable then for churches (e.g. St John, Walmley, Sutton Coldfield, p. 442). A rectangular box with two tiers of windows, still in the Georgian tradition. Four-stage tower showing the influence of Rickman's St Thomas (*see* p. 203). Quadrants on the belfry stage; octagon above with a pagoda top. Big, handsome doorcase. A Christian Science church from 1926; now offices.

BIRMINGHAM PROGRESSIVE SYNAGOGUE, Bishopsgate Street. 2009 by *Keith Reynolds Associates*. Alas not inspired. Brick, with tall windows, shallow roofs, and a recess for the entrance.

MAJOR BUILDINGS

HALL OF MEMORY, Centenary Square, E end. The city's First World War memorial, of 1922–5 by *S.N. Cooke & W.N. Twist*. A domed octagon, or chamfered square. Portland stone, new to Birmingham then, with a base of Cornish granite. The short diagonal faces are set slightly back, framing bronze seated figures representing the Services, by *Albert Toft*. Heavy Doric entablature and attic, and a low dome. Pedimented projections on the main sides, the SE one the entrance, originally facing the corner of Broad Street and Easy Row. Interior also Doric, in Beer stone, with curiously spreading pilasters. The focus is the central SHRINE, a Siena marble tomb crowned by a bronze casket made by the *Birmingham Guild* containing the Roll of Honour. Marble paving and seats in the angles, bronze flambeaux. Ribbed and coffered dome set below the outer one. STAINED GLASS by *Richard Stubington*, and three SCULPTED PANELS, high up, by *William Bloye*, showing soldiers joining up, in the firing line and returning wounded. Fine Primitivist work in low relief, showing the influence of Eric Gill. The returning figures particularly haunting, walking on angular ground against a background of receding graves.

BASKERVILLE HOUSE, Centenary Square, N side. 1939–41 by *T. Cecil Howitt* of Nottingham (competition 1935). Portland stone, to match the Hall of Memory in front, and Cornish granite. Academic classicism, but with real urban scale and dignity. The *piano nobile* with pedimented windows marks the most important offices. It represents the front half of the E wing of the proposed Civic Centre (the subject of an earlier competition in 1926–7), hence the big pavilion with columns *in antis* stranded at the NW corner. Stepped-up centrepiece with a big niche behind a free-standing Ionic order. Gutted for offices by *Rolfe Judd*, 2003–7. – STATUE in front, King Edward VII by *Albert Toft*, 1912–13. Moved to Highgate Park from Victoria Square in 1951, restored and installed here 2010, with replicas of the stolen bronze pedestal figures.

LIBRARY OF BIRMINGHAM, Centenary Square, N side. Birmingham's fourth central library. *Martin & Chamberlain*'s building of 1864, burnt out in 1879 and rebuilt splendidly by *J. H. Chamberlain* in Lombardic Renaissance, came down in 1974 after a long campaign to preserve it. The *John Madin Design Group*'s Central Library of 1969–74, NW of the Town Hall and W of the Council House Extension, the finest example of the Brutalist aesthetic in the city, was also demolished, in 2016, after a similarly long campaign to preserve it. A *Richard Rogers* replacement proposal at Eastside of 2002 was abandoned after a change in council political control in 2004. This library is by *Mecanoo* – founding partner, in charge, *Francine Houben* – of 2010–13. But *Capita Symonds*, the project managers, ran the competition which selected them, appointed the contractors (*Carillion*) and sat 'in the middle of the design and construction process'. The 'People's Palace' which Mecanoo envisaged is significantly compromised.

With its ten floors and a basement, the Library is a bulky addition to Centenary Square. It is sited, unfortunately, on the open courtyard originally intended for the Civic Centre schemes (*see* p. 169): not the architects' choice, and too small. It pushes out like a stack of boxes. The middle box and the drum at the top are clad in gold-coated aluminium. All the boxes are covered in a screen of thin interlocking metal circles, the building's 'signature'. For the architects, they symbolize the city's metal industries and the craftsmanship of the jewellery trades. They look very similar to their International Criminal Court project of 2008. The lowest box cantilevers far over the entrance. It is reminiscent of the stacked floors of Madin's inverted ziggurat, but covered in Nottingham lace. In front of the entrance is a circular opening in the pavement, revealing a lower level and below-ground performance space.

Circles are a main theme of the building, explicit inside. The tall entrance hall leads to escalators with views of the extensive yellow-painted lending and children's libraries in the basement. The escalators cross a series of circular spaces, offset from each other, and partially overlapping: a fascinating and involving spatial sequence. The main reference floor is at the bottom of the largest light well, centred on the 'Book Rotunda', with upper floors behind piers all round: the heart of the design. Reading areas are high and light (and sometimes draughty). Books run all round the rotunda including, disquietingly, above the escalators. The third and seventh floors open on to landscaped gardens on top of the stacked boxes. At the top, reached by lifts, is the twice-relocated SHAKESPEARE MEMORIAL ROOM from *Martin & Chamberlain*'s second library, opened in 1882. Their richest interior, a small room, like a casket, in refined Elizabethan Revival. The entrance culminates in a centrepiece topped with a shell. Small square panels of carved leaves, and a frieze of laurel. Tall oak bookcases run all round, their tops with patterned glazing. They stand on a panelled dado which projects in the middle of each side. Rich tympana at each end, with arcading, central niches and beautiful marquetry. The ceiling, with alternating plasterwork and glazing, was reconstructed in the 1970s from photographs.

The architects' vision has been further curtailed. The below-ground performance space is unused. First-floor meeting rooms have been commandeered by a language institute, opening hours reduced, and the public desk moved from its crucial central position in the Book Rotunda. But the building is still popular. Seven years after opening, visitors come to see the interior. What is its vision – a place of public education and scholarship, as Madin envisaged in 1974, or just the last local monument in the line of cultural institutions as anchors of urban regeneration, like the Lowry at Salford, the Public at West Bromwich (p.607) or the Walsall New Art Gallery (p.629)? Those inaccessible shelves in the Rotunda suggest that books here are a symbol of culture and identity, rather than things you actually use to study.

BIRMINGHAM REPERTORY THEATRE, Centenary Square, N side. 1969–71 by *Graham Winteringham* of *S.T. Walker & Partners*. A complex grouping of masses unified by functional relationships. A good Modernist analogy might be a ship (reflecting its architect's naval career). The flattened curve of the façade resembles the captain's bridge. Its reeded concrete uprights are linked by arches, and it follows the shape of the auditorium. No front entrance, because the 1958 Civic Centre scheme (*see* below) envisaged a water feature here. At the sides, now only visible on the W, sharply angled volumes cut in to the stage and fly tower at the rear. Now linked to the Library of Birmingham, and badly treated: flying front stairs removed, and the rear with its array of boxed-out dressing rooms obliterated. The unusual single-rake auditorium with wide proscenium was re-fitted in 1998. Rear parts rebuilt by *Mecanoo* as part of the Library of Birmingham project (*see* above), 2010–13. Major entrance alterations by *APEC Architects*, disfiguring Winteringham's front, under way in 2021.

INTERNATIONAL CONVENTION CENTRE and HYATT REGENCY HOTEL, Centenary Square, W side. 1987–91 by the *Convention Centre Partnership* (*Percy Thomas Partnership* with *Renton Howard Wood Levin*, acoustic consultants *Artec*). A complex of hotel, concert hall and conference facilities, the first such in the UK. Architecturally a huge disappointment. The 2,200-seat concert hall, SYMPHONY HALL, faces the square. Top drum with corner wings. Below, what was a heavy mass of grey granite and blue-tinted glass has been refronted by *Page/Park*, 2020–1. Shallow curved elevation with much glazing, and swooping floor lines. Convention Centre entrance to the N, under a blue metal canopy, with more halls and a theatre beyond. S across Broad Street, linked by a bridge, the hotel. A twenty-five-storey mirror-glass slab, pure commercial American. A mall-like route runs E–W through the Centre, another American concept. Awkward forty-five-degree angles inside and out. The concert hall is tall and narrow, with three tiers of balconies and big adjustable sound holes, acoustically superb but visually uncomfortable. – SCULPTURE. In the entrance canopy, Birdlife, neon tubes, by *Ron Hasleden*, 1991. N side of mall, Construction, delightful chromed bronze by *Vincent Woropay*, 1990. S side, high up, Convention, limewood relief by *Richard Perry*, 1992, overlapping tree forms.

BIRMINGHAM MUNICIPAL BANK (former), Centenary Square, S side. By *T. Cecil Howitt*, 1931–3. It has his grand sense of urban scale. Four giant fluted Ionic columns *in antis*, complex deep entablature, attic supported by big consoles laid flat. The main hall has a heavy square-panelled ceiling, with the motto 'Thrift Radiates Happiness', and an arcaded side passage to adjoining rooms. Converted for the University of Birmingham by *Glancy Nicholls*, 2021: ceiling opened to a glass roof.

IKON GALLERY, Oozells Square. Formerly Oozells Street School, by *Martin & Chamberlain*, 1877 (E wing 1898). Ruskinian Gothic. The confined site dictated a compact three-storey block. Renewed sash windows, stone and tile tympana in pointed openings, typical naturalistic sculpture. Converted by *Levitt Bernstein*, 1997, who reinstated the tower to the original design, and added glass N and S extensions for lifts and stairs: tough additions to a tough building. Inserted floors in the main classrooms and hall. Big wooden arch-braced roof with iron ties; the 1898 roof has iron arches.

NATIONAL INDOOR ARENA, Cambridge Street. 1989–91 by *HOK* and *Percy Thomas Partnership*. A huge uninspired lump with brick staircase projections. It seats 8,000 to 13,000.

REGISTER OFFICE, Holliday Street. 2006 by *Aedas*. Glazing and cladding panels, rather a mess.

PERAMBULATION

From Chamberlain Square, E, the approach is along CENTENARY WAY of 1989, the first-level bridge across the inner ring road. From it, a spectacular view S to the ATV development of 1969–73, on the site of the canal basin. A twenty-eight-storey tower, hotel and offices by *H. George Marsh* of *Richard Seifert & Partners*. A good example of Marsh's dramatic and angular style (cf. Centre Point, London). The tower cranks in the middle and has tapered ends, slit from top to bottom. They house the staircases. The window surrounds have tapered sides, and the angles are reflected in the ground-floor arches. Far too close to the W, No. 1 Centenary Square, by *Make*, 2017, twelve storeys, pivoting round at the top.

CENTENARY SQUARE is a long E–W rectangle, Broad Street forming its S side. It has a long history of projects for a Civic Centre, including a scheme of 1918 by *William Haywood* with a 'Municipal Tower'; another of 1926 by *Maximilian Romanoff*; and a spectacular *Haywood* Beaux Arts scheme of 1940–1, of which Baskerville House (p. 166) was to have formed the SE part. In 1958 this was recast more informally by *A. G. Sheppard Fidler*, with towers to the N. In front of us, the Hall of Memory. On the N side, Baskerville House, the Library of Birmingham, and the Repertory Theatre. Opposite, the former Municipal Bank. The square itself, created in 1989–91 by the *Birmingham City Architect*, with screens by *Tess Jaray* and sculptures by *Raymond Mason* (destroyed by an arsonist) and *Tom Lomax*, was redone by *Graham Massie & Partners*, 2019. It must have looked good on the drawings. Hard, empty formality. A grid of very tall, tapering lighting columns runs right across, looking like redundant radio masts. Stone benches. The delightful feature is a shallow paddling pool. At the W end, the Convention Centre, and the Hyatt hotel. *William Bloye*'s SCULPTURE of 1956, standing figures of Boulton, Watt and Murdoch in conversation, is to be reinstated (2020).

We walk through the Convention Centre mall. Beyond, a canal-side space, with a bronze SCULPTURE of 1990 by *Roderick Tye*, Battle of the Gods and the Giants, a cloud shape split vertically. To the N above a retaining wall, the BREWMASTER'S HOUSE of 1816, repaired 1983–4 for the Birmingham Conservation Trust. Built as the owner's house and office of a small brewery. Almost symmetrical three-bay façade. Typical Birmingham architraves on consoles. Doric porch with open pediment. Rear cartshed with cast-iron columns, glazed in and extended by the *Birmingham City Architect*, 1989. To the N, the brick ICC ENERGY CENTRE by the *Convention Centre Partnership*, 1986, and the brewery's MALTHOUSE, later C19, converted to a pub by *John Dixon & Associates*, 1995. Immediately N of the latter, KINGSTON BUILDINGS, built *c.* 1803 as Price's nail warehouse, on a courtyard plan. Symmetrical two-storey E front, arched central entrance with pediment. Sash windows, including some tripartite windows at the rear facing the canal, where former loading bays can be seen. Heavily restored by *David Robotham*, 1995. Across the canal to the W, the National Indoor Arena.

Now back S, and W across the canal into the WATER'S EDGE restaurants and shops, by *Benoy*, 1993–5. Postmodern industrial vernacular, the most obvious joke the steel-pipe column on top of a huge sloping buttress. It succeeds by strong detailing, e.g. brickwork with red stretcher rows alternating with blue headers. Part of the *Terry Farrell Partnership* masterplan of 1991 for this area, retained in the 1993 version by *John Chatwin* (see Birmingham Introduction, p. 110). A passage runs W to the main square of BRINDLEYPLACE, laid out in 1995. The masterplan's combination of informal relationships within strong townscape disciplines is evident in the buildings and the apparently casual layout with trees, pools and carefully aligned pathways, by *Townshend Landscape Architects*. At the centre is a CAFÉ by *Piers Gough* of *CZWG*. Small, angular, sculptural: a pointed oval of grey-painted steel and glass, its roof slopes extended like the wings of a bird about to fly. SCULPTURE in the W corner by *Miles Davies*, 1995, blackened arches. The buildings share a common scale, the use of brick, and a tripartite division into base, main storeys and attic. On the NE side, No. 3 by *Porphyrios Associates*, 1997–8, the most classical design, of seven storeys. Doric colonnade with intersecting arches hinting at both Gothic and Romanesque. Huge attic, like a temple set sideways. Clock tower with cornice on big consoles. It shows the influence of early C19 Germany, Schinkel and Klenze, filtered through Leon and Rob Krier. Inside, a Doric screen leads to an atrium with very Mannerist stretched Corinthian pilasters. On the SE, two plainer buildings by *Allies & Morrison*, also with colonnades. No. 2 of 1996–7, buff brick. No. 6 of 1998–9, red brick. Beyond them No. 7 by *Porphyrios Associates*, 2003–4, in red sand-faced brick. Open arcade, grey-clad attic with deep canopy. On the SW side No. 5 by *Sidell Gibson*, 1996. Buff brick with stone bands, asymmetrical, pulled together by the classical tripartite division. Deep glass atrium on the SE, flanked by a massive turret to the square and a bull-nosed end beyond. The base adds bands of blue brick. NW side, No. 4 by *Stanton Williams*, 1997–9. Moving beyond Postmodern, into the resurgent planar Modernism of the late 1990s. A louvred screen of metal and glass, a recessed entrance, and a l. block and cornice of pink flush-pointed Belgian brick. Crisp but coldly threatening, and unpleasantly bulky at the rear. To the N, between Nos. 3 and 4, the SEA LIFE CENTRE, an aquarium by *Foster & Partners*, 1996, of three-dimensional 'ray' shape.

Now between Nos. 2 and 6, and into OOZELLS SQUARE, S. On its NE side the Ikon Gallery (p. 168). Landscaping of the square, with a diagonal rill aligned on the gallery tower, by *Townshend Associates*. Granite sculptures by *Paul de Monchaux*, 1998. At the SW end, No. 8 by *Sidell Gibson*, 2002–3. Tall, with a gimmicky prow.

Back to the main square, and SW down Brunswick Street, from in front of No. 4. On the NW side, CAR PARK and SPORTS CENTRE by *Benoy*, 1998; steel panels covering the concrete structure. Attached beyond, facing Sheepcote Street, the CRESCENT THEATRE by *John Chatwin*, 1998. Brick with a blue-painted front, cut down from the original design. Opposite the theatre, Grosvenor Street West, with on its NW side the UNION MILL of 1813, perhaps by *William Hollins*. Originally the largest flour mill in the town. Simple two-storey front range with a pedimented gable over the central carriage arch. NW from the theatre in Sheepcote Street, NE side, SYMPHONY COURT, the Brindleyplace private housing scheme, 1995 by *Lyons+Sleeman+Hoare*. Friendly canal-side scale, and shaped gables. On the SW, retained C19 façades to a large private flats scheme, with white-clad end pavilions, by *Associated Architects*, 2000–2. Then a good Queen Anne office building by *Osborn & Reading*, 1890, fronting large flats by *Turner Woolford Sharp*, 2000–2. On the W corner with St Vincent Street, the former CORPORATION DEPOT of 1873–4 by *W.H. Ward*. Picturesque paired Gothic lodges. Inside, a more than semicircular range with a cartway running under its centre to the canal. Extensions along Sheepcote Street, probably 1890s. Being restored for a mixed-use scheme by *Burrell Foley Fischer*, 2020.

Now SE down Sheepcote Street from the theatre. The CITY INN (now Hilton Garden Inn) is by *Hulme Upright Weedon*, 2000; then No. 11, by *Glenn Howells*, 2009, already eroding the Brindleyplace design rules with a thirteen-storey tower and no division of the elevations. Ahead r., the former SOUTH STAFFORDSHIRE WATERWORKS CO. OFFICES, 1931–2 by *Crouch, Butler & Savage*. Brick and Portland stone. Heavy Doric porch, small top pediment with long consoles embracing a round window. Then the new Birmingham townscape of the C21. Two looming towers by *Glancy Nicholls*, 2015–19, seventeen and twenty-two storeys, the taller one at an unfortunate angle. Behind, facing us across Broad Street, a forty-two-storey tower by *Glenn Howells*, 2021. Cowering between them, on the N side of Broad Street, the former BIRMINGHAM AND DISTRICT BANK of 1898 by *C.E. Bateman*. A beautiful Norman-Shaw-classical piece with Arts and Crafts touches and a slight French air, e.g. the little iron balconies. Angled corner porch with Ionic columns. W from the Howells block, TRANSPORT HOUSE by *Culpin & Bowers*, 1927–9. Friendly, slightly overcrowded faience front with Ionic pilasters and a perky oriel. Then CUMBERLAND HOUSE, an office tower of 1963–4 by *Lewis Solomon, Kaye & Partners*, the podium dressed up by *Halpern Partnership*, 1998. Opposite, the former owner's house of the Islington Glassworks of 1815. Three storeys, three bays. Stone strings between the floors, Doric porch. Windows probably of 1863 by *J.J. Bateman*, who added the wings then, when it became the Lying-In Hospital. Railings with Gothic piers by *Martin & Chamberlain*, 1869. On the SE side, a large cinema and leisure complex by *Aedas*, 2000–2. Between them is BISHOPSGATE STREET with the CITY TAVERN (now Bulls Head), a terracotta pub of 1901 by *James & Lister Lea*, the Progressive Synagogue (p. 165), and HOUSING of 1968–72 by the *Birmingham City Architect*: low-rise courtyard blocks with deck access, unusual in Birmingham, over ground-floor garages. Metal roofs 2002–3. Back on Broad Street, the PARK REGIS development was Auchinleck House, by *J. Seymour Harris & Partners*, 1961–2, with a commanding fourteen-storey tapered end towards the junction. Hotel conversion by *5plus*, 2015, with a horrible lumpy top to the tower. Opposite to the w, the BROADWAY office complex by the *John Madin Design Group*, 1973–6, brick-faced, typical of their later manner. w from here is Edgbaston (p. 357).

In BROAD STREET NE of Sheepcote Street, SE side, the former LEE LONGLANDS furniture shop (No. 224) is by *Hurley Robinson*, 1931, in his distinctive squared-up Art Deco. E extension 1939. The TRAVELODGE, 1961–3 by *John Madin*, was badly re-clad *c.* 1990. On the opposite corner the former GRANVILLE pub, 1923 by *Arthur Edwards*. White faience. The Art Deco FIGURE OF EIGHT bar next door, by *Bernard G. Warr*, 1932, started as a car showroom. GRANVILLE STREET runs SE alongside the Granville, with GRANVILLE SQUARE on the SW side, red brick housing of 1978–80 by *Peter Hing & Jones*. Low-rise blocks surrounding a tower breaking into horns at the top. Back in Broad Street, NW side, the NOVOTEL by the *Percy Thomas Partnership*, 1988–9; No. 10 Brindleyplace, orange brick, by *Sidell Gibson*, 2003; then No. 9, by *Associated Architects*, 2000–1, rather reticent, the base signified by two-storey stone framing. It wraps round the former Presbyterian church (p. 165). Opposite the church, a sixteen-storey Seifertian tower and podium of 1974–5 by *Ian Fraser, John Roberts & Partners*, now the JURY'S INN. Tower fins tapering at the top. BERKLEY STREET runs SE alongside. At the far end, SW side, the CBSO CENTRE, offices and rehearsal rooms. Retained façade of Rowe's lead works, 1921–2 by *H. Peter Hing*, to a development by *Associated Architects*, 1997. Their SE front is a grid structure of dark grey steel I-beams with characteristically varied infill, including wooden trellising. Barrel-roofed hall behind. Opposite, the Register Office (p. 168).

Back in Broad Street, NW side, No. 1 Brindleyplace, a fine gateway building to Broad Street, by *Anthony Peake Associates*, 1994–5. Brick skin with deliberately unstructural detailing e.g. broken lengths of cornice. Slightly Chinese turrets. Then the BRASSHOUSE, a brassworks of 1781, the finest surviving secular building of the C18 town. Long low façade: seven bays, the ends slightly recessed. Two storeys, with a parapet over the central bays breaking into balustrades over the main windows, and supported by consoles at the ends. Wyatt windows in the second and sixth bays, divided by slender colonnettes; central Venetian window. Sills tied together by string courses. Romanesque central doorway by *Martin & Chamberlain*, 1866. Restaurant conversion 1987–8, with rear extensions, by *Temple Cox Nicholls*. QUAYSIDE TOWER opposite is a sixteen-storey slab of 1963–5 by *John Madin*, re-clad in 2003 by *Richard Johnson & Associates*. Podium enlivened by original textured abstract reliefs.

Beyond the canal, the former CROWN INN was William Butler's brewery tap (his C19 tower brewery survived at the rear until 1987). Small, irregularly spaced sashes on first and second floors, from the building of 1781. Reconstructed in 1883 and again in 1930, when *E.F. Reynolds* did the ground floor with its rusticated piers, the Brasshouse-style parapet, and the domed clock tower. Nouveau-classical SW façade by *Alan Goodwin & Associates*, 1991. Opposite, Nos. 264–265, 1887 by *Martin & Chamberlain*. Informal composition with one big gable decorated with brick mullions, balanced by two smaller ones. Nos. 266–271, slightly earlier, are Italian Gothic. Then a block of 2000 by *Level Seven Architects*.

Now back across the canal, and SE into GAS STREET. On the NE side, houses of *c.* 1810 with typical window architraves and doorcases. SW side, a house and factory of 1821 with segment-headed iron-framed windows and a massive doorcase. Behind, Postmodern offices of 1995–7 by *Peter Hing & Jones*. No. 46, diagonally opposite, is the former WORCESTER AND BIRMINGHAM CANAL CO. OFFICE of 1864 by *James Lea*. Severe and dignified, with a heavy porch in the angle. Rendered ground floor with cornice, blue brick above. Intrusive glass extension of 2016 by *Gillespie Yunnie*, r. Next, the former Birmingham Gas Light and Coke Co.'s works. First a plain brick range of 1857 with segmental roof, built as a store. Then the RETORT HOUSE of 1822, designed by its engineer *Alexander Smith*. Street front with windows in three-centred relieving arches. Its 'fireproof' iron roof survives inside: cast-iron trusses, wrought-iron tie-rods. The S side was originally open; some cast-iron supporting columns survive. Extended W 1828 with a similar roof; contemporary coal store to the N with louvred roof. Heavily restored in 1998–9 by *Richard Johnson & Associates* who also designed the flats beyond, red brick with grey-clad roofs. Now ST LUKE (GAS STREET CHURCH); conversion in 2015–16 by *APEC* included new floors and birch-plywood-clad 'pods' for storage.

A gateway in the wall opposite leads into the hidden GAS STREET BASIN, still a great surprise to enter. A small basin on the Birmingham Canal of 1772, it became important as the junction of the Worcester and Birmingham Canal from 1795. Its sense of enclosure was seriously compromised in the late C20; best now viewed from the traditional-style footbridge of 1988, to the l. as we enter. The Birmingham Canal enters from under Broad Street and its old E exit to the terminal basin is still visible. The WORCESTER BAR runs SW–NE across the basin, originally separating the canals. STOP LOCK of 1815, now crossed by the bridge. Surrounding buildings are taken clockwise, from the SW side. Here the Gas Street cottages have an extra lower storey facing the canal, and the rendered range alongside is revealed as a three-storey corn warehouse of *c.* 1830. Across the canal, backs of buildings in Broad Street, altered and extended in the mid 1860s for a foundry, hence the chimney. Then the dominating Hyatt hotel (p. 168). SE of the NE arm, late C20 replacements for C19 warehouses. The JAMES BRINDLEY (now Canal House) pub of 1985 by *Alan*

G. Goodwin here was crassly re-clad, with a fake crane, in 2017. Continuing SE, on the SW side after the lock cottages a long C19 factory. A cast-iron AQUEDUCT of 1870 carries the canal over Holliday Street, with brick vaults supported on decorative iron columns. Beyond is an exit to Bridge Street to the NW, and so N back to Centenary Square.

THE JEWELLERY QUARTER AND SUMMER LANE
NW and N of the centre

The boundaries are the inner ring road, the Dudley road (The Parade and Sand Pits) SW, the middle ring road NW and N, going slightly N of it along New John Street, and New Town Row and the Digbeth Branch Canal, E. Development started nearest the centre, as part of the Newhall estate (*see* p.159). The grid of streets focused on St Paul's Square was laid out, and the church built, in 1776–9. A surviving lease is dated 1791. The W part was developed in the early C19 with villas in private grounds, but industry arrived quickly. The N end, around Vyse Street, was built up *c.*1845–70 with houses and workshops, the latter taking over in the later C19. There was a great variety of manufacturing, especially of the metal 'toys', trinkets and boxes for which Birmingham was famous. From the mid C19 the precious metal trades became concentrated in the area, helped by the large number of interdependent skilled tasks needing close proximity. This encouraged related businesses and connected institutions: the Assay Office and the Municipal School for Jewellers. Pen factories were concentrated around Legge Lane. The Summer Lane area to the E was different, a tightly packed district of closes of houses and factories, the epitome of inner industrial Birmingham until mid-C20 slum clearance.

Manufacturing began in houses or small workshops at the rear, but by the 1830s combined houses and workshops were being built, a type that died out *c.*1880. Older domestic premises were rapidly converted, with rear 'shopping' wings and front extensions, producing a dense, small-scale industrial townscape. These simple brick structures with large iron-framed windows changed little throughout the C19. Many premises were let in small units, even single rooms. Elliott's button works of 1837 in Vittoria Street is probably the quarter's first purpose-built factory. By the 1860s factory designs were of increasing architectural effect, from the late C19 by more significant local architects such as *William Doubleday* and *Arthur McKewan*.

Early C20 factory planning became more sophisticated, with e.g. T-plans of long workshop wings and front cross-ranges, giving maximum light. Constitution Hill and Great Hampton Street were largely rebuilt in the C20 on a larger scale than the rest. After the Second World War the City Council planned reconstruction of the quarter with large flatted factories, while

INNER AREAS: JEWELLERY QUARTER   175

the Summer Lane area was rebuilt piecemeal. Only one flatted factory was built, the Hockley Centre (1970–1), which failed to attract the craft firms which still dominated the industry. An alternative strategy started in 1971 with small conservation areas, expanded in the 1990s to cover the whole Jewellery Quarter, with a comprehensive study by English Heritage (2002) and a management plan to stop unsympathetic development. But pro-development policies are currently endangering the area again, with residential schemes permitted even in its industrial heart.

PLACES OF WORSHIP

ST PAUL, St Paul's Square. The last survivor of Birmingham's C18 churches. 1777–9, by *Roger Eykyn* of Wolverhampton. Upper part of the tower and spire added in 1822–3 by *Francis Goodwin*. Bomb damage repaired by *J.B. Surman*, 1949–51. The site, near the NW end of the Newhall estate, was given by Charles Colmore, undoubtedly to stimulate development. Eykyn's design was altered after criticism by *Samuel Wyatt* and a *James Gibson* of London. It is very much a pattern-book church of the period, heavily dependent on Gibbs's St Martin-in-the-Fields and St Peter, Vere Street, London. Heavy five-bay stone box with pedimented square E chancel and W tower, and slightly recessed W corners enclosing porches. Rusticated quoins, bracket cornice and two tiers of N and S windows with Gibbs-style blocked surrounds, round-headed above segmental-arched. Big Venetian E window in a relieving arch. Pedimented doorways also with blocked surrounds. *Goodwin*'s work is faced in Tixall stone. His tower follows Eykyn's design in outline, but its details are fashionably Greek: the lower octagonal stage with Ionic columns set into the diagonals, and the angle pilasters of the lowest stage of the delicate spire.

The interior is equally Gibbsian. An elliptical plaster tunnel-vault, the aisles with groin-vaults. The Ionic arcade columns stand on square piers which support the galleries, their top mouldings continuing as the base moulding of the gallery fronts. W gallery with iron columns of 1779 in the centre, extended forward by *Hansom & Welch*, 1833. Elegant E window surround by *Samuel Wyatt*, 1791, with Greek Ionic half-columns and pilasters, and oval medallions. Its pediment is by *Surman*, 1950. – Many original FITTINGS. BOX PEWS with fielded panels and, a Birmingham touch, enamel numberplates. – VICAR'S and CHURCHWARDENS' PEWS in elliptical coved recesses, W; flanking the door, BEADLES' SEATS. – CHOIR STALLS incorporating C18 panelling. – FONT. White Ionic capital on a pink granite stem. By *Peter Hollins*, 1883. – ORGAN by *George Hollins*, 1838, moved and reconstructed in 1927 by *Marcus O. Type*, with an additional case facing the gallery by *H. Ravenscroft Richards*. – ROYAL ARMS by *John Poole*, 1996, but of George III. – STAINED GLASS. E window, the Conversion of St Paul, an important piece of 1791, designed by *Benjamin West* and made by *Francis Eginton*. In the Baroque style West used at Windsor

Castle in the 1780s. The technique involves a double thickness of glass painted on inner and outer surfaces. Much by *Pearce*, 1900–7. N aisle, 2000, by *Rachel Thomas*. S aisle easternmost by *Ward & Hughes*, 1880. Around it, a delightful contemporary MONUMENT by *Peter Hollins*, 1880, to William Hollins and family. Carrara marble. Bust in Roman dress (perhaps earlier), tablets with the vine and olive plants of Psalm 128, and sculpted surround. – Other MONUMENTS. Richard Mico Wise †1826, by *Seaborne*. Sarcophagus on lions' feet; cherub in the predella. – S gallery. Sarah, Eleanor and John Legge, †1805, 1807, 1824. Oval tablet with soul ascending to a heavenly crown, by *W. Hollins*. – NW corner, several with weeping branches, e.g. William Redfern †1820 etc. by *P. Hollins*. – Others by *J. Richardson*. – CHURCHYARD. Laid out by the City Council in 1895–6, retaining some early C19 tombs.

ST GEORGE, Great Hampton Row. *Thomas Rickman*'s church of 1819–22, a landmark in the Gothic Revival, was demolished in 1960. The churchyard retains characteristic tapering octagonal cast-iron GATEPIERS (cf. Hampton Lucy, Warwickshire), and Rickman's TOMB, designed by his partner *R.C. Hussey*, 1845: a big gabled structure, much battered and defaced.

ST GEORGE, Bridge Street West. The successor church, by *Reginald Smeeton* (*Bromilow, While & Smeeton*), 1971–2. Low, brick; shallow-pitched metal roofs. A rhombus shape topped by a flèche defines the worship space, which is oddly angled inside. – Contemporary VICARAGE.

CATHOLIC APOSTOLIC CHURCH (now GREEK ORTHODOX CATHEDRAL OF ST ANDREW), Summer Hill Terrace. 1873 by *J.A. Chatwin*, one of his finest buildings, a soaring design in tough brick Gothic. A progressive plan of the type deriving from Albi: broad nave and narrow passage aisles running through the tall stepped buttresses. The W apse rises above curved porch and meeting-room extensions. The interior has excellent Butterfieldian polychromy. 'Early French' arcades: stubby columns with scalloped capitals, heavy pointed arches, and leaf decoration on the bases, all in striped and banded brickwork. Cross-arches in the aisles the same. Brick patterning in the spandrels and above the tall clerestory windows. The most startling detail is the zigzag on their sills. The E apse has a chancel arch of typical Chatwin form, again of banded brick. – Original PEWS.

CONGREGATIONAL CHAPEL (now RAMGARHIA SIKH TEMPLE), Graham Street. Built as the Highbury Independent Chapel in 1844, the only survivor of the city's larger C19 chapels. Front with projecting centre and tall round-headed windows in a 1–3–1 arrangement, divided by rusticated pilasters which rise awkwardly up to the gable.

PUBLIC BUILDINGS

BIRMINGHAM CITY UNIVERSITY INSTITUTE OF JEWELLERY, FASHION AND TEXTILES (former Municipal School for

Jewellers and Silversmiths), Vittoria Street. Converted in 1890 by *Martin & Chamberlain* from a goldsmith's factory of 1865 by *J.G. Bland*, r. This has an attractive Lombardo-Gothic front, with insistent multicoloured voussoirs and some bright tilework. Top storey of 1906 by *Cossins, Peacock & Bewlay*, who in 1911 built the S extension. Red brick mottled with blue. Three wide bays, large windows. End towers with stepped tops. Minimal detail except for a rich stone cornice. In 1992–3 *Associated Architects* added a range further S, with piers and windows echoing the 1911 design, and rebuilt much of the interior, creating an atrium with gallery access to workshops enclosed by glazed screens. The long sides are linked by bridges. It works well, combining enticing spaces with light and attractive workplaces.

UNIVERSITY COLLEGE BIRMINGHAM. This was the College of Food and Domestic Arts, with a block of 1968 in Summer Row by the *Birmingham City Architect*. MCINTYRE HOUSE, in Charlotte Street, is by *Associated Architects*, 2015, with an aggressive cantilever. Large extensions behind down Holland Street to George Street by *Glenn Howells*, 2018–20.

ASSAY OFFICE, Icknield Street. By *Glazzard Architects*, 2015. Heavy blue-brick piers and cornice. (For the former Assay Office building *see* p. 178.)

POLICE STATION, Summer Lane, N of New John Street Middleway. By *Herbert Manzoni*, City Engineer and Surveyor, dated 1939. Chamfered corner with *Moderne* entrance.

ICKNIELD STREET SCHOOL (now BHAGWAN VALMIK ASHRAM), Heaton Street. 1883 by *J.H. Chamberlain* (*Martin & Chamberlain*). One of his finest Board Schools. A picturesque composition with tall three-storey gabled ranges, falling away to single-storey blocks facing Icknield Street, E. The tower is splendid, with a Germanic spire which has four subsidiary spirelets breaking out halfway up. The main hall has an inserted ceiling. In the smaller hall, particularly fine pierced cast-iron trusses starting just above the ground.

BREARLEY/TEVIOT CHILDREN'S CENTRE, Brearley Street. By *W.T. Benslyn*, 1939. A former nursery school. The most progressive example of the International Modern style of its date in Birmingham. The wings look like 1965, with cantilevered concrete balconies (originally open) and flying staircases. Only the central brick entrance hints at the real date.

PERAMBULATIONS

1. To Caroline Street via St Paul's Square

The start is the crossing of Great Charles Street Queensway and Newhall Street (*see* p. 162). NW down NEWHALL STREET, behind mid-C20 blocks on the NE side, the POST OFFICE TOWER (now BT), 1963–7 by the *Ministry of Public Building & Works* (architect in charge *M.H. Bristow*). The city's tallest structure (499 ft, 152 metres), but utilitarian compared with

London's. On the SW side, TELEPHONE HOUSE of 1934–7, top floor c.1975. Here FLEET STREET runs SW. On its NW side, flats by *Turner Woolford Sharp*, 2003–4. On the SE side, a remarkably unspoilt example of the typical late C19 factory of the area: the former NEWMAN BROTHERS, coffin-furniture makers (Nos.16–17), 1892–4 by *Roger Harley*. Rows of segment-headed iron windows. Back in Newhall Street, NE side, BRINDLEY HOUSE, straddling the canal, by *D.K. McGowan*, 1967–8, recast. On the SW side, NEWHALL SQUARE, apartments by *Associated Architects*, 2018–20. The development incorporates two bays of Elkington's pioneer electroplating factory of 1838 alongside, and a mid-C19 warehouse at the rear. Then No.144, seven bays, later C19, and the QUEENS ARMS pub by *Joseph Wood*, 1901. Projecting gables enclose canted first-floor bays with iron crestings. Rounded corner with big gold-and-brown terracotta panel, proudly displaying Mitchell's brewery's medals. On the NE side a former printing works by *Cherrington & Stainton*, 1946–7, altered 1987. Then the former ASSAY OFFICE of 1877–8 by *A.B. Phipson*, for official testing and hallmarking of precious metal products. Originally established in 1773 in New Street, following a campaign led by Matthew Boulton. Red brick with Darley Dale stone dressings. Pilasters and a big centrepiece: Tuscan porch and Corinthian aedicule with a segmental pediment; granite columns. First-floor windows with inset lintels on Corinthian colonnettes. Royal arms on top, enclosed in an extra storey by *Ewen Harper, Bro. & Co.*, 1914. In 1885 *Phipson* added the plainer three-storey building to the SE. Many extensions, including *Harper* work (1890, 1899, 1907). Converted to flats 2016 by *Glenn Howells*, with a new entrance between the blocks. Down Charlotte Street alongside, Nos.59–60, a warehouse of c.1878.

Beyond, we enter ST PAUL'S SQUARE. In the centre, St Paul's church (p.175). The original late C18 houses are three-storeyed, with Doric porches with panelled soffits and open pediments. The best survivors are Nos.35–37, NW side, restored 1985 by *Associated Architects*. Continuing clockwise, No.34 is two houses altered in the 1930s. One original doorcase; early workshop wing behind. Then a swagger factory by *Marcus O. Type*, 1936, with giant arches, big end pediments and rusticated ground floor, a later C19 three-storey range with careful terracotta insertions, and a grey metal-clad six-storey block by *Associated Architects*, 1993, with balconies and brise-soleil. Just beyond in Cox Street, Nos.36-37, c.1920, late Free Style.

The E SIDE starts with No.24, Early Victorian classical. Nos.21–23, c.1853, plain, seven bays, much altered. Then a pseudo-Georgian range by *Jacqueline Wall*, 1988. Nos.12–14 are late C18, with some original interior details, e.g. Adam-style cornices; No.11 is mid-C19, with five close-set bays. Doorcase with broken pediment. Nos.11–14 reconstructed and flats built behind, by *Inston Sellers Hickinbotham* and *Baron Design*, 1983–7. NE down MARY ANN STREET here, *Ewen & J.A. Harper's* extension works of Taylor & Challen (for their main works *see* p. 184). No. 3, 1904–5, Free Style, with giant arches and exaggerated triangular pediments. On the E corner with Livery Street a very fine big factory of 1913–16 (*Ewen Harper, Bro. & Co.*), with a whiff of Peter Behrens's AEG turbine factory in Berlin. Round the far corner in Water Street, a smaller block of 1910–11. On the opposite, W corner of Mary Ann Street a wartime block, then Nos. 89–91 Livery Street of *c.* 1908, with larky Free Style doorcases, and the GOTHIC WORKS by *Sidney H. Vaughton*, 1902, actually more Jacobean. Good lettering between the windows. T-plan, with a workshop wing. On the S SIDE of St Paul's Square, 1980s Postmodern and reproduction classical. No. 1 on the corner of Ludgate Hill, late C18. Unusual doorcase with half-columns and husk garland frieze. (Gutted 1981.)

LUDGATE HILL has modest C19 industrial premises. No. 21, on the SE corner with Water Street, is a warehouse of *c.* 1854, extended at the rear. Segment-headed windows recessed in tall panels, ground-floor openings recessed in arches, Italianate bracket cornice. GRIFFIN HOUSE is by *Holland W. Hobbiss* and *M.A.H. Hobbiss*, 1956–7. No. 17 is by *De Lacy Aherne*, 1912, with impressive giant arches. Flat conversion, top floor, E extension 1997 by *Mark Humphries*.

Back on the square, the w corner of Ludgate Hill has a former bank of 1898 by *Sydney Allcock* with Jacobean entrance and oriel. Then flats by *Turner Woolford Sharp*, 2005, and a late C19 generating station, converted to flats 2003. On the W SIDE, Nos. 55–56 represents at least two original houses. On the Charlotte Street front, l., a Venetian window with Gothick glazing. The doorway below is by *Holland W. Hobbiss*, 1934; also the ground-floor arches and cornice to the square, etc. Nos. 50–54 by *G.F. Hawkes*, 1902–3 for E.L. Gyde, jeweller, with big cornices and banded pilasters. At the rear, shopping ranges flank a narrow courtyard. Refurbished as offices by *Mark Humphries*, 1989. STEVENS TERRACE is six-storey flats by *Associated Architects*, 1980–2, the start of residential development here. Narrow bays, recessed balconies and small oriels. No. 42A on the Brook Street corner is a paper warehouse of 1890 by *Roger H. Harley*, with giant pilasters. Converted to flats with an extra floor by *Associated Architects*, 1984. On the N side facing, a big functional job of 1934, rebuilt in 1941–2 after bombing, now also flats.

Now SW along BROOK STREET. On the NW side, the ROYAL BIRMINGHAM SOCIETY OF ARTISTS, a former warehouse by *Marcus O. Type*, 1912–13. Strongly articulated, with typical Type round windows. Bronze lamp and plaques of 1912 by *Crouch & Butler*, from the former gallery in New Street (p. 150). Opposite, a little Gothic warehouse of *c.* 1868. On the NE corner with Newhall Street, BAKER & FINNEMORE'S plain Neo-Georgian factory by *Ewen Harper, Bro. & Co.*, 1911 and 1915. On the NW side facing, Nos. 200–202 and 204–206, 1900 and 1905, the latter Free Style with big lunettes with sun-ray voussoirs; both, surprisingly, by *F.H. Thomason*. Brook Street continues

SW as George Street with, at the far end, NW side, the big NEW HALL WORKS, a pin factory: r. end of 1847, l. part with central attic and royal arms of after 1861. Industrial classicism, with segment-headed windows in deep reveals.

Newhall Street also bends W, becoming GRAHAM STREET. On the N side SOVEREIGN COURT, quite convincing industrial-style offices by *Sinclair Architects*, 1990. On the S side 1990s flats, then the Ramgarhia Sikh Temple (p. 176). Next on the N side the VICTORIA WORKS, built for the pen-nib maker Joseph Gillott in 1839–40, perhaps by *Charles Edge*. First the yard wall, with pilasters, cornice and a later C19 medallion of Queen Victoria under a big curved pediment. To the r., the curved roof of a block by *Mark Humphries*, 1989–90, an early Birmingham example of High Tech. The factory is a dignified block with plain sashes and, on the second floor, small-paned iron-framed windows. Slightly projecting centre with heavy stone entrance surround. Shallow plan, with workshops lit from both sides. Across Frederick Street, the very large ARGENT CENTRE was Wiley's pen works, by *J. G. Bland*, 1862–3. Nine bays by fifteen with a later N extension. Lombardic style, in bright red, white and blue-brick and stone detail. First- and second-floor two-light windows linked under relieving arches. The corner turrets have restored pyramid roofs. Again, a shallow plan with full-width workshops. Office conversion by *Bonham Seager*, 1993.

We continue W along the narrow, ancient LEGGE LANE, until recent demolitions lined by C19 factories on both sides. The N side remains. No. 3 is a pencil-case works by *Essex, Nicol & Goodman*, 1893, terracotta, with a big shaped gable. Contrasting doorcases. No. 6, paired passage-entry houses and workshops by *William Tadman Foulkes*, 1885, late for this combination.

The lane turns N, with on the E the exceptionally well-preserved former ALABASTER & WILSON jewellery factory. By *J. P. Osborne*, 1892; E extension 1899. Moulded brick strings; W doorway with triplet lights above, under a pediment. To the SW, MANTON'S works of 1913 by *William Doubleday*. An eyecatcher entrance tower in cream faience with big entrance arch, foliage frieze and battlemented top. Flat conversion 2003. Beyond, N, a small square with on the E side a former FIRE STATION by *T. G. Price*, 1909–10. Bright red brick, stone dressings, Wren-style cupola. On the NW corner the former GEORGE & DRAGON pub. Early C19, extended and fitted out as a pub by 1875. Paired bracket cornice, Gothic canted bays. To the W, Nos. 103–106 (S side), passage-entry houses of *c.* 1855.

ALBION STREET continues E from the N side of the square. On the N side, flats by *Bryant Priest Newman*, 2003. Nos. 63–65, S side, is a factory by *W. T. Foulkes*, 1883. Round-headed windows, heavy attic-like top floor. Nos. 58–61, *c.* 1839, two pairs of passage-entry or 'three-quarter' houses, with side entrances from a central passage. Rear workshop ranges and canted bays to the street by *W. T. Orton*, 1900. Nos. 54–57 of 1837, similarly adapted. On the N side, Late Georgian survivors. No. 33 has

INNER AREAS: JEWELLERY QUARTER

pilasters with Soanian incised panels. Nos. 34–36, set back, of four bays with side extensions, has a Doric doorcase with open pediment and wheel fanlight. No. 50, S side, a workshop of c. 1870. Gothic doorway with heavy traceried fanlight. On the SW corner of FREDERICK STREET, No. 53, c. 1866, with round arches. On the E side, just S, Nos. 14–15, stucco Italianate of c. 1870 with unusual window heads decorated with circles, and bearded-head keystones. Nos. 19–20 are Edwardian classical by *T. G. Price*, 1908. No. 22 is a jolly Jacobean bank by *Hipkiss & Stephens*, dated 1901 in the semicircular gables. THOMAS FATTORINI, by *Mansell & Mansell*, 1894–5, is good restrained classical with sparing Jacobean detail. No. 25, on the opposite corner with Regent Street, was the Berndorf Metal Co. warehouse, by *Douglas J. Williams*, 1889. Impressively dour, with stilted segment-headed window arches. On the W side, No. 48, a mongrel of c. 1870. No. 47 is a manufactory and house by *Foulkes & Ryland*, 1879, its projecting bays pulled in and rising into dormers. No. 46, the QUALITY WORKS, by *Ewen Harper*, 1881, an even later house and factory, going Queen Anne. The first-floor windows lit warehouse space, with living rooms below and bedrooms above. No. 45, set back, has a front of 1882 by *Harper* hiding a house of c. 1820, originally in landscaped grounds. No. 43 was a civic restaurant of 1949–50 by *W. Norman Twist*. Opposite, No. 26 has an Italianate front of c. 1860. No. 27, fine Greek Revival of c. 1825–30 with coupled Doric columns. Roughly contemporary, Nos. 30 and 31, severe and cubic. No. 32 is a factory of 1914 by *Crouch, Butler & Savage*. Faience and green glazed brick (cf. their RBSA gallery in New Street, p. 150). T-plan, with a flat-roofed rear shopping wing.

At the cross-roads ahead a classical CLOCK TOWER of 1903, commemorating Chamberlain's return from South Africa. Bracket lamps reinstated to the original design 1990. On the SE corner a mildly Baroque BARCLAYS BANK by *Cossins, Peacock & Bewlay*, 1905. On the NE corner, the ROSE VILLA TAVERN of 1919–20 by *Wood & Kendrick*. Brick and terracotta, Jacobean style, but sober compared to pubs of c. 1900. The interior, confused by late C20 Victoriana, retains painted glass in the bar, with orange and purple ships on green waves, and original tilework, the best in the lobby and stair hall: cornices with garlands, and an alcove with a fireplace and a panel of maidens bearing flowers. On the NW corner, a much-altered and cut-down bank, retaining a rich doorway by *Daniel Arkell*, 1892. Tympanum with a glassblower and metalworker, and statue niche.

Now W down WARSTONE LANE. On the N side, the GATE-HOUSE of the CHURCH OF ENGLAND CEMETERY, 1847–8 by *Hamilton & Medland*. Puginian Gothic, with steep gable and stone oriel, but in beautifully toned Staffordshire blue brick. The chapel (dem. 1954) lay N, on the edge of a sunken amphitheatre, formed from an early C19 sandpit. Entrances to CATACOMBS in its retaining wall. On the S side, AQUINAS

House by *Thomas Frederick Proud*, 1882. Corner entrance with a diagonal spirelet. Impressive s factory wing with round-headed windows, articulated by pilasters corbelled out into chimneystacks. Original iron-framed glazing. Iron-beam and shuttered-concrete floors, an early use of the technique. Later C19 factories continue down TENBY STREET NORTH, e.g. Nos. 8–10 by *Osborn & Reading*, 1879.

E of the clock tower, Warstone Lane leads to GOLDEN SQUARE, a bleak grass and paved area of 2014–15. Landscape architects *Capita*, with the artist *David Patten*. Single-storey front block by *BPN*, in gold-coloured aluminium and cor-ten steel. Behind looms the HOCKLEY CENTRE (BIG PEG), an eight-storey flatted factory of 1970–1 by *Peter Hing & Jones*. Characteristic of the date the staircase projections with V-shaped tops. Opposite, Nos. 35–39, NORTHAMPTON PARADE, originally of *c.* 1830–40. Then two Venetian Gothic factories of 1870–1, No. 29 with juicy capitals and corbels, Nos. 27–28 with fanciful window details.

Now back and s down VITTORIA STREET. On the E side, Nos. 97–99 are of *c.* 1840–50, Nos. 85–87A a factory of *c.* 1870. Then a Brutalist intrusion by *Dron & Wright*, 1965, grey-brown brick with concrete floor bands. Beyond, Nos. 59–61 by *J.P. Osborne*, 1901, with large workshop windows. On the w side, the Institute of Jewellery (p. 176). Then Nos. 66–68 of *c.* 1875, with round-arched first-floor windows with little inset tympana. Nos. 60–64 is an early purpose-built factory of *c.* 1837–8, probably by *Charles Edge*, for William Elliott, button-maker. Plain brick with slightly projecting centre, recessed rounded corner. Extended up Regent Street by *Douglas Williams*, 1881. Also in Regent Street, No. 3, an ornate Italianate factory of 1872. Nos. 54–58, on the rounded sw corner, is by *Essex & Goodman*, 1904–5. Big windows divided by brick pilasters and a terracotta cornice. Nos. 48–52, early C19, retain round-headed doorcases with incised decoration. Then a run of bigger mid-C19 factories: Unity Works (Nos. 36–46) and Nos. 30–34, both *c.* 1866, No. 28 of 1859, early for Gothic; Nos. 22–24, a much-altered block of back-to-backs of *c.* 1840. Returning up the E side, No. 33 of *c.* 1881 has the wall effectively cut back to create giant pilasters with rich Gothic capitals. Nos. 35–37, 'three-quarter' houses of *c.* 1832 with a big Doric doorcase to the common entry. On the corner with Regent Place, STANDARD WORKS, an early flatted factory, by *Thomas F. Williams*, 1879–80. Plain giant pilasters above, five separate entrances, heavily rusticated and vermiculated, one on the rounded corner. Nos. 51–53 are former houses of *c.* 1830.

Now E down REGENT PLACE, with many good small factories. On the N side, Nos. 12–14, *c.* 1883, probably by *A.H. Hamblin*, in J.H. Chamberlain's Board School Gothic. No. 16, Free Style by *J.G. Dunn*, 1910, with Voysey-style piers rising above the parapet. Entrance with prominent segmental hood. Opposite, No. 17 by *Martin & Martin*, 1905–6, simple brick, Arts and Crafts-influenced, with windows recessed in giant arches. It encases part of a house of 1824. N again, 1820s houses including No. 20, l., a single bay with side entry (*c.*1824). No. 32, SQUIRREL WORKS, another *J. G. Dunn* design, 1912–13, its square piers rising clear of the cornice. Deep-arched entrance set flush. Residential conversion by *Sjölander da Cruz*, 2018. No. 53 is a paper warehouse by *J. H. Hawkes & Son*, 1906, restrained Free Style brick and terracotta. Further E on the N side, Nos. 60–70, an early purpose-built factory of 1852–3. Nine bays, the end entrance bays wider and with pediments to the first-floor windows.

Back W, then N up REGENT PARADE. Ahead, the bulky rear of HERITAGE COURT, flats by *Lawrence & Wrightson*, 2001–2, with corrugated and glazed roofs. On the NE corner, No. 14, a house of *c.*1840. The rubbed brick lintels and doorway with recessed bolection surround suggest *Bateman & Drury*. No. 15 round the corner, similar but altered. No. 16, a warehouse of *c.*1838. Beyond, on the SE corner with CAROLINE STREET, No. 65 of 1836, probably by *Fallows & Hart*, built as house and factory for a silversmith, George Unite. Three-bay front angled to the curve of the street; Ionic porch. No. 42, to the NE, housed PICKERING & MAYALL, case-makers, from *c.*1900 until the early C21. Built as two houses *c.*1826–7. One surviving Greek Doric doorcase. Workshop wing along Kenyon Street. SE down Caroline Street towards St Paul's Square, the BLOC hotel by *BPN*, blue brick, with carefully devised window openings, 2011. Opposite, Nos. 13–15, unusual early C20 Neo-Georgian of 1908 etc. by *Henry Hendriks*. Behind it, Nos. 67–71 Northwood Street, a late C19 brass foundry.

2. Constitution Hill, Great Hampton Street and the northern Jewellery Quarter

Constitution Hill and Great Hampton Street are the road NW out of Birmingham towards West Bromwich. The present wide, straightened road dates from turnpiking in 1727. We start at St Chad's Circus, by the cathedral, and go NW down OLD SNOW HILL. On the NE side by Shadwell Street, Focus Foyer by *Ian Simpson Architects*, 1997–8. On the SW side, No. 86, a cubic Neo-Georgian former YMCA by *Harry Weedon & Partners*, 1952–3, incorporating part of the structure of a music hall of 1885–6 by *W. J. Ballard*; QUEENS CHAMBERS by *J. H. Hawkes & Son*, 1902–3; and a former bank, Italian Renaissance by *Dempster & Heaton*, 1892. Opposite, flats by *Associated Architects*, 1996–7. Dominating the view on the acute corner ahead, the stunning circular red terracotta tower of the former H.B. SALE factory, by *William Doubleday & James R. Shaw*, 1895–6. Eclectic Gothic with Spanish touches and an almost oriental dome. Rich foliage band with raised lettering, and busts in roundels. Summer Lane (*see* p. 186) goes NE here. In Hampton Street, N, a factory by *G. E. Pepper*, 1911 (E side), with bold giant arches. We go NW, up CONSTITUTION HILL. On the sw side, the huge BISMILLAH BUILDING was Barkers' electroplating works, 1901–3 by *Newton & Cheatle*. Red terracotta, Free Style. Enormous details too: segmental pediment, giant order to l. and r., entrance with elongated voussoirs and broken pediment. End towers with segmental parapets and triangular pediments. Residential conversion 1993–5. On the NE side, Nos. 19–21 by *Henry R. Wintle*, next to an Italianate corner block by *William Davis*, with much yellow-and-cream glazed brick: both of 1881. The HEN AND CHICKENS pub of *c.*1875 on the next corner must be *Davis* as well. Beyond, Nos. 31–51, wild Italian Gothic of 1881–2 by *J.S. Davis*. Canted bays (cf. Nos. 391–396 Summer Lane, p. 186), cornice with pierced stone discs. On the sw side the former TAYLOR & CHALLEN works. By *E.F. Reynolds* the showroom and office with stripped pilasters of 1919–21, l., and single-storey showroom of 1915 with big pedimental gable, united by a giant arcade with typical imposts. Then a functional block of 1938 by *Watson & Johnson* with staircase tower. Nos. 60–62, *c.*1822–3, was a japanning factory; simple, handsome six-bay front. Original royal arms. Behind, a foundry of 1861 designed by *Joseph Taylor* and *S.W. Challen*. Further up, the former WHITE HORSE CELLARS (No. 106), restrained Queen Anne of 1890, *J.A. Chatwin*'s only known pub design.

GREAT HAMPTON STREET starts 150 yds beyond, with the former GOTHIC pub of 1867–8, very Ruskinian. Pointed arches with voussoirs of red, white and blue brick, a little oriel and steep dormers. Delightful seven-sided turret and spirelet. Beyond, the Quality Works of 1914 by *E.H. Wigley* (Nos. 9–12), minimal Tudor. The SYLVIA WORKS (now Hampton House) is Neo-Wren by *George E. Pepper*, dated 1912. Opposite, the former Cannings factory (now the UNIVERSITY OF LAW), by *Peacock & Bewlay*, 1936, a stripped block with a big rounded corner. Back on the NE side, No. 16, the excellent former J. ASHFORD & SON works of 1912 by *Arthur McKewan*. Free Style end bays linked by a giant arch, contrasted with a Wren-style rusticated ground floor. Enveloped by *BPN Architects*' flats, 2019. On the corner of Harford Street, the simple CHURCH INN, *c.*1840. On the next corner a bank by *J.A. Chatwin*, 1899. Buff terracotta, like a posh pub, with a domed octagonal turret supported on a big lion's-head and foliage corbel. Shaped gables, one pierced by chimneys. NE extension by *Associated Architects*, 1989–90. On the sw side here, three former factories all by *George E. Pepper*, 1919. Standard six-bay elevations with projecting ends, but varied treatment: CLAYTON-WRIGHT, rather Arts and Crafts with bold stone details; A.J. PEPPER & CO., cream faience with coloured diamonds; G.F. WESTWOOD & SON, heavily Baroque. Then a former Lucas factory of *c.*1926, converted to flats by *Nicol Thomas*, 2000–2. NE side, early C19 buildings extended over front gardens: No. 33, with a Greek Revival front with fluted pilasters; No. 34, the LORD CLIFDEN pub, with a street frontage of *c.*1910 with semicircular window mullion. Nos. 41–43, on the corner with Hockley Street, Italianate of *c.*1860 with a rich cornice. On the next corner the

INNER AREAS: JEWELLERY QUARTER

PELICAN WORKS, with its crest: an electroplating factory of c.1868. A tightly articulated palazzo with arcaded ground-floor windows and segment-headed lights above. Large workshop wing behind. Next on the SW side two Italian Gothic factories: Nos. 83–84, 1871–2; Nos. 80–82 (the GREAT HAMPTON WORKS, for button-making), by *Yeoville Thomason*, 1872, richer and more varied, with ornate brick voussoirs. Nos. 69–73, dates between 1824 and 1840, are partly refronted but preserve their domestic scale, set back behind gardens. Nos. 69–70, 1830, retain their simple architraved sashes and doorcases with open pediments and incised ornament. Restored 1995–6 for the Birmingham Conservation Trust by *Frank Brophy Associates*. Long rear shopping wings of 1872–5 with iron-framed windows. Opposite, the massive Nos. 60–64, CROWNGATE HOUSE: corner block to Well Street by *J.G. Dunn, Dallas & Lloyd*, 1913, extended by *Dallas & Lloyd*, 1919–22. Brick with terracotta bands and alternating voussoirs. A grand version of Dunn's Squirrel Works, with giant arches and entrance bays marked by piers rising clear of the parapet, the entrance arches flush with the pier fronts. Above, chequer faience panels and little shaped parapets.

HOCKLEY HILL is the continuation of Great Hampton Street. It starts on the N corner with a former bank by *Thomason & Whitwell*, 1892–3 (NE extension 1901), stirring together French classical, Jacobean and Baroque. On the SW side, altered early C19 buildings. The former HARRY SMITH ironmongers (Nos. 17–19) comprises two early C19 houses flanking a remarkable steel-framed block by *Arthur Edwards*, 1913, quite functional except for the simplest dentil cornice. Good original lettering. GEM BUILDINGS by *Wood & Kendrick*, 1913, is equally impressive. Four bays, huge windows, classical tops to the end towers. Finally a Neo-Wren POST OFFICE by *Edward Cropper*, 1911. Down an alley to its l. into KEY HILL for the remarkable functional white rear elevation of Gem Buildings, with more lettering, and the Nonconformist CEMETERY of 1835, with original railings and tremendous Greek domed piers by *Charles Edge*. In KEY HILL DRIVE, E of the cemetery, houses of c.1860. At the far end an alley runs SE into HYLTON STREET. This area, on a grid pattern – Spencer and Branston streets run NW–SE across Vyse and Hockley streets – is one of the most tightly packed in the quarter. Turning r., Nos. 38–40 of c.1866 is a well-preserved factory with three doorways for different occupiers. Nos. 16–24, 1920 by *W.J. Davis*, was an extension to Nos. 8–14 of c.1880, with round-headed arcading above iron-framed windows separated by pilasters. From 1916 W.H. Haseler Ltd and Liberty's store made 'Cymric' silver in partnership here. On the W corner to Vyse Street a good block of c.1847–50 with Ionic doorcases. On the NE corner of Spencer Street, opposite, ANVIC HOUSE, houses of c.1850–1 with an added third storey and E workshop wing, impressively glazed, with iron colonnettes, c.1875.

Going S down Vyse Street, Nos. 37–38 of 1847. Four central doorways in an Ionic surround, to shops and to living space above. On the E side Nos. 90–94, *c.* 1864, with big Doric doorcases and dentil cornice. No. 94 has a contemporary workshop range to Hockley Street with a third storey added early, and a seven-bay extension of 1887. (Early features reportedly surviving include narrow, ladder-like stairs and goods chutes.) Down HOCKLEY STREET, on the NW corner with Spencer Street, PLANTAGENET BUILDINGS of *c.* 1871, the most opulent Italianate design here: linked ground- and first-floor windows with canopied architraves, rich cornice with single and paired brackets. In SPENCER STREET, Nos. 93–107, modest mid-C19 houses and factories converted for the Duchy of Cornwall by *Derek Latham Architects*, 1989, into the JEWELLERY BUSINESS CENTRE. Entrance arch with sculpted steel gates by *Michael Johnson*. The JEWELLERS ARMS opposite, SE, is of *c.* 1840 with a modest mid-Victorian pub front, a rare survival.

Further down Hockley Street, and NW into BRANSTON STREET. On the SW side here, Nos. 114–124, houses of 1856–61, refurbished in the early 1990s. Nos. 115–121 opposite, houses and workshops of *c.* 1857–8. Nos. 75–79 on the S corner with Vyse Street, a modest Neo-Wren factory of 1909 by *George E. Pepper*, with a workshop wing down Branston Street; S extension, 1914, also *Pepper*. Converted in 1990–1 by *Dyer Associates* for the MUSEUM OF THE JEWELLERY QUARTER.

3. Summer Lane

Starting from Old Snow Hill, SW. On the NW side Nos. 391–396 SUMMER LANE, picturesque Gothic by *J.S. Davis*, 1883. On the SE side, at the corner of Loveday Street, a big former GENERATING STATION by *Ewen & J.A. Harper*, 1902 etc. Heavyweight classical detail. Opposite, a tiny former MORTUARY CHAPEL by *S.T. Walker*, 1930. Much further up, the BARREL pub by *J.P. Osborne & Son*, 1928. It turns the corner into Tower Street, W, with the former ST NICOLAS'S VICARAGE by *Bateman & Bateman*, 1913–14, N side. Central chimney and flanking bays. Back on Summer Lane, No. 308, *c.* 1830–40, the doorcase looking like *Bateman & Drury*. Running E along Brearley Street alongside, the former NEWEY BROTHERS works. Corner block of 1937, then seven bays of 1850, topped by a set of royal arms on an inscribed panel 'J.G. NEWEY PATENTEE'. The far range with basic pilasters and swept-up parapet is by *M.J. Butcher*, 1916. Brearley/Teviot Children's Centre (p. 177) is beyond. Further up Summer Lane, New John Street Middleway and the C. BRANDAUER & CO. WORKS (former). A big steel-pen factory of 1862. Three-storey S range with rows of round- and segment-headed windows, pedimented doorway and big cart entrance, all in polychromatic brick. Circular staircase projection behind. Long W side wing, with a N cross-wing. Front range extended E, to a more austere design, by *J.H. Hawkes*, 1896–8. Furthest N extension with chimney also by Hawkes, 1887. Empty since *c.* 2002.

OTHER BUILDINGS

SUMMER HILL TERRACE. No. 3, a five-bay villa of *c.* 1820 with Ionic porch. Late C20 wings.

Further up on the corner of Powell Street, CENTURY BUILDINGS, by *Hipkiss & Stephens*, 1901, incorporating a three-bay house of *c.* 1794.

HEATON HOUSE, Camden Street. An austere detached hipped-roof villa of *c.* 1823, now engulfed in flats by *D5*, 2021.

GREAT HAMPTON WORKS, corner of Great Hampton Row and Smith Street. Dated 1917. By *Marcus O. Type*. Brick and cream terracotta, still Edwardian classical, but with quirky detail.

THE GUN QUARTER
N of the centre

A smaller version of the Jewellery Quarter to the W. In the C18 the various trades were concentrated NW of Steelhouse Lane. The S part, around Whittall Street, went for hospitals and the inner ring road. But just N of St Chad's Queensway, wedged between big C21 developments, a small area survives with the feel of the pre-1960s quarter.

To the E of St Chad's Cathedral, the pavement slopes down into BATH STREET. In front, the GUNMAKERS ARMS, *c.* 1835–40. Architraved windows upstairs. Shop-like ground-floor front, perhaps original. To the r. a contemporary factory range, and a former WESLEYAN CHAPEL of 1839, now flats, with a severe parapeted front. Opposite, with its entrance in LOVEDAY STREET, E, the WELSH CONGREGATIONAL CHURCH (Eglwys yr Annibynwyr) by *Clifford Tee & Gale*, 1969. It faces a late C18 row, Nos. 44A–49, a unique survivor in the city centre. All one-bay and three-storeyed, Nos. 47–49 with C19 shopfronts. Adjoining them in Price Street, a workshop block of *c.* 1825–30 with iron-framed windows. All restored by West Midlands County Council, 1983–4 (project architect *M. Campbell*, County Architect/Planner *Alfred A. Wood*). Next in Loveday Street, the BULL pub, also late C18, with a minimal Venetian window on the first floor, and No. 44, slightly later, with a segmental-headed first-floor window. Both restored by Ansells Brewery (*J. S. Howell*), 1985–7. Behind the pub is a tiny, older cottage, here by 1781.

In Loveday Street N of the Wesleyan chapel is a former CATHOLIC SCHOOL of 1839, converted into a factory *c.* 1912. Big lancets still visible in the gable-end. Diagonally opposite, a smart three-storey house of *c.* 1845, with a N wing added for industrial use. Most of this wing, and the round-headed corner doorway, are from alterations of 1896 by *Jethro Cossins*.

SHADWELL STREET continues W from the cross-roads with a mid-C19 workshop range, then a gun factory, here by 1860, with a heavy doorcase. Round the corner in Little Shadwell Street, a range of 1839–40, built for a coachbuilder. Opposite, overweening flats by *GRID*, 2019–20: twenty-two-storey tower to the canal, lower ranges with 'industrial' gabled tops. Going E, PRINCIP STREET has a three-storey works range, probably mid-C19, remodelled by *G.T. Haylock*, 1878. Opposite (s side), No. 3, a handsome classical factory, probably 1840s. Minimal Wyatt window above the cart entrance. Then a gabled works and a smaller three-storey one, both mid-Victorian. No. 19, N side, is Late Georgian; Nos. 16–18, a works of the 1840s, with cart entrance running through to the canal. Lastly one big surviving doorcase of a rivet factory of 1895 by *William Jenkins*. To the s, at the corner of Price Street and Lancaster Street, a former INFANT WELFARE CENTRE by *Ewen Harper Bro. & Co.*, 1935, with two fine plaques of children by *Bloye*. Beyond, at Lancaster Circus, on the l. the former Halfords cycles' works and offices, now council offices, by *J. Alfred Harper & Son*, 1959. Behind it in Corporation Street the former KING EDWARD INN, by *Wood & Kendrick*, dated 1905, Jacobean style. Opposite, past the flyover, is Aston University (*see* Eastside, below).

EASTSIDE
NE of the centre

The city's major early C21 central regeneration area. The demolition of the elevated Masshouse Circus in 2002 broke the inner ring road and enabled development. The s boundary, beyond Curzon Street Station, will be the elevated terminus of HS2 (built from 2020). The masterplan of 2002 by *HOK International* was centred on a new library. When this went to Centenary Square instead, a new plan was drawn up by *Glenn Howells* in 2011. It seems that the idea of a new city park dictated the plan. Buildings fill spaces in a windy emptiness. Historic survivals, including the magnificent Curzon Street Station, are pushed into corners. The decline from Brindleyplace is precipitous. Apart from the park, the good things are the Conservatoire, the tower in Bartholomew Row and, surprisingly, the car park. Aston University to the N is treated first; other public buildings are in the perambulation.

ASTON UNIVERSITY
Gosta Green

The Birmingham Municipal Technical School began in 1895, with majestic buildings in Suffolk Street by *Essex, Nicol & Goodman* (dem. *c.* 1965). It became the Central Technical College in 1927, the first College of Advanced Technology in 1956, and a University in 1966.

The approach from the city is E across James Watt Queensway. To the N the former CENTRAL FIRE STATION of 1934–5 by *Sir Herbert H. Humphries*, City Engineer and Surveyor. Three-storey Neo-Georgian brick ranges; big stepped-up entrance tower in the short SW side, of Portland stone. Archway with side footways, top with Corinthian aedicules, owing something to the English Baroque of Hawksmoor. The interior courtyard is more contemporary, with long balconies to the accommodation blocks. In the centre a tall hose tower. Converted to student accommodation by *K4*, 2015.

Beyond, NE, is the University's MAIN BUILDING. A competition was won in 1937 by *Ashley & Newman*. After the war, construction began to a slightly amended design (*H. Fitzroy Robinson* and *Hubert Bull*) in 1949. Two-thirds was completed in 1955; the N side followed in 1956–62. Stripped Beaux Arts classicism, a huge buff-brick block with strip windows: impressive but not lovable. Full-height S and N wings by *Fitzroy Robinson*, 1958–61 and 1963–6: more up-to-date, with aggregate panels. The formal W entrance now faces the Lancaster Circus flyover, so *Hinton Brown Langstone* added a new glazed reception area at the SE in 1986, with full-height red and blue lifts.

A development plan of 1967 by *Robert Matthew, Johnson-Marshall & Partners* was abandoned in the 1970s. The CAMPUS hardly seems planned at all. The centre is now at GOSTA GREEN, E of the Main Building. FOUNTAIN by *Angela Conner*, 1994 (to be moved). On the N, an empty space where the Students' Union, by *Kelly & Surman*, 1964–6, has been demolished. On the E side, the front of the former DELICIA CINEMA, with an Ionic portico *in antis* and stepped attic, by *James & Lister Lea & Sons*, 1923, retained in the glass-walled EUROPEAN BIODIVERSITY RESEARCH INSTITUTE, by *Associated Architects*, 2013. The SACKS OF POTATOES pub, *c.*1790, survives from the first development on the old Aston road. Opposite, a new ten-storey building by *Hawkins/Brown* has been approved, 2021: shaped like three huge car air filters on top of each other. Lister Street runs downhill NE here. The pub with many arched windows and a steep hipped roof, on the SE side, was the offices of Holt's, Birmingham's largest early C20 brewer. By *C.H. Collett*, 1906. Beyond are the blocks of Aston Science Park, developed from the 1980s. Over the Digbeth Branch Canal, ASTON UNIVERSITY ENGINEERING ACADEMY, with dark horizontal cladding, is by *Feilden Clegg Bradley*, 2013. Opposite, the NATIONAL COLLEGE FOR HIGH SPEED RAIL, pale browns, lots of verticals, by *Bond Bryan*, 2016–17.

Back to Gosta Green and S down Woodcock Street, No. 10 (E side), a crisp office block with unusual oriels, by *Associated Architects*, 2011. For University buildings on the W side *see* below. Further S here, former swimming baths, now the WOODCOCK SPORTS CENTRE, an intriguing design by *Arthur McKewan*, 1924–6. Maroon and bluish brick, with recessed centre and screen with entrance arch. Tall chimneys and steep roofs, but contemporary window designs. Inside, a lovely surprise: the former FIRST CLASS BATH of 1902 by *Frederick W. Lloyd*, with pierced cast-iron roof trusses, cream tilework banded with blue and maroon, and studded terracotta arches to the cubicles. Extensions, including recasting of the E wing, by *Robothams*, 2011 etc.

Returning to Gosta Green, on the l., running round the corner, the NELSON BUILDING, by *Sir Basil Spence, Glover & Ferguson*, 1978 (after Spence's death), a large brick sandwich. W extension for ASTON BUSINESS SCHOOL by *ADP*, 2006: brighter brick, on pilotis. Set back on the S, the LIBRARY, again *Spence, Glover & Ferguson*, 1975, one of Spence's last buildings. Once the finest building here: a massive cube of brickwork articulated by broad piers all round, with just a curved turret on the N to hint at Spence's early Scottish Baronial idiom. Now disfigured by a full-height glazed extension, and glass infill elsewhere, by *ADP*, 2010.

The student residential area to the S is centred on Chancellor's Lake, with a triangular metal PEACE SCULPTURE by *William Pye*, 1985, moved here in 1991. The best part is LAKESIDE APARTMENTS, by *Feilden Clegg Bradley*, 1999, long sinuous brick blocks with bands of terracotta panels, and a S tower. The rest, replacing *Robert Matthew, Johnson-Marshall*'s sober ranges and towers of 1971 etc., is by *LOC Associates*, from 2007. New STUDENTS' UNION by *Robothams*, 2019.

PERAMBULATION

Going NE up MOOR STREET from St Michael's church (p. 123), on the SE side the angular black CLAYTON HOTEL by *pHp architects*, 2011–13, and two residential blocks from the first Masshouse development, twisty front one by *David McLean Design*, 2006, rear by *bluegreen*, 2007. Opposite, EXCHANGE SQUARE, a buff-brick complex of serviced apartments by *Stephenson Studio*, 2017–19, with deeply recessed windows. Beyond the cross-roads, SE side, UNIVERSITY HOUSE (Birmingham City University) by *Sheppard Robson*, 2004, partly of bronzed panels behind a mesh façade. Adjoining to the S, Nos. 9–12 BARTHOLOMEW ROW, a three-storey terrace probably of *c.*1855–60. The irregularity is because Nos. 9–10, r., are a refacing of two houses of 1749–51, very rare survivors of the period.* Inside, some original architraves, cornices and a staircase, perhaps moved. Later additions include a C19 malthouse with a lantern. Restoration in 2017–20 by *APEC* was funded by the linked tower of student residences (THE EMPORIUM), by *IDP*. A very big neighbour at fifteen storeys, but carefully set back, and clad in copper-coloured aluminium.

Moor Street continues NE as JENNENS ROAD. On the NW side the dominating quadrant front of BIRMINGHAM METROPOLITAN COLLEGE, by *Bond Bryan*, 2003–4. Beyond it, Aston University (p. 188). On the SE side JENNENS COURT, *c.*2006, more student flats, and ORMISTON ACADEMY, by *Nicholas Hare Architects*, 2009–11, clad in corrugated metal.

---

*They originally faced ST BARTHOLOMEW'S CHURCH, 1749–50 by *William Hiorne* (dem. 1943), a classical design with a little cupola.

Beyond, the ROYAL BIRMINGHAM CONSERVATOIRE, by *Feilden Clegg Bradley*, 2015–17. Clearly the best building here, but jammed between the dual carriageway and a poky rear yard. A cranked block faced in pale buff brick, with complex textures: vertical lines of projecting headers, more patterning above, and an array of small classroom windows. It is rather bleak, like a well-detailed warehouse; and for a monumental building, the entrance on the crank is trite and unimpressive. A through foyer nicely connects the levels inside. The hidden s front sharply delineates glazed foyer and brick auditorium. Beyond, set back, a fun CAR PARK, all metal sheets and projecting rectangles, with carefully placed opaque glass panels. By *Birmingham City Council Urban Design (Mark Sloane)*, 2009–10. Across Cardigan Street the brick and terracotta shell of the BELMONT WORKS, 1899 by *Frederick W. Lloyd*, awaits restoration (restoration and extension by *Aukett Swanke* proposed, 2020). Opposite, NW, the BLACK HORSE pub, by *James & Lister Lea & Sons*, 1907, brick and terracotta with semicircular-topped gables, retained in a mixed-use development by *Consarc*, 2015–19.

Now SE down Cardigan Street, into the new BIRMINGHAM CITY UNIVERSITY CAMPUS, a disappointing group. JOSEPH PRIESTLEY HOUSE, E side, by *Aukett Swanke*, 2016, with insistent fins, has been taken as the administration building. Gopsal Street runs E alongside, with the EAGLE AND BALL pub of *c*.1850. First floor with a nice contrast of pedimented windows. Penn Street beyond has been chopped off by the rear block of *Associated Architects*' CURZON BUILDING, 2015–17. Its Cardigan Street front has more insistent verticals, bright red in the big framed entrance. Opposite, the PARKSIDE BUILDING, 2013, also *Associated Architects*, also bristling with fins. Its s front has an angled forebuilding and darker masses behind. Full-height foyer with nice arrangement of stairs and balconies. But apart from the ground floor of Parkside, neither building acknowledges the Eastside park to the s (*see* below).

Here we reach CURZON STREET. Opposite, remains of the Grand Junction Railway station SCREEN WALL of 1838 by *Joseph Franklin*, with the bottoms of Doric pilasters. Its central composition had Roman triumphal arches. To the E, the DIGBETH BRANCH CANAL of 1799 runs below. On the towpath to the s, 'Curzon Street Tunnel', a series of RAILWAY BRIDGES. The splendid rusticated arch with huge dentil course is of 1837–8 by the engineer *Joseph Locke*, carrying lines into Curzon Street Station. N of Curzon Street and E of the canal, Stalinist student flats r. by *Glenn Howells*, 2015–17. All sense of enclosure, crucial to traditional Birmingham canalscape, has gone. The locks continue up N through Ashted Tunnel and the Aston University campus to Aston Turn.

LAWLEY MIDDLEWAY, E of Curzon Street, has the WHITE TOWER pub of 1931–2 by *James & Lister Lea & Sons*. To the s, the Lawley Street RAILWAY VIADUCTS. Widenings have hidden the original London & Birmingham Railway viaduct by

Robert Stephenson, 1838, which has been reconstructed, but the Grand Junction Railway viaduct by *Joseph Locke*, 1838, survives to the s, best seen from Viaduct Street, running E. Of brick, with Piranesian rusticated stone quoins, cornice and voussoirs. A second viaduct, of blue brick, abuts it on the N, of 1893, part of the widening of lines into New Street Station. At the same time the original viaduct was raised, with an additional set of arches above it, for the Grand Junction route to cross over the goods lines to Curzon Street Station.

Now we return to Curzon Street and EASTSIDE CITY PARK, by *Patel Taylor* with landscape architect *Allain Provost*, 2011–13. The narrow strip makes its mark by drawing on French traditions of formal gardening to create a succession of linked spaces. From the E, a lawn with lines of trees hides a long canal in front of the Parkside Building, with water jets from a stone wall. The canal continues in front of Millennium Point, which has a science garden. Then an area with stone steps and cor-ten steel towers (already a little passé), and another formal garden at the city end with a terminating pergola. MILLENNIUM POINT is of 1997–2001 by *Nicholas Grimshaw & Partners*, supervising architects *Mason Richards*. A steel-and-glass shed, 540 ft (165 metres) long. The W half, the THINK TANK museum of science and industry, has tilting terracotta sunscreen panels. The entrance is, awkwardly, two floors up; interiors low and claustrophobic. The N side, facing the Conservatoire, has a cylindrical Imax theatre, in grey cladding.

The original CURZON STREET STATION is in New Canal Street, just s of Millennium Point. Of 1838 by *Philip Hardwick* for the London & Birmingham Railway, the world's first long-distance railway. Built not as a passenger facility but a 'Principal Building', with offices and company board room,

Birmingham, Curzon Street Station.
Lithograph by J.C. Bourne, 1838

INNER AREAS: DIGBETH, DERITEND ETC. 193

but clearly designed to impress people with the new technology. Massively proportioned façade of fine ashlar, with giant Ionic columns, an appropriate counterpart to the Doric of the former 'Euston Arch', and a heavy central attic. Round-arched doorway with finely sculpted shields of the L&BR arms, and swags. First-floor windows with balustrades. The E elevation has giant corner pilasters and attached Ionic columns. Arches to either side, long demolished, led to a train shed with wide wrought-iron roofs by *John Joseph Bramah*. The l. arch was replaced in 1840 by a hotel block, itself demolished in 1981. Dramatic full-height stair hall with a screen of square piers on the ground floor and Greek Doric columns above. Conversion to visitor centre and exhibition for HS2 begun in 2021. To the S will be the new STATION for HS2, designed by *Grimshaw* with the engineers *WSP*.

Opposite, W, is the WOODMAN pub of 1897 by *James & Lister Lea*. Birmingham's first city pub to abandon the traditional pilastered ground floor. A subtle elevation of alternating wide and narrow bays, canted to the corner. Round-arched ground-floor windows, three-centred relieving arches above. Original bar back with round-headed panels of mirror glass, framed in marbled wood. *Minton* tiling, also in the smoke room.

DIGBETH, DERITEND, BORDESLEY AND HIGHGATE
SE of the centre

The area covered is SE of the Bull Ring and Moor Street (the inner ring road), N of the markets, and inside the middle ring road on its E and SE part, with a small part beyond in Highgate (Moseley Road). Digbeth, in ancient Birmingham, and Deritend in Aston parish, were built up by the late medieval period. They are divided by the River Rea. The streets to either side were developed from the mid C18 with tightly packed houses and workshops. St John, Deritend, described as 'lately built' in 1382 and rebuilt in 1735, was demolished in 1947 for road widening. Post-war slum clearance also led to much rebuilding. The area was never fashionable or rich, and one went quickly from the city centre into small-scale industrial streets. The area N of Digbeth and Deritend is a conservation area, but under threat; that S of it is being rapidly redeveloped with large apartment schemes, few of interest.

PLACES OF WORSHIP

HOLY TRINITY (former), Old Camp Hill, Bordesley. A Commissioners' church by *Francis Goodwin*, 1820–2. An excellent example of Late Georgian Perp. A simple rectangle in plan, with a shallow three-sided projection at the E end. There are octagonal angle turrets and pinnacled side buttresses, and at the W end a small central rose window above a dark recessed porch whose ceiling has a pattern of ribs. The splendid and ornate tracery of the E rose window is of cast iron. Redundant since the 1960s; interior gutted.

ST ALBAN, Conybere Street.* A major late work of *John Loughborough Pearson*, 1879–81, complex in plan, masterly in construction, yet simple in detail. Built for missionary Anglo-Catholic priest brothers, James and Thomas Pollock, among working-class terraced housing demolished in the 1960s. Brick with stone dressings and a little diapering. Two-light clerestory windows of paired lancets with circles above. Broad single lancets in the aisles. W front with octagonal turrets, rose window and porch. The transept ends have smaller turrets. E apse with ambulatory. Pearson's SW tower was completed by *E.F. Reynolds*, 1938. Massive and sheer with a saddleback roof, a reworking of Reynolds's unexecuted design for All Saints, Four Oaks (p. 440).

The interior is vaulted throughout, in quadripartite ribs. Bath stone, like the arcades. Complex arch mouldings with nice detail where they cross the pier shafting. Clerestory recessed behind high stone arches, with a triforium passage running all round. Pearson's use of the golden section in both plan and arcade elevation gives it spacious and noble proportions, at once aspiring and profoundly restful. The closest parallel is his St Michael, Croydon (1880–1). The S (St Patrick's) chapel has dogtooth on pier and ribs. Its E end has an intriguing spatial effect: a triple-arched vaulted stone canopy over the altar, linked into the vaulting above by ribs leading to a boss with a pelican. The ambulatory, also vaulted, starts as the l. bay of the triple canopy. W baptistery also canopied under the gallery. – FURNISHINGS. Original low stone chancel screen. Iron SCREEN on it by *Pearson*, 1897; CHOIR STALLS also his. – ROOD BEAM and FIGURES of 1913, designed by *Frank Pearson*, carved by *Nathaniel Hitch*. Brought from St Patrick's. – C18-style PULPIT by *Romilly Craze*, c. 1960. – Octagonal FONT by *Pearson*, 1881. Of stone with bright red veins. – Behind it a FRESCO of Christ with angels and children by *Clayton & Bell*, 1895–6. – S chapel REREDOS of beaten copper by *Myra Bunce* with painted panels by *Kate Bunce*, 1919; RAILINGS and GATES by *John Goodman*, 1916. – N chapel, iron *Bromsgrove Guild* SCREEN from St Patrick's, panelling of 1919 probably by *A.S. Dixon*. – STAINED GLASS. Apse window by *Henry Payne*, 1904, with sweeping angels' wings. Flanking it, two by *Sidney Meteyard*, 1926–7. *Clayton & Bell* glass in the ambulatory and chapels, 1883–96. S aisle easternmost by *Morris & Co.*, 1909.

ST BASIL (former), Heath Mill Lane. By *A.S. Dixon*, 1910–11, the finest example of his Arts and Crafts primitivism. Now the offices of the St Basil's homelessness charity. Red and bluish brick seconds. Round arches, tile bands, bellcote and a little projecting baptistery. The Romanesque style seems to grow out

---

*Now St Alban and St Patrick, reflecting another *Pearson* church of 1896, nearby in Frank Street, demolished c. 1970.

INNER AREAS: DIGBETH, DERITEND ETC.

of the functional buildings around it. The interior is more consciously Italian. Five-bay nave, infilled in the 1980s. The arcade columns are granite monoliths, with cushion capitals painted with scenes from the life of St Basil by *Humphrey Dixon*. The E end is intact and wonderfully evocative. Plastered walls, kingpost trusses, patterned stone floor. The apse has marble panelling recalling Lethaby, especially the piscina. Semi-dome with a mosaic. – SCREEN with linenfold panels, thick tapering square columns and a heavy beam with inscription and flower patterns. ROOD FIGURES by *George Jack*, influenced by late medieval German work. – Equally heavy ALTAR. – The LECTERN displays its construction.

ST ANNE (R.C.), Alcester Street. 1883–4 by *Albert Vicars*. Early English style in red brick with blue-brick and stone dressings: old-fashioned, but handled with confidence. SE (ritual NW) tower. Big Geometrical W window with many foiled circles. The tower turns octagonal, with diagonal buttresses to the belfry. Short spire with lucarnes and sandstone banding. Tall arcades with circular columns and arches with two chamfers; hoodmoulds with the Instruments of the Passion. Canted boarded roof supported by shafts on angel corbels. Lively tracery: E rose window, circular S aisle E window with a five-pointed star, very tall sanctuary lancets. Original PEWS and CONFESSIONALS in the S aisle, also the ALTARPIECES in the aisles with lots of cusping and crockets.

BIRMINGHAM CENTRAL MOSQUE, Belgrave Middleway. By *G. Langley-Taylor & Partners*, begun 1968 but delayed by a shortage of money. A cubic block of maroon brick. Narrow triplets of windows. Large plastic dome. Minaret completed in 1986 by *William Copeland*.

MUATH CENTRE, Stratford Road, Camp Hill. Built as the King Edward's Grammar Schools, 1883 (boys', N), and 1890 (girls', S). By *Martin & Chamberlain*, grander than their Board Schools, but in the same brick Gothic with big sash windows in shallow reveals with sparing stone tracery above. The boys' school has a fine octagonal tower which checks in to a little timber octagon and a stubby spire with lucarnes. The girls' school has a tall main block with stepped buttresses and a central gable. First-floor hall with hammerbeam roof. Alterations by *D5*, 2003–6, with glazed entrance link.

PERAMBULATIONS

1. Digbeth, Deritend and Fazeley Street

The start is the top of DIGBETH, opposite St Martin's and Selfridges (*see* pp. 122 and 138). S side rebuilt after 1953. The N side begins with a vacant plot, the site of several tower proposals (most recently a thirty-storey block by *Broadway Malyan*, 2015). Nos. 138–139 is by *S.N. Cooke*, 1936, with strip windows. No. 137 has an early C19 front much rebuilt in 1947, but retaining a good pedimented window. Inside, C18 doorways with plain architraves, an early C19 stick-baluster staircase and evidence of earlier timber framing. Nos. 135–136 of 1913 by *James Patchett* of Ombersley, unsophisticated but enjoyable Free Style. Green tiled frieze with the owner's name, G. MAKEPEACE, a second-hand-clothes seller. Then a former cold store of 1899 by *Ernest C. Bewlay*, impressively functional, with deeply chamfered paired windows with lunettes above. Opposite, WOLVERLEY HOUSE of 1955–6 by *Bertram Butler & Partners*. Porthole windows. Continuing on the N side, POLICE STATION of 1911 by *Henry E. Stilgoe*, City Engineer and Surveyor: slightly uncertain Baroque with a picturesque corner turret. On the Meriden Street corner the former CASTLE AND FALCON pub, *c*.1850, altered by *W.H. Ward* in 1906, including the corner lunette and blue- and yellow-brick bands. To the N in Meriden Street, W side, the former ASH & LACY works of 1905 by *J.G. Dunn*, a long crisply articulated brick and terracotta range. To the N, Coventry Street leads W to ALLISON STREET, with a factory of 1888 by *James Moffat*, a builder's version of J.H. Chamberlain's Gothic. To the N, a blue-brick RAILWAY VIADUCT chiefly of 1911–16 by the GWR Superintendent Engineer *W.Y. Armstrong* (cf. Moor Street Station, p. 136). Under the arch, an opening to the contemporary former lower-level railway goods depot, now a car park. An early reinforced-concrete structure on the *Hennebique* system. Impressive rows of piers supporting shallow segmental arches.

N of the bridge on the E side a former pig market, later bottling factory, by *Owen & Ward*, 1892, extended 1898–1900. On the W corner with BORDESLEY STREET, Nos. 8A–10, 1882–4 by *Jethro Cossins*, influenced by Philip Webb. Four storeys with steep corbelled gables and spare detail. The fenestration, shallow canted bays below tall casements, stresses the areas of brickwork. Opposite, the former Chamberlain & Hookham factory by *Arthur McKewan*, 1913. Big steel windows, sparing detail: diapering, tile lintels, recessed tympana.

Now E down Bordesley Street. On the corner of Meriden Street the horribly treated former SPOTTED DOG pub, *c*.1810, extended *c*.1830. Beyond, LADBROKE HOUSE of 1919–21 by *Ernest H. Wigley*. Opposite, the massive former TY-PHOO TEA FACTORY, by *Harry Weedon & Partners*: central section of 1929 (five l. bays) and 1937–8, making a symmetrical Art Deco composition; extensions 1947–51, l., and *c*.1954, r. (upper floors 1966 etc.); lift tower behind, 1932.

S into OXFORD STREET. Beyond the railway viaduct, W side, a fine Arts and Crafts factory of 1911–12 by *Buckland & Haywood-Farmer*. Three storeys, the wall surface cutting back between buttresses. Round-headed doorway with leadwork hood. Two-storey wing to Coventry Street. Interior with workshops round a double-height space, just like one of Buckland's school halls. Opposite, the mid-C19 former OLD WHARF pub.

Back on Digbeth and E, No. 86, a Gothic shop by *Edward Mansell*, old-fashioned for 1890: cf. the window of No. 85, Bonser's Lion Warehouse of 1860, by *J.R. Botham*. An impressive single-bay tower with classical entrance and truncated pyramid roof. No. 80, the former OLD BULLS HEAD pub, *c.*1880. The DIGBETH INSTITUTE of 1906–8 by *Arthur Harrison* is Edwardian Mannerist, with elements used unstructurally to indicate the steel frame beneath. Doric half-columns support only draped female figures. Baroque centrepiece, contrasting spiked central turret and Wren-style side cupolas. The BIG BULLS HEAD pub (No. 75), 1885, probably by *William Hale*, has canted bays effectively recessed between brick piers. On the opposite corner, brick shops and warehouse of 1869 for Thomas Fawdry, restored in 2003 as part of SOUTH BIRMINGHAM COLLEGE, by *Nicol Thomas*. This also incorporates the former FLOODGATE STREET SCHOOL to the N, a fine later work of *Martin & Chamberlain*, of 1890–1, with huge windows under gables. Strongly modelled ventilation tower with corner turrets. Buttresses with gabled tops enclosing open terracotta tracery towards Moore's Row. On the corner of Floodgate Street, mosaic MURAL commemorating President Kennedy by *Kenneth Budd*, 1968, re-created here by *Oliver Budd*, 2013.

Now E over the River Rea into HIGH STREET, DERITEND, a medieval settlement in Aston parish.* On the N side, DEVONSHIRE HOUSE was Alfred Bird & Sons' custard factory. Main four-storey frontage by *W.T. Orton*, 1902: six bays, buff terracotta arches and windows, ornate lettering and a rich shaped gable with a ship in tilework. Parapet like a piecrust, appropriate for custard. Plainer extensions of 1907–8, r., and 1913, l. Behind, low sawtooth range of 1887 by *Thomas Naden* (chimney by *Orton*, 1910), and functional later C20 extensions down Gibb Street, E. Converted into studios, shops and workshops by *Glenn Howells Architects*, 1994. On the E side of GIBB STREET a *Howells* building of 1997–8: brick stair-tower painted blue, and a delightful L-shaped block to its N with oval plate-like balconies suspended from steel masts. STATUE sprouting wire and plants, Green Man, by *Tawny Gray*, 2002. Next on the High Street a former Lloyds Bank of 1874–5 by *J.A. Chatwin*, domestic Gothic with power. To its N a former PUBLIC LIBRARY of 1866 by *Bateman & Corser*. Red brick with a little blue diapering, stone dressings and three-light Perp windows. Two gables, the taller rebuilt during repairs of 2003 by *Bryant Priest Newman*. Inside, four-centred arcades, also Perp, and a complex truss roof.

Next the OLD CROWN INN. The only complete medieval survival of the town of Birmingham, now shown by Stephen Price, Nicholas Molyneux and George Demidowicz to be the late C15 GUILDHALL AND SCHOOL of the Guild of St John the Baptist of Deritend. The street front indeed has a civic air, with its close-studded and jettied first floor and central entrance with gabled oriel on big brackets. Original round-headed side windows to the oriel. Ground floor underbuilt in brick in repairs of 1862 by *Joshua Toulmin Smith*, a local antiquary, who

---

*St John, a C15 chapel of ease rebuilt in 1735, was demolished in 1947.

saved the building from demolition and extended the E wing to the N. The great moulded bressumer supporting the first floor, faithfully restored by him, was removed in ham-fisted alterations of 1998. Cross-wings with unusual tie-beams decorated with blank arcading (cf. the Saracen's Head, Kings Norton, 1492, p. 408). But the appearance is misleading, as the centre of the r. side was originally recessed, in the so-called Wealden arrangement, hence the surviving brackets supporting the wall-plate to the r. of the oriel. This part was the schoolmaster's hall, with his parlour etc. in the E wing. The l. side housed the school on the ground floor, and the guild's hall above. Toulmin Smith's rear extension reconstructed as bedrooms in 1998, with a new entrance.

The much-renewed cross-passage has to its l. what was probably the SCHOOLROOM, with a beamed ceiling with a dragon (diagonal) beam supporting the SW corner. Post-Reformation stud partitions divide up the GUILDHALL above. Its roof survives above modern ceilings, with arch-braced collars and wind-braces. In one bedroom an C18 'buffet' corner cupboard. In the oriel a ceiling with original early plasterwork: six-pointed stars and simplified fleurs-de-lys. The master's hall, divided horizontally in the C16, also retains its roof, with tie-beams, convex struts and high straight collar. Smoke-blackening suggests an original open hearth. The extra internal wall-plate is evidence of the Wealden arrangement. Behind, an early C19 stick-baluster staircase.

Further E four brick and terracotta shops by *J.H. Hawkes & Son*, 1906. Then the former ST EDMUND'S BOYS HOME by *Mansell & Mansell*, 1912–14, derelict apart from the CHAPEL by the railway viaduct. Early Christian Revival, above a ground-floor workshop. Not quite as original as Dixon's or Ball's work, but with an impressive campanile, closely based on that of San Giorgio al Velabro, Rome. The interior has an inserted floor, but retains a rich painted roof with kingpost trusses on big consoles. Beyond, E, HIGH STREET, BORDESLEY starts. Bordesley was a medieval township, also in Aston parish. Two classical shop buildings of *c.*1860, and the former RAINBOW pub, *c.*1876, Gothic with good detailing.

Back to the Old Crown Inn, and N up HEATH MILL LANE. On the E side well beyond the railway, St Basil's church (p. 194). The FORGE TAVERN on the NW corner of Fazeley Street occupies part of the site of the medieval Heath Mill. Remains of the never-completed BORDESLEY RAILWAY VIADUCT of *c.* 1852, a casualty of early railway competition, on both sides of the road. Against the E side, a late C19 cast-iron URINAL. At the far end of Liverpool Street, E, a big BUS GARAGE of 1935–6 by *Crouch, Butler & Savage*. Wide entrance with the name across the lintel, and a long row of shallow giant arches enclosing two levels of windows. Beyond, in Adderley Street, the former WAGON AND HORSES pub. Early C19, with moulded window lintels. Late C19 ground floor probably by *James & Lister Lea*. Going

INNER AREAS: DIGBETH, DERITEND ETC. 199

E along Adderley Street, set back on the S side by the canal, a big former GAS RETORT HOUSE of 1909 by *Walter Chaney*, Corporation Gas Department engineer-in-chief.

Back NW to the Forge Tavern and, NE, a BRIDGE of 1854 over the Warwick and Birmingham Canal (surveyor *Edward John Lloyd*), its shallow-arched span constructed entirely of cast-iron plates. Panelled iron parapets. NW from the Forge Tavern in FAZELEY STREET, S side, a former UNITARIAN SUNDAY SCHOOL of 1865 by *A.B. Phipson*, extended 1868. A small brick temple front, but with lancet windows. Beyond, the sharp-gabled former CHAPEL of 1876–7 by *George Ingall*. Down Floodgate Street, S, the former MEDICAL MISSION of 1880, Italian Romanesque by *Edward Holmes*. On the N side of Fazeley Street, THE BOND has mostly early C19 houses with architraved windows and simple doorcases. The site was a gas works between 1837 and 1875; the house with a lunette window probably the works entrance. To the N a big warehouse in alternating courses of red and blue brick, of 1884–6 for Fellows & Morton by the builder *Edwin Shipway*. Segmental-headed iron windows, and a partly surviving hoist over the canal, N. Small canal side basin constructed *c.*1890, covered wharf with nice iron brackets, probably of 1896 by *Wigham*.

Further W on the N side, a large warehouse proudly inscribed 1935 and FELLOWS MORTON & CLAYTON; by *Watson & Johnson*. Then the former WARWICK AND BIRMINGHAM CANAL BASIN. The canal was cut here in 1796; the L-shaped basin, infilled but recognizable, *c.*1840. No.122 is the former canal company office and weighing-machine keeper's house, of 1843–4 by *Edward John Lloyd*. Simple, with architraved doorways and sashes, in fine plum-coloured brick. Also by *Lloyd* the basin entrance with big rusticated gatepiers, and probably Nos.106–110, 1850 for the Grand Junction Canal Co., in dark Staffordshire blues. Behind, a contemporary warehouse. Behind the basin on the canal-side, now best seen from the towpath, the so-called BANANA WAREHOUSE of *c.*1850, with a loading bay over the canal supported on iron columns. Its W wall incorporates earlier fabric, probably of Pickford's warehouse of 1811–12.

Now N into Andover Street, under the railway, and E into Banbury Street for the BIRMINGHAM GUN BARREL PROOF HOUSE. Set up by Act of Parliament in 1813 to 'prove', i.e. test, barrels and completed guns. ENTRANCE RANGE by *Jethro Cossins*, 1883. Simple Jacobean archway; caretaker's cottage, N, treated like a miniature C17 house; balancing S block linked to the ORIGINAL BUILDING of 1813–14, running W–E. This is a delightful piece of vernacular classicism by *John Horton*, architect and builder. The centrepiece shows off slightly clumsily, but the effect is lovable: three-centred Doric arch (infilled), big niche above with a splendid trophy of arms traditionally attributed to *William Hollins*, and a segmental gable with a clock. Five bays each side, the westernmost hidden by the 1883 work. Windows with segmental-headed architraves decorated with rosettes. Guardians' entrance, second bay from the E, with Doric half-columns, open pediment and five-petal fanlight. The symmetry is misleading: originally the W part had four widely spaced bays, not five, forming houses for the master and staff. In 1868–70 *Bateman & Corser* made it into workshops, tactfully re-spacing the windows; the second ground-floor window from the centre is theirs, with slight differences. Inside the archway, through an office, a semi-oval staircase of 1869 leads to the BOARD ROOM, E. This has paired doorways, one blank, at each end, with fluted architraves. Painted oval ceiling panel of 1836 and another on the W wall of 1835, both by *Jonathan Thorp* and copied from the façade sculpture. Fireplace probably 1868–70. Finance Room to the W, smaller but similar.

In the rear yard a simple COVERED WAY running N–S, with thin cast-iron columns, of before 1833. In the centre *Bateman & Corser*'s MAGAZINE of 1876; of specially fired bricks closely jointed, for safety. W and S extensions of 1868–70; short contemporary wing to the E. Beyond it, the original PROOF HOLE or proofing shed, rebuilt in tough simple Romanesque by *Charles Edge*, 1860. Inside, original iron deflecting plates below a slatted roof, to diffuse blasts. Behind, remains of the original canal-side WHARF.

2. *Bradford Street and Highgate Park*

S of Digbeth and Deritend. Mainly the estate of Henry Bradford, developed on a grid, mostly *c.*1775 to 1810, starting at the E end with Alcester Street. Industry, here from the start, took over in the early C20. Wireworks were concentrated here and a few survive.

In BRADFORD STREET, starting at the city end, No. 32 (S side), by *James & Lister Lea*, 1891, was a hide and skin market, an important Birmingham trade. Big ground-floor arches, central pediment. On the NW corner of Rea Street the ANCHOR pub by *James & Lister Lea*, 1902. Simple exterior with arched windows. Remarkably complete interior: bar front with fluted pilasters, Jacobean-style bar back with Ionic piers, rare surviving bar partition to the r. Diagonally opposite, an office of 1934 and three-bay factory of 1931, both for Fisher & Ludlow by *C.F. Lawley Harrod*. Beyond the River Rea, No. 54 by *J.P. Osborne*, 1908 (derelict). Pedimented end bays, off-centre Baroque doorcase. On the N side the WHITE SWAN pub by *James & Lister Lea*, 1899–1900. Inside, panelled dado and *Minton* tiles above. Original bar front and back. The smoke-room passage also has Minton tiles, particularly good, with a band of wreaths and a frieze of flowers. On the S side the big former brass foundry of Harrison & Co. by *Harrison & Cox*, 1908 (five E bays 1916–17). Top storey 1924. Plain except for a central broken pediment. Aggressive flat conversion with

INNER AREAS: DIGBETH, DERITEND ETC.

cantilevered corners by *BDG*, 2017. Further up, St Anne's church, s side (p. 195). On the NE corner with Alcester Street, big functional Fisher & Ludlow No. 10 factory by *John Christie*, 1936. Adjacent, the former Englands shoe factory, 1913 by *F. H. Thomason*, with giant arches (derelict). In ALCESTER STREET to the N No. 27, a coffin-furniture factory of 1899–1900 by *F. Dennison*, shows the persistence of the Georgian tradition. Rear heightened by *Joe Holyoak* and *BPN*, 2017–18.

Now s, past St Anne's church. On the corner of Cheapside the early C19 former FOUNTAIN pub. An optional diversion here E up Cheapside to Moseley Road and the MOSELEY ARMS pub of *c.* 1840. Windows with full entablatures, the cornices on consoles. Further up in Ravenhurst Street the former LENCH'S TRUST ALMSHOUSES of 1848–9 by *Hornblower & Haylock*. Brick, Tudor style. Three ranges round a courtyard and a wall in front with a tall central lodge. Four-centred-arched doorways and mullioned windows. The lodge has Jacobean shaped gables. E wing reconstructed after war damage, 1949. Back to Alcester Street and the ROWTON HOTEL, built as a Rowton House (lodging house for working men), 1903–5, by their regular architect *Harry B. Measures*. Bright red Ruabon brick. Big shaped gables, and octagonal corner towers, turning circular with conical copper roofs and terracotta dragons holding shields (by *Edwards* of Ruabon). Plain below, with sashes originally lighting 819 sleeping cubicles. Converted to a hotel *c.* 1990. Beyond, HIGHGATE PARK, laid out by *T. W. Coudrey* in 1876. LODGE on the E side.

Going w from the hotel in MOSELEY STREET. Nos. 82–84, *c.* 1820, restored; Nos. 72–74, much altered late C18. Nice details particularly on No. 74: segmental window lintels and moulded keystones with rosettes, severe doorcase. Further w on the corner of Birchall Street, the MARKET TAVERN by *James & Lister Lea*, 1899. In the other direction, immediately E of the hotel, a former POLICE STATION of 1877 by *Martin & Chamberlain*. Three tall gables split by tall, corbelled-out chimneys. Terracotta panels. At the top of Moseley Street, s into MOSELEY ROAD. On the E side, fine early C19 houses. No. 90, of three bays, has a doorcase with segmental pediment and thin paired colonnettes. Of *c.* 1813, perhaps by *John Horton*, as the lower architraves are like those of the Gun Barrel Proof House (p. 199). No. 94, taller, Italianate, *c.* 1850. No. 102 has a good doorcase with open pediment and fanlight (also Nos. 112 and 114). No. 106 with acanthus capitals to the piers of the porch. Finally No. 116 has three semi-elliptical bays with rusticated pilasters, very much Cheltenham Regency. Then a curving block by *Associated Architects*, 1993. Across a grassed space to the SW here, STRATFORD HOUSE. Porch lintel dated 1601 and initialled ARB, for Ambrose and Bridget Rotton. A timber-framed farmhouse, with characteristic West Midlands decorative framing. Four gables. The l. one is the parlour cross-wing. It projects slightly, and the smaller third one projects further, as a porch. Originally jettied, the front has been largely underbuilt in brick. Herringbone framing on the first floor, square panels with quadrant bracing in the gables. The cross-passage has heavy ceiling beams and studding. Other details mainly early C19. Restored 1951–2.

MOSELEY ROAD continues 100 yds SW, beyond Highgate Middleway. The former FRIENDS' HALL AND INSTITUTE by *Ewen & J.A. Harper*, 1897, for Richard Cadbury, is a tremendous Jacobean design, with shaped gables and projecting porch. Big canted upper bays light the lecture room. Coffee room and reading room below, meeting hall upstairs at the back. No. 232 next door, friendly Neo-Georgian of 1910 by *Cossins, Peacock & Bewlay*, was built as a remand home for Barrow Cadbury, Richard's son. The MERRY MAID pub is of 1931 by a Mr *Lynes* of Atkinson's Brewery. Opposite, E side, is Highgate Place, with an OVERBRIDGE of 1840 on the Birmingham & Gloucester Railway. Egyptian-style tapering pylons survive on the far side. No. 262 Moseley Road is like two bays of an Early Victorian stucco terrace, with two floors of pilasters. Other Victorian terraces beyond. On the W side a former FIRE STATION, dated 1911, by *Arthur Harrison*. Neo-Wren detail but Tudor gables. Contemporary accommodation block behind, more radical, spare and squarish, like early C20 London County Council work. On the E side, No. 320, an 1860s end-terrace house converted to a bank with Mannerist detail by *J.A. Chatwin*, 1900. Beyond is Balsall Heath (p. 303).

LEOPOLD STREET runs W from the Friends' Hall, back across Highgate Middleway.* Down the hill on the N side, the wonderful sight of SAMUEL HEATH & SONS (COBDEN WORKS), the last large firm of brass founders in Birmingham, and architecturally significant too. Offices in the centre, Jacobean, with swan's-neck pediment to the entrance, by *D. Henry Ward*, 1888. In 1888–9 Ward added a curving single-storey range r. After this everything is by *Bateman & Bateman*. In 1891 they recast the single-storey range and raised it to three storeys. Balancing range l., 1897, similar but simpler. Beyond, a two-storey block with chamfered corner, war damage replacement of 1946, and in Stanhope Street an impressive three-storey range with raised and quoined end bays, 1913–14. Going S down Stanhope Street, St Alban's church (p. 194). E of it, in Conybere Street, the LENCH'S TRUST ALMSHOUSES by *J.A. Chatwin*, 1878–80. A delightful Queen Anne group, a very early use of the style in Birmingham. Three ranges in an irregular U, with the warden's house in the centre facing the street. Brick with a few sandstone dressings. Steep little pediments with reliefs of flowers in vases, stepped-up window surrounds and big keystones, all in moulded brick. Star-shaped chimneys, sadly cut down.

---

*No. 25 Darwin Street, to the N, was the PEACOCK pub, Regency style by *J.B. Surman*, 1933–5 (altered).

INNER AREAS: SMALLBROOK & GOUGH ESTATE 203

OTHER BUILDINGS

A scatter to the E beyond Watery Lane Middleway. The former GARRISON LANE SCHOOL is by *Martin & Chamberlain*. Typical many-gabled main building of 1873 with powerful deep-set lancets. Mostly single-storey block, l., 1876. Just to the S in Witton Street, PARK VILLAS, two rows with big end chimneys and central archways, 1912–13 by *G.A. Cox*. S again in Lower Dartmouth Street, the timber-gabled former HEN AND CHICKENS pub by *James & Lister Lea & Sons*, 1908–9. Further E along Garrison Lane, BORDESLEY VILLAGE, private housing for the Heartlands Development Corporation. The centre has the former SPORTSMAN pub, with conical turret and nice name plaque, dated 1895. Behind it shops, apartments and community hall by *Bournville Architects*, 1996. Traditional brick, touches of Postmodern. For beyond the railway, *see* Small Heath, p. 284.

SMALLBROOK AND THE GOUGH ESTATE
s of the centre

Smallbrook Street was built up in the medieval period as the start of the route SW from the Bull Ring. The Hill Street area to its N was built up by the mid C18, the areas W of Suffolk Street and S of Smallbrook Street from the 1790s. New Street Station, built from 1849, cut the area off from the centre. Its extension S in 1881–5 included the cutting of Station Street, and caused substantial rebuilding. The area was badly bombed in 1940–1. Partly for this reason, the first stretch of the inner ring road, Smallbrook Queensway, was constructed here in 1957–60. The area was the city's 'theatreland', and developed as the gay quarter. Hurst Street was designated the city's Chinatown in the early 1990s. Smallbrook and Bristol Street are currently threatened with damaging high-rise projects.

PLACES OF WORSHIP

ST THOMAS (former), Bath Row. 1826–9 by *Rickman & Hutchinson*. Only the W end survived a 1941 bomb, the worn Bath stone now very poignant. An original Greek Revival composition. Tower with ground floor open to N, S and W, linked to the W wall by tightly packed Ionic quadrant colonnades. Above, a plain stage, then a square with pedimented aedicules, and an octagon, its ball and cross missing. Churchyard laid out as a Peace Garden in 1992, incorporating a Doric LOGGIA by *S.N. Cooke & W.N. Twist*, part of the Hall of Memory scheme, brought from Broad Street.

ST CATHERINE OF SIENA (R.C.), Bristol Street. 1964–5 by *Bernard James* of *Harrison & Cox*. Round nave, the first in the city to show the effect of the Second Vatican Council. Balanced outside by a tapering campanile. Open-air PULPIT with a canopy.

BETHEL PRESBYTERIAN CHURCH OF WALES, Holloway Head. By *James A. Roberts*, 1968. A complex and angular little design: triangular church on the first floor, with a copper roof, above a rectangular ground floor of hall, kitchen and caretaker's flat. The church interior is brick-lined, with a Parana pine roof.

CHRISTADELPHIAN CHAPEL (former), Suffolk Street. 1910 by *G.A. Birkenhead*. Baroque doorcase.

SINGERS HILL SYNAGOGUE (Birmingham Hebrew Congregation), Blucher Street. 1855–6 by *Yeoville Thomason*. Britain's earliest surviving 'cathedral synagogue'. Italianate, red brick with stone dressings; paired round-headed windows and big bracket cornice. Entrance front recessed behind wings, with a triple arcade and a rose window in the gable. Parapet of the arcade probably of 1937, when the whole gable wall was rebuilt one bay W by *Harry Weedon & Partners* (Oscar Deutsch, for whom Weedon designed Odeons, was president of the synagogue). In the wings, doorways with leaded hoods from alterations of 1957–9 by *Cotton, Ballard & Blow*. Two-tier side elevations of windows in shallow arches (cf. the Law Society, Temple Street, p. 155). Sumptuous interior. Seven-bay arcades with Corinthian columns above the galleries, and square piers with leaf capitals below. The treatment owes as much to Wren, e.g. St Andrew, Holborn, as to Italy. Barrel-vault with Thomason's interlaced heart ornament on the ribs. Apsed E end, beyond a grand arch with paired piers supporting freestanding columns; modern Ark. The rich mid-C19 impression owes much to the two tiers of original gilded CHANDELIERS. Galleries reconstructed and ground floor re-seated by *Weedon* in 1937; the deep W gallery also his. – BIMAH (pulpit) of 1988 using C19 pieces. – STAINED GLASS. An unusual series of *Hardman* windows, mostly late 1940s–1962. Figurative and mildly Expressionist, but all faces are concealed, e.g. Moses with the Tablets, upper S. Jewish festivals, lower N. Fascinating social documentation, e.g. the Exiles Return to Israel, lower S. Suitably religious C19 glass in the rose window.

JEWISH SCHOOL, also *Thomason*, immediately E. W part of 1862, originally two-storeyed. In 1884 the top storey was added, a first-floor council room formed, marked by round-headed windows, and the two-storey E block built. The hall reconstructed as a social centre in 1934 by *John Goodman*, who also re-fitted the council room.

ATHOL MASONIC HALL, formerly SYNAGOGUE, Severn Street. 1827 by *Richard Tutin*, the predecessor of Singers Hill Synagogue, to the S (*see* above). Modest classical front: pilasters, cornice, low attic. Windows and brick panels of 1891 by *Essex & Nicol*, who also reconstructed the lobby. Main hall articulated by plain pilasters, above a high dado. Deeply coved ceiling. At the S end the former synagogue Ark, a handsome niche with Greek Doric columns *in antis* and a rich entablature

INNER AREAS: SMALLBROOK & GOUGH ESTATE

with acroteria. Rear banqueting hall added for the Freemasons in 1871 by *Henry Naden*. Opulent ceiling with beams supported by big consoles. At each end a fireplace and a large mirror framed by Corinthian columns and a segmental pediment. The decoration includes five- and six-pointed stars, suitable for a lodge with many Jewish members.
For former PUBLIC BUILDINGS *see* Perambulations below.

THEATRES

ALEXANDRA THEATRE, Suffolk Street. *Owen & Ward*'s building of 1900–1 was rebuilt in 1935 by *Roland Satchwell*, except for the surviving office range at the rear. When the inner ring road was built, a new entrance façade and a new foyer, bridging John Bright Street, were added by the *John Madin Design Group*, 1967–9. Their stylish glass front was, sadly, replaced by *Day Architectural*, 2018. The 1935 front to John Bright Street, with its circular turret, is clad in silver panels. Satchwell's streamlined interior is largely intact, refurbished in 1992 by the *Seymour Harris Partnership*. Crush bar with typical panelling, a deep cove and a mirror-glass wall. Tall, shallow auditorium. Proscenium arch with plain and wavy mouldings running all round; similar balcony fronts. Deeply moulded, domed ceiling rose.

BIRMINGHAM HIPPODROME, Hurst Street. Started as assembly rooms of 1895 by *Essex, Nicol & Goodman*. In 1899 *Frederick W. Lloyd* added the 'Tower of Varieties', a combination of stage and circus ring, to the rear. Its tower – a miniature of Blackpool's – lasted until 1963. The concern failed and was reconstructed by Lloyd as the Tivoli Theatre in 1900. The auditorium was rebuilt again in 1924–5 by *Burdwood & Mitchell*. In 1980–1 the *Seymour Harris Partnership* rebuilt everything behind the proscenium. Then in 2000–1 *Associated Architects* with *Law & Dunbar-Nasmith* replaced the assembly rooms with a new foyer and studios, and added dressing and rehearsal rooms to Thorp Street, N. A glass front wall between dark green slate-faced piers of unequal heights, a silver canopy and a big projecting panel to the l. Along Inge Street, s, a long copper panel floating free of a dark metal-framed wall filled with orange unglazed terracotta tiles. All these materials well integrated, helped by the planar approach. The side wall of the 1899 building survives further along Inge Street, brick and terracotta with blind three-centred arches. Huge red metal fly tower of 1980–1. The 1924–5 auditorium is chaste Neo-Roman. Giant fluted Ionic columns enclose three bays of boxes on each side, with big segmental pediments above. Long elegant single balcony.

OLD REP THEATRE, Station Street. 1912–13 by *S.N. Cooke*. Austere monumental classic, fashionable for theatres *c*. 1910 (cf. Albert Richardson's Opera House, Manchester). Giant Ionic pilasters, delicately detailed, disappear into the tower-like end bays. Windows with heavy architraves, Greek-key and guilloche friezes. Semi-octagonal dormer like a look-out. Foyer and stairs have a heavy marble dado and a delicate Doric entablature. Small auditorium with an extremely steep rake, because of the shallow site. Doric proscenium with a huge frieze.

PERAMBULATIONS

1. John Bright Street, Bristol Street and Smallbrook

The start is the crossing of Hill Street and Navigation Street, over the tracks of New Street Station (p. 136). On Navigation Street, w, SIGNAL BOX by *Bicknell & Hamilton* with *W. R. Headley*, Regional Architect, British Railways London Midland Region, 1964–5, for the West Coast electrification. The restricted site produced a compact, forceful four-storey structure, clad in massively corrugated rough concrete. Deep fascia above the control rooms. Now s along JOHN BRIGHT STREET, cut in 1882. On the pavement a cast-iron COLUMN of 1908, from public lavatories in Hill Street, and stone SCULPTURE by *Lee Grandjean*, 1987. On the w side the rounded end of a big development including a tower facing Suffolk Street, by *BLB*, 2005–7. It incorporates the façades of a hotel of 1899–1900 by *A. B. Phipson*, round arches with nice brick detail, and the former Birmingham Athletic Institute, 1891 by *Benjamin Corser*, three bays with windows linked vertically. The GROSVENOR CASINO, E side, is by *Kelly & Surman*, 1963. Two buildings by *Marcus O. Type* mark the w corners of Lower Severn Street. GEOFFREY BUILDINGS of 1901, N, has a Free Style corner feature, a two-storey canted bay topped by a curved balcony, and a smaller bay in front of the shaped gable. ROSEBERY BUILDINGS of 1902–3, S, was showrooms for the early car maker Heron, with workshop at the rear. A quirky, slightly sinister design with flat-topped gables, canted windows and a corner turret with a sharp prow. On the SE corner, CAMBRIDGE BUILDINGS, 1884–5 by *Alfred Dickens Perry*. The former FUTURIST CINEMA (E side) is by *Arthur Stockwell* of Newcastle upon Tyne, started 1914, simplified by *Essex & Goodman* during construction, and completed 1920. A classical, rather civic design in pink-red brick and cream terracotta. Open Ionic arcade above the entrance. Then the Neo-Georgian BOROUGH BUILDINGS, 1909 by *Marcus O. Type*. Centrepiece with open pediment and oval window. The ground floor was another car showroom. Opposite, the former SKIN HOSPITAL of 1887 by *James & Lister Lea* (the date 1881 is that of the foundation). Its picturesque, asymmetrical Queen Anne front steps back to fit the tapering site. Concave leaded cupola over the entrance. Then a shop of 1898 by *Stephen J. Holliday*, with a giant arch, and another by *Newton & Cheatle*, 1899–1900, nastily re-windowed. Ahead is the Alexandra Theatre (p. 205), facing Suffolk Street Queensway, with the VICTORIA pub on the corner. 1883 by *Thomson Plevins*, cheerful and eclectic. Doorways with curly broken pediments, inset canted bays.

Steps opposite, sw, climb to SUFFOLK STREET QUEENSWAY. Subways to the s lead to the centre of HOLLOWAY CIRCUS, with a MURAL of the Horse Fair by *Kenneth Budd*, 1967, and a gloomy PAGODA of grey granite made in China, 1998. Looking s, the SENTINELS, two dominating thirty-two-storey tower blocks flanking Holloway Head. 1968–71 by *James A. Roberts* with the *Birmingham City Architect*. Simple square shapes with pale cladding, battered dark brick bases (altered in the 1990s). To N and S bleak offices and car parks by *Roberts*, 1972–4.

From the circus we can also see SMALLBROOK QUEENSWAY, NE, as a whole. The best piece of mid-C20 urban design in the city, and the only stretch of the inner ring road built as a boulevard, rather than an urban motorway. Much of the effect is due to the SE side. First the plain former SCALA HOUSE, offices and cinema by *James A. Roberts*, 1962–4. Then a single six-storey block by *Roberts* of 1958–62 runs as far as the Bull Ring. A good balance between thin concrete mullions, bands of windows, and relief panels with projecting concrete trough uplighters. Its central section bridges Hurst Street on raking concrete struts. Under threat, 2020. On the NW corner of the circus BEETHAM TOWER, by *Ian Simpson Architects*, 2003–6. Thirty-three storeys, on a curve, faced in blue fritted glass. Sited, unlike its Manchester namesake, absolutely in your face, on this major junction. Beyond it, the N side has the former ALBANY HOTEL, 1960–2 by *James A. Roberts*. Concrete frame rising clear at the top, brown-brick facings. Attached behind, a Travertine-faced BANQUETING SUITE, 1975 by *Roberts*.* CENTRE CITY is a twenty-storey tower by *R. Seifert & Partners*, 1972–5. The podium cornice line responds to its neighbours. Finally NORFOLK HOUSE, by *Hurley Robinson & Son*, 1958–60, a convincing piece of its time. Concrete-framed, windows separated by green slate panels. Charming wavy canopy with circular glass light-holes.

Now s from the circus along HORSE FAIR. The E side remains. Three survivors of four vigorous terracotta shops by *James & Lister Lea*, 1898–9. Big shaped gables and hints of giant arches. Then a much-altered C18 survivor (site lease of 1778), and the former WHITE LION pub of 1896 by *James & Lister Lea*. Brick with stone dressings. Giant fluted Corinthian pilasters, and a corner spirelet deriving from Burghley House. In Thorp Street behind, the BIRMINGHAM ROYAL BALLET, Postmodern studios by the *Seymour Harris Partnership*, 1990, with a rooftop extension by *Austin-Smith:Lord*, 2018–19. The KOH-I-NOOR restaurant, Jacobean of 1899 by *Ballard & Mantel*, was built for Simeon Theodore King, grocer (initialled cartouches). Next door, shops and the former Black Lion pub by *Osborn & Reading*, 1879–80. Canted bays slightly recessed. In Essex Street behind, the former QUEEN'S TAVERN (No. 23) by *J. & L. Lea*, 1894–5.

---

*On the site of ST JUDE'S CHURCH by *C.W. Orford*, 1850–1.

Horse Fair continues s as BRISTOL STREET. The Essex Street corner of 1890 by *Alfred T. Greening*, with brick pilasters, deep cove, tile bands and panels, was demolished 2021. Thirty-storey residential tower by *Glancy Nicholls* approved. No. 12, with a big concave gable, looks 1900 but is of 1926 by *T.D. Griffiths*. Further down, No. 36, a Neo-Georgian former Municipal Bank of 1929 by *W. Norman Twist*. Nos. 38–40 are early C19. Nos. 42–44 is by *Cherrington & Stainton*, 1929: first-floor office windows in stone architraves; workshops above with full glazing. Brick giant pilasters enclose both. Bronze entrance doors probably by the *Birmingham Guild* inside. On the SE corner of Bromsgrove Street two rare C18 three-storey survivors, probably of 1792–3. First-floor windows with typical segmental lintels with small keystones and stops. Also the WELLINGTON HOTEL, so named by 1818. The l. part represents a house of *c.* 1792. Now stuccoed, a storey added, and a big wing built towards Bristol Street with a shallow bow and Corinthian pilasters. This looks Regency but is all of 1890–1 by *James & Lister Lea* (also the shop, r.). Ground floor by *J.P. Osborne & Son*, 1930. Good billiard room of 1890 with coved ceiling and lantern. Nos. 76–94 are an excellent group of four-storey shops all by *J. & L. Lea*, mostly of 1896–7, in brick and variously coloured terracotta. Nos. 76–100 are an excellent group of four-storey shops all by *J. & L. Lea*, of 1896-1900, in brick and variously coloured terracotta. Nos. 76–78 have Dutch gables with fluted pilasters; No. 80 panelled pilasters and a built-up gable; Nos. 82–90 canted bays and windows with tympanum reliefs; Nos. 92–94, the richest, first-floor rounded bays in a golden terracotta arcade. All refurbished, with infill at No. 96, and extended down Wrentham Street by *St Paul's Associates*, 2013–17.

In Wrentham Street, No. 80, by *Rudolf Frankel*, 1944–5. An elegant, Miesian repair shop, challengingly modern for its date in the city. Steel frame and brick infill panels. Remarkably unchanged except for heightening of the l. end.

Back to Holloway Circus and NE along Smallbrook Queensway, where HURST STREET runs s under the long Roberts block. On the W side, shops of 1899–1900 by *Cox & Silk* turn the corner into Thorp Street, with the surviving front range of the WARWICKSHIRE RIFLE VOLUNTEERS' DRILL HALL. 1880 by *Osborn & Reading*. Toytown-castle entrance towers with arrow-slits and chunky corbelled turrets. ALBANY HOUSE, 1963–5 by *Marshman & Warren*, is a depressing dark aggregate slab. On the E side ahead, the ARCADIAN shopping centre by *FaulknerBrowns Architects*, 1990–2. Drum feature with free-standing columns and surrounding cornice. Inside, a Stirlingesque circular courtyard, but the quality is poor. Fronting Hurst Street, the OLD FOX pub of 1892 by *James & Lister Lea*. Beyond it, *FaulknerBrowns'* façade breaks up the street front by curving recessions. On the corners with Inge Street, w, the Birmingham Hippodrome (p. 205) and a unique survival: the last group of BACK-TO-BACK HOUSES in the city. Three,

Nos. 50–54, to Inge Street, and the entrance to COURT NO. 15, with a row of single-pile 'blind backs', Nos. 55–63 Hurst Street. The site was leased in 1789 but the earliest building, No. 50 Inge Street, was not erected until 1809, apparently as an ordinary house. Converted to a back-to-back pair c. 1821, and the others added 1827–31. Repaired and converted into a museum and holiday flats by *Derek Clarke* and *Bob Tolley* of *S.T. Walker & Duckham*, 2002–4, for the Birmingham Conservation Trust and the National Trust. A three-storey L-shaped group, their small scale so close to the city centre typical of Birmingham. Fronts mostly Flemish bond, courtyard walls cheaper Flemish stretcher bond. The back-to-backs have one room on each floor, linked by newel staircases placed against the middle partition walls. Courtyard entry on Inge Street. Sash windows, some recessed, some flush in moulded frames. Typical Birmingham moulded lintels to the first floor on Hurst Street. In the courtyard two late C19 ground-floor canted bays, and two much-rebuilt washhouses.

Further down Hurst Street, the former AUSTRALIAN BAR by *J. & L. Lea*, 1897. Neo-Georgian N extension by *Batemans*, 1930. W along Bromsgrove Street, the former ROSE & CROWN, 1900 by *William Jenkins*, with his favourite bargeboarded gables. Brick, four tall storeys. Nos. 119–133 Hurst Street, 1931 by *Alfred J. Dunn*, with pediments and banded piers, originally car showrooms. The VILLAGE INN, E side, is early C19 (ground floor 1887 by *C.J. Hodson*). Beyond, a large factory of 1935 by *C.F. Lawley Harrod*. Long banded windows.

Back to Smallbrook and N along HILL STREET. On the SE corner of Station Street, the CROWN INN, stucco classical of c. 1876, perhaps by *Thomson Plevins*. Original ground floor with Corinthian pilasters. STATION STREET has New Street Station on the N (p. 136). On the S the former Shaftesbury Coffee House and Temperance Hotel, a plain trabeated design by *J.P. Sharp & Co.*, 1890. The ELECTRIC CINEMA, 1909 by *Bertie Crewe*, was reconstructed 1936–7 by *Cecil E.M. Fillmore*. His front was restored from photographs in 2004. Then a former wine merchant's of 1890–1 by *J.P. Sharp & Co.* with upcurving cornice, and the Old Rep Theatre (p. 205). Finally the former MARKET HOTEL on the corner of Dudley Street. 1883 by *Plevins & Norrington*. Warm orange brick with sandstone dressings and terracotta panels. Big bays with rounded ends, pilasters with foliage panels and little curly pediments. Built as part-hotel, part-warehouse for H.E. Jordan, pram-maker; his initials and Plevins's appear.

2. Holloway Head to Severn Street

From Holloway Circus, HOLLOWAY HEAD leads W between the Sentinels (p. 207) and past Bethel church (p. 204). On the N side, LEE BANK BUSINESS CENTRE is a former City Council flatted factory of 1957–8 by *Philip Skelcher & Partners*.

Up BLUCHER STREET alongside, TREFOIL HOUSE (E) with a big semicircular bow, by *Holland W. Hobbiss & Partners*, 1962. Opposite, a former furniture factory by *J. Seymour Harris & Partners*, 1954–5, good Festival of Britain style, with curtain walling, rubble-stone-faced basement and brick staircases with projecting headers. The CRAVEN ARMS pub is of 1906 by *Arthur Edwards*, with splendid terracotta: blue ground floor, golden-brown fascia and plaques above. On the E side again, Singers Hill Synagogue (p. 204). COMMERCIAL STREET runs SW here with a Gothic factory by *Yeoville Thomason*, 1872, now apartments and nastily rendered. Further on, THE CUBE, by *Make* (*Ken Shuttleworth*), 2008–10. A glazed base, a fifteen-storey 'cube' clad in gold- and bronze-coloured anodized aluminium panels of varying size and depth, and pointed steel-and-glass structures flying out at the top like horns. The panels are patterned like an overcooked version of Lubetkin's Sivill House. It has an atrium plan, and the N side facing the canal is hollowed out, with the panels forming a screen wall: a pointless conceit. Ten years on, it seems the quintessence of the moment before the crash: unmissable, screamingly loud and utterly tasteless.

Back to the synagogue, and E round the corner into Severn Street. On the S side a three-storey house of *c*. 1809. Then the former SEVERN STREET SCHOOL, now apartments.* First, a *Martin & Chamberlain* block of 1879–80, excellent Italian Gothic in red brick with terracotta panels. Central gable with a cusped round window above three transomed lancets. Large upstairs classroom with a complex and beautiful roof: tie-beams, arched braces, Gothic arcading, and end braces supporting the purlins at the hips. Behind it a block of 1869–70 in similar materials by *Yeoville Thomason*. Upper classroom with a good clerestory roof. Then, set back, the original 1809 building, reconstructed and extended upwards in 1851–2. A massive ten-bay, two-storey design, industrial in appearance: red brick, blue-brick dressings, iron-framed windows. Big cornice, with 'BRITISH SCHOOL' cut in the frieze. Beyond, the Athol Masonic Hall (p. 204). On the N side, with its entrance on Suffolk Street Queensway, THE MAILBOX. A postal sorting office of 1970, the largest in England, by the *Ministry of Public Building & Works* with *Hubbard Ford & Partners*; reconstructed as shops, flats and two hotels in 1999–2001 by *Associated Architects*, with *Weedon Partnership* and *TCN*. The front quotes no historical motifs but is irresistibly reminiscent of a huge Renaissance palazzo: stone base, red rendered elevation with tall windows hinting at pilasters, big central entrance up steps, dark metal and glass attic.

---

*A Quaker Sunday (First Day) School, founded here in 1845 by the merchant and peace campaigner Joseph Sturge, taught literacy and numeracy to adults and poor children. Led for many years by Alderman William White, who chaired the Improvement Committee which built Corporation Street. George Cadbury taught here from 1859, and in 1903 mentioned meeting five former mayors at the teachers' Sunday breakfast.

Holloway Head continues w as BATH ROW. On the N side the former QUEEN'S HOSPITAL. What remain are the heavy original block by *Bateman & Drury*, 1840–1, with a porch on mutilated piers and surmounted by coat of arms, and an Italian Romanesque block of 1871–3 by *Martin & Chamberlain*, with a raised centrepiece and big arch.

SUBURBS: NORTH AND NORTH-WEST

All Saints, Summerfield and Winson Green	211
Churches	214
Public buildings	215
Other buildings	217
Aston	218
Churches	218
Aston Hall	221
Public buildings	227
Other buildings	228
Aston Cross	228
Newtown	229
Birchfield	230
Castle Vale	231
Duddeston and Nechells	232
Erdington	235
Churches	235
Public buildings	238
Perambulation	239
Other buildings	240
Handsworth	242
Places of worship	243
Public buildings	251
Perambulations	255
Other buildings	261
Kingstanding	261
Lozells	264
Perry Barr	265
Perry Beeches	268
Pype Hayes	269

ALL SAINTS, SUMMERFIELD AND WINSON GREEN

The western part of old Birmingham parish, much of it originally the common land of Birmingham Heath. The boundaries are the middle ring road, Hockley Brook, the city boundary and Edgbaston Reservoir. The usual history of C19 urban development and later C20 urban decline. The prison and asylum

BIRMINGHAM SUBURBS

5 km / 5 miles

- Perry Beeches
- Perry Ba[rr]
- West Bromwich (see p.601)
- Handsworth
- Birchfie[lds]
- Lozells
- All Saints, Summerfield & Winson Green
- BIRMINGHA[M]
- Ladywood
- Quinton
- Harborne
- Edgbaston
- Balsa[ll]
- Bartley Green
- Weoley
- Selly Oak
- Bournville
- Stirchley
- Kin[gs] Hea[th]
- Frankley
- Northfield
- Kings Norton
- Brandwo[od] with Druids Heath
- Longbridge & Rednal

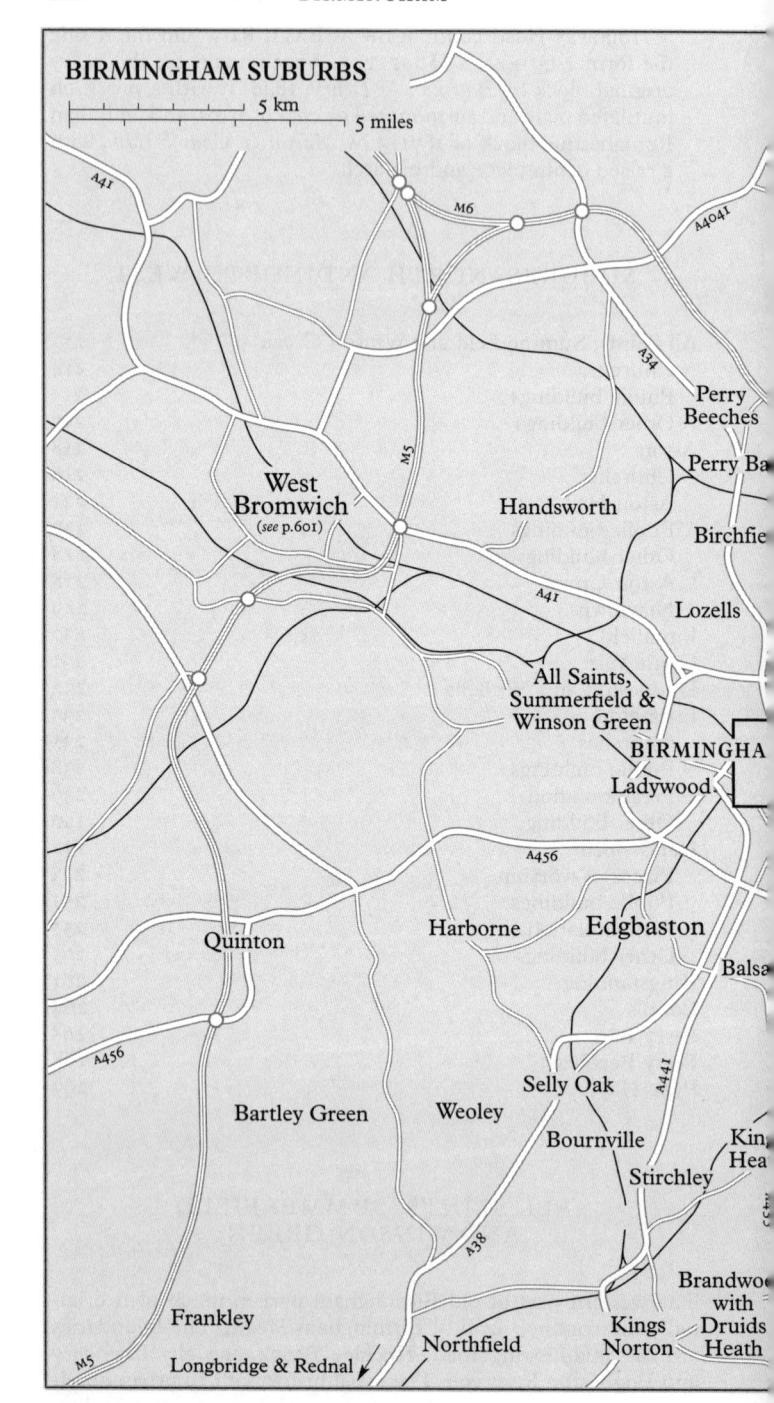

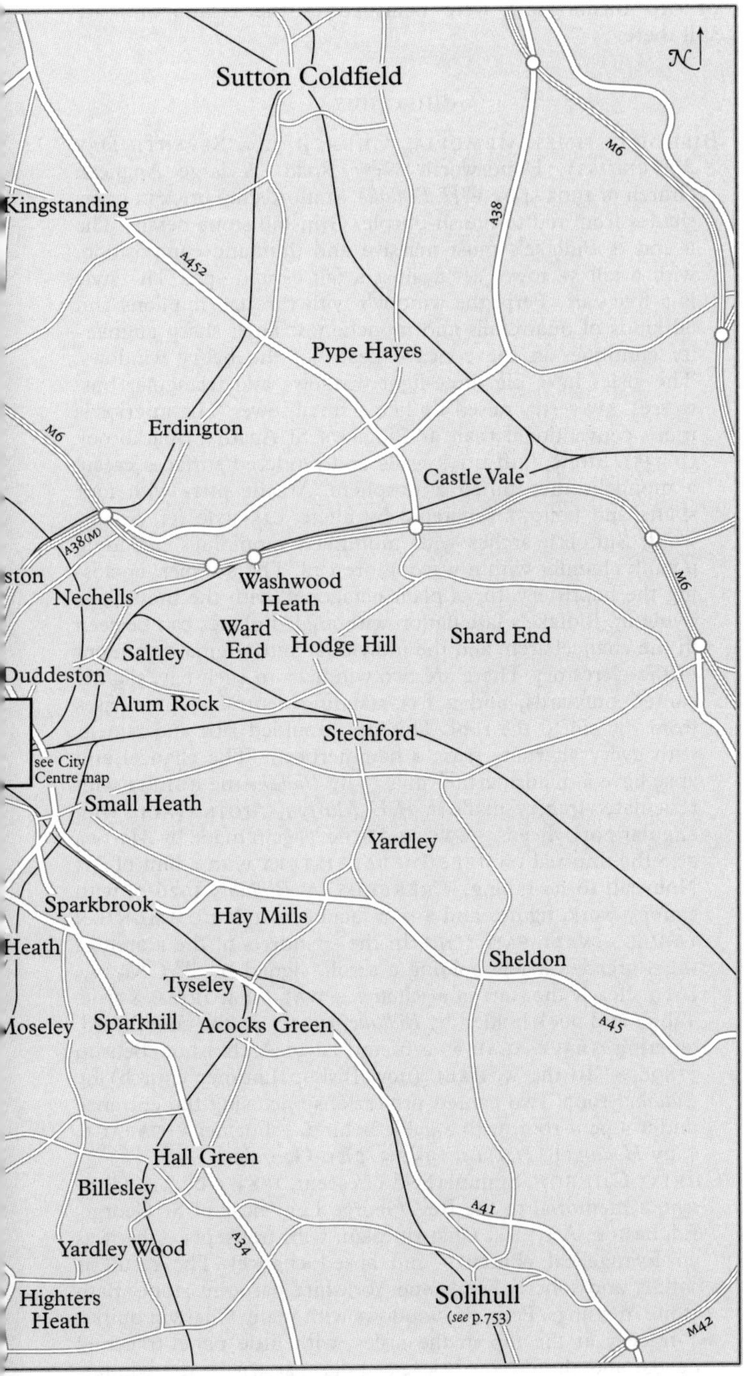
N
Sutton Coldfield
M6
A38
Kingstanding
A452
Pype Hayes
M6
Erdington
Castle Vale
A38(M)
ston
Nechells
Washwood
Heath
M6
Ward
End
Saltley
Hodge Hill
Shard End
Duddeston
Alum Rock
Stechford
see City
Centre map
Small Heath
Yardley
Sparkbrook
Hay Mills
Heath
Sheldon
Tyseley
Moseley
Sparkhill
Acocks Green
A45
Hall Green
Billesley
A41
A34
Yardley Wood
Highters
Heath
Solihull
(see p.753)
M42

of C19 Birmingham were banished to the Heath, and are still there.

CHURCHES

BISHOP LATIMER MEMORIAL CHURCH (now SEVENTH DAY ADVENTIST), Handsworth New Road. A large Anglican church of 1903–4 by *W.H. Bidlake*. Staffordshire brick in many shades from red to bluish-purple. Grinshill stone details. The E end is Bidlake's most massive and dramatic composition, with a tall SE tower set against a tall canted apse. The style is a free early Perp, the windows with through mullions and all kinds of quatrefoils and mouchettes. Their sharp angularity continues in the concave heads of the belfry windows. The aisles have big three-light windows and triangular buttresses. SW vestry raised up like a small tower. The interior is more conventional than at Bidlake's St Agatha, Sparkbrook (p. 335). Stone, buff-brick walls and rendered surfaces create a monochrome, muted atmosphere. Arcade piers with four shafts and hollows separated by fillets, C15-style (cf. Southwold, Suffolk); arches with multiplied mouldings including a sunk chamfer with a wave, more C14. The SW pier, enclosing the baptistery, turns plain octagonal, with the mouldings dying in. Bidlake's fascination with angled planes can be seen in the chancel arch, and the individual and original treatment of the clerestory. There are two windows to each bay, slightly canted outwards, and a free-standing central column rises from the sill to the roof. This has moulded ribs and panels, with every alternate truss a hammerbeam. The chancel and apse have a quadripartite vault. – By *Bidlake* the PULPIT with reticulated tracery, made by *H.H. Martyn*; CHOIR STALLS with angular poppyheads; PEWS; and FONT, again made by *Martyn*; also the unusual IMMERSION BAPTISTERY with a hint of Art Nouveau to its railing. – REREDOS by *Bidlake*, 1926–7, with canopy-work, figures and a rich Jacobean-style COMMUNION TABLE. – WALL PAINTING. In the spandrels of the E arch of the S arcade, angels holding a scroll, signed by *W.J. Neatby*, 1909, clearly the start of a scheme. – WAR MEMORIAL, S aisle. Tablet and book holder, by *Bidlake*, 1925. – In the churchyard, tapering GRAVE-SLAB as a memorial to Archbishop Benson †1896. – To the W, HALL (now Bishop Latimer church) by *Bidlake*, 1907. Two canted projections enclosing the entrance under a pent roof, with a gable behind. – Former VICARAGE, S, by *Holland W. Hobbiss*, 1932–3. Neo-Georgian.

CHRIST CHURCH, Summerfield Crescent. 1883–5 by *J.A. Chatwin*, a memorial to the Rev. George Lea, vicar of St George, Edgbaston. A typical Chatwin plan, with transepts – this was an Evangelical church – and apsed chancel. The result is solidly and soberly handsome. Yorkshire parpoint stone, Bath stone dressings. Perp, the windows with many Chatwin quirks: Y-tracery at the top in the aisles, with little panel-traceried heads; and the curious bicycle-spoke pattern in the window

SUBURBS N & NW: ALL SAINTS ETC. 215

over the W doorway. An intended NW tower was never built. Castellated porch instead by *J.A. Chatwin & Son*, 1907. Arcades with octagonal piers and double-chamfered arches; foliage and flower capitals. Typical chancel arch with shafts on corbels. A plainer arch separates the apse, of which the wall below the windows is panelled and treated as the reredos. Nave roof with segmental trusses, timber-vaulted chancel. HALL attached at the SE, by *S.N. Cooke*, 1921–2. – By *Chatwin* the COMMUNION RAIL with tracery, typical CHOIR STALLS, and Caen stone PULPIT, also typical, with figures under canopies. – Small octagonal FONT. – ALTAR by *Bidlake & Knight*, 1932.

ST PETER (now NEW TESTAMENT CHURCH OF GOD), George Street West. 1900–2 by *F.B. Osborn*. Bald brick Perp. SW tower of a rather pointed nature. Triple-gabled narthex, with a (former) baptistery. Statue on the W gable, and heads below and on the E arches of the arcades, carver *Thomas Catley*. Transeptal S chapel with a good tall arcade. The best feature is the transeptal N organ chamber, again with tall arches enclosing the ORGAN CASE, with an arcaded passageway below. Modern inserted ceiling. – Original REREDOS (moved forward), PEWS, CHOIR STALLS (now S chapel) and 'remodelled' FONT from *Rickman & Hutchinson*'s St Peter, Dale End, of 1825–7, which the church replaced. – STAINED GLASS. E window by *Heaton, Butler & Bayne*, 1902. S chapel E, the Annunciation, a lovely piece by *Mary Lowndes*, 1906.

ST PATRICK (R.C.), Dudley Road. 1894–5 by *Dempster & Heaton*. C13-style Gothic, rather French-influenced, with tall proportions. Red brick with stone dressings. Dark red sandstone arcades with plain capitals. Aisle roofs supported on half-arches running down to the ground. Only the very tall chancel arch is more ornate, with paired shafts and rich leaf capitals. – Tremendous original REREDOS in the E.W. Pugin manner, with scenes under canopies and a very tall spire. – Rich ALTAR and side chapel ALTARS with stubby columns; also low DADO SCREENS with bronze entrance gates. – Original PEWS. – PRESBYTERY, E. A stuccoed house of *c.*1830 with smooth rustication and panelled pilasters above.

CHURCH OF GOD OF PROPHECY, Aberdeen Street. 1979 by *Building & Urban Design Associates (Rob Ford)*. A big cut-off blue metal roof on a purply brick base. Inside, the focus is a stage-like area in the far corner.

PUBLIC BUILDINGS

SUMMERFIELD CENTRE, Winson Green Road. The former DUDLEY ROAD BOARD SCHOOL, by *Martin & Chamberlain*, 1876–8. One of their finest brick Gothic schools, showing J.H. Chamberlain's devotion to Ruskin. The main elevation faces E. Two-storey girls' and infants' school, l., with timbered gables; compact three-storey boys' school r., pulled together by a porch bay and a tower. Behind, an octagon rising to a spire with big lucarnes. The Dudley Road front has a semicircular bow, and gables with ogee windows and flower carvings. The boys' upper hall has a good hammerbeam roof. Similar, smaller ones in the flanking classrooms. Girls' hall with pierced iron trusses and a glazed screen dividing off the semicircular end. Original doors with chamfered timbers; matchboarded dadoes throughout.

PUBLIC LIBRARY, Spring Hill and Icknield Street Middleway. By *Martin & Chamberlain* (*Frederick Martin*), dated 1891, opened 1893. One of the finest buildings of the Birmingham terracotta school – here pinky-red, with red brick. Tall gabled blocks with big traceried windows, and a corner tower with two tiers of pinnacles and a short open spire. Lots of decoration, including a big coat of arms in the larger central gable to Icknield Street, and shield and crest in a triangular gable above the tower doorway. The interior has a pointed barrel-vault (with a splendid original gas fitting) with the main ribs on marble piers, and a gallery. Now linked by a glazed atrium to a supermarket of 2010.

Two more SCHOOLS by *Martin & Chamberlain*. FOUNDRY ROAD PRIMARY (now Academy) is of 1882–3. Low ranges with half-timbered gables. The infill, unusually, is abstract patterns of coloured tiles. BARFORD PRIMARY, Barford Road, is of the *Frederick Martin* period, 1887. Round-arched, with plain restoration after Second World War bombing. Cut-down tower with projections like elongated Corinthian pilasters, topped by steep gablets.

BENSON PRIMARY SCHOOL, Benson Road, is by *Thomason & Whitwell*, 1887–8. Heavy terracotta Perp windows and a more delicate Gothic spire, with traceried timber ventilation openings.

BIRMINGHAM CITY HOSPITAL, Dudley Road. This began as the Birmingham Union Workhouse, 1850–2 by *Bateman & Drury*; demolished c.1990–2017. Towards the rear of the site is a former BOYS' SCHOOL of 1869–70 by *Martin & Chamberlain*, basic brick Gothic, with disfiguring extensions. A very large INFIRMARY was added to the W in 1887–9 by *W.H. Ward*. This has a pavilion plan, with nine T-shaped ward blocks set alternately E and W of a corridor nearly a quarter of a mile long, the system of Blackburn Infirmary of 1857. Again basic Gothic. Alterations by *Martin & Martin & W.H. Ward*, including a first-floor CHAPEL of 1931–2, barrel-vaulted, with a pretty blue-and-gold reredos of 1940 by *Martin Travers*. Ward's front block, with a tall tower and spire, was replaced by *Martin, Martin & Ward*'s range of 1963–5. Bright blue panels, jazzy concrete grid above the entrance. To its E the BIRMINGHAM TREATMENT CENTRE by *Sheppard Robson*, 2006, metal-clad, with a glazed foyer. At the NE corner of the site, off Western Road, the BIRMINGHAM AND MIDLAND EYE CENTRE by *Abbey Hanson Rowe*, 1994–6, red and yellow brick with a Postmodern entrance.

BIRMINGHAM PRISON, Winson Green Road. This was the Borough Gaol of 1845–9 by *D.R. Hill*, a job which launched his career as a prison architect. Much of Hill's building is still there, a combination of radial and linear plan, with a long main N–S wing. Cut-down ventilation towers mark the central space and end wings. Many additions, including some by *Martin & Chamberlain*, c.1870. Hill's splendid gatehouse was demolished in 1989. Replacement entrance block by *Howell Killick Partridge & Amis* (partner in charge *Patrick Lawlor*), 1983–7. A Postmodern fortress, in orange-red brick and blue cladding. Entrance flanked by domed towers, in a reference to its predecessor. Security area behind, corbelled and cantilevered out, and a big tower with a low pyramid roof and blue-clad service projections. Rebuilt perimeter wall with flat buttresses, and another tower to the N.

E of the prison, accessed from Lodge Road, is the former BOROUGH ASYLUM, later ALL SAINTS HOSPITAL, now Prison Service offices. Also by *Hill*, 1847–50. A long Jacobean front with projecting centre and wings which have shaped gables and pierced balustrades, almost like a country house. Four-centred-arched doorway with an oriel above. N wing with canted end, part of extensions by *Martin & Chamberlain*, 1861–6 and 1874–8. The rest has been demolished and the site incorporated into the prison.

OTHER BUILDINGS

The best area is on Dudley Road. On the S side opposite the Summerfield Centre is SUMMERFIELD PARK, laid out by the Borough Surveyor *W.S. Till* in 1877–8. Facing Dudley Road, a lodge-like former POLICE STATION by *Martin & Chamberlain*, 1878–9, with half-timbered gables. BANDSTAND of 'Shell or Orchestra type' by the Baths and Parks Committee's engineer *Mr Cox*, 1907. Brick, with a terracotta gable supported on iron piers. W of the park entrance, in the angle of City Road, a former LLOYDS BANK by *J.A. Chatwin & Son*, 1901–2, Jacobean, with a semicircular oriel above the entrance. No. 381 Dudley Road, on the corner of Winson Street, is the former YORKSHIRE GREY pub, by *Henry Naden*, 1888, still stuccoed, with a scatter of swan's-neck pediments.

E of the park, the OLD WINDMILL pub (No. 84 Dudley Road), early C19 stucco, with typical segmental lintels with moulded keystones (cf. St Patrick's church presbytery immediately W, p. 215). The sculptural brick and concrete block on the NE corner of Western Road is a Midlands Electricity Board SUB-STATION of 1957–8 (board architect *A.W. Elliott*). Further E, in GEORGE STREET WEST by St Peter's church (p. 215), stucco terraces of four houses with round-headed doorways, and a pair with first-floor pilasters and entrances set back. They look c.1820–30, but map evidence suggests c.1850. The former vicarage is by *C.E. Bateman*, 1910–11. Neo-Georgian. In Steward Street S of Dudley Road, an altered former Board School by *Martin & Chamberlain*, 1872–3, extended by *H.T. Buckland*, 1925–6.

An interesting group on HANDSWORTH NEW ROAD, s of Bishop Latimer church (p. 214). Nos. 18–24 are by *Bidlake*, 1906, alas much altered. Beyond, the former HANDSWORTH NEW ROAD SCHOOL by *Buckland & Haywood-Farmer*, dated 1901. An original Free Style design, badly converted into flats. Gabled wings with half-elliptical windows, square porches with little recessed spires topped with finials. The hall block has simplified shaped gables.

ASTON

The manor of Aston wraps round central Birmingham to the N (the medieval parish which stretched E as far as Castle Bromwich and Water Orton). It developed rapidly in the C19 with tight-packed housing, and industry particularly in the Tame valley. Aston Manor was an Urban District (1894) and briefly a Borough, chartered in 1903 but absorbed into Birmingham in 1911. Its arms, with the motto 'Exaltavit humiles' ('He hath exalted the humble and meek'), can still be seen in several places. The commercial centre was at Aston Cross, ½ m. s, where the Birmingham to Lichfield road met a road running NW from Saltley. An unexpected group of civic buildings survives in the terraced streets W of Aston Hall and Park, around Witton Lane and Whitehead Road. The ancient village and the Holte almshouses of 1655–6 have gone. To the SE around Aston Cross, housing and factories disappeared in the late C20 for the Aston Expressway and industrial zoning. For Lozells, W of the Walsall road, *see* p. 264. In the C21 Aston means for many people a university, which is not in Aston (*see* p. 188), and a football club, which very prominently is.

CHURCHES

ST PETER AND ST PAUL, Witton Lane. A parish church on a grand scale, below the Hall to the E. Fine four-stage C15 tower with square angle buttresses, three-light windows and a most unusual bell-stage with rows of very worn trefoil-headed recesses containing two tiers of panels, two on each side forming windows. Tall octagonal spire without broaches, partly rebuilt 1776–7 by *John Cheshire*.

The rest was rebuilt from 1879 by *J.A. Chatwin*, largely paid for by John Feeney, owner of the *Birmingham Post*. Chancel and SE (Erdington) chapel were complete by 1883, nave by 1889; S aisle wall rebuilt 1893; N aisle and s porch not finished until 1908. The material is local sandstone. The result is Chatwin's finest church, rich, scholarly, eclectic and wonderfully spacious. The style is mid-C14: late Dec, turning Perp. The magnificent five-sided E apse must be inspired by St Michael, Coventry, its multi-stepped buttresses bristling with pinnacles, its height emphasized by three-light windows with continuous mullions. The chancel side windows have upper transoms, as do those in the nave clerestory. Continuous battlements. The aisle and Erdington chapel have Y-tracery, to incorporate glass from the previous chancel. Linked HALL at the NW by *K.C. White & Partners*, 1978–9.

The interior must also be inspired by Coventry: a single great space without a chancel arch, and dominated by the apse. Seven-bay nave arcades with alternating round and octagonal piers. Capitals with bossy foliage. Above them the wall checks in below the clerestory and the wall-shafts break free, stopping just above the labels of the arcade arches, a typical Chatwin detail. Opulent two-bay chancel arcades in Lincs. or Notts. Dec, e.g. Hawton. Their ogee arches have rich crocketing, cusping embellished with angels, and pinnacles breaking the sills above. The roof has alternating hammerbeams and arch-braced camber-beams. Chancel division marked by hammerbeam trusses with openwork tracery. The Erdington Chapel has a wooden barrel-vault and a big corbel of a knight, NE. Tall C15 tower arch with four continuous chamfers, alternating plain and hollow. Minimalist C20 N aisle room.

FURNISHINGS. All by *Chatwin*. The grandest set of his characteristic CHOIR STALLS with scrolled tops to the ends, here carrying biblical figures. – PULPIT. 1885. Alabaster and grey marble, with biblical scenes. – Mosaic FLOORS in chancel and Erdington Chapel. – Stone REREDOS. – Simple PEWS. – FONT, 1881. – STAINED GLASS. The climax of the apse is five glorious *Hardman* windows of 1885 representing the Adoration of the Lamb. More Hardman, of 1883, in the Erdington Chapel. N chapel E, behind the organ, by *Lavers & Barraud*, c.1860.*
S aisle, from the former church: second from E by *Hardman*, 1869; third by *Alexander Gibbs*, 1862–3; fifth by *Heaton, Butler & Bayne*, 1893. Tower W, *Lavers, Barraud & Westlake*, c.1884. Tower N, 1931, like a book illustration.

MONUMENTS. An important collection. Chancel. Alabaster effigy of a knight, c.1360, and sandstone effigy of a lady, c.1490, lying together on a stone and alabaster tomb-chest. This is probably Dugdale's 'faire monument of Arden removed from the priorye of Maxstoke'. – Mutilated sandstone effigy of a knight, early C15. – Sir Thomas Erdington †1433 and his wife Joan or Anne Harcourt †1417, he in armour, she in long skirt and mantle. Alabaster tomb-chest with very linear angels, and shields. Probably made c.1459, when Sir Thomas's son built a chantry chapel. – Erdington Chapel. Late C15 effigy of a knight, probably Sir William Harcourt, on a similar tomb-chest with finely carved angels. – Sir Edward Devereux †1622 and his lady. A fine altar tomb in alabaster and black marble, with a canopy of a heavy curved pediment on Corinthian columns. – John Frederick Feeney †1899 by *Sir George Frampton*. Arts and Crafts plaque in a classical surround. The

---

*The N window by *Francis Eginton*, 1798, is in store.

lower band has trees with his children named on hearts. – N aisle, E end. William Holte †1518 and wife. Sandstone effigies on a tomb-chest. Philip Chatwin suggested that a local workman was told to copy the Erdington and Harcourt monuments. – Charles King †1712, attributed to *Edward Stanton* (GF). Tablet with Corinthian columns and astronomical instruments in the predella. – Sir Thomas Holte †1654, erected *c.* 1715. By *Edward Stanton*. Corinthian pilasters and weeping putti. All carved with great spirit. – Sir Charles Holte †1722, attributed to *Edward Stanton & Christopher Horsnaile* (GF). Of similar type but later, more Baroque style. Free-standing columns, and standing children. – Sir Lister Holte, by the elder *Westmacott*, 1794. Sarcophagus on lions' feet. – N aisle W, inside room. Edward †1592 and Dorothy Holte. Big semicircular-headed recess with Corinthian columns. Conventional kneeling figures facing across a desk. – Sir Charles Holte †1782. Portrait medallion and mourning woman. – Henry Charles †1700, servant to Sir Charles Holte. Draped tablet with fringed canopy. – James †1821 and Ann Goddington, by *W. Hollins*, with typical drooping laurels. – George Yates †1828 by *Seaborne*. Tall tomb-chest. – S aisle, from E. Sir John Bridgeman †1710, erected 1726 and prominently signed by *James Gibbs*. An excellent, strongly architectural piece. Tablet with a semicircular top flanked by swans' necks. Cherubs stand on them and support an oval niche with urn. – Thomas and Catherine Caldecott †1774 and †1788. One putto with a Bible, the other a torch. By *Joseph Wilton*, perhaps from a design of *Sir William Chambers* (GF). – Robert and Laetitia Holden †1730 and †1751, by *Michael Rysbrack*. Simple pedimented tablet, but exquisite angels, just heads and wings, either side. – Edward and Sarah Brandwood †1731 and †1762, by *Eglington Sen.* – Booth family †1673–89. Big oval tablet; segmental pediment. Attributed to *Sir William Wilson* (GF). – Nave NW, Rev. Josiah Foster †1727 by *Thomas White*. – Tower, slab with 25-in. (63.5-cm.) figured BRASSES to John Holte †1545 and wife.

ALL SOULS (now CHURCH OF GOD UNIVERSAL), Wenlock Road, Witton. 1906–7 by *Philip B. Chatwin*. A powerful design with a big, low pyramid-roofed tower over the (ritual) W part of the chancel. Late Dec tracery at the E end, triplets elsewhere. The scheme included the HALL, W. Brick and stone (now painted) inside. Kingpost roof with wind-braces: simple, like a barn. Original PULPIT, CHOIR STALLS and REREDOS. – STAINED GLASS. Rich and glowing E window by *A.E. Lemmon*, 1933, 'The Spirit of Birmingham'. The Tree of Life blossoms between the Town Hall and Council House. The standing figures include bishops Gore and Wakefield.

ST JAMES, Frederick Road. 1981 by *S.T. Walker & Partners*.

SACRED HEART OF JESUS AND ST MARGARET MARY (R.C.), Witton Road. By *G.B. Cox (Harrison & Cox)*, designed 1914, built 1920–2. An exuberant Italian Romanesque basilica, Ultramontane to its core, and a fascinating contrast to contemporary Anglican churches in the same style. Brindled brick and grey stone. NW campanile, added in 1934–5. Its upper storeys are arcaded, inspired by Roman examples, Santa Maria in Cosmedin and San Giorgio al Velabro. In a niche, STATUE of Christ by *Gibbs & Canning*. Four-bay arcades of granite monoliths, with cream brick voussoirs, and an apsed sanctuary. Transepts for side chapels. Barrel-vaults of Colombian pine. NW tower baptistery. But what hits you is the decoration. Everywhere there is mosaic by *J. Linthout*, and marble carved by *R.L. Boulton* and *Fraleys*. The apse is faced in marble, with mosaics of saints in arcading and a panel of Christ and St Margaret Mary above. – HIGH ALTAR of Pavonazzo marble. – N (Lady) ALTAR with alabaster statue and rails of white and green Connemara marble. – S (St Joseph) chapel with RELIEF of the saint's death in an arch with Ionic columns, and ALTAR with relief of the wedding of St Joseph and Our Lady. – STATIONS OF THE CROSS painted on a curious hard surface. – Original CHOIR STALLS and PEWS.

WESLEYAN METHODIST CHURCH (former), Mansfield Road. 1883 by *G.F. Hawkes*. Gothic. Rock-faced front, big rose window.

CHRIST CHURCH BAPTIST CHURCH (former), Witton Road (Six Ways). 1864–5 by *James Cranston*. Now flats, after a devastating late C20 fire. A vigorous design with boldly contrasting red and blue brick. The tower cuts in above the ground floor and then has corner and middle buttresses with steep nosings, the middle ones shorter, stopping underneath the plate-traceried belfry windows. All the elements cut back from the wall-plane in the High Victorian way. The spire has big gabled lucarnes set at the angles. Rear school block of 1888 by *J.G. Dunn & F.W. Hipkiss*.

ASTON HALL*

The only major Jacobean mansion in the old county of Warwickshire, Aston Hall is now a stranded relic of Birmingham's rural past, prominently sited on a ridge overlooking the road between Birmingham and Lichfield. The house was built in 1618–35 for Sir Thomas Holte (1571–1654), a landowner with Court connections. In 1656 Sir William Dugdale called Aston Hall 'a noble fabric...which for beauty and state much exceedeth any in these parts'. Its exceptional height, elaborate articulation and strict symmetry, and the dramatic skyline of lead-capped turrets and shaped gables, recall such great Jacobean contemporaries as Hatfield (Herts.), Blickling (Norfolk) and Holland House in the London outskirts. The plan derives from drawings supplied by *John Thorpe*. Thorpe is best known as a surveyor, rather than as a designer of houses, but the ground- and first-floor plans for Aston Hall (in his 'Book of Architecture', now in the Soane Museum) are clearly design proposals rather than survey drawings.

---

*Description by Oliver Fairclough.

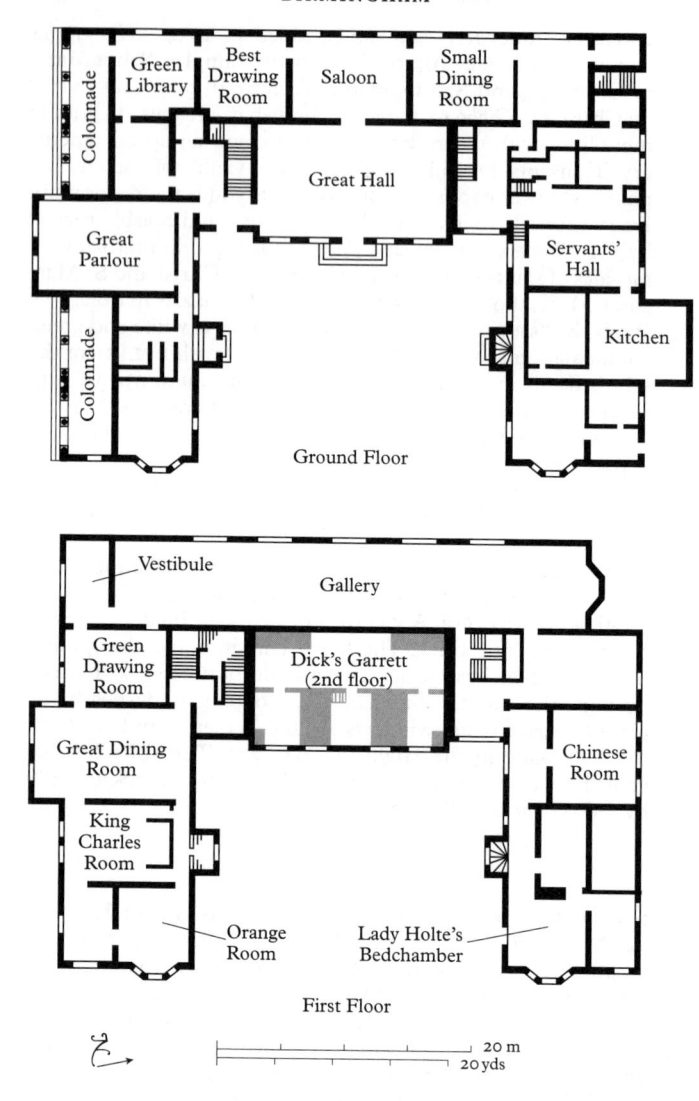

Birmingham, Aston Hall.
Ground- and first-floor plans

The last Holte to live at Aston was Sir Lister (†1770), and the estates were dispersed in 1817. From 1819 Aston Hall was occupied by James Watt Junior (1769–1848), son of the great engineer (*see* p. 245). *Richard Bridgens*, who had worked for George Bullock at Battle Abbey and at Sir Walter Scott's Abbotsford, designed antiquarian furnishings for him. Much of Aston Park was developed in the 1850s, and Aston Hall was saved from demolition by a

Birmingham working men's committee, which, as the Aston Hall and Park Co., opened it as a museum and place of entertainment, 1858–64. The house was acquired by Birmingham Corporation (the first major historic house in Britain to pass into public ownership) and is now a branch of Birmingham Museums and Art Gallery.

Exterior

The main block faces E, with projecting wings enclosing a forecourt. Red brick, in English bond with blue-grey diapering, and pale grey sandstone dressings (almost entirely renewed), including quoins, and string courses at the level of the window heads. The middle five bays of the EAST FRONT, corresponding to the ground-floor hall and three upper chambers, break forward slightly, with a balustrade parapet and, despite three-light transomed windows, have a more classical feel than the rest of the front. Flanking staircase bays with transomed windows of different sizes. Central round-headed doorway flanked by Doric columns. An inscribed panel above states that the house was begun in 1618, occupied in 1631 and completed in 1635. This sits a little uncomfortably below a broken pediment which seems more Mannerist than the surrounding ornament. A centrally placed entrance to the hall would be a progressive arrangement for the 1620s, but it has now been established that this part is a refacing, probably of the mid C17, replacing a porch at the lower end of the hall and an upper-end bay window, as indicated by Thorpe. The doorway appears to be the original, widened and re-set. The roof-line is enlivened by four shaped gables with pinnacles, and by a tall central tower with an elaborate ogee and square-dome lead cupola (clock added 1867). The house was largely reglazed in the C18 with octagonal panes in wooden frames, and some of these survived late C19 re-leading.

Aston's projecting WINGS, a conservative feature and longer than those of many late Elizabethan and Jacobean houses, give an impression of depth and recession, emphasized by the long forecourt walls. A square stair-turret projects from each inner face, slightly lower than the central tower, and with simpler ogee cupolas. Each has a doorway flanked by flat fluted pilasters, with a shell tympanum. The more ornate first-floor pilasters are ornamented with masks. These are recent replacements, but their form is recorded in early views. On either side of the turrets are transomed windows below shaped gables. The wings end in three-sided bay windows with strap-work cresting.

Originally the outer ends of the wings were only one bay wide. Sometime around 1700, these were extended outwards over a single-storey loggia, S, and service room, N. This programme also transformed the fenestration of the SOUTH (GARDEN) FRONT. At first-floor level this side contained the principal apartments. These appear to have been built to Thorpe's plan, with a two-storey polygonal central bay to the Great Dining Room, flanked by round and three-sided oriels. Only the shaped gables and the arcaded Doric loggia on either side of the Great Parlour remain after the remodelling, which swept away all the projecting windows and filled in the corners at first-floor level.

The WEST FRONT is of two storeys rather than three, with a flat roof over the Gallery, and an C18 parapet topped with urns. Behind rises the third storey of the hall range, comprising six shaped gables and a broad central chimneystack. This front has also been conservatively remodelled, removing three original projecting bays. The centre is now the tall Saloon doorway, with a window above flanked by niches.*

NORTH FRONT. The service and family wing is the most altered part of the house. The original bay window at the N end of the Gallery remains. The next bay E has been extended outwards to the line of the projecting central block, which on the ground floor contained the kitchen (subsequently servants' hall). The gables here are C18, the five first-floor sash windows of c. 1800. The present single-storey kitchen may be mid-C18, and its E extension probably a little later. The latter was remodelled for James Watt in 1835.

Interior

Thorpe's drawings, inventories of 1654, 1771 and 1794, sale catalogues of 1817 and 1849, and survey plans of c. 1824 do much to elucidate how the house was used. Much of the C17 interior was exuberantly decorated, and several outstanding plaster ceilings survive, together with a richly carved principal staircase and the fine panelled Gallery.

The ENTRANCE HALL – the great hall of Sir Thomas Holte's house – was substantially reorganized by the early C18. Original ceiling of the 1630s, with a frieze of animals added by James Watt. Round-headed stone archways on the S, W and N (only the first, to the main staircase, in its original position), in walls lined with reused early C17 panelling (that on the E wall evidently later). Two arches in the panelling on the W wall, flanked by Corinthian columns, contain large paintings of classical landscapes in the manner of *Jacques Rousseau*, while two more arches framed with pilasters on each side wall have grisaille paintings of warriors, also late C17 (could these arches have come from the Jacobean screen?). The fireplace was originally on the W wall, but the strapwork overmantel with a panel bearing verses on the merits of service may be from Holte's

---

*This was the principal entrance in James Watt's time. *Bridgens*'s porch of 1835 was replaced by a conservatory of 1858, removed 1887. Until 1958 the niches contained early C17 statues of David and Solomon, originally on the E front.

time. Behind the Hall on the w side is the SALOON with, to the s, the BEST DRAWING ROOM (C18, but with a fine resited Jacobean fireplace), and a room fitted up as a library *c.* 1800. N of the Saloon is the SMALL DINING ROOM, completed 1771. Its fireplace and the early C18 panelling in the room beyond (from a house in Old Square, Birmingham) were introduced by Birmingham Museum. Holte's GREAT PARLOUR (subsequently the chapel), beyond the main staircase to the s, retains some C17 panelling, but has lost its fireplace and bay window.

The STAIRCASE is one of the glories of the house. The twenty-two newel posts are carved with masks, scrolls and canopies up to the first floor, with a simpler strapwork design on the upper flights. The string bears a running pattern of wyverns and winged horses. In place of balusters are richly

Birmingham, Aston Hall, staircase.
Engraving, C19

carved panels pierced with flowing strapwork. All this closely resembles a contemporary staircase at Crewe Hall, Cheshire (burnt 1866). The staircase was once painted, and the first-floor landing still exhibits damage said to be from a Parliamentarian assault in 1643.

UPPER FLOORS. A massive early C17 stone doorway with a strapwork pediment leads S from the landing into the GREAT DINING ROOM, the principal state room of Holte's house; later the Great Library, during James Watt's occupation. It originally had a large polygonal window on the S wall. The ceiling is the richest in the house, with cherubs' heads in cartouches between the ribs, and grotesque masks, apparently after a series designed by Cornelis Floris and engraved by Frans Huys, at the intersections. The frieze of the deep entablature below is decorated with high-relief figures of the Nine Worthies standing in niches, taken from C16 Flemish prints published by Philips Galle. Additional, later figures in the centre of N and S walls. The Jacobean fireplace with the Holte arms remains, though the central panel of the overmantel has gone. Bolection-moulded panelling of *c.* 1700.

To the E are the ORANGE ROOM, with C17 ceiling with orange trees and frieze with beasts, and the KING CHARLES ROOM (the Best Lodging Chamber in 1654). Beaded and jewelled strapwork ceiling and high-relief frieze of real and mythical animals. Later bed recess, flanked by Gothick columns of *c.* 1760. On the other (W) side of the Great Dining Room is the WITHDRAWING ROOM, with a fine C17 ceiling and a resited stone, marble and alabaster fireplace. The rest remodelled in the mid C18. It leads into the GALLERY. With its S extension of *c.* 1700 the Gallery is 136 ft (41.5 metres) long. Apart from the removal of its projecting W bays it is largely as built, with an intricate strapwork ceiling, arcaded panelling articulated by fluted Ionic pilasters, and a stone and alabaster fireplace. At its N end are the family chambers in the N wing, and the SECONDARY STAIRCASE with large square newel posts and open well. These rooms are largely C18 in character, and LADY HOLTE'S BEDCHAMBER at the E end has a large bed recess added *c.* 1700. On the second floor, 'DICK'S GARRET' over the hall chambers, the turret rooms and the attic chambers have changed little since the C17.

Much also remains of the original SETTING. To the E, the forecourt walls connect with two square LODGES, of two storeys topped by an attic with shaped gables. Their projecting E bays, echoing those of the wings behind, originally had ornamental gunloops rather than windows on the lower floor. The forecourt, originally enclosed by a screen wall and gateway, and later by iron railings and gates, was flanked by a large walled garden, S, and a service court, N. The two-storey building on the E side of the service court is Sir Thomas Holte's STABLE BLOCK, substantially rebuilt in the mid C18, and again 1858–64. Converted to a visitors' centre, with new cupola, by *Stephen*

Oliver of *Rodney Melville & Partners*, 2007–9. A N range was demolished in 1869. At the rear is a terrace, nearly 500 ft (150 metres) long, with at its N end the remains of a Jacobean undercroft, perhaps that of the banqueting house listed in the 1654 inventory.

To the W, the remains of a formal garden laid out by the Parks Department, with a fine but mutilated FOUNTAIN by *William Bloye*, 1934: bowl with undulating edge, now infilled, and figure of Pan. Two large VASES by *Bloye*, 1937.

PUBLIC BUILDINGS

COUNCIL HOUSE AND LIBRARY (former), Witton Road and Albert Road. 1880–1 by *William Henman*. Queen Anne, an early example in Birmingham. Cut down from a scheme of 1879 with a large tower, but still a good design. It turns an acute corner excellently with an octagonal tower with concave spire and cupola. Well massed to either side with projecting gabled bays. Sashes with small panes and panels with little swans' necks on top. Gables plainly rebuilt.

FIRE STATION, Ettington Road. 1923–4 by *H.H. Humphries*, City Engineer and Surveyor. A commanding Neo-Georgian block in red brick and grey faience, three tall storeys and a parapet, with banded angles and chimneys. Small domestic wings with canted bays.

HIGHER GRADE BOARD SCHOOLS (now Eden Boys Academy), Whitehead Road. Aston's grandest public building. It could be the town hall of a large borough. 1898–1900 by *Crouch & Butler*, chosen after a competition assessed by E.R. Robson, the London school architect. Not much of the architects' usual Arts and Crafts manner, but a wonderfully eclectic design, unified by its materials, buff terracotta and red brick. Wrenaissance central block, with a big segmental pediment and giant banded Ionic columns. Hipped roof and tall cupola. But the flanking staircases are in octagonal turrets with domed roofs, and the porches have a hint of Art Nouveau in their curves. A doorway on the S (Ettington Road) side has its cornice broken by a more than horseshoe pediment enclosing a heart-shaped window, and free curves flow round the voussoirs of the arch below. N wing with a sculptural Jacobean cupola. The attached CARETAKER'S HOUSE, NE, has a sheer Tudor gable and another octagonal turret, linked by a convex porch.

PRINCE ALBERT PRIMARY SCHOOL, Whitehead Road. By *Edward Holmes*, 1880–1, extended 1885 and 1891. Severe brick Gothic with three big gables, in Martin & Chamberlain's way. In Albert Road, l., the former SCHOOL BOARD OFFICES, also *Holmes*, dated 1880. Unequal gables, the taller, r., with a stone oriel.

KING EDWARD VI ASTON SCHOOL, Albert Road. Original buildings by *J.A. Chatwin*, in educational Tudor: brick and terracotta ranges of 1881–3 with gables facing the road, linked behind in 1896. New front range between the gables by *Frost Bevan*, 1994. Large buildings at the rear by *Martin, Martin & Ward*, 1960 etc.

TRAMWAYS DEPOT (former), Witton Lane. Built as a steam-tram depot in 1882, altered and refronted 1904–6 for electric trams, with a wide shaped gable (builder *George Trentham*). Tram tracks still run across the cobbled floor and the sheathing for electric wires survives above. Used, wonderfully, as a bus museum until 2011; now a banqueting centre.

OTHER BUILDINGS

VILLA PARK, Witton Lane and Trinity Lane. The most celebrated football ground in the West Midlands, and an architectural disaster. It was the Aston Lower Grounds, developed between 1864 and 1872 as a park and recreation area. In 1878–9 *Thomas Naden* added a spectacular *Rundbogenstil* restaurant, aquarium and great hall. Aston Villa F. C. moved here in 1897. The impressive Trinity Road stand with brick frontage was by *Archibald Leitch*, 1923. Replaced in the late C20, by builders and an in-house design team: North Stand 1977, Witton Lane Stand 1993, Holte End 1994 (with a pastiche of Leitch's brick front), Trinity Road Stand 2000.

PUBS. In the fork of Witton Lane and Trinity Road, the HOLTE HOTEL, a good foil to the parish church and Hall. Mostly 1864–72, as part of the Lower Grounds development (*see* above), but the picturesque Jacobean front is of *c.*1897, almost certainly by *Owen & Ward*. Restored 2007 by *Dyer*. At the cross-roads of Witton Road and Witton Lane, the former ASTON HOTEL, by *James & Lister Lea*, 1909–11. Restrained Jacobean in brick and grey terracotta. Gabled wings with two-storey bays flank a diagonally set centre with porch. On Witton Lane a grander, triple-arched porch to the function rooms. Just N, the WITTON ARMS, Neo-Georgian of 1937 by *H. Peter Hing*.

ASSOCIATED ELECTRICAL INDUSTRIES works (later G.E.C.), Dulverton Road, E of Electric Avenue. The administration block survives, by *Wallis, Gilbert & Partners*, 1920–2. Beaux Arts classical composition, Egyptianizing detail: Art Deco before the Paris Exhibition. Giant pilasters; capitals with tasselled volutes. The central bay has tapering sides and attached fluted columns in the returns with Egyptian leaf capitals, resting on corbels again with tasselling. Small dome above.

ASTON CROSS

C19 housing, Ansells Brewery and the HP Sauce factory have all gone. Cast-iron CLOCK TOWER, stranded on a roundabout, by *Arthur Edwards*, 1891, with a slim column and pedimented faces. One remaining line of buildings, immediately NE along LICHFIELD ROAD. The former GOLDEN CROSS pub is by *William Jenkins*, 1890–1. Brick, with steep gables, buttresses, broken cornices, and tiles and terracotta panels around big golden crosses. It has lost its corner spire. The former PUBLIC LIBRARY, nicely lettered, is of 1903 by the Council Surveyor *G.H. Jack*. Ruabon brick, practical in an industrial environment. Free Style, with sweeping shaped gable and blocked architraves to the ground-floor windows. Then a late C19 shop with thin colonnettes to the first-floor windows and an arched ground floor for the MIDLAND BANK by *T.B. Whinney*, 1898, a very early job. At No. 11 a heavy former BARCLAYS BANK of 1892 by *Thomason & Whitwell*, with an elephantine doorcase. Finally No. 13, a former draper's, 1904 by *John W. Meredith*, with continuous first-floor windows.

ASTON MANOR POST OFFICE (former), Aston Road North. Dated 1890. Neat Queen Anne, with Dutch gable and swan's-neck doorcase.

¼ m. NE along Lichfield Road is the mid-C19 former VINE HOTEL, r. Further on by Aston railway station, the former BRITANNIA, by *Wood & Kendrick*, 1898–1900. A refined pub design. Mostly terracotta, chestnut on the ground floor, cream above. The centre is a big full-height canted bay, a statue of Britannia on the top. (Partly original interior, with *Maw*'s tiles.) Beyond the bridge, the SWAN AND MITRE by *James & Lister Lea*, 1898–9. Lively brick and terracotta, with a corner oriel crowned by a cupola and finial, and shaped gables to both streets. Three-centred arches over the ground-floor windows, semicircular ones over the doors. Keystone-like voussoirs. The public bar retains its original bar front and back, panelled ceiling and bench seating. The lobby has characteristic *Minton* tiles. In Alfred Street to the N, EAST TELEPHONE EXCHANGE. 1909–10 by *Bromley & Watkins*. Neo-Wren with a pediment, built for the National Telephone Co. Much extended. – HEN AND CHICKENS pub (former), No. 129 Rocky Lane, ¼ m. E of Aston Cross, among scrapyards. *Wood & Kendrick*, 1900–1. Jolly Jacobean front.

NEWTOWN

SW of, and historically part of, Aston, around the A34. A post-war Redevelopment Area. Industry and 1960s housing and shopping partly 'regenerated' in the early C21.

BARTONS ARMS, High Street. By Mr *Brassington* of *James & Lister Lea*, 1901. The grandest of Birmingham's Victorian and Edwardian pubs. Jacobean Revival in orange brick and stone, with a row of tall Dutch gables, an ogee-domed clock turret, and first-floor oriels. Big lanterns on brackets, some original. The plan largely survives, but some walls were broken through with arches in the early 1980s. This is 'the Chartres of tilework' (Richard Boston), all by *Mintons*. In the smoke rooms, panels edged with turquoise and red, and Jacobean-style fireplaces with mirrors. In the lobby a rare surviving snob screen with movable glass panels, to hide respectable customers. The former public bar retains its bar front with chunky pilasters, and central servery with pedimented centrepieces. Original fixed seating throughout. The staircase has an ornate iron rail, a vibrant red, olive, yellow and turquoise tile dado, and a tile picture of a hunting scene.

ALBERT HALL (now JAMIAH MASJID MOHIUDDIN SIDDIQUIA), Witton Road. By *Arthur Edwards*, 1899. Jacobean, with wide shaped gable. The main block facing Victoria Road, 1886–7 by *Daniel Arkell*, was demolished in 2016.

CROCODILE WORKS, Alma Street and Porchester Street. Some retained C19 industrial façades to a development of flats by *Glenn Howells Architects*, 2011.

BIRCHFIELD

The SE end of Handsworth parish, split by the Birchfield Road dual carriageway (A34).

HOLY TRINITY, Birchfield Road, below the flyover. *J.A. Chatwin*'s second church, of 1863–4. Geometrical style. Rock-faced Tower Hill (Hamstead) stone, Bath stone dressings. Many of his usual features, here particularly bold and fresh: S porch-tower and spire, perked-up windows near the W ends of the aisles, lively gargoyles and massive, low-set rose windows in the transepts. Arcades with circular piers, heavy foliage capitals and sharp double-chamfered arches. Chancel arch with massive short columns on corbels. Five-sided apse. Small, deep-set triplet lancets in the clerestory. Scissor-truss roof. SE vestry, extended E by *Joseph Wood*, 1897. Its gable conceals a flue which exhausts through the triple-cusped opening at the top. – FITTINGS by *Chatwin*: FONT with round-arched niches round the bowl and short red stone columns; PULPIT with red stone shafts and carved panels; REREDOS with central relief of the Crucifixion and flanking arcading, growing into sedilia on the S; and PEWS. – S transept ALTAR and panelling by *E.F. Reynolds*, 1922. – STAINED GLASS. Apse, 1864, probably by *Heaton, Butler & Bayne*. The rest mostly *Hardmans*: chancel 1864–5; S rose 1872; S aisle W 1894. W window, *Camm & Co.* with *J.B. Surman & Partners*, 1958.

Big Tudor-ish VICARAGE, N, by *Robert F. Matthews*, 1895.

CONGREGATIONAL SUNDAY SCHOOL (now REDEEMED CHRISTIAN CHURCH OF GOD), Westminster Road. Basic Gothic by *Ingall & Hughes*, 1885; chapel demolished.

BIRMINGHAM JAME MASJID, Birchfield Road. 1988 by *Edmonds Gooding Miller Appleby*, architecturally the most distinguished mosque in the conurbation. A massive block, with huge shallow openings with four-centred pointed arches. Brickwork beautifully laid in Sussex bond. The panels within the openings have bricks laid diagonally. Golden dome with a band of ornament, slim minaret. Prayer hall oriented at forty-five degrees, with the mihrab in the far corner. Tall shallow niches, and a zigzag pattern of beams supporting the dome.

MASJID AL-FALAAH, Trinity Road. 2008–10 by *RPS Design*, incorporating an earlier house.

CANTERBURY CROSS PRIMARY SCHOOL, Canterbury Road. By *Wood & Kendrick*, 1906–7, won in competition; the assessor was Beresford Pite. A delightful version of the traditional gabled classroom blocks and hall. String courses rising over the windows as hoodmoulds and lifting into eaves at the ends. Entrance with a spire over the archway, and flanking square projections with pastry-cutter parapets. Small cupolas on the classrooms, a larger one with corner columns on the hall.

WESTMINSTER PRIMARY SCHOOL, Westminster Road. 1906 by *J.P. Osborne*. Of brick banded everywhere with terracotta. The window voussoirs treated similarly. Two nice cupolas, one with an ogee top, the other with arches to each side.

POLICE STATION (former), Canterbury Road. By *Osborne*, dated 1904. Free Neo-Wren. Differing gabled ends, the r. one, containing the entrance, with a steep pediment and big keystones pushing into the window pediments.

TRINITY ROAD. Opposite Holy Trinity church, Nos. 8–16, Jacobean by *J.J. Raggett*, 1891.

CASTLE VALE

A large municipal estate of 1964–9, built for a population of 20,000. The plan was almost the last work of *A.G. Sheppard Fidler* as City Architect: a spine of multi-storey flats running W–E, with low-rise terraces to N and S on Radburn layouts, shopping centres at the ends, and the churches at the E. More high-rise blocks on the S edge. The houses built under *J.R. Sheridan-Shedden* reflected the council leader Harry Watton's tight control of house-building. *In situ* concrete towers and standard terraces, some with characteristic jettied upper floors and timber cladding. Much was built by *Bryants*. Following a masterplan by *Hunt Thompson*, 1993, all except two of the towers were demolished, replaced with high-density low-rise developments up to 2005. The shops and pubs all went too. The low-rise housing survives.

ST CUTHBERT OF LINDISFARNE, High Street. 1973 by *J.P. Osborne & Son*. A low complex of blue brick, originally Anglican–Methodist. At one end, free-form curves rise to a peak. The worship space has a flat ceiling and hidden lighting. – Original ALTAR, RAILS, CHOIR STALLS, cylindrical FONT and a late C20 version of a two-decker PULPIT.

ST GERARD (R.C.), Turnhouse Road. 1980–1 by *Cyril Horsley* (*Horsley, Currall & Associates*). Windowless brick volumes. The worship space has a slanting timber roof with a hidden lantern above the apse. Free-standing campanile with transparent toughened blue-glass cladding by *Daniel Hurd Associates*, 2000. It might be a mobile phone mast.

Several modest original SCHOOLS by *Sheridan-Shedden*. GREEN-WOOD ACADEMY, Farnborough Road, is by *Seymour Harris*, 2016–17, a bleak cube of buff-coloured brick.

HOUSING. The central towers were replaced by a park flanked by terraces with gabled and pyramid corner towers, by *Hunt Thompson*, 1996–8. Near the SW entrance, around Concorde Drive, neo-traditional houses by *Axis Design Collective*, 2000. Along Farnborough Road, replacing the S towers, jazzy terraces and pairs with lots of bright colour, by *Walker Troup*, 2002–4. Tucked away in Watton Green, a demonstration energy-efficient terrace by *PCKO*, 2000. Prefabricated insulated wall panels and roof cassettes, partly clad in brick and cedar boarding. Picturesque two- and three-storey grouping, with a north European feel. Replacement SHOPPING is an anonymous retail centre at the W; also High Street, E, by *Associated Architects*, alas not their best. SPITFIRE HOUSE of 2004–6, the library and community building, has a big piloti and acute corner cantilevered aggressively over a curve. To its E and S, blocks of 2003–9. Golden-brown brick, projections and slanting metal roofs. The C21 Birmingham planners' aesthetic is already evident.

DUDDESTON AND NECHELLS

'Duddeston-cum-Nechells' in C19 directories. Part of Aston parish; in Birmingham borough from its foundation in 1838. Briefly fashionable in the early C19. *Hansom & Welch* designed a villa here *c.*1833, and the district of Vauxhall is named after pleasure gardens, recalling London's. The area was built up with close-packed terraces and factories during the C19. Comprehensive redevelopment was first envisaged by *Manzoni* in 1937, with a full report and plan in 1943. This still defines the S part of the area, one of the city's post-war Redevelopment Areas, carried out *c.*1947–56. Industry NE of Lawley Street, housing along Vauxhall Road and in Bloomsbury further N. Much rebuilding again in the early C21.

ST CLEMENT, Stuart Street. *J.A. Chatwin*'s first church, of 1859, mostly demolished in 1977. It was cruciform, with a SE bell-turret and spirelet. What remains are part of the S aisle, with three-light Geometrical windows and some polychromy, and the S porch: big gable on little buttresses, elongated arch. Attached hall, W, by *William Jenkins*, 1887. MONUMENT, Rev. Henry Charles Milward †1896, by *Roddis & Nourse*, Baroque-cum-Jacobean. The remains are now part of the JAMES MEMORIAL HOMES by *Holland W. Hobbiss & Partners*: W and N ranges designed 1965, built 1970–1; E range, on the site of the church, 1978–9. Two-storey bays, Neo-Georgian doorcases. Small square office extension to the retained aisle, timber, with pyramid roof, by *J.P. Osborne & Son*, 1977–8. – To the W, ST CLEMENT'S PRIMARY SCHOOL (now Academy), by the *Birmingham City Architect*, 1970. V-roof and tile-hanging.

ST MATTHEW, Nechells Parkway. 1839–40 by *William Thomas* of Leamington. The first of five churches built by the Birmingham Church Building Society, and the only survivor. Still entirely Georgian, with broad nave, short chancel and W tower, in warm red brick. Big wide lancets. E window with Geometrical tracery. Rich E.E.-style W doorway, probably of 1862, when *J.A. Chatwin* made alterations. Gutted for offices and a worship space by *John Cunnington*, 1994. His is the SE extension with banded stone and brick. Closed 2019.

ST JOSEPH (R.C.), Thimble Mill Lane. Begun as the mortuary chapel of a Catholic cemetery opened in 1850; by *A.W.N. Pugin*. This survives as the chancel and N Lady Chapel. Limestone. Dec, with interesting tracery, e.g. the hexagons containing big trefoils and not-quite-vesicas. Two-bay arcade with C14-style flattened foliage capitals and shafted piers. Nave, N aisle and SE presbytery added in 1872 by *E.W. Pugin*. Red brick with some blue trim, and stone dressings. Typical tall proportions, and full-height two-light S windows. Steeply gabled W front and porch, even steeper bellcote. The extraordinary arcade has circular columns, keeled and gadrooned. The capitals continue these mouldings, but are brutally chopped off where they meet the downward projection of the hollow-chamfered arch mouldings. The chancel arch is similar. Aisle roof supported by struts from just above the capitals. War damage repairs and chancel roof probably by *Giles Gilbert Scott*, c.1950. – ALTARS. Both by *A.W.N. Pugin*, 1850, the nave one with a rare original wooden frontal. – Tall nave REREDOS of 1902. – Aisle REREDOS probably *Scott*, c.1950, Gothic, with angels in relief. – PULPIT, 1907. With small painted scenes influenced by local Arts and Crafts work, but not good. – FONT, probably 1872. – BENCHES by *Scott*. – STATIONS OF THE CROSS. 1904. – STAINED GLASS. Chancel E window, 1880. Lady Chapel E, Assumption by *J.E. Nuttgens*, assisted by *Anthony MacRea*, a very late work (c.1975–80). Our Lady rises in a mandorla held by angels. N aisle, three by *Hardmans*: 1878 (E), 1922, 1919. Then one †1896, pictorial.

ST VINCENT (R.C.), Francis Street. By *Louis Hayes* of *S.N. Cooke & Partners*, 1967–8. Concrete beams and brick infill. Octagonal baptistery. Inside, the roof rises gently to the centre. – By *Hardman Studios* the MOSAIC of scenes from St Vincent's life, and the contemporary FURNISHINGS.

PRESBYTERIAN CHAPEL (now CHURCH OF GOD OF PROPHECY), Long Acre. 1888–9, a rare survivor of *Crouch & Butler*'s early chapel work. Gabled front. Lancet windows, some climbing up the staircases, a big Perp window, and brick foliage panels with arty lettering 'Jehovah Jireh' ('The Lord will provide'). Mutilated entrance.

BLOOMSBURY LIBRARY (now nursery), Nechells Parkway. 1891–2 by *Cossins & Peacock*. A splendid reminder of Duddeston before redevelopment. Bright pinky-red terracotta, though the style is Queen Anne. Acute corner, marked by a tall tower with a dome. Large round-headed windows light the reading rooms, with carved tympana by *Benjamin Creswick* of work and sports scenes. In the last bay Art, Craft and Industry present their products to a classically draped female Birmingham.

PUBLIC BATHS (former), Nechells Park Road. An eclectic confection by *Arthur Harrison*, 1910. Paired porches (for men and women) with semicircular pediments rise into octagonal towers with open stages articulated by sloping buttresses and little domes. Another semicircular pediment between, with the city's arms by *Creswick*. Wings with Ionic half-columns. Even the end gable of the baths behind is treated as a broken segmental pediment. Converted to offices and community facilities by *TPS Consult* with *Bucknall Austin*, 2003–4, with square, wavy and circular side extensions.

HEARTLANDS ACADEMY, Great Francis Street. 2012 by *Archial*.

CROMWELL JUNIOR AND INFANTS SCHOOL, Cromwell Street. 1888–90 by *Jethro Cossins*. Gabled blocks, noticeably lower than in Martin & Chamberlain's schools. Windows with triple-cusped heads, not pointed, of deep red terracotta. Cut-down entrance with a rose window. Octagonal tower with a timber belfry, spirelet and picturesquely placed chimney.

NECHELLS PRIMARY SCHOOL (now Academy), Eliot Street. 1879. One of *J.H. Chamberlain*'s best Board Schools. A tall, austere block with rows of lancets. Tower checking in like the start of a spire, broken by big two-light windows, and finishing in a steep-gabled roof. Lower wing, w, with sashes. Many extensions.

STAR CITY, Watson Road. A huge cinema and entertainment complex by *Jerde Partnership* with *Geoffrey Reid Associates*, 2000. It looks like an ocean liner with a big funnel.

HOUSING. C19 survivors include Nos. 143–145, dated 1867, and Nos. 146–148, c. 1840, stuccoed, in Nechells Park Road. Two-storey flats between Barrack Street and Windsor Street South, of 1932–3 by the *Birmingham City Surveyor*. The blocks have linking archways and central courtyards. Post-war survivors include refurbished maisonettes around Cromwell Street, and four twelve-storey steel-framed towers of 1950–4 by *S.N. Cooke & Partners*: three – HIGH, QUEENS and HOME TOWERS – along Nechells Parkway and one – SOUTH TOWER – in Little Hall Road. Shaped like elongated Xs with pairs of diagonal wings at each end of the core. Slim glazed stair-turrets between them. Completely altered 2019 by *Michael Dyson Associates*: rendered, detail redone.

RAILWAY BUILDINGS. At Duddeston Station, Duddeston Mill Road, a many-gabled former Grand Junction Railway WAGON REPAIR SHOP of the 1840s. In Rupert Street and Avenue Road was the London & North Western Railway's WINDSOR STREET GOODS DEPOT, opened 1880. Plain wall and gates;

office block of 1901, hard red brick (LNWR engineer *G.M. Smith*, with *R. Lord* of *Rattison & Sons*, contractors).
OTHER BUILDINGS. VILLA TAVERN, Nechells Park Road, opposite the baths. By *Matthew Butcher*, 1925. Dour, with big segmental pediments. The interior is hardly altered: original bar, smoke room, tiled lobby, rear function room. In Cato Street North, E of the railway, a tower BREWERY of 1889 by *William Jenkins*. Thin five-storey gabled block with remains of top louvre and a hoist. Offices in front by *Bateman & Bateman*, 1911. Further up, the ALBION VAULTS pub of *c.* 1865–6 tapers to the acute corner of Nechells Place. Original three- and four-light windows with consoles and arched lights, original bar front (again with big consoles) and an early bar back.

ERDINGTON

A manor of Aston, separated from it by the Tame valley, the M6 and the Gravelly Hill Interchange ('Spaghetti Junction') of 1969–72, engineers *Sir Owen Williams & Partners*. The village grew through the C19, but its grandest period was from *c.* 1890 to the First World War; it was an independent Urban District from 1894 to 1911. Interwar development was municipal estates and small private houses, spreading W to Stockland Green and Perry Common. Larger houses around Orphanage Road and the border with Sutton Coldfield.

CHURCHES

ALL SAINTS, George Road, Gravelly Hill. 1900–1 by *R.B. Morgan*. Nave only. Bald brick Gothic, with a picturesque timber E bellcote.* The temporary E end survives, a spiky timber screen separating a small sanctuary and vestries. Double-collar-beam roof. W porch and NE vestry, now chapel, by *S.N. Cooke & Partners*, 1953.

ST BARNABAS, High Street. The first sight, apart from the high W tower, is of curving glass and roofs, with older Gothic bits sticking out. Tower and wide nave were a Commissioners' church of 1822–3 by *Rickman & Hutchinson*. In 1883 *J.A. Chatwin* added transepts and a chancel. Rebuilt in 2011–12 by *Brownhill Hayward Brown (Peter Brownhill)*, after a fire in 2007. The tower has diagonal buttresses, battlements and flanking vestries. Rickman's nave walls survive, with some cast-iron Dec tracery. Transepts and chancel are mature Victorian Dec, with good flowing tracery. But the new foyer and staircase dominate, sweeping above the old walls to join a whaleback roof. Inside, things are better, with pointed-arched trusses

---

*In 1914 *Morgan* and *W.H. Bidlake* proposed chancel and transepts, in 1938 *W.J. Knight* a more modest completion, but nothing was done.

complementing the old walls. The transept arches cant inwards because the chancel is narrower than the nave. – *Chatwin*'s rich REREDOS survives, with sculptured Last Supper and mosaic side panels. – STAINED GLASS. One surviving nave window of 1863. – All other FITTINGS of 2012, including a staring E window designed by *Pippa Blackall* and made by *Devlin Plummer*. – LYCHGATE by *Bateman & Bateman*, 1925.

ST MARGARET, Jarvis Road, Short Heath. By *Batemans* (*E.M. Marriner*), 1973. Brick box with a partly open concrete-framed tower.

ST MARK, Bleak Hill Road, Stockland Green. A mission hall by *S.N. Cooke*, 1928. Round-arched windows.

ST MARGARET MARY (R.C.), Perry Common Road. 1936–7 by *McCarthy & Collings*. Traditional plan: W tower, aisled nave, sanctuary. Brown brick, not attractive. But the style is challengingly modern by local standards: flat roofs, rectangular windows, triangular wall piers (their stone caps late C20). Only the tower with its double-stepped buttresses hints at Gothic, and even here the feel is Expressionist. The arcades just square piers and lintels; heavy beamed roof. The sources must be Germany and Austria. – ALTAR, PULPIT and RAIL with hints of classical and Art Deco, possibly later. – Linked PRESBYTERY with deep slated mansard roof.

ST MARY AND ST JOHN (R.C.), Gravelly Hill North. 1936–7 by *V.S. Peel*, dwarfed by the tremendous tower of 1961–2 by *G.B. Cox*, with brick ribs and angle buttresses cut back from the base, and topped by a statue of St John by *Raymond F. Kings*. The church itself is modest Dec with *Moderne* touches, red brick and Guiting stone. Aisles and chapels, with plain rendered arcades, nicely handled, creating intriguing vistas. S transept and W gallery by *Cox*, 1962.

ST THOMAS AND ST EDMUND OF CANTERBURY, ERDINGTON ABBEY (R.C.), Sutton Road. 1848–50, by *Charles Hansom*. Commissioned by Fr Daniel Haigh, a rich convert priest and antiquary. From 1876 until 1922 it housed Benedictines from Beuron, Germany; since then Redemptorists. Clearly no pains were spared to re-create a large C14 parish church. The exterior groups well, with a fine NW tower and broach spire. Three tiers of lucarnes. Red sandstone, with elaborate Dec tracery: E window with circles full of cusping, W window with three spherical triangles contained in a larger one. Additional short outer aisles or chapels, to give plenty of altars. The interior is more pedestrian. Cream-coloured limestone, recently unfortunately painted white. Arcades with octagonal piers and double-chamfered arches. Steep, thin collar-beam nave roof with cusped braces and wind-braces; chancel roof similar but richer. The aisles differ: N taller, with plain rafter roof; S with cusped timbers. Much carving on e.g. hoodstops and corbels. The original SW porch is now a chapel: two bays of rib-vaulting and bosses. Former sacristy E of the N aisle, now a chapel, with panelling of 1934 by *Frederick Winders*. New sacristy off the S chapel of 1933–4 by *J. Arnold Crush*,

SUBURBS N & NW: ERDINGTON

still Gothic. – Ornate REREDOS by *Joseph A. Pippet*, 1897, with painted panels. – Original probably the ALTAR (now forward) with attached marble columns and relief of the Recognition of Thomas, PULPIT with more reliefs, CHOIR STALLS, PEWS and FONT with standing figures. C19 S chapel REREDOS with sculptures and spired tabernacle, and N chapel ALTAR with recumbent figure behind an arcade. – STAINED GLASS. By *Hardmans*: E 1849, W 1850, both good; S aisle E (damaged) and S chapel 1850–4. – In the graveyard, a Breton crucifix of *c.* 1700 on a cross and canopy of 1938. – Front wall and LYCHGATE by *Hansom*.

The tall monastery buildings (now HIGHCLARE SCHOOL) run S along Sutton Road. Earlier part by *A.E. Dempster*, 1879–80, Dec, red sandstone, with many gables; S part, greyer stone, by *Redfern & Haigh* (that is, *Henry Haigh*, Fr Haigh's nephew), 1896–7, with a massive four-storey tower.

N of the church ABBEY HALL, of after *c.*1810: see the windows with architraves on consoles. Ionic doorcase. The r. bay an early addition, after 1833. Large plain hall behind by the *Rev. F. Askew*, 1928. Some way W is ABBEY PRIMARY SCHOOL. Main range with hipped roofs by *James & Lister Lea & Sons*, 1909–10, altered and minus its cupola.

ERDINGTON METHODIST CHURCH, Station Road. The church of 1902 by *Ewen & J.A. Harper* was replaced by a brick box with slit windows by *Denys Hinton & Partners*, 1971–2. Alterations, new roof and entrance area by *Bryant Priest Newman*, 2015.

STOCKLAND GREEN METHODIST CHURCH, Slade Road. The start is a chapel of 1906–7 by *Crouch & Butler*. Its pretty Arts and Crafts Gothic entrance front survives on the S, buried in extensions of 1932 by *Crouch, Butler & Savage*: new front with entrance tower and spire, large new church at the rear. Altered in 2010–11, leaving the original trusses and braced arcade piers in the café and corridor. Airy church interior of 1932 with wide-spaced arcade piers and barrel-vault. – Good PULPIT of 1907.

ERDINGTON CONGREGATIONAL CHURCH (now British Orthodox Church), High Street and Station Road. 1839. Set back behind its graveyard. Rendered, with big lancets throughout. Aisles part-way along each side.

ERDINGTON UNITED REFORMED CHURCH, Holly Lane and Orphanage Road. 1932–3 by *H.W. Way Lovegrove*. Low, brick, round-arched.

SLADE EVANGELICAL CHURCH (former Plymouth Brethren), Hunton Hill. By *Garratt & Simister*, 1913: see details like the round-headed l. former entrance. Heavy added porch.

WITTON CEMETERY, Moor Lane. Laid out 1860–3 as Birmingham City Cemetery, replacing many small older burial grounds. Layout by *Richard Ashwell*, superintendent of London Road Cemetery, Coventry, and former assistant gardener to Joseph Paxton at Chatsworth. Buildings by *Richard Clarke* of Nottingham. Local Towerhill sandstone and Bath stone dressings. Tall

Birmingham, Erdington, Witton Cemetery, chapels.
Engraving, 1862

buttressed GATEPIERS with spire-like tops. Intensely Gothic SUPERINTENDENT'S HOUSE to the l. Tower with open top stage and steep French pavilion roof. Modest Gothic LODGE, r. Long curving drives run up the hill to the CHAPELS, but only the Anglican one, to the S, survives. Like a substantial church: nave, chancel, S chapel, NW tower with angle buttresses and splay-footed spire. Dec tracery. Roof with high arch-braced collars. (Closed, fittings removed.) LODGE at the SW corner by Brookvale Road, dourly Old English, by *Daniel Arkell*, 1887. At the far NE corner facing The Ridgeway, the JEWISH CEMETERY. It includes an obelisk commemorating people re-buried here from Granville Street in 1876. (The later Jewish cemetery is across College Road, see Kingstanding, p. 263.)

PUBLIC BUILDINGS

HIGHCROFT HOSPITAL, Highcroft Road. The former Aston Union Workhouse, of 1886–9 by *Yeoville Thomason*. Receiving block, with a big Italian Gothic entrance arch, and main range behind. This has three overpowering storeys and a basement. Red brick banded with blue. Central tower more Germanic than Italian, with pyramid roof, spirelet and stubby corner pinnacles, actually chimneys. Modern hospital to the W.

To the E, entered from Fentham Road, the ASTON UNION COTTAGE HOMES of 1896–1900 by *Franklin Cross & Nichols*. Built to bring up poor children on 'homelike principles' under the care of foster-parents. The houses, in a slightly dour Queen Anne style, line an avenue, with a central timber clock tower. Lots of projecting gables with circular windows, some inset porches, dentil cornices, swan's-neck pediments. At the N end

SUBURBS N & NW: ERDINGTON

the former CHAPEL (now flats), with gabled windows pushing up into the roof. Facing down the avenue, a grander house with low wings and two chimneys linked by a flying arch.

SCHOOLS. The former OSBORNE PRIMARY SCHOOL, Station Road, by *William Henman*, 1884–5, was extended along Osborne Road by *Cooper Whitwell*, 1897–8. Simplified Queen Anne. SLADE PRIMARY SCHOOL, Broomfield Road, by *William Jenkins*, 1903, is old-fashioned multi-gabled brick and terracotta with tower and spire. The former FENTHAM ROAD SCHOOL is particularly good, though altered. By *Cossins, Peacock & Bewlay*, 1903–4, Free Jacobean. Later schools by *H.T. Buckland*: ERDINGTON HALL PRIMARY SCHOOL, Bracebridge Road, 1913, severe Free Style; and KINGSBURY SCHOOL (now Erdington Academy), Kingsbury Road, 1923, Neo-Georgian. STOCKLAND GREEN SCHOOL, Slade Road, is by *Associated Architects*, 2010–11.

For other public buildings, *see* the Perambulation.

PERAMBULATION

The old centre is the Green at the fork of High Street and Orphanage Road, with a MEMORIAL commemorating its enclosure in 1887. On the E side the PUBLIC LIBRARY, by *J.P. Osborne*, 1906–7. Single-storeyed but grand, with pedimented wings, banded Ionic columns and a semicircular-headed entrance intended as the base of a tower. Ionic columns separate the entrance area from the library proper.

HIGH STREET runs S to St Barnabas (p. 235). The interesting buildings start opposite the church with THE CHURCH HOUSE, smooth Tudor by *Collier & Davies*, 1911. HAZEL'S funeral parlour, dated 1933, by *E.G. Harrison & Tracey*, is also Tudor, but has a nice Baroque porch. Then a typical squared-up Deco former BURTON'S, 1936. Beyond York Road, YORK BUILDINGS, dated 1904, by *C.W. Bosworth* (mutilated). At the far end the roundabout at Six Ways, with a former municipal bank, 1924–5, probably by *W.E. Ballard*. Neo-Georgian, with a semicircular front. SUTTON NEW ROAD, the by-pass of 1938, runs N back to the Green, with a big Neo-Georgian former POST OFFICE, dated 1934.

Next, from the Green NE up ORPHANAGE ROAD. The FIRE STATION, S side, is by *Nicol, Nicol & Thomas*, 1938. Blocky modernized Neo-Georgian. Behind it the ERDINGTON SKILLS CENTRE, a lovely design by *Bryant Priest Newman*, 2014–15, with traditional brick gables gently subverted by asymmetrical oriels and a glazed ground floor. Back on Orphanage Road the LEISURE CENTRE, uninspired cuboids by *calderpeel*, 2017. Further on, the CONSERVATIVE CLUB, set back, has an early C18 five-bay NE range with two platbands and gables with kneelers. The SW wing may be of 1913 by *D.J. Roberts*. Further NE, hidden down an entry (r.) beyond Holly Lane, MASON COTTAGES, almshouses and hall by *Hurley Robinson*, 1938–9.

Cottage pairs with massive end chimneys. The hall has big semi-dormers.*

Finally N from the Green. High Street is immediately joined by Sutton New Road. After the former Congregational church (p. 237), at the crossing with Station Road, the former CROSS KEYS pub, with timbered gables: *Wood & Kendrick*, 1910. Erdington Abbey (p. 236) is on Sutton Road beyond. Ahead, the LYNDHURST ESTATE of 1958–60 by *A. G. Sheppard Fidler*, City Architect. One of his best schemes: a complete neighbourhood of towers, maisonettes, terraces and bungalows, well grouped in the gardens of demolished villas, with retained mature trees. Regeneration has re-clad the towers, demolished maisonettes and built unsympathetic high-density terraces (by *PRP*, N end, 2013 etc., and – better detailed – by *BM3*, S end, from 2015).

Down STATION ROAD, W, Nos. 19–21 are early C19. Nos. 23–25 were reconstructed in 1992 but retain a timber frame, probably C17. Opposite, the former Osborne School (p. 239). Beyond the railway bridge, close-packed late C19 terraces. The RED LION (No. 105) is a superior pub by *Wood & Kendrick*, 1899, smart Jacobean, with a corner tower with ogee roof. The main bar has a fine arcaded bar back with an original advertising mirror, and a wonderful ceramic bar front made by *Craven Dunnill*, with wreaths coloured in pink, green, mustard and grey. Original seating and etched glass. Another bar back with beaten copper panels between arches. Some way up GRAVELLY LANE, N, a row of shops (Nos. 168–180) with splendiferous corner oriel and ogee dome, by *Noah Weeks*, 1907.

SUMMER ROAD runs S from the Red Lion to Six Ways. Beyond the railway, the NEW INN, by *C. H. Collett*, 1907. Rich brown terracotta front with etched windows. Original bar, seating and smoke room.

OTHER BUILDINGS

THE YENTON pub, Sutton Road, beyond Chester Road. Big Tudor by *James & Lister Lea & Sons*, 1927–8. This was the Birmingham tram terminus from 1904. The little pavilion, minus its front arcade but with steep pediment and clock, is a former TRAMWAY WAITING ROOM by *H. H. Humphries*, U. D. C. Surveyor, 1910–11. Shops beyond by *Charles W. Bosworth*, boldly dated 1906.

ROOKERY HOUSE, in Rookery Park, Kingsbury Road, ½ m. S, looks early C19: rendered S front, 2–3–2 bays, the centre recessed. Off-centre Greek Doric porch. But this hides a house built for Abraham Spooner between 1725 and 1730, with the same front composition. Three-bay rear extension of *c.* 1760, also rendered. Many later alterations.

---

*JOSIAH MASON'S ORPHANAGE was further NE again, a huge Italian Gothic building by *J. R. Botham*, 1860–8 (dem.). A bronze BUST of Mason, cast by *William Bloye* in 1952 from a statue by *Francis Williamson*, is now on a pedestal ¾ m. NE, at the junction with Chester Road.

LAD IN THE LANE (formerly OLD GREEN MAN), further s, in Bromford Lane. A timber-framed hall house tree-ring dated to 1400 and (N wing) 1456–61. Only the wing looks old. Its gable has a tie-beam with curved brackets, collar-beam and close studding. The E gable similar. The hall range was rebuilt round the timber frame in 1916 by *James & Lister Lea*, with decorative timbering and big dormers. Inside, the two-bay hall is open to the roof, with a splendid central arch-braced cruck truss of impressively large blades, original tie-beam and central post. It is carefully chamfered on the N side, clearly the high-status end. A second, closed-cruck truss at the S end, separating a service bay. The roof has purlins and wind-braces, also impressively big. The N wing has a central truss with cambered collar-beam.

NAVIGATION INN (former), at the cross-roads of Bromford Lane and Tyburn Road. *Holland W. Hobbiss*, 1926. Tudor Revival with a much-timbered porch.

GRAVELLY HILL NORTH runs s from Six Ways, with classical villas on both sides. KINGSMERE, just s of St Mary and St John (p. 239), later a convent, is a picturesque composition, stuccoed, with a heavy Doric porch: here by 1833. Big post-war rear extensions; former chapel facing the road by *G.B. Cox*, 1933. Further s on GRAVELLY HILL, a handsome villa dated 1862, with the arched window lights and shallow square bays typical of the date.

At the bottom is the Gravelly Hill Interchange (*see* p. 235). Underneath it is SALFORD JUNCTION, where the Birmingham and Fazeley Canal of 1790 crosses the River Tame by an original AQUEDUCT. Seven low arches with stone voussoirs, and cutwaters. The Tame Valley Canal of 1844 runs NW; the Birmingham and Warwick Junction Canal, also of 1844, runs s, under an original ROVING BRIDGE and over a three-arch AQUEDUCT.

In WOOD END LANE, a line of single-storey C18 cottages with dormers. Opposite, Jaffray Crescent, with THE WHITE HOUSE, rendered, Voyseyesque, by *Benjamin Bower*, 1919.

SLADE ROAD runs N from Salford Bridge, through the w part of Erdington. THE BROOKVALE pub (former) at No. 144 is Neo-Georgian by *Holland W. Hobbiss*, 1934. Brick front wall raised to form the sign. Slade Primary School (p. 239) is just s. Down George Road is BROOKVALE PARK, laid out round an existing pool by the U.D.C., 1910, surveyor *H.H. Humphries*. Original paired octagonal KIOSKS with ogee domes, now behind shiny metal tree-like SCULPTURES by *Tim Tolkien*, 2003. Where Slade Road meets Reservoir Road and Marsh Hill, ¾ m. w of the centre, the massive former PLAZA CINEMA by *A.L. Snow*, 1927, and the STOCKLAND pub (now VILLAGE GREEN) by *Bateman & Bateman*, 1923–4, Cotswold Tudor in small bands of stone, with many gables.

In JERRY'S LANE, 1 m. NW, No. 192, a rare surviving farm labourer's cottage, probably late C18, brick, single-storeyed, with an attic and small extension. (Original plank door, range, and brick copper.)

WITTON HALL, off Brookvale Road. A tall, square three-storey house, probably early C18, though surviving details are later. N and S fronts of five bays, all sashed, the S slightly irregular; but the modest entrance is on the W, with a doorway of *c.* 1830–40. Windows here step up to light the stick-baluster staircase. Disturbed bricks on the N may mark the original entrance. Much extended, by *Peter Hing & Jones*, 1984, and later.

FORT DUNLOP, Fort Parkway. The Dunlop Rubber Co.'s works were started in 1915. What survives is the huge former Base Stores building of 1920 by *Sir Sidney Stott*, best known for Lancashire cotton mills, assisted by Dunlops' architect *W. W. Gibbings*. It could indeed be in Rochdale. Six storeys, rising to eight at the W, with a built-up centre. The bottom two storeys are treated as a base. Refurbished as offices for Urban Splash, 2008, by *shedkm*. A blue services spine projects at the E, with porthole windows.

HANDSWORTH

The ancient Staffordshire parish stretched from the Birmingham boundary at Hockley Brook to West Bromwich, and included Birchfield and Perry Barr (*see* pp. 230 and p. 265). It had dispersed farms and cottages, but no village centre. Industrial development began with Matthew Boulton's SOHO MANUFACTORY, founded in 1761. The principal building was by *William Wyatt*, 1765–7: a silver-plate works with showrooms, warehousing and living accommodation. Demolished by 1863, its site is covered by houses and gardens at the W end of South Road, below Boulton's surviving Soho House. Later C18 and C19 industry spread W and NW along the Hockley Brook valley, with housing on higher ground along Soho Road and Hamstead Road, and from the late C19 further N into Handsworth Wood, included here.

Handsworth had a Local Board from 1874 and became an Urban District in 1894, absorbed into Birmingham in 1911. The Board was responsible for *William Henman*'s Council House of 1877–9, the U.D.C. for *Bidlake*'s superb cemetery chapel of 1909. Much of Handsworth became an affluent residential area, and remained so until the 1960s. There is a wealth of fine Victorian and Edwardian architecture. The local architect *J. P. Osborne*'s career runs from High Victorian at Hamstead Road Baptist Church to Arts and Crafts-influenced Edwardian houses. Other Arts and Crafts houses are by the young *Harry Weedon*, later famous for cinemas, and *Arthur McKewan*. Afro-Caribbean and Sikh communities grew from the late 1950s.

C21 Handsworth is architecturally the saddest of Birmingham suburbs. Apart from Soho Hill, there are no conservation areas, and much has been lost to neglect and insensitive alterations. But there are still good things to see, and this account is necessarily selective, e.g. omitting such areas as around Radnor Road.

Church of England

ST MARY, Hamstead Road. The mother church of a large parish, and important as 'The Westminster Abbey of Birmingham' (Elihu Burritt), the final home of that brilliant group of late C18–early C19 industrialists, Boulton, Watt and Murdoch. The first impression is of a large medieval church, because of the S tower, one of a West Midlands group including Sedgley (p. 542) and Claverley, Shropshire. Its lowest part is of *c.* 1200, with clasping buttresses and two small, slightly pointed, deeply splayed first-floor windows, one with a C19 cusped head. Big multi-stepped SE buttress, perhaps C14. On the W side, now inside, a blocked round-headed lancet. Upper stages C15 or early C16, with angle buttresses, a big E stair-vice, a flat-headed two-light S window, and two-light cusped windows in the bell-chamber. Renewed double-chamfered tower arch. Blocked E doorway, Perp, with moulded jambs and shallow pointed arch. Also medieval is the NE (Wyrley) chapel, early C16, with a flat-headed E window of three lights and a similar N window.

In 1820 there were major alterations, designed by the rector, the *Rev. T.L. Freer*, using *Solomon Smith* as surveyor and *William Hollins* as builder. The N arcade and aisle were rebuilt, adding a broad N transept and NE vestry. Y-tracery windows with thin hoodmoulds, regular stepped buttresses and delicate battlements (those on the transept gable removed in 1878). The E front has the same early Gothic Revival character, but here the N gable is a modification of the Wyrley Chapel, with

Birmingham, Handsworth, St Mary.
Engraving by T. Donaldson after Stebbing Shaw, 1801

flat-headed E window, the S is the Watt Chapel of 1825–6 (*see below*) and the chancel E wall is a facsimile by *J.A. Chatwin* of 1878, when the building was extended E, re-creating the original intersecting tracery of *c.*1300. The rest is also *Chatwin*, of 1876–8, in reddish-grey Codsall sandstone. He rebuilt the nave and aisles, and extended the whole church w. Chancel arch with complex shafts on corbels. Early C14 Geometrical style, typically not clashing with the earlier C19 work. The outer N aisle, added at the request of the building committee. makes the interior dark, and the 'complex scheme of aisles and arches, columns and chapels...difficult to distinguish' (Rev. J.C.W. Tompkins, rector 1955–92). In the Wyrley Chapel a re-set C14 PISCINA, and at the W end a two-centred-arched N doorway with a convex sunk chamfer dying into the jambs. It must be *Chatwin*'s, but does it represent C14 work? Behind it is a four-centred archway of 1820 to the NE vestry, blocked in the C20. Reordering by *Acanthus Clews*, 2018–20, with new floors, nave altar and chairs, and bench pews.

OTHER FURNISHINGS. By *Chatwin* the CHOIR STALLS, 1878; REREDOS, 1883; PULPIT, 1890, with carved alabaster panels; wrought-iron chancel SCREEN, 1898. – HOLY TABLE, S aisle, dated 1725. – ROYAL ARMS, on wood; C20 gilding. The lilies and Queen Anne's motto 'Semper eadem' suggest a local carver of 1702–7. – SCREEN by *Douglas Hickman*, 1967, now under the tower. – STAINED GLASS. E window by *Ward & Hughes*, 1878. S aisle from E: *Burlison & Grylls*, 1881; *Herbert Bryans*, 1899, in his master Kempe's manner; *Hardmans*, 1878. W, *Burlison & Grylls*, 1881. N transept, *Ward & Hughes*, 1878.

MONUMENTS. A huge collection. Only the best can be mentioned. – Chancel. Matthew Boulton †1809, by *Flaxman*. An impressive mural monument with a bust in a circular recess. Two putti below, one with a picture of Soho. – William Murdoch †1839, by *Chantrey*. A classical bust set, oddly, under a pointed arch, on a tablet with chamfered sides and blank cusped lights, much less successful. – Joseph Grice †1833 with bust, by *W. Hollins*. – John Freer, sarcophagus in low relief with lions' heads by *Hollins*, after 1808. – Sarah Russell †1842 by *E.H. Baily*, with three Flaxman-type figures hovering over a sarcophagus. – Wyrley Chapel. William (†1561) and Elizabeth Wyrley. Recumbent effigies, he in armour with his feet on a dog, she in a ruff. Sandstone tomb-chest with coats of arms. – Thomas and Dorothy Wyrley, †1583 and †1597. Fragments of an incised slab. – Flanking the E window, two small illegible monuments, probably to Wyrleys: shield and cresting N, aedicule S. – John Fulnetby †1636, 'parson' of Handsworth and Archdeacon of Stafford. Brass tablet and stone 'predella' with defaced cherub. – C16 effigy in red sandstone on a C19 open tomb-chest containing the effigy of a corpse in a shroud. – Tower. C18 architectural tablets. – Nathaniel Clarke †1839 with bust, by *Peter Hollins*. – Other tablets signed by *W.* and *P. Hollins*, *J. & W. Bennett*, and *G. Biddle*.

WATT CHAPEL. A shrine built by James Watt Junior to his father's memory in 1825–6. *William Creighton*, head of the Soho drawing office, made sketches in 1824 fixing the Gothic style, access from the chancel, vaulting pattern, and position of the monument. Watt then brought *Richard Bridgens* in (cf. Aston Hall, p. 222), and the detailed design is his. *Rickman & Hutchinson* made working drawings and supervised the work. The builder was *William Hollins*, who made his own suggestions. The exterior matches the 1820s E end, as already noted. Also a blank Geometrical S window. Four-centred archway in the S chancel wall, with cusped panelling to the soffit. The interior is faced in beautiful, and expensive, creamy Roche Abbey limestone. It is delicately rib-vaulted in three bays, narrow–wide–narrow. E window with patterned glass, designed by *R. Thomson*, made by *J.A. Miller*. Watt's MONUMENT is carefully positioned towards the W. By *Sir Francis Chantrey*, dated 1825, and one of his finest pieces. The great engineer is seated in a chair, deep in thought, holding a pair of compasses, with a scroll on his knee. High pedestal with chamfered corners. The bare, isolated setting creates the feeling of a genius left alone with his ideas.

LYCHGATE to the NE by *J.P. Osborne*, 1908.

ARCHBISHOP BENSON CHURCH HALL (now UNITED CHURCH OF GOD), Austin Road. By *James A. Swan*, 1936. Mission hall with a big shaped gable.

ST ANDREW, Oxhill Road. A handsome urban church of 1907–8 by *W.H. Bidlake*, oriented N–S. A deceptively modest brick gable faces the road, with a big, elegant early Perp five-light window. Pent-roofed baptistery extension between stepped buttresses. Entrance towers set back on either side, flanked by low porches: a play of masses and planes. Two-light side windows, the tracery now Dec, and again pent-roofed projections, for aisles. Timber flèche over the crossing, and a little N transept turret. Linked N room by *Temple Cox Nicholls*, 1993. The interior has the soaring height of *Bidlake*'s later churches, and the typical three-dimensional, moulded effect of his internal elevations. The chamfered piers of St Agatha, Sparkbrook (p. 335) reappear, here with stone shafts up their narrow front faces. The blank plastered arches have hoodmoulds creating a framework in front of the wall, again like the earlier church. The piers run straight into arches; the shafts have capitals. Low passage aisles with paired round-headed arcades, bearing down as the arches rise above. Between arcades and arches, plain plastered wall. Then the space opens out into large transepts, the wall piers becoming high two-bay arcades, with transverse arches behind. Finally the chancel has arcades of pointed arches, leading to a N chapel and a S organ loft with gallery. The materials, maroon brick and Grinshill stone, are subtly integrated, with shafts and impost blocks of stone, and bricks and timbers continuing their mouldings into arches and roof.

Fine FITTINGS by *Bidlake*: panelled PULPIT with tester, bowl FONT, CHOIR STALLS with opulent poppyheads,

REREDOS (now in the S transept) with paintings by *Fred Davis*. Effective subdued colouring and well-grouped figures. The small scenes in the predella show Davis's study of Flemish and Venetian art. – By *Harold C. King* the ROOD and BEAM, 1919; REREDOS and ENGLISH ALTAR, 1931. – FONT COVER by *John Poole*. – STAINED GLASS. E window by *Geoffrey Webb*, 1922, Christ in Majesty, with characteristic blues. N chapel E by *Camm & Co.*, 1914, rich, with stylized landscape. Aisles, saints by *Pearce & Cutler*, 1935–6. Baptistery, 1909 by *Harvey & Ashby*.

ST JAMES, Crocketts Road. An amusing combination of very different churches. The first is of 1838–40 by *Robert Ebbels*, consisting of W tower and aisled nave. Inexpensive Gothic, with lancet windows. In 1878 *W.H. Ward* added a chancel and vestries in exactly the same pre-Pugin style, with slim plaster ribs to the ceiling. Then in 1894–5 *J.A. Chatwin* designed a new nave, chancel and S aisle, removing the original S aisle and making Ebbels's nave and Ward's chancel into N aisle and Lady Chapel. Lofty and grand, in C14 style. Brick exterior. Inside, Bath stone arcades with four-lobed piers, and plastered walls: a pleasantly cool combination which feels like early C20 Cotswold Arts and Crafts work. Perhaps the young *P.B. Chatwin* had a hand in it? Typical Chatwin chancel arch. Apsidal W baptistery and SW porch of 1921, but to the 1894 design. – By *J.A. Chatwin* the FONT and PULPIT, both alabaster. – Magniloquent alabaster REREDOS with flanking STALLS by *P.B. Chatwin*, 1909, in his father's manner. – CHOIR STALLS, 1907, and CLERGY SEATS, 1909, by *Jones & Willis*, at their best, with attractive poppyheads. – Lady Chapel SCREENS and PANELLING by *James A. Swan*, 1934, rich late Gothic (carvers *Pancheri & Hack*). – TOMB-CHEST between chapel and chancel by *Swan*, with bronze effigy of Eric Abbott †1917 by *William Bloye*, 1946. Astonishingly late for this kind of thing; but a fine piece. He is in army uniform with greatcoat and boots. – Chancel N SCREEN and ALTAR RAIL also *Swan*, 1940. – STAINED GLASS. E window by *Kempe*, 1906. Lady Chapel E by *Samuel Evans*, 1885. S aisle from E: *Walter Camm (T.W. Camm)*, 1926; *T.W. Camm*, 1898, a fascinating contrast of generations; *Heaton, Butler & Bayne*, 1919. Three baptistery windows by *Florence, Robert* and *Walter Camm (T.W. Camm)*, 1934.

ST MICHAEL, St Michael's Road. 1854–5 by *William Bourne*, the centrepiece of M.P.W. Boulton's development of the Soho Park estate. Competent, ample Dec, with a SW tower (broach spire completed 1866). Pink Hamstead sandstone, now eroded, with Bath stone dressings. Reticulated tracery in the aisles, cusped triplets under segmental arches in the clerestory. Arcades with octagonal piers, of Caen stone under the unfortunate 1960s whitening. – By *Bourne*, 1855: REREDOS, with good blank arcading; PULPIT; FONT, with tracery patterns enclosing flowers; and PEWS. – STAINED GLASS. Chancel E window, *Hardman*, 1866. Chancel N, *Ward & Hughes*, †1888 and (probable) †1875. S transept E *Hardmans*, 1866; S *Ward & Hughes*, 1905. N transept, *Florence Camm* (*T. W. Camm*), 1935. W, *Swaine Bourne*, 1869. N aisle W, *Henry Symonds*, 1884.

ST PETER (now CHURCH OF GOD SEVENTH DAY), Grove Lane. 1906–7 by *J. A. Chatwin & Son*. A typical Chatwin plan of apsidal chancel, nave and aisles. Red brick with stone dressings. Dec tracery with whorls. *P. B. Chatwin*'s hand can be seen in the powerful tower over the E part of the chancel, and the transverse wood vaulting of the two-bay aisles, treated as transepts. Two narrower W aisle bays were never built. The interior has been ceiled and subdivided. Square arcade piers with moulded brick arches.*

Roman Catholic

CONVENT OF THE SISTERS OF MERCY, Hunters Road, S of St Francis's church. It is hard now to appreciate the originality and careful detail of the first ranges, of two storeys with steep-pitched roofs. They are by *A.W.N. Pugin*, of 1840–1, following the directions on planning of Mother Catherine McAuley, the foundress. Stone dressings, brickwork patterned with devotional symbols in blue. Long range with three-light mullioned windows parallel to the road, and a projecting gabled wing in the centre. The wing has two-light windows with plate tracery. The style here is C13 or C14, deriving from buildings such as St Cross Hospital at Winchester, illustrated in Pugin's *Contrasts* (1836). Like his other Mercy convents, the design expresses both Pugin's re-creation of an ideal medieval Catholic world and his rational architectural approach. The money came from John Hardman, Pugin's stained-glass maker and metalworker, who lived opposite. The commandingly tall three-storey S wing was added by *Pugin* in 1850, noticeably different with its roof crowned with chimneys, and big mullion-and-transom windows. The S part of the roof of the older block was raised to match. The little entrance cloister on the extreme N is of 1876–7. At the rear on the S a characteristic little 1841 tower with pyramid roof. On the N, single-storey ranges enclose a courtyard, now with STATUES of Mother McAuley and Sister Juliana Hardman by *Philip Jackson*, 2005. Internal corridors are simply articulated by chamfered arches. Several cusped niches house C15 and C16 North European wood STATUES, some brought here by Pugin. E of these ranges the nuns' cemetery, with a floriated standing *Pugin* CROSS. A CLOISTER by Pugin, 1846, steps down the slope, with paired lights and buttresses, a perfect combination of picturesque and functional. It has a collar-beam roof on bold corbels.† Pugin's CHAPEL,

---

*The chancel decoration of 1923–7 by *Nora Yoxall*, *Elsie Whitford* and *S. Hall*, if it survives, is inaccessible. Their stained-glass windows have been moved.
†It led to a big Dec church with a brick tower, and school buildings, of 1846–7 by *A.W.N. Pugin*, extended 1857 by *Pugin & Murray*, destroyed in 1941.

projecting behind the front gabled wing, was replaced by a larger building: designed 1950 by *V.S. Peel* and *T. Morris*, built 1954–6, by *Morris & Whitehouse*. Still Gothic, but pale by comparison. The W and NW doorways of 1841 survive, and a three-light upper window for sick nuns to follow services. Original entrance DOORS with traceried panels. – STAINED GLASS by *Hardmans*, 1956 and 1987 (N chapel). – ALTAR of 1841, now in the N chapel. – C19 REREDOS on a corridor wall.

ST AUGUSTINE (R.C.), Avenue Road. 1938–9 by *G.B. Cox*, at his best; still Early Christian style, but streamlined and massive. Dark red-brown brick. Ritual NW tower, stepped in low at the corners, with a big STATUE of St Augustine on a bracket. Round-headed lancets in large areas of walling. Over the W door, relief PANEL by *Peter Bohn*, 1958. The interior is all semicircular arches: arcades with no capitals, just a single-step moulding all round, and a barrel-vault of Western red cedar, with panelled ribs. – By *Cox* the BALDACCHINO and ALTAR, and STATIONS OF THE CROSS. Sanctuary reordered 1977–8 by *Gordon Walker*. – STAINED GLASS. By *Hardmans*, N chapel, †1917. Saints by *Patrick Pollen*, angular, deeply coloured, c. 1967. – Contemporary PRESBYTERY.

ST FRANCIS (R.C.), Hunters Road. 1893–4 by *A.J.C. Scoles*. Red brick with stone dressings, E.E., large, bald and graceless. Ritual SW baptistery with spirelet. Arcades with octagonal piers. Mid-C20 narthex. – REREDOS and ALTAR by *Scoles*, carved by *A.B. Wall*, 1895, with TABERNACLE by *Hardman & Co*. Their pink marble fronts are an alteration of the 1980s when much work was done here. – Rich COMMUNION RAIL of 1901. – PULPIT probably also carved by *Wall*. – STENCILLING on ceilings and walls by *D.P. Dowling & Sons*, c. 1990, partly following a scheme of 1896 by *R. Jeffries Hopkins*. – STAINED GLASS. All *Hardmans*. E and W windows c. 1894; aisles early C20; porch 1927; S aisle W 1981 (*D. Cowan* and *R. Hickling*). N aisle easternmost 1895, by *W.J. Wainwright*, made by *Hardmans*. Annunciation with Adam and Eve below. Aware of Burne-Jones but going its own way, with taut writhing curves integrating the design. – The PRESBYTERY, S, was originally John Hardman's house (*see also* above). A stuccoed 1830s villa, extended E by *A.W.N. Pugin*, 1842–3. Late C20 render.

Other denominations and faiths

ASBURY MEMORIAL METHODIST CHURCH (now NEW LIFE WESLEYAN), Holyhead Road. 1884 by *J.L. Ball*. Brick Gothic with a big gable with a five-light window, and a ritual SW saddleback tower. Deep carved name panel above the door. Clerestory of paired lights. Wide C14-style three-bay arcades and chancel arch. W gallery on iron piers. – PULPIT with open-traceried panels. – STAINED GLASS by *T.W. Camm*: E window, a rich Transfiguration, †1897; W, small scenes and motifs in dense square and diagonal leadings, 1914. – ORGAN by *Nicholson*.

SOMERSET ROAD METHODIST CHURCH (now SINGH SABHA GURDWARA). 1893 by *Crouch & Butler*. Brick mission chapel, badly rendered and re-windowed. Diagonally set cupola. Former hall, N, by *Arthur McKewan*, 1910.

TRINITY METHODIST CHURCH, Rookery Road. 1913–14 by *Henry Harper* of Nottingham. Free Perp. Red brick and terracotta. Thin ritual SW tower with long sloping buttresses and a short spire.

VILLA ROAD METHODIST CHURCH. 1900 by *J. G. Dunn*. Brick and terracotta, more Jacobean than Gothic. Porch up side steps, rose window above, gable with a spirelet. Arcaded collar-beam roof. Now jointly used as the music department for King Edward VI School (p. 252).

CANNON STREET MEMORIAL BAPTIST CHURCH, Soho Road and Alfred Road. 1929–30 by *F.B. Andrews & Son*. Brick Romanesque. The exterior is a plainer, updated version of Andrews's Acocks Green church (pp. 301–2), with a gable between octagonal turrets. Brick patterning in the tympana in a Dixon or Ball manner, but the turret tops hint at Continental Expressionism. Wide, high interior, again all brick, with hammerbeam roof and big arches to the sanctuary and shallow transepts. The sanctuary arch has responds of bricks in twisted spirals. W gallery. – Original SEATING. – STAINED GLASS. Patterning in the apse by *T. W. Camm*, 1930.

HAMSTEAD ROAD BAPTIST CHURCH (now IKHEWA MASJID). 1883 by *J. P. Osborne*. A grand chapel in early Dec style, evoking the wealthy Nonconformity of the 'Civic Gospel'. Sandstone W front with limestone dressings. NW tower and spire. Porch with sandstone shafts, a trumeau, and an open cinquefoil above. The main gable answers this with a five-light window with a big sexfoil. Octagonal SW vestry, gabled all round. The rest, not so visible, is brick. Inside, three-bay arcades with circular columns and Dec knobbly foliage capitals, and big transepts. The chancel arch has dark stone shafts on corbels. Five-sided apse with spiky blank arcading. W gallery. Hammerbeam roof. At the rear, facing Hunters Road, SUNDAY SCHOOLS by *Osborne*, 1900. Simple brick gables between a Tudor oriel, l., and an engaging turret, r., which has lost its top. (Closed 2015, when *Osborne*'s fittings survived remarkably complete.) – STAINED GLASS. Apse windows by *Samuel Evans*, 1883; N and S transepts probably also *Evans*, slightly later. Nave N, First World War memorial by *Benjamin Warren*, made by the *Shottery Guild*. Nave S, *Camm & Co.*, †1932.

ELMWOOD UNITED REFORMED CHURCH, Hamstead Hill. 1966 by *McKewan & McKewan* (*Graham S. Madeley*). Oval plan with the ends cut off, the one towards the road a glazed wall.

ST GEORGE (former Presbyterian), now SHREE GEETA BHAWAN MANDIR, Heathfield Road. An extreme clash of cultures.

A chapel of 1896 by *J.P. Osborne*, Gothic with Jacobean touches (called both 'modern Gothic' and 'a modification of Renaissance' when built), covered in white plastic decorative porches and sikharas, by *MESH Architectural Services*, 2001.

UNITARIAN CHURCH (now BETHEL UNITED CHURCH OF GOD), Gibson Road. The w range is by *W.N. Twist*, 1915. Brick hall with minimal buttresses.

GURU NANAK NISKHAM SEWAK JATHA, Soho Road. 1993–6. Designed by members of the temple with *R.S. Bajaj*. A dominating presence, with a full-height porch topped by a dome. Architecturally, a decorated box. The NISKHAM CENTRE, added in 2002–3 by *Brian Bannister Projects*, is better, addressing the Villa Road corner with glazed walls, concave and convex curves, and posts projecting through the canopies with spiked finials.

SHRI GURU RAVIDASS BHAWAN, Grove Lane. 1990–2 by *Naseeruddin Kaiser*. A compact, well-articulated maroon brick block with cornice rising segmentally in the centre, chattris and dome. Ornate railings and gates by *Partington Associates*, 1999.

Cemetery

HANDSWORTH CEMETERY, Oxhill Road and Camp Lane. 1909–10, laid out by the U.D.C. surveyor *H. Richardson*. The exceptional CHAPEL is by *W.H. Bidlake*. An elegant Dec design in brindled brick and grey Ridge Park stone, with thin window mullions emphasizing its vertical quality. Small w towers with openwork spires, and a pair of turrets marking the division between what appears a simple nave and apse. The interior is a wonderful spatial surprise. Tall Hollington stone arcades, with complex mouldings and keeled shafts, define very narrow passage aisles. They rise to a tierceron-vault with carved bosses. Liernes are used only in the apse. Buff-brick

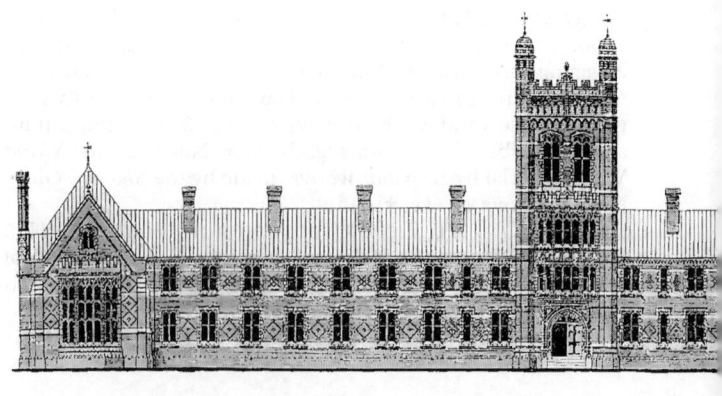

Birmingham, Handsworth Methodist College.
Elevation engraving, 1879

walls frame arcades and vault. At the W end, an octagonal MORTUARY CHAPEL behind two-light windows with through mullions. – Original *Bidlake* PULPIT and STALLS, arranged like a college chapel. – LODGE also of 1909–10 by *Bidlake*.

PUBLIC BUILDINGS

COUNCIL HOUSE (former) and LIBRARY, Soho Road. 1877–9 by *Alexander & Henman*, i.e. *William Henman*, the library extension, W, added in 1891. A vigorous, picturesque design in red brick and stone, with lots of what Victorians called 'Go'. The main references are Early French or north European Renaissance. Big mullion-and-transom windows. The central tower has a four-sided gabled timber top, the SW tower of 1891 a Chambord-style truncated spire, with a little many-gabled cupola. Two applied gables below with reliefs by *Benjamin Creswick*: Boulton and Watt discussing rotary motion and being overheard by a spy; another, part-hidden, over the library entrance. The band beneath has tiny miners in a seam among the foliage.

POLICE STATION, Thornhill Road. 1893 by *J.P. Osborne*. A tough version of Queen Anne. Entrance with massive consoles and balustrade, intended to impress. Big Dutch gable. Slightly French-looking former court room upstairs.

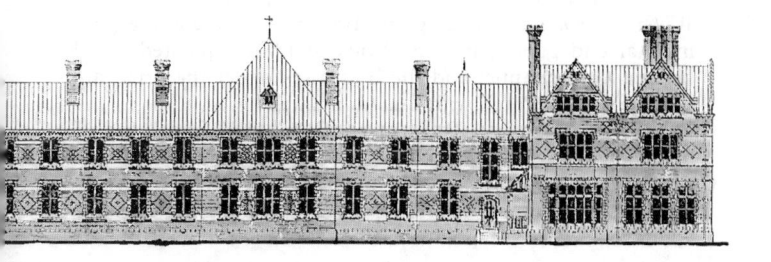

HANDSWORTH METHODIST COLLEGE (now HAMSTEAD CAMPUS), Friary Road. 1880–1 by *Ball & Goddard*, i.e. the young *J.L. Ball*. A large E-shaped building in a tough Tudor Revival style. Red-brown brick with blue diapering, buff terracotta dressings. The main NW front has a commanding entrance tower with a very big oriel and a crenellated parapet with corner cupolas. The motif of a segmental pointed arch runs through the design, in the repeated two-light windows, and the three-light Perp windows of the former LIBRARY at the N end. The ground-floor corridor has a seven-bay arcade running down it centrally, supporting the block's rear wall. The W side is rib-vaulted. The E side has a glazed roof and half-trusses with transoms and large brackets. The former LIBRARY, COMMON ROOM behind the corridor, and REFECTORY, S of the S wing, have heavy beamed and coved ceilings and rich fireplaces with piers or columns and swirling foliage capitals. – LODGE to Friary Road with a timber gable. – CHAPEL of 1932 by *Arthur Edgerton Leeson*, with open cloisters linking it to the 1881 wings, the central one extended. Tame Gothic in maroon brick with a pointed barrel-vault. Fresco, a copy of Fra Angelico's Annunciation, over the door, by *Nora Yoxall* and *Elsie Whitford*, *c*. 1932.

HANDSWORTH GRAMMAR SCHOOL, Grove Lane. The original buildings are High Victorian Gothic, of 1861–2 by *George Bidlake*. Red brick with blue-brick bands and Bath stone dressings. A line of acutely pointed gables with big Geometrical windows pushes up into a big roof. To the r. an entrance tower with a stilted pointed arch to the doorway, cutting in to cusped belfry windows and then out to a spirelet. Further r. a gabled block with big plate-traceried window. N extension by *Wood & Kendrick*, 1905 etc., recast, the upper storeys added, and extended along Dawson Road in basic Tudor by *Essex & Goodman*, 1927–8. – Sports centre to the S by *RPS Design*, 2008.

HOLYHEAD SCHOOL, Holyhead Road. 1973–5 by *S.T. Walker & Partners*.

KING EDWARD VI SCHOOL HANDSWORTH, Rose Hill Road. A girls' grammar school, by *P.B. Chatwin* (*J.A. Chatwin & Son*), 1908–11. A majestic design in a free late C17 style. Two short projecting wings. Steep roofs. Giant Ionic pilasters, and a big central aedicule with half-columns and a segmental pediment. · The interior is arranged round a barrel-vaulted HALL with fine plasterwork by *G.H. Cox*: bands of flowers and fruit along the ribs, shields on the pilasters and, below, lions in aedicules. Staircases at both ends, entered through arches and open through arches at the side, a nice effect. They have C18-style swept-up rails and newels with royal ciphers and ball finials. LIBRARY to the E by *Sidell Gibson Crouch Butler*, 2010–11, with monopitched roof and glass walling.

ST JOHN WALL R.C. SCHOOL, Oxhill Road. 1963–5 etc. by *F. Potter & Associate*, with *A.G. Sheppard Fidler*, City Architect.

TECHNICAL SCHOOL (former), Golds Hill Road. 1897 by *William Henman*. Already going Free Style, see e.g. the pedimental end gables; but the brick and white-painted wood suggest Queen Anne, and the buttresses under the oriels are Gothic echoes. Porch with quadrant sides.

GRESTONE ACADEMY (PRIMARY), Grestone Avenue. 1953–5 by *Baron C.S. Underhill*.

GROVE SCHOOL (PRIMARY), Grove Lane. By *Wood & Kendrick*, 1902–3. Big gables with shaped tops and round-headed windows. A pretty cupola. Rear block of 1913 in a spare Arts and Crafts-influenced manner, the end gable corbelled out above a window.

ROOKERY SCHOOL (PRIMARY), Rookery Lane. 1899 by *Edward Holmes*. Brick and terracotta, old-fashioned eclectic detail. Rear extensions 1908 by *Wood & Kendrick*.

WATTVILLE PRIMARY SCHOOL, Wattville Road. 1893–5 by *Wood & Kendrick*. An attractive Queen Anne design. Dutch gables with prominent middle transoms. Projecting apse end to the l. with big pedimented semi-dormers. The ventilation tower has an octagonal cupola. Main hall with big cast-iron trusses in the Martin & Chamberlain way, but with delicate quatrefoils in circles.

MATTHEW BOULTON PRIMARY SCHOOL (now Oasis Academy Boulton), Boulton Road. Started as an 'undenominational' school of 1884. What we see now are gabled blocks with triplet lancets facing the road, by *J.R. Nichols*, 1893, and the N extension with big round-headed window by *Wood & Kendrick*, 1901–2.

PUBLIC BATHS (former), Grove Lane. 1906–7 by *J.P. Osborne*. Front block in brick and terracotta, restrained Tudor style. Square tower with a spire on the N side. Now part of flats.

SOHO HOUSE, Soho Avenue.* The home of the manufacturer Matthew Boulton from 1766 to his death in 1809, restored by Birmingham City Council and opened as a museum in 1995. Boulton acquired the newly built shell of a modest L-shaped house with Soho Mill in 1761, and quickly fitted out the interior. He moved there in 1766, but did not develop the house further until the 1790s. The NW elevation to Soho Avenue is traditionally the 'back-front'; the SE elevation with the main entrance is now hemmed in by C19 housing.

The house today is the product of expansion and formalization in 1796–9, less subsequent demolitions. There was a rapid turnover of designers: *James Wyatt*, architect, 1796–7; *William Hollins*, architect, mason and clerk of works, 1797–8; *Samuel Wyatt*, architect and contractor, with his cousin *Benjamin Wyatt* of Sutton Coldfield, 1798–9.† It is not easy to distinguish the work of any individual. *James Wyatt*'s grandiose design was only partially implemented, raising the attic storey and adding a two-storey service wing, W (partly demolished). A frontage block to the SE was not built, so an internal wall became the main SE façade. This has seven bays, the central bay framed by giant Ionic pilasters with a Diocletian window in the attic above a tripartite flat-headed window, over a doorway flanked by narrow windows. Ionic pilasters also on the corners. Plain entablature and heavy cornice. Parallels for the central bay can be seen in *James Wyatt*'s unexecuted design for Badger Hall, Shropshire, but *Samuel Wyatt* submitted a drawing, now

---

*Adapted from the entry of 2005 by George Demidowicz in the *Birmingham City* guide, which also includes details of decoration and furnishings.
†Plans drawn by *Samuel Wyatt* in 1787 and *John Rawstorne* in 1788 were never implemented.

lost, of the SE façade to Boulton in June 1798. On balance the evidence favours Samuel, who was almost certainly responsible for encasing the house in slate, giving the appearance of finely jointed ashlar (cf. his portico at Shugborough Hall, Staffs.). The stone texture was achieved by adding sand to white lead paint. The present semicircular porch was apparently finished by *Hollins* c.1804 (rebuilt 1957). Most of the NW elevation is of 1766–96, including the three-storey canted bay window.

INTERIOR. Boulton made many compromises: the house never attained the desired size, and illusions of space were introduced where feasible. Two alabaster Doric columns in the ENTRANCE HALL opposite the main entrance frame the doorway into the dining room and cleverly inflate this modest volume. The painted floorcloths were made to the original 1799 pattern during the restoration. *James Wyatt*'s intended grand central stair, forward of the present façade, was never constructed, and the 'back stairs' off the l. side of the hall serve as the principal route to the first floor. Unpretentious, but with fascinating perforations in the risers as part of an innovative heating system installed throughout. Boulton experimented with 'central' heating in the 1790s, including by steam, but his son *Matthew Robinson Boulton* appears to have installed the earliest version of the ducted hot-air system in place today. A stove (cockle) can be seen in the cellar; other ducts fed warm air through grilles in the hearths.

James Wyatt converted the old kitchen into the DINING ROOM, incorporating two neighbouring rooms. Four Ionic columns replaced a wall, supporting a shallow groined ceiling spanning to pilasters opposite. Marbling was by the decorative painter *Cornelius Dixon*. It is likely that the meetings of the illustrious Lunar Society took place in this room. The BREAKFAST ROOM, r. of the hall, leads to the DRAWING ROOM. These rooms form part of the earliest house. Boulton's STUDY and FOSSILRY on the ground floor are reached along the narrow stair corridor. The restored first-floor rooms, spread along an equally tight passageway, include Anne Boulton's SITTING ROOM, BEDROOM and POWDERY and Matthew Boulton's BEDROOM, formerly a library.

As with much associated with Matthew Boulton, the house defies categorization. Boulton did not implement the grand plans to transform an overblown villa into a country mansion. He did, however, develop a large landscaped park from the heath around the house; unfortunately little is left. He was the probably the first industrialist in the country to bring together his home and nearby manufactory (*see* p. 242) on such a scale, and to see Palladianism as a legitimate style for his main working buildings.

HANDSWORTH PARK. A large park, stretching W–E down a valley from Grove Lane to Hamstead Road by St Mary's church, bisected by the Soho Loop railway. The Grove, W of the railway, was laid out by *R.H. Vertegans* and opened in 1888. In 1895–8 the former rectory grounds, E of the railway, were laid out by the Council Surveyor *Edwin Kenworthy*. Additions to the W followed until 1901. On Hamstead Road, mid-C20 GATES and RAILINGS. Grossly picturesque LODGE by *Kenworthy*, dated 1897, when the present POOL was created. Just E of the pool a domed octagonal cast-iron UMBRELLO of 1888, moved here in the late C20. On its S side a tall granite DRINKING FOUNTAIN of 1898. W of the railway an octagonal BANDSTAND of 1891 with ogee-domed roof, placed here *c.*1907.

PERAMBULATIONS

Handsworth is a difficult area to walk, because of its size and the scattered nature of its good buildings. The main perambulations go along Soho Hill and Soho Road (A41), and Hamstead Road (B4124), and necessarily include stretches of less interest.

1. Soho Hill and Soho Road

The old road to Wolverhampton, turnpiked in 1727. The start is the HOCKLEY FLYOVER of 1963–8. Underneath, three concrete MURALS by *William Mitchell*, 1968. Deeply moulded, with abstract patterns hinting at natural forms and occasionally breaking out into, for example, a big sunflower on the W side. Up SOHO HILL on the NE side the former NEW PALLADIUM CINEMA of 1927 by *L.L. Dussault*, with a half-octagonal recessed centre. Nos. 68–82 is a factory of 1906 by *W.J. Davis*, with bold faience bands and end towers with wavy parapets. Further up a taller and equally bold factory of 1912 by *Arthur Edwards*, with eye-popping voussoirs. In the fork with Hamstead Road, the early C19 former ROEBUCK INN.

Soho Hill beyond has contrasting sides. On the SW is the Soho Park estate, developed by M.P.W. Boulton from the early 1850s. RICHMOND ROAD was all built up *c.*1852–5. Nos. 12–26 are pairs with architraved windows with minimal pediments on the ground floor, the manner of the 1830s. Nos. 1–7 opposite are rendered minimal Tudor with thin hoodmoulds. Soho Hill itself has a long line of contemporary three-bay detached or semi-detached houses, many in poor commercial uses, some with eared architraves. PARK AVENUE has a picturesque mid-Victorian mixture of square classical villas on the W side, and Tudor cottages and Tuscan porches on the E. No. 8 is a good 1860s villa with Tuscan porch and windows with minimal pediments. Arched lights, the central ones unusually ogee-shaped. Beyond on Soho Hill, more Tuscan porches at Nos. 119, 121, etc. On the NE side a Neo-Georgian TELEPHONE EXCHANGE of 1929, then No. 176, the former SCHOOL BOARD OFFICES, by *Wood & Kendrick*, dated 1902, Jacobean with big grid windows. On the corner of SOHO AVENUE opposite, No. 127 of *c.*1870–5, replacing the lodge of Soho House: opulent Italianate. Down the avenue, Soho House (p. 253) on the E side. Further down, on the corner of Vicarage Road, the former

ST MICHAEL'S VICARAGE of 1873 by *W. Davis*, yellow firebrick with red and blue bands. No. 186 Soho Hill, the SUPREME WORKS, dated 1922, is by *Holland W. Hobbiss* for a goldsmith, J. H. Wynn. Arts and Crafts Neo-Georgian, simple but original, with a striking row of circular windows along the second floor. Pedimental gable with Mycenae lions and column in low relief by *William Bloye*, the lions' tails scrolling on to the side panels. Beyond, a lovable muddle of early C19 cottages, No. 188 dated 1826. Nos. 226–232, three-storey shops on the corner of Villa Road.

The junction here has St Michael's church (p. 246) on the S, the Methodist church (p. 249) on the N, and the Guru Nanak Niskham Sewak Jatha and Niskham Centre (p. 250) on the NW. In Soho Road on the SW side, good mid-Victorian classical villas. No. 1 has architraved windows and a pedimented doorcase; No. 3 is richer, with linked segment-headed windows; Nos. 5–7, more ornate, must be slightly later; Nos. 9–11 have smooth rustication and giant Corinthian pilasters. LANSDOWNE TERRACE (Nos. 13–19) continues the rustication, with vermiculated quoins. No. 21 has a doorcase with big consoles. On the N side, just before the railway bridge, the former IVY HOUSE HOTEL, by *J.J. Raggett*, 1892–3, lively commercial, all timber gables and oriels. Beyond the bridge the RHODES ALMSHOUSES of 1873. Red brick. A contrast in shaped gables: the big end ones rounded, the smaller ones with finials. Next to it the COMMUNITY ROOTS ENTERPRISE CENTRE by *Purvey May*, 2000. Nos. 100–112 by *Thomas Silver*, dated 1914, are Free Jacobean with a picturesque central gable. Then the Council House and library (p. 251). No. 128 is the former FRIGHTED HORSE pub, here in 1818, an extreme example of C21 total alteration. Up Stafford Road alongside, a former FIRE STATION, blocky Neo-Georgian by the *Birmingham City Surveyor*, c. 1938. In Union Row, W, a three-storey terrace, probably here in 1794, so the windows with moulded segmental lintels are early examples. Beyond, on the corner with Grove Lane, Shri Guru Ravidass Bhawan (p. 250).

Back to SOHO ROAD, and W. On the S side Nos. 205–207, Neo-Georgian by *J.B. Surman*, 1930–1. On the corner of Baker Street, N side, shops of 1891–2 by *J.G. Dunn & F.W. Hipkiss*, with a touch of French in the cut-off pyramid turret. CHOHAN'S (No. 223), S side, gabled with an oriel, is by *Clement A. Young*, 1912. At No. 233 a former BILLIARD HALL with big segmental pediment between miniature towers, by *Albert Bye*, 1915. Nos. 196–198, N side, are crude Art Deco of 1935; Nos. 200–202 a former Burtons by *Harry Wilson*, 1929. On the S side, faience classical by *Thomas Silver*: MAIRS dated 1914, and a former draper's with big upstairs windows, dated 1912. On the N side a long Early Victorian row, including the PUMP TAVERN. Further up on the S side, the CROSS GUNS pub of 1936–7 by *J.P. Osborne & Son*, cubic Neo-Georgian. Diagonally opposite, shops by *Oliver Floyd & Salt*, 1903, the corner feature with an oval window.

Continuing on the N side, No. 272 is the former RED LION pub, 1901–2 by *James & Lister Lea* (closed since *c.* 2005). 'With its Jacobean strapwork and heraldic lions, its inventive, faintly Flemish tracery, and several different types of pediment, the façade has an air of plunder about it; the designers at *Hathern Station Brick & Terracotta Company* have been ransacking the history books' (Alan Crawford). Plum terracotta on the ground floor, buff above. The most sumptuous pub interior in Birmingham. The PUBLIC BAR has its original bar front and back, all mirror glass and mahogany. *Minton* tiling here with blue flowers, and all along the r. STAIR HALL, mostly in cream and turquoise. The COFFEE ROOM beyond has full-height Jacobean-style panelling incorporating framed lithographs. SMOKE ROOM, down a corridor on the l. side, with more *Minton* tiling with a series of colour lithographs of maidens carrying baskets, and still-lifes. Nos. 292–298 are the former headquarters of the SOHO CO-OPERATIVE SOCIETY, by *George Randle*, 1919–21. Brick and faience. Big display windows, swan's-neck centrepiece. W extension by *E. J. Davies*, 1928. Then Cannon Street Memorial Baptist Church (p. 249). Finally HOLYHEAD BUILDINGS by *Ralph Heaton & A. H. Dight*, dated 1914. Brick and red terracotta, sparingly classical.

Determined walkers can continue NW into HOLYHEAD ROAD, past much-altered villas, and on the S side the Asbury chapel and Holyhead School (pp. 248, 252). At No. 65 a Neo-Georgian former POLICE STATION by the *Birmingham City Engineer and Surveyor*, 1938. On the N side the former NEW INN (No. 42), by *Wood & Kendrick*, 1900–4, originally a large and smart hotel, in refined Jacobean style. Nos. 163–167, Free Style shops dated 1907, by *Thomas Silver*.

2. Hamstead Road

This was the Walsall road, turnpiked in 1809. Its fascination is the feeling of a preserved main road, superseded by the modern A34 through Perry Barr. The first stretch is from the fork at the former Roebuck (*see* p. 255). Nos. 20A–46, E side, were originally the city's longest Georgian terrace; still impressive despite being broken in the late C19 to make Charleville Road. Standard open-pedimented Doric doorcases. A former carriage arch N of the break, infilled by a shop. Wyatt windows with slim colonnettes at the N end. Opposite, an Early Victorian house with a veranda, flats of *c.* 1956, and No. 41 of *c.* 1830, with a doorcase with panelled pilasters. N of the long terrace, Nos. 72–76, Early Victorian, and Nos. 80–84, plain Late Georgian, with one surviving doorcase. Then the former Baptist church (p. 249). Beyond it, a butcher's shop of 1895 by *Oliver Floyd*, a lively mongrel with Jacobean gable and Composite pilasters to the shopfront.

At the cross-roads of VILLA ROAD, NE, YE OLDE TOLL GATE HOUSE (currently ASIAN RESOURCE CENTRE), 1904 by *George E. Pepper*. Wonderfully overdone, with acres of fake timbering above – including birds and beasts in quadrant-braced panels – and Mackintosh and Art Nouveau below, with oval glass door panels and wavy transoms. To the E, 'The Village', a smart shopping centre until the 1960s. Two former pubs by *Osborne & Son*: No. 104, the BULLS HEAD, S, 1935, and the VILLA CROSS, in the fork of Lozells and Heathfield roads, 1937.

Back to the main road and W, the N side of Villa Road is all 1840s. First a pair with a balustraded extension for a former Lloyds Bank, *c.* 1900 by *J.A. Chatwin* (now a mosque). Then a long terrace with a string curving up as the road climbs. The last pair have pedimented Wyatt window surrounds (windows replaced). On the S side, No. 42 of *c.* 1860, rich classical, then Nos. 34–40, an unusual terrace of shortly after 1840: houses stepped *en echelon* to the road, each a single bay wide.

The main road continues N with solid late C19 villas on the E side (also in Radnor Road). Nos. 134–136 are undigested Old English, probably by *Thomas Guest*, 1891. No. 138, a very late classical villa by *J.G. Dunn*, 1883, with a full-height bay. Further N, No. 166A, with Art Deco doorcase, by *Edwin J. Griffin*, 1931. No. 168 was *A. Gilbey Latham*'s own house, 1921. Timbering, corner oriel, pyramid roof. Down Gibson Road, E, the former Unitarian church (p. 250) and No. 10, restrained brick by *J.P. Osborne*, 1914. Back on Hamstead Road, a pair by *Crouch & Butler*, 1896–7: No. 170 with half-timbering and a very free doorcase, No. 172, now rendered, with a big semicircular door hood. Opposite, No. 139, a doctor's surgery by *H.S. Scott & Harry Weedon*, 1911–12. Contrasting brick and render gables, and a tremendous chimney. Nos. 174–176 are by *Herbert R. Lloyd*, 1894, mangled, but once ruthlessly simple, almost like contemporary work by J.L. Ball. No. 178 is by *Osborne*, 1890–1, in Ernest George's Flemish-cum-Queen Anne manner. His No. 171, W side, is a grander version, 1885–6.

Beyond Handsworth Park we reach St Mary's church (p. 243). Opposite, a former 'Parish Room and Coffee House' by *William Davis*, 1889–90, with a spirelet. N of the churchyard a pair of picturesque brick Tudor 'school houses', by *Charles Edge*, 1850. Up the hill, on the E side, a square rendered villa, probably 1830s (now a mosque). Porch with paired fluted Doric columns. Ground floor altered for pub use *c.* 1930, with smooth rustication. Nos. 318–320 are of *c.* 1830–40, plain, with a Greek Revival architrave over the r. porch.

At the junction with Church Lane we go N along HANDSWORTH WOOD ROAD. On the NE corner another 1830s villa, stuccoed to imitate ashlar. Opposite, ENDWOOD COURT, flats by *John Madin*, 1960–1, and a much-altered early C19 former lodge. Nos. 34–36, E side, are Late Georgian, with Doric half-columns to the doorcases. Fanlights with central vesicas.

The last group starts ¼ m. N. On the corner of Handsworth Wood Road and Devonshire Road a group (now a Buddhist temple) by *J.G. Dunn & F.W. Hipkiss*, 1889–92, in the brick Gothic of their Walsall Science and Art Institute (p.629). Opposite, No.82 is by *J.G. Dunn*, 1898, with half-timbering and tile-hanging. No.84, dated 1906, is a perfect imitation of Bidlake's or Bateman's Arts and Crafts manner by *Osborne*, with good brickwork and rounded gable tops. No.88 is Oliver Floyd's own house, blowsy Norman Shaw style, of 1898–9; also his the contemporary No.92. Opposite, a fine Free Style group by *Crouch & Butler*. No.133 and No.2 Somerset Road, 1904–5, are rendered, with an octagonal tower and bold voussoirs. No.135, 1898–9, is influenced by Charles Rennie Mackintosh. Completely unmoulded rendered bay, plain wall to the r. with only small casements. No.137, THE ANCHORAGE, dated 1899, is less radical. Sheer brick gable and tower with fancy parapet to the l., arty oversailing timber upper floor to the r. The interior retains much, despite fire damage in 1977. Full-height hall with gallery on timber posts, the pegging very noticeable. This is as radical as any Morris follower, but the beamed ceiling and studding are more imitative. Elsewhere the style is free C17. The drawing room, s, has an inglenook fireplace with paired pilasters, but with swirling Art Nouveau leaves instead of capitals. Beaten copper fireplace hoods by the *Bromsgrove Guild*, stained glass in the hall by *Mary Newill*.* It is all beautifully crafted, but has none of the ideal simplicity of Bidlake or Bateman.

In SOMERSET ROAD, Nos.3–11 by *Ewen Harper*, 1881–2, forward-looking for the date. No.13 is a shock: white brick and boarding, by *Graham Durrant*, 2005. Then modest Arts and Crafts houses: weatherboarded No.17 by *H.S. Scott* and simple No.19 by *Harry Weedon*, both 1914; Nos.25–27 by *Arthur McKewan*, 1905. No.29 is a larger *Weedon* house of 1919. No.53 is again *Weedon*, 1911. On the N side, Nos.62 by *Scott*, and Nos.64–66, full-blown Neo-Georgian by *McKewan*, both 1914.

Back on Handsworth Wood Road, No.120 of 1910 (E side), large and loosely composed. No.126 is a surprise, a rustic early C19 lodge with rendered walls and overhanging roof on rough tree-trunk supports, with branches arranged to form primitive ogee arches. Ogee-headed doorway and windows as well, with Y-tracery.

NW from here, up Hamstead Hall Road, is the interesting but puzzling HAWTHORN HOUSE. The start is a three-bay rendered Late Georgian villa of c.1825–30 (render replaced 2013), probably for James Villers, a gentleman farmer. Finely detailed Doric portico with pairs of columns and small pediment. Altered and extended by Edwin Bullock, ironmaster, who was here by 1841 and died in 1870. Slightly projecting lower wings with separate hipped roofs and plain Wyatt windows. The l. wing has a semicircular side bow. A further

---

*Wall paintings in the hall by *Fred Davis*, destroyed in 1977, were replaced with copies.

wing set back r. The big r. canted bay must be later. Inside, a large hall opens to the l. through an opening too wide to be Late Georgian, yet that date fits its exquisitely detailed Greek Ionic columns and return pilasters. Staircase of 1862 (date formerly in the staircase window), with ornate cast-iron balusters and newel with bunches of fruit, probably from Bullock's *Spon Lane Iron Foundry*. Through arches to the r. a smaller original hall, but the overdoor reliefs of classical scenes are probably *c*. 1862.

3. Hunters Road

A hidden delight, reached N from Hockley Circus under a factory bridge of 1954–5. Up the hill the road changes character. This was Hunter's Lane, the old parish boundary between Aston and Handsworth. On the W side, the CARNEGIE INFANT WELFARE INSTITUTE, by *J.L. Ball*, 1922. A long three-storey block in dark red brick. Massive in a Lethaby way, articulated by shallow pilasters, with a band of chevron ornament below the parapet. Discs of stone and tile in the spandrels of the ground-floor arches. Central niche with statue of mother and child by *Bloye*. Projecting porch, r., only two storeys because of the slope. Beyond, the Catholic enclave of St Mary's Convent, E, and St Francis's church and presbytery, W (p. 248). Behind St Francis's in Wretham Road, the ST FRANCIS INSTITUTE of 1907–9 by *G.B. Cox*. Jacobean going Neo-Georgian. N of the convent, stuccoed classical houses, 1820s and early 1830s. No. 108 has an iron porch, Nos. 110–112 have end pilasters and good arched doorways with Greek Doric columns and entablatures in front. The same doorcase on No. 114 and on No. 116, which is of red brick. No. 118 has an Ionic doorcase, Nos. 120–122 have rustication below and panelled incised pilasters above. Doorways with diagonally patterned reveals. Nos. 136–138, THE LIMES, are of shortly after 1833, probably by *William Hollins*. Four wide bays, the ends projecting. Unusual porches, recessed at the sides. They taper inwards in false perspective, with Greek Doric columns inset at the back. No. 140, Tudor, is contemporary. On the corner ahead, THE OBSERVATORY, sole survivor of the area's little pubs, also of shortly after 1833. It tapers to a comically narrow front, like something from an Ealing film. Ground floor of 1891 by *James & Lister Lea*.

BARKER STREET runs NNE from here, developed by George Barker from the early 1830s. Much detail has gone. Mainly standard two-storey brick houses. Nos. 34–36, E side, are stuccoed, with smooth rustication and larger architraves. No. 33 has first-floor pilasters and a Greek Doric doorcase; Nos. 55–57 opposite have windows with rosette friezes. In John Street, running NE, WELLINGTON TERRACE, a close of *c*. 1850. Red brick banded with yellow, segment-headed doorways and casement windows, bargeboards.

OTHER BUILDINGS

THE GROVE pub, corner of Oxhill Road and Grove Lane. By *Sam Owen*, prominently dated 1891. Big moulded brick chimneys pushed through timber gables. In College Road, NW, Nos. 38–52, a very early terrace by *Crouch & Butler*, 1892–3, altered but retaining eyebrow dormers. Opposite, the OLD TOWN HALL, a C15 or early C16 four-bay cruck house. Much restored by the *Birmingham City Engineer and Surveyor* in 1946–7, when the side panels were altered and the brick infill renewed. Heavy collar-beams and ridge-piece, purlins with wind-braces. Restored C17 chimneystack attached to the E gable.

THE FARCROFT, Rookery Road, is an over-the-top timbered pub of 1919–20 by *J.P. Osborne & Son*.

LEA HALL, Wood Lane. A tall, square brick Neoclassical house, called 'lately built' for a Mr Spencer by Stebbing Shaw in 1798. In a manner similar to Lightwoods House, Smethwick (p. 588). Three storeys, five bays, projecting (painted) stone string courses between the floors, and cornice. Ionic porch. Lower W wing, with intersecting glazing to the ground-floor window heads. Contemporary stables further W with lunette windows to front, rear and (under a pediment) W side.

CALTHORPE COTTAGES, Wood Lane. C18, perhaps incorporating earlier fabric. In Butlers Road, W, No. 68 by *Harvey & Wicks*, 1937. Rendered, with classical detail but resolutely asymmetrical in a Baillie Scott way.

NW of Handsworth is still countryside, part of the Sandwell valley. PARK FARM BARN, difficult to find amid golf courses, is C17 or C18 but much rebuilt in brick and converted to a house. S of the track which runs NW from Silvercroft Avenue, an ANTI-AIRCRAFT BATTERY, *c.* 1940. Two octagonal concrete gun-pits, surrounded by earth banks, and with concrete ammunition lockers inside. Command post to the S, also with earth banks.

KINGSTANDING

The largest of Birmingham's interwar municipal estates, built in 1928–37. Named from the King's Standing, at the top of Kingstanding Road, probably a late Neolithic or Bronze Age round barrow, which may later have been used as an observation point (stand) for hunting in Sutton Park and Sutton Chase. The population in 1937 was 30,000. Endless curving roads with semi-detached pairs and terraces of four, by the *Birmingham City Engineer and Surveyor*, in pale facing brick and render. Exceptions in HURLINGHAM ROAD, and GREENWOOD PLACE off Finchley Road: streamlined and rendered houses, with hipped roofs, deep eaves and long recessed bands (much alteration alas). Small areas of owner-occupied houses around Rough Road and Old Oscott Hill. The centre is Kingstanding Circle, at the junction of Kingstanding Road and Kings Road. Some 1960s infill.

ST LUKE, Caversham Road. Early Christian Revival by *Percival J. Hunt*, 1936–7. The major work of this architect from a working-class family, who died aged forty-three from T.B., still living in his parents' council house. Chancel added by *Bromilow, While & Smeeton* (*Douglas Hickman*), 1965–6. Reoriented, chancel divided off as a meeting room, new staircase, and aisle roofs pitched (alas) by *Christopher Thomas*, 1995; N Lady Chapel by *Thomas*, 2000; S foyer by *Fiona Mottershead*, 2008. Hunt's design is now best appreciated from the W. Buff brick laid in monk bond. Bare volumes: sheer NW tower, unmoulded windows, semicircular projecting baptistery. Tower N doorway with tympanum of the bull of St Luke, carved probably by *Alan Bridgwater*: influenced by Herefordshire Norman work, but also Eric Gill. Head corbels below. Wide, unmoulded arcades and narrow passage aisles.

ST MARK, Bandywood Crescent. 1971 by *J.P. Osborne & Son*. A brick oval, with windows in set-backs. White walls and boarded ceiling inside, with a lantern over the altar.

CHRIST THE KING (R.C.), Warren Farm Road. 1962–3 by *Jennings Homer & Lynch*. Simple hall, its low-pitched roof echoed in the top of the tower. Front divided by brick fins, interior articulated by brick piers. – STAINED GLASS in the side chapels by *Norgrove Studios*.

OUR LADY OF THE ASSUMPTION (R.C.), Old Oscott Hill. 1956–7 by *G.B. Cox*, assisted by *Bernard James* (*Harrison & Cox*). Impressive, well-massed stripped Romanesque. *Westwerk* tower with semicircular-ended side projections. Statue by *Peter Bohn* in a big niche. Nave and aisles with low-pitched roofs. Plain round-headed arcades. Ritual W gallery. The E end opens out into former chapels, with nice spatial effects. Original PEWS. Altar area reordered *c*.1978.

KINGSTANDING METHODIST CHURCH CENTRE, Kings Road. By *Crouch, Butler & Savage*, 1934. Clerestoried hall surrounded by lower meeting rooms.

MARYVALE, Old Oscott Hill. Formerly Oscott House. The present name is John Henry Newman's; he lived here 1846–8. A convent and children's home from 1851 to 1980: now an institute of further education. The Catholic mission here was started by Fr Andrew Bromwich in 1688. The house was rebuilt in 1753 and is still recognizable between later ranges. S front of three storeys and three wide bays, divided by broad plain pilasters. In 1778 *Fr Pierce Parry* added a chapel to its E, almost certainly designing it himself. A seminary was established in 1794. For it Dr Bew added in 1800 the taller, almost barrack-like three-storey range to its W. *Bishop John Milner*, Catholic apologist and antiquary of Gothic, was in charge from 1808. He extended the chapel in 1809, adding a sanctuary and a sacristy to its E, and in 1816 added buildings to the S, including the semicircular ambulacrum (a hall above it was destroyed in 1860) and its Greek Doric colonnade, which extends round the 1753 house and 1800 block. His Sacred Heart Chapel above the sacristy was completed by 1820. Hall on the N by *Gordon Foster*, 1989, extended with a Quinlan Terry-esque classical front and cupola by *Brownhill Hayward Brown* (*Charles Brown*), 2003–4. By the same firm (*Peter Brownhill*) a CONVENT further N, 1999, and major restoration of the chapel, 2000.

The main hall of the 1753 house is articulated by pilasters. Elegant STAIRCASE with swept-up rail and column-on-vase balusters. The 1800 block has a large first-floor study room with marble fireplace. The CHAPEL has an original gallery with two pairs of Ionic columns, front and rear. Open-baluster front. Ionic altar surround of 1809, its pediment broken by the central of three round windows. Rich C18 altar. Big sashes with false drapery architraves. Panelled ceiling. Pews, dado rail and rear doors all of 2000. The SACRED HEART CHAPEL is reached up a precipitous original staircase. Long and narrow, pretty but rather old-fashioned Gothick: cluster columns supporting a plaster rib-vault. The window jambs have pointed arches in relief. Stained-glass roundel of the Sacred Heart, brought back from Italy by Milner in 1814.

The house is the centre of a Catholic enclave. Up the hill, E, CARDINAL WISEMAN TECHNOLOGY COLLEGE, by *G.B. Cox*, 1955. Low, flat-roofed blocks, much extended. Further up, Our Lady of the Assumption church (*see above*). To the S, MARYVALE PRIMARY SCHOOL. Basic Gothic of 1881, probably by *Henry Naden*. Large late C20 extension.

JEWISH CEMETERY, College Road and Warren Road. Octagonal OHEL dated 1937, by *Essex & Goodman*, with large Gothic windows. Witton Cemetery (p. 237) is opposite on College Road.

ODEON CINEMA (now bingo), Kingstanding Circle. 1934–5 by *J. Cecil Clavering*, the assistant to *Harry Weedon*. 'One of the most spectacular and brilliantly designed of all 1930s cinemas' (Allen Eyles). Buff brick. Front block defined by curved ends, and a curved-end forebuilding, clad in cream faience. A black faience base runs all round. The tremendous central feature has three tapered faience fins, illuminated at night, inspired by Iles, Leathart & Granger's Dreamland Cinema, Margate, Kent (1933–5). Curved entrance canopy below. Conversion has been fairly kind to the interior. Full-width foyer, staircases with chromium handrails. Simple auditorium with few stylistic references: shallow three-centred ceiling, dado with horizontal bands. The shape is reflected in the screen arch. Swinging balcony front, now built out.

Original SCHOOLS all of 1930–2. WARREN FARM SCHOOLS, Dulwich Road (now KINGSTANDING LEISURE CENTRE), are massive brick by *Wood & Kendrick & E.F. Reynolds*, partly replaced by a 1980s swimming bath. TWICKENHAM PRIMARY SCHOOL, Twickenham Road, rendered flat-roofed blocks by *H.T. Buckland*. KINGS RISE PRIMARY (now Academy), Peckham Road, by *Arthur McKewan*, has gambrel-roofed blocks. KINGSTHORNE PRIMARY, Cranbourne Road, by *J.H.*

Hawkes & Son, is low and also gambrel-roofed, including the centrepiece.

PERRY COMMON LIBRARY, College Road. 1934 by *J.P. Osborne & Son*. L-shaped, the corner recessed in a quadrant. Doorcase with streamlined mouldings, and a tympanum of books and torch designed by *William Bloye* and carved by his assistant *Thomas Wright*. Hexagonal lobby with a serrated-edged cut-out to the ceiling, a rare Birmingham touch of Art Deco. The main space is a quarter-circle with a ring of piers with fluted capitals, low clerestory and twelve-sided lantern. Original bookcases with quarter-curve top mouldings.

PUBS. The COLLEGE ARMS, College Road (now McDonalds), by *Holland W. Hobbiss*, 1930, is Neo-Georgian, long, low and loosely composed, with a mansard-roofed pavilion, tall cupola and prominent pedimented doorcases (minus their Doric columns). The DEER'S LEAP, Queslett Road and Cooksey Lane, at the far N end of the estate, by *Batemans*, 1937–8, is gentle Tudor Revival.

1960S HOUSING. A surviving 'live' project by *Birmingham School of Architecture Live Projects Dept* in association with *J. A. Maudsley*, City Architect, 1969. L-shaped bungalows in BANNERS WALK, with courtyards in the angle, on a stepped plan. Also the timber-boarded blocks in HEVER AVENUE and PEMBURY CROFT, again on stepped plans.

LOZELLS

The W part of Aston Manor, now separated by the A34 dual carriageway.

ST PAUL, Lozells Road (now ASSEMBLIES OF THE FIRST BORN). 1880 by *J.A. Chatwin*. Perp, like Christ Church, Summerfield Crescent (p. 214). Hamstead sandstone front with Bath stone dressings; the rest brick. Typical Chatwin apsidal chancel. Good ritual NW tower with prominent stair-turret.

ST PAUL AND ST SILAS CHURCH CENTRE, Lozells Road. 1985–6 by *S.T. Walker & Partners*. Brick, with a big lead-covered dormer lighting the worship area.

ST SILAS (now TRIUMPHANT CHURCH OF GOD), St Silas' Square, Church Street. 1854 by *F.W. Fiddian*. Delightfully situated in a little square of terraced houses. Bulky brick, with lancets and two-light Geometrical windows. W bellcote with louvres and a spirelet. Little pent-roofed transept porches by *Dunn & Hipkiss*, 1887; also the nice RAILINGS, gabled PIERS and LYCHGATE. NE organ chamber by *Cooper Whitwell*, 1898. Wide plastered interior. Collar-beam roof with big arched braces. W gallery. – Original PEWS. – FONT by *Peter Hollins*, 1854, cut back to the stem in deep concave shapes (cf. St Lawrence, Darlaston, p. 649). – PULPIT, 1868, and old-fashioned REREDOS, 1893, by *Jones & Willis*. – CHOIR STALLS. 1896, made by *Hill & Egginton*. – STAINED GLASS. E window by *Hardmans*, 1868; chancel lancets by *T. W. Camm*, 1881. – Former SCHOOL by *Fiddian*, W, dated 1852; W extensions by *J.A. Chatwin*, *c.*1875.

LOZELLS METHODIST CHURCH, Lozells Street. Large mission hall by *Crouch & Butler*, 1893–4. Up-to-date free Romanesque. Big gable with clasping buttresses which have domed tops, big triplet window with delicate shafted columns. Flanking porches with two-bay arcades. On the corner with Gerrard Street, S, LECTURE HALL by *W.H. Martin*, 1908–9. Conventional Free Jacobean with a dash of Baroque. The corner tower has a domed top. The earlier building was infilled to form offices and meeting rooms by *Christopher Thomas*, 2010. Cast-iron columns and trusses poke through floors. In the 1909 hall, now used for worship, an alabaster FONT of 1928.

NEW TESTAMENT CHURCH OF GOD, Lozells Road. 2009 by *Paul Henry Architects*. A brick and artificial stone lump, with vaguely Art Deco towers. It replaced Aston Villa Methodist Church, 1865 by *J.G. Bland*, a good Gothic design.*

LOZELLS MOSQUE. 1998 by *Gurmukhi Building Design*.

In LOZELLS ROAD a spectacular row of shops (Nos. 137–159) with huge oversailing timber-framed dormers, by *Joseph D. Wood*, 1897–9. To the W, FINCH ROAD PRIMARY CARE CENTRE, dominating grey, yellow and red, by *Panton Sargent*, 2005–7. At the E end near Six Ways the former ROYAL OAK pub by *Hobbiss*, 1926, 'Neo-William-and-Mary' (Alan Crawford). Compact, with a steep hipped roof, big mullion-and-transom windows, and Hobbiss's favourite off-centre chimney. The tympanum of an oak tree must be by *Bloye*.

PERRY BARR

The NE part of old Handsworth parish. The Urban District Council of 1894 covered the area N of the River Tame, but the name spread S to include the Walsall Road/Aston Lane junction area. Walsall Road N to Great Barr was built as a turnpike in 1831, the last in England. Hamstead, to the NW, developed round the colliery, opened in 1878. It closed in 1965, the last in the Birmingham area. Absorbed by the city in 1928, by the Second World War the area was covered by suburban development.

ST JOHN THE EVANGELIST, Church Road. In an unexpected position next to a factory. 1831–3 by *Robert Studholme* of Sutton Coldfield, built as a chapel of ease to Handsworth by John Gough of Perry Hall. Nave and W tower, in red sandstone ashlar. Conventional Late Georgian Gothic. Y-tracery windows,

---

*In 1874 it started a football team, which survives (*see* p. 228).

big lancets in the tower, and emphatic battlements. Stepped buttresses, alas without their pinnacles. *J.A. Chatwin* added chancel and N vestry, 1888, and transepts, completed 1894. Late C13 Geometrical style in matching stone. The interior is all plastered. Chatwin's chancel arch has head corbels; his transept arches are segmental. – PULPIT, 1833. Classical, but with cusping to the panels. Elegant curved stair rail. – Simple PEWS, also 1833. – Typical *Chatwin* CHOIR STALLS of *c.*1894, and red alabaster FONT of 1888, on stubby columns. – PAINTING, N transept. Lunette above the altar, a Virgin and Child with local scenes by *Marion Robison*, 1938. – ROYAL ARMS of 1833, W wall, small. – STAINED GLASS. Chancel E window 1890, N 1898, both almost certainly by *Heaton, Butler & Bayne*; good small lancet by *T.W. Camm*, 1898, vestry passage; S transept, *Hardmans*, 1906; N transept, *Pearce & Cutler*, 1938. – CHURCHYARD with several nice C19 tombs, C19 gatepiers and iron gates.

ST PAUL, Walsall Road, Hamstead. Built for the former mining village down the hill to the SW. 1891–2 by *William Davis*. Red brick and Bath stone dressings, early Dec style. Three-sided apse. A tall flèche was taken down in 1969. Crude SW extension of 1980. Davis was mostly a commercial architect, and the interior has some clumping details. The arcades have huge bells to the capitals and enormous torus mouldings on the bases. Attractive wall paintings above: scenes from the life of St Paul by *Andrew Wade*, 1994, in a mid-C20 mural tradition, with a light palette. N aisle prettily screened off as a CHAPEL by the *Bromsgrove Guild*, 1932, with altar and panelling; clearly also theirs, S aisle SCREEN with little figures. – Alabaster REREDOS, 1902. – PULPIT and FONT, like Gothick work of the 1830s. – PEWS. 1914. – STAINED GLASS. A good collection. E window 1894, probably by *Samuel Evans*. Three apse windows by *Charles M. Gere*, 1899, his only work in the medium. Arts and Crafts, with unusually pale borders and backgrounds, and wandering, 'uncertain' (Martin Harrison) leading. S aisle S by *George Cooper-Abbs* of *Wippells*, 1936, with little animals in the borders; W by *T.W. Camm* (*Walter* and *Florence Camm*), 1923, good, with small scenes and texturing. N aisle from the E: two lights by *T.W. Camm* (*Walter*, *Florence* and *Robert Camm*), 1930; two by *A.J. Davies*, 1932. – Churchyard WAR MEMORIAL. Celtic cross, 1920. – PARSONAGE by *William Hale & Son*, 1906, S.

ST TERESA (R.C.), Wellington Road. 1962 by *Morris, Smith & Partners*. Glazed gabled front, plain interior with arcades of square piers. The large mid-Victorian pair, l., now the presbytery, was the original church.

PERRY BARR METHODIST CHURCH, Aston Lane, by the A34 underpass. 1890–1 by *Thomas Guest*. Tremendous Gothic front with a triple arcade, rose window and lots of juicy stone foliage. Arch-braced collar-beam roof, ritual W gallery, original pews.

CREMATORIUM, Walsall Road. 1902–3 by *F.B. Osborn*, engineers *Willcox & Raikes*. Robust brick Gothic with lancets, like a church of c. 1870. The chimney is disguised as a NW tower with belfry windows and cut-off pyramid roof. S cloister columbarium, simple Gothic, by *Buckland & Haywood* (H.T. Buckland was a director of the company), 1926. Weak Gothic portico by *Philip Herbert*, 1956. – LODGE, 1903.

PERRY BRIDGE, Aldridge Road. Sandstone, four arches and cutwaters, probably of 1711. Massive concrete replacement by *Herbert H. Humphries*, City Engineer and Surveyor, 1931–2, E, with a touch of Art Deco.

PERRY HALL, Perry Avenue. Moated site of a substantial Elizabethan house, probably begun by Sir William Stanford (†1558) and finished c. 1576; dated 1569 on a gable. The moat is older. The house was owned by the Gough family from 1669. In 1850 *S. S. Teulon* made alterations, including a large N porch carried on a bridge over the moat. Demolished 1928. New bridges as part of a public PARK, opened 1929.

OTHER BUILDINGS. Opposite St John's church, the little PERRY VILLA ESTATE, flats and maisonettes by *A. G. Sheppard Fidler*, 1958. Perry Barr has retained its interwar PUBS; all Neo-Georgian, altered but still of interest. Going E, the squarish CHURCH TAVERN is by *Hobbiss*, 1936–7. On Aldridge Road just beyond the M6, the BOAR'S HEAD by *J.P. Osborne & Son*, 1934, with a swan's-neck doorcase. Splendid pole SIGN, the head carved by *Bloye*. On Walsall Road, W, the TENNIS COURT by *Hobbiss*, 1938–9. Hipped roof, giant Ionic end pilasters, set-back wings. ¾ m. NW, THE TOWERS by *E.F. Reynolds*, 1935–6, rendered, slightly Spanish. A little to its S, the former CLIFTON CINEMA by *Ernest Roberts*, 1937–8. A dramatic front, the foyer curving out between round-ended towers.

To the SE, the former Birmingham City University buildings in Aldridge Road and Wellhead Lane were demolished in 2019. In Franchise Street, the approach from the E, the former WELLHEAD TAVERN by *Matthew J. Butcher*, 1908, with an original lantern. On Wellhead Lane, E side, lodges of 1915 to the former KYNOCHS ammunition factory, founded 1862. Early *William Haywood* (*Buckland & Haywood-Farmer*): pedimented central block, side buildings with pyramid roofs and tall central chimneys. Behind, the EDEN BOYS' SCHOOL by *ADP*, 2015–16. Across Aldridge Road, NW, STADIUM, the former Alexander Stadium of Birchfield Harriers, now a greyhound track. Steel and red brick, by *Horace G. Bradley*, 1929. Relief of a hare perhaps by *Bloye*. Extensions by *Weedon Associates*, 2003 onwards. The modern ALEXANDER STADIUM is 1 m. NNW in Perry Park. Main stand 1978 (*Birmingham City Architect's Department*), extended S 1983 and N 1986. Back Straight Stand, smarter, by *Acivico*, 2010–11. To the W, the HIGH PERFORMANCE CENTRE by the *Urban Design Team*, 2003. Metal roofs and panelled walls. Beyond, BIRMINGHAM GYMNASTICS AND MARTIAL ARTS CENTRE by *CPMG*, 2008, similar but louder.

PERRY BEECHES

A large area of housing NE of Perry Barr, developed after Birmingham absorbed Perry Barr U.D.C. in 1928. The centre is on Aldridge Road around the church and college.

ST MATTHEW, Aldridge Road. By *Robert Maguire & Keith Murray*, 1959–63. An important church in the development of Liturgical Movement ideas in Britain, i.e. a building in which the whole congregation can participate more fully in worship. The first impression is an angular brick tower, supported by lower, pent-roofed extensions. Grey brick, laid in English bond, and exposed concrete beams: a nod to the polychromy of Butterfield. The entrance, at the NW, leads into a low baptistery. The interior is completely open, and more spacious than you expect. It rises in an anticlockwise spiral: a series of diminishing irregular hexagons, each partly cut off by a series of concrete beams, until it reaches a regular hexagon high up above the altar. Succeeding roof levels are defined by the succession of concrete beams in the walls. The design turns in on itself, and the altar is near the font where we started. It is a very carefully controlled architectural conceit, but firmly based in Liturgical Movement principles, with the congregation gathered round the altar. Light comes from the long thin windows under each roof slab. The blue-brick floor reflects contemporary interest in industrial architecture. Sanctuary raised on a single step. – Thin wooden PULPIT, LECTERN, ALTAR RAILS and CLERGY SEATS; bench PEWS; circular blue brick FONT. – LIGHTING by *Murray*: rows of hanging lamps with semicircular shades, aligned with the beams above. – At the rear, community rooms, with a separate entrance. – Former MISSION CHURCH, N, by *J.P. Osborne & Son*, 1939. Between it and the church, *Maguire & Murray* created a small enclosed garden.

BROOKLYN TECHNICAL COLLEGE (now JAMES WATT COLLEGE), Aldridge Road. 1954 by *S.N. Cooke & Partners* (*J.C. Goodman*). Five-storey slabs in buff brick. Many recent additions.

GREAT BARR ACADEMY (now FORTIS ACADEMY), Aldridge Road. Front blocks by *S.N. Cooke*, 1938–9: low, flat-roofed ranges in brown brick, with a minimal portico. Four-storey blocks behind by *A.G. Sheppard Fidler*, City Architect (*H.O. Williams*, Principal Architect, Schools), 1955–6, badly re-clad. MUSIC DEPARTMENT by *Glazzard Associates*, 2005. – GREAT BARR PRIMARY SCHOOL (now Academy), S. Also *Cooke*, 1938–9, altered and extended.

PERRY BEECHES CAMPUS, Beeches Road. The earlier buildings, including the main school, are by *Birmingham Design Services* (*Malcolm Leech*), 1998–2000. The most significant example of their characteristic late C20 style: white render and grey-painted metal, piercingly angular, with a crowd of monopitches. Later blocks by *Aedas AHR*, 2004, tamer, unimaginative versions of the same manner.

DRAKE'S DRUM, Aldridge Road, opposite the college. Pub of 1938 by *J. Alfred Harper & Son*. Recessed centre and shallow wings. Occasional round-headed windows. Altered and painted.

PERRY BEECHES ESTATE, W of the college. Developed by the First National Housing Trust, 1934–8. It stretches beyond the M6 to Tideswell Road, Rowdale Road, etc. Very plain pairs and terraces of four and six, with occasional gables, by *A. J. White & Styles*. On Thornbridge Avenue, shops with steep gables, by *Ernest Willson*, 1937–8. THE BEECHES pub opposite is by *J.B. Surman*, 1935. Large, austere Tudor with big stone windows. An impressive design.

PYPE HAYES

A large 1920s municipal estate, almost completely replaced in the late C20 and early C21 because of construction defects.

ST MARY, Tyburn Road and Padstow Road. The masterpiece of *E.F. Reynolds*, designed in 1927 and built 1929–30. It combines a wide nave with passage aisles, and a traditional cruciform scheme of chancel, transepts and crossing, arranged so that every nave seat has an altar view. A N chapel balances the vestry. Reynolds called his approach here 'not traditional in character but frankly modern', which meant a common-sense application of techniques to the needs of the building, with apparently historic motifs, such as round-headed windows and arches, chosen for practicality, not for their associations. Brick, laid in Reynolds's favourite Flemish stretcher bond, with white Hollington stone details. The massive nave is balanced by the transepts, its effect emphasized by the sloping buttresses of the clerestory, derived from Turkish mosques. S bell-turret, carefully placed where transept meets chancel. On the N side a modest gabled hall, attached by a cloister.

The interior is plastered. The nave is held in tension, structurally and metaphorically, by great segmental cross-arches (of steel and plaster, though they have the mass of concrete). Oregon pine roof with stencilled patterns. Its purlins run straight through from end to end. The cross-arches express the wide nave; the purlins express the long axis. They meet, therefore, with a clash of great underlying power. Red Hollington stone capitals to the arches. The same stone is used for the SCREEN, with its central arch, and for the chancel walls, with niches for sedilia. The nave cants in to the crossing. The N chapel has been boxed in, damaging the spatial effect. Twin

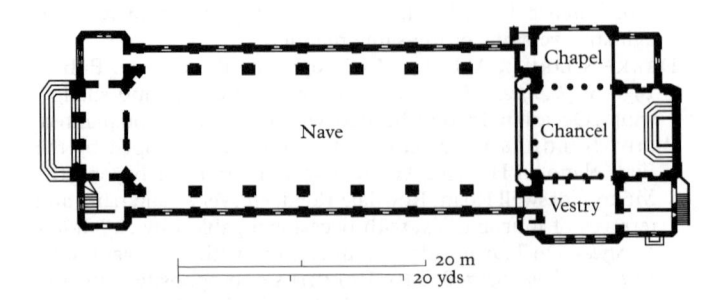

Birmingham, Pype Hayes, St Mary.
Plan

PULPIT and READING DESK, in niches, flanking the chancel arch. The aisle PAVEMENTS are a Reynolds trademark, York stone and green Westmorland slate, squares set diagonally inside larger squares. LIGHT FITTINGS with arched hangers mirroring the screen design, now modified for strip-lights.

St Mary's is not an easy or charming building, but its austere magnificence is compelling. It looks plain compared with the contemporary work of, say, Bernard Miller or F.X. Velarde, and it has nothing to do with Art Deco or jazz, but it may recall late Sibelius, or the Holst of *Egdon Heath*. (Reordering proposed by *Gavin Orton*, 2021.)

ST PETER AND ST PAUL (R.C.), Kingsbury Road. 1968–71 by *Harry Harper (Radford Harper)*. Brick. Low-pitched metal roof, clerestory lighting, and a perky hat for the lantern over the altar.

UNITED REFORMED CHURCH (formerly Congregational), Chester Road. 1929 by *J.R. Armstrong* of *Bournville Village Trust Architects*. Simple brick Early Christian, the entrance and rose window enclosed in a giant arched recess.

PYPE HAYES HALL. Decaying and inaccessible (2020). Probably built for the Bagot family who acquired the estate in the early C17, but heavily remodelled for the Rev. Egerton Arden Bagot who was here from 1806 to 1861; *James Trubshaw* has been suggested as the architect. H-plan, with a long central range. S front refaced in stuccoed masonry, with an odd array of little gables all along; probably early C19. Big five-sided bays, much rebuilt but perhaps original; small mullioned windows higher up, and bigger four-light windows with hoodmoulds. C18 Tuscan porch. Tall end chimneys. Early C19-looking bargeboards. At the rear a stuccoed Victorian Jacobean range. – STABLES. Ruinous. The older, lower part C18 (the VCH records a date of 1762). Gabled range and much alteration by *J.J. Raggett*, 1896. – The GROUNDS have been a municipal park since 1920. On Chester

Road a LODGE by *E.F. Titley*, 1902. At the junction of Chester Road and Eachelhurst Road, a pair of C18 cottages altered by Titley in 1902.

SCHOOLS. PAGET SCHOOL, Westmead Crescent, by *Holland W. Hobbiss*, 1928, has two-storey wings with hipped roofs linked by an entrance block with a minimal pediment and big off-centre chimney. GUNTER PRIMARY SCHOOL, Gunter Road, by *H.T. Buckland*, 1930, has prominent hipped roofs, and a hall block with a big domed cupola. BIRCHES GREEN INFANT SCHOOL, by *Arthur McKewan*, 1929, has a parapeted centre with tall end chimneys.

THE TYBURN, corner of Kingsbury Road and Chester Road, is of 1930 by *Batemans*. 'The simplest and subtlest of the Bateman pubs' (Crawford and Thorne). Single-storeyed, in warm, brown rubble stone with delicate Tudor mouldings. L-plan. Very shallow bays on each front give the building light and shade. A panelled room largely survives as part of the opened-out interior. *Batemans*' BAGOT ARMS, 1931, Neo-William-and-Mary with tall chimneys, is a splendid presence at the Chester Road/Eachelhurst Road junction. (Derelict in 2020.)

No. 924B Chester Road (down Saltney Close, almost opposite the Hall entrance), is a little C16 or early C17 timber-framed cottage. Square panelling.

SUBURBS: EAST

Alum Rock	272
Hay Mills	273
Hodge Hill	275
Saltley	275
Shard End	278
Sheldon	280
Churches	280
Other buildings	282
Small Heath	284
Places of worship	284
Public buildings	288
Other buildings	290
Stechford	291
Ward End	292
Washwood Heath	294
Yardley	295
Churches	295
Schools	297
Perambulation	298
Other buildings	299

ALUM ROCK

A manor in the parish of Aston. Little Bromwich is an alternative name.

CHRIST CHURCH, Burney Lane. 1934–5 by *Holland W. Hobbiss*, his finest church. This is Hobbiss's German church, in more than one way. The ritual W tower with its flanking cloakrooms is a *Westwerk*, broader than it is deep, and the sheer brickwork of its upper parts shows a knowledge of both medieval German churches and contemporary ones such as Albert Bosslet's Herz Jesu Kirche at Aschaffenburg (1928–9). Setting off this plainness is excellently integrated sculpture by *Bloye*: a solemn Good Shepherd above the entrance, and a cross incorporating an Agnus Dei above, flanked by little Art Deco angels. But the entrance itself is more Italian or Byzantine, with its heavy piers, stylized leaf capitals incorporating crosses, and entablature with a crushed pulvinated frieze. And it is placed in a big projecting rectangular panel of the type frequent in Norman churches in Worcestershire. The nave is still Romanesque, but in its own, different manner: two-light windows to the passage aisles, with stone balusters, cushion capitals, and arches turned in tiles, a material absent from the front. The nave is spanned by semicircular cross-arches, rendered but with brick soffits, every fifth brick extending further into the render, a jazzy and contemporary effect. Rows of narrower bricks are used to suggest imposts. The chancel, however, is deliberately different, with a flat beamed ceiling tapering down to corbels in the side walls. Side chapels open through simple arcades, two paired arches to each side, a spatial effect spoilt when they were glazed in the late C20. – FITTINGS by *Hobbiss*. FONT, complex and elegant in shape, a convex square block with concave corners. Excellent relief carving by *Bloye*, including a Christ Child's head, and waves round the base. – Also CHOIR-STALL FRONTS, PULPIT (1946) and matching READING DESK (1955). – Set back on the W, HALL of 1967–8 by *Noel Hastilow* (*Holland W. Hobbiss & Partners*). Brick, low and plain except for a tympanum with low-relief Byzantine peacocks. – VICARAGE, W, 1968.

COMMUNITY OF ST JOHN THE DIVINE, No. 652 Alum Rock Road. The Society of the Incarnation of the Eternal Son, founded in 1894 by Gertrude Bromby, moved here in 1910 at the suggestion of Bishop Gore. It was dissolved in 1972; the present sisters came in 1976. The Society took over MOAT HOUSE, the manor house of Alum Rock, rebuilt c. 1730. Three-bay S front with renewed segment-headed windows and a deep platband. The entrance is now on the E, with a Doric doorcase of c. 1800 with open pediment. Also of about this time the staircase with elegant slim balusters, and a marble fireplace in the SW room with half-columns and a fan motif. This room was given a semicircular W end with, upstairs, an ogee-headed window.

To the N the CHAPEL, 1911 by *Cecil Hare*. A Bodleyesque steep-gabled brick rectangle with late Dec three-light W (ritual E) window, and flat-headed lancets with ogee tracery. Small ante-chapel divided by a rich late medieval-style SCREEN, with stalls on its W. Reordered 1999 by *Derek Clarke* of *S.T. Walker & Partners*. – STAINED GLASS. Five windows of *c.*1911–20.

In 1931 *Holland W. Hobbiss* added the cloister between house and chapel, with nice timberwork inside, and extended the house W, linking it to former outbuildings. His work has a pretty N elevation with an oversailing tile-hung floor. Inside he created a REFECTORY. Its fireplace has bands of brick and tile, laid flat and zigzag. In 1937 Hobbiss added the residential and library block at the SW corner, Neo-Georgian, with a pedimented doorcase.

WASHWOOD HEATH ACADEMY (originally Comprehensive), Burney Lane. 1964–8 by *Martin Ward & Keeling*.

THORNTON PRIMARY SCHOOL, Thornton Road. By *H.T. Buckland*, 1929–30. The central block has a big gambrel roof with dormers

BROOKHILL TAVERN, No. 484 Alum Rock Road. 1926–7 by *G.B. Cox*. A powerful Tudor Revival 'reformed' pub, with a half-butterfly plan well adapted to its sharply angled site. The ends have big side chimneys, the main accents seen from the front. The l. chimney rises above a ground-floor door. The public bar retains a bar back and front with arcading. Ceiling with geometrical patterns and fruit on the beams, and the M&B brewery emblem. Of the important contemporary GARDENS behind, the hipped-roofed former BOWLING GREEN PAVILION and a toilet block survived in 2019.

The pub is at the entrance to the SUTTON TRUST ESTATE, pairs and groups of four laid out on tree-lined roads and around greens, by *E.C.P. Monson*, 1912–16. Simple Arts and Crafts designs, subtly different from the local Bournville idiom: many gables, much all-over render, a little brick. Commemorative Doric COLUMN with ball finial and raised lettering on the shaft.

In the fork of Alum Rock Road and Burney Lane, ⅔ m. E, the WARD END pub (now restaurant), brick Tudor by *S.N. Cooke*, 1926–7.

HAY MILLS

SW of old Yardley, down by the River Tame. Developed for industry from the C16, but mostly now of the C20. Much C19 housing on Coventry Road was obliterated by road widening in the 1980s.*

---

*In Kings Road was the factory of H. Pontifex & Co., whose managing director was Henry Yorke (the novelist Henry Green). The buildings of his time, 1929 etc., by *Ewen Harper Bro. & Co.*, and 1937 by *James A. Swan*, have mostly gone.

St Cyprian, The Fordrough. Built by James Horsfall at the gate of his factory, which is still there. 1873–4 by *F.B. Osborn*, incorporating as its chancel a chapel of 1861. Built on arches spanning the Hay Mill leat. Deliberately blunt and angular Gothic. Red brick with Bath stone dressings, and tumbled-in blue bricks for buttress nosings. Plate tracery with alternate sexfoils in the clerestory, lancets in the aisles, both under purposeful linked hoodmoulds. Ritual sw entrance tower with angle buttresses, tympanum of the Transfiguration, under a patterned triangular gable. Broach spire with banded slates and two tiers of lucarnes on alternate faces. E gable rebuilt in lighter brick by *J.B. Surman*, 1950, after war damage. Mortuary chapel of the Horsfall family, SE, added by *Osborn* in 1877. Big s cross-gable with sexfoiled window. 'Early French' arcades and clerestory windows with deep reveals. Naturalistic foliage capitals, all different. w gallery. The mortuary chapel has an impressive brick tunnel-vault and heavily chamfered brick tomb-recesses lining the walls. – By *Osborn*, 1873–4, the CHOIR STALLS, PEWS with poppyheads, and PULPIT with open arcading, foliage and saints under canopies, carved by *S. Ruddock* of London. Also by *Ruddock* the FONT, a Thorwaldsen angel holding a shell, †1879. – STAINED GLASS by *Hardmans* throughout: chancel 1869, clerestory 1874–88, aisles 1873, W 1874–80, mortuary chapel 1877. The total effect is wonderful.*

The church is down a narrow road by the river. Further E, workers' cottages of before 1856. Immediately s, James Horsfall's SCHOOLROOM of 1863. Beyond, the buildings of WEBSTER & HORSFALL LTD, wire drawers. The firm, founded in 1720, moved here in 1841–52. Present buildings are mostly plain C20, following a fire in 1919. One important survival: the DESPATCH SHOP, built in two months in 1864 to make the first Atlantic cable. Simple brick, with segment-headed windows and a dentil cornice, subdivided by cast-iron columns with moulded capitals; the subsidiary range, w, retaining original kingpost trusses.

RED HILL SCHOOLS, Redhill Road. By *Crouch & Butler*, 1893, with fancy triplet lancets and Jacobean-style cupola. To the N, the former REDHILL TAVERN by *G.B. Cox*, 1923–5. Domestic Tudor, memorable for the frieze with its long, slightly altered quotation from G.K. Chesterton in Morris-style lettering. Further E on Coventry Road, the former ADELPHI CINEMA of 1929 by *Satchwell & Roberts*, classical-cum-Art Deco with giant columns. The OLD BILL AND BULL pub is a grand former police station by *A.B. Rowe*, 1902.

In Berkeley Road, N, the former FRIENDS' INSTITUTE (now SEVENTH DAY ADVENTIST CHURCH) by *Cossins, Peacock & Bewlay*, 1905–6, with end bow and angled porch.

HAY HALL. *See* Tyseley, p. 344.

---

*Missing is *Hardmans'* wall decoration of 1874–8, including angels on the chancel ceiling and chancel arch, and processions of saints flanking the E window.

HODGE HILL

E of Washwood Heath, to the boundary at Castle Bromwich. Interwar housing and the 1950s Firs municipal estate.

(ST PHILIP AND ST JAMES, Hodge Hill Common. 1963–8, designed by the *Institute for the Study of Worship and Religious Architecture* at Birmingham University and the architect *Martin Purdy*. The first completely multi-functional church centre in the Church of England, demolished *c*.2010.)

ST WILFRID (R.C.), Shawsdale Road. By *Louis Hayes* of *S.N. Cooke & Partners*, 1965. Large, brick, with ritual NE campanile. W narthex with enormous W window. On its N, statue of St Wilfrid on horseback by *R.F. Kings*. The nave tapers outwards in the middle, and the chancel has hidden windows to light the altar. A convincing design. – Original FITTINGS, including a V-shaped altar canopy. – STAINED GLASS designed by *Hayes*, made by *John Hardman Studios*. – STATIONS OF THE CROSS by *Kings*.

HODGE HILL UNITED REFORMED CHURCH, Coleshill Road. 1952–3 by *Robert Stanley-Morgan* and *Sidney Lunn Whitehouse*. Effective simple gabled tower.

SALTLEY

The creation of Sir Charles Adderley, 1st Lord Norton (1814–1905), President of the Board of Trade under Disraeli, who inherited the estate at the age of twenty-one. The first plan was made in 1837, at Sir Robert Peel's suggestion, by the Commissioners of Woods and Forests. Adderley paid for a church, gave much towards St Peter's College, and provided Birmingham's first public park, Adderley Park, opened 1854.* The W part of the district became industrial from the opening of the Birmingham to Derby railway in 1842. Residential development was slow; the roads around St Saviour's church were built up only in the 1890s. There was a Local Board from 1876, and a short-lived Urban District in 1888, absorbed into Birmingham in 1891. Now home to a large Mirpuri community.

ST FRANCIS (former), Arden Road. By *P. Morley Horder*, 1907. A survivor of Fr Adderley's mission churches, long in industrial use. The tile-hanging and low boarded gable are original. Built, under the render, of Italian 'Patent Frazzi Hollow Fireproof Slabs'.

ST MARY AND ST JOHN, Alum Rock Road, Shaw Hill. 1934–5 by *Holland W. Hobbiss*. Now International Pentecostal Mission

---

*It had a Gothic reading room by *G.E. Street* (demolished).

Church. Buff brick. A simple block with the bellcote treated as a wide (ritual) S buttress. Italian Romanesque, but with eclectic touches, as always with Hobbiss: the middle clerestory windows have deeply shouldered segmental heads; the porch has columns with correct capitals, but they are baseless, as if they were Greek Doric. Perfectly plain unmoulded round-arched arcades. E end and CHURCH HALL to a new design, 1957–8, by *H.W. Hobbiss* and *Maurice A.H. Hobbiss*.

ST SAVIOUR, St Saviour's Road. 1849–50 by *R.C. Hussey*, generously planned with transepts, in a consistent Perp style. *The Ecclesiologist* was rude: 'we never saw a worse design; it has not one redeeming feature'. The material is a not very attractive purple-grey sandstone, and some details, like the diagonal buttresses, are thin. But it is grouped well around a S tower with deep-set belfry windows and a picturesque SW turret, and there is an impressive six-light W window. Four-centred-arched arcades, with plain and hollow chamfers, on octagonal piers. Chancel with a hammerbeam roof. Blank arcading flanking the five-light E window, incorporating the Lord's Prayer and Creed. SE organ chamber, now chapel, by *J.A. Chatwin*, 1886–7. Several of the FITTINGS date from the early C20 incumbency of the Anglo-Catholic socialist Fr James Adderley. – FONT. Plain bowl, probably medieval. The tapering base with attached corner shafts, perhaps C13, does not appear to belong. – SCREENS to S transept and former NW baptistery (now SW), by *J.C. Hawes*, a Benedictine of Caldey, 1907–8 and 1910. Simple, eclectic but not Gothic: cushion capitals and classical pediment and niche. – PULPIT. Jacobean style, made for St Margaret, Ladywood (dem. *c.*1956). Probably by *Hubert Adderley*, *c.*1925–30. – Matching bowed ALTAR RAIL carved by *Frank Fell*, 1963–4. – N transept altar with a painted REREDOS installed after 1947, and a painted CANOPY by *Hubert Adderley* (6th Lord Norton),* 1953. (– FRESCO, S transept, by *Emily Ford*, 1907, sadly painted over.) – STAINED GLASS. E central light and tracery by *Mary Lowndes*, 1910, the side lights *E. Showell Trickett & Son*, 1951. S chapel E, *Lawrence Lee* and *Alan Younger*, 1964, angular, good colouring. Nave NW, *Hardmans*, 1952.

OUR LADY OF THE ROSARY AND ST THÉRÈSE OF LISIEUX (R.C.), Bridge Road. By *George Drysdale*, 1932–4. Austere Italian Romanesque on a monumental scale, dominated by a massive crossing tower. It cost £43,000, raised by the parish priest Fr John Power. Brown brick with red quoins and cast-stone architraves. Few and small buttresses. Triple portal with tile-turned arches. This and the S transept were rebuilt in 1941–3 after war damage. Nave of three wide bays. Square marble-faced piers and plain round arches. Crossing arches with the simplest stepped imposts which return as a string along the nave. – A rich collection of FITTINGS. By *Drysdale* the dominating BALDACCHINO of Brescia marble with white

---

*Hubert Bowyer Adderley (1886–1961), pupil of Ninian Comper, parish clerk 1953–61, vice-chair of the Parochial Church Council.

Carrara capitals, based on that at Sant'Ambrogio, Milan; the main ALTAR and five others all of white Carrara marble; also PULPIT and READING DESK treated like ambones, and ALTAR RAIL. – SCULPTURE. A reproduction of Michelangelo's Pietà (s aisle w). The carving is by *Pietra Santa* of Carrara, and by *R.L. Boulton & Sons*. – Figurative MOSAICS by *John Hardman Studios*; mosaic DADO in the nave by *Richards Tiles* of Tunstall, including WAR MEMORIALS in the transepts. – CONSECRATION CROSSES in the nave, mosaic, by *Elphege Pippet* of Hardmans, 1934. – STAINED GLASS by *John Hardman Studios*, 1932–4 (repaired after war damage), clerestory and transepts 1944–6.

SALTLEY METHODIST CHURCH, Alum Rock Road. By *Arthur Harrison*, 1904. Jacobean, with a big five-light window and domed corner turrets. A terracotta rib runs naughtily up from the window keystone to the little segmental pediment on the gable.

ZIA UL-QURAN MOSQUE, St Saviour's Road. 1992–3 by *John Manning Partnership*. Simple, restrained brick.

ST PETER'S COLLEGE (former), College Road. A training college for Church of England schoolteachers, founded in 1847. The original quadrangle is by *Benjamin Ferrey*, 1850–2, in Pugin's manner, as one would expect from his biographer. Sandstone with limestone dressings, two storeys plus dormers, in C14 style, with cusped windows. Steeply gabled entrance with an oriel over the archway. The quad has four corner towers. Its E side consists of a low connecting wing. To the NW the former CHAPEL, by *J.L. Ball*, 1912. Five bays, of sandstone broken by zigzag patterns of tile (cf. Ball's St Gregory, Small Heath, p. 285). Tall SW bellcote. The interior has been gutted, but the Romanesque arcading on the E wall and the window surrounds, with immensely tall shafts, survive. Capitals with crosses and stylized foliage. W gallery with diagonal-pattern front. Beamed ceiling. Other later BUILDINGS by *Holland W. Hobbiss*, whose father was vice-principal. A long range faces the garden S of the quadrangle, of 1911–12: a teaching block faced in boldly tooled sandstone, with big mullion-and-transom windows, and former gymnasium, S, brick, with giant arches. Big S wing of 1928–9 with end towers which have stone and brick chequering. To the N, additions of 1959–62 (*Hobbiss & Partners*): link between quadrangle and chapel, sandstone-faced, with a cloister and a tiled Romanesque archway; and LIBRARY, square and flat-roofed, with buttresses. The extra floor to the quadrangle N range is also part of this work. To the E, former PRINCIPAL'S HOUSE, Neo-Georgian, 1931, and workshop block of 1934, both by *Hobbiss*. Closed in 1978, the college was converted to offices, workshops and flats, a good idea, but with poor detailing and extensions.

ROCKWOOD ACADEMY (formerly Park View School), Naseby Road. Front block by *Associated Architects*, 2019–20, in the heavy framed style of their Birmingham City University buildings. It has none of the fantasy of *Haworth Tompkins*'s 2012 transformation of the original 1968 buildings behind, with much slatted woodwork and angled roofs and fronts.

SALTLEY ACADEMY, Belchers Lane. *See* Small Heath, p. 288.

ADDERLEY PRIMARY SCHOOL, Arden Road. 1879 by *William Jenkins*. Blunt Gothic with saddleback-roofed entrance tower and stepped buttresses, obviously inspired by J.H. Chamberlain. Plain E extension by *H.T. Buckland*, 1903–4. Further extension by *Urban Design (Malcolm Leech)*, 2000, deconstructed Modernism.

NANSEN PRIMARY SCHOOL, Naseby Road. By *W.H. Ashford*, designed 1914, built 1921–3. A handsome design. Tall central block with brick piers supporting pedimental gables. The wings also have simple piers.

PARKFIELD COMMUNITY SCHOOL, Parkfield Road. 1936–7 by *E. Bower Norris*. Very plain, with hipped roofs.

SHAW HILL PRIMARY SCHOOL, Anthony Road. 1900–1 by *Martin & Martin*. The usual gabled ranges with round-arched windows separated by buttresses. To Alum Rock Road a smaller shaped gable, formerly an entrance.

NORTON MEMORIAL HALL, Ralph Road. 1906–7 by *Holland W. Hobbiss*, his earliest-known significant building. Two storeys, red brick with blue diapering. The gable is inset between little hipped-roofed corners. Deep gabled buttresses at the front, enclosing a pent-roofed projection (originally a seating alcove in the billiard room!), give it an ecclesiastical flavour, as does the pointed-arched entrance, r.

OTHER BUILDINGS. The centre was the cross-roads at SALTLEY GATE, now the E end of Saltley Viaduct, over the railway and canal. Tall shops of 1904 to the E, built and probably designed by *Alfred Ford*. WASHWOOD HEATH ROAD runs NE, with some Early Victorian survivors; also in Havelock Road, E. From the Gate again, ALUM ROCK ROAD, Saltley's main shopping street, climbs gently E. On the corner of Bowyer Road the former ROCK pub, now shops, standard Tudor Revival of 1928 by *James & Lister Lea & Sons*. In Adderley Road, on the W side opposite Hams Road, a factory of 1901–2 by *C.E. Bateman*. Arts and Crafts simplicity. Three gables with circular windows, seven bays. Sashes, and large round-headed lights on the ground floor. In Naseby Road, SHAW HILL HOUSE, early C19 (now a mosque). Four storeys, mutilated, but retaining a porch on slim Tuscan columns.

SHARD END

The most interesting architecturally of Birmingham's municipal estates. Historically part of Castle Bromwich (p. 768), and close to the old village and Castle Bromwich Hall, to the N. Land was purchased in 1937–9. The design is by the *Shard End Panel*, a group from the Birmingham and Five Counties Architectural

Association, including *H.T. Buckland* (*Buckland & Haywood*), *J. Brian Cooper*, a housing specialist and probably the main designer,* *Herbert Jackson* (*Jackson & Edmonds*) and *H.G.Wicks* (*Harvey & Wicks*). Their Beaux Arts-influenced, low-density formal plan of 1944 was reduced in execution, but the approach is clear in the straight Heath Way and semicircular Shard End Crescent. Technically consultant architects, the panel did everything apart from the contract drawings. Construction began in 1947 and was essentially complete by 1955.

ALL SAINTS, Ownall Road. 1954–5 by *F.J. Osborne*. Church and hall, set curiously at an angle, linked by a tower with a passageway through. A conservative design. The tower recalls the late 1920s Scandinavian fashion: hipped sprocketed roof with little cupola, tall statue niche over the passageway (cf. Östberg's Stockholm Town Hall), with a figure of Christ by *William Bloye*. Passage aisles; nine-bay arcades of tall brick columns, patterned with projecting headers arranged in spirals. Beamed ceiling. – Original PULPIT with tester, tapering FONT, ALTAR RAIL and CLERGY STALLS. – The HALL has a line of dormers; alterations, including new entrances, black and carbuncular, by *IDP*, 2013.

MOTHER OF GOD AND GUARDIAN ANGELS (R.C.), Freasley Road. 1953–5 by *Jennings Homer & Lynch* (*J.T. Lynch*). Low, broad W tower, a *Westwerk*. Nave articulated by thin buttresses. A touch of Art Deco in the detail: concave window hoods, W window with concave–convex top supporting a statue of the Virgin and Child. Wide nave with a shallow barrel roof. Reordered, retaining original PEWS and FONT with wave decoration. The Lady Chapel has its original patterned ceiling, heavy brick ALTAR, and STATUE in a semicircular-headed decorative band.

SCHOOLS. TIMBERLEY PRIMARY SCHOOL (now Academy), Bradley Road. 1949–50 by *Jackson & Edmonds*. One and two storeys, buff brick. Hall at one end, balanced by a long curving classroom range facing S. Extensions by *Acivico*, 2015. HILLSTONE PRIMARY SCHOOL, Hillstone Road, is *Harvey & Wicks*, 1951, very plain. GUARDIAN ANGELS CATHOLIC PRIMARY SCHOOL, N of the church, by *Jennings Homer & Lynch*, 1954. Single-storeyed, with framed windows.

OTHER BUILDINGS. Despite new porches and UPVC, there is much to enjoy. Good details in e.g. chimneys everywhere. PACKINGTON AVENUE has four-storey towers with asymmetrically placed three-storey bays, and arched staircases behind. More in Pithall Road. Up BRADLEY ROAD, maisonettes with two-storey arched recesses cut by balconies. The entrance to Timberley School is framed by another pair of towers. Opposite, corner bungalows linked by walls and archways. Across Timberley Lane is TURNLEY ROAD with maisonettes, this time

---

*Architect to King Faisal II of Iraq, showing his mastery of formal composition in the Royal Mausoleum, and the Parliament Building, in Baghdad.

with framed three-storey projections. TIMBERLEY LANE runs s to Shard End Crescent with the corners marked by gabled towers. Regeneration in 2009–13 by *IDP* replaced *Jackson & Edmonds*'s shopping centre of 1959 with rendered blocks and a grossly insensitive new library, a bright red cube with a big blue corner prow, and filled in behind and around All Saints' church with high-density, traditional-styled housing.

SHELDON

A rural parish until the early C20. The largest hamlet was not Sheldon itself but the vanished Mackadown, where the present Mackadown Lane meets Tile Cross Road. Absorption into Birmingham in 1931 marked the start of private development, N of Coventry Road. Post-war municipal estates filled the present Garretts Green and Tile Cross, further N. Sheldon also possesses three of the best post-war churches in the city.

CHURCHES

ST GILES, Church Road. A pretty little church of red sandstone, typical of rural Warwickshire. Early C14 nave, with seven s windows, two N ones of two cinquefoiled lights, s doorway and a PISCINA with wave-moulded jambs and trefoiled head in the s wall. The most impressive feature, however, is the C14 roof of four trusses with its curved braces to the cambered tie-beams, and principal rafters cusped in cinquefoils above the collar-beams. Two tiers of cusped wind-braces. Three-bay N arcade of two orders, with a plain chamfer and a sunk quarter-round, the mouldings continued into the heads without capitals. It is probably of *c.* 1349–50, when a chantry was founded by John de Peyto. The w tower was begun in 1461 and built by *Henry Ulm*, according to an inscription on the s wall. It has two stages with an embattled parapet, a w doorway with crocketed hoodmould, and a w window of four cinquefoiled ogee-headed lights, the other windows being of two trefoiled lights. At the same time the nave was extended westwards, as indicated by the C15 w truss of the roof. The attractive timber-framed s porch is probably late C15, as it has a camber-beam with arcading similar to the Saracen's Head, Kings Norton, and the Old Crown, Deritend (pp. 408, 197). Gable with cusping and quatrefoils, and more quatrefoils on the purlins. In 1820 *John Cheshire* rebuilt the top of the tower, but his 'Pinickles' disappeared in *Slater & Carpenter*'s restoration of 1867. They rebuilt the chancel, with a C13-style chancel arch, following original work including the s capital. The N aisle is mostly theirs. N doorway partly original with the same mouldings as the arcade. w window with flowing tracery and unusual five-sided E window, both apparently following earlier evidence. – FONT. C15. Octagonal bowl with shields in rather crude cusped panels. – C15 REREDOS, re-set in the N aisle wall. Two large canopied niches separated by a smaller niche with trefoiled head. Trefoiled gables and tall crocketed pinnacles to the main canopies. Flanking buttress-pilasters on carved foliage corbels. The niches held a representation of the Annunciation, but the figures have been cut away so that only their silhouette remains. – PULPIT and PEWS of 1867. – REREDOS by *Powell & Sons*, 1912. – STAINED GLASS. Twelve windows by *Ward & Hughes*, 1867; bright reds and blues. Nave S, *Hardmans*, 1924; *Walter Camm (T.W. Camm)*, 1937, The Sower, good, well leaded. – MONUMENTS. In the ringing chamber. Edward and Isabella Barford †1789. Oval tablet in an elegant pedimented aedicule with Ionic columns and vase finial. Stele with swag and cherub-like ascending soul. – Esther Leay †1808, with a fine cherub's head in the predella.

ST PETER, Haywood Road, Tile Cross. 1966–8 by *J.P. Osborne & Son (Keith Wainwright)*. A curious and complex building, of irregular roundish shape with a wall slicing through at an angle. Inside, this is carried on a lintel and defines the baptistery, which bulges out Coventry Cathedral-style, with a big, intense stained-glass window by *Kenneth Gordon Bunton*. Outside, it rises to a knife-thin tower with bell-openings. Everything curves: gallery, sanctuary space and the choir seating placed behind the free-standing altar. – ROYAL ARMS carved by *Fred Spriggs*. – More *Bunton* glass in a side chapel. – Hall to the S, also *Osborne & Son*, 1951–2.

ST THOMAS, Garretts Green Lane. 1958–60 by *S.T. Walker & Partners* with *B.J. Whiting*; design by *Graham Winteringham*. Fine but unpretentious Festival of Britain Modernism. The structure is reinforced-concrete portal frames. Brick walls in shades of buff to maroon, large stone grid windows. German-influenced NW porch-tower with rows of openings and a grid of them for the belfry (the disfiguring crosses double as microwave aerials). Undivided nave, narrower chancel with sloping walls. These reflect the frame shapes, as do the recesses, S, for clergy seats and balancing arcade to the Lady Chapel, N, with angled cross-shapes in the framing in front of the windows above. – CHOIR STALLS with the same angles, the rear row recessed behind sloping timber mullions. – FONT, a ribbed tulip shape. – Original hanging LIGHT FITTINGS. – PAINTING on the E wall by *Matvyn Wright*, 1960, St Thomas at the moment of his realization of the Risen Lord. The expression, astonished yet certain, is compelling. – HALL attached to the NE.

OUR LADY HELP OF CHRISTIANS (R.C.), East Meadway, Tile Cross. 1966–7 by *Richard Gilbert Scott*. Brutalism at its most expressive. A crown of sharply V-ribbed copper-clad concrete, sweeping down in curves, and stepping down again to a cantilevered porch, its roof also V-ribbed. In the corners, brick octagons topped by bell-shaped cupolas. The architect aimed to imbue the church with the sense of Gothic found in his father Sir Giles Scott's work, but in a modern idiom, and like a Gothic Revival church, this works from the inside out. The interior is not easily forgotten. The folds of concrete sweep up like immense curtains on three sides, to a five-sided timber roof structure set in from the walls, so light comes in around it. Between the folds, heavy angled piers of rough concrete support the structure, with a big beam running round, forming the ceiling of low passage aisles. The piers almost meet at the roof, where they support the concrete frame from which it springs. This architectural power is, surprisingly, underlain by the most formal of plans: nave and transepts form a T-shape centred on the altar, with the octagons forming balancing Lady Chapel (N) and baptistery (S). – Original ALTAR, and twin PULPIT and READING DESK in white marble. – STAINED GLASS. By *John Chrestien*, much of it symbolizing the victory over the Turks at Lepanto (1570), the origin of the feast of Our Lady Help of Christians; bright patterns of circles, crosses and rhombus shapes, red, blue and yellow.

ST THOMAS MORE (R.C.), Horse Shoes Lane. 1968–70 by *Richard Gilbert Scott*, and a fascinating contrast to Tile Cross. Again a combination of Brutalism and formal planning, this time a modified polygon. But here everything is low, massive and spreading except for the dramatic spire of two concrete blades, formed by upwards projection of the rear walls, and set slightly apart but linked at the top by a cross. Below, a shallow pyramid roof, paired corner buttresses and the close uprights of the long windows. The porch has a deep chamfered lintel on piers. The square U-section waterspouts between the buttresses are the most expressive detail. Inside, the roof rises in wide flat slabs, like primitive vaulting. Arcades of ascending piers, piercing the roof slabs, separate the Lady Chapel r., and baptistery l. This has its own character: semicircular, lined in maroon-blue industrial brick, and top-lit. – ALTAR, a deep block on low piers, in character with the church. – Cylindrical FONT with conical cover. – STAINED GLASS by *John Chrestien*, here with more figuration: St Peter's key and cock, and birds and other symbols above the arcades. – HALL, W, by *E. Bower Norris*, 1936–7.

OTHER BUILDINGS

FIRE STATION, Garretts Green Lane. By *A.G. Sheppard Fidler*, 1954. Sculpted panel of firefighters by *Robert Pancheri*.

TILE CROSS ACADEMY, Gressel Lane. The former Byng Kenrick and Central Grammar schools and Sir Wilfrid Martineau School, all of 1953–7 by *Jackson & Edmonds*. Single- and two-storey ranges with rows of windows and brick end walls. Reception block with glazed ground floor and brightly coloured grilles above, by *FAT*, 2011–12. Sports hall by *Acivico*, 2018–20, bright orange cladding and swooping curved roof.

CHARITY SCHOOL (former), N of St Giles. Of 1852. Five bays, with big, basic Gothic windows. Facing Church Road, a pair of

C18 COTTAGES.* SW of the church a former INSTITUTE with bargeboarded gables, as late as 1923.

SHELDON HALL, Gressel Lane, 2 m. NE. A manor house of rural Warwickshire, of unusual form and with a sad C20 history. It is shallow in plan, with the entrance front facing S. The hall block is brick, red but with some blue headers, laid in English bond. Four bays, the end ones projecting, the l. one with the porch. Stone mullion-and-transom windows with ovolo mouldings and string courses with a cyma. To the W is a gabled bay, and another two gables to the E, both rendered over timber framing. Also mullion-and-transom windows, of oak. The ends look like additions, or earlier survivals, but Stephen Price and Nicholas Molyneux have convincingly argued that the whole house is of 1617–19 (tree-ring dates on both ends, and the whole roof), probably for Sir George Devereux, and a fascinating example of the use of both brick and timber construction.† Brick chimneystacks at each end, with tremendous star-shaped chimneys, the E one leaning noticeably. The ceiling of the hall remains, with moulded beams in large squares. Its fireplace has been restored with a big plain bressumer. The main front room of the E wing, the former Great Parlour, has a large moulded stone fireplace with a shallow four-centred-arched head.‡ The panelling here is modern, but a rear partition survives with big studs and diagonal braces. On the first floor another moulded stone fireplace, in the W wing, and a plain staircase to the attics. The roofs are simply made, with tie- and collar-beams and trenched purlins. Converted to a restaurant, with a rear extension, by *Dean Walker Bateman*, 1996.

OLD RECTORY FARM, Ragley Drive. Now in a country park. Rendered brick, L-shaped. Renewed Georgian sashes, NE porch with an early C19 cast-iron column. But Thomas Bray, rector 1690–1729, lived here, and the plan suggests a C17 origin.

THE SHELDON pub (now THE CRANE & DRAGON), Warmington Road. 1937 by *Holland W. Hobbiss*. An unusual design. Entrance in a quadrant between two-storey wings. The main block, r., has a single storey with big mullion-and-transom windows. Another two-storey block at the far end. The wings have excellent plaques of musicians by *Bloye*, with a hint of Cubism.

WHEATSHEAF pub (former), Coventry Road. 1937 by *Hobbiss*. Brick, murdered by stuck-on timbering.

KENT'S MOAT, Sheldon Heath Road, 1 m. NW. A complete moat, roughly rectangular, with traces of an internal bank. Excavations in 1964 dated it to the C13. It enclosed a manor house rebuilt in the C14 with main E–W range, solar range to the S, and kitchen. Now surrounded by housing of 1946–7

---

*Demolished 2013, the Neo-Georgian RECTORY by *Baron C.S. Underhill*.
† Excavations showed that a timber building pre-dated the brick central range, and located the N and E arms of the moat.
‡ Until 1919 it had a rich timber overmantel with Ionic pilasters, and there was a staircase with heavily turned balusters, carved newels and arcaded panelling. The hall screen was removed c.1977.

and infilled with 1960s flats. *A.G. Sheppard Fidler*'s SHOPPING CENTRE of 1957–62 and the HOSTEL of 1963–6 by the *Architects' Co-Partnership* were demolished in 2019.

DRILL HALL, Barrows Lane. 1939 by *Batemans*. Neo-Georgian. Raised centre with doorcase linked to a window above with swan's-neck pediment (carver *William Bloye*).

SHELDON HALL ESTATE, 2 m. NE, W of Sheldon Hall. Simple terraces and pairs by *A.G. Sheppard Fidler*, 1954–6.

BABB'S MILL, 2 m. NE, down a track off Gressel Lane. C18 mill, now a house. Mill cottage attached, SW. Both two-storeyed.

SMALL HEATH

Inner SE Birmingham. Coventry Road was built up in the 1840s–50s, and houses spread across the area into the early C20. The process was slow: Small Heath Park was nearly in the countryside until *c.*1900. At the far SE end is 1920s municipal housing. The area has a fine selection of Board Schools, and was a heartland of Anglo-Catholicism, hence the fine churches. In the C21 the Muslim community has expanded, and there are several mosques.

PLACES OF WORSHIP

ST AIDAN (now ALL SAINTS), Herbert Road. By *Thomas Frederick Proud*, who was a member of the congregation: chancel and two bays of the nave 1894–5; the remainder 1898. Built by the parishioners, with Fr J.J. Agar-Ellis, the founder, as clerk of works. Perp in red brick and buff terracotta, the finest church of the Birmingham 'terracotta style'. The very tall clerestory has paired two-light windows to each bay, divided by shafts running up from the arcades. Generously broad aisles, chancel as high and wide as the nave. Little decoration, though the arcades have complex shafting. Hammerbeam roof with very flat braces. W baptistery with an ambulatory, behind an arcade of four-centred arches. Former CLERGY HOUSE attached, NE, a simple design by *A.S. Dixon*, 1903–4.

Drastic reordering of 1999 by *Duval Brownhill* reversed the orientation, making the chancel the entrance area, separated by a full-height glazed screen, and with a mezzanine floor on steel supports. New entrance porch. These changes broke up an important and beautiful set of English Use FITTINGS designed by *Frederick Bligh Bond* and *W.E. Ellery Anderson*. The principal remaining items are of 1911–12. – Splendid ROOD BEAM and figures, now stranded against the glazed screen. A reinterpretation of medieval rood lofts, with their vine trails eaten by dragons (e.g. Partrishow, Breconshire). Here the vine runs down brackets, to be consumed by dragons clamped to the chancel-arch piers. – CEILURE of decorated panels above. – Lady Chapel, N, with a SCREEN with Somerset-style ogee canopies above and below, and free little tracery panels, and REREDOS and rear riddel-posts of an English altar with painted panels, including much gold, by *Martin Travers*. – Good Shepherd Chapel, S, with SCREEN and LOFT by *Bond* with *Thomas Falconer*, 1914. Swirling tracery panels of Devon type, influenced by French Flamboyant work; figures of 1919–20. – ALTAR of 1894. – N wall, richly carved REREDOS of the former main English altar, by *Anderson*, 1921. The Lamb of God, flanked by saints under nodding ogee canopies. – FONT. C15, from St Stephen, Bristol. Cusped panels on bowl and stem. – STAINED GLASS. S chapel E window by *Bertram Lamplugh*, 1907. W, *Hardmans*, 1960. – PAINTING. Crucifixion by *Sidney Meteyard*, 1916, with a background of a rocky chasm in spectral lighting. Formerly at St Oswald (*see* below).

ST BENEDICT, Hob Moor Road. 1908–9 by *G. Salway Nicol* of *Nicol & Nicol*. A big church of red brick with Hollington stone dressings. Round arches throughout – 'an experiment' according to the architect – but the tall proportions are Gothic Revival, not Early Christian. There is none of the intensity which Dixon or Ball brought to this manner, but the E end is good, with big sloping buttresses on the apse. Projecting W baptistery, apsidal S chapel. Impressively lofty interior, with a wooden tunnel-vault. Sanctuary arch of moulded brick separated by a deep, plain canted stone surface. Nice brick corbelling supporting the roof, but the arcade details are weak. – Handsome PARCLOSE SCREENS by *Nicol*, S 1914, N 1922. – WALL PAINTINGS. After the diocese's Evangelical chancellor refused to allow a baldacchino, the parish commissioned *Henry Holiday* to decorate the apse in 1913–19. A more or less Byzantine scheme of excellent quality. Saints at the bottom. In the semi-dome, Christ in glory with flanking saints. In the central part, angels with outspread arms and wings, holding texts. Mainly reds and browns, but some telling areas of blue. The concentration, typical of Holiday, is on the figures: their formal, hieratic poses have links to both Early Christian art and the Pre-Raphaelites. – HALL to the W by *Nicol*, 1904–5, with a Diocletian window. VICARAGE, SE, also by Nicol, 1911–12, with a round-arched doorway and windows towards the church in a Lethaby manner.

ST GREGORY THE GREAT (now BETHEL UNITED CHURCH OF JESUS CHRIST), Coventry Road. Apse and three (ritual) E bays of the nave by *J. L. Ball*, 1911–12; the rest, and the W front, by *Ball* and *Holland W. Hobbiss*, 1926–8. The original part is a magnificent fragment, the grandest of the Arts and Crafts Early Christian group by Dixon and Ball in the 1909–13 period. Maroon-red brick with some greyer shades, mostly laid in a variant of English garden wall bond. Blank arcading to the aisle with differing patterns in the tympana: tile and stone squares, zigzags of tile through stone, and the same with stone diamonds added. The apse has more blank arcading, cogging and a band of zigzag. In the Ruskinian tradition, the materials are integral to the design, and the texture starts to approach the complex patterns and *cloisonné*-like work of later Byzantine churches. w front in keeping, but simpler. The interior continues this intensity with a hand-moulded plaster ceiling probably by *Robert Catterson-Smith*, of formalized flower patterns, and the narrowly spaced arcades of stone monoliths. Only at the NE were they carved: rich late Roman Corinthian capitals. A little decoration, of C5 Roman style, here: geometric patterns in circles. Typical Ball wooden beams link the imposts to the walls. A progressive plan liturgically, with the congregation coming up to the altar rails. The choir, originally on the N side, moved to the w gallery of 1928 with criss-cross balustrade. C21 offices in the aisles.

ST OSWALD OF WORCESTER (former), St Oswalds Road. Now a Muslim nursery, and inaccessible. By *W.H. Bidlake*, 1892, his first church; the w front added 1899. Brick, clearly under the influence of Pearson, see e.g. the paired lancets and Y-tracery clerestory windows. Five-bay nave, chancel with flanking organ chamber and S chapel. NW and SW porches, organ chamber and chapel all gabled N–S, a good effect but difficult to see. Three-light Dec E window flanked by lancets. The excellent w front has the angle buttresses and turrets with stubby pinnacles of the original design, but the centre is mature Bidlake: large five-light Dec window with slim mullions and tracery, panels with reticulation to either side at high level, and a free Gothic niche in the gable with a statue of St Oswald (carver *H.H. Martyn*). Instead of the intended SW tower and spire, a little cross-gabled and traceried ventilator with a flèche. Arcades with Hollington stone piers with big half-rounds to E and W, but moulded brick arches. Shafts rise to the arch-braced collar-beam roof. Chancel arch with similar slim shafts. Fittings removed (reredos painting now at All Saints, p. 284).

ST PAUL, Belchers Lane, Bordesley Green. 1967–8 by *J.P. Osborne & Son*. Blue brick, fan-shaped, with curving walls and a concave-sided SE tower and spire: a local Ronchamp, but somehow it does not quite come off. Subdivided by *Jenns Howl*, 1999, with curved foyer, meeting rooms and a dividable worship space. – FONT of 1968, a tapering block with curved top. – Former MISSION CHURCH by *C.E. Bateman*, 1912–13, W. Simple brick, with a nice combination of stepped buttresses, sashes and small dormers.

HOLY FAMILY (R.C.), Coventry Road. Original church by *George Drysdale*, 1927–8, a Greek cross, with round arches throughout, austerely detailed, in maroon brick. Uninspired extension to the road by *George T. Cotton* of *Jennings Homer & Lynch*, 1966–7. Drysdale's interior is on an impressive scale, with groin-vaulted crossing. The extension has a barrel-vault but no arcades, just enormous cased steel joists, yet the 'aisles' have groined vaults. – Big Gothic ORGAN by *Steele & Keay*, 1903, brought from Pitts Hill Methodist Church, Stoke-on-Trent, c.1993. – PRIMARY SCHOOL, W, facing Oldknow Road. Squarish rendered block by *Peacock & Bewlay*, 1948–50.

Birmingham, Small Heath, St Oswald.
Drawing, 1897

SMALL HEATH METHODIST CHURCH, Yardley Green Road. A school-chapel by *Harry Campbell Hawkes*, 1922, with a wide pointed window and porch with canted-in sides.

PRIMITIVE METHODIST HALL (now THE INSTITUTE), Jenkins Street. 1893–6 by *Ewen Harper*. Big and plain with enormous mullion-and-transom windows.

NEWBRIDGE BAPTIST CHURCH, Yardley Green Road. 1929–30 by *Sidney Lunn Whitehouse*. A school-chapel, with a very odd take on mullion-and-transom windows.

SMALL HEATH BAPTIST CHURCH, Coventry Road. 1891 by *Ingall & Son*. Basic brick Gothic. Entrance and classroom block in front by *Andrews & Hickman*, 1922–3, with fancy brickwork.

UNITARIAN CHAPEL (now RAMGARHIA GURDWARA), Waverley Road. Gothic of 1897–8 by *John A. Grew* and *S.H. Eachus*, terribly mutilated. HALL of 1923–5 by *Warwick Scott*, r., with pointed windows.

CENTRAL JAMIA MOSQUE GHAMKOL SHARIF, Golden Hillock Road, Poet's Corner. 1992–6 by the *John Manning Partnership*. Enormous, in red, white and blue brick, with a very tall minaret which has bands of bright green arcading.

MOSQUE, Chapman Road. 1997–9 by *Al-Abbas Associates*. A big octagonal prayer hall and a minaret which tapers outwards in yellow brick.

PUBLIC BUILDINGS

PUBLIC LIBRARY and SWIMMING BATHS (now GREEN LANE MASJID), Green Lane and Little Green Lane. By *Henry Martin*, 1893 and 1902. Frequently misattributed to Martin & Chamberlain – and no wonder. Red terracotta. The best part is the circular corner tower, with steeply pedimented panels on the clock stage and conical top. Main T-shaped block behind, Flemish Renaissance style, all panelled. The baths, E, are marked by big curvy gables and mullion-and-transom windows. Power station behind: tall chimney with ogee-capped turrets rising round its base. Mosque conversion by *Birmingham City Planning Department*, 1985. Interior recast by *Akram Bonham* (*Catalyst Regeneration*), 2012–13, revealing original details. Main library room, reached through a Gothic arcade, with a semicircular bow; upper room with an unusual roof with central posts. Bath with big pierced cast-iron trusses.

HEARTLANDS HOSPITAL, Bordesley Green East. This was Little Bromwich Hospital for Infectious Diseases, begun in 1895 with buildings by *W.H. Ward*. Greatly expanded in the 1930s, a general hospital from 1953. Late C20 and C21 rebuilding has produced a hotch-potch of little architectural interest. Earlier survivals at the S, above Yardley Green Road. Big Neo-Georgian NURSES' HOME, now management block, by *Dallas & Lloyd*, 1930, with a stepped-up centre and end wings. Dining-room block to the E with prominent chimney. Further E, two plainer blocks by *W.N. Twist*, 1936–7. The PRINCESS OF WALES WOMEN'S UNIT by *John Madin Design Group*, 1990, is a friendly design in brick and render, with ground-floor arches and oriel windows. Similar, smaller blocks nearby.

BRANCH DISPENSARY (former), No. 443 Coventry Road. By *William Doubleday*, 1895. Rich French Renaissance style in creamy stone, with an octagonal corner feature topped by a big spire. Mullion-and-transom windows with basket-arched tops.

POLICE STATION (former), Bordesley Green. 1907–8 by *Henry E. Stilgoe*, City Surveyor. Free Style. Pedimental gables and lunette windows

FIRE STATION (former), Bordesley Green. 1905–7 by *John Price*, City Surveyor (Stilgoe's predecessor). Similar, with lots of stone banding and a shaped gable.

SALTLEY ACADEMY, Belchers Lane. 1928 by *H.W. Simister*. Severe Neo-Georgian. The central block lost its l. end in the Second World War. Extended 1949–54 and more recently.

OLIVE SCHOOL SMALL HEATH, Waverley Road, but best seen from Small Heath Highway. The former Waverley Technical Board School (now Primary), by *Martin & Chamberlain*, 1891–2, a special job, and a fine terracotta design. The usual gabled blocks with large paired Gothic windows, but a Flemish treatment above, with roundels and little cusped windows. The caretaker's house has a tile-hung bay as well. The tall slim tower alas lost its top c.1990. Good SE block by *H.T. Buckland*, 1905, with gables and Gothic windows, but more sparely treated.

SMALL HEATH SCHOOL AND COMMUNITY CENTRE (now WELLBEING CENTRE), Muntz Street. 1975–7 by *W.G. Reed*, City Architect (principal architect *Stephen Mitchell*). A pioneering combined community and education building. Two storeys, the upper cantilevered over piers, and a partly pitched roof to cover services.

WAVERLEY SCHOOL, Yardley Green Road. By *Allford Hall Monaghan Morris*, 2014. Cubic blue-brick blocks with carefully randomized fenestration. Entrance marked by red-brick piers.

ALSTON PRIMARY SCHOOL, Alston Road. 1925–7 by *Holland W. Hobbiss*. Long ranges, economically designed. Big windows, corner pilasters and low-pitched roofs. Good low-relief plaque almost certainly by *Bloye*.

BORDESLEY GREEN PRIMARY SCHOOL, Marchmont Road. 1902 by *Martin & Martin*. Still brick and terracotta. Big sashes framed by pilasters with swan's-neck tops. Tower with a recessed octagonal top, hinting at something Scandinavian.

DIXON ROAD SCHOOL (former). By *J.H. Chamberlain* (*Martin & Chamberlain*), 1879, with a splendid Butterfieldian Gothic tower, the corners cutting back as buttresses. Two-storey and single-storey teaching blocks, caretaker's house set forward.

HOLY FAMILY R.C. PRIMARY SCHOOL, Oldknow Road. See Holy Family church, p. 286.

MARLBOROUGH INFANT SCHOOL, Green Lane. By *Martin & Chamberlain*, 1897–8. Gabled blocks with big paired windows and a tower with octagonal louvred stage and concave top. Lots of ball finials.

OLDKNOW ROAD SCHOOL (now ARK VICTORIA ACADEMY). Crowded on a small site. The original school by *H.T. Buckland*, 1905, is at the rear. A most unusual design, influenced by J.F. Bentley's Westminster Cathedral. The classrooms have big segmental gables with much brick dentilling, there are square domed porches, and fortified-looking clerestories mark the halls. Many checked-in arches in a Bentley way. Hoppers with grotesque gaping figures. Hand-moulded plaster ceilings in the halls, with flowers and complex, Byzantine-influenced scrollwork. The windows below have gouged-out brickwork. The segmental gables are reflected in plaster barrel-vaults inside the classrooms. Simpler *Buckland* block of 1905–6 at the front. Impressive Brutalist extensions of 1964 by *Reginald Smeeton* and *Douglas Hickman* (*Bromilow, While & Smeeton*). Exposed concrete framing (now painted), with prominent shuttering marks. Minimal staircases with curved wooden handrails. A slated pyramid covers the tank room. Classroom block by *Baily Garner*, 2015, with a narrow full-height atrium. Original RAILINGS.

ST BENEDICT'S PRIMARY SCHOOL, Heather Road. 1912–13 by *H.T. Buckland*. A massive two-storey range with Arts and Crafts brick detail and a Byzantine-domed cupola.

SOMERVILLE PRIMARY SCHOOL, Somerville Road. By *Martin & Chamberlain*, 1894. Their usual gabled blocks with big lancet-style windows. The stepped tower has lost its top. Large and small halls with decorative cast-iron trusses. Large NW extension by *Birmingham City Council Urban Design*, 2005–6.

STARBANK JUNIOR SCHOOL, Starbank Road. 1926–8 by *H.T. Buckland*, Neo-Georgian, with a pediment.

TILTON ROAD SCHOOL (former), off Garrison Lane. 1891 by *Frederick Martin* (*Martin & Chamberlain*). Mangled, and with its tower cut down. Now part of a mosque.

WYNDCLIFFE PRIMARY SCHOOL, Little Green Lane. By *Martin & Chamberlain*, 1878. Their usual brick Gothic, with blank tracery patterns, including bold reticulation, in the gables. More on the tower (minus its gable).

BIRMINGHAM CITY FOOTBALL CLUB (St Andrew's), Coventry Road. The club moved here in 1906. Main Stand (N side) of 1955. The rest rebuilt by the *Seymour Harris Partnership*, 1994–9.

SMALL HEATH PARK, Coventry Road. Laid out by the Borough Surveyor *W.S. Till*, 1877–9. It cost £12,315, of which Louisa Ryland gave £4,000. Large (over 40 acres), with a big pool. LODGE with a kind of box framing.

OTHER BUILDINGS

The main street is COVENTRY ROAD, now bypassed. The S side has a long line of early and mid-Victorian classical villas (also one Gothic house of *c.*1875, No. 527); the N side has three-storey houses and shops, mostly late C19. Highlights from the W. The former BRIGHTON ARMS pub, N side, is *Holland W. Hobbiss* Tudor Revival, 1928, now mangled. The former MALT SHOVEL pub on the corner of Muntz Street, by *Charles H. Collett*, 1906, has gables topped by aedicules with swan's-neck pediments. Nos. 510–512, red and yellow brick, are by *Joseph D. Wood*, 1891. BLENHEIM BUILDINGS (Nos. 548–560), with timber gables, by *Wood & Kendrick*, 1903. WORDSWORTH ROAD runs SW with, on the SE side, villas of the 1860s. The largest is No. 46, heavily eclectic, with matching coachhouse. By *F.D. Johnson*, 1864. Nos. 590–596 Coventry Road are by *Thomas Robinson*, 1907, with his trademark tiny pediment on a gable.

In Dora Road, No. 18, the former ST OSWALD'S VICARAGE. By Bidlake, dated 1899. Modest, L-shaped, traditional in feel but almost styleless. Unmoulded mullion-and-transom windows and canted bay. Platband. Doorcase with inscribed panel. Still as fresh and attractive as it was when built.

The IDEAL VILLAGE, bounded by Bordesley Green, Belchers Lane and Yardley Green Road, was developed by the Ideal Benefit Society in 1908–14. Houses were rented in the hope that tenants would eventually be able to buy them. Everything built seems to be by a minor Birmingham architect, *H. Ireton Hand*. The layout is like Bournville or Moor Pool, pairs and terraces of four along curving tree-lined roads, but detailing is coarser. The best houses are in FINNEMORE ROAD. Nos. 58–60 are an asymmetrical pair with a corner turret and diamond-shaped windows; No. 62 has a big gable flanked by angled porch and bay. W of the estate, No. 42 Yardley Green Road is the former SAMSON AND LION pub by *Arthur Edwards*, 1913–15, with full-height stone bays and projecting clock. In Green Lane the former AVENUE pub (No. 468), by *S. N. Cooke*, 1929–30. Brick, C17 style. Hipped roof with big chimneys. On Garrison Lane, N of the football ground, NORTH, EAST and WEST HOLME, municipal flats of 1926 by the *Birmingham City Surveyor*, the only ones of their time in the city. Steep mansard roofs expressed as double-pitched gables.

Small Heath was the site of a number of experiments with CO-OPERATIVE HOUSING in the 1970s–80s. A good example is Taywood Drive and Rochdale Walk, off Cooksey Road, of 1982–4. *Nicol Thomas Viner Barnwell* (*Rob Flower* and *Peter Broad*) worked in partnership with residents, who helped choose services and materials. Well-grouped houses and bungalows, with timber porches.

STECHFORD

The London and Birmingham Railway opened its station at Stechford in 1844. It became a junction in 1882 with the opening of the line to Aston. A village grew up round it. Victorian terraces survive W and SW of the station. Interwar housing to the E.

ALL SAINTS, Albert Road. 1897–8 by *J.A. Chatwin*. A typical later Chatwin church. Dec style, banded blue and red brick. Four-bay aisled nave arcades with octagonal piers and moulded brick arches, collar-beam roof. The best thing is the impressively tall proportions. In 1936–7 *P.B. Chatwin* added the tall W baptistery to a simplified version of the original design, also SW porch and NW vestries. – Original *Chatwin* stone PULPIT with open tracery, and alabaster FONT. – Chancel PANELLING and CLERGY DESKS of 1948 by *J.B. Surman*. – STAINED GLASS. By *Claude Price*: E 1969, semi-abstract, richly coloured; S chapel E 1975, S lancets 1980.

ST ANDREW (now SHILONITE GOSPEL CHURCH), Audley Road. 1938 by *Percival J. Hunt*, the best survivor of Bishop Barnes's mission churches. Brownish wire-cut brick, laid in monk bond. Round-headed windows high up. Heavy (ritual)

SE belfry.* Full-height folding screen, separating dual-use nave from sanctuary. – Brick PULPIT, ALTAR RAIL with piers set diagonally; also PISCINA with fishes, by *Alan Bridgwater* and *Charles Upton*.

ST RICHARD, Ridpool Road, Lea Hall. 1966 by *Denys Hinton & Associates*. Brick box with a sharply angled lantern.

CORPUS CHRISTI (R.C.), Lyttleton Road. 1970–1 by *Gerard O'Brien*. Octagonal, dominated by an eight-gabled central lantern. Reinforced-concrete frame with sloping buttresses at the angles, pinkish brick walls. Pine-boarded ceiling. Forward altar. Rendered upper walls enclose the flanking side chapels. – Original FITTINGS throughout. – CRUCIFIX behind the altar, and REREDOSES in the chapels, apparently made of fibreglass. – SCHOOL to the S by *Sandy & Norris*, 1933, much extended.

STECHFORD PRIMARY SCHOOL, Albert Road. 1895–6 by *Robert F. Matthews*. Basic Jacobean, with ball finals. Big extension by *Glancy Nicholls*, 2011.

LEISURE CENTRE, Station Road. By *calderpeel*, 2019.

HEALTH CENTRE, Church Lane. By *Cherrington & Stainton*, 1952–4.

LEA HALL ESTATE. Municipal housing of 1936–40. The usual pairs and terraces by the *Birmingham City Engineer and Surveyor*. They run S without a break into post-war housing round Kent's Moat (*see* Sheldon, p. 283).

COLE HALL FARM, Cole Hall Lane. A tall early C18 brick farmhouse. Five bays, the bay r. of the entrance now with only a narrow ground-floor window. Platbands. Three large dormers. Rendered SE wing with a platband. NE wing, almost detached, again with a platband. – C18 BARN to the NE.

RAILWAY BRIDGE, Hill House Lane. A tall, three-arched London & Birmingham Railway bridge of 1838, over a deep cutting.

WARD END

The historic centre is round the church and formerly Ward End Hall to its N. Its final, classical rebuilding was *c.* 1830. Demolished *c.* 1945. To its E were earthworks of an older building, including a double moat, destroyed for housing in the 1970s. Industry developed in the Tame valley to the N in the C20. The largest factory, Wolseley Motors (finally LDV) by *J.J. Hackett*, 1919, was demolished in 2011.

ST MARGARET, St Margaret's Road. From its setting, with roads and paths leading to it, a medieval origin is clear. A chapel was built here in 1517, or shortly before, by Thomas Boyd, a merchant of Coventry. The building was said to be in ruins in

---

*Early sketches were for a sweeping full-height curved support to a transverse belfry.

the early C18 and again in the early C19. Rebuilding by *John Frith*, 1833–4. A small, simple country chapel. Nave with N vestry and S porch set centrally, short chancel and W tower, which looks bald without its pinnacles. Lancet windows, the E window a triplet. Renovated in 1929 by *James R. Shaw*, with grey-buff render and a new W doorway.* Tall thin chancel arch, typical 1830s queenpost roof with basic cusping. Reordering by *Acanthus Clews*, 2011. – ROYAL ARMS of William IV, carved. – STAINED GLASS. Unexpectedly good. E window by *Claude Price*, 1953, figurative but with none of the anaemic character of much mid-C20 glass. Chancel N and S by *Lavers, Barraud & Westlake*, 1875. Nave S, *Hardmans*, 1874; *Powells*, 1893; nave N, two by *Morris & Co.*, 1902, with *Burne-Jones* female figures; also *Hardmans*, 1897. – MONUMENTS. William Hutton, the Birmingham historian, †1815 and family, by *Peter Hollins*, 1848. Ogee-headed niche with pinnacles, double-cusped and with cusped arches set behind. Good, expressive bust of Hutton, surrounded by books. – Solomon Bray †1850, also by *Hollins*, simpler Gothic aedicule.

WARD END METHODIST CHURCH (former), Washwood Heath Road. By *Crouch, Butler & Savage*, 1950–1. The end of the Early Christian round-arched tradition.

SLADEFIELD INFANT SCHOOL, Bamville Road. 1910 by *H.T. Buckland*, in his personal Byzantine style. Mansard-like eaves, domed staircase. Nasty C21 renovations.

WARD END PRIMARY SCHOOL, Ingleton Road. 1930–1 by *J.B. Surman*. A landmark in school design in the city. Brick early Modernism. Symmetrical, with lower wings angled back from a central hall block. Flat roofs throughout. The corridors, at the rear, were originally open. Staff rooms behind the central block with Dudok-influenced chimneys and big canted corners. Aggressively angled bright blue porch by *Bournville Architects*, 2008.

PERAMBULATION. The start is in front of St Margaret's church. s up St Margaret's Road, Nos. 5–9, cottages by *Hobbiss*, 1907, with a continuous pent roof over doors and bay windows. Opposite, NORMANHURST, a mangled late C18 house with a good Doric doorcase. It faces s to WASHWOOD HEATH ROAD. Facing, Nos. 563–573, 1909, also by *Hobbiss*, also horribly treated, but with good surviving brick details. Going w, on the N side, the LIBRARY, by *J.P. Osborne*, 1927–8. Heavy Neo-Georgian with a deep attic. Doorcase with Doric columns and architrave set in the arch in an Adam way. Big fanlight. Next door, MAITLAND HALL by *Arthur G. Anderson* and *F. Broadbent*, built in 1923–4 as a Conservative Club to counter 'insidious Socialist propaganda' in this working-class area. Crude English Baroque. Big Ionic doorcase with broken segmental pediment, and a sharp pedimental gable. Opposite, WARD END PARK, opened in 1904 in the grounds of WARD

---

*A scheme of 1916 by *C.E. Bateman* to make it the chancel of a church oriented N–S came to nothing.

END HOUSE, built c.1850 for George Marshall. Rich classical, but determinedly asymmetrical. Stuccoed, the ground floor smoothly rusticated. Porch with paired fluted Doric columns. Two bays r. with architraved and balustraded windows, one bay l. with a triplet window and the same details.

To the E along Washwood Heath Road, s side. No. 659, a former Co-op by *F.B. Andrews*, 1910, with nice brickwork and emphatic corner. No. 681, ROWLSTONE HOUSE, is strongly modelled Arts and Crafts Tudor by *Harry Weedon*, 1909–10. Also by *Weedon* Nos. 693–695 with timber gables, dated 1909; Nos. 697–699, brick with star-shaped chimneys, 1908–9. At the cross-roads with Bromford Lane the FOX AND GOOSE, dated 1913, by *Hobbiss*, an early 'reformed' pub, rich in texture and inventive in detail. A big timber-framed gable r. is balanced by the smaller, full-height porch, l., both with brick-nogging. The ground floor of the porch is all timber, with fox and goose standing on the posts, and chasing in the frieze. Elsewhere, stone banding and chequering. Big chimney, r., buttressed in all three directions. Corner doorway with a grinning head corbel among bunches of grapes. Interior altered.

WASHWOOD HEATH

The area N of Saltley (p. 275), with the same civic history. Late C19 development produced a centre on the Washwood Heath Road. Industry was to the N, in the river valley; the largest factory was Metropolitan-Cammell.

ST MARK, Washwood Heath Road. By *J.A. Chatwin*, built in three parts: chancel 1888–90; two nave E bays 1894; the rest, SW tower, NE vestry and SE organ chamber, 1898–9. As always with Chatwin, well proportioned: grandeur on a tight budget. Red brick with stone bands, stone broach spire with pinnacles. Cusped lancets, Geometrical tracery in the aisles, Y-traceried E window. NW choir and clergy vestries, with an apsed end, by *G.A. Cox*, 1919. Brick interior. Plain one-step arcades with circular stone columns, tall chancel arch. – FONT by *Chatwin*, 1899. – ROOD BEAM and FIGURES probably by *Hubert Adderley*, c.1930. Brought from St Margaret, Ladywood (dem.) in 1958. – STAINED GLASS. By *John Hardman & Co.*, s chapel 1921; N aisle 1925, a good piece with restrained colour.

VICARAGE, E of the church. 1913 by *Holland W. Hobbiss*, Neo-Georgian. To the W the CHURCH HOUSE of 1908–9, also *Hobbiss*, with his love of picturesque juxtaposition already apparent. Two-bay ends with clasping piers and low gables, suggesting pilasters and pediment. The details (casements in round-headed recesses with blank tympana) are A.S. Dixon-style. Sandstone frontispiece and frieze, the entrance showing the influence of Lethaby: big arch, limestone with marble jambs, voussoirs and wall bands.

HIGHFIELD JUNIOR AND INFANT SCHOOL, Highfield Road. 1878–9 by *William Jenkins*. Simple red brick Gothic, but with an eccentric tower. It has clasping buttresses rising to pinnacles, and a central buttress on each side pushing through a gable to a higher finial. Many early C21 extensions.

LEIGH PRIMARY SCHOOL, Warren Road. 1908–9 by *H.T. Buckland*. An excellent Free Style school. Two long ranges with gabled ends and stone canted bays rising clear of the eaves. Big grid-like mullion-and-transom windows. In the centre a sheer tower with big open niches with segmental pediments, and stone quoins. One can see the influences, but the result is an integrated and personal design.

w of the school are the former offices of METROPOLITAN-CAMMELL, railway carriage and bus builders, 1909–12 (the works, N, demolished 2019). Heavy plain Jacobean. All designed by the engineers *D. & A. Home Morton*.

YARDLEY

The historic centre of an ancient Worcestershire parish running NE–SW from Stechford to Yardley Wood. The parish became a Rural District in 1894, with its administrative centre at Sparkhill (p. 338). Absorbed into Birmingham in 1911. The old village centre is lovingly preserved, with parkland to its E. General development began in the late C19, and the rest was covered by housing from the 1920s to just after the Second World War.

CHURCHES

ST EDBURGHA, Church Road. A substantial medieval church. The earliest fabric is C13, part of the chancel S wall, with one narrow lancet. To its l., partly hidden by the vestry, a doorway with a crude ogee head; to its r. a window with two restored cusped lights. These are part of C14 alterations and enlargements, when transepts were added. Their arches are quite elegant, with two chamfered orders, the outer without capitals, and the inner with bell capitals with a wave moulding. The S transept retains a three-light Dec window with elongated tracery lights. The nave S windows with reticulated tracery must be slightly later, mid- to late C14. The simple S doorway may be C13, repositioned. The N aisle is C15, with a three-bay arcade of standard elements, awkwardly proportioned and looking like a crude version of the earlier arches. It is separated from the transept by a short piece of wall. The aisle windows are similar to those in the nave and were probably re-set from the former N wall, but the easternmost three-light window, with round-headed lights, is C17. Inserted N doorway with a four-centred, hollow-chamfered arch. The spandrels are carved with a pomegranate and a Tudor rose, the symbols of King Henry VIII and Catherine of Aragon, so probably of *c.*1509. C15 aisle roof, very low-pitched, with moulded beams and one boss with the Five Wounds. The W tower is of similar design to that at Sheldon (p. 280) so is probably of *c.*1460–70 and by *Henry Ulm*. Four stages, embattled, with diagonal buttresses. The tall crocketed hexagonal spire must be contemporary, as it has similar heavy crocketed canopies. Fine C15 oak porch with traceried sides, a camber-beam on heavy braces and collar-beam above, and bargeboards with complex cusping motifs.

Many C19 and C20 alterations. In 1850 *H. R. Yeoville* (*Thomason*) partly refaced the N arcade and rebuilt the base of the S porch: see the rock-faced stone. Chancel E end rebuilt in similar stone, probably also by *Thomason*, *c.*1875–80. In 1888 *J. A. Chatwin* repaired the tower, adding the crenellated parapet, and rebuilt the spire above the first tier of lucarnes. In 1890 he added the NE vestry and organ chamber, reusing a C13 lancet from the chancel N wall. But the major restoration was as late as 1926, by *W. H. Bidlake*. He rebuilt and heightened the C14 chancel arch, reusing the old capitals and probably the arch stones. The change of stone on the piers can be seen. His are the trussed-rafter roofs. He saved the aisle roof by placing a steel frame above; but the top courses of stone externally are his, with decorative shields.*

FURNISHINGS. PULPIT. C19, with C17 panelling, perhaps from a pulpit given in 1627. – FONT dated 1874, almost certainly by *Thomason*. – PEWS. 1861 by *Thomason*, still with doors. – LECTERN. Desk with carved angels on a refined Jacobean-style column. It must be by *Bidlake*. – CHARITY BOARDS (vestry). – STAINED GLASS. The finest is the W window, a Last Judgment thronged with figures, by *John Hardman & Co.* of 1892. E window also *Hardman*, 1895. Chancel S, from E, early C20 Arts and Crafts with small scenes; a typical *A. J. Davies*, 1916; *Hardman*, 1874. S transept, *William Holland*, 1861. – MONUMENTS. Thomas Est †1462 and wife (NW pier of the tower arch). Top of an alabaster tomb-chest with incised figures, much worn. – Izabell Wheler †1598 (chancel N). Incised brass. She faces us, praying, between three-quarter figures of her husbands. Architectural setting of rather provincial type with an alabaster surround. – Humfry Greswold †1671 (chancel S). Tablet framed by rather crude Corinthian pilasters, and broken segmental pediment. Attributed to *Thomas Cartwright I* (GF). – Rev. Dr Henry Greswold †1700 (chancel S). A most remarkable monument, consisting of a curtained cave containing the marble statues of the praying parson and his wife. Medallions of their eleven children frame the recess, treated like cameos, the profile figures particularly good. There is a wide broken pediment and the whole is flanked by stone

---

*A C17 inscription on the chancel N wall-plate records a re-roofing of 1637.

festoons, now in bad condition. Attributed to *Richard Crutcher*, probably using a design by *Francis Bird* for the monument to the 1st Duke of Bedford at Chenies, Bucks. (GF). – Edward Est †1703 (s transept). Black tablet with low-relief bust at the top. – Job Marston †1701 (chancel arch N side). By *Sir William Wilson*. Small oval black tablet with weeping putto above and three other cherubs' heads. – Rev. Marshall Greswold †1728 (chancel N). With Ionic pilasters and broken pediment. Probably by *Francis Smith* (GF). – Edmund Makepeace †1766 (N aisle). Old-fashioned, with Corinthian pilasters and segmental pediment; probably London work (GF). – Richard Hodgetts †1828 (chancel N). Greek tomb-chest, by *Matthew Seaborne*. – Edmund Greswolde †1836 (chancel s). Handsome marble vase signed *Hollins* (probably *Peter Hollins*). – Charlotte Horsfall †1862 (s transept) by *P. Hollins*. Draped urn and three cherub-like angels.

ST MICHAEL AND ALL ANGELS, Rowlands Road. 1964–5 by *Denys Hinton & Partners*. Previous church, 1929 by *Gateley & Parsons*, now the hall.

DIGBETH-IN-THE-FIELD CONGREGATIONAL CHURCH (now UNITED REFORMED), Moat Lane, ½ m. SSE. 1958–9 by *Jackson & Edmonds*. A period piece, its steep roof echoed in lines of jazzy triangular dormers. Inside, angular concrete trusses and exaggerated Vs where the dormers meet the roof, a startling effect. The rear gable wall is all window. Entrance hall with an abstract design in the floor. Original furnishings.

CEMETERY, Yardley Road, 1 m. SSW. Determinedly Gothic LODGE by *Alfred Smith*, 1882–3, with blue-brick bands and even a rose window with cusped tracery. A long way E, CHAPEL by *James A. Swan*: 1936. Massive, cruciform, in brown brick with a central tower. This has chamfered corners in the Giles Scott way. Gothic windows with decorative tilework above the arches. Extended E by Swan to form a crematorium, 1949–52. Rendered interior with unmoulded, slightly pointed crossing arches. The octagon is supported on squinches. – NE of the lodge, MAUSOLEUM of the Pickard family, †1917 and later, by *White & Sons*. A miniature Doric temple.

SCHOOLS

BIERTON SCHOOL, Bierton Road (now part of Starbank School), ½ m. SW. 1926–8 by *Harvey & Wicks*. Neo-Georgian in buff brick, with the formal Beaux Arts planning Wicks liked (cf. St Francis, Friar Park, p. 603). Hipped-roofed blocks flank a massive propylaeum archway: side pilasters topped with, it seems, acroteria which have slipped down, and a slightly angled parapet suggesting a pediment. Tympanum by *Bloye* with the city arms flanked by engineering and arts objects, now hidden by late C20 infill. Single-storey infants' range axially placed at the rear.

LYNDON GREEN JUNIOR SCHOOL, Wensley Road, ¾ m. SE. 1950–3 by *Graham Winteringham* of *S.T. Walker & Partners*.

Two- and three-storey ranges separated by a tower with a low-pitched roof and slightly bowed front with almost full-height window: an unusual combination, but it works.

YARDLEY PRIMARY SCHOOL, Church Road, ½ m. S. 1907 by *Arthur Harrison*. Plain, with a long row of gables.

PERAMBULATION

Old Yardley village 'retains more of its rural atmosphere than any other of the villages now incorporated within Birmingham' (Stephen Price, whose 1980 'Trail' is the basis for much of the following). S of St Edburgha's churchyard, the former YARDLEY TRUST SCHOOL. Early C16, probably the 'church howse' being rebuilt in 1512. Entirely of close studding, jettied along the W gable and N front. E end underbuilt in brick, probably in the early C19, when two cottages were added beyond. The central roof truss has tie- and collar-beams, with a crown-post, curved struts and upper raking struts. Simpler trusses to either side, partly hidden in walls. Many wind-braces to the purlins. Sympathetic restoration with new partitions and brick fireplaces, 1923. Opposite the school Nos. 423–425, a cottage of *c*.1710, with a former butcher's shop added *c*.1850, l. To the N, No. 431, three storeys, 'newly built' in 1796, now roughcast. The former COTTAGERS' INSTITUTE, dated 1882, is probably by *Alfred Reading*. Queen Anne style, with projecting centre, oval windows and decorative doorcase pediment. No. 435, PENNY COTTAGE, is of 1826, built by *George Cotton*. Nos. 445–447, an C18 malthouse converted to cottages in the 1850s. Then CHURCH FARM, rebuilt by a local contractor, *Samuel Thornton*. First a converted COWHOUSE of the 1820s. Behind, a BARN of 1848–9. On the N side, the farmhouse, 1837, with segment-headed casement windows, a simple dentil course and slightly off-centre entrance. N from the farm, a much-rebuilt but still active SMITHY. On the corner of School Lane, the mutilated former CHURCH SCHOOL of 1831–2 by *Joseph Bateman*, Gothick window hoodmoulds still visible. The l. wing is later. Further N, ALMSHOUSES, 1903, by *Cossins, Peacock & Bewlay*. Conventional Tudor, but gently and freely done. The rear block has a central pedimental gable, and a nice balance of warden's house and hall, with differing full-height bays. Down School Lane, IVY HOUSE, probably Early Victorian, with a later C19 house attached E. Behind hedges, HOLLY CROFT, *c*.1830. Windows with architraves on consoles. It seems to have started as a pair: see the off-centre doorcase with panelled pilasters, now with a Victorian porch. Behind is a slightly smaller parallel range, already here in 1780, in smaller bricks.

S of the Trust School, No. 390 (E side), the former TALBOT INN. Late Georgian, with restored canted bays and panelled doorcase. Past Blakesley Road, on the W side, No. 345, THE GRANGE, now flats. A rambling C19 house, mostly rendered. Big rear extension probably of *c*.1880 by *Osborn & Reading*. The NE wing contains C16 or C17 timber framing, with queenpost trusses. Victorian and Edwardian villas on the E side, the best Nos. 320–324 with facing gable chimneystacks, by *Essex & Nicol*, 1892–3.

OTHER BUILDINGS

BLAKESLEY HALL, Blakesley Road, ¼ m. WSW. A showy, though not large, timber-framed house, tree-ring dated between 1585 and 1610, built by Richard Smalbroke II.* L-shaped, still with the medieval arrangement: family rooms in the W cross-wing; a central hall; to its E, porch with Smalbroke's initials and a motto, leading into the screens passage; service rooms beyond. The S front makes a display of herringbone work and picturesquely grouped gables with quadrant braces. First floor continuously jettied, the brackets bold statements of geometry. Big brick chimneystack, W. The HALL has moulded ceiling beams and a bay at the W, dais end. The GREAT PARLOUR to the SW has a similar ceiling and a restored C17 overmantel brought from Little Aston Hall, Staffs., in the 1980s. Its floral patterns and grapevine are paralleled at Oak House, West Bromwich (p. 610), its addorsed dragons at Bells Farm, Brandwood (p. 308). The staircase is Neo-Jacobean, part of alterations of 1899–1900 by *Harry Quick* of Coventry. The first floor has a miniature LONG GALLERY, again a status symbol, across the S front. The tiny room over the porch was Smalbroke's 'Closet' or study. Opposite, a passage to a garderobe. In the SW corner the PAINTED CHAMBER, its walls covered in late C16 interlaced arabesque patterns, foliage and fruit; also texts, and a centaur holding a shield with Smalbroke's and his wife Elizabeth's initials. The N kitchen wing is mid-C17 (called 'new' in 1685). – VISITORS' CENTRE to the NW by *Niall Phillips Architects*, 2000–2. Two gabled ranges with glazed loggias, at right angles, linked by an entrance lobby with a circular lantern.

BLACKLEIGH CLOSE, to the W. Sheltered housing by *McKewan & McKewan*, 1976.

THE SWAN, on Coventry Road ¾ m. S, is a wasteland of late C20 and early C21 redevelopment. The eponymous pub has gone. SWAN CENTRE by *James A. Roberts*, 1962–7, with a ten-storey slab; much rebuilt by *Saunders Partnership*, 2011–12. Opposite, a tall S-shaped slab, recently reglazed, follows the roundabout. To the S in Yardley Road, SOUTH YARDLEY LIBRARY of 1938 by *J.P. Osborne & Son*. Neo-Georgian going cubic. Recessed entrance portico with fluted urns above; sculpture over the door by *Bloye*, cherubs holding a book. In Mansfield Road, W from the cemetery lodge, PINFOLD HOUSE has a stuccoed early C19 front which hides earlier fabric, probably C17. Outbuildings, converted to housing, with timber framing. JOURNEY'S END pub, Clay Lane, Neo-Georgian by *F.W.B. Yorke*, 1939.

---

*Earlier occupation is indicated by a C13 pebble surface found under the service range and a moat detected by geophysics to the N.

SUBURBS: SOUTH AND SOUTH-EAST

Acocks Green	300
Balsall Heath	303
Places of worship	303
Public buildings	304
Perambulation	306
Billesley	307
Brandwood with Druids Heath	307
Hall Green	309
Places of worship	309
Colleges and schools	311
Sarehole Mill	311
Perambulations	311
Other buildings	313
Highters Heath	314
Kings Heath	314
Churches	315
Schools	316
Perambulations	316
Other buildings	319
Moseley	320
Churches	320
Major houses and parks	323
Public buildings	325
Perambulations	325
Sparkbrook	335
Sparkhill	338
Churches	339
Public buildings	340
Perambulation	342
Other buildings	343
Tyseley	343
Yardley Wood	345

ACOCKS GREEN

The ancient hamlet was on the Warwick road; Flint Green Road marks a separate hamlet to the w. Development started with the opening of the Great Western Railway line to Banbury in 1852. Late Classical villas still line parts of Yardley Road, Warwick Road and Botteville Road. Interwar development to the s included the Fox Hollies municipal estate. Many attractive suburban roads, but the centre has little of interest.

> ST MARY, Warwick Road. A big lofty church that took many years in building. Nave and aisles of 1864 by *J. G. Bland*. Hampstead sandstone with Bath stone dressings, but brick-faced inside. Continental Gothic of the Burges or Clutton kind: plate

tracery, four-bay arcades with stubby circular columns with bold leaf capitals on high tapering bases, and alternating stones in the arch voussoirs. Chancel and transept arches of 1883 in the same style. Bland's sw steeple was never built, and his transepts never completed, hence the sections of brick walling which break their stonework outside. E end by *J.A. Chatwin*: vestry and organ chamber 1891, chancel 1893. Impressively tall, to match the nave, with continuous shafts dividing the N and S windows. The church was severely damaged by a bomb in 1940; the arcade piers are still pitted with marks. Restored 1945–9 by *P.B. Chatwin*. His is the clerestory, with big plain paired lancets, and the nave roof, where the pitch was lowered. – HIGH ALTAR 1898, REREDOS behind 1903, and chancel wall PANELLING 1914, by *Bridgemans*, ornate alabaster. – ALTAR by *Hurley Robinson & Son*, 1952, with paintings by *Donald Brooke*. – PULPIT and FONT by *Chatwin*, 1949, simplified Gothic. – CHOIR STALLS and SCREENS. *Nicol & Nicol*, 1930. – STAINED GLASS. E window by *Morris & Co.*, designed by *Burne-Jones*, 1895, restored from fragments 1950. Crucifixion, but the cross has become a Tree of Life. SS Mary and John and angels with much of the intense red typical of late Burne-Jones. N aisle, *Hardman*, 1962.

SACRED HEART AND HOLY SOULS (R.C.), Warwick Road. By *G.B. Cox*, the sanctuary and ritual E part of the nave 1923–5, remainder 1938–40. Gothic, not usual for this architect. Grey brick on a maroon base. The front is unbuttressed; the sanctuary richer, with statue of the Sacred Heart in a niche, gabled buttresses with many set-backs, and banded inscription. N and S projections with two-light windows. Dec tracery. The interior is a single space, much influenced by Bidlake, with moulded timber arches supporting the roof and a N chapel with tall two-bay arcade. – WEST GALLERY by *Ivor Day & O'Brien*, 1972.

HOLY SOULS SCHOOL (former), E of the church. Original part by *H.T. Sandy*, 1907. Brick, with a porch with prominent voussoirs and a segmental gable set asymmetrically under the main gable.

ACOCKS GREEN METHODIST CHURCH, Shirley Road. 1882–3 by *Loxton & Newman* of Wednesbury in 'the Gothic style of a Continental character'. Red brick with yellow voussoirs and Bath stone dressings. W windows with exaggerated cusping to the tracery, plate-tracery rose in the gable. The NW steeple cuts back from square to octagonal, and has little half-hipped gables. Flying buttresses along the N side. Much recast in 1927 by *J. Percival Bridgwater*, with a S extension with three-light window. Interior cut in two in 1969–71 but retaining moulded giant piers of 1927 with decorative caps. N arcade piers encased in 1927. – STAINED GLASS. Three good Arts and Crafts windows of *c.*1919 (sanctuary). – Behind, massive former SCHOOLS by *Arthur McKewan*, 1933.

ACOCKS GREEN BAPTIST CHURCH, Yardley Road. 1913–14. *F.B. Andrews*'s finest chapel, a strongly modelled Arts and

Crafts design with much bare maroon brickwork. Central gable between octagonal turrets, which have open belfry tops with cusped heads to the openings and big stone louvres. Five-light window in a deep stone arch, free Perp, with two big mullions. Side extensions for cloakrooms, with hipped roofs. Spacious and sober interior. Two-bay nave with passage aisles, wide crossing, shallow transepts and apse. The arches die into the piers. – PULPIT with foliage decoration, good PEWS and apse SEATING, SCREENS at the entrance end, and simple apse PANELLING. – ORGAN CASE with bold sprays of carved foliage.

Behind, facing Alexandra Road, the earlier CHURCH of 1903 by *Ingall & Son*, also with a gable and corner turrets, also with larky Perp tracery, but of hard red brick with terracotta dressings. Fancy little domes, shaped gable. Plain hall with arch-braced roof. On the corner between them, HALL of 1924 by *Andrews & Hickman*, with timbered gables.

MISSION HALL, Arden Road. 1908 by *Holland W. Hobbiss*. Red brick with blue bands and diapering. Doorway with a stepped-in arch.

ACOCKS GREEN PRIMARY SCHOOL, Westley Road and Warwick Road. 1908 by *A.B. Rowe*. Big broken pediments to the central gable and entrances. The flanking gables have rhombus-shaped windows.

PUBLIC LIBRARY, Shirley Road. 1926 by *J.P. Osborne & Son*. Neo-Georgian, with a Doric doorcase and dentil cornice. Glass screens, counter and shelves survive inside.

POLICE STATION, Yardley Road. By *A.B. Rowe*, dated 1909. A long front, Jacobean-cum-Baroque, in brick and red terracotta. The centre has paired banded Ionic pilasters. Flanking it, boldly broken segmental pediments (cf. the primary school). Domed turret, r. FIRE STATION behind by *H.H. Humphries*, City Engineer and Surveyor, 1922.

OTHER BUILDINGS. THE GREEN is now a traffic roundabout. On the SW, the former NEW INN by *James & Lister Lea*, 1930–1, eclectic but uninspired. In WESTLEY ROAD, W, the former WARWICK CINEMA by *Horace G. Bradley*, 1929, the bowed centre nastily panelled over. In WARWICK ROAD, NW, just beyond the primary school, STONE HALL, a stucco Early Victorian villa. Smooth rustication to the ground floor. The round-headed upper windows are picturesque Italianate. Nos. 1075–1077 are mid-C19 classical. No. 1071, formerly THE KNOLL, is of 1886–7, probably by *George Jenkins* of Coventry. Picturesque domestic details: brick with square sandstone bays and timber gables, segment-headed porch. The garden front has a big stone canted bay set back into a timber bay above. N of Warwick Road, ARDEN ROAD and GRESWOLDE PARK ROAD were mostly developed by the local builders *Williams & Boddy*, 1898–c.1909. Tall pairs, some with timbered gables and two-storey chamfered-in gables. Arden Road divides, delightfully, round a big tree. Earlier survivals on the S side: GLADSTONE COTTAGE, C18, painted brick, casement windows; Nos. 89–91, similar but lower.

N of The Green in SHERBOURNE ROAD, a good stretch starts S of the railway station with Nos. 46–50, W side. Classical villas and a Picturesque cottage of shortly after 1852. Beyond the station in YARDLEY ROAD, E side, the GREAT WESTERN pub, by *Hurley Robinson & Son*, 1955. Hipped roof and dormers, still in the Neo-Tudor tradition. Beyond the police station and Baptist church, shops by *H.C. Tomkins*, 1906 etc., with ornamental oriels and bargeboarded gables. On the E side, No. 50 of 1902–3 by *Essex, Nicol & Goodman*, was *J. Coulson Nicol*'s own house. Domestic Revival, but no hint of the Arts and Crafts. Rendered, with a tile-hung gable and terracotta doorcase and semi-oval bay. More by the firm in ELMDON ROAD here, e.g. ALTON LODGE of 1892–3 with continuous ground-floor bay, sashes and big hipped dormer, and ELMDON LODGE, 1899 by *G. Salway Nicol*, with projecting wings with half-hipped roofs. Nos. 34–36 beyond by *Essex & Nicol* too, c. 1895. Nos. 15–17 opposite by *E. H. Wigley*, 1902.

In SHIRLEY ROAD, No. 75, formerly a pair; pretty Domestic Revival by *Crouch & Butler*, 1888.

In FOX HOLLIES ROAD, opposite Greenwood Avenue, CURTIS GARDENS, a wooded area landscaped by *Mary Mitchell* on the site of the C19 Fox Hollies Hall, marked by its surviving GATEPIERS. Three *Sheppard Fidler* tower blocks of 1959–60 behind, still with their original brick and coloured-panel cladding. – Concrete 'PLAY SCULPTURE' by *John Bridgeman*, c. 1960, like a fish with a Hepworth-style hole.

BALSALL HEATH

The N tip of old Kings Norton parish, stretching W–E from the River Rea to Stoney Lane, bisected by the Camp Hill railway line. Developed intensively from the 1850s. A Local Board of 1862 was absorbed by Birmingham in 1891. Much original townscape remains, partly due to lively late C20 community campaigning. Architectural interest is concentrated W of the railway.

PLACES OF WORSHIP

BALSALL HEATH CHURCH CENTRE, Edward Road. 1978–80 by *Charles Brown* (*Hinton Brown Langstone*). A multi-purpose church centre. The worship area has a boarded ceiling and exposed roof trusses.*

ST BARNABAS, Ladypool Road. By *T. F. Proud*, 1898 (chancel and S chapel) and 1904 (nave), 'elaborated' after Proud's death by

---

*It replaced St Paul, a brick Gothic church of 1852–3 by *J. L. Pedley*.

William Hale & Son. Brick and biscuit-coloured terracotta. A fire in 1970 left only the chancel and chapel, and the lower part of one bay of the nave. Refurbished, with a new w wall, by *C.C. Gray & Son*, 1972. In 2002 the site of the nave was filled by a vicarage behind a high wall, by *APEC*. Red-purplish brick, a chimney with tumbling-in, and a little oriel.

ST JOHN AND ST MARTIN (R.C.), George Street. 1896 by *Albert Vicars*, completed after his death by *Ernest Avern*. Basic Romanesque. Front with paired entrances, big gable and little turret. Interior altered by *Jennings Homer & Lynch*, 1962–3, with steel columns supporting lintels to the aisles. – BRASS. Rev. John Dowling †1904.

MOSELEY ROAD METHODIST CHURCH (former). Dull gabled block by *F.J. Osborne*, 1949–52.

BAPTIST CHURCH, Edward Road. 1899–1900 by *Ingall & Son*. Richly decorated eclectic Jacobean, like Gothic with the arches gone round. Complex shaped gable, big buttressed porch. There was a spirelet. Schoolrooms behind. Inside, round-arched arcades (now partitioned off) and sanctuary arch, with Gothic leaf capitals. Wide nave, big transepts. – Original PEWS and PULPIT FRONT.

SPARKBROOK CONGREGATIONAL CHURCH, Ladypool Road. 1907 by *William Hale & Son*. Brick and cream terracotta. Tower with pyramid roof. Louche detail, e.g. the tricky ground-floor arches (for a shop) and the oddly shaped gable.

AL-ABBAS ISLAMIC CENTRE, Clifton Road. Mosque by *Marc Worrall*, 1982. Replacement buildings by *K4*, 2020 etc.; black brick block with a patterned screen and canopy.

MUSLIM STUDENTS' HOUSE MASJID, Moseley Road. A former Church of Christ chapel, converted from terraced houses by *Marcus O. Type*, 1911–12, with a turreted forebuilding.

PUBLIC BUILDINGS

LIBRARY AND BATHS, Moseley Road. The library is impressive Free Jacobean of 1895, by *Cossins & Peacock*. Brick and cream terracotta. Big three-centred mullion-and-transom windows with straightish Dutch gables above. The tower especially is an organic design. Rich entrance: banded Ionic columns and a partly broken concave pediment rising to a city coat of arms. Above, deep-set little windows with balustrades, a clock stage and a stubby concave spire. Baths, l., by *William Hale*, 1906–7, rather old-fashioned Jacobean. The pretty but bitty façade has an oriel and Dutch gable flanked by two octagonal towers. Again brick and terracotta, orange-buff, by *Jabez Thompson* of Northwich. Three doorcases, with banded columns and swan's-neck pediments, lettered for Men's First Class, Women's, and Men's Second Class baths. The tapering brick chimney is a landmark. But it is the interior which is important here: a rare well-preserved large Edwardian public baths, for swimming and washing. The nearest surviving comparison is Victoria Baths, Manchester. All faced in glazed brick, cream, turquoise and green, by the *Stourbridge Brick Co.* The foyer has a bowed oak attendant's kiosk. The private or 'slipper' baths, for washing, retain cubicles with some original equipment, e.g. ropes to help bathers out, and a bell system to summon attendants. The Gala (first-class) Pool is articulated by wide cast-iron trusses with slightly Art Nouveau infill panels. Ceiling, above a clerestory, on little colonnettes. Big end windows. Along the sides, original dressing boxes with arched entrances. Balcony with bowed iron handrail. Second-class pool similar but smaller and without boxes. Laundry with steam-heated, cast-iron drying racks. Huge iron water tank above.

POLICE STATION, Edward Road. 1862 by *Henry Rowe*. Heavily classical. 1–3–1 bays, but off-centre doorcase. Flemish bond, with stretcher rows darker than headers. Hipped roof. Extended 1881; this must be the taller range behind.

SCHOOL OF ART (former), Moseley Road. By *W.H. Bidlake*, dated 1899, his most significant public building. 'Wrenaissance', in red brick and Bath stone, with hipped roof and dentil cornice. Powerful two-storey porch, with paired columns (outer piers on the ground floor) and nearly semicircular pediment. The big windows behind the first-floor Doric colonnade light a long studio. Bidlake was a scholar, and his design is infused with Italian Renaissance motifs, e.g. the framed ground-floor windows. Entrance hall with free-standing Doric columns. Up the paired staircases – with swept-up rails – the columns support plain semicircular arches and a groined vault, suggesting Brunelleschi or Michelozzo: a Pre-Raphaelite art school. Repaired by *BPN* with *Donald Insall Associates* (front elevation), 2017–18.

MOSELEY AND KINGS HEATH INSTITUTE (former), Moseley Road. By *William Hale*, 1882–4, extended 1896. Ruskinian Gothic. Shafted doorcase with foliage and tympanum figures of the arts and crafts. Busts of Dickens and Shakespeare in roundels above. Shafted lancets to either side with more sculpted tympana. Big gabled triple-lancet windows with more foliage above.

JOSEPH CHAMBERLAIN COLLEGE, Belgrave Road. By *Nicholas Hare* with *BDP*, 2008. Planned round a courtyard, with a long, curving rendered range facing the tilting-out, pale blue-clad centrepiece, on pilotis. But the outside is a bleak fortress on a hill.

CLIFTON ROAD SCHOOLS (former), Hertford Street and Clifton Road. For the Kings Norton School Board. Strong, basic Gothic. Junior school of 1878 by *George Ingall*, single-storeyed with an apsed end and a spire. On the corner the Board's offices, 1884; along Clifton Road the tall senior school, 1883–5, both by *Ingall & Hughes*. Tower and spire with big lucarnes (under threat 2021).

ANDERTON PARK SCHOOL, Dennis Road. 1896 by *Martin & Chamberlain*. The usual gabled blocks, with a two-storey centre. The tower has an octagonal stage with slatted openings, and a slim cupola. Much extended.

NELSON MANDELA PRIMARY SCHOOL, Colville Road. By *Will Howland* of *Birmingham City Architect's Department*, 1987. Low and understated, with pitched roofs. Flexible layout, replacing classroom walls with folding doors and screens.

TINDAL STREET PRIMARY SCHOOL (now ARK TINDAL PRIMARY ACADEMY). The old parts are by *George Ingall*, 1880. Straightforward Gothic. Single-storey junior school, taller senior school, tower and spirelet between. On Cromer Road, E, a block of 1952 and two altered gables of 1906 by *Buckland*.

PERAMBULATION

Starting on MOSELEY ROAD, at the junction of Cromer Road. On the NW corner a former Post Office, with turret and spire, and adjoining houses, by *Oliver Essex*, 1884–6. Going S, the former Institute. Then a former TRAM DEPOT of 1906 by *F.B. Osborn*. Jacobean office range with gable and oriel flanked by tall chimneys, in poor repair. Car shed behind, with big pilasters, three-centred rusticated entrance arches and city coat of arms. Beyond, Victorian classical villas and terraces climb ALCESTER ROAD towards Moseley. Nos. 28–32, 1860s, have consoles extended down the top floor as pilasters. Nos. 34–56, BRIGHTON PLACE, *c.*1855, are still Regency: stuccoed, with smooth rustication, and eared architraves above.

Going N from Cromer Road, in Runcorn Road (E) a former Congregational Sunday School, Gothic of 1889 (chapel of 1862 in front, demolished). Slightly N, HOMER STREET runs W, with simple, quite progressive gabled terraces by *J.G. Dunn*, 1905. Nos. 529–535 Moseley Road, shops built over the garden of a classical terrace behind. The former NEW INN, on the corner of Edward Road, is by *William Jenkins*, 1901. Big round bays and gables. On the E side, the OLD PRINT WORKS, a complex of 1908–24 for J.H. Butcher & Co. by *Marcus O. Type*. The front range has end towers with stepped tops, in brick banded with Portland stone. Heavy doorcases with radiating voussoirs. To its r. a villa updated by *Type*, probably in 1909, with semicircular bays and semicircular-pedimented porch. Beyond, the former School of Art (p. 305) and former Moseley Road Methodist Church (p. 304), and (W side) the Muslim Students' House Masjid, the baths and the library (p. 304).

The old Moseley Road continues N, r. of the new A435. 300 yds N, the finest villas. Nos. 360–362 have Ionic porches, their entablature extended across a pair of Ionic columns in the middle. No. 356 has a Greek Doric porch, its pediment decorated with palmette and foliage. The line continues, with smooth-rusticated ground floors, to Highgate Road, becoming derelict.

W of Moseley Road, in TINDAL STREET, the OLD MOSELEY ARMS, 1927–8 by *W. Norman Twist*. Gentle Neo-Georgian. Bar with original furnishings, and two smoke rooms with panelling, now joined. No. 103 is one of a pair of 1850s cottages turned into the 'Zero Carbon House' by *John Christophers*, 2009. An extension fills in l. and wraps round behind. Large windows on the garden side fill the house with natural light. Walling of rendered compressed earth blocks; reclaimed materials, e.g. stair treads and bricks; and a heat-exchanging ventilation system. Intriguing curved stair fitted by the original side wall. The infill rises picturesquely to a s-facing pitch with solar panels. In GEORGE STREET, No. 17, the former BUILDER'S YARD of *John Bowen*, a fortunate survival. Front offices, brick and terracotta, dated 1882. Later ranges behind. Beyond, the Catholic church (p. 304). MARY STREET starts with the former COACH AND HORSES pub by *Osborne & Son*, 1938–9, streamlined Tudor with delicate twisted chimneys. Then late 1850s and 1860s terraces, still classical. No. 219, with *Bateman & Drury*-style doorcase, was here by 1854. No. 261, the grandest, ornate classical of *c*. 1864. At the top a stepping-up terrace with open balconies, looking almost New Orleans, by *J.F. Hartland*, 1892.

BILLESLEY

Interwar housing SE of Kings Heath and N of Yardley Wood.

HOLY CROSS, Brigfield Road, Billesley Common. 1935–7 by *Holland W. Hobbiss*. His usual basilican plan with passage aisles. Brown and red brick laid in English garden wall bond. This one has a rural French flavour, with a ritual SW belfry clambering up the wall. On the W front a fine plaque of the Agnus Dei by *Bloye*. Pointed arcades with incised bands round the arches. Heavy arcaded roof trusses. Later work by *Hobbiss & Partners*: chancel and vestries 1964–5 (*Holland W. Hobbiss* and *Maurice A.H. Hobbiss*), Lady Chapel 1969–70 (*Noel Hastilow*). Large (ritual) N meeting-room extension, creating a courtyard, by *APEC*, 2000. – PULPIT and FONT by *Hobbiss*.

BILLESLEY BAPTIST CHURCH, Brook Lane. 1927–8 by *F.B. Andrews*. Mission chapel made of terracotta blocks. Gambrel roof.

THE BILLESLEY, Brook Lane. Pub by *Wood & Kendrick*, 1927. Old-fashioned. Curved corner with conical spire.

HAIG PLACE, Wheeler's Lane. Ex-servicemen's homes, by *H.P.G. Maule*, 1930. Cottage rows centred on a green.

BRANDWOOD WITH DRUIDS HEATH

Interwar private housing and post-war municipal estates SW of Kings Heath. Historically part of Kings Norton parish.

ST BEDE, Bryndale Avenue. 1992–4 by *APEC*. Orange and purply brick octagon with pyramid roof and lantern, cut off for offices at the rear.

BRANDWOOD END CEMETERY, Woodthorpe Road. Attractive but old-fashioned CHAPELS by *J. Brewin Holmes*, 1897–9 (disused). Brick and terracotta, in the common arrangement flanking an open-arched central tower and spire. LODGE, also *Holmes*, dated 1897.

MONYHULL HALL, St Francis Drive. S of Brandwood Park Road, amid recent housing. Minus its pediment and heavily rendered. The core is 1730s, built for John Arderne. Three-storey house facing SE, with a linked house for a tenant facing SW, with framed doorcase and pedimental gable. Recast and other N extensions added in the 1870s, for Ezra Millward: see the typical angled brackets in the cornice and the corbelling-out of the applied portico at first-floor level. The SW entrance particularly looks like *J.J. Bateman*. In 1906–8 the house became the centre of an experimental colony for epileptics and the 'feeble-minded', housed in small ward blocks by *C. Whitwell & Son*; closed in 1999 and mostly demolished. Surviving chapel of 1917 by *Whitwell*, NW, now MONYHULL CHURCH. Brick, Dec, with paired gables marking transepts. These have two-bay arcades with terracotta columns. Diaphragm arches support the roof. Sharp-gabled extension by *D5*, 2014. Blocks of 1913–14 by *Whitwell* further NW, facing Monyhull Hall Road, are now part of LINDSWORTH SCHOOL. The colony also took over THE PLEASAUNCE (now a nursery), further SW at No. 132 Monyhull Hall Road. *W. De Lacy Aherne*'s own house, of 1898. Long and low, rendered except for two half-timbered gables, one with a little lantern.

The Stratford-upon-Avon Canal runs under the junction of Monyhull Hall Road and Broad Lane in the KINGS NORTON TUNNEL of 1796, engineer *Josiah Clowes*. The NW entrance, off Tunnel Lane, has a deep curved retaining wall, red brick with one blue band rising over the tunnel mouth. Upper part rebuilt in the C20, but retaining a pedimented aedicule with the company's crest, a head of Shakespeare.

DRUIDS HEATH is a municipal estate of 1963–6 (*J.R. Sheridan-Shedden*, City Architect; *Miall Rhys-Davies*, project architect), centred on BELLS LANE. Thirteen-storey flats built in the Bison Wall Frame system; terraces in the Bryant Low Rise system, many with jettied upper floors and timber cladding. Some tower blocks being demolished, 2020.

BELLS FARM (Community Centre), Bells Farm Close. An early to mid-C17 timber-framed house. What survives after devastating fires in 1977 and 1980 are two studded gabled bays facing W, and a rear wing at the N end. Brick chimney with three star-shaped stacks. Matching N gable chimney, and stone GATEPIERS with heavy moulded tops and balls, added in 1661. Repaired and extended S by *Christopher Pancheri* of the City Planning Department, by 1988. The N wing followed in 2011–12 by *Nick Joyce Architects*, lime-rendered. Bold studding in the ground-floor hall and parlour above, which has a sandstone fireplace. (Some C17 panelling remains in store.)

HALL GREEN

Part of Yardley parish, developed from *c.* 1920 as the archetypal Birmingham owner-occupied suburb, defined by tree-lined roads of substantial semi-detached houses, like the world of Alan A. Jackson's *Semi-Detached London*. Earlier survivals include an early C18 chapel of ease and a C19 planned estate, The Hamlet. UPVC and poor extensions have done serious damage. This account includes Sarehole and Gracewell, W of the River Cole.

PLACES OF WORSHIP

THE ASCENSION, School Road. Job Marston left £1,000 for a 'handsome convenient firm and durable chappell' for those living at a distance from Yardley parish church. Designed by *Sir William Wilson* of Sutton Coldfield, and built by *William* and *Francis Smith*. Dated 1703 in a plaque over the W doorway. Transepts and chancel added in 1860 by *J.G. Bland*. The original nave and W tower are slightly toy-like and of great charm. Red brick in Flemish bond, stone dressings. Four bays articulated by Doric pilasters on pedestals (a very early use on a church), full entablature with pulvinated frieze, and balustrade. The whole Wren-like classical treatment is applied to a building too small for it; cf. Wilson's own Moat House, Sutton Coldfield (p. 452). SUNDIAL, S side, inscribed *Joseph Peter* 1766. The tower has brickwork patterned with burnt headers; the bricklayer, *John Lee*, cut his name on a brick. N and S œil de bœuf windows, two octagonal stages and a copper dome. The 1860 parts are distinguishable by slightly larger, darker bricks and a blue-brick plinth. More œil de bœuf windows, and hipped roofs. The C18 coved ceiling is continued in the transepts and chancel. – FITTINGS. BOX PEWS in the nave, C18, cut down; 1860 ones in the transepts. The originals have fielded panels, the later ones are beaded. – DADO in the nave, partly C18. – WEST GALLERY. C18, extended in the early C19 on iron columns. – NORTH and SOUTH GALLERIES of 1860 on iron columns with leaf capitals. – PULPIT. Octagonal C18 top, ornate Victorian stair rail. Base probably C20. – FONT. Small, alabaster. 1933. – COMMUNION RAIL and CLERGY SEATS. 1932 by *Percy Yabsley*, with balusters; CHOIR STALLS probably also his. – E end PANELLING of 1951–2. – BENEFACTION BOARD, S wall, a good piece dated 1703, with Job Marston's arms in a semicircular top projection. His HATCHMENT opposite. – PEW ALLOCATION BOARDS, C18. – ROYAL ARMS, W gallery front. 1828 by *J. Thorp*, 'Herald Painter'. Fluently done, with a bear-like lion. – STAINED GLASS of 1866, chancel.

Original CHURCHYARD WALL with half-round sandstone copings. A number of TABLE TOMBS, the best Mary and Benjamin Steedman †1826 and †1840, with gadrooned corners. To the w, a brick HALL of c.1910, with entrance block of 1932 by *Batemans*.

ST PETER, Highfield Road. On a back plot behind semi-detached houses. 1961–4 by *Norman T. Rider*, a member of the church, for the Rev. Joseph Adlam, who was much involved in the design. So there are interesting ideas but the execution is uncertain. The dominating feature is the tapering w tower of bush-hammered concrete. Flat w face framed by deep flanges; concave N and S faces. The entrance is convex, a nice contrast. Criss-cross-pattern belfry windows, and a circular cap supported by four columns and surmounted by a copper cross. A remarkable and sculptural piece. Octagonal nave faced in concrete panels, subsidiary volumes in thin pink brick, an odd combination. Reinforced-concrete piers supporting a shell dome. A low passage aisle, separated by cross-beams, runs all round. Plastered blockwork above. Shallow E apse, screened S Lady Chapel, and NE vestries. – Original FURNISHINGS including paired PULPIT and READING DESK, and triangular FONT with curved corners. – STAINED GLASS. By *Tristan Ruhlmann*, made in Strasbourg. *Dalle-de-verre* technique, i.e. coloured pieces set in concrete. Five-light E window, Christ's call to St Peter. Dense, rich colours, Expressionist angularity. Many symbols and objects worked into the pattern. Clerestory windows, based on Persian prayer carpets. Lady Chapel, Virgin and Child (1970), again densely patterned.

HALL GREEN UNITED COMMUNITY CHURCH (formerly Methodist), Reddings Lane. By *W. Cyril Moss* of *Crouch, Butler & Savage*, dated 1924. With the heavy sandstone dressings of Moss's later churches. Short powerful tower with angle buttresses and small spire. Deep roof and dormers. Detail mostly C17 – Jacobean window in the tower, plain mullioned windows along the sides. Cool, aisled, barrel-vaulted interior. Arcades with sandstone Doric columns. Groin-vault over the crossing.

HALL GREEN BAPTIST CHURCH, Stratford Road. By *F.B. Andrews*, 1935. In a Free Style which would have been radical thirty years earlier. Gable window with heavy round-arched tracery and dividing buttresses, porch with immense round arch and corner turrets.

FRIENDS' MEETING HOUSE, Stratford Road. 1888, almost certainly by *J.A. Chatwin*. Built by John Simcox as the community hall for The Hamlet (*see* Perambulation 2, p.312). Simple brick with segment-headed windows, linked to the former caretaker's house.

FRIENDS' MEETING HALL (former), Creswell Road. By *J.R. Armstrong*, 1933. Round-arched entrance in a projection covered by a half-hip of the deep roof: a touch of Lutyens.

TRINITY UNITED REFORMED CHURCH, Etwall Road. 1929 by *Armstrong*. With a similar front projection, here with a big window.

COLLEGES AND SCHOOLS

SOUTH AND CITY COLLEGE, Cole Bank Road. 1958 by *S.T. Walker & Partners* with *A.G. Sheppard Fidler*, City Architect. Long, concrete-framed three-storey block (altered). The infill panels were originally cedar boards. Careful proportions, with large first-floor windows. Crass porch of *c.*2012.

HALL GREEN JUNIOR SCHOOL, Stratford Road. By *Arthur Harrison*, 1892–3. Queen Anne, with a rustic Baroque ventilation turret.

PITMASTON PRIMARY SCHOOL (now ROBIN HOOD ACADEMY), Pitmaston Road. 1931–2 by *W.H. Ashford*, with a Neo-Georgian centre.

SAREHOLE MILL

A working water mill in Cole Bank Road, now a branch of Birmingham Museums and Art Gallery. The buildings were heavily restored in 1964–9 by *F.W.B. Charles* (machinery reconstructed by *Derek Ogden*), and their history is difficult to unravel. The main three-storey building probably dates from 1764–8, and is almost certainly the mill described as 'lately taken down and new built' in 1773. Attractive orange-red brick, laid in English garden wall bond with three stretcher rows. Lucam on the E. To the S a single-storey range, in its present form probably mid-C19, which may have been a blade-grinding shop.* At the N end, at right angles, a former granary, probably early C19. At the NW corner a tall chimney, almost certainly of 1851. Main N wheel of high breast-shot type, enclosed within the building; smaller S wheel in the single-storey extension, of overshot type. To the E a single-storey C18 building, for many years a bakery; beyond, a much-rebuilt former stable. J.R.R. Tolkien, who lived at Gracewell Cottages between 1896 and 1900, remembered Sarehole as 'a thriving corn mill'. Milling ceased in 1919. – ¼ m. NW, in Moseley Bog, the DAM of the former mill pool and Bronze Age BURNT MOUNDS on Coldbath Brook.

PERAMBULATIONS

1. School Road

The start is The Ascension church. Diagonally opposite, E, the CHARLES LANE TRUST ALMSHOUSES of 1937, by *J.B. Surman*. High-quality Tudor Revival, austerely handled. Warm brownish brick with stone dressings. Single-storey blocks, irregularly shaped, with hipped roofs, round a grass court. Slightly canted gabled bays, chimneys alternating between diagonal pairs and big blocks with patterns of projecting headers. Good original lamp standards. In Fox Hollies Road, S, No. 592, the VICARAGE, by *Philip* and *Anthony Chatwin*, 1953. SCHOOL

---

*In the C20 it had a storey added to become the miller's house, removed in 1964–9.

ROAD to the E became a conservation area in 1988, as a good example of interwar housing. Much UPVC now, alas. By *H. Dare & Son Ltd*, interwar Birmingham's best commercial house-builders, 1933–6, as their 'Severne Estate' (including Studland Road, N, and Miall Road through to Lakey Lane, S). Nearly all semi-detached, nearly all with big round two-storey bays, mostly under square gables. Many round-arched porches. Red brick varied by purple-maroon Staffordshires. Much variation in e.g. the small bedroom windows: some little canted oriels, some dormers set in catslide roofs, a Dare's trademark. Dare's also offered *Moderne* or 'suntrap' designs, but Birmingham conservatism meant that only one such pair was built here, Nos. 144–146 School Road. Also on the N side Nos. 168–190, shops by *Dare's*, 1935, pure Metroland with huge steep gables and lots of fake timbering. Opposite, on the SW corner to Shirley Road, the THREE MAGPIES pub (now 'The Maggies'), by *E. F. Reynolds*, 1935. Bold brick Modern, influenced by Dudok. Square block with public bar and landlord's flat above, the entrance on the r. side; lower wing, l., with ground-floor cellar, and smoke room and lounge beyond, separately entered. This unusual plan allowed the owners of the Dare's houses to take their wives for a drink without seeing men in overalls. The unifying motif is a thick pier with a bull-nosed front. It divides the strip windows, and appears in the thin tower with a ball and cap on top. The public bar retains its bar back, divided by similar piers. The PAVILION of the pub's bowling green, S, has similar piers.

2. *Stratford Road and The Hamlet*

On STRATFORD ROAD S of the junction with School Road, E side, the HORSE SHOE pub by *Hawkes & McFarlane*, 1934–5, plain Tudor. SPRINGFIELD COURT, flats by *H. Peter Hing*, 1936, are flat-roofed, with balconies and rounded corners. VIGGERS COURT is by *Barratt, Shaw & Wheeler*, 1978–80. Then the Baptist church (p. 310). PETERSFIELD COURT is two- and three-storey flats of 1934 by the developers *A. E. Jennens & Co.*, their design improved by *F. W. B. Yorke*. Rendered, streamlined, and still *Moderne* rather than Modern Movement, but Yorke has put little flying canopies with column supports on the roof by the ends. On the W side further S, the Junior School (p. 311), and opposite it the Friends' Meeting House (p. 310) and the end of THE HAMLET. Houses in Hamlet Road etc. in a rather George Devey manner with tile-hung upper floors on big brick brackets, casement windows, half-timbered gables and star-shaped chimneys. Several are dated 1883. Almost certainly by *J. A. Chatwin*, for John Simcox, who owned Stratford House, Bordesley (p. 201), hence the liking for half-timbering; builder *Frederick Daniel Deebank*. The best are on FOX HOLLIES ROAD, to the E: No. 38 Hamlet Road on the corner, dated 1883, with a porch with elongated balusters;

to the N Nos. 639–647 (altered), to the S Nos. 651–653 and 657–659, the last dated 1892.

Back to Stratford Road and S, on the W side No. 1301 (CENTRE COURT), by *T. Wynne Thomas*, 1937–9. A big cubic block of flats with a raised centre and a large framed staircase window. The BULL'S HEAD pub, E side, is early C19 in the *Bateman & Drury* manner, with a round-headed doorway.

3. Sarehole and Gracewell

W of Sarehole Mill (p. 311), a road junction. WAKE GREEN ROAD runs N towards Moseley and Sparkhill. On the W side, GRACE-WELL COTTAGES, Domestic Revival going Arts and Crafts, by *C. E. Bateman*, 1892. On the E side the GRACEWELL HOMES (FOSTER TRUST), brick pairs in a hemicycle by *Batemans*, 1929–30. To the N a range with a circular building in the angle, by *Paul Burley* and *Graham Winteringham* (*S.T. Walker & Partners*), 1989. Gracewell Road runs N here into GREEN ROAD. On the corner, No. 132, four gabled E–W ranges, rendered, with bargeboards. It looks mid-C19, but is shown with the same shape on a plan of 1807. To the E, No. 143, THE CHALET. A C17 two-bay cottage, the street range E of the set-off added probably in the C18. Recast and the entrance bay added in the mid C19, with bargeboarded gables. Part of a timber-framed barn survives to the N.

S down Wake Green Road from the junction, Nos. 397–427 are a well-preserved group of PREFABS probably of 1945–6, of the rare *Phoenix* type. Steel portal frames, asbestos-panel walls. No. 405 has its original corrugated asbestos roof.

OTHER BUILDINGS

THE BALDWIN, Baldwins Lane. A pub of 1935 by *Batemans*. Brick, Dudok-influenced Modern. The blocks step up from r. to l., ending in a staircase and chimney. Buff brick in fashionable monk bond, carried round the semicircular front projection.

COLLEGE ARMS, Stratford Road and Shaftmoor Lane. An early 'reformed' pub by *Arthur Harrison*, 1900. Domestic Revival, with half-timbering and slate-hanging, paired central gables and angled corner porches. S porch with sprocketed roof.

SHAFTMOOR pub (currently SUMMER HOUSE), Shaftmoor Lane. By *E. F. Reynolds*, 1930. Massive Neo-Georgian; hipped roof.

ROBIN HOOD (now a Toby Carvery pub), Stratford Road and Shirley Road. 1848–9, perhaps by *J. J. Bateman*. An unusual design. Typical Early Victorian architraves, doorcases and deep cornice, and quite asymmetrical. But the ground floor is of red brick with blue bands, the frieze red brick with cream patterning and blue headers. On the W side of Stratford Road opposite, Nos. 1487–1493 by *H. S. Scott*, 1933, brownish brick; also Nos. 27–29 Robin Hood Lane, W. To the NE off Shirley

Road is the BUSHMORE FARM ESTATE of 1930–2, by *H.H. Humphries*, City Engineer and Surveyor. The usual cottage pairs and terraces; also in Redstone Farm Road some with tile-hanging and gambrel-roofed porches; on the corners of Wellfield Road blocks with half-timbering, and in that road some of the streamlined rendered type.

THE YORK, York Road. 1929 by *G.B. Cox*, whose 'reformed' pubs explore a range of styles. This is unconventional Jacobean, roughcast, with Cotswold stone dressings and rusticated base. Doorcase pediment broken by a panel with coat of arms, oriel above resting on a console with a bearded head.

SHERWOOD PUB (former), Highfield Road and Cole Valley Road. 1929 by *H. Peter Hing*.

HIGHTERS HEATH

The furthest s projection of Birmingham into Worcestershire. Semi-detached houses and cottage groups of the 1930s. Warstock, to the N, is similar.

IMMANUEL, Highters Heath Lane. 1938–40 by *H.G. Wicks* of *Harvey & Wicks*. An odd, memorable front, like a fragment of something great: low, brick, with a full-width gable of pediment pitch, a heavy round-arched doorway, and a massive semicircular stair-turret, l. Wicks planned a cloister to the r., and a huge campanile just behind it. The marks where these would have joined on are visible. Heavy buttresses, pierced for passage aisles, support a flimsy roof. Short chancel and Lady Chapel added 1964–5. – FONT. An C18 marble baluster, with gadrooned bowl and shallow-relief leaves. – PLAQUES with heads of bishops Barnes and Wilson on the nave piers.

HIGHTERS HEATH COMMUNITY SCHOOL, Highters Heath Lane, ¾ m. NE. 1931 by *S.N. Cooke*. Entrance with a pedimental gable.

KINGS HEATH

Kings Heath is as Late Victorian and Edwardian as Moseley, but more modest. Development on the Alcester Road had spread along the N part of the present High Street before 1840. Further s, Alcester Lanes End began to develop around 1860. The streets on either side of the High Street developed rapidly from *c.* 1890. The late C19 Cartland estate development has early *C.E. Bateman* houses, and his pioneering 'reformed' pub, the Red Lion. Interwar suburbs spread further s. The High Street is now the most important suburban shopping centre in south Birmingham, which has not helped its historic buildings.

CHURCHES

ALL SAINTS, High Street. 1858–60 by *Frederick Preedy*. Simple early Dec, in Bromsgrove stone, with a s aisle and sw tower with porch and stair-vice. Its broach spire is the single landmark of Kings Heath. Nice window details: chancel lancets with X-shapes of tracery, clerestory windows with five-cusped circles and cusped triangles. N aisle and NE organ chamber by *J.A. Chatwin*, 1883. W extension 1899, probably also *Chatwin*.* Plain, spacious interior. *Preedy*'s s arcade has octagonal piers and double-chamfered arches of alternating blocks of Bath and Bromsgrove stone. Chancel arch with leaf capitals. Chatwin's arcade matches the s one, but his organ-chamber arcade has richer foliage capitals. – FONT. 1860 by *Preedy*. Octagonal, on a circular concave stem with a band of leaf moulding. – Also *Preedy* the simple PEWS. – Ornate REREDOS by *C.E. Bateman*, 1889–90, made by *Farmer & Brindley*. Centre with top arcading, angel finials and mosaic Pietà. – Wrought-iron SCREEN also *Bateman*, 1893, a beautiful piece like a Spanish *reja*. Endless patterns of scrolls at the top, many flowerheads, a gilded leaf frieze and a cresting of cockerels. CROSS on top with central Agnus Dei, quite 'advanced' for 1893. – PULPIT. 1895. – STAINED GLASS. E window, Ascension, by *Mayer & Co.* of Munich, 1881. Chancel N by *H. Vernon Spreadbury* of *Maile Studios*, 1935; S, 1904. S aisle, E †1886, s by *Henry Payne*, 1927, the best here; N aisle, *O.C. Hawkes*, †1885. Now in a w room, *Ward & Hughes*, †1883; another, *c.* 1899.

Linked COMMUNITY ROOMS AND MEDICAL CENTRE, SW, by *Cottrell & Vermeulen*, 2004–9. Deliberate geometrical awkwardness: a simple brick ground floor, upper storey within a mass of free-form shingle-clad roofs. The well-tree'd CHURCHYARD was landscaped by *RGA Landscape Architects*, 2011: uncomfortable, with gravestones standing in the patterned paving.

ST MARY MAGDALENE (now HAZELWELL CHURCH, Anglican and Methodist), Vicarage Road. Well positioned above the road. It started as a domestic-looking brick chapel of 1915–16 by *Gerald McMichael* and *Howard C. Weston*, with low walls, segment-headed windows and big dormers. In 1936 *Holland W. Hobbiss* reoriented it, adding a chancel (w), an E extension and a s tower with a single set-back and low pyramid roof. The finest thing is Hobbiss's eclectic E doorway, with broad brick buttresses supporting a stone pediment filled with an angel's wings. Plain hall with scissor-truss roof of 1916, unmoulded chancel arch of 1936. – CHOIR STALLS. 1930, carved by a parishioner, *W.F. Huband*. – Linked behind, THE HUB, a community centre by *John Wormald*, 2001–3. Gable-end with two pitches, the lower extending inwards as a big scissor truss.

---

*A puzzle, as there is neither faculty nor building control plan; newspaper reports do not mention the architect.

ST DUNSTAN (R.C.), Kingsfield Road. By *Desmond Williams & Associates*, 1968. Pinky-buff brick with alternate courses slightly raised, like many platbands. The spiral plan is immediately visible, the long curving foyer rising slowly to the l., until we enter the semicircular sanctuary at the far end. This has heavy radiating roof beams. Behind the altar, Risen Christ by *John Poole*, pierced metal and wire, dominating, hieratic, anguished. – STATIONS OF THE CROSS in coloured glass around the rear. – Behind, the altered former church, now HALL, by *Jennings Homer & Lynch*, 1951–3.

METHODIST CHURCH, Cambridge Road and School Road. 1896 by *William Hale*. A vigorous brick and terracotta design in Flemish-tinged Gothic. Boldly cross-gabled, with plate tracery. Germanic SW tower with tall, deep belfry windows, an octagon with gables and corner pinnacles corbelled out like tourelles, and a spire. Wide nave with arch-braced roof. Passage aisles, the arcades with stone capitals and bases but complex brick arches. Reordered by *J. Alan Bristow & Partner*, 1982. – STAINED GLASS. E window by *Camm & Co.*, 1896; S †1960.

NEW LIFE BAPTIST CHURCH, High Street. 1897–8 by *Arthur Harrison*. Brick, with a pent-roofed forebuilding and paired gabled entrances. Early French rose window in the gable. Four-bay grey stone arcades, transepts and apse, all Dec. Collar-beam roof with big braces. – STAINED GLASS. Apse, saints by *Pearce & Cutler*, 1927. – SCHOOLS behind, also by *Harrison*.

SCHOOLS

KING EDWARD VI CAMP HILL SCHOOL, Vicarage Road. 1953–8 by *Jackson & Edmonds*. Curtain-walled teaching blocks and a brick tower. Many late C20 extensions.

COLMORE PRIMARY SCHOOL, Grove Road. 1910–11 by *Ewen & J.A. Harper*. Two long E–W ranges, separated by the playground. Brick and a little grey faience. Rows of close gables, segment-headed windows. One tower on the rear block with parapet enclosing a cupola, a hint of Harrison Townsend.

KINGS HEATH PRIMARY SCHOOL, Valentine Road. 1984 by *Birmingham City Architect's Department* (project architects *Gunars Zimbachs* and *Rod Hatton*).

PERAMBULATIONS

1. High Street

A mixture of Late Victorian and Edwardian buildings of some quality, and big late C20 and C21 intruders. The railway bridge at the N end is the start. On the E side, the STATION INN, mid-C19, with canted bays. Extensions l. (a gabled shop) and r. by *D. Henry Ward*, 1897. Opposite, the POLICE STATION, mainly late C20 but retaining one C19 hipped-roofed block. Then the LIBRARY, by *A. Gilbey Latham*, 1905–6. Edwardian Baroque, small but powerful and determinedly asymmetrical. Entrance at the l., with coupled Ionic pilasters and blocked half-columns, deep pediment and a built-up top. The three bays to the r. are treated as a separate symmetrical composition. Nicely calculated extension l. by *Birmingham City Architect's Department*, project architect *Philip Howl*, 1983, with porthole windows. Facing, shops by *William Hale*, 1898–9, restrained Jacobean with an ogee turret. 100 yds s, set back, the derelict front block of the former KINGSWAY CINEMA by *Horace G. Bradley*, 1925, blocky classical. Opposite, shops by *Oliver Floyd*, 1896. Each has a linked stone architrave with a double concave dormer top, like a chimneypiece climbing the wall, ugly but memorable. Nos. 56–66 by *Oliver Floyd & Salt*, 1911, with ball finials on piers dividing the shops. The CROSS GUNS pub (now THE OLD COURT) is by *Wood & Kendrick*, 1896: half-timbered, with projecting gabled bays and a continuous jetty on big consoles. s end of 1898 (below) and 1904, with billiard room.

Beyond the Baptist church (*see* left), HSBC bank by *Ralph Heaton*, dated 1898, Jacobean on a grand scale, with double-height ground floor. Tremendous doorcase with superimposed broken pediments, but he does not know what to do with the consoles, which trail down a long way. The E side has ASDA, with huge faux-classical aedicules, by *Gordon Benoy & Partners*, 1987; and a range with aedicules in yellow brick against red, by *John Day*, 1985. Opposite, the HARE AND HOUNDS of 1906–7, by *Sam Owen* for the Holt Brewery Co. A loose composition in brick and pinky-red terracotta with occasional square timber bays and a big octagonal corner with a dome. The lounge retains part of its bar front and back, and blue and cream *Maws* tiling; also in the stair hall, with Art Nouveau patterns of green, blue and mustard brown. Assembly room at the rear by *C. H. Collett*, 1911. Then on the E side Nos. 141–143, also by *Owen*, 1882, in that picturesque commercial Gothic which does not actually have many pointed arches. Oriel with an elongated corner spirelet, crucial in the streetscape. Answering W corner block by *A. Freeman Smith*, 1896–7, its turret with ogee cap. Back on the E side, SCOTS CORNER, shops by *Michael Brashier Associates*, 1983–4, quite restrained, gabled, in purply brick. Opposite All Saints' church (p. 315), a nicely detailed brick Neo-Georgian block, 1913 by *Ingall Bridgewater & Porter*, with pediment. Then HEDGES BUILDINGS by *Harry Campbell Hawkes*, 1905, with shaped gables, circular corner turret, shallow bays, and bands of pink terracotta. s of Drayton Road, two shops by *Crouch & Butler*, 1894–5, with another circular turret; very simple, with a dentil cornice. Finally the N corner with Addison Road: by *J. P. Sharp & Co.*, 1899–1900, with half-timbered gables.

2. The Cartland Estate

SW down Vicarage Road from All Saints' church. After 300 yds, on the NW side, KINGS HEATH PARK, the grounds of KINGS

HEATH HOUSE. The house has essentially its present shape on an 1840 map Six-bay N front, symmetrical except for an extra recessed r. bay. Porch with coupled Doric columns and a minimal pediment which looks 1830s. The two full-height semicircular bays, E, must be later C19. To the SW, King Edward VI Camp Hill School (p. 316), on the site of the Cartland family house, THE PRIORY. By Vicarage Road a castellated LODGE, probably by *J.J. Bateman*, *c.*1856. The area beyond was developed from 1887, principally by John Howard Cartland, who inherited the estate in 1889. At the junction with Howard Road is the RED LION, a very early 'reformed' public house by *C.E. Bateman*, 1903–4; used by Mitchells & Butlers, whose initials appear over the richly detailed l. doorway. Cotswold stone, beautifully laid in random blocks, with two full-height canted bays flanking the entrance. Tudor style, with big mullion-and-transom windows, foreshadowing innumerable interwar roadhouses. The planning also anticipated the interwar pub. The main entrance led originally into a large public bar, the l. entrance into a passage to the lounge. Inside, a lobby with panelling, and the staircase, every fourth baluster fret-cut. The door to the gents has studding and decorative hinges and nailheads. The rest gutted.

Further down Vicarage Road, early houses by *C.E. Bateman*, moving from Domestic Revival to the more austere Arts and Crafts idiom of *c.*1900. The corners of Stanley Road have asymmetrical semi-detached pairs of 1889. Brick with tile-hanging above, with a half-timbered gable, l. In STANLEY ROAD, Nos. 4–6 of 1891–3 have the whole upper floor half-timbered, with a long continuous roof-line and little white-painted oriel bays nestling underneath the central jetty.* No. 8, 1892–3, is smoothly rendered with a big tile-hung gable; the contemporary No. 10 is roughcast, also with a long upper casement, and has a swan's-neck pediment to the doorcase. At Nos. 12–14, 1893, the simple style of 1900 is almost there. Brick, with wide stone dressings set flush, the sills shaped in curved dripmoulds. Big central chimneystack with blank arches (Bateman thought that these should be 'miniature towers, not stalks').

Back on Vicarage Road, Nos. 247–249 of 1892–3 are like Nos. 4–6 Stanley Road, but with corner porches and no central jetty. Nos. 251–253 are early C19. Then on the corners of Melstock Road, asymmetrical semis by *Bateman & Bateman*, 1887, the year C.E. Bateman returned from London to join his father. Half-timbered gables here too, but handled thinly and decoratively. On the corners opposite, fine semi-detached pairs by *C.E. Bateman* of 1895–6. Brick, with stone details like those of Nos. 12–14 Stanley Road. The r. pair have a continuous roof-line, with a large r. gable to end the composition; the

---

*Bateman said in 1900 'at some time or other, everyone does a half-timber house, and wishes they had not after a later inspection': a harsh verdict on these.

l. pair have large and small gables to front and side. Down CARTLAND ROAD between, on the W side, pairs by *De Lacy Aherne*, 1903–6, with much half-timbering. An entry on the r., opposite Priory Road, leads to GABLE HOUSE, *C.E. Bateman*'s most unusual design here, dated 1896. L-plan, the base stroke cranked forward to the r. end, where it drops to a single storey. The main house to the l. is of brick, with stone windows, timber casements and a tile-hung bay. But the central feature is a low gabled tower, above an open archway with the entrance inside it. The tower steps in to a crenellated parapet with the gable proper rising above it, and a tall chimney corbelled out on its l. The sources are Shaw and Nesfield, much refined. Bateman never did anything like it again, but its publication in *The Builder* in 1902 must have influenced local architects such as George E. Pepper.

3. Alcester Lanes End

The start is at the KINGS ARMS (now THE CROWN), by *Arthur Edwards*, 1911, with a grid of windows below and a grid of half-timbering above. Further down on the E side, shops with giant terracotta pilasters and an octagonal turret by *Thomas Silver*, 1910. Going N, on the W side, APPIAN CLOSE, like a little outlier of Bournville: simple brick pairs and terraces by *S. Alex Wilmot*, 1929–31. Nos. 238–240 are an odd asymmetrical pair by *G. Repton Faulkner*, 1908, No. 236 a big Gothic villa of *c.* 1875. No. 216, 1904–5, and No. 214, 1903–4, are by *Gerald McMichael*: simple Domestic Revival, brick with a little render. Returning down the E side from further N, the MASONIC HALL by *Hawkes & McFarlane*, 1937, large but domestic. The CORKS CLUB to the S was ALCESTER HOUSE; mid-C19, horribly mutilated. The PAVILION pub also began as a house; *c.* 1870, with Frenchy architraves and a porch with segmental pediment. Nos. 243–245 are earlier, their plain round-arched porches and minimal entablature still in the Neoclassical tradition. No. 245 cannot be much later, but is oddly detailed, with a double cornice between the floors, the upper curiously breaking the first-floor sills. Nos. 261–265 are three almost identical linked villas by *Edward Holmes*, *c.* 1860–3, well proportioned and detailed. Doorcases with dentil courses; upper windows with entablatures on consoles, supporting minimal pediments, with central blocks.

OTHER BUILDINGS

Nos. 33–35 GREENHILL ROAD, on the Greenhill Estate. Arts and Crafts by *Holland W. Hobbiss*, 1908, the moment for decorative brick. Dentil courses and cogging in the canted bays, decorative cornice, banded and arched chimneys. The porch rises from a pent roof into round arches in sweeping curves.

MOSELEY

Moseley is the great Late Victorian and Edwardian suburb of Birmingham. Until the mid C19 it was a typical Worcestershire village, with a green below St Mary's church, a chapel of ease to Bromsgrove. The Hall estate lay to the w. The Birmingham & Gloucester Railway came in 1840, the station opened in 1867. Steam trams started in 1886. From *c.* 1870 Moseley developed rapidly as a high-class residential area, coinciding with declining development in Edgbaston. Its architecture starts Gothic, e.g. the village end of Oxford Road, but quickly adopts Old English, Domestic Revival and Queen Anne. *Essex, Nicol & Goodman* mixed all of these, and more; *Ewen & J.A. Harper* are refined by comparison. Building spread into Yardley parish, where the church, St Agnes, came first.

Late Victorian and Edwardian Moseley is centred on the Hall estate, developed from 1891. The grandest houses are in Chantry and Wake Green roads. There are a few by major Arts and Crafts names, but two local architects define the period. *George E. Pepper* was an architectural confectioner, whipping up picturesque and slightly over-sweetened houses with many gables and much timberwork and clever brick. *W. De Lacy Aherne* designed prolifically in a recognizable manner, again much timbered – gables mostly with protruding purlins – but with a repertoire including lunette windows and diamond-patterned render.

Later C20 Moseley attracted academics, and from the 1970s became Birmingham's radical left village, with wholefood shops and a significant gay community. Something of this atmosphere has survived C21 property prices.

CHURCHES

St Mary, St Mary's Row. A chapel is recorded in 1405. The present w tower was added in 1513. Small, of three stages, faced in pink-grey sandstone, but built of thin, long orange-red bricks (visible inside), laid in a kind of English garden wall bond. Three-light w window with a four-centred arch and deep hollow chamfer all round. Blocked internal stair door. Four-centred tower arch with two plain chamfers.

The church was rebuilt in 1780, in a simple Neoclassical style, and again in 1823–4 by *Thomas Rickman*, brick Gothic with cast-iron windows. The medieval, 1780 and 1824 rooflines are all visible on the tower wall inside. Rickman's building has all but disappeared in complicated alterations and extensions, nearly all by *J.A. Chatwin*. In 1873 he added a chancel, with a three-sided apse; in 1885 a N aisle; in 1887 an organ chamber, chancel N. Then in 1898 he extended the chancel eastward, with a square end, and added the s transept (Lady Chapel). Finally in 1909–10 his son *Philip B. Chatwin* added the s aisle and sw porch, and rebuilt the nave, adding the clerestory.* The result is a unified building, long and low, in sandstone to match the tower, with deep unbroken parapets. A half gable-end of *Rickman*'s church survives N of the tower, orange-red brick, with a cast-iron cusped lancet. Chancel and Lady Chapel E windows late Dec, with continuous mullions. Perp clerestory windows, set in shallow recessed panels, the only motif obviously of 1910. The aisle windows below are Dec, a historicist touch by *Philip B. Chatwin*. His S arcade follows his father's N one: Dec, with octagonal piers and capitals with bossy foliage. Tall chancel arch on clustered shafts. Philip's roof has alternating hammerbeams and arch-braced collars, the hammerbeams on clustered shafts which again die into corbels short of the arcades, a favourite motif of his father. It is not exciting, but spacious and satisfying.

FURNISHINGS. PULPIT by *J.A. Chatwin*, 1898, with figures of saints. – CHOIR STALLS also his, with typical traceried ends and scrolled tops. – FONT by *Frederick Preedy*, 1873. Tapering chamfered square bowl on alternating short columns. Relief of the Presentation, N. – PEWS. Made up from C18 box pews, with fielded panels. – C18 PANELLING in the Lady Chapel from St Bartholomew, Birmingham. – STAINED GLASS. Much was lost in 1940. The replacements are by *Hardmans*: E and Lady Chapel E (*Donald Taunton*), 1952–4, Lady Chapel E (S) and E 1955. Survivals in the S aisle, from E: a single-light Arts and Crafts window of 1916, perhaps by *Harvey & Ashby*; three by *Kempe & Co.*, 1910–c. 1913; *Pearce & Cutler*, 1927. N aisle easternmost, *Lawrence Lee*, 1981. Fragments elsewhere (original windows of 1895–1915). – MONUMENTS. Many tablets from the village church this was, the best in the N aisle: Elizabeth Russell †1821, by *E.H. Baily*, with mourning woman and urn; William Congreve Russell †1850, by *Peter Hollins*, with portrait relief. – S aisle, Samuel Barns †1829 and others, by *John Nutt*, with flaming urn. (– Mary Sayer †1823, by *William Hollins*.)

ST AGNES, St Agnes Road. A large church in Geometrical style by *William Davis*; chancel, transepts and two bays of the nave and aisles 1883–4, the remainder 1892–3. Rock-faced red Hamstead sandstone, Bath stone dressings. SE vestries by *William Hale*, 1903. The W tower was completed in 1931–2 by *C.E. Bateman*. The best part of the building: a fine free Gothic design in grey sandstone, with clasping buttresses and flat-headed belfry windows. Interior faced in Bath stone. Conventional details, but amply proportioned. Chancel arch on sandstone shafts. – PULPIT, CHOIR STALLS, CLERGY STALLS, COMMUNION RAIL, all in late medieval style by *James Swan*, 1937–9. – Original FONT; COVER of 1939 by *Swan*. His carvers were *Pancheri & Hack*. – REREDOS. Central arches original. The rest, including the figures, by *Boultons*, 1920. – STAINED GLASS. E window by *Ballantine & Gardiner*, 1897, rich and effective. N aisle W by *Henry Payne*, 1908, with carefully controlled colours including dark reds and blues. Replacements

---

*He also repaired the church in 1952–4, following war damage.

for wartime losses by *Claude Price*, 1951–5; not at his best, pale and watery. Also S aisle easternmost by *Hardmans*, 1949.

ST ANNE, Park Hill. 1873–4 by *Frederick Preedy*. Confident High Victorian, drawing on late C13 Geometrical and Continental sources. Red Hamstead sandstone with grey stone bands and dressings. The commanding NW tower, with powerful NW stair-turret, rises to emphatic pinnacles and a short stone spire with dark bands. Deeply recessed belfry windows with three orders of columns. Gabled N porch with contrasting coloured stones in the arch. Large SE choir vestry by *Ewen Harper*, 1898. Projecting W baptistery by *P.B. Chatwin*, 1922, in keeping. Inside, a subtle contrast of grey Bromsgrove and yellowy Corsham Down stone. Arcades with alternating circular and octagonal piers. The chancel S window surround extends down to form sedilia. – Original FONT, lobed, with stubby columns, PULPIT and CHOIR STALLS. – REREDOS by *P.B. Chatwin*, 1916. – STAINED GLASS. Nothing survived a bomb in 1940. E window by *Christopher Webb*, 1957; Christ in Majesty and small scenes linked by sinuous foliage. A fireman, lower r., as a memorial of 1940. W, *L.C. Evetts*, 1966, impressive: symbols and stylized angels and doves against an irregular lattice.

MOSELEY BAPTIST CHURCH (now CALVARY CHURCH OF GOD IN CHRIST), Oxford Road. 1887–8 by *J.P. Osborne*. The wealthy Nonconformity of the 'Civic Gospel'. Early Dec style, very similar to Osborne's Hamstead Road church (p. 249). Rock-faced Bromsgrove sandstone with limestone dressings. Tracery with lots of cusping and quatrefoils. The hoodmoulds extend downwards to the tracery springing. Ritual NW tower with angle buttresses and a spire prickly with lucarnes and crockets. Darley Dale and Bath stone inside. Four-bay nave arcades, with circular columns but correctly English Dec bossy leaf capitals. Wide transepts and sanctuary, five-sided apse. Contemporary (ritual E) SCHOOLROOM with gabled-apsed end. – Original stone PULPIT and REREDOS, also PEWS. – STAINED GLASS. A biblical feast. Apse from N, *Hardmans* (*Dunstan J. Powell*), 1898; 1888; two perhaps *Swaine Bourne*, †1887, †1884; the last 1888. N transept *Hardmans*, 1894; S transept, †1898, probably *Heaton, Butler & Bayne*; two certainly by them in the N aisle, 1910, †1907; S aisle, †1901, then two by *A.J. Davies*, richly coloured, 1932.

MOSELEY PRESBYTERIAN CHURCH (now ST COLUMBA UNITED REFORMED CHURCH), Alcester Road. The low building on the corner with craftsmanlike brick detail and an angled entrance is the SCHOOL of 1924 by *Andrews & Hickman*. Plain gabled CHAPEL behind by *Claud E.A. Andrews*, 1939–40.

HOPE CHAPEL, Alcester Road. 1908–9 by *J.P. Osborne*. built for the Swedenborgians. Perp. Brick with stone dressings. The end bays rise above the eaves.

Birmingham, Moseley Hall.
Engraving by W. Radclyffe after J.P. Neale, 1823

MAJOR HOUSES AND PARKS

MOSELEY HALL is now entered from Alcester Road, s of the village (*see* Perambulation 2, p. 328). Neo-Georgian LODGE of 1933 by *Ewen Harper, Bro. & Co.* Near it a late C18 DOVECOTE, brick, octagonal, with a blank round-headed arch to each side. Just N, a HAYLOFT, brick, also late C18.

The HOUSE is by *John Standbridge*, 1792–6, for John Taylor II of the banking family (Taylors and Lloyds). Severe, handsome Neoclassical in the Wyatt manner. Limestone ashlar. The plain five-bay central block incorporates the shell of a house burnt in the Priestley Riots of 1791, also designed for Taylor, and probably by *Standbridge*.* Projecting pedimented end wings with Ionic pilasters and rusticated ground floors. Wyatt windows with Ionic columns and segmental tympana below, repeated above with semicircular tympana. The apparent compression of the lower windows gives a subtle feeling of mass. Massive three-bay Doric portico of 1838–9 by *Charles Edge*, with paired columns and triglyphs placed punctiliously over them. The garden (N) front has a full-height central bow, and wings similar to those on the s. Long, thin E office wing. The entrance hall has Corinthian pilasters and garlands in the frieze. To its r., the staircase, with iron balusters alternately simple and with moulded leaves. Some surviving cornices, and fireplaces in the first-floor bedrooms.

Richard Cadbury leased the hall, then bought it for a children's home in 1891–2. A geriatric hospital since 1970.

---

*Standbridge certainly designed the earlier house's wings, with small Neoclassical pavilions, which were added in 1790.

Institutional use has not been kind. Early C20 full-height part-glazed extension on the W. By *Ewen Harper, Bro. & Co.* the octagonal bathroom tower on the N front, 1927–8, and top floor with mansard roof on the service wing, 1934. Many recent blocks close to the house.

The PARK originally stretched N and W past the village as far as Cannon Hill. John Taylor II employed *Humphry Repton*, whose Red Book is dated 1792. The fine stand of trees N of the house is probably part of his work. It now lines Salisbury Road, cut from 1891, with Chantry Road. Between them hides the private MOSELEY PARK, centred on the pool planned by Repton, though apparently not made until after 1840. In the N bank an ICE HOUSE, probably of 1792–6 by *Standbridge*.

CANNON HILL PARK, ½ m. NW. Opened in 1873; given by Louisa Anne Ryland, who employed *John Gibson* to lay it out. Original LODGE to Edgbaston Road, N. To the SW, lawns with paths and two Corinthian capitals of 1850, from *Charles Edge*'s completion of the Town Hall, removed in the alterations of 1891 (*see* p. 125). The BOER WAR MEMORIAL is by *Albert Toft*, 1906. A disquieting design: a big female figure representing Peace, standing over soldiers firing a gun. Tapering pedestal with corner volutes on which stood eagles, now lost. Beyond, a BOATING LAKE. The main drive continues S. To the E, a late C19 BANDSTAND. Beyond, the SONS OF REST clubhouse, by *W.J. Davis*, 1936–7. An odd conceit, rectangular but with square bays in the middle of the sides, and set diagonally at the corners, for the best views. On the W, the GOLDEN LION. A C16 timber-framed inn, originally on the S side of High Street, Deritend. Re-erected here in 1911, supervised by the Parks Superintendent *W.H. Morter*. Three gables with square panels and quadrant braces. The ground floor re-creates C18 bays inserted in the original building. Much behind is of 1911. Further W, the large SOUTH POOL, an early addition. At its S end a brick BRIDGE dated 1875, by *R. Morrison Marnock*. Gothic, with arcading in the parapets.

Between the pools, the MIDLANDS ARTS CENTRE. Original buildings by *Jackson & Edmonds*, 1962–4. Their Hexagon Theatre survives, with monopitch roofs going round like the blades of a propeller; also a maroon brick block at the S. Recast and the rest rebuilt by *Chetwoods Architects*, 2008–10, with tall blocks forming a courtyard, all clad in bright coloured squares, tiles and boarding.

CANNON HILL HOUSE (now NATIONAL INSTITUTE OF CONDUCTIVE EDUCATION), Russell Road, E of Cannon Hill Park. A grand Late Georgian house. Five-bay N front, the details puzzling. Three symmetrical r. bays probably of shortly after 1830, when the Rylands acquired the land. Greek Doric porch with paired columns, smooth inside fluted; smooth rustication; windows in shallow segment-headed panels, and framing pilasters and cornice. The narrower l. bays look an early addition. Three-bay W front, particularly good, with separately framed lower and upper windows, the latter with delicate architraves.

The staircase, with a good wrought-iron handrail, rises out of the hall. The main room has reeded architraves and a marble fireplace.

PUBLIC BUILDINGS

KING DAVID SCHOOL, Alcester Road. 1964–5 by *Holland W. Hobbiss & Partners*. Simple brick, of T-plan (long classroom range, hall behind), but dignified with a heavy brick portico with square piers *in antis*. Big half-round staircase projection, l. s extension, 1973. An extra classroom of 2009 by *Rush Davis* is boldly coloured and cantilevered from the façade. Behind, classroom of 2001 by *Harry Butterworth* (*Hawkins McGowan*), convertible to a small SYNAGOGUE.

MOSELEY SCHOOL, Wake Green Road. *See* Sparkhill, p. 341.

QUEENSBRIDGE SCHOOL, Queensbridge Road. 1951–5 by *Martin & Martin & W.H. Ward*. Buff brick. L-shaped. The entrance is a symmetrical seven-bay projecting block with a recessed portico *in antis*.

UFFCULME SCHOOL, Queensbridge Road. Built as an open-air school in 1911, by *Cossins, Peacock & Bewlay*. Much altered and extended, but the administration block and pyramid-roofed classroom pavilions stepping E survive.

PERAMBULATIONS

1. Moseley village

The centre is a triangular green on ALCESTER ROAD, enclosed by ST MARY'S ROW which climbs SE towards the church. From the N end, the FIGHTING COCKS, by *Newton & Cheatle*, 1898–1900. A superior pub from a firm notable for high-quality Free Style commercial buildings. Refined and austere Free Jacobean, in stone panels, articulated by thin raised strips, and handmade brick. Alan Crawford and Robert Thorne point out that the superb corner tower owes something to Charles Rennie Mackintosh, particularly his Glasgow Herald Building of 1893–5. The public bar retains its bar back, the usual elements but freshly treated: Ionic piers with reversed volutes, and segmental arches. Sea-green *Craven Dunnill* tiling. Going s, tall gabled shops by *J.P. Sharp & Co.*, 1887. The former BARCLAYS BANK, by *Peacock & Bewlay*, 1928, has an Ionic portico *in antis*. The BULL'S HEAD was rebuilt in 1886 by *Sam Owen*. Queen Anne, not routine: see the doorway with two pediments and the little row of gable windows. The castellated top to the stable is an alteration. Then simple Georgian houses stepping up the hill.

On the s side a row of shops with prominent dormers by *William Hale*, 1881, and former shops and garage by *Marcus O. Type*, 1906–7. Classical-cum-Jacobean, with a whiff of Lutyens. A dentil cornice plays hide-and-seek behind shallow oriel bays, and a nearly semicircular pediment addresses the corner.

Opposite, SW, a brick-and-render chemist's shop with oriel, by *Hipkiss & Stephens*, 1901–2.

The W side of Alcester Road was the Hall grounds, developed after 1891. N from Salisbury Road up ALCESTER ROAD, shops by *Oliver Floyd & Salt*, 1899–1902. No. 93A, with half-timbered upper floor and little gable and oriel, is by *George E. Pepper*, 1911. It fronted mews owned by F.J. Taylor, veterinary surgeon, of No. 93, a good restrained job with big grid windows by *Essex, Nicol & Goodman*, 1899. On the E side, SAINSBURYS occupies a Gothic house of *c.* 1870; extended l., and r. (*Bailey & McConnal*, 1907). The former LLOYDS BANK (No. 140) is by *J.A. Chatwin*, 1892, eclectic domestic classical, with swan's-neck pediments, brick strips in the gable, and ground-floor windows with pilasters with little figures carved in the capitals. Up WOODBRIDGE ROAD here, some small Early Victorian houses, S, opposite the former TRAFALGAR HOTEL (No. 142 Trafalgar Road) of *c.* 1870, with polychromatic brickwork. Ground floor and square bays above of 1894 by *James & Lister Lea*.

Back and across Alcester Road is the Presbyterian church (p. 322) and CHANTRY ROAD, with Moseley Park (p. 324) behind the S side. On the NW corner, an eclectic design – half-timbered, Queen Anne brickwork to the chimney – by *Ewen Harper*, 1894–5. The first houses on both sides are by *Essex, Nicol & Goodman*, 1892–6, developed partly by *Oliver Essex* himself and partly by their builder *John Parker*: heavy semi-detached pairs, still looking mid-Victorian despite timber gables and Queen Anne porch detail. The last ones, Nos. 46–52, S side, are simpler, a gables-over-canted-bays design with render and tile-hanging. Beyond are the grandest houses in Moseley. They start with more *Essex, Nicol & Goodman*. No. 38 (rendered) and No. 40 (timbered) are an eclectic mirror pair of 1899–1900. No. 36, 1894, is grander. Shaped gables above Queen Anne windows. No. 34, PENLEE, by *Daniel Arkell*, 1893–4, slightly overdone: panels with cusped braces, plasterwork with mermaids in the gable, old-fashioned porch. No. 32, BOSCOBEL, by *Arthur Harrison*, 1891, is one of the best, eclectic but controlled. Oriel above a square bay, r., little projection between doorway and projecting gable, coved cornice, against areas of plain brickwork. Timber gable with another little oriel. Rear observatory tower with ogee top. No. 30, BRACKLEY DENE, by *Alfred Reading*, 1891–2, a big Norman Shaw-style house with much half-timbering. Central gable jettied twice, a little tile-hanging in the gable to its l. No. 26 by *G.R. Faulkner*, 1892–3, the same style but loosely handled. No. 22 by *Ewen Harper*, 1891–2, still has a stone bay and tracery lights above the door, but is severely and simply composed. Nice detail: sunburst in the timbered gable, and the dormer to its r. Billiard room added by Harper in 1894 above the stableyard, with big mullion-and-transom window and ogee cupola. No. 20 is by *Owen & Ward*, 1892. Conventional jettied gable over a canted bay, r. On the l., a gable turns into a hipped dormer, all jettied over a little oriel. Extension l. by *Wood & Kendrick*, 1896. No. 18, less sophisticated, by *D. Henry Ward*, 1892.

Returning on the N, No. 5, with odd tile-hung gable and castellated porch, is by *J.A. Grew & Edwards*, 1906. The rest are big late C19 houses, mainly pairs, nearly all with some half-timbering. Nos. 7–9 by *J.P. Sharp & Co.*, 1895, asymmetrical; No. 11 also *Sharp*, 1894; Nos. 11A–19, probably *J.J. Raggett*, 1892; Nos. 21 and 23, a detached pair by *Sharp*, 1893–4. No. 25A, COURT HEY, charmingly undisciplined – cusped half-timbering, tile-hanging, oriel, balustraded porch – is *De Lacy Aherne*, 1896. No. 27 is *J.P. Osborne*, 1892. His trademark minimal pediment above the lower window of the square bay. No. 29 is probably *Riley & Smith*, 1894, as is No. 31, slightly smaller, 1897–8. Nos. 33–35, *Sharp*, 1896–7, overdone. No. 37, with lots of tile-hanging, is *Essex, Nicol & Goodman*, 1897–8. Nos. 39–43 by *Owen & Ward*, 1898, with tile-hung gables.

Back on Alcester Road and N, on the W side pairs of 1890–1 by *Thomas Wilkinson*. On the E, the plain mid-C19 PRINCE OF WALES pub. The smoke room, S side, retains its dado, fixed seating and fireplace of *c.* 1900. Nos. 104–106, Early Victorian, with big doorcases in *Bateman & Drury* manner. FIVELANDS HOUSE (No. 98) is a plain hipped-roofed classical villa of *c.* 1850.

PARK HILL runs WNW here. Nos. 11–13 by *Oliver Essex*, 1887, slightly more controlled than his Wake Green Road houses (p. 329). Nos. 14 and 24 (N side) have arched window

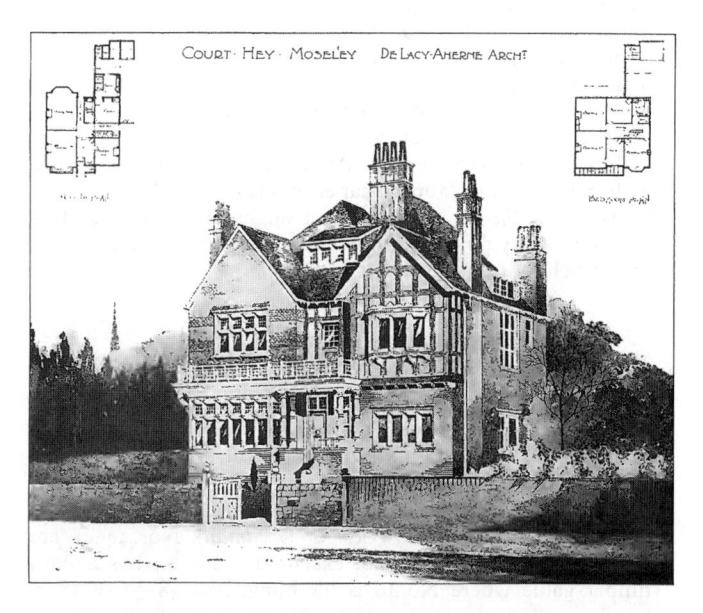

Birmingham, Moseley, Chantry Road, Court Hey.
Drawing and plan by James Akerman, 1898

lights typical of the 1860s. Nos. 28 onwards perhaps c. 1880, with heavy bays. Then St Anne's church (p. 322). Beyond Augusta Road, on the s side, No. 31, monster half-timbering by *J. Brewin Holmes*, 1897, and No. 33 by *T. W. F. Newton*, 1890, modest brick, timber and tile. Then a group by *Cossins, Peacock & Bewlay*, 1898-9, at their simplest and best: No. 35, brick and render with big mullion-and-transom staircase window; No. 37 all brick, No. 39 all render in the Voysey way, Nos. 43-45 brick again. Opposite, Nos. 80 and 86 by *J. P. Sharp*, 1885, in a loud version of J. H. Chamberlain's manner, and a Domestic Revival group by *T. W. F. Newton*, 1887-8 at Nos. 96-102.

2. South, along Alcester Road

From the main cross-roads, on the w side of Alcester Road the POST OFFICE, Neo-Georgian of 1913-15 by *Edward Cropper*. The delightful No. 155 is by *C. E. Bateman*, 1903-4. Brick and render. Steep little gable, the date in a plasterwork wreath. Five-sided bay below. No. 169 is a former social club of 1898 by *J. Brewin Holmes*, half-timbered. No. 171 by *Edward Holmes*, 1899-1900, with a timbered gable. The VILLAGE INN is the former MOSELEY CLUB, by *Owen & Ward*, 1894, the r. end added in 1897. Queen Anne-cum-Jacobean: brick with sandstone dressings, canted and square bays, tile-hung gables, entrance with cornice swept up to a pediment and French Gothic columns, looking out of place. The TELEPHONE EXCHANGE, dated 1960, is typical *Ministry of Public Building & Works* Modernism. Opposite, E, DOWELL'S CLOSE, an informal grouping of gabled blocks, brown brick relieved with purple, by *Anthony Chatwin*, 1966. On one wall, two ogee doorcase heads from the former almshouses of 1831 in Warner Street, Bordesley, with the Angel of the Annunciation and the Virgin Mary in relief. After the Moseley Hall entrance with dovecote and Hope Chapel (pp. 323, 322), Nos. 195-197 by *De Lacy Aherne*, 1898-9, like a single house, but the division marked by render and tile-hanging above. Opposite, King David School (p. 325).

3. Salisbury Road

Salisbury Road runs W from the green. A scatter of worthwhile houses. No. 16, N side, is by *George E. Pepper*, 1905, with an entrance tower ending in an octagonal turret with deep eaves on iron brackets. Opposite, Nos. 19-21, a pretty pair by *Owen Parsons*, 1901. Further down on the N side, Nos. 44-52 are all *John Goodman (Essex, Nicol & Goodman)*. Nos. 44-46 are a mirror pair of 1899-1900, except that No. 44 has a half-timber gable where No. 46 is tile-hung. Nos. 48-50 of 1897, heavier and more conservative. No. 52 of 1896, *Goodman*'s own house, is larger, with a gentler use of materials (the l. part later). No. 54 by *R.V. Gough*, 1897–8, old-fashioned, with an odd horseshoe porch. No. 56 is grand Old English by *Owen Parsons*, 1896. No. 58 of 1898, *Edward Holmes* following the fashion, with tile-hanging and jettied timber gable. No. 60 is early *De Lacy Aherne*, 1897–8, all close studding. No. 62 is by *Pepper*, 1911, Arts and Crafts timberwork (note the pegging) but still with a bit of tile-hanging. No. 64 is a rare survivor of *James & Lister Lea*'s domestic work, 1897–8, the l. wing with its tile-hanging and inset timber gable balanced by a domed octagonal tower, r. Opposite, No. 59 is by *Crouch & Butler*, 1897–8. A good example of their Arts and Crafts approach, nostalgic and associative rather than purist. A castellated porch-tower stands between a simple brick wing, l., and louder timber wing r., canted all up to the hipped roof.

AMESBURY ROAD runs S here. On the W side No. 2 by *Alfred Reading*, 1897. A nice pattern of brick and tile-hanging. No. 4 is by *Owen Parsons*, 1909. Large and complex, in beautiful red brick with some blue diapering. Two big brick gables, the l. one doubled with another set back to its r. This has half-timbering, like the porch. Tall, massive chimneys balance long rows of windows, l., above the porch, and below the timber gable. No. 6 is by *W. H. Bidlake*, dated 1908 in beautiful lettering on the door lintel, with the initials of the owner, the builder *John Bowen*. The materials very restrained, just narrow pink-grey bricks and grey stone dressings. A relaxed yet complex design, with four gables, all different: a big one at the r., with a powerful chimney; a full-height porch; a small gable gently emphasized by cutting back the wall-plane either side; and the l. one with a big staircase window. It looks simple but is of great mastery.

4. Wake Green Road and Oxford Road

E from St Mary's church, the road twists l. and r., then narrows. CHURCH ROAD runs N with some Victorian villas and a nice Early Victorian brick classical group, Nos. 104–110, W side, and facing to the N, No. 47 Woodbridge Road. Back to WAKE GREEN ROAD and E, on the S side, LENCH'S CLOSE ALMS-HOUSES by *Graham Winteringham (S.T. Walker & Partners)*, 1983. Attractively grouped and detailed. A long line on the E, stepped outwards twice. Deep pitched roofs run down into catslides over porches; tall leaded semi-dormers. No. 8, dated 1885, is rather obvious Queen Anne by *D. Henry Ward*. Awkward extension, 1990. On the N side No. 17, WINTERSLOE, by *Essex & Nicol*, 1891, large, with half-timber gables. The enormous Nos. 10–12 opposite are also *Essex & Nicol*, 1889, a salmagundi of Old English black-and-white gables, French pyramid roofs and Flemish Gothic terracotta porch heads. The r. turret added by *Osborn, Pemberton & White*, 1909, to house dressing rooms. No. 18 is smooth Old English by *De Lacy Aherne*, 1902–3, as was No. 20, before its Spanish makeover.

ANDERTON PARK ROAD runs N here into an area of good housing of *c.*1890–1914, spoilt by alterations. The finest is No. 103, by *Crouch & Butler*, 1903, with part-rendered gabled wing and Tudor and Baroque hints to the detail.

Back on Wake Green Road, going E, on the N side No. 29, simple, rendered, by *E. Stanley Mitton*, 1904–5. No. 31 is unmistakably *George E. Pepper*, 1909. A pair of half-timber gables perch on a shallow ground-floor bay. To their r. an entrance tower with a gable which has had a nasty accident with a semi-octagonal turret. No. 33 by *Hipkiss & Stephens*, 1903–4, is brick-and-render Domestic Revival in the Shaw–George tradition, but with the simplicity of *c.*1900. S again, Nos. 24–26 by *J. Brewin Holmes*, 1903–4, about his best. A favourite composition of large half-timber gables counterpointed by a smaller central projecting one, the central gable tiled. WAVERLEY COURT is another *Essex & Nicol* potpourri, 1891. A big shaped gable balances the corner feature, l. This starts simply with a low pyramid roof, but a taller pyramid roof grows out of it at forty-five degrees. Porch with a three-centred arch and attached Corinthian columns. Beyond Grove Avenue, No. 30 by *Alfred Reading*, 1893. Old English, carefully balanced with a large l. gable linked to a smaller projecting one for the porch. The large r. gable is distinguished by two timbered storeys. Former stables, l., projecting slightly via an angled oriel. Nos. 32–34, mutilated Queen Anne by *Oliver Essex*, 1889. No. 36, REVESBY, also *Essex*, 1889, an earlier and slightly gentler version of Waverley Court. Beyond Mayfield Road, Nos. 45–47, also *Holmes*, 1884, and Nos. 49–51, designed and built by *Thomas Wilkinson*, 1882, 'mixed Italian' with full-height semicircular bays. On the S, No. 38, a very big Old English house by *Osborn & Reading*, 1883, with an ogee-roofed lantern to the billiard room above the stables. A glance into COTTON LANE for No. 86 by *Pepper*, 1904. The r. gable is almost conventional, but to the l. is a mock-timber turret with candlesnuffer roof. To its l. on the corner with Wake Green Road, No. 40, restrained Tudor by *Owen Parsons*, 1911. Nos. 42–46, typical *De Lacy Aherne*, 1911, like overdone miniature Voysey. The central house has a huge lunette and an entrance tower. No. 50 is of course *Pepper*, 1907, with a gabled wing hinting at a tower, a complicated dormer and a wooden segment-headed porch.

Now back W and S down GROVE AVENUE, into townscape defined by tall gabled semi-detached houses, and particularly the oddities of *Stephen Holliday*. He liked conventional Old English gables jettied over canted bays, but offset from the centre line of the gables, an unsettling effect. His Nos. 2–4 are old-fashioned, brick with Gothic arches. Nos. 6–8, also 1894, introduce his Old English. Nos. 10–12 of 1895, again *Holliday*, with two-storey jetties above single-storey bays. Nos. 9–11, E side, are by *Alfred Reading*, 1897–8, but Nos. 13–15 are unmistakably *Holliday*, 1898–9. Here both gables and bays have all-over timbering. No. 17, *De Lacy Aherne*, and No. 14 opposite, *E. H. Wigley*, both 1898, brick and render. Nos. 16–18 of

1898 introduce the best architects working here, *Ewen & J.A. Harper*. Plain brickwork, a little tile-hanging in the gables, and sash windows; Queen Anne moving towards Arts and Crafts.

Then the cross-roads with OXFORD ROAD. To the E, on the S side, two more houses by the *Harpers*, in the same simple manner: No. 56 of 1904 with an angled porch facing the corner; No. 58 of 1897, *J.A. Harper*'s own house, the earlier date shown by much tile-hanging. Opposite, the Harpers' Nos. 63–65 of 1897, still with stone canted bays, and Nos. 67–69 of 1899, with jettied gables. On the SE corner with Cotton Lane, No. 50 by *J. Brewin Holmes*, 1908–9, a complicated mass of gables and hips. Oxford Road beyond here was developed from *c.* 1905, with much by *De Lacy Aherne*. At Nos. 110–112, of 1906–7, his self-conscious charm produces something memorable. Detached, but linked at the rear by their garages, with balanced asymmetrical gables, white-painted brickwork with black window frames, polygonal bays, side gables with chimneys perching on them, and delightful paired iron arches to the driveways. Nos. 114–116 beyond are by *Arthur Harrison*, 1906–7. Brick; open porches flush with the bay windows.

Back to Grove Avenue and S, the E side starts with No. 31, by *G.R. Faulkner*, 1911–12, its half-timbering perched above a rendered ground floor with Voysey-style sloping buttresses. No. 33 by *Gerald McMichael*, 1920–1, is good Neo-Georgian, or more accurately Carolean and Baroque, with swan's-neck doorcase. Then three pairs by *J.R. Nichols* (Nos. 35–45): centre one with Dutch gables, 1896, flanking ones of 1899–1900. Finally Nos. 51–53, 1896, *Faulkner*. Now back N down the W side. Nos. 58–60 are by *Ewen & J.A. Harper*, 1899, their usual brick and tile-hanging, here with rendered gables. Nos. 50–52 are *Faulkner*, 1898; Nos. 46–48 by *Proud & Faulkner*, 1891, still mid-Victorian, with stone bays and cusped lights; No. 44 by *J.F. Hartland*, 1893, also old-fashioned, with Gothic windows. No. 42 by *Osborn & Reading*, 1890, sparely handled. Nos. 34 and 32 by *Lewis W. Goold*, 1893–4 and 1890, try to be up-to-date with bits of timber, tile-hanging and coved cornices.

Now W down OXFORD ROAD. On the S side surveyors' designs: Nos. 46 and 50 by *R.G.W. Lee*, 1889–90; No. 48 by *John Meggatt*, 1890. Opposite, No. 51 by *Faulkner*, 1896–7, overdoes the picturesque. On the E corner of School Road, the GABLES HOTEL, by *Edward Holmes*, 1888–9 under stuck-on timbering. Going W again, No. 35, N side, by *J.P. Sharp & Co.*, 1883, with unequal gables. Nos. 31–33 are by *Holmes*, 1883–4, with lots of 'Go', as the Victorians called it. Ends with canted bays cutting back to square bays in the gables, small towers inside the gables, very decorative timber porches. No. 29 is by *Sharp & Co.*, 1883, altered. Beyond, a stretch with the road's earliest houses, nearly all by the *Sharp* firm, mostly 1875–82. Minimal Queen Anne brickwork in the gables on the N side; first timber gables, then brick sub-Gothic on the S. The exceptions are Nos. 17–19 of 1894, where the little pediments between the storeys on the gables give the architect away as *J.P.*

Osborne. Beyond, s, No. 2, classical of *c.* 1870, and the former Baptist church (p. 322), lead back to St Mary's Row.

5. *St Agnes*

The start is in COLMORE CRESCENT, at the w entrance to St Agnes's church (p. 321). Opposite, the VICARAGE, by *C.E. Bateman*, 1922–3, Arts and Crafts Neo-Georgian. Rendered, with a big hipped roof and prominent chimneys; the entrance side comfortably asymmetrical, so the door is near the road. Going round NE, ASHLEY LODGE, very large Tudor Revival by *Owen Parsons*, 1916 (an unusual date). N into ST AGNES ROAD, the w side starts with Nos. 25–27 by *W.A. Harvey*, 1904, the best pair here, with projecting steeply gabled ends, inset porches and eyebrow dormers. Then two pairs by *J. Brewin Holmes*, Nos. 21–23 of 1905 with plain gables and half-timbering between; Nos. 17–19 of 1904, with this reversed. No. 15 is an attempt at Bidlake's manner by *Anthony Rowse*, dated 1904: good, but slightly overdone. No. 13 is by *De Lacy Aherne*, 1900, early and unusually good. Brick with render above, and contrasting big canted bay and square one. No. 11, *Christopher Silk*, quantity surveyor, 1903, for himself, with an expanded Venetian window to the staircase. No. 9, WHITECROFT, is by *Aherne*, 1905, instantly recognizable. Boldly diapered tympana, long buttresses. No. 7, by *Arthur Harrison*, 1903, with a lot of 'features': corner oriel, angled porch, sprocketed gable with picturesque little window. No. 5, HILVER, the largest house in the road, was built in 1898–1900 by *Harry Lucas*, son of Joseph Lucas, of the industrial family. He probably designed it himself, which explains its slightly uncertain handling, with both tile-hung and terracotta gables, a domed corner oriel and perhaps too many windows. Returning on the E side, No. 8 is horribly cut-down Jacobean of 1896. *Owen & Ward* were involved, but the basic design may be the owner's: *G.W. Holt*, tube manufacturer. MAPLEDENE, by *Marcus O. Type*, dated 1913, is an uneasy mix of Free Style and Neo-Georgian. Much extended. No. 18, HAZELMERE, is by *H.H. Reynolds*, 1903, brick and tile-hanging. Facing the church, three sharply gabled pairs by *Frederick Urry*, 1903, and two equally old-fashioned Queen Anne ones designed by their builder, *R. Hughes*, 1904. No. 44 is hammed-up Arts and Crafts from *Pepper*, 1906. The composition is from Bidlake's No. 22 Ladywood Road, Four Oaks (p. 458), but this condensed version has stone bands, a five-sided bay, a bit of half-timbering, a set-back porch roof, and a tiny window with sloping jambs and heavy keystone. Nos. 46–48 of *c.* 1905–6 have much terracotta. No. 50 is by *Gerald McMichael* 1909, in the early Neo-Georgian manner of Ernest Newton. Projecting ends with hipped roofs. Darker brickwork quoins and jambs. Tudor chimneys, but classical doorcase and panel with sundial. Then two pairs with central gables by *G.F. Titley*, 1907, Nos. 50–52 (rendered above) and

Nos. 54–56. No. 60, a neat design by *James Moffat & Sons*, builders. Finally Nos. 62–68 by *Aherne*, 1907.

Back along the s side towards the church, No. 47 is uninspired Old English by *Frank Davis*, 1904. Nos. 41–43 by *Essex & Nicol*, 1890, have big two-storey canted bays and a line of four fancily timbered gables. No. 39, more modest, by *J.P. Sharp & Co.*, 1893–4; No. 37 by *T.W. Baker*, 1899–1900. This line of houses becomes DYOTT ROAD along the s side of the church. The first two here are by *Aherne*: No. 41 of 1900, with an enormous Venetian window upstairs; No. 39 of 1902. No. 37 is by *J.G. Dunn*, 1905, much extended. On the corner of Billesley Lane, the CHURCH HALL, by *E.F. Reynolds*, 1925–6. Severely plain, with deep half-hipped roof and simplified Romanesque doorway. Behind, a simple house of 1954, very early *John Madin*.

Finally OXFORD ROAD, running w from the church. On the s side No. 130 by *Owen Parsons*, 1907–8. Then No. 128C, for F.W. Lanchester, the motor engineer. The first design of 1921 was by *Lanchester, Rickards & Lucas* (H.V. Lanchester was F.W. Lanchester's brother), and the garage, l. (No. 128D). The revision of 1923 was by *Marcus O. Type*. F.W. Lanchester himself was certainly involved in the design. Modest and plain, with red-purple brick laid in Flemish stretcher bond. The house gable returns at the eaves (cf. Mapledene, above).

6. Queensbridge Road and Highbury

An extension from Perambulation 2, w along QUEENSBRIDGE ROAD. On the N side Queensbridge School, on the s, Uffculme School (p. 325). Then UFFCULME, built for Richard Cadbury when he moved from Moseley Hall. By *William Jenkins*, best known for pubs (an odd choice for a Quaker); dated 1890. Enormous, overblown Jacobean with big shaped gables, a full-height canted bay, and a *porte cochère* on partly banded Ionic columns. Small LODGE, E; STABLE COURT to the W and another, bigger LODGE.

HIGHBURY, in Yew Tree Road, running w, is the 'mansion' designed for Joseph Chamberlain by *J.H. Chamberlain*, 1878–80. He spared no effort (or expense) to produce a home worthy of the great man who was his friend, and the result is a *tour de force* of rich, hard Gothic. The contractors were *Barnsleys*. First impressions from the road are confusing: brick walls and an array of gables with all kinds of exposed timber trusses: double collar with upper braces, collar and king-strut, and more. True to Chamberlain's Ruskinian beliefs, the elevations are a truthful expression of the plan, and the plan reflects its use. This is like a capital 'J' with a very big top stroke, containing the main interiors; the stem is dining room and kitchen, the tail the service wing. Red brick with pointed arches everywhere and stone floral decoration. The show front is s, to the gardens: 'one of Chamberlain's favourite compositional strategies, of three dissimilar gables...which appeared later at the School of Art' (Joe Holyoak). The l. gable has a two-storey square bay; the central one is hipped, with a two-storey canted bay; the r. one is in a projecting wing (the extra storey here is of 1888). The entrance front, w, has a two-light window with a tympanum full of floral decoration. To the r. a projecting wing with a powerful chimney running up the gable. Here are hints of the coming Queen Anne manner: floral squares like 'pies', and fluting.

A panelled lobby leads to the spectacular full-height HALL. It has a gallery running all round, and a remarkable roof with hammerbeams and a clerestory, like nave and aisles of a church suspended in air. The staircase rises behind arcading at the E end, with Gothic arches in the wrought-iron handrail. There is hardly an undecorated surface to be seen. The maximum number of media are used to produce interiors of great heaviness and richness. The piers have matchboarding and pink granite above; the walls between have marquetry, tiling and timber display shelving. Complex mouldings everywhere. Plaster coving with typical Chamberlain naturalistic flower decoration. The drawing room (SE) has a stone arcade dividing one end, and a Jacobean pattern ceiling with marquetry panels. Joseph Chamberlain's LIBRARY (SW) is unaltered: full-height bookcases with canted top architraves like buttress set-offs, and a matching panelled overmantel. Doorcase lintel with a line of gablets. The DINING ROOM (SE) has a heavy beamed ceiling, again with marquetry, and rich fireplace. The STAIRCASE continues behind a three-bay first-floor arcade, spatially intriguing. The doorways along the gallery have architraves with canted tops like the library furniture, and flanking gabled shelving. – Entrance LODGE by *Martin & Chamberlain* on the corner of Moor Green Lane.

Highbury quickly appeared old-fashioned: the Liberal cartoonist 'FCG' drew it as a medieval mansion inhabited by 'Sir Joseph de Birmingham'. Yet its Ruskinism and its concern for materials and craftsmanship prefigure the Arts and Crafts, and it has exceptional architectural integrity.

To the E, seen first from Queensbridge Road, the former HOME FOR AGED WOMEN (now part of Uffculme School), 1937–9 by the *Birmingham City Engineer and Surveyor*. Brick with stone dressings. The main front, S, has a recessed loggia. Suggestions of both Östberg and Art Deco, but the handling is uncertain.

The GARDENS were laid out by *Edward Milner* (plan dated 1879). The ground falls to the S, and a *Chamberlain* VIEWING PLATFORM with cusped balustrade (restored 2012) is E of the lawn. The rest now forms part of HIGHBURY PARK, best accessed from Moor Green Lane, W. Mature trees were retained in clumps, and the original circular path is traceable. To the SW, a DUTCH GARDEN, originally planted entirely with bulbs, with geometric beds and a surrounding holly hedge.

On the N side of Yew Tree Road opposite Highbury, the former BRITANNIC ASSURANCE headquarters by *T.M.*

Ashford, 1960–3, individual as ever. A long curving range, each bay canted forward to a point. Converted to flats, with an added storey, and curving ranges to the E enclosing a courtyard, 1999–2000. Going N along Moor Green Lane, the surviving LODGE of Moor Green House, by *Arthur Edwards*, 1907; the Voysey moment. Then BOUNDARY DRIVE, with an accomplished Georgian Revival terrace by *Malcolm Payne Design Group*, 2000.

Further N at the junction with Russell Road, PITMASTON, the former Ideal Benefit Society headquarters. By *Holland W. Hobbiss*, 1930–1, his finest surviving commercial building. It replaced the C19 residence of Sir John Holder, so the design re-creates a country house: long two-storey range, raised three-storey centre, projecting wings. The centre is a complex Neo-Regency composition with Greek Doric porch and a shallow bow rising into the roof. Full-height sashes with balconies, a motif repeated more emphatically in the wings. Inset balustraded corner towers and *Hobbiss*'s favourite off-centre chimney complete the ensemble. To the E, the former MANAGER'S HOUSE, also *Hobbiss*, 1931, with a shell-hood doorcase. It faces RUSSELL ROAD, which runs N towards Cannon Hill Park. In GOODBY ROAD, running E, PITMASTON COURT, London-scale Neo-Georgian flats by *J. Stanley Beard & Bennett*, 1935–6. Further down Russell Road on the w, No. 60, GREYSTOKE, is by *Buckland & Haywood-Farmer*, 1906, a cousin of the Buckland houses in Yateley Road, Edgbaston (p. 393). The big half-timbered No. 54 was *J.P. Sharp*'s own house, 1900. Much extended and linked to No. 52, Tudor Revival by *Owen Parsons*, 1902–3.

SPARKBROOK

C19 terraced housing. One surviving C18 house of historical importance.

ST AGATHA, Stratford Road. The masterpiece of *W.H. Bidlake*, built in 1899–1901. It is in the free late Gothic Revival, deriving from C14–C15 medieval work, developed by Bodley and G.G. Scott Junior, and used with great freedom and invention, especially inside. Bidlake won a competition assessed by Sir Arthur Blomfield, beating John Douglas, Mervyn Macartney and Temple Moore. The church is built of special long and thin Staffordshire bricks. On the exterior these are reds with some blue burn, with dressings of Bath stone. The ritual W tower, 120 ft (37 metres) tall, dominates its surroundings. It starts with a projecting three-sided baptistery (a J.A. Chatwin habit). Then a three-light window, a blank stage with a big niche, and the belfry, its tall windows deeply set, with massive stone louvres. All is held together by octagonal buttresses, set back near the top, where they gain mullions and stone bands. Finally a pierced parapet, corner pinnacles resembling Sedding's at Holy Trinity, Chelsea, and a slender leaded 'spike'. Flanking porches, gabled N–S, hint at a cross-range running through the tower. Relief TYMPANA over the entrances: St Peter appearing to St Agatha in prison, l., St Agatha with her persecutor Quintilianus, r. The rest of the exterior is articulated by triangular piers, a motif used earlier by Leonard Stokes and also G. G. Scott Junior. Aisle windows straight-headed, with flowing tracery. Chancel and clerestory windows late Dec turning Perp.

The interior impresses immediately by its height and lightness. Yellow-grey brick with Hollington stone for the arches and mouldings. It is a study in angled and chamfered plane surfaces, a further development of Bidlake's St Patrick, Salter Street, Earlswood (p. 775). The immediate inspiration for both was Stokes's St Clare, Sefton Park, Liverpool (1889–90), for which Bidlake drew the interior perspective. The arcade piers are chamfered lozenges narrowing to a front face only 1½ in. (40 mm.) wide, and the side faces run back at an angle which contrasts with both the plane wall above and the differently angled recesses of the clerestory windows. The piers rise up clear to the wall-plate, where luscious flower corbels support the wooden tunnel-vault, also derived from Stokes. The arcade arches have a hollow chamfer and a big wave moulding. Their hoodmoulds curve up at the bottom, and appear to pass through the piers, like wires through a block. The angles and planes, the narrow pier fronts and this kind of detail create an interior of high nervous tension. N chapel with vestries to its E; larger S chapel divided into two at its E by an arcade. Its pier has a pensive angel corbel. This planning follows Pearson's St Alban, Highgate (p. 194). Three-bay chancel arcades, enriched by roll mouldings flanking the chamfer, to the S chapel and the N vestry passage.

The church was bombed in 1940, when the chancel was badly damaged. In 1959 a fire destroyed the nave roof and many furnishings. Repairs and reconstruction, by *Laurence Williams* of *Wood, Kendrick & Williams*, were completed in 1961, distinguishable by slightly yellower brick. The new roof is an exact replica. – PULPIT, the only survivor of *Bidlake*'s fittings. Octagonal, with the sacred monogram in tracery. The base has free-standing piers linked to the main block by little arches. – *Williams*'s forward ALTAR of 1964 is of green Westmorland stone. Tapering base, cantilevered top. – Small marble FONT on a Doric column, of 1865, brought from Christ Church, New Street (*see* p. 156). – STATUES: Virgin and Child, sanctuary, 1922; St Agatha, nave, *c.* 1930. – STATIONS OF THE CROSS. 1931. – STAINED GLASS. E window by *L. C. Evetts*, 1961, mildly Expressionist. Much clear but textured glass.

CHRIST CHURCH, Farm Road and Sampson Road. *Medland, Maberley & Medland*'s church of 1867 was demolished in 2007. Its replacement – together with the SPARKBROOK COMMUNITY HUB (health centre etc.) diagonally opposite on the old church site – is by *One Creative Environments Ltd*, 2012. The church has a big rendered monopitch roof and a bit of timber cladding; the Hub has nasty rock-faced artificial stone facing and a dominating angled canopy flying out.

EMMANUEL (former), Walford Road. 1900–1 by *W.H. Lloyd*, the nave never completed. Conventional Dec, brick with stone bands. Nice octagonal bell-turret on the N with a lead spirelet. Converted to flats 1993 by *APEC*, with Neo-Victorian w extension.

SPARKBROOK BAPTIST CHURCH, Stratford Road. *William Hale*'s church of 1878–9, Geometrical Gothic with a sw tower and spire, has gone. His severe Gothic former SUNDAY SCHOOL of 1882 remains, and the cross-gabled stair-tower which linked it to the church.

UKIM JAMIA MASJID SPARKBROOK, Sydenham Road. 2002–3 by *A 1*.

CONWAY PRIMARY SCHOOL, Conway Road. 1899–1900 by *Martin & Chamberlain* (probably *Frederick Martin*), a late school work. The usual gabled blocks, very plain. Ventilation tower with big louvred octagon, dome and tiny cupola.

MONTGOMERY PRIMARY SCHOOL (now Academy), White Road. 1878–9 by *Martin & Chamberlain*, extended 1911–13 by *H.T. Buckland* (E) and later. Two blocks facing s, the r. one single-storeyed, the l. one two storeys. Former caretaker's house recessed between. Big pointed windows with much moulded brickwork. Ventilation tower with porch and triplet Gothic windows.

LADYPOOL PRIMARY SCHOOL, Stratford Road. 1884–6 by *Martin & Chamberlain*, enlarged 1893 and 1896. One of their finest schools, built just after J.H. Chamberlain's death but in his style. Cusped lights with ogee hoodmoulds in red terracotta, timbered gables. On the corner, a chimney rises through the gable. A delightful slim tower and tall spire with corner pinnacles were lost in a 2005 tornado.

FARM, Sampson Road. Otherwise LLOYD HOUSE, built in 1758 by Sampson Lloyd II, Quaker ironmaster and co-founder of Lloyds Bank. From the s, the original entrance front, it is a tall little box: three storeys, five narrow bays, a pedimented doorcase with fluted pilasters, stone cornices above ground- and first-floor windows, parapet. Sampson Lloyd III almost doubled its size, in 1767 and probably in the 1770s. The entrance was moved to the W front. This is completely informal: a big full-height canted bay of 1767, r., a pedimented doorcase, three bays with platbands, and finally a later extension. N and E sides show a history of later C18 alterations and extensions. Out of repair in the later C20, the house was restored in 1982 and 1992–3 by *Gwyn Roberts*. Many details, including most lintels, are recent. The interior was heavily reconstructed. The ground-floor room with the canted bay has full-height panelling. Open-string staircase rising between fluted piers, three delicately turned balusters to each tread, swept-up handrail and dado. Another panelled room at the NE.

The grounds, now FARM PARK, retain mature trees, though Sampson Lloyd II's elm avenue has gone, as have the stables etc. SE of the house.

On Sampson Road diagonally opposite, No. 100, the former St Agatha's VICARAGE, by *W.H. Bidlake*, 1901. A house of his great period, contemporary with No. 22 Ladywood Road, Four Oaks (p. 458). Brick with stone dressings, restrained Tudor, with mullioned windows and rosettes and a little leaf decoration on the porch entrance. The plan is a U, with the plainest rear wing.

ARMOURER MILLS, Montgomery Street. Of *c.* 1872 for the National Small Arms and Ammunition Co. Red and blue brick, four big gables. To the l., a showroom and upholstery works for the Lanchester Motor Co., 1911 by *J.L. Ball*: a progressive architect working for a progressive manufacturer. Despite bashed-in entrances, much survives: big windows, alternating broad and slim brick piers, and a row of round-headed arches above. Another range by *Ball*, 1915–16, r., single-storeyed.

OTHER BUILDINGS. On Stratford Road, coming from the N (city) end. At No. 118 the former BLACK HORSE pub by *Sam Owen*, 1880. Timbering in the gables, steep triangular pediments to the doorways. In Kyotts Lake Road, E, were the city tramways' Central Works, developed from 1884 by *James Kincaid*. What remains is part of *F.B. Osborn*'s reconstruction for Birmingham Corporation, 1906–7: two shaped gable-ends and a plain block with a recent upper extension. Next off Stratford Road to the E, BRAITHWAITE ROAD, developed by Joseph Baxter between *c.* 1860 and 1871. Italianate villas. L-shaped corner houses, that on the N extended for a bank with smooth rustication and a grand Ionic doorcase. Then semi-detached houses on both sides. 300 yds S, LONG STREET runs W, with 1850s houses. On the corner of Ladypool Road the mangled former ANGEL HOTEL (currently Manjaros). A severely classical block with the attic breaking upwards on either side. A valuation survives of 1834 by *Joseph Bateman*, a good date for this, so perhaps he designed it. No. 200 opposite is a lively Gothic villa of *c.* 1873–4 with lots of cusped tracery. On the W side Ladypool School (p. 337) and St Agatha (p. 335). Beyond the Baptist church (p. 337), Walford Road runs E with various entertainment venues, much altered, e.g. a former BILLIARD HALL by *Albert Bye*, 1920–1.

SPARKHILL

Rural until the mid C19, with houses at the present junction of Stratford Road and Showell Green Lane, and a few cottages by the Mermaid inn at the junction of the Stratford and Warwick roads. Developed rapidly from *c.* 1870, becoming the largest settlement in Yardley Rural District. Its important architect was the underrated *Arthur Harrison*.* This account includes Springfield, to the S.

CHURCHES

ST BEDE (now SEVENTH DAY BAPTIST), Warwick Road, Greet. A tin church of 1894, unfortunately refaced 2012.

ST CHRISTOPHER, Springfield Road. 1906–7 by *Arthur Harrison*. Nave, aisles and S chapel; the chancel never built. Sutton Coldfield brick with Alton stone dressings. Free Gothic, with Perp tracery and larky details, fancy tops to the buttresses, and low dormers with little central buttresses. They look like W.D. Caröe. S porch with sculpted panel by *Benjamin Creswick*. Tall brick arcades with continuous mouldings and stone blocks instead of capitals. Collar-beam roof with intermediate trusses coming down in the middle of the dormers, another little lark. – FONT with leaf ornament, circular stem, and piers at the cardinal points. – STAINED GLASS. N aisle, by *Benjamin Warren*, 1924 and 1925. – To the NE, the SPRINGFIELD CENTRE by *Hickton Madeley*, 2007.

ST JOHN THE EVANGELIST, Stratford Road. By *Martin & Chamberlain*, 1888–95. Tower and spire 1905 by *Tom E. Dove*, a former Martin & Chamberlain assistant, who kept their basic design but altered details. An unusual church, an Evangelical preaching plan in uncompromising Gothic. Brick with Horsley Castle stone dressings and Bath stone tracery. Shallow transepts with blunt lancet windows. Deep nave roof with alternate bays pushing up into it as semi-dormers, and triangular dormers further up between them. Inside, huge pointed timber diaphragm arches rise from low clustered shafts, with leaf capitals individually carved by *Samuel Barfield*. At the crossing two of these big arches intersect diagonally. High up, above the dormers, are blank clerestories, with arcading where they meet above the crossing arches: dramatic and spatially memorable. Apsed chancel. The tower has a tall W projection (originally baptistery), angle buttresses, and belfry windows gabled up into the stone spire. A little tile-hung gallery on brackets links the tower to the roof. – PULPIT, PEWS and VICAR'S STALL by *Martin & Chamberlain*, 1888. The pulpit has naturalistic detail, especially the almost Art Nouveau leaves on the base, probably also carved by *Barfield*. – REREDOS also *Martin & Chamberlain*, 1896. – N transept ALTAR by *J.B. Surman*, 1949. – SCREEN by the *Bromsgrove Guild*, 1919–20. – STAINED GLASS. Apse windows by *Benjamin Warren*, 1915–16, Arts and Crafts work. Nave S also *Warren*, 1946–7. – The W end was partitioned off in 1987 with an enormous WALL PAINTING by *Katie Francis*. – Small CHURCH ROOM by *Arthur Harrison*, 1907, E.

---

*His INSTITUTE and PRIMITIVE METHODIST CHURCH, both of 1894, and his DISCIPLES OF CHRIST church, of 1903, have gone.

ENGLISH MARTYRS (R.C.), Evelyn Road. 1922–3 by *E. Bower Norris*. An Early Christian basilica, 'modelled on the lines of the famous church of S. Giorgio, Rome'. Apsed chancel and side chapels, ritual SW campanile. A handsome and considered design, though not with the originality of Ball or Dixon. Thin purple and brown brick. Two-light windows with arches turned in tile, and moulded stone shafts. Inside, the polished Siena marble columns and stone cushion capitals stand out from the rendered walls. Sanctuary and side chapels with marble panelling. – Rich marble ALTARS and FONT by *Norris*, also PEWS with nice fretwork panels. – MOSAICS: W, by *Gianese* of Venice; side chapels, by *Elphege Pippet*, 1946. – STAINED GLASS. Aisle windows by *Anthony J. Naylor*, 2008. – PRESBYTERY by *Norris*.

SPARKHILL METHODIST CHURCH, Warwick Road. By *Bromilow, While & Smeeton*, 1959–60 (the hall 1954). Buff brick. Sheer corner tower with a Scandinavian-influenced copper top with ball finials and a small central flèche. Inside, the church has a panelled ceiling, light carefully modulated through tall windows to focus on the altar, and a low segmental-arched arcade on the r. The access corridor to the hall has open timber frameworks below the ceiling near either end, articulating what could have been an unattractive space: an architectural lesson in a nutshell. – Original FITTINGS, the altar with projecting timber frame and decorative front. – STAINED GLASS. Above the entrance, three combined windows of *c*.1921 from the predecessor church, with deep reds and flowing small leadings.

PRIMITIVE METHODIST CHURCH (now CHRISTADELPHIAN), Springfield Road. 1904 by *A. Macer Wright*. Simple brick Gothic.

CONGREGATIONAL CHURCH (former), Stratford Road and Colgreave Avenue. 1932–3 by *W.H. Bidlake*, his only late church, elegant and original Romanesque. Dominating *Westwerk* tower. The central section, rising above square buttressed side turrets, has a very tall open arcade. Deep, concave-sided entrance niche with beautifully laid brick and tile bands. Big brick arches to the apse and transepts, more decorative arcades with stone columns and tile-turned arches. Restaurant conversion 2012. – Former SCHOOL behind.

SALVATION ARMY HALL (now LIGHTHOUSE CHAPEL), Stratford Road. 1909 by *Oswald Archer* of London. Jacobean, with little turrets.

PUBLIC BUILDINGS

LIBRARY AND COMMUNITY CENTRE, Stratford Road. 'Yardley Town Hall' is the finest municipal building of Birmingham's pre-1911 suburban local authorities. Built as offices and council chamber by *Arthur Harrison*, 1900–2. Spirited Free Jacobean. Central semicircular bay; entrances in the angles of the wings, which have big canted bays and Dutch gables. Sculpted figures by *Benjamin Creswick*. The l. end was the Surveyor's Department, the centre the Clerk's and the r. end finance. Big stone mullion-and-transom windows form a unifying grid. Symmetry is broken by a tower at the r., rising sheer to pedimented clock faces, octagonal cupola and ogee dome. A staircase with Art Nouveau wrought-iron handrail leads up to the former Council Chamber (now library) with a big double-collar-beam roof.

POLICE STATION, Stratford Road, immediately N. 1897 by *A.B. Rowe*. More conventional Jacobean, with many gables.

SPARKHILL POOL, Stratford Road, immediately S. 2017 by *Roberts Limbrick*. Perhaps the best of the city's recent pools, with a largely glazed upper storey over pilotis.

ADULT EDUCATION CENTRE (former COMMERCIAL SCHOOL), Stratford Road, on the corner of Newton Road. Bare, cubic Neo-Georgian by *H.T. Buckland*, 1929.

MOSELEY SCHOOL, Wake Green Road. Built in 1854–7 as Spring Hill Congregational College, the predecessor of Mansfield College, Oxford. By *Joseph James*; 'an astonishing performance for a man of twenty-five' (David Walker). With James's contemporary Square Congregational Church, Halifax, it is a landmark in the adoption of Gothic by Nonconformists. The original buildings form a U-shape with wings running back from a main S range. Red brick with blue-brick patterning and stone dressings. The style is late C14, with a wealth of ballflower ornament, crockets and window tracery. The through mullions of the library windows are 'late', but in every other way this is a confident expression of Pugin's manner. After the college moved to Oxford in 1886 the building became a hydropathic establishment, and from 1923 a school (alterations for this by *H.T. Buckland*, 1924). The central accent is a big crenellated tower with a stair-turret. Stilted entrance arch with corbels with three angels holding inscriptions, instead of capitals. Buttress to the r. with an open-traceried gablet and angels. Above, a two-storey stepped-in canted bay. To the l., full-height four-light windows mark the former library. To the r., the ground floor has flat-headed windows of the former refectory. The SW corner was the principal's house. Two-storey square bay windows, the S with a pent roof and a prow, the W with a ground-floor pent roof out of which the upper floor grows. Between them an octagonal entrance turret. The W wing has an equally sculptural two-storey entrance, and corbelled-out chimney flues like paired buttresses set at forty-five degrees. Both wings originally ended in spires.

Inside, the ENTRANCE HALL has recessed doorways with cusped timber framing set in the arches. Big ogee stone niche, now a war memorial. Beamed ceiling. High windows with original heraldic glass by *Chance Bros*. The former LIBRARY has an organ gallery on iron brackets. Hammerbeam roof. The cat's cradle of steel braces is by *Birmingham City Architect's Department*, 1994. The E–W corridor has double-chamfered cross-arches dying into square piers. In the PRINCIPAL'S HOUSE a staircase with pyramid finials, fireplaces with quatrefoil panels, and good foliage cornices. The main school staircase, E of the entrance, is of 1924, as is the HALL, to the NE. Shallow barrel-vault with plaster panels of muses and zodiac signs by *Bloye*.

Large NEW BUILDING further E by *Penoyre & Prasad*, 2012, tactfully low-lying.

GREET PRIMARY SCHOOL, Warwick Road and Percy Road. By *Arthur Harrison*, 1891–2. Queen Anne, with a delicate cupola. Gables rebuilt after war damage.

SPRINGFIELD PRIMARY SCHOOL (now Academy), College Road. 1899–1900 by *Robert F. Matthews*. Brick and creamy-yellow terracotta, with an array of Dutch gables. Even the caretaker's house on Springfield Road, N, has one. Infill N of the main block by *Arthur Harrison*, 1904–5; gables without terracotta bands.

PERAMBULATION

The start is the junction of Stratford Road and Baker Street. The ANTELOPE (now a restaurant) is a 'reformed' pub by *Holland W. Hobbiss*, 1922. A square Tudor pavilion on the corner, with massive chimneys, and a side wing with pretty semi-dormers but a rigorous window grid below. The entrance has tile banding and interlace, and a fine *Bloye* panel above, in Gill-like low relief.* The S wall has a sundial under a gablet. Good leadwork. The former public bar retains its stone fireplace, dado and bar front. Carved central wooden pier, originally a ventilation duct. Rear smoke room with an Adam-style ceiling. To the S brick and terracotta shops with a conical turret by *Arthur Harrison*, 1898–9. Opposite, a similar but more modest range also by *Harrison*, 1900–1. Going N on the E side, the former Salvation Army hall (p. 340), a typical BURTONS by *Montague Burton Architect's Department*, 1937, then St John's church (p. 339).

400 yds N, at the corner of Warwick Road, the former MERMAID. The C18 pub was rebuilt in 1894 by *Wood & Kendrick*, and their angled wings survive, with timber gables and terracotta porches. The centre was rebuilt plainly by *Hobbiss*, 1946–7, after war damage. On the E side beyond, set back, a Victorian classical villa with a framed round-arched doorcase. Next to it Nos. 384–386, a former CO-OP by *Ingall & Son*, 1904–5, with a tower with an oval window, triangular dormer and truncated spirelet. Nos. 380–382 are a former bank by *Ewen & J.A. Harper*, 1902–3, Jacobean-cum-Baroque. Doorcase with a shell-hood, shallow first-floor bow with Ionic part-blocked columns. The former PICCADILLY CINEMA is by *Satchwell & Roberts*, 1930. Nos. 352–356, dated 1894, brick and terracotta with shallow oriels and pedimented dormers, are by *Ewen Harper*.

Down WARWICK ROAD E of the Mermaid, the Methodist church (p. 340), and on the S side the SPORTSMAN pub (now MCDWYER'S) by *James & Lister Lea*, 1900. Angular shaped

---

*Mitchells & Butlers were proud of it: 'In years to come that sculptured doorway may well draw as enthusiastic admirers as many a doorway at Oxford and Cambridge.'

gables, octagonal corner turret with concave top. Also theirs the former WAGGON AND HORSES, 1924, ¼ m. E, opposite Greet school (p. 342).

OTHER BUILDINGS

In STRATFORD ROAD S of the library and baths, the BEAR, a corner pub by *Holland W. Hobbiss*, 1937–8. Tudor, narrow maroon brick, with moulded mullion-and-transom windows and very flattened four-centred arches. Relief by *Bloye* above the entrance. S of Formans Road, Nos. 726–738 are by *T. G. Price*, 1904. To the W in SHOWELL GREEN LANE, the ZINNIA CENTRE by *Nightingale Associates*, 2007–8. No. 123 is the former St John's vicarage, by *Arthur Harrison*, 1900. A castellated bay and a three-storey gable, linked by the porch. Ends with tile-hanging. No. 133 is by *Crouch & Butler*, 1892–3. Sweet and petite Queen Anne. Jettied upper floor, rendered and with pilasters and garlands, on long brick consoles.

TYSELEY

Tyseley developed rapidly with terraced housing following the opening of the Great Western Railway station (later junction) in 1906.

ST EDMUND, Reddings Lane. By *Hobbiss*, 1937–9, at his most eclectic. W front with a Lethaby-style Romanesque entrance, and tympanum by *Bloye*. The memorable feature is the NW tower. It has a slightly French flavour, rising sheer to groups of five round-headed lancets in the belfry. They are recessed, leaving the angles proud, like clasping buttresses, until these in turn check in just below the low pyramid roof. The side elevations have flat-headed lights divided by bull-nosed piers. Pointed arcades with a single step, and a more complex sanctuary arch. Apse by *T. Dunkley Hogg*, 1960. – Ornate ALTAR by *Jones & Willis*. – RAILS and CHOIR STALLS (N aisle) brought from Bishop Ryder Church, Gem Street, in 1960. – STAINED GLASS. Apse, angels in *dalle-de-verre*, by *Goddard & Gibbs*, 1960.
METHODIST CHURCH (now gurdwara), Warwick Road. By *Henry Harper*, 1909–10. Free Perp with fancy tracery, a corner tower, and a separate hall to the W, now refronted with three Hindu shikhars, by the *Shree Hindu Community Centre*, 2020.
YARDLEYS SCHOOL, Reddings Lane opposite Weston Lane. By *Aedas AHR* (*James Handley, Jonathan Cowper*), 2003. Low, curving, brick and metal.*

---

*Railings and piers with ball finials from *Arthur Harrison*'s lovely Yardley Grammar School, Free Tudor of 1908 (dem.), survive in Warwick Road, E of the former Methodist church.

FORMANS ROAD SCHOOL (now AL-FURQAN PRIMARY SCHOOL), Reddings Lane. 1906–7 by *Gerald McMichael & A. Dennis Thacker*. Nicely detailed in an Arts and Crafts way: see the little end gablets, relieving arches over the windows, and slim cupolas with tall weathervanes. Sandwiched between, flat-roofed blocks by *H.T. Buckland*, 1925–6.

RAILWAY STATION, Wharfdale Road. 1906, by the Great Western Railway's New Works Engineer *W.Y. Armstrong*. Remarkably complete, restored after an early C21 fire. Booking office on the overbridge, covered stairs, glazed red brick waiting rooms and platform canopies all in the railway's early C20 style. TYSELEY LOCOMOTIVE WORKS, W, a repair facility for preserved engines, retains the tall coaling stage of 1908 with canopied hoist and the turntable of its demolished roundhouse.

HAY HALL, Redfern Road. An unexpected survival among factories. The timber-framed C15 manor house of the Este family, of H-plan with its front facing SE, was encased in brick in the 1530s (a glass pane formerly in the house refers to a wedding of 1538). Following a fire in 1810, the house was turned round and a new front built facing NW. In 1917 it was bought and repaired for offices by what became the Reynolds Tube Co. (the architect *E.F. Reynolds* was of the family). More repairs in 1948–9. In 1984–5 *Associated Architects* restored the building.

The NE solar or family wing shows its high status with brick diapering and a plinth with stone top moulding. Two-, three- and four-light arched windows. A little gabled projection contains a tiny upper room. The original front, SE, is plainer and much reworked. One big timber post part-surviving in the hall range. Porch with studding above, of *c.*1500. The SW wing beyond was extended plainly in 1939. Finally the early C19 NW front. Tudor Gothic, three bays, with sash windows and a central door under hoodmoulds. Pointed relieving arches. End bays of the wings rebuilt to match, with plainer windows.

In 1984–5 a new entrance and stair hall were created in the NE wing. A piece of C16 wall painting is preserved on the landing here. At the same time the GREAT HALL beyond was opened out, its inserted floor removed. Much 1980s restoration, in paler timber. The three intermediate trusses are all visible. From the NE (dais) end, a simple collar-beam truss, a bigger tie- and collar-beam truss, and a heavily restored but impressive spere-truss. All have convex upper struts. Two C16 stone doorways, one angled at the N corner. The spere-truss divided off the screens passage, of which the far wall survives, with a blocked pointed-arched timber doorway. The SW wing has a first-floor room with tie- and collar-beam trusses. W corner room with an unusual ceiling with a rectangular timber frame and coving below. The early C19 range has ground-floor rooms with moulded wall panels and one fine marbled fireplace. Simpler fireplaces and barrel-vaulted ceilings above.

WORKS RANGE along Redfern Road, NW, including the bridged-over entrance, by *E.F. Reynolds*; mostly 1917–20, the end nearest the hall 1936.

OTHER BUILDINGS. On Warwick Road W of the station, the proudly named TYSELEY AND DISTRICT WORKING MEN'S CLUB AND INSTITUTE, 1923 by *A. Heatherley*. Doorcase with segmental pediment. ⅓ m. W, the former TYSELEY CINEMA of 1941–6 by *Hurley Robinson*, with a massive classical front. E of St Edmund's church the TYSELEY FARM ESTATE of 1927–8 by *H.H. Humphries*, City Engineer and Surveyor.

YARDLEY WOOD

0575

Yardley Wood began as a hamlet at the SW end of Yardley parish. The C19 church and school survive among interwar housing.

CHRIST CHURCH, School Road. 1849 by *A.E. Perkins*, paid for by the Taylor family of Moseley. Nave, transepts and chancel, in rock-faced sandstone, with lancet and two-light windows. W spirelet. Chancel extended E, and SE vestry added, by *Buckland & Haywood-Farmer*, 1909–10, a rare piece of church work by them. Matching stone, but the chancel, tellingly, unbuttressed, and the vestry massively treated. Inside, the plaster was removed in 1932, exposing rough stone and unmoulded crossing arches, an unsettling effect. Collar-beam roof with long arched braces. W gallery. – CHOIR STALLS by *Buckland & Haywood-Farmer*, 1910. – Most attractive PANELLING around the E end, with cherubs, festoons and swags. Part of *William & David Hiorne*'s altarpiece of 1753 from St Bartholomew, Birmingham (1749–50, dem.), reworked and inserted by *W.D. Kesby*, joiner, 1944–5. – PULPIT. Typical *J.A. Chatwin*, 1880. – PEWS probably original.– STAINED GLASS. Much by *William Holland*: S transept 1863, nave 1874–7; N transept 1875. Nave N by *Hardmans*, 1879 (Marys at the Tomb). Nave S by *Camm Bros*, 1877, quite different, pictorial. Nave SW by *Oswald D. Brooke*, 1922, with painted figures and patterning. – LYCH-GATE by *Chatwin*, 1880.

Opposite the church, COTTERILL'S ALMSHOUSES, a pair of cottages by *D. Holloway*, 1857. They once had pretty bargeboards.

OUR LADY OF LOURDES (R.C.), Trittiford Road. By *G.B. Cox*, 1964–6, his last church. Bulky Romanesque, still to a traditional plan, with a powerful low tower over the chancel. Ritual W doorway with mosaic tympanum. Wide nave; grey stone transverse arches with incised mouldings, linked to similar but smaller arcades. N and S chapels with two-bay arcades, more traditional, with columns and Byzantine capitals. – MOSAIC, E wall: the Coronation of the Virgin, designed by *Cox*, 1966. – STAINED GLASS in the chapels by *Hardmans*, 1980.

PRIMARY SCHOOL (now day nursery), School Road. By *Arthur Harrison*, 1893. A pretty Queen Anne design with a mixture of gables and semi-dormers.

LIBRARY, Highfield Road. By *J.P. Osborne & Son*, 1938. Neo-Georgian, on a half-butterfly plan. Big Doric doorcase in a brick aedicule, with a fine carved tympanum by *Bloye*.

DOG AND PARTRIDGE PUB (now HARVEST CHURCH), Priory Road. By *J.P. Osborne & Son*, 1929. Pyramid-roofed pavilions at each end. Rear assembly hall of 1937, also by Osborne.

SUBURBS: WEST AND SOUTH-WEST

Bartley Green	347
Bournville	348
Churches and public buildings	351
Perambulations	353
Other buildings	357
Edgbaston	357
Places of worship	359
University of Birmingham	365
Other public buildings	374
Streets	377
Rotton Park Estate	393
Frankley	394
Harborne	395
Churches	395
Major houses	397
Moor Pool Estate	399
Perambulation	400
Other buildings	405
Kings Norton	406
Major buildings	406
Perambulation	409
Canal structures	410
Other buildings	410
Cotteridge	411
West Heath	412
Ladywood	413
Longbridge and Rednal	415
Longbridge Motor Works and Austin Village	415
Other buildings, with Rednal	416
Northfield	418
Quinton	422
Selly Oak	423
Places of worship	424
Public buildings	427
Perambulations	428
Stirchley	433
Weoley	435

BARTLEY GREEN

Bartley Green and its neighbours were industrial hamlets involved in the nail-making trade. The centre lost its focus with the demolition of old St Michael's church (*see* below). WOODGATE was ¾ m. NW, along Woodgate Lane. CALIFORNIA, 1 m. NE towards Harborne, grew up in the mid C19 around the E end of Lapal Tunnel on the Dudley No. 2 Canal of 1798, and Smarts brickworks (dem.). The area is now mostly amorphous post-war municipal estates. Typical early post-war low-density development around Field Lane and Adams Hill; 1960s–70s estates to the S (Kitwell), NW and N of Clapgate Lane (Woodgate Valley South). BARTLEY RESERVOIR, S, was constructed by the city's Water Department in 1930 (chief engineer *F. W. Macaulay*).

ST MICHAEL AND ALL ANGELS, Field Lane. The original church by *Isaac Newey*, 1838–40, extended by *J. H. Gibbons*, 1878, was at the junction with Genners Lane. It had Y-tracery windows and a little spirelet. Demolished 1968, the site now shops, but the graveyard survives, W. Replacement on the corner of Romsley Road, of 1965–6 by *H. Norman Haines*. Square worship area with an enormous pyramid roof. Full-width glazed entrance gable. A triangular window cut into the pyramid lights the altar. – Original FURNISHINGS, including a square concrete FONT with shuttering marks. – SCULPTURE. Christus and Madonna, naturalistic but heavily tooled, by *John Poole*, 1967. – STAINED GLASS. *Dalle-de-verre* by *Rosemary Rutherford*, not quite abstract.

ST PETER (R.C.), Adams Hill. 1975–6 by *Paul Bonham & Associates*. Unappealing brick front like a fortress. This is the sanctuary, with a long high window. Nave tapering away behind. Better inside, lit by slit windows, and the high window lighting the altar.

METHODIST CHAPEL (now CALIFORNIA CHRISTIAN CENTRE), Stonehouse Lane. 1878 by *J. Hill* of Harborne, helped by '*Mr Heal*', probably *Henry Heal*, a Selly Oak builder. Small, with bargeboarded gable and lancets.

READING ROOM (now library), Adams Hill. 1905 by *W. F. Edwards*. Brick and terracotta. Jacobean-style gabled entrance.

NEWMAN UNIVERSITY, Genners Lane. Originally a Catholic teacher-training college. University status came in 2013. The original buildings in Genners Lane are of 1966–8 by *Weightman & Bullen*. Dull reddish-brown brick and expressed concrete floor slabs. Six-storey ranges in a staggered layout, linked by a two-storey range at right angles. Chamfered recesses linking windows create a little three-dimensional relief. Partly open staircase at one end. Staff houses to the NW, similar, two-storeyed. RECEPTION AND LIBRARY building of 2011, *Glenn Howells Architects* at their best, a graceful reworking of 1950s Modernism. Gently curved, brick-faced, with a long full-height canopy on round piers. SCULPTURE in front, Globe, with texts from John Henry Newman's 'Out of Darkness', by *Planet Art* (*Julie Edwards & Ron Thompson*), 2012. Five-storey brick hall of residence, N, by *ADP*, 2018.

BARTLEY GREEN SCHOOL, Adams Hill. 1914 by *Crouch, Butler & Savage*. Brick, of careful simplicity: recessed quoins, big semi-dormers with hipped roofs, stone bands at the top of the gables. Behind, DESIGN CENTRE of 1978 by *W.G. Reed*, City Architect (project architect *Stephen Mitchell*, with *G. Surridge*). Concrete panels and ground-floor piers. At the rear, flat-roofed secondary school buildings of 1954–5 by *Harrison & Cox*.

HILLCREST SCHOOL, Stonehouse Lane. Formerly Bartley Green Girls' Grammar, 1954. By *T.M. Ashford*. Modernist, but original and surprising, as one would expect from the architect of Ravensbury (p. 390). The S front has two three-storey classroom blocks, set at a slight angle. Full-height glazing, replaced 2018. The entrance hall, r., retains its staircase, angling up to a first-floor glazed observation balcony. Hall with stage and curved acoustic hood. Canteen further r. with canted-out servery. The classroom corridors l. of the entrance face a courtyard, including a stair-tower at the NW corner. Between the classroom wings another staircase, starting curved, then rising around a triangular well. Classroom doors with circular and, upstairs, rhomboid windows. At the rear at the W, balancing the further classroom block, the gymnasium.

KING EDWARD VI SCHOOL FIVE WAYS, Scotland Lane. This was the King Edward foundation's middle school, now a mixed grammar school. Present buildings by *S.T. Walker & Partners*, 1956–8; many additions and extensions.

WOODGATE PRIMARY SCHOOL, Trimpley Road. By *Wood, Kendrick & Williams*, 1953–4. Single- and two-storey ranges with flat roofs, classrooms set *en echelon*.

The most attractive municipal development is the HEATHY FARM ESTATE, N of Field Lane, of 1949–53. By the Public Works chief architect *D.H. Davies*. The normal terraces and pairs, but stepping nicely down Romsley Road. An unusual group at Nos. 10–32 Trimpley Road: bungalows with tall chimneys and cut-back eaves.

BOURNVILLE

A model village, now a garden suburb, created from 1894 by the Quaker chocolate-maker George Cadbury. It follows Bedford Park in London (begun 1875) and Port Sunlight, Cheshire (begun 1888), but comes before the work of Ebenezer Howard and the Garden City movement, which starts with Letchworth, Herts., in 1903. Another progressive private housing development, New Earswick near York, was developed from 1904 by the Rowntree family with advice from Cadbury, closely following

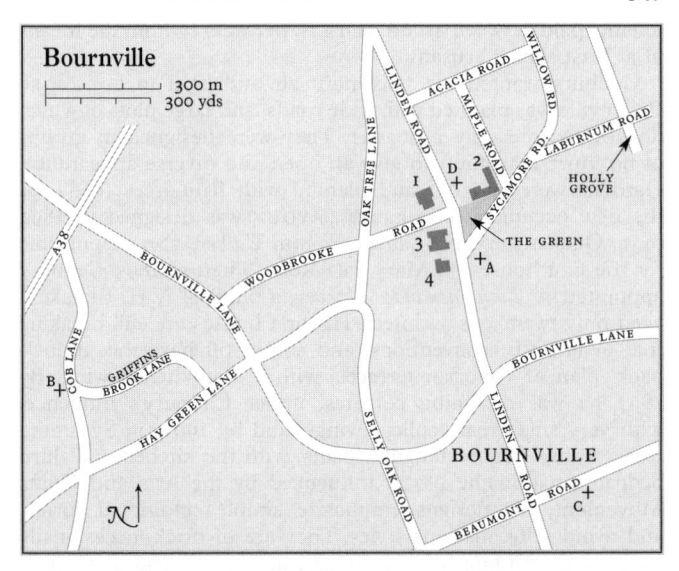

A	St Francis of Assisi	1	Ruskin Hall
B	Serbian Orthodox Church of the Holy Prince Lazar	2	Day Continuation School
C	United Reformed church	3	Junior School
D	Friends' Meeting House	4	Infants' School

the Bournville model. It also had Continental influence, through Hermann Muthesius's *Das englische Haus* (1904–5).

The brothers George Cadbury (1839–1922) and Richard Cadbury (1836–99) came from a family with a tradition of public service. George was also a deeply religious man; friends called him a 'practical mystic'. He knew working-class conditions at first hand from his teaching work at the Adult School (*see* p. 210n). Interested in many social issues, he campaigned nationally on the issue of 'sweated' labour, and in favour of Temperance. In 1879 the Cadburys moved their factory to a country site 3 m. SW of central Birmingham, between Selly Oak and Stirchley. They named it Bournville, because French chocolate was highly prized. It was laid out spaciously, and surrounded by recreation grounds. A few houses, designed by *George Gadd*, were built for senior workers (demolished). However, most employees had to travel from Birmingham, until in 1893 George Cadbury bought another 120 acres for housing, to be sold on long leases. When it became clear that many could only afford tenancies, the Bournville Village Trust was set up in 1900. The Estate was intended as a model for private development; even in the early years, less than half the residents worked at the factory, and there has always been a mixture of owner-occupied and tenanted properties. Early tenants paid between 4s. 6d. and 12s. per week, within the means of at least skilled artisans.

Cadbury wanted the maximum air and light in houses, so Bournville was planned with wide roads, and large plots of which houses covered only a quarter. They were designed in groups of no more than four, to give an open and diverse appearance. Gardens were laid out and planted with fruit trees ready for the new occupiers. The Estate LAYOUT was designed in 1894 by a Quaker surveyor, *Alfred Pickard Walker*, also responsible for the first houses, in Mary Vale Road. Then in 1895 Cadbury appointed *William Alexander Harvey*, a pupil of W.H. Bidlake's, aged only twenty, as architect. His first houses are still breaking free of late C19 conventions, and some still have the 'tunnel-back' plan of Victorian terraces, with a rear kitchen wing. By 1897 he was designing cottages, under Cadbury's influence, with very small rear scullery wings, and by 1900, in Sycamore Road, completely rectangular plans, with the kitchen and third bedroom within the block. Influenced by the Arts and Crafts Movement, his designs emphasize simple traditional forms, and avoid self-conscious styles. They are of brick, occasionally roughcast, with hipped roofs, overhanging eaves and most often casement windows. From about 1898 he used timber framing, increasingly structurally, for e.g. porches. His later work, such as the Bournville Tenants' Estate (p.357), has dentilled eaves and big Tudor or arched chimneys. He could hardly avoid imitation when designing so much so quickly, and few have committed architectural petty larceny so often but to so much effect: Edgar Wood at the Friends' Meeting House, Harrison Townsend at the mission church, Shaw, Voysey and Bidlake in details of the houses. The *Architectural Review* commented that 'in some of the houses one can scarcely see the architecture for the "features"'.

Development started from the s end of the Estate at Mary Vale Road, and the N end at Raddlebarn Road. By 1900 there were 313 houses. In 1904 Harvey resigned to go into private practice, though he was still employed to design the public buildings round The Green. His successor, *H. Bedford Tylor*, left in 1912. By 1914, with the original village nearly complete, the Estate had 894 houses. Later developments to the w and sw include some by independent societies using the Trust's architects: the Bournville Tenants' Estate of 1906–13, and the Weoley Hill Estate (Selly Oak) of 1915–39. The Shenley development of 1950–65, w of Weoley Hill, was built in partnership with the City Council. Tylor's successor, *S. Alex Wilmot*, specialized in planning, and most of the important interwar buildings were by his assistant *John Ramsay Armstrong*. Old trees, hedges and lanes were retained, and consistency achieved by careful control of materials and details such as window design. By 1999 there were 7,600 houses on the Estate.

In the C21 Cadbury's vision is fraying. Right-to-buy legislation threatens the balance of tenants and owners. The Trust, still a family preserve, has expanded substantially as a housing provider away from Bournville. The Architect's Department was outsourced in 2016.

CHURCHES AND PUBLIC BUILDINGS

ST FRANCIS OF ASSISI, Linden Road. By *Harvey & Wicks*. At the N the mission church of 1913, now CHURCH HALL. Simple Italian Romanesque, with a low, broad roof recalling Harrison Townsend's mission church at Blackheath, Surrey (1895). To the s the basilican church, planned in 1913 but not built until 1924–5, also Romanesque, linked by a cloister of 1937. More self-conscious than Ball or Dixon. Parapet arcading, W rose window, apse with stone arcading. The blocks at the gable-ends have cogging framed in plain brickwork. A campanile at the junction of church and cloister was never built. N and S porches 1933. The N has a tympanum by *Bloye* of St Francis's Sermon to the Birds, with flowers and trees forming wooden mullions separated by glass. S tympanum by *John Poole*, 1964: St Francis's Canticle of the Sun. Cool rendered interior with round-arched arcades, their piers Cornish granite monoliths. Lacy undercut capitals. SE chapel by *Selby Clewer*, 1965–6.

SERBIAN ORTHODOX CHURCH OF THE HOLY PRINCE LAZAR, Griffins Brook Lane. A wonderful exotic: a painstaking recreation of a C14 Serbian Byzantine church, of 1967–8 by *Dragomir Tadic* of Belgrade with *Bournville Village Trust Architectural Services* (chief architect *Selby Clewer*). Tall and compact, among trees. Creamy-buff and red brick. Cruciform with a dome, W forebuilding with a tower. Windows and door in round-headed niches; also on the drum, pushing up into the dome in a traditional way. The interior is plain architecturally – just one pair of columns with Byzantine capitals in the nave – but frescoed everywhere in traditional Serbian style by *Dusan Mihailovic*, including twelve Old Testament prophets and Christ Pantocrator in the dome. – Richly carved ICONOSTASIS with paintings of saints. Other fittings in the same manner. – MOSAIC over the entrance by *Fritz Kramer*. – CULTURAL CENTRE, S, by *Pedrag Ristich* (initial design) and *Bournville Village Trust Architectural Services* (project architects *K. Jones, D. Wood*), 1999. Serbian gone Postmodern: banded brick, render, and an octagonal tower with a canted-out top.

UNITED REFORMED CHURCH, Beaumont Road. 1914 by *E.B. Norris* of *Cossins, Peacock & Bewlay*. On a plot between houses. Gabled centre, entrance in a tall relieving arch between windows in tall arches with minimal Romanesque arcading.

FRIENDS' MEETING HOUSE, The Green. By *Harvey*, 1905. Big central gable and wings running out at forty-five degrees, a round-arched entrance, and an octagonal stair-turret with candlesnuffer roof: a more domestic version of Edgar Wood's First Church of Christ Scientist, Manchester of 1903–4. Deep red brick with dressings in limestone and rich-veined brown ironstone. A band of windows runs across the front, broken by the entrance, and the r. wing. Shaped lintels and sills, to act as hood- and dripmoulds. The gable-end of the S wing, facing The Green, has a niche with a bust of George Cadbury by *Francis Wood*, 1924, surveying his creation. Simple undivided interior, dominated by a roof with huge cruck-like trusses springing from ground level, linked to the wall-plates by horizontal braces resembling hammerbeams. W gallery. N extension by *BVT Architects*, 1970.

RUSKIN HALL (now BIRMINGHAM CITY UNIVERSITY), Linden Road. By *Harvey*, 1902–5, as the village institute. Conceived as a national memorial to John Ruskin, inspired by his friend J.H. Whitehouse. Original the big N wing and the range running S with swept roofs and small dormers. Entrance under a smaller gable. Tudor details, some slightly wilful, e.g. the peak in the bay-window parapet. S wing with cross-gabled corner tower by *Harvey & Wicks*, 1928. NW extension by *Harvey & Wicks*, 1956, extended E, with another gable to Linden Road, by *BVT Architects*, 1966. Moulded plasterwork in the library. Staircase with twisted iron uprights and a tapering wooden post with a band of rose decoration. Refurbished by *Associated Architects*, 2002, with glazed infill on the W.

DAY CONTINUATION SCHOOL (now BIRMINGHAM CITY UNIVERSITY), The Green and Maple Road. 1925 by *J.R. Armstrong*. Brick and stone dressings; rather like Lutyens. Two long, symmetrical Neo-Georgian ranges – two-storey centre, gabled end pavilions with canted bays – joined by a gatehouse, E, with big sloping buttresses, set on an acute corner. Through the archway, projecting ranges at angles, their entrances with stone and tile diapering. Refurbished by *Associated Architects*, 2002. Open wooden walks glazed in, and a new workshop block with a grey metal roof.

JUNIOR SCHOOL, Linden Road. By *Harvey*, 1905. A complex design of calculated contrasts. The focus is a powerful stair-tower in brick with stone dressings, the tallest accent on The Green, topped by the open lantern and ogee dome of the CARILLON, 1934. Its bluntness is relieved by window bands and small, delicate late Gothic elements, e.g. the oriel. Main hall aligned N–S behind, marked by a flat-topped turret. Other doorways with heavy foliage blocks interrupting delicate arch mouldings which die into the jambs. The carving is by *Benjamin Creswick*. This massive architecture contrasts with gabled classroom blocks, in a lighter style with big white-painted mullion-and-transom windows. Massive, heavily pegged hall roof with two collar-beams, the lower supported by arched braces which rise from corbels. Upper walls with frescoes of biblical scenes by *Mary Creighton McDowall* and *Mary Sargent Florence*, 1914. Light colours, rapid sketchy handling. Sargent Florence's figures are small, lost in space: McDowall's heavier, almost like Stanley Spencer – an impression heightened by the appearance of Bournville buildings in some scenes.

INFANTS' SCHOOL, Linden Road. By *Harvey*, 1910. Simpler than the Junior School. Big roofs, tall windows rising into gabled semi-dormers. Timbered bays, used as discrete elements in Harvey's mature way. S entrance with its gable clamped between buttresses, and a big chimneystack with star-shaped chimneys.

SUBURBS W & SW: BOURNVILLE 353

ROWHEATH PAVILION, Heath Road. 1924 by *J. R. Armstrong*. Long and low, rendered. The main elevation, S, has a row of arched entrances between narrow wings with gables. A similar little gable on the clock turret.

PERAMBULATIONS

1. The Green and the roads to the north

We start in the centre of THE GREEN with the octagonal REST HOUSE of 1913 by *W. Alexander Harvey*, based on the C16 yarn market at Dunster, Somerset. Paid for by Cadbury's workers to mark George and Elizabeth Cadbury's silver wedding. Continuous canopy, gables and lantern; a strong presence among the trees. Inside, a painted roof rises from crenellated capitals and the lantern has pendants with balls. Carved plaque by *Bloye*, 1932. To the N the Friends' Meeting House (p. 351). Going anticlockwise round The Green, Ruskin Hall (p. 352), across Woodbrooke Road the Junior School, with the Infants' School to the S (p. 352). Diagonally opposite the last, across Linden Road, the church of St Francis of Assisi (p. 351). Along the SE side of The Green, shops of 1905–8 by *H. Bedford Tylor*. Oversailing upper storey, quietly non-matching gables. To the NE, LLOYDS BANK, also *Tylor*, 1908, of pinky-red brick and brown ironstone, with the name and beehive symbols carved on the doorway. On the N side opposite, the Day Continuation School (p. 352). Facing it, E side of Maple Road, two houses re-erected from elsewhere by George Cadbury to add interest to his village: early examples of this kind of re-creation. Both were partly reconstructed by *Harvey & Wicks*, using other contemporary material. SELLY MANOR, from Raddlebarn Road, Selly Oak, was rebuilt 1912–16. Three gabled bays of timber framing face Sycamore Road, S. The W bay is C15. Close-studded and jettied; on its W side a porch with stairs to the first floor, reconstructed from a David Cox watercolour. Early C17 chimney-stack with star-plan chimneys. The central range, on the site of the open hall, is of *c.* 1600 and has the largest gable. Close studding and herringbone brick-nogging. The original main entrance opens here into a lobby against the chimneystack. The E wing, originally C16, has been reconstructed in square framing, without a floor. The first-floor interior of the W wing has plaster between the joists, and the central roof truss, which has been cut to afford access, resembles a hammerbeam. Good wind-braces. The other roofs have tie-beams and raking struts. To the N, MINWORTH GREAVES, re-erected 1929–32. Its three bays incorporate a two-bay C14 or C15 hall of cruck construction, originally with a C15 box-framed cross-wing. Only the wall framing and the crucks are original. Middle bay all C20, also both intermediate trusses.

Continuing N up SYCAMORE ROAD, a stretch by *Harvey*, 1902. Nos. 17–21, E side, have simple brick three-storey elevations but unusual plans: set below the road, with first-floor doors reached by bridges. Nos. 13–15 contrast curved ground-floor bays with little canted ones in the gables. Nos. 9–11 are a dormer bungalow pair with a big roof swept up over the doors and tall, tapering chimneys: a dramatic little design, reused with slight variations. Nos. 5–7 start a group which exemplifies Harvey's way of varying essentially similar houses, sharing the same simple plan with three pairs opposite on the NW. These are important historically because they are illustrated in Muthesius's *Das englische Haus*: Nos. 30–32 with eyebrow dormers; Nos. 26–28 with gabled semi-dormers and windows linked to front-door canopies; Nos. 22–24 with the same dormers as Nos. 5–7, but plain doors with tiny canopies. Continuing N, Nos. 14–20 have three storeys, with tall end gables separated by a big sweep of roof, a special version of a design Harvey used several times. Nos. 10–12 are a unique 'Dutch' pair with stepped gables, little Venetian windows over canted bays, and timber corner porches below dormers with little, very concave leaded roofs. The little triangular green opposite has a WAR MEMORIAL of *c.* 1920.

E along LABURNUM ROAD, more *Harvey* work of 1901–2. No. 32, N side, has a two-storey canted bay under the gable, and a side porch with convex braces. Nos. 28–30 are another small cottage variation; Nos. 24–26 a quiet but radical Arts and Crafts design in thin handmade maroon-grey brick. Gables with tumbled-in brickwork, stepped stone-capped chimneys with side smoke holes. HOLLY GROVE opens off the S side. W side by *Harvey*, 1900–1, decidedly picturesque; Nos. 1–4 have a timbered N end and a Voysey-ish rendered S one; Nos. 5–6 have a slate-hung first floor; Nos. 7–10 are Voysey-ish again, even to the shutters with heart-shaped piercings, but with a first-floor bressumer on brackets. Back across Laburnum Road, ELM ROAD runs N. On the W side Nos. 92–94, part of the Holly Grove group. No. 90 has diagonal buttresses and a semicircular porch hood. Beyond, simple terraces of four built from 1898, e.g. Nos. 73–79, E side, by *Tylor*, 1907.

Back to the triangle and N up WILLOW ROAD. Simpler *Harvey* pairs here, of 1902 onwards, e.g. Nos. 57–59, E side, with shaped gables; Nos. 52–54, W side, with chimneys in fours set diagonally. No. 30 has a timber gable on typical *Tylor* big stepped brick brackets, Nos. 26–28 are a *Harvey* three-storey block of four bays with end gables. Along ACACIA ROAD between, Nos. 1–7 by *Harvey*, 1898, rendered with shouldered dormers, and Nos. 9–11, 1906–7, showing *Tylor*'s simple, rather angular style. Nos. 12–18 (N side), *c.* 1900 by *Harvey*, are a beautifully simple version of his three-storey design. His Nos. 36–42, further W, have slightly projecting gables with chamfered corners; his contemporary, part-rendered Nos. 15–17 opposite have a similar gable; his Nos. 1–5 Maple Road, alongside (s), 1903–4, are three-storeyed with differing Venetian windows.

Further W, Acacia Road meets LINDEN ROAD. The corners are marked by a group by *Harvey*, 1903, NE, and Nos. 19–21 and 23–25, SE by *Tylor*, 1905, big rendered asymmetrical pairs. On the W side Nos. 24–26 by *Harvey*, 1898; No. 24 was his own house. A low, spreading U-shaped pair. His developing feeling for timber is shown in the partly structural end gables with small canted bays on brackets underneath, and the pent-roofed porches in the angles with tiny rooms above. Nos. 20–24, N, are a simpler version.

Between these pairs, a footpath leads to OAK TREE LANE. On its E side to the S, Nos. 139–141 and 143–147 by *Tylor*, 1908. W side, two exceptional single houses by *Harvey*. No. 168, 1908, is a big L-shape, rendered, with carefully random fenestration and brick chimneys. No. 172, dated 1907, is a smaller brick L-plan with a typical oriel, diamond-paned casements, and a timber porch in the angle. Detached cross-gabled garage by *Harvey*, 1909, with a very Herefordshire lantern and a round-arched entrance. On the NW corner with Woodbrooke Road is ST GEORGE'S COURT by *J.R. Armstrong*, 1924–5, Neo-Georgian flats for single professional women. U-shaped; quoins made by recessed brick bands. In the S continuation of Oak Tree Lane, Nos. 165–181 are a U-shaped court by *Tylor*, 1911.

Along WOODBROOKE ROAD, to the E. On the N side, two U-shaped bungalow ranges by *Tylor*, 1909. Opposite, SE corner of Thorn Road, a pair by *Harvey*, 1903. Central gable with Venetian window between chamfered piers. Darker, higher-quality red brick than usual, also used to the E on his contemporary Nos. 1–7. Beyond these, The Green.

2. The factory and south of The Green

From The Green, SE between Lloyds Bank and the shops, a path leads past the buildings of the FACTORY, basic classical with plain pilasters and big dentil cornices, of 1908 etc. At one place a glimpse of the RECREATION GROUND, W, of 1896, with *Tylor*'s half-timbered and turreted PAVILION of 1902. E of the ground a more decorative factory block with canted Tudor bays and Venetian windows, probably by *Buckland & Haywood*, 1922. The centre of its S side, to BOURNVILLE LANE, has been infilled by *Stanton Williams*, 2004. Immediately E, the BATHS of 1902–4, an original Free Style design by *G.H. Lewin*, the factory's architect. Brick with stone dressings and footings. Plan and handling suggest a progressive Nonconformist chapel: a 'nave' with shaped gable and round-headed window with blunt tracery, and a cross-gabled W aisle. SE tower with sloping buttresses enclosing tall windows with alternating brick and stone voussoirs, octagonal top with flat-topped angle buttresses, ogee lead cap with a delicate weathervane. Below the main gable window a large carved panel by *Benjamin Creswick*, with his distinctive luxuriant foliage.* On the S side opposite, a LODGE of 1895 by *A.P. Walker*. E of it an office complex of

---

*In the W wall DATESTONE of one of the original works cottages, 1879.

1959 by *Cadbury Bros Architects' Department* (remodelled 2015). Also by them on the N side, a seven-storey block of 1963–4 with a wavy roof. Beyond it, an early factory range with jettied half-timbered upper storey. No. 1 LODGE at its W end has a hexagonal roof with gabled projections. Returning W, on the S side, the WOMEN'S RECREATION GROUND has the brick wall of the former Bournbrook Hall and, set back, a tall brick pavilion with delicate lantern. On the NW corner with Linden Road, the OLD FARM HOTEL, a farmhouse remodelled by *Harvey*, 1900, as a Temperance inn. Altered, but retaining his E front and corner porch. To the N, early pairs also by *Harvey*, 1897.

Now S up LINDEN ROAD. On the W side early estate houses. Some, e.g. Nos. 124–126 and 132–134, are local builders' designs. Nos. 128–130 are *Harvey*'s earliest design, of 1896: still tunnel-backs, with conventional square bays, but handled more simply than their neighbours. On the E side three-storey pairs with end gables of 1898. On the NW corner of Mary Vale Road, shops and flats by *Harvey*, 1897–8, with timber gables and upper floors on brackets with grotesque heads carved by *Creswick*. Slightly overloaded compared with his mature work. On the NE corner the BOURNVILLE ALMSHOUSES of 1897 by *Ewen & J.A. Harper*, given by Richard Cadbury. Single-storey pairs and longer ranges, linked by walls and gates round a large grassed quadrangle, in a Late Victorian Tudor style reminiscent of John Douglas. Half-timbered gables and canted bays with ogee lead roofs. Gatehouse-like entrance on Mary Vale Road with domed octagonal turrets to the porch and main gable. To the E, the S side of MARY VALE ROAD is early C20, by *Grants Estates*. Conventional tunnel-back terraces with square bays, doorways with shaped pediments: a telling contrast with the Bournville Tenants' Estate. Going W, the conventional Late Victorian Nos. 222–232 (N side) are the earliest houses on the Estate, by the surveyor *A.P. Walker*, 1895. Nos. 234–236, shops by *Harvey*, 1899, show him trying out Voysey's manner. Also by Harvey No. 246 onwards, pairs of 1896 with shouldered gables, and Nos. 270–272, 1899, another Voyseyesque design. Harvey's No. 274, 1896–7 for J.H. Whitehouse, turns the corner into Selly Oak Road with clashing S and W gables, the former sweeping down to enclose the porch.

N along Selly Oak Road and E into BOURNVILLE LANE, with more early *Harvey* work; the best Nos. 97–99, S side, and Nos. 80–86, dormer bungalow pairs, N, all 1901, all slightly different. Also No. 3 LAUREL GROVE, S, with gabled timber upper storey and porch with shaped parapet: built as washing baths, 1896–7, for residents without their own. BEECH ROAD runs N near here with more early *Harvey* pairs, and a footpath leading E back to Selly Oak Road. On the E side U-shaped courts and a stepped-up terrace, Nos. 55–65, by *Tylor*, 1910; on the W, terraces and a pair by *Harvey*, 1902–3, obviously on a budget. Going N, a terrace of pre-Bournville houses, one dated 1879.

3. The Bournville Tenants' Estate

1 m. SW of The Green. Developed between 1906 and 1914, all designed by *Harvey*.* On HAWTHORNE ROAD, the houses around the triangular green at the junction of Kingsley Road are mainly of 1907–9. On the E side, pairs and groups of three, some partly rendered. Steep gables with dentilled eaves resting on slight capitals, suggesting open pediments. On the SW side the last houses on the Estate, 1912–13. S down Hawthorne Road, more of 1907–9. Nos. 11–13, W side, stand out, with arched central chimney, chamfered side projections for staircases, and concave lead-roofed porches. On the corners with Northfield Road two complex groups, each with a timber-gabled projection, a steep brick gabled wing with an inset two-storey flat-roofed porch, and a timber porch with big brackets. More houses E and W on the N side of NORTHFIELD ROAD.

KINGSLEY ROAD has long terraces of 1908–10, with varied fenestration. Nos. 51–57 are the show job here, rendered and with a centrepiece of timber projections linked by a balcony. Nos. 43–49 have diagonally set chimneys on the SW gable. Nos. 48–54 (N) have eyebrow dormers, Nos. 35–41 a wide segmental porch, Nos. 11–25 dentilled gables and rows of big dormers. The corners to Woodlands Park Road have terraces of four of 1907–8, the NW one stepping downhill. Just N in WOODLANDS PARK ROAD, E side, a timber PUBLIC HALL by *Harvey*, c. 1913. Doorcase with segmental pediment, oculus above.

The Estate has a quiet purity of design, which makes the spread of plastic windows especially damaging.

OTHER BUILDINGS

No. 212 Beaumont Road is a former Ten Acres and Stirchley Co-op SHOP, by *F.B. Andrews*, 1910. Free Style with a big semi-dormer, turrets and a little dome with a spike.

EDGBASTON

0580

'Unquestionably the most important suburb of Birmingham, the favourite place of residence for the professional men, merchants and traders of the busy town which it adjoins' (*Edgbastonia* magazine, 1881). Edgbaston is indeed a middle-class suburb unique in Britain in size, closeness to the centre, the low densities of its wealthiest roads, and the way it was developed by the landed Gough-Calthorpe family.

---

*Except for two pairs by the Estate Company's secretary, *David Glass*, on Woodlands Park Road.

Sir Richard Gough bought the estate in 1717, and his grandson was created Lord Calthorpe in 1796. A few leases were granted from 1786 in the triangle between the Hagley and Harborne roads, but it was George, 3rd Lord Calthorpe, who started replacing agricultural tenants with 'gentlemen and tradesmen' in 1810. By 1814 Calthorpe, Frederick and George roads had been cut, and Wellington and Sir Harry's roads off the Bristol Road. The area between Hagley and Westbourne roads followed after 1820. The 3rd Lord, a devout Evangelical, also encouraged charitable and educational foundations: the Institution for Deaf and Dumb Children in 1814 and the Botanical Gardens in 1831.

Many roads took years to complete; Wellington Road, for example, was almost empty, except the E end, until the mid 1830s. Artisans' houses were also built, in bigger blocks, on the edges of the estate, e.g. in Sun Street and Balsall Heath Road. Increasingly through the C19, a horseshoe-shaped area of lower- to middle-middle-class roads, such as the Frederick and George roads area and the district SE of Bristol Road, protected the upper-middle-class core. Development moved SW with Arthur Road (1848) and Ampton Road (1850). The 1880s boom saw a start on the Somerset and Farquhar roads area, but this failed to equal the growth of rival areas like Moseley. The estate passed in 1910 to the Anstruther-Gough-Calthorpe family, and some land sales began: to the University, and in the 1930s to the hospitals board and King Edward's School.

HOUSES are mostly detached, with some semi-detached pairs. Larger plots have ample, well-tree'd grounds. Only in the earliest development, e.g. the city end of Hagley Road, are there terraces. The 3rd Lord Calthorpe's conservatism can be seen in the long survival of the classical tradition. The earliest houses seem to be builders' designs, in the Wyatt-influenced local Georgian. Greek Revival appears c. 1820, and stucco often covers brick. Ground floors are frequently rusticated; sometimes there are pilasters above. *Charles Edge* probably introduced c. 1830 Soane's language of cut-back wall-planes, and then the Italianate manner used by C.R. Cockerell. *John Fallows* used Soane's incised ornament, and also 'Graeco-Egyptian' with tapering architraves, and picturesque Tudor. From c. 1840 *F.W. Fiddian, Samuel Hemming* and others adopted an increasingly rich Italianate manner, especially for cornices. They were developers as well as architects, as slightly later was *Yeoville Thomason*, who introduced brick polychromy. *J.J. Bateman* introduced c. 1845 the rural Italian villa, asymmetrical with a low tower, deriving from Nash and J.B. Papworth. *J.A. Chatwin*'s work looks Victorian from his very first design, Nos. 38–39 Frederick Road, 1850; in the 1850s he used a wild Jacobean. *Teulon*'s rogue-Gothic St James's church of 1850–2 is now flats. Full-blown domestic Gothic Revival arrived as late as 1855 with *J.H. Chamberlain*'s No. 12 Ampton Road. Around 1900 *W.H. Bidlake, J.L. Ball* and others designed good houses in the Edgbaston Park Road and Farquhar Road areas, in free Arts and Crafts-influenced styles.

John Madin's plan of 1957 responded to mid-C20 circumstances, with the larger houses impossible to keep up. The Five Ways area was redeveloped with offices, including towers. C19 mansions were replaced with flats and groups of smaller detached houses, retaining old walls and trees. Two shopping centres, the Eastern and Western 'Hearts', were created. The plan successfully retained the estate's character, but in the C21 this is threatened by heavy redevelopment near the city, damaging to Madin's maximum one-third plot densities.

PLACES OF WORSHIP

St Bartholomew (Edgbaston Old Church), Church Road. The first impression of a charming, low medieval fabric is misleading. A church existed by 1279. A N aisle was added c. 1500, a W tower in the early C16. Civil War damage took years to make good (briefs 1658, 1684). The upper part of the tower was rebuilt. In 1810 the N arcade was removed and the space roofed in a single span. In 1844–6 *Harvey Eginton* raised the walls, replaced windows and built a new N porch and vestry. A S aisle was added in 1856 by *F. W. Fiddian*, assisted by the young *J.A. Cossins*.* In 1885–6 *J.A. Chatwin* built a new chancel, N chapel, N arcade (redividing the space) and SE organ chamber, and raised the nave walls further to form a clerestory. Finally in 1889 Chatwin added an extra S aisle.

Our first sight is the much-patched medieval N wall, with *Eginton*'s simple porch and vestry, walling above the string course, and typical 1840s two-light Perp windows, themselves much renewed. C15 N doorway. Above, an oval plaque, probably C17, mysteriously inscribed '777'. Two-stage tower. W window with irregular Y-tracery, probably of c.1300, re-assembled badly in the C17. Large basic pointed C17 belfry windows, and small pinnacles which look C18 Gothick. W doorway of 1885. *Chatwin*'s work respects the Perp style and low proportions, echoing late medieval North Country churches. Big six-light four-centred-arched E window. The N chapel has *Fiddian*'s E window of 1856 repositioned, with an unusual eight-cusped vesica. Chatwin's N windows follow Eginton's. Clerestory with paired lights. Small SW HALL by *Anthony Chatwin*, 1969, linked by a canopy.

The INTERIOR is nearly all *Chatwin*'s, but influenced by *Fiddian*'s S arcade with thin piers with four shafts and hollows. Chatwin's N arcade follows it, but with slightly different capitals. His outer S arcade is similar. His chancel arch and stepped segmental N and S chapel arches are heavier, typical late C19, on rich leaf corbels. Camber-beam nave roof. The interior is faced in beautiful pink-grey sandstone ashlar. *Fiddian*'s S aisle roof survives, collar-beam trusses with many stop-chamfers.

---

*In 1850 *S. S. Teulon* had proposed replacement by a hall church with unusual outer passage aisles.

Late medieval tower arch with clumsy quarter-rounds and one deep hollow moulding.

Complete C19 FITTINGS. Typical *Chatwin* CHOIR STALLS of 1885, with scrolled ends supporting symbols of the Evangelists. – Contemporary PULPIT, PEWS and REREDOS. – FONT. Octagonal, limestone, Perp style, by *Eginton*, 1846. – Lady Chapel SCREEN and REREDOS by *P. B. Chatwin*, 1932(?). – STAINED GLASS. E window incorporating glass of 1859 from the former S aisle, by *J. Hardman Powell*, in hot colours. Chancel N and S by *Hardman*, 1886. N chapel E, the former E window, *Hardman*, 1859. More by them in the N aisle, 1887. Its W window by *Kempe & Co.*, 1909. Outer S aisle, window †1871, probably designed by *Chatwin*; also made by *Hardman*.

MONUMENTS. A selection. N aisle from E. Sir Richard Gough †1727. Ionic aedicule in grey marble. Heavy fluted base. – Sir Henry Gough †1774. Tablet with urn above. Nice cherub in the predella. – 1st Lord Calthorpe †1798, by *King & Sons* of Bath. Two oval tablets in a marble surround, weeping woman against an urn above. – Frances, Lady Calthorpe †1827. Chunky Greek Revival. Tall urn in semicircular-headed surround. – S aisle, from E. Gabriel Jean Marie de Lys †1831. By *Hollins*. With bust. – William Withering, the discoverer of digitalis, †1799, by *W. Hollins*. Oval tablet with a most lifelike snake twisting round a branch and a sprig of foxglove. – Joseph Ledsam †1816, by *W. Hollins*. Elegant tablet with reeded border. – W wall, Henry and Sarah Porter, †1710 and †1724. Lead tablet. – The CHURCHYARD has good C19 tombs W of the tower. By the porch, William Alexander Harvey †1951 and wife, by *H. G. Wicks*. Ribbed urn.

ST AUGUSTINE, Lyttelton Road. By *J. A. Chatwin*, 1867–8, the splendid tower and spire added in 1876–7. A confident and successful early Dec design. Bath stone with bands of Hamstead sandstone. Big stepped buttresses. A variety of Geometrical tracery. The S transept tower (a local tradition, e.g. Handsworth) has immensely tall belfry windows; the transition to the spire is well handled: an octagon flanked by pinnacles, and a corona above. Five-sided apse; two-storey NE vestry with a steep elongated pyramid roof, balancing the tower from the E. Cross-gabled W porch-cum-meeting room by *Anthony Chatwin*, 1968, from a design by *P.B. Chatwin*. Original W doorway reused, with tympanum of 1898. Rich but hard interior, a wonderful evocation of mid-Victorian Edgbaston. Sharply pointed arches with foliage capitals, hammerbeam nave roof on shafts with corbels of the Apostles (all sculpture by *John Roddis*). Chancel arch with complex mouldings, shafts on angel corbels. Chancel ceiling of painted metal panels, with angels and a Christ in Majesty, by *Hardmans*, 1877–8.

An impressive ensemble of FITTINGS by *Chatwin*. REREDOS with hanging arches and Last Supper in alabaster, 1877, with shafts and arcading on either side; CHOIR STALLS with typical rolled foliage ends, also 1877; PULPIT with the Sermon on the Mount and other reliefs, 1868; PEWS. – BAPTISTERY, N transept, by *George Pace*, 1964. Uncompromising, yet it fits well. Massive plain FONT of grey York stone with a punched claw finish, set below floor level. COVER with sculpture of the Baptism of Christ by *John Bunting*. Typical angular *Pace* iron CANDLESTICKS. INSCRIPTION on the N wall, stone BENCH. – Lady Chapel, S transept, with screens by *P.B. Chatwin*, 1936, extended by *Robert Pancheri*, 1962. – STAINED GLASS. Apse windows all *Hardman*, 1869–70, the Passion of Our Lord, with impressive reds and blues. S transept, *Osmund Caine*, 1954. W window by *Hardmans*, 1954, when they also 'thinned out' the aisle windows. S aisle from E: three *Hardman*, 1879, one *Heaton, Butler & Co.*, 1890. N aisle: W *Francis Spear*, 1968; second going E *Clayton & Bell*, 1881.

ST GEORGE, Highfield Road and Westbourne Road. Prominent on its island site. Grey-brown Alvechurch sandstone. Six-bay nave and aisles by *J.J. Scoles*, 1836–8, chancel by *Charles Edge*, 1855. In 1884–5 *J.A. Chatwin* built a new, bigger nave and S aisle, making the original nave his N aisle. His SE tower remains a two-storey stump. Edge's octagonal NE turret is overwhelmed by the new nave. Scoles's N elevation has typical 1830s big lancets, thin uniform buttresses and corbelled parapet. Chatwin tactfully repeats this on the S, but adds a clerestory of sharp paired lancets with trefoiled heads. His E window has five grouped lancets. His W front has plain lancets and an ornate rose window (but has lost its pinnacles). One tall 1838 pinnacle remains poignantly at the NW.

The INTERIOR is unexpectedly good. *Scoles*'s work is tall and airy. His surviving N arcade has very thin circular piers with attached half-shafts. Panelled canted ceiling. Edge's former chancel arch follows Scoles's C13 style with richer mouldings. N and W galleries with arcaded fronts probably by *Edge*, 1856, the N infilled for meeting rooms. *Chatwin*'s clerestory, raised above the older work, is nobly proportioned. Wall-shafts between its windows, ending on leaf corbels just above the arcade piers. The easternmost shaft ends in a curl of stone across the arch mouldings, the chancel arch has corbels with shafts stepping curiously inwards.

The wide E nave bay is a preaching space, confirmed by *Chatwin*'s stone PULPIT of 1885. Circular top linked by ribs to a polygonal base. Alabaster cresting. Matching low SCREEN. – CHOIR STALLS and CLERGY STALLS, typical Chatwin, with carvings of angels and Evangelists. – Mosaic CHANCEL FLOOR. – Big wooden REREDOS by *P.B. Chatwin*, 1903, made by the *Bromsgrove Guild*. – Oak SCREEN to the N (Lady) chapel, 1905–6. – ORGAN, chancel S, by *Brindley & Foster*, 1890. Case with trumpeting angels. – Good late C19 STAINED GLASS. Of 1888 the E window, *Burlison & Grylls*. Chancel S, *Heaton, Butler & Bayne*. S aisle from E, Resurrection, *Burlison & Grylls*; Life of Hannah, *Hardman*; three by *Heaton, Butler & Bayne* with Jacobean architectural surrounds (two dated 1891, 1892). W window, *Dunstan J. Powell*, 1898, made by *Hardmans*, a forest of intricate leading surrounding the figures.

N chapel E, *Kempe*, 1903, also the N lancet, 1907. – ROYAL ARMS of 1841, carved wood, W wall, signed *G.R. Collis*. – MONUMENTS. War memorial tablet by *P.B. Chatwin*, 1919, W end, N wall. – Opposite, circular metal tablet to James Dixon †1916, by *A.S. Dixon*. – S aisle, Raymond Lodge †1915 by *Oliver W.F. Lodge*. Alabaster tablet, tiny putti.

ST GERMAIN, City Road. 1915–17 by *E.F. Reynolds*.* A massive Early Christian basilica, in local brick, the style growing naturally from materials and construction in the Arts and Crafts way. Won in competition against Bidlake, Ball and others, it marks a change in Birmingham church architecture, the end of the Gothic Revival. Reynolds's personal handling can be seen in the flat brick buttresses of the chancel and the W front, where the brick cuts back in planes. Quoins are emphasized by lighter brick. Window arches turned in tile; cornices with brick vernacular detail, dentils and cogging. Reynolds proposed a tall NW campanile; when it was abandoned he added the delicate C17-style W cupola. The apse is five-sided outside. The ample white-plastered interior must have been a shock after Gothic Revival brick. The nave arcades are Shap granite monoliths with capitals of Portland stone. Richer chancel: columns of Swedish green marble with Ionic capitals of Carrara marble. All FITTINGS except where noted by *Reynolds*. – PULPIT, FONT and ALTAR RAILS with green marble panels. – ALTAR of 1918, beaten brass with grey marble panels, made by *F. Kedward-Sheldon*. – CHOIR STALLS (now in nave) of 1927 with Gimson-like gougings. – TRIPTYCH in the N (Lady) chapel by *Kate Bunce*, 1926.

ST JAMES (former), Charlotte Road. By *S.S. Teulon*, 1850–2. Redundant from 1973, converted to flats 2003–4. Lord Calthorpe was considering a new church in 'Middle-aged Gothic' in 1846, when *R.C. Carpenter*, *F.W. Fiddian* and *Charles Wyatt Orford* made designs. Not Teulon at his wildest, but there are many original touches. A cruciform preaching church, without aisles. E end above a basement, due to falling ground. SE organ chamber and vestry by *Thomas Naden*, 1886. Teulon's tower rises between it and the S transept, tapering into an octagonal belfry with alternating one- and two-light windows, and a short spire with lucarnes. Big sheltering roofs; the nave has conventional dormers and additional triangular ones above. Five-light Dec E window. Ingenious transept roses: the S has two huge quatrefoils, set at forty-five degrees to each other, so eight even points touch the edge; the N has trefoils set at sixty degrees, so six points and six spokes. W window a spherical triangle, almost cut by a sharp buttress. Teulon's roof survives, the nave trusses alternating scissors with complex hammerbeam and double-collar structures, the lower collar arch-braced, and big cusped hexagons between the two. The crossing has hammerbeams set diagonally supporting central

---

*Built during the First World War to satisfy the terms of the gift of the land by the Gillott family.

collar-beams, the lower one projecting to form the transept ridges. *Naden*'s organ chamber has a two-bay arcade with pink granite columns.

ST MARY AND ST AMBROSE, Pershore Road. 1897–8 by *J.A. Chatwin*. His usual Dec, striking here in red brick and terracotta. Unusual tracery: big segmental curves in the chancel, and whorls everywhere. NW tower with rectangular belfry windows; spire with flying buttresses. Typical Chatwin W apsidal baptistery, and the tall proportions inside. Red brick and Bath stone. Four-bay arcades divided into pairs by piers, with the E parts of the aisles wider, treated as transepts. S chancel chapel. The nave roof has arch-braced collars with alternate bays supported on stone shafts and rising to big wooden corbels like classical imposts. Odd carving, like courses of bricks, here and along the wall-plate. – Original CHOIR STALLS and PEWS; also big circular Caen stone PULPIT (carvers *Bridgemans*), and impressive Cornish-type FONT. – REREDOS by *Chatwin*, 1901. Much figure carving. *P.B. Chatwin* 'helped considerably in the draughtsmanship'. – SCREEN. 1920, probably *P.B. Chatwin*. – Painted PANELS by *Kate Bunce*, 1907, transepts. – STAINED GLASS. Good. E window by *Hardmans*, 1898, a rich crowded Christ in Majesty. W, three by *Kempe*, 1907, very characteristic. S chapel E by *Mary Newill*, 1906, typical Birmingham Arts and Crafts work. S, three lights by *Richard Stubington*, 1928, with heavy figures, hinting at Expressionism. N aisle, *Camm & Co.*, 1930.

ORATORY OF ST PHILIP NERI (R.C.), Hagley Road. St John Henry Newman established the English Congregation of the Oratory of St Philip Neri in 1849, at first where St Anne's Deritend now is (*see* p. 195). The Edgbaston site was bought in 1850. The buildings are tremendously Italian, befitting a Counter-Reformation order. Newman thought Pugin a bigot, and loved classical architecture, writing in 1850 'Now is not a *dome beautiful*, "poetical and solemn"? Is not a row of pillars beautiful? By my taste they are as beautiful, nay more so, than any thing in Gothic.' He lived here even after he was made a cardinal in 1879, until his death in 1890.

The street front, red brick with stone dressings, starts with the ORATORY HOUSE, a sober Renaissance palazzo by *Terence Flanagan*, 1851, with just a Michelangelesque doorcase and string course with Vitruvian scroll. To its W the former SCHOOL HALL, by *Henry Clutton*, 1861–2, beautiful Italian Romanesque, with arched windows above a blank ground floor. The entrance here leads into *Clutton*'s CLOISTER of 1872–3, strikingly treated with stone bands reinforcing the brick vaults, and short columns on high tapering bases. The side against the school, never completed, has part-arches supporting a corridor.

Opposite, the cloister runs behind the façade of the CHURCH. Newman obtained drawings in 1851 from a French architect, *Louis-Joseph Duc* (not, as was long thought, E.E. Viollet-le-Duc), and had a model of a basilica made. A temporary church of 1853 by *Flanagan* perhaps incorporated some of these ideas. In 1858 *John Hungerford Pollen* added a small S chapel and

St Philip's Chapel beyond it. The present church by *E. Doran Webb*, 1903–9, built as a memorial to Newman, reflects his tastes and early ideas. Latin-cross plan with seven-bay basilican nave, short transepts, dome on pendentives and apsed sanctuary. Sumptuous materials: arcades of pink Breccia marble on green Swedish marble bases; sandstone Corinthian capitals and continuous cornice. Corinthian pilasters on the aisle walls. The barrel-vault with big dormers defines an impressive but static space. The (ritual) w gallery and the side chapels betray Webb's preference for English prototypes, slipping into English Jacobean. Domed NE chapel (SHRINE OF ST PHILIP), by *G.B. Cox*, 1927, with columns of red Languedoc marble. Simple SE chapel. Beyond it, ST JOHN HENRY NEWMAN (formerly ST PHILIP'S) CHAPEL by *Pollen*, 1858. Triple-arched entrance screen.

What most distinguishes the church is its DECORATION and FITTINGS. Marble everywhere, richest in the sanctuary, which has red African and green Mexican onyx. Only important pieces can be listed. – HIGH ALTAR by *Dunstan Powell*, 1899, red marble, with curved ends and supporting cherubs. – BALDACCHINO by *Sensi* of Trastevere. – Apse MOSAIC of the Coronation of the Virgin. – CHOIR GALLERY, S transept, by *Sensi*. – N transept ALTAR, C17, from Sant'Andrea della Valle in Rome. Statue of the Virgin, C19, from Deritend, in a niche by *F.A. Walters*. The Algerian onyx columns were intended for Westminster Cathedral. – ALTAR RAILS here and in the sanctuary also from Sant'Andrea. – PULPIT. 1911. – FONT by *Dunstan Powell*, 1912. Oval alabaster basin carved by *Bridgemans*, bronze cover with St John the Baptist, made by *Hardmans*. – SE chapel REREDOS by *Pollen*, 1858. – ALTARPIECE in St John Henry Newman Chapel by *G.G. Scott Jun.*, 1880. Chellaston alabaster, with angels supporting the central frame.

The ORATORY HOUSE has Renaissance details matching the exterior. Panelled REFECTORY; cornice decorated with anthemia and corner pulpit. Newman's STUDY is preserved intact. The finest room is the LIBRARY, by *Pollen*, above his St Philip's Chapel. Long and narrow, with low clerestory lighting, continuous iron GALLERY and original SEATING.

METHODIST CHURCH (former), Sandon Road and Barnsley Road. Nave and aisles 1889–90 by *J.L. Ball* and *Ernest Barnsley*, with a square ritual W turret and spirelet. Chancel and small transept added by *Ball* in 1901. Deeply influenced by George Gilbert Scott Junior (e.g. St Agnes, Kennington; St Mark, Leamington Spa): both the exterior – red brick and bold stone bands – and the interior – stone arcades with mouldings dying into octagonal piers, which are encased in wooden dadoes, and boarded roof. Low passage aisles. Clerestory with lancets in broad relieving arches. To the E, the gable of the original school-chapel by *Ewen Harper*, 1882, and the parlour range, also *Ball*, 1901. – Original PULPIT with openwork panels, also PEWS in the W gallery. – STAINED GLASS. E window by *Pearce & Cutler*, 1920, a striking Sermon on the

Mount. Typical deep reds. Clerestory, three by *Swaine Bourne*, 1894–5, with extensive canopy-work. By *Pearce & Cutler*, clerestory S (two) 1930, W narthex 1938.

FRIENDS' MEETING HOUSE, George Road and St James Road. Dated 1893. By *William Henman*. *Rundbogenstil* in brick with stone dressings. Heavy pedimented entrance on the SW angle with a big arch and short fat columns. Lower W wing lit by a Venetian window in the gable.

CHRISTIAN SCIENCE CHURCH (now Methodist), Sandon Road. 1951–2 by *John Ramsay Armstrong*. Pale brown brick. Upper floor never completed. Finely detailed round-arched arcade.

UNIVERSITY OF BIRMINGHAM

One of the great Victorian academic foundations in provincial cities, comparable with those at Manchester and Liverpool. It started in Edmund Street as Mason College, a science college founded in 1873.* It became Mason University College in 1898, and received its charter in 1900, with Joseph Chamberlain as first chancellor. 'What we want to begin with is brains and not architecture', he told the steel magnate and philanthropist Andrew Carnegie. But Carnegie thought differently, and the £50,000 he offered to establish a 'first class modern scientific college' on the model of Cornell University was conditional on new buildings being erected.

In 1900 Lord Calthorpe gave a 25-acre site on the Bournbrook side of the Edgbaston estate, about 3 m. S of the centre. As architects, Chamberlain chose *Aston Webb & Ingress Bell*. They had both local and national work in their favour. Their Victoria Law Courts on Corporation Street (*see* p. 131) had earned praise, and they were engaged in new buildings for the Royal Naval College, Dartmouth and the Royal College of Science at South Kensington. The new campus was opened in 1909 by King Edward VII, though several buildings had already been occupied for a couple of years.

The site falls about 30 ft (9 metres) from N–S, so the architects placed their buildings on two terraces with a drop of 16 ft (4.9 metres) between. The basic plan was D-shaped, with the incomplete straight side running E–W along University Road. The curved side faced S, straddling the drop, from which on the lower side radiated two-storey T-shaped teaching blocks (only three of the intended six were built) and the Great Hall at the centre. At the semicircle each block meets a domed square pavilion with small domed corner turrets. The semicircle housed offices served by a spine corridor, two storeys high on the N side, three storeys on the S. The plan was adapted from pavilion hospitals, the curved spine achieving maximum light and ventilation with a minimum distance between individual buildings. But Birmingham was also the first formally planned British university, influenced by the Beaux Arts layouts popular at American colleges in the 1890s.

---

*Its Gothic building of 1875–80 by *J.A. Cossins* was demolished in 1964.

University of Birmingham

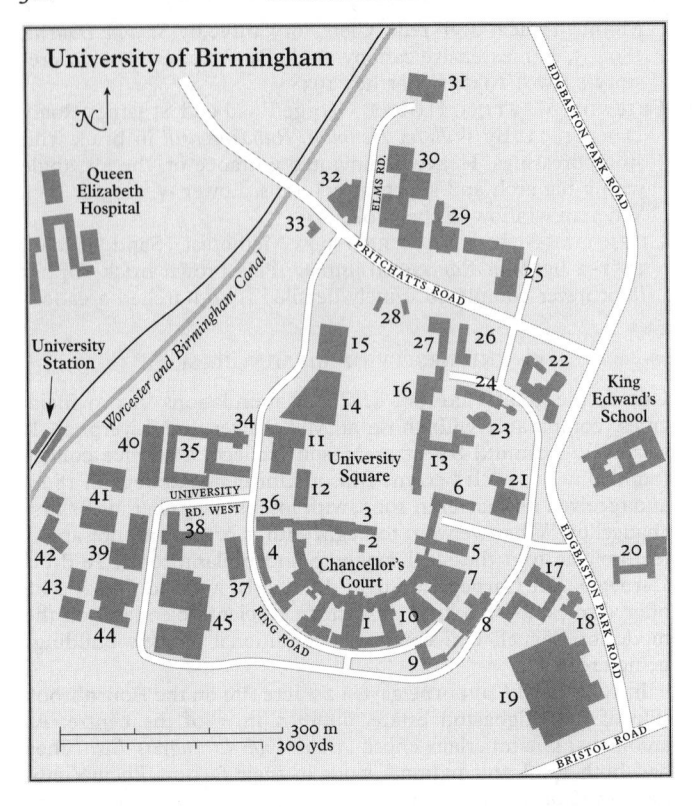

1. Great Hall
2. Chamberlain Tower
3. Harding Law Library
4. Hills Building
5. Poynting Building
6. Watson Building
7. Physics West
8. Physics East
9. Medical Physics
10. Bramall Music Building
11. University Centre
12. Staff House
13. Arts Building
14. Library
15. Teaching and Learning Building
16. Muirhead Tower
17. Guild of Students
18. St Francis' Hall
19. Sport and Fitness Building
20. University House
21. Barber Institute
22. Department of Education
23. Ashley Building
24. Strathcona Building
25. Gisbert Kapp Building
26. J.G. Smith Building
27. Alan Walters Building
28. Entrance lodges
29. Net Shape Building
30. Metallurgy and Materials
31. Computer Centre
32. European Research Institute
33. Institute for German Studies (former)
34. Geography etc.
35. Biosciences
36. Frankland Building
37. Old Gym
38. Haworth Building
39. School of Engineering
40. Collaborative Teaching Laboratory
41. Westgate Centre
42. Public and Occupational Health
43. Biochemical Engineering
44. Chemical Engineering
45. Mechanical and Civil Engineering

Interwar developments included *Holland W. Hobbiss*'s Guild of Students building and Queen's College, and *Robert Atkinson*'s masterpiece, the Barber Institute of 1936–9. *William Haywood* of *Buckland & Haywood* made plans to expand Webb & Bell's scheme in the same Beaux Arts manner, but little was done. *Verner O. Rees* was appointed in 1945 to prepare plans for bringing the remaining faculties to Edgbaston. His library (now demolished) blocked Webb's grand axis, to lasting regret. Meanwhile science buildings proliferated haphazardly around the w and s (Birmingham was one of the universities selected for expansion in technical subjects in the early 1950s).

In 1957 the University asked *Sir Hugh Casson & Neville Conder* to prepare a new development plan. Casson & Conder had won the competition for the new arts area at Cambridge, and at that moment were the leaders in campus design. They organized the teaching area into informal squares, with additional blocking buildings that enclosed views and kept out traffic. The University had meanwhile acquired the land stretching N, providing a remarkably extensive campus for an industrial city, and here larger buildings were set on either side of a new ring road. In 1960 the University committed itself to expand, and Casson & Conder revised their plan in 1963 to include a tall tower (Muirhead Tower). Some of the new buildings were by the firm, but what makes Birmingham exceptional is the employment of so many other major Modernist practices: only Oxford and Cambridge boast greater selections. The pity is that not every building was constructed, or completed as intended, while others have been altered or demolished. As a concentrated experience of 1960s university architecture, however, Birmingham remains hard to beat.* Recent developments, except for *Lifschutz Davidson*'s Sports Centre, are not to the same standard.

1. The original centre

It is difficult to describe the University in a manner that will make perambulation easy, partly because one has to start at the centre and fan out. The picturesque and romantic skyline of the first phase is best appreciated from the s, the viewpoint of most students as they arrived from the city. Sir Hugh Casson found it 'impossible not to admire...from certain aspects and in certain lights [it] can even look as magical as the domes and spires of Istanbul or Moscow'.

The original physical and ceremonial centre is CHANCELLOR'S COURT, the closest thing at Birmingham to an Oxbridge quad. However, in style and plan Webb & Bell's buildings distance themselves from Oxbridge colleges, as was felt to be required for the first English university primarily devoted to science.

---

*Descriptions of the original buildings are by Ian Dungavell; of the Barber Institute and most 1960s buildings by Elain Harwood.

The red bricks, stone stripes and saucer domes recall Bentley's Westminster Cathedral, London (1895–1903) – a style much promoted by W.R. Lethaby, who thought it rational and universal in character – and the buildings also play with the geometry of squares and circles, cubes and hemispheres, perhaps inspired by Lethaby's *Architecture, Mysticism and Myth* (1892).

At the centre of the s side is the GREAT HALL. The entrance pavilion is square, of three storeys, surmounted by an octagonal drum, ribbed dome and tiny lantern. Square turrets at the corners, capped by ribbed domes and a great round-arched mullioned window. In its spandrels the arms of the Midland counties. Above, in a ceramic frieze by *Robert Anning Bell*, the enthroned goddess Learning hands the wreath of scholarship to the new University, represented by a kneeling man in academic dress. Over the doorways a pantheon of immortals carved *in situ* by *Henry Pegram*, with the most famous Midlander at the centre: Beethoven, Virgil, Michelangelo, Plato, Shakespeare, Newton, Watts, Faraday, Darwin.

The Great Hall itself cannot be seen from this side, but from the s it is evident that its distant ancestor is the grand late medieval type with end gables flanked by turrets, such as King's College Chapel. Inside, first the domed and galleried Entrance Hall, a 50-ft (15.2-metre) cube topped by a hemispherical dome, now painted with rather heavy *trompe l'oeil* coffers. Geometric patterned floor of Pentelikon and Sicilian marbles. The hall itself is 150 by 75 ft (45.7 by 22.9 metres). The passages at ground and first floors are vaulted transversely. Gallery balustrade and pilasters of buff terracotta, carrying the ceiling ribs. Barrel-vaulted ceiling with plaster enrichments of the city and University arms by *George Bankart* of the *Bromsgrove Guild*. Stained-glass window designed by *T.R. Spence*.*

The pavilion fronts to the TEACHING BLOCKS are similar to that in front of the Great Hall, but of two storeys only, with round corner turrets. Their libraries, above, were top-lit by Diocletian windows in the octagonal drums of the domes. Ceramic friezes by *R. Anning Bell* represent in contemporary costume Midlands trades and industries. The linking curve is of two-storey offices with recessed windows under segmental heads pulled together by string courses at the level of the tops and transoms of the ground-floor windows.

The CHAMBERLAIN TOWER is in front of the Great Hall, a tall detached campanile which serves to emphasize the existence of the University; it was described in the *Birmingham Daily Post* as 'the intellectual beacon of the Midlands'. This has no stylistic connection with the buildings around it, though it too is of Accrington red brick. For it was Joseph Chamberlain and his wife who, during an Italian holiday, had settled on the Torre del Mangia at Siena as a suitable model. Webb & Bell obligingly did as they were told – though it is not an exact copy.

---

*To the sw, across the playing fields, *Webb & Bell*'s SOUTH LODGE faces Bristol Road.

The incomplete long straight wing along University Road is also of red brick with Darley Dale stone dressings. Above the entrance loggia at the centre is the HARDING LAW LIBRARY.

Webb's semicircle was infilled with less style for science, first on the W by *Maurice Webb*, 1935–7, with, filling in behind, the HILLS BUILDING (originally Chemistry) by *Wornum & Playne*, 1955. On the E, just N of the hemicycle proper, the POYNTING BUILDING, by *Webb*. N of it, *Verner Rees, Laurence & Mitchell*'s WATSON BUILDING for mathematics, 1958–61. S of it, the same firm's PHYSICS WEST of 1957–9. Behind Physics West, their PHYSICS EAST of 1965–7. Behind the latter, linked by a bridge, MEDICAL PHYSICS (RADIATION CENTRE) of 1968–71 by *Devereux, Mitchell, Price & Davis*. Next S round the hemicycle is the BRAMALL MUSIC BUILDING by *Glenn Howells*, 2013, completing the concept, with a matching dome but irritating detail differences.

Back to Chancellor's Court and N, we enter UNIVERSITY SQUARE, the centrepiece created by *Casson & Conder* that gave a grassy heart to the campus. On the W side is the UNIVERSITY CENTRE and connected STAFF HOUSE, with a small hexagonal office in the glazed link. All by *Conder*, 1958–62. In the University Centre, for students, concrete horizontals and plate glass predominate, dividing the elevation into five bands; the chief features of the green-rendered Staff House are vertical windows in broad painted architraves. The University Centre was remodelled with shops in 1991–2, but a cantilevered stair survives, floating free of the timber-lined walls. To the NE of the University Centre, SCULPTURE: Ancestor 1 of 1970–1 by *Barbara Hepworth*, part of the Family of Man series. On the E side of the square, the spreading four-storey ARTS BUILDING, by *Verner Rees, Laurence & Mitchell*. Red brick with a prominent copper attic.

The N side is now open, following the demolition of *Verner Rees*'s Library of 1957–60. It craves a formal avenue, to complete Webb and Bell's plan (the Pritchatts Road lodges (*see* below) are on the axis). Instead there is a 'Green Heart', a windy space with trees and banks of grass and footpaths: a spectacular missed opportunity. On its W side the new LIBRARY, by *Associated Architects*, 2016, with insistent patterns of vertical fins, grey relieved with gold. Behind it the TEACHING AND LEARNING BUILDING by *BDP*, 2017–19. On the E side, opposite, the mammoth MUIRHEAD TOWER for Arts, bridging the ring road (a location regretted by Conder). By *Philip Dowson* of *Arup Associates*, 1968–9; variously loved or loathed. A 'dark' floor of laboratories or lecture halls for every two glazed floors, and a large hall in its sloping underbelly. Refurbished 2009 by *Associated Architects* with full-height S sunscreen and silver-clad projecting café.

Walking E under the bridge between Arts and Physics, on the S side, facing Edgbaston Park Road, the GUILD OF STUDENTS building by *Holland W. Hobbiss*, 1928–30. E-plan front, with three big gables, inspired by Midlands manor houses. Brown brick with red relieving arches and stone dressings. A chimney breaks the symmetry. Central plaque by *William Bloye*. The back has giant Ionic pilasters of Kirby Hall type. Extensions by *Hobbiss & Partners*, 1948–51 and 1960, form three sides of a quad surrounding the MERMAID FOUNTAIN by *Bloye*, 1960. Inside, an impressive staircase leads to the DEBATING HALL with hammerbeam roof. Opulent fireplaces. To the E, ST FRANCIS' HALL, the University chaplaincy. First an octagonal building of 1968–9 by *Hobbiss & Partners*. Behind, the original *Hobbiss* building of 1936, with short 'nave' and low N–S gabled tower. To the S, facing Bristol Road, the SPORT AND FITNESS BUILDING by *Lifschutz Davidson*, completed 2017. The finest of the recent buildings, impressively articulated. From the road, an open colonnade, a gym and changing-room block in brick, beautifully laid in English garden wall bond to match Hobbiss, and the large swimming baths, glazed, with bronze trim. The N part houses a multi-storey car park, replacing one by *Casson, Conder & Partners* of 1964–5.

Opposite the Guild to the E, UNIVERSITY HOUSE, now BIRMINGHAM BUSINESS SCHOOL. By *Buckland & Haywood-Farmer*, 1908, friendly Arts and Crafts Neo-Georgian with linked stone windows and green slate roofs. Big boxy extension by *Architects Design Partnership* of Oxford, 2003–4. Further extension by *Glancy Nicholls*, 2019.

2. Buildings further east and north

N of the Guild of Students, King Edward's School and King Edward VI High School (p. 374). Turning l. from the Guild, the Barber Institute. In front, bronze equestrian STATUE of King George I. Commissioned in 1717 by the City of Dublin and installed there in 1722; bought in 1937. Attributed to *John van Nost the elder*, though probably executed by his assistants *Andrew Carpenter* and *Christopher Burchard* after his death. The heavily built king is in contemporary armour, but wears a laurel wreath.

The BARBER INSTITUTE is of 1936–9 by *Robert Atkinson*, for the visual arts and music. Atkinson was appointed in 1934; an impeccable choice, as an architect straddling modern and traditional tastes, and a noted connoisseur. The form is a central auditorium ringed by libraries, a ground-floor lecture hall, and an imposing sequence of top-lit galleries above. Brick dominates over stone, to be more in keeping with the neighbouring Guild of Students, with a plinth of Darley Dale stone. The styling owes much to Atkinson's growing fascination with Scandinavian classicism and also to the Boymans Museum, Rotterdam. *Rosemary Stjernstedt* was his principal assistant. Heraldic shields, and relief panels designed by *George Atkinson* (no relation) and executed by *Gordon Herickx*. The Boymans Museum also inspired the gallery interiors with their hessian wall coverings. The auditorium, panelled in Australian walnut with a proscenium of satin inlaid maple, is a skilful fusion of classical, Deco and Adamesque. The Institute is Atkinson's finest surviving work, and an exemplar of the influence of North European classicism in 1930s Britain. Only the glass roof by *Bickerdike Allen*, 1986–9, intrudes.

The best of the 1960s buildings were laid out along the ring road N of the Barber Institute. Facing us, the business-like DEPARTMENT OF EDUCATION by *Casson, Conder & Partners*, 1966–7. To the N, the Ashley and Strathcona buildings, now the DEPARTMENTS OF COMMERCE, SOCIAL SCIENCE, ACCOUNTING AND ECONOMICS, were early post-Casson & Conder realizations, in 1961–4. They were also early in the career of *Howell, Killick, Partridge & Amis*, appointed following their *succès d'estime* in the competition for Churchill College, Cambridge. The five-storey ASHLEY BUILDING brought together scattered departments, setting all sixty-nine tutors' rooms around a single atrium, through which coils a circular stair. It is the best 1960s space in the university, rough but full of panache. The exterior is clad in the full-height pre-cast panels that HKPA were among the first to use, here with distinctive sills to throw off rainwater. Next to it is the two-storey STRATHCONA BUILDING, a long curving tail designed to avoid a straight corridor, built of concrete blocks and housing lecture theatres and seminar rooms. Behind, the Muirhead Tower (*see above*). A bridge over the ring road leads to Pritchatts Road. On the NE, the GISBERT KAPP BUILDING (1964–8 by *Denys Hinton*) and No. 52 adjoining, were recast and tile-clad in 2010–11 by *Associated Architects*, who added the multi-storey CAR PARK r., 2014. Opposite (S side), the J.G. SMITH BUILDING, 1975–6, by *Casson, Conder & Partners*, for Urban and Local Government Studies. Then the ALAN WALTERS BUILDING, by *Berman Guedes Stretton*, 2016. Brick front, with a blank patterned wall, but glazed attractively to the W. Beyond it the former main University entrance, with *Buckland & Haywood*'s subtly curved LODGES and enclosing walls of 1930, and GATES by the *Birmingham Guild*.

Returning N across Pritchatts Road, the Interdisciplinary Research Centre has built the cool NET SHAPE BUILDING, 1996–8 by *Architects Design Partnership*, and has taken over the adjoining METALLURGY AND MATERIALS BUILDING of 1964 by *Philip Dowson* of *Arup Associates*. This has four linked laboratories, designed to be flexible internally and to provide a defining 'wall' at the campus edge. It was the first major building in England to use a 'tartan' grid to incorporate servicing, a concept developed in the US by Eero Saarinen and Louis Kahn. A column is placed at the corner of each pre-cast section, giving four columns internally where the corners join, allowing space for services between. These nodes are expressed externally by little roof vents. PLASMA LABORATORY behind by *Arup Associates*, 1970. Further behind, in Elms Road, W, the COMPUTER CENTRE, 1972–4 by *Casson, Conder & Partners*. Across Elms Road the EUROPEAN RESEARCH INSTITUTE,

2000–1 by *Feilden Clegg*, purple brick and prominent sunscreens. To the NW, No. 32 by *Harold S. Scott*, 1936–7. Opposite, the domestic-scaled former INSTITUTE FOR GERMAN STUDIES (No. 31) of 1994 by *Rathbone & Taylor*, its entrance in Hobbiss revival.

3. Buildings to the west

Walking s from Pritchatts Road, behind the Teaching Centre and Library, we reach a gross Postmodern addition of 1999 for GEOGRAPHY, EARTH AND ENVIRONMENTAL SCIENCES, by *Martin, Ward & Keeling*. Behind it, BIOSCIENCES of 1960 by *Playne & Lacey*, its ten-storey tower strongly modelled. Panels with bold pebble aggregate, projecting end window. Here is the W end of Webb & Bell's ranges (the Frankland Building) and, across University Road West, the OLD GYM of 1939 by *Peacock & Bewlay*, converted to offices by *Associated Architects*, 2017, and the HAWORTH BUILDING for Chemistry, also *Playne & Lacey*, 1957–61. Lower, with gently modern foyer. Beyond it, the SCHOOL OF ENGINEERING by *Associated Architects*, completed 2021. N of the road, the COLLABORATIVE TEACHING LABORATORY by *Sheppard Robson*, 2018, blue brick, with a pushing-out glazed front with diagonal fins. Beyond, the WESTGATE CENTRE, marking the entrance to the campus from University Station. On the S, COMPUTER SCIENCES, on the N, LEARNING CENTRE AND PRIMARY CARE, both by *Architects Design Partnership*, 1999. Between them *Eduardo Paolozzi*'s giant SCULPTURE of Faraday, a gift commemorating the University's centenary, 2000. To its S, PUBLIC HEALTH, 1996–8 by *Martin, Ward & Keeling*, and OCCUPATIONAL HEALTH by *Leonard J. Multon & Partners*, 1981–2.

Now we dive down paths behind the S side. Going E, BIOCHEMICAL ENGINEERING of 1955–7, extended 1987–8 by *David Rathbone*. Then CHEMICAL ENGINEERING of 1954–6 to its E, with another, behind, of 1925–6, both by the *Hobbiss* practice, and traditional. Mostly of three storeys. Finally the large MECHANICAL AND CIVIL ENGINEERING DEPARTMENTS, built in stages by *Peacock & Bewlay*, 1951–7. Additions by *Peter Neale* of the firm, 1962, three storeys, red brick and stone dressings, still traditional. Solid centrepiece with a big frame. SCULPTURE: frieze with lightning shot through a cogwheel, and groups of male students with their tutors, hieratic figures but in contemporary dress (including a duffel coat), by *Bloye*, 1954. Inconspicuous to the NE, Wrestlers, SCULPTURE by *E. Bainbridge Copnall*; 1950, sited 1974. From here we can return E up paths to Chancellor's Court.

4. Edgbaston Park Road and The Vale

N of Pritchatts Road, large houses taken over as University buildings. On the E side of Edgbaston Park Road, WINTERBOURNE by *J.L. Ball*, 1902–4. His finest house, for the housing expert J.S. Nettlefold. A long, low range with gabled porch and staircase projections. Strongly influenced by Lethaby but with an angular character of its own. The length reflects its Arts and Crafts single-pile plan. Wide hall and first-floor landing. Massive platbands continue the eaves line across the gables. Casement windows set flush. The garden front has end gables and a ground-floor loggia. The hall has a barrel-vault and fine plasterwork by *George Bankart*. Good early C20 gardens, now the UNIVERSITY BOTANIC GARDEN, including a Japanese garden with tea house and bridge. On the w, HORNTON GRANGE, brick Tudor, by *Arthur Edgerton Leeson*, 1928. Now part of the EDGBASTON PARK HOTEL AND CONFERENCE CENTRE by *Glancy Nicholls*, 2017. Tactful gables at the front, but very big behind. Then GARTH HOUSE by *W.H. Bidlake*, 1901, at his finest, for Ralph Heaton of the Birmingham Mint. Muthesius illustrated it in *Das englische Haus* (1904–5) and noted Bidlake's naturalness and simplicity. Red-blue brick below and roughcast above. Its seemingly random elevations are in fact carefully integrated, e.g. the garden front, s, with its big bay and paired gables balanced by a chimney which encloses a little window. It has an S-plan, carefully arranged round a low tower (with altered top) and the entrance hall, with its shallow barrel-vault and open-screened staircase. Casement windows quietly stress the transoms. The roughcast suggests Voysey, but his distinctive manner is felt only in the coachhouse range with its eyebrow arch and tapering chimney. Its entrance hall is a room in the Arts and Crafts way, with an inglenook and the stairs rising behind a screen of posts. Beyond, MEADOWCROFT, a restrained brick design by *Peacock, Bewlay & Cooke*, 1920. Opposite these, first WESTMERE, Italianate of 1858–60; then PRIORS FIELD, Domestic Revival by *Cossins, Peacock & Bewlay*, 1899–1900. Down a drive past a *Rundbogenstil* lodge, PARK HOUSE is a conservative stuccoed villa of 1852–3. Doric portico, badly treated. Later C19 stables with a massive extension by *A.S. Dixon*, 1914–15. Blank arches and tile banding, wonderfully patterned at one point with ventilation holes. Opposite, an early C19 cottage with hoodmoulds. No. 33, rambling and rendered, looks *c*. 1850 but has a C16 or C17 core. This shows on the SE front as a two-storey gable-end. Chimneystack to the l. probably also C17. On the E, going N, CENTRE COURT by *Benniman Design & Build*, 1990–1, and the TENNIS COURT flats, *Danks Rawcliffe*, 1981–8.

THE VALE is downhill on the l. *Casson & Conder*'s first commission at the University, in 1956, was to produce a layout for a new residential area here. The site was, in the architects' words, 'a mature, gracefully contoured and planted piece of parkland', which should be developed 'in the tradition of the English picturesque movement...but recreating it in contemporary terms'. Three large early C19 villas were demolished, and new landscaping mounded to shield the buildings to the NE. The low-lying damp centre became a lake. BRIDGE by

Neville Conder. The new parkland reflected that of Edgbaston Hall opposite (p. 377), and its Victorian exotics were enhanced with additional planting by *Mary Mitchell* to create a masterful piece of C18 landscape revivalism. Three halls of residence were set around the edge, only one of which survives. On the W MASON HALLS, massive curving ranges in glass and red terracotta by *Aedas*, 2006. At the rear WYDDRINGTON HALL and LAKE HALL, from 1998 SHACKLETON HALL, 1963–6 by *H.T. Cadbury-Brown*, remodelled 2003–4 as student flats by *Barton Fellows Ltd*. Further up, to the r., CHAMBERLAIN HALLS, tall angular blocks and tower, by *Glancy Nicholls*, 2015. Behind, MAPLE BANK by *Miall Rhys-Davies*, 1976–7.

OTHER PUBLIC BUILDINGS

BIRMINGHAM CHAMBER OF COMMERCE, Harborne Road and Highfield Road. By *John Madin*, 1959–60. The building which made his reputation, and now the only survivor of his greatest works, and Edgbaston's first post-war commercial tower. Four-storey block for the Chamber itself. Recessed ground floor with green Serpentino marble piers and blue and grey facings. Mullions of cream Travertine with Serpentino fillets. The W end cleverly disguises differing floor heights. Linked by a bridge, infilled by *Associated Architects*, 1996, to a simpler eight-storey block with aluminium mullions and a framing Travertine band, forming a T-shape. The foyer retains a *John Piper* MOSAIC: bright greens, yellows and oranges on a background of black and dark green with a little blue. An urban landscape, perhaps, with tall towers.

KING EDWARD'S SCHOOL for boys and KING EDWARD VI HIGH SCHOOL for girls, Edgbaston Park Road. By *Holland W. Hobbiss*, 1937–47. The boys' school was founded in 1552 in New Street, rebuilt there in 1731–4 and again splendidly in Tudor Gothic by *Charles Barry* with *A.W.N. Pugin*, 1833. FOUNDATION OFFICES flanked by square Nesfield-type lodges, their linking archways sadly removed. The BOARD ROOM has a marble chimneypiece of 1747 by *Peter Scheemakers* with crisp flowers and garlands, crowned by a bust of Edward VI. At the top of the drive the unfortunate DESIGN CENTRE by *Mason Richards*, 1987. Beyond, *Hobbiss*'s school buildings: a loose, subtly related brown-brick group, with stepped buttresses and big metal windows, pulled together by steep Lutyens-style roofs. The fenestration of BIG SCHOOL is a perfect example of Hobbiss's skill: full-height stone oriel, and tall windows under relieving arches, balanced by the long row of ground-floor triplets. Splendid oak hammerbeam roof with moulded pendants. Chief Master's CHAIR, canopied Gothic by *Pugin*, 1833, inscribed 'Sapientia'. DINING HALL with segmental barrel-vault and heraldic stained glass by *Moira Forsyth*, 1947. SWIMMING POOL, now covered, with colonnaded open loggia recalling Ernest Gimson. The detached CHAPEL is the re-erected Upper Corridor of *Barry*'s school, with a brick skin by

Hobbiss, 1952–3. The beautiful interior is Perp, in Darley Dale stone, with a lierne vault. Four-light windows in arched reveals, their mullions integral with the stone panelling. Details by *Pugin*. BENCHES made by boys, designed by *J. Bruce Hurn*. His impressive REREDOS is an Expressionist Crucifixion (restored by *Lissa Lester*, 2007–10, after overpainting). RUDDOCK PERFORMING ARTS CENTRE designed by *Haworth Tompkins* but delivered by the contractor, *Shaylor*, with architects *ADP*, 2013. Brick, with patterns of musical notation. Glazed foyer, dance studio above. Concert hall with recessed balconies. SPORTS CENTRE to the S, brown-clad, by *BDP*, 2017.

QUEEN'S COLLEGE (now the Queen's Foundation), Somerset Road. A theological college, founded in 1828, in Paradise Street from 1843, amalgamated with Handsworth Methodist College (p. 251) in 1970. L-shaped accommodation block by *Holland W. Hobbiss*, 1928–30, Neo-Georgian, with steep roofs and dormers with alternating plain and segmental pediments. *Hobbiss*'s CHAPEL was begin in 1939 but completed only in 1947. Charming, almost toy-like, Romanesque, with an apse. In the porch a relief by *William Bloye*. Hobbiss's twin amboes and altar (the first in the Church of England made for celebration facing the congregation) were swept away in the early C21. His chunky W gallery survives, with a very Eric Gill-like Christ and angels by *Bloye*. Office and lecture-room block, and students' flats, forming a loose quadrangle, by *John H.D. Madin & Partners*, 1965–6. To the W more flats, by the *John Madin Design Group*, 1972, heavier, with concrete balconies.

BIRMINGHAM CITY UNIVERSITY (CITY SOUTH CAMPUS), Westbourne Road. The former School of Education buildings by *A.G. Sheppard Fidler*, 1957–8, transformed and extended since 2010 by *Associated Architects*, *Robothams*, and *Sheppard Robson* (the prominent brick-framed block facing the road).

WEST MIDLANDS POLICE LEARNING AND DEVELOPMENT CENTRE, Pershore Road. 1964 by *A.G. Sheppard Fidler*, City Architect (job architect *Joan Zunde*). Cleanly detailed eight-storey tower, lower ranges round an informal courtyard. – STATUE. Sir Robert Peel, by *Peter Hollins*, 1855, standing as if debating. Moved here 1963.

QUEEN ELIZABETH HOSPITAL, New Fosse Way and Mindelsohn Way. Two contrasting hospitals. The first is by *Lanchester & Lodge*, 1934–8. Three buff-brick blocks set behind each other, in a formal Beaux Arts plan: University Medical School, the huge hospital proper, and nurses' home. The largest British medical development of its time, co-ordinating many services on one campus. The Medical School has an austere framed entrance, with a panel of Aesculapius by *Bloye*, 1938. On either side the façade plays with recessed planes. The hospital has balconies along the ward floors and at the ends of the wings (now glazed in). It steps up to a clock tower.

The new hospital to the W, also huge, is by *BDP*, 2008–10. Three pristine white curved blocks set side by side and linked by a wing behind, which contains the main end-to-end atrium.

At the E end, the main entrance, a lower wing and the end of the main block are united by a whizzy canopy sailing upwards. To the NE, the INSTITUTE OF BIOMEDICAL RESEARCH, orange brick, by *RMJM*, 2003. – SCULPTURES. Between the hospitals, Compassion, by *Uli Nimptsch*, 1963. Two figures, one with a bowl caring for the other. By the new hospital entrance, To The Future, by *Richard Thornton*, 2013, bright twisted metal.

METCHLEY ROMAN FORT, New Fosse Way. Investigated by excavations in advance of development. The first fort (10 acres), built between the late 40s and late 50s A.D., had defended annexes on all sides and a short-lived *vicus* (civilian settlement) outside it. It subsequently became a supply depot with enclosures and funnelling ditches to its W, probably for livestock management. In the 70s this was replaced by a smaller fort, again with livestock enclosures outside. It was abandoned by the mid C2. In the N part of the fort, between University railway station, the Medical School and the Queen Elizabeth Hospital, grassed banks of modern landscaping (2012) indicate the lines of ramparts of the first fort, its annexes and the smaller, later fort.

WARWICKSHIRE COUNTY CRICKET GROUND, Edgbaston Road. The county side moved here in 1886. Basic older stands. Cottagey scoreboard of 1938. ERIC HOLLIES STAND of 2003 by *Bryant Priest Newman*, with slim, angled aluminium roof. The PAVILION END and main entrance block is by *Broadway Malyan*, 2011, a cut-price Senedd with angled-out blue front on piers. Separate, facing Pershore Road, the EDGBASTON INDOOR CRICKET CENTRE, by *Bryant Priest Newman* with *David Morley Architects*, 2000. Gabled front with zigzag canopies, faced in terracotta tiles. Artwork, texts by *Renn & Thacker*.

CALTHORPE PARK, Pershore Road. Opened in 1855, given to the city in 1871 by Lord Calthorpe and then laid out by *W.S. Till*, Borough Surveyor. Dour Gothic LODGE on the corner of Speedwell Road by *D. Smith & Son*, 1872.

BOTANICAL GARDENS, Westbourne Road. Laid out 1831–2 in the grounds of the villa HOLLY BANK of 1822, now engulfed by later buildings. The original garden design by *J.C. Loudon* partly survives. ENTRANCE LODGE of 1831 by *Rickman & Hutchinson*, heavily altered. New ENTRANCE of 1986–7, when much rebuilding was done by *Peter Hing & Jones*. Arches mimicking the Terrace Glasshouses (*see* below). Inside, going S, the TROPICAL HOUSE, reconstructed 1991 by *Peter Hing & Jones*, incorporating the remains of *Charles Edge*'s LILY HOUSE of 1852. Beyond, the SUB-TROPICAL HOUSE is the remaining part of *F.B. Osborn*'s PALM HOUSE of 1871. It lost its clerestory in a gale in 1967, but retains a three-bay cast-iron arcade with twisted columns. On the S side, thin Corinthian pilasters. To the W, the TERRACE GLASSHOUSES of 1884, designed and made by *Henry Hope & Sons*. Tall round-arched central feature with original petal tracery. Behind, decorative chimneystack or 'Smoke Tower' by *Osborn*, *c*.1884. To the E, *Peter Hing & Jones*'s PAVILION RESTAURANT of 1990. The GARDENS have a main lawn and curving paths sloping downhill, part of *Loudon*'s design, conserved after 1978. To the S, FOUNTAIN of 1850 by *Charles Edge*, and octagonal BANDSTAND by *F.B. Osborn*, 1873 with columns like the Palm House. To the SE, eye-catching AVIARY of 1995 with four domed flights surrounding a lobby with tall square cupola finial. Concept by *Ian Morris*, design by *Ken Fairbairn* of *Peter Hing & Jones*. To the SW, a GAZEBO of *c*.1850, rebuilt here in 1994. In the Herb Garden in the far SW corner, a COTTAGE of 1847–8 by *S.S. Teulon*, who took over the foundations of a house begun by *Edge & Avery* in 1846. T-plan, shaped gables and mullion-and-transom windows, some stepping up the centre. It originally stood in the Guinea Gardens (p.390).

MUSEUM (now Birmingham Wildlife Conservation Park), Pershore Road, opposite Pebble Mill Road. By *A.L. Snow* and *Arthur Edgerton Leeson*, 1930. A classical box with a recessed small pediment, oculus and big Doric doorcase (currently hidden). Behind it a double avenue of 1920, the approach to the unusual BOY SCOUTS' WAR MEMORIAL, by *William Haywood*, 1924. A short triangular obelisk on a base with big consoles.

EDGBASTON HALL, Church Road, S of St Bartholomew. Now a golf clubhouse. Wall and brick LODGE, with odd perforated patterning, probably of 1850 by *S.S. Teulon*, but much extended. The HALL itself was rebuilt by Sir Richard Gough in 1717, perhaps by *Francis Smith*. Plain five-bay SE front. Three storeys, brick, in old-fashioned English bond, with grey stone quoins and lintels. Simple dentil cornice and parapet. An unusually early instance of a *piano nobile*, its windows enlarged in the C19. NE wing of 1751–2 by *William & David Hiorne*, with rubbed brick lintels. Central porch with pierced brick parapet, probably part of alterations of 1852–3 by *Sir Charles Barry*. The doorcase is probably the original, moved forward: grey stone Doric half-columns and sandstone entablature. Canted SW bay of 1852–3, heightened 1937 by *Harvey & Wicks*. The ENTRANCE HALL has a fine staircase of 1751–2 by the *Hiornes*, U-shaped, in three flights, with twisted balusters and swept-up corners marked by little fluted Corinthian columns. Matching pilasters to the dado. Contemporary arch on the first floor, with panelling and fluted pilasters. C18 panelling in the CALTHORPE ROOM (ground floor, E) and in the SNOOKER ROOM upstairs. Some reworking, probably by *Harvey & Wicks* in 1937. The LOUNGE, beyond the hall, and the MEMBERS' LIBRARY have refined Jacobean panelling and fireplaces, probably early C20. The LADIES' LOUNGE (NE wing) has good *Hiorne* fittings: doorcases with eared architraves and pediments, dignified fireplace.

STREETS

Streets are listed below in alphabetical order, and usually ascending number order, but some suggested perambulations may be helpful.

1. Hagley Road, W from Five Ways to St Augustine's Road, with a diversion N up Monument Road, and further W if desired to Barnsley Road.
2. Harborne Road W from Five Ways, with diversions S and N into Highfield Road, Vicarage Road and Chad Road, and, beyond the White Swan, S up Richmond Hill Road to Farquhar Road and Pritchatts Road.
3. An extension of Perambulation 2, from Harborne Road W and NW up Westfield Road, with a look at Norfolk Road, to Woodbourne Road and Hermitage Road. This can be combined with Perambulation 1 in a long loop.
4. Calthorpe Road, SW from Five Ways, with a look at Greenfield Crescent, to St George's church. Then W down Westbourne Road and back, and S along Church Road to Carpenter Road and Ampton Road, ending at the Old Church to the SE.
5. From the Old Church, NE down Arthur Road, diverting S and E by Carpenter Road into Gough and Charlotte roads, then St James Road. Ryland Road and Lee Crescent can be reached from here, with the return NW to Five Ways from St James Road, looking at George and Frederick roads.
6. From the Old Church, a loop E down Wellington Road and SW along Bristol Road to Priory Road, then back NW up Sir Harry's Road to the start.

AMPTON ROAD runs SE off Carpenter Road, to Wellington Road. No. 12 is *J.H. Chamberlain*'s first house, built for his uncle's partner Mr Eld in 1855. The first High Victorian house in the town, inspired by Butterfield and Continental sources. Insistently vertical among low, spreading villas. Red brick with lots of yellow and blue patterning, and Bath stone dressings. The SE front has a tall gable with a canted bay, balanced by a short wing with segmental windows above lancets. Big gabled doorhood in the angle. Quoins with nook-shafts. Contemporary stables, E. Well-preserved interior. A square lobby leads to a dizzily tall stair hall with a ceiling on brackets and big skylight. Iron balustrade with ivy leaves below the rail and supports with paired twisted and plain colonnettes. The main rooms have marble fireplaces with ivy and shamrock leaves.

Beyond, two Tudor villas by *Bateman*; No. 11 (1855) has been roughcast, and has a square bay of 1911. No. 10, dated 1860, looks like *Yeoville Thomason*. Ample stone dressings, wavy bargeboards. No. 9 rich Italianate, also No. 17. The WALKER MEMORIAL HALL was the parish school. Low Tudor ranges of 1847 etc. No. 18, the slightly later schoolmaster's house, is probably by *F.W. Fiddian*. Rogue Gothic with cusped windows outlined in blue and yellow brick. Nos. 5–7 pre-date the estate development: C18 cottages recast *c.*1840 with slight Tudor details. Beyond Arthur Road, NE side, big stucco villas of *c.*1852-3.

ARTHUR ROAD. The S continuation of Wheeleys Road. The interest is on the NW side. At the start, WARWICK CREST, a light sixteen-storey block by *Madin & Partners*, 1962-3, faced in blue brick and mosaic. Then two picturesque bargeboarded Tudor villas by *Yeoville Thomason*, 1854–5. Beyond Ampton Road, No. 3, stuccoed classical of 1855. Then Nos. 1 and 2 of 1849–51, almost certainly by *F.W. Fiddian* (cf. No. 43 Wellington Road, p. 389). No. 1B, EDGBASTON VICARAGE, is by *Hobbiss & Partners*, c. 1967.

BARNSLEY ROAD runs N from Hagley Road at the city boundary. A whole development designed by *J.L. Ball*. Not as radical as some of his work: stylistic gestures are restrained Old English or Queen Anne, but vernacular traditions lie behind. The start is Nos. 441–451 Hagley Road, with tile-hung dormers and pent-roofed porches and bays. In Barnsley Road, on the r., large semi-detached pairs of 1898 with hipped roofs, large dormers, massive canted bays and steeply gabled porch hoods. Opposite, smaller pairs of 1900–1 with roughcast above. Methodist church (p. 364) at the top. The houses continue E in Sandon Road with Nos. 42–52. Further E, No. 40, good Arts and Crafts of c. 1900, probably by *Arthur McKewan*, and Nos. 36–38 by *Newton & Cheatle*, 1899–1900.

BRISTOL ROAD. A turnpike road of 1771; it runs SW dead straight for a mile from the Wellington Road junction. The interest starts near the corner of Speedwell Road. All stuccoed. On the NW, No. 93 of c. 1840; Nos. 95–97, perhaps slightly earlier, with a veranda on wrought-iron columns. A narrow lane leads to plain No. 103, c. 1825 with rear wing by *M.O. Type*, 1917, and No. 99, slightly later, with delicate leaf first-floor architraves, hoodmoulds below, and an iron tent-roof porch. Up a further drive, Nos. 101 and 101A, long, low stuccoed houses of c. 1938 by *Peacock & Bewlay*, with a little Art Deco detail. In their garden a remarkable but puzzling Gothick GROTTO. Pedimented front with pointed windows, ogee-arched doorway, and short obelisk pinnacles. The rear is semicircular but only the lower wall survives. It is faced in blast-furnace slag, in small pieces, over brick. Doorway and windows have surrounds patterned in shells and animals' teeth. Shell frieze. Panels inside framed by vertebrae, probably from sheep and cows, and with more shells. In one place bones make a kind of Greek key ornament. Probably built for James Guest, a merchant, shortly after c. 1814 when development started here. In 1827, when a grove is marked on the tithe map, this was his 'Pleasure Ground and Plantation'. Opposite, No. 96 (The Corinthians) of 1850–1 has a Corinthian porch and Corinthian pilasters to the canted bays; round-headed upper windows linked by a string. The splendid conservatory is a little later. No. 98 of 1845–6 has architraved windows, channelled ground floor, and porch with detail suggesting *John Fallows*. VICEROY CLOSE, flats of 1938 by *Mitchell & Bridgwater* and *Gollins & Smeeton*, the city's most sophisticated of their time. Six-storey blocks in a mature landscape of trees and lawns. Symmetrical, with five-storey canted bays flanking the recessed porches. Centrally placed office with hipped roof. SCULPTURE by *Oliver O'Connor Barrett*: childlike PANEL on the office of the Temptation of St Anthony (who looks like Tintin), and masks grinning over the porches. Opposite, municipal housing of 1978 with prominent pent-roofed porches, by *W.G. Reed*, City Architect (*Nigel Davies*, project architect); Nos. 136–142, stucco pairs of 1829–32 with round-headed doorcases; and more municipal housing by *Reed* (and *Davies*), 1984–5. No. 160 is a Jacobean survivor with shaped gables, dated 1871. Opposite, early C19 cottages, then a Gothic pair of *c.* 1870. Further on, Nos. 211–217, long low pairs of 1850 etc., no longer stuccoed. Nos. 219–221 are earlier, *c.* 1830, stuccoed, with round-headed doorcases. Nos. 223–231 are a picturesque group of 1849 by *F.W. Fiddian*: a low villa, a larger classical house; a three-storey Italianate town house, and a cottagey Tudor Gothic pair.

Beyond Priory Road and further SW, Park Grove's early C19 LODGE, the drive now leading to the ELMHURST SCHOOL FOR DANCE, pedestrian and angular, by *Weightman & Bullen*, 2004.

CALA DRIVE runs N between Nos. 11 and 12 Carpenter Road. Distinguished infill by *J.H.D. Madin & Partners*, 1962–3. Detached houses step in and out downhill. At the bottom, a footpath into ESTRIA ROAD. Terraces and two-storey flats, with typical Madin recessions, here for open balconies and porches. Grey-buff brick and dark hexagonal tile-hanging. Brick piers support lapped timber roof canopies. The blocks are square, occasionally stepped; the roads and tree'd lawns curve round them.

CALTHORPE ROAD. Starting at Five Ways, on the corner of Islington Row, LLOYDS BANK, by *P.B. Chatwin*, 1908–9. Treated as two sides of a square Palladian villa, with a giant Ionic order and open central pediments. No. 60, in the fork with Harborne Road, is of 1814–15 by *George Jones*, builder, for himself. A catalogue of local Late Georgian details: porch with quadrants, flanked by windows with fluted pillarets; tripartite window above divided by slim fluted pillarets; *œil de bœuf* in the pediment. In front a late C19 Gothic CLOCK. Then poor late C20 blocks. No. 12, SE side, by *John Madin*, 1961–2, has an elegant slab linked to a lower block extending SW. Dark marble-clad verticals and mosaic panels. Characteristic recessed entrance between pilotis. Re-cladding and upwards extensions proposed 2021, by *Glancy Nicholls*. Beyond, NW side, semi-detached pairs of 1876 etc. built by *John Barnsley & Sons*, the central one removed for an inert office scheme by the *Weedon Partnership*, 1988. Opposite, villas of *c.* 1815–20. No. 20 is stuccoed, with a doorcase with incised ornament, and windows in segment-headed recesses; Nos. 24–25 have Doric doorcases, No. 26 a full porch. On the NW side, pairs of *c.* 1830 with incised giant pilasters. Then No. 36 of 1830 by *John Fallows*, set back, a three-bay villa with single-storey wings. Fluted baseless Corinthian columns to the porch, similar capitals to the first-floor pilasters. Tapering window architraves. No. 35, of 1829 by *Fallows*, faces SW to St George's church (p. 361). Greek Revival, with full Doric portico, but the detail is restless. Opposite, No. 31, now the core of St GEORGE'S SCHOOL, *c.* 1830, also by *Fallows*.

Round-arched windows below. Extended NE by *J.A. Chatwin*, 1893, and later. Rear hall by *Jackson & Edmonds*, 1961. Low Junior School block with small monopitched roof by *Kelly & Surman*, 1971.

CARPENTER ROAD. Starting from Church Road, W, on the N side a fine stucco group: Nos. 3–6, begun 1834, and Nos. 7–14, 1844–52. Nos. 4–5 still Regency with delightful concave-roofed iron porches. No. 7 has Soanian detail and a porch which looks like *John Fallows*. No. 12, with Ionic porch and segment-headed windows, is by *D.R. Hill*, 1849. On the S side, two houses of 1865: No. 51, chunky bargeboarded Tudor Gothic by *J.J. Bateman*; and No. 50, brick Gothic by *J.H. Chamberlain*. A stone blind arcade continues as the open cusped arches of the porch. No. 49 is heavy stuccoed classical of the 1860s. Carpenter Road continues to Wellington Road with some Victorian classical villas, e.g. Nos. 35 and 36.

CHAD ROAD runs N from Harborne Road to Hagley Road. Italianate villas of *c*. 1850: Nos. 8–9 a mirrored pair probably by *J.J. Bateman*; No. 6 a fine design perhaps by *Charles Edge*, with smooth rustication, doorcase with teardrop fanlight, and plaster panels above. Nos. 4–5 are by *Madin*, 1958, low, with exposed concrete floor-plate. No. 15 of 1838 (E side) must be by *Edge*, who did similar houses in the road, now demolished. Slightly projecting centre with Doric porch. Nos. 16–17, yellow London brick, are by *Deakin & Phipson*, 1853.

CHARLOTTE ROAD. Good stucco villas of 1847–9 etc. (GOUGH ROAD, running W, has more.) Nos. 13–14 are an Italianate pair with low end towers by *J.J. Bateman*, 1851, Nos. 17–18 a brick 'Lombardic' pair by *Yeoville Thomason*, 1853–4. No. 20, a large villa with Palladian alternating pediments.

CHURCH ROAD. The E side starts by St George's church, N end, with houses now linked and extended as retirement apartments, by *Quad Projects*, 2012–16. BEECHWOOD HOUSE is of 1823, an extended stucco villa with a Doric porch. THE CHAINS, by *Oliver Essex* for himself, 1894, Domestic Revival, with a Rococo terracotta name plaque. Then a fine stucco villa of 1818 with rusticated ground floor and sashes in round-headed recesses. Doric porch. Semicircular bows behind. Extensions of 1898–9 by *F.B. Osborn* for the former Royal Institution for Deaf and Dumb Children, with an attractive Venetian window breaking into the pediment, S.*

The W side starts with No. 53, the former CALTHORPE ESTATE OFFICES, by *Hobbiss*, dated 1935. HALLFIELD SCHOOL occupies BEECH LAWN, an ornate villa of *c*. 1860. Piquant Gothic LODGE. No. 45, *c*. 1828. Later square bays. Beyond, the University's Vale site (*see* p. 373). On the E, No. 10, mid-Victorian brick Gothic. Then No. 11 by *Buckland & Haywood*, 1936–7. An austere cubic brick block with metal windows and (formerly) a tilted glass canopy. Shaped gatepiers

---

*The Institution's main building of 1859 by *F.W. Fiddian* (replacing a Gothick original of the 1810s), and *Rickman*'s Master's House, Tudor Revival of 1829, lay to the SE. Demolished *c*. 1960.

(garden with FOUNTAIN by *Bloye*). No. 12 is Greek Revival of 1827 with mid-C19 alterations. No. 13, LAWNFIELD, 1855, built by *John Barnsley*, is rich Italianate with a Corinthian porch. No. 14, 1850, classical, with a Doric porch facing N. On the W, two grand C19 gateways and Nos. 33 and 34, lodges of *c.* 1850. Beyond the cross-roads are the Hall and St Bartholomew's church (pp. 377, 359). Opposite the church, a bungalow with monopitch-roofed wings: *Douglas Hickman (John Madin Design Group)*, 1980.

ELVETHAM ROAD. On the corner of the Middleway, LEOFRIC COURT by *Hickton Madeley*, 1982–3, with double-level balconies on light timber supports. Nos. 18–24, E side, stucco and brick villas of the 1860s–70s. Beyond St James Road, the former St James's church (p. 362), and Neo-Georgian vicarage of 1911–12 by *C.E. Bateman*. Opposite, along St James Road, WEST HOUSE SCHOOL occupies two stucco villas of the 1830s, one with a pyramid-roofed tower.

ENFIELD ROAD, off Islington Row. Former VESTRY HALL, by *F.W. Fiddian*, 1848. Neo-Norman.

FARQUHAR ROAD. At the N end No. 4, ornate classical Jacobean, and No. 6, more severe, both by the builder *John Briley*, 1879–80. No. 8 is by *Crouch & Butler*, 1898, Neo-Georgian in an Ernest Newton way. Nos. 3–5 opposite are a mirror pair, severe Queen Anne by *William Hale*, 1889. No. 7 is by *Crouch & Butler*, 1905, Arts and Crafts Tudor with big r. wing, recessed porch, full-height bay with steep gable, and wing l. with central end chimney. No. 10 is heavy latest classical, 1870s. No. 12, with bargeboarded bays flanking a picturesque centre, is probably *Talbot Brown & Fisher*, 1887. No. 18, Gothic, by *Briley*, 1879–80; No. 11 by *Harrison & Cox*, 1924. No. 15 is by *Buckland & Haywood-Farmer*, 1907, roughcast *à la* Voysey, but much more blunt. No. 17, dated 1907, is by *Martin & Martin*. Also roughcast, but slightly smoother. A smaller gabled wing tucked in r., then a gabled porch, a dynamic combination. No. 19, timber-gabled, is by *F.B. Osborn*, 1898. Then two by *William Withers*, No. 21 (1883) like late *Rundbogenstil*, No. 23 (1880) Gothic. No. 25 also probably *Withers*, 1878–9. No. 27, Jacobean-ish, is by *Essex, Nicol & Goodman*, 1903. Nos. 48 and 50 opposite are by *Henman & Cooper*, 1898, brick and render, with quirky columned porches; No. 48 was Henman's own house. No. 52 is a fine, austere Arts and Crafts design by *H.T. Buckland*, 1899–1900, also brick and render. Across Somerset Road (p. 388), on the l. WHETSTONE CLOSE, flats by *John H.D. Madin*, 1962 etc. Opposite, the side of Queen's College (p. 375), then Nos. 71–73, long, low tutors' houses by the *John Madin Design Group*, 1974–5. To their r. a cottage and stable by *Henman & Cooper*, 1899, with a little cupola piquantly at an angle. No. 76 opposite is a big brick Gothic house of 1879–80, very like *J.H. Chamberlain*'s early manner. Nos. 78 and 80 of 1880–1, Gothic becoming Queen Anne, built by *James Moffat* and perhaps designed by him. Opposite, No. 79, SEVEN GABLES, by *W.H. Bidlake*, 1914. Three of the gables form the dramatic street front, the centre one taller, recessed, with the entrance. Three mullion-and-transom windows above with patterned tilework tympana, all different, and a tile-hung gable. Almost sculptural chimneys, unusual for Bidlake. No. 81 is Tudor Revival by *Harry Weedon*, 1923.

FREDERICK ROAD. Small-scale and mostly residential, except for one big interruption on the SE: FIVE WAYS TOWER by *Philip Bright* of the *Property Services Agency*, 1979, a twenty-three-storey office tower and two-storey podium. It was an extension to FIVE WAYS HOUSE, round the corner in Islington Row, an eight-storey curtain-walled block of 1956–7 by *Eric Bedford* of the Ministry of Works (architect in charge *L. G. Pargiter*). Nos. 45–49 are of 1839–45. Slightly projecting doorcases with panelled jambs. Nos. 42–44, more obviously Victorian, are of 1853, probably by *J.A. Chatwin* (cf. Nos. 38–39). On the SE side, Nos. 14–15 of 1822, with good doorcases. No. 16 by *John Madin*, 1957, is a simple handsome statement with cantilevered Travertine-faced first floor. Characteristic recessed entrance, with a free-standing patterned slate slab. Beyond St James Road a good group all of 1828. Nos. 19–20 are so dated. Nos. 21–26 are consistent semi-detached pairs, with simple side entrances and early bays. Nos. 27–28 have teardrop fanlights which look like *Bateman & Drury*. No. 29 is a big villa of *c.* 1830, beyond its pedimented coachhouse. Beyond, down a drive, three Classical Revival houses by *Sinclair Architects*, 1994. Returning NE, on the NW side, Nos. 31–34, pairs of 1844–6 with Greek Revival detail. No. 32 tactfully extended in 1866. Then a group of 1850. Nos. 35–36 and 37 are Italianate. Nos. 38–39 are *J.A. Chatwin*'s first design, before he trained with Barry. Arched windows and heavy shell-hoods.

GEORGE ROAD. From Islington Row, on the SE, a brick pair of 1830–1 with fancy detail. Nos. 43–44 of 1830, probably by *Bateman & Drury*, have rubbed brick lintels and arched doorways. Opposite, Nos. 5–7, early development of 1820 including a pedimented pair. On the SE side again, stucco pairs of the 1830s and two handsome pedimented brick villas of *c.* 1833. Then an unusual Greek Revival villa of 1827 with recessed centre and doorcase with simplified Tower of the Winds capitals. Garden front, SE, with giant pilasters. Here is the Friends' Meeting House (p. 365) and St James Road. Beyond, on the SE, a stucco villa and terrace of three of *c.* 1820 with fluted Tuscan columns to the doorcases. No. 29 is of 1818, but its porch looks *c.* 1830 and by *John Fallows*. Opposite, No. 22, a mid-1830s stucco villa facing SW.* The façade, with recessed centre and small pediment, is the first of a series otherwise associated with *Charles Edge* (Apsley House, Wellington Road; No. 15 Chad Road). Up a drive beyond, No. 23, THE BOTHY, was its coachhouse, stable and garden room. Tudor Revival of *c.* 1860,

---

* Hansom & Welch built a house here in 1833 but went bankrupt before they signed the lease: either No. 22 or that adjoining, now demolished.

bargeboarded and battlemented. No. 25 is nouveau-Georgian by *Lapworth*, 2019.

GREENFIELD CRESCENT. Developed in 1875–6. N from Calthorpe Road towards Harborne Road, on the SW corner, No. 19, almost certainly by *J. H. Chamberlain*, with foliage panels above the ground-floor windows. Houses beyond mostly by *Henry Naden*. On the E side Nos. 1–2, probably by *G. T. Haylock*, Jacobean hinting at Queen Anne.

HAGLEY ROAD. Starting from Five Ways, on the r. the nineteen-storey METROPOLITAN HOUSE, 1972–4, offices by the *John Madin Design Group*, with wings offset from a central core, and canted glazed corner bays. Too close behind it, a featureless block by *BDP*, 2019, and the intrusive TRICORN HOUSE by *Sidney Kaye, Eric Firmin & Partners*, 1973–4. FRANCIS ROAD runs N here with façaded houses mostly of c. 1838. Nos. 75–79 are a single composition, the end houses with Ionic porches, the central one plainer. No. 73, probably later, is Italianate, with pedimented upper windows and heavy porch. Nos. 71 and 72 have delicately recessed windows and pedimented doorcases. Back on Hagley Road, opposite, the overblown Neo-Georgian MARRIOTT HOTEL by *Cotton, Ballard & Blow*, 1958–60. In front, STATUE of Joseph Sturge by *John Thomas*, 1859. Beyond, mid-C20 towers of Madin's plan, interspersed with Georgian survivors. On the N, HAGLEY HOUSE, *Madin & Partners*, 1963–5, exposed concrete structure and glass-mosaic facing panels. Nos. 93–95, early C19, have Tuscan porches with garland friezes. Nos. 97–107, a terrace, and No. 109 beyond, are part of a symmetrical scheme of 1819–20, unusual for Edgbaston; the balancing l. terrace was never built. Developer *John Harris*, plumber; *Thomas* and *Joseph Bateman* acted as surveyors and probably designed them. Handsome Greek Doric doorcases and giant pilasters above. Façaded by *Madin & Partners*, 1975. No. 111 by *Harry Bloomer & Son*, 1965, has a low circular forebuilding and office block behind. Nos. 119–121, early C19 with handsome semicircular bays. On the S side, No. 54 by the *Madin Design Group*, 1974–8; LYNDON HOUSE by *Madin*, 1962–4, its mosaic replaced by render. No. 64 of 1795, by the builder *Charles Surman Smith*, is the earliest survivor of the Edgbaston development. Doric porch, flanked by triplet windows with thin colonnettes. Then a *Madin* block of 1962. Opposite, No. 123 of 1965–7 was *John Madin Design Group*'s own offices, brown brick with long horizontals balanced by Louis Kahn-style stair-towers. The PLOUGH AND HARROW is by *John Fallows*, 1832, Tudor Revival for Lord Calthorpe, who disliked it as 'ultra-gothick'. Orange brick with eroded pink sandstone dressings. Three S gables, the central one shaped. Larger E extension, 1863–4. Bargeboarded STABLES behind of c. 1825, classical in form but with Tudor detail. Cupola with boar's-head weathervane.

Across Plough and Harrow Road, the Oratory (p. 363). Opposite, No. 76, Early Victorian with a Tuscan porch. Then a Late Georgian group: Nos. 78–84 with central bargeboarded gables; Nos. 86–92, pairs now linked, with doorcases with teardrop fanlights. These look like *Bateman & Drury*. No. 100 by *Madin*, 1965, shinily refaced and heightened by *online-architects*, 2009. Opposite, beyond the Oratory, buildings of the former ST PHILIP'S SIXTH FORM COLLEGE by *Paul Bonham & Associates*, 1968–9. WINDSOR TERRACE of 1845, perhaps by *J.R. Botham*, runs N. Stucco pairs with ground-floor windows in shallow reveals. Further W, the IVY BUSH pub on the NE corner of Monument Road, reconstructed 1929, probably by *J.P. Osborne & Son*.

Beyond, the N side has late C19 shops: Nos. 189–195 by *Bland & Cossins*, 1882; Nos. 197–199 by *Radclyffe & Watson*, 1888–9, brown terracotta and red brick, with giant fluted pilasters. ST CHAD'S COURT by *Diamond Partnership*, 1990–1, engulfs a good five-bay Late Georgian house with unusual detailing. No. 215, *c.* 1800, with a mid-C19 r. bay and porch. Original doorcase repositioned, facing Stirling Road. Beyond Stirling Road the WARWICKSHIRE MASONIC TEMPLE by the *John Madin Design Group*, 1968–71. A blank brick block sculpturally treated, the piers recessed between panels above, but splaying out below. Further W, the THISTLE HOTEL, a circular 'Dekotel' with lower-level car parking, by *Duke & Simpson*, 1970–1.

At the cross-roads beyond, two big Gothic pairs of the 1860s. Then a fine classical run. Nos. 198–200 are a big pair of 1853–4 with pedimented end wings. No. 202, 1852, asymmetrical. No. 204 of 1853–5, a conventional three-bay villa. Nos. 210 and 212, 1860s villas much extended. No. 214, *c.* 1840, stuccoed, with Doric porch. The N side here is much more Gothic. No. 257 has a triple-arched recessed porch. The picturesque *Bateman & Corser* pairs of 1872–4 in St Augustine's Road (p. 394) spread on to Hagley Road with Nos. 271–277. Much further W, Nos. 405–409, early Rotton Park estate villas of *c.* 1860, and No. 415, by *J.L. Ball*, dated 1902. One of his simplest and most radical houses. Plain brickwork, flush casements, gabled porch; plaster cove at the eaves. The end gables stand slightly proud of the roof. For houses further W *see* Barnsley Road.

HARBORNE ROAD. The start from Five Ways is between the backs of Hagley Road and Calthorpe Road. On the l., pairs of 1876–7 built by *John Barnsley & Sons*. Set back on the NW, NEVILLE HOUSE, by *Douglas Hickman* of the *John Madin Design Group*, 1975–6. A beautifully crisp Miesian glass box, the ground floor recessed behind piers, on a chamfered base of small square rough-textured stone. On the corner of Highfield Road, the Birmingham Chamber of Commerce (p. 374). Beyond on the r., No. 81, a grand classical villa of *c.* 1855. *J.J. Bateman* worked round here, and the linked ground- and first-floor windows look like his work. Opposite, Nos. 38 and 40 of *c.* 1829–30, villas with smooth rustication and solid Greek Doric doorcases. The wreaths in the friezes suggest *John Fallows*. No. 46 is probably also *c.* 1830, attractive orange-red brick. On the N side No. 89, roguish Jacobean Revival of 1851 for the builder

George Branson, almost certainly by *J.A. Chatwin*. Entrance with alternating banded Ionic columns, canted bay above, square bays with V-shaped projections. Opposite, Nos. 52–54 of *c.* 1830, with round-headed doorcases of *Bateman & Drury* type. Further on, s side, FERNDALE, by *Martin & Chamberlain*, 1868–9, a good survivor of J.H. Chamberlain's earlier houses. Two steep gables. Pairs and triplets of Gothic windows, on the ground floor at the l. with incised stone tympana. Gothic porch with a sexfoil in the gable. (For Harborne Road further sw, *see* Westbourne Road.)

HERMITAGE ROAD, From the SE end. WEST POINT, flats by *Madin*, 1959. Opposite, houses by *Bateman & Corser* of 1877–80. No. 19A a former lodge; Nos. 11 (much extended), 15 and 19 austere brick villas with some details in common: segment-headed windows, hipped roofs. Old-fashioned No. 9 is by *Walter Wright*, 1894. No. 7, OAK GRANGE, is by *Alfred Reading*, 1894, with Old English half-timbered gables, but a shell-hood porch. Opposite, Nos. 22–24, estate cottages of *c.* 1830–40, Tudor hoodmoulds, roughcast; and No. 20, by *F.B. Peacock* of *Cossins, Peacock & Bewlay*, for himself, 1899. A good simple progressive design, brick and render, with a bold full-height semicircular projection for the staircase. No. 18 by *Mansell & Mansell*, 1900. Nos. 6–8, more early C19 cottages.

HIGHFIELD ROAD. Going SE from Hagley Road, on the sw side a pair of 1838. Pediments with side consoles, iron verandas. On the NE side a Greek Revival villa of *c.* 1830. Past Harborne Road and the Chamber of Commerce, consistent, mainly semi-detached villas of 1830–45. At the far end on the l., No. 21, by *Norrish & Stainton* as their own offices, 1961. Nicely detailed. First-floor offices on piers above a car port and (extended) entrance area.

LADYWOOD MIDDLEWAY. N from Five Ways, on the l. the former LENCH'S TRUST ALMSHOUSES. Tudor Revival, with shaped gables, arranged round a courtyard. *Hornblower & Haylock*, 1858. Beyond, the retained façade of the former CHILDREN'S HOSPITAL, by *Frederick Martin* (*Martin & Martin*), 1913–14. Neo-Georgian but of a massive kind. The centre is like a triumphal arch, with a built-up attic, enclosing an oriel and the Doric entrance porch.

LEE CRESCENT. Open on the NE to the Middleway, but just detached enough. Starting from Ryland Road, first brick, then stucco villas climb the hill. Nos. 37–40 are three-storey passage-entry pairs. Round-headed doorcases, paired slim pilasters. Nos. 35–36, WINEYFORD BROWN'S BUILDING, dated 1830, shows a step beyond passage-entry layout, with close-set doors. Nos. 31–32 similar. Finally No. 30, detached, facing SE.

MONUMENT ROAD. From Hagley Road the start is tight-packed houses on either side, some Late Georgian or Early Victorian. Nos. 204–207 (E side), *c.* 1830, stuccoed, with pilasters and smooth rustication to the ground floor. Nos. 200–203, slightly more modest, and more altered. Opposite, flats incorporating the CHURCH OF THE REDEEMER by *Downing Smith Kendrick*

Hood, 1984. Beyond, Waterworks Road runs w. THE MONUMENT, or PERROTT'S FOLLY, is a Gothick tower of 1758. Six storeys of pointed windows – except the fifth, where they are circular – the top storey with blank arcading. Stone battlements and circular stair-turret. Further w, the WATERWORKS has cubic brick offices with big windows in chamfered reveals, by *S.N. Cooke*, 1932. Behind, the PUMPING STATION of 1862 by *J.H. Chamberlain*. A high Gothic hall with two tall windows, and a chimney which is Giotto's bell-tower come to Birmingham. Lancets, tall cusped lights in the top storey, and a top trying to look like a spirelet.

Back on Monument Road and N, a line of stuccoed Late Classical houses, w side. The L-shaped pair on the corner of Noel Road is probably *c.*1840, and with its strip pilasters and recessed panels looks like *John Fallows*. Nos. 268–275 are solid pairs (plots laid out in 1850). Nos. 268–271 have rusticated doorcases, Nos. 272–273 delicate doorcases and minimal Wyatt windows. The group continues round the corner in RESERVOIR ROAD with more 1850s pairs. Between them, RESERVOIR RETREAT, with terraced cottages, like a mews. The l. side is 1850s, the r. after 1862.

At the far end of Reservoir Road, ¼ m. NW, is EDGBASTON RESERVOIR, part of *Telford's* improvements to the Birmingham Canal. 1826, enlarged 1830 and 1835/6. Lodge on the r. by *Telford*, probably of 1826, with full-height canted end to see the water.

NORFOLK ROAD. *Madin* flats, STONEBURY and ELMHURST of 1958–60 N of Augustus Road, WOODBOURNE of 1960–2 (facing Augustus Road) to the S. Further S, No. 6, a large asymmetrical classical stucco villa of 1870–1, and No. 7, BLYTHE COURT, by *Buckland & Haywood-Farmer*, dated 1911, massive Neo-Georgian, L-shaped, with a tile band and porch with tile lintel and zigzag. Diagonally set chimneys. Opposite, No. 16, a grand Italianate villa of 1854–5, probably by *Yeoville Thomason*. Red brick with stone dressings, porch with Corinthian pillars, triplet ground-floor windows. Hipped roof and bracket cornice. Large extensions of 1900 by *Wood & Kendrick* for the brewer W.W. Butler include the fanciful tower on the SE corner with frilly parapet and ogee roof. (Fine interiors of 1900 including a large reception hall, a ballroom with segmental plaster vault and panelling, and a conservatory.)

PAKENHAM ROAD. The SE side has a long line of villas of 1870 etc. in varied classical and Gothic styles.

PRIORY ROAD. Going N from Bristol Road, on the l. two houses of interest, now part of a private hospital. No. 24 is by *Harris & Martin*, 1878–9, for J.T. Bunce, editor of the *Birmingham Post*. Very much in J.H. Chamberlain's manner, with a traceried oriel rising from a sculptural buttress. No. 28 is by *Cossins, Peacock & Bewlay*, 1897–8, with much timbering.

At the back of the site is PARK GROVE, formerly reached from Bristol Road (p. 380). A picturesque villa built for William Cazeley *c.*1815–17. Low, stuccoed, with a veranda on trellised wrought-iron supports. Semicircular bay window facing W. Cazeley went bankrupt in 1824 and the house was bought by Charles Grafton, who must be responsible for extending the W side c.1825–30. Gothick, with scholarly Dec windows. Stables, r., with cupola, classical but probably after 1825. Rear extension of 1878, brick Gothic, for (Sir) John Jaffray, by *J.H. Chamberlain*. Much of the interior is Jaffray's, including the staircase with octagonal posts and exotic finials. Metal-panelled C19 ceiling in the NW room, which also has a Gothick traceried door.

PRITCHATTS ROAD. S of Vincent Drive is part of the University. Going N, on the W, two by *E.F. Reynolds*, No. 13 of 1927 with inset towers, and No. 11 of 1926. No. 9 by *Cossins, Peacock & Bewlay*, 1905–6, a smooth version of Arts and Crafts radicalism. On the E, the MASSHOUSE. The front block, with hipped roof, dentil cornice and big platband, was probably added to an existing farmhouse in 1722. A Franciscan school started here in 1723. Later C18 sashes. Projecting entrance with early C19 doorcase. Alterations by *S.T. Walker*, 1932–3. (Fireplace by *A.S. Dixon*, brought from Chad Road.)

RICHMOND HILL ROAD. From the N (Harborne Road), on the r. flats and maisonettes by *John Madin*, 1958–62. Climbing the hill, on the l. No. 28, with round-arched porch, and No. 30, more Gothic, both probably *C.A. Edge*, 1877–8. Beyond Farquhar Road, big, timber-gabled No. 34 by *Ewen Harper*, 1898. No. 36 is again probably *Edge*, Gothic, of 1877–8. Opposite, HIGH POINT, by *Madin*, 1961, one of his best early developments, with maisonettes, some above a bridge on pilotis, and a twelve-storey tower, grouped among lawns.

RYLAND ROAD. Modest terraces on the fringe of the Calthorpe estate. Starting at the Middleway, the NW side was started in 1832. Nos. 37–42, a terrace, have pilasters, vestigial centre and end pediments, and tapering doorcases, all suggesting *John Fallows*. The SE side starts with stucco and brick houses, also of the 1830s. Nos. 74–75 are a pair treated as a *cottage orné*, with Tudoresque windows. Nos. 66–69 of 1854 are pairs of single-pile passage-entry houses, with rear houses reached through the passages.

SIR HARRY'S ROAD. Climbing NW from Bristol Road, on the l. Early Victorian villas. Nos. 6–7 are a stucco pair with recessed side porches. Two by *Samuel Hemming*: No. 9 of 1854–5, brick; No. 10 of 1852–3, stucco, with much frilly anthemion decoration. Nos. 11 and 12 are of c. 1852–3 by *F.W. Fiddian*, Italianate. The Priory School (*see* below) is beyond.

SOMERSET ROAD. Only No. 24 by *Ball*, 1906, now part of the Nuffield Hospital, and opposite, No. 25 and its lodge, Jacobean by *J.A. Chatwin*, 1861.

VICARAGE ROAD. From Hagley Road, the E side is of 1838–40. No. 3, particularly attractive, with incised pilasters and iron veranda. Nos. 6–8 have round-headed doorcases of the *Bateman & Drury* kind. Beyond Harborne Road on the r., a small roughcast lodge of c. 1905, perhaps by *C.E. Bateman*.

SUBURBS W & SW: EDGBASTON

WELLINGTON ROAD starts at St Bartholomew's church (p. 359) and runs NE. To the E the PRIORY SCHOOL, a good five-bay villa of 1829. Its single-bay pedimented centre with Corinthian columns suggests *Charles Edge*. To its l., a larger but sympathetic block of 1878–9 by *T. Chatfeild Clarke*. To the r. a big mid-C20 block with Gothic windows. Entrance hall grandly remodelled by *Martin & Chamberlain*, 1890. AMPTON ROAD runs NW here (*see* p. 378). Beyond, the road runs dead straight towards Bristol Road and the city centre. On the NW, villas of 1847–52. The finest is BEECH MOUNT, with projecting centre bay, giant Corinthian pilasters and 'debased' details. On the SE, Nos. 54–57 of 1936–8; No. 56 by *Hobbiss* in his King Edward's School Tudor style. On the N side again No. 44, 1845, and on the corner of Carpenter Road, No. 43 by *F.W. Fiddian*, 1840, its pedimented doorcase with a characteristic heavy architrave. Opposite, three large houses of 1828–30. No. 58 has incised pilasters and an off-centre pediment, behind a later forebuilding. No. 60, set back, with recessed entrance bay. No. 61, FIELDGATE HOUSE, has Corinthian pilasters with tall single-tier capitals. Its porch suggests *John Fallows*. Later C19 octagonal extension. Here a drive runs S, dividing into three. To the W, SPRING FOLLY, a mid-C19 sham ruin. Continuing S, HIGHLAND LODGE of *c.* 1830 with elegant shallow bays, then a lodge of 1864 by *J.J. Bateman*, and, set beyond a small lake, SPRING COTTAGE. The nucleus is of before 1827, but the long range with a shallow bow is of after 1855, probably also *Bateman*.

Back to Wellington Road and NE. No. 63 of 1845–7, almost certainly by *Bateman*, is like a rural Italian villa of the Nash or Papworth type, with a three-storey tower. Linked architraves with panels of foliage and little supporting consoles. Opposite, behind a wall, No. 39, APSLEY HOUSE, 1836. Three-bay front with small pediment. Projecting ground floor, with Ionic porch by *Edge*, 1850. Nos. 34–35, old-fashioned for 1850–1, with channelled rustication and pilasters above. On the SE, No. 68 by *E.C. Bewlay* (*Cossins, Peacock & Bewlay*), 1913. His own house. Arts and Crafts Neo-Georgian with a shell-hood doorcase.

No. 28, on the NW side, begins a line of stucco villas mostly of 1844–7. Opposite, No. 73 of 1816, a large house facing E, behind a stable wing with Tudor cupola. Later C19 Gothic lodge. Then a group of 1815. No. 74 has a Greek Doric porch with paired columns. Nos. 76–77 Doric doorcases and little tympana over the windows, No. 78 a doorcase with fluted pillarets in a moulded surround. Finally the ornate No. 82, *c.* 1860, with a Corinthian porch.

WESTBOURNE ROAD runs W from St George's church (p. 361). On the r., Birmingham City University (p. 375). Opposite, No. 5 of 1827, set back behind trees. FAIRLAWN is *Madin* of 1959–64, as is ST GEORGE'S CLOSE. Three-storey flats with characteristic recessions, and a retained Gothic lodge of *c.* 1870. Landscape with mature trees. To the SE No. 20, THE HOUSE, a Regency villa reinterpreted in mid-C20 blue brick, perfectly square with an exposed concrete floor slab, pyramid roof and central chimney. Back on Westbourne Road, the remarkable RAVENSBURY, of 1935 by *T.M. Ashford*, assisted, it is said, by the young *Robert Furneaux Jordan*. Tudor Revival collides with Art Deco. Conventional H-plan with end gables, the expanses of maroon brick relieved by an abstract pattern of protruding headers. Deep central eaves with big soffit discs. Garden front with full-height timber windows and a jolting central chimney with Art Deco sundial. Below its terrace, a formal garden with central canal, running to a boldly treated arch. The narrow full-height galleried lounge has a heavy beamed ceiling and a primitivist stone fireplace with stubby twisted Ionic columns, zigzag-pattern lintel and tapering hood. First-floor bathroom with black-tiled walls and floor with inset stainless-steel circles and waves. To the w, BEVAN HOUSE, by *Associated Architects*, 1998. Beyond, EDGBASTON HIGH SCHOOL FOR GIRLS, *H.W. Hobbiss & Partners*, 1960 etc.; alterations from 1991 and more recently. Opposite, the former lodge to OAKMOUNT, dated 1879 and inscribed 'REC', for Richard Chamberlain, Joseph's brother. Almost certainly by *J.H. Chamberlain*, and showing a move towards Shaw's and Nesfield's Domestic Revival. The roof folds over the hipped w gable, with its canted bay and tiny traceried window between half-timbered panels. Big chimney with flutes twisted halfway up. Then the Botanical Gardens (p. 376). Beyond them the road to the GUINEA GARDENS, a unique survivor of the C19 plots of allotments which surrounded the city. Then No. 15, severely beautiful Queen Anne by *Jethro A. Cossins*, 1887. Front sharply defined by the bold chimney and two contrasting gables. Hipped gable and dormer echoed in the coachhouse, l. No. 16 is a Gothic lodge, of *c*. 1870, to WESTBOURNE MANOR, a large restrained Italianate villa of 1839.

Beyond in HARBORNE ROAD, the former hamlet of GOOD-KNAVES END is marked by the WHITE SWAN pub. It looks Early Victorian, with gables and minimal Tudor hoodmould, but may hide earlier work. Opposite, CHAD SQUARE, houses and shops by *Madin*, 1958–64.

WESTFIELD ROAD. The interest is in the E end from Harborne Road, and the stretch further NW, s of Augustus Road. Starting from Harborne Road, on the s Nos. 120–130, Domestic Revival pairs and a single house, by *William Henman (Henman & Timmins)*, 1883–6. Opposite, the drive to BERROW COURT. A major house by *J.H. Chamberlain*, of 1879, for J.A. Kenrick, contemporary with Chamberlain's Highbury (p. 333) and in the same tough brick Gothic, with timbered gables. The NE entrance front has a l. gable split by a powerful decorated brick chimney and a r. one with a semicircular truss enclosing a triplet window. Deliberately varied fenestration: paired and triplet lancets, casements. Garden front, sw, with more gables. The l. end with an oriel is an extension of 1895 (*Martin & Chamberlain*). Full-height hall. The staircase and landing have extraordinary newels, part High Victorian, part exotically foreign. Panelling all round with marquetry. Roof with upper and lower collars, and arcading between.

Back on the road, a group of 1928–9 all by the short-lived firm of *Tanner & Horsburgh*, two of them probably the earliest flat-roofed houses in the city. No. 87 has been badly mauled, including a pitched roof; No. 79 is more intact, with semi-circular bay and straight-ended wing. This was Douglas Tanner's own house (he died in 1930). Nos. 77, 81 and 89 in contrast, are conventional Tudor Revival. Nos. 69–75 are big Gothic pairs probably of 1879–80 by *William Ross*. No. 67 is by *S. N. Cooke*, 1907–8, for his parents. Arts and Crafts Neo-Georgian, with curved bays and blank-arcaded chimneys. No. 65 is by *Hobbiss*, 1924, with a big oversailing timber porch. No. 63, simpler, by *Tanner & Horsburgh*, 1924. Opposite, No. 86, by *Frederick Martin* of *Martin & Martin*, dated 1907. A creditable Arts and Crafts design from the architect of the National Telephone Company building. Garden front with unequal end wings and a recessed centre with a little triangular oriel. Single-pile plan, the main rooms facing s. Wide hall and landing. Full-height staircase rising behind a timber screen, with delicate balusters. No. 84 (altered) is by *Ralph Heaton* for himself, 1908. Rendered.

Beyond Norfolk Road, No. 39 is by *A. W. Moore*, old-fashioned Gothic for 1897. Then a Domestic Revival group. Nos. 35 and 37 by *Essex, Nicol & Goodman*, 1895. No. 33, by *F. B. Osborn*, also 1895, with more tile-hanging, and timbered gables. No. 31, also *Essex, Nicol & Goodman*, 1893–6, in a C17 brick manner, with shaped gable and canted bay with stepped-up top. Opposite, No. 50, Neo-Georgian by *Henry Martin & Son*, 1905. No. 48 by *Harris, Martin & Harris*, 1881–2, with a pointed lunette in the gable. Nos. 42 and 44, heavily Gothic, by *William Withers*, 1878–80; Nos. 38 and 40 by the builders *James Smith & Sons*, 1876. Opposite, Nos. 25 and 27 by *J. P. Sharp & Co.*, 1890, starting to go timber and tile. Then two by *Osborn & Reading*, No. 19, spreading with assorted gables, 1884; and No. 17, their finest here, of 1890: austere Queen Anne, with friezes, surrounds and strapwork, of moulded bricks. Opposite, No. 36, plain except for blue-brick bands and the bargeboard, by *G. T. Haylock*, 1880. Nos. 34 and 34A are estate cottages, here by 1841: brick, with hoodmoulds and impressive grouped chimneys. No. 32, *Osborn & Reading* again, 1882, with some tile-hanging and tall moulded chimneys. Nos. 28, 26 and 22 (alas rendered) are by *T. H. Mansell*, 1875–6, Gothic; No. 24, timber-gabled, is by *Osborn & Reading*, 1882. No. 20, on the corner of Woodbourne Road, is early Neo-Georgian by *J. L. Ball*, 1893, austerely handled except for the Ionic doorcase. It spreads informally w, with square bays. Nos. 6–8 are more early C19 Tudor-style estate cottages.

WHEELEYS ROAD. From Islington Middleway going s, a survival of the more modest Early Victorian Calthorpe estate houses which surrounded the grander ones: Nos. 77–79 and 75, E, and Nos. 10–14, W, all of after 1843. Beyond Yew Tree

Road, Nos. 57–64, heavy stucco pairs, and Nos. 65–66, red and blue brick, all of *c.*1858–60 by *Thomason*. Nos. 17–18 of 1829 with first-floor Ionic pilasters. No. 19, contemporary, with a good reeded doorcase. Just in St James Road is the ROUND HOUSE. Its circular central block of 1818 was built as a garden house. Conical roof, deep eaves, Gothick windows in both floors. Turned into a residence *c.*1827 with flanking blocks, one retaining a Tudor-style window.

WOODBOURNE ROAD, from the E end. No. 2 by *William Davis*, 1880, Gothic without pointed arches. No. 4 is nouveau-Georgian by *PCPT*, 2008. No. 6 is the Tudor manor house of your dreams, with full-height half-octagonal bay and tremendous paired chimneys: late *Owen Parsons*, 1936–7. Big l. extension, unbalancing it, by *Lapworth*, 2010–11. Nos. 8, 10 and 16 are tall, bleak villas by *Charles Allerton Edge*, 1875–6. Opposite, Nos. 7 and 9, Gothic villas by *J. Statham Davis*, 1897–8. No. 15 by *A.B. Phipson*, 1885, opulent Jacobean, with a triangular-pedimented Dutch gable and two-bay arcade (added 1888) hiding the entrance. Beyond the railway, large houses set well back: No. 21 by *Yeoville Thomason*, No. 23 by *Henry Martin & Son*, 1909. No. 25, THE HOMESTEAD, is by *C.E. Bateman*, 1898–1900. One of his most important houses, and perhaps his most progressive, with its cool rendered walls and metal-framed casements. Yet it has steep-pitched roofs and a pointed arch to the porch – inscribed 'East, West, Home's Best'. Tapering chimneys in exposed brick. Approached up a drive and through a forecourt with low brick walls and piers with large stone balls. L-plan, on an awkward site, with the garden to the side of the drive, so the main rooms face S. Unusually for an Arts and Crafts house, this range is a double pile, with the billiard room behind, extended to get light through a SE window. Coach-house range at the rear, l. (The entrance has a passage to the hall, which faces S and has a fireplace on the exterior wall with decorative tiling. The dining room to its E has a full-width

Birmingham, Edgbaston, The Homestead.
Perspective drawing by C.E. Bateman, 1901

panelled inglenook with two square wooden piers. Drawing room to its W with a simpler inglenook with cambered soffit. The billiard room has a fireplace with stone strips rising into the overmantel, and a large wrought-and-scrolled five-branch hanging lamp of iron.)

YATELEY ROAD. From Harborne Road going W, four Domestic Revival houses by *William Henman*, 1889–91. The second (No. 7) has a r. extension by *A.S. Dixon*, 1895–6, absolutely plain, making the existing house look ornate. Then four important Arts and Crafts houses by *Buckland & Haywood-Farmer*. It is best to start with the far one, No. 21, of 1899, H.T. Buckland's own house. Compactly put together, with a central entrance rising through the hipped roof to a gable. Roughcast, with flush casement windows and a modest canted bay, the influence of Voysey. It has a cool, progressive quality, like Bidlake's contemporary Garth House (p. 373), but with an up-to-date Continental air. Round-headed doorway with abstract decoration round the arch (Roderick Gradidge suggested it is based on the zodiac). (Remarkably unaltered interior.) No. 17, 1901, and No. 15, 1907 – with windows linked in shallow reveals in a Ball or Dixon way – have the same quality. No. 13 of 1901, red brick, was extended by *Buckland & Haywood-Farmer* in 1908 and 1910, so the almost pyramidal roof comes down through two tiers of dormers. Fine chimneys.

YEW TREE ROAD. The NE side has modest brick pairs by *Bateman & Drury*: Nos. 2–5, 1836–8; Nos. 8–9, 1841. Doorcases with flattened fluted pilasters, teardrop fanlights. Breaking the row, Nos. 6 and 7 of *c.* 1834, stucco cottages with arched bargeboards. The SW side has No. 14, tall Gothic of *c.* 1860, probably by *Charles Edge*. Otherwise stucco and brick classical pairs of 1853–5, grander than those opposite, and with Italianate detail.

ROTTON PARK ESTATE

The area N of Hagley Road and W of Edgbaston Reservoir, up to the city boundary. It ran N to Summerfield Park (p. 217). The estate was bought by Joseph Gillott in 1851. Following the example of the Calthorpes, he developed it on ninety-nine-year leases which prohibited trade or business. The planning, with St Augustine's church as a focus, followed a suggestion by *J.A. Chatwin*. In the later C19 the area became less sought-after, and streets of terraced houses were developed to the N; interwar semis later, around Selwyn Road. Roads below are taken starting from Hagley Road.

The earliest houses are Italianate villas. In PORTLAND ROAD a line of 1862–3 with heavy porches. Nos. 15–19 are slightly earlier, of 1858–60, with Ionic porches and architraved windows. In CLARENDON ROAD Nos. 12–16, stuccoed, and No. 18, brick, *c.* 1873–4. No. 20, picturesque Gothic of *c.* 1874 (with a bit of half-timbering) was *Henry Naden*'s own house. There are *Bateman & Corser* houses here of 1877–8, probably Nos. 28–34 and 25–31. Nos. 36–38 are by *George Duvall*, boldly dated 1908. Closing the view, the former MAGDALEN ASYLUM (for 'fallen women'), by *Thomas Naden*, 1860–1, 'in the Italian style, of an inexpensive character'. Brick, with end wings and slightly projecting centre. Arched entrance with side openings.

ROTTON PARK ROAD, further w, starts with flats by *Essex & Goodman*, 1938–9. In YORK ROAD, on the r., Nos. 17–23, classical pairs of *c.* 1855–6, among the earliest on the estate. Beyond on Rotton Park Road, houses by *J. L. Ball*. Nos. 13 and 15 are severe Queen Anne of 1895. Nos. 17–19 (No. 17 was Ball's own house), 1895–6, but significantly more advanced. Cotswold cottages done in special two-inch brick, nearly all in stretchers. Flush casement windows, gabled porches, very shallow ground-floor bays. A nice detail is the coved plaster cornice stopped short of the ends.

ST AUGUSTINE'S ROAD, w again, leads formally to the church. Picturesque Gothic pairs with frilly bargeboards on the w side by *Bateman & Corser*, 1872–4. Pairs opposite by *Henry Heal*, 1877. Near the church, w, minimal Gothic houses by *J. S. Davis*, 1896. No. 15, E, is by *J. P. Osborne*, 1896.

FRANKLEY

A Birmingham overspill estate, planned from 1969, built 1975–82. Originally in Hereford and Worcester, transferred to Birmingham in 1995. Surrounded by fields on the N and W, and the Rubery Hill/Hollymoor site on the S, it still feels separate from the city.

ST CHRISTOPHER'S CHURCH CENTRE and HOLLY HILL INFANTS SCHOOL, New Street. 1977–8 by *Alan Meikle*, Hereford and Worcester County Architect. Single-storeyed, with a low pyramid roof over the central space. To the N, FRANKLEY CHILDREN'S CENTRE by *Glancy Nicholls*, 2006, all sharp angles. FRANKLEY COMMUNITY HIGH SCHOOL, s (now KING EDWARD VI BALAAM WOOD ACADEMY), is by *Meikle* with *R.W. Cheney* and *S. G. Taylor*, a long block of 1979–81.

HOUSING and SHOPS. All by *W.G. Reed*, City Architect, project architect *Will Howland*, with *Granville Lewis*. A good example is FABIAN CLOSE and MOWBRAY CLOSE, N of the Children's Centre: brick and tile-hanging, lots of Aalto-esque monopitches. Their most individual designs are GANNOW MANOR GARDENS and MITTEN AVENUE, s, of 1981: built into the hillside, with huge asymmetrical roof pitches and linking brick steps.

GANNOW GREEN MOAT. A well-preserved moat alongside the River Rea. Excavations revealed a dressed sandstone wall alongside part of the edge, and timber buildings and a hearth on the moat platform. To the W, dam of a former fishpond in Mull Close.

HARBORNE

Originally a Staffordshire parish, which also included Smethwick (p. 577). The village was round St Peter's church. The modern centre on the High Street was mostly Harborne Heath, by the late C18 almost completely enclosed. A network of small streets developed from the 1850s to the First World War, increased, especially N of the High Street, by the Harborne Railway (1874). There was a Local Board from 1864; absorbed into Birmingham in 1891. Harborne had its own architects: *Isaac Newey*, succeeded by his son *C. Isaac Newey*, and *A.B. Phipson*, assisted by his short-lived son *W.A. Phipson*. C19 residents included the banker and political leader Thomas Attwood, and the Kenricks, Joseph Chamberlain's relatives. Later private housing up to the 1960s has ensured it remains an affluent suburb. Away from the High Street it retains an intimate, small-scale character, with townscape qualities rare in Birmingham. For this reason, public buildings are covered in the Perambulation, and in Other Buildings. Buildings just E of the old boundary, e.g. in Harborne Road and Hintlesham Avenue, historically in Edgbaston, are also included.

CHURCHES

ST PETER, Old Church Road. Embattled three-stage W tower of red sandstone, with diagonal buttresses. Doorway with continuous mouldings and a very flattened arch. Close above it and off-centre, a three-light Perp window, the mullions not quite running through. Belfry with a two-light flowing tracery window, well off-centre because of the staircase. A carved corbel for an image on the NW buttress. Late C14 window in the S wall, cusped ogee-headed niche, perhaps an infilled window, in the N wall. All this suggests a lengthy C14 building programme.

The medieval church was much rebuilt in the C18. By the early C19 the S side had Y-tracery windows, though the N side probably retained medieval fabric. In 1827–8 *Rickman & Hutchinson* enlarged the building on the S. The shell of this greatly altered building survives, recast in 1865–7 by *Yeoville Thomason*. Rock-faced stonework. New transepts, S chapel and a three-sided apse with gables running round. Nave windows rebuilt with a show of different tracery – circles with sexfoils and spherical triangles. Plate-tracery roses in the transepts. Picturesque contrasting staircases to the transept galleries, the N a big catslide with stepped lancets. Inserted arcades with tall tapering bases, circular columns and striped sandstone and limestone arches. Flourishing foliage capitals and corbels; collar-beam roof. Galleries in the transepts with matchboarded fronts (nave galleries removed in the C20). Dormer windows by *Ralph Heaton*, 1896. The apse has blank arcading. NE vestry, the upper storey added by *Thomason* in 1873. Repairs after a fire by *Anthony Chatwin*, 1974–5. – PULPIT by *J.A. Chatwin*,

1885, carved by *Bridgemans*. – CHOIR STALLS probably by *Heaton*, *c*. 1895. – STAINED GLASS. Apse, *Hardmans*, 1874; transepts *Capronnier*, 1883; s aisle, *Hardmans*, †1984. – MONUMENTS. N transept. George Simcox †1831 and others, by *Bacon Jun*. Tomb-chest on a big base with projecting pedimented panel. – Rev. John Garbett †1858, Gothic aedicule. – Hannah Maria Simcox †1824 and others, with an ogee-arched canopy, by *J. Oakes* of Ombersley. – s aisle. Thomas Price †1782 etc. Roundel in a classical frame, pedimented tablet above, big predella below. – William Summerfield †1837 etc., with urn, by *R. Badham*. – Robert Lloyd Crosbie †1894, bronze cartouche by *Hart, Son & Peard*. – w wall, Rev. Edward Roberts †1891, with ivy border, designed by *J.A. Chatwin*, made by *Bennett & Son*.

ST FAITH AND ST LAURENCE, Croftdown Road. 1936–7 by *Philip B. Chatwin*, completed 1958–60 with chancel, sanctuary, Lady Chapel and vestries by Philip and his nephew *Anthony Chatwin*. Simple, refined Early Christian, in reddish-buff brick. The recurring motif is a triplet of round-headed windows, stepped in the clerestory and w gable. Sheer sw tower with dainty pyramid roof. The interior is especially successful. Perfectly plain semicircular cross-arches, steel-framed and rendered, and panelled ceiling, following E.F. Reynolds's St Mary, Pype Hayes (p. 269); perfectly plain semicircular arches to the low aisles. The proportions are very pleasant, as is the contrast between brick and rendered arches. – PEWS and tapering FONT, 1937; PULPIT and CHOIR STALLS, 1960. – STAINED GLASS. Aisles, *C.L. Dagley*, 1945–9; chancel and Lady Chapel, *John Hardman Studios*, 1959–60.

ST JOHN THE BAPTIST, High Street. 1959–60 by *Eric M. Marriner* of *Batemans*. It replaced a brick church in Early English style by *Yeoville Thomason* in St John's Road, bombed in 1941. A simple hall with shallow transepts. Patterned brick on the front, stone facing to the r. entrance. First-floor addition at the rear by *Kelly & Surman* (*P.B. Robbins*), 1985, a metal-clad half-hexagon with steeply gabled windows. Stepped hexagonal ceiling inside. More extensions by *Gould Singleton*, 2020.

ST MARY (R.C.), Vivian Road. The start is ST MARY'S RETREAT, formerly HARBORNE LODGE (*see* below), of 1828–9 by *Rickman & Hutchinson* for George Simcox, announced on the road by its gatepiers. Radical Neoclassicism: heavy tapering columns with Doric capitals and conical tops. The first church, for the Passionists, is by *Dunn & Hansom*, 1875–7. Brick with stone dressings, Dec, with a turret with an open arcaded top. A long wing of 1910–11 by *V.S. Peel* links it to the house. Replacement church for the Augustinians by *Brian A. Rush & Partners*, 1977–8, r. Fan-shaped, with a thin lantern above the altar, on which perches a thinner metal spire. Dark inside, with cheap-looking metal beams. *Dunn & Hansom*'s interior partly survives at one side; arcade with circular piers and juicy foliage responds. The junction is a car-crash, with a flat lintel across the former chancel arch. Nice two-bay arcade between the former chancel and Sacred Heart Chapel. – STAINED GLASS. Chancel 1898, Lady Chapel by *Hardmans*, 1917. – PARISH CENTRE of 1990, l.

St Mary's Retreat, at the rear, is a stuccoed Picturesque villa. Tall three-bay S front with pedimental gables to the end bays. First-floor windows in segment-headed recesses. Deep bracket eaves. Porch, E, with Ionic columns *in antis*. The drawing room has one end divided by fluted Ionic columns. Deep cornice. Sober marble fireplace. Staircase with alternating stick and fancy cast-iron balusters, made by the *Eagle Foundry*. Attached, W, a Gothick ORANGERY, added later. Its bays are divided by slim buttresses ending in finials. Pretty cresting between. Renewed cast-iron glazing with intersecting patterns, and coloured glass. Cast-iron roof trusses with unusual intersecting cusping.

METHODIST CHURCH (currently OASIS CHURCH), South Street. A relatively early work by *J.H. Chamberlain* (*Martin & Chamberlain*), 1868. His only surviving Nonconformist chapel in use, and still a shock among little terraces. High Victorian Gothic, the front a blunt arrangement of angular masses and planes. A big porch sits in front, equally sharply gabled. Ritual SW tower, cut back to an octagon and short blunt spire. Perilously steep buttresses. The moments of delicacy are the attenuated two-light gable window with quatrefoil, and the plate-tracery rose in the tower. High interior with a wiry collar-beam roof on massive cruck-like brackets. W gallery (infilled) on cast-iron columns. Chancel added by *J.L. Ball*, 1895, also impressively tall. Chancel arch with continuous mouldings, except that the innermost ones rest on angel corbels. The E wall is a single composition of reredos, traceried stone panels and Perp five-light window. Angular PEWS by *Chamberlain*, CHOIR STALLS and PULPIT by *Ball*. – STAINED GLASS. E window, 1896, sentimental pictorial scenes by *Alfred Long* of West Bromwich, made by *Samuel Evans*. Ball disliked it so much that he resigned as a trustee and left the chapel. Nave S, *Pearce & Cutler*, 1924. – SCHOOLROOM behind by *Ball*, 1887, severe Queen Anne.

COURT OAK METHODIST CHURCH, Earls Court Road. 1903 by *R.W.S. Chadney*. A Primitive Methodist school-chapel, with wide lancets. C21 porch.

MAJOR HOUSES

BISHOP'S CROFT, up a drive N of Old Church Road. Of *c.* 1780, for Thomas Green, a Birmingham manufacturer who became the squire of Harborne. A brick cube: three storeys, three bays, plain dentil cornice and parapet. Adam-style doorcase with half-columns and plasterwork garlands in the frieze. The side wings with pediments are original, but the linking blocks were enlarged, with characteristic little relieving arches, in alterations by *A.S. Dixon*, 1902–3, for Archibald Kenrick. The garden front has five close-spaced bays and an Ionic porch (the front capitals mutilated) with a good fanlight. Ground floor with linked round-arched windows, repeated in the wings. The r. extension of the main block, which quietly ruffles the symmetry, is the dining room (*see* below). The high chimneys rising above pediments are of course *Dixon*'s, as are the oval windows (of 1910). The entrance is off-centre in the hall, which has an Adam-style ceiling with delicate flowers, circular and diamond-shaped panels, and a frieze of lyres and garlands. The axial main corridor has a similar one. Dixon's open-well staircase rises to the r. of the hall. Small projecting lower flight, and alternating octagonal and twisted balusters. His DINING ROOM has full-height panelling and a buffet with a typical segmental arch. Excellent plasterwork by *George Bankart*, a deep frieze with garlands of roses and berries, and apples and lemons. Fireplace with metalwork panels, stylized leaves and flowers, made by the *Birmingham Guild*. Dixon also created a billiard room, now the study, in the W wing, with more fine *Bankart* plasterwork. He extended the E wing slightly in 1910. The first-floor landing has more delicate C18 plasterwork.

The house became the Bishop of Birmingham's residence in 1911, and in 1923 *Dixon* added a CHAPEL at the SW, in his favourite red-blue brick, in Sussex bond, and with stone blocks in the quoins. The stylistic references, classical for Dixon, evoke C17 Laudian Anglicanism: buttresses with consoles set upright on the tops, and simplified Dutch gables on the ends. The interior is wainscoted to doorhead height, and painted white above, the scheme of Philip Webb's Rochester Diocesan Institution Chapel of 1896. Lethaby-style plain groined vault. Fine LOBBY SCREEN and sparely detailed STALLS arranged like a college chapel.

House and garden are surrounded by a high C18 WALL, with *Dixon* gatepiers.

HARBORNE HALL, Old Church Road. The original house was of *c.*1800. Its S front is still recognizable, symmetrical and stuccoed. A semicircular bow faces E. To its r. a Tuscan porch, similar to that on the house now part of St Mary's (p. 396), so probably added *c.*1830 by *Rickman & Hutchinson*, for George Simcox. All swamped by alterations and extensions by *Martin & Chamberlain*, 1884, for Walter Chamberlain, brother of Joseph. The pedimented centre of the S front was replaced with a big stone bay, out of which sprouts the projecting centre of a half-timbered gable, flanked by dormers. Big rear extensions by the road, including a clerestoried billiard room with a spirelet. Very tall central hall with two levels of galleries, partly supported on iron columns. Wood and iron balustrades with standing flowers. Convent extensions, w, by *Hollins, Jones & Oldacre*: chapel with a blank apse of 1963, long residential block of 1956–8. To the E, heavily timbered LODGE by *Martin & Chamberlain*, 1890, and huge chamfered gatepiers.

TENNAL GRANGE, Tennal Road. A radical Arts and Crafts house, little known, by *A. S. Dixon*, 1903–5. Built for Claude Napier-Clavering, a businessman involved in the Birmingham

Guild of Handicraft. Disfigured (UPVC windows, fire doors) but not fundamentally damaged, by many years of military use. Tall, but on a spread-out plan, in the Lethaby way. Handmade maroon two-inch bricks, laid in Sussex bond. The E-plan N front has the entrance pushed l. into a pent-roofed extension. Steep-pitched roofs and dormers, and the slightly thin gabled wings, give it a stark, almost gawky quality. The E wing has a big chimney running up the gable, and no front ground-floor window, a tough gesture, matched by the stepping-up gables on the E side. The W wing was entirely for servants, their status reflecting the client's and architect's social views. The garden front, rendered above, has two larger gables with a linking loggia and balcony. Wide corridors, the first-floor landing a 'room' in the Arts and Crafts way. Main dog-leg staircase in the middle wing, its presence emphasized by a first short flight in the hall. Heavy, close-set square balusters, linked by equally heavy ties. Plasterwork probably by *George Bankart*, to ground-floor arches and beams; also the best fireplace overmantel, moulded with fruit trees in panels. Other fireplaces with Philip Webb-style panelling (SW room) and marble surround and blunt consoles (library).

For LOW WOOD, St Mary's Road, see p. 403.

STONE HOUSE, Stonehouse Lane. A mysterious three-storey gabled house, C17 or older, almost like a tower. Red sandstone with later S wings, now rendered, and a brick C18 E wing. It is close to Weoley Castle, across the brook to the SE (*see* Weoley, p. 435), and may have been associated with it; or it may simply be of reused stone from the castle.

MOOR POOL ESTATE

A venture by Harborne Tenants Ltd, begun 1908, completed 1912. The initial capital came from local benefactors, but the idea was that tenants would progressively buy shares and come to own the garden suburb, as an alternative to municipal house-building. The chairman and prime mover was the industrialist and housing reformer J.S. Nettlefold; the committee included Claude Napier-Clavering of the Birmingham Guild (*see* Tennal Grange, p. 398). The architect throughout was *Frederick Martin* of *Martin & Martin*. Despite the nearness of Bournville, the model was Parker & Unwin's Hampstead Garden Suburb. It shows in the simple brick and roughcast houses, with big roofs and prominent gables, a few with the plainest bay windows. Gardens and hedges were planted from the start, and it is the roughcast and the beech hedges which give Moor Pool its particular character.

The centre is The Circle. Narrow roads run out and round from it; the longer Moor Pool Avenue and Carless Avenue go E and W. The public buildings are round THE CIRCLE, with its central tennis courts. They use the same language as the houses, with especially ample brick quoins. Facing E is the former POST OFFICE. Three gables, the central one larger, with a long oriel below. On the N side, MOOR POOL HALL, with a complex and enveloping roof with hipped extensions to either side. Two-storey forebuilding, S. On the W side the ESTATE OFFICE, with a simpler roof descending in catslides over the ends, and an oriel breaking the eaves line. Hidden behind houses between The Circle and Ravenhurst Road, E, are a bowling green and a lake.

Three other places of note. In RAVENHURST ROAD, two-storey flats built into the side of the hill, ingeniously designed with full-height porches which have long sloping side buttresses. On Nos. 108–122 the porches are weatherboarded, with steps to the upper floors. Nos. 124–134 have rendered porches with thin slit-windows, and bridges to the upper floors. To the S, at the crossing of Moor Pool Avenue, Eastway leads uphill SE to EAST PATHWAY. Three terraces, all brick; almost symmetrical, with complex arrangements of gables and central oriels. The central terrace has a middle archway (to the station footpath); the side ones are cranked in the middle. Finally CARLESS AVENUE at the W end, the last part built. Larger semi-detached houses, at one point set round a circular widening now filled with trees.

PERAMBULATION

A long circular walk from the E end of High Street, the junction with Nursery Road, to St Peter's church and back.

The BLUE COAT SCHOOL is on the SE corner, running along Somerset Road. The C18 building was in St Philip's Place in the city centre (p. 152). The present school is by *J.L. Ball* and *H.W. Simister*, 1929–30. A long line of classrooms and house blocks facing SW behind an ample lawn, with more to the N. Neo-Early Georgian brick of a personal kind, the details tough. The central block has stone corner pilasters and a centrepiece with a Tuscan porch and a pair of round-headed niches. They follow the arrangement of the 1792–4 building in St Philip's churchyard, and contain copies by *Bloye* of statues of a boy and girl in school costume by *Samuel Grubb*, 1769. Square cupola. To the l., symmetry is broken by the DINING HALL. Serliana entrance with punchy Arts and Crafts brick detail. ASSEMBLY HALL some way to the SE, behind imitative extensions of 1988–9. The entrance hall has simple doorcases and just a guilloche moulding in the ceiling. Here are the original *Grubb* statues. Fireplace with Greek-key moulding framed by giant pilasters in the Board Room. CHAPEL, NW, 1932: Ball's last work. Arts and Crafts Jacobean, quite big. All brick except for the doorcase and mullion-and-transom window frames. Square timber ogee-topped cupola on the W gable. Panelled parapet; small pediments on the N and S sides. Deliberately prominent chimney. Plain interior with a panelled ceiling, W gallery, and seating with curved arm-rests, arranged college-fashion.

Next down HARBORNE ROAD, NE, towards the city. On the NW side Nos. 423–427, plain early C19, with central entrances. Nos. 407–411 are probably 1860s: see the arched lights. CLYDE VILLAS, dated 1867, Gothic in the manner of *Yeoville Thomason*. Nos. 395–401, early C19 like Nos. 423–427, but smaller and very charming. Nos. 391–393, probably 1830s, pretty stucco with end gables, wavy bargeboards and pointed arches to the upper window lights. Finally Nos. 385–389, High Victorian Gothic of 1869–70. Further down on the SE side HARBORNE ACADEMY, large and angular, by *Bond Bryan*, 2014.

Back and SW along HIGH STREET. It starts with the GREEN MAN pub by *Batemans*, 1938–9, with prominent stepped gables. Good carved sign, commissioned from *Bloye* but perhaps carved by *Alan Bridgwater*. THE PLOUGH is C18, but its details are probably from *Arthur Hamblin*'s alterations of 1899. Then an Early Victorian terrace, Nos. 20–26, SE, and contemporary cottages, Nos. 29–39, NW. Nos. 41–51 are a badly treated but interesting Free Style block in roughcast, by *E. G. Holtom & F. W. B. Yorke*. Domed corner turret, dated 1906 in the leadwork. Further along on the SE side, former BOARD SCHOOLS by *J. P. Sharp & Co.*, 1880–1. Gothic in the J.H. Chamberlain way, not with his finesse, but impressive. Big entrance tower and spire, with a gable l. like a church front, for the girls. Corner block with hipped roof for the boys; single-storey infants' school at the back with a spirelet. Refurbished as shops by *K4*, 2012–13; rear block by *Bryant Priest Newman*, 2015, wearing loud black zinc. On the NW side, flanking Station Road, Neo-Georgian shops by *Essex & Goodman*, 1910, and the mid-Victorian classical HARBORNE STORES pub. Beyond, depressing late C20 redevelopment. To the S, YORK STREET was laid out with the parallel Bull and South streets by Josias Bull York, *c.* 1850; mostly complete by 1864. Charming small-scale terraces, mostly classical. The WHITE HORSE pub, *c.* 1861, was refronted with canted bays and casements by *H. Peter Hing*, 1930. No. 21 is a Tudor-style brick cottage. Nos. 35–37, stucco with smooth rustication; No. 39 with Tudor hoodmoulds. Nos. 26–28, E side, are of 1865–6 by *A. B. Phipson*, with blue-brick trim.

At the top, across Greenfield Road, Metchley Lane leads SW to METCHLEY ABBEY. Late Georgian Gothick. Two storeys, with a heavy parapet and large pointed windows with iron tracery. Full-height porch, open-arched below. Details such as the stop-chamfers on the porch suggest a late date, perhaps *c.* 1827, when the owner William Neville was making 'ground improvements'. The SW end has a turret and lower portion, perhaps part of the C18 house. Hintlesham Avenue runs E from Metchley Lane, opposite. On the N side No. 23 by *Robert Townsend*, 1955, for Professor McKeown. A low, ground-hugging range, inspired by Frank Lloyd Wright. Long balcony faced in overlapping hardwood boards, stopped at the r. by a faceted brick panel. Long, low chimney. The interior has a full-height living space with a balcony landing. Further down Metchley Lane on the w side, the METCHLEY GRANGE estate. The first part is of 1964–7 (*J.A. Maudsley*, City Architect; *Don Fenton*, *Trefor Phillips* and *Ron Middleton*, job architects). Four towers, now rendered, and low-rise terraces, well grouped among lawns and mature trees, sloping down to the s.

Returning to the end of York Street, GREENFIELD ROAD leads w. Its N side was also part of the York development. DUNLEWEY, on the E corner with York Street, looks like *J.J. Bateman*, with its doorcase linked to the window above. No. 130 has a splendid fretwork porch. The s side is grander and slightly later, starting after 1860. Nos. 115 and 113 are classical. Nos. 109–111 are by *Martin & Chamberlain*, 1870. Red brick banded with blue. Bold Gothic door-hoods with dogtooth ornament, repeated on the lintels. Original gatepiers and r. gate. On the N side again, GREENFIELD HOUSE was the home from 1841 of the painter David Cox. Perhaps C18 in origin, but everything visible is picturesque Early Victorian. Nos. 93–99, s side, are by *A.B. Phipson*, 1865, with big flat-roofed bays and a bracket cornice. Harshly converted to flats, with a central archway. Later C19 canted bay, r. Nos. 83–91 with decorated bays and porch hoods are by *Alfred T. Greening*, 1890–1. Nos. 79–81, by *George Ingall*, 1864, brick Gothic lifted by fine detail: corbelling-out of the gable-ends, tilework floor band. Opposite, a terrace of six of 1868, probably also *Ingall*; mangled, but with surviving blue- and yellow-brick detail. Set back behind, BELL COTTAGE, probably 1840s, with Tudor-style windows. s again, Nos. 77 and 73, severe Queen Anne by *Phipson*, 1877 and 1881; No. 75 between, with wavy barge-boards. Opposite, the scale is smaller at first, with the earliest houses. On the corner of Margaret Road, four three-quarter houses of 1887 by *John Newey*, builder. At the cross-roads ahead, the NEW INN: 1830s but altered in 1878, the probable date of the fine bar back with paired Ionic columns and carving of leaves, flowers and fishes.

Back and s into MARGARET ROAD, developed after 1883. Almost immediately an alley leads w to WIGGIN COTTAGES, dated 1899: almshouses by the local builder *John Goodman*, for Sir Henry Wiggin. Queen Anne style, set *en echelon*, to fit the site and to have s-facing windows. Nos. 8–16 (E side) by *John Newey*, 1887, still have classical windows upstairs; ALBERT VILLAS (W side) by 'Mr *Thomas* of Sparkbrook', 1889, are mongrel Gothic-classic.

At the bottom is ST MARY'S ROAD, the grandest road in Harborne. On the NW corner No. 9 by *John Goodman*, 1907, with angled porch. No. 18 opposite (s side), by *William Haywood*, dated 1922, is Neo-Georgian in the asymmetrical, late Arts and Crafts way. Heavy porch with concave hood. On the N side going W, No. 17 is by *Harry Weedon*, 1923: also Arts and Crafts, but slightly stagey. Brick with tile lintels, porch with waney-edged boarding. No. 19 also *Goodman*, 1909; No. 21 by *Benjamin Bower*, 1907–8, mixing half-timber, render and Cotswold stone. No. 23, by *William Henman*, 1897, mixed timbering and tile-hanging.

Opposite, LOW WOOD (No. 32). A major Arts and Crafts house by *E.F. Reynolds*, 1910, for his brother John, tube manufacturer and amateur astronomer. H-plan, with gabled end ranges, derived from C17 Midlands manor houses. Segmental door-hood of Lethaby inspiration. The garden front has a loggia between the wings. Reynolds's favourite diagonal and rhombus patterns are everywhere, in woodwork, ceilings and even paving. Wide hall with full-height panelling, continuing into the dado of the staircase. Plasterwork of leaf patterns. Main rooms at the E and rear; W wing for kitchen and servants. The drawing room has a big fireplace with flanking niches and diagonal patterns, and low-relief plasterwork of sprays of flowers and leaves. One bedroom has a fine plasterwork overmantel of birds in a field. At the E is a MUSIC ROOM added by 1914, impressive but very classical for Reynolds, with barrel-vaulted ceiling, pilasters and cherub-like corbels. In the garden a circular domed OBSERVATORY, also *Reynolds*, 1911.

Continuing W, more half-timbering: No. 34 by *Lloyd F. Ward*, 1910; No. 36 by *Goodman*, 1909. Hidden behind a wall is No. 38, by *Fred Mark* of the *John Madin Design Group*, 1976–7, single-storey ranges around a rectangular pool. On the N side No. 25, FIESOLE, by a surveyor, *William Parrott*, 1890, a brick villa with lots of amateur-Ruskin decorative brick cornices. No. 27, THE GABLES, lives up to its name, with long curved braces and S-shaped studs at the top: by *J.P. Osborne*, 1896. No. 33 of 1899 shows *De Lacy Aherne* submitting to the Shaw fashion: large and small gables and lots of timbering, all regular studs.

At the W end is the dual carriageway of HARBORNE PARK ROAD. Immediately S, FIELD HOUSE. Three storeys, three wide bays. The core may be C17. The front range is marked on a map of 1790, and the tripartite first-floor windows look late C18. Later rear wing, here by 1827. Oriel, l., and extended ground floor probably of 1883–4, when alterations were made for (Sir) Henry Wiggin. Across the road to the S, the former DIOCESAN OFFICES of 1965 by *Bromilow, While & Smeeton*, a cool brick range with cantilevered glazed entrance l., balanced by a tiny piquant oriel.

Further S past Old Church Road is GROVE PARK, formerly the grounds of THE GROVE. A tile-hung LODGE by *Martin & Martin & W.H. Ward*, 1923, leads to a drive through mature Victorian planting, with many specimen trees. To the l., a curving lake. Further SW a magnificent cedar tree planted *c.* 1785. The house of 1877, a major Gothic work of *J.H. Chamberlain* (*Martin & Chamberlain*), for William Kenrick, Joseph Chamberlain's brother-in-law, stood immediately NW (demolished 1963).* A small ancillary building survives, with half-hipped roof and tapering-top chimney; also the remains of

---

*A panelled ante-room, made by *Samuel Barfield*, is preserved at the Victoria and Albert Museum.

garden terraces. The C18 predecessor was the home of Thomas Attwood in 1823–46.

Now back N up Grove Lane to OLD CHURCH ROAD, and two surviving grand houses, Harborne Hall and Bishop's Croft (pp. 398, 397). To the W, the road curves around the densely wooded churchyard. On the N side is ST PETER'S JUNIOR SCHOOL. Two gables in maroon brick by *Ralph Heaton*, 1903, with stone mullion-and-transom windows. The curious structure on the wall-head is the base of a chimney. Extended r. by *H.T. Buckland*, 1911–12: see the characteristic brick detail. Small contemporary l. extension also. Behind is the original building by *Thomas Johnson*, 1836–7. The rear wing, originally the master's house, survives unaltered: picturesque Tudor Revival with dormers, latticed windows and an unusual round-headed doorcase. N again, the former INFANTS' SCHOOL, perhaps of 1852, in the same style; N wing, now hidden by late C20 extensions, by *W.A. Phipson*, 1879. On the corner of St Peter's Road, an 1830s cottage. Beyond, No. 12, looking Early Victorian with dormers and mullioned windows, but probably older. Two Victorian cottages opposite, then the BELL INN, mostly early C19. The different gabled wings suggest an earlier core. The central corridor survives, and small rooms on the l.; the rear one with an inglenook and classical bressumer. St Peter's church (p. 395) is to the SE. On the corner opposite, ELMLEY LODGE, stucco classical of *c.* 1845.

Now back and N up ST PETER'S ROAD. On the W side Nos. 32 and 34, a raw brick mirror pair by *C. Isaac Newey*, 1890. Nos. 39–49, E side, also *Newey*, 1879, rather better, severe Queen Anne. In ALBERT ROAD, N, MANRESA HOUSE, mid-Victorian classical, much extended. On the E side Nos. 47–49, a Gothic pair by *William Jenkins*, 1879, with fancy brick and ironwork detail. At the N end Nos. 2 (now a shop) and 4, linked Italianate houses probably by *J.J. Bateman*, 1856. Rich doorcases and windows; inset behind, two Osborne-style pyramid-roofed towers. Here is the PRINCE'S CORNER roundabout. In Lordswood Road, NW, HARBORNE SWIMMING POOL, fashionably angular, by *Saunders Boston*, 2010–12. HIGH STREET runs E, at first with little of interest. In Serpentine Road, N, a former cinema by *Hurley Robinson*, 1913. Further E the former ROYALTY cinema by *Horace G. Bradley*, 1930, with a small dome. Circular entrance lobby. Auditorium retaining original jazzy Neoclassical decoration. Coving above the screen with lyre shapes in grilles. (Damaged by fire, 2018.) Beyond, flats and houses by *Weedon Partnership*, 2006–10. On the N side a long row of *c.* 1860, facing St John's church (p. 396), then COTTAGE ROW, stuccoed, of after 1840. The LIBRARY, as the inscription says, was the MASONIC HALL, of 1879 by *W.A. Phipson*. Simple Queen Anne. The JUNCTION INN is by *Wood & Kendrick*, 1903–4. A grand pub, in an important position in the fork with Vivian Road, and a smart one, in a refined version of the usual Jacobean. On the opposite corner a former LLOYDS BANK by *J.A. Chatwin*

& Son, 1906–7. Red brick, hipped roof, delicate classical details. Down ALBANY ROAD here, No. 4 by *A.B. Phipson*, 1896, half-timbered, and No. 6 by *William Henman & Timmins*, 1885, going Queen Anne. Then back down High Street to the Green Man, with some early and mid-C19 survivors above shopfronts.

OTHER BUILDINGS

PAGANEL PRIMARY SCHOOL, Swinford Road. *W.T. Benslyn*, 1938. Low, flat-roofed ranges, steel-framed with brick facings. Clerestoried hall.

QUEEN ALEXANDRA COLLEGE, Court Oak Road. Begun as a 'kindergarten' for the General Institution for the Blind, with a long Neo-Georgian range by *J.A. Chatwin & Son*, 1903–4. Extensions by *Paul Lister* of *Associated Architects*, including the prominent pyramid-roofed DINING HALL of 1995–6 and the timber-clad KARTEN CTEC CENTRE behind in Woodville Road, of 2001–3.

A scatter of interesting buildings in the terraced roads N of the High Street. In Gordon Road the former FIRE STATION by *Henry E. Stilgoe*, City Engineer and Surveyor, 1907. Neo-Wren, with rusticated arches for the engines, a Tudor bay and domestic firemen's houses. Tower behind with wavy parapet. In Station Road the former INSTITUTE of 1878 by *C. Isaac Newey*, like a big Gothic villa. Also HARBORNE PRIMARY SCHOOL. Main block by *H.T. Buckland*, 1911–12, plain, but with typical decorative brick tympana. SW part by *Martin & Martin*, 1901, with buttresses and terracotta detail. Down Wentworth Road, Nos. 18–28, Gothic pairs by *James S. Clarke* of Nechells. *c.* 1883. Nos. 25–35 opposite are probably 1860s, old-fashioned stucco Tudor. Finally in Park Hill Road the impressive Harborne Railway BRIDGE of 1869–74; engineer *J.H. Tolmé*, but probably designed by the contractor *Arthur S. Hammond*. Red brick, with a yellow-brick arch, splayed jambs, and recesses underneath.

By St Faith and St Laurence, the COURT OAK pub, 1932 by *G.B. Cox*. Spanish style: white-painted brick, green pantile roofs. Relief of an oak tree over the entrance. The garden survives, with box hedges, conifers and an arched LOGGIA. In Balden Road, N, the former TENNAL INDUSTRIAL SCHOOL, by *Arthur Edwards*, 1901–2. A long, bleak sash-windowed range. The centre has a big bow, a shaped gable and a tall clock turret. (Disused since 2011.)

In NORTHFIELD ROAD, two unusual terraces (Nos. 87–103), 1893–7, by *C. Isaac Newey*. Conventional timber gables, but hoodmoulds to doors and windows, and pointed arches to the entries, like Late Georgian Gothick. Further S, opposite Quinton Road, down a track, HOME FARM. Three-bay farmhouse, early to mid-C19. Farmyard mostly C19, but a barn with timber framing is probably C17. Brick infill with air holes in decorative patterns.

KINGS NORTON

The centre of a large, ancient parish which included Moseley, Stirchley, Rednal and Wythall. The late medieval village became a significant commercial centre, particularly in the wool trade: wealth still evident in the parish church – a chapel of ease to Bromsgrove until 1846, but the grandest surviving medieval church in present-day Birmingham – and the timber-framed Saracen's Head and Primrose Hill Farm. It received a market charter in 1616. The Pershore turnpike, constructed from 1825 (now A441), bypassed The Green but connected the village directly to Birmingham. C19 development spread along it, and became linked to the city. An Urban District with Northfield from 1894, absorbed into Birmingham in 1911. Late Victorian and Edwardian development W of The Green includes Arts and Crafts houses especially by *Gerald McMichael*. Post-war estates at Pool Farm and Primrose Hill by *A. G. Sheppard Fidler* are now much altered.

MAJOR BUILDINGS

ST NICOLAS, The Green. An impressive medieval church, set back in its churchyard. Its outstanding feature is the C15 W tower and spire, Leland's 'goodly piramis of stone'. The earliest fabric, however, is in the chancel N wall, with a C12 round-headed window and, below it, perhaps a lowside window. The arcades are mostly of standard elements – octagonal piers and double-chamfered arches – but towards the E some piers have quatrefoil shafts, those on the S with fillets. So, in conventional dating, they run from the late C13 on the N to the C14 on the S and towards the W. The E window has five stepped lancets, but the chancel arch is C14, of two chamfered orders, the inner with good ballflower ornament, and the chancel has multi-stepped buttresses at the NE corner, suggesting some rebuilding. C14 S aisle windows with renewed cusped reticulated tracery and bold label stops. Just E of the porch is a contemporary ogee-arched piscina, suggesting a former chapel. The tower is of four stages, with interesting arcading to the belfry stage consisting of two transomed two-light windows flanked by similar blind windows, with crocketed labels and finials to all, in each face. It is one of a local group, and particularly like Coleshill (Warwicks.) and Bromsgrove (Worcs.), its mother parish. The W doorway has a heavy, much-eroded crocketed label with a fleur-de-lys finial. Embattled parapet with angle pinnacles. From within this rises the crocketed spire, in three stages. Two-storey S porch, C15, with an arch with continuous mouldings, its hoodmould with fragments of a canopied image bracket above: all in the distinctive West Midlands manner with exaggerated details found locally at e.g. Romsley (Worcs.). The porch was vaulted, and the carved angle corbels remain.

The final major alteration was made in the C17, when three gabled roofs with plain mullioned windows were added to each aisle. The s ones survive. Small clerestory lights between the gables. The porch gable was also rebuilt, with a cyma moulding, and a cavetto on the cornice. All this is probably of 1659, the date on the rear porch tie-beam, during the curacy of Thomas Hall (*see* Old Grammar School, p.408). The chancel, much rebuilt in the C18, was restored by *Ewan Christian* in 1863. The E window, five stepped lancets under a four-centred arch, and s wall are his. In 1870–2 *W.J. Hopkins* restored the rest. He rebuilt the N aisle and reconstructed the N arcade, reusing original stones. A protest led by the historian J.R. Holliday stopped the same being done to the s aisle. The over-elaborate and badly constructed nave roof is Hopkins's. Organ chamber, s, with rose window, by *J.A. Chatwin*, 1874–5. Double-gabled NW vestry by *William Hale*, 1887.

FURNISHINGS. SCREEN. The upper parts of the late medieval rood screen set in a modern base to form a dado at the chancel entrance. Three pairs of lights each side, with good tracery heads, including X-shapes in the patterns, a Worcestershire or Gloucestershire type. Thickly moulded mullions, and frieze with stylized vine trail. – PEWS. C19, but made up of older work; some with C18 fielded panels. A C17 SEAT reconstructed like a settle from old pews, with arabesque panels, N aisle. – STAINED GLASS. E window by *Kempe*, 1889. Chancel N, *Hardmans*, 1872 (a fine angel) and 1879 (Abraham). s aisle, *Hardmans*, 1872–7; the E window, 1955, an interesting contrast. N aisle all *Swaine Bourne*: E 1881, the rest probably *c.*1892–5. – MONUMENTS. s aisle E end, a worn incised slab, to Humfrey Toye, chaplain, †1514. – The others now mostly under the tower. N side, Humfrie (†1624) and Martha Littleton, life-size figures incised on an alabaster slab. Attributed to the *Royleys* of Burton-on-Trent. The monument only gives the date of Martha's death, 1588, and presumably dates from that time. – In a recess, two kneeling figures under a semicircular canopy, *c.*1620. – s side. Alabaster tomb-chest with the recumbent effigies of Sir Richard Grevis †1632 and wife. Particularly good strapwork. Back divided with stages and panels to contain their four sons and four daughters, as well as contemporary poems. It is a handsome piece and has similarities with Burton-on-Trent work. – Many wall monuments, some signed by local sculptors such as *Charles Williams*. In the s aisle, John Middlemore †1698, with bulbous tablet and obelisk, by *R. Squire* of Worcester, *c.*1740; Mary Orford †1823, Tudor Gothic, probably by her son *Charles Wyatt Orford*, who is also commemorated.

CHURCHYARD. Near the Saracen's Head, s, the once-elegant Middlemore tomb. Late C18, tall, with an urn and Corinthian columns (two missing). – N side, Thomas and Elizabeth Hamper †1811, square, with deep cornice and fluted urn.

KINGS NORTON BAPTIST CHURCH, Wharf Road. Early C19, with lancets. Greatly altered and extended.

OLD GRAMMAR SCHOOL, N side of the churchyard. There was a 'free Schole' in 1547. The present building is of *c.*1662, when Thomas Hall, the Puritan minister of Kings Norton, recorded the parishioners' undertaking to build a library to house his intended gift of books. Two storeys, with a projecting s porch. Ground floor of brick, with stone quoins, foundations and small plain mullioned windows. The upper storey is of re-erected timber framing, perhaps from a previous school building (tree-ring dates between 1434 and 1460). Four bays. The central truss has big arched braces springing from sideposts, supporting a slightly cambered collar-beam. Diagonal struts above. To each side simpler collar-beam trusses. Three-light E window with two sexfoils and a top quatrefoil, all of timber. Heavily restored: by *William Hale* in 1892 and 1910, when the W staircase was built and much timber replaced (beams marked 'MCMX'); by *Owen Parsons* in 1931; by *Philip* and *Anthony Chatwin* in 1951 and the latter again in 1988; and lastly in 2007. Panelling inside, mainly C17.

LIBRARY, Pershore Road South. 1905–6 by *Benjamin Bower*. Charming small-scale Tudor-cum-Baroque, just a single storey on a basement. Doorcase with Gibbs surround and split pediment framing a cartouche. Tiny cupola.

KINGS NORTON PRIMARY SCHOOL, Pershore Road South, s of the library. In the middle, the Board School of 1878 by *William Hale*. Picturesquely massed, with tile-hanging in the gables but an octagonal Gothic turret with a spirelet over the entrance. Master's house separate to the N. By *Edward Holmes*, 1901–2, the former School Board offices (now nursery) attached to it, and the s part with four Dutch gables to the road; both Jacobean in brick and deep red terracotta. Linking entrance block by *Birmingham Department of Planning and Architecture*, 1994–6.

WYCHALL PRIMARY SCHOOL, Middle Field Road. 1957 by *Norrish & Stainton*. Two-storey main block, single-storeyed elsewhere. Some random stone-faced walls.

SARACEN'S HEAD (St Nicolas Place), adjoining the churchyard to the s. The N range and part of the E range of a timber-framed courtyard house of 1492–3, built for Humphrey Rotsey, woolstapler, lawyer and auditor.* The ostentatious N range was built first. A jetty runs all round. Corner post with a bracket tenoned into a dragon beam. Close studding to both floors on the N, where doorways mark a demolished two-storey porch. A later wing projects N at the W end. The E gable has the first floor coved outwards, and a cambered tie-beam with arcaded decoration (cf. the Old Crown, Deritend, and the porch of Sheldon church, pp. 197, 280). Of the E range, facing The Green, the N half remains, refaced in brick probably between 1756 and 1764, when the house became an inn. The square bays with Gothick

---

*Excavations revealed a C12 boundary ditch on the line of the N wall of the N range, remains of C13 and C14 timber buildings in the courtyard and under the N range, and part of a C15 decorated tile floor within the N range.

arcading may be part of this work. The s gable represents the original entrance to the courtyard, extended outwards *c.* 1860. s and w ranges of 2006–8 by *APEC*, a heavy intervention, glazed and grey-clad, with much restoration of the C15 ranges.

The grandest INTERIORS are in the N range. The ground-floor E room has richly moulded ceiling beams with a wave and hollow chamfer, and remains of wall paintings, particularly arabesques in red r. of the fireplace. To the w another room with moulded ceiling beams and close studding. Upstairs, the Queen's Room, E, has studding again and a fireplace with a moulded and brattished lintel. w rooms opened out, exposing a cambered collar-beam truss, a box-framed partition with wattle-and-daub infill, a tie-beam with square panels above, also with infill, and finally a big tie-beam truss on brackets, again panelled above. In the E range, timber framing is visible in the corridor, and part of the former central archway can be seen in the Gable Room.

PERAMBULATION

THE GREEN is tree-lined and triangular, sloping up to the church and the Saracen's Head at the top. The cottages seen in early C20 photographs were cleared by the City Council between 1936 and the 1960s. On the NW side the BULL'S HEAD, 1901, *James & Lister Lea* in their countrified manner, brick with render above and half-timber gables. Also half-timbered is No. 20, s side: by *Arthur Edwards*, 1907, as an off-licence for Holders Brewery, whose monogram is on the ends of the fascia. Nos. 16–19 are early C19; No. 10 (SPAR) retains the cross-wing of a timber-framed house of *c.* 1500 behind a much-altered C18 brick front. Camber-beam trusses, the front and rear ones with a collar-beam and close studding, the middle one open, with angle struts. One collar-beam truss of the front wing survives, with queen-struts and wind-braces. The E side is sadly opened up by a car park. At the SE corner, an exit to a roundabout on the main A441 road. To the E, at the start of WHARF ROAD, the former NAVIGATION pub, 1906 by *James & Lister Lea*, the same mix as the Bull's Head. On PERSHORE ROAD SOUTH, N, a former CO-OP by *H.W. Simister*, 1936 (w side). Brick Tudor with a hipped roof, and formerly a cupola. On the E side, the primary school, the former POST OFFICE of 1902 by *Fred J. Gill* of Smethwick, like a suburban semi of *c.* 1935, and the library (*see* left).

Back to The Green and w, REDNAL ROAD twists uphill to the SW. On the E corner of Westhill Road, No. 1, by *Gerald McMichael*, 1907, rendered, with sharp gables. More satisfyingly plain McMichael houses at Nos. 71–73, rendered, and No. 75 (brick), 1911. No. 87, in the same manner, is by local builders *Parry & Sons*, 1912–13. No. 89 is by *W.N. Twist*, 1913, brick with sprocketed roofs; r. wing by *E.F. Reynolds*, 1921. Diagonally opposite, WESTHILL is by *Payne & Talbot*, 1886, big, in brick and render. Further w a cross-roads. On the SE corner No. 2 Grange Hill Road, by *F.E. Bromilow*, 1939–40, rendered, with a bold green pantile roof; greatly extended 2019. BEAKS HILL ROAD leads N. Grassmoor Road, off its W side, has No. 21, by *John Madin*, 1953–5, nicely integrating render, boarding and a brick chimney. No. 53 Beaks Hill Road, flat-roofed, rendered and curved-cornered, is of 1935 by *T. Dunkley Hogg* of Smethwick. In Meadow Hill Road opposite, THE RED HOUSE, Neo-Georgian by *W.T. Orton*. 1908–10. Back in Beaks Hill Road, No. 25, by *A.W. Baylis*, a quantity surveyor, for himself, 1913, relieved by one little concave oriel. No. 21 (DELL COTTAGE) is by *W.A. Harvey*, 1909–10. Hipped roof, very tall chimneys (one cut down), off-centre doorway with good wrought-iron brackets A full-height bay, r., breaks the eaves. Extended by *Harvey & Wicks* behind, 1914–17, with a loggia and former garage (l.). Inside, a miniature entrance hall and good plasterwork on beams. Back to Rednal Road past the road's smaller earliest houses, mostly by *Orton*.

CANAL STRUCTURES

The WORCESTER AND BIRMINGHAM CANAL, here of 1794–7, engineer *Thomas Cartwright*, runs N–S through Kings Norton. The junction with the STRATFORD-UPON-AVON CANAL of 1795–6, engineer *Josiah Clowes*, is ½ m. NE, marked by a T-shaped TOLL HOUSE, dated 1796. A full-height canted bay with a Doric doorcase and big mullion-and-transom windows faces the canal. Along the Stratford canal, under the modern bridge of Lifford Lane, a GUILLOTINE LOCK of 1813 by *William Whitmore*, engineer. Two single gates, their chains running round pulleys to counterweights in brick chambers. It was the stop lock between the two canals. ¾ m. S along the Worcester canal, N of Shannon Road, the N portal of the 2,726-yd (2,493-metre) WASTHILL TUNNEL. Curved brick retaining wall with stone voussoirs to the arch. Above the tunnel mouth, TUNNEL COTTAGES, whitewashed brick. The casement windows may represent originals.

OTHER BUILDINGS

LIFFORD HALL, Tunnel Lane. A C17 house, now hemmed in by canals and lime-works, and reached by a bridge over the River Rea. A deceptive building; its location is the clue to its history. The L-shaped main block, with pairs of gables to N and W, is a classy miller's house built by William Turton in the 1670s. Orange-red brick laid in Flemish bond, restored C18 sashes. The gentrification was completed almost certainly by *Charles Wyatt Orford* (†1867), who bought the estate c. 1850. A two-storey bay window, N, covers the site of a mill-wheel. The wing to the E is the much-altered former mill. In its gable a smart C17 mullioned window with a moulded cornice. Flemish stretcher bond brickwork, clearly earlier than the house. Further E a crenellated C19 wall and folly tower with corbelled parapet.

LIFFORD RESERVOIR, to the NE, was constructed by the Worcester and Birmingham Canal Co. in 1812–13.

PRIMROSE HILL FARM, Meadowsweet Avenue, ¾ m. s. A substantial timber-framed farmhouse, with tree-ring dates from 1440 onwards. T-plan, with two-bay hall (1440) and three-bay W cross-wing extended and partly rebuilt in 1475 and 1521. (The sandstone sill of a former E cross-wing was found in excavations.) The hall has an impressive spere-truss with an arch-braced collar-beam, a tie-beam truss (infilled), with king-post and diagonal struts, and an arch-braced collar-beam truss. The cross-wing has tie-beam trusses with queenposts, except for the second from the N, which has a kingpost. S front faced in C18 brick, much repaired, W side with a grid of cross-beams and tightly packed studs. Two original windows with timber mullions, under the eaves. More studding on the N. In the mid C16 the hall was ceiled in, the beams dated to 1555. Two good stone fireplaces in the cross-wing probably date from this time. Restored in 1913–14 by *Owen Parsons*, who added the small N extension. Repaired again 2006–7, after fire damage, by Chris and Sue Higgins, with nicely grouped surrounding care houses by *Ian Keay*. – To the W, a box-framed BARN, dated to 1457. Framing in two rows of large panels on a brick plinth, an early example of this. Tie-beams with arched braces and diagonal struts above.

CARTLAND ARMS (former), Parsons Hill. Streamlined pub by *Watson & Johnson*, 1935.

LODGE to the former Moundsley Hall, Walkers Heath Road. C19, with bargeboards. Strapwork and cusping to the porch.

WALKERS HEATH FARM, Gay Hill Lane, nearby. W part with platband, probably early C18. The E part, with roughcast brick buttresses, may be C16 in origin. – Brick CARTSHED, NE, probably C18.

COTTERIDGE

N of the old village. A product of the Midland Railway (Kings Norton station, opened 1849). Its best building, St Agnes's church, free Perp of 1902 by *Cossins, Peacock & Bewlay*, was demolished in 1988.

METHODIST CHURCH (now THE COTTERIDGE CHURCH), Pershore Road South. 1901–2 by *Ewen & J. Alfred Harper*. Red brick and stone dressings. NW tower with octagonal spire. Dec. Extended and reordered by *APEC* (*Ken Fisher* and *Michael Brabbs*), 1990.

ST JOSEPH AND ST HELEN (R.C.), Northfield Road. 1932–3 by *G.B. Cox*. A modest, rather conservative brick church. C14-style window tracery. Big ritual W window with Free Style buttressed mullions. Satisfying interior with two-bay arcades to the side chapels (keeled shafts). Close-set rafter roof. – Gothic REREDOS with tympanum painting. – STAINED GLASS. W window, c. 1935, probably by *Sidney Meteyard*.

FRIENDS' MEETING HOUSE, Watford Road, 1962–4 by *Harry Harper* of *Clifford Tee & Gale*. Modernism and the gentle Bournville design approach. Single-storeyed, buff brick, low V-pitch roof. L-plan, facing a rear lawn through large windows. Spacious meeting room with an asymmetrical pine roof.

KINGS NORTON BOYS' SCHOOL, Northfield Road. 1909–11 by *Pritchard & Pritchard*. Plain Tudor, with many gables. A three-arch arcade marks the centre.

COTTERIDGE JUNIOR AND INFANT SCHOOL, Pershore Road. Front range by *J.P. Osborne*, 1908–11. Spare Tudor Revival. Terracotta bands, patterned brick tympana. At the rear the original school, by *Edward Holmes*, 1899–1900. A tall compact block of London type (cf. William Hale's at Stirchley, p. 434). Jacobean, with insistent pilasters. A half-hip on the Breedon Road end.

FIRE STATION, Pershore Road South. A big Neo-Georgian scheme with houses and flats, dated 1930. By *H.H. Humphries*, City Engineer and Surveyor.

The centre is N of the station, at the junction of roads from Birmingham and Selly Oak. NE of the former Methodist church, a classical former BARCLAYS BANK by *Peacock & Bewlay*, 1925. Opposite, NW, former Birmingham Gas Department offices, Neo-Wren by *Cossins, Peacock & Bewlay*, 1911, with paired Doric columns dividing the shop bays. To the l. an octagonal GOVERNOR HOUSE of 1910 by the Gas Department engineer *James Hewett*. In Walford Road, N, the former POST OFFICE, dated 1939. On PERSHORE ROAD, E, LLOYDS BANK by *W. Norman Twist*, 1930, and the GRANT ARMS pub by *E.F. Reynolds*, 1928–9, Neo-Georgian with a big hipped roof and swan's-neck doorcases.

MIDDLETON HALL ROAD runs W from the centre towards Northfield. Solid mid- and Late Victorian villas. ¼ m. W, on the corner of Selly Oak Road, No. 114, a rambling Arts and Crafts house in brick and grey render by *William Hale & Son*, 1905. No. 75 opposite, old-fashioned and steep-roofed, by *Hale*, 1898–9. No. 156, N side, dated 1901, is by *Ewen & J. Alfred Harper*. At the Northfield end, *Hale*'s No. 151 of 1900–1, and No. 153 of 1884, his own house, a loose composition around a big gable pierced by a chimney and flanked by decorative timbering (poorly extended).

CAMP INN, S of the railway in Camp Lane. Tudor Revival of 1927 by *James & Lister Lea & Sons*.

WEST HEATH

A large area of low-density mid-C20 housing. The churches face each other across a grassy roundabout.

ST ANNE, Alvechurch Road. 1965–6 by *Harold N. Wright* of *Harvey & Wicks*. Maroon brick, steeply gabled, with a half-oval plan. Inside, asymmetrical laminated trusses. Behind, its modest C19 predecessor, brick with terracotta Y-tracery.

ST JOHN FISHER (R.C.), Cofton Road. By *E. Bower Norris*, 1962–4. Late Byzantine Revival in yellow brick with red dressings. Low octagonal central tower. Big unmoulded round arches to nave, transepts and sanctuary, smaller ones in the diagonals, smaller still along the passage aisles, spatially satisfying. Sanctuary arcades with piers necked at top and bottom with gold mosaic. – BALDACCHINO of metal piers forming arches curving into the dome; circular PULPIT with disc tester; late Art Deco-style REREDOSES in the side chapels. – STAINED GLASS by *Jonah Jones*, lancets in the crossing with four aspects of Christ.

LADYWOOD

Ladywood was one of the city's five post-war Redevelopment Areas. Tight-packed mid-C19 streets were replaced by municipal housing. The first were completed in 1958, in Morville and Ruston streets: typical terraces and three-storey flats by *A.G. Sheppard Fidler*, City Architect. Cheaper mass housing of the late 1960s, maisonettes and tower blocks, equally typical of *J.A. Maudsley*, survives in Guild Close. In the 1990s the Ladywood Regeneration Framework replaced 1960s towers with cottagey low-rise housing. In 2019 major regeneration was again proposed.

ST JOHN THE EVANGELIST, Monument Road. 1852–4 by *S.S. Teulon*, extended by *J.A. Chatwin*, 1881. Dec, sandstone, with limestone dressings. Nave, aisles, ritual NW tower. Little of Teulon's usual inventiveness. Sexfoiled circular windows at the W, a castellated turret by the S porch. The arcade piers have sharply cut-back bases. Octagonal columns and capitals, double-chamfered arches. Chatwin's chancel, S chapel and two-bay transepts follow Teulon's details except for his chancel arch with shafts on corbels (with undercut foliage). His transepts have their own arcades, a nice play of arches and spaces. E window almost certainly Teulon's, moved: big spherical triangle containing a concave-sided triangle, little sexfoiled centre. – Teulon's FONT survives (S transept): small, with little blank gablets. – Typical *Chatwin* PULPIT, open tracery panels, statues under canopies, dated 1881. – The delight of the church is the S chapel (currently unused). ENGLISH ALTAR by *Hobbiss*, 1927. Big top cornice, octagonal corner columns with gougings *à la* Gimson, chunky square riddel-posts. – PEWS by *P.B. Chatwin*, 1932, with relief panels of the symbols of the Evangelists and, at the back, small lanterns on tall columns. – N chapel SCREEN by *Hobbiss*, 1940; the main ALTAR RAIL must be his too. – STAINED GLASS. E window by *Hardmans*, 1866, bright High Victorian colours. Flanking windows, 1893, perhaps also theirs. S aisle, SS John the Evangelist and Paul by *Pearce & Co.*, 1901. By *Kim Jarvis* two W roundels, 2000, and a two-light window in the S transept, 2002. – Reordering by *RRA*, 2003, already looking tired: vast open spaces, 'pod' in the S aisle, pool in the S transept. Hideous TV screens, 2018.

BIRMINGHAM BUDDHIST VIHARA (DHAMMATALAKA PAGODA), Osler Street. The golden-covered stupa with its projecting porches is of 1994–8 by *David Jones*, with the help of artists from Myanmar, *Win Tin*, *Khin Zaw U* and *U Aye*. Residential block by *Jones*, 2002.

LADYWOOD JUNIOR AND INFANT SCHOOL (now St John's and St Peter's Academy), St Vincent Street West. 1961 by *A.G. Sheppard Fidler*, City Architect (job architect *Mary Granelli*). A once crisp two- and three-storey range (the ground falls at the back). It has suffered by re-windowing and loss of the shaped roof structure for services.

LADYWOOD HEALTH AND COMMUNITY CENTRE, St Vincent Street West. 1965–6 by *Norrish & Stainton*, reinforced concrete and smooth brick, adapted in 1993 with an array of angled and curving metal roofs by *Axis Design Collective* (*Joe Holyoak*).

LADYWOOD LEISURE CENTRE, Ladywood Middleway. 2019 by *calderpeel*.

CHAMBERLAIN GARDENS, Skipton Road, SW of Ladywood Middleway. One of *A.G. Sheppard Fidler*'s most important housing schemes, of 1961–6 (project architects *Miall Rhys-Davies* and *B. Leicester*). Nine-storey blocks and two- to four-storey houses and maisonettes. Landscaping by *Mary Mitchell*, including an octagonal shelter.

ICKNIELD PORT LOOP. Part of *Brindley*'s Birmingham Canal of 1769, cut off by the straight line of Telford's improvements of 1829. It crosses under Icknield Port Road twice. In ROTTON PARK STREET, running NE, a factory of 1891–2 by *William Hale* for the Weldless Steel Tube Co., with a little Queen Anne detail, and a muscular former council depot by *Martin & Martin*, dated 1903: hard red brick, central gable with corbelled-out chimney. In 2019 regeneration is starting here, with high-density energy-efficient terraced housing. The first blocks are by *shedkm*, with prefabricated components, designed with flexible internal planning. Grey cladding, darker little gables, like their work in New Islington, Manchester: Khrushchyov-kas for the C21. Future blocks planned by *Glenn Howells*. W of Icknield Port Road, just N of the northern canal bridge, a CANAL MAINTENANCE DEPOT nestles under the dam of Edgbaston Reservoir (p.387). By the canal a two-storey office of *c.*1845 with Gothick windows and doorway. The hipped-roofed building behind is a COVERED DOCK, probably of the 1860s, as are the STABLES beyond. To the W a workshop range, probably 1870s.

LEDSAM STREET WORKS. G.E. Belliss & Co., engine and boiler (later compressor) makers, founded 1866, moved here in 1872–3. Belliss & Morcom from 1899, closed in the 1980s, now in various uses. The first buildings, by *T.H. Mansell*, have gone. The long front range is by *William Hale*, 1885–7.

Heavy pilasters and segment-headed windows. Taller classical office block, r., with workshops behind, by *W.T. Orton*, 1914–15. Large extension l. with framed windows by *Buckland & Haywood*, 1953.

In GREAT TINDAL STREET a dourly impressive warehouse of 1849 with rows of segment-headed windows sunk in reveals, and a dentil cornice. FRANK ALLART, mildly Postmodern, is by *Daniel Hurd*, 1995.

LONGBRIDGE AND REDNAL

LONGBRIDGE MOTOR WORKS AND AUSTIN VILLAGE

Longbridge was defined by one huge factory. Herbert Austin founded the AUSTIN MOTOR CO. in 1905, taking over a tin-box printing factory of 1894–5. This began the SOUTH WORKS, on the E side of Lickey Road. A machine shop was added in 1909, offices in 1913; the First World War saw the WEST WORKS, w of Bristol Road South, and the NORTH WORKS, opposite. Austin used *S.N. Cooke* as architect, but from c.1914 his own designers. More large extensions came in the 1930s, and again after 1945 for Austin Morris, later the British Motor Corporation. Nearly everything was demolished after closure in 2005; a smaller successor, MG MOTOR UK, is at the s end of the site, on Lowhill Lane. The EXHIBITION HALL of 1956, now conference centre, by *Harry Weedon & Partners*, is L-shaped, brick-faced, with a low round tower at the corner. Herbert Austin's office has been re-created inside. To its E the re-clad CAR ASSEMBLY BUILDING of 1952 by *C. Howard Crane*, originally with glazed walls and roof. The COMMERCIAL VEHICLE SHOWROOM to the w (the 'Elephant House'), 1965 by *Weedon*, now Sales Centre, is much more fun: circular, with an outer aisle roof waving up and down. Panels between originally fully glazed.

Regeneration of the rest is a paradigm of the latest Birmingham: badly planned, aggressive and vacuous. BOURNVILLE COLLEGE is of 2011 by *Broadway Malyan*, a six-storey ski-jump with a low, gold-coloured free-form block at the w end. Isolated to the E, a retail development of 2012–15 by *Holder Mathias*; N of Longbridge Lane, THE FACTORY (young people's centre), by *Associated Architects*, 2012, the best here, grey and pink strips over a glazed ground floor.

AUSTIN VILLAGE, ½ m. NE. A little bit of the Midwest in south Birmingham, built by Herbert Austin for wartime workers in 1917–18. It runs along Central Avenue, linked by side roads, with greens and trees, to Coney Green Drive, w, and Hawkesley Drive, E. Rows of prefabricated weatherboarded cedarwood bungalows by the *Aladdin Co.* of Bay City, Michigan: 200 in all. Wide front porches instantly identify them as American.

Semi-detached houses designed by the *Austin Motor Co.* (for managers) mark street corners; also some pairs with balanced asymmetrical gables.

OTHER BUILDINGS, WITH REDNAL

The rest is suburban development, 1920s to 1960s, to the foot of the Lickey Hills in the Birmingham part of Rednal.

ST JOHN THE BAPTIST, Longbridge Lane. 1956–8 by *George While* of *Bromilow, While & Smeeton*. A quirky, unusual church, drawing on C19 and older sources. Brick nave, shading from salmon-pink to brown; limestone-faced chancel. The roof is continuous from (ritual) E to W. Rectangular SE tower with a prominent copper double-saddleback roof. The famous one at Fingest, Bucks., is in its ancestry, but north German or Scandinavian Modernism is nearer. Segment-headed windows on the N, big mullioned windows divided by slim buttresses on the S. Semicircular N stair-turret, just where the rood stair might be. The large W window has copper mullions supporting five oak statues designed by *While* and carved by *Robert Pancheri*. Inside, the surprise is that there are no arcades. Deep girders span the lengths of the aisles, which are defined by lower, flat roofs. The focus is the E wall, covered in 'Black Country paviours' with smudged joints, and a fine cross with Agnus Dei. – Good and simple original FURNISHINGS by *While*, including the dark marble FONT, a stripped version of the Cornish type with four supporting legs. Copper disc cover with curving handles. LAMPS on a frame above. – Linked HALL to the N, enlarged by *Harrison Coton Harvey & Wicks*, 1982. VICARAGE beyond by *Bromilow, While & Smeeton*, 1955–6, modernized Neo-Georgian.

ST STEPHEN, Edgewood Road. 1951 by *J.P. Osborne & Son*. Flat-roofed dual-purpose hall and church, with a small tower.

OUR LADY OF PERPETUAL SUCCOUR (R.C.), Leach Green Lane. 1960 by *E. Bower Norris*. Buff brick. Still traditional. Pairs of rectangular lancets, piers and lintels for arcades.

LONGBRIDGE METHODIST CHURCH, Bristol Road South. 1964–7 by *John H.D. Madin & Partners*. Maroon brick with a little lantern. Altered – courtyard roofed over, triangular windows – by *Kenneth Holmes*, 1997. The worship area is an irregular octagon.

ORATORY HOUSE, Rowantrees, off Leach Green Lane, Rednal. Hidden in a wood, the country retreat of the Birmingham Oratory. A tall, plain house (builders *Thomas & Jacob Nowell*), 1854. Some upper rooms – bathroom, WC – hardly touched since. Attached CHAPEL by *John Hungerford Pollen*, 1856–7, taller than it is long. Brick Italian Romanesque, with much dentilling, a bold porch hood and a row of high windows. Sanctuary separated by a big plain arch. – In the Fathers' GRAVEYARD, simplified Celtic crosses; one for John Henry

Newman †1890 and his friend Ambrose St John †1875, who paid for the chapel.

LIBRARY (former), No. 129 Leach Green Lane. Dated and signed on a plaque with foliage: 1909 by *Benjamin Bower*. Arts and Crafts; the full-height timber bay and round-headed doorway are nods to Lutyens's Deanery Garden. Now a house.

SCHOOLS. COLMERS FARM SCHOOL, Bristol Road South, is by *G.B. Cox*, designed 1938, built 1948–50. A massive range with a blocky tower. REDNAL HILL JUNIOR AND INFANT SCHOOL, Irwin Avenue, is by *Nicol, Nicol & Thomas*, 1952 etc. Low flat-roofed blocks, with, at one point, circular windows.

RUBERY HILL HOSPITAL. The city's second lunatic asylum, by *Martin & Chamberlain*, 1878–82, mostly redeveloped for offices and housing. LODGE on Bristol Road South, almost on the Worcestershire boundary. A picturesque mix of segment-headed sashes, timber-framed windows and a bracket cornice. To the N, the tall SUPERINTENDENT'S HOUSE, dated 1879, with more typical Gothic woodwork. To its E the former CHAPEL. Paired lancets, stepped buttresses and an eye-catching E end with apse, gabled and buttressed turret above, and flanking spirelets. Hammerbeam roof.

HOLLYMOOR HOSPITAL, Tessall Lane. A large annexe to Rubery Hill mental hospital, by *Martin & Chamberlain*, who won a competition in 1898; opened 1905. Red brick with red and buff terracotta. Much demolition after closure in 1994. Impressively tall and massive water tower, with angle and central buttresses, belfry-like windows and a copper dome. Entrance block with an Ionic surround to the doorway and a pyramid roof above. Chapel with paired entrances, wide lancets separated by buttresses, triangular dormers, tapering cupola-cum-spirelet and three-sided apse. Hammerbeam roof with arched braces to a high collar. Small entrance lodge.

HAWKESLEY FARM MOAT ESTATE, N of St John the Baptist church, down Munslow Grove. One of *A.G. Sheppard Fidler*'s best housing schemes, of 1957–8. Three eight-storey blocks, now rendered, balanced by an L-shaped group of bungalows. Grouped round a retained moat, partly water-filled: the site of Great Hawkesley, a C14/C15 timber-framed house, and later an C18 farmhouse. Excavations in 1957–8 found remains of a timber gatehouse at the entrance gap, beam slots of a C14 building, post-holes and sandstone bases for more timber walls, and a C15–C16 coal-fired oven. Moat fencing of 1958.

On BRISTOL ROAD SOUTH, going W, No. 1730, a streamlined former CO-OPERATIVE shop of 1936 by *H.W. Simister*, with a circular tower. Small plaque by *Bloye*. Going NE towards Northfield, No. 1375, the former DANILO CINEMA, by *Ernest Roberts*, 1937–8. On the corner of Tessall Lane, the former KING GEORGE V pub by *J.B. Surman*, 1935. Tudor Revival, rendered, with ample Cotswold stone dressings. Butterfly plan, angled along both roads. The central block has a slightly projecting gable, so three gables at different angles face the junction. (Panelled first-floor assembly room with queenpost roof, function room with plaster barrel-vault.)

NORTHFIELD

A Worcestershire parish, which historically included Selly Oak, Longbridge and Bartley Green (qq.v.). The present centre is on the Bristol road, ½ m. NW of the ancient village. In the late C19 and early C20 houses spread along Bristol Road and Church Road, and from *c.*1900 settlement began around the railway station, to the S. The area was covered by suburban housing after the 1920s, started by the car factory at Longbridge. The MANOR HOUSE, 1¼ m. N, was by *John James*, 1701–3, greatly extended and altered for George Cadbury by *Franklin Cross* from 1893. It became student accommodation, with residential blocks by *Holland W. Hobbiss* of 1955–7 etc. Damaged by fire in 2014 and demolished.

ST LAURENCE, Church Hill. Tucked away in a tightly enclosed village setting, this church contains the finest E.E. work in the area. Grey local sandstone, much repaired, often in red. The original C12 building is represented by a round-headed doorway of *c.*1170, re-set in the N aisle wall. It is of two orders, the inner with chevron ornament and the outer with beakheads, now very worn. Also apparently early are four carved animal heads, inserted in the N and S faces of the tower. The glory of the church is the complete and unspoilt C13 chancel. Groups of three lancets under hoodmoulds, and broad buttresses. At the W end of the N wall a lowside window; in the S wall a doorway with a flattened trefoiled head, and a single lancet, without shafts, in plain walling. The interior is quite unexpected. The E window lights have moulded heads and shafted jambs, under an outer arch with shafted jambs and moulded label. The three groups in the N wall and the two in the S wall are treated similarly, each lancet having shafted jambs and moulded capitals and arches, with on the outer sides a blank half-arch. The segmental arches run like wide blank arcading, and at their ends are delicate slim shafts supporting the hoodmoulds. The tower is also C13, with a W doorway flanked by blank niches set higher, and two-light N and S windows. The second stage is blank. Perp top stage, battlemented. The S aisle is of *c.*1300, with intersecting and Y-tracery windows, three-light to E and W, two-light along the S. Doorway with big crowned heads for hoodstops, and almost certainly the original DOOR of four big planks, cross-braced inside. Outer skin renewed; decorative hinges also original. The S wall leans out markedly, and has additional C19 buttresses. In the E wall by the chancel is the jamb and part of the arch of a doorway which looks

Norman, part of an extension, perhaps a chapel or vestry, built off the original Norman nave. If it led to a building to its E, this might explain the irregularity of the chancel S wall. Late C14 or C15 S arcade, with octagonal piers and unsophisticated capitals. The timber-framed S porch looks C15 or even C14, on a sandstone base. N aisle added by *G.F. Bodley*, 1899–1900, in a smooth Dec style. Sympathetic N vestries by *Anthony Chatwin*, 1960.

Inside, an arch-braced collar-beam truss and another against the nave wall with boldly cusped struts. Brattished wall-plate; wind-braces. The main roofs, probably C15, also have lots of brattishing. Nave and S aisle have tie- and arch-braced collar-beams, the aisle with queen-struts. The chancel has collar-beams with moulded arch braces (repaired by *C. Hodgson Fowler*, 1894). Double-chamfered C13 tower arch, altered. The capitals, a simpler version of those of the S arcade, may be C19 restoration. To its S, remains seemingly of a former staircase. A most interesting feature of the interior is the absence of a chancel arch and its replacement by four separate roof trusses side by side: the end trusses of nave and chancel, and two more between. A flat timber-framed tympanum is still intact in the space between the tie-beam and principal rafters of the second truss from the nave end. It is grooved at the sides for wattle-and-daub filling, and the front angles rebated for boarding. Traces of painting on the boards, perhaps a Last Judgment, and holes almost certainly for rood figures, hidden by the present figures of 1956 by *Anthony Chatwin*, carvers *Robert Bridgeman & Sons*. Third and fourth trusses from the nave end share a moulded tie-beam. This elaborate structure possibly came about in the late C15, when the chancel roof was replaced. The two middle trusses probably carried the then nave roof, as well as filling up the space between roof levels. Then finally the nave roof was replaced by the present one. Much work is due to the Rev. Henry Clarke, Tractarian curate and then rector, 1839–80. Gentle restoration of 1854–5, by a local builder, *Edward Grove*.

FURNISHINGS. PULPIT of 1843, incorporating C15 woodwork, from a former screen: ogee-arched tops to panels, with quatrefoils and flowers. – CHOIR STALLS. 1887. – Chancel SCREEN of 1861, C15 style, richly carved. – SANCTUARY LAMPS. 1894. –PEWS of 1869 by *Dudley Male*; one on the N with C17 panels. *Bodley* made the aisle ones to match. – PANELLING in the N aisle by *Bodley*, 1900. – ROYAL ARMS. Hanoverian, period 1714–1801, S aisle. – STAINED GLASS. A fine C19 collection, almost all by *Hardmans*. The first is the chancel SE, 1850, designed by *Pugin*: St Michael and the dragon surrounded by angels, in medallions. Chancel E 1870; S central 1853; N 1853 and 1859 (two). The programme is the Ministry of Christ. S aisle: E 1863; S 1881, 1907, very different with much silvery-grey; 1868. N aisle, from E: 1870, 1878, 1870. By the *Kempe* firm, N aisle E 1903, W 1914. – MONUMENTS. Isabella Wolferstan †1680. Tablet with cartouche and pediment-like garlands. – Rev. John

Hinckley †1695, big tablet (renewed 1916) with segmental pediment. – Good *Hardmans* brass of 1846, chancel floor. – Another of 1869, S wall. – Many small C19 brasses.

In the churchyard a MEMORIAL CROSS to the Rev. Henry Clarke, 1884 by *J.L. Pearson*, with canopied niches containing saints. – LYCHGATE of 1863. Bold and simple timberwork.

(ST BARTHOLOMEW, Allens Cross. Brick Early Christian basilica by *S.N. Cooke*, 1938. Demolished 2008.)

ST DAVID, Shenley Green. 1969–70 by *Peter Carrick* of *Bournville Village Trust Architect's Department*. Fan-shaped, with a big angular lantern, faced in reeded bush-hammered concrete. Low narthex with a small bell-tower at one end. HALL also by *BVT Architects*, 1962. Rendered interior with boarded ceiling sloping up towards the altar. Original FITTINGS.

OUR LADY AND ST BRIGID (R.C.), Frankley Beeches Road. Massive stripped Italian Romanesque by *E. Bower Norris*, 1935–8, brick with Hollington stone dressings, on a constricted site. Tall apse, square blocky nave with narrow passage aisles, ritual SW campanile with an arcaded top and pyramid roof. Low unmoulded arcades. Narthex separated by arches with wrought-iron grilles. – PAINTING. The apse is filled by a Neo-Baroque Resurrection by *Neil Harvey*, 1990s. – Very fine STATIONS OF THE CROSS by *Benjamin Creswick*, dated 1920–9, vigorous, crowded, with expressive elongated figures in a Mannerist way. Strongly formal, e.g. the Entombment (XIV) with arch and body forming almost a complete circle. – Behind, PRIMARY SCHOOL of 1950–1 by *Sandy & Norris* and the former church, now HALL, 1930–1 by the *Rev. Francis Askew*, with a quirky Diocletian window turned in tile.

FRIENDS' MEETING HOUSE, Church Road. Set back up an access road by the park. 1929–30 by *Buckland & Haywood*. Neo-Georgian, big hipped roof.

HELIER CHAPEL (now CROSSWAY CHURCH), St Heliers Road. By *George While*, 1937–8. A dourly impressive brick box with a pedimental gable and classical doorcase.

ADULT EDUCATION CENTRE, Church Road. Built as a coffee house by George Cadbury in 1891, designed by *William Doubleday*. Two big gables. Much of its Domestic Revival timbering has gone. Powerful chimneystack at the rear, cut down. Semi-detached COTTAGES behind, also for Cadbury by *Doubleday*: a small precursor of Bournville.

LIBRARY, Church Road. By *C.E. Bateman* and *Alfred Hale*, 1914. Neo-Georgian. Porch with a big segmental pediment.

PUBLIC BATHS, Bristol Road South. *H.W. Simister*'s fine modern Neo-Georgian building of 1935–7 was demolished in 2017. Loud replacement by *calderpeel*, 2017–18.

ST LAURENCE CHURCH OF ENGLAND JUNIOR AND INFANT SCHOOLS, Bunbury Road. By *Holland W. Hobbiss & Partners*, 1958–71.

TRESCOTT JUNIOR AND INFANT SCHOOL (now MERRITTS BROOK ACADEMY), Trescott Road. Original buildings by *P.B. Chatwin*, 1929–31, low ranges with deep roofs and big dormers.

ROYAL ORTHOPAEDIC HOSPITAL, Bristol Road South. The start is THE WOODLANDS, an 1830s stucco villa perhaps by *Charles Edge*, who worked nearby. Purchased by George Cadbury in 1899 and given to the Crippled Children's Union in 1909; amalgamated with the hospital in 1925. *Bateman & Bateman* (*Batemans* after *c.* 1914) were the hospital architects up to 1939. In 1908 they added the prominent circular tower with a conical roof l. of the house, for lavatories and washrooms, and a smaller one behind. Interwar work is friendly Neo-Georgian: former NURSES' HOME at the rear, 1929, and RECREATION HALL. Linking COVERED WAY of 1933. To the r. of the house the former SURGEON'S RESIDENCE (now spinal unit) of 1935. Many recent extensions, including a big X-ray block and main entrance, 1997: angular, full-height glazing, render.

The old VILLAGE is by St Laurence's church. To the N, the GREAT STONE INN. C18 brick exterior with casement windows. Inside, the remains of a C16 or earlier hall house, of three bays. Tie-and collar-beam trusses, wind-braces. Infill box framing below one truss, probably C17. The S end was jettied, underbuilt in the C18. S wing probably C18, with a barn-like tie-beam roof. N of the inn in Church Road the village POUND. Mentioned from the C15 and marked on a map of 1714. Sandstone front with shallow triangular-arched openings and central entrance. Then ROSE COTTAGE, early C19. Opposite, the former RECTORY, rendered, by *J.H. Hawkes & Son*, 1932–4. It replaced a late C17 H-plan house with a cupola. To its E a box-framed wing, probably C16.

Going down Church Hill, on the r. a cluster of cottages; No. 6 on the corner L-shaped, C18. Then the former NORTHFIELD SCHOOLS. Front range dated 1837, with bargeboarded gable and lower wings. Rear block with lancet windows by *William Davis*, 1879. BISHOP'S COURT opposite (E side) is sheltered housing by *Associated Architects*, 1979.

On Bristol Road South at the junction of Church Road the industrial-looking GROSVENOR CENTRE (shopping) by *Halpern & Partners*, 1966–70. Opposite, quirky Free Style shops by *Bernard Perrins*, 1908. At the start of Bell Lane, two cottages: No. 5, probably C18; No. 7, perhaps early C19. At the S end the baths (*see* above) and Northfield's one stunning building, the BLACK HORSE pub of 1929 by *Francis Goldsbrough* of *Batemans*. His best pub, and perhaps the finest example of Brewer's Tudor in England. Very high-quality detailing, woodcarving by *Jean Hahn*, stone-carving by *Sidney Smith* in. The street front rises from the S end: the manager's house, on a Cotswold stone base, then the fully timbered hall and staircase wing, then the main block, with continuous casements under a massive roof, and finally a wing with a large gable jettied over a full-height canted bay. The timbering, now black, was originally stained a gentler grey. The ground floor has been opened out, but retains a fireplace in a kind of inglenook at the S with a rearing black horse in a circular border. This now leads to the assembly room, with a moulded beamed ceiling. The former 'Mixed Smoke' has a stone fireplace; the former 'Gents' Smoke' has roof trusses with vertical struts, ceiled above. First floor almost intact, with a barrel-vaulted lobby leading to the club room, which has roof trusses with free-standing posts in front of the walls, and the finest stone fireplace, left unfinished at Smithin's death, with an inscription to his memory. The committee room is Georgian style, with a domed ceiling. The garden-front roof sweeps down to a loggia, interrupted only by a line of casements, with the assembly room wing in Cotswold stone. Decorative timber gable to the l. Bowling green with a Cotswold stone PAVILION with hipped roof, and lines of stone pergola columns.

QUINTON

Properly 'The Quinton'; mostly in Shropshire until 1844, then Worcestershire. The old village was absorbed into Birmingham in 1909, with Ridgacre to the E. The W portion is now in Dudley, everything N of Hagley Road in Sandwell. Residential development filled the area between the 1930s and 1970s. The municipal estates are not of much interest.

CHRIST CHURCH, Hagley Road West. 1839–40 by *Rickman & Hussey*. Wide nave and apsidal sanctuary without structural division. Golden sandstone with redder trim. Lancet windows, regular two-step buttresses. Pretty W bellcote and spirelet. W extension, roughcast, by *Bromilow, While & Smeeton*, 1952. N vestry by *Abel Round*, 1906. Rendered inside, with a queenpost roof. Apse windows with nook-shafts. The side ones are flanked by blank lancets. W gallery lit by circular N and S windows. Chancel raised in 1890 by *F.B. Osborn*. – PEWS, 1890, by *Osborn*. – PULPIT by *Jones & Willis*, 1902. – REREDOS (now W end), by *James A. Swan*, 1928, with linenfold panelling and statues in niches. – STAINED GLASS. E lancets by *Gibbs*, probably *C.A. Gibbs*, 1862, brightly coloured. Four, S, by *Alexander Gibbs*, by 1871. N side from E, *Rupert Moore* of *Powells*, 1967; then *Hardmans*, 1909 (two), and 1992, watery. Gallery, three by *Gareth Morgan*, 2000, unusual and good; abstract splashes of colour and small figures.

ST BONIFACE, Quinton Road West. 1957–9 by *George While* of *Bromilow, While & Smeeton*. Early Modernism with a Scandinavian air. Gabled front with a splendid octagonal gabled copper turret, with finial, ball and cross. Above the doorway a relief panel by *Alan Bridgwater*. Undivided interior, beneath a steeply pitched boarded roof pierced by four dormers on each side. As at While's St John, Longbridge (p. 416), there are aisles without arcades, marked by low flat ceilings, here lit from hidden higher-level side windows. The (ritual) W end is raised, a relic of an idea of dual-purpose use with a stage. Altar wall of brick with an ornate silver cross, perhaps late C17 Italian.

The chancel side windows direct light towards the altar. Linked HALL, also *Bromilow, While & Smeeton*, 1968, renovated 1978–9 after a fire. – PULPIT, FONT, ALTAR RAILS and CLERGY SEATS by *While*. – ALTAR by *W.H. Bidlake*, 1909, from St Stephen, New Town Row (dem.). Richly carved, with saints in niches; paintings of angels almost certainly by *Fred Davis*.

SCHOOLS. FOUR DWELLINGS SCHOOL (now Academy). Part of the school by *W.N. Twist*, 1938–40, survives as a community centre on Quinton Road West. Flat-roofed, Dudok-influenced, nicely detailed. Secondary school in Dwellings Lane, big brick ranges with large windows by *J.B. Surman & Partner*, 1949–53 and 1956 etc. Primary school, an almost circular tile-faced building by *dRMM*, 2010. WOODHOUSE SCHOOL (now WOODHOUSE PRIMARY ACADEMY), Woodhouse Road, is by *H.T. Buckland*, 1931: gambrel-roofed classroom range.

HAGLEY ROAD WEST is the boundary with Sandwell. On the corner of Wolverhampton Road a big T-shaped block of 1972–3 by *Leonard J. Multon & Partners* occupies the site of *T. Cecil Howitt*'s Odeon, Warley, of 1934. Much-altered pub opposite by *J.V. Boswell & Co.* and *George A. Boswell*, 1936. ½ m. w is the HOLLY BUSH pub by *Batemans*, 1934, overlaid by fake timbering and clumping bays.* Shops on the N by *Marshall & Tweedy*, 1939. ½ m. w again is the OLD VILLAGE. S of Christ Church (*see* above) is an altered HALL of 1934 by *James A. Swan*, and a surviving part of the CHURCH SCHOOL of 1846 and later. On the corner of College Road, W, a former Municipal Bank by *Swan*, 1937. High Street, with modest late C19 and C20 houses, leads S to The Green. Here is THE COTTAGE (No. 497 Ridgacre Road West). Rubble sandstone, perhaps C17, though the upper brickwork must be C18.

SELLY OAK

0080

Selly, or Selley, was a manor in Northfield parish, a scattered settlement with its centre at the junction of Bristol Road and Harborne Lane. A large oak here, felled in 1909 (the stump preserved in Selly Oak Park), gave its name to Oak Tree Lane, then to the whole area. The Worcester and Birmingham Canal came in 1795, joining the Dudley No. 2 Canal of 1798 N of Bristol Road.†
An industrial village grew from the 1850s to house workers at brass and copper factories along the canal. Selly Park developed from the 1850s almost like part of Edgbaston, which it adjoins. Late C20 road widening destroyed much of the old village. The

---

***Holland W. Hobbiss*'s PUNCHBOWL pub, Ridgacre Road, 1937, was demolished in 2016; his MONARCH, Quinton Road West, was trashed in 2017, and a shell-hood porch by *Bloye* destroyed.
†A length of the latter is visible W of Harborne Lane, at the rear of Selly Oak Park, with a much-repaired bridge.

Birmingham West Suburban Railway opened in 1876. Working-class Bournbrook, E of the railway, is the poor man at the University's gate, developed from the 1890s; mostly now housing students.

PLACES OF WORSHIP

ST MARY, Bristol Road. Approached delightfully up an avenue. By *Edward Holmes*, 1860–1. A solid Dec design in Bromsgrove stone with Bath stone dressings. Slightly thin NW tower with economical belfry windows but a tall broach spire. Spherical-triangle window in the W gable, three spherical triangles in a circle in the S transept window. Three grouped quatrefoils set in a recessed panel in each clerestory bay. Interior distinguished by contrasting stones. Three-bay arcades and wide transept arches with Bath stone columns, alternating Bath stone and Weoley Castle sandstone voussoirs. Plastered walls with Weoley Castle stone bands. Segmental arches over the clerestory windows in the same stone. Bold sedilia, the mouldings of the lancet window over the central seat cut back to the capitals of the flanking arches.

'A treasure-house of Victorian fittings' (Douglas Hickman), despite some reordering in 2007. Finest is the massive sculptural FONT designed for the church by *William Butterfield*, 1861. Octagonal, with cusped-arched arcading. The arcade bases grow out of the deep chamfered base. The arch gables have star finials breaking into the top mouldings. – By *Holmes*, the PULPIT with traceried arches, foliage carving and deep-arched overhang, CHOIR STALLS, PEWS and arcaded REREDOS (bright colouring by *Stephen Dykes Bower*, 1961). Also the ORGAN SCREEN, 1869. – BRASS. George Richards Elkington †1865 and his wife Mary. By *Hardmans*. Kneeling figures under a double canopy, with a floriated cross above. – STAINED GLASS. All *Hardmans*, the finest windows the E (Ascension) and W (Transfiguration), both 1861. S aisle, 1866 and 1872.

ST STEPHEN, Selly Park Road and Serpentine Road, Selly Hill. 1870–1 by *J.H. Chamberlain* (*Martin & Chamberlain*), his only Anglican church in the city. Rock-faced Hamstead sandstone with Bath stone dressings. Geometrical tracery. Apsidal chancel. S porch-tower and spire, a landmark on the top of Selly Hill. Flat buttresses with long nosings, lucarnes with tall hipped gablets. S doorway in solid timber framing. Bold W stair-turret. NE vestry by *Martin & Martin & W.H. Ward*, 1925. *JBKS* added the dumpy conical-roofed W addition, 2015, together with N meeting rooms. Impressive open interior, a Low Church preaching space. Faced in 'best pressed brick' with a pitch-pine dado, the same materials as Martin & Chamberlain's School of Art. Collar-beam roof with cusped trusses. The chancel arch is a breath of Ruskinian Venice, with free-standing shafts on tapering corbels, angels holding scrolls for capitals, and alternating brick and stone voussoirs. A plainer arch separates the apse, an effective combination. Chancel stripped out in the late C20, pews in 2015. *Chamberlain*'s FONT, carved by *Samuel*

Birmingham, Selly Oak, St Mary
Brass to George Richards Elkington †1865

Barfield, has delicately undercut flowers. – STAINED GLASS. Apse by *Hardmans*, 1893.

ST WULSTAN (now ENCOUNTER CHURCH), Exeter Road. 1906–7 by *J.E.K. & J.P. Cutts*. Brick, old-fashioned, but details strong and simple. Lancets and plate tracery. Standard Cutts arcades with circular piers and moulded brick arches. Scissor-truss roof. Now divided horizontally.

ST EDWARD (R.C.), Raddlebarn Road. Nave and aisles of 1901–2 by *H.T. Sandy*; sanctuary of 1926 and (ritual) W front with flanking porches of 1937–8 by *E. Bower Norris*. Reddish-brown brick Dec, tall proportions, old-fashioned stepped lancets in the aisles. Norris's additions are in the same style. Their sheer massing, and the zigzag moulding round the apse, give the late date away. Grey stone arcades with octagonal piers, and shafts springing from corbels. The transverse aisle arches, which spring from the nave piers, are slightly pointed, and contain a stone circle: strength without excess weight. – PEWS probably of 1902; REREDOSES and hanging ROOD of 1926.

SELLY OAK METHODIST CHURCH, Langleys Road. 1965–6 by *Hulme & Upright*. Blue brick, low-pitched roofs.

SELLY PARK BAPTIST CHURCH, Pershore Road. By *Martin & Chamberlain*, 1876–7. Big gabled hall with paired lancets and stone octofoils above. Plate-tracery rose above the entrance. Extension of 1985.

WEOLEY HILL PRESBYTERIAN CHURCH (now United Reformed), Bryony Road. 1933 by *J.R. Armstrong*. Very Scandinavian, with a big stepped gable and cross-gabled porches. Interior spanned by pointed arches on corbels. Small sanctuary with a pointed arch. Original FURNISHINGS.

FRIENDS' MEETING HOUSE, Bristol Road. 1926–7 by *J.R. Armstrong*. Low, rendered, with a colonial feel. Buttresses with tile nosings.

CONGREGATIONAL MISSION HALL (now JALALABAD MOSQUE), Dartmouth Road. 1911–12 by *A.J. Dunn*. Small but monumental, with a big lunette.

HARBORNE HEALING CENTRE (Spiritualist), Weoley Park Road. Formerly Our Lady and St Rose of Lima (*see also* Weoley, p. 435). By *G.B. Cox*, 1933. Cottagey, with waney-edged boarding in the gable. Sloping buttresses along the sides.

CHRISTIAN LIFE CENTRE, Bristol Road. 1999 by *Brophy Riaz*. Straining domesticity to the limit.

COLLEGE OF THE ASCENSION (now AL-MAHDI INSTITUTE), Weoley Park Road. 1928–9 by *Christopher Wright*. Domestic lodge house and ranges in maroon brick, with big hipped roofs; chapel with tower-nave supported by big stepped buttresses.

CONVENT, Selly Park Road. The English Congregation of the Sisters of Charity of St Paul moved here in 1864, under their foundress Mother Geneviève Dupuis. They took over SELLY HALL, of *c.* 1780 (here by 1786). The architect was 'Mr *Wyatt*'; local connections and the austere handling suggest *Samuel Wyatt*. Three wide bays, the central one slightly advanced and with a pediment. C19 entrance. The side ground-floor and central first-floor windows are triplets with cornices on consoles, in relieving arches. Little sham balustrades under the upper windows. The garden front has an unusual composition, 1–2–1 bays with a central pediment and no doorway. Oval staircase, its rail with serpentine branches and leaves among plain uprights. The landing is Roman grandeur in miniature, with almost unmoulded arches to plain niches and to passages and doorways. Delicately moulded frieze. Another, with garlands, round the dome. Good fireplaces in the front ground-floor rooms. At the rear, the former dining room has a beautiful niche, its half-dome partly fluted with long stylized pointed leaves above. Severe fireplace with corner garlands. Good cornices here and in the drawing room, r.

The CONVENTUAL BUILDINGS started in 1877 with the gabled wings flanking the Hall, and probably the low N wing towards the entrance. Building control records name the chaplain, *Fr William Tandy*, though the architect *A. E. Dempster* was probably involved. The NOVITIATE BLOCK of 1880 to the N, running E–W and separating the Hall from the entrance courtyard, is certainly *Dempster*. Two tall storeys and a high roof with dormers, plate tracery to the ground-floor windows and an internal cloister walk on the S. It originally ended at the large gable. The Puginian LODGE with its arched entrance must also be *Dempster*'s. The Novitiate block was extended by *Cossins, Peacock & Bewlay*, 1898–1900. The plainer chimneys give the date away. W COURTYARD WING, with a massive tower, by *G.B. Cox*, 1932. CHAPLAIN'S HOUSE also by *Cox*, 1929. The CHAPEL is linked to the convent at the SE. By *H.T. Sandy*, 1914. Cruciform, with an apse. Conventional Gothic outside, with a piquant N turret and frilly Dec tracery. Impressive interior with stone arcades across the transepts, extended as blank arcading down the nave. The arches die into octagonal piers. Gothic side altars of 1924. Stained glass by *Hardmans*, mostly 1922–9.

LODGE HILL CEMETERY, Weoley Park Road. Laid out in 1893–5. Buildings by *F.B. Andrews*, in local sandstone. Free Perp chapels (derelict 2020) with ogee-roofed cupolas. Tudor lodge with foliage panels in the gables (later C20 extension). Domed gatepiers. Further W, crematorium, by *Holland W. Hobbiss*, 1936–7. Blocky Romanesque chapel with big clasping buttresses and tall windows. Impressive T-shaped open portico, with semicircular raised centre and baseless columns with capitals somewhere between crockets and Ionic volutes. Tympanum, a Tree of Life with Byzantine affronted birds, by *Bloye*. Rendered interior with unmoulded round arches and beamed ceiling. Crematorium proper at the rear, with massive tapering chimney.

PUBLIC BUILDINGS

SELLY OAK HOSPITAL (former), Raddlebarn Road. Originally the Kings Norton Union workhouse, basic Gothic of 1869–72 by *Edward Holmes*. Office range at the front with segment-headed windows and projecting gables with long buttresses. Main block behind. Central tower with four cut-down corner turrets. Octagonal WELL-HOUSE with lantern. Gatehouse by *C. Whitwell & Son*, dated 1902, and master's house of 1911. Some way E the former administration block of the Infirmary, by *Daniel Arkell*, 1895–7; further back, a bulky buttressed water tower. *Whitwell & Son*'s Nurses' Home survives, SE, at the junction of Willow Road, dated 1907, with Free Jacobean touches. The rest demolished 2015.

SELLY OAK LIBRARY, Bristol Road. 1905 by *J.P. Osborne*. Free Tudor. Brick and terracotta, with slightly shaped end gables. (Closed 2016.)

SWIMMING BATHS, Tiverton Road. 1905 by *E. Harding Payne*. Neo-Wren front with a hipped roof, aedicule with broken segmental pediment, and a segmental pediment on top. Converted to a gym 2019.

POLICE STATION (now Probation Service), Bristol Road. 1878–9 by *Henry Rowe*. Heavily classical. Recessed bays at the ends. The mansard is C20.

TECHNICAL INSTITUTE (former), Bristol Road, by Oak Tree Lane. 1898–9 by *Bertram V. Hirst*. Plain Jacobean. Now flats.

SELLY OAK TRUST SCHOOL, Oak Tree Lane. A former boys' secondary school of 1962–3 by *A.G. Sheppard Fidler* (schools architects *E. Mason* and *S.G.V. Milligan*, architects in charge *H.O. Williams* and *G.E. James*). Concrete-framed main block with load-bearing brick end walls, still with its attractive original blue cladding panels.

SELLY PARK GIRLS' SCHOOL, Pershore Road. 1909–11 by *W.H. Ashford*. Long ranges, one with segmental pediments, another at right angles with big pedimental gables. A severe design, even the squared-up cupolas.

UNIVERSITY OF BIRMINGHAM SCHOOL, Weoley Park Road. By *Associated Architects*, 2014–15. Buff brick. Arranged round a central forum with fully glazed ends.

RADDLEBARN PRIMARY SCHOOL, Gristhorpe Road and Umberslade Road. 1908–9 by *J.P. Osborne*. A big, well-detailed group with contrasting elevations, plain and stone-arched.

TIVERTON JUNIOR AND INFANTS' SCHOOL (now Academy), Tiverton Road. 1905–6 by *Edward Holmes*. Tall, old-fashioned brick and terracotta, with lots of gables. Entrance with bay window and coat of arms.

PERAMBULATIONS

1. Bournbrook

Commencing at the NE end, at the start of the by-pass, opposite the University S gate (*see* Edgbaston, p.365). On BRISTOL ROAD, No.480 on the corner of Alton Road is a former house and surgery of 1896 by *Arthur Edwards*, for (Sir) Guy Dain.*

---

*Later chairman of the British Medical Association and doughty opponent of Aneurin Bevan over the creation of the NHS.

1. Birmingham, Victoria Square, Council House by Yeoville Thomason, 1874–85, statue of Queen Victoria by Thomas Brock, 1901 (pp. 127, 156)
2. Wolverhampton, George Street, mainly later C18, with St John, by William Baker, 1756–60 (pp. 693, 677)

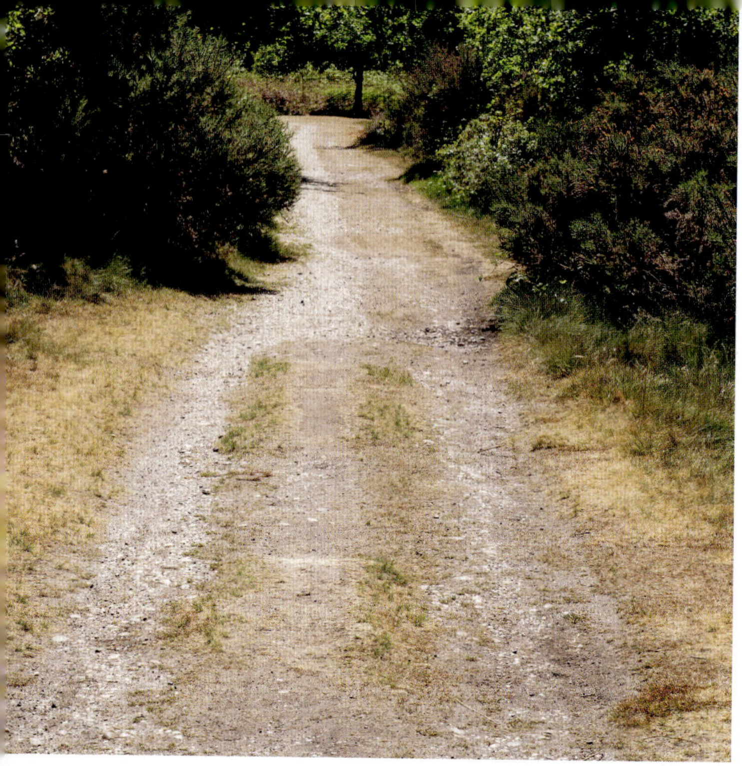

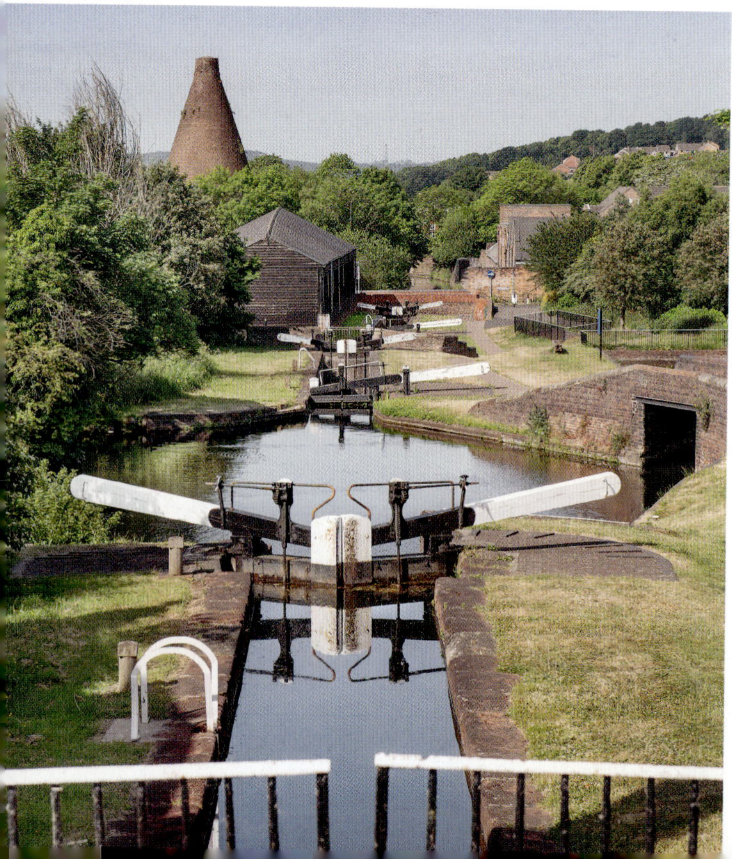

3. Sutton Coldfield, Sutton Park, Roman road (p. 449)
4. Dudley, Wordsley, Red House Glass Cone, *c.* 1790, and Stourbridge canal (pp. 560, 561)
5. Birmingham, Hurst Street and Inge Street, back-to-backs, 1809–31 (p. 208)
6. Wolverhampton, Castlecroft Gardens, by Kenneth Hutchinson Smith, 1927 onwards (p. 707)

3	5
4	6

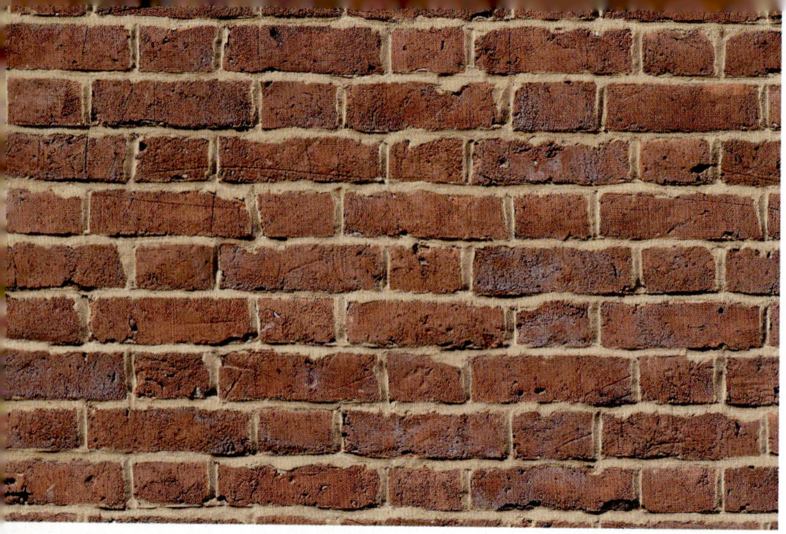

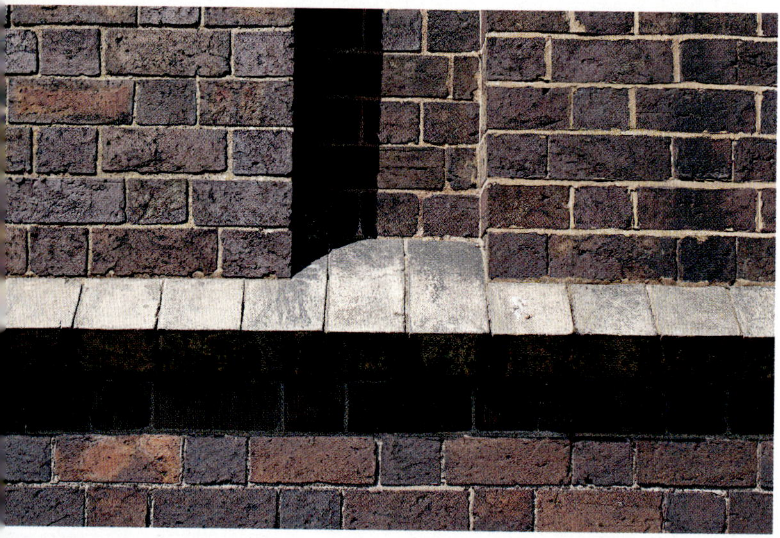

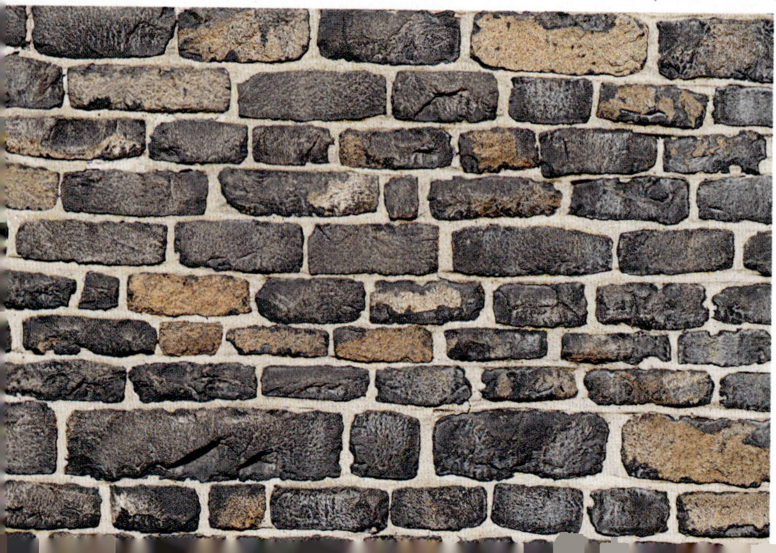

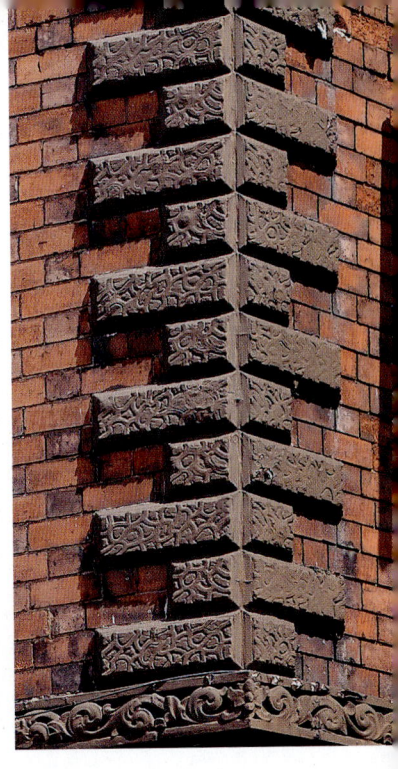

7. Wolverhampton, Giffard House, 1728–33, red brick (p. 679)
8. Dudley, Brockmoor, St John, by Thomas Smith, 1844–5, Staffordshire blue brick and firebrick (p. 500)
9. Walsall, Willenhall, St Anne, by W.D. Griffin, 1858–61, Pouk Hill dolerite (p. 664)
10. Dudley, Sedgley, Grand Junction Hotel, c. 1849, Gornal stone (p. 544)
11. Sandwell, Oldbury, Junction Inn, 1851–4, red brick and cast dolerite (quoins and string course) (p. 565)
12. Birmingham, Small Heath, St Gregory the Great, by J.L. Ball, 1911–12, brick and tile (p. 285)

7	10	11
8	12	
9		

13. Wolverhampton, St Peter, cross, C9 or C10 (p. 677)
14. Dudley, Kingswinford, St Mary, tympanum, late C12 (p. 523)
15. Dudley, Halesowen, St John the Baptist, nave, s arcade, *c.* 1175–99 (p. 512)
16. Birmingham, Northfield, St Laurence, chancel interior, C13 (p. 419)

13	15
14	16

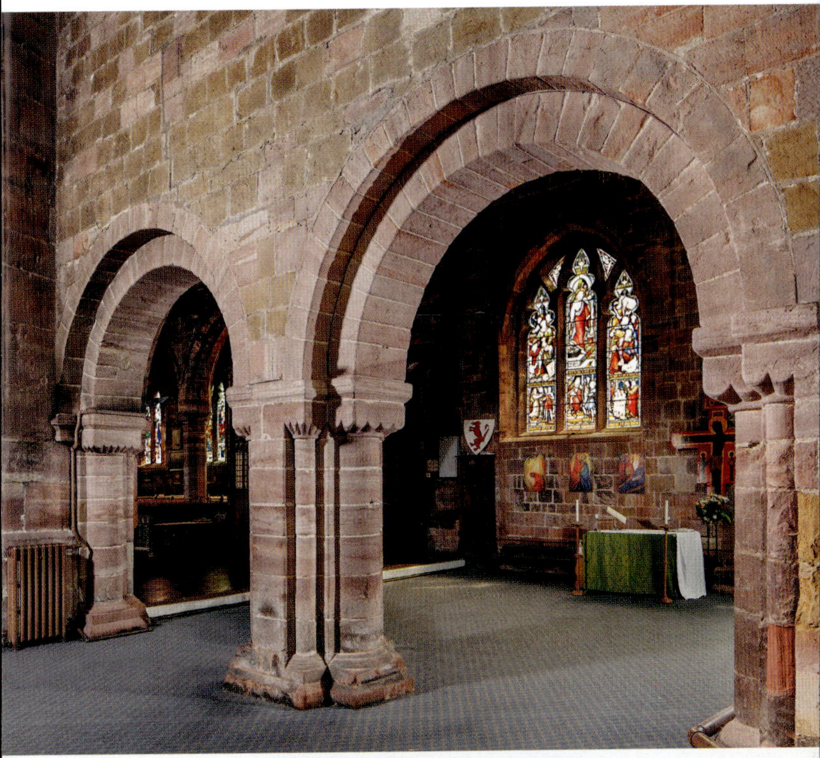

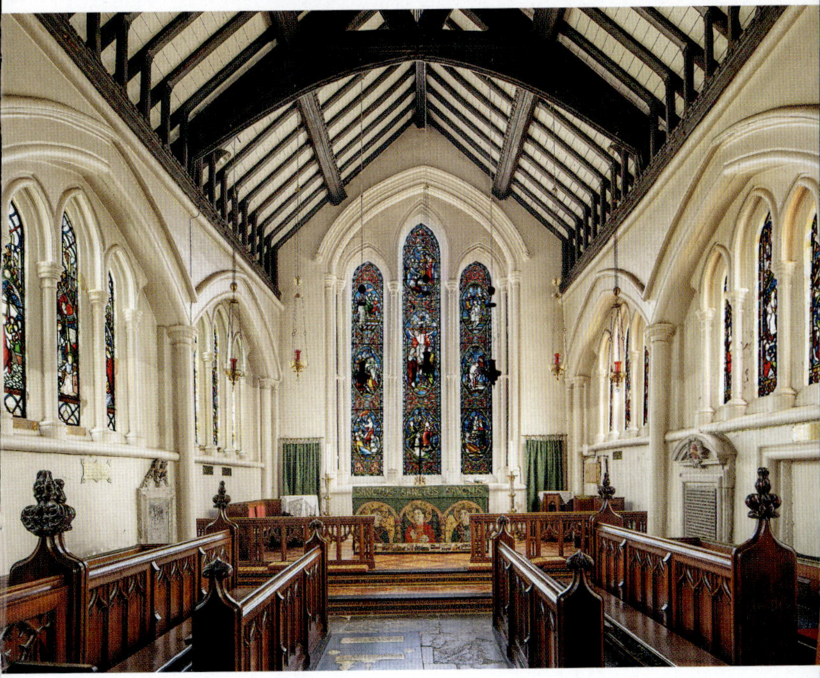

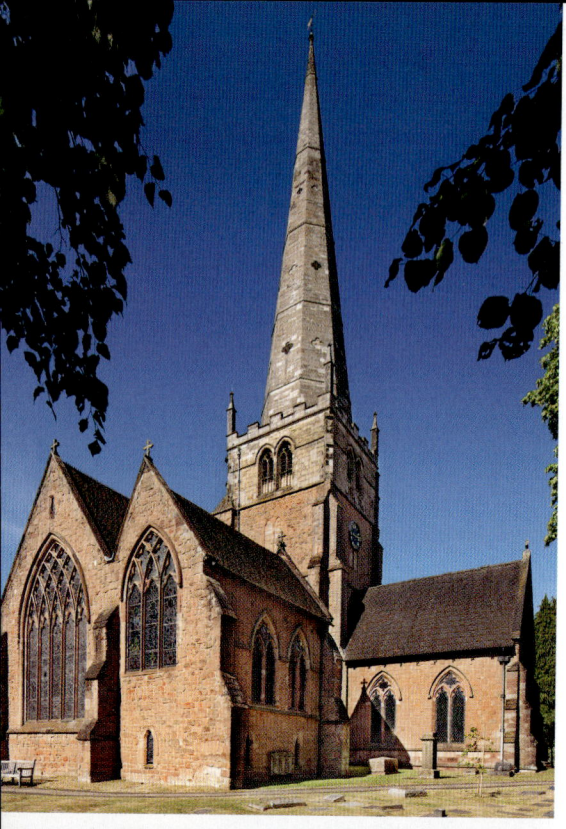

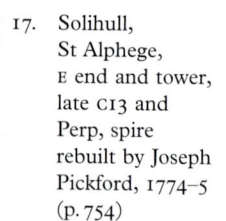

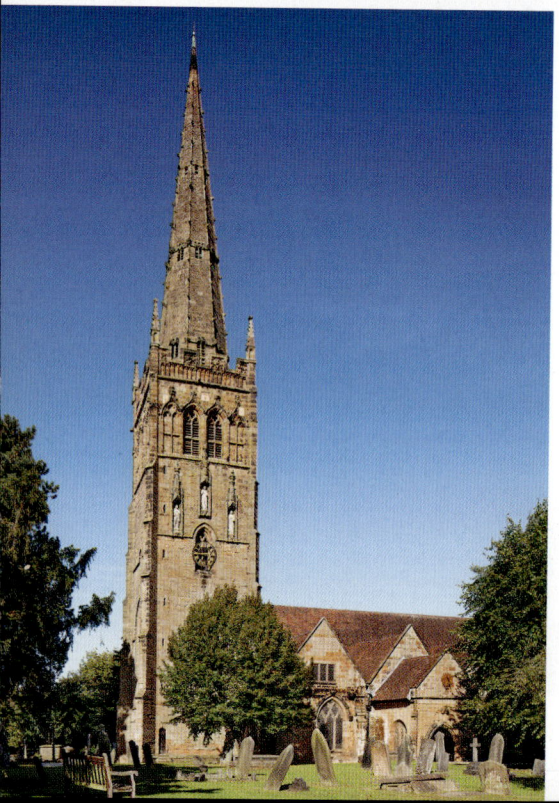

17. Solihull,
St Alphege,
E end and tower,
late C13 and
Perp, spire
rebuilt by Joseph
Pickford, 1774–5
(p. 754)
18. Birmingham,
Kings Norton,
St Nicolas,
tower and spire,
C15 (p. 406)
19. Wolverhampton,
St Peter, nave
and S transept,
mid-C15, and
tower, after 1475
(p. 672)
20. Solihull,
Bickenhill,
St Peter, N aisle,
screen, C15 or
early C16, detail
(p. 767)
21. Wolverhampton,
St Peter, pulpit,
mid-C15 (p. 675)

17	19	
18	20	21

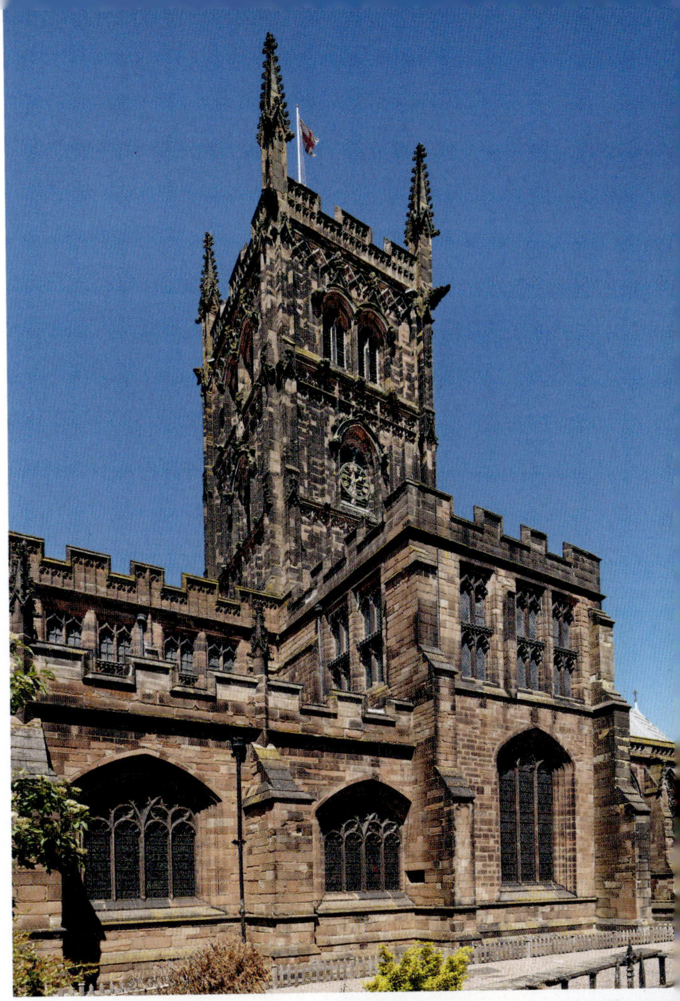
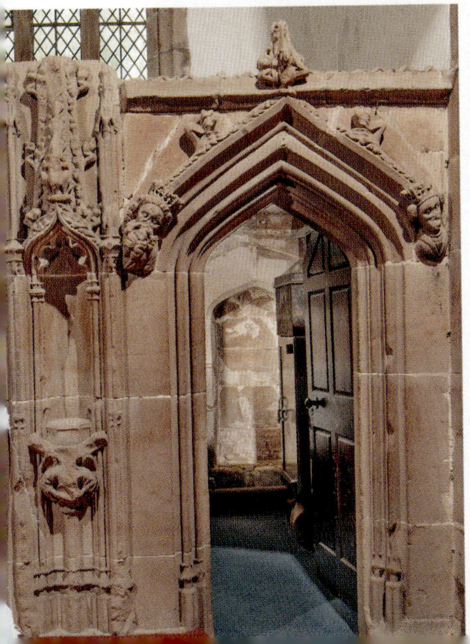
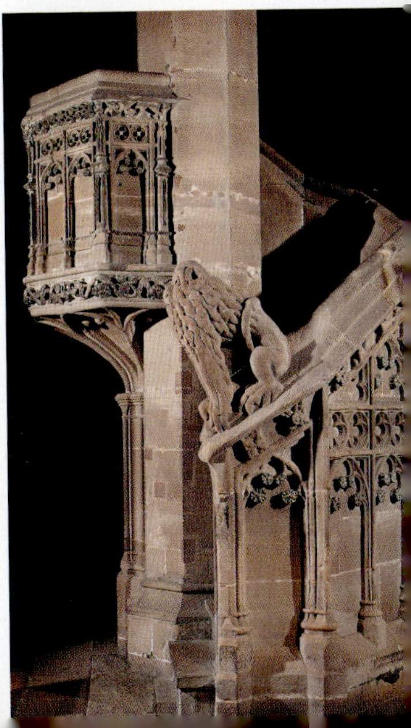

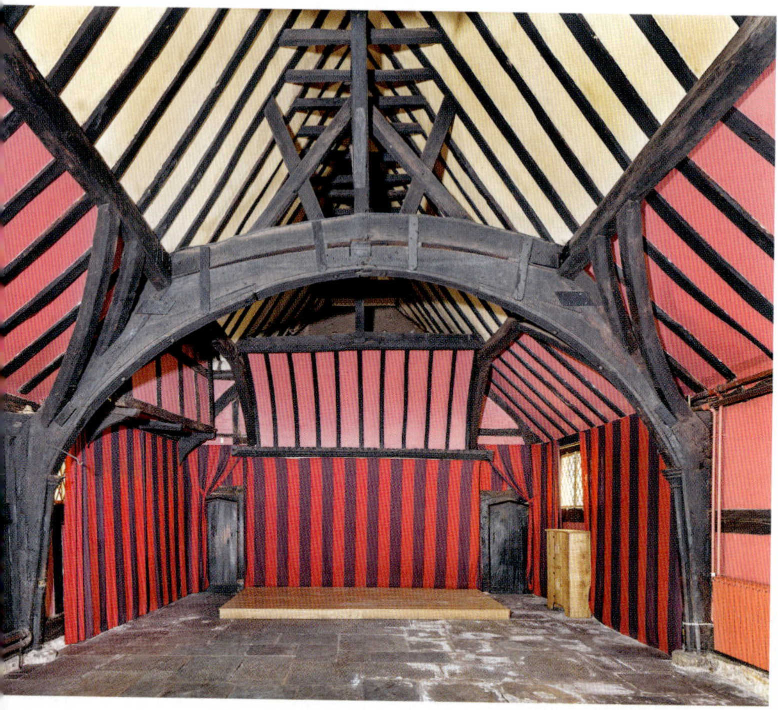

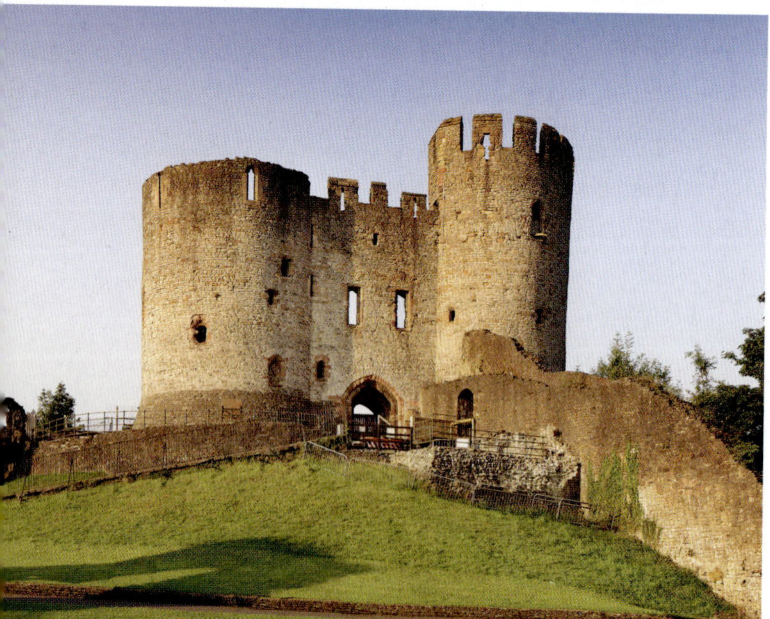

22. Sandwell, West Bromwich, Manor House, hall, 1270–88 (p. 609)
23. Dudley Castle, keep, early C14, from the N (p. 477)
24. Sutton Coldfield, Old Stone House (Vesey cottage), between 1527 and c. 1543 (p. 449)
25. Sutton Coldfield, Holy Trinity, chancel woodwork from Worcester Cathedral, 1556–7, detail (p. 439)

22	24
23	25

26. Dudley Castle, E range, c. 1537–53, with chapel, right, early C14, from the W (p. 478)
27. Birmingham, Yardley, Blakesley Hall, between 1585 and 1610 (p. 299)

28. Sandwell, West Bromwich, Oak House, between 1604 and 1629, NE front (p. 610)

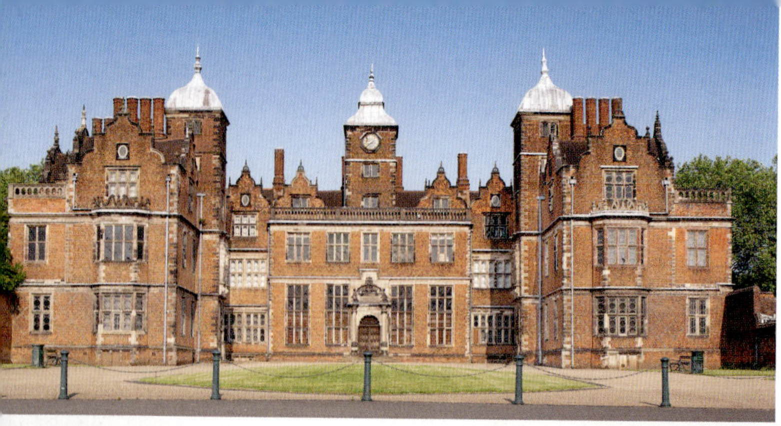

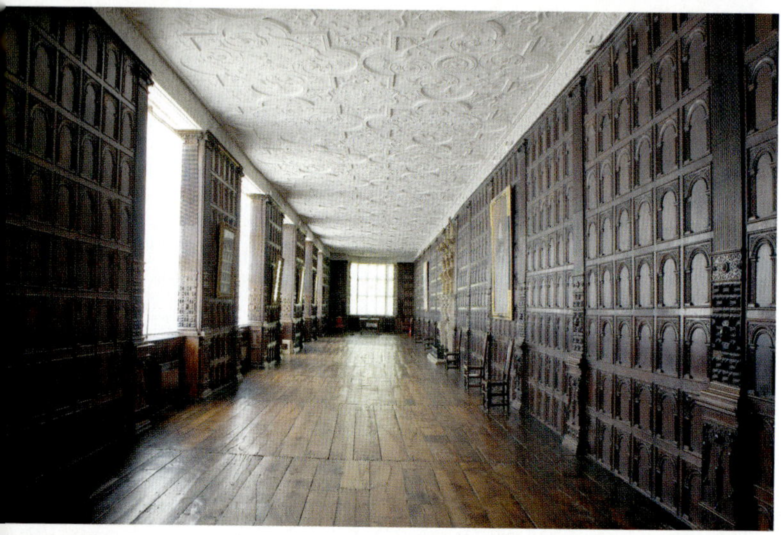

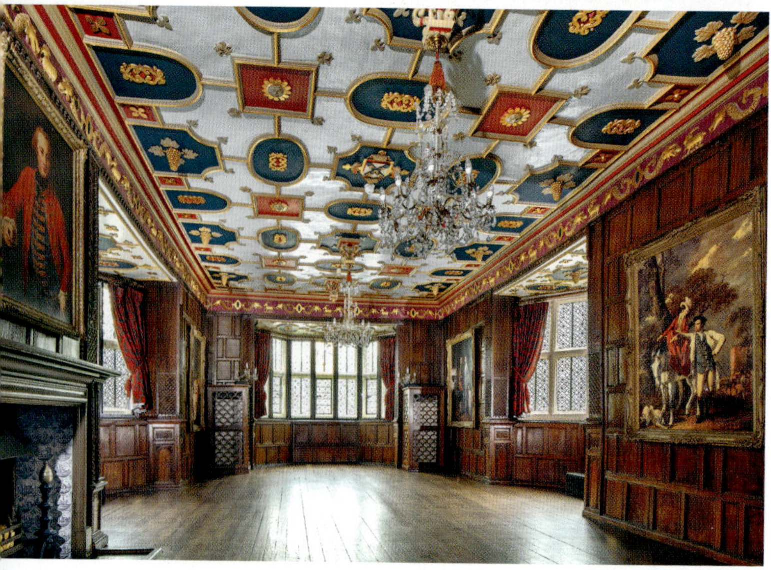

29. Birmingham, Aston Hall, by John Thorpe, 1618–35, E front (p. 221)
30. Birmingham, Aston Hall, Gallery (p. 226)
31. Sutton Coldfield, New Hall, Great Chamber, c. 1630–40 (p. 465)
32. Solihull, Castle Bromwich Hall, early C17, top storey by William Winde, 1697–8, porch, mid- to late C17 (p. 771)

33. Birmingham, St Philip's Cathedral, by Thomas Archer, 1709–25, w front (p. 111)
34. Dudley, Stourbridge, St Thomas, probably by William Westley, 1728–36, interior (p. 547)
35. Solihull, Castle Bromwich, St Mary and St Margaret, 1726–31, communion rail by Benjamin Taylor, 1744–5 (p. 769)

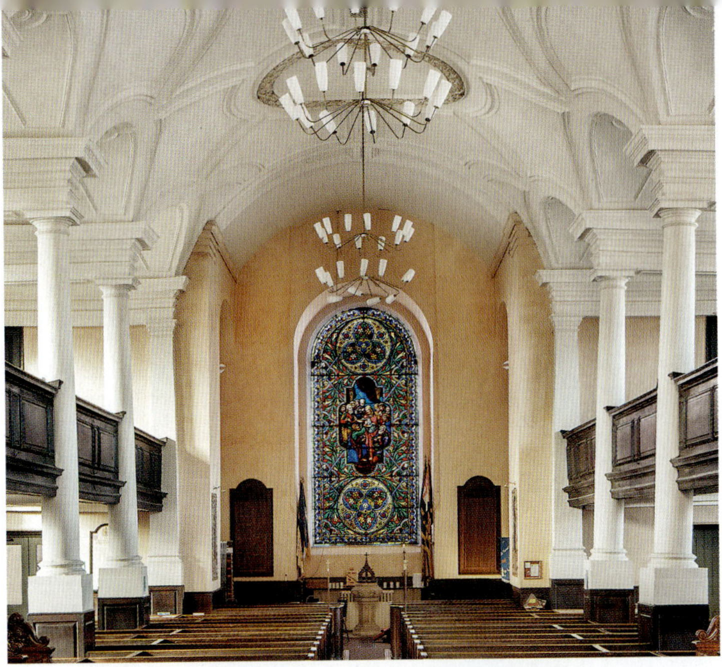

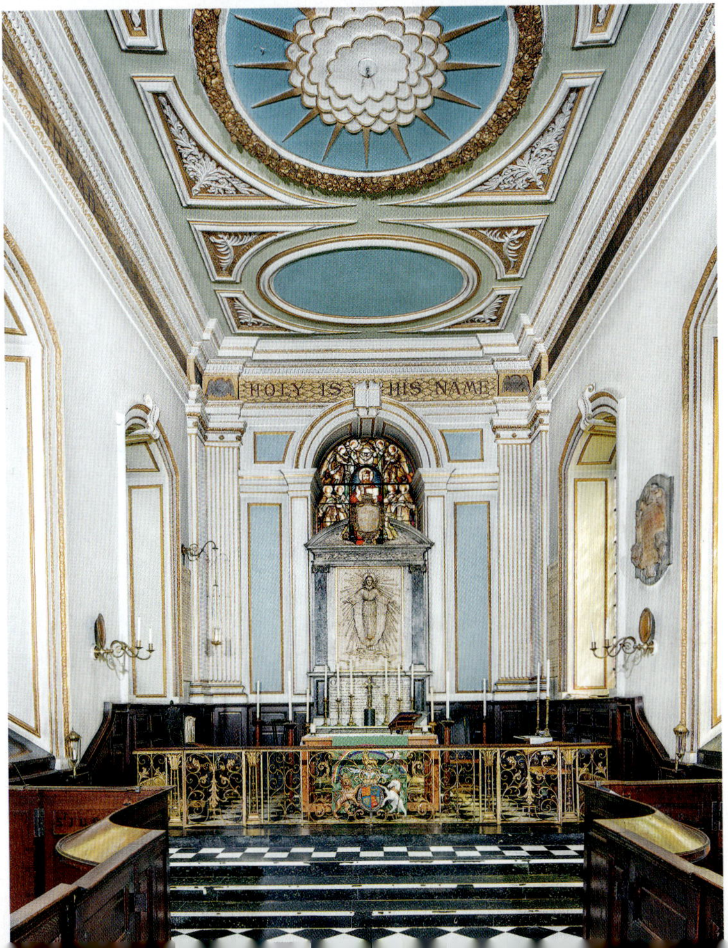
HOLY IS HIS NAME

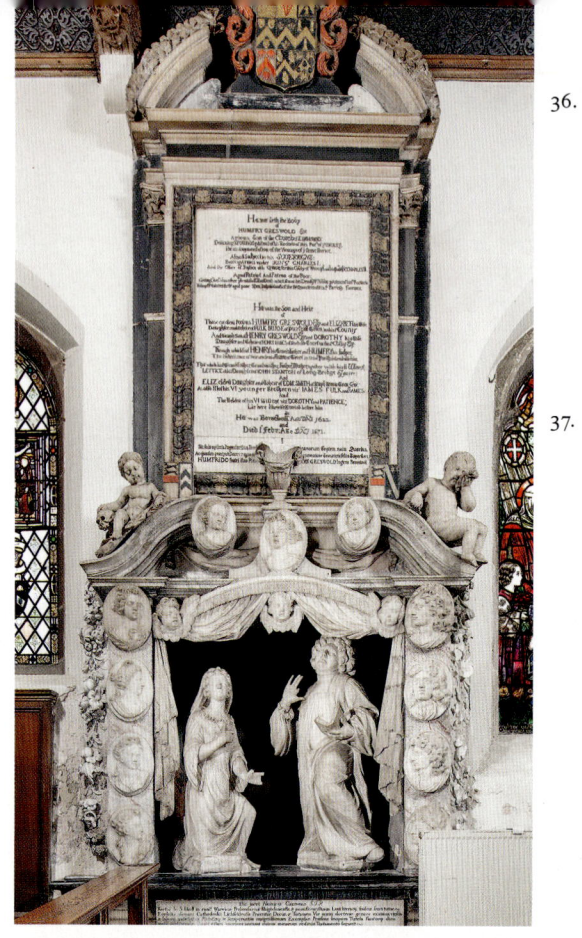

36. Birmingham, Yardley, St Edburgha, monument to the Rev. Dr Henry Greswold †1700, attributed to Richard Crutcher (p. 296)

37. Birmingham, St Paul, E window, surround by Samuel Wyatt, stained glass by Benjamin West with Francis Eginton, 1791 (p. 175)

38. Birmingham, statue of Lord Nelson by Sir Richard Westmacott, Bull Ring, 1807–9 (p. 138)
39. Birmingham, Handsworth, St Mary, Watt Chapel, by Richard Bridgens and others, 1825–6, monument to James Watt by Sir Francis Chantrey, 1825 (p. 245)

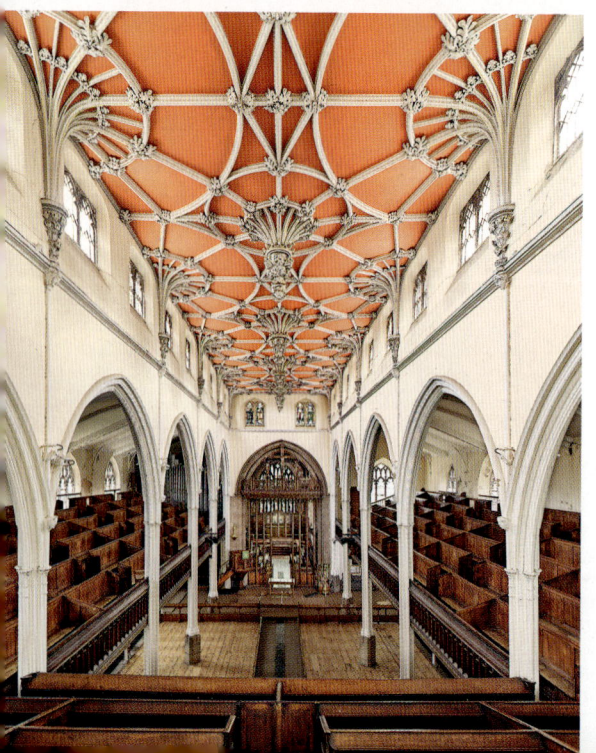

40. Dudley, St Thomas, by William Brooks, 1815–19, interior (p. 472)
41. Walsall, St Matthew, by Francis Goodwin, 1820–1, interior (p. 620)
42. Wolverhampton, Bilston, St Leonard, by Francis Goodwin, 1825–6 (p. 697)
43. Walsall, St Mary the Mount (R.C.), by Joseph Ireland, 1825–7, interior, decoration of 1880 and later (p. 625)

| 40 | 42 |
| 41 | 43 |

SINE LABE ORIGINALI CONCEPTA

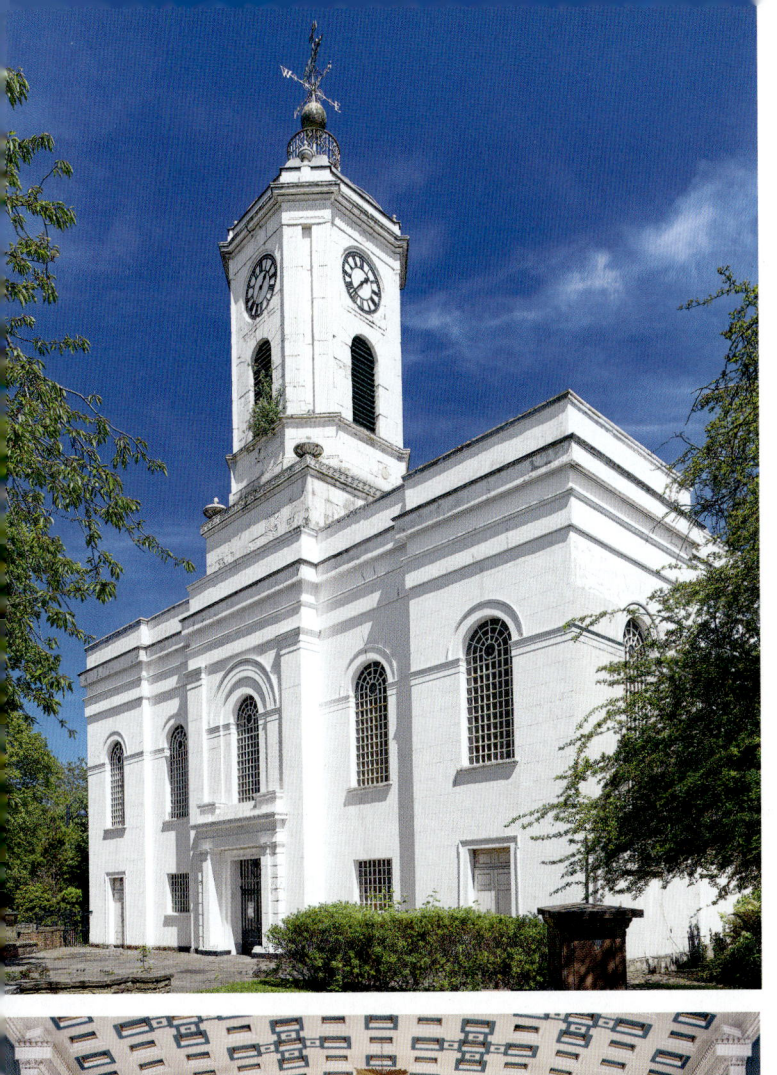

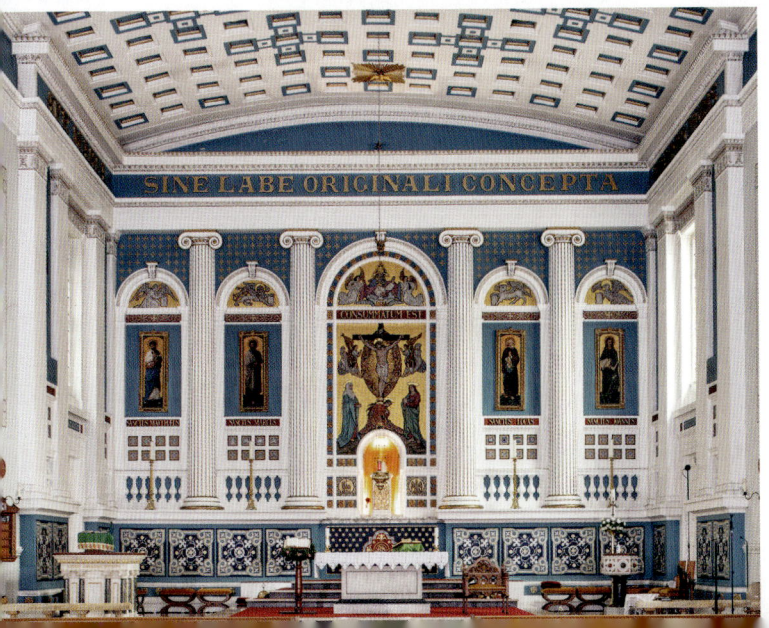

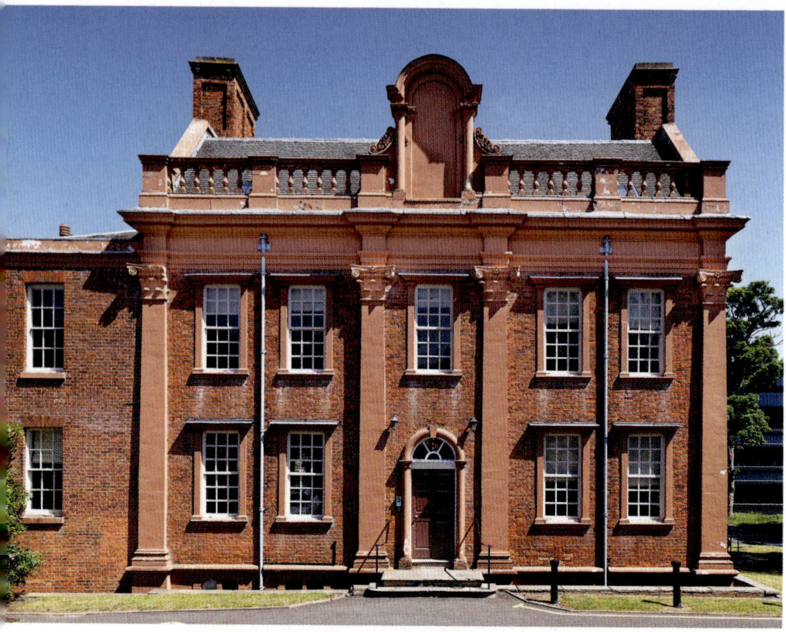

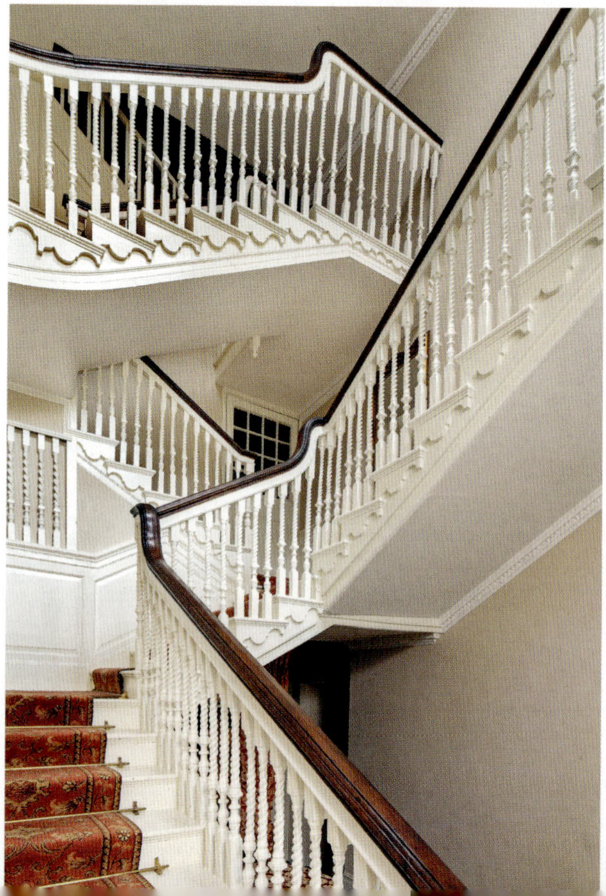

44. Sutton Coldfield, Moat House, by Sir William Wilson, after 1697 (p. 452)
45. Wolverhampton, Giffard House, staircase, by Thomas Evans and Nicholas Bache, 1732 (p. 679)
46. Wolverhampton, King Street, N side, after 1751 (p. 689)
47. Sandwell, West Bromwich, Sandwell Park Farm, probably by Sanderson Miller, 1750s (p. 611)

48. Birmingham, Edgbaston, Monument Road, Perrott's Folly, 1758 (p. 387)
49. Solihull, Warwick Road, barn, by John Soane, 1798 (p. 762)
50. Sutton Coldfield, New Hall Mill, mostly 1780s (p. 466)
51. Birmingham, Handsworth, Soho House, dining room, by James Wyatt, 1796–7 (p. 254)

	49
48	50
	51

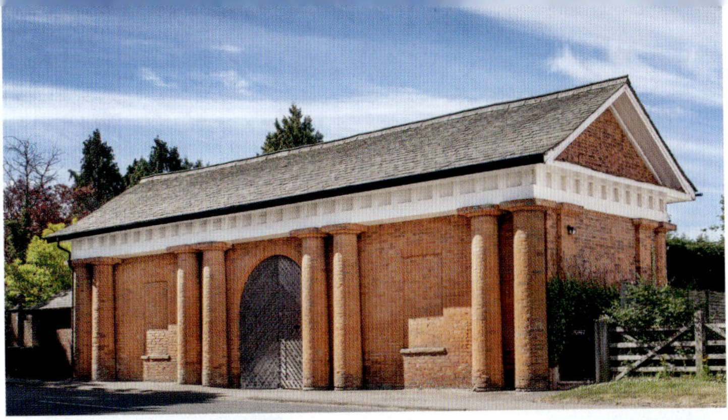

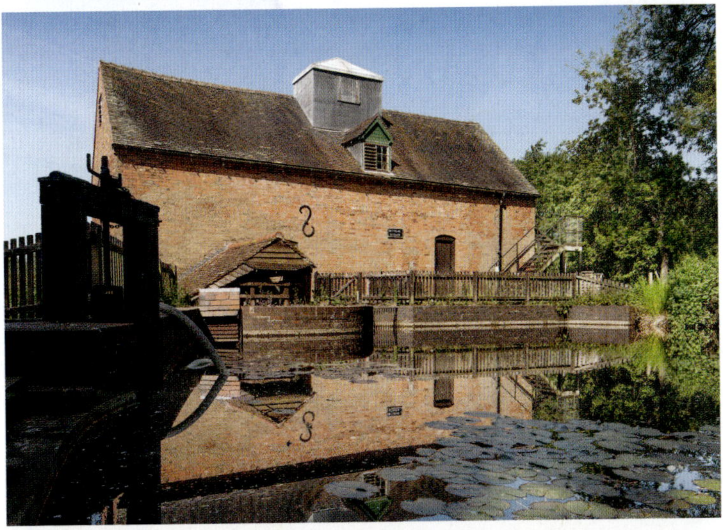

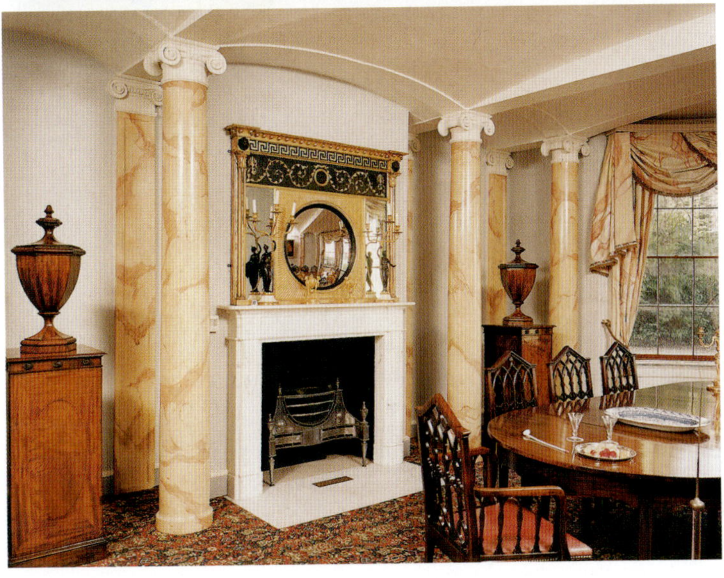

THE BONDED
STOURBRIDGE NAVIGATION TRUST
WAREHOUSE
FUNCTION ROOMS FOR HIRE

52. Dudley, Amblecote, Bonded Warehouse, by Thomas Dadford Jun., 1779, and Mr Kyte, 1799–1800, reconstructed by Robert Robinson, 1849 (p. 494)
53. Sandwell, Smethwick, Engine Arm Aqueduct, by Thomas Telford, 1827–9 (p. 587)
54. Birmingham, Kings Norton, Worcester and Birmingham Canal, guillotine lock, by William Whitmore, 1813 (p. 410)

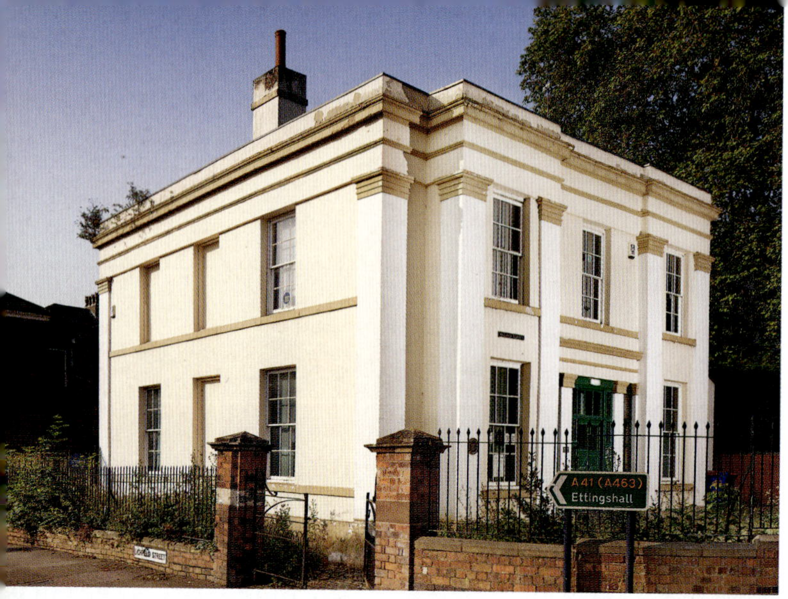
A41 (A463)
Ettingshall

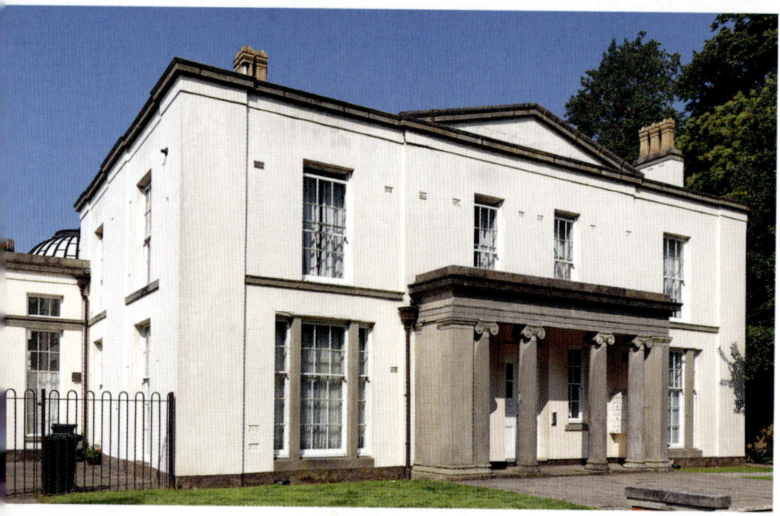

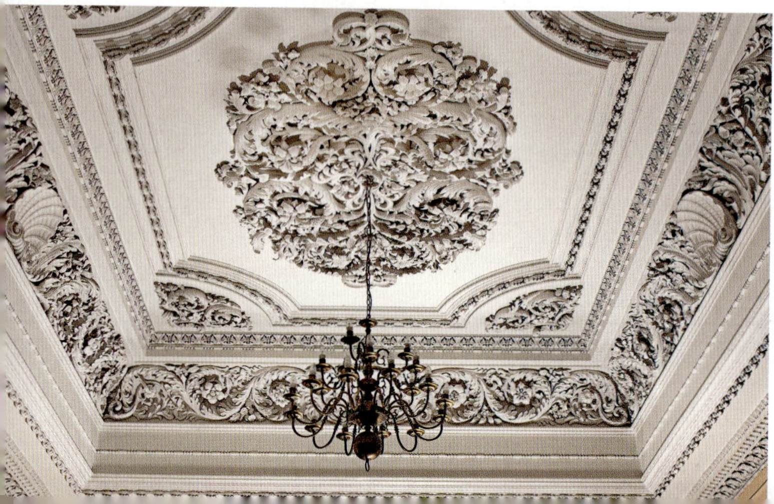

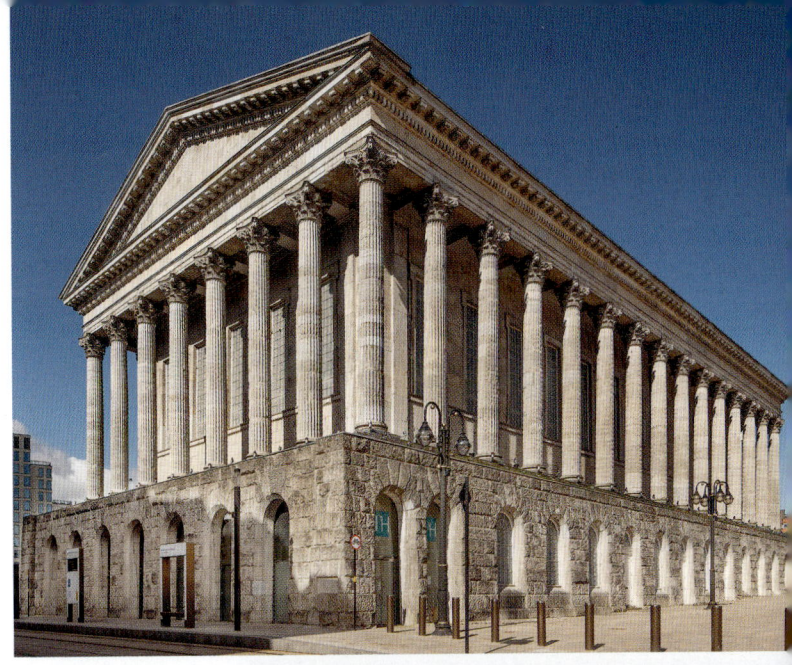

55. Wolverhampton, Bilston, Walsall Street, former parsonage, by Richard Tutin, 1822 (p. 699)
56. Wolverhampton, Oxley and Fordhouses, Oxley House, probably by James Morgan, *c.* 1830 (p. 732)
57. Solihull, Castle Bromwich Hall, drawing room ceiling, by R.C. Hussey, plasterwork by James Holmes, 1839 (p. 772)
58. Birmingham Town Hall, Victoria Square, by Hansom & Welch, begun 1832 (p. 125)
59. Walsall, St Matthew's Hall, probably by John Fallows, 1830–1 (p. 628)

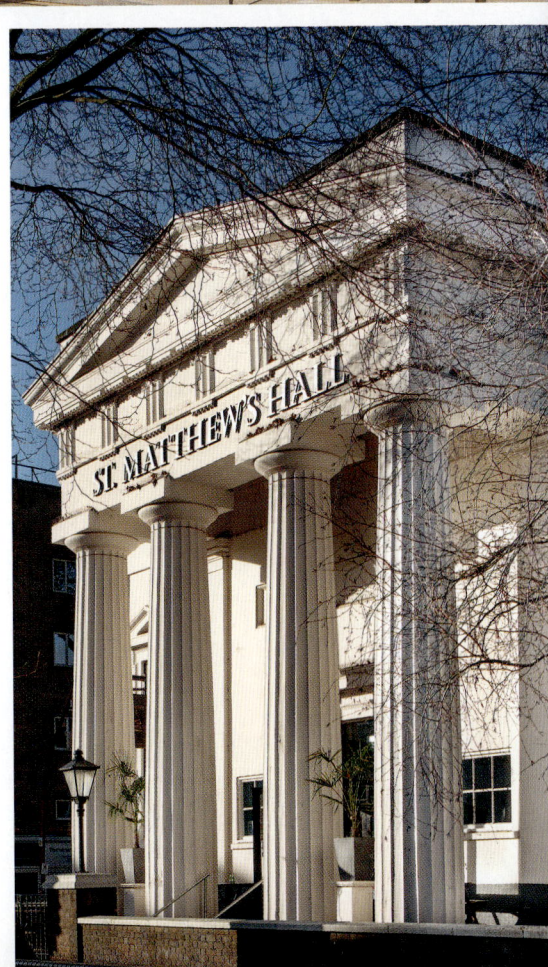

60. Sutton Coldfield, Oscott College, chapel by Joseph Potter and A.W.N. Pugin, interior, 1836–7, stained glass in apse by William Warrington, 1838 (p. 446)
61. Birmingham, Singers Hill Synagogue, by Yeoville Thomason, 1855–6, interior (p. 204)

	62
63	64

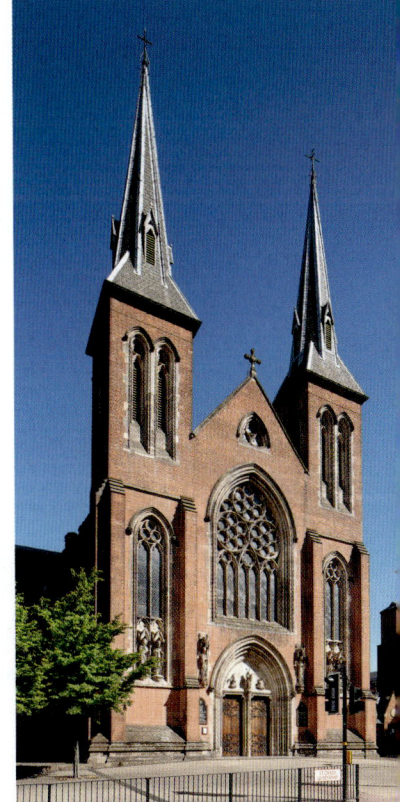

62. Birmingham, St Chad's Cathedral (R.C.), by A.W.N. Pugin, 1839–41, w front (p. 117)
63. Birmingham, Edgbaston, St Augustine, by J.A. Chatwin, 1867–77, w extension 1898 and 1968 (p. 360)
64. Birmingham, Sparkbrook, St Agatha, by W.H. Bidlake, 1899–1901 (p. 335)

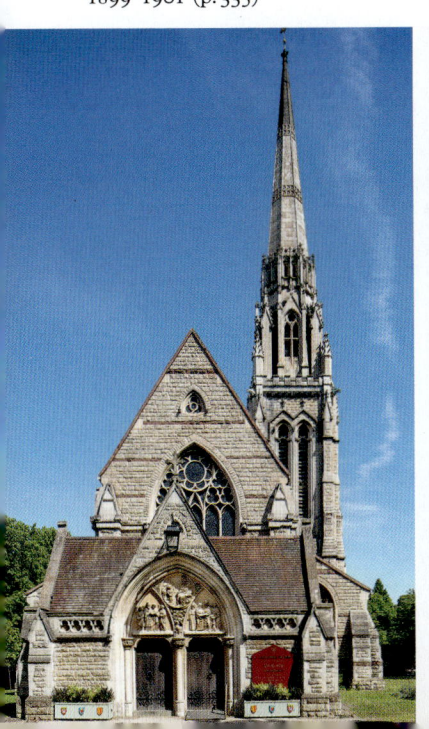

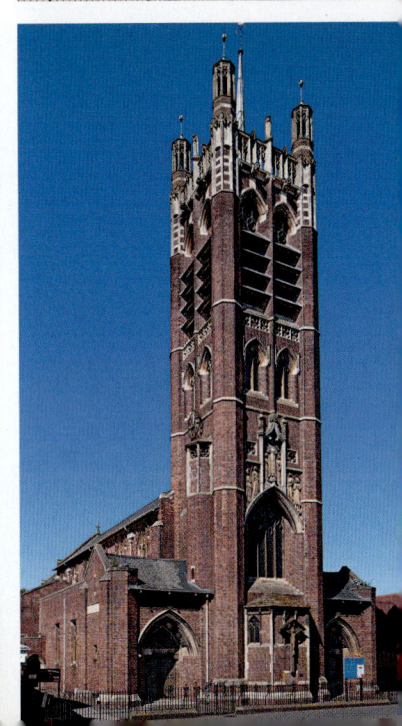

65. Birmingham, St Alban, Highgate, by J. L. Pearson, 1879–81, interior (p. 194)
66. Birmingham, Handsworth Cemetery chapel, by W. H. Bidlake, 1909–10, interior (p. 250)

67. Birmingham, Edgbaston, Oratory of St Philip Neri (R.C.), church, by E. Doran Webb, 1903–9, interior (p. 364)
68. Dudley, Coseley, Christ Church, Lady Chapel, by A.T. Butler, interior, with painting by Florence Camm, 1909–10 (p. 501)
69. Birmingham, St Basil (former), Deritend, by A.S. Dixon, interior, with rood figures by George Jack, 1910–11 (p. 195)

67	
68	69

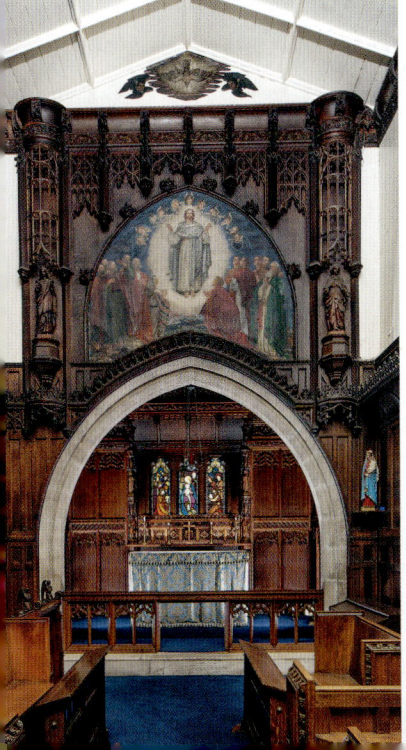

70. Walsall, Willenhall, Trinity Methodist Church (former), front, by Edward Banks, 1864 (p. 664)
71. Birmingham, Methodist Central Hall (former), by Ewen & J. Alfred Harper, 1900–3 (p. 123)

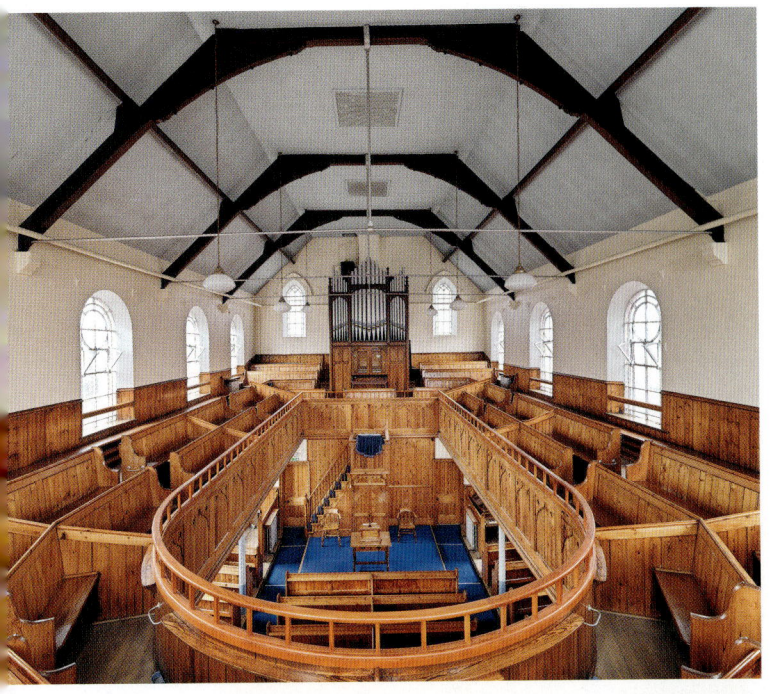

72. Sandwell, Rowley Regis, Blackheath, Cave Adullam Baptist Chapel, by William Willett, 1897–8, interior (p. 569)

73. Wolverhampton, Darlington Street Methodist Church, by Arthur Marshall, 1899–1901, interior (p. 680)

74. Birmingham, Erdington, St Thomas and St Edmund of Canterbury (R.C.), w window, by Hardmans, 1850, detail (p. 237)
75, 76. Birmingham, St Philip's Cathedral, stained glass by Edward Burne-Jones, Ascension, 1885, and Last Judgment, 1897–8 (p. 116)
77. Solihull, St Alphege, St Alphege's Chapel, E window, by Bertram Lamplugh, 1908–9 (p. 756)
78. Sandwell, West Bromwich, St Peter, Greets Green, E window, by A.E. Lemmon, 1930, detail (p. 616)

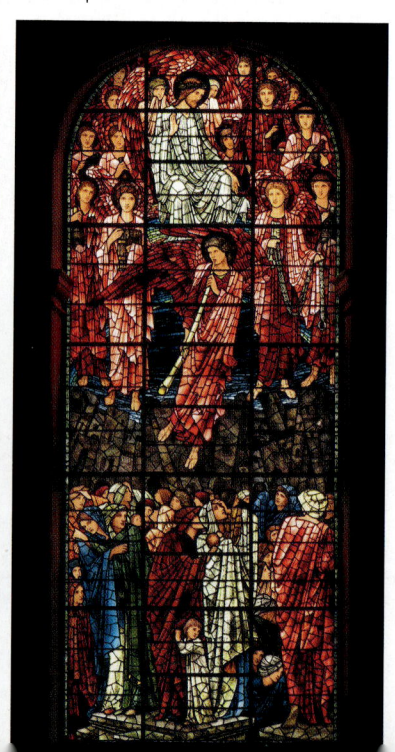

74	77
75 76	78

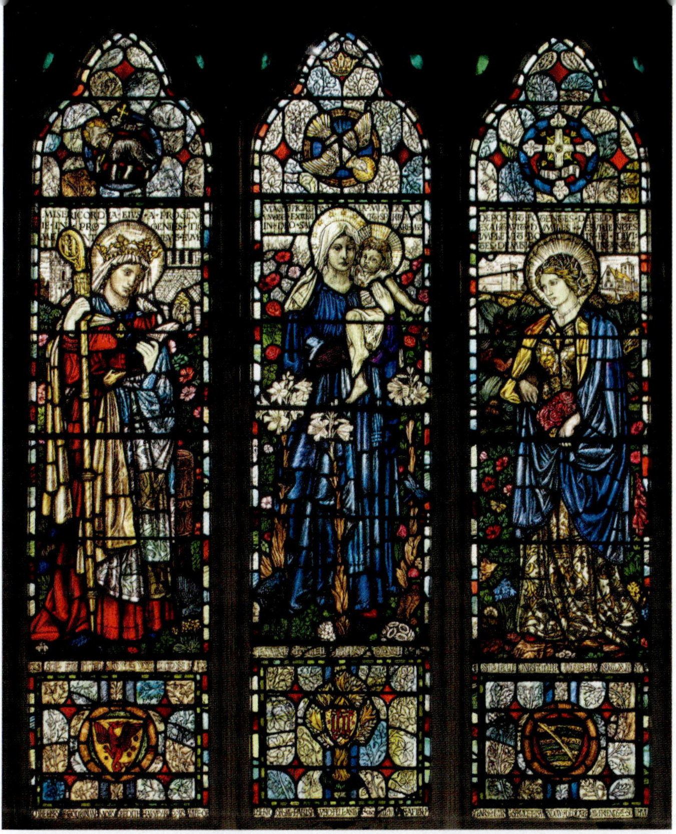

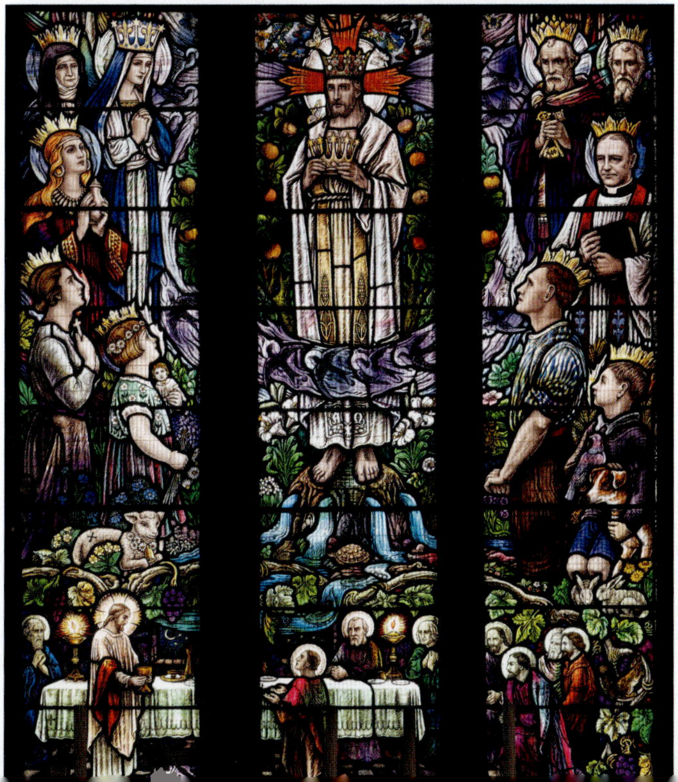

79. Birmingham Museum and Art Gallery, Industrial Gallery, by Yeoville Thomason, 1881–5, interior (p. 129)
80. Birmingham, Victoria Law Courts, by Aston Webb & Ingress Bell, 1887–91 (p. 131)

81. Sandwell, West Bromwich, Town Hall, by Alexander & Henman, 1874–5 (p. 605)

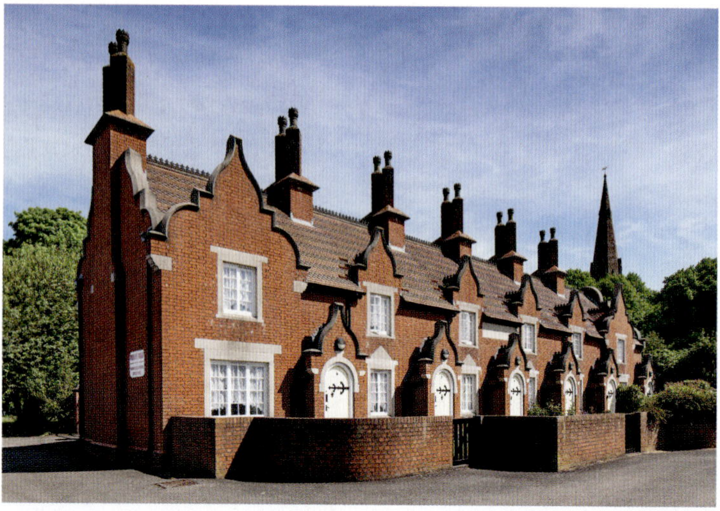

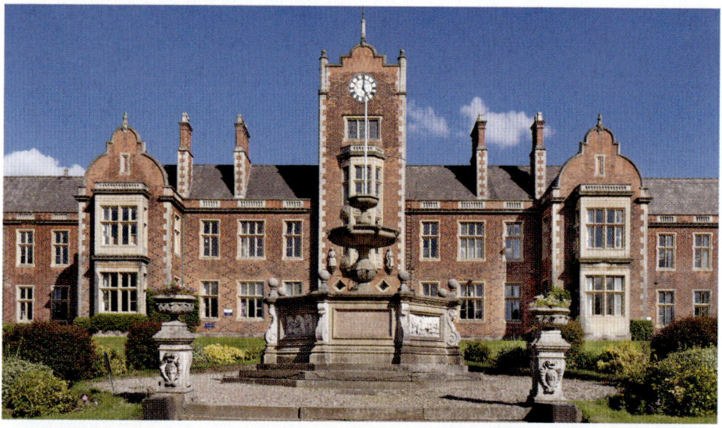

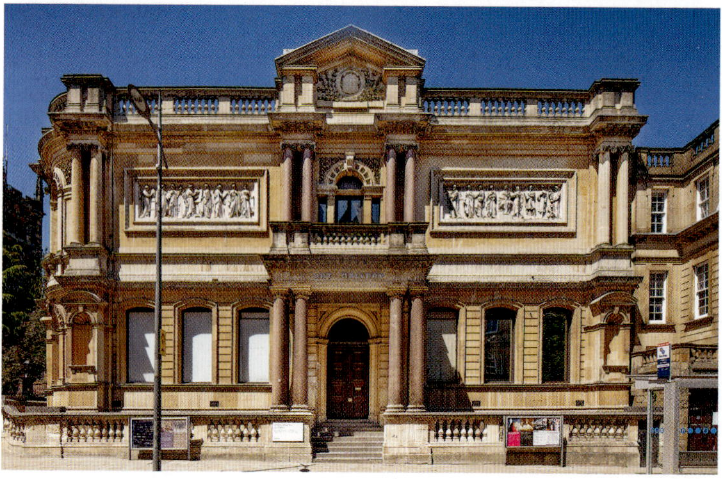

82. Wolverhampton, Heath Town, almshouses, by Edward Banks, 1850 (p. 730)
83. Wolverhampton, Graiseley and Penn Fields, Royal School, by Joseph Manning, 1853–4 and 1863–4, entrance front (p. 726)
84. Wolverhampton, Museum and Art Gallery, by J.A. Chatwin, 1883–5 (p. 683)
85. Birmingham School of Art, by J.H. Chamberlain (Martin & Chamberlain), 1884–5, w front (p. 133)
86. Walsall, Council House and Town Hall, by J.G.S. Gibson, 1902–5, staircase (p. 627)

82	85
83	86
84	

Lodge Primary School

DIEU ET MON DROIT

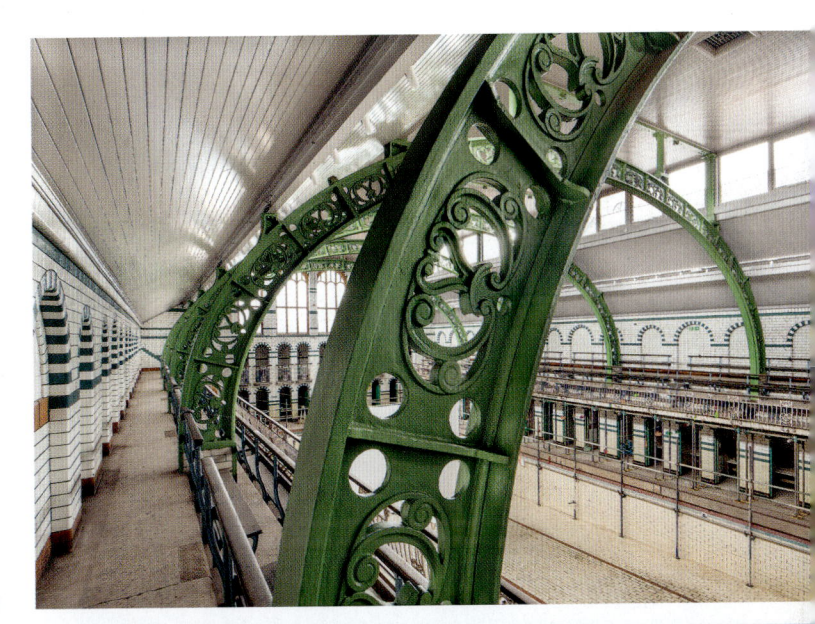

87. Sandwell, West Bromwich, Lodge Primary School, by Alfred Long, 1902–4 (p. 608)
88. Birmingham, Handsworth, King Edward VI School, by P.B. Chatwin, 1908–11, detail of hall, plasterwork by G.H. Cox (p. 252)
89. Birmingham, Balsall Heath, Moseley Road Baths, by William Hale, 1906–7, Gala Pool interior (p. 305)
90. Dudley, Library, by George H. Wenyon, 1908–9, left, and Town Hall, by Harvey & Wicks, 1926–8 (pp. 483, 482)

87	89
88	90

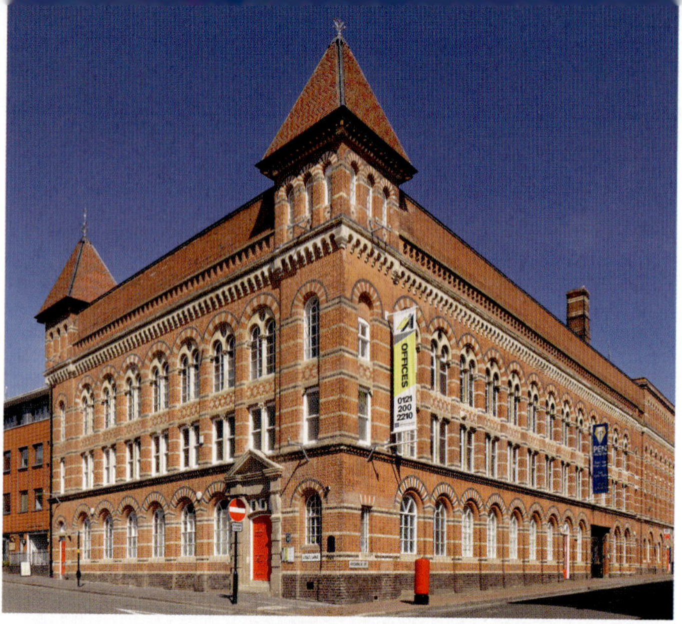
OFFICES
0121
200
2210

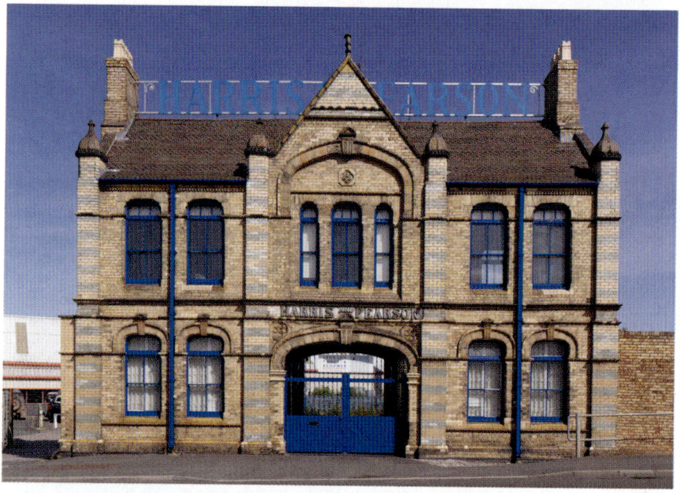

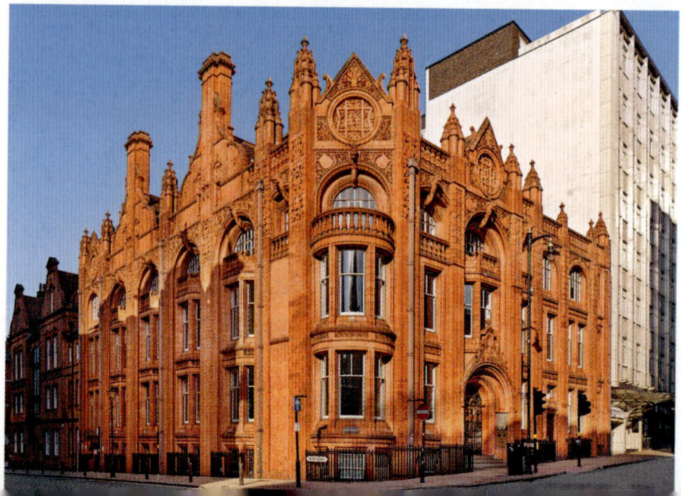

91. Birmingham, Argent Centre, Frederick Street, by J.G. Bland, 1862–3 (p. 180)
92. Dudley, Brierley Hill, former Harris & Pearson brickworks offices, by Rollinson & Beckley, 1888 (p. 499)
93. Birmingham, former National Telephone Co. offices and exchange, Nos. 17–19 Newhall Street, by Frederick Martin, 1896 (p. 159)
94. Birmingham, Grand Hotel, Grosvenor Room, by Martin & Chamberlain, 1893–5 (p. 144)
95. Birmingham, former Eagle Insurance, Colmore Row, by W.R. Lethaby & J.L. Ball, 1900 (p. 140)

91	94
92	95
93	

96. Wolverhampton, Finchfield, The Spinney, by W.J.H. Weller, 1908 (p. 708)
97. Wolverhampton, Tettenhall, Wightwick Manor, Great Parlour, by Edward Ould, 1893 (p. 739)
98. Birmingham, Edgbaston, Garth House, by W.H. Bidlake, 1901, garden front (p. 373)
99. Sutton Coldfield, Four Oaks, Bryn Teg, by C.E. Bateman, 1904, garden front (p. 459)
100. Birmingham, Bournville, Nos. 10–12 Sycamore Road, by W.A. Harvey, 1902 (p. 354)

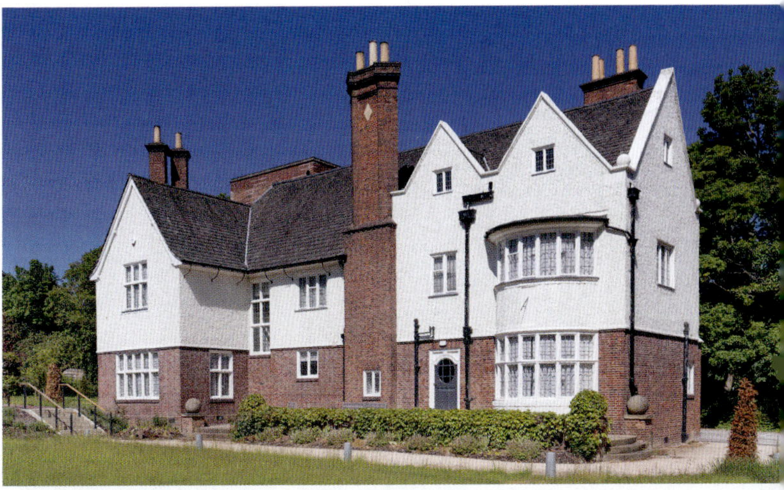

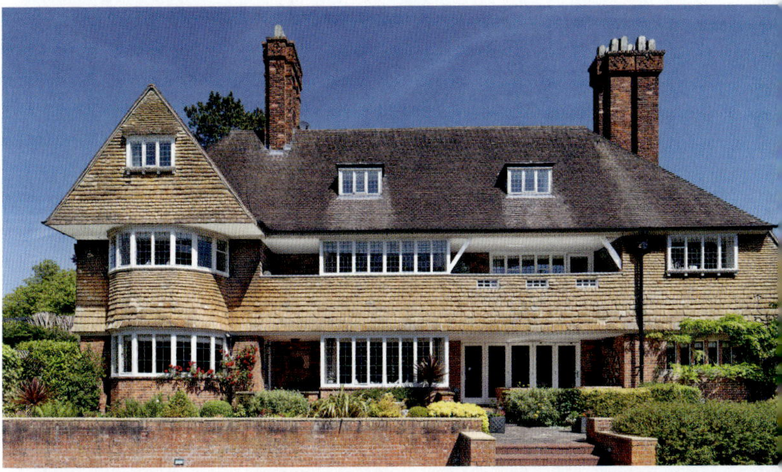

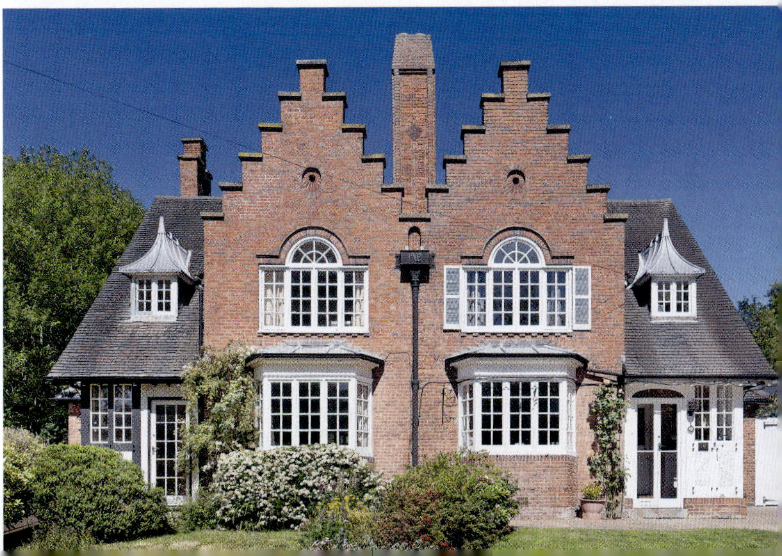

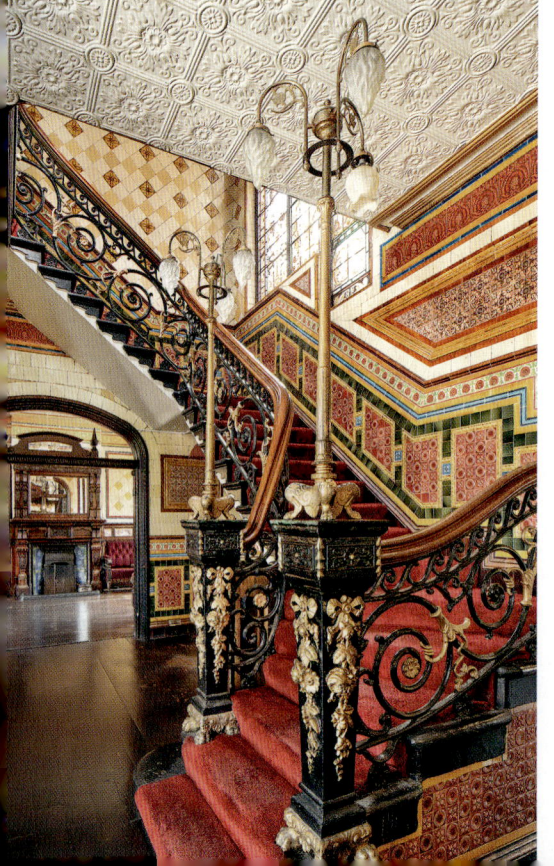

101. Walsall, Bloxwich, Turf Tavern, 1860s (p. 646)
102. Dudley, Crown Inn (former), Wolverhampton Street, by Joseph D. Wood, 1897–8 (p. 486)
103. Birmingham, Aston, Bartons Arms, by James & Lister Lea, 1901, interior (p. 229)

101 | 102
103

104. Wolverhampton, Royal London Insurance building, Prince's Square, by Essex, Nicol & Goodman, 1902–3 (p. 686)
105. Birmingham, Taylor & Challen works, Water Street extension, by Ewen & J.A. Harper, 1910–11 (p. 179)

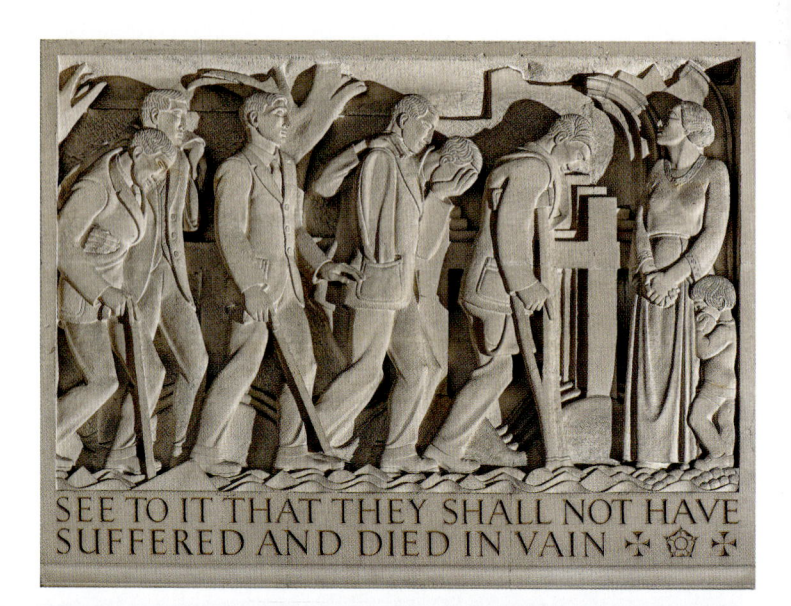

106. Birmingham, Hall of Memory, Broad Street, relief by William Bloye, 1925 (p. 165)
107. Birmingham, Moseley, Pitmaston, by Holland W. Hobbiss, 1930–1 (p. 335)
108. Sandwell, West Bromwich, former West Bromwich Building Society, by J.B. Surman and W.T. Benslyn, 1926–8 (p. 612)
109. Birmingham, Legal and General Assurance, Waterloo Street, by S.N. Cooke and Edward Holman, 1931–2 (p. 158)

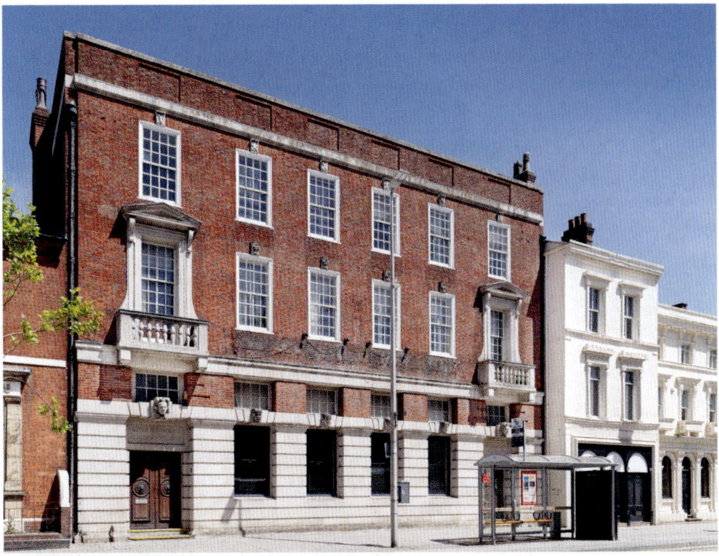

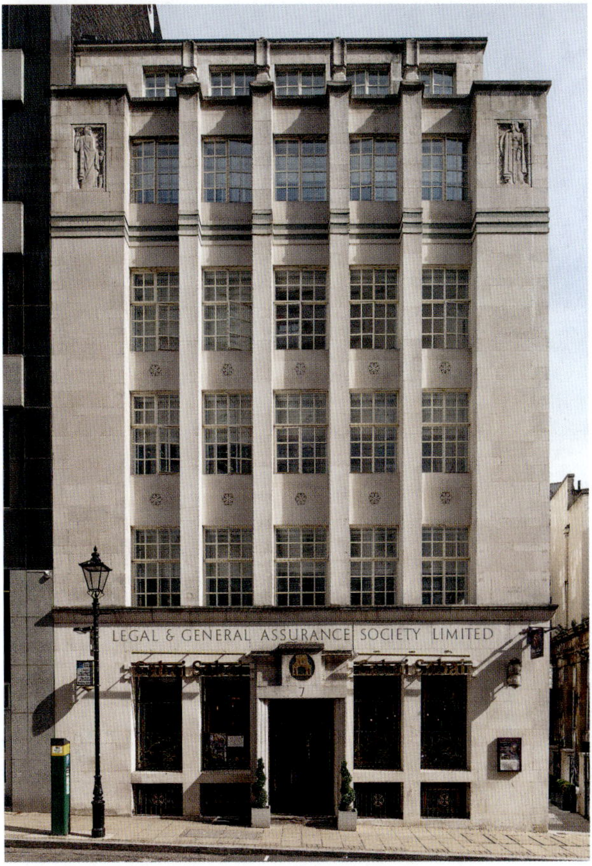
LEGAL & GENERAL ASSURANCE SOCIETY LIMITED

110. Birmingham, Northfield, Black Horse pub, by Francis Goldsbrough of Batemans, 1929 (p. 421)
111. Wolverhampton, Wednesfield, Vine Inn, by Watkin & Maddox, 1937, public bar (p. 750)
112. Birmingham, Kingstanding, former Odeon Cinema, by J. Cecil Clavering, 1934–5 (p. 263)
113. Sandwell, Smethwick Baths, by Chester Button, 1933, interior (p. 586)

110	112
111	113

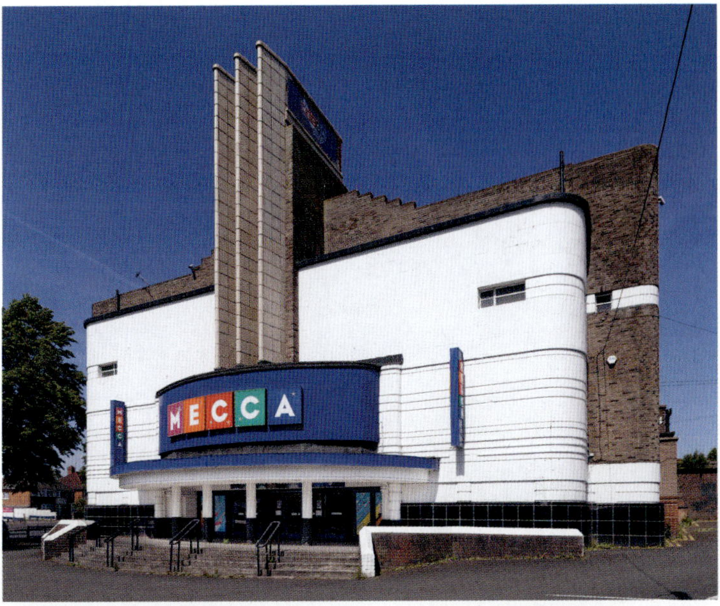
MECCA

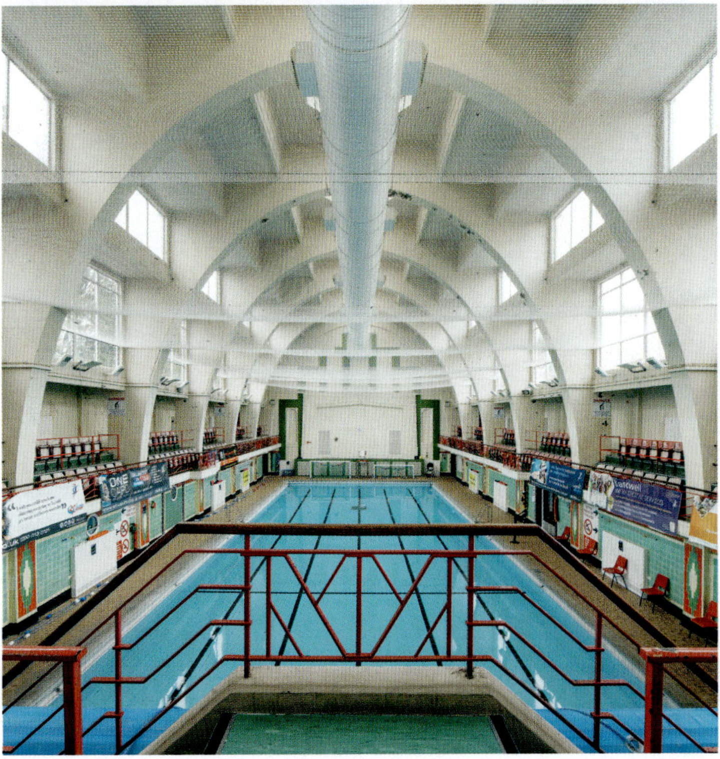

114 | 116
115 | 117

114. Birmingham, Edgbaston, University of Birmingham, Barber Institute, by Robert Atkinson, 1936–9 (p. 370)
115. Dudley Zoo, entrance gates, by Berthold Lubetkin and Tecton, 1935–7 (p. 479)
116. Birmingham, Edgbaston, Bristol Road, Viceroy Close, by Mitchell & Bridgwater with Gollins & Smeeton, 1938 (p. 379)
117. Sutton Coldfield, Beech Hill Road, No. 10, by Jackson & Edmonds, 1936–7 (p. 461)

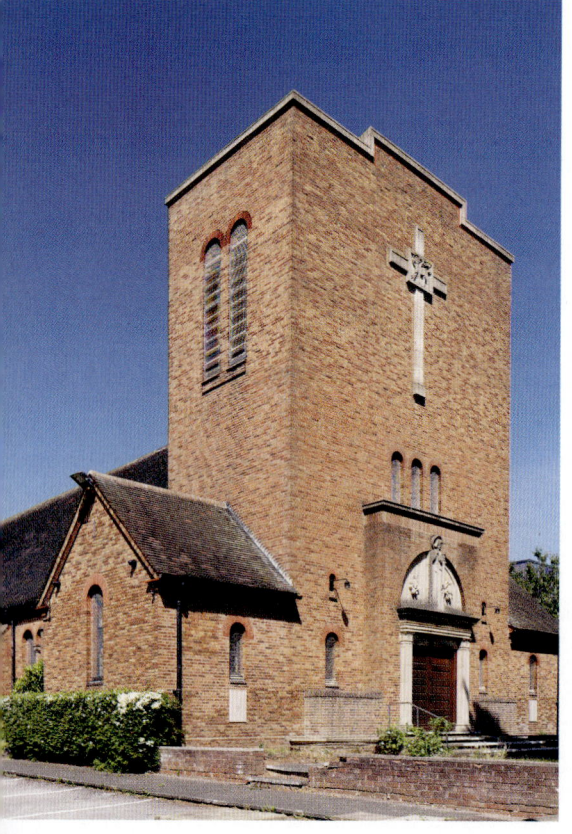

118. Sutton Coldfield, St Chad, by C.E. Bateman, 1925–7, interior (p. 441)
119. Birmingham, Alum Rock, Christ Church, by Holland W. Hobbiss, 1934–5, w tower (p. 272)
120. Sandwell, Oldbury, Warley, St Hilda, by E.F. Reynolds, 1938–40, interior (p. 567)
121. Sandwell, Oldbury, Warley, Our Lady and St Hubert (R.C.), by George Drysdale, 1934 (p. 567)

118	120
119	121

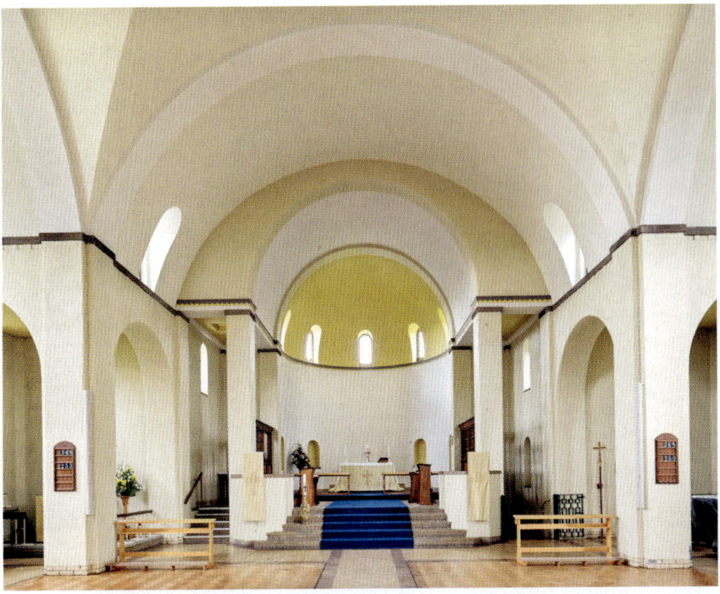

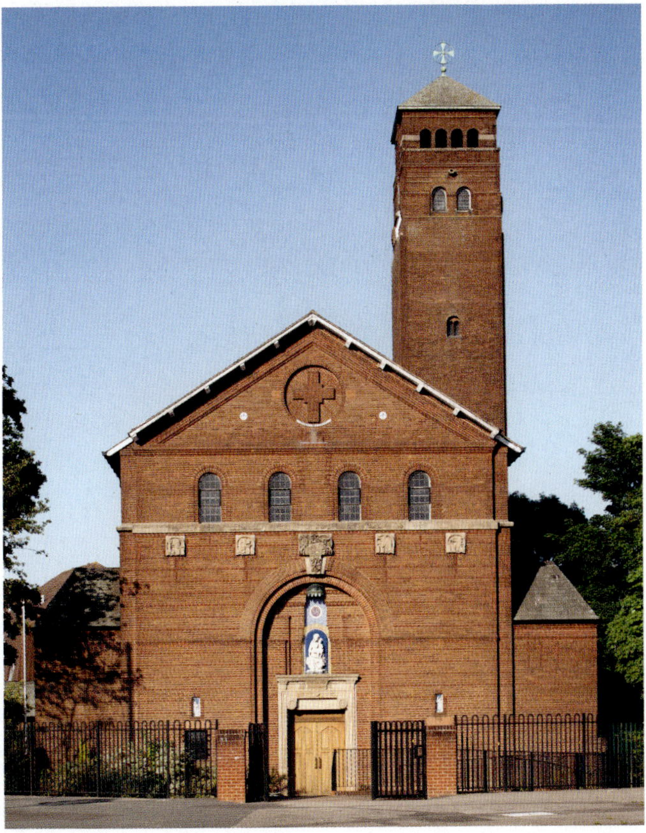

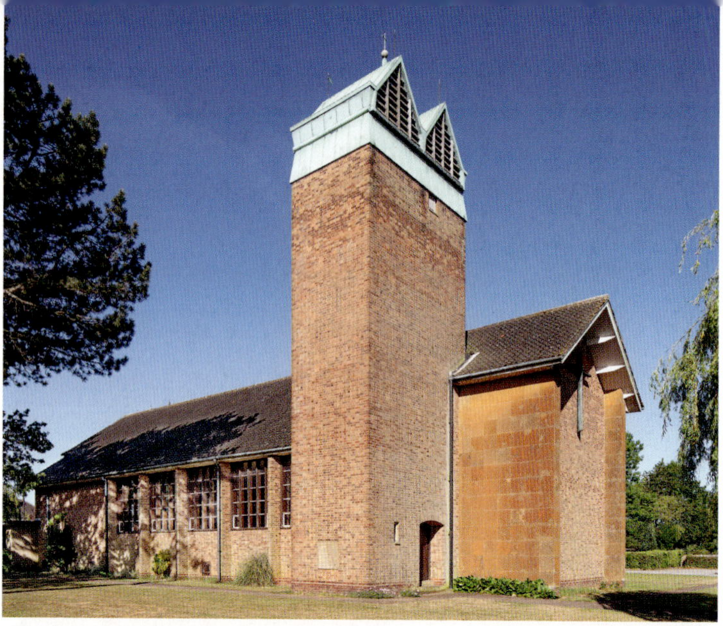

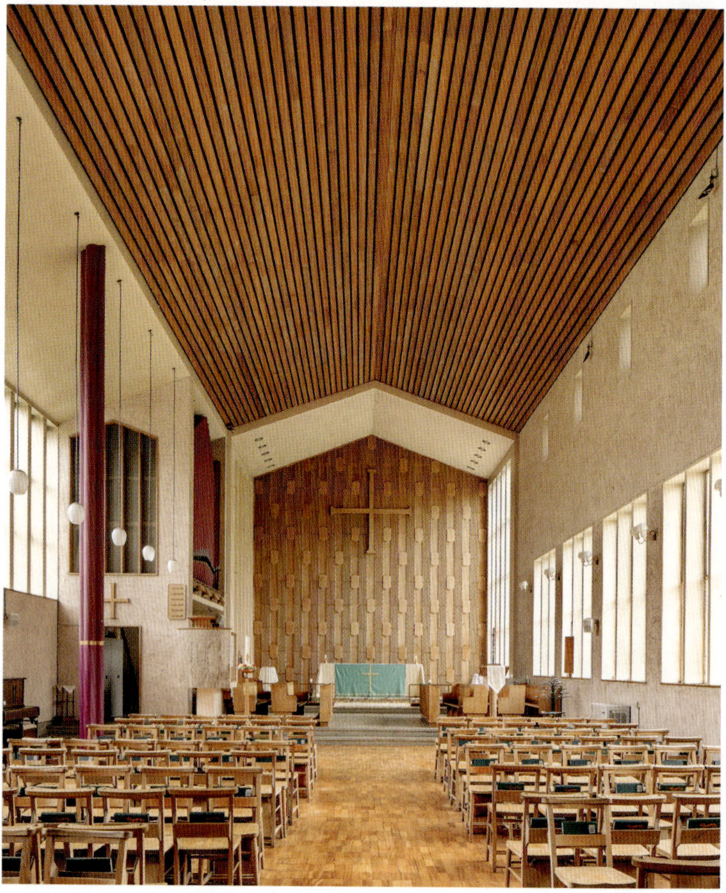

122. Birmingham, Longbridge, St John the Baptist, by George While, 1956–8 (p. 416)
123. Walsall, Darlaston, Bentley, Emmanuel, by Richard Twentyman, 1954–6, interior (p. 653)
124. Birmingham, Sheldon, Our Lady Help of Christians (R.C.), by Richard Gilbert Scott, 1966–7, interior (p. 282)
125. Wolverhampton, Whitmore Reans, St Andrew, w window, by John Piper and Patrick Reyntiens, 1967–8 (p. 752)

126. Birmingham, Shard End estate, by the Shard End Panel, 1947–55, Packington Avenue, tower (p. 279)
127. Birmingham, Edgbaston, Frederick Road, No. 16, by John Madin, 1957 (p. 383)
128. Birmingham, Edgbaston, University of Birmingham, Ashley and Strathcona buildings, by Howell, Killick, Partridge & Amis, 1961–4 (p. 371)

129. Wolverhampton School of Art, Ring Road, by Diamond, Redfern & Partners, 1968–9 (p. 684)
130. Birmingham, former ATV Tower, Broad Street, by H. George Marsh of Richard Seifert & Partners, 1969–73 (p. 168)

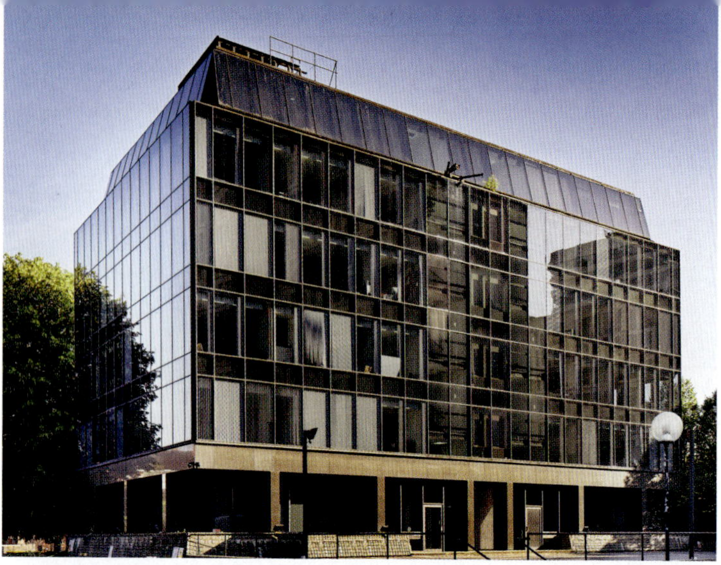

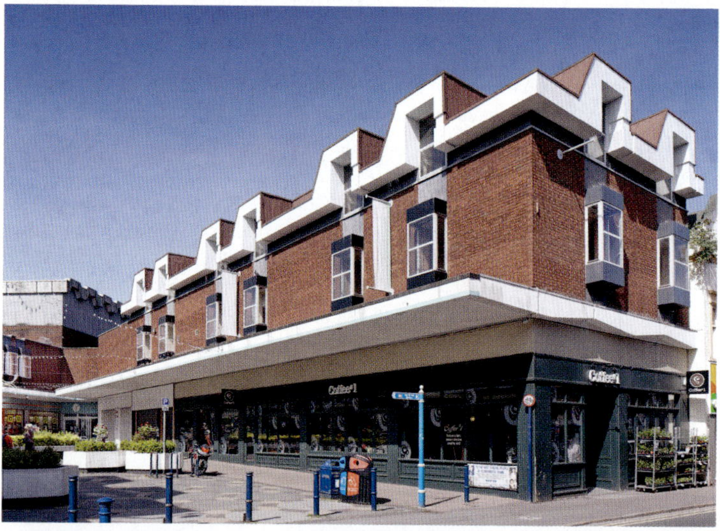
Coffee#1
Coffee#1

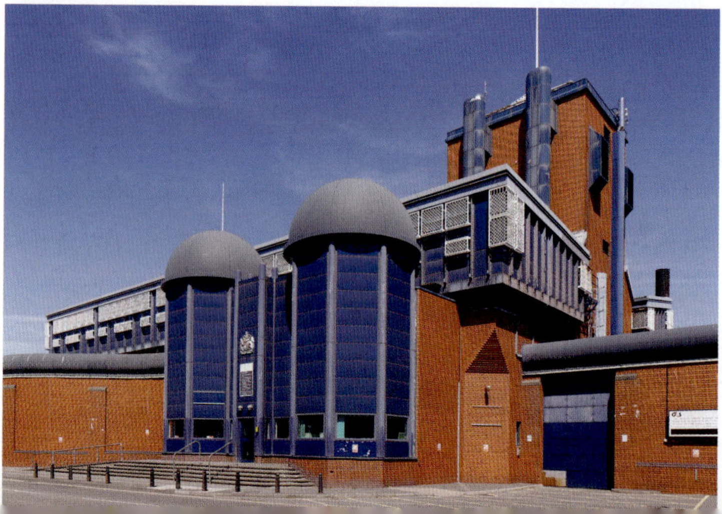

131. Birmingham, Edgbaston, Harborne Road, Neville House, by Douglas Hickman of John Madin Design Group, 1975–6 (p. 385)
132. Dudley, Stourbridge, Ryemarket Shopping Centre, by J. Seymour Harris & Partners, 1972–4 (p. 552)
133. Birmingham Prison, Winson Green, entrance block, by Patrick Lawlor of Howell Killick Partridge & Amis, 1983–7 (p. 217)
134. Sandwell, Rowley Regis, Tividale, Shri Venkateswara Balaji Temple UK, by Adam Hardy of the Prince of Wales's Institute of Architecture with Dr V.P.N. Rao and Associated Architects, 1997–2006 (p. 577)
135. Walsall, New Art Gallery, by Caruso St John, 1998–2000 (p. 629)

131	134
132	135
133	

136. Birmingham, Bartley Green, Newman University, reception and library building, by Glenn Howells Architects, 2011 (p. 347)
137. Birmingham, Library of Birmingham, by Mecanoo, 2010–13, interior (p. 166)

Next door, the former Technical Institute (*see* left). Further W, N side, terraces of shops by *Arthur Hamblin*, 1897–8. Also the former BOURNBROOK HOTEL, a commanding Late Classical block, here by 1839. Stuccoed, three storeys, the centre marked by pilasters; curved ends. Early C20 faience ground floor with concave-sided porch. Good NE extension by *H.T. Buckland*, 1898. The area to the N has been transformed into student housing; the best is JARRATT HALL, W, by *Associated Architects*, 2013: patterned blue and red brick, complex roof-line.* The BOURNBROOK PAVILION and associated residences, N, are by *MJP Architects*, 2017.

Where Bristol Road turns SW, the roads running SE (Tiverton, Hubert etc.) were developed by the Birmingham Freehold Land Society from 1898. Further on, the former SELLY OAK INSTITUTE (No. 648), 1893–4 by *Franklin Cross* for George Cadbury, built as a Quaker meeting house. Tremendously half-timbered. Three gables jostle each other, the biggest pushing out over a porch with a forest of free-standing columns and ogee domes halfway up. Name plaque with sunrays. Star-shaped chimneys. Opposite, a former WATERWORKS, by *Martin & Chamberlain*, 1878–9, an important work, using Gothic in an industrial context. Two LODGES face the road. Front gables hipped, with pushy semi-dormers; side gables with timber framing. The PUMPING STATION is set back, a convincing Gothic design with random – it seems – blank arcading and, as a charming foil, a projecting apse with conical roof. After the lodges, the library (*see* left), and the former STATION pub opposite, mostly of 1901 by *Edward Holmes*.

Beyond the railway and canal, at the highest point in the area, are the student flats which now dominate much of Selly Oak. One enormous block, eighteen storeys at one end, of pale brick, formed like a misshapen camel: astonishingly, by *Glenn Howells*, 2018. The SENSE building opposite, well scaled but loud, is also *Howells*, 2015–17.

2. Selly Park

The start is as Perambulation 1, opposite the University S gate. From Bristol Road, S up BOURNBROOK ROAD, with houses on the E side by *D. Smith & Son*, 1889–90, marked by exaggerated dormers. On the W side past St Edward's Road, Nos. 86–88 by *J.R. Ireson*, 1899–1900, have octagonal side towers with domes. Simpler pairs beyond by *Benjamin Bower*, 1906–7. No. 134A is the former St Wulstan's vicarage, by *C.E. Bateman*, 1914–15, a lovely Neo-Georgian design with a hipped roof, the centre marked by closer-spaced bays, and tremendous chimneys. St Edward's church (p. 426) is at the top of the road.

Now back, and E along OAKFIELD ROAD into the SELLY PARK ESTATE. In 1854 a local solicitor, Robert Dolphin, bought the land, divided it into plots with restrictive covenants

---

*Westley Richards' gun factory, by *C.E. Bateman*, 1898–9, was demolished in 2009.

and sold them for residential development. Each was at least ¼ acre. Only detached and semi-detached houses were permitted. Significant development started in the early 1860s. *William Martin* owned several plots by 1864, and he and his partner, *J.H. Chamberlain*, certainly provided designs for developers in 1871–3. Covenants specified large plot sizes and detached or semi-detached houses (they stopped a 1930s flats scheme by *Walter Gropius*). On the N side, No. 144, old-fashioned for 1889, and No. 142, with rendered bays pushing above the eaves, by *John A. Grew & Edwards*, 1907–8. Then basic mid-Victorian classical and Gothic villas, occasionally detached. Nos. 97–101 are by the builder *J. Cresswell*, 1877–8, with steep gables, bargeboards and timber porches. Nos. 114–116, thoughtfully detailed, with blue-brick bands and inset porches under pent roofs, are almost certainly a *Martin & Chamberlain* design of *c*. 1871. At the start of Selly Park Road, S side, another Gothic pair of *c*. 1870. No. 93, render and brick, big horizontal framing, is by *Sjölander da Cruz*, 2008–9. Nos. 94–96 opposite, classical of *c*. 1864–6. Nos. 79–89 are *Cresswell*, *c*. 1877. No. 76 of *c*. 1870–1 is also Gothic, with a crenellated porch and beautifully elongated cusping to the windows. Nos. 72–74, classical, *c*. 1871. No. 68, *c*. 1873–4, may be a *Martin & Chamberlain* design modified by a builder. No. 63 is again classical of *c*. 1868, with a *J.J. Bateman*-type doorcase. No. 56, austere Neo-Georgian, is by *Frank Wager* of *Peacock & Bewlay* for himself, 1939. Good doorcase. No. 52 is probably another *Martin & Chamberlain* design, *c*. 1871–3. The last stretch is more modest. Nos. 37–39 are 1860s classical; No. 36, Voysey style of 1922 by *H.J. Marshall*; No. 34, Queen Anne, by *G. Repton Faulkner*, 1900. Nos. 30–32, with canted dormers, are by *Franklin Cross & Brookes*, 1898–9.

Oakfield Road leads into PERSHORE ROAD. To the S, the SELLY PARK TAVERN, of 1901 by *Arthur Edwards*, for Sir John Holder of Holder's Brewery. Refined Tudor design, an early 'reformed' pub. Central gable framed by wavy parapets, counterpointed below by bays to either side. SKITTLE ALLEY behind of 1912. Holder sold the land to E and S, down to the River Rea, to *Grants Estates*, whose attractive terraced housing dates from 1905–10. Common combinations are Gothic doorways with square timber bays, and plain doorways with porch hoods and full-height canted bays. The grandest group, in THIRD AVENUE, has foliage tympana, and capitals to the bays. SIR JOHN'S ROAD and FOURTH AVENUE are nicely centred on a triangular green. Nos. 663–685 Pershore Road are stucco pairs of *c*. 1845–50 with smooth rustication. 300 yds S, Nos. 768–778, also Late Classical stucco, probably 1840s.

Back into Selly Park Estate here, up SELLY WICK ROAD. No. 15, S side, by *T.H. Mansell*, 1876, has minor additions, including a triangular oriel, by *James A. Swan*, 1922. Nos. 17–19 are *W.J. Davis*, 1904, in Bournville manner. No. 21, also Davis, 1908, is Voyseyesque. No. 30 opposite, with canted bays and shell-hood porch, is almost certainly by *S.N. Cooke*, 1913. No. 34 is by *Cossins & Peacock*, 1895, brick and Cotswold stone, drawing on Lethaby and Ernest Newton. No. 40 is by the builder *Chris Bryant* for himself, 1914. No. 46, brick Tudor by *Tanner & Horsburgh*, 1926. No. 48, BOSCOBEL, hiding behind its arched gateway, is by *Harvey & Wicks*, 1913. L-shaped, in warm orange-red brick. Entrance gable with waney-edged boarding, parapeted bay r. with Cotswold stone slates. House and garden are one composition, with a garden room (formerly open) at the corner: a Lutyens idea. Sprocketed roofs, blank wall to the W with tall paired chimneys. Entrance hall a room in the Arts and Crafts way; brick fireplaces, painted beams. No. 54, old-fashioned rendered Tudor by *Bloomer & Gough*, 1927. Opposite, SELLY WICK HOUSE, a stuccoed Regency villa with small pediment and pedimented doorcase, much extended W by *William Jenkins*, 1903.

Beyond, a junction with St Stephen's church. S down Selly Park Road, SOUTHBOURNE CLOSE, E side, was the grounds of Highfield, owned in the mid C20 by Philip Sargent Florence, friend of Walter Gropius and Nikolaus Pevsner. At the bottom, a LOGGIA constructed of stonework brought from *Thomas Archer*'s St Philip's Cathedral (p. 111) when its E end was altered in the 1880s. In poor condition, with details hard to make out. E and W sides have arches with the bulbous table-leg shapes of the Cathedral doors, and huge keystones, supporting cornices. Lengths of balustrade to N and S.

Nos. 47–65 Selly Park Road, ¼ m. S, are inventive semi-detached pairs of 1905 by *Owen Parsons*. The best include Nos. 59–61, rendered in the Voysey way, with separately gabled porch blocks pushing in front. No. 45 of 1927–8 is petite, with a big hipped roof, by the cinema architect *H. S. Scott* for his mistress. In KENSINGTON ROAD to the E, Nos. 38–48, by *C. K. Shepherd*, 1930, early Modern with flat roofs (some now pitched), but not inspired. No. 34, with gabled wings, the whole upper floor tile-hung, is by *J. P. Osborne & Son*, 1937.

Back N past St Stephen's, and NE into UPLAND ROAD. At the corner, No. 60, Gothic, probably a *J. H. Chamberlain* design of 1871. THE UPLANDS, SE side, was formerly a pair of Italianate houses of *c.* 1862–4, linked by a terrace above a vaulted colonnade; l. house replaced with flats, 1975.

Finally NW from St Stephen's church, down SERPENTINE ROAD. On the r., No. 21 is by *William Doubleday*, 1884, Old English, with a chimney thrusting through a gable. Nos. 17 and 19, a mirror pair, and Nos. 7 and 9, with canted bays, are by *Ewen Harper*, 1889 and 1890. Opposite, BEECHENHURST, 1870, grand but mangled. At the bottom we return to Oakfield Road.

3. The Selly Oak Colleges and Weoley Hill

Really part of the history of Bournville, adjacent to the SE. The colleges formed a loose federation of higher education institutions, many denominational, begun in 1902 with George

Cadbury's development of Woodbrooke (*see* below) as a Quaker college. Mostly absorbed by the University of Birmingham in 2001.

A perambulation can start on Bristol Road, at the corner of COLLEGE WALK. Down this on the l., the ASBURY OVERSEAS HOUSE of 1926 by *Beresford Pite* and *Arnold Silcock*. Important because of Pite's lifelong concern with mission buildings. 'In all Pite's architecture there is always something highly charged straining to express itself through a carefully contrived simplicity' (Brian Hanson). Here the most powerful motif is a pair of chimneys set at forty-five degrees to the front, expressing a cunning arrangement of corner fireplaces inside. Opposite, PROSPECT HALL, by *C. Wycliffe Noble*, 1970, romantically overgrown Aalto-esque ranges, with monopitch roofs, in brownish brick.

Back to BRISTOL ROAD and sw, the GEORGE CADBURY HALL is by *Hubert Lidbetter*, 1926–7. Portico with paired Tuscan columns and a big steep roof, not expressed inside. The former RENDEL HARRIS MEMORIAL LIBRARY is by *J.R. Armstrong*, 1931, Neo-Georgian, with a vestigial pediment clamped between hipped flanks. The CHARLES GILLETT CENTRE started as a stuccoed Frenchy villa of *c.*1860–70. Nos. 1020–1022, very picturesque brick, render and timber, dated 1901, are by *Harvey*. Down the drive to the l., FIRCROFT COLLEGE. Past a timber-clad block of 2005 by *Hugh Byrd Associates* is PRIMROSE HILL, George Cadbury Junior's house: a major work by *Harvey* of 1901, made confusing by additions. The main block has simple, blunt chimneys, stone mullion-and-transom windows, and gables with shaped stone copings. Entrance with a Lethaby-style segmental door-hood. The garden front has full-height canted bays. Contemporary timbered coachhouse wing, originally detached. Harvey extended the house SE in 1909, and linked it to the coachhouse with a timber overhang on long brackets in 1911.

Back on Bristol Road, w side, the angular and bulky ORCHARD LEARNING CENTRE of 1996 by *Ahrends Burton Koralek*. Dull pink brick. To its sw is ALAN GEALE HOUSE, Arts and Crafts Neo-Georgian of 1911–12, part of KINGSMEAD CLOSE, former student residences, all by *Harvey & Wicks*. NW block of 1915; across the lawns, three linked cottage-style blocks of 1912–13. A path through the r. link leads to the former WESTHILL COLLEGE. By *Harvey & Wicks*, 1914–15, with distinct Lutyens influence: three-storey porch, its doorway with a big curly pediment; main block articulated by giant arches with the upper storey partly open, mansard-roofed wings. Garden front with an impressively piled-up centre. To the NW, BARROW CADBURY HOUSE by *Clifford Tee & Gale*, 1961, with a circular porch on a central pier, and a little flying staircase.

Back and across Bristol Road to WOODBROOKE COLLEGE, past a LODGE of semi-detached houses by *BVT Architects*, 1924. A Quaker college since 1903. A grand house of *c.*1840–50 (not on a map of 1834), but altered. Main s front of seven bays, stuccoed, with a three-bay pediment and giant Corinthian pilasters. Five more bays l. which must be an addition, with the same pilasters, but four of them with a heavy attic. Lower addition r. Cubic white extension by *Bryant Priest Newman*, 2012.

Now w across Bristol Road again, into the WEOLEY HILL ESTATE, developed from 1915. Houses by *BVT Architects*, mostly designed by *S. Alex Wilmot*. The start of WITHERFORD WAY has the earliest, of 1915–17. All rendered. Gabled corner blocks, then pairs and terraces with some pedimental gables. More *Wilmot/BVT* houses up FOX HILL, NE. Also No. 12, by *Harvey & Wicks*, 1922–3. A fine late Arts and Crafts house, asymmetrical but with Neo-Georgian details, in the manner of Ernest Newton or Baillie Scott. Sumptuous Venetian window with relieving arch to the garden. WEOLEY HILL, at the top, has more *BVT* houses, the best No. 5 to the NE, by *Wilmot*, 1923, with a semicircular door hood. At the end is WEOLEY PARK ROAD. All the interest is on the SW side. Nos. 38 and 40 are by *Harvey & Wicks*, 1923 and 1922, Neo-Georgian of Arts and Crafts ancestry. Nos. 42–44 are by *J. Bernard Mendham*, 1914–15. Beyond, the former College of the Ascension, and Lodge Hill cemetery (p. 427). Going back SE past Weoley Hill, a picturesque early C19 cottage, then the Baptist INTERNATIONAL MISSION CENTRE, a Victorian house extended by *Harvey*, 1912, with a prominent stair-tower. Beyond, the University of Birmingham School (p. 428) and Bristol Road.

STIRCHLEY

Bournville's poor relation, E of the railway. The parish church of 1901, *William Hale*'s finest design, burnt down in 1965 and was replaced on the Pineapple Estate, ¾ m. NE. Edwardian public buildings remain, the best by *J. P. Osborne*.

THE ASCENSION, Pineapple Grove. 1972–3 by *Romilly Craze*. Octagonal, with a concrete frame and brick infill. Low-pitched roof and central lantern. Above the entrance, STATUE of the Risen Christ by *John Bridgeman*. Simple but pleasant interior, wide yet intimate. – ALTAR, ALTAR RAILS, PULPIT and FONT by *Craze*. – STAINED GLASS behind the altar by *John Lawson*, dalle-de-verre, with a bold Christ figure. – Hanging ROOD by *John Skelton*. – HALL, r., the former St Hugh's mission church of 1927–8 by *S. N. Cooke*. Its ALTAR and REREDOS with paintings by *W. Lawson* are in the Lady Chapel of the new church.

FRIENDS' MEETING HOUSE (former), Hazelwell Street. 1913 by *Osborne*. Low, purply brick, with stone dressings and Tudor windows.

PUBLIC LIBRARY, Bournville Lane. 1905 by *Osborne*. An interesting combination: two-storey canted bays, wide Mannerist doorway with a big keystone, grid of windows in the bays and above.

PUBLIC BATHS (now community centre), Bournville Lane and Hazelwell Street, immediately E. By *Osborne*, 1910. The building turns the corner in a quarter-circle, with the main bath block on the r. Edwardian Baroque. Small-scale entrance: Ionic doorcase with banded pilasters, split segmental pediment with cartouche in a garland, resting of course on the keystone, and a dome with a tall finial. Aedicules to the l., their broken pediments with scrolled ends. Functional interior with thin steel trussed roof. A nice touch is the balcony handrail with curvy balusters.

INSTITUTE (now Stirchley Community Church), Hazelwell Street. 1891 by *William Jenkins*. Front block like a house, hall at the back. Old-fashioned basic Gothic.

STIRCHLEY COMMUNITY PRIMARY SCHOOL, Pershore Road. Fronting the road, the village school by *William Hale*, 1878–9. Single-storeyed, with timber Gothic tracery in the gables. Behind, also by *Hale*, 1892, a tall block like a Robson school in London, with basic Dutch gables and a pretty cupola. Rooms with big curving tie-beam roof trusses, staircase with a gabled wall for the banister. At the rear, facing Charlotte Road, an infants' school by *Harvey & Wicks*, 1910–11. Bournville in Stirchley, with an entrance with dentilled pediment and big keystone. Its hall has pilasters and a dentil cornice, the ceiling boldly interrupted by dormers.

The earliest development is represented by STIRCHLEY COTTAGES at the N end of Hazelwell Street, dated 1838, with unusual doorcases. Going S, the former Institute faces the Friends' Meeting House and baths (pp. 426, 428). The BRITISH OAK, E side, is by *James & Lister Lea*, 1923–4; probably by *Mr Brassington* who designed the Bartons Arms, Newtown (Aston, p. 229), but here a 'reformed' pub in Tudor Revival. Long roof-line and symmetrical bays, red brick with diapering and tilework; heavier than Reynolds or Hobbiss. What matters here is the remarkably complete interior. The public bar retains its simple bar front and back. Smoke rooms with original seating and fireplaces, the l. one now opened out. Large rear hall with high panelling and fireplace. The rooms leading off retain their brass nameplates. Beyond, the assembly room, used originally for meals, and a garden. PERSHORE ROAD continues dead straight S. No. 1429 is a former LLOYDS BANK by *J.A. Chatwin*, 1900, with nice brick detail.

THE WORTHINGS and BARN CLOSE, off Fordhouse Lane. Municipal housing by *Arthur McKewan*, completed by 1926.

PILLBOX, on the Worcester Canal, 200 yds NW of the Pershore Road crossing. An unusual Second World War pillbox consisting of a concrete pipe with slits, intended to look like an industrial chimney.

WEOLEY

Completely rural, except for the castle ruins, until the Weoley Castle Estate was built in the 1930s.

ST GABRIEL, Marston Road. 1933–4 by *Edwin F. Reynolds* (*Wood & Kendrick & E.F. Reynolds*). Only the nave was built, in buff brick laid in Reynolds's favourite Flemish stretcher bond, with round-headed windows set high up. The interior is unexpected, with square piers separating narrow passage aisles. Barrel-vault delicately panelled in plaster, with little cartouches and birds at the intersections by *William Bloye*. More decoration along the cornices. – Octagonal FONT with little sculpted doves.

OUR LADY AND ST ROSE OF LIMA (R.C.), Gregory Avenue. 1959–61 by *Adrian Gilbert Scott*. Impressive ritual W tower, a rectangular mass of grey brick, with a hipped roof behind a parapet. Characteristic of Scott the way the tower cuts back at the corners, and also the big entrance niche with a parabolic arch. Classical doorcase in a modernized Gothic frame, and fine iron GATES. Flanking baptistery and staircase extensions. The church is equally massive, with brickwork held down by big sloping roofs. Traditional interior, with a long nave and passage aisles, almost untouched. Elliptical arcades and sanctuary arch. Jazzy triangular-arched narrow arcading in the canted sides of the nave roof, in the canopy of the sanctuary and in a double-ended pattern on the back of the high CIBORIUM. Square piers and dado faced in brownish limestone blocks. SE chapel REREDOS with a carved Nativity by *Ferdinand Stuflesser* of Ortisei. – Original ALTAR, RAILS and PEWS. – SCHOOL, W of the church. Low ranges by *E. Bower Norris*, 1935–6, with an originally dual-use hall and sanctuary.*

WEOLEY CASTLE. Remains of a fortified manor house, rather than a fortress: as if the C13 Stokesay Castle, Shropshire, were chopped off just above ground level. Hidden off Alwold Road, N of the council estate (*see* below), by the Bourn Brook. Archaeological investigations in 1932–40 and 1955–62 showed that a smaller area was previously surrounded by a moat with a palisade and timber-revetted bank, and included a timber great hall, a kitchen and a chapel. These were buried by the upcast from the present moat in the C13. In 1264 Roger de Somery received licence to crenellate, but the house was not mentioned at his death in 1272. Most of what we see now is probably late C13 and early C14, the work of his son, also Roger, and grandson John (†1322), contemporary with their work at Dudley Castle (p. 475). There may have been substantial late C14 rebuilding; the present remains closely resemble a description of 1424. After 1531 it fell into disuse, and by the mid C17 was described as a 'ruined castell'. A farmhouse of *c*. 1690

---

*The first church, of 1933, was on Weoley Park Road, Selly Oak, p. 426.

to the s (dem. 1955) used stone from the castle. Repairs and consolidation, and new VISITORS' CENTRE, by *S.T. Walker & Partners* (*Bob Tolley* and *Derek Clarke*), 2008–10.

The present approach is from the sw, along a modern causeway. An inspection should however start by walking round the complete dry moat. The revetted base of the walls, of red Frankley sandstone, is of high quality, and virtually complete below the former water-line. Going clockwise, first the base of a turret, then the original entrance, at the NW corner. Here the base of a spiral staircase, and the tremendously battered base and fragments of the piers of the gatehouse. The base of the barbican at the outer end of the drawbridge is visible. On the long N side a turret with splayed buttresses, and another at the NE corner. E wall similar; SE corner with the buttress of a turret. The s wall has another turret.

In the courtyard only base courses of buildings survive, identifiable from the 1424 survey. Going clockwise again, first a warehouse or granary. Then the entrance group, with the bottom of the spiral stair, and the side walls of the gatehouse. Along the N side, first stables, then the chapel, with the bases of the altar and of a wall W of it, perhaps a screen. S vestry, projecting into the courtyard. To the E the great chamber, with nursery chamber to its N. At the NE corner the only complete surviving construction, cellars and garderobe, with a C13 archway of two plain orders. S of this complex the great hall, probably rebuilt in the late C14, with the base of the central fireplace visible. In the SE corner the kitchens, with the tile-built, back-to-back base of the hearth. Finally on the S side another chamber and, near the causeway, a polygonal turret, and a bakehouse with circular oven.

Outside to the E is the large depression of a medieval fishpond. W of the drawbridge was an outer court, now vanished. The Stone House Farm to the NW (*see* Harborne, p. 399) may be related to it.

The WEOLEY CASTLE ESTATE is a superior development by *Herbert H. Humphries*, City Engineer and Surveyor, 1931–7. The centre is Weoley Castle Square (actually an ellipse), with roads running in four directions and others in concentric circles. The houses have deep eaves and decorative porches. The N side of Shenley Fields Road, adjoining the Bournville Trust Estate, has special designs with tile-hanging, tilework eaves, corbelled chimneys, gambrel-roofed porches and even some half-timbering. Contemporary schools, single-storeyed: PRINCETHORPE JUNIOR AND INFANTS, Princethorpe Road, by *Crouch, Butler & Savage*, 1931–2, H-plan; JERVOISE, Jervoise Road, by *H.W. Simister*, 1933–6, with a buttressed hall. One pub, the big hipped-roofed WEOLEY CASTLE, Shenley Lane, by *S.N. Cooke*, 1934–5 (altered).

For Weoley Hill *see* Selly Oak, p. 431.

SUTTON COLDFIELD

Introduction	437
Churches	438
Oscott College	445
Public buildings	447
Vesey Cottages	449
Perambulations	450
Outlying buildings	461
Minworth	466

INTRODUCTION

An ancient town, 'Sutone' in Domesday, and 'Sutton Co'fil' in Shakespeare's *Henry IV Part I*. The medieval manor was owned by the Earls of Warwick. Its C16 development was the result of John Harman, who took the surname Vesey. Born at Moor Hall Farm about 1462, he was Bishop of Exeter from 1519 to 1551, and President of the Court of the Marches from 1526. Reinstated as bishop by Mary I in 1553, he died in 1554. He lived at Moor Hall from 1527 until his death. He established a fair and a weekly market, and built a grammar school, a town hall and fifty-one stone cottages. In 1528 he obtained a charter creating Sutton a Royal Town, administered by a Warden and Society, which elected into itself. It survived until 1885, when Sutton became a Municipal Borough, absorbed into Birmingham in 1974. It gained a town council in 2016.

The first settlement was on Manor Hill, s of the Ebrook (Plants Brook) valley. A new development began by the late C13 to the N, with the church, Holy Trinity, on top of a steep hill. The town grew N of it, its centre where High Street and Coleshill Street meet. Parade and Lower Parade, the modern centre, were the Dam (so called) across the Ebrook valley, developed in the C19, as Sutton became a middle-class commuter town for Birmingham. A town planning scheme of 1913, developed by the town clerk, *R.A. Reay Nadin*, enforced low building densities, creating an exclusive residential neighbourhood. The most prestigious area was the Four Oaks estate. Parade was redeveloped, not well, and a ring road built, following a scheme of 1962 by *Max Lock & Partners*.

C.E. Bateman lived in Sutton from 1902 and 1924, and did much. *Crouch* and *Butler* both lived in Driffold, and Sutton has much of their work. Other late C19 and early C20 local architects were *E.F. Titley* and *Marston & Healey* (Marston was the Borough Surveyor). An interesting local man between the wars was *J.W.Wilson*.

One lost building must be mentioned here: the RECTORY, of 1701 by *William Smith the elder* for John Riland, in what is now Rectory Park. It had a five-bay front and hipped roof, still in the late C17 way. Demolished 1936.

CHURCHES

Church of England

HOLY TRINITY, Coleshill Street and Trinity Hill. From the N, across the Vesey Gardens and on its hill, the church looks mostly Victorian. But from the SE, old fabric is visible: nave and aisles, chancel with N and S chapels, W tower. C13 work survives in the triple-chamfered plinth of the chancel E wall and the restored flat buttresses above. Perp S aisle: see the concave string course (in 2016 evidence was found of an earlier, narrower aisle). Its S windows are replacements, probably C18, the partly blocked W window probably the one enlarged in 1759. In 1533–4, according to Dugdale, Bishop Vesey built 'two Iles to the Church'. Leland says: 'the north and south part or aisles'. These must be the chancel chapels, since Leland describes Vesey's monument as 'in the wall of the north isle'. Three-light S windows, flat-headed, with delicately moulded surrounds. The chapels' E windows are similar but of four lights, under flattened four-centred arches. C19 timber S porch, its GATES an iron rail of 1728 formerly in front of Vesey's tomb.* The simple S DOOR may be from the pre-C16 aisle. The clerestory was rebuilt by *G.T. Robinson*, 1865. The windows and steep-pitched roof are his. He also rebuilt the chancel E wall, accurately re-creating the reticulated tracery. The low, broad and substantial W tower looks early Perp. W window with restored reticulated tracery. SW stair with a much-crocketed conical stone roof among the battlements. But Leland says Vesey 'built alsoe ... the Steeple'. W doorway by *Yeoville Thomason*, 1880; ugly DOORS of 2017. Low, massive NW vestry, with inventive late medieval tracery, by *W.H. Bidlake*, 1898. The N side is all *Thomason*'s outer N aisle of 1880, boldly cross-gabled, with tall four-light Perp windows. NE vestry also Thomason, 1875. Glass and timber porch between tower and NW vestry, part of the dogmatic reordering of 2015–18 (architects *Brownhill Hayward Brown*).

Inside, arcades of five bays with convincing Perp-style octagonal piers but single-chamfered round arches. The chancel arch is the same. They are by *William Hiorne*, 1759–60, after part of the nave collapsed. Chancel arcades of 1533–4, also round-arched. They have familiar Perp four-shafts-and-four-hollows, and capitals trying to wrap themselves round this moulding, as if they were of rolled-out dough. A simplified mitre, surely for Vesey, on the middle N capital. *Robinson*'s nave roof has under-fed hammerbeams. Outer N arcade of 1880; similar piers to Hiorne's, but pointed arches. The glorious PAINTED CEILINGS are by *C.E. Bateman*. Chancel 1914, with Tudor roses and foliage, and gilded Tudor roses surrounded by leaves as bosses. Angels in the E bay, a ceilure above the

---

*Before the C21 reordering, the shock of entering here into a church twice as big as expected, and then seeing the ceiling paintings and the woodwork, was unforgettable.

former altar. Nave, 1929 with big Tudor roses. The E bay has rose bosses and gilded flower patterns. More angels on the hammerbeams. Vesey (N) Chapel roof also 1929: blue panels with golden diagonal ribs, and again angels at the E.

FURNISHINGS. Marian WOODWORK of exceptional importance, even after its dismemberment in 2015. As the Vesey Chapel inscription says, removed from Worcester Cathedral in 1864 and installed here 1875, when *Thomason* made up a complete set of chancel furnishings. Its present treatment is deplorable, with pieces scattered around purposelessly, and some apparently lost. The woodwork was part of choir fittings of 1556–7, a model Catholic reordering of a cathedral under Mary I, who contributed to the cost and inspected the work. Confidently classical, progressive for mid-C16 England; possibly by *Robert Trunquet*. The present REREDOS, most of the N and S CHANCEL SCREENS, PANELS now fixed to the S aisle wall, and the S AISLE SCREEN come from the rear and return canons' stalls. Former frontals with panels with symbolic affronted fishes, sprouting foliage from mouths and tails: of different designs, and exquisitely done. They flank shields, some repainted for C17 canons, but on the reredos with Instruments of the Passion, surely part of a larger Marian set and, explicitly Catholic, the Five Wounds of Christ. Return panel on the S with St Katherine, probably honouring Katherine of Aragon, the queen's mother. Between the panels, boxes with candelabra, and ribbons and other decoration wreathed round them; below, Composite colonnettes. In e.g. the Vesey Chapel frieze, panels with an opened scroll with slightly rolled ends, kept tight by nicked ribbons fed through slits, a typical mid-C16 motif (cf. the Gardiner Chapel at Winchester). The slim columns in the screens are richly treated with fluting, and foliage arabesques below; some have little putti heads, separately carved. The S aisle screen is a complete section of frontals and columns, probably from the back of the return stalls. The former stalls now jammed in front of the reredos, and parts of the set now in the S aisle, from the front longitudinal stalls at Worcester, have small fluted Composite pilasters. C19 bench seats, on C16 lion's-paw feet, to a design from Serlio. The arcaded lower panels of the chancel N screen (Vesey Chapel) are from the Worcester organ loft of 1612–13, joiner *Robert Kettle*. Crown and thistle for James I on one panel.

The tower inner DOOR has four complete Marian columns; also early C17 woodwork from St Michael, Coventry: a lion and unicorn above from a royal arms, now flanked by female and male centaurs, and gryphons. More of these on the N gallery front. In the new porch, two figures holding shields: late medieval? Discarded to the N gallery, pieces of the altar rails of 1634 from Worcester. – SOUTH GALLERY. A faculty exists of 1754, but the severely detailed front and slim iron columns look later C18. – NORTH GALLERY and (relocated) staircase by *Thomason*, 1880; front panels a good imitation of the Worcester work. – PULPIT. A lovely piece, almost certainly of 1760–1 and presumably by *Hiorne*. Octagonal, on a tapering shaft; tester with openwork ogee top and dove finial. Much marquetry, and foliage and fretwork decoration. *Thomason* supported the tester on slim Worcester columns of 1556–7. – FONT. Norman, of flower-pot shape. Intersecting arches and above them four heads with thin sprigs of foliage coming out of their mouths, as if they were smoking clay pipes. Found at Over Whitacre (Warwicks.) and brought here in 1856. – SCREEN to the Vesey Chapel by *Bateman*, 1929, a beautiful Free Jacobean piece; contemporary TYMPANUM with symbol of the Trinity. – ALTAR. Florid Neo-Jacobean of 1891. – ROYAL ARMS. Large, Stuart, in the tower.

STAINED GLASS. E window by *Alexander Gibbs*, 1863. Small-scale drawing, bright metallic colours. N chapel E by *James Ballantine & Son*, 1871. S chapel: E by *Yoxall & Whitford*, 1964, small scenes and plain glass. S from E, *Yoxall & Whitford*, 1955; *Mary Lowndes*, 1907. S aisle near the W, perhaps *Heaton, Butler & Bayne*, †1893; S aisle W, *Ballantine*, †1865 and †1875. W (tower), *Ward & Hughes*, 1896. Outer N aisle, *Geoffrey Webb*, 1916, with his typical blues.

MONUMENTS. N chapel. John Vesey, Bishop of Exeter †1554. C16 effigy in full pre-Reformation vestments including mitre, and with a crook. The effigy is painted. Pevsner said 'handled over the centuries with too much care', but it is as shown in the 1730 edition of Dugdale. Gothic tomb-chest of 1876, incorporating a panel of 1748 (which misdates Vesey's death). – Henry Pudsey †1677. Busts of Pudsey and his wife, slightly turned towards one another. Big segmental pediment on pilasters. Opened curtains. Plausibly attributed to *Sir William Wilson*, who married Pudsey's widow. – Henry Jesson †1705, aged six. A little boy, only the bust visible, holds an inscription drape. Added drapes record deaths †1708 and †1710. – Sir William Jesson †1719 and family. Ionic pilasters and segmental pediment. Contrasting stones. – Chancel. Katherine Holden †1688, with scrollwork and cherubs' heads. – Oval tablets by *Edward Grubb* to Richard Bisse Riland †1760 and William Ash †1759. – S aisle W. Sir George Sacheverell †1715. By *William Woodman the elder* (GF). Tablet in a rich aedicule with Ionic columns, segmental pediment, urns, cartouche. Below, foliage, flowers, cherubs and a winged skull. – Many simpler tablets. – BRASSES. Chancel, Barbara Eliot †1606 (N), Josias Bull †1621 (S). Small figures, inscription panels.

ALL SAINTS, Four Oaks Road. Brick nave and aisles of 1908 by *E. F. Reynolds*, his first church, with his massive handling already evident: see the heavily buttressed porch and solid bellcote. Alton stone arcades without capitals, and with little pointed arches across the passage aisles. The front piers rise to support the panelled ceiling. Chancel etc. by *Wood, Kendrick & Williams*, 1965, in keeping. The octagonal S vestry with its delightful copper spire and gablets gives the date away. W choir vestry by the same, 1954. – FONT and PEWS of 1908, CHOIR STALLS etc. of 1965. – Hanging ROOD by *John Poole*,

1998. – STAINED GLASS. Aisles, nearly all by *Osmund Caine*, 1992–9, a significant collection. Choir vestry, two by *Yoxall & Whitford*, 1955 and 1961. – MONUMENT. Rev. C.S. James †1931. Designed by *Reynolds*, carver *Bloye*, enamelled shield by *Bernard Cuzner*. – HALL of 1974, N.

EMMANUEL, Birmingham Road, Wylde Green. By *W.H. Bidlake*, 1909; chancel E bay and apse completed 1925–7. Bidlake intended a tower with a short spire over the chancel. The apse is the striking external feature. It has all of Bidlake's refinement and the tall proportions of his later work, but its ancestry is High Victorian: four-sided, with four-light windows under gables. Delicate Geometrical tracery. Tall clerestory windows too, above low, narrow aisles. Bidlake's characteristic triangular wall piers. Round arcade arches. No capitals, but a nice sculptural detail where the cross-arches of the aisle groin-vaults meet the rear of the piers. Hammerbeam roof with pendants and arches between. Small W gallery with vaulted baptistery underneath. Low NE extension, muscular Lady Chapel and simpler parish room, by *George While* (*Bromilow, While & Smeeton*), 1967. – Bidlake fittings: ROOD BEAM and figures, ENGLISH ALTAR with riddel-posts, and FONT of alabaster with green marble free-standing columns, all of 1927; ALTAR RAIL by *Bidlake & Knight*, 1930. PULPIT with tester by *W.J. Knight*, 1938. – STAINED GLASS. S aisle, *Sidney Meteyard* 1935, *A.J. Davies* 1930; N aisle W, *Meteyard* 1938; baptistery 1911.

ST CHAD, Hollyfield Road. 1925–7 by *C.E. Bateman*. A big Hornton stone barn, with wooden mullion-and-transom windows at high level. Extensions by *Batemans*: SW hall 1959, SE chapel 1975. Unfinished W end. The interior is a wonderful surprise. Massive circular arcade piers faced in Hornton rubble stone support a plaster barrel-vault divided into panels by bands of vine trail and ears of corn. – FITTINGS. REREDOS with gilded vine-trail borders, enclosing the E window – the STAINED GLASS and mosaics probably by *James Powell & Sons* – and flanking PAINTINGS of SS Chad and Winifred. – Oak PULPIT with tester; octagonal Cotswold stone FONT.

ST COLUMBA, Chester Road North, Banners Gate. 1957–60 by *N.F. Cachemaille-Day*. A late work, combining innovative use of concrete with the post-war interest in radical Neoclassicism. Light brick with concrete framing. Square, with a Soanian, domical concrete shell-vault on four segmental lunettes. The symmetrical windowless entrance wall also has classical ancestry. Asymmetrically placed bellcote and vestries. ALTAR with three-sided rails, between staircases leading to an upper room (originally Lady Chapel) behind. PULPIT and READING DESK at the staircase corners. – SCULPTURE. Trumpeting angels by *Kathleen Parbury* flank a cross and lead up to an over-life-size Christ in Glory by *A.E. Buss* of *Goddard & Gibbs*. The lunettes have random grilles of concrete and abstract STAINED GLASS, also *Buss*.

ST JAMES, Mere Green Road, Hill. Nave and ritual W tower by *D.R. Hill*, 1834–5, typical of the moment. Rendered, with lancets and thin buttresses. The tower has a crenellated parapet and big pinnacles. Wide nave with queenpost roof. Chancel and transepts by *C.E. Bateman*, 1907–9, his most important early church work. Smooth red Hollington stone. The chancel walls rise sheer, and the s vestry is like a tower house, with chamfered corners and crenellations. Only the transepts have single buttresses. Dec and early Perp tracery, delicately done; the vestry window has a complex arrangement of blank panels, crenellated transom and a vesica-like design at the top. Bateman's interior is plastered, with high windows in the chancel. Leaf friezes run along the walls and around the window reveals, and the pointed barrel-vault ceiling is panelled, with similar ribs (all by the *St George's Guild* of Kings Heath). Bath stone transept arches with mouldings dying into the jambs, and foliage panels on the soffits. The E wall is a decorative ensemble, a theological progress with angels, from Entombment (mosaic by *Powells*) on the ALTAR, to Resurrection on the REREDOS, and Christ in Glory in the richly coloured STAINED GLASS by *Harvey & Ashby*. Flanking saints and patterning. Chancel N window also *Harvey & Ashby*. – Contemporary *Bateman* CHANCEL FITTINGS. – Sumptuous ORGAN CASE and BALCONY of 1919–22 by *Bateman*, with much foliage. – N transept, ENGLISH ALTAR of 1935, also *Bateman*; window above by *Harvey & Ashby*. – N window also theirs, 1909. – FONT. C19, with cover and bracket by the *Birmingham Guild*, 1909. – PEWS by *Bateman*, 1935. – ROYAL ARMS of William IV, small, of *papier mâché*: a rarity. Dated 1835, signed *Jennens & Bettridge*.

ST JOHN THE EVANGELIST, Walmley Road, Walmley. 1843–5. Designed by *H.J.Whitling*, who left the country in 1844 'having got into pecuniary difficulties'; completed, with alterations, by *D.R. Hill*. The Neo-Norman fashion of the 1840s, done with gusto in Staffordshire blue brick with stone dressings (Pevsner: 'a fascinating horror'). Incorrect but splendid w rose window. Triplet E window. Tremendous chancel arch with scallop capitals and disc, zigzag and a kind of billet moulding. Rather thin hammerbeam roof. Large N extension for a new worship space by *K.C.White & Partners*, 1987. The old part, alas, is now subdivided and partitioned. – STAINED GLASS. E window by *William Holland*, 1858, good patterns. Old nave N, *Claude Price*, 1956; the rest mostly 1886–93 by *Jones & Willis*. – MONUMENTS. Tablets in the former chancel, the best to members of the Webster family, †1843–†1856.

ST MICHAEL, Boldmere Road and Church Road, Boldmere. Originally of 1856–7 by *J.F.Wadmore*. S aisle and chapel added by *J.A. Chatwin*, 1895–6. A fire in 1964 left only Wadmore's tower and spire and Chatwin's aisle. The tower is early Dec in Rushall limestone with Hollington stone dressings. Chatwin's aisle follows suit with Geometrical windows. The rest is by *George While* (Bromilow, While & Smeeton), 1966–7, his last major work. Brutalism in dark blue brick. Consistent monk bond. A square block with projecting piers containing slit windows. Inside, a honeycomb concrete roof supported by steel corner piers. Lighting from a narrow clerestory. A building of integrity, but very gloomy. Chatwin's aisle is now meeting rooms. – FURNISHINGS all by *While*. – STAINED GLASS. S chapel E window, *Morris & Co.*, 1912. A lovely piece, with many angels from *Burne-Jones* cartoons. S aisle, all *Ward & Hughes*, †1889, 1892, 1892, 1901 (*T.F. Curtis*); W, also *Curtis*, †1915. Fragments of C19 windows above the altar.

ST PETER, Maney Hill Road, Maney. By *E.C. Bewlay* of *Cossins, Peacock & Bewlay*. The body of the church is Free Perp, of 1904–5. Red and purple-blue brick, and *Doulton*'s grey-buff terracotta. The interior has lighter red brick and Quarella stone from the Forest of Dean. The chancel has a lower sanctuary arch to the E. The ground falls away, so the sanctuary is an impressively blunt mass outside. Octagonal arcade piers, the arch mouldings dying in. These start in stone but carry on in brick. Brick cross-arches in the aisles. Hammerbeam roof. Lady Chapel, N. Fine SW tower and nave W bay added in 1935 by *Peacock & Bewlay* (*Bewlay* and *Edward Berks Norris*). The later date shows in the massive, planar quality. Remarkably unchanged interior, with original FITTINGS; but the TESTER, with rich late medieval decoration, is by *C.E. Bateman*, 1916. – Alabaster REREDOS with reliefs by *Bridgeman & Sons*, 1916. – ORGAN CASE by *Bateman*, 1924. – Lady Chapel REREDOS by *Bateman*, 1933, with paintings by *Sidney Meteyard*; contemporary painted CEILING also *Bateman*'s. – STAINED GLASS. E window (above the sanctuary arch) and apse windows by *William Pearce Ltd*, 1918. Lady Chapel N by *Harvey & Ashby*, 1924. W rose by *Sidney Meteyard*, 1938, the small figures below also probably his. Another *Meteyard* window, 1935, in the porch. – VICARAGE, W, by *Bateman*, 1911–12. Ample, spreading Arts and Crafts Tudor. The front facing the church steps uphill. Five gables behind. Big canted bays pull the elevations together.

Other denominations

HOLY TRINITY (R.C.), Lichfield Road. By *G.B. Cox* (*Harrison & Cox*), 1933–4. Tall and massive tower set above the road. The design veers between Cox's usual round-arched brick style and 'Venetian Gothic', as it was called when the church opened (fussy Italian detailing on the tower). Good sculpted tympana. Inside, moulded pointed arcades without capitals, and a heavy compartmented ceiling. Sanctuary reordering has left only the fine marble floor. – Former SCHOOL behind, simple Tudor Gothic of 1872.

HOLY CROSS AND ST FRANCIS (R.C.), Springfield Road and Signal Hayes Road, Walmley. By *Paul Bonham & Associates*, 1975. Red brick, curving stone narthex. Wide worship space, heavy ceiling beams.

SACRED HEART (R.C.), Lichfield Road, Four Oaks. By *Cyril Horsley* (*Horsley Currall*), 1986. Brick, angular, big monopitch roof.

ST NICHOLAS (R.C.), Jockey Road, Boldmere. 1951–3 by *Victor S. Peel* and *T. Morris*, entrance bay completed 1958 by *Morris & Whitehouse*. The end of Early Christian-cum-Romanesque. Better inside, a hall church with tall arcades and narrow aisles, with nice spatial effects into the chapels.

FOUR OAKS (WESLEYAN) METHODIST CHURCH, Lichfield Road and Four Oaks Road. By *Crouch & Butler*, 1902–9, a stately design on a cruciform plan with a crossing tower. The church of a wealthy suburb, in a commanding position in the fork of the roads, and a wonderful expression of early C20 Nonconformist status and High Wesleyan ideas. Weldon limestone ashlar, with areas of bare stonework and careful control of e.g. buttress stepping. The details Perp, with the many unmistakable licences in tracery and carving of the Arts and Crafts. The interior is more conventional, with arcades of grey Forest of Dean stone. Passage aisles with flying buttresses to the arcades, W gallery with convex buttress-like uprights. The Sunday School projects to the SE. Bay window to the church parlour. N extension by *kke*, 2018, aggressive convex roofs hidden by an awkward screen wall. – Contemporary FURNISHINGS by *Crouch & Butler*, including the PULPIT with a band of fine carving and a marquetry Good Shepherd.

Also by *Crouch & Butler* the former PARSONAGE HOUSE facing Four Oaks Road, 1907–8, Voysey-ish, rendered, with stone-mullioned windows, staircase tower, and doorway with four-centred arch; and a COTTAGE facing Lichfield Road, 1908–9.

METHODIST CHURCH, South Parade. 1936 by the young *George While*, with *W.C. Moss* of *Crouch, Butler & Savage*. The domestic-looking nave is mostly Moss, the powerful brick W tower certainly While's. It rises sheer to a set-off below paired round-headed windows (cf. While's St John, Longbridge, p. 416). – SCHOOLS, S, by *W.H. Martin*, 1926.

BAPTIST CHURCH, Victoria Road. The former Town Primary School. The W building is by *Yeoville Thomason*, 1870–1. Good Ruskinian Gothic, with tall gabled two-light windows and an arcade underneath. Entrance r. with open archway and two-light opening above. Vigorous contrasts of brick and stone. Extensions up Trinity Hill by *E.F. Titley*, 1902. Rebuilt behind by *Brian Bannister & Associates*, 1984–5, a creditable job. Worship space with big cambered laminated trusses. E of Trinity Hill, the former Junior School by *Crouch, Butler & Savage*, 1907, with broad gables, stone banding and square cupola.

CHESTER ROAD BAPTIST CHURCH, on the corner with Boldmere Road. By *F.B. Andrews*, 1912–13. Free Perp, with Bodleyesque tracery in the entrance gable and transept windows. The original touch is the front porch with diagonal buttresses rising to square pinnacles, and flanking brick parts with hipped roofs. CLASSROOMS of 1928, W; gabled link by *Sarum Partnership*, 2003.

UNITED REFORMED CHURCH (formerly Congregational), Brassington Avenue. 1879–80 by *George Ingall*, Gothic with a tower. Sanctuary arch with foliage capitals. Big roof trusses.

WYLDE GREEN UNITED REFORMED CHURCH, Britwell Road. 1904 by *Ingall & Son*. Brick, rather bald. Dec-going-Perp windows.

OSCOTT COLLEGE

ST MARY'S COLLEGE (R.C.), Chester Road, New Oscott. A fascinating place, set in lovely grounds which still keep the traffic at bay and create the feeling of peaceful monastic seclusion, the spiritual cradle of much learning and activity among the newly emancipated Roman Catholics, and an important preaching ground for *A.W.N. Pugin*. Introduced to the college in 1837 by the 16th Earl of Shrewsbury, Pugin made it a centre for his early experiments in ecclesiastical furnishings and the home of a theological library and museum of medieval artefacts. In his first lecture at Oscott as Professor of Ecclesiastical Antiquities, he declared 'Now is the time to direct the attention of all back to days of former glory, and from the inexhaustible source which the talents of the middle ages furnish, draw the materials of all future works.' The original buildings, however, are nearly all the work of *Joseph Potter* of Lichfield as architect and builder, together with *Dr Kirk*, the missioner at Lichfield. They date from 1835–8. The main front, facing sw, is all of red brick with stone dressings and in a basic Tudor style. The central tower has a big oriel window and octagonal staircase turret. Four bays of three storeys with gables to either side. Behind is the cloister, to the r. the chapel and to the l. the refectory and kitchens. The style is plain and pleasant, uncomplicated and not worried by any didactic purpose. The STATUE of the Virgin set high under a magnificent canopy on the terrace in front of the central tower, however, reveals a new intensity and seriousness. It is by *A.W.N. Pugin*, undeniably beautiful and very thoroughly medieval. It is in fact a copy of a German late C15 statue in St Chad's (p. 121). Potter's CLOISTER has two-storey side ranges and a single-storey NE range with four-light windows (glazed in the C20). All plain inside. Behind is the gable of the NORTHCOTE HALL, begun in 1860 by *E.W. Pugin* but not completed until 1879–81 by *P.P. Pugin*. Its roof has timber beams with big braces enclosing open cuspings (ornate Gothic pulpit). Potter's REFECTORY has bay windows with *Hardman* heraldic glass of 1862 etc. The masters' end is divided by a plain four-centred arch and has a heavy fireplace by *E.W. Pugin*.* Tactful Gothic extensions flank the Northcote Hall at the rear: to the NW, the GLANCEY LIBRARY of 1928 by *E. Bower Norris*, with galleried interior (the upper supports are C21); to the SE, common rooms and bedrooms of 1932 by *G.B. Cox*, more massive and up-to-date. Later extensions to the NW including the 1920s INFIRMARY.

---

*Some splendid *A.W.N. Pugin* FURNITURE, in his earlier chunky style and looking exactly like the illustrations in his books, survives in the refectory (tables) and elsewhere.

To the SE, linked by a corridor, the CHAPEL. Here Pugin and Potter coincide. *Potter*'s building, begun in 1836, is a simple rectangle of a Georgian preaching-box with a gallery, with Perp windows, stepped buttresses and a five-sided apse. *Pugin* came to Oscott in 1837 when it was nearly finished. What he did is not clear. According to Greaney's history, 'He at once knocked out the east end wall and inserted the present chancel arch. He added the Apsidal Sanctuary, with its beautiful groined roof.' But Roderick O'Donnell has pointed out that there is no sign of a break in the brickwork. The rib-vault in the apse is certainly *Pugin*, as his drawing survives for the carved angel bosses, which are drawn from the Litany of Our Lady. He decorated the roof, with its shallow pitch and simple trusses, in panels with red central motifs (prominent Ms for Mary) on a blue background: rich glowing colours. The splendour of the chapel is indeed due to its decorations and FURNISHINGS, mostly by *Pugin*, but with a history of reorderings. – REREDOS. A complicated structure of wood, designed to hold works of art that Pugin and Lord Shrewsbury had collected on the Continent. Central tabernacle with a niche for the monstrance and cross. To either side, Flemish C15 painted relief panels, one of the Annunciation and the Nativity, the other of the Magi and St Hubert. Above are Flemish C15 free-standing figures; below, small but fine C16 Limoges enamels in grisaille. The wings have paintings by *J. R. Herbert* of St Augustine and St Athanasius. On the side walls of the apse four Doctors of the Church, also by *Herbert*. – PULPIT. High up on the N side, accessed from behind. Front panels with angels holding scrolls and a cross, decorative canopy, another angel on the corbel beneath. – CHOIR STALLS. The E blocks on either side are by *Pugin*. They incorporate C17 French rear stalls with delightful carved heads on the uprights, with expressions ranging from the devout to the mischievous. W blocks added in 1925, carved by *Ferdinand Stuflesser* of Ortisei. – ALTAR RAILS, now W of the stalls. Flemish Baroque, dated 1680, with swirls of openwork foliage containing figures, and little Ionic pilasters with caryatids between.* – STAINED GLASS. Apse. Designed by *Pugin* and made in 1838 by *Warrington*, the most impressive and ambitious part of the C19 decoration. The central window, Virgin and Child crowned with a glory, 'shows just how quickly Pugin had grasped the essential qualities of the medium, and is a milestone in the history of the revival' (Martin Harrison). Side windows with the twelve Apostles. S windows all by *Hardman*: from the E 1855, 1860, 1867, 1869.

Through an arch to the S, the CHAPEL OF ST GEORGE AND ST PATRICK. ALTAR by *Pugin*, 1842. At the rear a C17 Baroque CONFESSIONAL, brought here by Pugin with the altar rails: lots of fruit, the four Evangelists as caryatids, and

---

*The exceptionally fine Netherlandish eagle LECTERN of *c.* 1500 attributed to *Jehan Aert van Tricht* was sold to the Metropolitan Museum of New York in 1967.

a broken segmental pediment enclosing a cartouche. Beyond, the WEEDALL CHANTRY, by *E.W. Pugin*, 1861–2. Four chapels, two to each side, separated and divided by four-centred arches. – STATUE of Our Lady Seat of Wisdom by *John Hardman Powell*, exhibited at the International Exhibition of 1862. Alabaster, on a stone base with niches containing small statues of Old Testament women. – BRASS to Bishop Milner by *Pugin*, 1841, the metalwork by *Hardmans*. His first important attempt at a revived medieval brass, based on that to Bishop Trillek †1360 in Hereford Cathedral. Figure under a cusped and sub-cusped arch, with pinnacles. – Behind the statue, small brasses by Hardmans, of 1867 etc., originally on a painted MORTUARY TREE, with branches to either side. – Much *Hardman* glass of the 1860s and later.

Two very attractive LODGES by *Pugin*, each with an arched gateway in a gabled structure built in red brick and stone: on Chester Road, *c.*1839–40, with a central niche containing a statue of the Virgin, and a simpler building on Court Lane, dated 1838.

PUBLIC BUILDINGS

COUNCIL HOUSE AND TOWN HALL, King Edward Square. The Council House, l., was built as a hotel in 1865 by *Edward Holmes*. Extended 1869 by *Holmes* and 1889 by *William Jenkins* (the three-storey block, r., next to the Town Hall). Brick Gothic. Big Geometrical window over the entrance, divided by a stepped-up brick part where the staircase rises. Show elevation at the back, with polychromatic stone windows and triangular dormers. Holmes's fantastic central spire has been cut down. The council bought it in 1901, added the porch, and heightened a section to its r. Converted to flats 2014–17 by *Holloway Foo*, with a S extension, painfully dominating at the back. The Town Hall was added in 1905–6 by *Arthur R. Mayston* (*Mayston & Eddison*). Neo-Wren in brick and Monks' Park (Bath) stone. Single-storey front with triplet windows divided by Doric columns, and a balustrade. The tower rises sheer to a banded brick and stone clock stage, and a small lantern and dome, a convincing silhouette. The assembly room has a shallow barrel-vault and pilasters with garlands and cartouches. Supper room, similar but simpler, with a pedimented aedicule above the fireplace. N extension by *Tom Porter*, Borough Surveyor (head architect *Graham Jones*), 1964–5, when the domed porch was alas removed from the frontage.

SUTTON COLDFIELD COTTAGE HOSPITAL, Birmingham Road. Basic r. wing by *E.F. Titley*, 1897 and 1907; l. wing, minimal Tudor by *Buckland & Haywood-Farmer*, 1907–8. Stripped Tudor central tower and rear extensions by *Bateman & Bateman*, 1923–4.

GOOD HOPE HOSPITAL, Rectory Road, ½ m. E. A house by *Yeoville Thomason*, 1882, now demolished, was extended as a convalescent home and then a hospital from 1943. Much extended from 1963 by *S.N. Cooke & Partners*, including the seven-storey Richard Salt Unit of 1971. Recent developments are by *Highbury Design*: ward block, 2011; critical care centre, 2015.

MUNICIPAL ELECTRICITY WORKS (former), Coleshill Road and Riland Road. By the engineer *W.C.C. Hawtayne*, 1901. The generating hall survives, with large iron windows, and offices on the corner.

CEMETERY, Rectory Road. Laid out in 1880. LODGE and LYCH-GATE by *T.W. Cutler*, in Norman Shaw's Old English manner. Small timber-framed mortuary chapel.

CREMATORIUM, Tamworth Road, 3 m. NE. 1964 by *Tom Porter*, Borough Surveyor. Low, brick. Chapel with laminated trusses.

BISHOP VESEY'S GRAMMAR SCHOOL, Lichfield Road. Founded 1527, near Holy Trinity. The present school starts with the five-bay Georgian house facing the road, of 1728–9. Segment-headed windows, their keystones meeting the string courses. Ground floor extended in the C19. Three gables behind, and an extension by *G.T. Robinson*, 1859–61, with narrow gabled bays. This has mostly been swallowed up in the large S extension by *Jethro Cossins*, of 1886–7. Queen Anne style, with shaped gables. Windows with broken pediments and rubbed brick lintels and aprons. It runs back E and ends in a little tower. Extensions further E by *A.C. Bunch*, Warwickshire County Architect, 1938–9. Neo-Georgian gone *Moderne*. Science and mathematics block by *rja*, 2016. Monopitch roof.

SUTTON COLDFIELD GRAMMAR SCHOOL FOR GIRLS, Jockey Road. By *A.C. Bunch*, Warwickshire County Architect, 1929, extended 1938–9. Long Neo-Georgian front with pedimented centre. Many additions.

Sutton Coldfield, cemetery lodge.
Perspective drawing and plans, 1880

SUTTON COLDFIELD, Railway Road. 1884 for the London & North Western Railway. Lofty booking hall with classical doorcases. A covered footbridge leads to the Birmingham platform, with original wooden buildings and canopy.

SUTTON PARK. A large area (over 2,200 acres) of heathland and woods W of the town centre. A deer park within Sutton Chase, mentioned in 1126 when Henry I gave the manor to Roger de Newburgh, Earl of Warwick, it passed to the Warden and Society in the charter of 1528. Encroachments since the C16 have reduced the original area. The extensive archaeology includes a well-preserved 1½-m.-long stretch of the Ryknield Street ROMAN ROAD, built in the C1 as a military road between forts at Metchley (p. 376) and Wall (near Lichfield, Staffs.). Intermittent side ditches flank the *agger* (raised road surface), composed of gravel, which is exposed in places. The gravel surface was derived from quarry pits, visible beyond the ditches. The ensemble of *agger*, ditches and pits is clearest near Lord Donegal's Ride and across the nearby golf course, and in woodland E of Streetly Gate. Also many BOUNDARY BANKS AND DITCHES. The C12 deer-park boundary, along the present SW, W and N boundaries, is visible from Streetly Lane to Chester Road North. The POOLS were made for fish, and later for mills. All have substantial dams.* Few significant buildings. TOWN GATE, at the end of Park Road, has early C20 timber-framed lodges. MIDLAND LODGE, with timber gables, ½ m. further NW, is by *William Jenkins*, 1880. The thatched timber SHELTERS which were a feature of the park have nearly all disappeared. PARK HOUSE, near Town Gate, was a mill house, rebuilt in the C18. The big extensions, timber gables and former entrance tower, are of 1899–1900 by *E.F. Titley*. At Bracebridge Pool is an early C19 COTTAGE ORNÉ with bargeboarded gables and ogee-headed doorway, hugely extended for a restaurant.

VESEY COTTAGES

The simple houses of local sandstone must date from between 1527 and *c.* 1543, when according to Leland, Vesey built 'dyvars praty howsys of stone in the forest, and plantyd his pore kynesmen in them'. Of fifty-one cottages, five survive. They have walling of roughly squared blocks, dressed quoins, and doorways with flattened four-centred arches. First-floor access is by a spiral staircase round a stone newel. Collar-beam roofs, with a curious weakness where the collar is mortised into the principal rafters near where these are cut for the purlins. The OLD STONE HOUSE in Maney Hill Road is the largest. Two rooms on each floor, divided by studded partitions. Original window openings. The W gable retains most of a projecting chimneystack with characteristic asymmetrical weatherings.

---

*POWELL'S POOL was made by Sir Thomas Holte *c.* 1730; in 1733 John Wyatt erected a mill here to carry out experiments in spinning cotton.

Doorway with chamfered arch; another blocked doorway opposite it. The first floor has a screen of good oak panelling. WARREN HOUSE FARM on Walmley Road, 1½ m. SE, is much extended, with a S wing which may originally have been a granary. Chimneystack again with asymmetrical weatherings. STONE HOUSE, on Wylde Green Road near New Hall Mill, has three surviving windows with replaced mullions. VESEY GRANGE in Weeford Road, 2¼ m. NE, has been roughcast, and is much altered and extended. The cottage is the S part, with the staircase at the SE corner. Lower N part, timber-framed and probably C17, perhaps originally a barn. HIGH HEATH COTTAGE, 1¾ m. ENE, is the smallest survivor, with just one room on each floor. Stair at the SE corner, its small window just l. of the door. Brick N extension, now cut back.

PERAMBULATIONS

1. The old town, and Anchorage Road

The start is the roundabout where High Street, Mill Street and Coleshill Street meet. C18 and older buildings on the S were replaced in 1936–9 by the formal VESEY GARDENS, designed by *C.E. Bateman* with the Borough Surveyor *Tom Porter*. At the top, a double staircase to a balcony and wrought-iron gates to Holy Trinity churchyard (p. 438). CHURCH HILL, along the SW side, has the cottagey SONS OF REST, by *Batemans*, 1939–40. The E side starts with one of *T.B. Whinney*'s earliest designs for the Midland Bank, 1902, picturesquely combining a half-timbered gable and a Baroque corner clock tower. No. 2 High Street is mid-C18. Doorcase with consoles and inset cornice. Then COLESHILL STREET begins, with Nos. 1–5, rebuilt *c.* 1748 for Richard Riland. First a six-bay house with giant end pilasters, fancy windows and a swept-up parapet. Inside, C18 dado panelling and staircase. Outbuildings beyond, converted to houses probably in the early C19. Inside the cartway arch a blocked mullioned window, remains of a late medieval or C16 stone house, later an inn (the Swan). S of the church on the W side, No. 16 is Tudor Gothic of *c.* 1844. Splendid imported panelling in the dining room. Mostly C16, perhaps Flemish, with pilasters, portrait heads in profile in roundels, geometric shapes, vases of fruit, and beasts. By the window C16 linenfold. C17 overmantel with Ionic columns, fan-headed niches and delicate figure sculpture. C18 dado of fielded panels round the entrance hall, probably former box pews. Opposite, Nos. 43–45, ALBION HOUSE, sandstone ashlar, Late Georgian, windows with architraves on consoles. Nos. 47–49 have an Early Victorian Tudor front but three parallel rear wings, late C17 or early C18. At Nos. 57–59, C19 brick (laid surprisingly in monk bond), hides a two-bay timber-framed hall house, probably C16. A rare original smoke-hood survives in No. 57 (panelled in). Lower down, the KING'S ARMS by *Batemans*, 1935. Half-butterfly plan.

Now back N, to HIGH STREET. The narrow street with its plain Georgian brick houses is much more like a small Staffordshire town – Brewood or Gnosall – than a Warwickshire one; but it also has affinities with Birmingham architecture of the C18. On the corner of Midland Drive, E side, a former Lloyds Bank, slightly French with channelled rustication, and two shops with big square bays, all by *J.A. Chatwin & Son*, 1900–2. Opposite, No. 1 has a mid-C18 seven-bay front with console doorcase, moulded string and delicate cornice set in. It masks the former White Hart inn, 'being built' in 1619. Its sandstone N wall is visible, and parts of the S wall (with the end of a demolished cottage). It replaced in turn a timber-framed building, probably C16, of which the NW corner survives. VESEY HOUSE started as 'the Brick House' in 1634, still visible in the courtyard and at the rear. Late Georgian or Early Victorian refronting in the Jacobean fashion, with three narrow canted bays. In 1933–4 *A.J. White & Styles* converted the ground floor into shops and reduced the bays to oriels. Restoration and rear extension by *Roy Thornton*, 1987–9. The main first-floor room has full-height square panelling with a decorative frieze, and a stone fireplace. Overmantel with short tapering pilasters (the panels between are modern) and a frieze of affronted beasts. Nos. 9 and 11, plain Georgian. No. 20, opposite, is the loveliest house in the street, similar to houses begun in 1697 in Old Square, Birmingham. Four narrow bays, giant end pilasters, steep roof with dormers. Moulded window architraves, the ground-floor ones linked to the string above; round-arched doorway with eared architrave. Fine C18 wrought-iron railings. (Original staircase, panelled front room.) The THREE TUNS, W side, has a plain rendered five-bay front of *c.* 1820–30 with a central carriage arch, but the different rear wings indicate an earlier building, at least C18. The former smoke room retains an C18 buffet. Brick-vaulted cellars.

Diagonally opposite, No. 36 (CULL'S HOUSE). A five-bay Baroque front in red brick with sandstone details: swept-up parapet and odd windows with pediment-like heads broken by the keystones. Doorcase with swan's-neck pediment (cf. William Westley's now demolished houses in Temple Row, Birmingham, 1719). A date *c.* 1720–40 would fit well. It hides a C16 or C17 stone house, perhaps originally two. Timber-framed rear wing with square panels, perhaps contemporary with other C17 survivals: a basement stair with fret-cut balusters, and in a first-floor room, now an extended landing, a three-centred timber barrel-vault with a primitive acanthus frieze. C19 armorial glass in the window below. The main staircase looks later C18, with ornate octagonal newels and delicate balusters. No. 38 must be slightly later, as it borrows a pilaster for symmetry. Four bays and one giant pilaster, l. No. 44, Late Georgian with plain end pilasters. No. 46 has a three-storey mid-Georgian front: windows with lintels incorporating keystones. Some earlier timbering inside. Then a picturesque group including a cottage flying over an alley. Last on this side, No. 56, mid-C18, five bays plus one with a carriage arch, r. Again moulded lintels, and platbands. The ROYAL HOTEL opposite (currently 'The Townhouse') begins with the grand but unsophisticated house of *c.* 1751, r. Seven bays, the central three awkwardly narrower, and under a gable. Segment-headed windows with moulded heads, and circular windows too. The l. range, pub-classical below, is by *Robert F. Matthews*, 1896.* Assembly hall behind by *Thomas G. Price*, 1897, with a Jacobean-ish doorcase.

The old centre ends at the railway bridge. Beyond is LICH-FIELD ROAD. Set back on the W side the POLICE STATION and former MAGISTRATES' COURT (now SUTTON MASJID) by *G.R. Barnsley*, Warwickshire County Architect (group architect *E.H. Thurlow*), 1958–60. Long, low, formal not-quite-Modernism. On the E side, after late C20 blocks for Birmingham Metropolitan College, MOAT HOUSE. Built almost certainly by *Sir William Wilson* for himself, probably shortly after his wife's death in 1697. Five bays, two storeys. Giant Corinthian pilasters to the ends and the central bay. Balustraded parapet which rises up as a central round-headed Doric aedicule. Original cross-windows survive on the side; C18 sashes on the front. Wilson liked giant orders; he used one at Hall Green church (p. 309) of 1703. The rear elevation, with semicircular-headed dormers and a steeply pedimented centre, is more old-fashioned. The l. front bay and the semicircular bow to the rear were added probably shortly after 1794, in the austere manner associated with Samuel Wyatt. Entrance hall with an C18 fireplace and fielded panelling. The room to the r. has finer panelling and a fireplace with eared architrave. Open-string staircase with turned balusters and moulded handrail. STABLES beyond, with the same concave-sided gables Wilson used on Four Oaks Hall (p. 456), and some altered C18 cottages.

Next the former CATHOLIC CHURCH of 1834, pre-Puginian Gothic: Y-tracery windows, ogee-arched doorcase and rather Jacobean fat cut-down pinnacles. Plain classical PRESBYTERY attached at the side. The former TECHNICAL SCHOOL immediately N is a lovely Neo-William-and-Mary design by *Crouch & Butler*, 1903. Brick, hipped roof, cupola. Sashes in relieving arches, stone panels with garlands above. Converted to housing, 2020. Then Bishop Vesey's Grammar School (p. 448). Opposite, semi-detached Gothic villas of Wellington Terrace, completed by 1885, and Holy Trinity R.C. church (p. 443). Then late C19 houses on either side, the E ending with an emphatic Gothic terrace with huge Neo-Elizabethan chimneys, and a corner house by *Thomas Guest*, 1889–90, with octagonal turret and spire.

ANCHORAGE ROAD, developed by Richard Sadler from 1870, runs W here. First a good early C20 group. On the N side two late Arts and Crafts designs, No. 10 by *W.J. Davis*, 1923–5, and No. 12 by *C.F. Marston*, 1923. No. 14, 1905, *George*

---

*The lunettes had delightful painted-glass scenes of sportsmen, footballers and rowers; destroyed in the late C20.

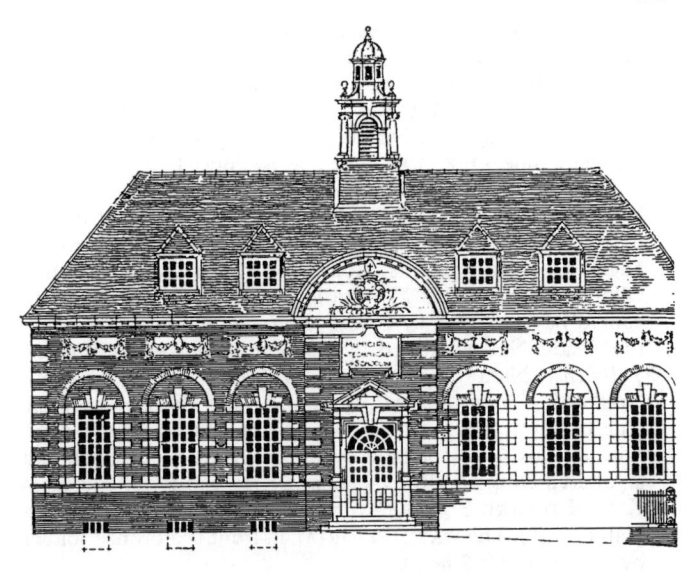

Sutton Coldfield, Technical School.
Elevation drawing, 1903

E. Pepper's attractive but slightly coarse version of Bidlake or Bateman's manner. No. 16, altered, is by *Ewen & J.A. Harper*, 1906. On the S side No. 1, 1902–3, *Marston & Healey* at their best: dark roughcast, a little timbering, and a picturesque corner tower with a splay-footed spire. No. 3, by *C.E. Bateman*, 1903, rendered, is petite but quirky.

MULROY ROAD branches off W here. On the N side, timbered houses of 1922–3, No. 2 by *Harry Weedon*, No. 4 by *C.F. Marston*. No. 12, BARN HOUSE, is a country cottage in old brick by *Bateman & Bateman*, 1925. No. 14 is by *Tanner & Horsburgh*, 1927. No. 22 is brick Tudor by *Scott & Weedon*, 1914. On the S side, No. 11, with a big dormer trying to grow into a tower, is by *Arthur Edgerton Leeson*, 1920–1, extended on both sides. No. 15 is by *J.H. Sellers* of Manchester, 1925–6, built for the estranged wife of his former partner Edgar Wood. Rather dour, asymmetrical but with a classicizing centre, minimal pilasters and pediment.

Back in Anchorage Road, curving S towards the centre, Nos. 5–7 are *Bateman* again, 1903–4. One of his semi-detached pairs designed to look like a single house, in a Midlands or Cotswold manor-house tradition. Dark roughcast front, brick at the rear. Carefully random windows, with blunt stone bays below. No. 7 was Bateman's own house. Opposite, No. 18, render and timber, by *Everard Healey*, 1907. No. 20, rendered with paired gables, is by *L. Collier*, 1904–5. No. 22 of 1901–2, and No. 24, dated 1903, are a remarkable near-mirror pair, tall, gabled, rendered, with aware details like No. 22's Mackintoshy oriel, but also something European: Douglas Hickman wrote of their 'Austrian flavour ... as if they have slipped out of a book by Hermann Muthesius'. Often attributed to Bateman or Buckland & Haywood-Farmer, they are by *Marston & Healey*. On the w side, OAKHURST, the biggest house here, by *William Jenkins*, 1896. Hard red brick banded in blue, timber gables, big canted bay with frilly iron cresting. Extension set back l. dated 1909, by *Crouch, Butler & Savage*, with a porch in the angle. Opposite, the first houses on the road: four Gothic villas of 1872–3. THE MANSE is Neo-Wren but with severe canted bays, of 1911 by *Crouch, Butler & Savage*. Beyond on the w side, Nos. 44–46, gristly Jacobean of 1895–6 by *Matthew J. Butcher*; No. 48 of 1891 by *Roger Harley*; No. 50, Arts and Crafts by *William J. Davis*, 1913; and more *Butcher*, a Gothic pair of 1896 and a mongrel design of 1894–5. Beyond the railway, Nos. 62–64 of 1899 by *E.F. Titley*, nastily treated; and an altered Domestic Revival house by *Titley* of 1896. This faces KING EDWARD SQUARE, with the Council House and Town Hall (p. 447). The WAR MEMORIAL in front is a bronze soldier by *Francis Doyle-Jones*, 1922.

2. Parade and Birmingham Road

From the roundabout at the Vesey Gardens, MILL STREET descends s. The w side is nearly all a big office development of 1989–92 by *Weedon Partnership* in basic traditional styles. It retains the front of the former Post Office, by *Essex & Goodman*, 1909. Opposite, the former parish workhouse of 1739, recast with Tudoresque detail in 1886–8. The Masonic Hall beyond was built as the Town Hall. By *George Bidlake*, 1858–9. Italian Gothic in red brick with dressings of coloured brick, tile and Box Ground stone. Big paired and triplet lancets. Most unfortunately its s tower, which had a French pavilion roof, was cut down in the 1970s. The GATE INN opposite, *c.* 1880, has slim colonnettes dividing the ground floor. Restrained brick rear extension by *Arthur Edwards*, 1922–3. To the w, Station Street leads to the railway and the STATION pub of *c.* 1884, recast by *William Jenkins*, 1898–1900.

PARADE, s of Mill Street, was redeveloped in the later C20. The ring road to E and w is part of *Max Lock & Partners*' plan of 1962. To the w, the uninspired GRACECHURCH CENTRE shopping precinct by *Harry Weedon & Partners*, 1969–74. LOWER PARADE immediately to its E, with the former schools, now Baptist church, at the N end (p. 444), has a low McDonalds by the *Seymour Harris Partnership*, 1985. Then a retail block, with the LIBRARY at the rear, by *James A. Roberts Associates*, 1974. Further s, the NEWHALL WALK shopping centre, neo-traditional with a little clock tower at the far end, by *Leslie Jones*, 1995–6. Decorative metal trusses across the side passage by *James Blunt*.

Beyond the ring road to the s, older shops, e.g. a former Co-operative shop and hall by *C.F. Marston*, 1915, on the corner of Holland Street, E side. The BOTTLE OF SACK pub opposite is an extended house of 1895 by *Titley & Jones*. BIRMINGHAM ROAD beyond has a scatter of worthwhile buildings. LLOYDS BANK, E side, is a former Birmingham Corporation gas office, Neo-Georgian of 1932 by *Peacock & Bewlay*. On the w side, the former CUP INN by *Robert F. Matthews*, 1894, timber-gabled, a very early 'reformed' pub. Much extended by *Cemka Group*, 2013. Then the Cottage Hospital, E side (p. 447). On the w side after the shops, No. 50, Arts and Crafts brick by *Crouch & Butler*, 1902–3. In While Road opposite, Nos. 7–9, also *Crouch & Butler*, 1900–1, with a pent-roofed porch with long brackets linking its canted bays. Nos. 62–64 Birmingham Road (VESEY MANOR) is a substantial farmhouse, probably early C17. Sandstone ashlar. Three gables with finials and kneelers, the details reminiscent of the Sacheverell work at New Hall (p. 463). Attic windows under short moulded strings rather than hoodmoulds. The l. bay is C19. Made into two houses by a builder, E.J. Charles, in 1900, probably with *Arthur McKewan* as architect. The charming ogee-roofed porches, bow windows and first-floor casements are his; also the internal doorcases with slim pilasters hinting at Mackintosh, and the heavy but impressive staircase. Fine imported late C18 fireplace with a relief of Cupid and Psyche. The ODEON (currently EMPIRE) cinema opposite is by *J. Cecil Clavering* for *Harry Weedon*, 1935–6, one of the finest of the chain. Brick slab tower to the l., enclosing a tile-clad fin which originally rose higher. To the r. the round-ended staircase, with the taller brick auditorium behind. Tower and staircase block are linked by the curving foyer. Interior much altered. No. 66, w side, originally single-storeyed and timber-framed, was bulkily rebuilt by Charles in 1899–1900. The timber-framed No. 68 survives, much restored. Beyond Church Road the OLD SMITHY. A much-altered two-bay cruck cottage of 1442–4 (felling dates); the truss facing the road replaced by a C17 sandstone wall with an C18 brick gable. The w truss is intact behind, the blades joined by a ridge-piece. The cruck trusses are wind-braced to the purlins. C17 NW wing with tie- and collar-beam trusses. Brick NE extension 1898, further extended 1966.

MANEY HILL ROAD runs E here. On the s side the Old Stone House, one of the Vesey cottages (p. 449). Behind it, the COOPER MEMORIAL HOME, just cottages with an eyebrow dormer, by *Arthur Edwards*, 1920–1; to the E, St Peter's vicarage and church (p. 443). Back on Birmingham Road, w side, the HORSE AND JOCKEY pub, with big timber gables, is by *Matthew J. Butcher*, 1905–6. In Pilkington Avenue, running SE here, No. 37, late brick Arts and Crafts by *Holland W. Hobbiss*, 1932. Extended at both ends.

DRIFFOLD, the road running NW behind the Old Smithy, is the best place to study *Crouch & Butler*: inventive, picturesque, using materials with skill, certainly Arts and Crafts but, compared to Bidlake or Bateman, overladen with features and half-timbering. The first three are of 1898–9. N of the railway on the S corner of Digby Road, SEVEN GABLES, Joseph Crouch's own house, with lots of studding and a brick porch-tower with a little corner oriel. On the N corner opposite, a house with louder timbering and symmetrical wings with two-storey bays. No. 14 next door, TOP O' THE HILL, was Edmund Butler's house. A heavily timbered projecting wing with a canted end pulls together a more casual range, r., with a decorative timber gable, and a set-back brick range running l. No. 12, WYNDHURST, 1900, has a big half-timbered l. wing balanced by a brick one r. Opposite, Nos. 11–13, a crusty brick pair of 1879, where the very young *Joseph Crouch* may have been involved. Tile-hung gables, aggressive triangular gablets over the ground-floor windows. Nos. 7–9 are *Crouch & Butler* again, 1895. Brick with semicircular gables, timbered side wings with early eyebrow dormers. Big villa opposite, *c.* 1880, with timber gables. Ahead, Manor Drive leads to THE MANOR, on the site of the medieval manor house. C17, stone, with C19 brick-and-render extensions in front. Manor Hill runs E from near here, back to the town centre.

3. Four Oaks

1 m. NNW of the centre. The important area architecturally is FOUR OAKS PARK, a private estate. It was the grounds of Four Oaks Hall, built *c.* 1700 by *Sir William Wilson* for Simon Luttrell, a rather old-fashioned house with shaped gables at each end. It was recast in the early C18 in Palladian style with corner towers, and demolished in 1895, after the estate was purchased for development by Hubert de Burgh-Canning, 2nd Marquess of Clanricarde. Purchasers of individual plots had to agree to spend a minimum amount on construction (depending on the size of the plot) and to observe a building line. Building carried on until the 1920s. Many houses were demolished from the 1960s, including *Lethaby*'s The Hurst. The estate was declared a conservation area in 1986, but its character is still being eroded. Many houses have been replaced by badly proportioned and inflated 'traditional' designs.

The start is the Methodist church (p. 444). NW up FOUR OAKS ROAD, on the NE side, No. 12, WESTMOOR, by *W.J. Davis*, 1900, a minor architect managing Arts and Crafts severity. Davis's No. 5 opposite, of 1922, jams together a big asymmetrical gable and a full-height canted bay. No. 7 is *Cleland & Hayward*, 1925, conventional, timbered. No. 9 is by *Holland W. Hobbiss*, 1919, casually and functionally composed. No. 15, balancing a gable with central chimney and a two-storey curved bay, is by *J.P. Osborne*, 1910. No. 17, *George DeVall*, 1906, old-fashioned; No. 19, *W. De Lacy Aherne*, 1900–1, not inspired. Then two of *Crouch & Butler*'s finest houses, both of 1900, both roughcast. No. 21, AVONCROFT, is L-shaped, tall and compact. E wing close-studded, with a chimney up the gable; S wing plainer, with a ground-floor bay and a sundial inscribed 'I Count the Sunny Hours'. In the angle the porch, and a tower with a curvy parapet and finial. Coachhouse to r. At the l. side a curving buttress, one of a pair framing the garden front and its veranda. Big through entrance hall with stone fireplace and stairs rising up through a typical screen. Dining room with wide inglenook (1950s panelling here and in the hall). No. 23, CRESSINGTON, down a drive, is similar in style and again L-shaped. Large s extension by *Ewen Harper, Bro. & Co.*, 1921, with close studding. The garden front's most original feature, the door enclosed in a swelling chimney-breast, is now masked by an extended veranda. Good staircase.

In HARTOPP ROAD, off to the SW, No. 1, REDLANDS, an important house by *C.E. Bateman*, 1903–4. Old orange-brown bricks, said to come from the owner Frank Parkes's previous house in Northumberland. 'Mr Bateman has eschewed anything like a conscious feature ... He has relied on the dignity which is always secured by a long level roof' (Lawrence Weaver). Flush casement windows. Stables at right angles, forming a forecourt. Two unequal gabled wings, the r. one with the single architectural feature, a barrel-vaulted porch extended into a Serliana, with fluted Doric columns. SW end extended by *Bateman*, 1930. Behind the stables an octagonal dovecote. The garden front has been altered; before 1930 there was just the l. of the two full-height projections, with shaped gables and relief patterns in the brickwork. Large hall, with reused C17 panelling, and a frieze of leaves and arches linked by a ribbon. Angular geometric motifs on the doors. The main rooms face the garden. Stone fireplaces in dining room and drawing room; the latter has a heavy compartmented ceiling. The staircase starts with a short flight and turns into a dog-leg. Lovely slim balusters.

Opposite, No. 4, brick and render, by *E.F. Titley*, 1905–6, and No. 6, BRIARWOOD, extravagantly timbered, by *Cossins, Peacock & Bewlay*, 1896, with stables, r. (No. 6A). No. 7, YEW TREES, is by *Harry Weedon*, 1923. No. 9, WICKHAM, is by *E.F. Reynolds*, 1920. Roughcast, almost symmetrical, with variations on hipped roofs: see the tiny gablets on the ends.

Now back down Four Oaks Road, and SW along LUTTRELL ROAD. On the NW, Nos. 2 and 4 (extended), both *Titley*, 1910, brick. Opposite, No. 5 by *Owen Parsons*, 1927–8. No. 9 by *Hobbiss*, 1923, a good roughcast design spoilt by a huge recent garage. Panelling and a piecrust moulding on the front gable.* No. 8, HOLLINGTON, opposite, *F.W.B. Yorke*, 1924–5, smoothly Tudor. No. 10 is *Hobbiss*, 1924. No. 11, CARHAMPTON HOUSE, opposite, is announced by a pair of C18 sandstone gatepiers, probably from Four Oaks Hall, as are the reused bricks of *C.E. Bateman*'s house of 1902. A lovely piece of Arts and Crafts Neo-Georgian. Symmetrical, except for the off-centre pedimented Ionic doorcase. Carefully articulated by

---

**Hobbiss's No. 7, Neo-Georgian of 1927–8, was scandalously demolished in 2017.

varied window size and spacing (the window r. of the door is an addition). Hipped and sprocketed roof. The garden front varies the same idea, with wider central windows than those at the sides. Open and closed loggias on the SW side. Staircase with tapering balusters and swept-up rail. Panelling in the W corner, formerly a separate room; Ionic pilasters framing the fireplace. The morning room has reused C18 panelling and delicate plasterwork. No. 15 is by *W.J. Davis*, 1912–13. Opposite, two houses by *Crouch & Butler*, in grey roughcast: No. 16, 1907, and No. 18, ARDENCOTE, 1906, with a red brick chimney.

Beyond is a junction of roads, and the Tennis Club. First s down Hartopp Road for No. 34, by *W.R. Lethaby & J.L. Ball*, 1905, the former stables and coachhouse for *Lethaby*'s The Hurst (1893–4, demolished). Single storey plus attics, with an asymmetrical gable. Tactful extension, r. Then back and E along BRACEBRIDGE ROAD. No. 57, KENWOOD, set back in extensive grounds, is by *Harry Weedon*, 1927. Smooth late Arts and Crafts. Opposite, No. 16 is by *Owen Parsons*, 1900. No. 14 (HAWKESFORD, now SWANSTON HALL) is by *C.E. Bateman*, 1902, for his father. Like Carhampton House, this is Neo-Georgian, of reused brick, with a symmetrical seven-bay front and hipped roof with central and side chimneys. But the centre is a full-height canted bay, the entrance on the E side: a very Arts and Crafts transposition. No. 12 is by *Edward Haywood-Farmer* for himself, of 1902–3. A fine but angular design, with four different steeply pitched gables. Delightful coachhouse of 1905–6, r. Opposite, No. 51, WOODSIDE, by *W.H. Bidlake*, 1897, a slightly experimental design. Brick, diversified by render in the main gable, a long ground-floor timber projection, l., and a little timber side gable poking out behind the main one. On the corner of Ladywood Road, part of the shell of No. 22 (REDCROFT, later ST WINNOW), one of *Bidlake*'s greatest houses, of 1901, treated at length in Muthesius's *Das englische Haus*. Despite neglect and a devastating fire in 2015, it is still possible to appreciate the drama of the N front, with the sheer gable of the E wing, its first floor kept windowless, set originally against a sweeping roof and timber porch.

N along LADYWOOD ROAD, on the E side, No. 19, by *Bateman*, 1907, but reduced to a single storey. Opposite, No. 18 by *Hobbiss*, rather colonial. L-shaped, rendered, but with brick pilasters. Narrow asymmetrical entrance front with an Ionic porch. Then a group by *Weedon*: No. 16 of 1926, rendered, with waney-edged gables; No. 14, also 1926, timbered (much extended); No. 11 opposite, 1923, also restlessly gabled, but all brick. No. 9, brick with a timber porch, is by *J.B. Surman*, 1924–5. Going s, past the ruin of No. 22, No. 21, simple brick Tudor by *Crouch & Butler*, 1909–10; No. 25, render with brick treated like pilasters, by *A.A. Simpson*, 1926–8; and No. 27, as good as recent 'traditional' designs here get, by *Swan Architects*, 2015. On the fork with Hartopp Road, WOODGATE, 1897: *W.H. Bidlake*'s own house, and his first in the spare style, influenced by Midlands C16 and C17 manor houses, of his maturity. Brick, with some render on the ground floor. Typical Arts and Crafts plan, one room deep, the main rooms facing s. The entrance front has a slim three-storey stair-tower and a lower, asymmetrical gable to its l. To the r. the roof sweeps down to a timber porch. A long dormer lights the landing. The s front is quieter, with two broad gabled bays rising through the roof. Blunt chimneys, one on the s stepped. At the s end of HARTOPP ROAD, a run of the more conventional early houses: Nos. 50 and 46 by *Titley*, 1901; No. 48 by *Thomas G. Price*, 1902; No. 42 by *Titley & Jones*, 1891–2.

Now back to Bracebridge Road and E. On the s side No. 35, BRYN TEG, by *Bateman*, 1904. All faced in stone slates – a mixture of Hollington, Grinshill and Penkridge, beautifully laid in diminishing courses – over a brick base: a remarkable sight. Four carefully grouped gables. The garden front contrasts a big curved bay with offset overhanging gable, and long lines of windows. A deep band of slates sweeps across between the floors, with the windows first recessed, then flush, above and below. The source is Voysey (Norney, particularly the preliminary design of 1897, and Greyfriars). Also a hint, perhaps, of Frank Lloyd Wright. No. 8 opposite is by *Owen Parsons*, 1929, rendered, with a timber-framed bay with brick infill. No. 25, HINDECLIFFE, is an accomplished early house by *Parsons*, of 1905–6. A complex composition with a l. wing pushing out of a taller bay behind, and a balancing wing r. Rendered over a brick ground floor. Stable wing l. with a big eyebrow dormer. Further E, on the N side, tall timber-gabled villas of 1899–1900, for *George Barker*, a consulting engineer, designed either by him or his builder *Benjamin Dyke*. Opposite, No. 6, HOLMWOOD, big and much timbered, by *Titley*, 1899–1900; and No. 4, a heavyweight bungalow probably by *John W. Wilson*, 1934. No. 2, THE DENE, is *Bidlake*'s earliest house here, 1895–6, still in a refined Norman Shaw style.

99

Sutton Coldfield, Four Oaks, Hindecliffe.
Perspective drawing, 1906

Tile-hanging, big timbered gable, plain inset entrance tower. Its little timber gable is set picturesquely inside the parapet, topped with an arty finial. Back to the cross-roads, where WENTWORTH ROAD, S, has No. 7, a plain job by *Crouch, Butler & Savage*, 1920–1. Nos. 9 and 11 are more George Barker houses, of 1901. No. 15 is by *Cossins, Peacock & Bewlay*, 1907–8, harled *à la* Mackintosh, the angled staircase in dark sandstone. At the end, No. 25, cool Tudor Revival by *Cleland & Hayward*, 1923 (extended r.). To the N, Wentworth Road has two timber-gabled villas by *F.B. Andrews*, No. 16, 1906–7, and No. 14, 1905. No. 5 opposite, brick with a stair-turret, is by *Cecil E.M. Fillmore*, 1926–7. No. 3, SILVERBIRCH, rendered with a big timbered wing, is by *W.J. Davis*, 1926–7. Opposite again, No. 10, SUNNYCROFT, is by *Titley*: half-timbered end gables, central porch. No. 1, and No. 4 opposite, are of 1892 by *Titley & Jones*. Finally No. 2, *Titley*, 1898–9, plain brick, but already much smoother and more contemporary-looking. Beyond, the Methodist church.

On the W side of LICHFIELD ROAD S from the church, No. 147, hidden away, is the former lodge of Doe Bank House, the C16 and C17 dower house to Four Oaks Hall (demolished 1965). A *cottage orné* of *c.* 1860, with bargeboards and decorative chimneys. The S end, with a blocked mullioned window and a tremendous stepped stone chimney, is older, probably C16. Part of a queenpost truss behind. No. 141, 1896, is by *Titley*; No. 139, plain brick, is of *c.* 1900. Nos. 135–137 are by *Marston & Healey*, 1906; No. 133, probably also theirs; No. 131, by *Everard Healey*, 1907–8. OAKLANDS ROAD, running E, is largely by *J.W. Wilson*, 1931–5, half-timbered houses with his touch of Expressionism. Back on Lichfield Road, No. 129 is a timbered monster by *G.F. Hawkes*, 1899–1900, for E.L. Gyde, jeweller, whose works at Nos. 50–54 St Paul's Square (p. 179) are also by Hawkes. The big l. wing, with a chimney rising out of the gable, was the billiard room.

Further S, No. 107, THE LEASOWES, by *Ernest Newton*, 1893. Domestic Revival, showing the way to the Arts and Crafts radicalism of *c.* 1900: a house with historical awareness but almost without style. Characteristic Newton full-height porch-tower, with crenellations and a dome. Full-height curved bay to the l. Two gabled bays r. They gently defy expectations: timbering to the first floor, but weatherboarded gables. The garden front is looser – gabled bay r. with a complex faceted window, full-height bay l., veranda between – but pulled together by three big chimneys. Single-storey N service wing. Simple plan with cross- and long corridors. Staircase with heavy pyramid-topped newels. The GARDEN was laid out by *C.E. Bateman*, 1910. Sunken path leading to a deeper sunken pool and classical aedicule. SUMMERHOUSE with sloping door jambs and buttresses. STABLES of 1894, now derelict, to the NE.

Further W, a scatter of worthwhile houses. In BARKER ROAD, Nos. 4 and 8 are by *E.G. Harrison*, 1929. No. 12, old-fashioned

Old English, is by *Matthew Butcher*, 1905. No. 11, with tile-hung wings linked by a balcony, is by *Crouch, Butler & Savage*, 1910–11. No. 17, WITHENS, is by *Bidlake*, 1898–9, severely impressive. E-shaped front, the completely blank brick l. gable balanced by one with a big plain curving bay and minimal Venetian window. Central feature with an oriel rising from a big datestone which breaks the door architrave, and bold alternating quoins. No. 26, BEACONHURST, is by *Newton & Cheatle*, 1900–1 (l. end 1908). A good design with a grid of windows on the ground floor. Arty tapering chimney pots. No. 32, THE GATE HOUSE, is by *Cossins, Peacock & Bewlay*, almost as spare as Bidlake. Minimal Venetian windows in the gables, contrasting oriel and large canted bay below. BEACONSFIELD ROAD, N, has more early C20 timber-gabled houses. No. 2, 1902, was *Matthew Butcher*'s own house; No. 8, 1903–4 (extended), is also his. No. 5, an arty design with pie-crust parapet and oval windows, is by *Barratt & Jones*, 1907. No. 6, carefully composed, by *Newton & Cheatle*, 1900. HALLOUGHTON ROAD, further W, has No. 4, hung with stone slates, by *Owen Parsons*, 1931; and No. 2, big brick Tudor by *E. Langley*, 1934.

FOUR OAKS VILLAGE is further N, on Belwell Lane below All Saints' church. The FOUR OAKS pub is of *c.* 1870–80, with big gabled front bays by *Charles Hodson*, 1896. Also his, the shop immediately E, 1897. Early C19 brick cottages with basic hoodmoulds in Park Drive, opposite. At MERE GREEN, E, where Belwell Lane meets Lichfield Road, the former BARLEY MOW pub is by *Thomas* and *Joseph Bateman*, 1829, much altered by *Ansells' Brewery Architect's Dept* in 1935. Opposite, a shopping development by *K4*, 2016. In MERE GREEN ROAD behind it, the former Hill School (the OLD SCHOOL HOUSE pub) by *Thomas Bateman*, dated 1826. Single-storey front block, two-storeyed behind. Pedimental gables and windows in shallow round-headed niches.

4. Wylde Green

1½ m. S of the centre. The best area is down GREENHILL ROAD, E from Birmingham Road. Most of the S side is by *Owen Parsons*, including Nos. 10–16. No. 14, HOLMWOOD, 1912, was Parsons's own house. Red-brown brick. A gable with a big chimney projects from a short range forward of the main block. Doorway recessed under a segmental arch. In BEECH HILL ROAD, No. 5 is also *Parsons*, of 1923–4. No. 10 is good early Modern: rendered, cubic, with metal windows and rounded corner, by *Jackson & Edmonds*, 1936–7. No. 17, PANTILES, heavily Spanish, is by *J. W. Wilson* for himself, 1933–4.

OUTLYING BUILDINGS

Taken roughly clockwise from N to S. Distances are from Holy Trinity.

In HILLWOOD COMMON ROAD, 3½ m. N, No. 9, by *C. Edmund Wilford* of Leicester, 1936. The Dudok moment: buff brick, cubic volumes. Central tower with an angled oriel.

MOOR HALL, Moor Hall Drive, 2 m. NNE. Bishop Vesey's C16 residence was rebuilt in the late C18 to a severe astylar design. The porch of this house survives at Ashfurlong Hall. The present building, dated 1905, is by *Henman & Cooper* for Edward Ansell of the brewing family. Not their best: loose classicism with an old-fashioned tower. NE of the house an C18 COCKPIT, circular, with sandstone walls. Turned into a sunken garden in the late C19, with a miniature triumphal arch as entrance, and a pool with a fountain on a rock-carved base. Paired curving steps to a covered gate on the far side.

OLD MOOR HALL FARM, Moor Hall Drive, 1¾ m. NNE. A C15 stone house. Main house two rooms long, with a picturesque staircase projection behind. The lower part, l., with the present entrance was originally stables. A tiny original ogee-headed window survives l. of the entrance. Plain rectangular windows at the rear.

VESEY GRANGE, Weeford Road, 2¼ m. NE. See p. 450.

FOX HILL HOUSE, Fox Hill Road, 2½ m. NE. Built for John Valentine, who bought the estate in 1826 and went bankrupt in 1833. The builder was *Solomon Smith*. A stuccoed Regency villa, gabled E–W. Quite a sophisticated S front: three bays with shallow giant arches enclosing sash windows, the entrance bay narrower. Small pediment with a Gothick-glazed lunette. 100 yds W, a brick BOTTLE KILN, *c*. 1830.

COLLETS BROOK FARMHOUSE, Tamworth Road, 3 m. NE. A former toll house, built between 1792 and 1807. The usual canted bay to see approaching traffic. The end walls have shallow three-centred arches rising into the gables. (Derelict 2019.)

ASHFURLONG HALL, Tamworth Road, 2 m. NE. A fascinating house, hidden in wooded parkland. S front of sandstone ashlar, 2–3–2 bays, with pediment on slim Doric pilasters, the manner suggesting *John Standbridge*. Probably for Thomas Vaughton, who was here by 1801, and High Sheriff in 1804. Late C19 porch. Early C20 alterations for Colonel J.H. Wilkinson. Bow window to the l. probably by *J.P. Osborne*, 1901. At the rear the scale reduces to a vernacular sandstone range, in two parts, with a mullioned window facing E, probably C16. Inserted N windows part of alterations by *Crouch & Butler*, 1894. E of the main front, a LOGGIA by *Osborne*, 1911, with an Italian Mannerist air: three bays, hipped roof, pilasters, rusticated stonework. Set back on the W, a single-storey extension by *Bateman & Bateman*, 1924. (The entrance hall has an imperial staircase of the 1800s. Wrought-iron serpentine balusters.) On the drive, a GARDEN ROOM, probably by *Osborne*, incorporating the late C18 porch of Moor Hall (*see* above), moved here by Colonel Wilkinson in 1904. Fine Ionic columns.

WHEATMOOR FARM, off Tamworth Road, 2 m. NE. Brick, with a Gothick front with central full-height bay and crenellated parapet. Probably designed to be seen from Ashfurlong Hall, so perhaps *c.* 1800.

REDDICAP HILL, ½ m. ESE, has houses on the S side developed by Charles Adams between 1884 and 1903. No. 59 is a small stone cottage, probably C17, much extended.

FALCON LODGE, 1½ m. E, is Sutton's largest municipal estate, of 1947–59 by *Tom Porter*, Borough Surveyor. Not special architecturally, but the planning, with closes linked by footpaths, and retained hedgerow trees, is pleasant.

LANGLEY HALL, Ox Leys Road, 2 m. ESE. The fortified manor house of the C14 at least (licence to crenellate 1327) was pulled down *c.* 1817. The former STABLES of *c.* 1685 survive, almost certainly by *Sir William Wilson*, whose wife's family, the Pudseys, lived here. Brick with sandstone dressings, hipped roof. Big cross-windows with moulded architraves. Slightly projecting centre with a big arched opening which has panelled pilasters. Not quite symmetrical: five bays to the l. of the archway, four to the r. plus two (infilled) arched entrances. Converted to housing by *Roger Dudley & Sons*, not well, with a courtyard behind, 1988. The house stood to the N; parts of its moat survive.

THE GROVE, Grove Lane, 3 m. ESE. In appearance a low, unassuming brick farmhouse of the early C19. Simplified brick hoodmoulds. A pair of gables flank a late C19 porch. Crow-stepped gables. Three parallel short N wings, the W one with a tie- and collar-beam truss. This is the one hint of the interior: a four-bay hall with splendid cruck trusses, datable to the late C14 or early C15. The present hall is the second and part of the third bay from the E. Its E truss has a saddle and a short post to the ridge-piece, visible in a bedroom behind. The next truss, in the hall, is probably similar, as its blades are slightly S-shaped. The roof has principal rafters set in, behind the trusses, and large wind-braces. W of the hall is two-storey infill with later framing, perhaps C16, suggesting a hall-and-solar arrangement. Another truss partly visible in a bedroom here. The N wing has a rustic tie- and collar-beam internal truss, probably C16 or later. Substantial alterations – staircase, dado panelling – probably early C20.

NEW HALL, 1¼ m. SE, off Walmley Road. A major but puzzling mansion, in a water-filled medieval moat. First mentioned *c.* 1327; owned in the C16 by the Gibbons family, relatives of Bishop Vesey; bought by Henry Sacheverell in 1590. The Sacheverells and their relatives the Chadwicks owned it until 1903, Alfred Owen and his son Sir Alfred from 1923 to 1982. A hotel since 1986.

The old courtyard of the HOUSE is reached by an C18 bridge over the moat, its piers topped by huge acorns, and with a picturesque roof of 1870. The oldest work is the S range and the S end of the main range. The stone used is grey. It is difficult to date. Pevsner thought it medieval; P. B. Chatwin, C16. The plain mullioned windows are original, if restored; the arched

p. 464

Sutton Coldfield, New Hall.
Engraving by T. Radclyffe, 1830

lights C19 replacements. The gable-end is in good ashlar, but there is rougher stone further back; so perhaps the answer is medieval, part of a larger house, reconstructed in the C16. The large W bay of the S wing, with mullion-and-transom windows and crenellation, dated 1590, marks the start of the Sacheverell contribution. Contemporary or slightly later, perhaps early C17, comes the wing running E, which makes a small courtyard with the older ranges. Red sandstone, with a canted bay window on a big moulded corbel. More canted bays to N and S. The staircase block projecting into the courtyard at its NW corner is part of this work (except its top storey), as is the courtyard entrance into the main range, with continuous mouldings, a big lintel with the Sacheverell motto 'En Bon Foy' ('In good faith'), and a panel with their arms and goat emblem. The main range was also extended N, almost to its present extent.

Later work is of two main phases. 1796, in the time of John Chadwick, is inscribed on the brick tower with lancet windows against the S front and the bigger tower on the W front. This work also includes the pyramid-roofed N end of the main range. But the biggest extensions are of 1868–70, for John de Heley Mavesyn Chadwick, by *Yeoville Thomason*. An extra storey was added to the main range, with an array of red sandstone mullion-and-transom windows on the W front, and the N end block was recast to match. Darker sandstone walling, recognizable also in the top storey of the courtyard staircase. Extensions N of the old courtyard included another E-facing wing, with canted bay and pyramid roof. There is an ogee-topped cupola. At its N end this work bridges the moat. The present entrance is here. In 1986–7 *Peter Inston Design* added a large extension N again, for hotel bedrooms, round three sides of a new courtyard, in the old kitchen garden. Sympathetic simple red brick Tudor, a tactful solution.

The important interiors are all Sacheverell work. Starting from the courtyard entrance, first a panelled corridor, perhaps an echo of a screens passage. To the l. the DINING ROOM, in the rear of the s range. Panelled all round, including in the 1590 bay. Pilasters with an unusual palm or fern motif running right up. Rear fireplace, its overmantel, probably reconstructed, with many motifs, including blank arcading. A narrow corridor, clearly in pre-existing fabric, runs N from the entrance passage. The STAIRCASE is E off this, cramped but grand. Openwork panels, and carved standing beasts on the posts. It runs up two storeys. On the first floor, a panelled ante-room leads to the GREAT CHAMBER, in the N range of the old courtyard. A remarkably rich and coherent interior. Fully panelled – the rows, unusually, offset from each other – with pilasters, most with fluting above and scallop shapes below, but the pair flanking the fireplace with the palm motif of the dining room. The frieze has addorsed sea monsters linked by strapwork, separated by Sacheverell goats. Compartmented ceiling with suns and little cartouches, and modest pendants, some architectural, others fruit. A different version of the Sacheverell arms in the central panel. All quite innocent of anything Jonesian, but the classicizing frieze and the ceiling motifs suggest a date some way into the C17, say c.1630–40. Painted glass with the Sacheverell arms in the bay windows; text scratched on window panes, biblical verses, by George Sacheverell, some dated (16)89.

CHAPEL COTTAGE, NE, is rubble stone, probably C16. Two- and three-light mullioned windows in both gable-ends, corbelled-out chimney. GARDENER'S COTTAGE, further NE, is C18 brick on a stone base. Still further NE, a former COACH-HOUSE AND STABLE BLOCK, brick Gothic, early C19.

On the drive from Walmley Road, C18 GATEPIERS with stone balls. THE HIGHWAY, on the s, is a house by *Batemans*, 1932. L-shaped, brick, with Cotswold stone slates in the gables and render for the upper floor of the inset porch.

PEDDIMORE HALL, off Peddimore Lane, 3½ m. SE. The double moat of a C13 house of the Arden family survives. The present house was built by William Wood, who bought the site in 1659. It was complete by 1671. Red brick with stone quoins and a stone base with a cyma moulding. The W front has a pedimented doorcase inscribed 'Deus Noster Refugium' (from Psalm 46). Its plain segment-headed windows date from 1809, when the upper parts of the house were largely rebuilt by *Samuel Bennison*. Originally the front had three gables. Simple dentil cornice of 1809. Stone mullion-and-transom windows survive on s, E and N. The C17 house had a direct-entry plan (the s wall of the present entrance hall is an insertion). Unsophisticated but lively detail. Dog-leg staircase, originally rising straight out of the hall. The newels have bulbous finials, shallow carving of flowers and leaves, and odd horizontal fluting. The rails have this fluting as well. No balusters, but some diagonal bracing. Rare original dog gate with more shallow carving and splat balusters. Stone fireplaces in the bedrooms with four-centred arches and ogee-moulded top shelves. Several stone doorcases with double ogee mouldings and stop-chamfers, with carved trefoils. In the SE room downstairs some hefty square framing is exposed.

50 NEW HALL MILL, off Wylde Green Road, 1½ m. SSE. The present warm brick mill house is mostly as rebuilt in the 1780s by William Twamley, but the ground floor at the N end has big sandstone blocks, perhaps the base of an earlier mill. The cottage attached on the W, of timber framing in square panels, is probably as late as of 1710, when George Sacheverell agreed to build 'a convenient dwelling house...for the use of the said mills'. Machinery of 1861; the overshot wheel, in a covered wheelhouse, later C19. Still workable, owned by a trust. C18 STABLE and later COWHOUSE to the S, now a visitors' centre.

NEW SHIPTON FARM BARN, The Avenue, off Walmley Ash Road, 2 m. SSE. A four-bay cruck-framed barn, tree-ring dated to 1424. The trusses all have collars and arch braces. A full set of wind-braces.

WALMLEY village centre is on Walmley Road, 2 m. SSE. The church (p.442) is on the E. The FOX INN, smoothly traditional, is by *John P. Osborne & Son*, 1931–2. In the angle with Fox Hollies Road, the Sutton Coldfield Charitable Trust ALMSHOUSES. Gothic pair of 1863 facing the junction; Tudor pair behind by *E.F. Titley*, 1898–9; long single-storey E-shaped range facing W by *H.E. Farmer*, 1926–7.

PENNS HALL, Penns Lane, 2½ m. S. In 1618 blade and fulling mills here were worked by John Penn. The Webster and Horsfall families, here from *c.* 1750 to 1948, used the mill for metalware and wire drawing, but in 1859 moved manufacture to Hay Mills (p.273), and turned the mill house into a country home. Entrance lodge, Frenchy classical of 1888, by *William Davis*. Much-altered narrow ranges with gable-ends facing S represent the C18 mill house. The W block is of *c.* 1860 at the rear, perhaps by *F.D. Johnson*, extended S and recast by *Davis*, again Frenchy classical, in 1888–9. Big E hotel extensions and gruesome porches, 1960s and after. The mill itself was at the S end of the pool, now a beautiful lake.

BOLDMERE, 1½ m. SW, has little interest. On the corner of Boldmere Road and Jockey Road the prominently gabled PARK HOTEL, mostly of 1898–9 by *A.H. Hamblin*.

MINWORTH

A village on the Kingsbury Road (A4097) 3½ m. SE of Sutton, and E of Castle Vale (p.231). The Birmingham and Fazeley Canal of 1786–9, engineer *John Smeaton*, runs just N of the main road. The centre, unexpectedly, is a large green. Minworth is defined by the large sewage treatment works built by the Birmingham Tame and Rea District Drainage Board, formed in 1877, which spread 2 m. SE. Its land to the SW is now covered by early C21 commercial development.

St George, Old Kingsbury Road. 1909 by *Sir Charles Nicholson*. A sweet brick Gothic mission church with a catslide roof and a Cape Dutch belfry. Boarded canted ceiling, wall recesses divided by large piers. Rear extension, 1986–90. – Font. The worn stone bowl is C17 or C18, with rustic cherubs. – Altar. Early C20, finely carved.

Minworth Junior and Infants' School, Water Orton Lane. 1900–2 by *Arthur S. Clarson*, for the Lea Marston United District School Board. Very simple, with a little Queen Anne detail. Extensions of 1926 etc.

On Kingsbury Road at the Green, the Hare and Hounds pub of *c*.1930, timber gables and dormers, but stone bays. Minworth Hall, at the S end of the Green, has an early C19 front with heavy Doric porch, added – hence the end gables – to an C18 farmhouse behind. Barns to the N. Much housing for Drainage Board employees, officially by the Board engineer *John D. Watson*, probably designed by a *Mr Roberts*, on his staff.* Semi-detached pairs, on the E side of the Green and in closes going S, down Water Orton Lane, of 1920. Wakefield Cottages, further S, 1924–5, are rendered with boarded end gables. Further S and along Park Lane, the two most characteristic designs, 1925–8, one with eaves chimneys separated by a long dormer, the other with a central boarded gable. More of these N of Kingsbury Road (and over a canal bridge) in Cottage Lane, 1925–9. The earliest houses are Sutton Square, ½ m. E along Kingsbury Road, of 1919–20, pairs with hefty round-headed double porches. Further E, Minworth Greaves, a late C18 farmhouse with ground-floor canted bays and a moulded doorcase. To its l. a four-bay barn, now housing, with a kingpost roof. Tree-ring dates 1453–76.

Wiggins Hill is a hamlet in the fields ¾ m. NE. Wiggins Hill Farm is late C17. Big Dutch end gables, as on the White Hart, Caldmore, Walsall (p. 638). Its stable wing has a sandstone base, pilaster-like buttresses and a cogging band. Quaker Cottage was a Friends' meeting house, built in 1724. Much extended and altered. A dormer window on the S, near the W end, lit the gallery. Just E, the arched head of a tall window which lit the main room. The Old Barn is probably C17, with heavy weatherboarding. Behind it, Old Barn Farm, probably C16. Square framing, tie- and collar-beam roof with raking struts.

---

*In 1919 a sub-committee of ten women, wives of Board employees, was formed to consider the designs, and 'in almost every instance the proposals made were embodied in the new plans'.

THE BLACK COUNTRY

Dudley Metropolitan Borough	469
Sandwell Metropolitan Borough	563
Walsall Metropolitan Borough	617
City of Wolverhampton	669

DUDLEY METROPOLITAN BOROUGH

Dudley	470
Churches	472
Dudley Castle	475
Dudley Zoo	479
Dudley Priory	480
Public buildings	482
Perambulations	484
Other buildings	490
Hartshill, Woodside and Holly Hall	491
Amblecote	492
Perambulations	493
Brierley Hill	495
Places of worship	495
Public buildings	497
Perambulations	497
Other buildings	499
Merry Hill	499
Brockmoor	500
Coseley	500
Woodsetton	504
Cradley	504
Gornal	507
Halesowen	511
Churches	511
Halesowen Abbey	514
Perambulation	516
The Leasowes	517
Other buildings	519
Hill and Cakemore	520
Lapal	521
Lutley	522

Kingswinford	522
Churches and schools	522
Perambulations	524
Other buildings	526
Lye and Wollescote	526
Churches and major buildings	527
Perambulations	528
Other buildings	530
Netherton	530
Churches	530
Public buildings	532
Perambulations	532
Canal structures	533
Oldswinford	533
Pedmore	537
Pensnett	538
Quarry Bank	540
Sedgley	542
Stourbridge	545
Churches	547
Public buildings	549
Perambulations	550
Other buildings	555
Wallheath	556
Wollaston	557
Wordsley	559
Churches and public buildings	560
Perambulations	561
Other buildings	562

DUDLEY

The town has Anglo-Saxon origins, and appears in Domesday. Since the Norman Conquest it has existed in the shadow of the castle. By the C13 it was regarded as a Borough, and had a mayor from the C16. Coal mines are mentioned in 1272. Thomas Habington, writing his C17 survey of Worcestershire, approached Dudley 'over hylls resembling with theyre black couller the Moores who are scorched with the Sun'. The town was an island of Worcestershire until 1966, though the castle was in Staffordshire until 1928. The manor was owned by the lords of the castle – FitzAnsculph, the Paganels, the Somerys and the Suttons. Dudley had Town Commissioners from 1791 and a Board of Health from 1853, and became a Municipal Borough in 1865. It is the largest town in the metropolitan borough created in 1974, but does not dominate it as Wolverhampton and Walsall do.

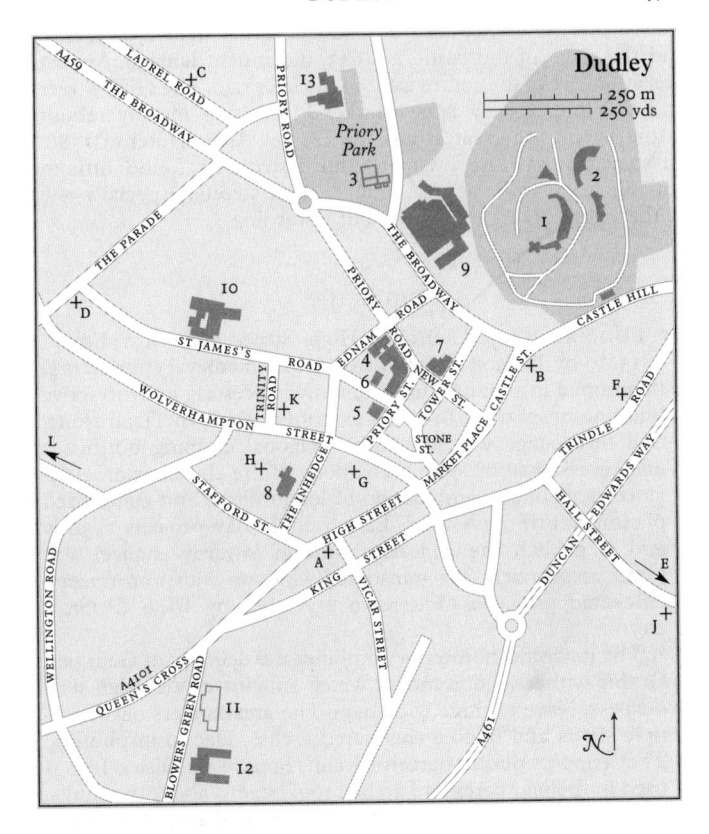

- A   St Thomas
- B   St Edmund
- C   St Francis
- D   St James
- E   St John the Evangelist
- F   Our Blessed Lady and St Thomas of Canterbury (R.C.)
- G   Old Meeting House (Unitarian)
- H   Central Methodist Church
- J   Dixon's Green Methodist Church
- K   Trinity Presbyterian Church (now United Reformed)
- L   Park Congregational Church

- 1   Dudley Castle
- 2   Dudley Zoo
- 3   Dudley Priory
- 4   Civic Centre
- 5   Art Gallery
- 6   Library
- 7   Police station
- 8   Magistrates' Court
- 9   Dudley College
- 10 Dudley Grammar School (former)
- 11 Claughton Centre
- 12 Blowers Green Primary School
- 13 Priory Hall

Ironworks and furnaces existed from medieval times, and the celebrated Dud Dudley experimented with smelting iron with coke in the early C17. The industry lasted until the mid C20. All kinds of metal manufacturing – bedsteads, structural steelwork, motor-car parts – replaced it, and a few firms survive. The town, apart from the castle, has no buildings earlier than 1700. Fires, and the siege of the castle in 1643, did much damage. Almost everything SE of the centre went in the later C20. The High Street and the impressively large Market Place were meanly rebuilt in the 1960s, the greatest loss the Dudley Arms Hotel of 1786. Pevsner, who saw the town after this destruction, found 'little to encourage perambulations'. But the best streets, especially NW of the High Street, are shabby but rewarding.

CHURCHES

ST THOMAS ('Top Church'), High Street and Vicar Street. 1815–19 by *William Brooks*. It replaced a medieval church, first mentioned in 1182. An uncommonly interesting and attractive building of its date. Brooks's exterior is Perp, in Tixall stone. Tall three-stage W tower with octagonal clasping buttresses and recessed stone spire.* The body of the church is an elongated octagon, a combination of longitudinal and centralized planning. Five bays long. Each middle bay projects slightly and is gabled, the end bays cant in towards chancel and tower respectively. Big transomed windows with iron tracery, crocketed pinnacles. Extensive E vestries by *Webb & Gray*, 1951–2.

The magnificent interior combines the delicacy of Georgian Gothic with a solid grandeur which anticipates Victorian seriousness. Nave of three wide bays. The arcade piers have multiple shafts and double-chamfered arches, Dec in inspiration. They support plaster tierceron-vaults in nave and aisles. Iron is used in the pier cores and arched roof beams, above the vaults. The canted W bays are reflected in narrow diagonal arches at the angles. A continuous gallery with crenellated front runs round between the piers. The chancel arch is triple-chamfered and has even more shafts. Brooks, a Low Church man, originally designed an E alcove for the altar, with organ above; the presence of a short chancel is due to Viscount Dudley and Ward, the lay rector. It has a richer vault with arches between the ribs. CRYPT underneath, medieval, of finely laid stonework with projecting base courses. A three-centred arch between the two chambers. Iron roof beams, inserted by the builder, *Daniel Evans*, to strengthen the structure (resulting in a legal action between him and the church and architect). Reordered 2019 by *Donald Insall Associates* (*Matthew Vaughan*): pews removed, new flooring, partitions etc.

FITTINGS. Attractive original REREDOS with hanging ogee arches and pyramid-shaped canopies at the ends. Fine, strongly modelled relief of St Thomas recognizing the Risen Lord, by *Samuel Joseph*. – CREED and COMMANDMENT BOARDS to N and S, in ogee surrounds. – STATUES of Faith and Hope in

---

*Ritual E is roughly SSE here. Repairs and decoration by *William Bourne*, 1862 (tablet in the W porch). In 1909 *P.B. Chatwin* designed a large, unbuilt E extension.

canopied niches above, probably also *Joseph*. – Stone ALTAR (rare, and illegal, at that date), with paired buttresses, quatrefoil panels and top of greenish 'Dove marble'. – PULPIT. Octagonal top of the original three-decker, N. Carved angels at the corners. – Handsome CHOIR STALLS by *Webb & Gray*, 1932; their backs look early C19, reused. – STAINED GLASS. E, Transfiguration by *Joseph Backler*, 1821, an important Late Georgian window. Painted in enamels on rectangular panes, with billowing clouds and much brown, the Christ taken from Raphael's famous painting. Larger standing figures below. – Original ORGAN by *Thomas Elliott* of London, much altered, in large towered and castellated case. – FONT, a rich medieval re-creation of 1867 by *Edward Blore*, carved by *James Forsyth*. Tapering square bowl with reliefs (Baptism of Christ, E). Ornate open-spired cover. – Minton TILES, probably also 1873. – Good CHOIR STALLS by *Webb & Gray*, 1932.

MONUMENTS. Elizabeth Green †1740. Arched top, garlands and volutes, cherub below. – Francis Downing †1825. With a tapering angled top which looks almost Art Deco (both W wall). – Anne, Phillis-Anne and Elizabeth, successive wives of the Rev. Luke Booker, who rebuilt the church. 1827 by *Booth* of Nottingham (N aisle E). – Several tablets by *Peter Hollins*, the most charming Edward Guest †1826, S aisle E, with tomb-chest and elevation of the church in the predella; the later ones still classical but richer. – Samuel Spittle †1917, monogram *DJB*. Beaten copper.

ST EDMUND ('Bottom Church'), Castle Street. The dedication suggests a late Saxon foundation. The principal medieval church of the town, was described in 1674 as 'totally demolished in the time of the late war'. Rebuilding began only in 1724, dated by bricks by the W door inscribed by John Homer and Moses Hinton, probably the churchwardens. Tower and nave roof timbers have been tree-ring-dated to 1723. The first baptism was not until 1739. Brick with stone dressings, in typical local Baroque of the date. W tower with big eared doorcase with a segmental pediment, and a curious double niche with swan's-neck pediment above. Similar but smaller doorcases to the aisles, linked to oval windows above. Medieval stonework survives inside. The top stages of the tower check in sharply, with diagonally placed consoles. Nave and aisles have tall arched windows with keystones linked to the string course above. Unusually long chancel for the C18, perhaps on the medieval foundations. Serlian E window, partly blocked in the C19. An impressive yet incoherent design, designed by someone who knew Archer's St Philip, Birmingham, and also St Alkmund, Whitchurch, Shropshire (the double niche), built by William Smith the elder; *Smith* himself is possible (Andor Gomme).

W lobby with large doorcase to the nave, again with a segmental pediment. The interior seems at first glance original, but has had many alterations. Arcades with moulded keystones, a simpler version of St Philip, Birmingham. In 1876 *Davies & Middleton* altered the piers by cutting back the corners into sunk quadrants, with anthemia at the top. Their chancel arch imitates the arcades, but stands on half-piers of Gornal stone, now painted, with naturalistic foliage corbels. – GALLERIES of 1814–15, the fronts with fielded panels. – REREDOS by *Cherrington & Stainton*, 1948, with elegant Corinthian pilasters, also N aisle (Lady Chapel) REREDOS and CLERGY STALLS. – PANELLING in the chancel by *W.E. Ellery Anderson*, 1929, following a 1927 scheme by *J. Coates Carter*. – CHOIR STALLS and PEWS by *William Bourne*, 1864–5. Classical, probably reusing earlier work. The colonnettes on the stalls betray the date. – FONT by *Cherrington & Stainton*, 1943. – STAINED GLASS. E window by *Geoffrey Webb*, 1929, calm Christ in Majesty. Chancel N, *Jones & Willis*, 1877. N aisle *Samuel Evans* †1898.

MONUMENTS. A good large collection; this was the fashionable church of Dudley in the Georgian period. Chancel, George Bradley, ironmonger, erected 1791. Urn on a tall base. His 'Piety and Munificence erected this Temple' (inscription); his brother Richard also contributed. – Abiathar Hawkes †1800. Elegant gadrooned urn on a tomb-chest with projecting inscription panel. – N aisle: by *Peter Hollins*, John Badley †1870 with relief head, and Thomas Badger †1856, weeping woman. – S aisle. Joseph Wainwright †1810, by *William Hollins*, with sword and snake. – John Finch †1759, with well-draped urn. – John Finch †1791, by *Charles Peart*. – Jane Simpson †1802, by *William Thompson*. – Edward Dixon †1807, by *Thomas King & Sons*. Weeping woman and urn at the top.

ST FRANCIS, Laurel Road. 1931–2 by *Webb & Gray*. Simple Early Christian in brick, masked by late C20 additions. Inside, typical *Webb* segmental cross-arches. – STAINED GLASS. 1961–2 by *Francis Skeat*, commemorating the footballer Duncan Edwards (*see* pp. 484–5). – PAINTING. Large, probably C19.

ST JAMES, The Parade. By *William Bourne*. Squared grey limestone with Gornal sandstone dressings. Of 1838–40 the tall tower and nave, originally unaisled, with typical repeated buttresses and lancets. The tower has lost its battlements. In 1868–9 Bourne extended the chancel and inserted the nave arcades and clerestory, in Early French Gothic with shaft-rings and bold foliage capitals, with galleries retained behind them. – Of 1869 by *Bourne* the Caen stone PULPIT with statues of the Evangelists (sculptor *Thornton*), FONT, CHOIR STALLS and PEWS. – Gallery PEWS probably 1840. – War memorial REREDOS by *C.E. Bateman*, 1921, now in the W gallery. Big central ogee arch, Crucifixion with saints, emblems of martyrdom. – Iron SCREEN, 1902. – STAINED GLASS. E window *c.*1870, perhaps *Lavers, Barraud & Westlake*. – In the churchyard, MONUMENT to John and Elizabeth Stokes, by *Abraham Ramsell*, 1906. Broken column on an enormous pedestal, a single granite block.

ST JOHN THE EVANGELIST, St John's Road, Kate's Hill, S of the centre. A twin to St James: tower and nave 1838–40 by *William Bourne*, extended chancel, arcades and clerestory by his successors *Davies & Middleton*, 1872–3. Early French-style arcades again, with juicy foliage capitals, all different. Gothic arcading round the gallery front. – Original PULPIT with the Four Evangelists, and CHOIR STALLS. – Iron SCREEN, 1888. – FONT by *Tom Grazebrook*, 1908. – ORGAN by *Conacher*, 1886. – REREDOS by *Davies & Middleton*, 1873. – STAINED GLASS. Good High Victorian E window probably by *T.W. Camm*, 1873; chancel s, *Jones & Willis*, 1873. Twelve nave windows by *Powells*, 1918–40, are in store. – LYCHGATE of 1920. – Closed 2004, owned by a local trust.

OUR BLESSED LADY AND ST THOMAS OF CANTERBURY (R.C.), Trindle Road. 1839–40 by *A.W.N. Pugin* (consecrated 1842). Aisled nave, chancel and N chapel. Baldly tooled Gornal stone. Lancet windows. Typical simple arcades with octagonal piers and single-step arches. Flat-roofed narthex and s vestries, s chapel with ugly arch, screen and pews removed, nave ceiled, all done by *Jennings Homer & Lynch*, 1964–5. – STAINED GLASS. E window by *Hardmans*, 1862. Later Hardman figures elsewhere with backgrounds removed.

OLD MEETING HOUSE (Unitarian), Wolverhampton Street. 1717. Gornal stone ashlar. Two tiers of small cast-iron windows, hipped roof. An early chapel on a back plot. Entered up an alley, past the former SUNDAY SCHOOL of 1865, red brick with blue and cream detail and round-headed windows. The chapel has an odd Italianate tower-like entrance porch with coved top, part of alterations by *Boden & Grove*, builders, 1869. They reorientated the interior. Galleries on iron columns of 1869, but their tiered seating looks C18. – PULPIT with Gothic arcading, probably early C19.

CENTRAL METHODIST CHURCH, Wolverhampton Street. 1977–8 by *Tony Hodder* of *Webb & Gray*. Big slated pyramid over the worship space.

DIXON'S GREEN METHODIST CHURCH, Dixon's Green Road. 1869–70 by *Holton & Connor* of Dewsbury, cut down and refronted by *Webb & Gray*, 1950. Original windows along the sides.

TRINITY PRESBYTERIAN CHURCH (now United Reformed), Trinity Road. 1949 by *F.J. Parkinson*.

PARK CONGREGATIONAL CHURCH, Grange Road. By *Ewen & J.A. Harper*, 1906. Modest, with a shaped gable.

DUDLEY CASTLE

Dudley Castle is the most important secular medieval and C16 building in the area, with work of national significance for both phases. Its keep dominates the wooded hill, and stands on a motte constructed by William FitzAnsculph shortly after the Norman Conquest. Fragments of C12 work by the Paganel family survive, though much was dismantled in 1175. The major surviving medieval fabric, including the curtain wall, the keep or great tower, and most of the Triple Gatehouse, has traditionally been dated to the early C14, but recent research suggests it is earlier. Roger de Somery began work in 1262, and his buildings were

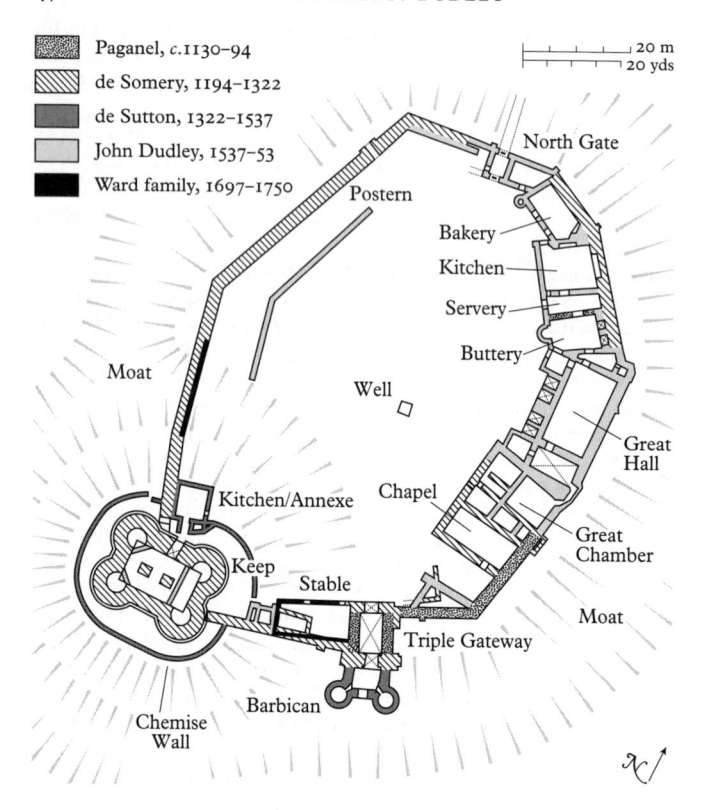

Dudley Castle.
Plan

called 'newly commenced' at his death in 1272.* By 1291 when his son, also Roger, died, the castle was 'the chief edifice of the barony'. The work seems to have been completed under the second Roger's son, John: the chapel is mentioned at his death in 1322. John de Sutton, lord of Dudley from 1422 to 1487, extended the gatehouse with a barbican. The other important period is the mid C16. John Dudley, Duke of Northumberland and Lord President under Edward VI, was in possession by 1537 and was executed in 1553. He rebuilt much of the E range, including a new Great Hall. The first signs of the Renaissance in the area appear here. Dudley was part of a circle centred on Lord Protector Somerset who were interested in the new architecture. He sent John Shute to Italy in 1550 to measure buildings, and knew Sir William Sharington, who was responsible for Renaissance work at Lacock Abbey (Wilts.). In June 1553 Sharington wrote to Sir John Thynne of Longleat, apologizing for having been unable to send him *John Chapman*, a mason, who had

---

*See Malcolm Hislop in *Antiquaries' Journal* 90, 2010.

instead been sent for by the Duke of Northumberland. The letter also refers to a 'chimney' (chimneypiece) that he was working on for Dudley. This must be almost the end of the work, as Northumberland fell and was executed shortly after. Materials are consistent throughout the medieval and C16 work: white or pale grey Silurian limestone from the Wenlock shales, quarried locally at Wren's Nest, with dressings of local red sandstone. In the keep walling some sandstone is also used.

Later work is less important. The outer gatehouse and watch tower are later C16, traditionally for a visit of Queen Elizabeth in 1575. In the Civil War the castle was held for the king, captured in 1646, and slighted: the Triple Gatehouse was reduced, and the S side of the keep demolished. Partial rebuilding afterwards included the block between gatehouse and motte. In 1750 a fire reduced the E range to a ruin, which it has remained, despite evidence of C18 repair in brick. From 1799 the Earl of Dudley cleared up the site and rebuilt the NE tower of the keep. Restoration in the early 1980s included the replacement of all the E range windows in dark grey Pennant sandstone. Mouldings were carefully reproduced (architects *S.T. Walker & Partners*), but the result is grim. The present condition of the buildings is not good.

Access to both castle and zoo is now from Castle Hill, or, by car, far E on Tipton Road. The VISITOR CENTRE is by *Tecton* (*see* p. 479), 1936, originally the Station Café. Concrete slab roof on pilotis, floating clear of the walls. The W façade has framing rising round doorways (some now blocked). Beyond, *Tecton*'s striking former ENTRANCE GATES, now sadly out of use. The most immediately attractive of all their buildings. The ticket booths are sheltered by S-shaped concrete canopies, overlapping each other as we climb the slope. Further on is the site of the old castle entrance behind the Fellows (p. 488). Steep steps lead from here to the late C16 LOWER GATEHOUSE, with a simple segmental vault. Contemporary walling to either side and a circular WATCH TOWER to the S, crenellated, with a picturesque roof. In the outer bailey beyond we see the MOTTE and the main entrance, the TRIPLE GATEHOUSE. Of the C15 BARBICAN in front, only the lowest parts of the flanking circular towers survive, but the entrance arch remains, with a Perp shaft and hollow moulding. The gatehouse itself has depressed arches with three convex quadrant mouldings. The portcullis groove also survives. Negative evidence for a C13 date here and in the keep is the absence of Dec mouldings such as waves or sunk chamfers. The side walls are C12 work; the W wall, visible from the walkway around the keep, has a blocked archway.

Through the gatehouse we are in the INNER BAILEY. The gatehouse façade here has paired lancets. We first turn W. The two-storey block here has typical late C17 mullion-and-transom cross-windows. Beyond, modern steps climb the C16 encircling wall to the KEEP. The S side was reduced to the lowest courses in the Civil War, the N side stands to full height. In the middle is a doorway with the same details as the arches of the gatehouse.

The NE tower has a staircase to the first floor. The plan is a rectangle with thick round angle towers. There was one room on each floor, the first floor being the hall. The crenellated top of the NW tower is of 1810. Recent work by Malcolm Hislop argues for a start *c*.1262, possibly involving the king's mason *Robert of Beverley*, and links it to Harlech and Caerphilly. The keep is in a line of development of keeps on pre-existing mottes between Clifford's Tower in York, begun in 1244, and the multi-faceted late C14 keep at Warkworth. Dudley was clearly influential: Nunney in Somerset, for example, is similar, but a century later.

Now we return past the gatehouse to the EAST RANGE. The first part is early C14, the end of the Somery work. The CHAPEL has a large W window with fragments of flowing tracery, and a prominent ogee S window. It is 50 by 23 ft (15.2 by 7 metres) and stands on an undercroft. This is tunnel-vaulted in brick, probably C18 rebuilding. The GREAT CHAMBER range beyond was altered in the C16, with big windows and on the N wall, formerly in an upper bedroom, a fireplace with columns. The C12 CASTLE WALL continues along all the buildings on the E side.

So we come to John Dudley's work of *c*.1537–53. With its mullion-and-transom windows and gables it is remarkably progressive, and could easily be dated thirty or forty years later. The Renaissance first appears in local architecture here. The buildings are difficult to read at first. Uneven survival has made the kitchen block to the N more prominent than the hall range. The GREAT HALL is 78 ft by 31 ft 6 in. (23.8 by 9.6 metres), and has a remarkably original formal composition. In front is a LOGGIA on a high basement. It rests on transverse tunnel-vaults, two to each side, with four-centred arches. In the centre was a lost stairway. The loggia itself had Ionic columns on tall bases – a link to Lacock. The responds survive, very eroded. The roof-beam holes are prominent in the hall wall, and they and a blocked arch show that there was a central feature and entrance under the hall. To either side are flanking towers, originally of three storeys. The S one stands to full height. The original main entrance was in the N tower; much of its doorway, including angled jambs, survives, and a window above. The W front of the hall itself has a symmetrical arrangement of windows, the vertical lights going 3–4–4–4–3: all clumpingly restored, but surviving pieces of moulding on the towers and hall wall already have cavetto-like profiles. The N and S walls of the hall partly survive, the E wall has gone. If *Chapman* made his chimneypiece for it – the likeliest place – that has gone too. In the N wall the three usual service doorways survive.

NW of the hall, the KITCHEN AND BEDROOM RANGE also played on symmetry, with three gables, the r. one now missing. But the composition was disrupted by a semicircular staircase projecting from the r. bay; only its lowest part survives, looking like a bay window. Walls here all survive, though floors have gone. In the room behind the staircase, on the N, a stretch of

C12 walling and a round-headed arch. So there were early stone buildings along this side. The next room N has a small doorway and a large former hatch on the N (now a full-height opening) with a moulded three-centred arch, rather grand. The kitchen beyond has two large fireplaces. The bedrooms above retain much-eroded and restored but distinctly classical fireplaces. Beyond this range is a block with pantries and more bedrooms, marked by a tall octagonal corner tower, an obvious parallel to Sharington's tower at Lacock. Finally a short wing ends in the North Gate. The C14 wall returns along the W side of the bailey to the keep, with a postern gate, and evidence of structures, including a projecting garderobe, at the N end.

DUDLEY ZOO

By *Berthold Lubetkin* and *Tecton*, of 1935–7. Early Modernism also of national significance, happily mixed up with the castle's outer bailey. The mixture comes off well; after all, medieval castles sometimes had wild beasts in the moat. But it is difficult to perambulate, because of the steep contours. The zoo was promoted by the 3rd Earl of Dudley, Ernest Marsh (of Marsh & Baxter, *see* Cradley), and Captain Frank Cooper, of the jam-making firm but also a Fellow at London Zoo. London's director, Geoffrey Vevers, suggested *Tecton*. The results, though less well known than London's, are 'the most sustained example of Tecton's work in this genre' (John Allan). Lubetkin's classical training, and the social commitment and formal adventures of Constructivism, are all displayed here. The job was exceptionally difficult because of the short time-scale and the unmapped old mine shafts and quarries on the hill. The job architect was *Francis Skinner*, the structural engineers *J.L. Kier* (that is, largely the young *Ove Arup*). A first phase of restoration, by *Bryant Priest Newman* (structural engineer *Stuart Tappin*), took place in 2014–16.

The PERAMBULATION covers all the Tecton structures, going clockwise.* The start is in the outer bailey, just through the Outer Gatehouse. To the NE is the former REPTILE PIT, a rockery enclosed by a tapering low oval wall, profiled so that animals cannot escape and visitors cannot touch.† Past the Triple Gatehouse, on the r., is the former ELEPHANT HOUSE. From the path we see a walkway and a low clerestory roof. Down steps we see the whole, with animal houses recessed below a big concrete transom. Now back past the reptile pit, and on past a C19 COTTAGE to the W side. N here at the lower level is first a KIOSK, with oval canopy on pilotis. The oval is bisected by a diagonal, expressed as the rear wall of the

---

*An alternative is to go W to the polar bear pit, then through the castle and postern gate to the restaurant and its neighbours, and finally return to the entrance and N to the bear ravine.
†As a child the sudden discovery that this innocent-looking rockery was crawling with snakes was exciting and scary (AF).

servery. Beyond is the POLAR BEAR PIT, with the central bear pit flanked by ravines for lions and tigers. Viewing walkways go round, stepping up to different levels. A concrete 'iceberg' in the pit. The handrails are a *Tecton* design used throughout: a low wall with elliptical steel struts supporting a broad top, so that adults can lean, and children can look through. From here steps lead up to a level outside the castle's outer walls. Here is the MOAT CAFÉ (now education centre), with a long serpentine front, formerly open on pilotis. Then on the r., sunk in the moat, the SEA LION POOL, with wavy canopies and viewing platforms. Its symmetrical 'butterfly nut' plan centres on a bridge carrying a path from the Postern Gate on a straight axis to the CASTLE RESTAURANT (currently Oak Restaurant). Low roof-line, to fit below the castle. Symmetrical arrowhead plan to fit the N end of the escarpment. Concrete entrance arch, more than semicircular. The walls are a trellis of windows, for views, canted outwards in the seating area itself. Looking downhill E of the sea lion pool we see the APE HOUSE, a sympathetic addition by *Philip Skelcher & Partners*, 1963, with three high-walled semicircular enclosures. The C14 E wall of the castle is above, with the C16 E range structures on top, and the moat continues S.

Back to the restaurant and N on its E side, we come to *Tecton*'s BIRD HOUSE, the most fascinating of their formal structures. Circular with a low domed roof, and a porch with a concave front splaying out in front: a Baroque contrast of convex and concave. Inside, a circular passageway with glazed roof runs round the central cages. Around the exterior a walkway. N and then E down a steep pathway with steps, we see that the walkway is cantilevered out over a sloping enclosure below. The BEAR RAVINE is seen from above here. Equally formal, with a curving viewing platform on mushroom-headed columns. It is reached up steps from a second central projecting platform below. The symmetry is broken by the lower entrance, along an 'arabesque' curving wall to the r. and below. Here is another oval KIOSK, with a diagonal axis defining the servery space. A path runs S back to the entrance.

DUDLEY PRIORY

The priory of St James was founded for Cluniac Benedictines by Gervase Paganel, sometime between 1149 and 1160. It was a daughter house of Much Wenlock, but had close links to the lords of the castle. We hear at no time of more than five monks, but the Cluniacs strictly regulated the number of monks in their priories. The remains are at the S end of Priory Park, by Paganel Drive, off The Broadway: an aisleless cruciform church, and monastic ranges to the N. What stands up high are parts of the CHURCH. The first phase, of the later C12, was chancel, crossing and transepts with E chapels. Chancel and chapels all had apses. The lower walls of the S transept survive, with broad clasping buttresses at the angles. The arch to the

Dudley Priory.
Engraving by Samuel and Nathaniel Buck, 1731

s chapel has jambs with big half-round mouldings. The arch itself is much rebuilt, partly with bricks, probably C18. The shape of the original apse is in the ground. Part of the s wall of the chancel is there and, some way N, the NE angle of the N transept, with the bottom of the spiral night stair. The nave is early C13: see the typical E.E. flat buttresses and string course. It had a porch: see the marks above the W doorway. Also in the C13 the chancel was enlarged, with a square E end, almost all gone. A stiff-leaf capital, probably from its sedilia, was found in 1939. Three de Somerys were buried in the church, Roger †1272, his son Roger †1291 and his wife Agnes †1309. This may explain the early C14 alterations, new Dec windows in the nave, a big new W window which involved removing the porch, and probably the much-eroded W doorway. In the later C14 the Sutton Chapel was built (SE), with a stair-turret – its lowest courses survive – which had an ogee cap. An ogee-headed doorway links it to the chancel. Finally in the later C15 the chapel was rebuilt, probably by John de Sutton †1487. It was divided in two by the wall which stands to full height, and the E part was vaulted in three bays: see the remains of the ribs. Ashlar blocks, a contrast to the rubble masonry elsewhere. Large Perp E window with image niches on either side, the r. one complete.

The CONVENTUAL BUILDINGS are only bases of walls. N range late C12, with the chapter house, a large day room, and reredorter at the N. The rest C13. The S wall of the buildings pre-dates the nave and was extended upwards as its N wall: see the change in stonework. The W range comes forward of the W front of the church. The priory was dissolved in 1539. By the C18 a cottage occupied the Sutton Chapel and a factory the W range. In 1825 the drive to the Priory Hall destroyed the crossing of the church. The remains became part of the park in 1932.

PUBLIC BUILDINGS

CIVIC CENTRE, St James's Road, Priory Street and Priory Road. A large complex in two parts, both by *Harvey & Wicks*. The Town Hall, Coroner's Court and War Memorial Tower, at the w end, were won in competition in 1923, and built in 1926–8. The Municipal Buildings, facing Priory Road, followed in 1934–5. Between them, facing Priory Street, the retained façade of *Harvey Eginton*'s Police Buildings of 1847. *Harvey & Wicks*'s competition design was conventional Tudor Revival, but before construction it was redesigned under the influence of Östberg's Stockholm Town Hall of 1909–23, and the result is a landmark of interwar Scandinavian influence on British architecture. Good sculptural detail by *Bloye* complements the massing.

The TOWER rises sheer to a parapet of two drip-courses. The ground floor is the War Memorial Chamber, open through wrought-iron gates, with a ribbed vault. Above, a big mullion-and-transom window with tiny balcony and tall swan's-neck Östberg pediment. Panel with inscription composed by Thomas Hardy. Bold clock, red and blue, in a square set diagonally. A gabled wing l., with the staircase entrance to the Coroner's Court, leads to the equally sheer TOWN HALL entrance block. Loggia of three four-centred arches with deep hollow chamfers. Big window above with Östberg-style tympanum carved with the Borough arms. Inside, more Stockholm motifs: CRUSH HALL with shallow three-centred barrel-vault, and main HALL (now 'Concert Hall') with shallow ribbed vault and tall windows with spiral jambs and openwork pediments. Mural by *Hans Feibusch*, 1948: Sir John de Somery caught by the king's men while hunting. The bright contrasts of orange with pink, yellow with blue, come from 1930s German Expressionism.* CORONER'S COURT with oak seating and dado, desk with spiral columns, and a cornice with interlace ornament on the soffit and big corbels. BANQUETING ROOM with deep coved ceiling decorated with intersecting diagonals. Arcade with criss-cross ribs on columns; similar door jambs. The effect is almost Moorish.

Outside, r. of the tower, *Eginton*'s fortress-like Gothic GATE-HOUSE of 1847 (originally to the police station) with massive tapering towers, the language of contemporary prisons, and to the r., another octagonal tower. Beyond, the MUNICIPAL BUILDINGS. The Priory Road front combines a composition of centre block and lower wings with more Östberg detail and inventive sculpture: three-bay loggia with tapering granite columns and capitals with corner heads, window above with balcony and swan's-neck pediment, rounded l. corner with another doorway with exaggerated swan's-neck, and tympanum

---

*Alderman T.E. Bennett and the town clerk, A.V. Williams, escaped from a local government conference in Eastbourne in 1946 and saw Feibusch's murals in St Elisabeth there, hence the commission. They and other local figures are portrayed as huntsmen.

of scenes from Dudley's past. Apsed ENTRANCE HALL. Pavement with incised Borough arms. Hemicycle of black marble columns, behind which paired staircases rise to an upper hall. More columns here, and tympana, of Dud Dudley smelting, and the town seen from Wren's Nest. The COUNCIL CHAMBER has arcades of black columns, here octagonal and paired, like the Great Gallery at Stockholm. Original furnishings by *H.H. Martyn & Co.*; canopy over the mayor's chair, also a Stockholm feature.

ART GALLERY, St James's Road and Priory Street. 1883 by *Bateman & Corser* of Birmingham. Queen Anne, but the heavy doorcases and details still feel mid-C19. The nicest feature was the corner oriel, but it has lost its domed turret.

LIBRARY, St James's Road. 1908–9 by *George H. Wenyon*. Fine early C18 English Baroque. Upper floor with banded piers, Ionic columns *in antis*, and panels and windows in circular wreaths. Centrepiece with big segmental pediment over a round-headed window, with a seated figure above. Doric doorcase below with Michelangelesque figures reclining on its broken pediment, and tremendously banded columns. Flanking ground-floor canted bays. Interior altered but retaining more Michelangelesque features: Mannerist inner doorcase, and grand staircase to the main floor with a hint of the Laurentian Library. Barrel-vaulted main reading room, now subdivided.

POLICE STATION, Priory Road and Tower Street. 1939–41 by *G.F. Webb*. Following the Civic Centre in combining traditional and modern: a sheer brick block with corner entrance recessed in a quarter-circle. But the restrained detail – classical doorway, linked small-paned windows, balcony with chubby balusters – is more English Neo-Georgian and Jacobean. Above the entrance, statues of a nightwatchman and policeman carved by *Alan Bridgwater*; flanking the door, lions carved by *Charles Upton*; all to designs by *Webb*. Taller and more utilitarian former fire station down the hill.

MAGISTRATES' COURT, The Inhedge. 1976 by *Dudley M.B.C. Borough Architect* (successively *John T. Lewis* and *Philip Whittle*). Brutalist but modest, concrete-faced, with cantilevered upper floor.

GUEST HOSPITAL (former), Tipton Road. Almshouses by *William Bourne*, 1860, converted into a hospital by him in 1871. Redeveloped for housing from 2015. Survivors are *A.T. Butler*'s massive brown stone ADMINISTRATION BLOCK, designed 1934, built 1938–40, with entrance tower, and a steeply gabled LODGE, 1860.

DUDLEY COLLEGE, The Broadway. 1933–6 by *G.C. Lowbridge*, Staffordshire County Education Architect, with *A.T. & Bertram Butler*. 'How can so unrelievedly utilitarian a brick block have been accepted bang between the priory ruin and the castle hill?' (Pevsner, 1974). Extensions 1990–3 by *Dudley M.B.C. Architect's Department*, with courtyard layout by *Steve Field* and SCULPTURES, The Objects of Technology, by *John Vaughan*.

DUDLEY GRAMMAR SCHOOL (now CASTLE HIGH SCHOOL), St James's Road. 1898 by *Woodhouse & Willoughby*, the Manchester school specialists. Tudor Gothic. Hard Ruabon brick and terracotta. Three big gables. Windows with three-centred arches and bits of curly tracery. The r. corner has a turret and little porch. Extended 1936, by *G.C. Lowbridge*, and later.

DUDLEY EVOLVE (Further Education College), Priory Road. By *Metz Architects*, 2013.

CLAUGHTON CENTRE (originally UPPER STANDARD SCHOOL), Blowers Green Road. 1903–4 by *Barrowcliff & Allcock* of Loughborough. Basic Jacobean. Brick and creamy-brown terracotta. Three large gables. Girls' entrance with short fat columns.

BLOWERS GREEN PRIMARY SCHOOL, Blowers Green Road. 1935–6 by *Butler, Jackson & Edmonds*. Central hall block, teaching wings to the rear, originally with open-air corridors. Brown Himley brick with some patterning and blue headers; pantiled roofs. On a concrete raft, to counter mining subsidence. Good detailing, e.g. concrete lintels incorporating tiles. Torch of Learning over the entrance by *Bloye*.

PRIORY HALL AND PARK, Priory Road. House by *Thomas Lee*, 1825, the agent's house for the Dudley estate. Tudor Gothic, picturesquely composed. The entrance front (s) has a tower, a three-storey section l., and two storeys r. All originally battlemented. On the garden side (E) a two-storey canted bay. Clustered chimneys. Plain classical rear service extensions. An octagonal LODGE guards the yard entrance. The PARK surrounds the hall. Laid out by *E.P. Mawson*, 1932, as part of the Priory Estate scheme to the N (p. 490). Below the Hall on the E a formal ITALIAN GARDEN; to the SE a SUNKEN GARDEN with lily pond. Between, a curving SHELTER with loggia by *A.T. Butler & Partners*, 1954. To the S, the Priory ruins (p. 490).

PERAMBULATIONS

1. The Market Place and north-west

We start in the MARKET PLACE. The old Town Hall stood in the centre from the C17 until 1851. Its replacement is the FOUNTAIN of 1867 by *James Forsyth*, sculptor of the Perseus fountain at Great Witley, Worcs. The Dudley fountain was shown at the Paris Exhibition of 1867. The 1st Earl of Dudley paid for it. It is a lush and very enterprising design, Free Italian Renaissance, with two busts of horses on two prow-like corbels, dolphins below, standing figures inside an open arch, and a figural finial. Well restored by *S.T. Walker & Duckham*, 2014–15. On the NW side, the FOUNTAIN ARCADE, dated 1926; but the r. bay was the District Bank of 1909 by *Cossins, Peacock & Bewlay*, Free Style, with a half-conical-roofed oriel and semicircular gable. In 1926 *George Coslett* doubled it l., not quite identically, and added the central bay. To its l. a good Early Victorian classical block. To the NE, STATUE of Duncan Edwards, the footballer killed in the Munich air crash, by *James*

Dudley, Market Place, fountain.
Engraving, 1868

Butler, 1999. To the SW, the former CRITERION cinema by *Joseph Lawden* and *Howard Cetti*, 1923, with a deep pediment on broad pilasters. It faces down STONE STREET. W corner 1841, by *George Hilton*: stuccoed, with giant pilaster strips. Beyond, the GRIFFIN pub, 1935, cottagey stone Tudor, almost certainly *A.T. Butler*.

Back on High Street and SW, BARCLAYS BANK is by *Peacock & Bewlay*, 1930–1. Grand entrance, set diagonally: a full-height Portland stone pedimented aedicule, with Corinthian columns *in antis*. SE down Union Street is the OLDE FOUNDRY pub by *O.M. Weller*, 1936, with semicircular gables. Then along King Street, SW, the former ST THOMAS'S SCHOOL, by *William Bourne*, 1847. A dour three-storey block like a factory, in cream London-type brick, with plain pilasters. Stair-tower at the E corner. Below, l., its successor of 1936 by *Holland W. Hobbiss*, single-storeyed, flat-roofed, quite progressive. Back to High Street and SW, the TRIDENT CENTRE by *Alan Young & Partners*, 1971. No. 69, S side, was CRANAGE'S teashop, 1914 by *A.T. Butler*, with C17-style oriel and plasterwork. Also some minor C18 survivors. At the top, facing St Thomas (p. 472), a streamlined former CO-OP, 1939 by *Webb & Gray*, with faience tiling (recently restored). SE down VICAR STREET, behind the church, Tudor-style VICARAGE by *Webb & Gray*, 1929–30. Beyond, No. 63, *c.* 1840 with Doric doorcase, No. 62, later Georgian. On High Street opposite the church, former REGENT CINEMA by *W.E. Trent*, 1928, with heavy cornice. Immediately beyond the churchyard, Nos. 81–82 were the Dudley estate offices. Early Georgian, with swept-up parapet, but refaced. No. 83, also Early Georgian, but recast *c.* 1821: see the wreaths on the pilasters. On the NW, the THREE CROWNS pub, Tudor, 1924, probably *Butler*.

Back to Barclays Bank and NW down WOLVERHAMPTON STREET. Many altered Georgian survivors: Nos. 1–3A, l., including the SHREWSBURY ARMS, and Nos. 214–216, r., Nash style, with giant pilasters. No. 22, l., contains the arched entrance to the Old Meeting House (p. 475). Then a set-back range by *F.R. Fisher*, 1958, with entrance loggia to the Inhedge burial ground. Opposite, on the corner of PRIORY STREET, the former CROWN INN, by *Joseph D. Wood*, 1897–8. The later C19 Birmingham type with canted bays rising into bargeboarded gables, and picturesque corner tower and spire. On the facing corner, No. 200A, the former POST OFFICE, by *John Rutherford*, 1909–11. Hollington stone. Baroque central window and cartouche, but also a distinctly French elegance. Ionic pilasters and pediment, smooth rustication. Nos. 199 and 200, Early Victorian Italianate; No. 198, handsome Late Georgian with Tuscan doorcase; No. 196, good mid-C18 with swept parapet and pedimented doorcase.

On the SW side, No. 25, a former Lloyds Bank, Gothic by *Martin & Chamberlain*, 1875. Shallow giant arches with decorative tympana. Nos. 28–30, FINCH HOUSE, is dated 1707 in a cartouche enclosed in a pedimented aedicule with twisted columns. A double house. Eight bays, two storeys. Four-bay pediment. The elevation is tied together by platbands linked to the window keystones. Side elevation with Georgian bow window. No. 195 is 1860s, Nos. 193–194 of *c.* 1830, with Greek Doric doorcase. Further W, Southalls Lane runs SW, with the former KING AND QUEEN pub by *H.E. Folkes*, 1906.

Diagonally set corner tower, concave spire roof. Opposite, the former SHAKESPEARE, a Beer Act beerhouse, built for James Tomlinson in the early 1830s. Late Georgian first-floor windows with delicate pediments and bracketed lintels. Ground-floor bays inserted before 1883. The remarkable interior has evolved in a vernacular way. Central corridor with original six-panel doors, and floor tiles. Front bar separated by a later C19 matchboard partition, rare survival of a Black Country type. Original fireplace with bressumer; humble pilastered bar front, an early alteration. Rear-room fireplace with similar pilasters; flanking cupboards. (Closed 2013 but believed intact.)

Back to the Crown and down PRIORY STREET, N. On the l. the former COUNTY COURT, by *Charles Reeves*, 1857–8. The usual Italianate palazzo, nicely done. Big round-headed windows with console keystones, rusticated ground floor with head keystones. No. 31 opposite was *A.T. Butler*'s own office, 1911. Neo-Georgian details, Free Style composition: cornice stopping short of the corners, off-centre entrance and round window. Nos. 27–28, *Gammage & Dickinson*, 1907–8, English Baroque style. Opposite, Nos. 3A–5, much-restored Late Georgian, with one late C19 two-storey shopfront. No. 6 perhaps *c.*1800, with depressed window arches. No. 7 has a datestone 1703 with the initials of Hugh Dixon, glassmaker, and wife. Five bays with a central pediment. Platband. Similar to Finch House, but simpler and slightly heavier, e.g. the wide architraves. The cornice breaks forward over the quoins. Here we enter a small square. On the S, Domestic Revival blocks of the former FIRE STATION by the Borough Surveyor, *John Gammage*, 1892; side wall altered for a restaurant, 2015–16 by *Brownhill Hayward Brown*. Opposite, the SARACEN'S HEAD AND FREEMASONS' ARMS. Front with minimal pediment of *c.*1830, perhaps by *Edward Marsh*, with segment-headed windows in big frames.* NW wall of rubble stone and thin brickwork, C17 or C18.

NW down ST JAMES'S ROAD, past Town Hall and Library r., Art Gallery l. (pp. 482–3). Beyond, the former BOARD OF GUARDIANS OFFICES by *Wood & Kendrick*, 1888. Queen Anne, its powerful corner spirelet removed. Here is the Priory Fields estate, laid out from 1876–7 as a middle-class residential area. On the S side THE GABLES, two pairs by *Meredith & Pritchard*: Nos. 11–13, 1908; Nos. 15–17, 1900. Opposite, EDNAM HOUSE, by *Davies & Middleton*, 1877–8, Jacobean, and TIXALL HOUSE, also 1877–8 and picturesquely composed, but classical. Further on, the former Grammar School and mostly interwar houses, the best No. 30, TREBANT, by *Butler*, 1926, individual Neo-Georgian.

Back and NE along EDNAM ROAD. On the SE side a group almost certainly by *J.T. Meredith* (Nos. 4–8), of dates between 1881 and 1885. Opposite, No. 1, 1877, with canted bay and

---

*Also used in rebuilding the Griffin, Stone Street (*see* p. 485), 1835, where Marsh was certainly involved.

canopied balcony on top, and No. 2, 1882. On the corner of Priory Road No. 3 of 1864–5. Hipped roof, like a Regency villa, but heavier detail. Beyond, No. 9, Neo-Georgian by *Cherrington & Stainton*, 1919–20, and No. 10 by *Webb & Gray*, 1923, with inset brick porch-tower. Opposite, CORONATION GARDENS, laid out in 1937. STATUE of Apollo by *William Bloye*, 1939, his first large-scale bronze.

SE up PRIORY ROAD. On the l. PRIORY HOUSE, a big villa of probably *c.* 1820: see the upper windows with architraves on consoles. Between them, paired pilasters with wreaths in the cornice. Ground-floor Venetian windows, segmental porch. Rear extension for the Conservative Club by *Walter Wright*, 1912. Opposite, CHARLTON HOUSE, Late Georgian, with Tuscan doorcase. Behind it in PRIORY STREET, an Early Victorian classical range and an early C19 picturesque cottage.

Priory Road continues as NEW STREET. On the l. the former GLADSTONE LIBERAL CLUB, by *Webb & Gray*, 1937, unexpectedly Art Deco. Then the police station (p. 483). Beyond, the COURT HOUSE pub by *A.T. & Bertram Butler*, 1936, Tudor Revival. TOWER STREET runs across here. Looking SW, Nos. 59–60, altered C18, and Nos. 61–65, taller mid-C19 classical. Then down NE. Set back on the r., the former BAYLIES'S CHARITY SCHOOL of 1824. Severe trabeated Neoclassical, stuccoed, with slightly projecting centre and ends, articulated by plain pilasters. End porches with *Coade* stone figures of charity children in niches above. Beyond, the MALT SHOVEL pub of *c.* 1800, with moulded three-centred arches to the first-floor windows. Back and SE up New Street, on the r. Neo-Georgian blocks of 1933–8 by the Borough Surveyor, *F.H. Gibbons*, consultant *A.T. Butler*. At the top is the Market Place, and two very different buildings by *Butler*: NEW STREET CHAMBERS, 1923, breaking out above the cornice with pediments and circular dormers; and opposite, the Neo-Georgian former HEN AND CHICKENS pub, 1932–3.

2. East of the Market Place

CASTLE STREET runs E from the Market Place. On the corner of Fisher Street the streamlined former ANGEL INN by *Holland W. Hobbiss*. On the l. No. 267, NATWEST, modernized classical by *Harvey & Wicks*, 1937–8. Opposite St Edmund's church (p. 473), Nos. 270–272, probably late C18. Tuscan doorcase. Older stonework visible in GREEN MAN ENTRY, l. STATUE of the 1st Earl of Dudley in peer's robes by *C.B. Birch*, 1888. Tall circular pedestal. THE BROADWAY runs NW, with on the r. the old entrance to the Castle. Also a group of buildings of *c.* 1845: the FELLOWS pub, castellated; cottages facing; and beyond both, the ESTATE OFFICES, Tudor Revival, perhaps by *William Bourne*, with a small castellated tower.

Now NE down CASTLE HILL. On the r., KING CHARLES HOUSE, probably of 1786–7. Handsome three-storey 1-3-1-bay villa with pedimented centre. Elegant Ionic porch with quadrant ends. Windows with cornices on consoles, the end ones plain, quite up-to-date. Opposite, the early C19 castle wall and a small mid-C19 Tudor lodge, then No. 5, an Early Victorian classical villa. On the s side the former ST EDMUND'S CHURCH SCHOOL (now CENTRAL MOSQUE), by *William Bourne*, 1848–9. L-shaped group, Tudor Revival. Limestone and Gornal sandstone. Long, comfortable roof-lines give it a rural feel, despite the loss of its corner tower and cupola, and many cut-down chimneys. Facing *Tecton*'s Zoo entrance (p. 479), the former ODEON (now Jehovah's Witnesses), 1937 by *Harry Weedon & Partners* (assistant in charge *Budge Reid*). A 'near-perfect expression of the circuit style' (Allan Eyles). Cream faience frontispiece, banded with dark green (now mostly black); five deeply recessed windows behind rounded piers. Rounded corners echoed in the brick auditorium behind. Diagonally opposite, the former HIPPODROME theatre by *Hurley Robinson*, 1937–8. Brick, with curved corners and huge first-floor window divided by giant brick mullions. Heavily banded attic. On the s side, curving round the corner, the STATION HOTEL, by *A.T. & Bertram Butler*, 1938. Neo-Georgian, with shallow bows and fan tympana. Up TRINDLE ROAD. On the l., pedimented factory by *Butler*, 1917 (altered). On the r. the former RAILWAY TAVERN by *Hobbiss*, 1939, with classical doorcases and hipped roof. At the top one of Hobbiss's finest pubs, the former EMPIRE TAVERN, 1938–9. Restrained Tudor, with the special moulded bricks he used at King Edward's School (p. 374). Symmetrical except for the picturesque array of chimneys.

3. South-east of the centre: Hall Street and Dixon's Green

From the E end of the Market Place s along Fisher Street and Birdcage Walk alongside the CHURCHILL PRECINCT by *John T. Lewis*, Borough Architect, 1961–9, altered by *Geoffrey Woodward*, 1992. Sculpted frieze with miner and chainmaker flanking a mother and child, by *E. Bainbridge Copnall*, 1963. Across the bleak King Street and SE down HALL STREET over the by-pass to the former BEAN CAR FACTORY OFFICES by *A.T. Butler*, 1916. Long brick block, entrance with Ionic pilasters. Framing piers, repeated on the rear, hint at Mackintosh. Entrance hall with Ionic columns. To the E, CENTRAL CLINIC by *John T. Lewis*, Borough Architect, 1960. No. 109, 1877, was the minister's house of Dixon's Green Methodist Church beyond (p. 475), probably by *Holton & Connor*. Then later C19 villas, first plain, then in Norman Shaw Old English. Opposite, No. 8, a Late Georgian cottage, and No. 10, c. 1830. BEAN ROAD runs SW here, with No. 25 by *G.F. Webb*, 1910, very Bournville. Further SE the OLD BUSH pub, basic Jacobean of 1904–5, perhaps by *George Coslett*. OAKHAM ROAD runs E with interwar villas. The best are No. 30, Neo-Georgian of *c.*1930, almost certainly *Butler*; No. 63, brick Tudor; and No. 110, THE THATCH, *c.*1931 by *Webb & Gray*, with decorative thatched roof.

OTHER BUILDINGS

N of the centre, the PRIORY ESTATE of 1928–32, planned by *E.P. Mawson*, with municipal houses (now largely demolished). PRIORY CLOSE, off The Broadway, ½ m. NW, was planned by *Cherrington & Stainton*, 1934. Nos. 21–31, with slightly *Moderne* detailing, are by *Webb & Gray*. Further W up THE PARADE, the former St James's vicarage, brick, 1852. Probably by *William Bourne*, extended 1874 by *Davies & Middleton*. In CASTLE VIEW opposite, simple LODGE of *Crouch & Butler*'s Neo-Georgian DUDLEY TRAINING COLLEGE of 1909 (dem. 2003), the town's greatest recent architectural loss.

CEMETERY, Stourbridge Road, ½ m. SW. 1903 by *John Gammage*, Borough Surveyor. BOER WAR MEMORIAL, solider on pedestal, by *H. O. Burgess*, 1904. Further SW on a large roundabout, immense Pegasus STATUE by *Andrew Logan*, 2001.

BLACK COUNTRY LIVING MUSEUM, Tipton Road, ½ m. N. Established in 1975, a museum of buildings which show the area's social and industrial history. The emphasis is different, therefore, from pure building museums such as Avoncroft in Worcestershire. ENTRANCE BUILDING incorporating the front block and iron trusses of public baths from Rolfe Street, Smethwick, by *Harris, Martin & Harris*, 1888, Chamberlain-style Gothic. To the r., the polychromatic brick façade of *c.* 1870 from the Old Patent Tube Works, Wednesbury.

Inside, l., WAR MEMORIAL of 1923 by *Robert Jackson Emerson*, from Springfield Brewery, Wolverhampton. Bronze soldier. By it, a pair of iron MUNICIPAL HOUSES from Dudley, 1925. Going N, ENGINE HOUSE with a replica of *Newcomen*'s pioneer beam engine of 1712 at Tipton. At a road junction, mid-C19 COTTAGE from Coopers Bank, Gornal, reconstructed to show the effect of mining subsidence. To the l., OLIVER SHOP (small forge) from Blackheath, C19. Then r., past a TOLL HOUSE of 1845 from the Sedgley–Tividale turnpike. Canted central bay to see approaching traffic. Further N, ST JAMES' CHURCH SCHOOL from Dudley, by *W. Bourne*, 1842. Small limestone blocks but a Gornal sandstone lining. Lancets; big plate-tracery window in the gable. Full-height glazed partition dividing boys and girls. 'BIRMINGHAM ROAD', W, represents an interwar street with e.g. Hobbs's FISH-AND-CHIP RESTAURANT from Dudley. The WORKERS' INSTITUTE from Cradley Heath is by *A. T. Butler*, 1911–12. Built with funds left after the 1910 women chainworkers' strike. Picturesque Free Style, characteristic Butler details: wings pushing out at the sides, round windows. Small, good staircase and main hall with light steel trusses. Then, a 1920s BUILDER'S YARD with a STONE-CUTTER'S HOVEL in Peldon stone.

The main VILLAGE is further N, across a cast-iron BRIDGE from Wolverhampton, 1879. It crosses Lord Ward's Canal of c.1775. To the l., massive LIME KILNS of 1842. Beyond, C19 shops line the narrow street. At the end on the l., PROVIDENCE METHODIST NEW CONNEXION CHAPEL of 1837 from Darby Hand, Netherton. Standard low gabled Georgian front, replica doorcase. Replacement bricks (the originals were perished) came from Wolverhampton Street Methodist Church, Dudley (1828–9). Galleries of c.1870 on iron columns.

Opposite, a hardware shop of 1827 from Wolverhampton with typical architraved windows. The BOTTLE AND GLASS pub from Brockmoor, slightly earlier: see the upper windows with delicate architraves on consoles. A traditional Black Country 'two-room drinker', with added canted bays. Interior mostly late C19. Behind it, the Dudley Canal, running SW to DUDLEY TUNNEL, 3,172 yds (2,900 metres) long, constructed 1785–92. It has an open basin at Castle Mill, and served limestone quarries underground as well. Going E, on the l. COTTAGES and a COBBLER'S SHOP, and small NAIL MAKER'S WORKSHOP, on the r. back-to-back COTTAGES from Brook Street, Sedgley. Behind them, a re-created BRASS FOUNDRY and ROLLING MILL. Beyond, a LIFTING BRIDGE leads to a BOAT DOCK. The view across the village from Birmingham Road looks authentically of before c.1970. To be re-erected (2021): Woodside Library (p.492); replica of the ELEPHANT AND CASTLE pub from Wolverhampton, by *Hickton & Farmer*, 1905.

HARTSHILL, WOODSIDE AND HOLLY HALL

Industrial hamlets, now indistinguishable, on the Stourbridge road 1½ m. SW.

ST AUGUSTINE, Hallchurch Road, Holly Hall. 1882–4 by *H.G.W. Drinkwater* of Oxford. Economical but impressive. Brick with stone dressings. Bellcote on the nave E gable (SW tower never built). Apsidal W baptistery. Lancets; plate tracery E and W. Arcades with circular piers and nice contrasts of brick and stone. W end infill by *Robin Hurley*, 1988–9. – ALTAR by *A.S. Dixon*, 1913–14, segmental arches between posts, ruthlessly simple. His RIDDEL-POSTS have gilded angels made by *Barkentin & Krall*. – PULPIT and FONT by *Drinkwater*. – STAINED GLASS. E window by *Bell & Beckham*, 1884. S chapel E by *G.H. & W. Randle*, 1914. Scenes from the life of Our Lady, very good and unusual, with pale but expressive faces, especially the Last Sleep, r. N aisle, *Florence, Walter* and *Robert Camm*, 1929; W apse, good Arts and Crafts figures by *Walter* and *Florence Camm*, 1914.

WOODSIDE (WESLEYAN) METHODIST CHURCH, Hallchurch Road. 1890 by *J.B. Marsh*.

WOODSIDE PRIMITIVE METHODIST CHURCH (now NEW TESTAMENT CHURCH OF GOD), The Square. By *S. Bennett*

492 BLACK COUNTRY: DUDLEY

& Son of Brierley Hill, builders, 1882. Gothic with paired octagonal towers, a bigger version of their Wordsley chapel (p. 560). Badly rendered.

WOODSIDE LIBRARY (former), Stourbridge Road. Friendly Jacobean-cum-Queen Anne by *Tom Grazebrook*, 1894. Turret with concave spirelet. (Moving to Black Country Museum, 2021.)

WOODSIDE PARK. MONUMENT to Job Garratt, made by *C.R. Davis*, 1911. Bust, short column, splendidly ugly pedestal.

LOW TOWN, Pensnett Road. Overgrown remains of an C18–C19 industrial hamlet.

RUSSELLS HALL HOSPITAL, Pensnett Road. Rebuilt 2000–6, architects *Percy Thomas Partnership*. Huge low-rise complex faced in white panels.

AMBLECOTE

9085

Immediately N of Stourbridge across the River Stour. Historically, the Staffordshire part of the parish of Oldswinford. A 'coal pit' is mentioned in 1649, a 'glasshouse' in 1650. Williamson's map of 1769 shows many glass cones. The River Stour was made navigable in 1665–7 by *Andrew Yarranton*. It was superseded by the Stourbridge Canal, projected by *James Brindley* in 1766 and built in 1776–9 by *Thomas Dadford Jun.*, with the basin of its Town Arm by the river. The SE part, up Vicarage Road, remained open land with derelict mines until replaced with housing in the 1970s. Amblecote was an independent Urban District from 1898 to 1966 – claimed to be the smallest in England – but the widened High Street (A491) has little sense of a town centre. The glass industry disappeared in the late C20.

HOLY TRINITY, High Street and Vicarage Road. 1841–2 by *Samuel Hemming* of Birmingham. A solid Commissioners'-type design, in yellow firebricks made by *J. & W. King* of Stourbridge. W tower with diagonal buttresses, flanked by full-height angled porches with crenellated parapets. Lancet windows. SE vestry of the restoration by *Tom Grazebrook*, 1902–6. Wide aisleless interior with a queenpost roof. Original W gallery on iron columns. Short chancel entered by a tall arch with two continuous chamfers. – FONT by *Grazebrook*, also perhaps the chancel WALL PAINTINGS. – PULPIT by *Harold C. King*, 1916. – STAINED GLASS. E window doubtless by *O'Connor*, 1854. Aisles: four by *William Morris & Co. (Westminster)*, 1948–9. St Francis, S, by *John Hardman Studios*, 1965, cartooned by *Patrick Feeney*. Two by *Claude Price*, 1968–9. – MONUMENTS. Two by *Peter Hollins*. Anna Amery †1844, signed. Large tablet with a putto by a sarcophagus. He extinguishes a torch. Lyndon J. Grier, 1858 (behind the organ), Roman altar tablet. – Rev. J.W. Grier †1866, draped tablet, probably also *Hollins*. – The churchyard has original RAILINGS and W GATEPIERS.

METHODIST CHURCH, High Street. 1993 by *Frank R. Humphreys* of *Ronald Baker, Humphreys & Goodchild*. Traditional, with pedimental gables. Yellow brick with red and blue dressings. Dwarfed alas by the A491. – Rear HALLS by *Sidney Davies*, 1932.

PERAMBULATIONS

1. High Street

The start is Holy Trinity church. Up VICARAGE ROAD, the CORBETT OUTPATIENTS CENTRE by the *Percy Thomas Partnership*, 2004. Semicircular, with overlapping S-shaped roofs. Opposite, Nos. 26–46, council houses of 1920–1 by *Tom Grazebrook*, one group pleasantly enclosed. Back and N along HIGH STREET, on the site of a glassworks on Deeley's map of 1688, STOURBRIDGE WAR MEMORIAL ATHLETIC GROUND. Monumental brick ARCHWAY by *Frederick Woodward*, 1928, with stepped-up top. At the rear, PAVILION of 1928 by *Alfred Long*. On the E side was the CORBETT HOSPITAL, mostly demolished 2007: an C18 house, The Hill, converted and extended by *Thomas Robinson*, 1892–3. Robinson's brick and half-timber LODGE survives, with plaster relief of the Corbett crest, and GATES with attractive lettering. Further N, HILL HOUSE, the former superintendent's house, also *Robinson*, 1900. Big black-and-white s gable. Beyond, early C20 villas: the best No. 40A, ORCHARD HOUSE, Voysey-ish of 1913, perhaps by *G. F. Webb*, and No. 36A, WOODCROFT, *c.* 1930, Neo-Georgian. HARLESTONE HOUSE on the W side, Early Victorian classical, built as the master's house of a glassworks. Opposite, beyond School Drive, plain brick ranges, the former DEPOT of the Kinver Light Railway (1901, closed 1930).

At the cross-roads, on the W, the former FISH INN. 1760s, the classical detail and s porch probably from a 1923 recasting. Clock of 1951 celebrating the Festival of Britain. Behind it, the RUSKIN GLASS CENTRE. The former Coalbournhill glassworks, founded 1691, closed 2000. 1930s front block with big chimney, earlier ranges behind. Conversion 2008 by *BPN*. Opposite, the former LITTLE PIG pub of 1929 (No. 120) by *J. S. Redman*, with timber gable and Tuscan corner columns. In COLLIS STREET, running E, the INSTITUTE of 1908 by *G. F. Webb*, his first known work. Altered front. Its billiard-room roof has impressive segmental braces. Simple staircase. Glass of 1920 by the *T. W. Camm* workshop in some internal windows: playing cards and billiard balls.

N up High Street, on the W side No. 135, Early Victorian classical. Opposite, the tiny early C19 former LODGE of Dennis Hall (*see* below), with Greek Doric columns *in antis*; its pilasters and cornice repeated on the picturesque classical villa attached on the N, of after 1839. On the W, the Methodist church (*see* above). Opposite, on the corner of BRETTELL LANE the former WHITE HORSE pub, 1840s Tudor Revival with a sharp corner gable. Horseshoe-shaped w doorway, probably from alterations by *Rollinson & Beckley*, 1892–4. Opposite and N, the former OLD DIAL, 1830s. In Brettell Lane, E, modest Late Georgian survivors, e.g. No. 145.

Dennis Park, E of High Street between Brettell Lane and Collis Street, was developed slowly from 1833 in the grounds of DENNIS HALL, which survives in Cameo Drive. Built by Thomas Hill, between 1762 and 1769. Three storeys, 2–3–2 bays, slightly projecting pedimented centre, stone strings. Stone-arched segment-headed windows with fluted keystones. The central bay has a first-floor aedicule and second-floor eared architrave. Bracket cornice. Semicircular porch on thin Doric columns with plain entablature – the only progressive feature. Part of Thomas Webb's glassworks from 1854 until 1990; a C19 chimney projects on the N. Extended and converted to flats by *Lewis & Percival*, 2003.

KING WILLIAM STREET has attractive mid-C19 classicism at Nos. 122–129. Next to No. 124 a former MISSION HALL by *Tom Grazebrook*, 1889. No. 136, part of an eclectic mid-C19 block with a corner tower.

2. Stourbridge Canal Basin

At the s end of High Street by the river, adjoining Stourbridge and its ring road. A Regency classical range, and the former MOORINGS TAVERN (now OLD WHARF INN), early C19 but with an C18 cottage behind, flank the cobbled CANAL STREET. Down here on the l. the canal company's OFFICES etc., 1849 by *Robert Robinson*. *Rundbogenstil*, brick, L-shaped, with pedimental gable in yellow refractories. Heavy bracket cornice. The first-floor committee room has a three-centred vaulted ceiling. Reconstructed outhouses, W, on the probable site of *Yarranton*'s river wharf of the mid C17.

Opposite, the BONDED WAREHOUSE. Ground floor, with inserted sandstone blocks, probably of 1779 by *Thomas Dadford Jun.*, perhaps incorporating earlier fabric from C18 warehouses for the river navigation. Second floor and the unexplained E apse of 1799–1800 by 'Mr *Kyte*'. In 1849 *Robert Robinson* reconstructed the building, extended it N to the edge of the canal, and added the third storey and lucams. His is the grand architectural gesture, the Doric cast-iron colonnade facing the canal. All three phases visible on the W. The earlier phases loosely bonded, with English garden wall bond used for strength in e.g. the W gable; *Robinson* uses this bond consistently. Lower floors supported on cast-iron piers with slotted sides to allow flexible subdivision for storage. Massive fir queenpost roof. *John Greaves Smith* repaired the almost derelict warehouse in 1989 for the Stourbridge Navigation Trust, adding an elegant steel and wood staircase, and the offices in 1992. Until the 1960s the canal extended E under High Street to wharves.

W along the towpath, cast-iron BRIDGE of 1838 made by *John Bradley & Co.*, re-erected here in 2000.* Further on, the arch to a former DRY DOCK, also by Bradley, dated 1873, and the ruinous former MANAGER'S HOUSE of the Stourbridge ironworks (for the New Foundry, *see* p. 559), retaining windows with late C18 segmental cast fluted lintels.

On High Street towards Holy Trinity, the former JONES & ATTWOOD factory, dated 1893, probably by *Thomas Robinson*. Tall thin Dutch corner gable. Oval and round windows mark the offices. Down OLD WHARF ROAD here, the former SUTTON'S HOLLOWARE offices by *Webb & Gray*, 1922, with lunette windows.

BRIERLEY HILL

First mentioned 1642. Early settlement was along the High Street and at Black Delph. The Stourbridge Canal of 1776–9, and the enclosure of Pensnett Chase in 1784, encouraged houses and industry to spread. Lord Dudley's timber yard, established before 1822, was transformed in 1855–7 into the huge Round Oak ironworks (later steel), N and E of the centre. The most famous glassworks was Royal Brierley. Local Board 1868, Urban District 1894. From 1934 this included Kingswinford, Pensnett, Quarry Bank and Wordsley (qq.v.). The late C20 recession was hard: Round Oak closed in 1984, and the Merry Hill development has eclipsed the old centre. A by-pass was completed in 2008.

The local architects were *Rollinson & Beckley*, founded 1870. Mark Rollinson chaired the Local Board, Josiah Beckley was its surveyor. *Henry Jennings* was the firm's designer from c. 1902, recognizable by his liking for ball finials. The firm survives as *Jennings Homer & Lynch*.

PLACES OF WORSHIP

ST MICHAEL, Church Hill. Built as a chapel of ease to Kingswinford in 1765. Brick. In 1822–3 aisles were added, treated externally like transepts, with staircases in the W angles, vestries in the E. Their designer is not certain; *John White* of Stourbridge was involved, perhaps only as surveyor; also *W.M. Geary*. Chancel extended by *Lewis Vulliamy*, 1836–7. In 1899–1900 *Jethro Cossins* of *Cossins, Peacock & Bewlay* re-cased and largely rebuilt the C18 W tower, extended the chancel and S vestry, added a NE organ chamber, and recast the interior.

Cossins's tower is a solid design with big angle buttresses, in Adderley Park brick with Penkridge stone dressings. His cupola was sadly never built. Mixed early C18 and Jacobean

---

*From Ketley Road, Kingswinford, on the Standhills branch of the Stourbridge Extension Canal.

detail: belfry windows with swan's-neck pediments, corner pinnacles with ogee tops. The transepts have two tiers of windows, both segment-headed, like a grand factory. Big brick quoins. The chancel has quadrant corners of 1900 and a three-light E window.

The interior is a surprise: a delightful mixture of Georgian, Cossins and later C20 classicism. Galleries with two tiers of arcading of 1822–3, Ionic over Doric. *Cossins* inserted the little balconies with splat balusters, and the arches linking the upper columns. His chancel arch is a Serliana, with Ionic columns supporting the cross-wall, linked back by the entablature. An identical arrangement separates the sanctuary. E window of three stepped round-headed lights, probably a reference to the late C17 church at Ingestre, Staffs. – PULPIT and PEWS by *Cossins*, 1900. – FONT by *Jones & Willis*, 1901. – ALTAR, REREDOS, CHOIR STALLS and arcaded SCREEN, S aisle, by *Harold C. King*, 1935; also the nave PANELLING, 1944–9. N aisle partitioned by *Robin Hurley*, 1994. – PAINTINGS. Medallions of SS Michael and Gabriel above the chancel arch, 1910 by *Sidney F. Smith*; survivors of a scheme designed by *Robert Baker*. – STAINED GLASS. All by *Samuel Evans* or *Samuel Evans & Sons*. E window, 1900, incorporating side windows of 1885. S aisle, from E: 1900 with earlier work, 1919 (the 'Christian Warrior'), 1913. W lancets 1911.

ST PAUL, Hawbush Road. 1954–5 by *Jennings Homer & Lynch*.

ST MARY (R.C.), High Street. 1872–3 by *E.W. Pugin*. Red brick with Bath stone dressings. Nave and chancel, the division not expressed externally, N aisle and chapel. Contemporary, sharply gabled NE sacristy by *Alfred Emery*. Stump of a SW tower with pyramid roof. W doorway with tympanum of Christ's head crowned with thorns. S windows with plate tracery, E window with seven sexfoiled circles. Inside, typical E.W. Pugin attenuated proportions. Four-bay arcade with grey Aberdeen granite columns. Chancel arch with red granite columns. The N chapel has Cork marble. Bath stone capitals, some with foliage carved by *William Griffiths*. Reordered in the late 1960s. Original W gallery, behind late C20 panels. – REREDOS probably of 1873, the painted saints and flanking panels by *J.A. Pippet*, 1899. – FONT by *Emery*, 1873. – STAINED GLASS. E windows by *Hardmans*, 1899.

BRIERLEY HILL METHODIST CHURCH, Bank Street. 1969–71 by *John P. Osborne & Son*, replacing a chapel of 1829. Low, maroon brick, a monopitch roof marking the worship space. This has a folded pine ceiling. – STAINED GLASS probably by *Percy Bacon Bros*, *c.*1910.

CONGREGATIONAL CHAPEL (now ALBION STREET CHURCH). 1882 by *Thomas Robinson*. An impressively tall Gothic front. Brick and terracotta. Cusped lancets. Kneelers and projections on the gable.

BAPTIST CHURCH, South Street. 1963–4 by *Roger Hodges*, replacing a chapel of 1853–4. Its square, blue-brick meeting-room block survives behind.

FAT YUE TEMPLE (Buddhist), Cottage Street, E of the by-pass. Former youth centre by *Jennings Homer & Lynch*, 1963, with big asymmetrical roof.

PUBLIC BUILDINGS

CIVIC CENTRE, Bank Street. A competition in 1938 was won by *H.P. Crallan*, but war stopped work. The present incoherent flat-roofed group is by the U.D.C. architect *J.P. Moore*: offices 1952–4, Council Chamber and committee rooms 1955–8 (altered), Civic Hall 1960–2. Buff brick. The Hall lobby opens to side staircases, a nice spatial effect.

LIBRARY AND TECHNICAL INSTITUTE (now INTERNATIONAL GLASS CENTRE), Moor Street. 1903–4 by *J. Lewis Harpur*, U.D.C. Surveyor. Jacobean, in brick and pink terracotta. Many small accents: corner dome, gable with statue niche, cupola, entrances with big convex mouldings. Figures modelled by *Arthur Gibbons* and *Albert Oakden*.

TEMPERANCE HALL (former), Trinity Street. 1909 by *Henry Jennings*, with his characteristic ball finials.

PRIMARY SCHOOL, Mill Street. 1909–10 by *John Hutchings* (or his assistant *G.C. Lowbridge*). Severe Neo-Georgian, with a small cupola. Many additions.

PERAMBULATIONS

1. High Street and Church Street

We start at the cross-roads in front of the Civic Centre. In DUDLEY ROAD, N, the former LIBERAL CLUB by *John Yorke*, dated 1902, and massive former DANILO cinema of 1936, next door, probably by *Ernest Roberts*. S down HIGH STREET, small-scale, with poor late C20 shopfronts. On the W side, Nos. 181–183, *c.* 1840, with pilasters and pedimented windows. Further down on the E side, a block of 1973–6 by *Kenneth W. Norton*; boxed-out oriels light the present LIBRARY. It replaced *Josiah Beckley*'s Town Hall of 1873–5, disjointed but lively Gothic. W side, MOLYNEUX HOUSE of 1957 (Nos. 129–137) by *Webb & Gray*; Nos. 121–125, Late Georgian; Nos. 109–111 of *c.* 1880 by *Rollinson & Beckley*, yellow brick; and Nos. 99–101 by *Jennings & Homer*, 1936–7. Opposite, the MARKET HALL of 1930, also by *Jennings & Homer*. Façade with urns and broken segmental pediment; steel-truss-roofed hall behind. No. 94 was Marsh & Baxter's butcher's shop, almost certainly by *Henry Jennings*, *c.* 1911. Four storeys, in maroon terracotta and brick. Jacobean. Oriels with quadrant corners, ball finials.

At the junction the former ALMA pub of 1937–8, probably by *Watkin & Maddox*, with a corner chimney. Opposite, the MOOR CENTRE by *John Edwards & Partners*, 1982 (replacing Marsh & Baxter's pork factory). Set in its High Street front a little DRINKING FOUNTAIN of 1868 by *William Griffiths*. Stubby columns, shell-hood. Off Moor Street, W, ALBION STREET runs N. Here a boldly lettered 'Iron & Steel Warehouse' by *Rollinson & Beckley*, c. 1875, with patterned iron glazing.

Back and S down High Street. On the E side the former POST OFFICE of 1894, plain Queen Anne by *E.J. Searchfield*, on the W side the RED LION pub by *A.T. Butler*, 1926, characteristic brick Tudor Revival. Nos. 30–32, next to St Mary's church (p. 496), are Late Georgian. Across the by-pass, CHAPEL STREET ESTATE of 1962–5 by *Adelphi Architects*.* The climax of Brierley Hill U.D.C.'s post-war housing, a *ville radieuse* with thirteen- and sixteen-storey towers, and maisonettes, all in pale buff brick. *G.F. Webb* designed the S towers, crisply detailed, with brick piers delineating the end bays and glazed top screens. – NINELOCKS COMMUNITY CENTRE, a V-roofed former church hall, 1965.

Now SW down CHURCH STREET. On the SE side Nos. 3–5, early C19 with alterations. Opposite, a steep terrace and the CHURCH HILL 'promenade', an improvement of 1883–4 by *Josiah Beckley*. On top the WAR MEMORIAL, 1921. By *George Brown & Sons* of Kidderminster, 'elaborated' by *Francis Lane*, local industrialist, from a sketch by Councillor *J.T. Fereday*. Limestone and marble. Tiers of corner columns. Houses to the SW, including Frenchy No. 2, all post-1884, probably by *Rollinson & Beckley*. Across North Street, No. 22 is Late Georgian (before 1822). Tuscan doorcase, between mid-C19 bays. Nos. 24–26 were the early C19 WHIMSEY INN, much altered; taller brewery building behind. On the E corner of South Street, S side, the former TRAVELLERS' REST by *A.T. & Bertram Butler*, 1937.

BANK STREET runs NW from the Civic Centre. Nos. 8–16 by *G.S. Gough*, 1898–1900, for the Methodist church. Nos. 127–135, 'ONE MANS PROPERTY ERECTED 1891', with brick detail suggesting *Rollinson & Beckley*. Former BRIDGE INN, 1937 by *A.T. Butler*, with shallow bow.

2. Delph

DELPH – no longer 'Black Delph', but still of interest – is the area reached down MILL STREET, SE from the Moor Centre. The former WATERLOO pub (No. 41), of before 1822, has canted bays of c. 1890 by *Rollinson & Beckley*. Beyond the by-pass, the top of the DELPH LOCKS on the Dudley Canal of 1776–9, engineer *Thomas Dadford Sen*. Called the 'Nine Locks', eight since reconstruction in 1856–8 by *Walker, Burges & Cooper*. At the top, lattice-parapet FOOTBRIDGE made by the *Horseley Co.*, 1856. Below, much-restored STABLES, probably contemporary. Remains of original locks in undergrowth, SE. Beyond them a former LOCK-KEEPER'S COTTAGE (No. 42 The Goss),

---

*A consortium of local practices under *Alan Young & Partners*. Pevsner said of the towers in 1974, 'As if a place like Brierley Hill needed any.'

probably of 1779, now roughcast. Three-sided end facing the canal. Simple dentil cornice.

The bottom lock is crossed by a *Moderne* concrete bridge of 1934–6 carrying DELPH ROAD. The Stourbridge Canal continues SW. The BELL INN, W, recast by *O.M. Weller*, 1937. Going E, the TENTH LOCK pub (formerly STORES) by *A.T. & Bertram Butler*, 1937. Up the hill, DELPH MILL, small-scale C19 industrial, and the 1830s BLACK HORSE pub. Further up, the VINE pub, with behind, the tower of BATHAM'S BREWERY. The façade retains mid-C19 first-floor windows, but is mostly of the rebuilding of 1911–12; r. part originally a butcher's shop. Surviving traditional plan of rooms flanking a central entrance passage. At the roundabout Mount Pleasant runs E into Quarry Bank. Back N up Mill Street, the former COTTAGE SPRING pub (No.172) by *Henry Jennings*, 1907. Jacobean, with curly gable and, of course, ball finials.

OTHER BUILDINGS

STEVENS & WILLIAMS WORKS (later ROYAL BRIERLEY CRYSTAL), Moor Street. 1870. Irregular blue-brick ranges. Ground floor mostly warehouses, storerooms and board room above. Porch and extension 1925. A surviving chimney, S. Converted to housing 2008–9.

HARRIS & PEARSON BRICKWORKS OFFICES (former), Brettell Lane, ¾ m. SW. By *Rollinson & Beckley*, dated 1888. The firm's glazed firebricks: yellow walls with cream and blue banded pilasters and central gable. The firm's name in terracotta over the archway, and in bold iron letters on the roof. Repaired for West Midlands Historic Buildings Trust 2004–5, by *Bob Tolley* of *S.T. Walker & Duckham*. To the E, the former OLD CROWN pub, early C19, with one hipped roof end.

PUBS on DUDLEY ROAD, ½ m. N. Former ROUND OAK (No. 141), painted faience below, probably *Scott & Clark*, 1939. The BLUE BRICK (No. 153), large mid-C19; faience front of 1929.

MERRY HILL

Developed partly on the site of Round Oak steelworks. The most significant late C20 commercial development in the Black Country, but architecturally dire. SHOPPING CENTRE of 1984–9 by *Building Design Partnership*, the main mall concept by *Leslie Jones Architects*. To the N, the WATERFRONT development. Masterplan and most buildings by *Level Seven Architects*. A new basin on the Dudley Canal separates WATERFRONT EAST, 1988–90, an immense series of yellow-brick hipped-roofed blocks (project architects *Percy Thomas Partnership*), from WATERFRONT WEST, 1990–2. POINT NORTH (also with *Percy Thomas*), stepped roofs, 1991–3. The worthwhile building is WATERFRONT HOUSE, with barrel roof slung from pylons, 1994–5. BUSINESS PARK to the W, 1993–5.

BROCKMOOR

NW of Brierley Hill, with a similar pattern of industrial development, encouraged by the Stourbridge Canal of 1776–9. It ran between the two most important factories, the Leys ironworks (pronounced 'Lays') and the Cookley iron and tinplate works, later Richard Thomas & Baldwins.

ST JOHN, High Street. By *Thomas Smith*, 1844–5. Cost £2,153; the Commissioners gave £500. Attractive Neo-Norman. Plum brick with primrose-yellow firebrick dressings, an early example of Smith's polychromatic work. Cruciform, with low proportions. Quadrant porches in the transept angles; heavy bellcote with chamfered piers. Interior white-painted and reordered by *W.E. Homer* of *Jennings Homer & Lynch*, 1991–2, with rooms built in at the W. Chancel arch with trumpet-scallop capitals, transept arches (now blocked) big chevron. Tie-beam roof, but one hammerbeam truss at the E. – STAINED GLASS. Good E window by *T.W. Camm*, 1897. Nave, three by *G. Maile & Son*, 1954. Now on the W stairs, *Goddard & Gibbs* of 1965 and 1974. – War memorial LYCHGATE, 1917.

WESLEYAN REFORM CHURCH (former), Campbell Street. 'Erected 1861, Restored 1905.' Rendered, with Y-tracery windows, like a Georgian chapel gone oddly heavy.

The HIGH STREET has modest C19 terracing. In NORWOOD ROAD, running SW, the OLD STAR pub by *Henry Jennings*, c. 1904, with tiled front. Behind the church the former VICARAGE, by *Thomas Smith*, 1847. Tudor Revival, blue brick with Gornal stone dressings. Further W, survivors of the Cookley works, by *Webb & Gray*: CHILTERN HOUSE, the offices, 1937–8, cubic, flat-roofed, with small entrance tower; machine shop of c. 1950. Behind, the Fens branch of the Stourbridge Canal, and BROCKMOOR JUNCTION, from where the Stourbridge Extension Canal of 1837–40 ran NW. Only a short length remains. Back on High Street and W again, at MOOR STREET, the former HAPPY RETURN pub by *Scott & Clark*, 1935–6.

On PENSNETT ROAD, ¼ m. NE, the former BULL'S HEAD, similar to the Happy Return but larger, 1938, by *Scott & Clark* (*Thomas Galbraith*). N, the former BROCKMOOR BASIN, landscaped in the late C20 as WIDE WATERS. Beyond (properly in Pensnett), former canal reservoirs, originally made in 1779 or shortly after: to the W, GROVE POOL; to N and E, MIDDLE POOL and FENS POOL. The path between these is the trackbed of the Pensnett Railway of 1844–5.

COSELEY

The eastern part of the ancient parish of Sedgley, with 'innumerable little villages' (John Roper, 1952): Roseville, Wallbrook,

Coppice, Hurst Hill (Can Lane) and Sodom,* the last three marked by surviving chapels. Roseville became the main centre in the C19, it and Wallbrook were redeveloped in the late C20. The largest engineering firm was Cannon Industries, famous for gas cookers (closed 1994). Coseley had an Urban District Council until 1966. Its offices of 1895 (*C.W. Sidebotham*, Surveyor) were demolished in 1968, its swimming baths of 1962 (*Scott & Clark*) in 2010.

This account includes Hurst Hill and Woodcross, part of the U.D.C. but in Wolverhampton since 1966.

CHRIST CHURCH, Church Road. 1827–30 by *Thomas Lee*. Tooled Gornal ashlar. Broad lancet windows and single-step buttresses. w tower with a strong profile created by set-back buttresses and heavy pinnacles. Chancel E wall reconstructed with new window, curvilinear Dec but with straight mullions, by *A.T. Butler*, 1905–6. Tall C15-style arcades with capitals to the shafts but characteristic Late Georgian 'drops' between. Galleries with blank ogee arcaded fronts. The chancel is separated by a tie-beam on decorative brackets. – FONT. 1830. Cover by *James A. Swan*, 1930. – PULPIT, 1830, cut down 1888. – Ornate CHANCEL SCREEN and loft by *Advent Hunstone*, 1904, with figures by *William Glasby*, 1924. – Chancel PANELLING by *Swan*, 1930. – STAINED GLASS. E window by *William Morris & Co.*, 1906, Our Lord in Glory, not typical, with rather pale figures. Figures from its predecessor by *Warrington*, 1847, now in the porches. Aisles, an important series by *Nathaniel Westlake* (*Lavers, Barraud & Westlake*), 1867 etc. Figures above, biblical scenes below, marking a move towards pictorial composition following his studies of European C17 glass. s aisle, *John Hardman Studios*, 1957.

The LADY CHAPEL is enclosed behind a chancel s screen by *Wood & Kendrick*, 1897. Formed by *W.A. Bonney* in 1888, but what we now see is a rebuilding and re-fitting by *A.T. Butler*, 1909–10. Lobby with spiral stair to the tiny w gallery. Panelling to head height. Butler added a small altar recess through a plain chamfered arch. Contrastingly ornate wooden superstructure enclosing a PAINTING of the Ascension by *Florence Camm* (*T.W. Camm*). – BENCHES and ALTAR RAIL by *A.T. & Bertram Butler*, 1934. – STAINED GLASS. The Resurrection, by *Walter Camm* (*T.W. Camm*), 1910.

ST MARY, Gorge Road, Hurst Hill. Nave and aisles of 1872 by *George Bidlake*, chancel of 1882 by his partner and successor, *T.H. Fleeming*. A solid, severe, unified E.E. design in rock-faced Gornal stone. Impressively tall chancel with E window of five cusped lancets and stepped-up string course. NE organ chamber by *F.T. Beck*, 1911. Wide and high inside. C13-style arcades. Aisle roofs with effective diagonal braces. – FONT carved by *H.C. Frith*, 1872, with castellated cover. – REREDOS.

---

*Marked on parish surveys of 1826 and 1843, but the name was suppressed later in the C19.

Centre by *Fleeming*, 1882; canopy and tracery sides, chancel PANELLING, by *James A. Swan*, 1930–1. – PULPIT and CHOIR STALLS probably *Fleeming*. – NAVE ALTAR by *Leonard Woodhams*, 2001, with intersecting parabolic supports, handsome but alien. – s aisle REREDOS by *Beck*, 1920. – N aisle SCREEN with paintings of saints also his, *c.*1915. – STAINED GLASS. E window, *Samuel Evans*, 1900. Last Supper with Crucifixion. s aisle, *J. Wippell* (*George Cooper-Abbs*), St Martha 1956, King David 1959; five lights by *A.E. & P.E. Lemmon*, 1947–52.

ST CHAD, Oak Street. 1882–3 by *T.H. Fleeming*. A tough, cheap brick church, a simpler version of St Mary. Clerestoried nave, low aisles with lancets, tall unbuttressed chancel with bold plate-tracery E window and again a nicely managed string course. A tall flèche on the nave roof was unfortunately removed in 1967. Chancel reordered in 1980 by *Hinton Brown Langstone*. – Original PULPIT and bench PEWS. – STAINED GLASS. E window, *John Hardman Studios* (*Donald Taunton*), 1945. Aisles, the best *Heaton, Butler & Bayne*, †1897, s.

ST JOHN FISHER (R.C.), Yewtree Lane. 1960 by *Jennings Homer & Lynch*.

COPPICE BAPTIST CHAPEL, Caddick Street. Begun 1804. Strict and Particular Baptist (Gospel Standard) since the pastorate of William Bridge (1816–61). Simple block with rendered front, pedimental gable and two tiers of round-headed windows. The original build is the first two bays. Central doorway, a later C19 modification. Section behind added probably *c.*1825. Rear cross-wing containing schoolrooms, dated 1875. Gallery at the entrance end of *c.*1825 with iron columns, panelled front and original elegantly stepped PEWS. Another facing it, probably originally of the same date; reconstructed with Gothic panelling in 1992 when the organ was altered. – PULPIT. Upper part 1804, with reeded panels; base *c.*1825. – PEWS. 1884.

EBENEZER BAPTIST CHAPEL, Birmingham New Road. 1857–8. A landmark on the A4123. Rendered façade with tall windows, giant pilasters and a show pediment. Plain brick sides articulated by pilaster strips. Gallery on iron columns, with original seating. Reordered, with inserted ceiling.

HURST HILL METHODIST CHURCH, Hurst Road. 1864–5, builders *Elliott & Whitfield*, designer perhaps *Hamlet Durose*. Four-bay pedimented box with plain giant pilasters and bluebrick cornice. Tall round-headed windows and recessed panels underneath. Schoolroom behind, 1910, by 'Mr *Price*'. Gallery round four sides, original PEWS. – PULPIT, RAIL, TABLE and LECTERN of 1921. – FONT. Odd, like an octagonal High Victorian pinnacle with the top chopped off.

OLD MEETING HOUSE (Unitarian), Old Meeting Road. 1874–5 by *T.H. Fleeming*, replacing a chapel of 1717. A small Dec gabled hall in rock-faced stone. Four bays, one with side gables lighting the gallery. Doorcase with tiny lights in the tympanum. Four-light window with heptafoiled circle in the tracery. Collar- and arch-braced roof. – Original PEWS and GALLERY with iron columns and heavily stop-chamfered front. – Square

PULPIT. – STAINED GLASS. One E window, 1930. – Behind, SUNDAY SCHOOL originally of 1753, but with Late Georgian iron-framed windows and C19 roof.– In the graveyard, tea-caddy TOMB to James Maullin †1765 etc.

PROVIDENCE BAPTIST CHAPEL, Hospital Lane. 1870–1 by *T. Richards*. Savagely cut down. It had two storeys, and paired towers, in a kind of Lombardic Romanesque.

ROSEVILLE METHODIST CHURCH, School Street. 1980 by *John Greaves Smith*, replacing a chapel of 1853. A simple cubic brick block with narrow clerestory windows, but also allusive traditional details: walls cut back with chamfered sills and weathered buttress-like projections; corbelled brick cross. An unexpected and fascinating combination.

UPPER ETTINGSHALL METHODIST CHURCH ('Sodom Chapel'), Upper Ettingshall Road. 1850. The original part has three bays, with two tiers of windows. Plain front with pedimental gable. Doorway with heavy architrave and minimal pediment. Sunday School behind, added 1853. Horseshoe-shaped gallery on iron columns. End wall with big arch of 1853. PULPIT and RAIL by *O.A. Turner*, 1957–8.

CHRIST CHURCH PRIMARY SCHOOL, Church Road. *G.E. Hamilton*'s picturesque school of *c*.1830 has been demolished. The surviving, minimally Tudor range N of the church appears on a map of 1843, so may perhaps also be his. Much altered.

MANOR PRIMARY SCHOOL, Ettingshall Road. 1931 by *J. Percy Clark*. With hipped roof, sculpturally treated, and low wings,

MOUNT PLEASANT SCHOOL (former), Mount Pleasant. 1878–9 by *A.P. Brevitt*, but substantially rebuilt in 1904 by *S.H. Eachus*. Converted to housing by *Dudley M.B.C. Construction & Design*, 2019.

SILVER JUBILEE PARK, Birmingham New Road and Mason Street. 1936. Original KEEPER'S COTTAGE, tile-hung, with pyramid roof and central chimney, by *J.P. Clark*.

Opposite Christ Church in CHURCH ROAD, a terrace of *c*.1845–50, PORTLAND PLACE, rendered, basic Tudor. Going s, mid-C19 terraces. In PEAR TREE LANE, W, Nos. 14–21 by *A.T. Butler*, 1908–9. Voysey style, rendered, with long buttresses; the moment for this fashion (cf. Fallings Park, Wolverhampton).

COSELEY HALL, Avenue Road. Three-bay central block of *c*.1845–50 for Edward Sheldon.* Probably by *Hamlet Durose*, known to have worked for the Sheldon family. Shallow giant pilasters, paired bracket eaves and low hipped roof. Tuscan porch. Canted bays added *c*.1900. It had symmetrical single-storey wings. To the l. now, recessed, a later C19 block with taller roof. Converted to flats, in a poor state. Also in Avenue Road, No. 44, N side, a three-bay villa of *c*.1850, and the PAINTERS ARMS opposite, of the same period.

HORSE AND JOCKEY pub (former), Ivyhouse Lane. 1938–9 by *F. Morrell Maddox*.

---

*John Roper thought that the parts now demolished were mid-C18, but no building is marked on the Sedgley parish maps of 1826 or 1843.

WINDMILL, Oak Street, w of St Chad. Only the tower, now a house. Rendered, with one window to the w. Probably late c18, certainly here by 1807. Comical c20 hipped roof.

BIRMINGHAM CANAL. The Coseley tunnel, made in 1835–7, has its N portal off Ivyhouse Lane and S portal off School Street. Plain arched brickwork; double towpath with horse treads. Immensely deep approach cuttings.

WOODSETTON

A scattered hamlet to the sw.

MOUNT TABOR METHODIST NEW CONNEXION CHAPEL (former), Sedgley Road. Dated 1859. A tiny single-storey front with a heavily shouldered pedimental gable. Windows with red and blue voussoirs. – WAR MEMORIAL outside.

WOODSETTON METHODIST CHURCH (former), Parkes Hall Road. 1882 by *Charles Round* of Tipton. A gabled hall with lancets, bluntly articulated by recessed panels and blue-brick bands. Contemporary SCHOOL behind.

CHURCH OF JESUS CHRIST AND THE LATTER-DAY SAINTS, Tipton Road. 1962 by *Watson & Coates* with *Graham & Baldwin*.

The present centre, SWAN VILLAGE, grew up in the mid c19 on the Tipton to Sedgley turnpike of 1843–5. Terraces and two pubs of this period. In Park Road, the mid-c19 PARK INN and behind, c20 buildings of HOLDEN'S BREWERY. The older settlement is further up the hill towards Sedgley. The grandest houses here, Woodsetton House and Woodsetton Lodge, have gone. Others of after 1845 survive on TIPTON ROAD. ST FAGAN'S, N, Jacobean with shaped gable. Nos. 173–187, a mid-c19 line, with Tudoresque windows at No. 183. Nos. 157–159, heavy, almost styleless.

CRADLEY

A manor in the parish of Halesowen, though always in Worcestershire. The ancient settlement was on a steep N-facing slope where the old High Street twisted down from St Peter's church to the River Stour. Netherend was a separate hamlet. The present centre at Colley Gate and Windmill Hill grew up in the c19 along the Halesowen to Stourbridge road.

Cradley (pronounced with a long 'a') was part of the Black Country chain-making area, with many small domestic workshops. The largest firm was Jones & Lloyd (1837–*c*.1970).* Coal mining expanded from the 1860s; the last colliery, Beech Tree,

---

*One of its chainshops survives, re-erected at the Avoncroft Museum of Buildings at Stoke Prior, Worcestershire.

closed in 1958. The C19 Ragged School movement was active here, and two examples associated with the Hingley family survive, now used as chapels. The finest chapels have gone: *Edward Pincher*'s Trinity Wesleyan Methodist, 1873–4, Gothic, with a landmark spire, dem. 1998; and *A.T. Butler*'s Baptist chapel, 1900–1, Free Style, dem. 1968.

Cradley was part of Halesowen Rural District from 1894, and later a Borough. Its School Board, formed as late as 1899, built in Colley Lane before the County Council took over in 1903.

ST PETER, Church Road. Above Colley Lane in a fine position. It began as a Countess of Huntingdon's Connexion chapel of 1789 by *Mark Jones*, with a pedimented front flanked by angled sections containing gallery staircases. It became Anglican in 1798–9. Parts of the C18 nave walls survive, with large round-headed windows. The ritual W front was replaced by a bold High Victorian tower by *John Cotton*, 1874–5, in red and blue brick with Grinshill stone dressings. Pairs of shafted lancets, frowning hoodmoulds, and balustrade. Not without subtleties, e.g. the way the bands stop lower down on the big stepped buttresses than on the main walls. A short wooden spire with gables was lost in 1933. The church was badly affected by mining subsidence, and in 1931 *G.F. Webb* proposed a rebuilding: a massive cruciform Romanesque design with a tower over the W part of the chancel. Instead, in 1932–3 he rebuilt the E end of the nave with sloping buttresses, put a concrete raft underneath, heightened a small NW vestry of 1907 to make an organ chamber, and added the three-sided E apse.

Inside, there are galleries on three sides and flat aisle roofs, essentially of 1789 but reconstructed by *Webb*. Nave roof by *Cotton*, 1875, with heavy tie-beams and kingposts. Webb's apse is straightforward Romanesque, with triplet windows. But he remodelled much else, stirring in hints of Art Deco and *Moderne*: e.g. the not-quite-Georgian tiers of octagonal gallery columns (around original iron cores) and the organ chamber grille on the r. of the chancel. – PULPIT and PEWS by *Cotton*, 1875; FONT probably also. – C18 tiered SEATING in the N and S galleries and BENCHES in the ritual W. – PELMET and wooden PIERS around the apse by *Webb*, 1954. – STAINED GLASS. Apse, saints by *Stourbridge Stained Glass Works*, 1934. Late Arts and Crafts, but with unsentimental faces. – MONUMENTS. Tablets by *W. Hollins* (†1831) and *Jackson* of Hagley (†1833).

PARK LANE CHAPEL (UNITARIAN), Netherend, ½ m. W. The original chapel is of 1795–6; 'building operations were personally and closely supervised by Mr. *Pargeter*, of Foxcote'. Three bays of large round-headed windows with timber Y-tracery. Two identical S bays and the tower and small spire added in 1864. Plain hall with a recess for the pulpit. Rear corner galleries on iron columns, panelled fronts perhaps of 1796 reused. Fittings in C18 layout, but mostly of 1864: BOX PEWS with chunky stop-chamfering, similar ORGAN CASE, LECTERN and FONT, arcaded iron COMMUNION RAIL. DADO made from

C18 pews. – Bow-fronted C18 PULPIT. – MONUMENTS. Many classical tablets. A series by *Peter Hollins* moves from Late Georgian simplicity (†1829 and †1831) to a heavier mid-C19 aesthetic (†1864). – STAINED GLASS of 1993–4 by *Richard Stokes*. – SCHOOLROOM of 1825–6 across Parsonage Drive, S. Round-headed windows, stone key blocks and imposts. Iron roof trusses with central circles.

PROVIDENCE METHODIST (NEW CONNEXION) CHURCH, Colley Gate. A fascinating contrast: two buildings forty years apart by *G.F. Webb* (*Webb & Gray*). Simple Modernist chapel of 1962–3 with shallow-pitched roof and recessed entrance. Inside, abstract STAINED GLASS by *William Pardoe*. To the W, big SUNDAY SCHOOL of 1925, still Free Style. Entrance between broad pilasters, grey faience frontispiece with moulded top. Inside, transverse segmental arches carry the roof, with dormers between. Timber partitioned classrooms survive along the sides. – Across the narrow lane of Colley Orchard, its predecessor SCHOOL. 1886, by *Isaac Meacham* of Cradley Heath.

CRADLEY BAPTIST CHURCH, Church Road. Former British School of 1871, designed by the builder *T. Lewis* and the minister, the *Rev. M. Morgan*. Low gables with bright polychromatic brickwork, behind a late C20 forebuilding. The lost chapel of 1900–1 was below, facing Colley Lane.

HIGH TOWN RAGGED SCHOOL, Mapletree Lane. 1863. A gabled brick hall with three-centred lancet windows. The rear part may be an early addition. Simple space with collar-beam roof, subdivided by a folding glazed partition. On the N, separate men's classroom dated 1883, perhaps by *Isaac Meacham*. Kitchen extension by *L.J. Southall*, 2002–3. – STAINED GLASS. Three windows by *Walter Camm* (*T.W. Camm*), 1953.

TWOGATES RAGGED SCHOOL (INDEPENDENT METHODIST), Two Gates. Dated 1867. Simple, with renewed round-headed windows and small porch.

PERAMBULATION, from the junction of Colley Gate and Colley Lane. The former TALBOT HOTEL was built in 1875 for the Oliver family, maltsters and brewers. Heavy, domestic-looking classical, with a hipped roof. Brewery range behind. Rare contemporary bar back with thin columns, leaf capitals and a frieze with gilded lettering in panels; also bar front, and staircase. Converted to a nursery in 2017.

E along COLLEY GATE, on the N side Nos. 118–120, heavy classical, dated 1872: Black Country conservatism. Opposite, the OLD VICARAGE of 1899–1900 by *Meredith & Pritchard*, Domestic Revival with half-timbered gables. On the N again, the GATE pub of 1901 by *Wright & Sons*. Past Toy's Lane, WINDMILL HILL has altered C19 houses, and at the top the ROUND OF BEEF. A rare survivor of a Black Country combination, the pub and butcher's shop (now in separate ownership). Pub of 1864, with arched lights to the sashes. The shop is a separate build, but must be close in date. Tall chimneys, a local way of removing smoke, also fast disappearing.

Beyond, down the hill and l. into COLMAN HILL, the GRANGE (now nursing home) is a smooth buff-brick house of 1938, perhaps by *Jennings & Homer*. Opposite, OAK BUNGALOW by *Webb & Gray*, 1922. L-shaped, with a timbered gable in the angle.

Back and N along Colley Lane. On the W side CRADLEY PRIMARY SCHOOL by *Ellis Williams Architects*, 2001. Opposite, former INFANTS' SCHOOL of 1902 by *Meredith & Pritchard*. Beyond, the LIBRARY of 1936 by the Halesowen U.D.C. Surveyor, *George Spurr*. The LIBERAL CLUB is of 1911 by *Philip L. Best*, with a big Baroque semicircular pediment. Down Church Road, across Blue Ball Lane and sharp r., is CRADLEY C. OF E. SCHOOL. The near (S) part is by *A.T. Butler*, 1897, with a carefully placed hipped dormer. Behind, the original school of 1855–6 by *Francis Smalman Smith*. Three half-hipped gables, the centre one taller. A row of tiny stone openings nestles under the hip. Main windows redone in 1928. Beyond, former teachers' houses, also by *Smalman Smith*, 1855–6. More half-hipped gables, Tudor-arched doorways and quirky detailing. Then the Baptist church, and St Peter's church (pp. 506, 505).

Below the churchyard, WAR MEMORIAL of 1928 by *Stanley Griffiths*. Off Colley Lane opposite, the curiously named INTENDED STREET of 1902: terraced houses by *L. Adams*. To the N, Colley Lane (the former High Street) drops steeply to the river. On the W side, the ROSE AND CROWN pub by *A.T. Butler*, 1902. A 'two-room drinker' in Free Style. Inventive detail everywhere: tall keystones, moulded doorcase with roses and crowns, piercings in the parapet where the roof flows down to corbelled-out gutters. C19 terraces beyond. Below in LYDE GREEN, No. 15, the former manse of Trinity church, by *Rollinson & Beckley* (perhaps *Henry Jennings*), c. 1900. Tall chimneys, bracketed side porch.

GORNAL

A group of hamlets or small villages, historically part of Sedgley parish and Urban District. They tumble down the escarpment from Upper Gornal on the Dudley to Sedgley road at the top, through Lower Gornal, to Gornal Wood at the bottom, with views W to the Welsh border. Gornal is *echt* Black Country, where in the story a man put his pig on the wall to watch the band go by.* The Gornal stone quarries were at Ruiton, the only stone village in the region. Baggeridge, the last Black Country colliery (closed 1968) was just over the modern Staffordshire boundary, but its former Miners' Welfare is still a landmark.

---

*The German word is appropriate, for here 'I bin' can mean *Ich bin* rather than 'I've been'.

ST JAMES, Church Street, Lower Gornal. The start is a simple four-bay chapel of 1815–17, with lancet windows and tall w tower. The Earl of Dudley's surveyor *John Piddock Roberts* drew site plans, but a more likely architect is *Robert Ebbels*, who was paid an old debt in 1831. Present appearance mostly due to *William Bourne*, who 'considerably enlarged and re-fitted' it in 1849. Stepped buttresses, like those of Bourne's Dudley churches, and small NW and SW porches.* In 1888–9 *T.H. Fleeming* added the chancel with polygonal apse, N vestry and S organ chamber, with red Straits sandstone dressings. Three-light windows under heavy lintels. The W tower, cut down and then 'reconditioned' *c.*1900, was again recast and reduced by *J.C. Thompson*, 1929–30, with new windows and parapet. Standard roof of queenpost trusses. W gallery on slim square wooden piers, survivor of three by *Edward Marsh*, 1837. Chancel lined with Straits stone. – Tall REREDOS by *Warwick Scott*, 1948. Saints under canopies. – PULPIT and simple FONT by *Fleeming*, 1889. – S (Lady) altar and vaulted REREDOS by *J. Eadie Reid*, 1916, with PAINTING of the Virgin and Child with SS Alban and Bernard in a symbolic landscape. – CHOIR STALLS and PEWS by *Johnson & Giles*, 1956 etc. – STAINED GLASS. Apse NE *Comper*, 1903; apse SE perhaps by *Camm & Co.*, †1901. Nave N and S *T.W. Camm*, 1956. Nave W quatrefoils (gallery), patterning by *Drury & Smith*, 1849. Tower W, *Hardmans*, †1957.

ST PETER, Kent Street, Upper Gornal. 1840–2 by *Robert Ebbels*. A Commissioners' church. It cost £2,353. The W front has two polygonal turrets *à la* King's College Chapel, and four-centred arches to doorways and the three-light window. Its tracery is by *Harold C. King*, 1947, when the turrets were cut down. Six-bay lancet hall behind. Much of 1872–4 by *Davies & Middleton*: open roof, slightly extended chancel, N vestry, PEWS and arcaded CHOIR STALLS. The chancel arch looks original except for the shafts with big rings on tapering corbels (cf. St Edmund, Dudley). – STAINED GLASS. E window perhaps of 1854, small scenes in patterning; S window 1901 by *Jones & Willis*, as is the FONT. – PARCLOSE SCREENS to N chapel and S vestry by *F.T. Beck*, 1922; REREDOS also his, lowered 1948.

ST PETER AND THE ENGLISH MARTYRS (R.C.), Temple Street, Lower Gornal. 1966–7, by *Harry Harper* with *Blantern Radford*. Harper's most dramatic church, with a cantilevered porch supported by a single concrete pier rising into a large cross. Main structure expressed by external transverse beams. Their supports have characteristic 1960s paired thin mullions. Glass wall by the entrance lighting the baptistery. Quiet, low-lit interior, with V-profile lantern over the altar. A satisfying piece. – STAINED GLASS. Lancets by *Patrick Feeney* of *Hardmans*. – Contemporary PRESBYTERY.

---

*The porches have been ascribed to 1837 but do not appear on Thomas Peploe Wood's drawing of 1841.

Dudley, Gornal, St Peter.
Watercolour by Thomas Peploe Wood, 1841

RUITON CHAPEL, Hermit Street. 1830 by *Edward Marsh*. Gornal stone ashlar, in large blocks. A severe and handsome classical design with pedimental gables and a doorcase with panelled pilasters. Round-headed windows, on the front with moulded architraves, on the sides plain. Original tall PULPIT, and gallery on iron columns.

FIVE WAYS METHODIST (NEW CONNEXION) CHAPEL, Ruiton Street, Lower Gornal. Dated 1841, but a recasting of an earlier building, probably a barn. Typical gabled front with three round-headed upper windows. Front extension of 1988 by *D. Harrison* with balancing monopitch roofs. The street range converted from cottages in 1911. Intimate interior with gallery. The choir galley with unusual triple arcade may also be original, but with a late C19 front. – PULPIT and PEWS also late C19.

PROVIDENCE BAPTIST CHURCH, Robert Street. 1874 by *Bidlake & Fleeming*. An austere brick box with High Victorian detail.

HIMLEY ROAD METHODIST CHURCH, Gornal Wood. 1895 by *J.H. Gibbons*. Gabled, with lancets, Y-tracery and round windows. Tough red brick. Hall with false hammerbeam trusses. Original gallery, organ gallery and PEWS. WAR MEMORIAL with bronze panels signed by *Fraleys*. – SCHOOLROOM of 1901.

LAKE STREET (PRIMITIVE) METHODIST CHURCH, Lower Gornal. 1926 by *Joynson Bros*. Still the Edwardian type. Front with gable clamped between buttresses. Big window with fancy Perp-ish tracery.

ST PAUL'S PROTESTANT CHURCH, Lake Street, Lower Gornal. 1923. Very conservative. Brick and biscuit-coloured terracotta, with much corbelling and a toy tower. Older stonework behind.

ZOAR METHODIST (NEW CONNEXION) CHAPEL, Abbey Street, Gornal Wood. 1906 by *P.H. Ashby Bailey* of Dudley. Dominating the village centre. Brick and grey terracotta. Ritual SW tower with characteristic Edwardian spirelet. Eclectic detail: big Perp window and stone frontispiece below, the name panel with foliage background, but round-headed paired lancets to either side, one pair with a steep C17-style pediment. Clearly a deliberate attempt to move beyond Gothic, as the almost unaltered interior has the same mixture. Pointed roof trusses, organ-chamber arch with short columns on corbels, galleries with classical fronts gone delicate. The FURNISHINGS also mix classical, Jacobean and hints of Gothic. PULPIT STAIR with unexpected Art Nouveau wrought ironwork, by *G.W. Pridmore & Son* of Coventry.

CREMATORIUM, Coopers Bank Road. 1958–60 by *John T. Lewis*, Dudley Borough Architect. A steep-roofed Scandinavian design in thin handmade brown brick. Bold diagonal glazing in the entrance wall. Curving open colonnade, r.

PERAMBULATION, Gornal Wood to Lower Gornal. Starting at Zoar Church, up ZOAR STREET past RED HALL SCHOOLS, by *A.P. Brevitt* for Sedgley School Board. S side of 1878–80 with lancets, N of 1891 with terracotta-tiled gables. Caretaker's house of 1891. Then good townscape, terraces stepping up the hill. Black Country bye-law chimneys, straight stacks halfway up the roof slopes, not at the ridge. The OLD BULL'S HEAD, 1904, has a working brewery behind. Zoar Street continues as Temple Street, then NNW as CHURCH STREET, with the Catholic church, the MEMORIAL HALL by *F.T. Beck*, 1924–5, and St James's church, to the FIVE WAYS junction. No. 4 Lake Street, r., double-pile, rubble stone. Opposite, J.R. JONES, also Gornal stone. Both are on a plan of 1817.

RUITON. Vale Street has the WINDMILL (former) and MILLER'S HOUSE (No. 63). Of between 1826 and 1833, perhaps by *Edward Marsh*. The mill has segmental-arched windows; the house has kneeler gables, concave cornice, and minimal doorway pediment. Also No. 119, Late Georgian (altered); Nos. 98–102, also stone, c. 1840; and Nos. 76–80, formerly all RUITON HOUSE (altered). Nos. 42–46 by *Douglas Billingsley* of *Mason, Richards & Partners*, 1965, are the best 1960s houses in the district: two with monopitch roofs (one horribly altered), another beyond, low and long, with high strip windows.

BRITANNIA INN, Kent Street, Upper Gornal, ½ m. NE. Of c. 1840–50. Brick front (now rendered), Gornal stone side walls. One rear room still with a servery without a counter; perhaps originally a semi-private space, for invited customers.

BAGGERIDGE SOCIAL CLUB, The Straits, Gornal Wood, ½ m. W. 1939–41 by the Miners' Welfare specialists, *Warner & Dean* of Sutton-in-Ashfield. Big Lutyens-style roof, tall chimneys. Symmetrical, with a recessed centre, the windows in long bands.

COOPERS BANK FARM, Coopers Bank Road, ½ m. S. T-plan farmhouse, probably early C18, with platbands. Now rendered. Late Georgian sashes and doorcase. Big BARN, probably C18 with alterations, with a wonderful array of ventilation holes. CARTSHED to its r.; ruinous STABLE, l., with ground floor of Gornal stone.

STICKLEY ESTATE, ¼ m. N. Planned by *T. Alwyn Lloyd*, from 1945. Simple pairs in Stickley Lane etc. by *McKewan, Fillmore & McKewan*, 1947–9.

HALESOWEN

9580

The centre of a large ancient parish, which included Cradley, Hunnington, Oldbury, Quinton, Romsley and Warley; a detached part of Shropshire until 1844. Halesowen Abbey, founded in 1215, owned the manor and obtained a borough charter in 1270.

The iron and steel industry started with the medieval Hales Forge. Coombs Wood tube works of 1860, later Stewarts & Lloyds, closed in 1990. Halesowen was part of the Worcestershire nail-making area which stretched SE to Bromsgrove. Nailshops were small, often attached to family houses, as with the nearby chain industry.

In the C19 the town lagged behind its neighbour, Stourbridge. Civic development came late: Rural District 1894, Urban District 1924 and Borough 1936. From the 1950s, the Borough Council, which included three local builders and a demolition contractor, encouraged the piecemeal but almost total destruction of the old town centre. A Development Plan of 1948 produced Queensway, opened in 1962, and the Precinct (now Cornbow Centre) on fields S and W of the church. The worst losses were the Congregational chapel of 1811, and late medieval and C18 houses in Great Cornbow. The by-pass of 1958 cut the town off from the countryside to the S.

CHURCHES

ST JOHN THE BAPTIST, High Street. An impressive church, large, in a prominent position, and with a slender Perp tower crowned by a fine recessed spire. To understand the highly confusing exterior and interior a chronological approach is best. There was probably a Saxon minster here, as two priests are recorded in Domesday. The present church starts with a C12 rebuilding, probably *c.*1175–99 when the advowson was owned by Pershore Abbey. Much late Norman work remains, including E and W gables, so the building was as long as it is now. Yet the church is not at all Norman in character. C12 W doorway of two orders, the outer with three layers of chevron, and an incised inner order also with some chevron. One order of colonnettes, N with scallop capital and S with interlaced loops. The nave buttresses l. and r. are Norman again, and the base of a buttress further N marks the NW corner of the Norman N aisle. The lancet in the gable shows the change of style at the end of the C12. The S doorway is Norman too, with two orders of columns. The arch has chevron again. Scallop capitals on the l., thin trails on the r. The E gable has an intersecting blind arcade carried on cushion capitals (cf. the S transept at Pershore, Worcs.).

Enter for a moment, and W of the tower are two bays of the Norman nave. Composite piers, sturdy, with big scallop capitals. Four big demi-shafts and four thin ones in the diagonals. The arches have a single step. The blocked doorways high up probably led to an C18 gallery. In the chancel a Norman N window with deep rere-arch, now inside. A change from smooth to rough masonry on the N and S walls, and a blank arch in the E wall, suggest there was originally a barrel-vault here, again a Pershore Abbey feature. The E wall of the N aisle has early stonework, perhaps the E wall of a C12 N chapel. The Norman church may have had a crossing tower, but there is no evidence except perhaps a slight thickening at the bottom of the chancel arch S pier. In the C14 a tower was begun in a most unusual position, halfway down the nave. The roof-line shows that the Norman nave survived to its E, as well as W, when it was built.* The arches have two sunk chamfers, a motif also of Ludlow and Hodnet, so probably a Shropshire connection. The upper parts are fully developed early Perp, the windows with super-transoms. Second stage open inside, under a tierceron star-vault. The tower is red sandstone, the battlements and spire grey, so later, C15 ('me'dyng the led of the stepull' is mentioned in accounts of 1499–1500). Three tiers of decorative lucarnes. S aisle of *c.*1300, windows with three elongated cusped lights. The N aisle appears early Perp, despite rebuilding in 1838–9. Blocked N doorway with a sunk chamfer and delicate roll mouldings; windows with through mullions on the N and a crossover pattern at the W. The E nave probably C15: two large bays with standard octagonal piers and capitals, but arches still with sunk chamfers.

In 1531 a 'bargeyne' was made with '*Edward Nicols* and hys felowe' to build a new aisle, probably the chancel S aisle with its rather crude, late-looking arcade: octagonal piers and single-chamfered arches. The low clerestory with small two-light windows is probably of 1533–4 ('an ale...at ye Reryng of ye churche roffe', and payments for 'leydde'). In 1543–4 there was a 'Newe Warke', with a large payment, £3 2s., for 'glasy'g of ye wyndowys'. Apart from *Nicols* the craftsmen were

---

*The VCH, and Pevsner in 1968, suggested that a Norman crossing tower fell on to the nave, causing the rebuilding of the nave E arcades and the new tower. But the present tower must come before these arcades.

Edwarde Moysley and *Thomas While*, mason. Can this be the N transept? The detail, with huge (renewed) beast-stops, and crocketed ogee arches, is common in the West Midlands, e.g. at Romsley, and mostly late C15. But the big four-light window looks late Perp, with flat curves in the tracery and uncusped lower lights. This was a conservative parish, and the 'Newe Warke' may have accommodated the suppressed abbey's rood, 'organs' and images, purchased in 1538. There is a rood-stair turret W of the window.

In 1820 *Francis Goodwin* advertised for tenders for rebuilding E of the tower, and in 1825 he proposed new pews and galleries (as did *William Walker* in 1837), but nothing was done. Then in 1838–9 *Rickman & Hussey* rebuilt the aisle walls, raised the chancel arch and removed the N porch. E window replaced *c.*1850, with thin Geometrical tracery. In 1871–2 *Henry Curzon* removed plaster and raised the Norman chancel arch again. Its details – cable mouldings on the arch, shafts on head corbels – all seem C19. In 1873–5 *Sir Gilbert Scott* lowered the floors and paved them with *Godwin* tiles, removed galleries and partition walls, and re-roofed E and W naves. Outer S aisle by *John Oldrid Scott*, 1882, with three-light windows. Aisle roofs also his.

FURNISHINGS. FONT. Norman. Big round bowl on a fat central column and four slim outside ones, not a Worcestershire type, but similar to Devon and Cornwall ones. Round the bowl crudely cut, very snaky interlace of a decidedly Viking style. The outer columns have small figures with ribbed drapery. Interlace and drapery are related to the S tympanum at Romsley, so perhaps *c.*1170. – SCULPTURE. Gabled cross-head, carved with the Crucifixion and the Virgin and Child, probably C14 (S aisle). – PULPIT and LECTERN by *Gilbert Scott*, 1875. – PEWS also his; identical outer S aisle ones by *Oldrid Scott.* – Former chancel SCREEN with coved top by *Harold Brakspear*, 1922, now between inner and outer S aisles. – BENEFACTION BOARDS. C18. – STAINED GLASS. Much by *Hardmans*: E window (Crucifixion and Ascension), W lancet, both 1875; S aisle, 1875, 1881 (W) and 1884. Outer S aisle E by *William Pearce*, 1893; S going E, *T. W. Camm*, 1911, the Dignity of Labour, with Hiram building Solomon's Temple, good; *Powells*, 1906, Moses; Ascension, perhaps by *Daniel Bell*, 1883. N aisle W by *Samuel Evans*, 1895; N aisle N by *Swaine Bourne*, †1903. Tower, St George by *Walter W. Randle*, 1924. – ROYAL ARMS. Large, of George II.

MONUMENTS. S aisle W. Coffin of a priest, C14, with recumbent effigy under a canopy, badly preserved; also another stone coffin. – Elijah Underhill †1732, S aisle. Crude cartouche with skull and crossbones. – N aisle W. John Halliday, by *Thomas Banks*, 1797. Now stranded behind late C20 cupboards and partitions. Large and grand. Big obelisk with a very high pedestal in front, on which stands a Grecian urn with a fine relief of a seated young woman and a naked boy. To the l. of the pedestal an over-life-size man in a large mantle. His gesture expresses grief. To the r. a kneeling young woman, holding the small dog to save which Halliday was drowned. – Humfri Peshall and others, the last †1770. Convex tablet with cartouche under. – N aisle. William Shenstone †1763, the poet, of The Leasowes (*see* below). Simple free-standing wooden urn on a pedestal. – Edward Lyttelton †1614, with paired Corinthian columns.

In the churchyard, SW of the church, William Shenstone's simple GRAVE. SE of the church, Neoclassical tea-caddy tomb to Thomas Partrdge (*sic*) †1857, with fluted urn. Near the gates, former MARKET CROSS. Medieval base, C18 capital and ball finial. Shaft of 1912, when re-erected here. On the N side of the churchyard, the CHURCH HOUSE by *J.T. Meredith*, 1897, with lancets and half-timbered gable. To its W, HALESOWEN C. OF E. PRIMARY SCHOOL. Tudor Revival range facing the churchyard, of 1838. Probably by *Thomas Smith*, who extended it r. and added the tiny master's house in 1844–5. To its W, gable-end of 1887, probably by *Tom Grazebrook*, and infants' school of 1859 by *Francis Smalman Smith*, mutilated Gothic, with canted end. N side mostly of 1887, with extensions of 1964 by *J.C.T. Cole & Partners*. At the W end of the churchyard, CEMETERY CHAPEL of 1858–9 by *Francis Smalman Smith*, with roguish belfry.

ST MARGARET, Hagley Road, Hasbury. 1907–8 by *J.E.K. & J.P. Cutts*. Brick, Perp. Low old-fashioned exterior with heavy spired bellcote. Spacious interior. Six-bay arcades, stone piers but brick four-centred arches. Typical Cutts W baptistery under a wide arch. – CHOIR STALLS by *A.T. Butler*, 1913. – STAINED GLASS. E window by *A.E. Lemmon*, *c.* 1935. S aisle by *T.W. Camm* (*Walter Camm*), 1952. W by *Swaine Bourne & Son*, 1908. Lady Chapel E by *A.J. Davies*, 1949, S by *Alfred Wilkinson*, 1953, and *D. Cowan*, †1976 and 1977.

OUR LADY AND ST KENELM (R.C.), Siviter Street. 1967 by *Rush Granelli & Partners*.

HALESOWEN UNITED CHURCH (United Reformed and Methodist), Hagley Road. 1960–1 by *Cecil E.M. Fillmore*. SUNDAY SCHOOL behind by *A.T. Butler*, 1909.

EBENEZER PRIMITIVE METHODIST CHURCH (former), Birmingham Street. 1868. Standard gabled front with round-headed windows, but pilasters and string course decorated in yellow firebrick. Schoolroom, r., 1889. Now a restaurant.

SHORT CROSS METHODIST CHURCH, Attwood Street. 1934–5 by *T. Stanley Beach*. Interior with shallow barrel-vault. – STAINED GLASS of 1928 from the previous church by *Paul A. Mantle*.

HALESOWEN ABBEY

The remains are ¾ m. SE, down a track off Manor Way (A456). Peter des Roches, Bishop of Winchester, Justiciar of England, and crusading ally of the Emperor Frederick II, founded a Premonstratensian house in 1215, dedicated to the Assumption of the Blessed Virgin Mary and St John the Evangelist. The first

Dudley, Halesowen Abbey.
Engraving by Samuel and Nathaniel Buck, 1731

canons arrived in 1218. Henry III gave sixty tie-beams from the Forest of Kinver towards the works in 1223, and fifteen oaks to make stalls for the choir in 1233. In addition, the king made annual payments towards building costs from 1218 until at least 1241/2. The master of the works in 1232 was *Brother Richard*. The abbey was suppressed in 1538. In 1558 the site and manor were bought by John Lyttelton, whose family owned it until the C20.

The plan of the CHURCH is known from excavations.* It had an aisled nave, probably of seven bays, crossing, transepts and a long rectangular chancel flanked by vestries or chapels. Building payments are recorded from 1218 until 1241–2. Just enough survives to give an idea of its scale. The materials are red, grey-green and orange sandstones, all probably local. First, a high fragment of the N wall of the chancel, up to the bottom of the arch of a tall lancet, and the jamb of its E neighbour. Relieving arches above the windows, and the springers of quadripartite vaulting on moulded corbels. On the N a robbed buttress, and to its W the end of a tall cross-wall. At the E end the jamb of a doorway. At the NW corner a corbel survives of low vaulting to a N room, perhaps a vestry. Then the W wall of the S transept, with a pair of lancets, complete. Their arches have two chamfered mouldings and a chamfered hoodmould to the W. Again, springers of the vault. To either side, the ends of a relieving arch. Immediately W was a two-storey building, probably part of the frater. A small portion of the S wall has an upper doorway, probably to the dormitory. All this is fine but austere E.E. work. Part of the S aisle wall, with blocked archways, is embedded in the present farm buildings.

The farmyard is on the site of the cloister. The CHAPTER HOUSE in its E range was excavated in 1938. A tall section of the S range, probably the REFECTORY, survives by the farmhouse

---

*In 1870–1, 1906, 1928–30 and 1938. Birmingham University Field Archaeology Unit surveyed the monastic buildings and landscape in 1987–95. In 1870–1 a small area of tile pavement was found in situ at the W end of the nave, including several tiles depicting the Romance of Tristram.

garden. Small windows lit an undercroft, and scars of its vault remain. Good high paired lancets above with deep rere-arches. The inner jambs have shafts with moulded capitals, the arches have roll mouldings. Rebuilt buttresses on the S. To the W, a ruinous low range with fine ashlar on the W face of its E gable, probably part of the W cloister range. The rest C17 and later, in brick and robbed abbey stone.

A good deal further E is an oblong BUILDING, its original function uncertain. Its W wall must belong to an earlier N–S range, perhaps the infirmary. The W part is of c.1290–1310. In 1293 *Richard the mason* had not finished a hall he was building for the abbot, perhaps this. Paired lancets with transoms, one on the N with a sculpted head in the spandrel. Mutilated but high-quality four-bay roof. The middle trusses have finely moulded crown-posts braced to crown-plate and collars. The E part is late medieval, with rectangular chamfered windows and a simple collar-and-rafter roof. The joint is visible on the S. This part was quickly divided into two chambers and the upper one given the fireplace on the S, corbelled out externally. Many later alterations, mostly in brick, including cart doors for agricultural use. Late C20 internal supports. – SCULPTURES. In the S wall a miniature figure of a knight, probably C14, with crossed legs, perhaps made for a heart burial. Medieval grave-slab with a kneeling figure below a Crucifixion, now in the E reveal of the fireplace.

Extensive EARTHWORKS of fishponds, perhaps also mill ponds, and dams, run E up a small valley from N of the church. More to the SE.

MANOR FARM is by *Yeoville Thomason*, c.1863: tall, Gothic, brick, with good corbelled chimneys. Tactful early C21 renovations. Its predecessor, demolished in the early C19, was probably the abbot's house.

PERAMBULATION

The start is the church gates. Opposite, a former BIRMINGHAM MUNICIPAL BANK by *E.C. Bewlay*, 1939–40, Neo-Georgian. N along HIGH STREET. Down Church Lane, r., Nos. 6–8, WHITEFRIARS. A box-framed cottage row, probably C16. Quadrant braces to the central cottage and E wall. IVY HOUSE is Late Georgian, with Doric doorcase. Back past the Church House and school, on the roundabout the GEORGE INN, c.1730–40. Upper windows with moulded keystone, doorcases with pilasters, lintels with little keystones.

Across the roundabout, the former HALESOWEN GRAMMAR SCHOOL (now EARLS HIGH SCHOOL), founded 1652. Its older buildings went for the road. Massive hipped-roofed block of 1931 by *A.T. Butler* with pilasters and blue-brick detailing. The HALL has plain pilasters and stained glass by *Florence Camm* (*T.W. Camm*). To its r., a delightful Free Style building of 1908 by *Bailey & McConnal* with huge semi-dormers. Former hall, now LIBRARY, with contemporary stained glass no doubt by *William Pearce Ltd*. Behind, the former TECHNICAL

SCHOOL of 1937–9, by *A.V. Rowe*. Neo-Georgian; rich Doric doorcase but also big grid windows.

A detour here up FURNACE LANE. In Whittingham Road, HALESOWEN COLLEGE. *Corstorphine & Wright* from 1996, and something tougher from *Glenn Howells Architects*, 2003 etc. Original buildings of 1967, nearly all replaced, by *Richard Sheppard, Robson & Partners*. Back and N, in MELBOURNE ROAD, r., two houses by *A.T. Butler*: No. 4, 1915, mangled; No. 51, 1919, in Bournville manner. Further N the LOYAL LODGE, with date plaque 1736, probably *in situ*. Early C19 casements.

Now W up STOURBRIDGE ROAD. On the l., former BAPTIST CHURCH by *Arthur Harrison*, 1898–9. It had three stepped lancets under the relieving arch. Then the former ZION METHODIST CHAPEL, dated 1842. Standard pedimented front with round-headed windows. On the corner of Islington the WAGGON AND HORSES pub, originally of 1867, set back and much rebuilt by *Wood & Kendrick*, 1898–1901. Free Jacobean with generous pedimented doorcases. Nos. 8–30 opposite are much-altered nail-making workshops with housing above, the row not quite complete in 1901. Cart arches for access to rear shops survive at No. 30 and, much disguised, at No. 12.

Little else has to be visited in the town centre, mostly redeveloped from the 1960s. CORNBOW CENTRE by *Bernard Engle & Partners*, 1965–7, with library tower of 1971. Remodelled by *Seymour Harris & Partners*, 1988–9, and again with dominating car park by *WCEC Architects*, 2005–8. In BUNDLE HILL and HALES ROAD, W, housing of 1962–4 by *Remo & Mary Granelli* and *Miall Rhys-Davies*. Two ten-storey blocks, and smaller blocks of three to five storeys in lively grouping. Red brick and rough-faced concrete. Nicely detailed, with inset balconies and occasional corners recessed behind pilotis. Unfortunate late C20 pitched roofs. In HAGLEY STREET No. 23, a former LLOYDS BANK, by *J.A. Chatwin*, 1876. His powerful secular Gothic. Up HAGLEY ROAD, the former NELSON pub of 1937 by *Hobbiss*, Neo-Georgian. In GREAT CORNBOW, a nice row on the s, now public offices. No. 24, 1817, has an Ionic doorcase. No. 25, c. 1820–30, originally two houses, has a W wing with stepped gable. No. 26, 1860s classical. Further E, SWIMMING BATHS by the Borough Surveyor, *T.W. Tivey*, with *D.J. Lane*, Chief Assistant Architect, 1963.

On the corner of Laurel Lane and Powell Street, a rare surviving C19 NAIL WAREHOUSE. Hipped roof, segment-headed iron-framed windows. Inside, the upper floor is carried on thin iron columns. In GRANGE ROAD, Nos. 28–30 of 1905 with decorative timber balconies. In HAGLEY ROAD, near St Margaret's church, No. 260, an C18 farmworker's cottage with a later side workshop, probably for nail-making. Now derelict.

THE LEASOWES

William Shenstone was born at Halesowen in 1714. He went to Oxford but took no degree, and about 1743 returned to the Leasowes and farmed the estate, while writing essays, letters and

Dudley, Halesowen, The Leasowes.
Engraving by James Mason after Thomas Smith, 1748

poetry. He was of sweet and vulnerable temperament and wore his own hair and no wig. 'Water gruel bard' was Horace Walpole's description. Shenstone's passion was the beautifying of his estate, and his ambition to be admired for it. Partly for economy, he developed a simple and natural style, creating an early *ferme ornée*, which drew on the work of Alexander Pope at Twickenham and William Kent at e.g. Rousham (Oxon), and was influenced, like them, by the landscapes of Salvator Rosa and Poussin. Effects were carefully calculated, his twisting paths leading to broad prospects and narrow vistas which were composed and balanced, using objects such as seats, urns, small buildings and 'water... as an irregular lake or winding stream'. After Shenstone's death in 1763 the estate went through many owners, and his structures disappeared. Dudley Metropolitan Borough Council have been restoring the landscape since 1999.

The present entrance to the gardens is from Mucklow Hill, ½ m. E of the church. A short walk can start by the path leading E to a bridge at the bottom of VIRGIL'S GROVE, begun in 1744. Along the paths, many new seats with carved inscriptions Shenstone himself used. His plantings – beeches, oaks, birches, alders – are now mature. E along a small pool to a single-arch bridge. Beyond, the stream twists in a rough rock channel, then a view of the restored HIGH CASCADE framed by trees. Beyond, the path continues to the dam of the BEECHWATER. In its present form the layout here is of the late 1750s. The path follows its r. side to a bridge, across and round a small promontory between two valleys. This was the LOVERS' WALK, which had an 'assignation seat'. Back to the bottom of Virgil's Grove, and down to the large PRIORY POOL, Shenstone's last work, of 1760–2. It is Y-shaped, and a second landscaped valley runs SE. On the hill between, now just in the golf course, footings of the PRIORY RUIN.

THE LEASOWES, now HALESOWEN GOLF CLUB. Shenstone's house was rebuilt in 1776–8 by Edward Horne. Three-bay rendered villa with hipped roof. E front with semicircular Ionic porch flanked by Venetian windows. Three Wyatt windows to the W, now mangled. Single-storey links to two-storey wings running E–W, probably built as kitchen and stables. The hall leads to a cross-passage and beyond, in the NW corner, the former saloon, with nice plasterwork and a semicircular end with niches. The room to the S, now thrown in, has a fireplace with triglyph frieze. Staircase with stick balusters, perhaps Late Georgian. Its continuation to the attic is original, with Doric column-newels. In the S wing, unexpectedly, a fine oval staircase with wrought-iron balusters. Shenstone's Gothic STABLES were demolished c. 1960.

OTHER BUILDINGS

THE GRANGE (now SOMERS SPORTS AND SOCIAL CLUB), Grange Hill, ½ m. S. Early C18, probably built by William Lea, who inherited in 1709. The original two-storey block, five bays by two, has a steep C17-style hipped roof with dormers whose pediments alternate triangular–segmental–triangular. Baroque façade with giant angle pilasters, entablature with pulvinated frieze, and an unusual doorway: Doric half-columns with oakleaf necking and tiny zigzag on the abacus, pulvinated frieze, and segmental pediment broken back in the centre. It is linked to the upper window, which is flanked by Ionic pilasters. Later C18 S wing, with plain frieze. It is separated by a two-storey semicircular bay, probably later still. Interior lost in the mid C20. – C19 STABLES.

At HASBURY, ½ m. SW, along Hagley Road, SCHOOL, W of St Margaret's church. 1869–71 by *Arthur W. Burr*, Gothic, altered. At the rear, former infants' school by *J.T. Meredith*, 1897–8. C20 extensions.

HAYLEY GREEN ISOLATION HOSPITAL (former), Hagley Road, 1¼ m. SW. 1900–2 by *H.T. Hare*, assisted by *A.T. Butler*. Closed 1996, redeveloped for housing. The ADMINISTRATION BLOCK survives, rendered below, brick above, with a tiny high oriel and an Arts and Crafts chimney rising flush from a side gable. Some way S, small single-storey WARD BUILDING.

HUNTING TREE pub, Elizabeth Road and Wall Well, ½ m. W. Built as the button-maker G.F. Grove's house. 1908–9 by *A.T. Butler*. Recessed corner porch with the angle carried on a Tuscan column. In Alexandra Road, N, Nos. 95–103, also *Butler*, 1915 etc.

NEW HAWNE COLLIERY, Hayseech Road, ¾ m. NW. Rare surviving buildings of a mid-C19 colliery, opened 1865. Red brick with yellow firebrick voussoirs; heavy cornices. The largest building is the WINDING-ENGINE HOUSE. Immediately

N, a tall FAN HOUSE (for ventilation) and CHIMNEY BASE. Along the road, STABLES AND WORKSHOPS, their upper floor added 1895.

CANAL BUILDINGS. The Dudley No. 2 Canal of 1794–8 runs E of the town. The present limit of navigation is HAWNE BASIN. The canal agent's house, HEYWOOD HOUSE, survives on the N side of Mucklow Hill. Early C19, extended 1833. Three storeys, large sashes. To the S, the canal runs on a tall embankment across the Leasowes park. The course crosses Manor Way, and swings E beyond to the filled-in W entrance of LAPAL TUNNEL.

HILL AND CAKEMORE

The E part of Halesowen, high above the town on Mucklow Hill. At the N it almost reaches the centre of Blackheath in Rowley Regis (p. 569); at the E it joins Birmingham at Quinton (p. 422). A common Black Country fringe pattern of farms and small hamlets, C19 small-scale industry and terraces, and C20 residential development.

ST PAUL, Long Lane and Church Street. The parish church of Blackheath. 1868–9 by *W.J. Hopkins*. Brick, with lancets and Geometrical tracery. W tower never built; the W window with crude tracery was meant as a tower arch. Porch by *W.F. Edwards*, 1934. Tall, austere, impressive interior. Six-bay arcades, the end bays narrow, with short round piers carrying early Gothic capitals. Big dormers in the second bay from the E. A rood loft must have been intended. Bold chancel arch springing from the walls without capitals. Roof with big timber arches. – Original FONT and PEWS. – *George While* designed the elegant CHOIR STALLS, 1961–2 (ball finials with lovely undercut leaves) and COMMUNION RAILS, 1963. – Caen stone REREDOS by *H.O. Burgess*, 1898. – ALTAR of 1916. – NAVE ALTAR by *Garry Dyhouse (APEC)*, 2005. – STAINED GLASS. By *Martin Dunn*: E window 1902; aisles 1926–7. S aisle by *John Hardman Studios*, 1976.

BLACKHEATH CONGREGATIONAL CHURCH (now CHURCH OF GOD), Long Lane. 1908 by *A.T. Butler*. Severe front with three wide lancets, domestic side elevations with deep mansard roof. – STAINED GLASS. Central W lancet by *T.W. Camm*, 1908.

COCKSHEDS (PRIMITIVE) METHODIST CHURCH (former), Malt Mill Lane. *W.F. Edwards*, 1907. Perhaps his best. Tall gabled front with clasping buttresses. Now flats.

HURST GREEN METHODIST CHURCH, Narrow Lane. By *H. Marcus Brown*, 1936. Early Christian revival. Low front with narthex. Extended 1982, 2006. To the S, No. 116, the original CHAPEL of 1900. Round-headed windows, blue-brick voussoirs.

LONG LANE METHODIST CHURCH (former), Long Lane. 1909 by *Ewen & J.A. Harper*, a later work, simple Birmingham Arts and Crafts. Intended as the Sunday School to a large chapel on the N, never built. Big gable with five-light Gothic window clasped between piers. Continuous gallery.

(HOLT ROAD JUNIOR AND INFANT SCHOOL. *A.V. Rowe*, 1907. Gabled, with big sashes. Demolished 2016.)

FAIRFIELD, Hurst Green Lane. By *A.T. & Bertram Butler*, 1937. Their finest pub. Three big canted stone bays push up into a big sheltering roof of green slate, counterpointed by five dormers above. Tall off-centre chimney. Just N, on the corner of Culmore Road, No. 21 of 1934, *Cherrington & Stainton*'s personal Neo-Georgian.

The hamlet of COCKSHEDS at the top of Malt Mill Lane is marked by the former Methodist CHAPEL and the VICTORIA pub, *A.T. & Bertram Butler*'s Neo-Georgian, 1938.

At the cross-roads of Halesowen Road, Long Lane and Kent Road, the STAG AND THREE HORSESHOES pub by *Scott & Clark*, 1936, with shaped gables. W along MUCKLOW HILL, down a drive, GREENHILL HOUSE. Front of c. 1780 for Edward Green, nail ironmonger. Gables with bold crenellations, Tuscan porch. This was added to a C17 timber-framed house, with two ranges running N–S, now much rebuilt. The best survivals are in the r. range. Inside, a partly visible jointed cruck truss, and part of a second truss to its N. The N gable has tie- and collar-beams, and king- and queen-struts. The ground-floor front room has full-height panelling, probably C19 but incorporating much C17 work with blank arcading. Beamed ceilings here and in the l. range. Former rear door with rounded jamb. Rear extension of 1974 by *Paul Mellors*, full-height windows and rubble stone fireplace, a period piece. To the W, POTTERY FARM, probably C16, box-framed, L-plan. The gable-ends have collar- and tie-beam trusses. BARN behind, now ruinous, with the remains of a collar-beam roof with wind-braces. Perhaps late medieval, underbuilt in brick.

The W end of QUINTON (*see also* Birmingham, p. 422) is in Halesowen. QUINTON CEMETERY was laid out by Birmingham Corporation, 1923. OFFICES and LODGE by *James A. Swan*; his CHAPEL (1935–6) demolished. Further E, METHODIST CHURCH (*Bournville Trust Architectural Department*, 1967) and the former DANILO cinema (*Andrew Mather*, 1938–9).

LAPAL

SE of the town. Suburban development of the 1930s onwards.

ST PETER, Hiplands Road. *Peter Falconer*, 1964. Grey-brick hall with sawtooth walls and slit windows. Fibreglass spire, a Falconer speciality. Boarded ceiling, timber altar canopy.

CARTERS LANE BAPTIST CHURCH. 1938–9 by *T. Stanley Beach*. Romanesque, with a tower. Hard red brick, windows with little hoodmoulds.

HOWLEY GRANGE PRIMARY SCHOOL, Howley Grange Road. *Richard Sheppard, Robson & Partners*, 1956–7. Purple-blue brick, shallow-pitched roofs.

Royal Oak, Manor Lane. *Scott & Clark*, 1937. Half-timbered.
Lapal House, Lapal Lane. Mid-C19, with hoodmoulds and bargeboards. Alterations by *A.T. Butler*, 1902: see the round window with *T.W. Camm* glass. The lodge also looks *Butler*'s.

LUTLEY

A hamlet in fields and woods, 1½ m. w of the town. A manor by the C11, long owned by the collegiate church of Wolverhampton.

The Grange in Lutley Lane, tall and compact, looks C18 but is partly older, see the smaller C17 brickwork in English garden wall bond on the l. side, also stone quoining and architraves. Two gabled ranges at the rear. (C18 staircase with slim twisted balusters, plasterwork dated 1616 reported in 1975.) White House Farm is H-plan with an infill range at the rear. Heavily rendered with massive platbands, probably early C18, and with a pedimented doorcase, but clearly over earlier timber framing. Big stone front buttress. An array of chimneys. Four Elms Farm, probably C17, has a box-framed main range and close-studded r. wing. Garish recent brick-nogging.

Old Boggs Farm, stranded in housing ½ m. se (The Hayloft, off Portsdown Road). Brick-faced, probably over C16/C17 timber framing; sandstone l. wing with an impressive stepped chimney, and box framing at the rear.

Lutley Mill, ¾ m. ne, off Huntingtree Road. Four-storey early C19 mill house. Windows with cast-iron Gothick glazing. Derelict wheel. Further l., the side leat falls into a deep chasm.

KINGSWINFORD

The ancient parish included Brierley Hill, Wordsley, Pensnett and Quarry Bank. The settlement by the church, 'Townsend', was always small. A select residential area from the C18. Industrial development was concentrated to the n and e, encouraged by the Shutt End railway of 1829. Brickworks were prominent: Ketley, Planet. In the later C19 the present shopping centre developed along the Wolverhampton to Stourbridge road. A Rural District Council in 1894, absorbed into Brierley Hill in 1934. Suburban development grew in the 1920s; *David Gray* of *Webb & Gray* designed several houses. Occasional terraces of workers' cottages remain in a pleasant middle-class area, its industrial history gone.

CHURCHES AND SCHOOLS

St Mary, The Village. Originally Holy Trinity. Replaced by the new church at Wordsley in 1831 (p. 560), but retained as a chapel of ease, and made a parish church again in 1868. A priest is recorded in 1186, and the lower parts of the W tower are Norman. The ground floor, with blocks of greenish sandstone, looks earlier than the stage above, mostly rubble stone, with round-headed belfry windows. The top storey, sandstone ashlar with two-light windows, is convincingly Perp but dated 1668. The rest looks Late Georgian and Victorian at first sight, but includes parts of an aisled C13 church. The first sign is the jambs of the doorway from tower into nave, with nook-shafts and crude bell capitals. Then the N arcade columns, circular, with cut-back bases; one with primitive blank arcading, perhaps of 1735, when the aisle was rebuilt with round-headed windows. In the chancel N wall a C13 lancet, then two Y-tracery windows, the first early C19, the second much repaired but apparently medieval. It suggests that the C13 chancel was lengthened in the early C14. In 1808–9 *William Roberts* recast the church in thin Gothick, at the 3rd Viscount Dudley's expense. He rebuilt the S aisle, added the tower buttresses and W vestries, refashioned the chancel, and rendered the exterior, over a Gornal stone base. Further work in 1832. In 1866–7 *William Bourne* restored the church, in 'early English...as far as possible'. He put plate tracery in the N aisle windows, and triple lights in the E, and the S aisle. The E.E.-style S arcade and the arches of the N arcade are his. In 1939–40 *J.C.Thompson* removed the render from the tower, renewed windows and replaced Roberts's pinnacles with the present parapet. On the NW, attached PARISH ROOM by *Jennings Homer & Lynch*, 1974. S aisle now with late C20 stone cladding(!).

FURNISHINGS. In the SW vestry, over the door, a Norman TYMPANUM of St Michael and the Dragon. Probably originally over a S door, moved here in 1808. Pink sandstone. The saint stands in profile with head turned towards us, his wings dramatically filling the arch. They are echoed in the feathered wing of the dragon, which has a coiled body, with big leg and claw, and long tail. The beading here and on the saint's shield suggests a late C12 date. Probably by a local sculptor, influenced by the Herefordshire school. – FONT. Dated 1662. Octagonal, with delicate but misunderstood classical detail. Gilded COVER by *Comper*, 1955, open Tuscan octagon with a spire. – PULPIT and PEWS by *Bourne*, 1867. – REREDOS by *Wood, Goldstraw & Yorath*, 1948, with relief carving. – N aisle ALTAR and REREDOS, with relief of the Nativity, by *Thomas Robinson*, 1915. – CHEST. C17, probably of domestic origin. Inscribed 'FR'. Standing figures between arches. On the r. a double-headed eagle. – STAINED GLASS. A good selection. By *Hardmans* the E window, 1876, Crucifixion and Resurrection, and chancel lancets, 1874 (N), 1884 (S). N aisle N, probably *Clayton & Bell*, c.1880; E, *Kempe*, 1907. S aisle S, *Hardmans*, 1881, and *Comper*, Presentation in the Temple, 1935, with deep red setting off his characteristic blue. – MONUMENTS. Crude cartouche dated 1654. – Rev. Thomas Hodgetts †1741, by *Richard Squire*. Tablet with nicely contrasting marbles. – John Hodgetts †1741, with tomb against an obelisk.

In the churchyard, medieval CROSS. Shaft and base, much weathered. Later lantern-shaped head. – Good headstones, C17 onwards, s. – LYCHGATE by *David Gray* of *Webb & Gray*, 1931.

OUR LADY OF LOURDES (R.C.), Summer Hill. By *S.A. Stanley* of Leeds, begun 1981, completed by *Andrew Moody*, 1983. Low, hexagonal, in purple brick. More attractive the former church, now HALL, by *Joseph T. Lynch* of *Jennings Homer & Lynch*, 1951, with a concave copper door-hood.

KINGSWINFORD METHODIST CHURCH, Stream Road. By *Desmond T. Crews & Partners*, 1965–6. Church and hall joined by an entrance link. The worship area has a folded roof and a narrow surrounding aisle with plain steel piers. So the architect knew St Paul, Bow Common. But the layout is traditional. –STAINED GLASS. *Dalle-de-verre*. Also, in the entrance area, glass by *Camm & Co.*, 1903, and *Abbott & Co.* of Lancaster, 1951, from former chapels in Moss Grove and Mount Pleasant.

CRESTWOOD SCHOOL (formerly BRIERLEY HILL GRAMMAR SCHOOL), Bromley Lane. 1956–9 by *Yorke, Rosenberg & Mardall*. Low blocks clad in maroon brick and (tactfully replaced) cladding panels, grouped round a hall with a clerestory roof and tall chimney. The main accent is a four-storey classroom block, its long sides cut back, with concrete balconies, a satisfying Brutalist touch.

KINGSWINFORD SCHOOL, Water Street. 1938–9. Late C20 additions.

SUMMERHILL SCHOOL, Lodge Lane. By *Ellis Williams Architects*, 2001.

PERAMBULATIONS

1. The Village

By St Mary's church, ½ m. E of the main centre at the Cross. The church is approached from the s along a triangular green. On the w side Nos. 2–6, by *J. Homery Folkes*, 1936, on the E Nos. 9–11, Georgian cottages with wooden Gothick windows. Behind, facing the churchyard, No. 8, THE RED HOUSE, probably mid-C18, with Gothick doorway and windows. To the S, HIGH STREET (DUDLEY ROAD) runs w towards the Cross. Immediately on the s side the OLD COURT HOUSE INN. The former manorial court house, a puzzling building. It looks C17 or early C18.* Brick, heavily painted. Gabled timber porch, much renewed. Primitive wooden Tuscan columns, twisted colonnettes and tiny central 'drop'. C20 balustrade. The windows and quoining look C19 Tudor. Iron tie-rods just below the eaves. W extension, probably the brewhouse added in 1810 by *William Roberts* for the 1st Earl of Dudley. Little of the interior survives.

---

*William Bradley leased a cottage called 'Courthouse' in 1660 and agreed to 'erect and build...one good and sufficient stock of Chimneys'.

2. The Cross, Summer Hill and Moss Grove

At the Cross, on the NE corner, the CROSS INN, Early Victorian Tudor Revival (altered). Main w front with end gables. Large windows with hoodmoulds. On the sw corner an unusual small SHOPPING CENTRE by *Jennings Homer & Lynch*, 1962–4. Circular detached former showroom with outward-raking concrete piers and low dome. Behind, a simple quadrant range.

In HIGH STREET, running E, Nos. 701 etc., originally one house. Mid-Georgian, probably rebuilt by Mary Homfray shortly after 1760. Three-storey, five-bay centre, now MANOR HOUSE. Grey roughcast over earlier render scored to imitate stone. Big keystones, pedimented doorcase, stone cornice. Two-storey wings. The l. wing, now MANOR LODGE, was perhaps the kitchens; r. wing much altered.

The main street, MARKET STREET, runs s. To the w of the Cross is SUMMER HILL. On the N side No. 1 by *Webb & Gray*, 1924, with half-timbering; late C20 extension. THE GLEN is by *A.T. Butler*, 1906, recognizable by the triplet window and wavy parapet. Still on the N side, beyond the Catholic church, SUMMERHILL COTTAGE of *c*. 1790, perhaps round a C17 core. Roughcast. Pedimented Doric doorcase, w. Alterations 1922–4 by *Webb & Gray*, including *T.W. Camm* glass. In BUCKINGHAM GROVE, N, rows of linked detached houses by *Desmond T. Crews & Partners*, 1962. At the corner of Summer Hill and Swindon Road, SUMMERHILL HOUSE (now hotel). Built *c*. 1790 for the Briscoe family. Three storeys and parapet, five bays. Still the Early Georgian type, but the details show the late date. Slightly projecting central bay with small pediment supporting a large urn. Below, a lunette and a narrow Venetian window, divided by delicate colonnettes. The rest articulated by plain pilasters. Wider Venetian windows flank an Ionic doorcase. Late Georgian former STABLES (now restaurant).

Back to the Cross and N up MOSS GROVE. On the E side No. 6, 1924, *David Gray*'s own house.* A symbol of England, perhaps, for a returned soldier. Half-timbered front, half-hipped gable, brick-nogging, timber porch. The sitting room has a canted fireplace with coving above, integral with the ceiling beams, articulating the whole space. Much *T.W. Camm* glass; arrangements of spare pieces, but also an Annunciation. On the w side No. 11, a rendered three-bay house of *c*. 1800. Doric doorcase with teardrop fanlight. On the E more *Webb & Gray*: No. 18, and Nos. 30 and 32, both 1924, the latter with oriel with *Camm* glass. On the w, No. 41 by *Jennings Homer & Lynch*, 1946–8, with shaped gable, extended. No. 45 is by *F.E. Bromilow*, 1939. A powerful design, with something Expressionist in its contrast of a very sharp gable with massive curves on the ground floor. No. 47 by *Webb & Gray*, *c*. 1929, No. 71 by *Jennings & Homer*, 1937.

---

*Originally named Melverley, after the Shropshire village where Gray fished. The glass was a wedding present to him from the Camms.

PENZER STREET, parallel to Moss Grove on the E, developed from 1924 with semi-detached pairs and small terraces, the earliest (Nos. 52–66) by *Webb & Gray*, much altered.

OTHER BUILDINGS

BROADFIELD HOUSE, Compton Drive. The dignified E front is of shortly after 1822, almost certainly built for Robert Dudley, nail maker. Brick, five bays, three storeys. Diocletian window in the Wyatt tradition, porch with pairs of unfluted Ionic columns. This building incorporates an early C19 two-storey house facing w. Fine Venetian ground-floor windows to this house, their piers with entasis. Early C19 lobby with shallow three-centred arches. Beyond, the staircase of Dudley's house, with iron balusters. In the main rooms, deep friezes of swirling Renaissance foliage, apparently moulded in *papier mâché*. Early C19 stables. A museum of glass from 1980 to 2015. In 1994 a structural glass pavilion with bonded joints was added, by *Brent Richards* of *Design Antenna* (structural engineers *Dewhurst Macfarlane*). Conversion to housing and demolition of pavilion approved, 2019.

In STREAM ROAD, the S continuation of Market Street, on the corner of Compton Drive, STATUE of Pegasus by *Andrew Logan*, 1999. On the E side, S of Greenfields Road, houses by *A.T. Butler*: HOLLY BANK, Neo-Georgian of 1913, and HIGHFIELD, of 1903, with typical concave-roofed bay. THE COTTAGE between, probably also *Butler*. In BROMLEY LANE, No. 11, THE HOMESTEAD, a simple restrained design by *G.F. Webb*, 1910. Brick gable, and a timber gable treated as a discrete feature. Nos. 12–14 by *Butler*, contemporary, with similar chimneys.* Pedimented dormers and domed canted bays. STREAM PARK runs back to Stream Road. Municipal houses of 1919–20 by *Butler*, with many quiet Arts and Crafts touches.

LYE AND WOLLESCOTE

Lye and Wollescote were scattered hamlets until the C18, when coal mining and brickmaking developed, and squatters' cottages covered Lye Waste, S of the present High Street. In 1781 William Hutton called it 'Mud City'. The last mud-walled cottage lasted until the early 1960s. The C19 brick industry specialized in yellow refractory furnace bricks, particularly for glassmakers. Nail making was important, first in domestic workshops), then in factories. Lye and Wollescote became an Urban District in 1897, but were absorbed into Stourbridge in 1933. Their distinctive architecture of around 1900 owes something to *Owen Freeman*, also manager of a refractory brick works, who made much use

---

*Webb was working in Butler's office, as well as on his own, at this time.

of his own products. A large housing programme was started in the 1920s by the U.D.C., with *H.E. Folkes*, Surveyor from 1912. The Waste was redeveloped from 1964. The end of the C20 saw the High Street, partly bypassed, become the Black Country's 'balti belt'.

CHURCHES AND MAJOR BUILDINGS

CHRIST CHURCH, High Street. Nave and W tower of 1812–13, built by Thomas Hill of Dennis Hall, Amblecote. A simple brick box with big, minimally pointed windows, some retaining wooden Y-tracery. S porch probably an early addition. Transepts and chancel added by *Thomas Smith*, 1846–7: solid, with diagonal buttresses, but the paired transept windows still have iron tracery. In 1885 *Owen Freeman* added a yellow-brick spire, demolished in 1985. In 1907 *P.B. Chatwin* proposed a new aisled nave, but only removed the original galleries and created a W baptistery, swept away in 1980s reordering. N transept converted to offices by *Martin Morris*, 1980–2; interior gutted 1984–6 by *David R. Mills*, who added the unfortunate meeting room and foyer W of the tower, 1987–90. *Smith*'s chancel has arch-braced roof trusses. Panelled nave ceiling perhaps by *Chatwin*. – STAINED GLASS. E window 1885, Crucifixion, probably by *T.W. Camm* when working for *R.W. Winfield*. S transept S, patterns, by *Camm & Co.*, 1908. Nave N, war memorial windows by *Pearce & Cutler*, 1920. By *A.E. & P.E. Lemmon* the S transept E 1950 and nave S 1952, a fine St Andrew.*

ST ANDREW, Oakfield Road. Cubic mission church in buff brick, by *G.F. Webb*, 1938–9. Unsympathetic cut-off tower by *J.C.T. Cole & Partners*, 1983.

MOUNT SION METHODIST CHAPEL (now GHAUSIA WELFARE ASSOCIATION), High Street. Dated 1827. Rendered, with a pedimental gable. Segment-headed windows in shallow wide reveals.

SALEM WESLEYAN REFORM CHAPEL (former), Pedmore Road. 1893 by *Owen Freeman*. An attractive Italianate design with tiers of arcading, and stepped windows above.

BETHEL CHAPEL (Independent), Hill Street. By *Owen Freeman*, 1900. Lancet Gothic in red brick boldly banded in yellow. Meeting room by *Ivan Coombs*, 2002.

UNITARIAN CHAPEL (former), High Street. 1857–61 by *Francis Smalman Smith*, in his characteristic 'rogue' Gothic. Red brick with banding of blue and yellow, and stone dressings. Four bays with windows – surprisingly, round-headed – deeply inset between buttresses. Plate-tracery lights in the W gable. Huge steep roof. Tall thin Italian tower, bereft of its spire. Former chapel of 1805 retained to the E, its round-headed windows with simple impost blocks. *Smalman Smith* added a heavy bellcote and exaggerated gatepiers in front. E schoolroom extension

---

*ST MARK, Stambermill, by *Thomas Smith*, 1870, was demolished 1987.

mostly by *Tom Grazebrook*, 1907. Converted to offices *c*. 1995, with triangular roof-lights.

CHRISTADELPHIAN MEETING ROOM, Pedmore Road. By *Folkes & Folkes*, dated 1932.

CEMETERY, Cemetery Road. By *Thomas Robinson*, 1877–9. The usual paired Anglican and Nonconformist CHAPELS separated by an entrance tower. Dec style, handsomely done. The tower has an ornate top with open zigzag parapet, pinnacles and big stone spire. Contemporary SUPERINTENDENT'S HOUSE, NE.

WOLLESCOTE HALL, Wollescote Road. A farmhouse stood here in 1508, and a jetty post with sunk panels is preserved inside. The present house has a S front of three gabled bays. The two r. ones represent the house built by Edward Milward shortly after 1660, a two-storey double pile with a N entrance under an originally central domed stair-tower, shown on Bache's Oldswinford map of 1699. The W bay was added *c*. 1760 by Thomas Milward. In the 1850s Stephen Hipkins, brewer, raised the attics, to form a third storey with the present gables, and the tower, adding its ogee roof. Square bay windows to the end bays of *c*. 1880 for Elizabeth Kings, mine-owner. All this work was in C17 style, difficult to distinguish. The original build has small local bricks laid in English garden wall bond. C18 illustrations show two-light mullioned windows; the present windows are C19. The Hall was bought by Ernest Stevens in 1930 and presented to Lye and Wollescote U.D.C. After falling into disrepair it was restored by *Dudley M.B.C. Planning & Architecture Department* in 1990–1. The STAIRCASE has C17 newels and rail but has been re-assembled, with C18 balusters and lozenge-work on the valence which looks C19. Delicate late C18 archway on the first-floor landing. Most detail elsewhere now late C20. Rich C17 fireplace in the central S ground-floor room, with fluted Ionic pilasters and overmantel with blank arcading and little aedicules. Is it also reconstructed? – Late C19 STABLES with tapering clock tower.

Extensive landscaped grounds, opened as STEVENS PARK in 1932, stretch N towards Cemetery Road.

HOB GREEN PRIMARY SCHOOL, Hob Green Road. By *Yorke, Rosenberg & Mardall*, 1961.

PERAMBULATIONS

1. High Street

Humble C18 and C19 survivors, contrasting with grander commercial development of *c*. 1880–1914. In front of Christ Church, WAR MEMORIAL of 1926 by *George Brown & Sons* of Kidderminster. Immediately E, BANK BUILDINGS by *Thomas Robinson*, dated 1901, with contrasting Dutch gables. Further on, the former CLIFTON CINEMA by *Roland Satchwell*, 1936–7. On the S side here, the redeveloped Lye Waste. Masterplan by *Herbert Jackson*, 1958. First phase, N, 1964–6 (builders *Wates*), mostly four-storey maisonettes; second phase, back to

Cemetery Road, by *Webb & Gray*, 1969–74, mixed with houses and bungalows. To the w, on the corner of Chapel Street, the PUBLIC LIBRARY, 1935 by *Frederick Woodward*, Stourbridge Borough Surveyor. Neo-Georgian. Doorcase with broken pediment and heavy attic. Returning w, No. 174, DENZIEL HOUSE, by *Thomas Robinson*, 1905–6. Dutch gable, Venetian window. Original shopfront. W of Christ Church, Nos. 31–40, RHODES BUILDINGS, of 1881–2, almost certainly by *Owen Freeman*. Grandiose but naïve. Yellow brick and red terracotta bands with flowers and pies. Oriels, and shields on the gabled ends inscribed from St Paul 'Be not slothful' and 'Diligent in business'. At LYE CROSS, NW corner, CENTRE BUILDINGS by *Freeman*, dated 1903. Amateurish but memorable. Much corbelling; canted oriels with iron cresting. Original shopfronts.

2. Cemetery Road

C19 terraces, industry and glimpses of Worcestershire hills. Starting from Pedmore Road, small former BOARD SCHOOL of 1884–5 by *Tom Grazebrook* in the fork of Chapel Street. Opposite, the HOLLY BUSH pub, probably mid-C19. On the N side the late C19 former Perry & Brooks nail works, with projecting pedimented bays. Further up, S, STAMBERMILL HOUSE, the former Stambermill vicarage of 1880 by *C. E. Davis* of Bath, Tudor Revival with brick diapering. Then the cemetery (*see* left). In Springfield Avenue on its E side, Neo-Georgian former POLICE STATION of 1938 by *A. V. Rowe*. Up Belmont Road, the TOP BELL pub of 1938 by *O. M. Weller*, with hipped roof covered in bright green tiles. Small streamlined bar front.

3. Industrial Wollescote

The area roughly bounded by Cross Walks, Brook Street, Balds Lane and Belmont Road is a rare survival of pre-1960s Black Country townscape, houses and factories jammed together in irregular narrow streets. CRABBE STREET is especially atmospheric, with the former WOLLESCOTE BOARD SCHOOL, dated 1882, by *S. A. Jackson*. Window arches turned in yellow brick and outlined in blue. Central block with small pediment, wings with half-hipped roofs. Rear extensions by *Hickton & Farmer*, 1898. Now industrial units. Opposite and running up Pearson Street, SPRINGFIELD WORKS, built for J. & D. Croft, nail makers, between 1885 and 1903. Beyond, facing the end of Crabbe Street, WOLLESCOTE PRIMARY SCHOOL, probably by *Hickton & Farmer*. Three gables, with terracotta bands inscribed 'Diamond Jubilee Schools 1897'. NE down Balds Lane, MONARCH WORKS, late C19 with an extension to the corner by *H. E. Folkes*, 1919, with big semi-dormers. Then S up CARELESS GREEN, with the former THOMAS PERRINS

CHAIN WORKS; 'Established 1770' and 'Rebuilt 1906' inscribed on its gables. Probably by *Thomas Robinson*. Opposite, the former RED LION pub by *Scott & Clark*, 1938. Further up, Lye's first council houses, of 1921 by *Folkes*. At the top, facing, CARELESS GREEN HOUSE, built *c.* 1800 by Thomas Perrins, and to the r. the HARE AND HOUNDS pub, mid-C19.

OTHER BUILDINGS

HODGE HILL ESTATE, ¾ m. S. The first part is by *J. Homery Folkes*, 1931–3. The nicest groups have minimal end pilasters and weatherboarded first floors: Nos. 1–7 Oakfield Road and Nos. 8–14 Coppice Avenue.

FOXCOTE FARM, 1 m. SE. C18 farmhouse. Pedimented doorcase with rusticated jambs.

NETHERTON

Always part of Dudley – literally, the lower town – but quite separate, 1 m. S. The greatest enterprise was Noah Hingley & Sons' ironworks, famous for the anchors of the *Titanic*. Dudley Wood, S, was part of the chain-making area centred on Cradley Heath. Netherton's chapels survive in greater numbers than almost anywhere else in the Black Country.

CHURCHES

ST ANDREW, Hill Street. 1827–30 by *Thomas Lee*. Conspicuous on a hill, ¼ m. W of the centre, in a large churchyard. A Commissioners' church of the First Grant, ample and solid. Gornal stone, conspicuously tooled. A typical 1820s mix of Gothic: W tower with angle buttresses and Perp belfry windows, nave with lancets but Tudor-style doorways with squared hoodmoulds. Short chancel. E vestries by *Maurice Jones*, 1938. Spacious interior, with 'considerable alteration and repair' by *William Bourne*, 1868. Original galleries with a full set of benches; most of the original BOX PEWS. Chancel separated by a beam on foiled brackets (cf. Christ Church, Coseley). Bourne remade the gallery fronts, added nook-shafts to the piers flanking the chancel, and decorative parclose screens. – FONT. 1879. – Alabaster PULPIT by *Jones & Willis*, 1903. – Frilly iron SCREEN by *J.B. Davies*, 1892, made by *Noah Hingley & Sons*. – REREDOS by *H.G.W. Drinkwater*, 1883. – CHOIR STALLS by *Bourne*. – S chapel formed by *Tom Grazebrook*, 1918. – STAINED GLASS. E window by *Wailes*, 1865. N aisle, the best, by *Sidney Meteyard*, 1924 and 1928. S aisle, two by *Samuel Evans*, †1883 and 1892. Several by *Jones & Willis*, 1903, 1911, 1917. Good Shepherd by *Powells*, 1938, old-fashioned. – WAR MEMORIAL in front.

Granite cross by *G. Maile & Son*, 1924. – Pedimented TOMB to Elizabeth Grainger †1827 etc., s side.

ST JOHN THE EVANGELIST, St Anne's Road, Dudley Wood. 1931 by *Sir Charles Nicholson*. A thoughtful design. Low, red and blueish brick, with a cranked roof, and the architect's favourite Cape Dutch-style belfry. C17 detail: brick doorcase, two-light round-headed windows. Inside, the roof turns out to express nave and aisles. Round-headed arcades with brick piers and rendered arches. Original PULPIT, CHOIR STALLS, PEWS and classical REREDOS. – STAINED GLASS. E windows almost certainly by *A.K. Nicholson*, 1931. Others altered and re-set from elsewhere, 1971–91: W (*Jones & Willis*, 1897, from St Luke, Dudley); N aisle (*C.E. Moore*, 1933, also SS Andrew and George, by *Patrick Feeney* of *Hardmans*, 1949–50, both from St Michael, Stourport), etc.

ST PETER, Darby End. 1912 by *Edward Hale*. Brick, with tile bands to the porches. Arcade of diagonally set brick piers. Extension 1957. – STAINED GLASS. Two single lights by *Sidney Meteyard*, 1929.

COLE STREET METHODIST CHURCH, Darby End. 1959 by *W.E. Homer* of *Jennings Homer & Lynch*. The hexagonal concrete framing is a period piece.

DUDLEY WOOD METHODIST CHURCH, Quarry Road. *W.F. Edwards*'s free Gothic chapel of 1907 was demolished in 2005. Sunday School, now chapel, by *Stanley Griffiths*, 1960.

EBENEZER BAPTIST CHAPEL, St Andrew's Street. Tall pilastered box by *H. Grosvenor*, 1864. Tall three-centred arch framing the pulpit. Gallery with original pews.

NOAH'S ARK (PRIMITIVE) METHODIST CHAPEL, Cradley Road. 1925, replacing a chapel of 1841. Converted to housing 2008. The little masterpiece of a minor Birmingham Arts and Crafts architect, *Harry Campbell Hawkes* (*J.H. Hawkes & Son*). Elegant but tense. Planes of brickwork contrast with big stone Perp windows with transoms. Gable projections. Sunday School behind by *Wood & Kendrick*, 1896.

PEOPLE'S MISSION (Baptist), Swan Street. By *W.F. Edwards*, 1934.

PRIMROSE HILL CONGREGATIONAL CHURCH, Chapel Street, ¼ m. S, among the factories. 1887 by *Alfred E. Hill* of Bristol, replacing a chapel wrecked by subsidence. Early Dec four-light window with quatrefoils, flanked by pinnacles. Below, a stone band with quatrefoils, broken by the entrance. Rear end rebuilt by *A.T. Butler*, 1919–21. Tie-bars all round. Inside, the roof trusses have two tiers of collars. Giant arch with rich Corinthian capitals. FITTINGS almost intact: gallery with a theatre curve, original pews, desk-like pulpit (moved to the side), angled rail. – HALL by *Stanley Griffiths*, 1931–2.

ST JOHN'S METHODIST NEW CONNEXION CHAPEL (now FAITH UNITED CHURCH OF GOD), St John's Street. 1848, probably by *Mr Sadler*, who enlarged it in 1850. New front 1903, by the builder *William Deeley*. Gallery on slim iron columns with panelled front (the 1850 join visible). Later C19 PULPIT, RAIL of *c.* 1890 with exceptionally ornate ironwork. – SCHOOL-ROOM of 1849–50 behind, with circular windows.

SWEET TURF BAPTIST CHAPEL (former), St Giles Street. 1820. Brick, round-headed windows, the front rendered. Unfortunate late C20 forebuilding. SUNDAY SCHOOL at the rear, dated 1898, by *George Coslett*.

TRINITY (WESLEYAN) METHODIST CHURCH, Church Road. 1912–13 by *Alfred Long*. Simple hall with lancets and big Perp window.

PUBLIC BUILDINGS

LIBRARY AND TECHNICAL INSTITUTE, Northfield Road. 1893–4 by *Tom Grazebrook*, given by the 2nd Earl of Dudley (cf. Woodside, p. 492). It looks exactly like a town hall. Queen Anne materials – moulded brick, terracotta and sandstone – and classical detail, but with an old-fashioned Second Empire pyramid-roofed clock turret.

PRIMARY SCHOOL, Northfield Road. 1890–1 by *Edward Pincher* of West Bromwich. Attractive U-plan block, conventional red brick Gothic, with sharply gabled bays and a tall spirelet. To its l., a severe Neo-Georgian quadrangle by *J.P. Osborne*, 1913. Very different brick, in grey and pink shades. Tall windows and shallow hipped roofs, porches with grey faience doorcases and deep attics. Built as an open-air school, originally with open corridors.

DUDLEY WOOD SCHOOL, Dudley Wood Road. 1931 by *Scott & Clark*. Blocky Neo-Georgian.

PERAMBULATIONS

1. Central Netherton

A proper urban centre, with a triangle of streets and the JOE DARBY OBELISK by *Steve Field*, 1991. ST JOHN'S STREET runs up W past St John's chapel. Further up, the BULL'S HEAD, early C19. Beyond, good townscape of C19 and early C20 housing. On the E side the OLD SWAN (Ma Pardoe's). 1863, with arched-light sashes. The bar retains its C19 back, front, and a remarkable ceiling in painted enamel panels, with a big central swan. Rear smoke room with fixed seating. Tactfully extended in 1986 by the *John Madin Design Group* into the shop, l. Contemporary BREWHOUSE at the rear. Opposite, former CHURCH SCHOOL by *Tom Grazebrook*, 1908. Former JUNCTION INN, s, dated 1905, probably by *H.E. Folkes*.

2. Mushroom Green

'Musham' in traditional speech and on early C19 maps. A surviving squatters' hamlet, of small cottages reached down narrow lanes. Most surviving buildings are C19. The entrance is 1 m. s, off QUARRY ROAD. Facing w, a much-altered workshop range, with pulley wheels in the walls to help load finished goods. The Pensnett Railway ran in front of it. Down the southern lane a CHAINSHOP of *c*.1850–60, carefully rebuilt by *Dudley M.B.C. Architect's Department*, 1975–6. Three chimneys each side, corresponding to the anvils ('tommy hammers') inside. Window shutters. Pulley over the entrance. Tiny two-storey cottage attached, NW. Below, No. 9 is perhaps C17, much altered. Other survivors down the northernmost lane: mid- to late C19, with segment-headed windows, singly and in groups. Many have a central doorway, e.g. Nos. 52 and 83. No. 85, a deep single-bay cottage on a narrow plot. No. 80, with modern but probably reliable date 1857, is single-storeyed.

CANAL STRUCTURES

Netherton Tunnel is in Rowley (*see* p. 576). In Highbridge Road, the HIGH BRIDGE crosses the Dudley No. 2 Canal. Part of the Birmingham Canal Navigation's improvements of 1857–8 (engineers *Walker, Burges & Cooper*), when the short Brewin's Tunnel was opened out.

OLDSWINFORD

9080

The ancient parish included Stourbridge, Wollaston, Lye and Amblecote. It first appears in a grant of land by King Eadred *c.* 955. The village survives inside the built-up area of Stourbridge. The old centre is hidden down Church Road and Rectory Road; the settlement around the Cross developed from the late C18. The name Glasshouse Hill is a reminder that industry came this far s; but it is now a comfortable residential area.

ST MARY, Rectory Road. At first glance a unified building, of red sandstone, set on a bank behind massive GATEPIERS of 1930 by *Sir Giles Gilbert Scott*. Then we see three very different parts. Late C14 W tower of three stages, with diagonal buttresses. Two-light windows. Its spire was taken down in 1983–4. The body of the medieval church was rebuilt in 1842–3. A design of 1839 by *Richard Oakley Couch* of Stourbridge was amended in 1841 by *Robert Ebbels*, who supervised construction. Pedmore sandstone with grey Alveley stone for battlements and pinnacles. Nave with close-set buttresses and tall two-light windows with cusps and quatrefoils, apparently Ebbels's design. Polygonal SW vestry. Chancel, S chapel and N vestry and organ chamber of 1898 by *J.A. Chatwin* in Bromsgrove stone. His seven-light E window has early Perp tracery, the N and S ones Dec. Circular E vestry window with characteristic Chatwin cross-pattern tracery.

Octagonal entrance lobby created in 1843, with a rib-vault. Inside, a dramatic contrast between wide unaisled pre-Ecclesiological nave and Late Victorian E end. Nave roof with bold queenpost trusses, cusped and quatrefoiled. Tie-beams supported by elongated braces. W gallery on iron columns, with crude front of 1955. *Chatwin's* chancel has his usual tall proportions and richly moulded chancel arch. E responds of his intended nave arcades.* C14 tower arch with two plain chamfers and complex moulded capitals. – BOX PEWS. – Rich PULPIT by *Chatwin*, 1903. – ALTAR of 1894 with painted panels by *H. G. Hiller*. – S chapel REREDOS by *Sir Giles Gilbert Scott*, 1931. Many BENEFACTION BOARDS in the tower lobby. – STAINED GLASS of 1843 in the nave N window tracery. E window, Lady Chapel E and chancel N by *Clayton & Bell*, 1902–3, 1924 and *c.* 1915. S chapel E, *Jones & Willis*, 1910; W, Christ Walking on the Waters, by *William Morris & Co.* (*J.H. Dearle*), 1915–16, a beautiful piece. A calm still Christ lights up dark waters and reaches towards an imploring St Peter and eager sailors. Unusual small scenes, a portrait of Commander Grazebrook and his ship, in the lower corners. – MONUMENTS. S chapel. James Foster †1853 by *Peter Hollins*. Sarcophagus, bust on top. – Rev. Simon Ford †1699, oval panel in cartouche. – Chancel N, high up, Robert Foley, probably of after 1717. Segmental pediment and twisted Salomonic columns. – Chancel S, also high, William Hunt †1843 by *Hinchliff* of London; kneeling woman. – N aisle. Francis Walker †1844 by *P. Hollins*. – Lodvick Verelst †1704. Heart-shaped cartouche with cherubs making a rhombus shape, crude but charming.

Detached HALL by *Desmond T. Crews & Partners*, 1967–9, SE, with overhanging roof.

OLD SWINFORD HOSPITAL. The school was founded in 1667 by Thomas Foley. The original block, now FOUNDER'S BUILDING, was being built in 1669, when Thomas's son Philip supplied 'timber for the hospitall'. Tall and compact, of three storeys, the top one in three gables. Small thin bricks in English bond, two-light mullioned windows. The top storey was rebuilt by *Charles Stephens*, 1886–7, in larger bricks laid in English garden wall bond, with three-light stepped windows. The C17 gables were lower, with two-light windows. C19 turret with segmental pediment enclosing a clock, and octagonal C20 cupola. On the roof-line also two lines of eight chimneys each. The E doorcase is an impressive but rustic C17 classical piece, related to the style known as Artisan Mannerism. Round-headed arch on plain pilasters, set against rustication. Full entablature which breaks forward under a segmental pediment. But the architrave turns up to enclose a central label, and at the sides are huge volutes rising the whole height of the doorway. Original door. Front garden with original GATEPIERS.

---

*In 1910 *P.B. Chatwin* proposed rebuilding the nave with N and double S aisles. In 1939 *Sir Giles Gilbert Scott* proposed inserting arcades and reconstructing the windows. N and S galleries removed in 1955.

Inside, the original teaching and dining hall, now the LIBRARY, runs across behind. In the NE corner the OAK ROOM, now headmaster's study, the finest interior, with C17 panelling. Fireplace with eared architrave, and Ionic pilasters above enclosing a portrait of Foley by *William Trabute*. Original heavy STAIRCASE rising all the way up. Square newels with ogee tops, and bulbous balusters. The top-floor room at the SE corner, probably 'Mr Foley's Room' of a 1672 inventory, has a roof with collar-beams, arched braces and central decorative drops, probably C17.

The school's later buildings have been influenced by this C17 start, not always to their benefit. To the N of Founder's, a screen and archway dated 1882 by *Charles Stephens*. Then MAYBURY HOUSE of 1883–7, also Stephens (altered). Further N, the GREAT HALL, by *Tom Grazebrook*, 1905–6, Edwardian Jacobean. Stained glass of 1999 by *Clare Johnson*, made by *Norgrove Studios*. W of Founder's is BARN HOUSE, C17 outbuildings reconstructed by *Joseph Griffiths*, 1836, with Tudor-style windows, and again by *Batemans*, 1930.

Distant at the SW corner, FOSTER HOUSE, the former infirmary, 1875–7 by *Francis Smalman Smith*.* An enjoyable High Victorian version of C17, with vigorous gables, doorway with segmental pediment, and cupola with ogee top. Neo-Georgian former SANATORIUM, 1925, by *Tom Grazebrook*, again with C17-style doorcase. A masterplan by *Sir Frederick Gibberd*, 1952, was not followed up. Several late C20 boarding houses. SPORTS HALL, N, by *Webb Gray & Partners*, 2000. New teaching block and boarding house, 2009, by *Associated Architects*.

PERAMBULATION. To the W of St Mary's church, the RECTORY of 1700. A handsome late example of the Carolean type. Hipped roof, end chimneys, platbands, deep modillion cornice. Flemish bond brickwork. Late C18 Ionic doorcase. The garden front has larger sashes, probably early C19. Original staircase with bulbous balusters and square newels. Late Georgian reeded doorcases on the first floor. COACH HOUSE altered for community purposes by *Bowles Whittick Young*, 1996. More *Giles Gilbert Scott* gatepiers.

N up CHURCH ROAD. On the W side, SWINFORD OLD HALL. The central five bays are a mid-C18 villa, still the Early Georgian type, three storeys, with giant pilasters and parapet. Three-bay pediment, heavy bracket cornice. The l. bay was raised from a low wing in the C19 and much rebuilt in the late C20; the r. bay probably has the same history. Most of the windows have broken curly pediments with keystones. Venetian middle window and Diocletian window above.

OLDSWINFORD CASTLE, on the E side beyond, looks surreal at first sight: 1960s flats on top of a timber-framed house. The core seems to be C17, of the hybrid NE Worcestershire timber-and-sandstone type identified by Stephen Price and Nicholas Molyneux. The house is called 'Castle' on Bach's

---

**Martin & Chamberlain* made designs in 1870.

map of 1699. W front with two gables. Despite its history, it seems mostly original. Ground floor with close studding, first floor with herringbone bracing and windows with carved sills and headstops. The tops of the gables are reconstructed. On the S, a big chimney with inscribed panel 'SH' and paired star-shaped brick stacks. More close studding to the first floor. The first castellation, with an added storey at the W, was done for Edward Hickman after 1782. After 1855 James Evers-Swindell added the heavy crenellations and bays on the S, an extra floor, and the steep-gabled feature on the N. The details suggest *Francis Smalman Smith*. Converted to flats by *Leslie Tibbetts* in 1955–6, when the Hickman work at the W was removed to expose the framing, leaving a tile-clad top floor. Inside, exposed box framing on the ground floor and a four-centred-arched fireplace.

Continuing N, Nos. 6–16, Late Georgian Gothick cottages. Windows with intersecting tracery, doorcases with reeded jambs. Repaired and extended *c*.1972. At the cross-roads with Brook Road the former LABOUR IN VAIN pub. Late Classical. E block of after 1837; segmental window pediments linked by string courses. Along BROOK ROAD, on the N side Nos. 3–9, *c*.1905 with horseshoe-arched porches, and the SEVEN STARS by *William Jenkins*, 1904–5. The late C19 Birmingham pub type, bright red brick with canted bays and ornate bargeboards. *Maws* tiling inside, and an original bar front and arcaded back. Opposite, the entrance to STOURBRIDGE JUNCTION STATION. Platform buildings and canopies of 1901 by *Mr Monckton* of the GWR, Wolverhampton engineer's office. In the car park on the far side of the tracks, CLOCK TOWER by *Anuradha Patel*, 1996. A colourful toy version of the tower in Giorgio de Chirico's painting Nostalgia of the Infinite, appropriate near trains. De Chirico's corner pennants have become railway signals which wave up and down on the hours.

Back W to the Labour in Vain, and up GLASSHOUSE HILL to the Cross. THE CROSS pub was rebuilt in 1951–2 by *Jennings Homer & Lynch*. Well massed, traditional. N along HAGLEY ROAD. On the W side No. 80, by *Thomas Smith* for himself *c*.1845–50. L-shaped, with a little tower in the angle. He must have seen Pugin's Bishop's House in Birmingham. Nos. 111–121 opposite are probably also *Smith*: banded brick, scissor trusses in the end gables. Beyond them, WEST HILL of 1897, with ogee dome. On the W side, the Hospital (*see* above) has taken over the former Stourbridge College buildings. Entrance range by *Pick Everard*, 2014–15. Behind, a curtain-walled block by *Sir Frederick Gibberd*, 1956–7.

W from the Cross in Craufurd Street, off Corser Street, two former TEACHERS' HOUSES of the demolished National School. 1860 by *Thomas Smith*. Gothic, blue-brick. S from the Cross, the BIRD IN HAND pub, shortly after 1886; surely by *Thomas Robinson*: see the characteristic scatter of tiny pediments. STANFORD HOUSE, W side, *c*.1830; Doric doorcase, window architraves on consoles. Nos. 182–202, a nice group of early C19 cottages. On the E side the MARY STEVENS HOSPICE. Main building of 1932 by *W.H. Martin*, set back. Neo-Georgian, the garden front with angled wings, i.e. a half-butterfly plan. Hospice building, 1992 by *Butler Wones & Partners*.

PEDMORE

The church is tucked away on the S side of Pedmore Lane. What old village survives is on Hagley Road (A491), just S of the roundabout.

ST PETER. Perp W tower, sandstone, with diagonal buttresses and restored two-light belfry windows. C18 swept-up parapet. The rest rebuilt by *Frederick Preedy*, 1869–71. Sandstone from Bromsgrove and Pedmore, with diagonal tooling; plain quoins on the buttresses. C13-style window tracery: quatrefoils, cinquefoils, spherical triangles. Arcades with double-chamfered arches, the S with octagonal piers and the arches dying into projections of them above the capitals, the N with one octagonal and one circular pier. Former Norman chancel arch, now between chancel and organ chamber: three plain orders. S doorway also Norman, mid-C12, with columns, scalloped capitals, angled chevron and lozenges round the arch, and an impressive TYMPANUM, an outlying work of the Herefordshire school (cf. Kilpeck, Brinsop etc.). Christ in Majesty, with a Mongol-style moustache, hand raised in blessing, in an almond-shaped mandorla, surrounded by the symbols of the Four Evangelists, with deeply ribbed wings and the beasts with prominent toes and claws. St Matthew, indebted to the angels at Rowlstone, holds on to the mandorla; the lion of St Mark has echoes of Shobdon and the W doorway at Leominster. Two grotesque heads at Christ's feet. C14 PISCINA, S aisle. N vestry extension, 1928–9 by *Tom Grazebrook*. – *Preedy*'s FITTINGS are intact; his REREDOS (with mosaic panels) and PULPIT have carved figures by *Boulton*. – FONT. Octagonal, with odd loop patterns. Said to be C15 but just as likely C17. – Tower SCREEN by *Grazebrook*, 1929. – SCULPTURAL FRAGMENTS re-set inside the tower: a cat-like beast, probably contemporary with the tympanum; bearded head; bell capital. – STAINED GLASS. Chancel E and S by *Preedy*, 1871–2; S aisle no doubt by *Clayton & Bell*, 1892 (two), †1905. – War memorial CROSS in the churchyard by *Harold S. Rogers*, 1921.

Former RECTORY, E. By *Roger Ives* of Halifax, 1857, incorporating an earlier house, r. Classical, six bays, brick (rendered). Heavy modillion cornice. Off-centre Doric porch of Halifax stone.

PEDMORE HALL, Pedmore Hall Lane, was rebuilt in the late C20 (portico 2009). On Hagley Road, PEDMORE LODGE, *c.* 1870, now rendered; steep gables and inset tower with pyramid roof, suggesting *Thomas Smith*. Opposite, PEDMORE CHURCH OF ENGLAND PRIMARY SCHOOL. Modest Tudor of 1859–60 probably by *J.L. Hornblower*, much extended; with the former parish hall, l., 1902 by *Tom Grazebrook*, with nice bellcote.

Late Victorian houses in REDLAKE ROAD, and on HAGLEY ROAD towards Oldswinford; Nos. 266–268 with eccentric bays, perhaps by *Francis Smalman Smith*.

In DINGLE ROAD, off Hagley Road, No. 21, 1925–6, and No. 16, with deep mansard, 1920s, both by *H.E. Folkes*; the latter extended by *J. Homery Folkes* 1958–9, who also did No. 2 of c. 1930.

THE GROVE, Wollescote Road. By *W.J.H. Weller*, 1908–9, one of his finest houses. w front with two big structural timber gables – not identical, the r. one has more timbering – linked by a loggia at first-floor level, on square tapering wooden piers. The balustrade has uprights with Voyseyesque cut-out hearts and diamonds. All this is clamped between massive brick ends with pairs of chimneys and corbelled-out diagonal corner projections. N entrance in a porch under an angled timber projection. (Full-height hall with gallery and staircase. Similar balustrades and piers. The loggia is supported on more square piers, uniting interior and exterior. Good fireplaces.).

PENSNETT

Pensnett Chase is mentioned in 1230. It covered all the E part of Kingswinford parish, including modern Brierley Hill and Quarry Bank. An inquisition of 1291 already refers to coal pits. By the C17 the area contained many colliers and nailers. The enclosure of the Chase in 1784 stimulated industrial development further. Collieries, ironworks and brickworks were concentrated W and N of the village, served by the Stourbridge Extension Canal, the Pensnett Railway of 1844–5 and the Kingswinford branch railway of 1858. By 1840 there was a settlement at the E end of the present village, and in the late C19 it spread W to the present centre at High Oak. The village still feels separate, despite the huge Russells Hall hospital complex linking it to Dudley. The large Pensnett Trading Estate, to the W, was developed from the 1930s. Few early industrial structures survive. The best secular building, the Conservative Club by *G.F. Webb*, Free Style of 1914, was demolished in 2007.

ST MARK, Vicarage Lane. 1846–9 by *J.M. Derick*. A large, serious, impressive Early English design. It cost £6,700, of which Lord Ward (later 1st Earl of Dudley) gave £5,500. The massive exterior, with buttresses and string courses cutting back to the wall-plane, anticipates the High Victorian manner. Yellow-grey Gornal sandstone ashlar, long blackened by industry. A full

Dudley, Pensnett, St Mark.
Engraving by James K. Colling, 1840s

Camdenian plan of high aisled nave with clerestory, transepts, long chancel and s chapel (originally Lord Ward's pew). Lancet windows, E gable roundel and w spherical triangle; two-light E window of the s chapel. sw tower and spire never completed; the present top, with an effective gambrel roof, by *Webb & Gray*, 1926. Arcades with circular red Gornal sandstone piers and alternate leaf capitals. Steep double-chamfered arches, recalling Pugin's Irish manner. Chancel and transept arches with attached shafts; the chancel arch has head corbels (carver *W. Dempster*). Roofs with high collars and tall braces. w end reordered with meeting rooms by *Roy Pugh* of *Jennings Homer & Lynch*, 2006.

FURNISHINGS by *Lewis Stride*, after Derick was removed from the work for 'misconduct': arcaded SCREENS, CHOIR STALLS, PULPIT (with paintings of the Evangelists by the *Rev. C.W. Dicker*, 1882), and FONT with all-over foliage (lettering and alabaster shafts by *Hardmans*, 1882). – REREDOS with Art Deco angels and chancel PANELLING by *Webb & Gray*, 1925, with WALL PAINTINGS of the Instruments of the Passion by *T.W. Camm* (probably *Florence Camm*). – STAINED GLASS. E window of 1862, perhaps by *O'Connor*. N transept lancets by *Brian Thomas*, 1966, densely worked images of Staffordshire and Lichfield Diocese. S transept, 1963 and 1969, and S aisle W, 1968, by *Francis Skeat*. S chapel, 1938, by *Charles E. Moore*. Several in the aisles by *T.W. Camm*, 1937–60.

ST JAMES WESLEYAN REFORM CHURCH, High Street and Chapel Street. 1983 by *Tony Shenton* of *Webb & Gray*, replacing a chapel of 1837.

INDEPENDENT METHODIST CHAPEL (now CHURCH OF GOD OF PROPHECY), High Oak. 1894 by *J. Marsh*. Gabled terracotta front, round-headed windows.

BROMLEY METHODIST CHURCH, Bromley. By *Stanley Griffiths*, 1960, brick. SUNDAY SCHOOL, 1910, by *Humphries, Slater & Co*.

PERAMBULATION. The OLD VICARAGE N of St Mark's church is by *William Bourne*, 1858–60. Tudor, with blue-brick diapering, and blue-and-red relieving arches. From the top of BARROW HILL, N, the view of fields scattered with old industrial buildings gives a good impression of rural parts of the Black Country before the late C20. Up Vicarage Lane to HIGH STREET and the WAR MEMORIAL – an unusual tapering triangular pillar by *G.F. Webb*, 1928. On the S side, No. 222, a former Methodist manse, buff brick, by *Webb & Gray*, 1938. Going W, on the S the FOX & GRAPES pub, 1934 by *O.M. Weller*, with characteristic squared-up door surround. Past St James's church, on the corner of Swan Street, the LIBERAL CLUB, formerly the SWAN pub, by *A.T. & Bertram Butler*, 1936. On the next corner the HIGH OAK, again *Butler*, 1933, with decorative plaque. N side, Neo-Georgian former CO-OP by *Webb & Gray*, 1929; POST OFFICE by *Jackson & Edmonds*, 1939; former FOUR FURNACES pub, c. 1900, perhaps by *George Coslett*.

For Wide Waters and the canal pools, *see* Brockmoor, p. 500.

QUARRY BANK

Part of the chain-making area centred on Cradley Heath. The little town – an Urban District from 1894 to 1934 – has a sharp topography. The High Street twists down from the church to Cradley Forge, where the Mousesweet Brook runs into the Stour. To its S, streets run into the shallow valley of the Bower. To the

N the land rises to the woods of Saltwells. Mount Pleasant, at the top, to the w, is now isolated by the widened Dudley to Worcester road. Until recently Labour, Conservative and Liberal clubs – modest architecturally, alas – lined the High Street.

CHRIST CHURCH, High Street. Nave and transepts by *Thomas Smith*, 1846–7. He is trying to do Victorian Gothic, but fails wonderfully. Tall, bulky, with regular lancets and buttresses. Also tall, the triple-stepped w bellcote. It is supported on a shallow projection, pierced by a circular window and rising from the porch, a spectacularly awkward composition. Octagonal NW and SW corner pinnacles. And all of this in yellow firebrick. Tactful chancel by *Thomas Robinson*, 1899–1900. Hammerbeam and collar roof with tricky passing braces. – PULPIT, FONT and PEWS of 1846. – REREDOS. 1926. – STAINED GLASS. E window by *O.C. Hawkes Ltd*, 1900. Much late *T.W. Camm* work, 1930s–50s.

CRADLEY FORGE METHODIST (NEW CONNEXION) CHAPEL, Hammer Bank. 1928 by *Sidney Davies*. A school-chapel. Low front with big lunette window, porch with stone bands. Undivided interior. Original platform and pulpit.

MOUNT PLEASANT (WESLEYAN) METHODIST CHAPEL. A plain chapel of 1828, recast in 1927 by *Alfred Long*. His are the forebuilding and doorcase with open segmental pediment, the twin round-headed windows above, and top pediment; also the rear extension. The date panel is original. Inside, segmental 'chancel arch', gallery and furnishings of 1927. Reordered and pews removed 1994–5. – STAINED GLASS by *Pearce & Cutler*, 1927, Christ Walking on the Waters.

BIRCH COPPICE METHODIST CHAPEL, Coppice Lane. 1958 by *Stanley Griffiths*.

QUARRY BANK CONGREGATIONAL CHURCH, High Street. 1935 by *Gething & Rolley*. Small, still Gothic.

LIBRARY (former), High Street. 1939 by *R.J.H. Comber*, Surveyor to Brierley Hill U.D.C.

STEVENS PARK, Park Road. Opened in 1921, given by Ernest Stevens. Laid out by *F.A. Furber*, Quarry Bank U.D.C. Surveyor. Iron BANDSTAND by the *Lion Ironworks*, Kirkintilloch, 1925. – PEACE MEMORIAL. Stevens was a lifelong Liberal; Ralph Homer, Labour leader of the U.D.C., was a senior foreman at Stevens's Judge works. Both were Methodists. In 1931 they produced this moving expression of the anti-war feeling of the time, the era of the Peace Ballot and the Oxford Union 'King and Country' debate. Slightly over-life-size statue of a pleading Christ by *George Edward Wade*. Tall tapering pedestal and stone surround with names of war dead, by *Alfred Long*.

MOUNT PLEASANT PRIMARY SCHOOL. 1888 by *G.B. Nichols & Son*. The usual gabled blocks, nicely done with blue-brick trim, cogging on the gables, and a spire with open Gothic arcade. Extension 1992.

QUARRY BANK PRIMARY SCHOOL, High Street. 2011 by *Dudley (M.B.C.) Property Consultancy*. Gothic CARETAKER'S HOUSE by *Thomas Smith*, 1877, from the first school here.

SEDGLEY

Recorded in Domesday. The ancient parish included Coseley, Gornal, the Ettingshall area of south Wolverhampton, and rural areas to the w. The small town escaped large-scale industry, though nail making, a home industry, was important in the C19 (cf. Bromsgrove, Worcs.). It was an Urban District until 1966. Sedgley Hall and Turls Hill House, C18 and earlier houses, were demolished in the later C20. The centre retains its small scale despite some aggressive 1960s shops.

ALL SAINTS, Vicar Street. Rebuilt in 1826–9 by *Thomas Lee*, paid for by the future 1st Earl of Dudley. A very impressive design. Gornal stone ashlar in large blocks with diagonal tooling and drafted margins. Tall nave and aisles and slightly projecting chancel. The unusual s tower is medieval, retained but refaced. Inside, remains of two round-headed C12 windows (first floor). The spire is *Lee*'s: tall lucarnes set diagonally. W porch. The massing looks Perp, as do the four-centred-arched doorways, but the windows all have Geometrical tracery – long two-lights in the aisles, five-lights E and W. Doorways with big headstops, and smaller ones on pinnacles and buttress gablets, rare examples of Gornal stone figure sculpture. Perp-style arcades with wide hollow chamfers. Plaster tierceron-vault, showing the influence of St Thomas, Dudley. N and s galleries removed by *A.P. Brevitt*, 1883. W gallery, front by *Ashton Veall*, 1903, on iron columns of 1829. W end reordered by *Twentyman Percy & Partners* (*George Sidebotham*), 2002–3.

FURNISHINGS. PULPIT by *F.T. Beck*, 1901. – FONT of 1829, wooden COVER by (*Sir*) *Charles Wheeler*, 1947, carved with a mother and child. – PEWS by *Brevitt*, 1883. – CHOIR STALLS by *Warwick Scott*, 1948. – STAINED GLASS. E window. Small upper lights, with armorial bearings of the Earl of Dudley, from the original by *J. Helmle* of Freiburg, 1831. The rest, saints against clear glass, replaced in 1970–1 by *D. Brooke* (*Weir's Glass*). S aisle from E: *T.W. Camm* for *R.W. Winfield & Co.*, 1883 (upper lights), *Chance Bros* 1866 (lower); *Hardman*, 1870; *Pearce & Cutler*, 1922; (vestry) *Hardmans*, 1920. N aisle from E: *Camm* for *Winfield*, 1884; the same, *c.* 1883 (upper lights), *Chance* 1866 (lower); *Alan Younger*, 1974; *Rosemary Rutherford*, 1972.

ST CHAD AND ALL SAINTS (R.C.), High Holborn and Catholic Lane. 1821–3, probably designed by the parish priest, *Fr Thomas Tysan*, and his builder, *John* or *Thomas Guest* of Dudley. A broad nave in squared Gornal ashlar with wide lancet windows, and an oblong W tower over the chancel. Gabled E entrance end by *G.B. Cox*, 1924, more sophisticated, translating the lancet style into a rather North Country E.E. Rood above the doorway, under a relieving arch. The nave has a very shallow barrel-vault. Chancel arch on piers with Gothick panelling. The chancel has a delicate plaster tierceron-vault, clearly another imitation of St Thomas, Dudley (q.v.). – ALTAR and REREDOS by *A.B. Wall*, 1890. – STAINED GLASS. Chancel lancets, 1914; nave N and S 1923, all *Hardmans*. – Attached, N, former SCHOOL HOUSE of 1837. To the S, PRESBYTERY of 1823, rendered. Doorcase with fluted half-columns.

CONGREGATIONAL CHURCH (now ST ANDREW, UNITED REFORMED AND METHODIST), Bilston Street. 1856–7 by *Bidlake & Lovatt*. A steeply gabled Decorated Gothic hall and SW tower with short pyramid-roofed spire. Rock-faced Gornal stone. Powerful detail, especially the buttresses with deep low set-offs. Big gable window with flowing tracery. Roof trusses with big diagonal members hiding iron cores. Gallery with chunky front and iron pillars. Extended with organ chamber and choir gallery (*Hilton & Caswell*, builders), 1905. Lobby and meeting rooms extension by *Bob Chesworth*, 1983. – Disfiguring porch, 2014 (architects *Sutton & Wilkinson*). – PULPIT. Dated 1937. Extreme Black Country conservatism: it looks *c.*1870. – STAINED GLASS. S window by *Pearce & Cutler*, 1926. One E by *Abbott & Co.*, †1939.

PRIMITIVE METHODIST CHURCH (former), Tipton Street. 1857–8 by *Hamlet Durose*. Striking front; the standard pilastered box turned Early Victorian Jacobean. Instead of a pediment, a wide shaped gable. Tuscan porch, with a shaped parapet. Flemish bond brickwork finely laid with white mortar (bricklayer *Mr Tomlinson*). Office conversion 2008. SUNDAY SCHOOL of 1881 behind.

QUEEN VICTORIA PRIMARY SCHOOL, Bilston Street. By *A.P. Brevitt*, 1896–7. Girls' and boys' blocks, linked by a late C20 entrance. Ruabon brick and Hollington stone. A lively design with Brevitt's typical patterning in the gables. Heavily corbelled chimneys.

DORMSTON SCHOOL, Mill Bank. Unremarkable blocks of 1957 (*J. Kenneth Dancer*) and 1971 etc. (*Scott & Clark*). The important work is the THEATRE, ART GALLERY and SPORTS HALL by *Maguire & Co.*, 1997–2000. Blockwork with alternating large and small courses. A roof-lit atrium forms the entrance, with a spiral staircase leading to a sculpture gallery with curved walling and a steel roof with long ties.

PERAMBULATION. The centre is the BULL RING, dominated by the former CLIFTON cinema, by *Roland Satchwell*, 1937. Rendered, with rounded corners, simple deep cornice, and tall windows cut straight in. Opposite, the Late Georgian RED LION pub, with dentil cornice. BARCLAYS BANK is by *E.C. Bewlay* (*Cossins, Peacock & Bewlay*), 1909, in domestic Free Style. Stone Baroque doorway, canted bay above, hinting at Harrison Townsend and Mackintosh. In GOSPEL END

STREET, l., the former COURT HOUSE INN. Front probably by the mason *Joseph Beddard*, who worked here in 1818–19. Stucco scored to imitate ashlar was removed c.2015. Tuscan doorcase. Random stone rear range, perhaps C17. The SWAN INN looks early C19, but the rear again shows earlier fabric. Further on, THE PRIORY runs E, with Nos. 1–3, mid-Victorian classical. Behind is PRIORY COTTAGE: street wing of c.1830, main block at right angles, probably earlier. At the start of VICAR STREET, E, the POLICE STATION is a reconstruction by the builder *Charles Hartland*, 1863–4, of the front block of the parish workhouse of 1734. Its top storey was removed. Heavy mid-C19 classical detail. The r. end rebuilt by *W.H. Cheadle*, Staffordshire County Surveyor, 1904, domestic. Beyond, All Saints' church. On the s side, GRAVEYARD of 1808 with Soanian gateway. At the end, DUDLEY STREET. Opposite, DORMSTON HOUSE. A *mondaine* Neoclassical three-bay villa in golden limestone, for James Culwick, surgeon, c.1815. Smooth rustication to the ground floor, windows with delicate architraves on consoles, porch with eroded Soanian columns.

Going s, in a fork of roads, the former GRAND JUNCTION HOTEL, c.1849. Finely laid Gornal stone. Typical Early Victorian windows with full architraves on consoles, doorcase with pilasters. In Tipton Street, l., the former Methodist church (p.543). In HIGH HOLBORN, r., ASDA, by the *Seymour Harris Partnership*, 1986, original as ever: here with a hipped roof and flying buttresses down to the pavement. Then the former COUNCIL HOUSE by *A.P. Brevitt*, 1882–3, a simple block in brick and Bath stone, with characteristic brick detail. Converted to flats and extended by *Mason Richards*, 2003–4. Opposite, the HOLBORN CENTRE by *Alan Cotterell Partnership*, 1991. Beyond on the w side, the Catholic church (p.542) with, set back, a Gothic SCHOOL of 1876, with plate-tracery windows. The street continues as DUDLEY ROAD, with late C19 Old English villas. Further s, No. 4, Early Victorian, Tuscan doorcase. On the E side Nos. 63–65, Late Georgian. Doric doorcases flanked by large semicircular bays. Back towards the Bull Ring, w side, the WHITE HORSE pub, c.1850–60. Giant pilasters, eared architraves. Canted bays of c.1900.

Now N from the Bull Ring up HIGH STREET. On the w side Nos. 5–13, Late Georgian. On the E Nos. 36–38, c.1830, with plain pilasters. BRICK STREET runs E with an early C19 former NAIL WAREHOUSE. Gornal stone rubble, round-headed windows. TOWNSEND AVENUE runs w from High Street with municipal housing by *Richard Twentyman*, 1949–52, including Nos. 13–27, two-storey flats with windows linked by strips and a sculptural arrangement of entrances and balconies. Back on High Street and N, the MOUNT PLEASANT pub, older than its C20 half-timbering. After High Street becomes Wolverhampton Road, more *Twentyman* housing of 1949–52 in THE VISTA, E, and in GIBBONS HILL ROAD.

Back S, and E from High Street along BILSTON STREET. On the N side a long row of humble early C19 cottages, then the Congregational church and OLD MANSE of c.1870. Opposite, the primary school (p.543). Further on, S side, a former WESLEYAN CHAPEL of 1864, a small pedimented and pilastered box. Beyond, on the N, GREENWAY leads into charming small-scale municipal housing by *T. Alwyn Lloyd*, 1920–3. Further E, the BEACON HOTEL, built in 1864 for Abraham Carter: window architraves on rich consoles, sashes with arched lights. Central corridor, flanking rooms. Glazed central servery, probably 1930s. Tower BREWERY behind, also 1860s, rebuilt 1921, restored to use 1987. BEACON LANE leads N alongside up to Sedgley Beacon, with its TOWER of 1846. Circular, with crenellated parapet. Small ogee-headed lancet windows.

STOURBRIDGE

9080

Stourbridge began as a hamlet called Bedcote, on the steep S bank of the River Stour in the parish of Oldswinford. 'Sturbrug' first appears in an Assize Roll of 1255. It grew fast because of its strategic location. By the C15 the main street had many timber-framed buildings, of which Nickolls and Perks's shop survives.* The Town Hall, at the junction where the Market Hall is now, was probably similar to that at Bridgnorth, Shropshire; extended in 1538, it was demolished in 1773. Glass-making began with immigrants from Lorraine in the early C17. Stourbridge Ironworks, spreading along both banks W of the bridge, also began in the C17. In the C18 it was owned by the Bradley family. As Foster, Rastrick & Co. it was famous for early railway engines. The surviving foundry is just in Wollaston (p.559). The river and canal navigations (*see* Amblecote, p.494) also helped trade. Until the C19 the town remained part of Oldswinford parish. An Act of 1866 created Improvement Commissioners. Stourbridge became an Urban District in 1894, and a Borough in 1914, absorbed by Dudley in 1974.

The town had significant architects from the mid C19. *Thomas Smith* boldly used polychromy from the 1840s. His brother *Francis Smalman Smith* liked 'rogue' Gothic, and used a characteristic Jacobean-cum-Baroque style in secular work. *Thomas Robinson*, who succeeded to Thomas Smith's practice, was a competent designer particularly in Queen Anne, his favourite motif small pediments on dormers and keystones. *H.E. Folkes*'s career ran from c.1900 to after 1945, but from about 1932 most *Folkes & Folkes* designs are by his son *J. Homery Folkes*, who worked until

---

*Timbers in Nos. 107–108 High Street (demolished) were tree-ring dated to c.1483.

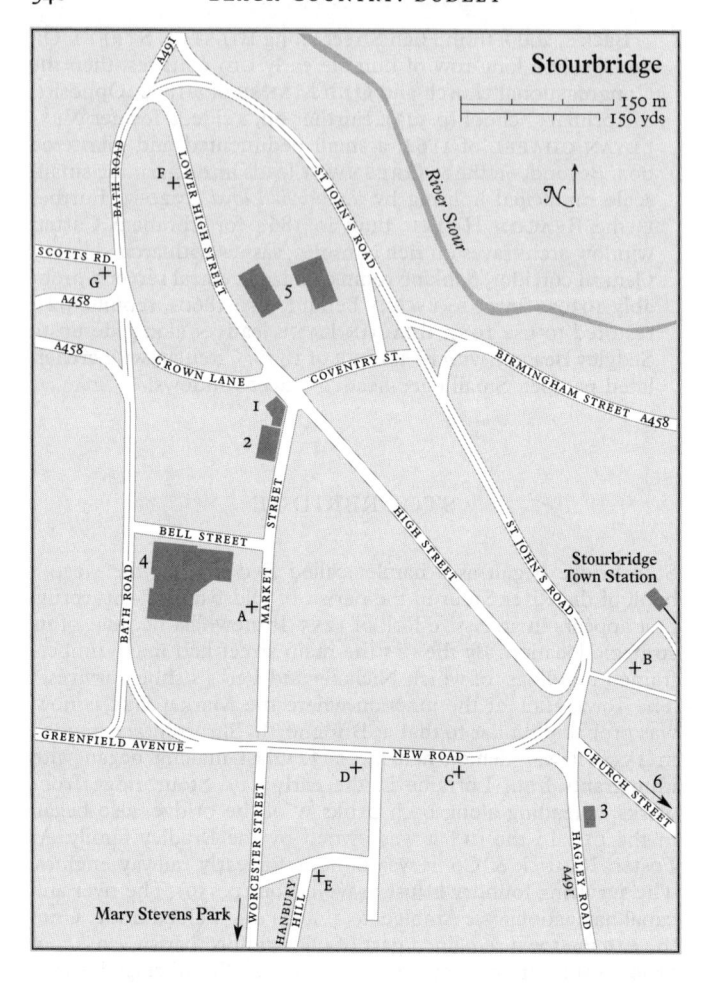

A St Thomas
B St John the Evangelist
C Our Lady and All Saints (R.C.)
D Methodist church
E Baptist church
F Presbyterian (Unitarian) chapel
G Friends' Meeting House

1 Market Hall
2 Town Hall
3 County Court (former)
4 Crystal Leisure Centre
5 King Edward VI College (formerly Stourbridge Grammar School)
6 Redhill School

the 1980s. His best work, reflecting his training with E. F. Reynolds, is in brick, slightly austere and beautifully crafted.

The disastrous ring road of 1964–9 cut the centre off from the suburbs, and destroyed the river bridge area. The delightful Ryemarket Shopping Centre of 1972–4 by *J. Seymour Harris &*

STOURBRIDGE

Partners is some compensation. The late C20 saw a lot of small-scale demolition of historic fabric, but much remains to enjoy.

CHURCHES

ST THOMAS, Market Street. Nave, aisles and W tower of 1728–36, brick with Bromsgrove stone dressings. Probably by *William Westley*, who contracted to build it 'according to the form and Modell in which it is now begun'. Erected for the Governors of the Grammar School, using £2,000 raised by subscriptions and a £300 bequest. It is a solid, competent, Early Georgian design – a pity it is not more prominently placed! Four-bay nave with round-headed windows. Aprons with panels underneath. The tower, unfinished in 1742, was completed by 1759. A recess runs up its W face with an arched top balustraded as part of the parapet, which is swept up to each corner. Transeptal projections N and S of the chancel of 1836 by *John Fallows*, originally for staircases. Their E walls have swept-up parapets and balustrading, with oval windows and doorcases with concave pediments below (now blocked), following the original design. In 1889–90 *Cotton & Bidlake* added staircases flanking the tower, and the E apse, turning the 1836 staircases into vestry and organ chamber. The scheme is by *John Cotton*, the detail drawings by the young *W.H. Bidlake*. The staircases are bluntly designed but the apse is a sophisticated Neo-Baroque piece, aware of contemporary London developments, and excellent street architecture. The parapet sweeps up to a segmental centre interrupted by keystone and finial, and the cornice sweeps up below this, producing the characteristic contrast of concave against convex. NE vestry by *Troyte Griffith*, 1911, with frowning keystone.

Inside, the arcades have giant Doric columns on high pedestals, and above them Wren's system at St James, Piccadilly, with transverse barrel-vaults in the aisles penetrating into the main vault. Galleries between the column shafts with panelled fronts swept up at the ends. The Westley family were carpenters – *John* and *William Westley* were paid for 'carpenter work and sawing' – which may explain the bolection moulding lurking in the cornice. The vaults are all panelled in a restless rhythm. Relief of the dove of the Holy Spirit at the entrance to the chancel. W tower open to the nave, a *Bidlake* alteration of 1890. – Mosaic REREDOS by *Troyte Griffith*, 1918, made by *Powells*; also by them two *opus sectile* PANELS of SS George and Alban at the W, 1920–2. – Chancel N SCREEN by *Bidlake*, 1891, successfully mixing classical and Gothic. – PULPIT. Base by *Simeon Bateman*, 1911, top by *Bridgemans*, 1978. – Lady Chapel REREDOS by *J. Homery Folkes*, 1962–3: Neo-Georgian, with pediment. – BOX PEWS, cut down in 1836. – ORGAN. By *George Pike England*, 1809. – STAINED GLASS. Apse windows by *Samuel Evans*, 1891. W, the former E window of 1859 designed by *Sebastian Evans* and made by *Chance Bros*, with good High Victorian colours. Nave, Good Shepherd (S) and Crucifixion

(N) by *Henry Payne*, 1911. s panel of angels also *Payne*, 1932, and probably also the N one (Suffer the Little Children).

ST JOHN THE EVANGELIST, St John's Road. 1860–1 by *G.E. Street*. Built by subscription, including £1,000 from the 1st Earl of Dudley. A cheap church, for people who could not afford pews in St Thomas's, in Street's most radical manner: hardly any decoration, but ruthless originality. Sandstone with limestone dressings and red brick voussoirs. Plate tracery; clerestory with circular windows. Buttresses with huge nosings, and a bold string. The W front is unbuttressed, so the awkward shape of high gable and aisle half-gables is stressed. Early French rose window and five excessively narrow lancets below. No tower, just a W flèche. Tall chancel and picturesque N vestry. French Gothic arcades with circular columns and foliage capitals, but absolutely plain soffits and responds. – Original FONT and PULPIT, both typical *Street*, also PEWS. – STAINED GLASS. By *Burlison & Grylls*, E 1912, W 1919, aisles 1926 etc. – REREDOS by *R. Bridgeman & Sons Ltd*, 1963. (Closed 2016.)

ST MICHAEL (former), Heath Lane. 1929–30 by *Webb & Gray*. Low, massive, Early Christian revival. Now a funeral parlour.

OUR LADY AND ALL SAINTS (R.C.), New Road. By *E.W. Pugin*, 1863–4, the steeple carried out to his designs by *G.H. Cox* in 1888–9. Tall enough to hold its own against the traffic of the ring road. Red brick banded with stone. Characteristic of the architect the tall, thin proportions, the Dec window tracery – especially the E rose with cinquefoiled circles round the edge – and, inside, the slim Scottish granite columns, alternating grey and pink, on high bases. The uncarved capitals weigh them down. A particularly tricky E.W. Pugin roof, with scissor trusses continued down as arched braces, and extra purlins clasped between them and lower diagonal struts, connected to the normal purlins by lines of small extra struts. You fear it may concertina up. – By *Pugin* the octagonal FONT, now supporting the forward altar, and the REREDOS, 1875, with saints and canopies. – STAINED GLASS. All by *Hardmans*: the E rose 1875, the rest 1893–1927.

GIGMILL METHODIST CHURCH, Glebe Lane. 1932–3 by *Stanley Griffiths*, trying to be original. Gabled front with full-height flat-roofed porches projecting at angles.

METHODIST CHURCH, New Road. 1927–8 by *Crouch, Butler & Savage*. Romanesque, dominated by a massive tower with angle buttresses. Self-conscious detail, two-light windows and entrance portal. Interior gutted, with inserted floor, and new porch, by *PB associates*, 2008.

BAPTIST CHURCH, Hanbury Hill. 1836. A standard Late Georgian box. Pedimented porch, part of alterations by *Thomas Smith*, 1860–4.

PRESBYTERIAN (UNITARIAN) CHAPEL, Lower High Street, set back. Brick. Three bays with a pediment. Porch also pedimented, and inscribed 'Hoc TEMPLUM Aedificatum 1788'. The architect was *Thomas Johnson*. Large iron-framed windows with patterned glazing of 1823, signed *J. Scott*. Inside, a 'drawing room of the Lord': a simple well-proportioned space with original box pews. Small w gallery of 1794 on fluted timber columns, with original benches. Pulpit end altered in 1862 by *Francis Smalman Smith*, with a big semicircular arch, now filled by a rich SCREEN of 1897 by *Pearson & Brown* of Manchester, and ORGAN above with screen by *Percy Worthington*, 1913. – PULPIT rebuilt in the corner by *Smith*, 1862, retaining the original front and some panelling. – MONUMENTS. Samuel Parkes †1811. Tablet with zigzag sides and projecting stylized half-flowers, by *Chantrey*, 1820. – Many tablets by Birmingham sculptors: *Michael Allen* (†1816, †1834, †1852, †1856), *John Nutt* (†1827), *William* and *Ann Lodge* (†1832) and others. – Alfred Worthington †1907 by *W. Forsyth*, with swan's-neck pediment.

FRIENDS' MEETING HOUSE, Scotts Road. Unremarkable at first sight. E end, up against the ring road, of 1994 by the *Alan Cotterell Partnership*; w gable a mid-C20 rebuild. Classroom to the s of *c.* 1967 with roof of 2004. Enter through the graveyard, now garden, and behind the w gable is the original meeting house of 1688–9. Roughcast, with a brick dentil course, casement windows and two semi-dormers at the E. Inside is a simple rectangle, its gallery with a front with fret-cut balusters. Panelled lobby underneath. Many original or very early fittings. Fixed SEATING around the walls. The ELDERS' SEAT, W, has a front with a bench and moulded mullions above, the main seat up steps, with a high back and shaped ends. Movable BENCHES, each strengthened with an extra chamfered back bar. The roof has tie- and collar-beam trusses: in the main room with king- and queen-struts; above the gallery, with side braces (boxed in) and a stud partition. A longitudinal strengthening beam runs w from the gallery collar-beam. The casements have a wonderful variety of C17 window furniture.

PUBLIC BUILDINGS

MARKET HALL, Market Street and New Street. By *John White*, 1827. Three-bay stuccoed front with giant Doric columns above. N doorcase with fluted columns and teardrop fanlight. It now fronts a big retail development by *Saunders Partnership*, 2010–13.

TOWN HALL, Market Street. By *Thomas Robinson*, 1887. Queen Anne, the civic style of the moment, in red brick and terracotta. It cost £4,500, raised by public subscription. The tower, near the s end, breaks the symmetry. Its open top stage and short spire are an excellent landmark. The main hall is set back behind a single-storey front, which rises to two storeys at each end. Robinson's design is seen obliquely in a narrow street, and its picturesque massing works in the same way as that of Webb & Bell's Birmingham Law Courts. Typical of the architect the many pediments, often semicircular: on the skyline and over the entrance, small ones on the ground-floor pilasters and on the keystones. Re-fitted for a new library and offices by *Mason Richards Partnership*, 1983–5, as part of a now replaced retail development behind.

COUNTY COURT (former), Hagley Road. A typical Italianate design by *Charles Reeves*, 1863–4, nicely tied together. Round-headed windows in pedimented aedicules above; smooth rustication below, with segment-headed windows with big keystones linked to the dividing string course.

CRYSTAL LEISURE CENTRE, Bell Street. 1990 by the Dudley M.B.C. Borough Architect (*Alan Powell*), job architect *Peter Ellerton*. Gimmicky brickwork and bright cladding.

KING EDWARD VI COLLEGE (formerly STOURBRIDGE GRAMMAR SCHOOL), Lower High Street. The present buildings start with a Gothic rebuilding of 1860–2 by *Thomas Smith*. His picturesque tower has buttresses with shields flanking the entrance, and royal arms over. Above, a three-quarter-round corbelled-out stair-turret, and bold battlements. Former hall, l., with a three-sided apse and big Perp windows. Pale yellow-grey firebrick with limestone dressings. Further l., extensions of 1907–8 by *Tom Grazebrook*, chaster Elizabethan. To the r., the present HALL by *Webb & Gray*, 1930–1, buff-yellow brick, with three impressive stone canted bays rising from a deeply chamfered base. The old hall, now LIBRARY, has a hammer-beam roof and stained glass by *William Pearce Ltd*, 1908; the HALL has big smooth segmental cross-arches, and glass by *T. W. Camm*. Behind the main buildings, the LYCETT BUILDING (chemistry), gabled, Tudor, by *Grazebrook*, 1897–9.

REDHILL SCHOOL, Junction Road. The older (N) part of 1929 by *A. V. Rowe*, with wide pedimented bays.

PERAMBULATIONS

1. North and east from the Market Hall

Opposite the clock, NICKOLLS AND PERKS'S shop, the former BOARD INN. The front, now rendered, has two linked shaped gables of C17 type, with plain rounded tops in the Black Country way (cf. the White Hart, Caldmore, Walsall). C18 sashes and canted bays, Gothick-glazed ground floor by *J. Homery Folkes*, 1948–51. Behind this façade is a two-bay late medieval house, its tie- and collar-beam truss roofs best visible in the S range, where the central truss has box framing visible below. One rear ground-floor room has an C18 ceiling with rosettes and consoles in the cornice. S side, two more shaped gables, one cut by a big C19 chimney, and an C18 doorcase. Lower E extension, perhaps C16, its cart entrance with more box framing. Immediately N in Lower High Street, a two-bay early C19 refronting of an older Georgian building with one elegant surviving first-floor fireplace.

A brief look E along COVENTRY STREET. Nos. 1–3 have modest C20 fronts hiding older brick buildings, probably C17. Nos. 5–7, Free Style of *c*.1910; linked dormers, suggesting *Thomas Robinson*. The DUKE WILLIAM, dated 1903, is probably by *H. E. Folkes*: brick and terracotta, fancy broken pediment at the corner, brown glazed-brick fascia.

Now back w, and N down LOWER HIGH STREET. The interest at first is on the w side. The MITRE on the corner is by *Scott & Clark*, 1932–4. Brewers' Tudor, with no expense spared. Pink-grey handmade brick with Cotswold stone dressings, half-timber above with beams deliberately cut twisted, and fancy bargeboards. Heavily corbelled chimneys, the architects' trademark. Leaded glass by *Samuel Evans & Co.* Surviving original lantern, w. No. 156, *c.* 1870–80, with ornate arched ground floor. Then the former SCALA CINEMA by *Joseph Lawden*, 1919–20, faience classical. Opposite King Edward VI College (*see* left) is STOURCOTE, a five-bay house of *c.* 1760–70. Modillion cornice breaking into a three-bay pediment on consoles, all builder's Palladian, but the central window below has a Gothick ogee head (cf. Nos. 6–7, below). Early C20 shop conversion, with canted first-floor bays. Nos. 164–165 are mid-Victorian; No. 168 must be by *Francis Smalman Smith*, *c.* 1875–80, with characteristic Baroque doorcases (cf. Oldswinford Hospital, p. 534). The curved JOB CENTRE by *Abbey Hanson Rowe*, 1993, breaks the street line. No. 170 is Regency, with ground-floor bow windows, seemingly original. No. 171, Early Victorian, four-storeyed. Nos. 172–173 retain cast C18 segmental lintels. Then the Presbyterian chapel (p. 548). Its former SCHOOL by *Tom Grazebrook*, 1907, r., is domestic Free Style, nicely massed, with shaped street gable. No. 176 is mid-Georgian, with modillion cornice and doorcase with Tuscan half-columns. Flanking the doorcase, pairs of narrow canted bays, their delicate cornices original. Early C19 first-floor oriels. No. 177, probably early C19; doorcase with pilasters and open pediment.

Opposite, the two best houses, both very enjoyable, built for the Bradley family of Stourbridge ironworks. STOURHURST on the r., *c.* 1750–60, was probably the 'great house I now live in' of John Bradley's will of 1766. Two canted bay windows with Venetian windows wrapped round them and Diocletian windows above. Wild top parapet with straight pediments flanking a segmental one with a round window. Doorcase with segmental pediment on Ionic columns. Nos. 6–7, l., is probably the 'New Built Messuage or tenement' in the will of Gabriel Bradley, John's son (1767). The same composition, extended by small end bays, but Gothick: all the windows have ogee heads. Even the parapet sprouts out in two ogee gables with finials. In the attic two quatrefoil windows. Doorway with clustered shafts instead of columns.* To the l., stables with ogee entrance arch and blank windows. Beyond, the former WOOLPACK INN, 1926, almost certainly by *A.T. Butler*.

The subway under the ring road leads to the modern Stour bridge and canal basin (*see* Amblecote, pp. 494–5).

---

*The juxtaposition of classical Venetian and Diocletian windows and Gothick ogees is the same as the S and E fronts at nearby Broome House (Worcs.), which Andor Gomme suggested were contemporary, and the work of William & David Hiorne of Warwick.

2. South from the Market Hall: High Street, the Hagley and Worcester roads, and Market Street

HIGH STREET winds nicely, but was too much rebuilt in the late C20. On the l. the former OLD BANK by *T.B. Whinney*, 1916–20, in French-influenced Neo-Georgian. Opposite, plain corner block by *Hugh E. Folkes*, 1927–8. CMD has an Art Nouveau shopfront of 1914. Then an Art Deco BURTONS by *Harry Wilson*, 1932.

On the SW side, the TALBOT HOTEL has a front of *c.*1794 with shallow first-floor oriels bracketed off the tops of Wyatt windows. It hides a grand and stylish timber-framed courtyard mansion probably of the early C17 for the Foley family, which was an inn by 1685. Original open-well staircase: heavy square newels with stopped hollow chamfers, but elegantly turned balusters. The WINDSOR ROOM on the first floor has full-height panelling, and a plaster ceiling with broad ribs finely moulded so they appear to pass through each other. They run in boldly intersecting curves with strapwork underneath. It resembles work of the 1630s at Crewe Hall, Cheshire. Fireplace with fluted Ionic half-columns and a remarkable but puzzling plaster OVERMANTEL (garishly painted). In the centre, Abraham sacrificing Isaac, with Baroque movement and swirling draperies, from the engraving by Egbert van Panderen (after Peter de Iode) of *c.*1600. Naïve and fascinating background of rolling hills and miniature representations of local buildings: on the r. probably Dudley Castle and a spired church, perhaps the medieval St Edmund; l. perhaps St Thomas, Dudley, and apparently Old Swinford Hospital (1669). Is this a late C17 addition (it is in poor perspective), or is the whole piece old-fashioned work of the 1670s? Caryatids at either end. A bedroom above (No. 19) has the liveliest timberwork, close studding and concave-sided lozenges, in what was originally the N gable. In the courtyard the S side has two tiers of semicircular and three-centred C17 arcading. A post in the bedroom behind (No. 9) suggests the arcades were originally open. On the N side, simplified Wyatt windows, one dated 1794 by the glazier (hence the suggested street-front date). The rear range has a jettied second floor and a gable, and timberwork of much heavier scantling inside. ASSEMBLY ROOM of 1924 by *A.T. Butler*. Neo-Adam interior with shallow barrel-vault.

Back on the NE side, PEPLOWS (No. 48) has a Neo-Georgian front with a fascia of 1936 by *Folkes & Folkes*. No. 49 is mid-Victorian with an oriel; Nos. 51–52, late C19 patterned red and yellow firebrick, looks like *Owen Freeman*. No. 53 retains an arcaded shopfront with alternating voussoirs by *Thomas Smith*, 1866. Opposite, an Early Victorian classical terrace, and LLOYDS BANK, crisp Neo-Wren by *James & Lister Lea & Sons*, 1913. Then on the NE side the POST OFFICE, 1885, by *Thomas Robinson*. Terracotta Jacobean; his usual scatter of miniature pediments. On the SW side the courtyard entrance to the RYEMARKET SHOPPING CENTRE by *J. Seymour Harris & Partners*, 1972–4, the best of its time in the area, tightly fitted into the urban fabric, scale and detail perfectly calculated. Maroon brick above the shop canopies, with little boxed-out oriel windows, and lines of asymmetrical semi-dormers: jokes that still make you smile. The dormers are reflected in the slanting roof of the arcade. (For the W front, *see* below.)

On the NE side, the former CRANAGE'S teashop, by *A.T. Butler*, 1926–7. Bronze and glass shopfront with central half-dome and quarter-domes in the corners. Above, pilasters divide deep-set canted bays. SW side, the former ROYAL EXCHANGE pub, late C19 half-timber. NE side, on the l. corner with Foster Street, BORDEAUX HOUSE, by *Thomas Robinson*, 1892–4, for Edward Rutland, wine merchant. Cut down, but still impressive with banded pilasters, terracotta frieze, balustrade and urns. On the r. corner, BARCLAYS BANK, a three-bay Early Georgian house. Windows with alternating straight and segmental pediments broken by consoles. Swept-up parapet.

An optional extra here goes up Foster Street to the BUS STATION, by *Jefferson Sheard*, 2009–12. Across the railway, HIGHFIELD HOUSE was the vicarage of St John's church (p. 548), by *Thomas Smith*, 1874. High Victorian with stone and yellow-brick trim.

Back on High Street, SW side, PARGETERS shop is mid-C18, with giant pilasters, with a rendered range N of *c.* 1830–40. The CHEQUERS is by *Fred Hunter Lynes*, 1906, a successful urban use of Voysey's roughcast manner. Two big gables and a small canted oriel with castellated parapet and tall arty finial. It plays with symmetry but avoids it, with a second-floor jetty, r., which steps down to the lower bay. Bold Shaw-style ground-floor windows.

Across the ring road, the former LIBRARY AND TECHNICAL INSTITUTE, by *Frederick Woodward*, Council Surveyor, 1903–4. Free Jacobean, with a tall gabled block enclosing a five-sided two-storey bay. Doorcase with stubby Ionic columns and two seated figures representing Arts and Crafts, the pediment broken by a cupid holding open a book. More obviously Free Style extension, r., also *Woodward*, 1908–9, with a square tower with octagonal domed cupola. First l. up CHURCH STREET. No. 1 is mid-C18, with doorcase with fluted pilasters. Nos. 7–17, CHURCH STREET CHAMBERS, are a picturesque range by *Thomas Robinson*, dated 1885. Further up on the corner of Junction Road, No. 1, a cottage with a shaped gable which looks C17. Beyond, in RED HILL, l., Nos. 1–3, probably by *Robinson*, with a part-butterfly plan, and Nos. 5–7, definitely his, 1905 (No. 7 was Robinson's own house), with oriels with tall finials and his trademark pedimented dormers. No. 9 is by *H.E. Folkes*, 1911–12, rendered with close studding above, but a canted-in porch with deep segmental lintel. No. 11 also *Folkes*, altered. Further on, W side, WHEELERGATE of *c.* 1711, five bays, hipped roof. The doorcase looks mid-C18.

Back to the former library and S down HAGLEY ROAD. The SWAN pub of 1905 is probably by *Robinson*. The end pilasters have addorsed swans for capitals. Then the County

Court (p. 550). Beyond, minor Late Georgian ranges, and a long series of Early Victorian terraces on the E side. Especially nice the round-headed doorcases with fluted columns on Nos. 79–81. No. 89 is a picturesque classical villa.

Back again and W along NEW ROAD, widened as part of the ring road. On the S side the former CONSERVATIVE CLUB, modest Latest Classical. Then the Catholic church (p. 548). Behind, former PRESBYTERY, brick Gothic by *E.W. Pugin*, 1864, and simple former SCHOOL by *Bailey & McConnal*, 1911. Going W from the church, sharply Gothic former CONVENT by *Pugin*, 1867. Beyond, the S side seems mostly *c.*1830–40. The Methodist church (p. 548) follows, then its former SCHOOL of 1886–7 by *Thomas Robinson*, Gothic with a side-buttressed central gable. On the N side and further back, first the POLICE STATION by *A.V. Rowe*, 1911, a long Neo-Wren range. No. 40, *c.*1830, has two pairs of giant Ionic three-quarter columns *in antis* above. Modern roughcast, as on the contemporary No. 42, which retains an inset doorway with fluted Doric columns. Beyond, a low range, slightly later, with panelled pilasters. Porches on odd columns.

WORCESTER STREET runs S here. On the corner the former DISPENSARY by *Tom Grazebrook*, 1893, Free Jacobean. Further up, Victorian villas and Nos. 46–56, a Late Georgian terrace. At the corner, GREENFIELD AVENUE runs W with houses on the S side of *c.*1900. The best is CLAREMONT, by *A.T. Butler*, 1902, with a Shaw- or Ernest George-type chimney.

Finally back across the ring road and N down MARKET STREET, with the Town Hall tower ahead. On the r. a Late Georgian terrace with severe details, then No. 65, with big workshop windows above. No. 63 is probably late C18. Prominent string courses and doorcase with spindly pilasters. On the W side St Thomas's church and hall (p. 547). Beyond, the BELL HOTEL and shops, by *A.T. Butler*, 1931–2, his best refined Tudor. Opposite, the end of *Seymour Harris*'s Ryemarket (*see* p. 552). Here the semi-dormers have gone symmetrical, and are linked to the oriels below. Display windows with curved corners like contemporary TV screens.

Across Bell Street, on the E side, groups of lively brick and terracotta shops of 1910–12, probably *H.E. Folkes*. Opposite, the INSTITUTE of 1936–7 by *G.F. Webb*. Symmetrical *Moderne* front, like a restrained cinema. Centrepiece with a turned-up pediment enclosing a relief. No. 10, *J.H. Folkes*, 1962. Then the Town Hall (p. 549).

3. West of the centre

Across the ring road an attractive area of mid- to late C19 housing, with small villas and short terraces. Nos. 59–61 Green Street are a grander 1860s classical pair. WINDSOR TERRACE in Brook Street is dated 1879; STRATFORD TERRACE on the corner of Cross Street is classical, as late as 1882. On the corner of

Cross Street and Cleveland Street, the GARIBALDI pub by *A.T. & Bertram Butler*, 1937, one of their best designs. Big corner chimney between gables at right angles. Deep-roofed ranges with big dormers. Canted bays nestling underneath.

4. Mary Stevens Park and Norton Road

The start is ¾ m. SW, at the far end of Worcester Street. Late Georgian cottages on both sides. Past Heath Street on the N, the first houses of the Heath Estate. *Francis Smalman Smith* was working here in 1863, and No. 138 is certainly his, with characteristic Baroque doorcase. It faces the entrance to MARY STEVENS PARK, opened in 1931. Piers and bronze lanterns by *Frederick Woodward*, wrought-iron gates by the *Birmingham Guild* (designer *C.A. Llewelyn Roberts*). On the main avenue, WAR MEMORIAL of 1923. Tapering pillar by *Ernest Pickford*; bronzes by *John Cassidy*. Figure of Victorious Peace cast by the *Bromsgrove Guild*, reaching forward while holding a furled flag: 'New Sculpture', all movement; well-detailed and accurate relief panels of soldiers. The park was the grounds of STUDLEY COURT, just W. Early Georgian, five bays, with giant pilasters, doorcase with segmental pediment, and windows with swan's-neck pediments. In the C18 it was the master's house of a glassworks, with a cone behind. Horrible front office extension of *c.* 1962. Early C20 extensions further E, and a square Council Chamber block by *Frederick Woodward*, 1937.

W of the park gates, on South Road, the OLD WHITE HORSE of 1939, by *F. Morrell Maddox* (*Watkin & Maddox*). NORTON ROAD runs SSW. The best houses are beyond the park, on the SE. Nos. 29–33, Old English villas of *c.* 1890, perhaps by *Thomas Robinson*. IVY HOUSE, a tough domestic Gothic piece of *c.* 1880. AVONDALE, old-fashioned Jacobean with hints of Old English by *H.E. Folkes*, 1907–8. No. 47, also Old English. OSMASTON is by *A.T. Butler*, 1905–6. Brick-and-render front, playing games. Where is the entrance? Not the half-Baroque dome, it's a stair-turret, but the classical porch to its r. Restrained Jacobean staircase hall. *T.W. Camm* glass in the staircase window. The dining room (now kitchen) has an alcove with a lovely Lutyens-style segmental arch on Ionic columns, and a Voysey-ish fireplace. Contemporary stables behind. Nos. 53–55 and 57 are by *Robinson*, 1898; mostly Jacobean detail. Finally No. 61, AMBERSHAM HOUSE, *c.* 1935, probably by *J.H. Folkes*. Arts and Crafts Neo-Georgian, five bays with the end ones gabled, like a modest country house. Swan's-neck doorcase.

Much further on, No. 113, THE LIMBERLOST, by *Webb & Gray*, 1926. Rendered, with sweeping roof. Porch on heavy carved consoles.

OTHER BUILDINGS

BIRMINGHAM STREET is crossed ¾ m. E by the fine ten-arched VIADUCT of 1881–2 by the GWR engineer *W.D. Rowbotham* of Wolverhampton, contractors *Kellet & Bentley*. Blue-brick with stone springers and copings. The arch span is 46 ft 6 in. (14.2 metres).

WALLHEATH

A former industrial village ¾ m. NW of Kingswinford. Some C19 character survives in the maze of little streets SE of the High Street, and the roads laid out *c.*1860–70 to the NW.

THE ASCENSION. Well positioned at the central junction of High Street and Dudley Road. Charming mission church by *Charles Lynam*, 1892. Brick, with wooden windows with ogee tracery. Timber-framed W gable facing the cross-roads, with a lead spirelet. SE extension by *Twentyman Percy & Partners* (*George Sidebotham*), 1991–2, well grouped with similar roof pitches, pinky-purple brick. Double hammerbeam roof in the nave, single in the chancel. Old-fashioned chancel arch with shafts on corbels. – STAINED GLASS. E window by *Camm & Co.*, *c.*1900; W by *Alfred Fisher*, 1968.

UNITED REFORMED CHURCH (formerly Congregational), Kidderminster Road. 1895 by *F. T. Beck*. Also brick and half-timber. Nice diagonally set wooden turret with ogee cap.

HIGH STREET is mostly Early Victorian. The PRINCE ALBERT pub has a hipped roof and doorcase with inset pediment. Nos. 22–23, stuccoed, have delicate pedimented windows with rosettes. The WALL HEATH TAVERN is early C19, altered by *Farmer & Farmer*, 1937. In FOUNDRY ROAD to the SE, No. 44, *c.*1830–40 with an unusual doorcase.

High Street continues SW past the United Reformed church as KIDDERMINSTER ROAD. After ¼ m. the former KINGFISHER pub, the front range of a former lido of 1937 and a joke of *G. F. Webb*: a thatched roof, with a raised centre enclosing a segment-headed dormer. Restored after a fire, 2017.

In High Street NE from the cross-roads, NW side, BERVIE HOUSE is a big mid-Victorian villa of tooled Gornal stone with fretwork bargeboards. THE HAWTHORNS is tall Latest Georgian. Segment-headed windows with oddly splayed lintels. Bracket cornice. GROVE FARM is also tall, with shallow full-height square bays and prominent gable chimneys. Opposite, GROVE PARK, municipal housing by *A. T. Butler*, 1920–1, with his trademark round windows.

HOLBECHE HOUSE, Wolverhampton Road, ½ m. NE. Sir John Littleton purchased the house from the Holbache family in 1581. In 1605 it was the last refuge of the Gunpowder Plot conspirators. Their leader, Robert Catesby, and others were killed in a siege, and an explosion 'blew up the roof of the house'. Repairs were being made in 1616, but in 1618 the house was sold to Edward Lyddyatt. The present building is probably his. The 3rd Viscount Dudley purchased it in 1803; the masons *Joseph*, *Jeremiah* and *William Beddard* did much work for him in 1819–23.

Low W front with projecting wings, rendered to imitate masonry (*Zachary Round* was paid for 'Roman Cementing' in 1820). The windows with Tudor-style hoodmoulds, the porch and the shaped gables of the wings, their Gothick lancets smaller versions of those in the porch, must all be of 1819–23. If the gables represent older work, it is most likely of after 1618.*
On the S side a vertical joint with the early work of thin darkish brick, in irregular Flemish stretcher bond. More Tudor-style windows here, and another shaped gable, definitely early C19. On the N, two rendered canted bays, one a porch, and at the far end a C17 chimney with diagonal shafts, perhaps for a kitchen. Altered C18 brick BARN to the SE.

Ancient main door, with huge planks visible inside. The wide main hall is of 1819–23: Tudor-style doorways with four-centred arches. Contemporary semicircular staircase behind, with cast-iron balusters and a Gothick lantern. The NW room has full-height C17 panelling, and a length of frieze with affronted and addorsed beasts. All very reworked; perhaps brought in. Another panelled room to the S. The main roof is old, with collar- and tie-beams. Cellars with shallow vaults, their small bricks indicating early work.

WOLLASTON

The ancient hamlet, in Oldswinford parish, was around the junction of High Street and Vicarage Road. To the S stood Wollaston Hall, a major timber-framed house dated 1617, with magnificent star-shaped chimneys (demolished 1926). Its estate was sold for development in 1848, the start of the modern village with its attractive mixture of C19 and C20 villas and short terraces. The best earlier C20 building has also gone, *J. Homery Folkes*'s strikingly modern New Inn of 1937–8 in High Park Road. In Stourbridge Borough until 1974.

ST JAMES, Bridgnorth Road. By *George Bidlake*, 1859–60, given by William Orme Foster.† Blue-brick with Bath stone dressings. Dec, with decidedly personal details; 'rogue architecture'. W window with angular tracery, triplet lancets in the aisles, big dormers to the clerestory. Triangular hoodmoulds punch up into string courses in the commanding NW porch-tower and

---

*Cf. Wollaston Hall (dem.), rebuilt *c.*1617. The 'priest holes' identified by romantic visitors are part of the cellars. Marks in the front wall, called musket holes, go through 1820 render and are probably where hooks were inserted for creeper.

†Pevsner's 'unified composition with school and parsonage' (actually the master's house) was wrecked *c.*1991 when the r. gable of the school was demolished, and a road driven through between (*see* below).

the w front. NE vestry by *Tom Grazebrook*, 1885, extended by *Webb & Gray*, 1935. Hall beyond, tactfully in blue brick but bulky, by *Frank Brophy Associates*, 1995.

The interior is a preaching space with a wide nave, and transepts. Arcades with alternating circular and octagonal piers, and lots of angel-stops. The roof has high collars and arch braces. W gallery on octagonal timber piers, with cross-braced supports. The atmosphere is still mid-Victorian, thanks to the original PULPIT, FONT, traceried CHOIR STALLS, square CLERGY DESK and PEWS. – REREDOS, flanking PANELLING and ALTAR RAIL by *Webb & Gray*, 1935. – STAINED GLASS. E window by *Clayton & Bell*, 1860, Crucifixion (some detail lost); also W, an unusual Twelve Apostles, heads only, in circular patterning. Transept windows by *Powells*, 1914, good. Aisles, a pair by *Jones & Willis*, 1921.

STOURBRIDGE CEMETERY, South Road. By *Francis Smalman Smith*, 1877–9. Tough CHAPEL in rock-faced sandstone. Cusped lancets. Short central tower with battlements (replacing a spire) and prominent stair-vice. Alterations for conversion into a crematorium, 1960. – LODGE, also rock-faced sandstone.

RIDGEWOOD HIGH SCHOOL, Park Road West. 1957–8 by *Yorke, Rosenberg & Mardall*. A satisfactory, straightforward job. Exposed steel framing, glazed panels (some replaced) and others of thin white brick. Extensions by *Dudley M.B.C. Architects*, 1992 etc.

The present centre is the junction of High Street and Bridgnorth Road. ESE in BRIDGNORTH ROAD, on the l., No. 46, the former MASTER'S HOUSE and, beyond, the remaining part of the many-gabled former SCHOOL, both by *George Bidlake*, 1858–9, also given by William Orme Foster. Blue brick with stone dressings, like the church. The school has a large gable forming one feature with the porch-tower and little spire. The demolished r. gable was similar. On the r., early C19 cottage in the fork of King Street. W along Bridgnorth Road, the streets to the s were laid out in 1848, but development was slow. The earliest houses are in COBDEN STREET (Nos. 2–18, E, Nos. 9–15, W). The stuccoed Nos. 22–26, designed to look like a terrace, were servants' houses to No. 28, THE HOLLIES, all of *c*. 1850. No. 31, *c*. 1870, must be *Thomas Smith*: vigorous Gothic with blue- and yellow-brick trim. DUNCOMBE STREET is plainer and later; No. 1 probably 1870s, with semicircular bays, No. 19 by *H.E. Folkes*, 1902, but unremarkable. A nice group of 1860s three-bay villas by the corner of Bright Street (Nos. 29, 30, 32). Nos. 36–46 (VICTORIA TERRACE), dated 1895, have tiny pediments so must be by *Thomas Robinson*.

Back on Bridgnorth Road and W, on the corner of HIGH PARK AVENUE the Late Georgian GATE HANGS WELL pub, three storeys. Next on the S side, Nos. 173–181, *c*. 1902, with shaped gables and domed canted bays. Probably by *A.T. Butler* (cf. Claremont, Stourbridge, p. 554). No. 2 High Park Avenue is similar. N side, Nos. 130–148, an attractive terrace of *c*. 1900 with paired porches. The PLOUGH INN, dated 1898, must be *Thomas Robinson*, with of course a tiny pediment. Steep plain and shaped gables, fascia with paired pilasters. CRADLEY HOUSE (No. 162), incredibly old-fashioned, is dated 1902. Nos. 235–247, s side, chunky brick mid-Victorian Tudor.

VICARAGE ROAD, ¼ m. NW. Nos. 89–123, s side, cottage terraces by *Tom Grazebrook*, 1905–7, for the Stourbridge Workmen's Dwellings Syndicate, an initiative to provide affordable rented housing. Brick with tile-hung gables and mullion-and-transom windows, under the influence of Bournville. Some self-consciously cottagey planked doors with fleur-de-lys hinges survive. Nos. 9–19 further E, dated 1904, must also be by *Grazebrook*.

NEW FOUNDRY (formerly Foster, Rastrick & Co.), Lowndes Road, ¼ m. E. Built in 1820–1 and designed by *John Urpeth Rastrick*, it increased cast-iron production six-fold. Reddish-brown bricks, clamp-fired on site. The principal front faces the river and canal, N. Seven wide bays, articulated by plain broad pilasters which act as structural piers. Heavy pediment with central oculus. Pairs of round-headed windows, central full-height round-arched opening. S front plainer: nine irregular bays, most with three-centred-arched recesses to the ground floor. The roof has six massive, cambered cast-iron beams spanning the whole width. The corners have two cast-iron beams placed diagonally. All this is braced and supported by two tiers of wrought-iron tie-bars running E–W, N–S and diagonally. On completion in early 1821 it was the widest unsupported cast-iron single span in the world (197 ft by 49 ft, 60 by 15 metres). It was originally covered in cast-iron plates, not slates, to make it fireproof. Original hearth hoods are visible on the S. The foundry was worked by John Bradley & Co. from 1831 until 1982; at its closure in 2004 it was the foundry building with the longest continuous use in Europe. Converted to a medical centre by *Abacus Architects*, 2012–14, with glazing in the central opening, and a grey-clad range added to the NW.

WORDSLEY

The largest ancient settlement in Kingswinford parish; from the C17 the centre of the Black Country glass industry. By the late C18 many works were operating near the Stourbridge Canal, s of the village. *The Beauties of England and Wales* in 1813 praises the 'elegant villas' of the 'capitalists of the glass trade'. The new parish church and school were built here in the early C19.* Much C20 suburban development, municipal and private. The closure of Stuart Crystal in 2001 marked the end of significant domestic glass production.

---

*The most significant Victorian building, the School of Art by *Thomas Robinson*, 1899, was demolished in 2000; the finest pub, the Tudor Revival OAKFIELD TAVERN by *Eric Farmer*, 1939, in 2011.

CHURCHES AND PUBLIC BUILDINGS

HOLY TRINITY, High Street. 1829–31 by *Lewis Vulliamy*, built as the new parish church of Kingswinford (Act of 1826). Builders *John Smith* and *Thomas Nadin*. Commanding Late Georgian Gothic, in biscuit-coloured stone. Nave, aisles, low clerestory and small N porch. W tower with tall belfry (disfigured by steel bands of *c.* 1947), crenellated parapet and pinnacles. All Perp in feeling, though the big two-light aisle windows have Y-tracery. Chancel tactfully lengthened in 1886–7 by *Alfred Perry* of Birmingham, with organ chamber and vestry.* Five-light E window of 1831, repositioned. The interior has tall Perp-style arcades with octagonal piers. Aisle roofs with Gothick trusses. Galleries between the piers, with panelled fronts and castellated staircase entrances. Perry's roof has decorative four-centred trusses on corbels with musician angels, delightfully in keeping. Reordering by *Jack Cotterill* of *Norman & Dawbarn*, 1996. – PULPIT (stored, W), and LECTERN by *G.F. Webb*, 1932. – PEWS. By *Tom Grazebrook*, 1914. – FONTS. One of 1831, chancel, one by *J.B. Davies*, 1883, SW corner. – REREDOS. By *J.A. Chatwin*, 1891, a rich piece with saints under canopies, carved by *Bridgemans*. – ALTAR TABLE, 1831, N aisle. – STAINED GLASS. E window by *Arthur F. Erridge* for *J. Wippell & Co.*, 1958, Ascension and Last Supper, replacing the same subjects by *Powells*, 1865. Chancel N and SE by *Samuel Evans*, SW by *Winfield*, all 1891. N and S aisles easternmost by *Evans*, 1893; N aisle westernmost by *Walter Camm* (*T.W. Camm*), 1911. – MONUMENT. N aisle, beautiful enamel and bronze tablet to Oswald Meatyard †1907, by *Sidney Meteyard*. – CHURCHYARD with grand C19 tombs, many of glassmakers.

METHODIST CHAPEL (former), New Street. Dated 1882. Designed by the builders, *S. Bennett & Son* of Brierley Hill. Gabled front in red brick with yellow dressings. Octagonal corner towers ending in spires. Delicate iron Gothick windows.

WORDSLEY HOSPITAL (former), Stream Road, ½ m. N. The Stourbridge Union workhouse. A parish workhouse here, probably C18, was altered and extended by *Robert Robinson* in 1836–9 (with *Josiah Griffiths*) and 1843–5. The surviving blocks are chiefly of the rebuilding by the workhouse specialist *Arthur Marshall* of Nottingham, 1903–7. Absolutely plain, except for the centre building with two shaped gables and a tower with a domed Baroque top. Near the road, former board room and offices by *Francis Smalman Smith*, 1874–5. Gothic. Gables with yellow-brick relieving arches enclosing chequering. All converted to housing *c.* 2009.

RED HOUSE GLASS CONE (Museum), High Street and Bridge Street, ¼ m. S. A glassworks founded by Richard Bradley in 1788. The cone, the only complete survivor in the Black Country and over 50 ft (15 metres) high, was built by 1794.

---

*Unexecuted earlier proposals by *Francis Smalman Smith*, 1876, and *J.B. Davies* (*Davies & Middleton*), 1882. It is tempting to suggest that *J.A. Chatwin* had something to do with an extension which so carefully enhances the original work.

Converted and reopened as a museum in 2002, after closure of Stuart Crystal's works. We enter at the street corner, through a wall of *c.* 1834. Curving glass-walled foyer of 2001–2 by *Horsley Huber & Associates*. Behind, the CONE itself. Slightly convex in profile, with bricks laid in English garden wall bond with five rows of stretchers. Used until 1936, it was both working space and the flue of the central FURNACE, reconstructed in replica in 2002. To one side the rare surviving LEHR, a low brick-vaulted tunnel used for slow cooling (annealing) of fired glass, leading to the open SHROWER, originally with table for inspecting products. On the N a visitors' range in traditional style by *Clarke Baker*, 1991, and the former WHARF to the Stourbridge Canal.

PERAMBULATIONS

1. The village centre

At the church entrance the WAR MEMORIAL, a stepped cenotaph by *A.T. Butler*, 1921. Behind, the former SCHOOL by *Vulliamy*, 1836. Brick, with stepped end gables and mid-gable. Tudor style. Two-bay r. extension, also Vulliamy, 1841. Later additions. Opposite, modest C19 shops lead N to the OLD CAT INN, much altered, perhaps with an C18 core. Along LAWNSWOOD ROAD here, N side, the RICHARDSON HALL. Dated 1907, but actually the refurbished drill hall of 1884 by *Tom Grazebrook*. A massive design with heavy end piers and a porch with banded brick pilasters. The primary school beyond is a standard Staffordshire County Council design, dated 1910, by *John Hutchins* (or his assistant *G.C. Lowbridge*). Back on High Street and N, the NEW INN. Mid-C19 windows but an older core. A nice Late Georgian/Early Victorian row starts at No. 126. Then WHITE LODGE, a rendered Early Victorian villa.

S of the church, down the hill, the ROSE AND CROWN, Late Georgian; architraves on consoles. In KINVER STREET opposite, former mill buildings, C19 and later.

2. The Stourbridge Canal area

E of the Red House entrance, off Bridge Street, JOHN STREET has consistent terracing of *c.* 1850–60 onwards. S of Red House at the corner of Camp Hill and Brook Street, flats of 1985 by *Coventry Churches Housing Association*. Sloping walls, two tiers of steep triangular windows. Now N from the works entrance to GLASSHOUSE BRIDGE on the Stourbridge Canal of 1776–9, engineer *Thomas Dadford Jun.* Beyond, W, buildings of the Wordsley Flint Glassworks, established before 1774. No. 52 was probably the lodge of Wordsley Manor. Victorian bargeboards, Late Georgian or earlier core. LOBLEY HILL, now RED BRICK COURT, a house by *Webb & Gray*, 1939.

Now on to the canal, W of the bridge. The 'Stourbridge 16' locks rise from W to E. On the S side, the former White House glassworks, first built 1779–85. Mostly later C19 and probably by *J. R. Veall*, but one earlier block. Back E under the bridge and past the Red House is DADFORD'S BRIDGE, C18 but widened. The towpath rises steeply to pass Lock 12, with horse steps in the paving. N up Mill Street, on the W side is WORDSLEY HALL, an odd late C18 house. The front has a truncated gable, originally with urns, and windows with delicate pediments. Late C20 porch.

Back on the canal and E, on the S side a mid-C19 timber warehouse hides a basin made before 1822. The area beyond, which still feels rural, is DOCK, a canal settlement named after an infilled dry dock S of Lock 11. On the N, an L-shaped group by *Joseph Webb*, 1825 or shortly after: the DOCK STORES, with casement windows, linked to a cottage with later canted bays. Beyond, closely spaced locks 9 and 10, 'The Staircase' (converted from a double lock in 1827 by *A.W. Provis*). S side, L-shaped LOCK-KEEPER'S COTTAGE of 1776–9 by *Dadford*, with later C19 extension. An iron SPLIT BRIDGE (to accommodate towing ropes) crosses the tail of Lock 9.

Much further E, by Lock 4 at Buckpool, on BRIERLEY HILL ROAD, the 1830s SAMSON AND LION. Restored front, doorcase with open pediment. Later C19 stable, r. Opposite, WORDSLEY SCHOOL. Low ranges in purple-maroon brick and glass, by *Coda Group Architects*, 1973.*

OTHER BUILDINGS

WORDSLEY MANOR, Meadowfields Close, ¼ m. S. Originally Park House. Probably of 1757. Palladian S front: three storeys, 1–3–1 bays, slightly projecting pedimented centre. Doric porch with pediment. Segment-headed windows with fluted lintels. The E side has a big Serlian first-floor window. Stable and kitchen wings recessed l. and r., now partly ruinous, with canted projections with quatrefoil Gothick windows. They must be early additions (the stable wing cuts a window). Their style suggests *William & David Hiorne*, as does the quite different N front, with full-height canted bays and Gothick glazing. Single central bay with pedimented Doric doorcase. Inside, a central hall leads to a staircase with slightly tapering stick balusters, perhaps early C19. Good fireplaces throughout, including simple Adam-influenced pieces; one has a heavy Early Georgian design with fluted Corinthian columns (dining room), now with a rich Victorian pedimented overmantel. Above, a cornice with acanthus and knotted-garland frieze. The kitchen has an unexpectedly 'polite' range with plain entablature and side panels, which looks early C19. In the 1930s Eldon Firmstone converted two top-floor rooms into a miniature cinema, and installed a *Christie* cinema organ in the dining room. *Christopher Firmstone* carefully repaired the house in 1992–4.

In the grounds surviving HA-HAS to N and S.

---

*Consortium of Dudley Architects': *Jennings Homer & Lynch*, *Webb & Gray* and *Alan Young & Partners*. The successor of *Adelphi* (*see* Brierley Hill, p.498).

WORDSLEY · SANDWELL METROPOLITAN BOROUGH 563

ASHFIELD HOUSE, Lawnswood Road, ¼ m. NW. Plain Early Victorian.

DIAL GLASSWORKS (PLOWDEN & THOMPSON), Stewkins, ¾ m. S. The last traditional glassworks in the area still working, making specialist industrial glass. The bottom of a huge CONE survives, 80 ft (24.4 metres) in diameter at the base. Elegantly lettered datestone: 1788. Built for John Piddock to replace the works on Brettell Lane. Blue brick, an early example.

In OAKFIELD ROAD, ¾ m. SE, Nos. 28–29 by *Webb & Gray*, 1923–4, with plaster panels and staircase windows with *T.W. Camm* glass. No. 21, *Jennings & Homer*, 1937.

SANDWELL METROPOLITAN BOROUGH

A creation of 1974, incorporating six towns in the centre of the Black Country. Named, curiously, after the former Sandwell Abbey and Hall in West Bromwich, near the Birmingham boundary.

Oldbury	564
Oldbury	564
Langley	566
Warley	567
Rowley Regis	569
Blackheath	569
Cradley Heath	570
Old Hill	572
Rowley	575
Tividale	576
Smethwick	577
Places of worship	578
Public buildings	581
Perambulations	582
Industrial buildings	587
Other buildings	588
Tipton	589
Churches	589
Public buildings	590
Perambulations	591
Other buildings	593
Wednesbury	593
Places of worship	593
Public buildings	598
Perambulations	598
West Bromwich	600
Places of worship	602
Public buildings	605
Major houses	608
Perambulations and other buildings	611
Canal structures	616
Great Bridge	616

OLDBURY

A medieval manor in Halesowen parish. A chapel of ease existed by 1529. It stood roughly where the Civic Centre is now. Urban District from 1894, Borough in 1935. Early industry included nail making, in small workshops, and tool making. Coal mining started in the C17. The Birmingham Canal of 1769 came close, and the Titford branch of 1837 penetrated the area. The huge chemical works of Albright & Wilson (now Solvay) was established at Langley in 1850. Oldbury town centre is near the N of the borough and, as often in Sandwell, is now hidden inside a ring road. It is surrounded by industrial areas. Further S are Langley and Warley, now mostly later C19 and C20 residential. Warley was a separate ancient manor, with a complex history. The three parts are described separately.

OLDBURY

CHRIST CHURCH, Birmingham Street. Rebuilt on a new site in 1840–1 by *Thomas Johnson*. Important for its townscape value, but clearly a cheap church. Nave, aisles and short chancel, all brick. Lancet windows, paired along the sides. Thin NW tower, heightened by *Wood & Kendrick*, 1887. Glass NE porch by *Robert Bacon (Derek Latham Associates)* from 1992, when the W part was turned into offices. – REREDOS, probably part of alterations of 1867 by *Edward Holmes*, now flanked by contemporary former FLOOR TILES by *Godwin* of Lugwardine. – FONT apparently of 1841. Small, with reliefs including an Ark. The supporting columns look later. – STAINED GLASS. E window by *Powells*, 1914, designed by *James Crofts Powell*.

ST FRANCIS XAVIER (R.C.), Simpson Street. By *S.N. Cooke & Partners (Louis Hayes)*, 1965. Tall, plain, brick-faced, concrete-framed. Extension 2001.

WESLEYAN METHODIST CHURCH (now NEW TESTAMENT CHURCH OF GOD), Church Street. Dated 1853. A big, dour brick design. Round-headed windows above and below, massive corner pilasters.

SANDWELL CIVIC CENTRE, Church Street. A design-and-build contract with *Conder Projects* (design architect *Roger Swaab* of *Hickton Madeley*), 1989–91. Unbelievably bad. Bulky, spreading, with Postmodern pedimented excrescences and a recessed brick entrance with a sort of minimal triumphal arch arrangement. How could a local authority have done this?

PUBLIC BUILDINGS (former), Freeth Street. *Wood & Kendrick*, 1891. Queen Anne, brick and terracotta, with shaped gables and an octagonal corner tower with a short spire. Good doorway with swan's-neck pediment. Now linked to a supermarket of 1980 to the SW.

COURT HOUSE (now a pub), Church Street. Dated 1816. Built under an Act which established a civil court for small claims covering much of the Black Country. *William Harris* and

Thomas Whitehouse, 'carpenters and builders', gave a plan and estimate. Five bays, with recessed round-headed windows. They have relieving arches with little keystones, linked as strings. Plain taller block behind by *Charles Reeves*, 1862, with upper lunette windows. Long wing beyond of *c*.1904 for Worcestershire County Council. Pedimented doorcase with blocked surround.

CAUSEWAY GREEN PRIMARY SCHOOL, Penncricket Lane. By *Yorke, Rosenberg & Mardall*, 1951–3. Hidden away. A loose U-shaped group of single and two-storey buildings on changing levels, the plan dictated by ground conditions (old marl pits and shafts). Chimney with circular hot-water tank wrapped round at high level, a lovely shape, perhaps derived from Connell, Ward & Lucas's demolished water tower at High and Over, Amersham (Bucks.), of 1929.

ROUNDS GREEN PRIMARY SCHOOL, Brades Road. By *Alfred Long*, 1910. Gabled blocks with segmental pediments over the windows.

PERAMBULATION. By the former Public Buildings (*see* above), the CENOTAPH, of Cornish granite, 1926. Designed by a local sculptor, *W.G. Jones*, with the Council Engineer *W. Greenwood*.* On the SE side, humble early C19 fronts, then JACK JUDGE HOUSE (library etc.) by *Sandwell M.B.C. Urban Design & Building Services*, 2011, with strident blue fins and a purple sail shape over the entrance. Now NE up Church Street, with the Civic Centre (*see* above) on the W side. No. 15 is early C19. Moulded lintels to the first floor. The WAGGON AND HORSES and attached shop are by *Wood & Kendrick*, 1899. A small but smart pub, Queen Anne style, with a corner oriel with a glazed timber top and little cupola. Brick, stone and orange terracotta. Splendid tilework in the bar and rear corridor. Original bar front and arcaded back. Rear smoke room with original seating. Then the former Court House (*see* above). On the W side, the BIG HOUSE. Built for a landowner, William Freeth, traditionally in 1705, more probably *c*.1725–30: see the alternating quoins. Narrow windows with broad architraves. Unusual rustic Baroque doorcase with reeded columns and a swan's-neck pediment (with later wooden additions). Open-well stair inside. Opposite, the former Methodist church (*see* above), then STEEL HOUSE, a police station of 1881 by *Henry Rowe*.

From the square again, SE down Birmingham Street. The flavour, as often in Black Country towns, is Late Georgian and Early Victorian. On the r. No. 1, *c*.1840, with bracket cornice, and No. 5, with giant Corinthian pilasters. Then shops with gables and pedimented dormers by *Wood & Kendrick*, 1899. No. 21 on the corner of Church Square is of *c*.1845–50, slightly old-fashioned. The street splits, Unity Place forking l., the square around Christ Church (*see* above) r. In the fork, the classical JUNCTION INN. A rare survival, with details – string courses,

---

*The best building, *Bateman & Drury*'s Talbot Hotel of 1840, was demolished in 1970.

quoins, architraves with decorative panels above, sills – made of cast Rowley Rag (dolerite), produced by *Chance Brothers* between 1851 and 1854. To its l. No. 30 was Lloyds Bank's first branch outside Birmingham, of 1864, the probable date of the ground floor with banded Corinthian doorcase and pilasters. Plain Late Georgian above. Then in Unity Place the Neo-Georgian former Post Office by the *Office of Works*, 1932. Across Albert Street, No. 12, of *c*. 1840, must be by *Bateman & Drury*: see the characteristic doorcase.

Back in BIRMINGHAM STREET, No. 38 on the N side, *c*. 1860. Rounded acute corner, rich cornice. It answers No. 17 (Barclays) diagonally opposite, here by 1845, also with a rounded corner. Five-light arrangement with pediment on the first floor. Ground floor by *Thomason & Whitwell* of 1888, when it became a bank. Now round CHURCH SQUARE. The sense of enclosure is the important thing here. W side, Nos. 2 and 3, here by 1845, with Tudor hoodmoulds; No. 3 also with a Doric porch with stepped-up cornice, looking like *Hamlet Durose*. S side, mostly flats of 1994; also No. 10, mid-C19, but the windows with tiny swan's-neck pediment keystones probably part of alterations by *Thomas Merryfield*, 1891. E side, No. 16, here by 1845, its heavy pedimented doorcase already Victorian. Further E on Birmingham Street, S side, No. 35, Neo-Georgian of 1933, signed by *Cecil E. M. Fillmore*.

LANGLEY

ST JOHN THE EVANGELIST (now St John and St Michael), St John's Road. Arts and Crafts mission church by *S. N. Cooke*, 1915–16. Big gable with bracketed-out bellcote, buttresses down the sides.

ST MICHAEL AND ALL ANGELS (now IGLESIA NI CRISTO), Causeway Green Road. Of 1890, by *Osborn & Reading* and *Wood & Kendrick* jointly (the committee liked features of both their designs, submitted in competition). Big but economical. Brick with stone dressings, lancet style. Thin NW turret, pent-roofed porch. Circular stone arcade piers, moulded brick arches. Nave roof with scissor trusses, alternate ones with heavy arched braces. All rather old-fashioned. – Original REREDOS.

LIBRARY, Cross Street. By *Abel Round*, 1908. L-shaped, breaking out at the corner into a brown terracotta frontispiece with Ionic columns *in antis* and big segmental pediment. Slim cupola.

LANGLEY SWIMMING CENTRE, Vicarage Road. *Crouch, Butler & Savage*, 1937. Long, low and massive, the entrance marked by an extra storey, a Hollington stone top and a minimal segmental pediment.

ROOD END PRIMARY SCHOOL, Rood End Road. By *Alfred Long*, 1905. Lively but uncouth. Undersized porch-tower with a comical umbrella-like cupola. Gabled ranges more Jacobean, with three-centred-arched windows and gables with urns.

OTHER BUILDINGS. The ALBRIGHT & WILSON factory (now SOLVAY), Trinity Street, has a block of *c*. 1937 and an entrance lodge probably of *c.*1950. The High Street, s, has little except LANGLEY PARK, opened 1886, with late C19 timbered LODGE. At the corner of Vicarage Road and Dog Kennel Lane, the MERRIVALE pub of 1937–8 by *J. Percy Clark (Scott & Clark)*, with his usual tricky timbering and corbelled-out chimneys. Derelict in 2020. On Vicarage Road a Neo-Georgian former DRILL HALL by *A.V. Rowe*, 1938. In Rood End Road, opposite, the schools (*see* above) and the unusually long classical BRISTNALL TERRACE, Nos. 67–121, dated 1879. To its N the BELL INN, 1859. Polychromatic brickwork, gables, rounded acute corner. Plan and early seating survive.* In Langley Road, off Joinings Bank, LANGLEY HALL. All the details are of *c.*1840, e.g. the sashes with architraves on consoles – but the H-plan suggests a C17 origin. In Titford Road, by the A4123, the NAVIGATION pub, by *J.P. Clark*, 1931, a typical design with wonky first-floor timbering and corbelled chimneys. Much of the interior panelling and plasterwork survives.

LANGLEY MALTINGS, Western Road, by the canal. One of the last traditional maltings built in England, of 1898 by *Arthur Kinder & Son* for Showells Brewery. Closed 2005, now derelict. Two three-storey blocks with stepped buttresses, containing malting floors, face the road. Of the kilns behind, two at the s end retain their pyramid roofs and louvres. The BREWERY, founded 1870, survives E of the railway in Crosswells Road. Now a distillery. Classical front office range.

FACTORIES, nearby in Tat Bank. The BIP WORKS in Tat Bank Road, brick and cubic, are by *S.N. Cooke & Partners*, 1946 etc. The Neo-Georgian former BRITISH CYANIDES offices in Pope's Lane are by *Arnold Crush*, 1919. Bowed centre with giant pilasters. Now a gurdwara.

WARLEY

ST HILDA, Abbey Road, Warley Woods. By *E.F. Reynolds*, 1938–40, his last church. Slim belfry tower (now partly masked by a porch of 1994 by *Christopher Thomas*). Piled-up masses behind: transepts, apse, smaller corner projections. The interior reveals these as a cross-in-square plan, inspired by Reynolds's research into early Ottoman mosques. Plain central groin-vault with a cross. Square brick corner piers, arches dividing off the subsidiary spaces. The sanctuary, reached through a similar arched arrangement, is raised up steps with vestries beneath. W gallery. – Original FURNISHINGS, including brick PULPIT and READING DESK, ambo-like twins, and sandstone FONT.

OUR LADY AND ST HUBERT (R.C.), Wolverhampton New Road. By *George Drysdale*, 1934. Early Christian Revival, handled with confidence. The tall SE tower, with its huge white-rendered crosses recessed into the brickwork to N and S, is a striking landmark. The massive basilica itself has a rich,

---

*A very rare C19 PLEASURE GARDEN, with octagonal Gothic pavilions, survived behind until *c.*1990.

unusual texture: English garden wall bond, with three rows of thin brownish stretchers separated by rows of normal-sized maroon headers. w front with pedimental gable, carvings of the Evangelists' symbols, and Della Robbia-style plaques. Round-arched arcades, their piers faced in Hornton stone, which continues round the apse as a tall dado. Integral paired stone PULPIT and READING DESK. The E end is an intricate spatial delight, with N and S chapels, at different levels, open to the sanctuary, and a narrow ambulatory separated by lintelled openings with pairs of columns. Their capitals with three chamfered projections suggest Art Deco, but also Early Christian precedent. Much of the detail has this double resonance: the angel on the sanctuary lamp bracket, the nave lamp brackets. The carvers are unrecorded: the builders were *W. & J. Whittall*, a local firm. Reordering in 1967 retained the original REREDOS, CHOIR STALLS, FONT (now by the pulpit) and PEWS.

GEORGE ROAD COMMUNITY CHURCH. A Wesleyan chapel of 1884 by *Edward Pincher*. Brick Gothic with lancet windows. Entrance front with paired porches and triplet windows with Dec tracery.

WARLEY INSTITUTIONAL CHURCH (now Salvation Army), Pound Road. 1924–5 by *F.W.B. Yorke*, his only church.* A gabled hall, progressive, rendered, with a big Tudor window. Now altered. Inside, arcades with delicate square piers, and plasterwork cross-arches.

WARLEY WOODS. A municipal park since 1902. From Abbey Road on the N, the sweeping open view across the grassed valley, and the copses on the hill, masking the boundaries, are a lovely surprise: due to *Humphry Repton*, who laid it out for Samuel Galton. His Red Book is dated March 1795. Galton may have employed Repton because of the link to Great Barr Hall (p. 657). It was, unusually, a new estate rather than the improvement of an existing one; the house on Repton's intended site, WARLEY ABBEY, came later, in 1819, by *Robert Lugar* for Hubert Galton. It was Georgian Gothic, with a tower with a short spire (demolished 1958; Lugar's lodges have also gone, and *Repton*'s Doric temple). The drive from Abbey Road winds up the W side of the valley. A pond, now infilled, was on the l. The house was some way up, on the r. and looking E across the valley. Remains of a kitchen garden behind.

OTHER BUILDINGS. Interwar suburban development E and SW of the new Wolverhampton Road; further W, the BRANDHALL ESTATE, 1960s. The other significant buildings are PUBS. THE WERNLEY, Wolverhampton Road, is by *E.F. Reynolds*, 1933–4. Cool, restrained Tudor, now painted. H-plan. Bowling green and former pavilion at the rear. The GEORGE, George Road, 1937, is almost certainly by *Scott & Clark*, with big shaped gables. The PHEASANT, Abbey Road, 1938 by *F.J. Osborne* (*J.P.*

---

*Built for a breakaway Methodist group committed to the social gospel, hence the foundation stones (one laid by George Lansbury).

Osborne & Son), rendered; horribly mangled. THE PLOUGH, George Road, is a rural survivor, probably late C18 and early C19.

ROWLEY REGIS

A group of industrial villages. Rowley, with its medieval church foundation, is the historic centre. Urban District 1894, Borough 1933. Old Hill was the civic centre of the borough in the C20.

BLACKHEATH

A settlement grew up in the C19 around the crossing of the Halesowen to Oldbury road and the lane from Rowley towards Quinton. A small triangular green at the junction became the Market Place. The parish church, St Paul, is just in Halesowen (*see* p. 520). The late C20 brought the usual brutal Sandwell M.B.C. relief road.

METHODIST CHURCH, High Street. Box by *Stone Ecclesiastical*, 2001–2, with ugly spired porch. It replaced *Gerald McMichael*'s church of 1902 (Primitive Methodist), Arts and Crafts with a Free Perp tower.

METHODIST NEW CONNEXION, Birmingham Road (now KINGSWAY INTERNATIONAL CHRISTIAN CHURCH). 1906 by *Ewen & J.A. Harper*. The remaining landmark building of Blackheath, now isolated N of the relief road. Brick and grey terracotta. Gothic. Well-proportioned tower with paired lancets and spire. Only the rounded tops to the side gables hint at progressive work. Interior altered by *Kenneth Holmes & Partners*, 1987, and *Paul Henry Architects*, 2007, retaining part of the gallery. – STAINED GLASS. Ritual E window by *William Pearce*, 1906.

CAVE ADULLAM BAPTIST CHAPEL, Beeches Road. 1897–8. By *William Willett*, 'sculptor & builder' of Old Hill. Gabled box with round-headed windows. Red brick and terracotta. Conservative interior, untouched and wonderfully evocative. Original BOX PEWS and PULPIT, also GALLERY all round, on fluted iron columns. Schoolroom at the rear (extended 1912), with its own pulpit and full-height glazed folding screen.

PERAMBULATION. The start is the MARKET PLACE, now a roundabout. On the NW side the SHOULDER OF MUTTON pub, C19 and perhaps earlier behind, with C20 half-timbering; a former BURTONS store of 1939; and HSBC by *Gotch & Saunders*, 1921, single-storeyed, with pedimented end bays and coupled Doric columns between. It turns the corner into HIGH STREET, the usual mix of humble Late Georgian survivors and larger C19 development. The Neo-Georgian VINE pub is by *A.T. & Bertram Butler*, 1935–6. The LIBRARY is by

Russell Hobbis, 2005, an assemblage of raked piers, barrel roof and tilting turret. At the w end, Nos. 42–43, with oversailing tile-hung gables. Across the relief road, former CONSERVATIVE CLUB by *W.F. Edwards*, 1905, a loose mix of Jacobean and half-timbering. Further w and N in ROSS is the former PUBLIC LIBRARY, now a nursery. By *Wills & Anderson*, 1909. Friendly Baroque, as at their Cradley Heath library (*see* right), but more freely grouped. Corner reading room, an octagon on top of a Venetian-windowed square. Entrance with Ionic columns and pediment in a low block behind, offices at the rear. Inside, the octagon has its cornice bridging the corners, with lunettes above. Opposite, THE HAWTHORNS pub by *Scott & Clark*, 1926–8, with typical half-timbering.

ROWLEY REGIS CEMETERY, Powke Lane, ¾ m. w. CHAPEL by *Leonard J. Taylor*, Borough Surveyor, 1935–7. *Moderne* tower, brick with projecting rendered bands. Extended as a crematorium by *Harper & Sperring*, 1962, and again 2014–15 by *Martin Critchell*. – WAR MEMORIAL, 1920. Obelisk by *Tom Woodward*, with soldier carved by *A. Hopkins*.

HIGHFIELDS JUNIOR AND INFANT SCHOOL, Beeches Road. 1894–5 by *J.T. Meredith*. His usual gabled blocks with expanded Venetian window arrangements in the ends.

THE BRITANNIA, Halesowen Road. Smooth brick pub by *Scott & Clark*, 1938–9.

CRADLEY HEATH

Open land until the mid C19, with small industry and scattered hamlets. A station on the Stourbridge Railway of 1863–6 encouraged rapid development. By the early C20 it was the most important shopping centre in Rowley, and the focus of the Black Country chain trade. The local architect was the young *A.T. Butler*, who moved to Dudley in 1911. The town's appearance remained consistently Late Victorian and Edwardian for a century, until disastrous demolitions – mostly of 2006–7, but more since.* Some buildings of interest survive, but the town's architectural character, and its industrial and social history, have been destroyed. Cradley Heath is a former place.

*The major losses were refused listing by English Heritage. ST LUKE, by *William Bourne*, 1845–7, pre-Ecclesiological, with apse of 1878 by *John Cotton*, Lady Chapel of 1913–14 by *Butler*. CHRIST CHURCH METHODIST NEW CONNEXION CHAPEL, 1884 by the Liverpool-Welsh chapel architect *Richard Owens*, its blunt spire, the *Stadtkrone* of Cradley Heath, dominating the Five Ways junction. GRAINGER'S LANE PRIMITIVE METHODIST CHURCH of 1906 by *Ewen & J.A. Harper*, progressive late Perp, with stained glass of 1921 onwards by *Henry Payne* (now in Birmingham Museum). SALVATION ARMY FORT of 1893, with attached Junior Soldier Barracks of 1900. WHITLEY MEMORIAL SUNDAY SCHOOLS, 1910–11 by *J.H. Hickton*, Baroque. ROYAL THEATRE, 1910. The HOLLY BUSH pub, Jacobean of 1906 by *Hugh E. Folkes*. LIBERAL CLUB, *Moderne* of 1924–5 by *T. Stanley Beach*. *Butler*'s D. & F. Fellows offices of 1911, English Baroque. ERNEST STEVENS FACTORY, Neo-Georgian by *Cherrington & Stainton*, 1930. In the former Bank Street, a tiny Georgian COTTAGE and attached CHAINSHOP, only survivor of the earliest development. The WORKERS' INSTITUTE of 1911–12 by *Butler* has been re-erected at the Black Country Museum (p. 490).

BAPTIST CHURCH, Corngreaves Road. 1904–5 by *Bailey & McConnal* and *A.T. Butler*. The remaining landmark building of the town. Butler supervised construction, and the lively Free Style design, Jacobean lightly spiced with Baroque, looks his. Big W window with round-headed tracery, tall Dutch gable ending in a tiny broken pediment. Naughty SW tower and spire. Its aedicules with swan's-neck tops, facing unexpectedly N and S, add movement. Inside, a good roof, with short hammers, collars, queen-struts linked by concave pediments and with drops below – an arty touch – and contrasting curved and S-shaped braces. Tall sanctuary arch with free Ionic pilasters and keystone with another tiny broken pediment. Five-sided apse, bow-fronted gallery. – PEWS with shaped ends, PULPIT with twisted columns. – CHANCEL FITTINGS. 1926, probably by *Stanley Griffiths*.

PUBLIC LIBRARY, Upper High Street. 1908 by *Wills & Anderson*. Sophisticated but friendly Edwardian Baroque. Red brick and grey faience. The four-bay front with off-centre entrance shows both Wills's Beaux Arts training with McKim, Mead & White, and the freer manner of the Norman Shaw school. Shallow giant arches enclose lunettes and framed windows. Balustrade and cupola. Barrel-vaulted reading room, entered through Ionic columns and articulated by matching pilasters.

CORNGREAVES PRIMARY SCHOOL, Plant Street, behind the library. Built by the British Iron Co., 1848–9. Simple big gabled range with yellow brick trim. Extended by *J.T. Meredith*, 1890–1, U-plan, now disrupted by a big chimney. Meredith's usual 'Venetian' arrangement in the gables, here with paired lancets in the central arches.

ST LUKE'S CHURCH SCHOOL (former), Newtown Lane. 1874–5 by *William Keen*, a mining engineer. Stepped lancets with shouldered lintels.

PERAMBULATION. In UPPER HIGH STREET N of St Luke's churchyard, the former UNITED COUNTIES BANK of *c*.1873 by *Yeoville Thomason*, a handsome arcaded Gothic design with rounded corner. NE, the new SALVATION ARMY HALL by *James Totty Partnership* and LIBERAL CLUB by *Gould Singleton*, both 2007. SW down HIGH STREET, LLOYDS BANK, with circular corner oriel, *c*.1905, perhaps by *Butler*. The former Midland Bank is by *F. Barry Peacock* of *Cossins, Peacock & Bewlay*, 1910. Domestic hipped roof but strongly modelled elevations, with smooth rustication below banded brick and stone. A Doric porch nicely turns the angle. Supermarket opposite by *Saunders Partnership*, 2006–7. SCRIVEN & THOMPSON (Nos.101–102) almost certainly *Butler*, *c*.1915; Nos.79–83 by *Butler*, 1911, plain but with tile zigzag of Birmingham Arts and Crafts kind. At the Five Ways junction CRADLEY ROAD runs S. On the W side the former MAJESTIC CINEMA, Art Deco by *Webb & Gray*, 1930. Opposite, POST OFFICE by *Henry Jennings*, 1907, with his trademark ball finials. Further down on the W, SHAKESPEARE BUILDINGS, *c*.1820–30, with window architraves on consoles, and an altered porch. On the corner of Station Street, BEECHER HOUSE by *Osborn & Reading*, 1881. Glass by *T. W. Camm*. Rear semicircular bay by *A.T. Butler*, 1901.

Back to Five Ways and SW down LOWER HIGH STREET into LOMEY TOWN. On the N side is Mary Macarthur Park, named for the leader of the women chainworkers' strike of 1910 (laid out on the waste land where she spoke to the workers), and the site of the Workers' Institute (p. 490). SYDNEY ROAD, running N, was early C20 Cradley Heath's smart residential area. Good builders' work, e.g. Nos. 35–36, *c.* 1905 by *Harper* of Blackheath. No. 20 was the Methodist New Connexion minister's house, by *Butler*, 1899, with steep hipped roof, square bays and chimneys with characteristic supporting gablets. Nos. 26–27, also by *Butler*, 1907–8, his most inventive houses, lively Free Style with a dash of Art Nouveau. Doorcases with sweeping voussoirs and tall keystones. One surviving gatepier. No. 28, r., also *Butler*, 1906, but much more conventional.

CORNGREAVES HALL, Corngreaves Road, ¾ m. S. Built *c.* 1780 for the ironmaster James Attwood. The Gothick front, with full-height canted bays and battlements, is probably an alteration of *c.* 1820. Quatrefoil windows in the second floor. On the W side tall blank E.E.-style arcading, also an early C19 alteration; likewise the Tudor-style hoodmoulds to the upper windows of the W wing; its far end later still. Restoration by *Sandwell M.B.C. Building Services c.* 1985, followed by dereliction, left little more than the shell, converted to flats by *Ian Guest & Associates*, 2011–13. The house is reached by a steep twisting drive through paired GATEPIERS with blank Gothick arcading.

OLD HILL

A scatter of cottages until the mid C19, when urban development began near the Cross, then from the 1870s around Holy Trinity church. Mines and quarries were all around. From the later C19 the town became the civic focus of Rowley Regis (Municipal Buildings by *Stanley Griffiths*, 1937, dem. 2012). Late C20 decline was accelerated by demolitions at the Cross for road widening in 1987.

HOLY TRINITY, Halesowen Road. By *J.T. Meredith*, 1875–6, extended W in 1877. An Evangelical breakaway from St Luke, Cradley Heath. So the plan is a wide nave and transepts for preaching, no aisles, and a short chancel. Rock-faced Penkridge sandstone with limestone dressings, well massed with a powerful SE tower. Geometrical tracery. W extension by *Colin Greenwood* of *A.T. Butler & Partners*, 1975. Vigorous High Victorian roofs with hammerbeams on tall braces, and high collars. The crossing has two collars set diagonally, and doubled braces in the corners. A double truss marks the 1877 extension. Full-height glass W screen of 1975 dividing off internal rooms – Original PULPIT (now painted) with alabaster shafts; also PEWS, including a CANOPIED PEW in the N transept,

probably for the choir, and COMMUNION RAILS. – GASO-
LIERS with conical drops. – ROYAL ARMS. 1801–16 period,
said to come from St Paul, Birmingham (p. 175).
ST JAMES WESLEYAN REFORM CHURCH, Highgate Street.
1989–90 by *Gould Singleton*, replacing a chapel of 1876 at the
Cross.
MACEFIELD'S MISSION, Claremont Street. 1904 by *William
Bloomer*. Big hall with pointed windows. Striking façade with
fat octagonal ogee-topped pinnacles and a cartouche.
EBENEZER STRICT BAPTIST CHAPEL, Station Road. 1903
by *Clarence A. Bloomer*. A conservative gabled front with
round-headed windows. Red brick. Original pews and
gallery. – PULPIT enlarged in 1910 for a stout minister, with
decorative back-board.
SPRING MEADOW BAPTIST CHAPEL, Spring Meadow. 1841.
Its delightful stucco Gothick façade was replaced in the 1980s
by brown render.
POLICE STATION (former), Halesowen Road. 1878–80 by *Robert
Griffiths*, Staffordshire County Surveyor. *Rundbogenstil*, unpretentious but clever. Red brick with Hollington stone dressings.
Recessed centre; the l. wing wider, with full-height windows
marking the former court room. But the side elevation is also
symmetrical, with hipped roofs and small projecting wings.
FIRE STATION, Halesowen Road and Barrs Road. By *Savills
Commercial*, 2014. Prominent but without interest.
PERAMBULATION. The start is at Holy Trinity. Down Halesowen
Road, s, the SPRING MEADOW, C19, rendered, with a later
pub front with a canted bay. s of the church in Lawrence
Lane, OLD HILL PRIMARY SCHOOL by *Edward Holmes*,
1876–7. Red brick with blue-brick banding and framing to the
pointed relieving arches. Back on Halesowen Road, opposite
the police station (*see* above), the former METHODIST NEW
CONNEXION SUNDAY SCHOOL of 1867, tough red brick
with yellow dressings. Going N, REGIS HOUSE by *Albert Bye,
Simms & Gifford*, 1933–5, was the headquarters of the Rowley
Regis Building Society. Cubic classical. Big framed display
window. Doorcases and parapet both with urns. On the w side
the POST OFFICE, dated 1911, by *A.T. Butler*. Symmetrical,
with gabled ends and canted central bay pushing through the
eaves. In Mace Street, running W here, former FIRE STATION
of 1942 by *Leonard J. Taylor*, Borough Surveyor. Neat buff-
brick design, *Moderne* with a touch of classicism to the former
vehicle entrance. Next w is Trinity Street, with REDDAL HILL
PRIMARY SCHOOL by *J.T. Meredith*, 1890–1. Arched windows
with keystones linked to string courses across the gables. Back
on Halesowen Road and N, only the former FIRE STATION,
dated 1910, W side. Small gabled front, tall tower. By *W.H.
Brettell*, Council Surveyor.
HADEN HALL, Haden Hill Park, ½ m. s. Land was granted to
the Haden family in 1290. The present building is perhaps
partly C16 and certainly C17 – a map of 1716 shows the
present footprint – but has been compromised by early C20

decay, repairs by *Stanley Griffiths* in 1936–7, a fire in 1977, and subsequent heavy restoration by *Sandwell M.B.C. Building Services* using trainee workers, completed in 2005. It is a confusing building. The main E entrance, with a studded door, is recessed between wings. To its N is a vertical joint. The block N of this may be the oldest part, perhaps C16. The N wing has first a large gable with kneelers, perhaps Late Georgian alteration (though its canted bay is all C20), and further N, at an angle, a smaller, much-renewed C17 projection with a crowstepped gable – a common Worcestershire motif – and little decorative arches above the windows. The S wing has similar details, but its symmetrical S front with full-height bays flanking a chimney was rebuilt in the late C20. The C17 details suggest a local builder imitating grand Jacobean houses.

The interior was destroyed in 1977 except for parts at both ends. At the N, C18 doorway from the ground-floor parlour into a small storeroom. A kitchen on the W has a brick inglenook fireplace with flattened arch. The S wing was altered in 1936 when *Griffiths* made two rooms on each floor into one. In the upper room his stone fireplace, with a C17-style overmantel copied from that at Stokesay Castle, Shropshire.

To the N, a DOVECOTE, linked by a wall to the house. Perhaps C17. Gabled brick S front in regular English garden wall bond. Six rows of pigeon holes in the gable, their ledges treated decoratively with corbelling or cogging. N and E sides, away from the house, of rubble stone.

Attached to the W, HADEN HILL HOUSE, built in 1878 by George Haden Haden-Best. Uninspired Jacobean. The hall has oak panelling and *Minton* tiles. Ornate fireplaces. To the N, big C19 STABLES. Further W, the CRICKET GROUND, its pavilion by *Clarence A. Bloomer*, 1911, now clad in plastic.

In REDDAL HILL ROAD, ¼ m. NW, CRADLEY HEATH COMMUNITY CENTRE, a former Church School. 1876, probably by *William Keen* (cf. Cradley Heath, p. 571). Low, with square-headed stepped lights with shouldered lintels. Further on, the WAGGON AND HORSES pub by *Frank C. Lewis*, 1907. A late and big example of the Black Country 'two-room drinker'.

TEMPLE MEADOW PRIMARY SCHOOL, Wrights Lane, ½ m. E. *Meredith & Pritchard*, 1898–1900. Grouped around a glazed lantern with ogee lead roof. The street front nicely balanced by a gable with semicircular top, and one big dormer.

BARRS ROAD, ½ m. S. Nos. 130–131, N side, are by *Butler*, 1920. Opposite, No. 2 by *Stanley Griffiths*, 1928, with ogee corner dome. Around the fire station, nice early C20 housing. Nearby houses on Halesowen Road (NW corner) and in Beauty Bank (W) look like *Butler* too.

The best INDUSTRIAL REMAINS are in the upper part of Station Road, the old road to Halesowen, ½ m. SE. The Dudley No. 2 Canal of 1794–8 runs by the road, to the N end of Gorsty Hill Tunnel, rebuilt 1881. Near the tunnel mouth, the former BOAT INN of c. 1841, with kneeler gables. Further S Nos. 136–138, cottages, probably 1840s. In the front garden of No. 171 a blue-brick VENTILATION SHAFT.

ROWLEY

The hilltop village, a narrow twisting street of brick and stone cottages, was flattened in the 1960s, leaving grassed spaces round the church. The hills behind, now topped by ugly concrete masts, produce Rowley Rag, a blue-black dolerite, hugely quarried in recent years for roadstone, but used in the past for cottages and field walls. The best things now are the parish church and the views w far into Worcestershire and Shropshire.

ST GILES, Church Road. The medieval church, a chapel of ease to Clent, was replaced in Commissioners' Gothic in 1840–1 by *William Bourne*, and again in 1904, after mining subsidence, in unremarkable brick Perp by *Lewis Sheppard & Son* of Worcester. Largely destroyed by fire in 1913, it was rebuilt once more in 1922–3 by *A. S. Dixon*, assisted by *Holland W. Hobbiss*. The result is the finest Arts and Crafts church in the Black Country. Local brick, shading from red to blue. The blunt high w tower, its sharply cut-off parapet contrasting stone and diagonally patterned tile, is a landmark. The chancel and transept walls of 1904 survive, with conventional Perp windows. So Dixon used pointed arches, the only ones in all his work: paired lancets in the nave, wider spaced in the clerestory. s porch added in 1926, with upper arcade and shafted doorway with Romanesque cushion capitals. Small, sympathetic w extension, now the entrance, by *Bryant Priest Newman*, 2000.

A screen with traceried top leads into the tall, narrow nave of three bays. Squared piers with a single set-back, in long thin handmade pinkish brick. Everything else plastered, including the matching single-stepped arches. Underneath this the chancel is mainly of 1904, its arch with shafts on half-conical corbels. Perp-style sedilia. The Lady Chapel, s, is *Dixon*'s. Complete contemporary FITTINGS. The PULPIT looks like *Dixon*, Free Perp timber top and stone base with tile bands and big corbels. The CHOIR STALLS look more like *Hobbiss*, a smoother design, with little figures. – FONT. 1929 by *Hobbiss*, with square tapering bowl with four excellent reliefs of the Evangelists' symbols carved by *William Bloye*. The eagle of St John, with sharp beak and halo set against its wings, is unforgettable. – STAINED GLASS. Three good late Arts and Crafts windows by *Benjamin Warren*: chancel E 1923, S transept 1929, Lady Chapel E 1930. Heavy diagonal leading and textured glass.

Churchyard WAR MEMORIAL, big Celtic cross by *J. H. Willetts*, 1920. LYCHGATE by *Hobbiss*, 1936, exquisitely detailed; the roof has braces with low-relief angels which rest on beams carved with angels' heads and wings.

ENGLISH MARTYRS (R.C.), Oldbury Road, Whiteheath, ¾ m. E. By *Jennings Homer & Lynch*, 1960–1.

KNOWLE METHODIST CHURCH, Dudley Road. 1907 by *W.J. Cornwell* of Barrow-in-Furness. Brick, with a big Perp window. Original pulpit, pews and gallery. Hammerbeam roof.

PROVIDENCE STRICT BAPTIST CHAPEL, Bell End. By *William Keen*, 1875; boldly dated in the gable. Classical façade with a 'Baalbek' arch, in red brick outlined in cream and blue, and pale stone. A stark building for High Calvinist theology: it should have been painted by John Piper. Tactful late C20 porch. Original pews and gallery. Rear SCHOOLROOM of 1926, identical in style.

At BELL END, ¼ m. SE, the mangled BRITANNIA INN is mid-C18: see the quoins. MYRTLE VILLA'S (*sic*) are proudly dated 1904, by *J. Hughes*, builder. On Birmingham Road, the SIR ROBERT PEEL pub, 1830s, with ground-floor canted bays.

In MINCING LANE, ½ m. E, Nos. 7–10, Jacobean-style cottages, probably 1840s, with cut-down octagonal chimneys.

At Knowle, ½ m. NW, the COCK INN by *T. Stanley Beach*, 1936, rendered.

COBB'S ENGINE HOUSE, 1 m. NW, in Warrens Hall Country Park. Shell of a three-storey winding-engine house of 1831, the survivor of three built to drain mines in the area. English bond brickwork, typical kneeler gables. It housed a *Watt* condensing engine, its beam projecting through the large round-headed opening on the S, with a timber structure covering the shaft. Detached tapering CHIMNEY, 95 ft (29 metres) high, braced with iron bands and corner rods.

Below, a crossing of four canals, created in 1857–8 when NETHERTON TUNNEL was built for the Birmingham Canal Navigation (engineers *Walker, Burges & Cooper*). Three iron BRIDGES with bold lattice parapets, cast at *Toll End Works*. The S portal, blue brick and double width, is 200 yds N. The tunnel, 3,027 yds (2,768 metres) long, was opened by Queen Victoria on 21 August 1858, and has towpaths on both sides.

At Portway, 1 m. N, the FOUR WAYS pub, 1936 by *Scott & Clark*, with big shaped gables. Going up PORTWAY HILL, on the NE, OLD PORTWAY FARM, C16 or C17, the SE end an addition. Box framing remains in the NW wall, the rest rebuilt in brick. Tie- and collar-beam trusses with raking struts, one visible in the gable wall. In the NE wing, rare surviving Rowley Rag walling. Restored by *Christopher Thomas*, 2006–8, with new windows and porch. To the SE a much-altered BARN, probably C17.

At the top, the WHEATSHEAF pub, 1935 by *T. Stanley Beach*, with flat roof and angled wings. ¼ m. further NW, WARRENS HALL FARM (now nursing home), probably C18, now rendered.

TIVIDALE

Rowley Regis N of the Rowley hills, between Dudley and Oldbury. An architectural wasteland.

ST MICHAEL, Tividale Road. *Davies & Middleton*'s church of 1877–8 was demolished in 1994. It was their best: big-boned brick E.E., NW tower with huge pinnacles. Its replacement, hidden S of the road, was the church hall, by *F.T. Beck*, 1914. Interior with segmental cross-arches. Chancel, modest saddleback tower and meeting rooms by *Twentyman & Percy* (*George Sidebotham*), 1996.

TIPTON ROAD METHODIST CHURCH. 1931. Brick.

SHRI VENKATESWARA BALAJI TEMPLE UK, Dudley Road East. Tucked away, but said to be the largest Hindu temple in Europe. The main TEMPLE is by *Adam Hardy* of the *Prince of Wales's Institute of Architecture* and *Dr V.P.N. Rao*, with *Associated Architects*. Designed 1993, foundation stone 1997, opened 2006. The model is the Sri Venkateswara temple in Tirupati, Andhra Pradesh. Indian granite. The temple, entered by a grand staircase, reproduces the distinctive horseshoe-roof style of Dravidian architecture. Much carving of Hindu deities on walls, pillars and ceilings. The worship area, on the first floor, has a main shrine and four subsidiary ones. By *Essex Goodman Suggitt*, big COMMUNITY CENTRE in a simpler manner, 2003–4; similar GATE TOWER (with accommodation for priests), 2007; smaller shrine buildings, 2003 etc. Circular GANDHI PEACE CENTRE by *darnton egs*, 2018.

SMETHWICK

Smethwick started as the northern part of Harborne parish. The earliest settlement was in the low-lying area where the Thimblemill Brook crosses the High Street, near the present Council House. The Old Church of 1729–32 stood originally in fields, serving scattered farms and hamlets.

Industrial development started with the Brasshouse Works of 1778, encouraged by *Brindley*'s Birmingham Canal of 1768–9. The canal's summit level here was lowered by *John Smeaton* in 1790, and the huge parallel cutting of the New Line made by *Thomas Telford* in 1825–9, with impressive iron bridges. Boulton & Watt's Soho Foundry was begun in 1795. French Walls works was owned from 1842 by G.F. Muntz, whose alloy of copper and zinc was used on ships' hulls. Chance Bros' glassworks, started in 1824, closed in 1981. London Street perpetuates the name of the London Works of Fox, Henderson & Co., founded in 1839, bankrupted in 1856, after fabricating the Crystal Palace for Paxton in 1851, and the original roof of Birmingham New Street station. Important C20 firms included Guest, Keen & Nettlefolds; Tangye's hydraulic engineering works; and W. & T. Avery, weighing-machine makers, who bought the Soho Foundry in 1895. Henry Mitchell's Cape Hill brewery of 1877–9 (Mitchells & Butlers from 1898), one of the largest in England, closed in 2002. Smethwick also became a centre of stained-glass manufacture from the late C19 to the mid C20, with firms including *T.W. Camm*, *Camm & Co.* and *Samuel Evans*.

Until the late C19 the town was considered almost part of Birmingham, its leading families also active in the city. It had a Local Board from 1856 and the Harborne School Board from 1873.

Rapid civic development followed: Urban District 1894, Borough 1899 and County Borough (unitary authority) 1907. The town centre developed along the Birmingham to Oldbury road, from Cape Hill to West Smethwick. Its architecture reflects growing civic pride. The 1880s schools and cemeteries, by second-rank Birmingham architects, follow the city's civic Gothic, the manner of J. H. Chamberlain. After 1900 local architects, especially *Fred J. Gill*, and outsiders like *A. E. Lloyd Oswell* of Shrewsbury, designed in a lively stylistic mix, noticeably different from Birmingham. Architects were among the civic leaders: Gill was a councillor, and *George Bowden* was mayor in 1905.

Interwar Smethwick was architecturally progressive. Public buildings by the council's architect *Chester Button* move confidently from Neo-Georgian to something approaching the Modern Movement. The same happened in the pubs of *E.F. Reynolds* and his partner *Spencer Wood* for Mitchells & Butlers, national leaders of the Reformed Pub Movement, though most have gone.

In the 1950s Black and Sikh communities grew rapidly. Comprehensive redevelopment replaced the oldest housing with unremarkable tower blocks, in the Soho area and elsewhere. Sandwell M.B.C.'s insensitive policies produced the by-pass of 1982–3 (involving the demolition of much on the NE side of the High Street), the intrusive Windmill Shopping Centre and the neglect of historic buildings. The exception is the canals, repaired and made accessible from 1982. A recent loss was the town's finest late C19 house, *Arthur Harrison*'s Hill Crest of 1894–5.

PLACES OF WORSHIP

SMETHWICK OLD CHURCH, Church Road and The Uplands. 1729–32, almost certainly by *Francis Smith* of Warwick, who sculpted Dorothy Parkes's monument (*see* below). Her will also left money for a chapel, a school and a minister's house. Repairs, including new windows, by *Thomas Elvins*, 1786. Refitted by *John Thomas Brown* of West Bromwich, 1853. In 1963, after a fire, *Anthony Chatwin* repaired the building and rebuilt the NE vestry.

A good simple Early Georgian church. Brick with sandstone dressings. W tower, four-bay nave with round-arched windows, and apsed sanctuary. The parapet goes all round, and characteristically curves up over the E end. Interior articulated by giant pilasters, those along the sides with little decorative brackets on top of the capitals. Coved ceiling. WEST GALLERY of 1759 with fluted Doric piers, reconstructed by *Chatwin*, 1963, but still with some box pews. – PEWS of 1853. – STAINED GLASS. C18 glass in the circular windows flanking the apse. E window, Ascension, by *Heaton, Butler & Bayne*, 1898. N side from E: fused glass by *Claude Price*, 1966; *Hardman & Co.*, 1921; *T.W. Camm*, 1934. S side from E: two by *Samuel Evans*, 1898; *Osmund Caine*, 1992. – MONUMENTS. On the soffit of the chancel arch, Dorothy Parkes †1727. She left 'the sum of

30 or 40£ at the most in making and erecting a monument for me'. Tablet with urns, marble obelisk above, and cartouche in the base. *Francis Smith* and his son *William Smith the younger* were paid £32 2s. for it in 1736. – Opposite, John Hinckley †1740. So similar, it must be by *William Smith*. – Thomas Turner †1760, with a pretty Rococo cartouche at the foot. – Thomas Hanson †1800 by *William Hollins*. – ORGAN by *J. Perritt*, 1904.

HOLY TRINITY, High Street and Trinity Street. Thin W tower and spire by *Thomas Johnson* of Lichfield, 1838. The rest rebuilt in 1888–9 by *Francis Bacon* of Newbury, 'relying on the Early English for inspiration' – but there isn't much. The best thing is the view of the three E gables from High Street. Tixall stone, much of it of 1838, reused. E window with thin Geometrical tracery and a wheel head. Paired lancets along the sides, reusing the old window dressings. No clerestory; dormers by *Holland W. Hobbiss*, 1934. Wide arcades with circular columns and capitals carved by *Dutton & Smith* of Cheltenham; infilled to create meeting rooms by *Christopher Thomas*, 1997–8. – PULPIT. 1877, altered 1914. – FONT. Alabaster, by *Jones & Willis*, 1915. – ALTAR by *Hobbiss*. – Good small Perpstyle SCREEN in the S chapel by *W.E. Ellery Anderson*, 1921. From St Stephen, Lewisham Road (dem.). – SCULPTURE. Heads of Archbishop Benson and Bishop Maclagan of Lichfield by *Earp*, 1888. – STAINED GLASS. E window by *Samuel Evans*, 1892–3, at his best: a Crucifixion, broadly treated across six lights, thronged with figures, like a painting by Frith. Lady Chapel E, fragments of an Annunciation by *Evans*, 1897. S aisle, St George, 1920; Good Shepherd, by *Camm & Co.*, 1938; W, 1899. Pieces in the glass screen between nave and S aisle, mostly *T.W. Camm*, 1908, also from St Stephen, Lewisham Road. S aisle W by *A.J. Dix*, 1899, thinned out. Nave W, *T.W. Camm*, c. 1930. – Concrete LYCHGATE of 1914 by *W.R. Walker*, a member of the church's Men's Brotherhood, who built it.

ST ALBAN (former), Devonshire Road. 1905–6 by *F.T. Beck*. Brick with Bromsgrove stone dressings. Now a community centre.

ST DUNSTAN (former), Marlborough Road. *S.N. Cooke*, 1911. Mission hall with half-hipped roof. Altered.

ST MARK, Hales Lane, Londonderry. 1935–6 by *E.F. Reynolds*. Nave and aisles only. Stylistic references are simple Gothic: mullioned windows and arcades with pointed arches. Extended tactfully N, under a catslide roof, and reordered by *Maguire & Murray*, 1962: a simple, low-cost job, with ALTAR on the S side of the nave, curving RAILS and SEATING. Three timber CORONAS, the central one defining the altar space.

ST MARY, Bearwood Road. 1887–8 by *J.A. Chatwin*, one of his good low-budget churches. It cost £3,400. Brick, with typical W baptistery, and incomplete SE tower. W window with plate tracery, otherwise lancets. Impressively tall interior. It also shows the bricks. Arcades with short circular Bath stone columns. High chancel arch on slim triple shafts. Tie- and collar-beam roof with crown-posts and upper braces. Original

PULPIT, CHOIR STALLS and FONT. – REREDOS and ALTAR by *Hobbiss*, 1928, good late Arts and Crafts work. Low-relief angels and octagonal corner posts with little sculpted depressions, deriving from Gimson. Carvers *Pancheri & Hack*. – STAINED GLASS. E window by *Kempe*, 1904; s aisle by *T.W. Camm*, 1905. Baptistery, four small windows by *Florence Camm (T.W. Camm)*, 1910. – SUNDAY SCHOOL to the W by *J.H. Hawkes*, 1897.

ST MATTHEW, Windmill Lane. 1854–5 by *Joseph James*. Dec style with nicely varied flowing tracery, 'rogue' touches like the central W buttress rising to a corbelled-out bellcote, and spiky detail: the timbering of the porches, the side gablets on the bellcote. Arcades of short round columns on high octagonal bases. W room 1980. Re-fitted 1895 by *Wood & Kendrick*, with alabaster PULPIT, FONT and REREDOS, and oak CHOIR STALLS and COMMUNION RAIL all made by *Robert Bridgeman*, and MOSAIC chancel floor by *J.F. Ebner*. – STAINED GLASS. Good E window by *Samuel Evans*, 1895, a Crucifixion. Chancel S †1865, perhaps by *Chance Bros*.

OUR LADY OF GOOD COUNSEL AND ST GREGORY (R.C.), Three Shires Oak Road. 1933–4 by *Philip B. Chatwin*, assisted by his nephew *Anthony Chatwin*. A fine eclectic design. The first impression, from the pediment and upper window, is of Roman classicism; but there is also a pyramid-roofed turret and a *Moderne* central doorway. Small r. entrance porch, its flat roof unfortunately pitched in 1995. The interior is articulated by plain giant pilasters, under a shallow barrel-vault with deep ribs. Doric aedicule with segmental pediment on the l. side. Coffering over the altar, beautiful BALDACCHINO with thin fluted columns and a pediment.

ST PHILIP NERI (R.C.), Messenger Road. By *Alfred J. Pilkington*, the nave 1892–3, transepts added later, and Lady Chapel and sacristy of 1904. An unusual design in the 'Early French' beloved of Burges and Clutton, with shallow-pointed arches, reflecting the taste of its creator, the Oratorian Father Charles Ryder. Brick and cream terracotta. A deep parapet on big corbels runs all round, with bartizans at the corners, and there are odd projections like low bastions l. and r. of the portal: a fortress of the Faith. Inside, a short marble-faced chancel with, against the E wall, an upper blind colonnade. The transepts are two bays deep and two bays long, with arcades of tall paired columns with thick shaft-rings. – STATIONS OF THE CROSS by *Mayer*, early C20.

PRIMITIVE METHODIST CHURCH (now CHURCH OF GOD OF PROPHECY), Regent Street. 1887–8 by *J.P. Sharp & Co.*, incorporating material from the previous chapel of 1873 in Rolfe Street by *Stockton & Son*. Lombardic Renaissance, the quatrefoils, carved foliage, acanthus frieze etc. now coated by heavy render.

AKRILL MEMORIAL METHODIST CHURCH (now GURDWARA AKAL BUNGA SAHIB), Londonderry Lane. 1928–31 by *Alfred Long*. Old-fashioned Perp in red brick with stone dressings, though the tower is good townscape. – SUNDAY SCHOOLS by *G.H. Plant*, 1932.

WEST SMETHWICK METHODIST CHURCH, St Paul's Road. 1928 by *Webb & Gray*. Small, massive Early Christian.

WESLEYAN METHODIST CHURCH (former), Waterloo Road. Now GURDWARA NANASKAR. 1896 by *Ewen & J.A. Harper*. Gothic, with a (ritual) NW steeple; Geometrical tracery. – SUNDAY SCHOOLS by the *Harpers*, dated 1907.

WESLEYAN METHODIST CHAPEL (former), New Street. The shell of a big pedimented box of 1855–6 by *G.B. Nichols*, predecessor of the Akrill church (*see* above).

BAPTIST CHURCH, Regent Street. 1877 by *Thomas Flewett*, surveyor to the Local Board, who gave the drawings gratis. Majestic Baroque front with giant fluted Corinthian columns and pediment. Two-tier frontispiece with double doorway and its own Corinthian order with pulvinated frieze. Interior recast by *Charles Brown*, 1969, with first-floor worship space, retaining the upper parts of a giant Corinthian order.

BEARWOOD BAPTIST CHURCH, Bearwood Road and Rawlings Road. 1965 by *Andrews & Hazzard*. – SUNDAY SCHOOL behind by *G. Bowden & Son*, 1903.

BEARWOOD CHAPEL, Bearwood Road. 1896 by *G.F. Hawkes*, for Swaine Bourne, the stained-glass maker. Domestic front with half-timber gable, now partly masked by a late C20 forebuilding.

GURU NANAK GURDWARA, High Street. The first Sikh temple, opened in 1962, was a conversion of the Congregational chapel of 1855. Rebuilt in stages by *G.H.W. Ensor*: meeting halls 1986, dining halls 1994 and the temple itself in 1996–7. Its tall façade dominates the street, a triumphant assertion of the Sikh community. It is poor architecture, hardly articulated, too flat, despite expensive materials (grey marble, with yellow detail and pink base). But the onion-shaped dome, above three-centred pediments, is a wonderful landmark, as if the Brighton Pavilion had come down on a visit.

GURDWARA BABA SANG JI, St Paul's Road. The former EMPIRE CINEMA, by *George Bowden & Son*, 1910. Baroque, with a big segmental pediment.

JAMIA MASJID ANWAR-UL-ULOOM, Windmill Lane. By *Arc-Hi-Structure*, 2004–17. Very big, of yellow brick. Four corner minarets, green dome.

UPLANDS CEMETERY, Manor Road. Laid out 1886–90. The chapel by *Harris, Martin & Harris* has gone but their Gothic LODGE survives.

HOLLY LANE CEMETERY. Gothic LODGE by *Harris, Martin & Harris*, 1886.

WEST SMETHWICK CEMETERY, St Paul's Road. 1857. (Chapel by *W. Wigginton* demolished in 2008.)

PUBLIC BUILDINGS

COUNCIL HOUSE, High Street. 1905–7 by *Fred J. Gill*. A confident, impressive building in Accrington brick and golden-brown *Doultons* terracotta. The style is the Baroque manner of the late C17 Office of Works. Two tall storeys, central portico and projecting wings. The portico has Ionic half-columns with drops, and a pulvinated frieze. The end wings have pilasters and big segmental pediments. The delicate but awkwardly proportioned cupola with its clock was an afterthought. Inside, an imperial staircase rises behind an arcaded screen with deep brown faience piers. Similar screen on the first floor. Semicircular COUNCIL CHAMBER with Ionic pilasters and rich panelled ceiling, the central panel open to a glazed dome. Doors with broken segmental pediments. Plasterwork by *Mallin & Co.*, glass by *Samuel Evans & Sons*.

FIRE STATION (former), Rolfe Street. 1909–10 by *C.J. Fox Allin*, Borough Surveyor. Firemen's flats by *Chester Button*, 1932–3.

ABBEY JUNIOR SCHOOL, Abbey Road and Barclay Road. 1909–10 by *W.F. Edwards*, at his best. Brick and buff terracotta, with an octagonal corner tower and spire. Larky details, e.g. the upturned consoles on the gable shoulders.

SHIRELAND HIGH SCHOOL (now SHIRELAND COLLEGIATE ACADEMY), Waterloo Road. 1907–8 by *Fred J. Gill*. Economical Neo-Wren.

HOLLY LODGE FOUNDATION HIGH SCHOOL, Holly Lane. Former girls' school, 1927, and boys', 1931–2, by *George Randle & Son*. Neo-Georgian, still with Baroque centrepieces. Rear block and low glazed front range by *Aedas Architects*, 2010. To the SE, RUSKIN HOUSE (formerly Holly Lodge), by *J.J. Bateman*, 1860–2, classical but asymmetrical. Characteristic details include the round-headed doorway with smooth rustication, and the linked windows.

SMETHWICK HALL SCHOOL (now DEVONSHIRE JUNIOR AND INFANTS), Smethwick Hall Park. 1939 by *George Randle & Son*.

UPLANDS MANOR SCHOOL, Addenbrooke Road. 1931–2 by *G. Randle & Son*.

WEST SMETHWICK PARK, West Park Road. Laid out in 1895 by the glassmaker Sir James Timmins Chance. His memorial by *William Henman* at the entrance is a big brick and terracotta aedicule with paired banded Ionic columns and concave broken pediment. It contains a portrait head by *Hamo Thornycroft* (replaced in resin). Also by *Henman*, picturesque LODGE with veranda, and in the SE corner, MEMORIAL to John Homer Chance, a domed Doric temple of 1905.

Other public buildings are mentioned in the perambulations.

PERAMBULATIONS

1. The town centre

The start is in HIGH STREET at the corner of Stony Lane, with the BLUE GATES pub by *E.F. Reynolds*, 1932, in his severe Neo-Georgian. Keystones with carved fruit, side wing with cupola. (In the assembly room a screen with Ionic pilasters probably made by *Peter Waals*.) The opposite side has gone for the by-pass, except for a TOLL HOUSE of *c.* 1820, with canted end and round-headed windows, but pointed upper recess to display the charges. Going NW, the best buildings are Nos. 66–68, a Neo-Georgian former Birmingham Municipal Bank by *J.B. Surman*, 1939, and Nos. 26–50, with lively skyline of bargeboards and broken pediments, dated 1904. Back and SE, the LIBRARY is the former Local Board offices by *Yeoville Thomason*, 1867. 1–3–1 bays with a central pediment, but attractively dressed in 'mixed Italian'. Round-headed windows in heavy pointed architraves, linked by stone strings and blue-brick bands. In 1928 *Chester Button* added the r. wing, and inside, a Shrine of Memory, with glass by *Samuel Evans & Co.* Beyond, on the corners of Brewery Street, two banks mark the former commercial centre. LLOYDS BANK, NW, is by *A.E. Lloyd Oswell*, 1905–6, Jacobean, but a Baroque flavour. Octagonal corner turret with small dome. The former MIDLAND on the SE is by *T.B. Whinney & Son*, 1911, in Whinney's characteristic Baroque classicism. Balancing circular turret with oval windows and dome. E is the Guru Nanak Gurdwara (p. 581). Opposite, STATUE of a Sikh soldier by *Luke Perry*, 2018. The OLD TALBOT on the corner of Trinity Street is *c.* 1830–40. Then Holy Trinity (p. 579). On the far corner, a mid-C19 house converted to a bank by *Wood & Kendrick*, 1899, combining Jacobean strapwork and Baroque corner porch.

Sandwell, Smethwick, Lloyds Bank.
Drawing, 1906

Up SOUTH ROAD is PAXTON HOUSE, a much-extended Early Victorian villa. Beyond, on both sides, Latest Classical pairs and terraces by *John Harley*, 1876–7. Doorcase cornices linked to round-headed windows above. Nos. 38–39 by *Fred J. Gill*, 1906, with timber gables.

Back on High Street, No. 215, the blunt Gothic former SCHOOL BOARD OFFICES by *J.P. Sharp & Co.*, 1883–4. Now E down PIDDOCK ROAD. POLICE STATION by *J.P. Osborne*, 1905–7, brick and grey terracotta. Baroque style but asymmetrical, with a French touch to the smooth-rusticated pilasters. Beyond, on the corner of CROCKETTS LANE, the former MAGISTRATES' COURTS by *Chester Button*, 1931, massive Neo-Georgian. Opposite, from the l., a good basic Gothic former infants' school with a steeple by *J.P. Sharp*, 1884–5, then the former Girls' School by *Gill*, dated 1898, still in tough Chamberlain-style Gothic, and the former TECHNICAL SCHOOL by *Gill*, 1910, Wrenaissance with a segmental pediment under a shaped gable. All converted to housing, 2017–19.

Back W to the High Street and on into COOPERS LANE. HOLLIES FAMILY CENTRE is by *Button*, 1937–8, spare Neo-Georgian. CROCKETTS COMMUNITY PRIMARY SCHOOL is by *Sandwell M.B.C. Urban Design*, 2008–9. HARBORNE COTTAGES, almshouses by *Batemans*, 1927–30, are Arts and Crafts Tudor in brownish brick, around a courtyard. In the centre a rustic column in Cotswold stone. Further SW in Londonderry Lane, a former DRILL HALL (now HARRY MITCHELL CENTRE) by *James & Lister Lea*, 1899, refronted in 1954. Cricket-ground PAVILION by *Fred J. Gill*, 1903. Beyond, the Akrill church (p. 580).

Back again to High Street, and S. On the E side the former MUNICIPAL GAS SHOWROOM by *L. Stanley Crosbie* of London, 1930–1 (altered). On the W the RED COW, by '*Mr Edmunds*' of Ansells Brewery, 1936–7. Neo-Georgian, not sophisticated. Past the Council House (p. 581), the WAR MEMORIAL by *Robert Lindsey Clark* and *H.H. Martyn & Co. Ltd*, 1926. Tapering shaft, standing bronze figure of Peace in front, reliefs on the base. VICTORIA PARK, behind, was laid out in 1887–9 by *J.C. Stuart*, the Local Board Surveyor. Attractive LODGE by *Harris, Martin & Harris*, 1891. Opposite, a Free Style range by *Henry Martin & Son*, 1896.

High Street now divides, the r. part continuing S as BEARWOOD ROAD. No. 2 is a former nurses' home by *George Bowden*, 1903–4, Jacobean. At Newlands Green, facing High Street, the former PARK HOTEL, Queen Anne by *Wood & Kendrick*, 1892. Next S, municipal flats by *Chester Button*, 1951–3. Beyond in Bearwood Road the former MITCHELL'S PEN FACTORY, now nursing home, by *F.B. Andrews*, 1910. Wrenaissance again. Rich doorcase with segmental pediment.

Continuing SE along High Street, on the corner of Edgbaston Road a block with octagonal tower and spire by *George Devall*, 1897. Further E, the disruptive and vapid WINDMILL SHOPPING CENTRE by *Browne Smith Baker*, 2003–5. Beyond, the road junction at CAPE HILL. A remarkably complete Late Victorian and Edwardian centre. On the S side Nos. 6–22, simple Arts and Crafts-influenced shops. An almost identical range in Waterloo Road behind. Both by *Henry Martin & Son*, 1906. On the W corner of the junction, a splendid Baroque former LLOYDS BANK by *A. E. Lloyd Oswell*, 1907–8. Its corner turret has Ionic aedicules with banded columns and steep broken pediments, and a dome. The WATERLOO HOTEL by *Wood & Kendrick*, 1907–8, is an excellent foil. Shaped gables enclosing cartouches, concave corner. Minor orders defining triplet windows. Excellent galleon weathervane. The public bar has its original front, and a back with bowed centre and clock. Tiling by *Carters* of Poole, including the ceiling. The glory of the pub is the basement GRILL ROOM. The walls have seagreen tiles with occasional moulded birds and dolphins, and a gorgeous frieze of galleons. Original bar front and back again, entrance screen with more galleons in leaded lights.*

On the N side, flanking the start of Windmill Lane, rows of gabled shops by *George Bowden*, 1896 and 1891 (including the SEVEN STARS pub). Down Windmill Lane the former RINK CINEMA by *W. T. Benslyn*, 1930. Massive bowed front, following the curve of the road. Brown brick, severely detailed, with square end towers and raised centre with big name panel, except for the line of first-floor windows with architraves rising into shell-hoods with standing peacocks on crowns. Art Deco auditorium, with *Bryans* 'Adamanta' plasterwork, vivid zigzag on the coving of the proscenium, and rows of stepped Moorish niches along the sides with more big shells, like miniature balconies.

Now E down Cape Hill. On the corner of Salisbury Road, N, a former UNITED COUNTIES BANK by *Wood & Kendrick*, 1902–3. Stourbridge brick and buff terracotta. Delightful skyline with concave gables set against balustrading, octagonal turret with spirelet. Beyond, the former DUDLEY ARMS on the corner of Rosebery Road is by *James & Lister Lea*, dated 1915; pale terracotta below (painted) leaded roofs to the upper bays. The former GENERAL DISPENSARY is by *Fred J. Gill*, 1907–8. Neo-Wren detail but asymmetrical composition, a domed tower balancing the pedimented ends of the main block. The CAPE SCHOOLS are by *G. H. Cox*, 1887–8, picturesque Queen Anne. Central block facing the corner at an angle, with a big Dutch gable against a hipped roof. Side ranges with hipped gables. Extended along Durban Road by *Fred J. Gill*, 1901.

At the Birmingham boundary on the S, the Mitchells & Butlers' brewery site, redeveloped for housing. The former FIRE STATION of 1925–7 survives down Barrett Street, S, rather domestic, with the company's WAR MEMORIAL, a cenotaph of 1922: both by *Wood & Kendrick*. W of the roundabout, N side, the former GROVE CINEMA by *Roland Satchwell*, 1937.

---

*Description as in 2009.

2. Bearwood

Early C20 development 1 m. s, on the Birmingham boundary. At the cross-roads of Bearwood Road and Sandon Road, the BEAR TAVERN by *C.H. Collett*, 1907. Domed turret unforgettably decorated with bears' heads. Opposite, shops by *Wood & Kendrick*, 1908. w down Three Shires Oak Road, past St Gregory (p. 580), the ABBEY pub, on the corner with Thimblemill Road. By *E.F. Reynolds*, 1929–31. His characteristic austere Neo-Georgian, with segment-headed dormers. The bar has its original front and elegant classical back, perhaps made by *Peter Waals*. Original seating here and in the smoke room.

Going N up Thimblemill Road, on the E side flats by *Chester Button*, 1938–9, still with hipped roofs, but Modernist detail including concrete balconies. Beyond, SMETHWICK BATHS by *Button*, 1933. Brick and 'Vinculum' cast stone. *Moderne* classical with stepped front, flat-roofed side blocks, and inset portico. The entrance hall has green cast-stone piers with inlaid mosaic. Impressive main bath with parabolic trusses, green-and-orange tiled dado, and former proscenium (it doubled as a dance hall in winter) with stepped Art Deco surround.

THIMBLEMILL LIBRARY is also by *Button*, 1936–7, by now fully Modernist. The reading room is a big half-round single storey facing the corner. Concave two-storey office range behind with tall triangular staircase window. Further NW, on the l., a former lodge by *C.E. Bateman*, 1912. Mackintosh influence: harled, with a blank semicircular stair projection, set next to a short flat-capped chimney and against a deep roof.

Back at the Bear, a scatter of buildings N up BEARWOOD ROAD. On the W side a primary school by *J.P. Sharp & Co.*, 1881–2, now without its spired tower. Former boys' school facing Ethel Street, N, by *Fred J. Gill*, 1893. Further up on the E side, the former WINDSOR CINEMA (now snooker club) by *Horace G. Bradley*, 1929–30, with bold circular corner tower. N again on the corner of Dawson Street the former BARLEYCORN pub by *Spencer Wood*, 1939. Now horribly metal-clad, but a remarkable design. The flat-roofed main block turns a quarter-circle round the corner. Balancing small square blocks to either side. Buff brick underneath, except for the tall red chimney at the l.

3. The Birmingham Canal

From High Street at the Blue Gates, NW, a footbridge crosses the by-pass into Brasshouse Lane, with bridges over the cutting where the canals run parallel just N of the centre. Looking NW, we see the deep cutting of the 1825–9 New Line, the 1790 Old Line higher up to the r., and traces of the original 1768–9 summit level on the slope beyond. On the bank between New and Old lines, SMETHWICK NEW PUMPING STATION of 1892 by the canal engineer *G.R. Jebb*. Banded brickwork with bright orange voussoirs, hipped roof. Repaired and the tall chimney rebuilt, 1982–2000. NE up the hill, the former COCK pub, by *J.P. Osborne & Son*, 1939, Tudor, and the Neo-Georgian former BEACON CINEMA by *Harold S. Scott*, 1929.

Back to the canals and SE, following the Old Line at its higher level. On the r. the attractive ENGINE ARM AQUEDUCT over the New Line, by *Telford*, 1827–9, its arch all of iron, with a continuous Gothic arcade fronting the water trough. The towpath crosses the arm by a miniature roving bridge. Beyond, the three SMETHWICK LOCKS by *Smeaton*, 1790. The top lock has a split bridge at the tail and a reconstructed TOLL HOUSE. Remains of *Brindley*'s 1769 locks to the N. At the bottom SMETHWICK JUNCTION, where the Old and New lines join, with two iron footbridges dated 1828 and made by the *Horseley Iron Co*. Lattice-pattern parapets with quatrefoils at the ends.

The finest canal monument is ½ m. NW from Brasshouse Lane, reached along the New Line towpath through a modern concrete tunnel. GALTON BRIDGE, dated 1829, was designed by *Telford* and also made by the *Horseley Iron Co*. A wonderfully delicate iron arch, of 154-ft (47-metre) span, 70 ft (21.3 metres) high, of four lattice-pattern girders. The parapets have intersecting iron railings and sandstone piers with blank cusped Gothic arcading. It carries Roebuck Lane, now a footpath, which crosses the Old Line, just N, by SUMMIT BRIDGE, dated 1790, with a huge brick abutment.

53

INDUSTRIAL BUILDINGS

SOHO FOUNDRY, Foundry Lane. Established in 1795–6 by Boulton & Watt (James Watt Jun.); initial plan by *William Wilkinson*. The first purpose-built steam engine manufactory in the world. William Murdoch conducted gas lighting experiments here, and in 1798 installed the first fixed gas lighting in a factory. In 1848 the firm became James Watt & Co., and in 1895 the Foundry was acquired by W. & T. Avery, weighing-machine makers. Much early surviving fabric, found in the early 1990s: the only standing buildings at any of the Soho undertakings.

Big classical front range and entrance by *William Haywood*, 1925. Immediately behind, now attached, a Boulton & Watt terrace of cottages of 1801–2 and 1809–10. The earliest structures lie at the W end of the site, currently covered by a temporary roof of 2008–9. The main FOUNDRY BUILDING (1795–6, 1801–2, 1895) will never delight the aesthetic senses, but the greater interest here is historic. In the vast interior, now abandoned, the cylinders and other parts of the Boulton & Watt engines were made. The earliest fabric, of 1795–6, forms the E gable and half of the S elevation; the Belfast-truss roof over all is Averys' (1896). The casting pit at the E end leads at 'basement' level, via 100 yds (90 metres) of tunnel buried in foundry slag, to the surviving brick vaults of the former PATTERN STORES (1799, 1809). E across a yard, attached to the main foundry, the ERECTING SHOP of 1847; another huge space, with original iron roof by *H. Smith* of the Vulcan

Foundry, West Bromwich, an impressive rhythmic lattice of wrought and cast iron.

The Foundry also made coining machinery. s of the main complex of buildings lies the MINT of 1860. Converted to a smithy c.1896, losing its internal walls. Its roof is a copy of that of the erecting shop. (Description by George Demidowicz.)

CHANCE'S GLASSWORKS, Spon Lane South, ½ m. W, between the Old and New Line canals. Prominent seven-storey L-shaped warehouse block of 1847, its original windows with segmental heads. Later three-storey block linked to its S end. Along the New Line canal to the S, from the E, first two warehouses of 1853, single-storeyed on the factory side, then the blue-brick and sandstone double-deck CHANCE'S BRIDGE, and partly surviving railway bridge beyond, linking to now demolished buildings to the S. Then a two-storey mid-C19 range, and beyond, HARTLEY BRIDGE over the canal, probably c.1828. Attractive sandstone, with honeycomb patterning to the voussoirs. W again, two three-storey warehouses, of twelve and fifteen bays. Seen from the canal, all the warehouses have impressive battered bases. Further S, in Crystal Drive, part of CHANCE'S SCHOOL of 1850 by *Charles Wyatt Orford*, a picturesque Tudor Gothic porch with a stone belfry. To its E a slightly later Gothic house.

At the W end of the site the New Line canal crosses the Old Line on the STEWARD AQUEDUCT. 1828 by *Telford*, brick and sandstone, with two low elliptical skew arches. To the N, under the huge concrete piers of the M5, *Brindley*'s three SPON LANE locks of 1769 link the canals.

HAWTHORN HOUSE, Halfords Lane. The former HENRY HOPE & CO. offices, by *John H.D. Madin & Partners*, 1963–4. Crisp curtain walling, on pilotis at the street end. Projecting oval stair-tower in blue brick, S – a hint of Brutalism.

OTHER BUILDINGS

LIGHTWOODS HOUSE, Adkins Lane. This was a radical Neoclassical villa of 1785 for Jonathan Grundy, Birmingham merchant (date and name on a brick E of the porch). The side blocks survive, ruthlessly simple, with blank lunettes in pedimental gables. Perhaps by *Samuel Wyatt*? George Caleb Adkins, who lived here 1858–87, added side bays to create a 1–3–1 composition, and dressed up the front with heavy architraves, quoining and porch. Many extensions at the rear, also a fine original Venetian window. It lights an open-well staircase, probably altered in the C19.

The grounds were laid out by Birmingham Corporation in 1902 as LIGHTWOODS PARK.* Ornate BANDSTAND made by the *Lion Foundry*, Kirkintilloch. FOUNTAIN dated 1903 with comical timber and tile canopy. SHAKESPEARE GARDEN of

---

*Transferred to Sandwell M.B.C. in 2010.

1915, the former kitchen garden, with plants mentioned in the plays.

OLD CHAPEL INN, The Uplands, by the Old Church. Apparently early C19, minimal Tudor Revival.

ST PAUL'S VICARAGE (former), No. 109 St Paul's Road. *J.J. Bateman*, 1857–8. Red brick Tudor with diapering. Extended by *Walker Troup*, 2000.*

TIPTON

An ancient parish, in Domesday as 'Tibinton', important for early industry. *Thomas Newcomen*'s first successful engine was installed at the Coneygre colliery here in 1712. The most famous enterprise was the Horseley Iron Works, celebrated in the C19 for canal bridges. An Urban District from 1895, Tipton became the last Borough created in the Black Country, in 1938, when the celebrations were ruined by rain. That seems to symbolize a sad place with many losses, including all its major industrial sites, C19 Board Schools, and the Toll End Library of 1907 by *George Wenyon*, the town's only significant architect. His career was short, from *c*. 1904 until the First World War, but his buildings show a mastery of Edwardian Free Style and Baroque.

CHURCHES

ST JOHN THE EVANGELIST, Upper Church Lane, 1 m. N. The ancient parish church, replaced nearer the centre of population in 1795 (*see* below) but brought back into use in the C19 (cf. Kingswinford). Small three-stage W tower with paired trefoil-headed belfry windows. Dated 1683 on the sundial with a segmental pediment. String courses with cavetto mouldings confirm the post-medieval date. One wide W lancet, perhaps C13, reused. Low four-bay hall of 1850, built and probably designed by *Thomas Cox*, in contrasting brick: red buttresses and cornice frame blue panels with paired lancets. SW porch, unusually gabled E–W. Vestry and organ chamber by *F.T. Beck*, 1921, now rendered. Plain interior with queenpost trusses. Wide semicircular C17 tower arch, infilled. C19 iron spiral stair to the belfry. – STAINED GLASS. E lancets by *Samuel Evans & Co.*, 1903, with characteristic twisting foliage.

ST MARK, Ocker Hill Road. 1848–9 by *Hamilton & Saunders*. Dark blue brick, C13 style. S aisle separately gabled, with two-light plate-tracery windows; N aisle a lean-to, with lancets. Three shafted lancets, with dogtooth, below the W bellcote. Clerestory with cusped spherical triangles. Arcades sharply pointed, with circular columns. Chancel rebuilt and extended

---

*Church by *G.B. Nichols*, 1857–8, rebuilt except for the tower by *Denys Hinton & Associates*, 1965–6, 'a handsome solution' (Pevsner, 1968). Demolished *c*. 1995.

by *J. Percy Clark*, 1909–10, still in blue brick. Perp, well proportioned inside, with a five-light E window, set high to accommodate a C19 stone REREDOS from the Lady Chapel of Winchester Cathedral, with big central vesica and side panels with grids of flowers. – *Clark*'s CHOIR STALLS and PULPIT are free late Gothic. – Original FONT with thin blank arcading, and COMMUNION TABLE (now in S aisle) with hanging Gothic arches, still Georgian in feeling. – STAINED GLASS. By *Chance Bros*, 1849, patterned lights in aisles and clerestory, and the main figure and small scenes in the E window, in 1910 borders.

ST MARTIN (former), Lower Church Lane. Five-bay nave of 1795–7 by *John Keyte* of Kidderminster, with linked arched window surrounds. Tower and chancel rebuilt by *A.P. Brevitt*, 1874, and again in plain Neo-Georgian by *C.C. Gray*, 1963–5. The cupola, removed in 1963, was replaced by a thin-ribbed glass dome in an uncomfortable house conversion, 2002–6. *Brevitt*'s PULPIT is now a garden feature.

ST MATTHEW, Dudley Road, Tipton Green. Designed in 1876 by *J.H. Gibbons*, 'from the modified design of [his] St Margaret, Edgbaston' (dem.). Built 1878–80, supervised by *Davies & Middleton*. Red brick with Bath and Hollington stone dressings. Tough lancet Gothic without graces, called 'Early French' when consecrated. Ritual SE tower with big gargoyles and pinnacles, oddly situated away from the street. W doorway with a tympanum of St Matthew, and shafts with foliage capitals and rings. Evangelical preaching-box interior, with narrow passage aisles and W gallery. Arcades of fat Forest of Dean stone columns (now alas painted), their foliage capitals all slightly different. Five-sided apse with STAINED GLASS by *Samuel Evans & Co.*, completed 1920. – Original PULPIT, FONT with angular projections, and PEWS. – WAR MEMORIAL, tablet by *Sidney Hunt* of F. *Osborne & Co.*, 1922.

ST PAUL, Owen Street (closed 2015). 1837–9 by *Robert Ebbels*. Brick, with a ritual W tower and lancets. E and W windows with Perp tracery. Crudely subdivided horizontally in 1985. The galleries remain, on iron piers, with their pews in the unused upper space. – COMMANDMENT BOARDS of 1839.

SACRED HEART (R.C.), Victoria Road. 1940 by *E. Bower Norris*. Brick, with a blocky Germanic *Westwerk* front, probably influenced by Hobbiss's Christ Church, Burney Lane (p. 272). Tall round-headed paired side windows. Low passage aisles.

PUBLIC BUILDINGS

LIBRARY (now CARNEGIE CENTRE), Victoria Road. By *George H. Wenyon*, 1905–6. Quite a spectacular building compared with what else Tipton has to offer. A confident Free Style design, the motifs mainly Elizabethan–Jacobean, but with a Baroque sense of movement. Brick and very yellow terracotta. Big mullion-and-transom windows, alternate bays gabled with supporting reversed consoles. Dominating, asymmetrically placed tower, with Westminster Cathedral Byzantine influence in its tall niches and cupola. Entrance hall with deep-blue tile dado and barrel-vault. The former reading room has complex roof trusses with brackets and side-posts mimicking hammerbeams.

NEPTUNE HEALTH PARK, Sedgley Road West. By *Penoyre & Prasad*, 1998. A community health centre, including social services. The first sight is a glazed prow rising behind curving brick walls. This is the clerestory of a high concourse, with shops and café. Behind it a drum-like projection links this axis to that of a long range along the canal.

ALEXANDRA HIGH SCHOOL (now Q3 ACADEMY TIPTON), Alexandra Road. 1926 by *Scott & Clark*, best survivor of their work for Tipton Council. Low Neo-Georgian, E-plan. Squared cupola on the rear wing. Tile and terracotta detail.

RSA ACADEMY, Bilston Road. By *John McAslan & Partners*, 2010. One of the best new schools in the area. Three teaching blocks, their framing extended to form covered balconies, linked by a glazed spine corridor, with courtyards between.

VICTORIA INFANTS' SCHOOL (now SILVERTREES ACADEMY), Silvertrees Road. By *Tony Carter* of *Sandwell M.B.C. Architect's Department*, 1995. Long, low, curving, with an enormous shallow roof of coated aluminium.

VICTORIA PARK, Victoria Road. Laid out by *William Barron & Sons*, 1899–1901. Domed iron drinking fountain of 1903, the standard product of *Macfarlane & Co.* of Glasgow. WAR MEMORIAL, obelisk of 1921.

PERAMBULATIONS

1. Owen Street to Factory Junction and Park Lane West

The main street, OWEN STREET, lost much of its character in the late C20. Next to St Paul's church, a Gothic former bank of 1876–7 by *Yeoville Thomason*, now nastily rendered, with some loss of detail. Going SW, the TIPTON AND COSELEY BUILDING SOCIETY is flat nouveau-classical by *Building Design Practice* of Wolverhampton, 1991. Opposite, Neo-vernacular housing around HORSESHOE WALK by *Diamond Redfern*, 1978 etc., intimately grouped, with segment-headed semi-dormers. By the canal, the FOUNTAIN INN, 1820s, but cut down and with original pilasters etc. lost.

The most interesting local stretch of canal goes NW from here, past Neptune Health Park (*see* above), to FACTORY JUNCTION, where the Birmingham Canal Old Line meets *Telford*'s New Line of 1835–8. On the W approaching the junction, C19 STABLES, converted by *Sandwell M.B.C. Architects* from 1983 into a canal activities centre. An iron footbridge crosses the New Line. On the N side, a BOATMEN'S MISSION CHAPEL of 1892–3, builder *Willcock* of Wolverhampton (now a factory). Brick, now painted, with overlapping courses to gable and eaves. To the E, the New Line descends three locks. By the top lock, a former BOAT GAUGING STATION, dated 1873. Bold brickwork with red stretchers and blue headers. Hipped roof. Blocked boat arches on the W side.

Returning to the Neptune Centre, we walk through it to PARK LANE WEST. The dedicated can go W here along SEDGLEY ROAD WEST. At the Five Ways junction the fancy gable of the PIE FACTORY (formerly DOUGHTY ARMS), 1923. DUDLEY ROAD runs S here with late C19 villas. N of St Matthew's, heavy Gothic former VICARAGE by *J.R. Naylor* of Derby, 1883–4. Continuing W, former DRILL HALL, by *C.G. Cowlishaw*. Dated 1910. Very red brick, conventional castellated centre. Beyond, the former MUNICIPAL BUILDINGS of 1917. A long range of reinforced concrete, faced in artificial stone. Built as offices for the car makers Harper, Sons & Bean, so almost certainly by *A.T. Butler*. The Free Style doorcases look his.*

Back at the Neptune Centre, we go SE past the roundabout. In CASTLE STREET, running SW, No. 7 is a former lock-keeper's cottage (with company numberplate). Beyond, a much-restored villa of *c.* 1800 with standard Tuscan porch. SE, across the canal bridge, the RED LION, late C18, much altered.

2. Upper Church Lane

A depleted group round the former St Martin's church (p. 590). ST MARTIN'S PRIMARY SCHOOL is by *John Weller II*, 1861. Symmetrical, with pedimented centre, but *Rundbogenstil* rather than classical. The OLD COURT HOUSE INN is probably mid-C19. POLICE STATION by *Malcolm Payne Group*, 2007, with bulky piers and glowering roof. It replaced a police station and courthouse by *Robert Griffiths*, 1864 (cf. Old Hill).

3. Dudley Port and Horseley Heath

A scatter of buildings on the Dudley to West Bromwich road. In DUDLEY PORT by the canal and railway bridges, the ROYAL OAK, probably of *c.* 1840. Altered by *George Wenyon*, 1909–10, with ornate Shaw-style bays and a back room with Jacobean-style fireplace. Also *Wenyon's* the contemporary MASONIC HALL behind. From the road we glimpse a circular window with prominent symbolic keystone. At the rear, gables with turned-up ends and a large shallow oriel. Barrel-vaulted and panelled HALL, the ends with dropped shaped panels implying pilasters.

Going NE, the HORSELEY TAVERN is Early Victorian. Tuscan doorcase with original sans-serif lettering. In HORSELEY HEATH the former POST OFFICE, by (*Sir*) *Henry Tanner*, 1896. Bright red Ruabon brick and buff *Gibbs & Canning* terracotta, with half-timbered gables.

---

*The area W of the former railway, transferred to Dudley M.B.C. in 1974, is described here for convenience and historical reasons.

In HORSELEY ROAD, to the N, the RISING SUN of *c.* 1897–8, probably by *William Jenkins*. Red brick, timber gables. For Great Bridge beyond, *see* West Bromwich (p. 616).

OTHER BUILDINGS

PUPPY GREEN AQUEDUCT, Park Lane East. Red brick. 1835–8, on *Telford*'s New Line.

In PARK LANE WEST, ¼ m. SE of the Red Lion, set back, house and offices for a former South Staffordshire Water Co. reservoir by *Henry Naden*, 1881–2. Queen Anne, with big semi-dormers flanking a pedimented name plaque.

WEDNESBURY

The name is probably from the Old English for 'Woden's burh', suggesting pagan links (cf. Wednesfield). Recent excavations on the hill around St Bartholomew's church suggest the existence of just such an Anglo-Saxon *burh* or fortified place. An iron mine is mentioned as early as 1315, a coal mine in 1377. Wednesbury Forge at Wood Green was in existence by the C16; developed for edge-tool making in the C19, it closed in 2005. The largest ironworks, Old Park, closed as early as 1877, the last coal mine in 1914, and heavy engineering took over. Tube-making grew after the invention here of the butt-welded tube in 1825. The largest employer was the Patent Shaft and Axletree Company, founded 1836, closed 1980. The leading local architects in the late C19 and early C20 were *C.W.D. Joynson*, mayor of the borough in 1899–1900 (*see also* Darlaston, p. 649), and the firm of *Scott & Clark*, especially for interwar pubs. The town had a Local Board from 1851, and became a Borough in 1886, absorbed into West Bromwich in 1966. The northern relief road begun in 1969 divides the centre from the old parish church.

PLACES OF WORSHIP

ST BARTHOLOMEW, Church Hill. A prominent and interesting church, first mentioned in 1210. The first impression is half early C19, half late C19, but the medieval building dictates much of what we see. The W tower was added in the C14, and the rest rebuilt in the C15 or C16, with an unusual polygonal apse (cf. St Michael, Coventry; Barton-under-Needwood, Staffs.). Nave, aisles and N transept were refashioned in 1827–8. Tall three-light aisle windows with cusped intersecting tracery and transoms. The designs were by *Edward Ingle*, but the work was supervised by *George Dickinson*, on whose advice the external walls were largely rebuilt. Their present smooth appearance is the result of almost complete refacing from 1874 by *Bidlake & Fleeming*.

Wednesbury

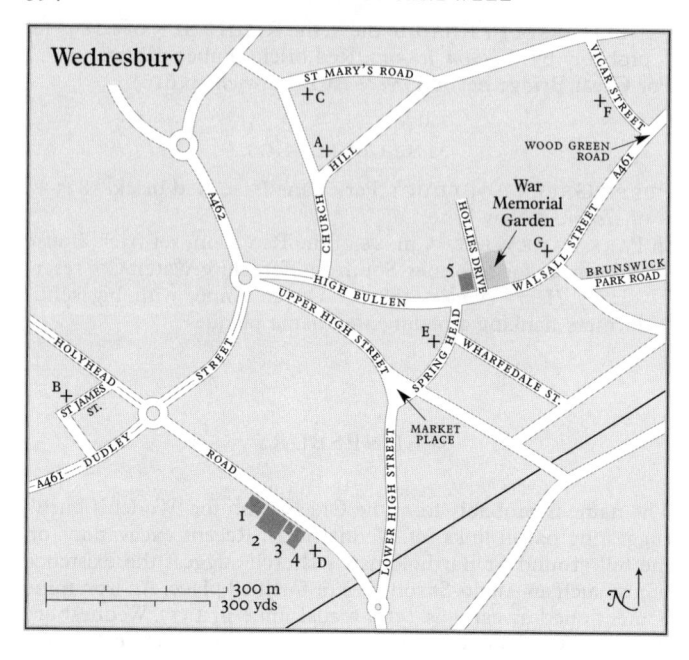

- A St Bartholomew
- B St James
- C St Mary (R.C.)
- D Baptist chapel (former)
- E Central Methodist Church
- F Primitive Methodist church (former)
- G Trinity Congregational Church (former)

- 1 Art Gallery
- 2 Town Hall
- 3 Science School (former)
- 4 Post Office (former)
- 5 Public library

Inside, in the N wall, a window with three cusped lights and chamfered arch, probably C13. The doorway to the N porch looks C14, with segmental arch. Tall five-bay nave arcades with octagonal piers and single-chamfered arches. They are essentially C15, but in 1827–8 the piers were taken down and reworked – see e.g. the plain chamfered bases – and the mouldings of the nave arches were replaced in plaster. These have little drops, typical Late Georgian. The easternmost piers have projections into the nave suggesting a crossing was intended, now topped with Hollington stone statues by *Bateman & Bateman*, 1917. Tower of three stages; much altered in 1855–6 when the belfry, with its two-light windows with quatrefoils, was moved down one stage to accommodate the clock, then also refaced by *Bidlake & Fleeming*, who rebuilt the recessed spire. W doorway with C14 mouldings, one sunk and two hollow chamfers, apparently following original stones. Segmental tower arch, with two plain chamfers. The E

Sandwell, Wednesbury, St Bartholomew.
Engraving by R.W. Basire after Stebbing Shaw, 1801

end is by *Basil Champneys*. In 1890 he rebuilt the apse further E, re-creating its distinctive five-sides-of-a-hexagon plan and four- and five-light Perp windows. In 1902 he doubled the size of the N transept, and added the S transept in 1904. Inside, his work is finely detailed and spacious. Sanctuary arch with plain chamfered jambs and moulded capitals, following the original. Two-bay S transept arcade; slim column with keeled shafts.

Rich FURNISHINGS, especially of the early C20. – Striking WALL PAINTINGS, a Christ in Majesty above the chancel arch, and angels in the apse, painted on fabric and set against bright stencilled patterns and texts, by *C.E. Bateman* and *C.G. Gray*, 1912 (cf. Holy Trinity, Sutton Coldfield). – ALTAR by *Bateman and Gray*, 1919, white alabaster with mosaic panels. – Alabaster sanctuary PANELLING and ALTAR RAILS by *Bateman*, 1908. – CHANCEL SCREEN by *Bridgemans*, 1953. – PULPIT. 1611. The usual blank arches, and above three arabesque panels. – LECTERN. A remarkable wooden C14 or C15 piece with a gamecock, not an eagle. It has bold breast feathers. Base with blank arcading. – LADY CHAPEL (SE) created by *Bateman*, 1913–14. – COMMUNION TABLE. C17, S aisle. – PAINTING (W gallery). Descent from the Cross, attributed to *Jean Jouvenet*, 1698; big and dark. – STAINED GLASS. An important series of sixteen windows by *Kempe* and his successors, 1898–1912. The N windows mostly Christ's miracles, Old Testament figures above; the S, Acts of the Apostles, saints above. Apse, Annunciation, Nativity, Pentecost. Much canopy-work, and rather standard greens, reds and blues, but the re-creation of a complete medieval effect is memorable.

MONUMENTS. Chancel. Thomas Parkes †1602. Oval relief tablet with two kneeling figures facing one another. – Addison family, after 1840. With a weeping woman and John Addison's portrait on a medallion. By *Peter Hollins*. – S transept. Francis Wortley †1636. Tablet with pilasters; shield above in drapery, and bird crest. – Philip Williams †1829. Gothic. – Edward Crowther †1829 by *W. Hollins*. Draped urn. – S aisle. Richard Parkes †1618 and wife. Alabaster effigies, she with a widow's hood. Heavily moulded tomb-chest with four small figures of children and three tiny figures, stillborn children, in shroud. Some nice ribbonwork, also an hourglass. – Rev. Isaac Clarkson †1860, by *P. Hollins*. Bust in gadrooned niche. – Elizabeth Watkins †1791. Simple tablet. – Francis Wastie Haden †1828, by *B. Baker*. Draped urn. – N aisle. Samuel Allison †1817, by *W. Hollins*. Angel by a sarcophagus, his upraised arm broken.

ST JAMES, St James Street. 1847–8 by *William Horton*. From 2016 the Eternal Sacred Order of the Cherubim and Seraphim; interior description as an Anglican church. Wide aisleless nave with lancet windows, in local Coal Measures sandstone. W tower never completed, now capped with a pyramid roof. The E end grew slowly, reflecting increasingly High ritual. All Dec, faced in Codsall sandstone. Chancel and S organ chamber by *Griffin & Weller*, 1857; apse by *Samuel Horton*, 1870; chancel raised to the height of the apse by *Horton & Scott*, 1881; N chapel and vestries round the apse also *Horton & Scott*, 1887. Much of the interior character is due to *S.E. Dykes Bower*, 1936–8. He whitened the walls (now, less effectively, partly cream) and laid the fine black-and-white marble pavement. Original nave roof with queenpost trusses and much cusping. W gallery of 1848, on iron columns with decorative spandrels. The chancel has arched trusses of 1881 and statues in niches by *Robert Bridgeman*, 1892–3. N chapel arcade with circular columns and moulded capitals. Two-light windows with big internal columns (cf. Moxley). In 1921 *Cecil G. Hare* turned the organ chamber into a small Holy Angels Chapel, in Bodley-like rich late Dec: REREDOS and PANELLING in clunch stone, figures of saints, and iron SCREEN. – C19 FONT from St John, Lower High Street (dem.). – HIGH ALTAR. Early C20, with PAINTINGS by *Dykes Bower*, 1938. – C19 STALLS from St Bartholomew, incorporating three C15 MISERICORDS: an elephant and castle with archers, owls, and a green man. – N chapel REREDOS by *E.A. Fellowes Prynne*, 1892. – Hanging ROOD by *Lane & Cardus*, 1948. – STAINED GLASS. N chapel N, from the E *Hardmans*, 1892 and 1895, *Charles G. Gray*, 1906. Chancel S, *Swaine Bourne*, 1898.

Across the street, s, former SCHOOLS. by *William Horton*, 1844–5, much extended: 1860 by *J. G. Palmer*; 1866 ('lecture room') probably by *E. M. Scott*, who did more work in 1870.

ST PAUL, Wood Green Road. By *E. F. C. Clarke* of London, 1872–4, tower and spire completed 1887. Hammerwich sandstone, 'Early Geometrical' style. High Victorian, with volumes cutting back to the wall-plane like early Street. N tower and spire with tall broaches and lucarnes. N aisle unbuttressed, with plate tracery, and circular clerestory windows with cinquefoils; s with massive stepped buttresses and three-light windows with bar tracery, repeated in the clerestory. Arcades with circular columns, moulded capitals, and arches with plain and sunk chamfers. Dressings of Bath stone. W lobby by *Leonard Woodhams*, 1999. – REREDOS by *Bridgeman*, 1904; iron SCREEN by *Jones & Willis*, 1903. – S aisle REREDOS by *Scott & Clark*, 1913, Perp, sandstone. – FONT. 1888. – LECTERN and ALTAR RAILS with Art Nouveau low-relief trees by *Haughton* of Worcester, 1906. – STAINED GLASS. Chancel E window by *Samuel Evans*, 1883; s, *C. Evans & Co.*, 1888. S aisle from E: *Shrigley & Hunt*, 1906; *Samuel Evans*, 1901; *William Pearce Ltd*, designer *Richards*, 1919. N aisle, *S. Evans*, 1919. – Simple brick VICARAGE by *Scott & Clark*, 1923, N.

ST MARY (R.C.), St Mary's Road. 1873–4 by *Gilbert Blount*. Like E.W. Pugin: brick Gothic, drawing on English C13 and German sources, all rather tall and wiry. Paired lancets in the aisles, triplets in the clerestory. Polygonal apse with plate-tracery windows, rising into spiky gables. NW steeple with open belfry and copper spire. Careful dark-blue brick detail. Painswick stone arcades with octagonal piers and tall tapering bases. – PULPIT. 1923. – ALTAR and REREDOS by *F. Bligh Bond*, made by *Boulton & Sons*, 1904. Rich Gothic, its Caen stone and marbles alas overpainted. – STAINED GLASS in apse and side chapels by *Hardmans*, 1910–12. Aisles, later *Hardmans* glass, 1920s–60s, and one (SS Bartholomew and Patrick) by *W. Daly*, 1929. S aisle W, Baptism of Christ by *R. L. Hendra* and *G. J. Harper*, 1947. – Former SCHOOL of 1872 by *Gilbert Blount*, W.

BAPTIST CHAPEL (former), Holyhead Road. 1827–30. Horribly mangled. Front with round-headed windows. More, with prominent keystones, along the side. – SUNDAY SCHOOL at the rear by *'Mr Robinson'*, 1881.

CENTRAL METHODIST CHURCH, Spring Head. 1967–8 by *Hulme, Upright & Partners*.

PRIMITIVE METHODIST CHURCH (now BAPTIST), Vicar Street. 1912 by *Scott & Clark*. A powerful Free Perp design in maroon-red brick with blue headers. Stubby ritual SW tower, lower than the nave roof. Interior now subdivided. Arcades with four-centred arches and piers with rounded corners which are convex sunk chamfers. – ORGAN by *Thomas Hughes*, 1912.

TRINITY CONGREGATIONAL CHURCH (now MEDINA EDUCATIONAL CENTRE), Walsall Street. By *C.W.D. Joynson*, 1904. Free Perp, with a short tower. Stourbridge brick and *Doultons* terracotta.

PUBLIC BUILDINGS

The civic buildings, except the library, are on the SW side of Holyhead Road, here described from NW to SE.

ART GALLERY. By *Wood & Kendrick*, 1890–1, in *King & Co.*'s Stourbridge terracotta. A stiff Queen Anne design with heavy, steeply pedimented doorcase and balustraded parapet. Heads of Wren, Reynolds, Flaxman and Newton by '*Mr Evans*, of Liverpool', and busts of Aldermen Williams and Lloyd by *George Tinworth*. Inside, an imperial staircase. The main RICHARDS GALLERY has a coved ceiling with exposed tie-beams and roof-lights in the centre.

TOWN HALL. Neo-Georgian front by *Scott & Clark*, 1913, on *Loxton Bros*' Public Offices, 1866–7, and Hall, 1871–2, at the rear, with coupled Corinthian pilasters and a coved ceiling. Council Chamber mostly 1890–1 by *Wood & Kendrick*, formal but unpretentious, with classical cornice and Neo-Jacobean fireplaces. – Stained glass by *Samuel Evans*, including painted industrial scenes.

SCIENCE SCHOOL (former). By *C.W.D. Joynson*, 1896. Small, Jacobean with a shaped gable.

POST OFFICE (former). 1883, upper floor 1910–11.

PUBLIC LIBRARY, Walsall Street. By *Crouch, Butler & Savage*, 1907–8. The best secular building of Wednesbury. Ruabon brick and Monks' Park stone. Free Style, but classical detail. The front has four bays of arched windows below, and paired windows recessed behind Doric columns above. Entrance on the long, partly asymmetrical side elevation. Doorway with big part-banded pilasters, cartouche, and three-light pedimented window on top. The entrance area is divided from the reading room by giant Ionic columns. Staircase rising over the lobby in a shallow bow, not expressed on the exterior. Upstairs, barrel-vaulted former REFERENCE LIBRARY with moulded plasterwork.

WAR MEMORIAL GARDEN, facing the library across Hollies Drive. 1926 by *Batemans*. With small obelisk, and big Doric aedicule enclosing an altar.

PERAMBULATIONS

1. The Market Place and south

In the Market Place, CLOCK TOWER of 1911 by *C.W.D. Joynson*, square, with a Baroque stone top. On the NE side, the former TALBOT HOTEL (John Taylor Duce & Sons) by *A.P. Brevitt*, 1879–80. Confident Italian Gothic in orange brick. Big upper windows with trellis-pattern spandrels, firm's name in a tile frieze, and corbelled cornice. To its l. No. 26, late C18, and the GOLDEN CROSS pub by *W.S. Clements*, 1938, with a big semi-circular bay. The WEST BROMWICH BUILDING SOCIETY was the Prudential Assurance, by their surveyor *J.H. Pitt*, 1916. Slightly crowded Neo-Georgian, faience and pinky-red brick.

Beyond, a former BURTONS, 1937. The SE side has a long mid-C19 classical range with segment-headed windows, and an inserted ground floor (HSBC) with Doric half-columns by *Gotch & Saunders*, 1922. Immediately S, Nos. 31–33, a good four-bay mid-C18 house. Giant pilasters at the ends, moulded lintels with keystones.

LOWER HIGH STREET starts here. On the E side Nos. 42–45, early C19 stucco. Opposite, a long three-storey Late Georgian row, interrupted by Nos. 32–33, older two-storey cottages. Then the TURKS HEAD HOTEL of 1903, probably by *A. Irving Scott*. Ground floor with majolica pilasters. Set back further S, with access from Russell Street, the MASONIC HALL. An unusual former Congregational chapel of 1850. Local sandstone ('Peldon stone'). It looks like a North Country rectory: tall, with paired chimneystacks on the gables with blunt square caps.

2. Spring Head, Hollies Drive and Wood Green Road

SPRING HEAD runs NE from the Market Place. On the SE side a horribly renovated range with C18 or even C17 fabric. A possible malt kiln behind.* No. 13, RYDERS CHAMBERS, *c.* 1888 has pointed windows but quasi-Corinthian pilasters. No. 12 by *Horton & Scott*, 1882, provincial Queen Anne. Opposite, the Methodist church (p. 597). In WHARFEDALE STREET, E, Nos. 6–10 by *Joynson Bros*, 1886–7, with unusual Gothic detail. At the top of Spring Head, on Walsall Road next to the library (p. 598), the CONSERVATIVE CLUB by *A. Irving Scott*, 1904–5. Ruabon brick and painted stone dressings, Jacobean going Early Georgian. HOLLIES DRIVE, alongside the library, was developed 1898–1912 with terraces and villas. No. 16, 1905, has big framed windows suggesting *Horton & Scott*. No. 5A by *Scott & Clark*, 1910, with ornate canted bay.

Now NE along WALSALL STREET. On the S side the garden wall of Oakeswell Hall, C15 and C17 (dem. 1962). Beyond the former Congregational church (p. 597), No. 52 starts a nice line of Old English villas, all probably by *C.W.D. Joynson*, who certainly did No. 53 of 1897–8 (extended 1902). Opposite, severely Neo-Georgian SONS OF REST (social club) by *Arthur Booth*, 1938. Beyond, BRUNSWICK PARK, laid out in 1886–7 by *William Barron & Sons*. Old English-style LODGE; inconspicuous former FOUNTAIN by *Crouch, Butler & Savage*, 1938, with low-relief panels of animals and birds.† CLARKSON ROAD runs N, with more villas probably by *Joynson*, to YE OLDE LEATHERN BOTTEL in Vicarage Road. The traditional date is 1510. Chamfered beams in the bar and E room may be C16. Recast in render with timber gables by *A. Irving Scott*, 1912–13. Down E

---

*The SE gable had early brickwork until *c.* 2015.
†E of the park in Crankhall Lane, the BRUNSWICK pub, 1937–8 by *O.M. Weller*. Timber gables, not his usual style.

back to WOOD GREEN ROAD. Opposite, CEMETERY of 1868.*
Going NE, the HORSE AND JOCKEY by *Wood & Kendrick*,
1898–9, mixes Queen Anne and timber gables. Exceptional
bar front, almost certainly by *Craven Dunnill*, a rare survivor.
Brown pilasters with gargoyles, green-and-cream frieze with
scrolly panels. Richly moulded bar back. The COTTAGE is
probably *c.* 1840, bargeboarded with central gable. SE down
BRUNSWICK PARK ROAD. The QUEEN'S HEAD pub, 1936,
and the former ST PAUL'S CHURCH INSTITUTE, Jacobean
of 1906, are both by *A. Irving Scott*. Further SE, former South
Staffordshire Water Co. PUMPING STATION by *Henry Naden*.
Impressive square main block of 1879. Italian Romanesque in
red, blue and a little cream brick. Windows with shouldered
stone lintels, round-arched openings above. Chimney with
blue-brick base.

3. Market Place to St Bartholomew

At the NW end of the Market Place a junction with Union Street,
l. with a Late Georgian building with window architraves, and
Walsall Street, r. with the former GAUMONT CINEMA by *W.E.
& W.S. Trent*, 1938, with off-centre tower. Further NW across
the dual carriageway, CHURCH HILL rises N. WODEN INN
by *Wood & Kendrick*, 1898. Facing St Bartholomew's church,
Nos. 42–46 of 1863, built by *William Stevenson*, heavy classical.
To the E, ARUNDEL HOUSE, 1843, with later C19 porch and
bays. To the NW in Hall End the OLD BLUE BALL pub, early
C19, with canted bays. To the SE down Reservoir Passage, the
ROUND HOUSE, built with reused parts of local buildings:
gatehouse with West Bromwich coat of arms; square lantern
tower from Park Lane Schools, Tipton (*Alfred Long*, 1903);
rear loggia with iron columns and decorative capitals from St
Michael, Tividale (*Davies & Middleton*, 1877–8).

WEST BROMWICH

West Bromwich is a major industrial town, an ancient parish, and
a settlement mentioned in Domesday. It was a County Borough
from 1889, and had Improvement Commissioners from 1854. It
has a confusing geography. The present centre grew up on former
common land, the Heath. The Enclosure Commissioners in 1804
allocated a 60-ft (18-metre)-wide strip to the Birmingham to
Wolverhampton turnpike, and the accidental result is the grandest High Street in the Black Country, quite straight and over a
mile long. The old village was around the parish church, 1 m.
N. The Manor House is ¾ m. N again, among suburban semis.
The ancient parish is largely enclosed in a loop of the River

---

*Chapels by *Samuel Horton* demolished.

West Bromwich

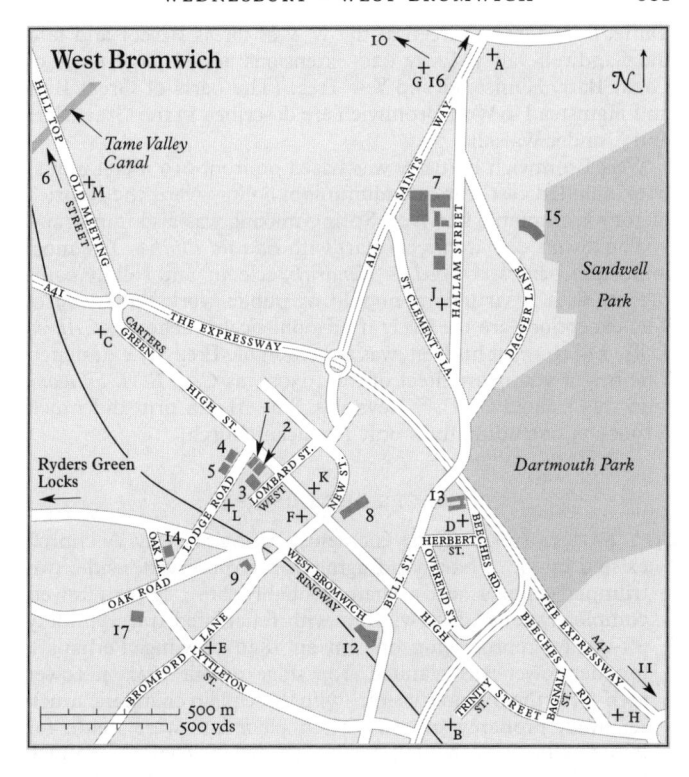

- A All Saints
- B Holy Trinity
- C St Andrew
- D St Philip
- E Good Shepherd with St John
- F St Michael and the Holy Angels (R.C.)
- G Holy Cross (R.C.)
- H (Wesleyan) Methodist church
- J (Wesleyan) Methodist chapel
- K Wesley Methodist Church
- L Unitarian church (now Shiloh Apostolic)
- M Shree Krishna Mandir

1. Town Hall
2. Library
3. Magistrates' Court (former)
4. West Bromwich Institute (former)
5. Ryland Memorial School of Art (now Sandwell College, Fashion, Art and Design Building)
6. Hill Top Library
7. Sandwell General Hospital
8. The Public, now Central St Michael's Sixth Form
9. Police station
10. Menzies High School (now Phoenix Collegiate)
11. Sandwell Academy
12. Sandwell College
13. King George V Primary School
14. Lodge Primary School
15. Eaton Valley Primary School
16. Manor House
17. Oak House

Tame, from Greets Green at the w, N as far as Bescot and E to the Sandwell valley. Early c20 extensions added large parts of Great Barr, Hamstead and Yew Tree. (The parts of Great Barr and Hamstead in West Bromwich are described in the Great Barr entry, under Walsall.)

West Bromwich industry was based on iron. c19 metal industries included cast-iron and aluminium hollow-ware; the Kenrick factory is a notable survivor. Spring-making was also important.

The town's c19 architects start with *Edward Pincher*. The most important firm was *Wood & Kendrick*, eclectic and solidly competent, with a virtual monopoly of public work *c.*1880–1910. The exceptions are the lively if unsophisticated schools of *Alfred Long*. *J.W. Allen*, at his best, was a memorable Free Style designer. The bright young architect of the 1930s was *Cecil E.M. Fillmore*, who was trained by E.F. Reynolds. The *Madin* firm did much *c.*1960–75, including their only Anglican church.

PLACES OF WORSHIP

ALL SAINTS (formerly St Clement), All Saints Way. A church existed by 1140. Norman fragments are preserved inside: two trumpet capitals and a shaft, probably late c12. c14 tower, completely refaced. W window with reticulated tracery, oddly off-centre, reproducing one on an 1840 drawing. Perhaps a broader tower was planned. Top stage rebuilt 1823–4. Tower arch (only the top now visible) with three plain chamfers: much renewed, probably in 1788 when payments were made for 'building the arch that fell down' and 'making center to gothick arch'. A 'new Chauncel or Chapelle' was added in the mid c16, and a s (Whorwood) chapel in 1619. Nave and chancel were rebuilt in 1786–8 by *Charles Norton* of Birmingham, with a Venetian E window. The present church is a second rebuild, by *Somers Clarke Jun.*, 1871–2, for the Rev. Frederick Willett. A packed Easter Vestry in 1871, suspicious of Willett's High Church practices, insisted on increased seating, and the result has nave, s aisle (with the tower at its w), short chancel with s chapel, N organ chamber, SE vestry, and extra S vestry replacing the Whorwood Chapel. Rock-faced sandstone. Imposing E end with five-light Dec window set high up, blank gabled organ chamber. Wide nave with scissor-truss roof, s arcade with octagonal columns and double-chamfered arches. Repetitive paired two-light Dec N windows, a weak motif. S vestry with flat-headed c17-style windows; repositioned datestone of 1619. Extensively reordered by *Hinton Brown, Madden & Langstone*, 1977–8, with meeting rooms at the w end and up the s aisle.

FURNISHINGS. FONT. c15, octagonal, with shields in quatrefoils. – By *Wood & Kendrick* the PULPIT, 1903, PEWS, 1889, and CHOIR STALLS, 1898, with figure groups on the ends. – COMMUNION TABLE. Dated 1626, with simple decoration. – MOSAIC, nave W. Christ blessing children, by *Burke & Co.*, 1928–9. – PAINTING, s chapel. Copy of Rubens's Crucifixion, given 1873. – Simple geometric c14/c15 TILES. – Mosaic

FLOOR in the chancel. Designed by *Wood & Kendrick*, made by *Burke & Co.*, 1888. – STAINED GLASS. Chancel lancets, W window and S aisle (Old Testament figures), 1871–3, designed by *H.E. Wooldridge*, made by *James Powell & Sons*: important Aesthetic Movement work. E, *Camm Bros*, 1873. In 1903 *G.F. Bodley* designed a scheme to be made by *Burlison & Grylls* for the nave N windows, but only the easternmost was made then. Others 1931, 1934, 1953. – MONUMENTS. Two alabaster effigies, an Elizabethan lady and a man of *c.* 1650, now unhappily against the S aisle wall. Probably Anne Whorwood †1599 and Field Whorwood †1658.

Massive sandstone LYCHGATE by *Clarke*, 1874, with half-hipped sprocketed roof. Near the S doorway, BODYSTONES or grave-markers, †1803, †1828, †1842.

HOLY TRINITY, Trinity Street. 1840–1 by *S.W. Daukes* of Cheltenham. Red brick. The W tower has a memorable silhouette, with high set-back buttresses topped by prominent gablets, and a tall belfry. It looks bald without its pinnacles. Six-bay nave, lancet windows, short chancel. Gallery on three sides with pretty arcaded cresting. Elegant reordering by *John Greaves Smith*, 1996–7; semicircular COMMUNION RAIL, pair of READING DESKS, and FONT. – REREDOS. 1920 by *Boulton & Sons*. Flanking it, pairs of blank canopied arches at right angles, probably of 1841 for Creed and Commandments. – Former FONT by *Bridgemans*, 1946. – STAINED GLASS. E window by *Chance Bros*, 1864, perhaps designed by *Sebastian Evans*. Passion scenes, deeply coloured; good. Several by *Martin Dunn*, 1914 onwards; one by *Samuel Evans & Co.*, 1918 (nave S); later *Hardmans* work, 1958 etc. – MONUMENTS. George Silvester †1860, by *Peter Hollins*, weeping woman against draped Roman altar; big, well modelled. – Many tablets. – Behind the church, VICARAGE by *Thomas Cox*, 1843. An interesting example of the almost styleless villa of the period. T-shaped, with a wing running back to the road, awkwardly extended on the W. Doorcase with a fanlight. The garden front has two slightly projecting bays with big tripartite windows.

ST ANDREW, Carters Green. 1922–5 by *Wood & Kendrick*, W end completed 1939–40 by *E.F. Reynolds* (*Wood & Kendrick & Edwin F. Reynolds*). Old-fashioned brick Gothic, but a pleasantly spacious interior. Wide five-bay arcades, sandstone columns and brick arches. Extension and nave reordering by *Bower Mattin*, 1993. – Original PULPIT, FONT and CHOIR STALLS. – STAINED GLASS. The best by *Hardman*, Crucifixion and Annunciation, 1892, from the previous church of 1867.

ST FRANCIS OF ASSISI, Freeman Road, Friar Park. 1938–40 by *Harvey & Wicks*, and *H.G. Wicks*'s most important church. Romanesque style with Continental influences, and a formal plan, reduced from the first scheme of 1937, flanked at the W by vicarage and (never built) hall. Grey ashlar. The dominating E tower has a steep concave roof and a gilded statue of St Francis. N and S porches with hieratic sculpted Apostles. Arcades of tapering octagonal baseless piers with volute capitals. N chapel with separate arcade set behind, a good spatial effect. Instead of a chancel arch, piers with STATUES of SS Mary and John looking up at a hanging ROOD, all designed by *Wicks* and made by the contractors *John Dallow & Sons*.

ST JAMES, Hill Top. Modest brick box by *Twentyman Percy & Partners*, 1994, replacing *Robert Ebbels*'s church of 1839–41.

ST PAUL, Bagnall Street, Golds Hill. 1881 by *Edward Pincher*, replacing a school-chapel of 1855 by *S.W. Daukes*. Simple brick mission church with lancets. Timber bell-turret over the chancel arch. Big SE organ chamber, gabled E–W. Plastered interior, hammerbeam roof. – Original FURNISHINGS. – W end SCREEN of 2003. – STAINED GLASS. E window apparently dated 1859 and from the earlier chapel. Nave N, 1911 by *Samuel Evans*, and two by *Martin Dunn*, 1922. W, *William Pearce Ltd*, 1908.

ST PHILIP, Beeches Road. By *Wood & Kendrick*: nave and aisles 1898–9, chancel, Lady Chapel and vestries 1913–14. Brick and golden-brown terracotta, quite grand. External detail C17 as much as Gothic: E window Perp-ish but with big sexfoil, flat-headed lights elsewhere. Arcades with circular columns on high bases, and foliage capitals, all different. – By *Wood & Kendrick* the FONT, 1899; CHANCEL SCREEN, 1919; and PULPIT, 1925. – REREDOS by *Jones & Willis*, 1937. – STAINED GLASS. E window by *Gerald E.R. Smith*, 1952; the rest mainly *Martin Dunn*.

GOOD SHEPHERD WITH ST JOHN, Lyttleton Street. 1967–8 by *John H.D. Madin & Partners*. Dark brick. Hexagonal church linked to hall and lounge by an angled lobby. Entrance through an open courtyard. Low-pitched roof with laminated timber trusses supported on timber piers of cross section. – Original concrete ALTAR and FONT, the latter on thin dark metal legs, metal ALTAR RAIL, STALLS and SEATING. – Contemporary ORGAN CASE. – STAINED GLASS. Re-set figures and pieces from the predecessor churches, mostly early C20.

ANNUNCIATION, Redwood Road, Yew Tree Estate, 2 m. N. 1956–8 by *Hickton, Madeley & Salt*. Low brick hall, asymmetrically gabled.

ST MICHAEL AND THE HOLY ANGELS (R.C.), High Street. 1876–7 by *Dunn & Hansom*, replacing a Gothic church by *Joseph Ireland*, 1830. A standard Catholic job of the time: red brick with Bath stone dressings, C13-style Gothic, with English and Continental sources. Rose window over the altar. Landmark tower and spire by *Edmund Kirby & Sons*, 1911. The same style, but smoother and more massive, with big gabled belfry windows and lucarnes. Arcades with boldly dogtoothed arches and blue Pennant stone columns, whitewashed in a 1970s strip-out. Carving by *Boulton*. Rear meeting rooms by *D.T. Rathbone*, 1975, with steep gables.

HOLY CROSS (R.C.), Hall Green Road, Stone Cross. 1968 by *L. Brocki*. Big, low, T-shaped, with jazzy gables and ugly, part-open copper spire.

(WESLEYAN) METHODIST CHURCH, Beeches Road. 1871–2 by *Edward Pincher*. Smart Italian Renaissance. Stone centrepiece with pediment and big round-headed window with Lombardic tracery. Now offices. Guild room, l., 1906 by *Ewen & J.A. Harper*. Further l., classroom block with half-hipped gable by *Ewen Harper, Brother & Co.*, 1931, now the church.

(WESLEYAN) METHODIST CHURCH, Ryders Green Road, 1 m. w. 1873–4 by *Edward Pincher*. A rare intact large mid-Victorian chapel. Dour, impressive brick block with round-arched windows, tightly articulated by blue-brick bands. Four-bay front, the centre slightly projecting, raised and corbelled out. Five-sided gallery on iron columns, with panelled front and tiny discs in the frieze. Big organ opening with paired pilasters, ROSTRUM with a central arched opening. – Behind, SCHOOLROOM dated 1856, rebuilt into a day centre by *Bower Mattin*, 1994.

(WESLEYAN) METHODIST CHAPEL, Hallam Street. 1883 by *Edward Pincher*. Red and blue brick; lancet windows.

WESLEY METHODIST CHURCH, High Street. By *Botteley & Chaffer*, engineers, 1972–4. It replaced a chapel of 1835 by *Joseph Cutts*, refronted 1905–6.

PRIMITIVE METHODIST CHURCH (now TRIUMPHANT CHURCH OF GOD), Harvills Hawthorn, 1¾ m. NW. 1912 by *Scott & Clark*. Gothic; now heavily rendered.

UNITARIAN CHURCH (now SHILOH APOSTOLIC), Lodge Road. 1874–5 by *A.B. Phipson*. Gothic hall with eccentric detail, now badly rendered. Steep-gabled front with narrow lancets. Triple-gabled porch.

SHREE KRISHNA MANDIR, Old Meeting Street. By *ARP Associates*, begun 1998, completed 2010. Bansiphardpur sandstone from Rajasthan. Single storey on a high basement, with much traditional Hindu sculpture, carved in Ahmedabad. Low domes and at the rear a *shikher*, which marks the shrine of Vishnu. An archway in front. Inside, a low central dome, elaborately corbelled. To the S, the former Ebenezer Chapel SUNDAY SCHOOLS, Jacobean-cum-Baroque by *J. Withers*, 1906.

PUBLIC BUILDINGS

TOWN HALL, High Street. 1874–5 by *Alexander & Henman* of Stockton-on-Tees. The design is almost certainly *William Henman*'s; he moved to Birmingham on the strength of it. The red brick corner tower still dominates, despite late C20 competition. It rises sheer, broken only by perfectly placed stone balconies, to a slightly corbelled-out top stage with an open trefoiled arcade. Short steep spire with big dormers; a chimney (cf. Burges's clock tower at Cardiff Castle), now cut down, and cupola. The entrance range is consciously Italian Gothic. Triple entrance arcade; foliage capitals with sculpted heads representing the Months, carved by *John Roddis*. Gabled oriels above and dormers further up, a fussy effect. The l. end is the former LIBRARY by *Weller & Proud*, 1874–5; gable with rose window.

Inside, small lobby-cum-corridor with *Maw & Co.* tiles. Staircase, r., its window with heraldic stained glass by *Dunn &*

Broughall. The main HALL, 81 by 48 ft (24.7 by 14.6 metres), takes up most of the interior. Impressive ironwork construction: two tiers of columns separated by a gallery and linked at the top by arches with sectional decorative trusses supporting the roof. Cross-arches link the upper columns back to the walls. Late C20 decoration, following the original scheme by *S. Broadbank*. Apse filled by an organ by *Forster & Andrews* of Hull, 1878, in Gothic case.

LIBRARY, High Street. 1907 by *Stephen J. Holliday*. Not large, but monumental. Ruabon brick and Portland stone. Giant fluted Ionic columns and a one-bay open pediment, enclosing an arch with tremendously exaggerated voussoirs. The lower windows have pediments and arches in the glazing bars in a Norman Shaw way. Small cupola. Stair hall with tiling and mosaic panels by *Maw & Co*. Main hall with arcades of three-centred arches on square piers. What marks the interior is the amount of wall painting: lunettes of local history and scenes from Chaucer by *Patricia Arnett*, c.1946–9; panels on the staircase by *W. Grant Murray*, 1909, *S.C. Rowles* and *L.M.B. Hall*, 1913–14, and *B. Willis*, 1924; and in the barrel-vaulted upper reading room more panels by *Arnett*, 1946 and (much more loosely worked) 1991.

MAGISTRATES' COURT (former), Lombard Street West. 1890 by *Wood & Kendrick*. An odd classical design, aware of the Queen Anne fashion but unsure how to follow it. Stone-framed arched windows with little swags above, becoming triplets in the end bays. The centrepiece has a pediment on big consoles which also support stubby Corinthian half-columns framing the upper window. Above, a piece of attic with four round-headed windows, and a pedimented centrepiece flanked by big Vanbrughian chimneys.

WEST BROMWICH INSTITUTE (former), Lodge Road. 1884 by *Wood & Kendrick*. Brick and red terracotta, mostly Jacobean, but a central Gothic doorway, flanked effectively by oriels.

RYLAND MEMORIAL SCHOOL OF ART (now SANDWELL COLLEGE, FASHION, ART AND DESIGN BUILDING), Lodge Road. 1903 by *Wood & Kendrick*. Free Style, still with Jacobean features, but an instructive contrast to the Institute. Tall spare gabled blocks with three-light windows, the lunette shapes on top making huge round-arched openings. Contrastingly rich entrance with ogee doorway arch, segmental lintel above with raised centre set against plain rectangular windows, and then a frieze of workmen offering their art to Athena. A pretty cupola disappeared in the late C20.

HILL TOP LIBRARY, Hill Top. 1897–8 by *Albert D. Greatorex*, Borough Surveyor. Eye-catching but incoherent Old English-cum-Jacobean.

SANDWELL GENERAL HOSPITAL, Hallam Street. Originally West Bromwich Union Workhouse, by *Briggs & Everall*, 1855–8. Their buildings have gone, but the INFIRMARY by *William Henman*, 1884, survives facing Lewisham Street. The r. wing retains original gables. At the rear, diagonally set projecting

Sandwell, West Bromwich Institute.
Engraving and plan, 1884

towers with Rhenish-helm roofs. They housed lavatories and washrooms. Isolated to the w, tiny CHAPEL by *Cecil E.M. Fillmore*, 1938–9. Thin bricks in Flemish stretcher bond, tall round-arched windows with steep tile sills. Further back, *Henman*'s CONTAGIOUS BLOCK of 1881, with more diagonally set towers. N along Hallam Street the Guardians' BOARD ROOM AND OFFICES by *Henman & Timmins*, 1887, big steep gables and Jacobean details. Further N, depressing six-storey blocks by *Leonard Multon & John Keeling* with *Clifford Rosser*, 1963 etc. (All under threat, 2021.)

THE PUBLIC, now CENTRAL ST MICHAEL'S SIXTH FORM, New Street. A magnificent example of early C21 architectural hubris. Community arts and entertainment centre by *Will Alsop* (*Alsop Architects*). Conceived by the local Jubilee Arts organization, begun 2003, with lottery, European and Arts Council funding. Completed, after financial problems, by *Flannery & de la Pole*, 2007–8. The gallery failed and closed in 2013. Converted 2014 by *Bond Bryan*. The exterior is a dark-clad rectangular shed, 113 by 21 metres, the façade broken up by irregular curvy pink-framed openings. Set back from, but aligned with the street, and with inconspicuous entrances. On the E, the box is disrupted by protruding shiny aluminium slug-like 'Pebble' and angular 'Rock', housing toilets and kitchens respectively. The interior, conceived as a 'Box of Delights', was open up to the third floor, with a now truncated ramp twisting up and round a suspended black gallery, the 'Sock', now a lecture theatre, at the N. Steel 'trees' by *Ben Kelly Design* remain, with panels of etchings, monitors etc. for 'leaves'.

DARTMOUTH PARK. Opened in 1878. WAR MEMORIAL by *Alfred Long*, 1922–3, winged Victory on a high pedestal. – PAVILION by *Bryant Priest Newman*, with the artist *David Patten*, 2012.

A huge playground castle. Steel post-and-beam structure clad in irregularly spaced vertical green oak planks, forming a long ramped walk, surrounding a brick office and café. Entrance area with flying stairs and walkways.

POLICE STATION, Bromford Lane and Oak Road. 2010–11 by *Lyons+Sleeman+Hoare*. With a central bow, a disquieting echo of the MI5 headquarters in London.*

MENZIES HIGH SCHOOL (now PHOENIX COLLEGIATE), Marsh Lane and Clarke's Lane. By *Richard Sheppard, Robson & Partners*, 1960–4. Four- storey teaching blocks faced in buff brick and glazed panels, linked by single-storey wings. The bold touch is concrete bridges linking the blocks E to Marsh Lane. To the W, LEARNING CENTRE by *Bryant Priest Newman*, 2005. Elegant and well-proportioned front in yellow brick. The parapet tops pay homage to Sheppard Robson. Entrance to the r., balanced by a long strip of upper windows with a rainscreen. The full-height entrance hall plays wonderful spatial games, with a flying bridge and unexpected lines of recessed windows in the ceiling.

SANDWELL ACADEMY, Halfords Lane. 2003–6 by *Barnsley Hewett & Mallinson*. Low, semicircular plan.

SANDWELL COLLEGE, West Bromwich Ringway. By *Bond Bryan*, 2011–12. With an enormous swooping roof.

KING GEORGE V PRIMARY SCHOOL, Beeches Road. By *Alfred Long*, dated 1892. Brick and buff-grey terracotta. Two long blocks forming an L-shape, articulated by large and small kneeler gables. Dominating SE entrance tower, corbelled-out double-pyramid top with heavily projecting gables.

LODGE PRIMARY SCHOOL, Oak Lane. 1902–4 by *Alfred Long*. Exuberant Jacobean in brick and buff terracotta. The tower, with truncated pyramid roof and ogee-topped lantern, is jostled by unequal gables, and the long front is articulated by more gables, shaped or with finials. If it looks crude on close examination, the sheer verve still carries you on.

EATON VALLEY PRIMARY SCHOOL, Dagger Lane. 2007–9 by *Lyons+Sleeman+Hoare*. Fashionable curving plan, fashionable low-angled roofs.

MAJOR HOUSES

MANOR HOUSE, Hall Green Road. An astonishing survival, among modest interwar housing. The C13 to C16 timber-framed home of the Marnhams and their Freebody and Stanley descendants, rediscovered underneath later fabric when on the point of demolition in 1950. After a report by *W. Maurice Jones* in 1953, West Bromwich Corporation decided to preserve it. It was heavily restored by *James A. Roberts* in 1957–60, including the removal of all structures later than c.1600.† A pub from

---

*It replaced a *John Madin* building of 1970–2.
†The house was measured and analysed from 1956 by Stanley Jones, whose comprehensive article in *Transactions of the South Staffordshire Archaeological and Historical Society* 17, 1975–6, is the basis of this description.

1960 to 2009, it is being repaired as a museum by Sandwell Council.

A GATEHOUSE, tree-ring dated to 1590–2, built by Walter Stanley, receives the visitor. It has a jetty, close studding on the ground floor (restored) and, above, the familiar concave-sided lozenges. More close studding, mainly original, on the N. A moat, reinstated in 1957–60, surrounds the house. One enters a small courtyard and faces the doorway into the HALL, tree-ring dated to 1270–88, built by Richard de Marnham. A spere-truss with cambered tie-beam divides screens passage from hall. A severe piece, the only decoration plain chamfers on the arch braces. On either side, long raking struts (the W restored) run down through the partitions to the side-posts. The hall itself has two ample bays with a base-cruck truss – a very early example – which supports twin tie-beams. Its blades have semi-octagonal shafts carrying capitals with three projecting chamfered mouldings, an up-to-date Dec motif. The middle moulding has an eroded band of ornament, like dentils, or perhaps nailhead. The N end has its canopy of honour. The four r. ribs are original, the rest restored. Deeply coved, but simpler than well-known Lancashire examples such as Rufford Old Hall. In the C16 (tree-ring dated 1530s), the W wall was replaced in close studding, with a full-height gabled rectangular bay-window projection (largely restored) at the N end, and a room above jettied back into the hall (this part mostly original).

The E wall is all C20, but follows the evidence of the surviving wall-plate. Original crown-post roof, the central post above the base cruck, but two others, braced only longitudinally, on tie-beams unusually placed: one slightly short of the spere-truss, the other forming the top of the canopy.

The N and S cross-wings were added in the early C15, probably by William Freebody. Walls of plain square panels. Ogee-headed doorways in the screens passage and the hall N end. Each wing has an upper chamber with a four-bay roof. The central decorative trusses are slightly different, the S with collar-beam, king-strut and raking struts, all cusped, the N raked struts cut to form a large quatrefoil flanked by smaller foiled openings. This, the 'SOLAR', was the high-status room (tree-ring dated 1412–37), and was heated: the projecting stone chimneystack survives on the N. Here alone the panels are distinguished by quadrant braces. The S or service wing has kitchen and buttery on the ground floor (identified in a 1552 inventory). Each wing has a lower W annexe, the N one rebuilt by *Roberts*. Shortly after construction, the N wing was extended E to form a CHAPEL, a tall, short space with close-studded walls throughout, and a two-bay roof. Its central truss has cusping and raking struts. Restored E window, designed by *Stanley Jones*: five lights with timber mullions. Upper W gallery for the owner and family. Its diagonally set uprights are original at the N end. In 1956 evidence was found of a N wing earlier than the present one, which may originally have been attached to an earlier hall range.

At the SW, a much-renewed late C16 close-studded KITCHEN range, originally detached; now linked by a single-storey *Roberts* extension with a curved rubble-stone wall.

In 1720 the house was bought by the horticulturist Sir Samuel Clarke. His alterations, including a new E wall to the hall with mullion-and-transom windows, and a staircase in the NE angle, were removed in 1957–60, but his WALLED GARDEN survives W of the house, now appropriately used as allotments. Pointed entrance arch, and to its l. two domed piers flanking an odd infilled arched opening.

NE of the house, a separate BUILDING retains a timber-framed W wall with square panels and a tie- and collar-beam roof with raking struts.

OAK HOUSE, Oak Road. A spectacular, if not large, early C17 timber-framed house. Recent tree-ring dating suggests the main phase is a single build of between 1604 and 1629, probably for the Turton family, who owned it by 1634. The original building was U-shaped, with wings to the rear. The NE front has three gables, close studding throughout, middle rails to both floors, a jetty which continues on the NW, and dragon beams. The porch is a very early addition (the wall-plate is cut for it inside), or an alteration during building. It has S-curved struts. Above is a remarkable timber-framed and gabled belvedere or look-out tower, a later C17 addition (felling dates between 1647 and 1673).* At the rear are substantial additions in brick (felling dates between 1646 and 1671). The space between the wings was filled by a tall block with two shaped gables, and the rear of the NW wing rebuilt. Also the kitchen was extended on the SE, with a stepped gable. Thin bricks laid mainly in English garden wall bond. Fine star-shaped chimneys. The house was restored by *W.H. Kendrick* in 1895–8, when Reuben Farley gave it to West Bromwich Council for a museum.

The HALL forms the ground floor of the centre block, with a former screens passage at its r. end. *Kendrick* opened the room up into the main bedroom above, making this a landing, a handsome arrangement. The panelling is his, and the first of a series of good Neo-Jacobean fireplaces. In the r. wing the PARLOUR, with full-height C17 panelling. Behind, the DINING ROOM with similar panelling, but above the fireplace a line of panels with decorative arches and diamonds. In the l. wing the KITCHEN, much restored. Open-string STAIRCASE of the framed newel type, in the brick rear block. It has decorative splat balusters which change as you go up from circles and diamonds to hearts. Next to it the MORNING ROOM, with raised strapwork patterns in all the top panels. Upstairs the finest panelling is in the front bedroom of the r. wing. The fireplace has panelled pilasters with carved fruit, a line of arched panels above and an entablature with vine-trail frieze.

---

*There was a similar tower, probably C17, at Oakeswell Hall, Wednesbury, dem. 1962 (*see* p. 599). The date 1488 on the front is C19 mythology.

To the w, two BARNS, one C19 with lines of ventilation holes, the other with C17 timber framing in square panels (tree-ring dated 1655/6).

SANDWELL PARK. Sandwell Priory was founded *c.* 1160 by William de Offini. Suppressed in 1525, the 'priory house' was owned by the Whorwoods from 1569. In 1701 they sold it to William Legge, created Earl of Dartmouth in 1711. The house was rebuilt by *William Smith the elder* in 1705–11, incorporating some medieval fabric. Its two-storey s front, roughly along the line of the nave N wall, had 2–9–2 bays. An engraving of *c.* 1810 shows three-storey corner towers with pyramid roofs, the Palladian scheme popular in the 1750s at e.g. Hagley Hall and Croome Court. These were added for the 2nd Earl, perhaps in 1757 (when he raised a loan of £6,000). The architect is uncertain; *Sanderson Miller*, a friend of the earl, was probably involved. A portico was added by 1821, perhaps by *Henry Hakewill*. Demolished 1928. The area is now a country park, and much of the LANDSCAPING remains, including a large lake, unfortunately divided by the M5.

The major survivor is the rectangular planned home farm, SANDWELL PARK FARM, down Salters Lane. Two-storey brick ranges with three-storey Palladian corner towers, again built for the 2nd Earl, probably in the 1750s and with *Miller* involved. The front range, smartly built in Sussex bond (the rest is Flemish stretcher), has three-centred arches to the wagon entrances. To the l. an early C19 COTTAGE. To the r. low brick VISITOR CENTRE of 1983 by *Sandwell Borough Architects* (*R. Gelder*, Chief Architect), and a BARN with two-bay round-headed arcade, perhaps of *c.* 1840.

½ m. E, beyond the motorway, the PRIORY foundations are exposed. It was always small. Cruciform plan with nave and s aisle. Five apses at the E, sanctuary and paired transeptal chapels each side: the plan of the C12 Worcester cathedral priory. Surviving vaulting ribs have profiles similar to those at Wenlock and Buildwas (both Shropshire), suggesting the same craftsmen were employed. The E end was probably complete by *c.* 1250, the rest by *c.* 1300. Blocking walls show where the chapels were demolished, probably in the C15. Monastic quarters to the N. The SAND WELL is immediately s. (For Arch Lodge see p. 615.)

PERAMBULATIONS AND OTHER BUILDINGS

1. *High Street*

The essential stretch starts at St Michael's R.C. church (p. 604). SW in ST MICHAEL STREET, a BILLIARD HALL (now pub) by *Albert Bye*, dated 1913. Big segmental pediment and flanking towers with moulded faience cues and balls. The SANDWELL HOTEL is mid-C19, the jolly Jacobean plasterwork probably added by *Edward Pincher*, 1880. Rear wing and ground-floor frontage by *Wood & Kendrick*, 1895.

NW up High Street, on the r. Wesley Methodist Church (p. 605), and LLOYDS BANK, classical by *J. Lewis Harpur*, 1937. Then loud Postmodern blocks by *pd architects*, 2003–4. They surround the former FREE PRESS offices by *Wood & Kendrick*, dated 1883. Dignified Queen Anne in brick and red terracotta. Diagonally opposite, more Queen Anne by *Wood & Kendrick*: Nos. 272–280 of 1898 and Nos. 282–288 of 1893 (horribly rendered), with similar gables and a domed corner turret. Further up, No. 303, the former ANCHOR INN of *c.* 1840. First-floor windows with architraves on consoles. BARCLAYS BANK incorporates the five-bay building of the Dudley and West Bromwich Banking Co. by *Bateman & Drury*, 1839. Reconstructed and extended by *Wood & Kendrick*, 1892. Theirs are the full-height pedimented canted bay, l., the pediment above the porch, the eared first-floor architraves, etc. No. 317 is of *c.* 1870–80 with ornate classical detail. Then the WEST BROMWICH BUILDING SOCIETY, quietly monumental Neo-Georgian of 1926–8 by *J.B. Surman* and *W.T. Benslyn*, who won a competition assessed by W.A. Harvey. Six bays, the end ones with the entrances, and windows above in pedimented aedicules. The ground floor smoothly rusticated up to a band with sculpted heads running across the windows, suggesting a mezzanine, with another band above which can be read as the cornice of a complete entablature. No. 325 was the POST OFFICE, of 1916–18 by *H.A. Collins*. Good revived Early Victorian classicism, with banded stone ground floor, *piano nobile* and solid cornice. Opposite, the library and Town Hall (pp. 606, 605). On the NE, a memorial LYCHGATE of 1980 and lime avenue lead to plain offices by *Lane Lister*, 1994–6, on the site of CHRIST CHURCH, West Bromwich's greatest late C20 loss. 1821–9 by *Francis Goodwin*, a Commissioners' church of the first grant. It was Perp, with a high W tower with tall belfry windows, nicely balancing the Town Hall. Closed 1978, gutted by fire 1979, dem. 1980.

SW into LODGE ROAD, alongside the Town Hall. A *Wood & Kendrick* townscape. On the r., their Institute and School of Art buildings (p. 606). Across the car park, l., in EDWARD STREET, their former MASONIC HALL, 1889, Queen Anne, with a big shaped gable. Lodge Road continues SW with nice terraces: Nos. 9–17, NW side, again by *Wood & Kendrick*, 1906. Opposite, the former Unitarian church (p. 605).

Back to High Street and NW. The angular HEALTH FUTURES block is by *Associated Architects*, 2015. No. 374, formerly the West Bromwich Building Society, is by *Hurley Robinson Partnership*, 1976–8. A fortress for your money, in corporate American Brutalism. First floor cantilevered out with heavy concrete framing. It addresses the wide High Street surprisingly successfully. Opposite, set back, HIGHFIELDS (now REGISTER OFFICE). It appears a unified but odd Late Georgian range, with central bow and flanking Tuscan porches with reeded friezes, but was four separate houses, of dates between shortly after 1804 (three r. bays of the centre) and

1839 (the balancing r. end). Restored by *Sandwell M.B.C. Architect's Department*, 1990–1.*

Across Sandwell Road, modest, much-altered Late Georgian and Early Victorian, e.g. Nos. 386–400, SW side, HEATH TERRACE, fifteen bays. A resident is recorded in 1819. One surviving round-headed doorcase with teardrop fanlight. The WHEATSHEAF of *c.*1840, NE, has a canted-out ground floor of 1876 by *Elliott J. Ettwell*: iron columns with leaf capitals. Ahead is Carters Green, and the FARLEY CLOCK TOWER of 1897 by *Edward Pincher*. Square, brick and red terracotta, with eclectic Continental detail (called in the opening brochure 'the Gothic Renaissance style'). Openwork cupola. Relief panels and portrait of Reuben Farley by *Albert Hopkins*. To its SW, the YMCA, nearly all of 2014–15 by *BPN*, with a tower far too close to the clock tower.

Returning SE we can turn l. into Sandwell Road, and r. into BRATT STREET. On the r., the OLD VICARAGE by *Wood & Kendrick*, 1891, Domestic Revival. To its r., contemporary former CHURCH HALL. Large end window with deep coving above; big semi-dormers. Opposite, Nos. 113–123, Free Style by *J. W. Allen*, 1907. Every house has a big curving bay but only the four centre ones have gables. Horseshoe-shaped recessed porches with stubby columns. Nos. 95–101, plainer, by *Allen*, 1897; Nos. 91–93, a showy pair with pilasters and broken pediments biting little balconies; almost certainly also his, *c.*1895. NE from the end of the street in PROVIDENCE PLACE, a cleanly designed block for British Telecom by *webbgray*, 2011. Lombard Street runs SW back to High Street.

E from St Michael's a pedestrianized stretch, with The Public (former; p. 607), and SHOPPING CENTRES by *John Madin Design Group*, now altered (masterplan 1962–5). QUEENS SQUARE (N), 1969–71, retains its top-lit atrium with black granite piers; KINGS SQUARE (S), 1972–5. Further E, FOUNTAIN by *Walter Macfarlane & Co.* of Glasgow, 1885, with ornate domed canopy. Just SE, iron CLOCK of 1912. W of Kings Square, BUS STATION of 1999–2002, with SCULPTURE, Beacon of Light, a cone surrounded by spiral tubing, by *Steve Field*, 2002. N of the High Street here, the big New Square shopping centre designed by *Lyons+Sleeman+Hoare*, with a Tesco supermarket by *Haskoll*. STATUE of the black footballers Cyrille Regis, Brendan Batson and Laurie Cunningham, N of The Public, by *Graham Ibbeson*, 2019.

2. North of the centre

Beyond the by-pass, W of Hallam Street, narrow streets centred on the HORSE AND JOCKEY of 1875 by *Samuel Horton*. In ST CLEMENT'S LANE, Nos. 44–56 by *J.W. Allen*, 1893, altered, with minimal broken pediments over pairs of doorways.

---

*The houses were purchased in 1922 as a site for new Municipal Buildings. A scheme by *Cecil E.M. Fillmore* was approved in 1937, but the war stopped construction.

E of Hallam Street, DAGGER LANE, along part of the W boundary of Sandwell Park, the N part of which was the smart road of the town from c.1900 until the Second World War. The best group starts with Nos. 64–70, dignified pairs by *J.W. Allen*, 1907. Nos. 72–74 also *Allen*, 1907, with terracotta lintels. No. 76 is by *W. Hadderton*, 1903, still Queen Anne. Nos. 78–80 by *Wood & Kendrick*, 1907, the grandest pair, with half-timbered gables over two-storey segmental bays. Diagonally opposite, No. 41, GATEHOUSE, by *Cecil E.M. Fillmore*, 1929–30, his own house. A quiet, refined design, with a big gable balanced by deliberately thin dormers, a good tile entrance arch, and gabled chimneys with side smoke holes. It is less than 6 ft (1.8 metres) high to the timber lintels, but Fillmore was a small man.*

Near the N end of Dagger Lane is HILL HOUSE. Brick front of c.1700, with three gables and platbands. It hides a timber-framed house tree-ring dated to c.1598, with a hall block between cross-wings. Timber framing is exposed in the E wall. The present entrance leads into the front room of the W wing. Close studding in the wall to the hall, box framing to the rear. The hall is much subdivided. Staircase to the rear with elegant turned balusters, probably C18. A separate entrance to the E leads into what was probably the screens passage, with C17 square panelling. The front room of the E range has more, and an overmantel with diamond panels and lines of squares. The hall block roof has collar-beam trusses and trenched purlins. A six-chimney stack at the W. Single-storey W extension of c.1900, probably by *Wood & Kendrick*.

Dagger Lane continues N as CHURCH VALE. VALE TERRACE is by *Wood & Kendrick*, dated 1885, very old-fashioned. N of All Saints' church (p. 602), the only hint of the old village is the late C19 terraces of NEWTON STREET, off Hollyhedge Road, with the ROYAL OAK pub (1898 by *J.W. Allen*).

WIGMORE, Pennyhill Lane, to the NE. Surviving gatehouse of schools for pauper children by the Walsall and West Bromwich Poor Law Unions. 1872, minimal Tudor, by *S.E. Bindley*. Ogee-capped cupola.

3. North-west and west of the centre

OLD MEETING STREET runs NNW from Carters Green. On the W side, No. 100 is the former St Andrew's vicarage by *Wood & Kendrick*, 1894, with Queen Anne detail but still a Gothic porch. Opposite, the AKRILL MEMORIAL HOMES are old-fashioned Tudor cottages of 1933 by *George H. Plant*. Beyond, Shree Krishna Mandir (p. 605). To the N in BLACK LAKE, the former NEW TALBOT by *A.T. Butler*, 1920, a 'reformed' pub, Free Jacobean, much altered 2021. Further up, the SOW AND PIGS, a 'two-room drinker', C18 and later.

J.B. & S. LEES (currently Liberty Performance Steels), Albion Road, ¾ m. W. By *Cecil E.M. Fillmore*, 1938. Long office range,

---

*No. 25, TWISTED CHIMNEYS, also by *Fillmore*, 1930, was demolished in 2014.

two-storey centre, entrance with stepped-in jambs. Gatepiers with tapering centres.

4. East of the centre

In Herbert Street, off Overend Street, the former SPON LANE TRUST ALMSHOUSES (now SILVESTER COURT). Tough High Victorian, red brick banded with blue. Near one of 1867, matching rear one by *J.W. Allen*, dated 1888.

Along the road towards Birmingham, beyond Trinity Way, the LEWISHAM HOTEL with fancy Jacobean front, mostly *Alfred Long*, 1895. BIRMINGHAM ROAD was a superior late C19 residential area, though few buildings stand out. Nos. 83–87, N, by *Long*, 1902 etc. No. 81 by *Edward Pincher*, 1876, but the half-timbering probably *Wood & Kendrick*, 1909. No. 79, with heavy Doric porch, also *Pincher*, c. 1875. Nos. 73–77 on the corner of Bagnall Street, by *Wood & Kendrick*, 1896, are an eyecatcher: octagonal corner tower with open top storey and dome; lively square bays beyond. To the N, the Beeches estate, developed from 1867 by *G.B. Nichols*. On the S, set back, No. 172, MARY SPOONER HOUSE, an unusual stuccoed Late Georgian villa: pedimented end bays with paired pilasters and smooth rustication below, doorcase with minimal pediment and wreaths in the frieze. Beeches Road Chapel (p. 604) on the N.

ARCH LODGE, the gateway of Sandwell Park, 'this Ozymandian relic' (Andor Gomme), is further E, stranded on a big roundabout over the M5. A pedimented triumphal arch with horizontal rustication, which continues across the columns at each end. Ribbed tunnel-vault inside. The style makes it later than the house, perhaps c. 1725–30.

THE HAWTHORNS (West Bromwich Albion football ground) is further E again. The club moved here in 1900. All stands now late C20: Halford's Lane by *Seymour Harris & Partners*, 1981; Birmingham Road and Smethwick End (S) by *Tim Ralphs Design Group*, 1994; East by *Ward McHugh*, 2001. The quality is not high. The former HAWTHORNS HOTEL (now café) was STREET HOUSE, rebuilt by Henry Halford, an iron merchant, between 1833 and 1846. Thin basic pilasters, hipped roof. Behind, Sandwell Academy (p. 608).

5. South of the centre

Former OFFICES AND WAREHOUSE of Archibald Kenrick & Sons, hardware manufacturers, Hall Street South. By *Martin & Chamberlain*, 1875–8. *J.H. Chamberlain*'s most important surviving industrial building, now jammed against the elevated M5. High Victorian sublime: fourteen-bay front with steeply cut-back buttresses, and seven unequal gables, the last shouldering the corner belfry tower. Another rhythm of linked two-light windows, with very tall stone mullions, against single lights.

In Union Street, open to Kenrick Way, former OFFICES of Taylor & Farley's Summit Foundry. 1882 by *Wood & Kendrick*.

Petite; hipped roof, Queen Anne pilasters and terracotta pies, but two-light windows still with Lombardic tracery.

CANAL STRUCTURES

In Ryders Green Road, N of the Methodist church, the top of the RYDERS GREEN LOCKS on the Birmingham Canal's Walsall branch of 1786, with the EIGHT LOCKS pub, mostly a rebuild of 1899 by *Wood & Kendrick*.

The TAME VALLEY CANAL of 1839–44, cut by the Birmingham Canal Navigation to connect the Black Country directly to the Grand Union Canal and London, takes a dramatic level route across the N parts of the borough. Several original BRIDGES. From W to E, GOLDS HILL BRIDGE (off Shaw Street, in industrial dereliction) has cast-iron parapets. HYDES ROAD BRIDGE has a deep iron trough, cantilevered parapets, and decorative railings. Old WALSALL ROAD BRIDGE (now Navigation Lane) is similar but with round nosings. Three-arched AQUEDUCT over the Grand Junction Railway, blue brick with stone voussoirs. The junction with the RUSHALL CANAL of 1847 (by the M5/M6 junction) has a towpath bridge with cross-girdered parapets. Further E, three more 1844 bridges, with bold saltire-cross iron parapets. The impressive single-arch AQUEDUCT over Spouthouse Lane (near the Birmingham boundary) has rock-faced masonry, with massive imposts and voussoirs. The blue-brick infill is later C19.

GREAT BRIDGE

Until the C18 'Grete Bridge', where the West Bromwich to Tipton road crosses the River Tame. A settlement grew up from the C16. Its modern centre is just on the Tipton side; the C19 church is ½ m. SE.

ST PETER, Whitehall Road, Greets Green. 1857–8 by *Thomas Johnson & Son* of Lichfield. A comfortable, low-proportioned design in cream sandstone. The features are consistently of *c.* 1300. W tower with angle buttresses with deep set-offs just below the top (was a spire intended?) and low pyramid roof. Wide nave, arcades of octagonal piers and arches with two wave mouldings. Their hoodstops, all different, must be portraits. – Original FONT, PULPIT and PEWS. – STAINED GLASS by *A. E. Lemmon*: E window, 1930 (Te Deum), 'a wall of colour' (Roy Albutt), with figures including the vicar, Father Lamplugh, and a workman with sleeves rolled up; N aisle 1938; S 1942. Others by *William Pearce Ltd*, 1901–12.

The MARKET SQUARE is dominated by the former LIMERICK INN of *c.*1837, with quoins and coved parapet. Just W, the former NAGS HEAD of 1906, probably by *George Wenyon*, Free Style. Going SE, the BRIDGE was rebuilt in 1780. Its N side survives. Semicircular arch with rusticated voussoirs and keystone for the main channel. From the road it is flanked by two Neo-Georgian buildings. The former BARCLAYS BANK is a small pavilion of 1930 by *E.C. Bewlay (Peacock & Bewlay)*. The WEST BROMWICH BUILDING SOCIETY, by *Cecil E.M. Fillmore*, 1935, has half-columns sinking into a curved sill, with Soanian capitals.

FARLEY PARK, s of St Peter's church. Opened in 1892, together with the READING ROOM by *Alfred Long*. Brick and half-timber. The porch-tower cuts sharply into an octagon and has a French pavilion roof.

In Sheepwash Lane No. 42–44, a three-quarter pair, with No. 73 Cophall Street on the corner. Unremarkable but by *George Wenyon*, of 1910–11, showing the bread-and-butter work of even good early C20 Black Country architects.

WALSALL METROPOLITAN BOROUGH

Walsall	618
Places of worship	620
Public buildings	626
Perambulations	632
Caldmore	638
Palfrey	639
Birchills	639
Pleck	639
Other outlying buildings, east and south-east	640
Aldridge	640
Blakenall	644
Bloxwich	645
Brownhills	647
Darlaston	648
Places of worship	649
Public buildings	651
Perambulations	651
Other buildings	652
Bentley	653
Moxley	654
Great Barr	654
Pelsall	658
Rushall	659
Streetly	661
Walsall Wood	662
Shelfield	663
Willenhall	663
Places of worship	663
Public buildings	665
Perambulations	666
Other buildings	667
Short Heath	668
New Invention	668

WALSALL

An Anglo-Saxon name – 'Wealh's hall'. It may also be the 'Walesho' in Wulfric Spot's will of 1002–4. In 1159 it was granted by Henry II to Herbert le Rous. A market was held by 1220, and the first charter was granted *c.*1235. By 1377 the division was established between the borough area and the 'foreign', the rest of the parish, with its biggest settlement at Bloxwich. Walsall became a Municipal Borough in 1835 and a County Borough in 1889. In 1966 it took in Willenhall and Darlaston, and in 1974 became a Metropolitan Borough, including Aldridge, Brownhills, Pelsall and Rushall.

The town shared in the growth of Black Country industry from at least *c.*1300, but its particular trade is leather. Tanneries existed by the mid C15, and a currier is recorded in 1752. In 1900 there were seven tanneries and more than thirty curriers. The grandest architectural statement is Brookes's saddlery factory in Leicester Street, right by the Council House. The local metal trade specialized in ancillary items such as bits and bridles. A much reduced industry survives.

Notable local architects begin in the later C19 with the workmanlike *Samuel Loxton*, and *H.E. Lavender. F.E.F. Bailey* and his later partner *H.H. McConnal*, active by *c.*1890, mark a step up in quality. The best firm was *Hickton & Farmer. Jeffries & Shipley*, later *Shipley & Foster*, and *Gordon Foster* alone, did solid work through most of the C20. The Borough Architect *Austin T. Parrott*, and especially *Julie Lindon-Morris* on his staff, did good work in the 1960s. The best, the police station of 1964–6, was demolished in 2019.

Walsall.
Engraving by T. Donaldson after Stebbing Shaw, 1801

WALSALL

Walsall

250 m / 250 yds

Birchills

Caldmore

Palfrey

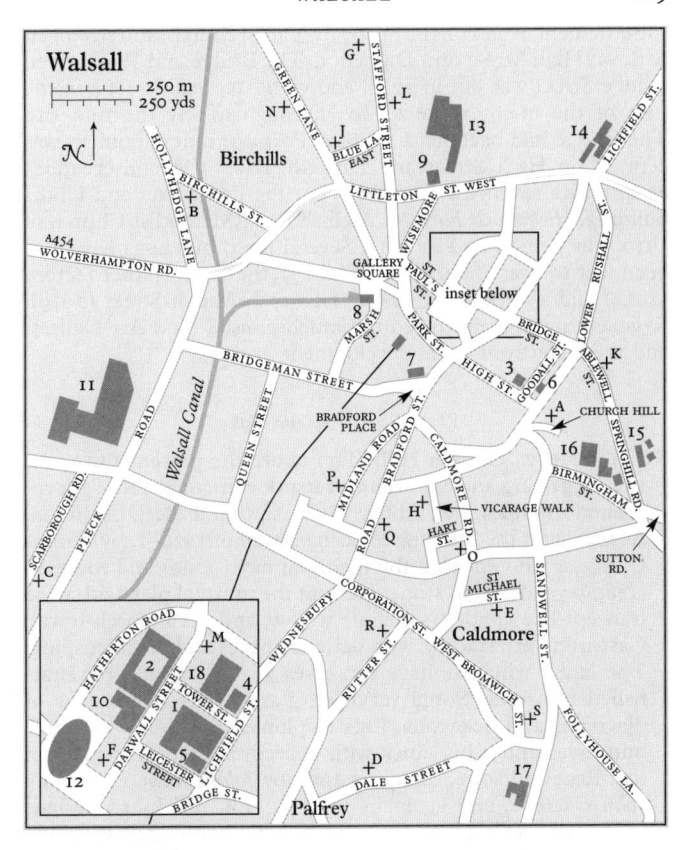

- A St Matthew
- B St Andrew
- C St John the Evangelist
- D St Mary and All Saints (former)
- E St Michael and All Angels
- F St Paul
- G St Peter
- H St Mary the Mount (R.C.)
- J St Patrick (R.C.)
- K Methodist Central Hall
- L Methodist chapel (former)
- M Hatherton Presbyterian Church (former)
- N Baptist church
- O Vicarage Walk Baptist Church (former)
- P Baptist chapel
- Q Glebe Centre (United Reformed)
- R Aisha Mosque and Islamic Centre
- S Guru Nanak Sikh Temple

- 1 Council House and Town Hall
- 2 Civic Centre
- 3 Guildhall (former)
- 4 Library
- 5 St Matthew's Hall
- 6 Library and police station (former)
- 7 Science and Art Institute
- 8 New Art Gallery
- 9 Leather Museum
- 10 Post Office
- 11 Walsall Manor Hospital
- 12 Bus station
- 13 Walsall College
- 14 Queen Mary's High School for Girls
- 15 Blue Coat Junior School
- 16 Blue Coat Secondary School (now Academy)
- 17 Whitehall Infant and Nursery Schools
- 18 Gala Baths

Settlement began on the hill by the parish church, and stretched w down High Street and Digbeth to The Bridge and Park Street. Bridge Street was cut in 1766, and with Ablewell Street became part of the major route SE to Birmingham. By the mid C19 The Bridge had become the centre. Post-war redevelopment was centred on High Street and Digbeth. Later C20 conservationist attitudes saved the Guildhall, but the finest Arts and Crafts building, *Hickton & Farmer*'s Mellish Road Methodist Church of 1910, was demolished in 2011. Several listed buildings have also been lost to fire: Shannon Mill (2007), the Boak leather factory (2012) and a *Hickton & Farmer* factory in Marsh Street (2019). Regeneration has produced the much-praised New Art Gallery, and the Waterfront canal development to its w.

PLACES OF WORSHIP

ST MATTHEW, Church Hill. High above the present town, the site suggesting ancient origins. First documented 1200; appropriated to Halesowen Abbey from 1248 until the Dissolution. At first sight the building looks nearly all of 1820–1, by *Francis Goodwin*, who encased the medieval nave, aisles and tower in creamy-yellow Bath stone. He kept the unusual plan with wide transept-like chapels set some way w, and a sw porch-tower. Cast-iron Perp tracery, with flattened ogees and much cusping. The larger windows have e.g. roses at the top, and big brattished transoms. Some surviving glazing bars in patterns of diagonals and hexagons. Lots of pinnacles. Tower with angle buttresses and a big clock with a sleepy little devil seated on top. Recessed spire, rebuilt in 1699 by *John Brown*, in 1777 by *John Cheshire*, and again in 1951 by *H.W. Shipley* to designs by *Sir Charles Nicholson*. Grand w porch with open-traceried parapet and gabled jambs, with niches. E extensions of the transepts by *Ewan Christian*, 1880, for staircases.

Perp chancel, rebuilt as part of work of 1462–74, which included the tower from 1465, and the original NW chapel of 1468. The master mason was *John Nightingale*, followed by *William Wotton* from 1467. Four bays long, and on a grand scale. Sandstone, mainly from Sutton Coldfield, but some from Hamstead and Brewood. Much restored by *Ewan Christian* in 1879–80. Five-light E window and three-light N and S ones, with tracery copied from a blocked window which Christian rediscovered inside. A super-transom in the central lights. Stepped buttresses, much renewed, but the NE and SE diagonal ones have original cusped panelling. The string course has carvings, some original: an angel holding a shield, and a deer(?), both N. Parapet and pinnacles of 1880. A vaulted passage runs under the E bay, clearly a processional way, needed because the chancel was built up to the old churchyard boundary. Arches with big hollow chamfers, resting on corbels. N vestry of 1880, extended by *Fleeming & Son*, 1908.

Goodwin's interior has slim iron Perp arcade piers with four attached shafts, on Gornal stone bases. Three-sided gallery with arcaded front and original seating. Until 1880 it ran round with a horseshoe curve at the E. The flat ceiling is delightfully decorated in a still Georgian tradition, with fans, central pendants and corbels. Nice detail in unexpected places, e.g. the arcaded brackets supporting the aisle roofs and chapel galleries. Many corbel heads, all different. In 1837 *George Basevi* strengthened the gallery. The smaller columns underneath are almost certainly his. Chancel arch by *Christian*, 1880. Beyond on the N, the surviving C15 window. Chancel window jambs C15, with big hollow chamfers. Between them, remains of image niches, the W ones with little vaulted canopies, the E pair restored. N and S doorways, also restored. SEDILIA with ogee arches and PISCINA, also a LECTERN, a stone surface on a panelled corbel in the chancel N wall, all restored 'with scrupulous fidelity'. They look completely C19. Kingpost roof also by *Christian*.

Beneath the three W bays of the chancel is a CRYPT, in two parts. The W section corresponds to a shorter, earlier chancel. Two bays of quadripartite vaulting, the ribs dying into the walls. Lancets in the E wall (one now a doorway). Their tops hint at ogees, so *c.* 1300 or early C14. The E section is contemporary with the C15 chancel, with a beautifully constructed four-centred tunnel-vault. On the S side a staircase to the chancel, and a blocked fireplace, suggesting domestic use at some period.

FURNISHINGS. REREDOS by *C.E. Bateman*, 1911–12. Glowing *opus sectile* panels, borders of angels and roses, and four standing archangels. – PULPIT by *Christian*, 1880. – STALLS. C15 or early C16. By tradition, brought from Halesowen Abbey at the Dissolution, a credible story (cf. Halesowen parish church's purchases, p. 512). Eighteen MISERICORDS, the largest set in the area, lively and inventive. They include (N) a Pelican in its Piety, a man playing a viol seated on a dragon, a double-headed eagle, and a standing warrior or perhaps Green Man, holding a branch or club; (S) two hybrid beast-men firing arrows, and three good monstrous heads. The arm-rests have heads but also clambering beasts. – BENCH-ENDS, perhaps from the 'settes' paid for in 1496–1506. With tracery, brattished transoms and flowers in the small top lights. Much-eroded poppyheads with birds' wings. All incorporated into CHOIR STALLS by *Christian*, 1880. – SCREEN by *Bateman*, 1914–15, a lovely piece with slim mullions filling the chancel arch. The cresting has writhing branches, clearly a Crown of Thorns. Rood figures expressively elongated and twisted, in a German late medieval way. Fine wrought-iron GATES. – FONT. Made in 1473 by *William Masyn*. Octagonal. Shields held by angels, with coats of arms including Stafford and Beauchamp, and (N) the Instruments of the Passion. Traces of colour. Fluted and gadrooned alabaster top, and lead bowl, dated 1712, with the initials of *Nathaniel Short*, plumber. – N chapel REREDOS by *Bateman*, 1920. – PAINTING. W end. By *Anna Lea Merritt*, 1900. Large. – STAINED GLASS. Chancel, nearly all *Burlison*

& Grylls, 1880–1904. Typical blues, greens and browns. The best is the E window (Sister Dora), 1880, with well-characterized small figures in the tracery. Also N side E by *Clayton & Bell*, †1908. Over the chancel arch two good Arts and Crafts windows by *Harvey & Ashby*, 1915. S aisle E, *Burlison & Grylls*, 1921; the rest *Goddard & Gibbs (A.E. Buss)*, 1960–5 and 1975 (S chapel). W window, central and tracery lights by *Chance Bros*, 1852. Bright, metallic colours and still almost Georgian patterning.

MONUMENTS. S aisle. Mutilated recumbent effigy, traditionally Sir Roger Hillary †1399 but probably an earlier Hillary, *c.*1330–50. Head on r. elbow, l. arm holding shield. The face is lost, and most of the legs. Dugdale in 1639 drew it complete with crossed legs. – John Burrowes †1746, old-fashioned tablet with urns. – Two oval tablets on tapering obelisks with urns, †1785 and †1790, by *James Eglington*. Mary and Thomas Scott, †1781 and 1793, delicate pedimented tablet and obelisk by *Percivall & Ricketts*. – Thomas Carless †1812, tablet by *William Hollins*. – S chapel, William Purvis, ornate alabaster tablet by *Jones & Willis* to a Light Brigade survivor, 1900. – W end. Charles Forster †1815, with book and crown. – Anna Maria Forster †1829, with draped tomb and cross, by *John Seeley*. – Mary Pedley †1859 and William Jones †1855, good draped tablets by *Peter Hollins*. – N chapel. Thomas Nicholls †1711, cartouche with fringed draperies. – Elizabeth Blackham †1798, Jacob Smith †1800, oval tablets on obelisks. – Henry Windle †1859, rich Gothic aedicule, by *P. Hollins*.

In the churchyard a WAR MEMORIAL, tapering cross on a gabled base and an open-air pulpit, of 1922, W; and a big LYCHGATE of 1927, like a small cottage; both by *James A. Swan* with *F.T. Beck*.

The MEMORIAL GARDENS and ST MATTHEW'S CLOSE form the church's precinct to the S. Gardens and buildings all by *Geoffrey Jellicoe*, a major work, gentle but tightly structured Modernism, with classical echoes. The GARDENS, SW on the crest of the hill, are of 1951–2. High brick walls, pierced by openings with minimal pediments. On the SE these form three entrances; at the N corner they open on to balconies with views of church and town. The idea of an Italian-style 'secret garden' was important to Jellicoe at this time. A grid of paths inside with irregular planting and trees. At the E corner a CHAPEL (Shrine of Remembrance), added 1964. Tougher, but quirky, with twin pyramid roofs, the end projecting on piers. At the W corner a former GROUNDSMAN'S COTTAGE rises above the wall. Square, rendered, with a pyramid roof and window balconies mirroring the garden itself. In front a finely lettered SLATE with scrolls, by *Gordon Herickx*. Beyond the garden to the NW, a stepped TERRACE. To the S, two-storey FLATS of 1955–7. Recessed entrances and balconies. Stepped-up central entrance, full-height carriageway flanked by lower footways, marked by a pair of chimneys. At the SE, the CHURCH HALL of 1961–2, its end on pilotis.

St Andrew, Birchills Street, Birchills. Set back behind PARISH BUILDINGS by *Fleeming & Son*, 1902: single-storeyed, simple, with big semi-dormer windows. Gothic entrance archway. The church is of 1884–7, by *J.E.K. & J.P. Cutts*. A typical Cutts design, rather old-fashioned: big, plain, of red brick with lancet windows, steep roofs, gabled corner pinnacles, small flèche, and w baptistery behind a triple arcade. C13-style arcades, circular sandstone piers and stepped brick arches. What impresses are the huge, tall space – six-bay nave, two-bay chancel, separated only by a double roof truss – and the cut-back layers of brick in the clerestory. – REREDOS by *Jones & Willis*, 1931. – SEDILIA by *Harold C. King*, 1935. – PULPIT by *Bridgemans*, 1950. – Original FONT with fine early C20 COVER, free Gothic, standing angels with Art Nouveau wings. – STAINED GLASS. All by *Hardmans*. E window 1911. Aisles, clerestory and porches, a remarkable series of saints reflecting the Anglo-Catholic tradition of the parish, 1902–28. – CALVARY outside on the E wall, carved by 'Italian workmen', 1920.

St Gabriel, Walstead Road, Fullbrook. 1938–9 by *Richard Twentyman*, his first church, progressive for its date in the Black Country. Brick with Clipsham stone dressings. Nave and low aisles, and a tower over the chancel, in a massive Dudok-influenced manner with few historic references. Parapets hide the roofs, and the tall clerestory windows are plain rectangles. The tower has a SW stair-turret ending in plain fins and lights between. SW porch with a minimal gable. Round-arched, unmoulded arcades and chancel arch; characteristic heavy stepped beamed ceiling. – Original FITTINGS: REREDOS, hinting at attenuated classicism; SEDILIA divided by steel columns; STALLS; massive, curving twin PULPIT and READING DESK with reliefs by *Donald Potter*; RAILS with up-and-down timbers linked to the top rail with balls; tapering and fluted FONT. – W end with a *Potter* LUNETTE of the Nativity, now screened off. – STAINED GLASS. Aisles, by *Hardmans*, 1980 etc.

St John the Evangelist, Scarborough Road, Pleck. By *Charles Brown*, 1976. Low asymmetrical-roofed church-and-hall complex in buff brick. It replaced a Gothic design by *Griffin & Weller*, 1858; an archway and wall survive on Pleck Road.

St Mary and All Saints (now the Orthodox CHURCH OF THE NATIVITY OF THE MOTHER OF GOD), Dale Street, Palfrey. 1901–2 by *J.E.K. & J.P. Cutts*. A pedestrian design. Large, brick, low; no tower, just a W bellcote. Late Gothic with Tudor and Jacobean features, used without consistency. Standard Perp-style arcades. – Original SCREEN now at the W, as a partition. – PULPIT. 1893, from Christ Church, Gailey. – MOSAICS. Prophets under the E window, Theotokos on the W front, by *Eirini Katsoulis*, 2006–9. – STAINED GLASS. E window *c.* 1910. W, by *Abbott & Co.*, 1946. – PARSONAGE, E. 1909 by *Fred J. Gill*. Economical Tudor.

St Michael and All Angels, St Michael Street, Caldmore. By *J.R. Veall*, 1870–1 (aisles and S chapel 1878–81). Sandstone with Bath stone dressings. C20 repair with tile stitching has created an unusual texture. Lancets, paired in the clerestory, and plate tracery. N transept and NE sacristy by *W.H. Bidlake*, 1924, in keeping. Unfortunate flat sacristy roof of 1967. C13-style arcades with circular piers, big spreading foliage capitals, all different, and plain arches except for an angle roll. Chancel arch with big half-shafts. Much of the internal character comes from the restoration by *Lavender, Son & Close*, 1965–7, after a fire. White-rendered walls, shallow curved nave roof with panelling. Chancel roof part-domed. – Original PULPIT; also the FONT, with a tall C20 classical cover. – CHOIR STALLS, 1967, refined Neo-Jacobean. – REREDOS by *Joseph Pippet*, 1901, a rare Anglican work by this Catholic artist, renovated 1967. Late medieval style, with many saints under tracery canopies, and painted groups flanking a central Christ in Majesty. – STAINED GLASS. All *Hardmans*, aisles mostly 1885–6, clerestory all 1907. Restored and thinned out in 1967, also by *Hardmans*, with new E windows, abstract, blues and yellowy-browns. (Closed 2018.)

ST MARTIN, Sutton Road. 1960 by *Gordon Foster* (*Shipley & Foster*). Steep-gabled hall in a Scandinavian way. The bold and successful motif is the recessing of the l. half of the front, with concrete framing exposed, creating an entrance. SCULPTURE here, Christ with children in low relief, by *R.F. Kings*; surrounding scenes incised into the stone. Portal frames inside, with top lighting.

ST PAUL, Darwall Street. By *J.L. Pearson*, 1891–3, a late work. A large town church, Dec style, with broad aisles, in local red sandstone laid in narrow courses. Mostly Geometrical tracery. SW porch-tower never completed. Transepts treated differently, the S taller and with petal tracery. Apse. Chancel chapels, the S with a smaller apse. Sharp little lantern and new W entrance, part of the partial transformation by *Michael Reardon & Partners*, 1994–5, into a shopping arcade, 'The Crossing'. Tall arcades with lobed piers and Pearson's personal hoodstops, now cut by shopfronts and floors. Staircase in the crossing with glazing and insistent verticals; hanging glass CROSS by *Daniel Cremin*, 1990. Worship spaces above the nave, with Pearson's close-set rafter roof, and the apse, with tall two-light windows. S chancel chapel retained, with PEWS and REREDOS. – STAINED GLASS. By *A.J. Dix*, 1903, apse, and two in the S chapel. More there by *Hardmans*, 1894, 1897, 1918.

ST PETER, Stafford Street. 1839–41, by *Thomas Smith*. *Isaac Highway* acted as surveyor and supervised construction. Brick, completely pre-Ecclesiological. Ritual W tower with angle buttresses below, polygonal clasping buttresses above, and cut-down pinnacles. Broad nave with lancets. Chancel by *Fred T. Beck*, 1910, with unmoulded lancets, a nice updating of the idiom. N chapel by *Beck*, 1918. The nave has a queenpost roof with cusping, and a W gallery. – REREDOS, CHOIR STALLS and PANELLING by *Beck*, 1912. – SCREEN by *C.E. Bateman*, 1906–7, altered to fit. Richly carved, with fleurons on the top band and down the mullions. Cusped lights. – PULPIT by

Bridgeman, 1904. – PEWS by *G.B. Nichols*, 1868. – STAINED GLASS. All by *Hardmans*: chancel 1918, nave †1919 to 1961.

ST MARY THE MOUNT (R.C.), Vicarage Walk. 1825–7 by *Joseph Ireland*. A pure white Grecian pedimented box set on a hill. Doric pilasters at the windowless W and E ends, plain side walls. Tall W doorway and straight-headed side windows. Wide, aisleless interior with a beautiful shallow coffered tunnel-vault. The E wall is treated as a splendid reredos, with giant attached fluted Ionic columns in five bays. Between them, round-headed arches and little decorative balustrades. The order returns N and S as pilasters with anthemion friezes, defining the sanctuary. W gallery on plain columns. – PAINTINGS, E end. Evangelists and little square panels below, part of an 1880 scheme by *Henry Naden*. Crucifixion by *Dunstan Powell* of *Hardmans*, 1909, also probably the inscriptions; *Hickton & Farmer* may have been involved. All restored in the late C20 after mutilation in 1962–7. – PULPIT, small, of 1906 by *Boultons*. – STATIONS OF THE CROSS by *Raffl* of Paris, 1880. – MONUMENT. Rev. Francis Martyn †1838, bust. – STAINED GLASS. N and S windows by *Hardmans*, 1909, mostly saints, in architectural surrounds.

Linked PRESBYTERY at the SE, also of 1827 by *Ireland*. It repeats the temple design smaller, a father-and-son effect. Inside, simple original doorcases and stick-baluster staircase. Extensions by *Hickton & Farmer* (including the bay window), 1909, and *Jeffries & Shipley*, 1937 (S).

ST PATRICK (R.C.), Green Lane and Blue Lane East. By *Bernard V. James* of *Harrison & Cox*, 1965–6. A curious design, with sawtooth side walls, Coventry Cathedral-style, but with the suspiciously old-fashioned feature of a sanctuary apse. Panelled ceiling. – Original FURNISHINGS, and STAINED GLASS in the small apse windows, intense red flames. Also C21 work by *Louis Healey*, bright but obvious.

METHODIST CENTRAL HALL, Ablewell Street. 1859 by *William* and *Samuel Horton*. Big, red brick, still in the Georgian tradition. Its pediment is visible behind the coarse *Moderne* classical block added in 1929–30 by *Arthur Brocklehurst & Co.* Interior recast with an inserted floor by *B.W. Blanchard & Partners*, 1972–3. Plain SUNDAY SCHOOL of 1958–60 by *Crouch, Butler & Savage* (*C. Stanbury Madeley*), N, replacing the chapel of 1829 by *John Fallows*.

METHODIST CHAPEL (now SHRI GURU RAVIDASS TEMPLE), Stafford Street. Rebuilt in 1860 by *Job Wilkes*, but the grand front block of 1889 by *H.E. Lavender*. Pediment with Romanesque three-light window below. Flanking staircase towers with small pediments too. Heavily rendered, and details lost. SCHOOL BLOCK, l., 1874.

HATHERTON PRESBYTERIAN CHURCH (now United Reformed), Hatherton Road. 1881–2 by *John Cotton* and *H.H. McConnal*. Vigorous Gothic in brick with stone dressings. Front with a big Geometrical window and ritual NW tower which turns octagonal but has lost its spire. Side gables with plate tracery. SUNDAY SCHOOL behind, its upper floor and turret of 1903–4 by *Bailey & McConnal*. Cream brick interior with red brick trim. Tall iron columns carry a roof of arch-braced trusses, and half-trusses with brattished tie-beams at the sides. Big organ arch, w gallery. – Original PULPIT and PEWS, curious box-like CHOIR STALLS of 1882 material, reconstructed in 1926.

BAPTIST CHURCH, Green Lane. 1972 by *Charles Brown (Brown Matthews)*. Cubic block in dark blue brick, with clerestory lighting.

VICARAGE WALK BAPTIST CHURCH (now MANDIR BABA BALAK NATH), Caldmore Road and Hart Street. By *W.F. Markwick*, 1878–9. A 'mingling of Classic and Italian' in contrasting brick and stone dressings. Big central pediment. Former SCHOOL by *H.E. Lavender*, 1883, l., also pedimented. Interior mostly lost on conversion.

BAPTIST CHAPEL, Midland Road. 1909–10 by *F.W. Harrison*. Small. Very red brick.

GLEBE CENTRE (United Reformed), Wednesbury Road. 1973–5 by *Stone, Toms & Partners*. An octagon with the cardinal faces extended, mostly grey brick, cantilevered over a lower storey. Sawtooth lantern. Contemporary office slab behind.

AISHA MOSQUE AND ISLAMIC CENTRE, Rutter Street. 1983–8 by *Solar Design*.

GURU NANAK SIKH TEMPLE, West Bromwich Street. 2007 by *Reade Buray Associates*.

PUBLIC BUILDINGS

Civic, cultural, medical and transport

COUNCIL HOUSE AND TOWN HALL, Lichfield Street. By *J.G.S. Gibson*, 1902–5 (competition 1901). The finest municipal buildings in the conurbation. 'The general style [is] English renaissance, based on the works of Wren, Gibbs, and Vanbrugh'

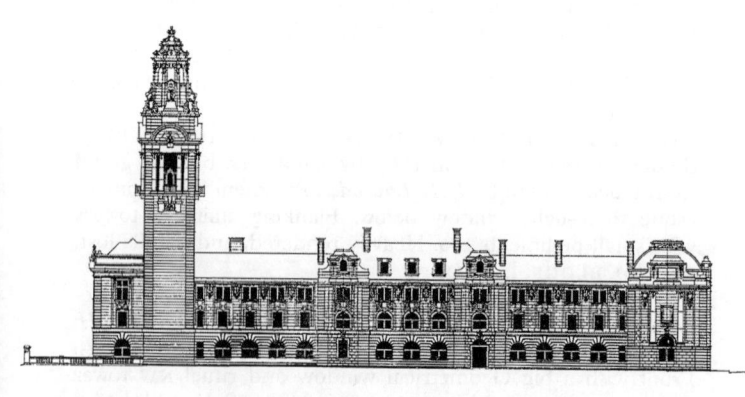

Walsall, Council House and Town Hall.
Elevation drawing by Sprague & Co., 1900

(Gibson), that is, Baroque, but with Free Style and Jacobean inflections. The effect is slightly purer than e.g. Lanchester, Stewart & Rickards's almost contemporary Cardiff City Hall. Sculpture, by *H.C. Fehr*, is integral to the design, contributing to its massing and silhouette. The brief specified offices for all council departments except police, and a hall to seat 1,500.

The material is grey-pink Hollington stone. Giant Ionic order on a rusticated basement, end blocks with open pediments and trophies. The centrepiece is the most Baroque feature. Big Ionic doorcase with Michelangelesque crouching cloaked female figures on its pediment representing Day and Night. They support a second, broken segmental pediment above, with a seated figure of Justice holding a child. Above, paired giant pilasters support a big segmental pediment and a built-up attic with a helmeted Britannia riding two horses. Panels between the windows to either side with figures representing local trades, including tanning and glass-blowing, in leafy cartouches. Original balustrade walls of Grindleford Bridge stone in front. The tower is set back on the r. It rises sheer, with smooth-rusticated quoins, to complex Doric aedicules with big segmental pediments and pairs of columns set slightly forward and enclosing pedimented niches and balconies. Then a stage with concave corners and big crouching figures. The crown, an excellent landmark, abandons Baroque for fanciful Free Style: an octagon, in browner Grindleford Bridge stone, with arches between piers, but all tapering inwards. To the l. some way down Leicester Street, the separate hall entrance. Concave corners and a big semicircular arch for the doorway, all with smooth rustication.

We enter from Lichfield Street into a low barrel-vaulted lobby. Green marble dado with split panels laid symmetrically. Long main corridor. On the r. an alabaster war memorial from St Paul's church, by *Bridgemans*, 1921. At the end the TOWN HALL. Shallow barrel-vault with coffered ribs on broad piers, pedimented windows. The plasterwork, here and elsewhere by *Gilbert Seale*, includes rich cornices, crowned cartouches, and Adam-style relief figures and garlands on the vault. Gallery over the entrance. Stage with pedimented organ case by *H.H. McConnal*, 1908, flanked by large paintings of First World War scenes by *Frank O. Salisbury*, 1921, realistic and sombre-toned. Bronze memorial plaques, 1921 by *Frank Baker & Sons*. Relief panel of Charles Swinnerton Heap by *Albert Toft*, 1901.

Halfway along the corridor we have passed the finest architecture here, the STAIRCASE. It starts modestly, on both sides, through arched openings, rising behind piers. The piers reveal arches giving glimpses above, where the upper flights are discovered as an imperial stair, i.e. with a single broad second flight returning as two to the top floor. Above, a dome on pairs of Ionic columns with elegant flattened capitals, and barrel-vaults in all four directions, a reduced paraphrase of Wren's St Stephen Walbrook. On the bases, good profile bronze memorial plaques by *Robert Jackson Emerson*, 1920 and 1923. The second flight leads to a boldly rusticated doorway with carved maidens in the tympanum, through a groin-vaulted lobby and into the COUNCIL CHAMBER. Another St Stephen Walbrook paraphrase, but with a larger dome on more conventional Ionic columns, and coffered arches to the arms. Seating in a horseshoe, centred on the mayor's chair. Finally the MAYOR'S PARLOUR, with a rich veneered fireplace with marble surround. Again good plasterwork. In the corridor, an excellent marble relief from *F.J. Williamson*'s Sister Dora monument, 1886 (p. 632): the Pelsall colliery disaster, with expressive figures and industrial background.

CIVIC CENTRE, Darwall Street. 1973–6 by *Stanley W. Bradford*, Walsall M.B.C. Director of Architecture (group leader *David Owen*). Buff brick with big piers, linked by a bridge to a similar block on the rear of the Council House, E.

GUILDHALL (former), High Street. On the site of the hall of the Guild of St John the Baptist, used for the assembly of burgesses by 1426. The medieval structure was rebuilt *c.* 1773. Present hall of 1865–7 by *G.B. Nichols*. A Venetian Renaissance palazzo, not large, but impressive: almost symmetrical, with projecting end bays. Ground floor all stone, with smooth rustication, upper floor red brick with ample stone dressings. Both storeys articulated by half-columns, Doric below Ionic, with swags. Windows of Sansovino's type: round-headed, with attached secondary orders of columns whose entablatures run between the main columns. Rescued from dereliction by *Gordon Foster*, 1985–6. Now a restaurant.

LIBRARY, Lichfield Street. 1906 by *J.G.S. Gibson*. A good counterfoil to the Council House immediately to the S. Brick, with a modest version of its Baroque centrepiece: segmental pediment, built-up top, projecting pedimented Ionic porch. Barrel-vaulted interior with dome. Attached to the N, the E.M. FLINT ART GALLERY of 1965 by *Austin T. Parrott*, Borough Architect, job architect *Julie Lindon-Morris*. A fine, understated design, a rectangular block faced in Portland roach on green slate piers. Glazed entrance and staircase link by *Baart Harries Newall (Mark Newall)*, 2004. SCULPTURE in front, Seaman Carless V.C., by *R.J. Emerson*, 1920: bronze bust on tapering pedestal.

ST MATTHEW'S HALL, Lichfield Street. Built in 1830–1 for the Walsall Subscription Library, which could not maintain it. The County Court from 1855 until the late C20; now a pub. Greek Revival, not large, but with a magnificent presence. Doric portico with fluted columns with noticeable entasis. The order is carried round the building, with pilasters. Cornice with full mutules. Doorcase and pedimented windows all with tapering architraves. Intrusive C21 glass porch. The architect is alas unrecorded, but the architraves strongly suggest *John Fallows*, whose Methodist chapel of 1829 was nearby. Rear wing on Leicester Street of 1869 by *T.C. Sorby*, for the County Court. Red sandstone, impressive Doric pilasters.

LIBRARY and POLICE STATION (former), Goodall Street. *See* Perambulation 4, p. 637.

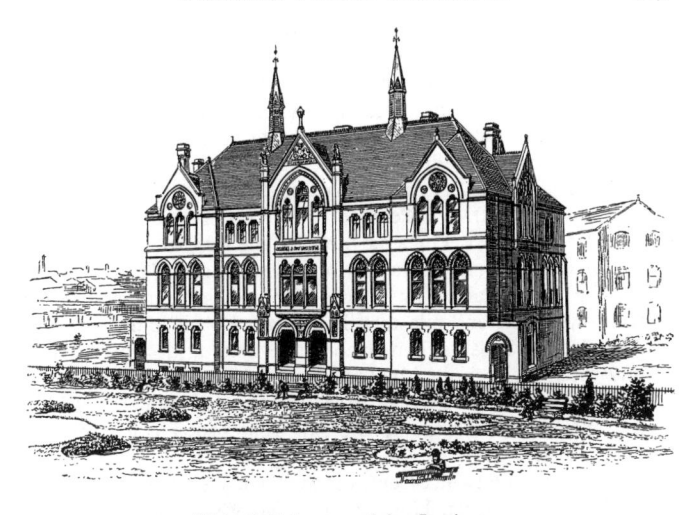

Walsall, Science and Art Institute.
Perspective engraving, 1889

SCIENCE AND ART INSTITUTE (former), Bradford Place. 1887–8 by *J.G. Dunn & F.W. Hipkiss*. Red brick and biscuit-coloured terracotta. Ruskinian Gothic, a child of J.H. Chamberlain's Birmingham School of Art (p. 133), but quite symmetrical, with three gables, the central one larger. Terracotta work by *King & Co.* of Stourbridge, including reliefs of plants on the central buttresses, and royal arms in the gable, modelled by Chamberlain's sculptor *Samuel Barfield*.

NEW ART GALLERY, Gallery Square. By *Caruso St John*, their first major work: won in competition 1995, built 1998–2000. The principal monument in the conurbation to the late C20 idea of a cultural institution as the anchor of urban regeneration (cf. the Lowry at Salford and Sage at Gateshead). Its main purpose was to rehouse the collection of Kathleen Garman, Jacob Epstein's second wife, and her friend Sally Ryan. A tall, square block, faced in overlapping pale grey terracotta tiles. Apparently random windows. An oblong turret projects upwards at the NE corner, inspired by the turret-like water tower of the Ravenscraig Works, Bridgeman Street (dem.). The tall mass was also intended to answer St Matthew's church on its hill to the SE. The building is aligned on the Town Arm canal at the W, but curiously disengaged. On this side, a single-storey extension. It is not an attractive or appealing composition: 'A tough building by uncompromising architects' (Andrew Saint). This is immediately apparent at the entrance, cut deeply in at the NE corner with the whole mass, including the turret, cantilevered above it. Large entrance hall with a concrete beamed ceiling, the start of an interior which fascinates but also frustrates. A broad flight of stairs rises to the first floor then stops, twists back and narrows. The Garman–Ryan collection occupies the next two floors, with small rooms set intriguingly round a double-height main hall. The upper level is reached by a partly concealed staircase, and at one point re-enters the main space in a corner balcony. The exhibition galleries above are reached, awkwardly, by a separate staircase, narrow and enclosed, from the first floor. Large, bare spaces with mostly clerestory lighting. A roof terrace at the top.

LEATHER MUSEUM, Wisemore. Two former industrial buildings, both of 1891. The s part, nearer the ring road, is by *H.H. McConnal* for J. Withers & Son, metalworkers allied to the leather trade, making bits, spurs and bridles. Segment-headed windows, basic end pilasters. The N, more basic, part is by *J.G. Nicholls*, for S. Llewellyn, who made belts and straps. Much renovated and rebuilt (the top floor of the s block completely) in 1988 by *Walsall M.B.C. Property Services*. They also added the entrance block facing the ring road, 1994 (job architect *Dave Priest*).

POST OFFICE, Darwall Street, s of the Civic Centre. By *Archibald Bulloch*, dated 1927. High-quality Neo-Wren. Linked round-arched windows, hipped roof of Westmorland slate with pedimented dormers. Single-storey sorting office, r., with circular windows.

WALSALL MANOR HOSPITAL, Pleck Road, 1 m. w. Largely rebuilt in 2007–10, by *Steffian Bradley Architects*. By the road approach the BOARD OF GUARDIANS OFFICES by *H.E. Lavender*, 1898, for the former Central Union Workhouse. Tudor Revival, like a grammar school, with an ogee-roofed tower.

BUS STATION, St Paul's Street. 2000 by *Allford Hall Monaghan Morris*. A big elliptical concrete canopy, pierced by circular lights, on branching steel supports. At the s, a glass box, also elliptical, houses offices. Bus stands like glazed pens. A difficult place for users and employees, and the canopy is aggressively close to St Paul's, E. To the N, the former TRANSPORT DEPARTMENT OFFICES, Neo-Georgian of 1937 by the Borough Engineer, *John Taylor*.

Colleges and schools

WALSALL COLLEGE, Littleton Street West. By *Dyer Associates*, 2007. Big rendered blocks with random strips of windows and a full-height sloping glass wall for the foyer.

QUEEN MARY'S GRAMMAR SCHOOL, Sutton Road. Founded 1554, in Church Hill. In 1815 it moved to Park Street. In 1850 its site was purchased by the London & North Western Railway, which paid for new buildings in Lichfield Street (*see* High School for Girls, below). The present school is of 1962–6 by *Robert Matthew, Johnson-Marshall & Partners*. A quadrangle with wings. Coming from the road to the NW, what hits you is the Main Hall, lit by windows in steep triangular gables tapering outwards to either side, like dragons' spines. To the r., the bell-tower reflects them in a wing top. Concrete podium and cantilevered porch (the dining hall, l., extended in the early C21). Boarded hall roof, dominated by the angled shapes of the top lights. Ground-floor corridors originally open, an interesting late example of an 'open-air' school. The rear SE range is the first-floor library, on pilotis, with tall thin windows. Interior altered, but with a nice flying stair. At the E the COVERED PLAY AREA, and beyond it the SWIMMING POOL, completed 1970. To the SW, contemporary former HEADMASTER'S HOUSE, a fine design: yellow brick, split-pitch roof, open-plan living area with sculptural fireplace. The most significant addition is the COLLIER CENTRE (sixth form) to the N, by *Rush Davis*, 2012, with an asymmetrical flying roof as a nod to the 1960s hall.

QUEEN MARY'S HIGH SCHOOL FOR GIRLS, Lichfield Street. The former Grammar School buildings of 1849–50 by *Edward Adams*. Educational Tudorbethan, a massive, dour block with four-centred ground-floor arches (infilled), tall mullion-and-transom windows, and big end chimneys. Flanking blocks with pairs of shaped gables, originally headmaster's and second master's houses. Later work in the same style, details and handling changing with time. In 1874–5 *Bidlake & Fleeming* built a parallel range to Upper Forster Street, behind. The piquant lodge house with its porch-tower tapering into a little cupola must also be theirs. Much by *Bailey & McConnal*: rear extension of the S end of the original range, 1890–1; range parallel to the 1874–5 work, set back from Lichfield Street, 1893–6 (W end heightened by *Jeffries & Shipley*, 1913); laboratories range attached to the lodge house, also 1893–6. In 1904–5 they linked the N end of the original buildings to the 1890s range, and added a block at the S, now facing the ring road. S of the C19 buildings in Upper Forster Street, plain Neo-Georgian block by *Jeffries & Shipley*, 1931–3. Fashionably free-form RICHARDSON BUILDING at the NE, by *Tweedale*, 2009.

BLUE COAT JUNIOR SCHOOL, Springhill Road. A charity school founded perhaps *c.*1656, certainly by the mid C18. In the early C19 it was in Digbeth. In 1859 it moved to a new building in St Paul's Close, by *Henry Cooper* of London, in E.E. style. The present buildings are of 1932–3 by *Jeffries & Shipley*, plain brick, symmetrical, with hints of Georgian and Jacobean. Cupola with little curvy gables. For the Infant School *see* Perambulation 4, p. 638.

BLUE COAT SECONDARY SCHOOL (now Academy), Birmingham Street. Present buildings by *Gordon Foster* (*Shipley & Foster*). Low-rise blocks of 1964–6, with blue-brick facings and Corbusier-style segmental concrete arches. Extensions S of the road, 1973–5.

WHITEHALL INFANT AND NURSERY SCHOOLS, West Bromwich Road, Caldmore. Former Board Schools by *Bailey & McConnal*, 1898–9, mixing Jacobean and Queen Anne. Gable with a lantern behind, tower with polygonal clasping buttresses, steep pediments and cupola. Rear range of 1902–3 facing Weston Road.

Leisure and parks

GALA BATHS, Tower Street. 1961 by *Austin T. Parrott*, Borough Architect. A simple clean shed with a forebuilding. Staircase nicely handled inside.

ARBORETUM, Lichfield Street and Broadway. Walsall's principal park. The site was flooded C18 limestone quarries. Laid out by the Walsall Arboretum and Lake Co. in 1873–4, designer *Mr Lowe* of Wolverhampton, with the pits turned into a lake; much extended E and SE. Original buildings by *Robert Griffiths*, 1874–5. Entrance with clock tower flanked by archways and lodges. Brick, with stepped gables everywhere. LODGE further up Lichfield Street in the same manner. After purchasing the park in 1884 the council added a BOATHOUSE, a half-timbered PAVILION by *H.E. Lavender*, 1902, and a BANDSTAND, 1924. Twee landscaping of 1931 E of the lake with channelled stream, bridges and boulders, now a period piece.

PERAMBULATIONS

The start for all is THE BRIDGE, a square since *c*.1815 when Walsall Brook was culverted; in 1855 described as 'the centre and the most strikingly beautiful portion of the town'. Present layout by *Eachus Huckson Landscape Architects*, 2000–1, with a FOUNTAIN by *Tom Lomax*. Back-to-back bronze discs and protruding heads, raised up steps. Just W, STATUE of Dorothy Pattison (Sister Dora) by *F.J. Williamson*, 1886, claimed to be the country's first commemorative public statue of a woman not of royal blood. Stiff figure, recast in bronze 1956. High plinth with good relief panels, including colliery and ironworks accidents (*see also* p.628).

1. Park Street, Townend and the New Art Gallery area

PARK STREET, running NW from The Bridge, impressively wide, became Walsall's main shopping street in the C20. It starts well with LLOYDS BANK, by *J.A. Chatwin & Son*, 1901–3, on the N corner. Italianate ground floor, more Wrenaissance above with two-storey pedimented canted bays recessed between giant Corinthian pilasters. After a few C18 or early C19 survivors, an Art Deco block of 1933 by *F.W. Woolworth Construction Dept* (*H. Wimbourne*). On the SW side, Nos. 35–39 by *Hipkiss & Stephens*, 1902, with Dutch gables. Diagonally opposite, flanking Butler's Passage, a shop of 1928 by *Jeffries & Shipley* with rounded oriels, and another with a giant Doric order by *Hickton & Farmer*, 1911. The former PRIORY HOTEL was a steeply gabled Queen Anne design by *E.F.C. Clarke*, 1876, the front redone by *Hickton, Farmer & Farmer*, 1928, with mock-timber put on the gables, and merry monks in mosaic. On the SW side beyond, late C20 regeneration, two long gabled Postmodern red and blue-brick ranges, and a similar gabled block closing the street. They are by *Temple Cox Nicholls*, 1994–6. Between the SW blocks, the RED LION, by *H.E. Lavender*, dated 1896 on the fanciest of Jacobean shaped gables, with classical maidens on the domed tops of the side-shafts. Name plaque with vines and grapes. Opposite, PARK PLACE, a podium-and-slab in maroon brick by *Ardin & Brookes & Partners*, 1968–71.

Now W into GALLERY SQUARE, with the overwhelming presence of the New Art Gallery (p. 629). First l. in front of the gallery, down MARSH STREET. On the r. curving flats by *Associated Architects*, 2002–5, responding to the Gallery with careful fenestration. (Beyond was the CROWN WORKS, by *Samuel Loxton*, 1889, with full-height pilasters, heavy cornices, round and segment-headed windows. Demolished *c.* 2019.) W of the gallery, the CANAL BASIN. On the N side the WHARF BAR, single-storey with a complex asymmetrical hipped roof, by *Sergison Bates*, 1996–8. Beyond it, a HOTEL by *shedkm*, 2012. Further W a long line of flats with spindly metal balconies by *S.P. Faizey*, 2010–12.

Now back to Park Street and N through the gap by Park Place. STAFFORD STREET runs N with early C19 survivors and the PRINCE pub by *Hickton & Farmer*, Jacobean-classical of 1902. Next to it Nos. 237–238, the earliest here, *c.* 1800, single-bay houses with segment-headed first-floor lintels. More early C19 development beyond Littleton Street (relief road). The narrow streets running W are worth a look. In Blue Lane East, small C19 workshops and ST PATRICK'S PRESBYTERY, by *H.T. Sandy*, brick Tudor with Arts and Crafts refinement, dated 1909. In Short Acre Street, a tall C19 former MILL. In Long Acre Street, the boldly lettered VICTORIA CORN MILLS, rebuilt for J.E. Dolman by *F.E.F. Bailey*, 1890. Three-storey mill with hipped roof, and lucam facing the narrow yard. Across r. is the warehouse and stables, with more inventive brickwork decoration. N again on Stafford Street, St Peter's church (p. 624). On the E side, the former PRESIDENT LINCOLN pub, by *H.E. Lavender*, 1897, with fancy lettering. Returning down Stafford Street, to the E on the dual carriageway the Leather Museum, Walsall College (both p. 630) and new commercial development, e.g. No. 100 by *Tyler Parkes Partnership*, 2010–12. N of the museum, a track leads to WISEMORE HOUSE, a three-bay villa probably of *c.* 1845–50.

Back to the start of Stafford Street, then W and NW again into GREEN LANE. Nos. 5–8 are by *G.H. Vernon Cale*, 1902, progressive Free Style, alas heavily rendered. Next, a former SALVATION ARMY HALL by *Alex Gordon*, 1902. Shouldered gable with ball finials, minatory inscribed panel. Back and W again into Wolverhampton Street, leading to Wolverhampton Road, with the former ALBION FLOUR MILLS, dated 1849. Four-storey mill r. (upper floors rebuilt after war damage); warehouse l., the two top floors of 1878 by *W.F. Markwick*. Central range straddling the former access road also late C19. Further W a former BOARD SCHOOL by *Samuel Loxton*, 1882–3, with a good High Victorian tower corbelled out to a big, steep roof.

2. Bridge Street, Lichfield Street and the civic area

BRIDGE STREET was built under an Act of 1766, bypassing the steep High Street. At the start, a Neo-Victorian CLOCK of 1983. S corner by *Inskip & Wilczynski*, 1979–80, post-Brutalist in buff brick. The pale stone TUDOR HOUSE next door is by *Jeffries & Shipley*, dated 1926. Neo-Georgian former Walsall Observer offices by *Farmer & Farmer*, 1931–2, with a bow and a raised centrepiece with gryphons. On the N side a consistent Late Victorian commercial row. HSBC is by *Bailey & McConnal*, 1898–9, its copper dome and big Baroque doorcase a good corner accent. It incorporates the classical STAFFORDSHIRE BANK of 1864 by *George Bidlake*, facing St Paul's Street, W. Then a six-bay range with giant arches by *H.E. Lavender*, 1902; two Gothic blocks, probably 1870s; another, with gables and a cut-off pyramid tower by *Lavender*, 1882; and IMPERIAL BUILDINGS, stone-faced, Jacobean-going-Baroque, with Dutch gables, by *F.E.F. Bailey*, 1891–2. The former Taylor's Music Shop, by *Samuel Loxton*, 1891, has its tall Italianate front covered in carvings by *John Lea* of composers' heads, musical instruments and musical biblical scenes. Last, a simpler *Loxton* range of 1890.

The junction here is a real urban focus. On the l., St Matthew's Hall (p. 628). Facing us, offices by *Bailey*, 1890, red brick and terracotta, curving round the corner, with a lovely wrought-iron crown. On the r. on the corner of Freer Street, LEICESTER BUILDINGS (OLD SQUARE), by *S.N. Cooke & W.N. Twist*, 1932–3. Cool Neo-Georgian, with a concave centre, a hint of Art Deco, and a Swedish-style clock turret.

Next SE up Bridge Street. On the S side minor C19 fronts, on the N side the former WALSALL CO-OPERATIVE SOCIETY central shop: the long l. part by *Jeffries & Shipley*, 1930–4, watered-down classical; the r. end the cut-down original store by *R. Worcester* of the C.W.S., 1910. Beyond, dour former WALSALL ELECTRICAL COMPANY offices, 1925, also *Jeffries & Shipley*; a half-timbered shop dated 1896 by *H.E. Lavender*; and three houses of *c.*1830–40. S side, a former leather factory of *c.*1870–5, with round-headed windows and polychromatic brickwork. KINGSCOURT, shops by *Bailey & McConnal*, dated 1904. Brick and terracotta. Beyond, TAMEWAY TOWER, a grey podium-and-slab of 1971–4 by *Crouch Butler Savage Associates*. Across Goodall Street, a curving block with pale blue curtain walling by *Scott & Clark*, 1958–60. Opposite, Nos. 77–89, low and Dudok-influenced, *c.*1935, and a rare survivor, a garage of 1936 by *Lavender, Son & Close*, with a quadrant curve and canopy on slim supports.

LOWER RUSHALL STREET runs NE here with much-restored survivors on the l. Nos. 6–8 were here by 1782. Pedimented doorcases, moulded lintels with stepped keystones. No. 15, *c.*1800, has a pedimented doorcase with reeded pilasters, flanked by Wyatt windows. Beyond, a five-bay house which has lost its doorcase, but a window with projecting cornice survives above. HOLTSHILL LANE runs up E. On the corner of Balls Hill the HATHERTON WORKS, a particularly good leather factory of 1901 by *Hickton & Farmer*. Free Style corner feature with window with elongated stone voussoirs, echoed in the doorway. At the top, the SPRING COTTAGE pub by *Thomas Pryce*, 1899, amateurish but memorable, with a Dutch-gable-topped window l., and an enormous ground-floor lunette r.

Returning to the E end of Bridge Street, ABLEWELL STREET runs s. The former BOROUGH ARMS is by *Hickton & Farmer*, 1905, a prestige job. Brick and orange-red terracotta, exuberant Free Jacobean, with big voussoirs. The interior retains a former smoke room with a good fireplace and seating in bays. Nos. 91–93, mangled shops by *H.E. Lavender*, 1889. The WATERING TROUGH pub is Tudor Revival by *J. Percy Clark*, 1926–7. Beyond, a fancily gabled row by *Lavender*, 1905. Opposite, the Methodist Central Hall (p. 625). Then on the E side TANTARRA STREET, with sheltered housing by *Foster, Ralphs & Mansell*, 1988–9, incorporating part of a former Board School dated 1872 by *George Bidlake*. Back on Ablewell Street, Nos. 72 and 69 (a pair) and 65–67, later Georgian.

Then back w down Bridge Street to St Matthew's Hall, and N up LICHFIELD STREET, constructed under an Act of 1830 (leases from 1831); in 1856 described as 'not only the most picturesque but the most fashionable portion of town'. On the w side the Council House and library (pp. 626, 628). Opposite, a rich but loose Jacobean block by *H.E. Lavender*, 1896. Beyond, many original buildings. Of 1831–2 No. 133, Cheltenham Regency in style, with projecting centre, and No. 132, the developer John Walhouse's own house, 1–2–1 bays with giant Corinthian pilasters. No. 131, slightly later; good Ionic porch. Nos. 129–130 are Gothic of *c.* 1870 with tower-like ends. Of *c.* 1831–2 on the w side Nos. 15–16 with paired ground-floor pilasters, and No. 18, a villa with a porch with paired Ionic columns. No. 23, slightly heavier Early Victorian. More of the same period beyond.

Across the big ring-road junction, Lichfield Street continues with the Arboretum, E (p. 632), and the High School for Girls, w (p. 631). Beyond the school, a consistent Early Victorian stretch. FODEN HOUSE has a top floor by *Bailey & McConnal* of 1910, when it was a nursing home. No. 58 has bay windows with angled Ionic pilasters, No. 72 has an odd Ionic porch with heavy cornice. Opposite, VICTORIA TERRACE runs SE, overlooking the Arboretum. Four attractive pairs of villas, called 'recently erected' in 1856, built for and probably designed by a surveyor, *Henry Farrington*. The first pair have the end bays recessed. Ionic porches breaking into miniature pedimental gablets; original bays, delicately done. At the N end of Lichfield Street, Butts Road runs w, with the BUTTS TAVERN by *Jeffries & Shipley*, 1935, and the former BUTTS SCHOOL (now flats), by *Bidlake & Fleeming*, 1879; Queen Anne, with a three-storey tower.

Back down Lichfield Street to St Matthew's Hall, and NW into LEICESTER STREET. On the l. a block by *Samuel Loxton*, 1890. Then, in this prestigious location, the grandest leather factory of all, that of W.H. Brookes, saddler and bridle-cutter, by *F.E.F. Bailey*, 1890, the three r. bays added by *Bailey & McConnal*, 1897. Projecting bays rise to decorative gables. Articulated by two-storey relieving arches, the structure clearly expressed by piers and cornices. Then Nos. 17–23 by *J.G. Nicholls*, 1894; Nos. 25–27, free classical by *Bailey & McConnal*, 1895; No. 29, less sophisticated, by *Loxton*, 1884. Here we reach Darwall Street. On the NE corner a former Post Office, severer classical, by *James Williams*, 1879. Turning N, on the E side the present Post Office (p. 630). Returning S, another free classical building, by *Hickton & Farmer*, 1903–4, then the former St Paul's VICARAGE by *Thomas Taylor*, 1885, and the church. Opposite, CAXTON CHAMBERS, with stuck-on timbering, by *S. Doddimeade Edmunds* of St Albans, 1899. The former IMPERIAL CINEMA has a striking front by *Hickton & Farmer*, 1914, its central arch enclosing a balcony supported on Doric columns. It started as the Agricultural Hall, 1869 by *G.B. Nichols*, altered 1879–80 by *Loxton*. Beyond, the TSB bank by *Hickton, Madeley & Partners* with *R.E. Cordin*, 1972, articulated by full-height slim brick piers. Here we return to The Bridge, SE.

3. South-west of The Bridge: Bradford Street

Developed by the 2nd Earl of Bradford. The street was cut in 1831. From The Bridge, on the W side the SADDLERS CENTRE by *R.G. Fernie & Partners*, 1978–80. Red brick façade, malls on two levels inside. Outside, SCULPTURES by *Tom Lomax*, 2000, part of The Bridge landscape scheme. Giant hand clasping a saddle, and conical pillar (S) with Walsall names. The ARCADE (E side) is of 1896–7 by *Jonathan Ellis*. A jolly front with upper gallery on piers, and iron columns with frilly brackets. Swirling iron balustrade. Square oriels above. It should be by the seaside. Inside, shops in the same style and a glass roof (restored after war damage) lead to a central octagonal space with grand arches and a dome.

Beyond, the street opens out into BRADFORD PLACE. In the centre the WAR MEMORIAL, a cenotaph by *H.H. Martyn & Co.*, 1921. On the N side the former Science and Art Institute (p. 629). On the E side the former TURF TAVERN by *Wood & Kendrick*, 1905, with shaped gables and shallow oriels. Brown and golden terracotta ground floor with Ionic pilasters and blue panels. This is the start of BRADFORD STREET, with Nos. 16–17 by *Bailey & McConnal*, 1903, the top with pediment and ball finials, refronted below. Beyond is a development by *John Eglington* (lease 1832), a fifteen-bay terrace, described in 1837 as 'very magnificent'. Three-bay end pavilions with giant Corinthian pilasters. The centre has strip pilasters but has lost much detail. Newport Street, l., with the former Stand pub, leads to LOWER HALL LANE, with more of c.1830, including Nos. 12 and 13 (stepped lintels, round-headed doorcases), Nos. 15–19 (doorcases with Composite columns), and two stucco villas opposite.

Back on Bradford Street, *Eglington* houses continue from No. 31, with giant pilasters. Diagonally opposite, the big gabled building with round-headed first-floor windows and lunette was a Spiritualists' hall, 1889 by *W. Jackson*. In Midland Road behind, a former PUPIL-TEACHERS' CENTRE of 1894–5 by *Bailey & McConnal*, with a French or perhaps Scottish Baronial rounded tower in the angle. No. 67 Bradford Street (w side) is the former SCHOOL BOARD OFFICES by *Samuel Loxton*, 1886, with tall upper windows and slim pilasters. Opposite, No. 36, a villa with later bays and doorcase. Nos. 44–47 are a good *Eglington* terrace with central pediment and Ionic pilasters.

Beyond, the street becomes WEDNESBURY ROAD. On the E side was the SISTER DORA HOSPITAL, opened in 1878. The only survivor is the tall former NURSES' HOME by *Bailey & McConnal*, 1902, with Baroque doorcase and all spiny with finials, again slightly Scottish. On the corner of Tasker Street, w side, the HENRY BOYS ALMSHOUSES, 1886 by *F.E.F. Bailey*, a pretty, long U-shape round a courtyard. Repeated motif of window architraves stepping up in the middle. Central and end gables with sculpture and cartouches. Opposite, the Glebe Centre (p. 626).

4. High Street, St Matthew's and Birmingham Road

s from The Bridge to the ancient town centre. First the side entrance to the Arcade (*see* Perambulation 3), with a giant arch. Beyond, the DIGBETH redevelopment. Masterplan by *Geoffrey Jellicoe*, 1959–60. Mostly rebuilt since c.2010; the 'loggia' separating it from High Street was a particularly sad loss. Shops by *Birch & Caulfield*, 1966–9, survive. HIGH STREET beyond is desperately sad. On the N side the BLACK COUNTRY ARMS occupies a three-bay house of c.1830–40, with the narrow building next door. This was the Dragon Inn. An agreement of 1769 required its rebuilding within five years with parapet and stone cornice. Full-height canted bay. Then the Guildhall (p. 628). Attached in Goodall Street, s, former POLICE STATION, 1865–7, part of *Nichols*'s Guildhall scheme. Projecting pedimented centre and ends; three-part windows, the central ones dignified by attached columns. No. 30, probably 1860s, with unusual recessed windows with concave pediments. Then the former LIBRARY (later School of Art), by *Nichols & Morgan*, 1859. Sansovino-style central window under the pediment. In George Street an apparently modest thirteen-bay terrace, of the early 1830s (incomplete in 1832), with a complex composition: two symmetrical five-bay units each with a projecting centre and a blank central round-headed recess, linked by a three-bay recessed centre. Back on High Street, modest C18 and C19 buildings, opposite an angular supermarket by *Brownhill Hayward Brown*, 2007–8.

The steep cobbled CHURCH HILL climbs up to St Matthew's church (p. 620), ahead. s of the Memorial Gardens in Birmingham Road, the WHEATSHEAF pub occupies two buildings, both looking late C18. Houses in Grove Terrace alongside include a block of four, built by 1832, with pilasters and central pediment. More of *c*. 1830 on Birmingham Road, e.g. Nos. 7–8, and No. 5 opposite. No. 16 is a Gothic villa of 1887 by *H.E. Lavender*. Up HANCH PLACE, s, THE TERRACE (now Blue Coat Infant School), a showy but mangled villa built in 1834 by John Forster. Big semicircular bow with giant attached Ionic columns, formerly with a dome; two bays either side with paired end pilasters. Nos. 1 and 2 beyond are of *c*. 1840–50, with round-arched windows. Mid-Victorian villas and Late Georgian cottages continue w along Birmingham Road.

CALDMORE

Pronounced 'Karmer'. An intricate area of mainly C19 housing s of the centre.

The best way from the centre is down BATH STREET. At the N end the modest brick HARPER ALMSHOUSES, dated 1878. The CEMETERY, now a bare green space, was consecrated in 1756. In Little Caldmore, w, a restored leather workers' cottage terrace of 1824. The BATH STREET WORKS ('The Old Foundry'), a long two-storey range with one taller section, once a house, is of 1877 by *James Adkins*, builder. Three-storey r. extension by *P. Adshead*, 1887. Beyond Windmill Street, the street becomes BATH ROAD. On the l. a former buckle works by *H.H. McConnal*, 1890, with windows in relieving arches. Opposite, a leather warehouse by *F.W. Cross*, 1897, again with relieving arches. Then St Michael and All Angels' church (p. 623). Down St Michael Street, w, the former VICARAGE by *Bailey & McConnal*, 1912. Further down Bath Road, E side, the former MARSH ALMSHOUSES, 1894, vigorous old-fashioned Jacobean by *H.E. Lavender*. In Little London, E, the WHITE LION pub by *Wood & Kendrick*, 1897. Eclectic, with classical doorcases but half-timbered gables. Hidden behind houses to the E (access off Highgate Road), a WINDMILL TOWER of *c*. 1770. Crenellated top of *c*. 1864–8, as a smoking room. Up Sandwell Street, N, DOVERIDGE PLACE, on the W side at right angles to the street. Tall three-storey mid-C19 house, smaller houses of *c*. 1781 adjoining.

Now back to Little London, and sw into WEST BROMWICH STREET. The stuccoed former CROWN AND ANCHOR pub on the corner looks Early Victorian. To the NW, the triangle of CALDMORE GREEN, with the semicircular-arched entrance of a former cinema by *Hickton & Farmer*, 1914, E side. On the NW side a remarkable survival, the WHITE HART. A substantial late C17 brick house, probably built for George Hawe (†1679). Very conservative in style: not a symmetrical composition, no hint of classicism. The main range runs SW–NE and has two shaped gables ending in semicircles, a local C17 motif (e.g. the Old Still, High Street, dem. c.1960). Two-storey canted bays. Single gabled bay of the same kind facing SW, two more behind. Projecting cross-wing, r., with a bigger gable. Inset two-storey porch. The bricks, red through to blue, are 2½ in. (6.4 cm.) thick – a sign of late date – laid in English garden wall bond. In the early C19, probably c.1814 when it became a pub, the cross-wing was extended and the gable rebuilt forward. In 1884 H.H. McConnal described the house as recently altered and restored 'almost out of recognition'. The chimneys and terracotta string courses are probably part of this. Of 1906 by *Hickton & Farmer* the cross-wing bay, and the r. end at the rear. Interior damaged by fire 1986, restored as flats by *Associated Architects* 1992–5. A rear staircase has original newels, one with a concave-sided finial, and some balusters. Roof of queen-strut trusses with trenched purlins.

PALFREY

S beyond Caldmore. Late Victorian and Edwardian terraces and 1920s cottage estates. The centre is on Milton Street, with PALFREY JUNIOR SCHOOL by *Samuel Loxton*, 1884. Long, with decorated gables and a spirelet. The BRADFORD ARMS, 1931–2, is by *Wood & Kendrick & Edwin F. Reynolds*. PALFREY PARK, E, is of 1886.

RAC CONTROL CENTRE, Brockhurst Crescent, by the M6. By *Gennaro Picardi*, 1989. Best seen from the motorway. A big monopitch roof, supported by masts, with a full-height angled and glazed front. Administration block by *Picardi Architects*, 2009.

BIRCHILLS

NW of the centre. At the N end of Hollyhedge Lane, a former NATIONAL SCHOOL of 1855, basic Tudor. At the crossing, N, the curving, boldly lettered former FOUR WAYS INN, by *Hickton & Farmer*, 1896–7. The jolly Jacobean ROSE AND CROWN in Old Birchills, NE, 1901, is a rare pub by the Methodist *C.W.D. Joynson*. Further E the Walsall Canal, with Walsall top lock immediately N. By it, a former TOLL HOUSE of 1841, a rare survival, with Gothick-glazed canted bay window; and a BOATMEN'S REST of 1900 by the canal engineer *G.R. Jebb*, for the Incorporated Seamen and Boatmen's Friend Society. The Gothick windows lit a chapel.

PLECK

1¼ m. SW of the centre, with interesting PUBS. The former BROWN LION, Wednesbury Road (No. 336), by *Hickton &*

Farmer, 1905, is Free Style with a super terracotta façade: green pilasters, yellow name panels, black base, grey gables. The former FOUR HORSE SHOES, Wellington Street, 1928, shows *A.T. Butler*'s ability to address an acute corner. The BRADFORD ARMS, Pleck Road, by *Jeffries & Shipley*, 1934, is sweetly tile-hung. THE GLOBE in Darlaston Road, W of the M6, is probably early C18: see the platband and the bowed roof. – Former POWER STATION (South Staffordshire Tramways Co.), Darlaston Road. Massive, pedimented, dated 1892.

OTHER OUTLYING BUILDINGS, EAST AND SOUTH-EAST

MAYFIELD (now Preparatory School), Sutton Road. Tall, square stuccoed villa of *c.* 1830. Greek Doric porch with unfluted columns and spider's-web fanlight. Narrow lights flank the door, and the reveals have Soanian incised decoration, details which suggest *John Fallows*. STABLES to the N.

HIGHGATE BREWERY, Sandymount Road. A complete group of 1898 by *Alfred Long*. Five storeys; single-storey repair shops to the r. To the S in Belvidere Road, HOUSES by *H.E. Lavender*. BEACONSFIELD HOUSE, 1881, has a pyramid roof; then a house with French cut-off pyramid-roofed tower, also 1881; then No. 24, Queen Anne, 1885.

CROSSWAYS, Highgate Road. By *Newton & Cheatle*, 1899. Much half-timbering, including a projecting two-storey porch. Altered as a nursing home.

No. 135 SKIP LANE, 2¼ m. SE. By *Lavender, Son & Close*, 1936. Remarkable in this area as an early Modernist house. White stucco, with rounded stair-tower.

ALDRIDGE

'Alrewic' in Domesday. Surviving houses testify to the prosperity around 1800. The area to the N developed as part of the Cannock coalfield from the C19, but the village remained small until the 1930s, when suburban development started to the S. It became an Urban District in 1934, united with Brownhills from 1966. In 1952 it was designated an overspill area for Walsall and Birmingham, and the centre was completely rebuilt.

ST MARY, The Green. C14 W tower of three stages with diagonal buttresses. Sandstone, also some limestone on the N and S faces. Ogee-arched W doorway, richly crocketed, 'carefully restored' in 1853. Tower arch with two plain chamfers and capitals only to the inner one. Re-set C13 S doorway, with fat angle rolls, no capitals, and torus base mouldings. Another, plainer, to the NE vestry, taken from the old N aisle. The rest looks Victorian outside, but is older. Stebbing Shaw (1798) shows a short nave

Walsall, Aldridge, St Mary.
Watercolour by J.C. Buckler, 1847

with S aisle, and a very long chancel. The N arcade confirms this. Octagonal piers, double-chamfered four-centred arches, plainly chamfered bases. The two W bays wider, their capitals with complex wave mouldings, representing a C14 Dec aisle. The E pier has a simpler capital, with nailhead, so here was an earlier, C13, N chapel. No chancel arch. The S arcade has a C14 W bay, but the other three are a crude imitation of 1841, when the aisle was extended E. The piers are brick underneath. This work is by *Scott & Moffatt*, i.e. the young *George Gilbert Scott*.* His exterior is better: two-light windows with reticulated and petal tracery, porch with diagonal buttresses. The major Victorian work was by *Anthony Salvin*, 1851–3. He widened the N aisle and extended it E by one bay; added a NE vestry; and rebuilt the C13 chancel larger, partly following its C14 E window with complex leaf and petal shapes. The N aisle E window has French Flamboyant tracery copied from St Jean at Caen, exceptional in Salvin's output (Jill Allibone). Unusual N aisle roof with collars, queen-struts and what look like crown-posts, but are bracketed to the ridge purlin and principal rafters. Chancel roof with arch-braced collars. SE vestry by *H.F.B. Close*, 1975, reusing 1841 windows. Reordering by *Ralphs & Mansell*, 1991 and 1995, with oppressive carpeting.

FITTINGS. FONT by *Salvin*, 1853. Caen stone, octagonal, with S-curved sides and Dec tracery. – PULPIT. Jacobean, with blank arches and stiff ornament. – REREDOS by *Jones*

---

*He said that his 'awakening attempts' of this period were 'as bad, or nearly so, as the rest'.

& Willis, 1936, old-fashioned. – BREAD CUPBOARD. With the usual balusters; inscribed 'TD 1694'. – STAINED GLASS. E window by *Henry Hughes* (*Ward & Hughes*), 1866, with nicely leaded landscape. N aisle E, 1853, and probably also chancel S (two, late 1850s), by *William Holland*, 1853. N aisle N, all *Ward & Hughes*, 1866–c.1870. S aisle, *Powell & Sons*, 1865, the artist for the Christ and St Peter medallions *Henry Casolini*. Also *Hardman & Co.*, 1948, and *Jones & Willis*, 1936. W window, 1885, and belfry window, 1865, by *Hardmans*. – MONUMENTS. Chancel S, defaced effigy under a wide arch with two plain chamfers. On the external S wall until 1852. Said to represent Nicholas de Alrewych, founder of the church, but the dress suggests a priest, and it looks early C14. – S aisle E, knight, C14, cross-legged, his feet on a damaged lion. Said to be Sir Robert Stapleton. – Thomas and Eleanor Lacy †1703 and †1705. Pedimented, with fringed drapery, but something like strapwork in the predella. – Katharine Leigh †1711, a rustic Baroque piece surely by the same sculptor. – Elizabeth Twyford †1727, cartouche with cherub head. – Rev. John Dolman †1746, with obelisk. – John Scott †1755, oval in an obelisk shape. – LYCH-GATE by *Fred T. Beck*, 1908.

ST MARY OF THE ANGELS (R.C.), Whetstone Lane. 1961–4 by *Eric Farmer*. Gabled narthex almost as tall as the nave, ritual S tower with low pyramid roof. Low passage aisles, with lintels, not arches. Tall clerestory windows with segmental tops and bottoms. The only up-to-date feature is the full-height concrete-framed sanctuary window. – REREDOS in *ciment fondu* and Westmorland slate. By *R.F. Kings* to a sketch design by *W. Stagg*, who also designed the STATIONS OF THE CROSS.

METHODIST CHURCH, Anchor Road. 1935–6 by *A. Brocklehurst & Co.* Gabled front flanked by pavilion wings, crushed by the canopy of 1994 by *Cornfield & Walsh*.

POLICE STATION, Anchor Road. 1937–9 by *K.L. Murray*, Staffordshire County Architect. Neo-Georgian.

ALDRIDGE YOUTH THEATRE, Little Aston Road. 1977 by *Ralphs & Mansell*. Neo-vernacular.

PERAMBULATION. The best area is around the parish church. In front, with The Croft to the S, Celtic cross WAR MEMORIAL by *G. Stretton & Sons*, 1919. W of the church, the MASONIC HALL, brick, the upper floor cantilevered. By *Barratt, Shaw, Wheeler* and *Lavender, Son & Close*, 1973. On Little Aston Road, NW, the MANOR HOUSE, probably early to mid-C18. Plain five-bay front, now stuccoed, done for Edward Tongue *c.*1813–16, almost certainly by *John Webb* who laid out a vanished front garden. Only the top-floor sashes are in their original form. In 1893 *F.E.F. Bailey* added the big *porte cochère* with paired Ionic columns and the pedimented aedicule with flanking pilasters to the window above. N of the church, the OLD RECTORY of 1826. A severe, elegant four-bay front. Off-centre Greek Doric porch. Later C19 COACHHOUSE and STABLES. Now SE from the church. MOOT HOUSE has a late C18 stuccoed front. Three bays, the outer ones with a Venetian, a tripartite and a lunette window and a pediment. Recessed centre with segmental porch on attenuated Doric columns. The unusual composition reflects older fabric, partly perhaps C17. Immediately SE, THE MALTINGS, an L-shaped former industrial building, perhaps late C18 or early C19, of more than one build. ERDINGTON ROAD runs S. On the W side, No. 2, a much-altered C18 brick cottage. Further S on this side, THE SHRUBBERY. Three-bay front, perhaps early C18: segment-headed sashes, platbands, pediment with lunette. Doorcase with Tuscan half-columns, probably late C18. Half-round staircase addition, S. Rear block perhaps earlier than the front; the Venetian S window must be a late C18 insertion. E along Little Aston Road, N side, ALDRIDGE COURT (formerly Portland House), c. 1864. Brick with stone dressings, the E front with canted bays and a frilly iron porch.

High Street, to the W, has nothing of interest. At the W end, the ALDRIDGE SHOPPING CENTRE by *Watson, Stokes & Partners*, 1972–3, then the ELMS HOTEL (currently THE CROWN), 1939, perhaps by *Jeffries & Shipley*, with bulky canted bays and Tudor chimneys. To the S on Anchor Road, past the Methodist church (*see* above) the former AVION CINEMA, by *Roland Satchwell*, 1938. Massive, with curved corners, streamlined bands, and big set-backs to either side.

OTHER BUILDINGS. ½ m. SW down Walsall Road, the WHITE HOUSE pub by *Jeffries & Shipley*, 1938. An eye-catching solution to the acute corner, with a whiff of Lutyens. Rounded corner, from which two chimneys rise through the tall dormered roof. To the E in Bosty Lane, a FARMHOUSE, probably C18, with mid-C19 detail (derelict in 2019). C19 barn in front; an C18 barn behind was burnt out in 2019.

In WALSALL WOOD ROAD, N of the centre, three houses. LEA HOUSE is Late Georgian, its doorcase with an open pediment. CEDAR COURT, further N, is the grandest house in Aldridge. Said to date from 1792, and certainly built by 1803. The main front faces E, away from the road. Three-bay, three-storey centre with Doric doorcase, two-storey two-bay wings. Tall staircase window, W, probably a modification. By the road, NW, C19 former STABLES. The centre block has a tall gable and chimneys, a two-bay loggia and a boldly detailed blue-brick string. SHUTT CROSS HOUSE (No. 70) has a good three-storey front of *c*. 1800 in dark red or purple brick. Sashes with moulded lintels, Doric doorcase with open pediment and fanlight. The rest perhaps early to mid-C18, with blocked segmental-headed windows and a platband.

W of the centre, large industrial estates. The only factory of note is the very large MCKECHNIE BRASS WORKS in Middlemore Lane, 1953–7 by *J. Alfred Harper & Son*. Buff brick with typical projecting window surrounds. Long two-storey block to the r. with strip windows; glazed hall at the l.

OLD IRISH HARP pub, Chester Road, Mill Green, 1 m. E. Three storeys, brick, perhaps early C18. Engulfed in late C20 extensions.

MOUND, ¼ m. NE of St Mary's, behind a cricket pitch. Probably a windmill mound, but it may reuse a prehistoric barrow.

BLAKENALL

Properly Blakenall Heath, with just a scatter of cottages until the interwar period. Mid-C20 municipal and private development was rapid. Some C21 replacements including low-rise flats.

CHRIST CHURCH, Blakenall Lane. By *Thomas Naden* of Birmingham, 1868–70, NW tower added 1881. Geometrical Dec, in small courses of local limestone, with Bath stone dressings. Big E and W windows with headstops, a recurring motif; circular clerestory windows. The tower has cusped lancets top and bottom, and quatrefoils in square recesses in between. A planned broach spire was not built, and the pinnacles look abrupt. Arcades with short fat circular columns on high bases. Transept arches separated by walling with again big sculpted heads, of the Evangelists. Richly moulded chancel arch. – Original PULPIT, FONT, CHOIR STALLS and PEWS. – REREDOS. By *C.E. Ponting*, 1891, from his restoration of Edington Priory, Wilts. (carver *Nathaniel Hitch*); installed 1951. Lush late Gothic with swirling foliage, and shields with the Instruments of the Passion. Gold-ground panels painted by *Eleanor Warre*, 1892, Crucifixion and figures associated with Edington, e.g. William of Wykeham, rather formal and hieratic. – S chapel REREDOS and PARCLOSE SCREEN, refined Gothic by *Cecil Hare*, 1919. – STAINED GLASS. Chancel E window 1876, N and S, with much clear glass, 1879, all probably by *Ward & Hughes*. Transepts definitely theirs, S 1879, N 1880, with characteristic streaky skies. Aisles, *Norgrove Studios*, 2005–10, sentimental. – PARISH ROOM, S. Plain Gothic by *H.E. Lavender*, 1888.

ST THOMAS OF CANTERBURY (R.C.), Dartmouth Avenue, Harden, ¾ m. SE. 1959–60 by *Jennings Homer & Lynch*. Large, Early Christian, in buff brick, with a campanile, but paper-thin, the end of an era. Not a basilica: the interior is a wide space with a flat ceiling. – Original FURNISHINGS. – STAINED GLASS. Apse by *Hardmans*, good, angular, richly coloured. – Contemporary PRESBYTERY behind.

COALPOOL METHODIST CHURCH, Coalpool Lane. 1896.

SURE START CENTRE, Blakenall Lane, S of Christ Church. By *West Hart Partnership*, 2004. An assemblage of big monopitch roofs, wavy rendered walls and curving timber-clad walls.

PUBS. KINGS HEAD, Ingram Road, E of the Sure Start Centre. Tudor, with wavy-roofed porches; by *Richard J. Barnes*, 1928. – NEW INN, Blakenall Lane. With much half-timbering. By *Ind Coope & Allsopp Surveyor's Department* (*William Blair*), 1937.

BLOXWICH

The largest community in the 'foreign' of the parish of Walsall (*see* p.618), in existence by *c*.1300. The earliest settlement was probably s of the present centre around the Pinfold and Old Lane. The High Street was built up from the late C18. From the 1850s growth was rapid. In the C20 it continued with council estates E and W, and later, private housing, N. Large-scale industry was concentrated to the W, where the Walsall to Rugeley railway opened in 1858. Little Bloxwich, ¾ m. NE, also mentioned *c*.1300, has disappeared as a historic settlement.

ALL SAINTS, High Street. Founded probably in the early C15, as a chapel of ease to Walsall. Rebuilt in 1791–2 by *Samuel Whitehouse*, with a W tower. Completely recast, retaining only the nave walls, in 1875–7 by *Davies & Middleton*. Eclectic Continental Gothic, effective and convincing, nearly all in brick. The Georgian box is visible, still unbuttressed. Sandstone is used only for the plate-traceried side windows. W tower with a Germanic pyramid roof and pinnacles. Inserted arcades in French C13 style, with massive circular columns. Plain brick arches. Galleries between with cusped arcading on the fronts. Wallshafts rise from the capitals to support the roof. E window with Geometrical tracery. – Chunky REREDOS. – Original PULPIT with portrait heads, circular FONT (both carved by *John Roddis*), and PEWS. – STAINED GLASS. E window, 1877, and chancel S lancet both probably by *Ward & Hughes*. Many nave windows by *Powells*, 1894–1905 and (s) 1929; also one s (kneeling soldier and Christ) by *Hardmans*, 1920. – WAR MEMORIAL, ornate oak tablet by *Advent Hunstone*, 1924. – CROSS, S of the church. Square base and tapering octagonal shaft with capital and ball finial, probably C17. – The churchyard is bounded on the E and S by a HA-HA.

ST JAMES, Old Lane. Mission church by *Bailey & McConnal*, 1904. Brick, with twin porches, just like a Nonconformist chapel.

ST PETER (R.C.), High Street. *Bucknall & Donnelly*'s church of 1869 was in C13 French style. Their three-sided E apse is still recognizable, and the nave clerestory with circular windows. The rest rebuilt in 1952–4 by *Jennings Homer & Lynch*. The W front is a cut-price cathedral in dingy maroon brick: twin towers with pyramid roofs, central gable. Arms of St Peter carved into the brick, an early work of *John Poole*. *Bucknall & Donnelly*'s arcades survive, with huge simplified capitals. But the internal character, grandiose and uninspired, is entirely of 1952–4. Wide aisles with panelled ceilings. – DECORATION. In the apse by Bucknall's friend *Alfred Stensell* of Taunton, 1869 (cf. Pontargothi, Carmarthenshire). Only one band of figures survives, without backgrounds, much restored by *Hardmans* in 1954. Draperies all theirs. – REREDOS, castellated Gothic, 1898. – Of 1954 the alabaster PULPIT and FONT, and

PEWS. – STAINED GLASS by *Hardmans*: apse 1898–1901 etc., aisles 1954.

ST CATHERINE (R.C.), Edison Road, 1 m. s. By *Jennings Homer & Lynch*, 1963. A gabled octagon with a spirelet.

METHODIST CHURCH, Victoria Avenue. Heavyweight brick and concrete box by *Hulme, Upright & Partners*, 1966. Domestic SUNDAY SCHOOLS to the w by *Johnson & Baxter*, 1910. (Previous chapel by *Loxton Bros*, 1864–5, on the High Street corner, w.)

POLICE STATION, Elmore Green Road. 2000–2 by *Mason Richards*. It replaced the delightful Queen Anne PUBLIC OFFICES of 1884 by *F.E.F. Bailey*.

WALSALL ACADEMY, Lichfield Road. *Richard Sheppard, Robson & Partners'* T.P. Riley School of 1956–61 has been replaced by an angular machine of 2003 by *BHM Architects Ltd*.

BLOXWICH C. OF E. PRIMARY SCHOOL, The Green. By *James Cranston*, 1861–2. Gothic, E-plan, the central gable mutilated. Former MASTER'S HOUSE, N, piquant Gothic, with half-hipped gables with swooping bargeboards.

ELMORE GREEN SCHOOLS, Elmore Green Road. E range (now a nursery) by *Samuel Loxton*, 1881–2, basic Queen Anne (l. end by *Bailey & McConnal*, 1894, to match). W range, simple Jacobean with a low, wide central shaped gable, by *H.E. Lavender*, 1902–3.

FRANK F. HARRISON SCHOOL (now Bloxwich Academy), Leamore Lane. By *Austin Parrott*, Borough Architect, 1966. Four-storey and lower blocks, much plum-coloured Staffordshire brick.

PERAMBULATION. The HIGH STREET, the A34 Walsall to Cannock road, runs due N from All Saints' church. A few remaining Georgian cottages and many Early Victorian buildings, all now shops. In front of All Saints, the WAR MEMORIAL, standard *Reginald Blomfield* Cross of Sacrifice, 1922. To the s is BLOXWICH HALL, *c.* 1835–40. Stuccoed. Gables with ball finials, but Tudor-style windows with hoodmoulds. Restored from near-dereliction 1985. BLOXWICH HOSPITAL beyond is a big brick classical house of *c.* 1850. On the E side of High Street going N, former CO-OP, dated 1904, by *W. Dagley*, brick and terracotta with a shaped gable; then the former GROSVENOR cinema of 1921 by *Hickton & Farmer*, 1921–2, white Neo-Grec. N of the church the former VICARAGE, originally a school as well. s block with hipped roof possibly C18; N wing, with heavy chimneys and pyramid-roofed tower, *c.* 1850–60. Diagonally opposite St Peter's church, the PRINCE OF WALES pub by *Hickton, Farmer & Farmer*, 1928, with a black-and-white gable flanked by curvy parapets..

WOLVERHAMPTON ROAD runs NW. On the corner with High Street a former MUSIC HALL, dated 1857, built and probably designed by *William Wootton*. Like a small Nonconformist chapel, with plain pilasters and a pediment. On the SE side facing the common, the SPOTTED COW pub, probably 1860s, and the TURF TAVERN, a little earlier: a Black Country terraced-house pub of a type now rare. A 'two-room drinker' with central entrance, the bays early C20 additions. Bar, r., complete with plain bar back, bar front and fixed seating. The smoke room has fixed seating with individual arm-rests. Brewhouse behind. Dominating to the NW among trees, multi-storey blocks by *Austin T. Parrott*, Borough Architect, 1962 etc.

Back to the music hall and N, High Street continues past the Primary School (p. 646). Here it opens into The Green (cf. Pelsall, p. 658). On the E side, PARK ROAD runs NE with the half-timbered former BULL'S HEAD pub of 1927 by *Hickton, Farmer & Farmer*, and the shell of a former Methodist chapel of 1832, in commercial use. Beyond, VIROLA COURT, good infill of 2007–8 by *Baker Goodchild*. Further N at the cross-roads the BELL pub of 1894 by *Samuel Loxton*, quite progressive, with half-timbered gables. Up Stafford Road, N, the former ROYAL EXCHANGE pub. Probably C18, with a platband. Billiard room of 1881, r. (*Sam Wootton*, builder). Compact two-storey former BREWERY behind by *F.W. Harrison*, 1913.

ROMPING CAT, Elmore Green Road. A superior pub of 1898 by *Hickton & Farmer*. Big timber-framed gable projecting from a brick elevation which curves round the corner. Deep plaster coving. Good etched glass. Original bar front with pilasters, bar back, seating (also in Smoke Room); off sales.

FIELD HOUSE (now golf club), Stafford Road, N. Built *c.* 1830 by Joseph Harrison, Austere brick, with hipped roof behind a parapet.

YIELDFIELDS HALL, off Stafford Road, 1 m. N. Probably early to mid-C18, for the Purcell family, recusants. A double pile. Five bays. Two storeys, and an attic above a platband. Segment-headed first-floor windows with moulded lintels. Later Georgian canted bays, C19 fretwork porch. N extension of 1891 by *Sam Wootton*.

SOUTH STAFFORDSHIRE WATER CO. OFFICES, Green Lane, 1 m. SSE. By the *Harry Bloomer Partnership*, 1985. Heavily chamfered brick, with a hipped roof.

BROWNHILLS

The 'Brown Hills' were originally an area in the parish of Norton Canes. Mining developed in the first half of the C19, and an urban centre grew up along the Chester road (now A452), after the opening of the South Staffordshire Railway in 1849. It had a Local Board from 1877, and was an Urban District from 1894, amalgamated with Aldridge in 1966 and into Walsall in 1974. Brownhills Common, NW, Newtown, NE, and Clayhanger, S, are still separate hamlets. In 1974 Pevsner said 'it is not an entity, let alone a town': still true.

ST JAMES, Church Road. 1850–1 by *G.T. Robinson*, construction supervised by *H.J. Paull & G.T. Robinson*. Local sandstone. Wide aisleless nave, short transepts and chancel.

Paired pointed windows with elongated cusping. Three-light E window with Geometrical tracery. Small, half-projecting W tower, with a big pointed niche between buttresses, now unhappily filled by the extension of 1991 by *Wood, Goldstraw & Yorath*. They also rebuilt the Gothic belfry and spirelet in 1983, with plain boarding. The nave has big arch-braced collar-beam trusses, the chancel a hammerbeam roof with decorative corbels. Iron ties to prevent subsidence. C14-style chancel arch with nook-shafts. – REREDOS by *Jones & Willis*, 1916. Old-fashioned Gothic. – PULPIT. 1885. – STAINED GLASS. Bright, well-drawn E window by *R.B. Edmundson & Son* of Manchester, 1869. St James with staff and shell, and scenes from the Life of Christ. Transepts, fragments by *T.W. Camm*, 1869. – Large brass PLAQUES, Rev. James Downes †1893, etc. – VICARAGE (former), E, 1855–8 by *Robinson*, and also with elongated cusped lancets.

CONGREGATIONAL CHAPEL (now a house), Coppice Lane. 1858. Still Georgian. Delicately moulded doorcase and windows.

METHODIST CHURCH, Silver Street. 1968 by *Birch & Caulfield*. Steeply gabled.

COUNCIL OFFICES (former), Chester Road North. 1882 by *John Siddalls*, Local Board Surveyor. Bald but forceful red brick Gothic. Many windows have segmental arches of paler brick, with stone sills, keystones and end voussoirs. Bell under a gable on the SE wall, for summoning the fire brigade. – CLOCK of 1911 on a wrought-iron bracket.

CENTRAL SCHOOLS (former), Chester Road North, opposite the Council Offices. 1892–3 by *G.H. Cox*, the finest building in the town. Queen Anne, friendly but picturesque. Corner entrance set at forty-five degrees, flanked by little five-sided apses (cf. Cox's Cape Schools, Smethwick, p. 585). The wings have shallow projections, then big semi-dormers. Unified by the hipped roofs on every part.

RAILWAY BRIDGE, S of Pelsall Road, ⅔ m. W. Carrying the former South Staffordshire Railway of 1849 over the canal. Cast iron, with decorative arcading along the parapets.

PUBS. SHOULDER OF MUTTON, Church Road. 1840s. Central entrance, later C19 bay windows. – HUSSEY ARMS, Chester Road North. C19, recast in 1935 by *H. Peter Hing*.

STATUE, on the traffic roundabout at the end of Lichfield Road, ¼ m. W. The most noticeable Black Country example of the early C21 fashion for colossal sculpture: a miner by *John McKenna*, 2006, 46 ft (14 metres) high, of faceted stainless steel, holding a pick and lamp aloft, and terrifying.

DARLASTON

The village was industrialized from the later C18. The 1840 tithe map shows a small 'TOWN', running S from the parish church along the present King Street. Rapid growth in the later C19, centred on nut- and bolt-making, developed in the C20 into heavy engineering, notably Guest, Keen & Nettlefolds and the local firm of Rubery Owen. Local Board 1869, Urban District 1894. Absorbed into Walsall in 1966, but still physically separate, divided by the River Tame and the M6. Factory closures have left it one of the poorest communities in the region.

The most interesting early building was the Octagon Methodist Chapel of 1790 (dem.). *A.P. Brevitt*'s office was here, and the town has good examples of his tough High Victorian Gothic. From the late C19 the architectural history is largely that of *Charles William Davies Joynson* and his firm, *Joynson Bros* (*see also* Wednesbury, p. 593), whose public buildings, houses and factories still define its character, moving from a free Norman Shaw manner to Neo-Georgian. Joynson was a devout Methodist, and the sad losses are his confident Free Style chapels: Kings Hill, 1907–8, and Slater Street, 1909. *Richard Twentyman*'s All Saints, Darlaston and Emmanuel, Bentley, traditional in layout but confidently Modernist in style, are two of England's finest 1950s churches.

PLACES OF WORSHIP

ST LAWRENCE, Church Street. The medieval building had a wooden 'steeple', replaced by the present slender W tower (cf. Wednesbury) in 1606. Refaced in Hollington stone, and the spire rebuilt, by *W.H. Bidlake*, 1906–7. Two-light windows with cinquefoil heads, as before. The spire is completely Bidlake's, with a dramatic open octagon supported by stepped buttresses.

The body of the church was rebuilt in 1806–7 by *Thomas Jackson* of Wolverhampton as a plain brick box with two tiers of windows to light galleries. The structure, with the window openings, is still there, recast and given a new chancel in 1871–2 by *A.P. Brevitt*. High Victorian Gothic. Rock-faced Codsall sandstone, Grinshill dressings. Plate-tracery windows, the lower tier with bold cream and pink voussoirs. Any number of headstops, and one upper window with serpents' heads growing out of the hoodmould. Cross-gabled vestries with big round windows, cinquefoils with surrounding quatrefoils. W meeting-room extension, with cottagey hipped roof, by *E.F. Reynolds*, 1931. Remarkable interior, at first sight all of 1871–2. *Brevitt*'s tall five-bay arcades recall e.g. S.S. Teulon at St Mary, Ealing: circular iron columns with spiral banding, brackets supporting the gallery fronts, and huge bell capitals with square imposts.* Chancel arch with paired columns on massive corbels with angels. Scissor-truss roof in the nave, tie-beam and kingpost in the chancel. Behind the arcades, however, the galleries are still those of 1806–7, with simple tiered seating. N vestry turned into a chapel by *Bidlake*, 1913–14, reordered 1989.

FURNISHINGS. PULPIT, Painswick stone and Devonshire marble, alas painted, by *Brevitt*. – FONT by *Peter Hollins*,

---

*They had 'iron foliage', removed by *Bidlake* in 1913–14.

1848. C13 style. – SCREENS all by *Bidlake*, 1908 and 1914, with elegant tracery motifs. – REREDOS by *Jones & Willis*, 1930. – N chapel REREDOS by *Bidlake*, 1914. – PANELLING with Baroque W doorway, 1933. Probably by *Bridgemans*, who extended it N and S as a war memorial, 1946. – PAINTING, W wall. Big Crucifixion, C19, signed '*Beebee*, Decorator, Bilston'. – STAINED GLASS. E window (four Evangelists), by *Wailes*, 1872; S aisle also 1872, probably theirs. N aisle, †1964, metaphysical poets. By *Brian Thomas*, with characteristic heavy hatchings. – MONUMENTS. Chancel. Rev. John Waltham, by *John Bacon Jun.*, 1816. Tablet with urn on a base with a relief of shepherd and sheep, and a church in the background. – Two by *Peter Hollins*: Richard Dorsett †1842 etc., draped tablet, urn, and souls rising above; John Smith Dorsett †1844 etc., with draped urn and foliage. – Nave, attractive tablets by *T. Wilmot* (†1800, †1810, †1818); also Jane Walton †1843 by *P. Hollins*. – Churchyard. STATUE, Mother and Child, in the Gill style, by *Thomas Wright*, 1958. – LYCHGATE and flanking benches by *Warwick Scott*, 1943.

ALL SAINTS, Walsall Street. 1951–2 by *Richard Twentyman* (*Lavender, Twentyman & Percy*), a very impressive church of an unusual date. It replaced one of 1871–2 by *Street*, destroyed by a landmine. Modernist, but of relatively traditional liturgical arrangement. Nave and chancel with a concrete frame and barrel roof with copper covering, articulated by the S tower at the join, a composition probably influenced by E.F. Reynolds's St Mary, Pype Hayes (p. 269). The nave has a grid of tall windows set high, divided by Portland stone mullions. Sussex bond brickwork. S porch with barrel roof echoing the nave, cross-shaped finial and sculpted architrave by *Donald Potter*. SE chapel with shallow-domed roof, formerly with a delightful six-pointed finial, projecting in front of the impressively blank E wall of the chancel. Linked CHURCH HALL, W, 1956. The nave has passage aisles punched through the piers, here with segmental arches, echoing the shallow barrel-vault. The chancel narrows in slightly but with no division. Complete contemporary FITTINGS, including PULPIT with Agnus Dei by *Potter* and black, tapering FONT with bold gilt intersecting ornament. – TAPESTRY on the E wall by *Stephen Lees*, 1975. – STAINED GLASS. A window by *Francis Skeat*, 1964.

ST ANDREW (former), Darlaston Road, Kings Hill. 1893–4 by *C.W.D. Joynson*. W front like a chapel, with pent-roofed extension containing paired porches. SW spirelet. Wide arch-braced roof. Converted to flats 2014.

ST GEORGE, The Green. *Thomas Johnson*'s lancet Gothic church of 1851–2 was demolished in 1975. In the churchyard, STATUE of St George and the Dragon, 1959, by *Thomas Wright*.

ST JOSEPH (R.C.), Church Street. 1980 by *Horsley, Currall & Associates* of Stafford. Hexagonal, in yellowy brick. Exposed girders and timber roof inside. – FONT. 1930s, probably by *E. Bower Norris*. Hints of Art Deco: wavy bands, fluted base. – PRESBYTERY of 1938, almost certainly by *Bower Norris*.

Methodist Church, Slater Street. Former Sunday School, 1910. Brick and biscuit-coloured terracotta. Late Perp tracery and chubby pinnacles. By *C.W.D. Joynson*, whose chapel was to the r.

Zia-e-Madina Mosque, Walsall Road. 2007 by *A. Ward*.

Masjid-e-Umar Mosque, Bills Street. 1986 by *R. Amin Zaki*.

PUBLIC BUILDINGS

Town Hall, Victoria Road. Built as the Local Board offices in 1887–8. A fine design by *Jethro Cossins* of Birmingham, in austere Queen Anne style. U-plan, deriving from C17 Midlands manor houses. Windows mostly with three-centred arches. Central cupola and an effective off-centre chimney. The main hall has a roof with large brackets and a central coved section raised on tie-beams and queenposts, all elegantly slim. The rest re-fitted 1951. Plain former Council Chamber in the w wing. Stained glass from St Andrew, Kings Hill (*see above*) by *Florence*, *Robert* and *Walter Camm* (*T.W. Camm*), 1919 and 1922.

Swimming Pool, Victoria Road. By *Hodder Associates*, 2001. Big curving asymmetrical roof. It replaced baths of 1938 by *Joynson Bros*.

Grace Academy, Herberts Park Road. 2013 by *Sheppard Robson*.

Rough Hay Primary School (now Woods Bank Academy), Rough Hay Road. 1940 by *G.C. Lowbridge*, probably designed by his deputy *A.C.H. Stillman*. Flat-roofed block, lower wings with semicircular ends.

PERAMBULATIONS

1. Town centre

In Church Street, N of the churches of St Lawrence and St Joseph, the Green Dragon pub, c.1830–40 (E side; altered), with rusticated entrance. S of St Lawrence, W side, tall Late Victorian shops. Immediately S, The Fold, a Late Georgian close with the former White Horse (now offices), of c.1810–20. Pilastered doorcase with rosettes on the capitals. Teardrop fanlight.

Now E down Victoria Road. On the S side the Swan pub etc., c.1830–40, with minimal window pediments. Pub ground floor c.1900. Beyond, the Town Hall. Opposite, the Rectory of 1835 by *Isaac Highway* was replaced in the late C20; the stable and coachhouse by *A.P. Brevitt*, 1872, survive behind, with a pyramid-roofed tower with lancet windows. Pardoe's Cottage, next, with bargeboarded dormers, must be c.1840. The Post Office by *C.W.D. Joynson*, 1912, is handsome Neo-Georgian. A cross-roads here with the War Memorial of 1927 by *Joynson Bros*, made by *Bridgemans*. Bronze soldier on tall granite pedestal. Rectory Avenue, N, developed

1898–c.1904, is all by *Joynson*, including the toy-like former JANE MILLS INSTITUTE of 1901, with half-timbered gable.

Victoria Road continues E through VICTORIA PARK, opened 1903. Part of the cutting of the former Darlaston branch railway is landscaped as part of it. Across the park to the SE, Late Victorian and Edwardian terraces in Avenue Road and Gordon Street, probably by *Joynson*. On its W side, CRESCENT ROAD, with the former POLICE STATION by *Joynson Bros*, 1899–1902, free Neo-Georgian. Pedimented wings with oculi, not quite symmetrical. Heavy entrance in the r. wing in the style of Norman Shaw's New Scotland Yard, with blocked half-columns and segmental pediment. Then ILMINGTON, a big gabled villa of c.1894, with timber-clad extension for Sure Start by *Baart Harries Newall*, 2005. At the end, WALSALL ROAD. Going W, on the N side, former MIDLAND BANK by *T.B. Whinney*, 1922. Darley Dale stone, with Doric half-columns set against smooth rustication. Here we reach the BULL STAKE, the traditional centre of Darlaston, now a bleak road junction. On the S side the former THREE HORSE SHOES pub, 1896. Beyond it at the start of Pinfold Street, a row of humble Georgian survivors. KING STREET runs N back to St Lawrence, the historic main street of the town, systematically wrecked since the 1960s. On the W side the PUBLIC LIBRARY, 1987 by *Walsall M.B.C. Director of Architectural Services*. On the E, one brick and terracotta survivor of c.1900.

2. Kings Hill

The worthwhile part is down OLD PARK ROAD, ½ m. SE. KINGS HILL SCHOOL is by *Joynson Bros*, 1931–2. Neo-Georgian with paired pedimented centrepieces. In JOYNSON STREET opposite, No. 1 was the caretaker's house of Kings Hill Board School, 1887 by *Edward Pincher* (dem.). Pent-roofed porch in the angle, big semi-dormers, bargeboards with circular ends. In FRANCHISE STREET, to the E, No. 2, the severe former All Saints vicarage, with blue-brick bands, by *A.P. Brevitt*, 1874. Nos. 17 and 19–25, with timber gables, are almost certainly by *Joynson*, 1910.

OTHER BUILDINGS

SALISBURY PRIMARY SCHOOL, Station Street, ½ m. ENE, amid good C19 and C20 industrial streetscape. Plain gabled blocks dated 1910, by *John Hutchings* or his assistant *G.C. Lowbridge*.

ATLAS WORKS, Salisbury Street, ½ m ENE. Office range by *Joynson*, 1919 etc., gabled features with Baroque doorways but castellated oriels above them. Machine shops also early C20; bigger gables.

JAMES BRIDGE AQUEDUCT, Bentley Mill Way, 1 m. NE. Typical early canal period: heavy brick superstructure with two low arches, dated 1797.

RUBERY OWEN OFFICES AND INSTITUTE (former), Booth Street, ½ m. N. 1912 by *Joynson*. Pinkish brick and creamy-grey faience. A grander version of his police station (*see* left), more Baroque in its massive pedimental end gables with oculi and coupled pilasters. Off-centre main entrance, nice pedimented doorcases.

WHY NOT INN, St George's Street. 1937–8, almost certainly by *Scott & Clark*: see the characteristic corbelled chimneys.

HERBERTS PARK TAVERN, Forge Road. 1937, probably by *Farmer & Farmer*. Nice brick detail.

BENTLEY

A large low-density estate developed by Darlaston U.D.C., 1948–56. Architect, *Thomas Galbraith* of *Scott & Clark*. The main road, QUEEN ELIZABETH AVENUE, runs N from the old Walsall–Wolverhampton road, with ample grass verges. Plain brick pairs, terraces and occasional three-storey maisonettes. Further N, shops with curving end blocks. On the E side, a large natural mound, reached by the narrow CAIRN DRIVE: the site, now marked by a cairn, of the Lane family's BENTLEY HALL, famous for sheltering the fugitive Charles II in 1651. Rebuilding or refronting gave it an Early Georgian façade of five bays, with depressed arches to the windows. Made unstable by coal mining – including a pit shaft, complete with winding wheel, on its front lawn – it was demolished in 1929. On the mound now, the finest building in Bentley.

EMMANUEL, Cairn Drive. 1954–6 by *Richard Twentyman* (*Lavender, Twentyman & Percy*), perhaps his best church. Fully developed Modernism with Continental references, but still with a traditional plan. Built as a memorial to Alfred Ernest Owen of Rubery Owen, paid for by his family. Like All Saints, Darlaston (p. 650), it expresses the conservative but confident spirit of the 1950s Church of England.* SW hall, small NW chapel shaped like an elongated hexagon, and NE vicarage. Concrete frame faced in golden-buff brick laid in Sussex bond, now very grey. It looks sprawling on plan but is held firmly together by the W tower. This is influenced by German 1930s work, with four pairs of off-centre belfry openings and a N batter nicely reflecting the asymmetrical roof of the nave with its single N aisle. Long lines of windows, low on the S with small lights higher up.

The interior is airy and light, with the aisle divided by slim four-lobed concrete piers. The sanctuary steps in very slightly. Specially chosen materials: Painswick stone entrance wall in the porch, Hornton stone floor here and in the sanctuary, nave floor of sapele-wood blocks and ceiling of fluted African walnut boards. E wall panelled in walnut, a pattern of alternating

---

*The Owen family were 'low' Anglicans, and Sir Alfred Owen, A.E. Owen's eldest son, hosted large church youth camps on his estate at New Hall, Sutton Coldfield.

reeded and plain strips with raised panels. CROSS and other FURNISHINGS of African mahogany. – PULPIT with bowed polished stone front. – FONT. Tapering Portland stone bowl on slate pier.

On the Wolverhampton road, s side, BENTLEY HOUSE, five bays, perhaps mid-C18 in origin but the front now *c.*1820 with Tuscan doorcase and lintelled windows. Further w, the CEMETERY of Willenhall U.D.C. Twin chapels by *Benjamin Baker*, 1898, minimal Gothic.

MOXLEY

An industrial village which grew up in the C19 on the borders of Bilston, Darlaston and Wednesbury, along the Birmingham to Wolverhampton turnpike. It became a parish in 1845. Its modest centre was almost completely destroyed in the late C20 for a big junction on the Black Country New Road.

ALL SAINTS, Church Street (E of the road junction). 1850–1 by *William Horton*. Tall, wide aisleless nave and short chancel. Pairs of lancets, nicely treated inside with big tall detached shafts. Four-light Geometrical E window. Collar-beam roof. NW tower and spire by *A.P. Brevitt*, 1877, whose vigorous manner shows in panelled buttresses, big blunt pinnacles, and curious stepped gablets enclosing the clock faces. W gallery with arcaded front. – PULPIT coming out of the wall, FONT with Perp-style top but hanging arches. – REREDOS and tile panelling in the chancel by *Mintons*, 1884. – STAINED GLASS. E window by *Hardman*, 1877, with saints in characteristic circles of foliage. Others by *Samuel Evans*, 1884, †1897 (nave N).

In HIGH STREET, w of the junction, WAR MEMORIAL, gabled cross with enclosing wall. By the *Bromsgrove Guild*, 1922. Further w, No. 64 (N side), the former VICARAGE, by *Horton*, 1858. Tudor, L-shaped, angle porch. No. 46, mid-C19 classical.

GREAT BARR

Built up mostly between *c.*1920 and the 1960s. Now subdivided between Walsall (including the old village, with church and Hall), Sandwell and Birmingham (SE). The boundary is mostly the M6. All is included here.

ST MARGARET, Chapel Lane. A chapel of ease to Aldridge until 1849. Rebuilt 1677 and 1786, spire added *c.*1800, perhaps by *John Nash* (*see* Great Barr Hall); the buttressed base of the medieval tower survived. The present church is largely a rebuild of 1862 by *W.D. Griffin*. Small courses of roughly tooled limestone – not very attractive – with sandstone dressings. The style is early Dec. Trefoils and quatrefoils everywhere in the tracery. Arcades with circular piers and double-chamfered arches; deeply undercut foliage capitals, all different. Chancel arch with big angel corbels. Boarded roofs with arch-braced trusses, decorated in the chancel. Big NE vestry by *F.T. Beck*, 1906–7. The tower was rebuilt round an older core in 1893, perhaps by *Beck*; C18 brickwork survives inside. The same C13 style, but sandstone ashlar, solid and impressive. Nice recessed spire. Large, poor S extension by *J.N. Barratt*, 1971–2. – Rich FURNISHINGS, with much panelling, mostly by *Bridgemans*, some as late as 1949. – FONT by *Griffin*, 1863, wineglass-shaped but eight-sided. Spired COVER by *Advent Hunstone*, early C20. – PULPIT by *Walter Tapper*, 1895. Alabaster, with Dec tracery. – Wrought-iron SCREEN by *Hardman, Powell & Co.*, 1911. – CHOIR STALLS by *Hunstone*, ornately carved. – REREDOS, 1907. By *Bridgeman*; also the STATUES on the E wall. – PAINTING. S chapel. Virgin and Child, Italian C15, much restored. Traditionally attributed to Baldovinetti, but probably from the circle of *Filippo Lippi*: see the characteristic flattened faces. – STAINED GLASS. A full late C19 and early C20 set, marred by some bad restoration. E window, †1884 by *Burlison & Grylls*; S chapel E and S also theirs, †1904. S aisle from E, *Mayer & Co.*, †1859, patterned glass 1871, †1887. W wall *Hardman*, †1908. N aisle from E *Swaine Bourne*, 1894; *Mayer*, †1886; then *Hardman*, †1902, 1910 and W wall 1910. – WAR MEMORIAL, N of the tower. By *Harvey & Wicks*, 1921. Tabernacle on a chamfered square column.

ST BERNARD, Broome Avenue, off Hamstead Road. 1972–3 by *Shipley & Foster*. A period piece. Big mansard roof with deep eaves, folded in an asymmetrical V, and broken by a heavy spire like a rectangular box sliced diagonally in half. It looks dangerous.

HOLY NAME OF JESUS (R.C.), Birmingham Road. By *E. Bower Norris*, 1938. A blocky, cubic front in pale grey-brown brick, with cinema-style fins. Ritual NW tower with stepped-in top. Aisles tactfully added 1957. Five-sided apse. Interior much altered. Perfunctory steel piers for arcades. Ceiling with streamlined plasterwork. – PRESBYTERY, 1954, behind.

GREAT BARR METHODIST CHURCH, Birmingham Road, diagonally opposite. 1868 by *Samuel Loxton*. Limestone, with sandstone dressings. Geometrical gable window, plate tracery down the sides. – Mansard-roofed HALL by *A. Brocklehurst*, 1938.

Q3 ACADEMY, Wilderness Lane. 2008–10 by *Ellis Williams Architects*. A contrast to Grove Vale (below). Red cladding. Unwelcoming, even menacing, angled glass front divided by timber piers.

GROVE VALE PRIMARY SCHOOL, Monksfield Avenue. By *H.T. Cadbury-Brown*, 1961–4. A friendly group of low linked pale-brick blocks, running along a hill. Octagonal assembly halls surrounded by classrooms, with much play of chamfered shapes, obtuse angles and angled roofs.

GREAT BARR HALL. Disused since 1978. A ruinous and melancholy house and landscape. The core is probably mid-C17: the 'Nether House', below the 'High House' or Old Hall. From 1777, (Sir) Joseph Scott enlarged and re-clad it in Strawberry Hill Gothic. Much enlarged in the 1830s for Sir Edward Scott, including a large service wing, E, with a tower. In the 1850s *George Gilbert Scott* built two lodges for Sir Francis Scott, and shortly before 1863 a three-bay S extension, meant as a chapel but used later as a billiard room. From 1914 the house became part of the Great Barr Colony (*see* below). Service wing demolished in the late C20. What remains is mostly 1830s, heavy Late Georgian Gothic, rendered, two storeys with remains of castellated parapets. The repeating motif is an ogee-headed window with a Tudor-style hoodmould and cusping or panelling between. N porch with partly surviving attached piers. The W front, facing the lake, has a projecting centre of three wide bays flanked by single-storey wings with big canted bay windows. The main block behind is the C18 house, refaced. The interior has gone. *Scott*'s S block is of red brick boldly diapered with blue – the manner of his St Michael, Crewe Green, Cheshire (1857–8). Three big windows rising into gables, one missing. Circular window with cuspings in the N gable.

The PARK was landscaped from the mid C18, centred on the valley SW of the house. To the NE a large KITCHEN GARDEN, created in 1744; wall partly surviving. The southern Big Pool was created at about the same time, and there was a cascade

Walsall, Great Barr, Old Hall.
Engraving by R.W. Basire after Stebbing Shaw, 1801

on the river. Major work by *Humphry Repton* followed Joseph Scott's return in 1797, after having leased the house. The Upper Pool was created at this time, and the Walsall (NW) and Handsworth (S) drives.* Weddall's map of 1830 shows a typical Repton landscape, with belts and clumps of trees framing and hiding views N, W and S from the house. From 1914 the estate became the Great Barr Colony, a mental hospital; architect *Gerald McMichael*. Its main buildings were E of the Hall and the Upper Pool, with others to the N and NW. Nearly all demolished from 2004 and replaced by pseudo-traditional housing. In 1970 the M6 cut off the SW end of the park. The POOLS remain, surrounded by dense woodland. To the NW some open land hints at Repton's schemes. Three LODGES also survive (*see* below). Survivors of the Colony just a heavily altered Voyseyesque LODGE and hefty GATEPIERS on Queslett Road, and one ruinous 1930s hospital block just SE of St Margaret's church.

OLD HALL, Old Hall Lane. Substantial C17 timber-framed house on a compressed H-plan. Entrance now on the N. The original main front faces E. Two big jettied gables and a short central range, all with diagonal bracing. One row of close studding below. Ground floor underbuilt in brick all round. The N side is all square panelling. Porch probably C19; brick NW wing, probably C18. The W side has more square panels and a timber-mullioned stair window, SW. Central chimney with six diagonal shafts. (C17 panelling in the SE room.) Long BARN to the N, mostly C18 and C19 brick, but with C17 timber framing on the N side.

RED HOUSE, Hill Lane. 1841, for Robert Wellbeloved Scott of Stourbridge. Handsome red brick with limestone dressings. A compact block with hipped roof and porch with coupled Ionic columns. The symmetry is broken by the big service wing, full-height and with chimneys as bold as the main house.

The old VILLAGE is very small. NW of the church the former GIRLS' SCHOOL of 1830. Single-storey range with filled-in arcading. The cottage behind, l., was the SCHOOL HOUSE. To the NE, THE OLD FARM HOUSE, probably C18. The Walsall drive of the Hall crosses the road just W of the church. AVENUE LODGE, much altered, is probably by *G. G. Scott*, pre-1858: see the diapered brickwork. The former VICARAGE in Vicarage Rise, off Chapel Lane, ¼ m. SW, is of 1847, said to be by *Ewan Christian*. Red brick banded with blue, big star-shaped chimneys, mullion-and-transom windows. ST MARGARET'S C. OF E. PRIMARY SCHOOL, just W, 1854–5, is similar in style, but much extended and rendered. A little spirelet. Just N, on the A34, the BEACON HOTEL, by *Jeffries & Shipley*, 1939–40.

---

*According to Stebbing Shaw, Repton 'furnished a variety of sketches...(and) very hastily and injudiciously planted several beautiful knolls...which the more considerate eye and hand of the skilful owner has since entirely removed'. Repton's partner *John Nash* designed a GARDEN GATE by the church in 1801, and *Scott* added a BOATHOUSE (both demolished). Around 1825 *Robert Lugar* designed a greenhouse for the flower garden SE of the Hall, which was not built.

Neo-Georgian. The clean, parapeted front (nastily timber-clad) shows the late date. Further up the A34, WALSALL (or SHUSTOKE) LODGE, definitely *Scott*, dated 1854, alas now rendered. With steep gables and chimneys tapering at the top and with little gablets.

NEWTON ROAD, S of the M6, towards West Bromwich. No. 23 (BARR HOUSE) is Late Georgian. FAIRYFIELD HOUSE, tucked up a drive further W, is delightful Strawberry Hill Gothic. Five bays, hipped roof. Central first-floor window an ogee. Porch with slim triple shafts and quasi-Doric frieze with quatrefoils. Similar doorcase on the E elevation. They derive from a plate in Batty Langley's *Ancient Architecture Restored and Improved* (1741–2). Perhaps *Thomas Farnolls Pritchard* of Shrewsbury, who made designs in a similar manner in the 1760s–70s, was involved. ½ m. W, BISHOP ASBURY'S COTTAGE, simple C18, associated with Francis Asbury (1745–1816), one of the first two bishops of the Methodist Episcopal Church of America.

HANDSWORTH LODGE, Queslett Road. Strawberry Hill Gothic of Joseph Scott's time, for Great Barr Hall (*see above*). Ogee-arched former doorway and side lights enclosed in a decorative arch of tracery; ogee windows. Originally some way N; rebuilt here in the 1830s.

PINFOLD FARM, Pinfold Lane, ½ m. NE. L-plan C17 timber-framed house, now rendered, with mullioned windows with hoodmoulds. These and the Gothick chimneys look early C19 but are reportedly mid-C20.

COXFOLD FARM, ¾ m. NE. Also probably C17 and timber-framed, partly replaced in brick, but all rendered. Lobby-entry plan.

WAR MEMORIAL on Barr Beacon, 1¼ m. NE. 1933 by *Batemans*. Octagonal, on baseless Doric columns.

PELSALL

A former mining village, memorable for its hourglass-shaped common, nearly ¾ m. long.

ST MICHAEL AND ALL ANGELS, Church Road. Rebuilt in 1843 by *George E. Hamilton*, replacing the medieval church, a chapel of ease to St Peter, Wolverhampton, in Paradise Lane. Basic wide nave with lancets, buttresses with gabled tops, queenpost roof. N vestry and former S porch treated like transepts. W tower added in 1860 by *Philip Horsman* of Wolverhampton, builder, 'Monumental and Architectural Sculptor', and later the major donor to the city's Art Gallery. Spindly pinnacles, blue-brick bands, decorative spherical-triangle windows. It looks like an ornament for a mantelpiece. Chancel, 1889 by *T.H. Fleeming*, a cheap brick job. Oversized angular S extension by *Duval Brownhill*, 1983. – REREDOS by *Jones & Willis*, 1936,

GREAT BARR · RUSHALL 659

alabaster, very old-fashioned. – Original REREDOS of 1843–4, N wall. Crocketed gables. – TABLE, small, C17, from the old church. – PULPIT, 1883. – STAINED GLASS. E window, 1905, and chancel S, 1912, by *Hardmans*. Nave, all by *Arthur S. Walker* (*G. Maile & Son*), 1951–4. – MONUMENT. Thomas Wright Dickinson †1859, by *Morgan* of Birmingham. Ornate Gothic, with relief head. – Rich Victorian TOMBS W of the church, especially Phoebe Bloomer †1860, by *J. Blunt*, and Edward Barnett †1896 and family, with portrait medallion.

METHODIST CHURCH, Chapel Street. 1970 by *Ralphs & Mansell*. Brick with clerestory lighting and a hint-of-Ronchamp curved end. – SUNDAY SCHOOL, 1866 by *Loxton Bros*, red brick with blue and cream detail, the bellcote cut down.

VILLAGE CENTRE, High Street. Library, surgeries and clinic by *Baart Harries Newall*, 2013. A long, low brick range with projecting roofs and a central clerestory, playing with symmetry but avoiding it; the entrance canopy continues r. as a shop fascia.

FINGERPOST, cross-roads of Lichfield Road and Norton Road, N. Early to mid-C20, the arms replaced 2007. Original pointing hands above each.

On the W side of the common, the CORNER HOUSE, *c.* 1800, with decorative lintels, spoked fanlight and canted bays. No. 1 CHURCH ROAD, S, must be contemporary, Nos. 2–4, humbler and a little earlier. In STATION ROAD, No. 44, the former STATION INN, late C18. Canted bay window with modillion cornice. Nos. 68–74, a terrace of cottages up a side lane, must be *c.* 1849. Red brick, blue-brick trim.

PELSALL HALL, Paradise Lane and Mouse Hill, ½ m. W. C18 outside, with plain sashes, but the three parallel steeply gabled ranges suggest older fabric.

CANALS. The WYRLEY AND ESSINGTON CANAL of 1794–7, engineer *William Pitt*, runs around the N edge of the village. W of the Norton Road is Pelsall Junction, with a C19 cast-iron FOOTBRIDGE. The CANNOCK EXTENSION CANAL of 1863 runs due N, under the contemporary FRIAR BRIDGE. Beyond, also of *c.* 1863, a pair of CANAL COTTAGES on the E side, and derelict STABLES, W, with two-storey tack-room and hayloft attached, N. The Wyrley Canal runs W from the junction to PELSALL WORKS BRIDGE. Shallow iron arch dated 1824, inscribed by the *Horseley Coal & Iron Co*. It served Pelsall Ironworks, founded in 1832 immediately N.

RUSHALL

The ancient village, with a hall and church group which goes back at least to the C13, is tucked away at the N end of Leigh Road, now on the NE fringe of Walsall town. It is probably of Saxon origin, and there is an earlier moated site N of the Hall.

The modern settlement, quite separate, ¾ m. N, was centred on Rushall Square, now a busy road junction.

ST MICHAEL THE ARCHANGEL, Leigh Road. A church is recorded in 1220. Rebuilt by *James Cranston*: church 1854–6, SW tower and spire 1867–8. Small blocks of grey limestone. 'Rogue' Gothic, in the manner of S. S. Teulon or E. B. Lamb, with a Low Church plan: cruciform, wide nave, short chancel. Tower and spire have a flowing, dynamic outline because the buttresses run straight up into the broaches. One tier of big lucarnes, with what look like square Corinthian piers. The rest early Dec style, with cusped lancets. E and W windows with quatrefoils. NE vestry by *Hickton & Farmer*, 1905. Large S extension by *Brownhill Hayward Brown*, 2000. – FONT. C13. Circular bowl with vertical bands of dogtooth. A wavy stem with three-leafed foliage round the base. – PULPIT and PEWS by *Cranston*, 1856: also former COMMUNION RAIL (N transept) and arcaded COMMUNION TABLE (W end). – PAINTINGS, E transept walls and above the chancel arch. 1906 by *E. R. Frampton*. A long line of angels and, below, the four archangels, separated by a band of foliage. Art Nouveau-style trees with slim trunks. Subdued colours. Figures going beyond Burne-Jones towards Symbolism. – STAINED GLASS. E window by *Ward & Co.*, 1857. C19 and early C20 glass, S transept and nave.

CHRIST THE KING, Lichfield Road. Tin mission church of 1887, built for mineworkers.

RUSHALL HALL, Leigh Road, E of St Michael. Much of the limestone enclosure WALLING survives of a fortified manor house, probably late C13 or C14. The GATEHOUSE is later, with the coat of arms of the Harpur family who held Rushall

Walsall, Rushall Hall.
Engraving by R.W. Basire after Stebbing Shaw, 1801

c. 1430–1540. Stebbing Shaw showed it in 1795 with three storeys and a castellated top. Only the ground floor, part of the first floor, and the S wall of the second floor remain. Very flat segmental arch, perhaps restored. Part of a blocked mullion-and-transom window above, probably C17 repairs after Civil War damage. E arch also segmental, C15, with a hoodmould. Evidence of buildings to N and S, including remains of fireplaces. The HALL sits along the N wall, in the NW corner. A C14 arched entrance just to its S. Victorianized, with fake timbering, but probably C17. The shorter parallel N range is Early Victorian: see the windows. – MOUND, NW of the Hall. Barrow, probably prehistoric in origin. A later burial is suggested by the discovery of human bones and Saxon coins at a shallow depth on one side. – FARMHOUSE, SW of the gatehouse. Probably C18, with one whopping tie-beam truss. NE of it a BARN of limestone rubble, c. 1700. Now ruinous, but retaining two tie-beam trusses.

CHAVASSE ALMSHOUSES, Rushall Square, ¾ m. N. By the builder *Cresswell* of Walsall, 1886. Twisty chimneys, tile-hung gables, scrolling inscription. Immediately N, Nos. 153–157 Lichfield Road, mutilated late C17 or early C18: hipped roof, platbands, rear wings.

STREETLY

C20 suburbia NW of Sutton Park. The Methodist church (1909–10 by *Ewan & J.A. Harper*) and Little Aston Park estate are in Staffordshire.

ALL SAINTS, Foley Road East. Modest Dec, brick with stone dressings. S aisle (intended as such) by *F.T. Beck*, 1908–9. His usual quirky details, e.g. the turret above the porch and the buttress coming through the roof to the E. Nave and chancel added to match by *Wood, Goldstraw & Yorath*, 1953–4. NW hall by them, 1957, poorly extended along the N side to 2005. Arcade without capitals. Beck's aisle roof is Jacobean style. – FONT of 1909, PULPIT 1937, PEWS 1954. – STAINED GLASS. E by *Evans & Co.*, 1955. Modest early C20 glass in the chapel.

ST ANNE (R.C.), Bridle Lane. Plain hall by *Joseph Lynch* of *Jennings Homer & Lynch*, 1959.

CREMATORIUM, Little Hardwick Road. 1984 by *C. Savage*, in succession to *S. Bradford*, Director of Architecture, Walsall. An arrangement of monopitch roofs.

WALSALL WOOD

Historically, a detached part of the 'foreign' of the parish of Walsall, outside the borough. The village grew in the C19 with nailers and chain-makers, then coal mining (Walsall Wood Colliery, 1873–1964). In Brownhills Urban District from 1894, Aldridge-Brownhills from 1966. A mixture now of late C19 terraces, council housing and recent private development. The centre hardly registers as such, on the bleak wide A461.

St John, High Street. 1836–7 by *Isaac Highway*, but all we now see is his thin w tower and gable. Blue brick, with lancets. The nave is engulfed in extensions by *H.E. Lavender*: s aisle and short sanctuary 1886, N aisle 1895.* Red brick with paired lancets, the arches with a kind of billet moulding. Arcade columns of cast iron, with almost classical capitals with two orders of flat leaves and small volutes, odd and rather old-fashioned. s porch with a sharp glazed gable, and w rooms wrapping round the tower, by *Duval Brownhill*, 1986–7, aggressive and confusing. They stripped the interior. – STAINED GLASS. E window 1925 by *J.H. Walker Ltd*, very old-fashioned. N aisle, *Arthur S. Walker* of *G. Maile & Son*, 1953; *Claude Price*, †1964 (two); *Alan Younger*, 1969, mostly abstract, but a miner and dog at the bottom.

Walsall Wood Methodist Church, Lichfield Road. Former Sunday School, 1908 by *T.W. Sanders*. Brick, with a few fancy Free Style details. The chapel, of 1891, stood to the N.

In High Street only the Master's House of the former National School of 1859 by *James Cranston*. The rest demolished 2012. Brick, Gothic, with mullion-and-transom windows. Zigzag blue bricks in the relieving arch.

Castle Old Fort, Castlebank Plantation, Castlehill Road, 1 m. E. A univallate hill fort, probably early Iron Age, oval, 500 ft (170 metres) across from N to S, all now in a wood. The bank stands up particularly high on the S, near the road, and the E. The ditch is prominent on the S also. Secluded within, a house of 1936 by *Kenneth Hutchinson Smith*, reusing old timbers, said to be C17 ones from Lymore Hall, Montgomery. Jettied, with tall panels above and recessed central entrance. Octagonal angle posts with brackets and dragon beams. Hipped roof with the higher gable of a r. wing. It looks like an Essex or Suffolk building, not a Welsh Borders one. Extensions by *Andrew Gifford*, 2008–11, timber-framed. Some way sw, a small outbuilding with a re-erected cruck frame. Further E down Castlehill Road, Nos. 197 (formerly two cottages) and 203, much-altered Georgian.

---

*Lavender produced schemes in 1885 for a complete rebuilding, with sw tower.

SHELFIELD

1 m. sw towards Walsall, almost contiguous with Rushall. A hamlet which became an industrial village, now dull and suburban.

ST MARK, Green Lane. 1965 by *A.G. Stanley*.
ST FRANCIS OF ASSISI (R.C.), Mill Road. 1932 by *Wilfred Mangan* of Preston. Modest but nicely detailed. Front with pediment and recessed centre.
SHELFIELD METHODIST CHURCH, Lichfield Road. 1906–7 by *T.W. Sanders*. Gabled hall with Free Style detail. Hard red brick.
SHELFIELD COMMUNITY ACADEMY, Broad Way. Mostly rebuilt 2010–13 by *Sheppard Robson*. Metal-faced.
FOUR CROSSES INN, corner of Green Lane and Mill Road. Early C19. Early C19, with a lovely early C20 painted panel sign.

WILLENHALL

'The town of locks and keys', in the words of its historian N.W. Tildesley. An ancient settlement in the parish of Wolverhampton, 'Winehala' in Domesday. Lock-making was established by the C16. It remained small-scale until the late C19, carried out in workshops at the rear of houses, often in appalling conditions. The Children's Employment Commission of 1843 described 'regular menageries...a pigsty under the workshop window...the accumulated dust and dirt of the floor'. Poor hygiene led to a devastating outbreak of cholera in 1849. Large factories were built from the end of the C19, including Squires, Legge, Parkes ('Union') and Vaughan (later part of Yale and Towne). The only survivor is Assa Abloy. Willenhall had a Local Board from 1854 and was an Urban District from 1894. Included with Walsall since 1966, but divided from it by the M6, it seems depressed and unloved, though a townscape scheme of 2012–15 has improved the centre.

PLACES OF WORSHIP

ST GILES, Walsall Street. 1866–7 by *W.D. Griffin*, the third church on the site. The medieval church, a chapel of ease to St Peter, Wolverhampton, was 'half-timber' with a 'middle aisle'. A tower was added in the C16. The rest was rebuilt plainly in 1748–50. Griffin's church is in rock-faced Codsall sandstone. An ample plan, with long chancel and N transept. Geometrical tracery. NW tower projecting to the W, an amendment to Griffin's first design, which retained its predecessor. What one remembers is its unusual silhouette, produced by angle buttresses with steep set-offs, stopping short of the parapet. Prominent triangular hoodmoulds over big two-light belfry windows. Matching S transept and S chapel by *Benjamin Baker*, 1896. NE vestry by

Batemans, 1927. The interior has broad aisles, and arcades with a wide bay for the transepts, then three normal bays. C13 style, with alternating circular and four-lobed columns, and naturalistic foliage capitals, a Griffin feature. Roof with high collars and arched braces with big quatrefoils. Narrow W bay on the N side with a strainer arch, by *Batemans*, 1927, when a gallery was removed. *Baker*'s S chapel arcade outdoes Griffin with spreading foliage capitals. – FONT. 1867. – By *Batemans*, 1927, the PULPIT (carver *Advent Hunstone*), the canopied SEATS at the W end, and the tall openwork FONT COVER. CHOIR STALLS perhaps also theirs. – STAINED GLASS. E window by *Clayton & Bell*, 1867. Lady Chapel E by *Hardmans*, 1933, a Fra Angelico Annunciation. S transept S perhaps *Clayton & Bell*, c.1897; single lights E and W by *Holland*, 1867. S aisle, style of *Percy Bacon*, †1894.

ST ANNE, Ann Street, Spring Bank, ½ m. N. By *W.D. Griffin*, the N aisle 1858–9 as a mission chapel, the rest 1861. This explains the odd plan with the aisle wider than the nave. Built, uniquely, of small blocks of dark Pouk Hill dolerite, with dressings of Brewood and Codsall sandstone. Early Dec tracery. W porch-tower with ugly C20 flat roof. It had a short spire. Simple Bath stone arcades and collar-beam roofs; curving upper braces in the nave, cusped ones in the aisle. NE vestry and organ chamber, with internal arcade, by *J.P. Baker*, 1904. – PULPIT 1902, FONT and REREDOS 1907, ALTAR RAILS 1909, all by local builders *W. Hopcraft & Son*. – SCREEN by *Nicholson & Lord*, the Walsall organ builders, 1906. – STAINED GLASS. By *A.K. Nicholson Studio*, E 1946, S 1947, N aisle 1948 (signed *Gerald E.R. Smith*).

ST STEPHEN, Wolverhampton Street. By *Wood, Goldstraw & Yorath*, 1977–9, replacing a church of 1853–4 by *Griffin*.

ST MATTHIAS (now MAHA SHIV SHAKTI MANDIR), Fletcher Street, Shepwell Green. 1907–8 by *J.P. Baker*. Brick hall with nice tapering bellcote and odd castellated porch.

ST MARY (R.C.), Leveson Street. 1906 by *A.J.C. Scoles* and *G. Raymond*. A studiedly plain pinky-red brick hall. Paired lancets and two-step buttresses along the sides.* Four-light Geometrical ritual W window arranged 1–2–1. – Original frilly REREDOS. – GALLERY, 1925, rather crude. – STAINED GLASS. Chancel N and S windows by *Hardmans*, 1964. – Attached PRESBYTERY by *Scoles*, 1897–8.

TRINITY METHODIST CHURCH (now LIFE AND LIGHT CHRISTIAN CENTRE), Union Street. Of 1837, with a spectacular front of 1864 by *Edward Banks*. Pedimented centre, projecting corner towers with tapering eight-sided Baroque domes. Two orders of pilasters, Doric and Corinthian with flat leaves, run all round. Also *Banks*'s the large rear transepts. The entrance part is now a hall, but the rest of the interior survives. The side galleries on fluted iron columns must be of 1837. Everything else is 1864. Tall piers support three-centred arches,

---

*It replaced a church of 1864 in Hall Street by *E.W. Pugin*.

linked by smaller arches between. Large PULPIT with CHOIR GALLERY behind, and PEWS above and below, going far back in the transepts. – STAINED GLASS. In the choir gallery, designed by *T.W. Camm* and made by *Chance Bros*, 1864.

LITTLE LONDON BAPTIST CHAPEL (now MOUNT OLIVE APOSTOLIC CHURCH), Temple Bar. 1851. Probably by *Henry Hall*, who built a minister's house (dem.) of 1852. The incoherent façade looks like a builder's design. The best part is the Greek Doric doorcase with pilasters flanking half-columns. A small central pediment was removed c. 1970. Virtually complete interior with galleries, BOX PEWS (including some large square ones) and an elegant PULPIT with reversed consoles at the base.

MOUNT CALVARY BAPTIST CHAPEL (now NEW TESTAMENT CHURCH OF GOD), Upper Lichfield Street. 1862 by *Charles Manton*. Temple front in an attractive rustic Doric. Triglyphs only over the pilasters. Thin shouldered pediment, eared segment-headed window below. Intrusive octagonal porch added and original interior destroyed 2018.

PROVIDENCE BAPTIST CHAPEL (closed), New Road. Dated 1879. Gabled front with a Baalbek arch outlined in coloured brick, enclosing a tablet, so perhaps by *William Keen* (cf. Providence Chapel, Rowley, p. 576).

PRIMITIVE METHODIST CHAPEL (now LIGHTHOUSE MISSION), St Anne's Road, Spring Bank. 1873 by *Benjamin Baker*. Small, with a big octofoiled circular window.

METHODIST CHURCH (former), Froysell Street. Of c. 1856. Still a Georgian pilastered box, but the blue-brick cogging gives the date away. Now a factory.

GURU NANAK GURDWARA, Walsall Road. 2006 by *Reade Buray Associates*, consulting engineers.

PUBLIC BUILDINGS

COUNCIL HOUSE (now PUBLIC LIBRARY), Walsall Street. 1934–5 by *Gordon Kidson* with *G.A. Waite*, U.D.C. Surveyor. Neoclassical of a hard kind. Brick and grey faience. Three-bay centre with raised attic and small pediment. Big, almost industrial, steel windows. Set back r., former FIRE STATION. Behind, BATHS also by *Kidson* with *Waite*, 1938–9.

WAR MEMORIAL, Field Street. Obelisk of 1920 and flanking name plaques of 1922 by *G.A. Waite*.

POLICE STATION, John Street. 1937–9 by *K.L. Murray*, Staffordshire County Architect. Neo-Georgian.

ST GILES' C. OF E. PRIMARY SCHOOL, Walsall Street. 1907 by *Johnson & Baxter*. Red brick. Big windows, delicate Jacobean detail: shaped and Dutch gables, tapering cupola.

CENTRAL SCHOOLS (former), Stafford Street. 1883 by *Benjamin Baker*. Queen Anne, early for the Black Country, handled rather heavily. Big tower with steep pediments above the clock faces. A variety of gables with fluted pilasters, and big windows with aprons. Converted to offices by *Tweedale*, 2020.

PORTOBELLO BOARD SCHOOL (former), Somerford Place. 1877–8 by *Benjamin Baker*. Picturesquely gabled, with two-light windows. Housing conversion by *Reedesign*, 2007–9, with an awkward glazed tower top.

PERAMBULATIONS

The centre is an intricate network of narrow streets. A fire of 1659 destroyed the medieval town. A few Georgian survivors, and a lot of minor Early Victorian, three-storeyed with architraved upper windows. Willenhall must have been prosperous *c.*1830–60.

1. The Market Place, east and south-east

The MARKET PLACE is really a street running N–S. Ungainly but memorable Jacobean CLOCK TOWER of 1892 by *John Roddis* of Birmingham, a talented sculptor, clearly not so competent a designer. Diagonally set corner lamp brackets. Walking N, the interest is on the E side. No. 34 has an early C19 front perhaps masking an older structure. No. 33, set back, is of *c.*1750–60. Pedimented doorcase, lintels with fluted keystones. THE BELL (No. 32) is said to date from 1660. Large Georgian canted bay, heavy C19 shopfront with big consoles. Rear wing with an upper casement, probably C18. At No. 29 a heavy classical three-storey block of *c.*1860. S of the clock tower, the square is closed by a plain three-storey Georgian range (No. 44 etc.). Further S, Nos. 45–46, five bays, mid-C18. First-floor windows with shaped lintels and keystones with leaf decoration. Giant pilasters at the ends. Right-hand bay added *c.*1900.

Beyond, a junction where the Walsall to Wolverhampton turnpike of 1748 meets the road from Bilston. On the NW corner the former HSBC Bank of *c.*1900 with a corner turret and spire. The former DALE CINEMA, SW, is by *Hurley Robinson*, 1932. Low curved front, with grooved piers rising above the parapet in an Art Deco way. Now a pub. Immediately S in Bilston Street, DALE HOUSE, later C18, very smart, with rubbed brick lintels and an Adamish doorcase with slim colonnettes and fan tympanum.

NEW ROAD runs W from the junction, an improved turnpike of *c.*1818. On the N side an original TOLL HOUSE (No. 8), with Gothick window surviving in the W wall. Most development took place in the 1840s–50s. Nos. 11–14, N side, Tudor Revival. 100 yds W, the former CASTLE pub, with giant corner pilasters, here by 1851. Nos. 71–76 (S side), heavy classical, must be *c.*1870. No. 54 opposite, the LOCKSMITH'S HOUSE MUSEUM, *c.*1840–50, was a family lockmaker's, Richard Hodson & Son, until 1972. Typical Early Victorian doorcase. E gable with chimneystacks linked by upwards extension of the end wall, a characteristic Black Country feature. The house retains its plan with staircase in the middle against the W wall, and many original details. Above the rear kitchen is the firm's office; behind, single-storey varnish and stamping shops. Across the yard, the main workshop. The ground floor is the smithy, with corbelled-out hearths (cf. Mushroom Green chainshop, Netherton, p. 533). Assembly room above. Towards the road, a former stable. Nos. 55–56, much altered, were another lockmaker's.

WALSALL STREET runs E from the junction. On the N side the ROYAL GEORGE, probably of 1847. Heavy central doorcase, smooth ground-floor rustication. The CROWN pub is probably Georgian, refaced, incorporating a smaller cottage r. On the S side the library and baths (p. 665). The COUNTY pub is by *W.A. Hutchings*, 1924, with his typical pedimented doorcases. Then St Giles's church and school (pp. 663, 665). Opposite, on the corner of Doctor's Piece, the CHOLERA GRAVEYARD of 1849. Small railed-in space with trees, desperately sad. Brick niche with tablet recording 292 deaths. To the E, the PRINCE OF WALES pub, brick Tudor, dated 1939, probably by *Jeffries & Shipley*. Behind it a C19 lock works. No. 54 is a three-storey Late Georgian house and workshop; No. 53, *c.* 1830–40, has a doorcase with delicate garlands. Opposite, Nos. 31–32, Early Victorian with semicircular pilastered bays. No. 40 is a much-altered toll house, formerly circular. Old photographs show a stone ground floor and Gothick windows. MANOR HOUSE is a much-extended villa of *c.* 1840–50. To its E a Tudor villa of the same period.

2. East and north-east of the Market Place

First down CROSS STREET, with Late Georgian survivors, e.g. Nos. 1–3 (N side). Nos. 27–29, S side, are of *c.* 1850–60 with decorative quoins. N into UPPER LICHFIELD STREET, where the W side has the former LION HOTEL, *c.* 1900 with half-timber gable. Then a blunt, tall Late Victorian warehouse, and a lower range of *c.* 1910 with timber gables and canted oriels. Nos. 14–15 are former lockmakers' houses, Late Georgian (shown on a map of 1838). Then Mount Calvary chapel (p. 665). The WORKER'S REST pub is mid-Victorian, with heavy Tuscan doorcase. Then W down Union Street, past Trinity Methodist Church (p. 664). At the end, STAFFORD STREET. The THREE CROWNS pub, 100 yds N, is probably Late Georgian; Nos. 69–70, with Free Style detail, are of *c.* 1905, perhaps by *J.P. Baker*. Then the former TIGER pub, Early Victorian, altered. To the S, much-altered C18 cottages, and the former PLOUGH pub of *c.* 1905 (W side), Free Style with an arty octagonal turret. On the SW corner, a low C18 or earlier building with remains of pilasters to the upper floor, facing a row of gabled shops of *c.* 1880–90.

OTHER BUILDINGS

VICTORIA WORKS, New Hall Street, NE of the centre at the corner with Stringes Lane. Early C20, with large upper workshop windows. Opposite, a modest former CO-OPERATIVE shop of 1871 by *George Bidlake*. Stone quoins, blue-brick bands. Staffordshire knot and clasped hands above the entrance.

SHORT HEATH

Amorphous suburbs and factories to the NE, around the A462. An independent Urban District until 1934. Its coal-mining past has disappeared.

HOLY TRINITY, Coltham Road. 1854–5 by *William Horton*. C13 style, with plate tracery. Geometrical E and W windows. W and N doorways with windblown stiff-leaf, in gabled surrounds. SE bell-turret. The fun is the sculptural decoration: beasts on hoodmoulds, masks on gable-stops. Plain arcades inside. – Original PULPIT, FONT, PEWS. – ALTAR by *Jones & Willis*, 1917. – STAINED GLASS. E window by *A.J. Dix*, 1905.

METHODIST CHURCH, Coltham Road. 1881–2 by *Benjamin Baker*. Brick Gothic. Ritual NW tower, ending in an octagon and short spire. Two-light windows. Three-sided apse. Interior much altered in 1952 and 1966. The best thing is the roof, with scissor trusses, diagonal braces and huge arched braces almost like raised crucks.

WILLENHALL LAWN CEMETERY, Bentley Lane. CHAPEL by *Johnson & Giles*, 1967–9. Steep-pitched roof, the rafters projected down as flying buttresses.

The centre is at Lane Head, around a bridge over the Wyrley and Essington Canal of 1792–7. The BRIDGE TAVERN, horribly rendered, must be contemporary. Just s, the former SHORT HEATH BOARD SCHOOL of 1880 by *Benjamin Baker*. Gothic, with contrasting plain and half-hipped gables. Windows with plate tracery, bright red voussoirs and relieving arches. Further s in SANDBEDS ROAD, the simple domestic former BROWN JUG pub by *J. Percy Clark*, 1938.

On COLTHAM ROAD a surviving area of miners' houses (dates 1880, 1895) and the cottage-like DUKE OF CAMBRIDGE pub, probably C18.

NEW INVENTION

Further N again. A bleak shopping precinct (*E.E. Bannington*, U.D.C. Architect, 1961–3), faces bleak flats on the site of Squires lock factory, demolished *c*.2006.

PRIMITIVE METHODIST CHAPEL, Lichfield Road. 1898 by *Johnson & Baxter*. Old-fashioned, with pinnacled buttresses halfway up the gable. Window with frilly Dec tracery.

NEW INVENTION INFANTS' SCHOOL, Cannock Road. 1908 by *Hutchings* (or *Lowbridge*). Simple blocks, much extended.

CITY OF WOLVERHAMPTON

Wolverhampton city centre	670
Collegiate Church of St Peter	672
Other places of worship	677
Public buildings	681
Perambulations	684
Other buildings	695
Bilston	696
Churches	697
Public buildings	698
Perambulation	699
Other buildings	701
Bradley	701
Blakenhall, Ettingshall and Parkfield	702
Bradmore, Finchfield and Castlecroft	705
The houses of Kenneth Hutchinson Smith	706
Other buildings	708
Bushbury	708
Chapel Ash, Tettenhall Road and West Park	712
Churches	712
Public buildings	713
Perambulations	714
Other buildings	719
East Park, Moseley and Portobello	720
Fallings Park and Low Hill	721
Fallings Park Garden Suburb	722
Low Hill	724
Graiseley and Penn Fields	725
Churches and major buildings	725
Perambulation	727
Other buildings	729
Heath Town	729
Merry Hill	731
Oxley and Fordhouses	732
Penn	733
Tettenhall	736
Churches	736
Other major buildings	738
Perambulations	743
Other buildings	748
Compton	748
Aldersley	749
Wednesfield	749
Ashmore Park	751
Whitmore Reans and Dunstall	751

WOLVERHAMPTON CITY CENTRE

Wolverhampton is a major provincial city (population 236,000 in 2021), larger than Plymouth or Derby and not much smaller than Leicester or Nottingham. It became a Borough in 1848, and gained city status in 2000. Wolverhampton is named after the lady Wulfruna, to whom King Æthelred granted it in 985. Its physical remains start with an Anglo-Saxon cross. It had a concentration of heavy industries, but was also the shopping and social centre for much of rural south Staffordshire and east Shropshire. Yet it is unjustly neglected, and its architecture has largely been ignored.

The city centre is on a hill with St Peter's church at the summit. The Saxon minster here probably lay within a monastic compound, and the medieval town developed around the market place, High Green (now Queen Square), to the S. This division still exists. The N part of the centre has churches, council offices and the University. The commercial centre is to the S.

The medieval and Georgian town was quite small. Taylor's map (1751) shows it extending N–S from Molineux to Bilston Street, where the Old Hall stood, and E–W from the present School Street to the bottom of Lichfield Street. Town Commissioners, created by an Act of 1777, cut Darlington Street and enlarged High Green, but as in Birmingham the main civic improvements followed the Artisans' Dwellings Act of 1875. A scheme confirmed in 1877 demolished the slum of Caribee Island, and created the widened Lichfield Street and Prince's Square.

Medieval Wolverhampton grew on the wool trade, with tailors, weavers and fullers. From the C17 metal trades increased, especially lock- and buckle-making. The earliest directory, of 1770, lists 118 lockmakers. The Birmingham Canal was completed in 1769. The railway history is complicated, but the Queen's Building of 1849 reminds us of its importance. The Great Western Railway's second locomotive works (after Swindon) was opened in 1859 and closed in 1964. C20 industry spread outside the centre, to include cycle manufacturing and later cars (Sunbeam) and buses and lorries (Guy Motors).

Wolverhampton's Georgian architects tended to be outsiders – *William Baker*, *William Hollins* of Birmingham, *Lewis Vulliamy*. The change came with *Edward Banks* (1815–66). He was an Alderman and magistrate: the first of the C19 Black Country architects who were also civic figures. A fine classicist – his Old Library of 1857 in Waterloo Road is a real loss – he also became, after criticism from *The Ecclesiologist*, a fine Puginian Goth. Late C19 architects, especially *Fred T. Beck*, were influenced by the half-timbered work of *Edward Ould* at Wightwick Manor; Wolverhampton's most important Arts and Crafts architect, *W. J. H. Weller*, used much structural timbering. Beck's successor *James A. Swan* created fantasies at The Dippons and the inner porch of St Peter's. *Richard Twentyman* (1903–79) was an impressive early Modernist.

Wolverhampton

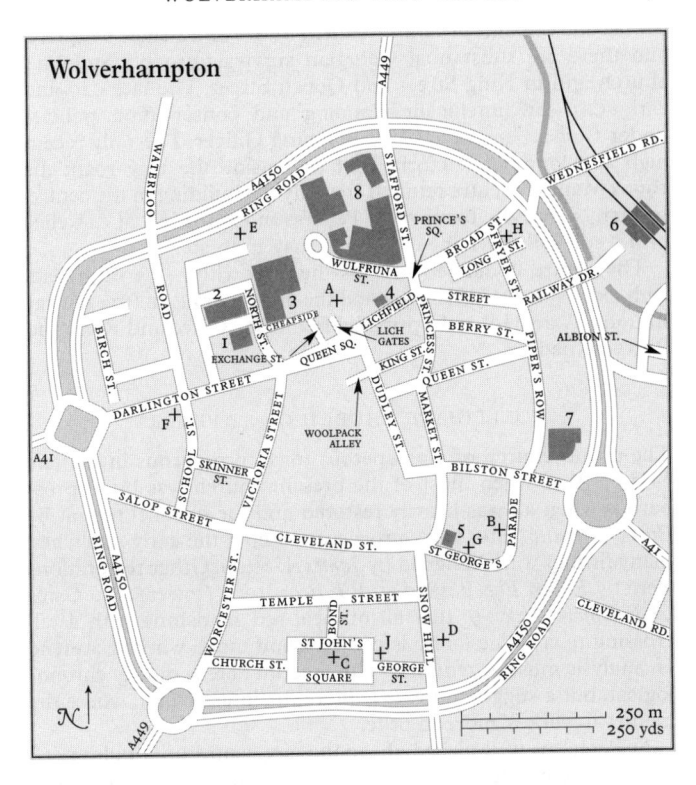

A Collegiate Church of St Peter
B St George (former)
C St John
D St Mary and St John (R.C.)
E St Peter and St Paul (R.C.)
F Darlington Street Methodist Church
G Salvation Army hall (former)
H Synagogue (former)
J Convent of Mercy (former)

1 Town Hall
2 Civic Hall
3 Civic Centre
4 Museum and Art Gallery
5 Library
6 Station
7 Wolverhampton Combined Court Centre
8 University of Wolverhampton

Despite the damaging ring road, completed in 1986, the centre suffered less in the late C20 than that of Birmingham. A large block S of Queen Square went for the Mander and Wulfrun centres, and Dudley Street was rebuilt. Losses included the old Grammar School, by *William Smith the elder*, 1712–14; St James' Square; *Beck*'s Queen's Arcade of 1907; and *George Bidlake*'s finest chapel, Queen Street Congregational of 1863–6. Recent losses include the Retail Market of 1960 by *Albert Chapman*, Deputy Borough Architect, with its concrete shell roofs. But Queen Square is still there, fine Late Victorian and Edwardian townscape remains around Lichfield Street and Prince's Square, and there are substantial Georgian survivals around St John's church and in King Street and Queen Street. The late C20 and early C21 saw intelligent planning and conservation policies under *Costas Georghiou*, Chief Planning Officer. The only recent high development, Victoria Hall, is outside the ring road; the 1960s Mander Centre remains the only tall building in the centre. In many views the tower of St Peter's, an expression of C15 civic pride, still sails over the city. Long may it do so.

The centre is defined here as the area within the ring road, with extensions N (Molineux and the area behind), E (the railway stations, Corn Hill and Springfield) and SE (Cleveland Road and Bilston Road).

COLLEGIATE CHURCH OF ST PETER

The proud church of a prosperous town, prosperous in the late Middle Ages when most of the present church was built, prosperous when all was heavily restored and the chancel rebuilt by *Ewan Christian* after 1852, prosperous still in the early C20 when many fittings were designed by *James A. Swan*. Other restorations were by *Robert Ebbels*, 1837–9, *F.T. Beck*, 1907 (tower), and *Caröe & Passmore*, 1937–9. It is all of local red sandstone with a tall crossing tower. The fabric is complex and much worked over, so an analysis must be tentative. The account here is mostly chronological, but a suggestion is to explore the interior first, where the medieval work is more in order.

St Peter's is well placed above the city centre on a hilltop (cf. Walsall, Wednesbury, Sedgley). Documentary history begins in the C10. If Wulfruna's charter represents a genuine document, then she endowed the monastery *c.* 994 with lands including Bilston, Willenhall and Wednesfield. From later medieval times, the college, the Royal Free Chapel of Wolverhampton, was administered by a dean – a post held from 1479 jointly with that of Dean of Windsor – and eight prebendaries. The college was abolished in 1846, when St Peter's and the outlying areas became separate parishes.

The flat buttresses of the Norman nave survived in the W wall until the C19. The earliest surviving fabric is the late C13 CROSSING. The arches have three round shafts, the middle ones keeled, with circular bases, and capitals with complex mouldings. The arches have three chamfered orders. The two-storey SOUTH PORCH comes next, probably still C13. Its exterior is all *Christian*, of 1855–6 (it had been refaced in the C17 or C18). The panelled parapet and pinnacles are a recurring motif of his. But inside is a rib-vault, with alternating plain and filleted ribs, rising from restored bell capitals in the door arch, and a fat quarter-round inside the entrance arch. The SOUTH TRANSEPT (Lady Chapel) is early C14: see the moulded jambs and arch of the E window. This was originally a four-light flowing Dec design. The present Geometrical tracery is of after 1865 but before 1905, almost certainly by *Christian*. Above, the gable of the original roof-line, suggesting that this was at first an aisle which clasped the tower, rather than a separate transept. C14 PISCINA in the S wall with finely moulded cusped arch, but the hoodmould cut away. Perp S window with straight mullions and cusping. The inserted arch from S aisle to transept, which rests awkwardly above the easternmost aisle window, is C15, and goes with the nave arcades. The heightening of the transept is slightly later, clearly contemporary with the nave clerestory. Large windows with mullions and transom, in an irregular arrangement: a single window and a pair, divided by a buttress.

The S aisle S windows were Perp, with mullions and cusping like the survivor in the transept. Their inner arches survive, with large and small hollow chamfers, but their Dec petal tracery is again *Christian*'s, of 1854. Also his the blank arcading of 1880. The aisle W window was Geometrical, replaced with petal tracery. Why did Christian do this, when he replaced the flowing E window with Geometrical patterns?

The NAVE has Perp arcades of the mid C15. Henry VI appointed a commission to provide 'the stone required to build the church' in 1439, and there is a bequest of 1457 towards the work. Tall octagonal piers and arches with repeated hollow chamfers. Octagonal capitals and fully Perp bases. Hoodstops of bearded kings emphasize the church's royal status. There may have been a break in the work, because the clerestory has a grid of straight-headed windows with cusped lights and transoms in an irregular arrangement which does not match

Wolverhampton, St Peter.
Engraving by Thomas Jefferys after Isaac Taylor, 1751

the arcades below: eleven lights, five pairs and a single one w, above five arcade bays. The s transept has a similar irregularity. Perhaps this reflects a change of masons; the clerestory grid certainly looks like Cheshire work. The N aisle has windows with three cusped lights in a rectangular frame. They look renewed – *Christian* restored the aisle in 1856–7 – but may represent their original form.

The display on the WEST FRONT is *Christian*'s, of 1852–5. The central window has early Perp tracery and a crocketed ogee hoodmould, like those on the tower. Above, a panelled parapet and pinnacles, like the porch. The parapet continues along the nave clerestory.* The low-pitched roofs are also all Christian's except for the N transept. They have slightly cambered tie-beams. The aisle roofs are more original, with short posts on top of the side walls and lines of small wooden clerestory windows. They originally lit galleries. NW VESTRIES also *Christian*'s, 1884–6.

A contract for the TOWER was made in 1475 between the mason *John Worseley* and the 'Gentilmen Wardens Yomen & Comyns' of Wolverhampton, to be built in three years: a civic project, not that of the dean and prebendaries. The contracted design was to be octagonal, like that at Nantwich (Cheshire), and with a spire, but the tower as built is rectangular. The mason's name suggests he came from south Lancashire. It is quite slender, because of the dimensions of the existing crossing. Panelled all over, with bands of quatrefoils, in circles between the stages, and squares set diagonally below the parapet. The belfry windows have big ogee hoodmoulds and big beasts for hoodstops. Slim angle buttresses, NE stairvice, and the stipulated 'batellynge and fenyals'. The hoodstops are typical late C15 West Midlands work, but the hoodmoulds are clearly related to the towers of Chester Cathedral and Nantwich, now dated to the 1380s, so this seems a deliberate re-creation of the style. Restored by *Christian* in 1854, it seems accurately.

The NORTH TRANSEPT (the 'Lane chancel', now war memorial chapel) is the puzzling part. The arch to the N aisle is unusual, with continuous mouldings. The huge E and N windows are all but round-headed. They have continuous mouldings of a normal Perp kind and blank arcading below, but their form is unusual: a single broad mullion runs straight up from sill to apex, without any other tracery or division. Bold wall panelling. The buttresses outside have drip mouldings like classical cavettos, so C16 or C17. Yet above the windows is a late medieval roof, low-pitched, with moulded ribs and square panels. What date is this? The C17 antiquary Huntbach copied C16 accounts, now lost, which hinted at work done by 1527.

---

*Taylor in 1750 shows decorative nave battlements but plain ones on the aisle and porch. Robert Noyes's early C19 drawings show plain battlements, but Turner's watercolour of 1796 shows very decorative ones. It seems that *Christian* restored the nave battlements to their earlier form, and rebuilt the others to match.

Topographical evidence is also confusing. Ebbels's plan of 1837 shows the present arrangement, but Noyes's drawing of 1846 suggests more mullions. In 1947 the E window sill was found to be altered, and remains of a former mullion were discovered. So the likeliest answer is early C16 work, rebuilt and the windows altered, possibly after Civil War damage.

The medieval CHANCEL was replaced in 1682–4 by Dean Trevor with a small classical design, which was altered with Neo-Norman windows, probably by *Robert Ebbels*, 1839. *Christian* replaced this in turn in 1862–5 with a long narrow chancel with a polygonal apse, on a scale appropriate to the medieval work. Late C13 Geometrical Dec, to match the crossing and s transept, with three-light windows. Hammerbeam roof with high collars. Christian does not fail at the climax, a seven-sided apse with two-light windows, and two tiers of timber vaulting rising from slim stone shafts with foliage capitals.

PULPIT. 'The most notable stone example throughout the kingdom' (J. Charles Cox). Perp, probably mid-C15, and integral with the first s arcade pier from the E. The pulpit and its staircase, which climbs around the pier, are panelled all over, with cusped heads, the cusps formed into rosettes. A band of flowers and leaves round the top, vine leaves and grapes round the base. The stem has moulded shafts and the vaulting mouchette-shaped cusped panels, again with rosettes. On the N side the Swynnerton arms; Thomas Swynnerton was a member of the 1439 rebuilding commission. Remains of colour. At the foot of the staircase is a large seated lion, with boldly modelled mane and fur. He looks rather like a guard dog, with paws gripping the stair rail and tail wrapped round his body.

OTHER FURNISHINGS. FONT. Octagonal stem with statuettes of saints. They include St Anthony, associated with Windsor, so the likely date is *c.*1480, after the uniting of the deaneries. Bowl dated 1660 and 'restored 1839', with typical C17 stylized motifs: leaf, a bell, a sun. Rich Gothic COVER by *James A. Swan*, 1928. – SCREENS. Two in the s transept chapel. The five-bay one to the s aisle was moved here in 1857, when narrow extra bays were inserted. Dado panels with blank tracery, moulded mullions, and good tracery heads to the lights, with ogees rising to vesicas. Elegant thin arch to the doorway. Everything is decorated with rosettes, like the pulpit, so probably mid-C15. The screen to the crossing is different in design, with framed bays. Both have replacement vaulting and cresting, probably C20 and by *Swan*, who designed the N chapel crossing and aisle screens in 1937–8. – STALLS. C15 or early C16, brought from Lilleshall Abbey in 1546. Much restored after the Civil War, when they were called 'rotten and out of order'. Eight are now in the s transept, three in the N. Heavy tops and moulded arms with typical Perp bases. Plain misericords with stylized leaves and shields, probably C17. The delightful details are the figures as elbow rests: some original, including the man in a tall hat (s) and the praying angel (N), but most C17: many grotesque bearded heads, and

a fish (N). Additional stall, N, 1947 by *Lavender & Twentyman*.
– PRAYER DESK, S transept, made up from two C15 or C16 bench-ends, with bold and crude leaf-heads. Said to come from Halesowen Abbey. – CHOIR STALLS by *Christian*, 1865, with open arcaded fronts. – INNER SOUTH PORCH. A spectacular Perp revival piece by *Swan*, 1929–32, double-storeyed, in limed oak, with innumerable canopies, open-traceried lights and pinnacles; also the PANELLING at the W end of the aisle. – WEST GALLERY. According to its inscription, built in 1610 by the Merchant Taylors of London, trustees of the Grammar School. Balustraded front, richly decorated with egg-and-dart, and a band of vine leaves and fruit. Piers also carved, with consoles like succubi. The rest largely rebuilt in 1939 by *Caröe & Passmore*. – COMMUNION TABLE, S transept. Probably the one consecrated by Archbishop Laud in 1635. Richly decorated but not sophisticated, with stubby, patterned Ionic columns and hanging arches. ALTAR SURROUND perhaps by *F. T. Beck*, 1905. – BENEFACTION BOARD, S transept. C18, of the former Blue Coat School. With a Virgin and Child above and two charity children below. Also C19 BOARDS here and in the S aisle. – LECTERN. By *James Fowler* of Louth (carver *Masey*), 1874. Big eagle on a ball, and a gabled base. – N chapel REREDOS and ALTAR by *Lavender & Twentyman*, 1947, when they re-fitted the transept. Perp, with canopies, astonishing at this date. – ORGAN over the E nave arch by *Henry Willis*, 1860.

STAINED GLASS. In the chancel side windows Flemish and German C16 glass, small scenes and medallions, from St Mary, Stafford Street (1840, demolished). – Apse, seven windows by *O'Connor*, 1865. Deep colours, strongly modelled figures with expressive faces. S transept E by *F.C. Eden*, 1921, a Tree of Jesse, W by *Wailes*, 1855. N aisle, three by *A.J. Davies*, 1913–21; the others *Heaton, Butler & Bayne*, 1876, and *Powells*, 1939. – S aisle by *Kempe*, 1890, 1895; W by *Powells* 1947. – WALL PAINTINGS on the chancel W wall, Moses and Elijah, by *Heaton, Butler & Bayne*, 1873, survivors of a scheme which ran along the N and S walls.

MONUMENTS. S transept. John Leveson †1575. Alabaster. Couple on a tomb-chest with small figurines and twisted colonnettes. – Admiral Sir Richard Leveson †1605, but made 1633–4. By *Hubert le Sueur*, whose price was £300. What remains is the bronze standing effigy, derived from le Sueur's Earl of Pembroke of 1629 at Oxford; a cartouche; and two separate cherubs. A swagger piece: r. leg slightly bent, l. hand on hip, r. hand holding his baton of office. You expect him to buttonhole you about his latest victory. – N transept. Thomas Lane †1585 and wife, perhaps by *Robert Royley* of Burton-on-Trent. Alabaster couple on a tomb-chest with small figures and some minimum Renaissance motifs. – Col. John Lane †1667. By *Thomas Cartwright I*, probably mid-1670s (GF). Standing wall monument. Black and buff. The base has a finely carved panel with a relief of trophies including a grisly severed leg, and on the l. a crowned oak tree with a horse disappearing round it, a reference to Lane's concealment of Charles II after the Battle of Worcester. Another horse r. The scale is all wrong, but easier to eyes accustomed to Surrealism. Open swan's-neck pediment. – N aisle. South African war memorial, 1902–3. Designed by *F.T. Beck*, made by *Bridgemans*. An imitation late C17 cartouche. – Some nice C18 tablets.

WOLVERHAMPTON CROSS, outside on the S. A mighty round shaft, 14 ft (4.3 metres) high, on a 1 ft 8 in. (50 cm.) base. It is of fine hard sandstone, not local, now badly weathered.* Gerald Mander suggested it might be a reused Roman column, perhaps from Wroxeter. It may be in its original position; excavation in 1949 showed that it rests on four circular steps. The cross has 'a quality of carving and distinction of iconography unmatched in cross sculpture in the Midlands' (Rosemary Cramp). The decoration is in zones, two of luxuriant foliage scrolls alternating with two containing lively Anglian beasts, with their heads turned back. Between the two lowest zones a band of acanthus. Below the bands are pendant triangles with animals and foliage. Michael Rix dated it *c.* 850 and argued that much of its inspiration comes from metalwork, relating it to C8 and C9 sources: the Copenhagen fragment, the Trewhiddle hoard, and brooches from Beeston Tor in the Peak District. David Horovitz suggests the later C9 or C10, perhaps as a commemorative memorial, possibly erected by Wulfruna herself. – Outside the W front, STATUE of Lady Wulfruna by *Sir Charles Wheeler*, 1974. Slightly over life-size, and heroic in a gentle way. – WAR MEMORIAL to the SW, by *C.T. Armstrong*, 1922. Slender cenotaph in red Hollington stone, with statues of servicemen and St George by *W.C.H. King* in niches near the top.

OTHER PLACES OF WORSHIP

ST GEORGE (former), St George's Parade. 1828–30 by *James Morgan*. A Commissioners' church (cost £10,268). Classical, simple, elegant but slightly thin, with a W tower clasped by the aisles. Recessed octagonal spire rising straight above the balustrade in the manner of Nash's All Souls, Langham Place (Morgan was Nash's assistant). Arched windows, but the E window Venetian. Grand W doorway with paired Doric columns. Also aisle W entrances. They are hardly visible behind the glass and metal entrance of Sainsbury's store (closed 2014), an unfortunate conversion and extension of 1987–9 by *Tweedale*. Semicircular arches and coving, already with a period flavour.

ST JOHN, St John's Square. By *William Baker*, 1756–60.† Spire completed *c.* 1775. The builder was *Roger Eykyn*. Perton

---

*A cast made *c.* 1877, now in the Victoria and Albert Museum, shows the decoration much better.
†Hugh Owen's *Account of...Shrewsbury* (1808) ascribed St John's to Thomas Farnolls Pritchard, quoting his memorial in St Julian's church there, but Baker was paid for plans in 1755, and regularly thereafter up to 1759.

sandstone ashlar, much renewed by *Anthony Chatwin*, 1968, in Hollington stone. The fine W tower has many elements from James Gibbs's *Book of Architecture*: bell-stage with coupled Ionic pilasters, octagonal stage with applied columns, clock stage with segmental pediment, and spire. Doric doorcase with heavy, intermittently blocked columns. Side windows in two tiers, all with Gibbs surrounds. The short chancel has a pediment and a blank Venetian window. The interior follows Wren's St James, Piccadilly in having square pillars supporting the galleries, and Doric columns above. These have detached pieces of entablature in the Gibbs way, with triglyphs. Aisles groin-vaulted, nave with three-centred tunnel-vault. Original seating in the galleries.

FURNISHINGS. REREDOS and chancel PANELLING by *James A. Swan*, 1929, Doric, with pedimented centre flanked by fluted pilasters, framing a copy of Rubens's Descent from the Cross, done for the church by *Joseph Barney* in 1780. – PULPIT on a tall stone base with detached granite shafts, and PEWS, by *J. Drayton Wyatt*, 1869. – FONT by *Wyatt*, 1866. – CHAIRS (chancel). Two, probably C17 and Flemish, with carved reliefs: Crucifixion and Resurrection. – ROYAL ARMS. 1778–9, probably carved by *William Ellam*. – COMMANDMENT and CREED BOARDS, C18, S porch. – BENEFACTION BOARD, N porch, dated 1768. – ORGAN. Made by *Renatus Harris* in 1682 for the Temple Church, London; actually placed in Christ Church Cathedral, Dublin; brought here in 1762, often restored since. Three-towered case with crown and mitres. – STAINED GLASS. Chancel N and S, 1852. S aisle from E: *Graham Chaplin*, 1983; *Ward & Hughes*, 1884; †1893; *G.J. Baguley*, 1895; *Samuel Evans*, 1901. N aisle from W: *Camm & Co.*, 1911; *T.W. Camm* (*Florence, Walter & Robert H. Camm*), †1912. A nice contrast between the Camm firms, the first traditional, the second Arts and Crafts with much texturing. Then two by *A.J. Davies*, 1918 and 1912. Galleries, two by *Gibbs & Co.*, 1880. – MONUMENTS. SW corner, Joseph Reed †1831, Henry Wood †1815, both by *Thomas Wilmot*. – N gallery, Ann Simpson †1833 and family, Gothic aedicule by *John Waudby & Son* of York, 1850–8.

ST STEPHEN, Hilton Street, Springfield. 1907–8 by *F.T. Beck*.* Brick and red terracotta. Standard stuff at first sight, but the details are thoughtful and personal. W window with intersecting tracery. Spreading composition with SE vestry, castellated NE Lady Chapel and NW baptistery, and pent-roofed W porch with segmental-arched entrance. The clerestory windows are pointed lunettes. No tower, but a satisfying E end: tall pinnacles, S gable enclosing a bellcote, and a little timber lantern. Interior mostly rendered. Octagonal arcade piers and tall arches of Alveley sandstone, with mouldings dying above the capitals.

---

*C.R. Ashbee made a magnificent design for St Stephen's in 1905, in an Arts and Crafts Romanesque style (cf. the churches of his friend A.S. Dixon), but grandly scaled and dramatic.

The arches enclose the clerestory windows and the segmental brick arches of the aisles. ROOD and BEAM by *Charles G. Gray*, 1915. Sanctuary arch on plain piers. – REREDOS and side panels with saints, early C20, from St Mary, Palfrey, Walsall. – CHOIR STALLS by *J.C. Brock*, 1958. – STAINED GLASS by *William Aikman*, E 1921 (the best), Lady Chapel 1929, baptistery 1930. Aisles, *John Hardman Studios (Patrick Feeney)* 1949, 1952, 1954. W window by *Holland*, 1855, from St James, Horseley Fields (dem.). – PAINTING. Crucifixion by *George Phoenix* (†1935), W wall. – Lady Chapel screened off by *Twentyman Percy & Partners* with ETCHED GLASS by *Gerry Powell*, 1986.

ST MARY AND ST JOHN (R.C.), Snow Hill. An ample Dec design in Gornal stone by *Charles Hansom*, 1852–5 (chancel and side chapels 1879–80). A SW tower was not built. Wide nave, otherwise a Puginian plan with a long chancel. Nave windows with flowing tracery, spherical triangles and petal shapes, clerestory windows with segmental arches and vesica shapes. Bath stone inside. Arcades with four-lobed piers and knobbly leaf capitals. Three-sided apse and smaller flanking apses to the side chapels, gabled all round, a fine sight. Slightly earlier Geometrical tracery here. – Rich Gothic REREDOS and HIGH ALTAR of 1880, designed by *Fr John Ullathorne* and made by *Boulton* of Cheltenham, with spires and saints in arched niches. – Similar REREDOS in the Lady Chapel, N. – Sacred Heart Chapel, S, with altar by *A.B. Wall*, 1893–4. – STATUE. Copy of the seated St Peter in the Vatican, 1920s. – SCREENS between chancel and chapels by *Hansom*, 1880 onwards. – STAINED GLASS all by *Hardmans*, 1880–94.

ST PETER AND ST PAUL (R.C.), North Street. A major Catholic monument of the Penal years. The history begins with GIFFARD HOUSE, facing the street. A post-Reformation mass house here was rebuilt with the house between 1728 and 1733, directed by *Peter Giffard* of Chillington, his chaplain *Edward Dicconson* and *Thomas Brockholes*, the priest at Wolverhampton. The master mason was *William Hollis*.* Giffard's initials and the date 1728 are on the hoppers. Very characteristic Early Georgian. Five bays and three storeys. Brick, all windows segment-headed. Heavily restored in 1988 by *Weightman & Bullen*. The excellent staircase was made by *Thomas Evans* and *Nicholas Bache* in 1732. It has three thin twisted balusters to each tread, and divides into two arms at first-floor level, to front and rear. The room at the NW corner has full-height fielded panelling, much restored. Good iron GATES in front, probably original, but restored.

The C18 house-chapel, roughly where the present sanctuary is, was rebuilt and much enlarged into a church in 1826–8 by *Joseph Ireland*. The exterior was hidden behind houses until the 1960s. Unattractive render of 1988. Austere, with plain

---

*The building accounts (hidden in a book of Giffard estate rentals) offer no evidence that Francis Smith of Warwick was involved, as often asserted.

pilasters, lunette windows, and severe transept and w windows. s porch with an equally severe doorcase, and STATUES of SS Peter and Paul on the cornice. Sacristy by *Edward Goldie*, 1901, with heavier sash windows. *Ireland*'s interior is articulated by pilasters with exquisitely decorated capitals including anthemion friezes, and a deep plain entablature. Shallow barrel-vault with coffered ribs, coffered dome over the sanctuary. In 1901 *Goldie* turned the s transept into a beautiful domed chapel with fluted Ionic corner columns. Panelled N chapel by *E. Bower Norris*, 1930–1, entered through a Doric arcade. Very good redecoration and reordering of the sanctuary by *Stephen Oliver*, 2009. – ALTAR, the support a Greek Doric capital and short fluted column, AMBO and TABERNACLE, all designed by *Oliver* and carved by *Katie Worthington*. – CRUCIFIX by *Rory Young*, 2009, of polished aluminium. – FONT by *Oliver*, 2012, again on a fluted Doric column. Carvers *Fairhaven & Woods*. – S transept ALTAR and RAIL by *Goldie*, rich Italian Baroque. – Former HIGH ALTAR (N wall), very Italian with much marble, 1885. – MONUMENTS. S wall, Bishop John Milner, the antiquary, †1826. By *A.W.N. Pugin*, made by *Hardmans*, after 1851. Sumptuous brass with canopies to the side and above, and figures of saints, God the Father and a Crucifixion at the top.

DARLINGTON STREET METHODIST CHURCH. 1899–1901 by *Arthur Marshall*. A chapel on the grandest scale, in English Baroque classicism, recalling Wren's St Paul's. Twin-towered front and central copper-clad dome, a triumphant assertion of late C19 Nonconformity. Pushing up into the dome are four aedicules with broken pediments and heavily blocked Ionic columns. These recur in the windows and turrets. The twin entrance doors say 'chapel', not church, and have lovely Art Nouveau furniture. The interior is marvellously complete, rich but sober. Three-bay nave, transepts and apsed sanctuary. Horseshoe-shaped gallery, echoing the apse, with balustraded front. The orders are combined in a convincing way: Doric under the gallery, Ionic above, and giant Ionic crossing piers supporting the dome. Barrel-vault in the nave, groin-vaults in the aisles, with plasterwork everywhere; swags of fruit in the drum of the dome. MOSAICS in the spandrels by *J. Rust*: foliage and wreaths. Full-height panelling. Gallery doorcases with steep broken pediments. – Wide PULPIT with Jacobean panels, little Ionic columns, and consoles flanking the desk. – ORGAN by *Nicholsons*, 1902. – Original PEWS (tip-up seats in the gallery), and fine hanging brass LIGHT FITTINGS, touched with Art Nouveau. – STAINED GLASS. N aisle, †1931 by *Henry James Salisbury*. (Closed 2019.)

Behind in School Street, VESTRIES of 1885–8 by *Samuel Loxton*: vaguely Queen Anne, with a cross-gabled tower. In the wall between chapel and vestries a large Venetian window survives from the chapel of 1824–5. It had an amateurish four-bay front with a small pediment; perhaps by *Robert Perks*, edge-tool manufacturer and member of the congregation.

SALVATION ARMY HALL (former), St George's Parade. By *Oswald Archer*, 1910. Typical gabled brick block.

SYNAGOGUE (former), Fryer Street and Long Street. Rebuilt in 1903 by *Fred T. Beck*. Small, simple Jacobean style, with prominent alternating voussoirs. Gable with broken pediment and finial.

CONVENT OF MERCY (now REDEEMED CHURCH OF GOD), St John's Square. 1860 by *E.W. Pugin*. Two tall brick ranges running W–E, set back from the NE corner of the square and entered through a brick archway, with low connecting ranges forming a small courtyard. The S range contains the CHAPEL on the first floor. Three bays of Dec two-light windows, polygonal apse, arch-braced roof. The tall octagonal SW turret with candlesnuffer spire, the main accent of the buildings, contains the plaster-vaulted access stair. S along the square, a Late Classical two-storey range, then a corner block reconstructed with steep pedimental gables, but retaining a good C18 Doric doorcase with three-quarter columns to George Street. E of this a late C19 Gothic block with chimneys corbelled out of buttresses, probably by *Fleeming & Son*.

PUBLIC BUILDINGS

TOWN HALL, North Street. Now magistrates' courts. By *Ernest Bates* of Manchester, 1869–71. Second Empire French with hardly a trick missed, in lovely creamy Cefn stone. Cut-off dome in the centre, cut-off pavilion roofs at the ends, all with frilly ironwork. Heavily rusticated plinth, and a giant Corinthian order with smooth rustication. Fifteen bays. Segment-headed windows below, round-headed above. The rear was the police barracks: red brick, very utilitarian. Octagonal main hall,

Wolverhampton, Town Hall.
Engraving by H. Abbott, 1869

grand but not large, with giant Corinthian piers which taper inwards noticeably. T-shaped staircase to the courts. – STATUE of G.B. Thorneycroft, ironmaster and first mayor, by *Thomas Thornycroft*, 1856.

CIVIC HALL, North Street, N of the old Town Hall. By *Lyons & Israel*, their first work, won in competition in 1934 and built 1936–8. A convincing fusion of progressive Swedish classicism and the emerging Modern Movement. The façade, with its portico of octagonal simplified Ionic piers *in antis*, and the main hall rising above like a recessed attic, is a version of Tengbom's Stockholm Concert Hall of 1926 (the resemblance was closer in the competition design, with Corinthian capitals as at Stockholm). The clean piled-up masses behind are generated from ingenious planning to accommodate the requirements – a large hall seating at least 1,800 and a small hall for 800 – on a small street block. The MAIN HALL runs E–W behind the entrance, and the small WULFRUN HALL is set N–S behind, with N side entrance, at lower level. The drop in level also provides storage under the main hall. Both foyers are articulated by unmoulded brick piers. The main foyer has a gallery running behind the piers, a nice spatial effect, and an incised mural panel of Wulfruna by (*Sir*) *Charles Wheeler*. The main hall is a sober but impressive volume, alas without its curving proscenium hood (acoustic consultant *Hope Bagenal*). Continuous gallery along three sides. Side corridors with massive half-piers. The Wulfrun Hall is equally straightforward but relieved by convex panelling flanking the stage, with murals of very freehand drawn figures by *Muriel Gilbert*. A smaller hood survives above. What consistently lifts this plain architecture is the quality of detail: the veneered doors with porthole windows; the patterned radiator grilles; the wheel windows on the rear staircases down from the main hall; the elegant handrails, best in the cloakroom staircases in the Wulfrun Hall foyer, where they end in spirals. The building was refurbished to a high standard by *Penoyre & Prasad*, 2003, with glazed crush bars at gallery level on the sides, elegant and logical. More alterations by *Jacobs*, consulting engineers: extra galleries, top extensions, 2021.)

CIVIC CENTRE, North Street, opposite the Civic Hall. By *Clifford Culpin & Partners*, 1974–9. A bulky L-shaped complex. Long E–W block and S wing, framing a square towards Cheapside, S, with St Peter's on its E side. Maroon brick, mostly of three storeys to the square, four to North Street because of the levels. Deep brick bands between the floors with big heavy chamfers, and thick circular pilotis, inside and out. The result has integrity, but is a massive, almost threatening presence. The N entrance, away from square and church, has a flight of stairs to the first floor. Big central three-storey well with balconies – maroon brick, chamfered, again – but stairs here are hidden away. Then at the top a bit more grandeur, an imperial staircase. It leads to the Council Chamber, an irregular hexagon, claustrophobically low.

MUSEUM AND ART GALLERY, Lichfield Street. 1883–5 by *J.A. Chatwin*, mostly paid for by the local builder Philip Horsman. An excellent design in the tradition of Barry and especially Cockerell. The solid two-storey block of the front with its relatively narrow centre and small pediment is Italianate, but with roots in the Antique. The centrepiece has a porch with paired Doric columns, paired Ionic columns breaking forward above, and a section of attic with plain short pilasters, before the pediment. The paired Ionic columns repeat at the ends, but below them a Mannerist touch, hollowed-out niches under the stress of the columns. Rounded l. corner. The design continues facing St Peter's, w, with a subsidiary entrance, originally to the School of Art. This is a variation on the Lichfield Street entrance, with Doric columns supporting the Ionic ones, and the columns-and-niches combination flanking them. The elevations express the plan: offices below, top-lit galleries above. The blank first-floor walls are decorated with FRIEZES carved by *R. L. Boulton & Sons*: classically draped female figures of the Arts, l., and male figures representing Sculpture, r. On the side elevation, figures in modern dress of Industry and Sciences. 84

A lobby leads to the top-lit main hall, grand but sober, with plain panelling, the only enrichments a decorative stair rail and the top cornice below the lantern. The stair climbs to a balcony and into the main galleries, also simply done, with plaster friezes in flower patterns.

In 2004–7 *Niall Phillips Architects* extended the building N with an angular entrance block clad in unglazed terracotta tiles, to Wulfruna Street. Inside, tricky narrow spaces and a stair and balcony, all in white, the C21 museum aesthetic.

LIBRARY, St George's Parade. 1900–2 by *Henry T. Hare*, a library specialist. In Hare's career it comes between the refined Jacobean of the Oxford Town Hall and his Edwardian Baroque work. Free Jacobean, combining powerful massing and delicate detail. A big gable and flanking domed turrets face the corner. Entrance in a triple arcade. The wings have round-headed ground-floor windows and freer details above, little windows with broken pediments linked to circular lights, E; larger windows flanking an oriel, S. Panels carved with the names of poets. The main staircase rises behind screening Doric columns in a domed oval hall. Chubby balustrade. The best interiors are on the first floor. LENDING LIBRARY facing Garrick Street with a barrel-vault and galleries, hence the tiers of windows to the E. The vault is cut by arcades. REFERENCE LIBRARY facing Bilston Road with a domed cross-in-square plan, the side spaces defined by free-standing Ionic columns.

RAILWAY STATION, Railway Drive. Replaced as part of the West Coast main line electrification in 1964–7 under *R.L. Moorcroft*, British Railways London Midland Region Architect. Main buildings again rebuilt in 2018–20, architects *Austin-Smith:Lord*.

WOLVERHAMPTON COMBINED COURT CENTRE, Bilston Street and Piper's Row. 1990 by *Norman & Dawbarn* with

PSA Projects. A monumental lump of banded grey and red blockwork, with some blue-framed dark glazing.

UNIVERSITY OF WOLVERHAMPTON, Wulfruna Street. The Wolverhampton and Staffordshire Technical College, founded in 1914, became a polytechnic in 1968 and a university in 1992. The original buildings occupy the site of the late C17 deanery. By *John Hutchings,* Staffordshire County Education Architect: the r. block 1926, centrepiece and remainder 1931–3, under *G.C. Lowbridge* (Hutchings's successor), with *Fleeming & Son.* Solid Neo-Georgian, good townscape, but not very inspired. Grandiose stone centre with rusticated corners, giant Ionic order, heavy attic and shallow pediment. Brick flanking ranges, stone end pavilions with segmental pediments and shallow through-storey bows. The l. end turns a quadrant to St Peter's Square. The main floor has a corridor with Soanian columns. An imperial staircase rises in a rear semicircular projection with a half-dome, to the Council Room, which has a dome too. The BOARD ROOM has full-height panelling, said to be reused from the deanery. Nice eared panels with pediments, but only the garlands of fruit look original. The fireplace looks more reliable and also has garlands at the sides.

Much recent building. Facing St Peter's Square an elegant ENTRANCE BLOCK with sunscreens linked by steel rods, by *Bond Bryan,* 2001–3. Inside the courtyard behind the old range, the MI BUILDING (Information Technology) by *BDP,* 2003. To the NE, on the corner of Stafford Street and the ring road, the MILLENNIUM CITY BUILDING, cubic, in red brick, by *RMJM* (project architect *Kevin Lloyd*), 2002. S of it facing Stafford Street, a new SCIENCE BUILDING by *Sheppard Robson,* 2014. Also theirs, BUSINESS SCHOOL of 2015.

Across the ring road to the N, the SCHOOL OF ART, by *Diamond, Redfern & Partners* with the Borough Architect *Albert Chapman,* 1968–9. A good design. Eight storeys, the shape straightforward, but the treatment shows the sculptural taste of the late Sixties. Concrete frame, the openings canted in at the corners, set in front of the curtain walls, and industrial blue brick for the plinth and staircase cores on the E and W. For other public buildings *see* Perambulations, below.

PERAMBULATIONS

1. Queen Square, Lichfield Street, Prince's Square and the east and north-east

This walk includes the finest Victorian streets. QUEEN SQUARE was High Green, the medieval centre. It was enlarged on the S after 1841 (*Edward Banks,* surveyor), demolishing the late medieval timber-framed High Hall. Renamed after the unveiling by Queen Victoria in 1866 of the STATUE of Prince Albert, by the equestrian specialist *Thomas Thornycroft.* Well-modelled horse; the figure slightly stiff, but the head good. The high plinth gives it the right scale, though the present road arrangement diminishes it.

The best buildings are on the N side. LICH GATES leads up to St Peter's. On its l. corner a handsome Early Georgian house, dated 1726 on a hopper. Rusticated angle piers, segment-headed windows with keystones, modillion cornice. The house behind, towards the church, must be Early Georgian as well: see the cornice and giant pilasters. Both much altered, with some renewed brickwork and Victorian ground floors. Opposite, BARCLAYS BANK, by *T.H. Fleeming*, 1875–6. Bold Gothic in Waterhouse's manner. Limestone, with brownish sandstone shafts to the windows. Details push out at you: canted corner bay with triple-arched porch, oriel on the l. on a heavy segmental arch. The E front, with an octagonal turret facing the gardens (*see below*), is by *Fleeming*, 1892.

Walking W, an ornate mid-C19 classical building on the E corner of Exchange Street. Next the NATIONAL PROVINCIAL BANK (now NatWest) of 1913 by *Bromley & Watkins*. Baroque classical, with a giant Ionic order and smooth rustication with big console keystones below. Doric corner doorcase with Michelangelesque pediment figures (carvers *G. Seale & Son*). In EXCHANGE STREET, on the r., set back, a surviving C16 box-framed rear wing of the 1726 house in Lich Gates. Much restored, the ground floor underbuilt in brick. Diagonal patterning in the jettied gable. Another mid-C19 classical block on the NE corner. Back on Queen Square and W, the former WOLVERHAMPTON FREEHOLDERS' BUILDING SOCIETY is in revived Nash style, by *Cleland & Hayward*, 1932–3. Giant fluted Doric columns, attic pediment set in from the ends. Then the former MARTIN'S BANK, by *Essex & Goodman*, 1936, Neo-Georgian with *Moderne* touches; and a little classical terracotta design of *c.* 1900.

The S side of Queen Square retains some buildings of after the 1840s widening, probably by *Banks*. The best is a four-storey three-bay Italianate stone front with pedimented windows to the *piano nobile*, round-headed upper windows and a console cornice. More round the l. corner, in Dudley Street. Going E, the half-timbered former SHAKESPEARE pub echoes the lost High Hall. Of *c.* 1928, probably by *W.S. Clements*. On the E side, LLOYDS BANK by *J.A. Chatwin*, 1878. Three-and-a-half storeys, Italianate, sparing in motifs, and of high quality. Rusticated pilasters to each storey, vermiculated on the ground floor, and the first and second floors treated as a giant order. Pedimented or round-arched windows. Uncouth late C20 extension, N. Then a three-bay range with blocked windows by *T.B. Whinney*, 1900, and a block of 1885 with corner dome, built and perhaps designed by *Philip Horsman*.

Now E along LICHFIELD STREET, widened from 1877, fine and consistent Late Victorian and Edwardian. On the S side, GRESHAM CHAMBERS by *F.T. Beck*, 1896–7. Tudor Revival in red brick with a little diapering. Differently treated paired oriels at each end, asymmetrical central oriel and turret, originally crenellated and with a little spire. Then a two-bay block of 1893 with a similar oriel, so also *Beck*, and a tall block of *c.*1900. On the N side, GARDENS with a memorial FOUNTAIN to Philip Horsman by *Farmer & Brindley*, 1896, with dolphins and putti, and MEMORIAL to Seaman Harris by *Robert Jackson Emerson*, 1918, bronze bust on a pedestal with bronze relief. Further back, WAR MEMORIAL by *J. J. Brownsword*, 1922. A heavy stone cross with a muscular crucified Christ, controversial when proposed for its 'Catholic' nature. Then the Art Gallery (p. 683).

On the S side again, within an eclectic 1880s limestone range, the POSADA, by *Beck*, 1900–1, a rare surviving city-centre bar of the period. Norman Shaw influence in the Ipswich-style bay window with curved corners and rounded-headed light. Arty lettering in the fascia and end pilasters. Interior gently opened out by *David Horne Associates*, 1983, retaining many original features, in a refined Jacobean style. Snob screen to the former side corridor. Tilework in orange-brown and cream. Smoke room behind. Opposite, the former METROPOLITAN BANK of 1912–13, by *F. Barry Peacock* of *Cossins, Peacock & Bewlay*. Massive Baroque classicism, with a giant Ionic order. Ends with smooth rustication, segmental pediments and built-up attics. Corner entrance of St Mary-le-Bow type.

Beyond is PRINCE'S SQUARE, the most complete Late Victorian and Edwardian urban space surviving in the conurbation. Going clockwise from Lichfield Street, on the curved NW corner the ROYAL LONDON INSURANCE building, by *Essex, Nicol & Goodman*, 1902–3. English Baroque with picturesque Jacobean echoes. Giant Ionic columns on the first and second floors, with canted bays recessed between. The cupola with its small Ionic aedicules gives the square the accent it needs. The ground floor retains its banded pilasters. On the next corner N the former GEORGE HOTEL (now part of the University), by *A. T. Butler*, 1930, carefully articulated Neo-Georgian. Opposite, E, the former VINE HOTEL of 1891 by *A. P. Brevitt*, showing his Ruskinian Gothic developing towards Queen Anne and Domestic Revival. A vibrant mix of pointed windows, gabled oriels with half-timbering and plasterwork, pilasters with terracotta flowers, and corbelled chimneys. Then a curved corner block by *William Edwards*, with Dutch gables and shaped parapet, dated 1899, and a tall block with shaped gables of *c.*1900. On the SE corner to Princess Street, the former CRITERION HOTEL, of *c.*1883. Finally, on the SW corner back to Lichfield Street, a block of *c.*1890 probably by *Beck*, with gables flanked by buttresses with ogee caps.

Next the remaining streets off Princes Square, also taken clockwise. First WULFRUNA STREET, NW, with the University (q.v.), and on the S side an Early Victorian classical block, the Art Gallery extension (p. 683), and the former BOARD OF GUARDIANS OFFICES by *William Doubleday*, 1879–80. Brick, windows round-headed or with stilted segmental arches, picturesque corner oriel with spirelet. STAFFORD STREET, running N, has a former DRILL HALL (E side), castellated Gothic by *Daniel Arkell*, 1885–6, and gabled domestic former SCHOOL BOARD OFFICES, dated 1885, by *T.H. Fleeming*. Then the former CO-OP, by *Thomas Hind* of Leicester, dated 1891. Simple and progressive: brick and render, segment-headed windows. Relief sculpture by *John W. Ash*. Tapering corner cupola with tiny flanking pinnacles, restored from photographs in 2010, designer *John Bradbury*. Then simple Free Style shops with shaped gables by *William Edwards*, 1902.

Now NE down BROAD STREET. Stepping down the S side, shops by *T.A. Lowry*, 1900–1. The N side includes a simple gabled row (Nos. 21–35) by *William Edwards*, 1904–5. On the S side at the bottom, a long brick and terracotta range with a well-placed corner spire, by *Fleeming*, 1897–1904. Beyond, the big former CHUBB LOCK WORKS (now LIGHT HOUSE MEDIA CENTRE etc.) best seen by walking round the ring road side. 1898–9, by *C.N.H. Mileham* of London, with *F.T. Beck*. The language of northern mills, five storeys of repeated windows and a proudly lettered parapet. Slim entrance tower with octagonal turret (formerly castellated). Extensions for the arts centre, 1990, by *Robert Seager Design*. They covered in the yard as an atrium, in a good industrial manner, with iron columns and girders.

Fryer Street, beside the Chubb building, leads past the former synagogue (p. 681). On the l., Railway Street and the PRINCE ALBERT by *George Wormal*, 1900–1, Wolverhampton's principal monument of the pub boom. Jacobean, slightly overcrowded, with ogee corner turrets, a row of steep gables, and a pent roof above the first-floor canted bays. Here is Wolverhampton's C21 development. Opposite (and very close to) the pub, the i9 BUILDING by *Glenn Howells*, 2021, brick-faced frame, top floor nicely recessed. Railway Drive leads to the station (p. 683). Beyond, the curving white-clad i10 BUILDING, by *Austin-Smith:Lord*, 2014–15. Its red brick rear forms a square with the same architects' bus station and the back of the Queen's Building (*see* p. 688). To the r., the curving pilastered front of the BRITANNIA (formerly VICTORIA) HOTEL of 1890–2, and the former SIR TATTON SYKES pub of 1888, with a big shaped gable, both by *A.P. Brevitt*. Between, up LICHFIELD STREET, the former CO-OP (N side), rebuilt 1939–50 etc., all it seems by *G.S. Hay*, C.W.S. architect. Cream faience. CARLTON CHAMBERS, probably of *c.* 1900 by *William Edwards*. Opposite, the GRAND THEATRE, by *C.J. Phipps*, 1894. Brick and stone, with tall central arcade (now glazed) and mansard-roofed ends. Foyer recast by *RHWL*, 1998. Phipps's splendid auditorium survives. Three U-shaped tiers, his usual circular ceiling, and boxes treated as Corinthian aedicules with curvy broken pediments. Much plasterwork including Rococo panels. The former POST OFFICE beyond is by *Sir Henry Tanner*, 1895. Symmetrical composition with cupola, like his grand Leeds Post Office of 1892–6, but Northern Renaissance in creamy-buff terracotta, with steep pedimented gables. Opposite again, flats by *Jesmond Group*, 2009, and one of the new street's earliest developments, Queen Anne-style shops of 1884, Ruabon brick and terracotta, by *George H. Willoughby* of Stockport, later well known for schools.

Back in Prince's Square, s down Princess Street then E into BERRY STREET. On the corner a tall Queen Anne block by *Joseph Lavender*, 1889, with a square turret. Beyond, a range of *c.*1880, a warehouse with pedimented gable, and houses with old-fashioned details, all of 1890 by *H. Goddard*. Opposite, the Grand Theatre fly tower, then a long mid-Victorian row. Facing its far end, the QUEEN'S BUILDING, by *Edward Banks*, 1849. Built as the offices and station entrance of the Shrewsbury & Birmingham Railway. Italianate. The central arches were originally open for the station drive. Side bays with detached Doric columns on the ground floor, three-quarter columns above, and sections of attic. To its r. the BUS STATION by *Austin-Smith:Lord*, 2009–11. Big horseshoe-shaped bays which separate buses and pedestrians. Sweeping canopies. The brick administration block forms a street with the rear of the i10 Building (*see* above), leading to a new ring-road bridge (*see* p. 694) and the railway station (p. 683).

Back W up QUEEN STREET. The s side, developed from 1812, has some fine early C19 survivors. Former MECHANICS' INSTITUTE (now Army Careers) of 1835–6 by *William Walford*, stuccoed, five bays, with Doric pilasters on the ground floor and heavy Doric doorcases to each side. The attic looks altered. Nos. 44–45 have typical Doric doorcases and fanlights of a distinctive local type with rectangular panels enclosed by a 'spider's web'. The former DISPENSARY is by *William Hollins*, 1825–6. Seven bays, stuccoed. Three-bay projecting centre with a rusticated ground floor which has segment-headed openings, a Hollins trademark. Greek Doric half-columns above. A central parapet has disappeared. Nos. 47–49 are like Nos. 44–45. The former COUNTY COURT started as a single-storey library and assembly room of 1814–15, severe Greek Doric with a three-bay projecting centre and side porches. Round-headed windows. Upper floor of 1829 by *Lewis Vulliamy*, with a superimposed Roman Ionic portico and pediment. The combination may offend purists, but is carefully proportioned, and integrated by round-headed windows in the end bays. The N side was laid out between 1754 and 1758. Nos. 29–31 are by *A. E. Dempster*, 1907; red terracotta, bowed ends, balustrade and ball finials. Then original houses with characteristic mid-Georgian lintels and keystones, with one three-storey Early Victorian interruption. s again, the EXPRESS AND STAR offices by *H. Marcus Brown*, 1934. *Moderne* classical, with a tower with huge Ionic aedicule and sculpture of Mercury by *Robert Jackson Emerson*. Extension r. by *H. Marcus Brown & Lewis*, 1965, with flared canopy. Opposite, Nos. 18–22 by *Fred Hunter Lynes*, 1900, a tight grid of chamfered pilasters and heavy cornice. Steep gables. Finally No. 56, S side, again like Nos. 44–45.

Now N up PRINCESS STREET. On the NW corner a late C19 shop straight from Amsterdam, then a range by *George A. Boswell* of Glasgow, 1932, with an impressive tower at the end. Art Deco birds on its corners. HENN'S, opposite, *Moderne* with touches of Swedish and Spanish, is by *Frank Birch*, 1935. The DUKE OF YORK pub, Victorian Gothic, rendered. Boswell's tower turns the corner into KING STREET, cut in 1750–1. The important side is the N. First the OLD STILL pub, a delightful intrusion, with a Jacobean front of 1896–7, probably by *A. P. Brevitt*. Then a long line of original houses. They mostly have first-floor windows with moulded five-piece stone lintels. Some modillion cornices. Good eared doorcases at Nos. 15 and 10. C18 cart and gully entrances with three-centred arches. One survivor on the S, No. 25, five bays, slightly grander, with swept-up parapet. Again an eared doorcase. The GRAIN STORE, N side, is an early C19 warehouse. At the end is Dudley Street. Opposite, a corner block of *c.* 1900 with octagonal turret. Down WOOLPACK ALLEY alongside, mid-Georgian houses with rusticated quoins and moulded string above the keystones. Dudley Street leads N back to Queen Square.

46

2. Victoria Street, Darlington Street and the west

We start at the W end of Queen Square. Here is BEATTIE'S department store. Its Art Deco rounded corner with Egyptian capitals is a former Burton's, by their architect *Harry Wilson*, 1931. In Darlington Street, r., a streamlined extension by *Richard Twentyman*, 1939, bronze-framed windows with Travertine surrounds. Block beyond probably also *Twentyman*. In Victoria Street, l., a long range by *Gerald de Courcy Fraser*, 1929, with tall windows and a hemicycle recess (its ground floor infilled *c.* 1948).

Also in VICTORIA STREET the MANDER CENTRE (E side), 1964–8 by *James A. Roberts & Partners*, principal architect *Stanley Sellers*. Cleverly planned, using the slope for basement access. Two levels of shops above. Sellers's interior has been ruined by refurbishments. The best survivor is the ten-storey tower, faced in Portland roach, with deeply recessed windows. SCULPTURE inside, Rock Form (Porthcurno) by *Barbara Hepworth*, 1968, a tall rounded bronze with four holes making it almost hollow. Opposite, Neoclassical shops by *Nicol & Nicol*, 1927–8, frame the GIFFARD ARMS, by *James A. Swan*, dated 1929. A very high-quality reformed pub in a tight setting. Cotswold stone, with a full-height canted bay which has a grid of three-centred-arched lights, and moulded shafts at the angles. Flanking door-hoods with ogee arches. Carved hanging sign. Opposite, two five-bay Georgian houses. No. 17 has rusticated giant pilasters and window keystones linked to strings.

No. 18 has plain pilasters, swept-up parapet, and a central lunette and pedimented triplet (cut by the shopfront): the vocabulary of *William Baker*, so probably 1750s–60s. Then the remaining part of ST JOHN'S STREET, with a timber-framed house, C15 or C16, heavily restored 1979–81. W gable with close studding and cambered tie-beam with braces; S side box-framed. Brick plinth and W ground floor. More Neo-Georgian shops on the W side, by *Nicol & Nicol & Thomas*, 1933; lively shops of *c*. 1870–80 with banded brickwork on the E side.

SKINNER STREET, off Victoria Street to the W, has the former ODEON by *Harry Weedon & Partners* (*P. J. Price*), 1937, sleek and cubic with a thin tower. Then S into SCHOOL STREET, with, on the corner, a long block by *Nicol, Nicol & Thomas*, 1956–8, with lots of gimmicks. Opposite, a C19 warehouse. In front the NEW MARKET SQUARE. Frilly iron cloister dated 2003. Big traditional revival block of 2001–4 by *Nicol Thomas*, the original concept by the head of planning, *Costas Georghiou*: brick and terracotta with an arcade and central tower. The details are coarse but it has real presence. W down SALOP STREET, two good undemonstrative designs, the former NEW INN by *Bertram Butler & Co.*, 1959–60, and former AVERY showroom and offices by *Richard Twentyman*, 1951–2. Beyond, the Neo-Georgian former WEIGHTS AND MEASURES OFFICE, 1934–5, probably by *Wallace Wood*.

Now back up School Street to DARLINGTON STREET, cut in 1823 by the Town Commissioners as a direct route from High Green to the Shrewsbury and Whitchurch roads. On the W side, dominating the cross-roads, the Methodist church (p. 680). At the NW corner CLOCK CHAMBERS, by *Twentyman*, 1939. The first fully Modernist complete commercial building in the conurbation. The massing is exemplary: a three-storey block, with a two-storey projection along Waterloo Road. Cantilevered canopy all round. Concrete frame, Portland stone facing. Bronze-framed windows, now painted. On the NE corner an 1820s building with elegant swags in panels.

WATERLOO ROAD runs N, cut in 1840, developed from *c*. 1845. *William Walford* was active as resident, developer and designer. Now a mixture of Early Victorian villas and terraces and 1960s office blocks. The E side first. Nos. 8–10, by *Twentyman*, of 1959, have nicely framed upper floors. Extended N by him in 1966, taller, in black tiles. Then an original row. Nos. 16–18, grey brick, with projecting end gables. No. 20, red brick, L-shaped, with hoodmoulds. Nos. 22–32, a stucco terrace with ironwork balconies. On the W side No. 31 by *Kenneth Wakeford, Jerram & Harris* of Bristol, 1972. Behind in BIRCH STREET, two high blocks, CROWN BUILDINGS by *Norman & Dawbarn*, 1972, and CONSTRUCTION HOUSE by *Mason, Richards & Partners*, 1972. Returning S, Nos. 21–27 Waterloo Road, 1850s; No. 13, Late Victorian with a castellated bay; No. 11, probably 1850s, eclectic, with a doorcase combining classicism and Gothic nook-shafts; No. 9 by *Twentyman*, 1966, with slim black mullions. It replaced the finest early building, *Edward Banks*'s Old Library of 1857 with Corinthian portico. Nos. 3–7, stucco of *c.* 1850 with Grecian scrolls on the first-floor architraves, a band of Greek key above, and part-surviving iron balcony.

Back to Darlington Street, and up E to Queen Square. The N side has many simply detailed Late Georgian buildings, mostly stuccoed. Nos. 85–86 are good Arts and Crafts by *W.J.H. Weller*, dated 1912. Brick with stone-framed windows, oriel, and parapet with modest cut-outs. No. 87 has a fancy Greek Revival attic, No. 88 has angle pilasters. The S side includes No. 19, a modest *Moderne* block of *c.* 1935, perhaps by *Cleland & Hayward*, and Nos. 16–17, *c.* 1890–5, surely by *F.T. Beck*, with shallow oriels and a Dutch gable.

3. North Street and Molineux

From the W end of Queen Square again, N up NORTH STREET. No. 1, W side, *c.* 1830, with windows framed by plain pilasters in the end bays. Former TOWN HALL TAVERN, Gothic with blue tile frieze, dated 1874. Opposite, Early Victorian classicism, including the former QUEEN'S HOTEL, N corner. Then the Town Hall and Civic Hall on the W side, and the Civic Centre opposite (p. 682). N of the Civic Hall the TELEPHONE EXCHANGE by *N.H.A. Gallagher* of the *Ministry of Public Building and Works* and *Clifford Culpin & Partners*, job architect *Leslie Parrett*, 1971 etc., in the same brick idiom as the Centre, extended from the Neo-Georgian block of 1932 by the *MPBW* in Mitre Fold, SW.

Further N down North Street, Giffard House and the church of St Peter and St Paul (p. 679). E of them, through the subway under the ring road, and l. MOLINEUX is a historic house and a famous football ground. An existing house was bought by Benjamin Molineux in 1744. The family sold it in 1860 to Oliver McGregor, who turned it into a hotel, and the grounds into pleasure gardens, taken over by Wolverhampton Wanderers FC, founded in 1877. The hotel closed in 1979 and remained empty. Some fittings were salvaged in 1999, before a fire in 2003 left it a shell. To its great credit, Wolverhampton Council was determined to save the building. In 2004 *Donald Insall & Partners* were appointed, and a full restoration as the CITY ARCHIVES was completed in 2009.

The façade, facing S across the ring road, looks *c.* 1740–50. Five bays, three storeys. Brick with sandstone dressings and quoins, the keystones nicely integrated with string courses. In the 1750s Benjamin Molineux added a new N front with a two-bay E extension slightly higher than the original. It has two Venetian windows. Smaller but wider wing to the S, probably contemporary. Large but tactful brick extension by *Insalls*. Their clock turret follows a lost one of *c.* 1876. The main staircase was re-created from surviving pieces and photographs. It has three thin twisted balusters to each tread. The OAK

ROOM to the r. has panelling similarly re-created, with fluted Corinthian pilasters and fielded panels. The ROCOCO ROOM, behind the Venetian windows of the 1750s extension, has sumptuous plasterwork probably by *Francesco Vassalli*, again re-created, partly from remaining pieces. It includes cresting to the windows, garlands and a delicate ceiling.

Behind is the WOLVERHAMPTON WANDERERS ground, redeveloped in 1991–3 by the *Alan Cotterell Partnership*. Blue-brick base, corrugated metal cladding and big steelwork frames in yellow and orange, to reflect the club's colours. The Stan Cullis stand is by *AFL*, 2012. STATUES: Billy Wright, 1996, and Stan Cullis, 2003, both by *James Butler*, who has made the great manager look like a bemused commercial traveller.

4. South-east to St George's and Cleveland Road

Starting from the s end of Princess Street, where MARKET STREET leads s. In Castle Street, E, an early 1850s iron merchant's warehouse (partly rebuilt), with a surprising Romanesque portal in coloured brick. On the corner of Market Street and Tower Street the WHEATSHEAF pub, 1923 by *A.T. Butler*, cool Neo-Georgian. Market Street continues s as Garrick Street, with the WULFRUN CENTRE, W side, by *Thomas & Peter H. Braddock* and *Bernard Engle & Partners*, 1966–9. Low, white, with many fins and some angular relief panels. Interior refurbished and roofed by *Chapman Taylor*, 2000. RELIEFS of Wesley preaching and Wulfruna receiving her charter, 1968–9. On the E side the library (p. 683), with OLD HALL STREET on its N side. In it the former PUPIL TEACHERS' CENTRE by *T.H. Fleeming & Son*, 1899–1901. A remarkable building in a radically simple Arts and Crafts manner. Gabled main block with both round-headed and three-centred-arched windows, in the A.S. Dixon way. Big semicircular bay and reduced Venetian semi-dormer to the house end, r. Beyond, the former ST GEORGE'S VICARAGE by *Edward Banks*, 1851, basic Tudor Gothic. To the SE, the former St George's church (p. 677). Facing it across St George's Parade, the curving FOYER building by *Howl Associates*, 2001–3: red brick and a long copper panel set forward at first-floor level: the materials of the moment.

Further S, running down Tempest Street, well-detailed flats also by *Howl*, 2008. To the E, a path leads to a crossing of the ring road and into CLEVELAND ROAD. On the s side a late C19 boot factory. Then the former ROYAL HOSPITAL by *Edward Banks*, 1845–9. Solid Early Victorian classicism. Five-bay central block with a tetrastyle portico which has Doric piers, not columns. Pilasters along the lower wing and surviving r. pavilion. The l. end was replaced by the EDWARD VII WING of 1912 by *A.W. Worrall*, repeating the elevation but pushing forward to the road. Behind, NURSES' HOME also by *Worrall*, 1907–8, heavy Neo-Georgian. Further down Cleveland Road the former FORDER CARRIAGE WORKS of 1886–7 by *Oliver*

Essex. Four storeys, with a skyline of pedimented dormers and a cut-off tower.

Dedicated walkers can cross the widened Bilston Road beyond, then E down Sharrock Street to Commercial Road, with the enormous former MUNICIPAL POWER STATION by *A.P. Brevitt*, 1895. Two gabled halls. Front office block, its upper storey added by *William Edwards*, 1901. To the N around WALSALL STREET, several C19 factories and the HARP INN, Neo-Georgian by *A.T. & Bertram Butler*, 1932–3.

5. Snow Hill and St John's Square

From the library, S down SNOW HILL. On the W side a row of late C18 houses. The Temple Street corner retains first-floor windows with swept-up lintels. To its l. a surviving giant pilaster. Further S, a long consistent row. Most have five-piece first-floor window lintels, often with fluted keystones, and several a modillion cornice. Nos. 33–34 were stuccoed *c.*1850–60, with most details replaced. On the E side No. 26, a former Barclays Bank by *John H.D. Madin & Partners*, 1969, with slim fins and much glazing. Then the former Whitehead Bros' printing works (hence the reliefs of heads), 1954 by *Johnson & Giles*. Beyond, St Mary and St John's church (p. 679). At the end of the C18 row, GEORGE STREET runs W, with consistent Georgian houses. Details similar to Snow Hill, so again late C18. St John's church (p. 677) is a perfect focus at the W end. No. 14, the corner house on the N side, has elegant Wyatt windows with fluted capitals to the slim three-quarter columns. The opposite corner house looks early C19, with windows in shallow reveals. Then houses on both sides with swept-up first-floor lintels. Standard doorcases with open pediments. Shallow ground-floor bays on Nos. 2–5, S side. This side is complete, with some moulded cornices and plain windows from No. 6 onwards, so probably slightly later. The N corner house by the church has a good pedimented doorcase with leaf capitals and Doric frieze, the S corner belongs with the Convent of Mercy (p. 681).

ST JOHN'S SQUARE itself is a let-down, the S side open to the ring road. Going anticlockwise N, past the convent, sensitive replacement ranges by *Richard Twentyman* (*Lavender, Twentyman & Percy*), 1966, with red rendered storeys over a brick base. They flank BOND STREET, running N, with Georgian houses on the W side. CHURCH STREET runs W from the square with one surviving Georgian pair, N.

6. The railways and canal, Corn Hill and Springfield

The shallow valley E of the centre was a natural through route, and the present townscape is dominated by the Birmingham Canal of 1770–2, one surviving railway – the London & North Western route – and one former one – the Great Western

– which all run SE–NW. Springfield, to the NE, has C19 terraces, but its factories have mostly gone.

The start is the railway station (p. 683), reached from the W across a curving bridge with angular canopy by *Austin-Smith:Lord*, 2011, over the ring road, then along RAILWAY DRIVE over the canal. By the station entrance, a subway leads under the tracks and we turn r. along a blue-brick colonnade, part of extensive reconstruction of the High Level embankment *c.* 1880. Here is the former LOW LEVEL STATION by *William Wilson*, working under *John Fowler*, engineer of the Oxford, Worcester & Wolverhampton Railway (later GWR), 1854–5. Blue-brick and limestone dressings. Five-bay pedimented centre and end pavilions, the details not scholarly. Conversion and extension by *Tweedale*, 2011–13, retaining an early C20 canopy and part of the footbridge. The glass porch is a pity. Continuing SE, by the railway bridge in CORN HILL, the GREAT WESTERN pub, here before 1852. Early C20 sashes, probably by *W.A. Hutchings*. Under the bridge, an evocative climb: cobbled street, blue-brick walls and pavements. Above the r. wall a former HYDRAULIC ENGINE HOUSE. Two gabled blocks. Its boilers powered the cranes in the former MILL STREET GOODS DEPOT, set back opposite, of 1849–52. Five bays wide under two pedimented roofs, nine bays long. Blank round-headed arches. Another nine bays to the SE, reconstructed with an extra storey probably in the 1880s.*

Beyond the canal, S, flats of 2003 etc. by *BLB Architects*, with the noticeable monopitch roofs of the early C21. Down ALBION STREET through them, on the N side the 1830s former ALBION FLOUR MILL, three storeys plus dormers, and a basement to the canal, with a row of gables to the E and a restored N lucam. Two-storey range to the SW. Further E is UNION MILL STREET, with a partly surviving industrial group of *c.* 1840 including a good three-bay MANAGER'S HOUSE, articulated by massive plain pilasters. At the far end, backing on to the canal, the CHEESE AND BUTTER WAREHOUSE, two storeys, with iron columns inside. Later C19 projecting r. wing.

Now S from Union Mill Street, and E along Horseley Fields. WULFRUNA COAL CO. OFFICES, heavy Neo-Georgian of *c.* 1947. At the canal bridge a track N leads on to the towpath of the Birmingham Canal, then NW and W under Corn Hill and a multi-storey car park. Beyond is a small branch canal, entered under a mid-C19 iron footbridge with lattice parapets, and then a brick WAREHOUSE built for the Shropshire Union Canal in 1869–71.

Under the bridge beyond we can turn back r. on to WEDNESFIELD ROAD, then E under the railway girder bridge, dated 1880, engineer *Henry Woodhouse*, makers *Horseley Co. Ltd*. Dominating in front, Wolverhampton's only monument to the early C21 high-rise fashion: VICTORIA HALL, student flats by *oconnell east*, 2009. Twenty-five-storey tower in grey, white and

---

*Beyond on the r. was the impressive OLD STEAM MILL (dem. 2015) of 1851, by *William Fairbairn & Sons* of Manchester.

pale brown cladding, with three-storey sections cantilevered out to the E. An uncomfortable design, but its grain does respond to its surroundings. N along Lock Street, with lower blocks of the Victoria Hall scheme. At the end, r. down the steps and NE along Grimstone Street. The former SPRING-FIELD BREWERY begins with the four-storey brick block with stone trim, running N–S, of 1873–4. It is crowned by a pyramid roof, originally ventilating the maltings. In front is the two-storey BREWER'S HOUSE, with pedimented doorcase. This belongs to extensions by the brewery engineer *Robert Cooper Sinclair*, 1880–1. His largest addition is the range running SW–NE parallel to the street, of two tall storeys with blank arches and round-headed windows. A similar range runs N behind, with partly surviving clock on the rooftop. Absorbed by Mitchells & Butlers in 1960, the brewery closed in 1991, and suffered a serious fire in 2004. Converted and extended as the SCHOOL OF ARCHITECTURE AND THE BUILT ENVIRONMENT of the University of Wolverhampton, by *Associated Architects*, 2018–20. New sawtooth ranges in bronze-coloured metal cladding, and a big glazed link. Forceful glazed top floor to the four-storey range.

Two ranges of stables were built along CAMBRIDGE STREET at the E, with brick relieving arches and clerestory roofs. Between them a delightful gatehouse. Brick blocks with stone trim flank a three-centred timber arch with shallow gable. Decorative iron gates, ironwork in the gable with William Butler's eagle symbol. Further N, extension buildings of 1895.

On the opposite corner of Cambridge Street, a former MISSION CHURCH-cum-school by *T.H. Fleeming*, 1879–80, with large windows from alterations of 1898. It was the predecessor of St Stephen's church, beyond (p. 678).

Back to Lock Street, w under the railway, and across the canal by Little's Lane Bridge, a pair of C19 LOCK COTTAGES and the top LOCK of the Wolverhampton flight. This descends N through twenty-one locks to the Staffordshire and Worcestershire Canal at Autherley Junction. S of the cottages is Broad Street Basin, landscaped by the council in 1980–1.

OTHER BUILDINGS

A scatter of buildings S of St John's church, beyond the ring road. ST JOHN'S RETAIL PARK is by *Mason Richards Partnership*, 1996. In Dudley Road an austere Gothic former BOARD SCHOOL. Ground floor of 1872–3 by *George Bidlake*, upper storey and gables by *T.H. Fleeming*, 1887. To the W, at the corner of Frederick Street and Thomas Street the former STAR MOTOR CO. factory of 1896. Under the nasty render are pilasters and a central straightened Dutch gable. Further W is SUNBEAMLAND, the former Sunbeam cycle factory. The part facing Paul Street comes first, in 1896. Later work by *A. Eaton Painter*: along Jeddo Street, rebuilt in 1914, and Pool Street, not completed until at least 1922. Plain three-storey elevations with prominent chimneys.

CHILLINGTON CANAL INTERCHANGE BASIN, Bilston Road, SE. Last survivor of many similar basins in the Black Country. They came about because after 1846 the Birmingham Canal Navigation fell increasingly under the control of the London & North Western Railway, which with the Great Western Railway encouraged the use of canals for short journeys, with railways working longer-haul traffic. The Chillington basins began as a branch canal into the Chillington ironworks, made in 1829 and improved in 1848, the date on the ROVING BRIDGE over the entrance. The interchange was built in 1902. Two gabled open SHEDS on steel piers, one still served by a canal arm. On the N side the remains of a 1930s TRAVELLING CRANE.

MONMORE GREEN SCHOOLS (former), Bilston Road, SE, beyond the railway bridges. Gothic, of 1873–4.

LEAPING WOLF pub, in the fork of Waterloo Road and Staveley Road, N. In origin a tall, steep-gabled house almost certainly by *George Bidlake*, 1864. HATHERTON ARMS, North Road, N. By *A.T. Butler*, 1927. Rounded corner with tall windows; dramatically tall chimneys, l.

BILSTON

Part of the royal peculiar of Wolverhampton, and mentioned in Wulfruna's charter of *c.* 994. An iron-making centre from the later C18, many of the works lining the Birmingham Canal. The most important, and last survivor, was Spring Vale, later Hickmans, then Stewarts & Lloyds. It closed in 1979. Bilston was an Urban District from 1894 and a Borough from 1933, absorbed into Wolverhampton in 1966.

The Borough Council was progressive, influenced by the socialist alderman Ben Bilboe (1902–51) and A.V. Williams, Town Clerk 1941–6. Early evidence is *Lyons, Israel & Elsom*'s health centre of 1938–9. For post-war housing *Otto Neurath* of Vienna was consulted in 1945, and *Ella Briggs* designed a scheme round a communal green. In 1946 *Sir Charles Reilly* proposed housing estates designed round similar curving greens, with detailed designs by *Derek Bridgwater*, *Bernard Miller*, *F.X. Velarde*, *Clough Williams-Ellis* and *Lionel Brett*, all Reilly pupils or associates. However, the Stowlawn Estate was built from 1947 by *McKewan, Fillmore & McKewan*, and smaller estates by the Borough architect *W.G. Lofthouse*. Many of the greens in Stowlawn were infilled in the early C21. Survivors of this idealistic programme are the *Briggs* scheme, and *Miller*'s mission church. *Lofthouse*'s HOUSES include some flat-roofed designs, e.g. on the corner of Wolverhampton Street and Shale Street, and Station Road SW of Oxford Street.

1970s demolitions for the Black Country Route separated Oxford Street from the town centre immediately to its N. Surprisingly, the centre retains its character, helped by an early C21 Townscape Heritage Initiative.

WOLVERHAMPTON · BILSTON 697

CHURCHES

ST LEONARD, Church Street. The very hub of the town. Medieval stonework survives inside the tower, a SW staircase with small blocked windows, and the ringing chamber doorway with a pointed arch and single plain chamfer, C14 or C15. The rest was rebuilt by *Francis Goodwin* in 1825–6 to a classical, not a Gothic, design. Long round-arched windows along the sides, broad five-bay front with two tiers of windows and a square, chamfered tower with a shallow dome, a little Soanian in detail.* *Ewan Christian* made alterations in 1882–3, including it seems to the cornice. Inside, a panelled segmental vault with rosettes in squares. Segmental sanctuary arch with Ionic columns at gallery level on tall projecting piers, and flanking pilasters with Greek ornament. The sanctuary has a semi-dome with delicate ribs. Galleries with cast-iron piers which have more Greek ornament; cut back by *Christian* in 1882–3, with Jacobean-style baluster fronts. – ALTAR RAIL, semicircular, by *Bernard Miller*, 1946. The REREDOS may be his. – PULPIT and CHOIR STALLS by *J. Drayton Wyatt*, 1869, the stalls rich and heavy, with round arches and balusters. – PEWS by *Christian*, 1883. – FONTS. A small octagonal pier with a tiny bowl, dated 1673. Elegant gadrooned and fluted bowl on a marble stem, probably of 1748. – STAINED GLASS. E window by *Shrigley & Hunt*, 1908. – MONUMENTS. A nice group flanking the sanctuary. N side, Sarah and John Willim, †1834 and †1837, by *Edward Gaffin*, with a weeping woman against a tomb; tablets with urns by *J. G. Bubb, William Weale, Peter Hollins* and *G. Legg*, †1822–†1863. S side, tablets by *Hollins* and *Weale*, and two more ambitious memorials by the latter: Brueton family, †1844 etc., with an urn in low relief, and Sarah Riley †1835, with an angel conducting her to heaven.

Churchyard with good TOMBS, the best on the N. Job Smith †1822 etc., chest tomb with reeded corners and frieze with cherubs' heads. – George Beards †1817 etc., a tea-caddy with delicate cherubs' heads and symbols. – Charles Gallimore †1816 etc., another tea-caddy, with Gothic cusped panels. – Also, W, iron memorial slabs.

ST MARY, Oxford Street. 1829–30 by *Goodwin*. A Commissioners' church, in a pretty Gothic style typical of the moment. It looks Perp, but the long two-light windows have cusped lights of an early C14 kind. Large blocks of limestone. The tower has big diagonal buttresses, an octagon with lancet windows, and crocketed pinnacles. Unusually it is an E tower, built over vestries behind the altar. There is even a doorway to confuse the unwary. The interior has a very shallow ribbed vault, panelled in the centre, and an equally shallow sanctuary arch with frilly cusping. Galleries with plain panelled fronts, on iron columns. Fine original REREDOS: centrepiece with octagonal turrets, like

---

*Iron bollards set into the doorway, with the architect's name and date, were stolen in the late C20.

a miniature King's College Chapel front, flanked by narrow bays with panels for Creed and Commandments. – FONT and PEWS by *F.H. Chettle*, 1919, but looking *c.*1870–80. – PULPIT. By *James A. Swan*, 1929, a good piece with relief and late Gothic canopy-work, but cut down.

ST CHAD, Connaught Road. 1953–5 by *Bernard Miller*. Buff brick. Tall three-sided apse, impressively blank except for a relief panel of Lichfield Cathedral. The roof sweeps down over the nave, with well-placed rows of dormers (now UPVC). Apse, flèche, SE belfry and windows all have sources in G.E. Street and his contemporaries. To prove the point, the laminated roof has scissor trusses and long passing braces down to wall-posts. – ALTAR with chunky beam-ends and a sun in relief.

HOLY TRINITY (R.C.), Oxford Street. Original church of 1833–4, a big box with lancet windows. Street front altered in 1926 by *G.B. Cox*, with a pent-roofed extension, Gothic porch and three-light window. Chancel by *Pugin*, 1845–6. His Dec E window has fancy tracery, spherical triangles in a circle. Gallery of 1834 with iron columns and railing. – PULPIT by *Cox*, made by *Jones & Willis*, 1927. – FONT perhaps by *Pugin*. In the porch, a small early C19 cast-iron octagonal bowl on a stem, perhaps its predecessor. – STAINED GLASS. Bright E window by *Wailes*, 1846.

Adjoining on the r., former SCHOOL of 1834 with an odd Baroque front of 1895. PRESBYTERY and SOCIAL CENTRE behind by *W. Chavasse* of *Jennings Homer & Lynch*, 1969.

METHODIST CHURCH, Bow Street. 1969–70 by *Diamond, Redfern & Partners*, brick, with vertical piers. Big SUNDAY SCHOOL, 1896 by *Richard J. Rowe*, with prominent semicircular-headed semi-dormers. Plainer block behind probably of 1868.

ASHLEY'S CHAPEL (Congregational; now Mission Hall Apostolic Church), Chapel Street, off Oxford Street. 1870 by *George Bidlake*. Romanesque, with plate-tracery windows, but a pointed arch to the doorway. Now heavily rendered, and the bellcote cut down.

PUBLIC BUILDINGS

TOWN HALL, Lichfield Street. 1872–3 by *Bidlake & Fleeming*, extended W by *T.H. Fleeming*, 1880–1. Stone-faced. S tower, a fine accent in the fork of the streets. 'What can one call this style?' (Pevsner, 1974). The ground floor is distinctly Second Empire: smooth rustication, a doorway with stilted arch and chunky sandstone shafts, segment-headed windows and early Gothic capitals. The fluted keystones on the tower, however, suggest Jacobean. Unfortunate glass porch by *Brownhill Hayward Brown*, 2008.

CITY OF WOLVERHAMPTON COLLEGE, Wellington Road. By *Bond Bryan*, 2000–2.

BUS STATION, Market Street. By *DGI International*, 1990–1. High Tech, with canopy and masts, but rather crude.

GIRLS' HIGH SCHOOL (former), Wellington Road and Windsor Street. 1929–30 by *G.C. Lowbridge*, clearly a special job. Impressive but heavy William and Mary front, with a five-bay central block which has a three-bay pedimented centre, and end wings. All the projections marked by giant simplified Composite pilasters. Doorway with a big scrolly pediment. Housing conversion 2013.

LOXDALE PRIMARY SCHOOL (former), Chapel Street. By *C.W.D. Joynson*, 1929. Gables with round-arched windows which have cornices curved up round them.

VILLIERS PRIMARY SCHOOL, Prouds Lane. Also by *Joynson*, 1932. Neo-Georgian, with a blocky centrepiece.

For other public buildings *see* Perambulation.

PERAMBULATION

The centre is an intimate group of streets around St Leonard's, and one long street running w. From the Town Hall, SE of the church, first SE down LICHFIELD STREET. Set back on the NE side a former bank of 1973–5 by *Lloyds Bank Premises Dept*, with a cantilevered upper floor supported on vaulting ribs. Opposite, MORTONS, C17 or early C18, hides its history under fake timbering. Elegant mid-C18 side doorway. This faces THE ORCHARD, with mutilated Georgian cottages on the w, and at the end, PIPE HALL. An early history refers to rebuilding 'about the year 1693'. Three rear gables. A sandstone ashlar front to Hall Street, now painted and mutilated, was added *c*.1800–10, its odd shape masking the side gables. First-floor Venetian window in a three-centred relieving arch; central pedimented niche with pilasters. Back on Lichfield Street, the OLDE WHITE ROSE has a stuccoed front of *c*.1820–30 with paired Corinthian pilasters. Opposite, a mid-Georgian pair with first-floor windows with fluted keystones. Ahead is BARCLAYS BANK, Early Georgian, three storeys with a parapet. Keystones and pedimented doorcase linking to string courses. Single-storey banking hall by *Yeoville Thomason*, 1881, r., attractive if mongrel brick classicism. Then an Early Victorian house with canted bays, in the fork of Bow Street. Further SE the former OAK AND IVY pub of 1934, almost certainly by *Watkin & Maddox*, with sculpted roundels.

Now NW from the Town Hall. On the NE the former SPREAD EAGLE, C17 or C18, altered, and former MIDLAND BANK of 1923–4, probably by *Woolfall & Eccles*, unfortunately rendered, with a good three-light central window and lunette. The former WOOD'S PICTURE PALACE by *Hurley Robinson*, 1921, has a big lunette window under a pediment. It extends into a Late Georgian house, r. Opposite, on the corner of Walsall Street, the former PARSONAGE, by *Richard Tutin*, 1822.* Severe Greek

---

*Francis Goodwin claimed the design in his *Rural Architecture* of 1835, but Tutin's drawings and affidavit in Staffordshire Record Office match the building in all but a few details. Tutin died in 1832, before Goodwin published.

Revival, its composition a bit out of the ordinary. Giant pilasters and a recessed centre. The entrance has its own minor order. Ends also recessed, with corner pilasters.

WELLINGTON ROAD, running NW here, was cut by an Act of 1821. A good original row on its NE side. The corner building is resolutely asymmetrical, with a Greek Doric porch. WELLINGTON HOUSE is typical of c.1830, with architraves on consoles and a recessed porch with minimal pediment and Doric columns *in antis*. In the fork of Prouds Lane the former HEALTH CENTRE (now Community Centre), by *Lyons, Israel & Elsom*, 1938–9. 'The moment of Dudok inspiration in England' (Pevsner). Light brown brick and horizontal windows. A low, single-storey building, the taller, recessed main hall with clerestory lighting. The concave front addresses the acute corner. Porch on angled steel piers, nicely integrated with access ramps.

Now back to the cross-roads by the parsonage and NE up MOUNT PLEASANT. On the NW side late C18 houses, including No. 4, with big leaf-decorated keystones and end pilasters. The former DRILL HALL (now pub) is by *Henry T. Hare*, 1901. Enjoyable Free Style classicism. The centrepiece is a full-height Doric aedicule with open pediment and royal arms, its bases tied to the imposts of the big round-arched windows. Where it breaks up into the roof there are larky scrolls. Opposite, former POLICE STATION of 1846–7 by *Joseph Potter Jun*. Three bays, hipped roof, heavy doorcase. On the NW side part of the former Wolverhampton District Electric Tramways depot, used until 1965 for municipal trolleybuses. Transformer station of c.1910 (now a gurdwara), and the former offices of 1902, neat brick and cream terracotta. Side pilasters with consoles setting back to the frieze. Magnet-and-wheel emblem of the British Electric Traction group. Beyond, the former TECHNICAL SCHOOL of 1897 by *C.L.N. Wilson*, U.D.C. Surveyor. Red brick and *Doulton*'s terracotta, with balustrade and small pediment. Doorcase and flanking windows with panelled pilasters. The blank end walls have terracotta roundels. On the SE side the LIBRARY AND ART GALLERY, a brick and tile-hung house of 1905 with a big shallow bow, extended r. as the library in 1937 (*W.G. Lofthouse*, Borough Architect). NW side, the former BELDRAY factory offices of 1937, with long bands of windows.

Finally W from the Town Hall, down CHURCH STREET. On the corner of WALSALL STREET a block with rounded corner, c.1830. HORSE AND JOCKEY pub of 1921, almost certainly by *A.T. Butler*, brick Tudor, with little flattened oval windows above the doors. Much-altered C18 houses beyond. On the NW old-fashioned terracotta shops of 1924. The MARKET TAVERN is c.1830, with paired window architraves. To its l. a former chemist's shop, also stuccoed, with giant pilasters and on the parapet a bust of Aesculapius, with snake and torch. The shopfront is partly original. In BROAD STREET, N, one surviving house of c.1820.

Church Street continues as HIGH STREET, with mangled Georgian houses and shops on the SE side. On the corner of Dudley Street the former SEVEN STARS pub of 1907, almost certainly by *Hickton & Farmer*. Half-timbered gables, corner cupola. Nos. 30–36 have Victorian bargeboarded gables. The splendid GREYHOUND AND PUNCHBOWL is not quite what it appears. The W range is genuine C15. Two close-studded gables to the W and one to the N: a remarkable display, for what must have been an important house.* *James A. Swan* transformed the rest in 1936 into an English inn of the type cherished by pub reformers. The E range is his, reusing old timbers. The front of the W range as restored seems essentially genuine, with two jetties, studding and small braces. Its front room has a C17 plaster ceiling with birds among branches bearing leaves and fruit. Stone fireplace of 1936, reused C17 panelling above. In the room behind, a C17 overmantel with plants in pots and standing figures, and addorsed dragons above. Small outdoor drinking area behind, typical of 'reformed' pubs, with a LOGGIA by *Swan*.

OTHER BUILDINGS

VILLIERS ARMS (former), Villiers Square. 1925–6. It must be by *W.A. Hutchings*, whose Neo-Georgian style is unmistakable. Rich doorcase with Tuscan pilasters.

LAWNSIDE GREEN, off Green Park Avenue, is the best survivor of Bilston's post-war housing. Pairs and terraces of four, all rendered, by *Ella Briggs*, 1946, laid out round a long, thin curving green. Special treatment is reserved for the terraces: Nos. 1–4 and 9–12, W side, with full-height flat-roofed bays; Nos. 49–52, E side, with cantilevered end balconies.

BRADLEY

A village 1 m. S of Bilston. The 'a' is pronounced long. John Wilkinson built the first furnace in the Black Country for smelting iron with coke here in 1757–8.

ST MARTIN, Slater Street. *George Bidlake*'s fine Gothic church of 1866–8 was demolished in 1977. The parish uses the former SCHOOL of 1900 by *Richard J. Rowe*, with a Jacobean-style central entrance.

WILKINSON PRIMARY SCHOOL, Walter Road. By *Architype*, 2014.

DAISY BANK CENTRE, Ash Street. A former Board School of 1878 by *A.P. Brevitt*. Also in Ash Street, the GREAT WESTERN pub. Converted from a house of *c.* 1835–40, probably in 1854 when a railway station opened next door (dem.). The stuccoed front must be part of the conversion.

---

*The Victorian historian of Bilston, G.T. Lawley, identified it with the manor house of Stow Heath.

BLAKENHALL, ETTINGSHALL AND PARKFIELD

s of Wolverhampton city centre. C19 terraces and factories in Blakenhall, centred on St Luke's church. To the E in Thompson Avenue, interwar municipal housing. The area of low-density post-war housing s of Parkfield Road and Goldthorn Hill was mostly in Coseley U.D.C. until 1966.

ALL SAINTS, All Saints Road. Nave and aisles of 1877–9 by *T. Tayler Smith* and *G.F. Roper* of London, won in competition. Big, impressively bony 'Early French'. Rock-faced local sandstone. The W front has a trumeau and a plate-tracery rose window. Big two-light clerestory windows, small lancets in the aisles. Side-buttressed NW porch. Chancel in the same style, added 1892 by *F.T. Beck*, with a big five-light E window, NE Lady Chapel and SE vestries. Reordered 1989–90 by *Twentyman Percy & Partners*. Arcades with circular columns, now cut by an inserted floor. Chancel and Lady Chapel used for worship, with a new N porch. Chapel arcade with four-lobed piers and double-chamfered arches, sedilia with cusped round-headed arches. – FONT with four-lobed bowl. – REREDOS by (*Sir*) *Charles Nicholson*, 1907, with saints in panels under canopies, large canopy, and transoms ending in riddel-posts. Now garishly painted. – The ROOD BEAM and figures saved from Nicholson's screen of 1937 are now at the back of the worship area. – WALL PAINTINGS, *c.* 1910. – STAINED GLASS. E window by *Hardmans*, 1892.

ST LUKE (former), Upper Villiers Street. 1860–1 by *G.T. Robinson* of Leamington, who evidently could be what Goodhart-Rendel called a rogue architect. Everything about the building has an exuberant originality; Pevsner called it 'furiously unruly'. Red brick with much banding and decoration in blue and yellow. SW steeple with angle buttresses, and deeply recessed segment-headed triplets in the bell-stage. Then it corbels out in alternating yellows and blues, turns octagonal (originally with corner pinnacles) and ends in a short spire with lucarnes. Circular SE stair-turret with a sharp spirelet. S portal with interlocking T-shapes of yellow and blue in the arch, circular RELIEF of St Luke, and gable jabbing up into the window above. NW portal even richer, with stepped T-shapes in red and blue and marble shafts, and a relief of Christ and disciples. Flying buttress above. Gabled clerestory with spherical triangles enclosing roundels. The nave windows and the attenuated three-light window of the SE vestry have the T-shapes again. The apse has – you expect it by this point – the 1860s fashion of gables running all round.

The interior, despite mid-C20 whitewashing, is just as extraordinary. Paired arcade piers with very thin bell capitals of cast iron. They end in pastry-cutter shapes below the impost blocks. The chancel arch is a stepped triplet with the same piers and steep, sharply pointed arches. All the arches have patterns of red, blue and yellow again. The roof is very steep and as tricky as E.W. Pugin, but plays with curves more. Enormous arched braces come down to corbels just above the arch imposts. Diagonal braces rise up to the principal rafters, with alternate bays enclosing the clerestory gables. The main braces support scissor trusses. Closed 2013, now an antiques centre.

Most FITTINGS still *in situ*. Massive limestone FONT on a central column and four corner ones of sandstone; REREDOS with carving of the Last Supper; some PEWS. – PULPIT by *Bridgemans*, 1909. – N chapel REREDOS by *F. T. Beck*, 1919. – CHOIR STALLS of 1926, probably *Beck*. – COMMUNION TABLE by *Frank Dredge*, 1929, ornate, with angels at the corners. Original COMMUNION TABLE, nave W. – STAINED GLASS. Apse, *Lavers & Barraud*, 1861, High Victorian, strong reds and blues. Lady Chapel N, 1924. – CHURCHYARD WALL in contrasting bricks, with gabled piers and quatrefoil piercings.

ST MARTIN, Dixon Street. A fine progressive design by *Richard Twentyman*, 1938–9. Still, just, a brick basilica in the interwar way, but moving fast towards Modernism. Maroon-red brick laid in Sussex bond. Plain central W tower, like a German *Westwerk* (cf. Hobbiss's Christ Church, Burney Lane, p. 272). Two set-backs near the bottom, another higher up, a row of unmoulded round-arched lancets near the top. The flat-roofed aisles project slightly on either side. Big round-arched W doorway, minimal Romanesque. Over it a STATUE of St Martin by *Donald Potter*, in the Gill manner. The clerestory and chancel have more unmoulded lancets, and the E end is absolutely plain except for a raised brick cross. The whole has a massive presence. Cool rendered interior. Low passage aisles, arcades without capitals. Heavy beamed ceiling, a Twentyman trademark. Bullnose piers divide off the S chapel. – Original PULPIT with curved corners and *Potter* sculpture of a lamb; LECTERN with tapering stand; CHOIR STALLS; ALTAR RAILS with a pattern of timbers separated by little red-coloured balls; ALTAR RAILS and PANELLING in the chapel; FONT with stylized dancing children and sprays of oak again by *Potter*, and elm COVER with a child held in a hand.

HOLY TRINITY, Farrington Road, Ettingshall Park. 1960–1 by *Caröe & Partners*. An odd building, set into the hillside, with the altar end facing the road. Gable with a big hipped-roofed aedicule enclosing the E window. Two levels of flat-roofed blocks either side. Entrance into basement community rooms, with stairs to the church. This has elliptical arches, but a semicircular chancel arch.

ST TERESA (R.C.), Birmingham New Road. By *Mason, Richards & Partners*, 1968. Very much of its moment, but a satisfying job. A picturesque array of dark maroon and blue-brick walls and piers. They resolve into a long lobby and spacious, almost square worship area to its l. Exposed brick inside, the floor too. Deep concrete roof beams. Lighting from a big (ritual) W window. – Original FITTINGS.

ST JOHN'S METHODIST CHURCH, Dudley Road. 1962 by *Malcolm Upright* and *Kenneth Gallimore* of *Hulme Upright*.

LANESFIELD METHODIST CHURCH, Laburnum Road. 1960–1 by *Richard Twentyman* and *Geoffrey Percy* (*Twentyman Percy & Partners*). Brick, long sloping roof, timber ceiling.

JEWISH CEMETERY, Cockshutts Lane, off Thompson Avenue. A narrow strip hidden behind houses, given by the Duke of Sutherland in 1851. Walls and OHEL (mortuary chapel) of 1884; the latter has oculi and a steeply pedimented plaque with foliage-pattern tiles. Fireplace with tiling, inscribed tablets.

PARKFIELD PRIMARY SCHOOL, Bowen Street and Dimmock Street. 1912–13 by *Ewen & J.A. Harper* of Birmingham. A conventional gabled design, but sparely and well detailed.

PARKFIELD HIGH SCHOOL (now LAWNSWOOD CAMPUS), Wolverhampton Road East. 1961–3 by *Norman & Dawbarn*. Miesian main block, lower ranges N and W.

ST LUKE'S CHURCH OF ENGLAND PRIMARY SCHOOL, Park Street South. By *Architype*, 2007–9. Their usual timber cladding and monopitch roofs.

PERAMBULATION. Starting at St Luke, Blakenhall. In UPPER VILLIERS STREET opposite, W, the J. ROPER factory by *A. Conrad Eckstein*, 1906. Going S, on both sides the former SUNBEAM MOTOR WORKS, an important early survival. John Marston, a cycle manufacturer in Paul Street (p. 695), started car building here *c.* 1900, at first on the E side. A machine shop was built behind in 1903, the three-storey office range in front with wide Dutch gables and a Baroque doorcase in 1905. Then in 1906–8 a large single-storey factory was built on the W side. The architect in 1903–8 was *Joseph Lavender*. Further extensions followed on the W, with the front range extended upwards as drawing offices in 1916, by *A. Eaton Painter*. His top floor has simpler Dutch gables flanking the archway. Car production continued until 1934, trolleybuses and aircraft until 1953. On the corner of Cross Street South, the former VILLIERS ARMS of 1920–3 by *W.A. Hutchings* (assistant *H. Marcus Brown*). Typical Hutchings Neo-Georgian doorcase.

GOLDTHORN HILL, ¼ m. S down Villiers Street South. HILL COTTAGE, on the E corner, has a platband suggesting the C17 or early C18. To the E, a tall brick PUMPING STATION of *c.* 1851 by *Henry J. Marten*, Wolverhampton Waterworks Co. engineer, advised by *Thomas Hawksley* of London. Impressive industrial architecture, with round-headed relieving arches, giant pilasters and rows of circular windows. On the corner of Fowler Street, BARONS COURT (now a hotel), by *W.J.H. Weller*. The original house of 1909, r., is of brick with a hipped roof. Big canted bay r., octagonal turret l. The big timber-framed section with recessed balcony and the diagonal end wing are of 1913 (the external staircase is late C20). Inside, the staircase has a handrail with stylized flower piercings. The finest room is in the diagonal wing: much timbering, inglenook fireplace. Beyond on the S, the GOLDTHORN PARK ESTATE, laid out from 1927 for the 2nd Earl of Dudley by *A.T. Butler*, who provided model house designs. Also his the corner houses to Ednam Road, and clearly a few others, e.g. the L-shaped house with porch in the angle on the corner of Honor Avenue.

PARK HALL (now hotel), Park Drive. A tall five-bay house, probably of c.1705–7. Display is reserved for the lively but old-fashioned central bay: doorcase with Doric pilasters and broken curly segmental pediment; first-floor window framed by part-fluted Ionic half-columns and very steep broken pediment; second floor with Corinthian half-columns. Angled metal and glass canopy slapped in front, unbelievably, in 2014. Crude C19 hipped roof; originally there was a parapet and urns. Neo-Georgian wings, early C20. Sedgley Park, an important Catholic school of the penal years, was here from 1763 to 1873.

NIPHON WORKS (now apartments), Lower Villiers Street. Four-storey range with a big shaped gable of 1898–1900.

BRADMORE, FINCHFIELD AND CASTLECROFT

Leafy, mostly C20 suburbs w of the town.

GOOD SHEPHERD, Windmill Lane, Castlecroft. 1954 by *Richard Twentyman*. A remarkably untouched dual-purpose mission church. The chancel is higher, with a grid of little windows. A metal screen divides it off when the nave is in community use. Stage for drama performances at the (ritual) w end. – Complete original FITTINGS, all timber, with a motif of flutings.

ST THOMAS (now WINDMILL COMMUNITY CHURCH), Oak Hill, Finchfield. By *J.R. Veall*, 1875. A small mission church. Rock-faced sandstone. Dec tracery. Steep s bellcote marking the division between nave and chancel.

ST COLUMBA UNITED REFORMED CHURCH, Castlecroft Road. By *Cecil Fillmore & Partners*, 1965–6, simple Modern. Oversized early C21 porch and spirelet.

SMESTOW SCHOOL, Windmill Crescent, Castlecroft. By *Yorke, Rosenberg & Mardall*, 1964–5. Buff-faced, load-bearing brick cross-walls divide a long two-storey block with slightly recessed timber-boarded panels (cf. Blythe Bridge High School, Staffs.): a solid effect. Single-storey craft rooms r., with clerestories. Front block by *Carillion TPS*, 2013.

UPLANDS JUNIOR SCHOOL, Finchfield Road West. By *Albert Chapman*, Borough Architect, 1969–70. Cubic brick blocks, single chimney as a vertical accent.

BANTOCK HOUSE (museum), Finchfield Road. Two gabled ranges, aligned N–S. The three-storey w part is the earlier, a mid-C18 farmhouse, with STABLES and altered BARN at the rear. The grander E range, five bays, with two tall storeys of the same height as the original three, was added c.1840. Stone porch with Soanian columns *in antis*, slightly later. Baldwin

Bantock, alderman, made alterations after 1895: an octagonal s turret, a CONSERVATORY at the SW corner, and a small pediment added to the early C19 front. The ground floor of the C18 block was opened out into a stair hall, with full-height panelling and inglenook. In 1900 a first-floor billiard room was created at the NW, with a very Wightwick-style inglenook. The architect for this, and probably all the work, was *Moses Johnson*. The drawing room and dining room in the front block were panelled, with delicate strapwork ceilings and fireplaces with Dutch tiles, in 1906, again very Wightwick (cabinet maker *George Pugh*). The house and grounds, now BANTOCK PARK, were given to Wolverhampton Council in 1940.

MERRIDALE CEMETERY. Laid out in 1848–50 by the Wolverhampton Cemetery Co., surveyor *Henry Beckett*. Large and now well tree'd, with curving paths. The original chapels and lodge by *Edward Adams* have gone, but his wall survives to Jeffcock Road, W, with heavily pedimented GATEPIERS. LODGE here of the 1880s. Towards the S a line of CATACOMBS, the earliest dated 1855, with 'Egyptian' entrances with tapering jambs. – MONUMENTS. Mary Steer †1878 etc., High Victorian Gothic. Gabled aedicules on a high base, with a pier growing out above with a Gothic capital and a statue of Faith, with anchor, on top. – John Shaw †1858 and others, a table tomb with aedicules all round, the central ones breaking into the top. This must be by the same designer (*George Bidlake*?). – Above the catacombs, the finest monument: Joseph Foster †1861 etc., a domed Ionic rotunda enclosing an urn on a high base. Capitals with shroud-like drapes between the volutes.

WINDMILL, Windmill Lane, Castlecroft, W. According to a stone on the SE, built by John Chamberlin in 1720. Tower only, brick, laid in irregular Flemish stretcher bond, and notably convex in section. Much rebuilt after an explosion, 2018. Small C19 porch, late C20 single-storey extension. An eye-catcher from Wightwick Manor, it was bought by Geoffrey Mander and given to Tettenhall U.D.C. in 1949.

THE HOUSES OF KENNETH HUTCHINSON SMITH

Kenneth Hutchinson Smith (1895–1945) was a Canadian army major who served in the Royal Engineers, and with this experience set up as a house builder after the First World War. He wanted to create a vision of continuing England, employing traditional craftsmen and many reused materials. He bought stone, old bricks, tiles and especially timber from demolished buildings, including Bradley Hall, Kingswinford, and Lymore, Montgomeryshire. He fits into a Wolverhampton tradition of timber framing stretching back to Wightwick Manor, but his work also relates to Arts and Crafts architect-builders such as Harold Falkner of Farnham and the Fallings Park radicals (p. 722).

FINCHFIELD GARDENS, off Finchfield Road opposite Bantock Park, was Smith's first development, the land purchased

c. 1920. Some plots have standard builders' houses; his own earliest surviving building is THE GREY COTTAGE, a bungalow for himself at the far end (altered). Then he built a number of distinctive small houses with mansard roofs, of which ST BEDE of 1922 is from a design by the young *Wallace Wood*, simplified in execution. THE DORMERS and RIVINGTON are almost certainly Wood's in origin, also one hipped-roofed Neo-Georgian house of 1923 on the E side, much altered.

CASTLECROFT GARDENS followed from 1927, Smith's most substantial development, off Castlecroft Road, entered down two narrow entries. Every house mentioned here is his.* Starting at the E end, No. 34 of 1931 contrasts a rendered wing with half-timbered gable with brick and timber l. wing. Down the side lane here, GREYSTONES of 1932 is tile-hung over render and brick. Big end chimneys, old timbers in the gables. STOW HOUSE has a rendered timber-framed wing and tile-hanging; PORCH HOUSE, 1929, lots of box framing and a big mullion-and-transom window. The window above has gargoyle-like corbels, probably C17.

Where the main lane turns W, in front is No. 32, MAGPIE LODGE, rendered, with hipped roof. Then ORCHARDS, of 1932, H-plan, rendered, with timber in the porch. BROOMY BANK, 1929, a double pile with hipped roofs. LITTLE OAK on the N side, probably late 1930s, is rendered but with structural timbers in the gable-end. Opposite, No. 26, tile-hanging and render, in a walled garden, of 1936. Nos. 20–24 beyond, 1935, plain. On the N again, GREY BEAMS is a re-erected C17 cottage from Trescott, finished *c.* 1943. Box framing to the upper storey and gable. BROOM, probably late 1930s, has framing in long wide panels. No. 15 of the same period shows *Smith*'s increasing mastery, its H-plan mixing reclaimed brick, tile-hanging, timber and creamy-buff render. Nos. 9 and 11, LYNDHURST and TIMBERS, 1937, are the only semi-detached pair, said to incorporate the structure of a Surrey barn. Carefully asymmetrical, balancing a plain gable with curving braces below against a half-hipped gable with smaller panels. No. 16, INGLE NOOK, 1932, at right angles to the road, has plaster left rough and brick-nogging. On the N again, PENNINGS, designed in 1928, has two large gables. Opposite, No. 14, white-painted brick and tile-hanging, and HOLLY COTTAGE of 1928, set back, similar to Broomy Bank. Opposite, THURLESTONE is also of 1928; lacking reused timbers, it looks blatant next to its neighbours. No. 3 is the C15 BUTTERMARKET from Shifnal, Shropshire, re-erected in 1936. Very much a West Midlands building, with its close studding, diagonal braces between the windows, and quadrant braces in the gable. Finally CORNER HOUSE to Castlecroft Road, built first, in 1927, to advertise the development. Rendered r. wing with timber gable, brick and tile-hanging l.

---

*Elevations of Orchards and Ingle Nook are signed by *Margot Ulrik*, whom Smith seems to have employed as a draughtswoman.

This description cannot convey the total impression of the curving lane, the houses of old timber, tile and brick, and their grouping among trees and lawns. It is perfect but slightly unreal. Inspector Barnaby may be around the corner.

OTHER BUILDINGS

THE SPINNEY, off Finchfield Hill. By *W.J.H. Weller*, dated 1908 on the sundial. Brick and timbering, a dramatic house. The entrance is recessed under a huge two-storey gabled timber oriel, all rectangular panels except for one big arched brace, and flanked by walls set at forty-five degrees. To the l. an octagonal glazed tower with pyramid roof. This forms the r. end of the former garden front, with a balancing turret l. and a central full-height canted bay flanked by covered open balconies, all under a great sweep of roof. Now engulfed in pastiche extensions, early C21.

WESTACRES, Finchfield Hill. A robust Jacobean house of 1895, with an array of gables and chimneys, now a pub.

GUNMAKERS ARMS, Trysull Road. By *A.T. Butler*, 1926–7. Brick, with stone dressings stressing the plain surfaces of walling and gables.

BRADMORE ARMS, Birches Barn Road and Trysull Road. 1928. A very odd design, brick with a half-timber gable, but the doorway surrounds rising to pointed arches. The heavy door architraves on brackets suggest *A.T. Butler*.

BUSHBURY

An ancient parish now mostly in Wolverhampton. Big municipal estates, interwar at Bushbury Hill and 1950s at Northwood Park, and more recent private development. Parish church and hall remain, with some interesting buildings in the rural N. Low Hill (p. 721), and Oxley and Fordhouses (p. 732), are dealt with separately.

ST MARY, Bushbury Lane. W tower, aisled nave with N chapel, and chancel, all of local sandstone. Chancel and tower are medieval, nave and aisles C19. The chancel is early C14, with three large windows on N and S with cusped intersecting tracery. Dec N doorway with ogee arch, no capitals and repeated hollow chamfers. Restored tomb-recess, N; PISCINA and triple SEDILIA, S, again with ogee arches and continuous mouldings, but here the main one is a sunk quadrant. Hammerbeam roof in which the hammerbeams turn up into the posts, two tiers of circular wind-braces: perhaps C17. The chancel arch must be later C14, with two plain chamfers and early Perp capitals and bases. The tower arch has similar mouldings, and an early Perp W window with very narrow upper lights. A S aisle by *James*

Wolverhampton, Bushbury, St Mary.
Engraving by R.W. Basire after Stebbing Shaw, 1801

Morgan, 1830–3, disappeared when nave and aisles were rebuilt by *Edward Banks*, 1851–3. Puginian Dec. Three-light windows with Geometrical tracery, slightly varied. s porch with diagonal gabled buttresses. Banks's arcades have octagonal piers and double-chamfered arches. The church had a late C14 N chapel, and *Banks* rebuilt it with the original materials – the difference is noticeable – further N: two-bay arcade with early Perp details like the tower, two-light windows with ogee tracery. Just w, a much-restored doorway with restored Norman arch with blank tympanum, from the former nave N wall. The quirkiest feature is the tiny gabled HORDERN CHAPEL, attached diagonally to the SE corner of the S aisle. By *Robert Raikes*, 1904, for H.S. Staveley-Hill M.P., to contain memorials of his Hordern relatives. Inside, a sandstone rib-vault.

FURNISHINGS. REREDOS by *Banks*. – WALL PAINTINGS all round the chancel, stems and foliage, in red, by *Thomas Chittenden*, 'the able master of the Wolverhampton School of Practical Art', 1853. – Balancing PULPIT and READING DESK made by *Henry Poole & Sons*, 1878, Gothic, either side of the chancel arch, an arrangement popular in the 1830s–40s.– ROYAL ARMS of Charles II, dated 1660, faded. – NAVE ALTAR and RAIL by *Twentyman Percy & Partners*, 1989. – FONT. Cup-shaped, divided by a broad zigzag band into triangles, filled with large fanned leaves, alternating upright and reversed, a larger version of those at Little Missenden, Bucks. (Malcolm Thurlby). In one triangle a small figure, perhaps Christ, the head restored, with hand upraised in blessing. A band of stylized trefoils around the rim and another round the base. Probably of *c.* 1200 but re-cut. – WAR MEMORIAL by *Bridgeman & Sons*, 1922. – STAINED GLASS. E window by *Henry Hughes* of *Ward & Hughes*, 'aided by suggestions from the Revds *J.L. Petit* and *H. Moore* and *Charles Winston*', 1853. It uses glass made to medieval specifications by *Powells* under Winston's direction. Small scenes from the Life of Christ, set in patterning, with oak leaves in grisaille. The prominent colour is a cool, attractive blue. Chancel side windows also almost all of 1853 by *Ward & Hughes*, with grisaille patterns and borders of castles and fleur-de-lys and maple-like leaves, following their medieval predecessors. C14 fragments in the central s window: Christ in Majesty and below, a priest praying and infant Christ. Also of 1853 the w window by *Ward & Hughes*, designed by *Winston*; S aisle E perhaps also theirs. S aisle w signed *O'Connor*, 1870, richly coloured. N aisle: N, *Gordon Webster*, 1964; W, *Alan Younger*, 1991. – MONUMENTS. Chancel. John Goughe †1645. Black-edged tablet, gristly surround with symbols of mortality, boars' heads above. – Two mutilated alabaster slabs, probably C17. – Edward Littleton †1724. Fluted Ionic pilasters, segmental pediment. – S aisle. Thomas Whitgreave †1711. Corinthian pilasters, segmental pediment. – Hordern Chapel. James and Jane Hordern, †1825 and 1813, by *Robert Blore II*. With Neoclassical busts in niches, turned towards each other. Opposite, Gothic aedicule to later family members.

The CHURCHYARD has much of interest. S of the church the base of a CROSS. Circular, like those at St Peter, Wolverhampton and at Penn, so optimistically attributed to the C11; but mostly late medieval: see the chamfered mouldings. Nearby, Greek Revival tomb-chest of 1813 to the Hordern family, and a tall Gothic memorial to the Rev. William Lister †1861. By the S aisle some simple C17 gravestones; another further E with cherubs (Jackson), also a finely lettered stone to a Catholic priest, John Carter †1803. W of the S porch a much-eroded medieval grave-slab. N of the church, tall square Greek Revival monument to Thomas and Sarah Bradburn, †1850 and †1858, weighed down by an enormous entablature.

W of the church the much-extended former SCHOOL, dated 1835.

CREMATORIUM, Bushbury Lane. 1953–4 by *Richard Twentyman*. Cool and gentle Modernism in yellow-buff brick and Clipsham stone. Low-pitched roofs, grouped around a tower-chimney with a pitched roof and stars on the main sides. *Porte cochère* on plain piers. Tall chapel block, its N end with stone panels and a large angel above, signed by *Donald Potter*, 1953. Inside, *Potter* doves above the catafalque. Arcade of circular piers, and windows on to an internal garden. The N side has a curving cloister ending in a circular tool store with conical roof with copper finial, and big *Potter* eagle on the W. Extended E by *Richard Twentyman*, with *George Sidebotham* and *John Hares* (*Twentyman Percy & Partners*), 1971–6, deliberately different, with an S-curve wall, and mansard roof behind.

BUSHBURY HILL PRIMARY SCHOOL, Old Fallings Lane. By *Architype*, 2011–12.

BUSHBURY HALL, Bushbury Lane, E of St Mary's church. The manor house of the Bushbury and Grosvenor families. Charles I stayed here in 1645. Front range rebuilt in the late C18, probably for William Huskisson (†1790). Three storeys, five bays, the central one wider. Ground- and first-floor windows with odd thin basic pediments. Late C20 doorcase. Two gabled rear wings with differing roof pitches, perhaps incorporating C17 fabric.

To the N, late C18 BARNS (roofless in 2020), making a U-shape open towards the house. E and W ranges with gabled centrepieces, one with a circular window and lunette.

MOSELEY HALL, Moseley Road. The home of the Moseley (Mollesley) family from the C14 to the later C18. We enter past brick COTTAGES with a platband, probably late C17, and fine C18 GATEPIERS with brick bands and big ball finials. Another set along the lane to the N. A simpler version of Old Fallings Hall, so probably Early Georgian; shown on an estate plan of 1728. Brick with stone dressings, five bays by three, with a hipped roof, modillion cornice and panelled doorcase. Three-row platband. Open-well staircase with swept-up rail and dado. The STUDY has C17 full-height moulded panelling with arcading to the corner fireplace, perhaps from the earlier house, which was further N. The DRAWING ROOM at the SW has fielded panelling with a dado, and a buffet in the NE corner. Neoclassical fireplace with vases and garlands. The main room on the S front has a large square bay, part of late C19 alterations. These include the two-bay extension with a steep gable l. of the main front and the extra bay beyond, now a screen, the kitchen behind having been demolished. They link the house to a range at right angles. Box-framed partition walls inside, probably C16. This timber building was encased in brick in the late C17 or early C18: two-row platband, as on the cottages, and noticeably thinner bricks than those of the main front. The windows are probably later insertions. Finally it was turned into a polite stable range in the mid C18, with a projecting central entrance with rusticated arch, pediment and cupola.

Landscaped GROUNDS to the S, probably late C18, with a lake. To the SE, a gabled SUMMERHOUSE.

(MOSELEY OLD HALL, ¼ m. N, is in Staffordshire.)

NORTHYCOTE FARM, Underhill Lane. A timber-framed lobby-entry house of *c.* 1600, drastically restored by F.W.B. *Charles*, 1984–7. The l. (w) bay, in render and tile-hanging, is entirely his, as are the timbering of the projecting gable, the close studding to the r., the wooden windows and the Tudor-style chimney, which he rebuilt from a stump. Collar- and tie-beam trusses inside, more reliable. One ground-floor room has reused C17 panelling and a stone fireplace, perhaps C18. Brick N wing dated 1758. Later arched link at first-floor level.

Behind, footings of a Gothick R.C. CHAPEL of *c.* 1821, built by G.T. Whitgreave of Moseley Court (dem. *c.* 1960), which lay ¼ m. NE.

CHAPEL ASH, TETTENHALL ROAD AND WEST PARK

This was the fashionable C19 residential area, NW of the centre, away from industry. It grew piecemeal along the Tettenhall and Compton roads from *c.*1830. West Park, opened in 1881, confirmed the status of the area. Schools and colleges began with the Grammar School's move to Compton Road in 1874–5, and multiplied in the 1960s.

CHURCHES

ST JUDE, Tettenhall Road. 1867–9 by *George Bidlake*. Competent Geometrical Decorated. Rock-faced Codsall stone with Box Ground dressings. Evangelical plan, with transepts and short chancel. SW tower; spire with flying buttresses added by *T.H. Fleeming*, 1877. Big four-light E and W windows. Buttresses with steep elongated nosings. SE parish room also *Fleeming*, 1890. Arcades with slim Aberdeen granite shafts and big leaf capitals. Scissor-braced roof. – Original REREDOS. PEWS, PULPIT with marquetry, and FONT. – Brass LECTERN of 1886 with angels on columns. – IMMERSION FONT. C20. – STAINED GLASS. E window by *Lavers, Barraud & Westlake*, 1870, small scenes with bright reds and blues; W by *Heaton, Butler & Bayne*, 1894, pictorial. – MONUMENT. Mary Davis †1886. Gothic aedicule, by *John Roddis*. – VICARAGE, see Perambulation 1, p. 717.

ST MARK (former), Chapel Ash. 1848–9 by *Charles Wyatt Orford*. Lancet windows. W tower with C13-style belfry windows and gablets marking the clock faces. Octagonal spire with lucarnes. Short chancel with three-sided apse. Vestries by *Joseph Lavender*, 1900. Arcade piers alternating quatrefoil and octagonal. Steep roof. Converted to offices 1988 by *Tweedale*.

CATHOLIC APOSTOLIC CHURCH (now RHEMA FAITH CHURCH), Bath Road. 1892–3 by *H. Whiteman Rising* of London. Lancet style, red brick with Hollington stone dressings. Apse with an ambulatory, spirelet over the chancel arch supported by buttresses clambering up the roof. Grand interior faced in white stone. Arcades and ambulatory with short circular columns and leaf capitals. – ALTAR and FONT, Victorian Perp, from the predecessor church in Dudley Road.

UNITARIAN CHURCH (now WEST PARK CHURCH, Evangelical), Park Road West. By *J.L. Ball*, 1911. A nicely detailed Gothic hall. Brick. Dec tracery in the SW gable, but the window above the entrance Bodley-style early Perp. Inserted floor by *Twentyman Percy & Partners*, 1986; narrow passage aisles survive.

ZION CITY TABERNACLE, Compton Road. A former Christian Science church. Low-pitched Modernism, by *John S. Scott*, *c.*1960.

FRIENDS' MEETING HOUSE, Summerfield Road. By *Clifford Tee & Gale*, 1969. Low, purple brick, monopitch roofs.

PUBLIC BUILDINGS

CITY OF WOLVERHAMPTON COLLEGE, Paget Road. By *Albert Chapman*, Deputy Borough Architect, with *N.C. Dowell, R.P. Callear, C.E. Hanley* and *J. Martin*. A five-storey curtain-walled block of 1959–62. Lower wings to the S of 1968, clad in prefabricated panels.

WOLVERHAMPTON GRAMMAR SCHOOL, Compton Road. Founded in 1512 by Sir Stephen Jenyns (Jennings), a local man who became Lord Mayor of London in 1509. The building in St John's Street, by *William Smith the elder*, 1712–14, was demolished for the Mander Centre. Present main buildings of 1874–5 by *Giles & Gough*, conventional scholastic Tudor Gothic, but solidly treated and well massed. Entrance tower with battlements and tall stair-turret. It housed boarders' bedrooms. To its l., BIG SCHOOL (for teaching), with tall, flat-headed two-light windows separated by multi-stepped buttresses, and a big five-light Perp w window. Hammerbeam and collar-beam roof, the members thin; two grand fireplaces with big stepped hoods. SE wing like a small version of Big School. To the r. of the tower a short wing and former headmaster's house beyond. SE of the original block, former GYMNASIUM of 1914 by *A. Eaton Painter*, with hipped roof and segment-headed doorcase, and the MERRIDALE BUILDING of 1930 by *G.C. Lowbridge*, William and Mary style (cf. his Bilston Girls' High School, p. 699). Giant pilasters and central pediment, heavy Doric doorcases. S extension of the old buildings, facing the playing fields, basic Tudor by *Stanger & Stanger*, 1897. Many post-war buildings, the best *Richard Twentyman*'s DERRY BUILDING of 1960. Also *Twentyman* the HALLMARK BUILDING of 1969, a chunkier brick job. – In Big School, STAINED GLASS from St Andrew Undershaft, London, including heraldic lions and symbols. Probably of *c.* 1530, like remaining glass in St Andrew, and linked to its rebuilding started by Jenyns *c.* 1520. Armorial w window by *Powells*, 1933.

WOLVERHAMPTON GIRLS' HIGH SCHOOL, St Jude's Road West, off Tettenhall Road. 1910–11 by *Fleeming & Son*. E-shaped, the main front facing SW. It shows the influence of the Birmingham Arts and Crafts school. Plain red brick with stone dressings. A long range in a simple Tudor or Jacobean manner, with a pair of full-height semicircular-gabled bays marking the centre. Just asymmetrical, the three bays r. of the centre wider than those on the l. The chimneys also differ. Chequer-pattern gables in the Lethaby and Ball way. Steep roofs. The main hall projects as the central stroke of the E, marked by alternate gabled bays with round-headed windows. Gutters like simplified dentil cornices. Barrel-vaulted interior, reconstructed after a 1970 fire. Recent buildings by *George Sidebotham (Twentyman Percy & Partners)*: GRAYSON TECHNOLOGY BUILDING 1992–3, SCIENCE BLOCK 1996, SPORTS HALL 2002–3.

COMPTON PARK SCHOOLS. A large campus running N from Compton Road. Two schools by *Richard Twentyman*. ST EDMUND'S CATHOLIC ACADEMY was the TECHNICAL TEACHERS' COLLEGE, of 1964, in fawn brick. Much alteration by *Turley Associates*, 2011–13. ST PETER'S COLLEGIATE SCHOOL, further N, is of 1965, extended 1970s. Similar but gentler, in golden-buff brick. Two-storey teaching blocks. Their shallow-pitched roofs are echoed in the angled end walls. Many additions, most recently by *Tweedale*, 2013.

WOLVERHAMPTON AND MIDLAND COUNTIES EYE HOSPITAL (former), Compton Road and Merridale Road. Original building by *T.H. Fleeming*, 1886–8, economical Gothic. W front with central tower and spire, wings with stone oriels and brick ribbing in the gables. Extended E by *Richard Twentyman*, 1935–8, his first major work, very progressive for the area. Grey-red handmade brick with Hollington stone details. Flat roofs and big metal windows. Shallow concave front block facing the road junction, with the main consulting room block behind. Unaffected and convincing. Closed 2007. Residential conversion proposed 2020, retaining part of the 1880s building.

SWIMMING BATHS, Bath Avenue. 1990 by *Rush Davis*. The red brick moment. Not inspired.

DRILL HALL, Park Road East. By *C.G. Cowlishaw*, 1910, his usual brick castellated job, but grander in this smart location. Stone-framed entrance arch with panels of trophies.

WEST PARK, Park Road East and West. A splendid Late Victorian municipal park, covering 50 acres inside an oval of roads. The site was Wolverhampton's first racecourse, of 1825 (with stands of 1827–31 by *Robert Ebbels*); laid out by *R.H. Vertegans* of Edgbaston, opening in 1881. Decorative RAILINGS all round (some restored). The main entrance opposite Southgate has stone Gothic piers, concave flanking walls, and a brick and half-timber LODGE. Similar piers at the other entrances, and another LODGE, N. The main feature is an hour-glass-shaped lake crossed by a cast-iron BRIDGE with Romanesque arcaded parapets. – STATUE of C.P. Villiers by *William Theed*, 1879, moved here 1931. Now sadly weathered. He is depicted speaking. Tall pedestal. – CONSERVATORY, N of the lake, by *Dan Gibson*, 1896. Brick base and Ionic pilasters, paired for the projecting entrance. The rest timber, including the pediment and big arched windows. Oblong domed cupola. Aisled interior with iron columns and brackets, supplemented by recent steel supports. – BANDSTAND given by Villiers in 1882, made by *Steven, Bros & Co.*, enlarged 1905. Frilly ironwork and ogee dome. – CLOCK TOWER of 1883.

PERAMBULATIONS

1. Chapel Ash and Tettenhall Road

CHAPEL ASH (the road) starts at the ring road with strident colours: Coniston House, S, re-clad by *Tweedale*, 2019, and

CHAPEL ASH, TETTENHALL ROAD & WEST PARK 715

Marston's brewery offices, N (p. 719). Going W, on the S side a former showroom by *A.T. & Bertram Butler*, 1948–9, streamlined with a tower. Then St Mark's church (p. 712), an excellent landmark. Set back behind, former VICARAGE of 1875 by *J.R. Veall*. Mullioned windows, square porch cutting into a semicircular turret. BARCLAYS BANK, adjacent, is by *Bertram Butler & Co.*, 1960, a well-detailed stone and glass block. On the N side, a row of four shops of *c.* 1850 with quoins, end pediments and central attic (Nos. 26–32), and the CLARENDON HOTEL, Victorian, with raised lettering; ground floor remodelled in 1906, almost certainly by *Joseph D. Wood*. Up Brewery Road alongside, a terrace of *c.* 1850. On the corners of Meadow Street a nice 1840s block with fancy Grecian window pediments, and a long plain row mostly of the 1850s. On the S side an 1850s stucco terrace with big architraved first-floor windows between narrow entrance bays. Its acute W corner has a fancy top beyond any classical discipline. Opposite, Neo-Georgian shops with a pretty cupola on the acute corner of Bath Road, looking 1930, but of 1949 (*Cleland & Hayward*), then a block with timbered gables and corner turret by *M.V. Treleaven*, 1908–9.

Here is the fork of the Tettenhall and Compton roads, with a tall cubic villa of shortly after 1852 between. Along TETTENHALL ROAD, the NE side starts with an early C19 brick terrace, including a little pub, the COMBERMERE ARMS, which retains three small bars accessed by a narrow corridor. The terrace belonged to CHAPEL ASH HOUSE (now SALISBURY HOUSE), W. Early Victorian at first sight, with big canted bays, rich cornice and lots of quoining: all here by 1852, and probably done for G.B. Thorneycroft, Wolverhampton's first mayor. But the central lunette shows that the house is C18 (leases are dated 1776–7). Beyond, a picturesque brick villa, and an 1860s pair with full-height canted bays which have broken segmental pediments at the top. Then two villas now part of West Park Hospital: No. 10, *c.* 1855, stuccoed, asymmetrical, with an elephantine side doorcase; No. 12, *c.* 1835, brick, with Ionic porch and end pilasters. Ionic bays of after 1871.

Now the SW side, with nicely varied terraces. First 1850s Tudor and classical, then a stucco row of the 1830s. Nos. 27–31 are Late Georgian. BLENHEIM TERRACE, *c.* 1850, has segmental-arched windows and Grecian doorcases suggesting *Edward Banks*. LANSDOWN TERRACE is 1840s, the bays added by 1870; PEEL TERRACE is 1850s, the details slightly fancier. ELY HOUSE is the best here, an austere three-bay villa of 1841–2, with end pilasters, deep cornice and pedimented doorcase. Late C19 bay. Built for Paul Law, Catholic, Tory and proprietor of the Star and Garter Hotel. Then Nos. 55–57 of before 1840, perhaps by *G.E. Hamilton*. The bays are later C19. Nos. 63 etc., an 1840s row with round-headed doorcases, the corner house grander, with a lintelled window; then a plainer pair with pilasters (Nos. 69–71). On the NE side, a Late Georgian group, some of the earliest in the road. No. 24 has a recessed panelled round-headed doorway. Then a terrace with standard Tuscan doorcases with open pediments. Two retain the distinctive panel-and-web fanlights of Nos. 44–45 Queen Street (p. 688). Nos. 34–36 are a three-quarter pair, but with a slightly grander Doric front doorcase. No. 38 is stuccoed, with a heavy Grecian porch. Nos. 40–42 have delicate pedimented doorcases. Beyond Middle Vauxhall an Early Victorian row with pilasters. Further on, DEANSGATE, formerly POPLAR TERRACE, of *c.* 1860. Heavy classical detail, round-headed upper windows. Perhaps by *Edward Banks*. Restored and extended SE by *Bloomer Tweedale*, 1991–2. Nos. 72–74 are a large 1830s stucco pair.

On the SW side, starting back at Larches Lane, houses by *Fred Hunter Lynes*: LARCHOLME, Jacobean Revival of 1900, and two pairs of 1901 with canted bays and tiled gables. Then BERRINGTON LODGE, by *George Bidlake*, 1866, beefy High Victorian. The side entrance tower is an extreme design: a Gothic porch with a massive circular column r. and two slim ones l., with foliage capitals, then a viciously corbelled oriel and a pyramid roof with tiny spirelet.

PARKDALE, on the NE, was developed by John Clarkson, financier and furniture agent, from *c.* 1878 until 1884, when he went bankrupt. His architect was *John Weller II*. A long green space curves N and E away from the road. The larger houses are in PARKDALE EAST, complete by 1881. No. 34, MONTFORD HOUSE, is the best, an eclectic design. A big semicircular

Wolverhampton, Chapel Ash, Parkdale, Montford House.
Drawing, *c.* 1878

bay rises to a turret, all glazed, with a conical spire (balcony altered). Hipped-roofed wing r. with an Aesthetic Movement half-timbered and pargeted upper floor. No. 35 is tall austere Gothic, with a cut-down tower. Nos. 36–37 are a rendered Tudor pair with steep gables and a long veranda. PARKDALE WEST has tall pairs of 1882–4, with gables and big square or canted bays. Some nice details, e.g. Nos. 5–6, with top-floor balconies under hipped dormers, a Weller trademark, and the frilly Gothic porches on Nos. 11–12. One later pair, Nos. 19–20, by *A. Eaton Painter*, 1903.

On Tettenhall Road beyond, an area of late C19 villas, interrupted by a cross-roads with the former HALFWAY HOUSE pub, C18, with characteristic lintels. To the N, SLADE HILL, flats of 1964 etc. by *Mason & Richards & Partners*. On the S side, it is worth picking out No. 161 of 1912 by *Fleeming & Son*, a pretty, rendered house with a complex front bay; No. 169, dated 1898, perhaps by *John Weller II*, picturesque but old-fashioned, with a spirelet; and Nos. 175–177 by *F. H. Lynes*, 1901, contrasting a rendered turret with a gabled wing with tile-hanging. Opposite, ST JUDE'S COURT flats by *S.D.W. Timmins*, 1934. Next to St Jude's church, the former VICARAGE by *John Weller & Sons*, 1897–9, perhaps *W.J.H. Weller*'s first design. Very red brick, with mullion-and-transom windows and a Gothic-arched doorway. Nos. 104–112 are by *F.T. Beck*, dated 1892, a terrace of gabled pairs, in Domestic Revival style; Wightwick Manor influenced local houses quickly. At the end, Balfour Crescent runs NE with Nos. 2–6 by *W.J.H. Weller*, 1909. Timber gables, sweeping roofs with little corner dormers. Continuing NW, on the SW side Nos. 213–215, *c.* 1855, a severe pilastered pair with recessed centre. Then Nos. 217–243, an even grander *Beck* composition, again of 1892. Two blocks of seven treated as a single composition with pairs of stone and timber bays, all different, and octagonal end turrets with copper ogee domes.

Now back SE, and SW down NEWBRIDGE CRESCENT. On the S side, flats by *Gotch & Partners* of London, 1961. On the N side, CRESCENT HOUSE, 1830s, stucco, with two full-height semicircular bows on the E front. FERNDALE is 1840s, with linked canted bays. NEWBRIDGE AVENUE, running S, was made in 1910. The language is still mainly half-timbering and render. E side first. THE COIGN is probably by *E. Hartill*, 1912, open porch. THE GABLES, *A.J. Walker*, 1914, not inspired. THE TUDOR HOUSE is by *W.J.H. Weller*, 1919, modest after his earlier work. Nos. 7–9 are by *G.J. Robinson*, 1923; No. 15 by *E. Hartill*, 1914, with timbering, brick quoins and segment-headed stone porch. Nos. 17 and 19, FAR CROFT, are by *Owen Parsons*, 1911, the latter particularly good, with an open timber porch, and a long casement band under the timber gable. A footpath link here to Compton Park. Back up the W side, No. 18, THE COTTAGE, is by *W.J.H. Weller*, 1911, excellent but not typical. Rendered in the Voysey way, tall and compact, with a fine play of masses and steep roofs, gables returned suggesting open pediments, and carefully placed casement windows.

No. 16 is early *H. Marcus Brown*, 1913. Nos. 10 and 8 are an unusual mirror pair by *Beck*, 1913, Arts and Crafts after a German holiday. Rendered, with bold quoins and a pattern of diagonals in the gables. Entrances treated as two-storey turrets swallowed by the façades. Nos. 4–6, old-fashioned Shaw style by *Charles Sharp-Smith*, 1910.

Further NW along The Crescent is the WOLVERHAMPTON LAWN TENNIS CLUB. A grand Gothic house of the 1860s, surely by *George Bidlake*, with a pyramid-roofed tower clamped between gables. Two similar but more modest pairs beyond. The Crescent rejoins Tettenhall Road at the grossly half-timbered NEWBRIDGE pub, by *Atkinson*'s *Brewery Surveyor's Department*, 1929.

Tettenhall Road continues NW. Set back, BREDON HOUSE, of *c.* 1840. A three-bay villa with an extra bay r. Clearly by the same architect as Ely House: see the side pilasters and heavy central chimneys. Delicate Ionic porch. Beyond is the STAFFORDSHIRE AND WORCESTERSHIRE CANAL of 1766–72 by *Brindley*, *Simcock* and *Dadford Sen.* (*see* Tettenhall, p. 736). Down l., the original Wolverhampton to Tettenhall road BRIDGE. Brick arch, widened on the S in the early C19.

Back down Tettenhall Road for just short of a mile, and S into LARCHES LANE. Consistent terraces of the 1870s onwards. At the W corner to COMPTON ROAD, LARCH PLACE, a charming L-shaped group probably of just after 1864, with fancy classical details. The road was originally closed by *George Bidlake*'s Trinity Methodist Church, vigorous Gothic of 1862–3. Its WAR MEMORIAL cross remains (*W. Hopcraft & Son*, 1920). Turning W, on the N side, flats by *S. D. W. Timmins*, 1937. Opposite, ASHTON HOUSE, with pilasters like Ely House, i.e. *c.* 1840. On the N side again, MERRIDALE HOUSE is Late Georgian, stuccoed, with pilasters, probably built for Edward Cooke. Two full-height semicircular bays to the garden, full-height W porch. Then Zion City Tabernacle (p. 712). WESTLANDS is a villa with Ely House-style pilasters but heavier detailing, perhaps *c.* 1850. Opposite, MERRIDALE LANE runs S, with the Grammar School (p. 713) on the W. Houses of *c.* 1860 down the E side. FAIR VIEW VILLAS are probably slightly earlier and by *John Weller I*, who died here in 1869. At the end on the r., OLD MERRIDALE, a much-rebuilt house restored from dereliction in 2003 etc. and now flats. Modest rendered exterior, with platbands, and C21 brick (replacing shopfronts). L-plan, the N cross-wing C15 or C16, the top storey altered in the C17 when the hall range was rebuilt. Walls underbuilt in brick in the C18, when the little S extension was added (the far end is C21). Gabled stair-turret in the rear angle. Archaeological investigation in 2001 revealed stone walls, C13 or older.

Now back N to Compton Road, and E. On the N side the entertaining ROYAL OAK, by *Joseph D. Wood*, 1906. Still Late Victorian, but details like the oval window show the date. Beyond, Late Georgian stucco terraces: Nos. 42–43 with local-style fanlights; Nos. 12–34, a long row with pilaster doorcases.

Restored 1977 by *Peter McAlster*. Opposite, the former Eye Hospital (p. 714).

Finally a glance down MERRIDALE ROAD, running SW. THE OAKS, on the SE, is a three-bay C18 villa with quadrant flanking walls. Central Venetian window and lunette above, still the William Baker type, but the handling looks later. C19 ground-floor window architraves. Nouveau-Georgian block l. by *Ronald Baker, Humphreys & Goodchild*, 1988. Opposite, the former Eye Hospital STAFF HOUSE, Neo-Georgian by *A.W. Worrall*, 1927–8 (demolition proposed). On the SE side, OAKS CRESCENT, cut shortly after 1840, with houses here by 1852: clockwise, Nos. 17–22, bargeboarded Tudor pairs; WITHYMOOR COURT, a tall stucco pair; and No. 34, a *cottage orné*.

2. West Park

The start is from the brewery on the S side of the park. Bath Road, running W from the N side, crosses SUMMERFIELD ROAD, with on the W side Nos. 1–4, an 1850s stucco terrace; Nos. 5–6, perhaps later, with pedimental gable and twin round-arched porches; and Nos. 7–8 a large 1840s stucco pair with big canted bays, No. 8 with a Jacobean-style side doorcase. The Friends' Meeting House (p. 712) is behind. To the N is PARK ROAD WEST, with the park railings on the r. On the corner, RAVENSHOLT, 1892 by the builder *Henry Lovatt* for himself. Beyond Connaught Road, the former Unitarian church (p. 712), then a pair of houses with canted wings and hipped roofs by *W.J.H. Weller*, 1914; No. 24 with timber gable and semi-dormers by *A. Eaton Painter*, 1924; and No. 23, simple, rendered, by *A.W. Worrall* for himself, 1923.

Back round the park from Ravensholt, in PARK ROAD EAST, linked pairs almost certainly of 1898 by the developer *J. Carding*, who may have used *H. Goddard*. Then large houses mostly of 1890–5. The house on the corner of Park Avenue has an octagonal corner turret. No. 42 is probably *John Weller II*, with a characteristic dormer. Nos. 43–45 must also be his, as they share the unusual stepped dormers. Lastly up Park Avenue and S into BATH AVENUE, with the swimming baths (p. 714) and KINGSTON HOUSE, a clean curtain-walled block with concave entrance by the *Ministry of Works Architects*, Birmingham, 1956.

OTHER BUILDINGS

MARSTON'S BREWERY, Chapel Ash. Thomas Banks established the Park Brewery here in 1875. From 1888 to 2007 Wolverhampton and Dudley Breweries, controlled by the Thompson family. Part of Marston's plc since 2007. By *Butler Wones* the big BOTTLING STORE of 1973 facing the ring road, E, and the brick OFFICES of 1976–7 to the S. Multicoloured new ENTRANCE by *Axiom*, 2015–16. To the W, one surviving late

C19 block, probably by *Joseph D. Wood*, 1897. Beyond it big mid-C20 blocks by *A.T. & Bertram Butler*.

HALFACRE, in Waterdale, off Compton Road. 1938, the best-preserved of *Richard Twentyman*'s early houses. Buff brick, hipped roof. Completely asymmetrical, Modernist arrangement of windows in lines. Big staircase window above the doorcase.

EAST PARK, MOSELEY AND PORTOBELLO

C19 survivals along Willenhall Road, but mostly C20 and later housing and industry, much on old industrial land. East Park was quite separate from the built-up area until the 1930s.

ST MATTHEW, Willenhall Road. By *Brian Bailey* of *Cecil Fillmore & Partners*: hall (behind) 1963–4, church 1968–9. It replaced a church by *Edward Banks* of 1846–9, ½ m. to the W. Cruciform, with low-pitched roofs and big mullion-and-transom windows. Plain, high interior with a flat ceiling.

ST JOSEPH (R.C.), Willenhall Road and Stowheath Lane. 1967 by *Joseph R. Chavasse* of *Jennings Homer & Lynch*. Almost a cartoon 1960s church, though impressive. A brick pentagon with a copper-clad roof rising to a tall five-sided spire with lucarnes. Contemporary PRESBYTERY, S. Inside, the angled walls focus attention on the altar. Behind partitions of timber and glass, Sacred Heart Chapel, N, and Lady Chapel, S. – Complete original FITTINGS by *Chavasse*. ALTAR and RAIL with much green Connemara marble, also used for the wall panels behind, all carved by *Sean Cullen* of Dublin, with *Willie Boylan*, *Mick Kelly*, *Mick Cullen* and others. – STAINED GLASS by *Hardmans*, large figures and much clear glass. – ETCHED GLASS in the vestibule by *Gerry Powell*.

ST MATTHEW'S PLACE, Willenhall Road. Sheltered flats by *Wolverhampton City Council Property Services*, 2003.

EAST PARK. Laid out on derelict industrial land as a second park for the town. A straight-sided oval, over 600 yds (550 metres) long NW–SE. A competition in 1893 was won by *T.H. Mawson*, but the entries all exceeded the cost limit. Instead, the Borough Surveyor produced a reduced plan with the help of 'an expert...to advise and assist...in maturing the scheme': clearly *Mawson*, who was described as 'landscape architect' at the opening in 1896. His original plan, illustrated in *The Art and Craft of Gardening* (1900), is close to what was done. The entrance on Hickman Avenue has a good LODGE and GATEPIERS.* An avenue of planes leads to a terracotta

---

*The lodge was attributed to Mawson's partner *Dan Gibson* in Pevsner's *Staffordshire* (1974), but there is no suggestion in the council papers that he was involved.

terrace. BANDSTAND to the SW, *c.* 1900 made by *W. Macfarlane & Co.* Paddling pool below the terrace, the remnant of a large U-shaped lake, now lost. CLOCK TOWER of 1896–8 by *Joseph Lavender*, slim, with tapering base and pedimented clock faces.

On WILLENHALL ROAD, going E from Lower Walsall Street, the former ROEBUCK, pub (S side), 1938–9 by *O.M. Weller*. Buff brick, with rounded corner. Opposite, part of the former BOARD SCHOOL by *Bidlake & Fleeming*, 1875–6, with the name on the transoms of a big window. The tiny BETHEL CHAPEL, now a mosque, S side, is dated 1890. The former MALT SHOVEL pub opposite looks late C19. The former BRITISH OAK pub (No.155, N side), bright red brick with stone bands, is by *A.P. Miller* of Hanley, 1902.

MANDER KIDD LTD OFFICES AND WAREHOUSE (now FLINT GROUP), Old Heath Road. 1962 by *Richard Twentyman*. L-shaped. Main floor articulated by vertical fins, cantilevered over a blue-brick basement.

PORTOBELLO, a mining village and part of Willenhall until 1966, has almost disappeared. The ROYAL OAK pub in NEW STREET is Tudor Revival of 1937–8, almost certainly by *A.T. & Bertram Butler*.

FALLINGS PARK AND LOW HILL

Separate areas historically – Fallings Park was in Heath Town U.D.C., Low Hill in Bushbury parish – but their C20 development belongs together. They were part of the estates of the Paget baronets of Old Fallings Hall, whose garden suburb scheme of 1908 formed the basis of the housing layout until the Second World War.

GOOD SHEPHERD, Second Avenue. A prefabricated building, extended in 2000 by *Twentyman Percy & Partners*.

OUR LADY OF PERPETUAL SUCCOUR (R.C.), Cannock Road, Old Fallings. 1933–4 by *E. Bower Norris*, at his best. A blocky brick mass with big round-headed window in the gable, and square open belfry. Flanking semicircular stair-turrets with projecting bands. Blank windowless clerestory. Inside, grandeur on a tight budget. Huge round-headed arcades in pale brick with a darker base, the simplest imposts, and cross-walls behind with the passage aisles arched through. Parts of the original ALTAR in the present small late C20 one.

METHODIST CHURCH, Wimborne Road. By *Frank Birch*, 1936. Low, domestic, rendered with a brick porch. Odd elevations, with projecting bays.

OLD FALLINGS UNITED REFORMED CHURCH, Cannock Road and Old Fallings Lane. 1965 by *Mason & Richards & Partners*.

OLD FALLINGS HALL, Old Fallings Lane. Now OUR LADY AND ST CHAD CATHOLIC ACADEMY. The Paget family house, a school since 1923. Early C18, of five bays and two storeys, in brick and sandstone. Hipped roof in the late C17 way, but other features are more up-to-date. Angle pilasters with lush Corinthian capitals, taken from Scamozzi's order as illustrated in John Evelyn's translation of Fréart. The entablature is only expressed on the pilasters, and the upper windows push up into where it would go. Centrepiece with a doorcase linked to a window with leafy side consoles. The moulded string above the ground-floor windows curiously stops short of it, a detail paralleled at Hales Hall, Cheadle, Staffordshire; both were attributed by Andor Gomme to *Francis Smith*, who is known to have worked for a 'Mr Huntbach' at Bushbury. Small s extension in hard Gothic of c.1860.

The hall has panelling with plain pilasters and fielded panels, and a heavily moulded fireplace. The main staircase has twisted balusters and a rail which rises into humps at the corners, reflected in the dado. To the l. a room with full-height bolection panelling and a keyed-arched doorcase. Simpler rear stair. A number of plain, apparently original, fireplaces survive. Repairs by *Tony Collier & Associates*, 1991, when the panelled room became a chapel.

To the W a SCHOOL RANGE of 1928 by *E. Bower Norris*, with hipped roofs and recessed centre. Dark brick patterning to the surrounds.

FALLINGS PARK GARDEN SUBURB

Sir Richard Paget (†1908) and his son Sir Arthur, Tory in politics but progressive landowners, tried from 1906 to develop their estate on co-partnership principles, as used at Letchworth Garden City: the first such scheme to be promoted by a private landlord. Tenants were to receive shares of the profits, in the form of reduced rents or services and amenities. The Pagets' agent was the pioneer urban planner *Thomas Adams*, first secretary of the Garden City Association and first director of construction at Letchworth. J.S. Nettlefold, the leading advocate of co-partnership (*see* Moor Pool Estate, Harborne, p.399), was on the committee. The plan was by *Detmar Blow*, Arts and Crafts radical, friend of William Morris, but also a partner in the fashionable Edwardian house architects *Blow & Billerey*. It was a Beaux Arts plan, reflecting Billerey's Paris training, with a *rondpoint* at the junction of Cannock Road and Old Fallings Lane, long straight avenues, and houses set slightly back behind greens.

A built housing exhibition in 1908 attracted designs from architects involved at Letchworth, such as *C.M. Crickmer* and *Pepler & Allen*, and some at other garden suburbs, such as *Speir & Beavan* of Cardiff, as well as two radical Arts and Crafts architects with links to both Blow and Letchworth, *Randall Wells* and *Basil Stallybrass*. The 'cottages' have in common simplicity, lack of ornament, and sweeping roofs. The Letchworth architects use

Wolverhampton, Fallings Park, Victoria Road, Nos. 34–46.
Drawing by Randall Wells, 1908

Voyseyesque render rather than exposed brick. After the exhibition the project stopped, a victim of recession in the building trade. The houses remain, alas with much UPVC.*

A walk round the exhibition houses can start at the junction of Cannock Road and Victoria Road. In VICTORIA ROAD, N side, Nos. 34–46 are by *Randall Wells*. Hipped roof and full-height square bays. The planning is clever: two-bedroom cottages on the ends and in the middle, separated by two pairs of three-bedroom ones which share the bays. The first-floor windows break the eaves as 'eyebrow' dormers, and are reflected in segment-headed door-hoods. Wells almost certainly acted as his own clerk of works, and worked on site (as he did at Letchworth).

BICKFORD ROAD, running S here, has houses of 1920–2 by *A.W. Worrall* (*see* below) for Heath Town U.D.C. Mostly simple rendered terraces, some round a green on the E. At the far end, NEW PARK VILLAGE by the Borough Architect, *Albert Chapman*, 1969–72. An interesting contrast of low-rise terraces with chunky pent-roofed porches, and sculpturally treated Brutalist plum brick four-storey maisonettes, with some elevated walkways.

On Victoria Road, the 1908 houses continue with Nos. 14–32 by *W.J. Oliver* of Wolverhampton, round a green now enclosed for gardens. Rendered, with brick bases and battered buttresses. Nos. 6–12 by *Speir & Beavan* have wings with half-hipped roofs, and a pent roof over the ground-floor porches and bays. Nos. 2–4 by *Pepler & Allen* have asymmetrically gabled fronts and an arty moulding delineating the ground-floor windows and doorheads.

---

*The only complete loss is *Blow & Billerey*'s Neo-Georgian farmhouse for the Pagets.

Continuing E up THORNEYCROFT LANE, Nos. 9–19 by *C.M. Crickmer*, to a design also used at Letchworth. The roof sweeps down to enclose the end gables, and cuts back in the middle. Beyond, Nos. 25–27 by *Boswell & Tomlins*, and Nos. 29–31 by *Frank W. Chapman* of Sheffield.

Back and N up BUSHBURY ROAD. On the E some rather old-fashioned entries, all very altered, e.g. Nos. 220–222 by *Fred T. Beck*, with tiling gable. The best local design is Nos. 232–234 by *A.W. Worrall*, rendered, with the gables sweeping down to enclose the entrances. No. 238, formerly NEWBOLDS farm, is a three-bay Early Georgian house with giant pilasters.

Back to the cross-roads and NW up a footpath, The Avenue. The grassed area on the l. was the suburb's recreation ground. At the far end is CANNOCK ROAD. Turning r., houses on the SE side by *Worrall*, 1920–2. Further N, the GOLDEN LION pub by *Lavender & Twentyman*, 1935, with hipped roof and large steel-framed windows. Going S down Cannock Road, the 1908 houses continue with Nos. 446–448, probably *Pepler & Allen*. Nos. 422–444 are by *Basil Stallybrass*, grouped round a green behind a hedge. Simple at first sight, but an original composition. The rear row of six has a deep hipped roof which encloses the first floor and projects as a pair of hipped gables in the centre, where it is carried on posts. Small canted bays with battered bases project under the roof. The side ranges simpler. Beyond, Nos. 414–420 by *Speir & Beavan*, like those in Victoria Road, and Nos. 410–412 by *Pepler & Allen*, again with projecting gables.

LOW HILL

Described in 1926 as by far the largest of Wolverhampton's municipal housing schemes. Built mainly 1925–9, under the 'Wheatley Act' of 1924 (Housing Director *W. Harrald*, designs by his architectural assistant *Wallace Wood*). It uses an enlargement of *Blow*'s 1908 plan, with the *rond-point* further NW. To E and W roads curving to form almond shapes; smaller circular roads to N and S. Houses mostly rendered, pairs and groups of four, typical of the period but showing Fallings Park ancestry. The *rond-point*, SHOWELL CIRCUS, has a grassed centre with the remains of an avenue, part of the Old Fallings Hall grounds. Among the surrounding buildings, shops by *Wood*, 1928–30, with big hipped roofs. The former BUSHBURY ARMS is by *W.A. Hutchings*, 1928, a grand Tudor job, instead of his normal Neo-Georgian. Main block faced in grey stone, wings in brick with half-timbering. Converted to flats, 2015. LIBRARY of 1930 built under the Borough Engineer *H.B. Robinson*, almost certainly designed by *Wood*. Octagonal, with a big classical doorcase and a low octagonal cupola. Main reading room, with square columns supporting an upper octagonal storey and the cupola, an unusual conceit and very effective. Behind, the LOW HILL COMMUNITY CENTRE of 1936–7, almost certainly *Wood*.

In OLD FALLINGS LANE opposite the school, garden suburb outliers of 1908: Nos. 16–18 by *Moses Johnson*, with full-height canted bays, and Nos. 20–22 probably by *Worrall*. The pairs with deep-roofed central blocks rising to big chimneys are municipal houses of 1928 etc. by *Wood*, a design he used elsewhere.

GRAISELEY AND PENN FIELDS

The area SW of central Wolverhampton. The earliest development has gone, but Penn Road has substantial houses built from the mid C19 to the 1910s, and the campus of the Royal Wolverhampton School. *W.J.H. Weller* built his own house here and several others, the best collection of his work. To the N around Great Brickkiln ('Bricklin') Street, working-class housing and factories. Terraced housing to the W around Lea Road, with the hidden Graiseley Old Hall. Some development over the boundary in Penn Fields (Penn parish) is treated here.

CHURCHES AND MAJOR BUILDINGS

ST CHAD, Owen Road. 1907–8 by *Fred T. Beck*. Brick and terracotta with stone dressings. Steep W bellcote above corbelled-out buttresses which enclose a big transomed window and a niche. Cusped round-headed triplet windows in three-centred relieving arches. Apsed chancel. Arcades with stone piers and brick arches, the mouldings dying in without capitals. Brick chancel arch on rendered piers. Collar-beam roof with many struts. In 1979–80 the W part was divided off as a community centre, the S aisle partitioned, and the N glazed in, decently and simply, by *George Sidebotham (Twentyman Percy & Partners)*. – By *Beck*, 1908, PULPIT, FONT, CHOIR STALLS and PEWS. – REREDOS by *Arthur Beech* and *S. Blower*, 1933. – STAINED GLASS. E window by *Samuel Evans & Co.*, 1930. N aisle: E, central light by *T.W. Camm*, 1947, side lights by *A.J. Davies*, 1950; W, central light, 'The Sower' by *T.W. Camm*, 1957, said to be *Florence Camm*'s last design. Good background of blue birds against a landscape. – In the dividing W wall, three lights by *Jones & Willis*, 1920, from St Mark, Chapel Ash (p. 712).

HALL to the S (now BUDDHIST MAHA VIHARA), 1898 by *Beck*. Good Free Style, with buttressed walls spreading forward as porches, and a hefty bellcote doubling as chimneys.

ST PHILIP, Church Road, Penn Fields. 1858–9 by *Griffin & Weller*. A capable Dec design in rock-faced sandstone. SW porch-tower, big transepts, narrow aisles. Five-light E window with much cusping. Piquant NE vestry with chimney in the gable. In 1996–7 *George Sidebotham (Twentyman Percy & Partners)* inserted a floor throughout. Upper worship area with the double-chamfered arcade arches, chancel arch with big angels on the capitals, roof with high collars and solid braces pierced only by little trefoils. – STAINED GLASS in the N transept by *Samuel Evans*, 1881, now mostly in an internal screen. – Former CHURCH ROOM of 1898 by *Joseph Lavender*, s, now a house.

SS VOLODYMYR AND OLHA UKRAINIAN CATHOLIC CHURCH, Merridale Street West. 1986–8 by *J.K. Pittaway*. A re-creation of a traditional Ukrainian church, in maroon brick. Not large, but cruciform and aisled with a central space and apse. A pair of onion domes on the front and a larger one in the centre – a remarkable sight over surrounding buildings. Plain piers and wooden barrel-vaults. A full traditional scheme of painting by Ukrainian artists, where criticism is best stilled by faith: ICONOSTASIS with saints by *Roman Vasilyk*; MURALS by *Wasyl Steblina* (apse) and *Bohdan Kaminsky* (main walls).

BECKMINSTER METHODIST CHURCH, Birches Barn Road. By *Crouch, Butler & Savage*, dated 1926. Heavy Gothic-cum-Jacobean, the handling like the firm's chapel in Stourbridge (p. 548). Big ritual W tower with angle buttresses which have four set-backs, and an arcaded parapet. Diagonally set porches. Transepts and apse with deep hipped roofs. Narrow passage aisles with round-headed arcades of circular stone columns, and a slightly pointed main tunnel-vault with plaster ribs. – HALL to the NW.

UNITED REFORMED CHURCH, Lea Road. By *Brian Jeffries*, 2006. Octagonal, Postmodern: red and blue brick, with Terry Farrell-style balls on piers. It replaced, alas, a church by *Crouch & Butler*.

ROYAL SCHOOL, Penn Road. Founded in 1850 by John Lees, merchant, as an orphanage; now a Free School. Set back behind generous sloping lawns, the long original block of 1853–4 by *Joseph Manning* of Corsham, Wilts., a friend of the founder. Jacobean Revival, in the manner of Blore or Salvin. Nine bays, central tower with tall oriel, wings with big square bays. Shaped gables. Extensions either side, and SW LODGE, all *Manning*, 1863–4. Headmaster's house, r., in the same style, probably by *W. Johnson*, dated 1885. On the lawn a FOUNTAIN of 1864 by *P.E. Masly* of London, octagonal, with relief panels of the Corporal Works of Mercy, sculptor *W. Farmer*. Surrounding urns on pedestals. The central HALL of 1854 is quite small but with a full hammerbeam roof. Big fireplace with Perp niches and four-centred arch. Panelled gallery front. Underneath, two excellent Arts and Crafts brass plaques, †1900 and †1901, by *Albert E.V. Lilley*.

Later blocks in the cramped space behind, plus a S wing, all basic Tudor-Jacobean. N range (Stripling Wing) by *Johnson*, 1875, the rest by *Beck*, 1900–12. Across Goldthorn Road, E, former GYMNASIUM by *Bertram Butler & Co.*, 1960–1. Behind, SPORTS HALL by *Thorne Architecture*, 2006.

Detached CHAPEL to the SW by *Fred T. Beck*, 1894–5, in his favourite late Gothic-cum-Jacobean style. Cruciform, with Perp windows and ogee-capped cupola. Attractive C17-style roof with S-shaped braces. – Original PEWS, PULPIT, CHOIR STALLS. – Gothic REREDOS, 1913. – STAINED GLASS by *Kempe* or *Kempe & Co.* in nearly every window, 1903–†1925. Their standard patterning and canopy-work. Rich and deep colours particularly for garments, the cumulative effect very impressive.

W of Penn Road the Neo-Georgian JUNIOR SCHOOL by *Joseph & H.E. Lavender*, 1931–2, extended W by *Lavender & Twentyman*, 1936–8.

GRAISELEY PRIMARY SCHOOL, Graiseley Hill. 1909 by *Fleeming & Son*. Simple, with a gabled centrepiece.

GRAISELEY OLD HALL, Carlton Road, off Lea Road. Hidden among trees, behind the Royal School junior buildings. De Graseleys are mentioned from 1282. The house was owned in the C16 by the Ridley family, then in the C18 the Jessons. A long rambling E–W range including two attached houses at the W, all faced in C18 or early C19 brick. The main part has a S wing and Gothick windows. Porch in the angle, part of alterations of 1911–13 by *George Green*, Wolverhampton Borough Surveyor, who lived here. The centre and S wing are an L-shaped timber-framed house, late C15 or C16. Gothick entrance doorway; large hall with an open-well staircase on the N: Gothick newels with curved stop-chamfers and stepped pyramid tops. They look quite late, 1830s–40s. A churchy screen by *Green* divides off the S wing room. This has box framing with pieces of C16 WALL PAINTINGS, including foliage patterns, guilloche and architectural elements. The main room in the E–W range has a rich late medieval panelled ceiling with main and subsidiary beams moulded with ribs and hollow chamfers. Early C20 *Green* fireplace. Box framing on the N, with a door arch. The room behind has a mid-C18 fireplace with eared architrave and big egg-and-dart moulding. The former library, W, has a later C18 Adam-style fireplace with Dutch tiles. Upstairs, more box framing and blocked door arches in the S wing and along the main corridor.

PERAMBULATION

One good stretch of PENN ROAD. The start is at Marston Road. Going SW, on the SE side CLAREMONT HOUSE, brick of *c.* 1845–50 with elegant shallow square bays. The unstressed centre suggests *Edward Banks*. Behind a spinney, GOLDTHORN TERRACE of *c.* 1855–60, red brick, now painted. Ends and centre marked by pairs of pedimental gables. Round-headed paired doorcases, Greek Revival detail. Then the Royal School (*see* above). Beyond, HIGHFIELDS, two large rendered pairs of 1860 with big canted bays and paired bracket cornices.

On the NW side beyond Lyndhurst Road three fine houses. No. 148, dated 1898, must be by *Fred T. Beck* (cf. Gresham Chambers, p. 685). Romantic Jacobean-cum-Scottish Baronial. Bold centrepiece with a four-centred-arched doorway and a stepped mullion-and-transom staircase window leading to a little semicircular oriel with a tiny copper spirelet. Stepped gables to either side, the r. one running into a circular tower with a concave copper spire. No. 150, ELMSWOOD, is *c.*1895–1900. Domestic Revival with fancy timbering and tile-hanging. Details such as the stepped gable oriel suggest *John Weller II*.

No. 152, LONGFIELD, is *W.J.H. Weller*'s own house and perhaps his finest, of 1903–5, in his personal Arts and Crafts Free Style with distinct Wightwick influence. Shielded from the road by a stone wall with his trademark lychgate-like stone doorway. Brick, with two short timber-framed wings, the l. one narrower, taller, and all canted, the r. one square over a canted ground floor. Recessed porch with chunky octagonal posts supporting a balcony. This has another post to the roof, and decorative balustrade. End chimneys with stone lintel tops. The interior is a little box of spatial tricks. Entrance hall a proper room in the Arts and Crafts way, entered diagonally at the s corner. The ceiling steps down before the fireplace, and the bressumer continues as a transom over the staircase immediately r. This rises up a barrel-vaulted tunnel, then turns l. under a shallow oriel and an arcade of octagonal posts and segmental arches. Main living room r., shaped by the canted front bay and angled rear one. Art Nouveau door furniture with complex curves. Garden front much plainer, all brick, with a big r. gable balanced by a long dormer, and again a recessed entrance like a loggia, influenced by Edward Ould, with an angled bay l. The garden steps down to *Weller*'s most radical work, a hipped-roofed stone LOGGIA with a tall finial which has a disc top. Towards Copthorne Road, s, it has an arched gateway with canted sides. The l. side runs up into the loggia in an organic conception, reminiscent of H.H. Richardson or Harrison Townsend.

Across Copthorne Road, Nos. 154–158 by *P. Colin Campbell*, 1902. GRAISELEY LODGE (No. 172) is rendered Early Victorian with a yellow-brick front extension and castellated bay by *T.H. Fleeming*, 1898. Opposite, set back, No. 181, THE HATTONS, by *W.J.H. Weller*, 1926. Altered, probably by Weller himself – front infilled, entrance moved to the rear – but the grid effect of the flush unmoulded windows, the cool brickwork, and details, like corner windows flanking the r. chimney, are still effective. Nos. 185–187 by *A. Eaton Painter*, 1912, brick and timbering; Nos. 189–191, before 1903, with decorative brick detail; Nos. 193–195, render and brick base, by *V.S. Peel*, 1913. No. 197, *Weller* again, 1914, addresses the corner with three big timber-framed gables set at forty-five degrees. In Stubbs Road, w, a Neo-Georgian TELEPHONE EXCHANGE by the *Ministry of Public Building & Works*, 1931.

Continuing sw down Penn Road, WELLESLEY HOUSE, NW side, formerly a pair, is stucco classical, probably 1850s, with nice detail; Nos. 190–194 similar. On the SE side, *Moderne* houses by *S.D.W. Timmins*: No. 217 of 1934; No. 221, with eaves chimneys, *c.*1936. Opposite, No. 224, INGLEWOOD, by *W.J.H. Weller*, *c.*1903–4, with his typical gateway. Brick, hipped roof, big casements. No. 226 is 1860s classical, No. 228 a little earlier.

Opposite, LEYLANDS, by *Weller*, 1905–6. The front is a grid of timbering, in the full-height gabled bay and again l., relieved by a rendered oriel over the porch, and a brick stair-tower, l. Also by Weller No. 288, NW side: brick, an unusual composition, damaged by uPVC. The MOUNT pub opposite was rebuilt by *O.M. Weller*, 1941. MOUNT ROAD runs up SE. Nos. 18 and 20 are of 1904 by *G.H.T. Robinson*; also almost certainly the Voysey-ish No. 24, slightly later.

OTHER BUILDINGS

A worthwhile scatter N of Penn Road. In MERRIDALE STREET the unusual former ST PAUL'S SUNDAY SCHOOL (now Jubilee Christian Centre), by *A. Eaton Painter*, 1930, a massive windowless façade with side piers and small pediment. On the corner of RETREAT STREET, W, the former ST PAUL'S NATIONAL SCHOOL by *Edward Banks*, 1850, mangled. In Great Brickkiln Street the former BRICKKILN PRIMARY SCHOOL, by *Bidlake & Fleeming*, 1878. Their typical heavy mullion-and-transom windows under hipped gables. In Dale Street and Graiseley Street, S, Wolverhampton's first post-war REDEVELOPMENT SCHEME, of 1956–60, attractive houses and flats faced in grey-red Himley bricks, by *Albert Chapman*, Deputy Borough Architect, with *H.T.D. Smith* and others. The gaps were eight-storey blocks, early C21 demolitions. In Pelham Street a FACTORY of *c.* 1900 with lunette windows and shaped gables.

BECKMINSTER HOUSE, Birches Barn Road. Large brick Tudor, *c.* 1845–50.

GATEPIERS, Marston Road, S side. Four (one now missing), linked by quadrant walling, from Tong Castle, Shropshire (dem. 1954). Extraordinary designs, with truncated pyramid tops with lots of crocketing, niches and small carvings: harp, anchor, Staffordshire knot etc. They go with the fantastic Gothick of the Castle, of 1745 by Lancelot 'Capability' Brown, but an inscription on the missing pier dated them 1821.

HEATH TOWN

Named from Wednesfield Heath. The Grand Junction Railway of 1837, which ran nearest to Wolverhampton here, encouraged industrial and housing development to the W, but open land remained elsewhere until the C20. Heath Town was an Urban District from 1894, absorbed by Wolverhampton in 1927 (for its municipal housing *see* Fallings Park, p. 723). C19 terraces were largely replaced in the 1960s by Brutalist municipal housing.

HOLY TRINITY, Church Street. 1850–2 by *Edward Banks*, mostly paid for by Henry Rogers, merchant. A perfect Puginian or Camdenian design: nave, aisles, long chancel, and SW tower with broach spire, 'in the decorated English style', all in sandstone ashlar. Picturesque NE vestry.* Arcade piers with four shafts and double-chamfered arches. Chancel arch with shafts, capitals with knobbly foliage, and complex mouldings. Arch-braced roofs with free-standing shafts on figure corbels, the only ornate feature of the design, and perhaps the least successful. – Original PULPIT, FONT and PEWS. – Much else reflects the incumbency of Prebendary James Morison, 1882–1928. REREDOS and SCREEN by *Bridgeman*, 1902. – STAINED GLASS. E window †1881; chancel 1905–22 etc.; S aisle 1891 etc.; N aisle 1904, 1910, all apparently by *Samuel Evans & Sons*. W window, Four Evangelists, by *William Morris (Westminster)*, 1930. – NW vestry SCREEN by *Lavender & Twentyman*, 1936.

Ample churchyard with many trees, approached through a Hollington stone LYCHGATE with paired lights on the sides, 1920 by *Fred T. Beck*. Some distance W an attractive row of six ALMSHOUSES. Also founded by Henry Rogers, and also by *Banks*, 1850. Jacobean, with an array of shaped gables on porches, dormers and ends; each house with chimney to W and door to E. Much repaired from dereliction 1994–5 by *S.T. Walker & Partners (Paul Burley, David Warren)*.

The green space extends E across Church Street as a park, with a WAR MEMORIAL of 1920 by *A.G. Walker*. A soldier leaning stoically on his rifle, naturalistic and moving. Side reliefs of a biplane and naval gunnery.

ST BARNABAS (now NEW TESTAMENT CHURCH OF GOD), Wednesfield Road. 1882 by *T.H. Fleeming*. Lancet style.

ST PATRICK (R.C.), Wolverhampton Road. 1972 by *Andrew Moody*. Low, spreading, brick.

BATHS AND LIBRARY (former), Tudor Road, S of the churchyard. 1931–2 by *Wallace Wood*, directed by *H.B. Robinson*, Borough Engineer. Impressive front with hints of modern Tudor and Art Deco. Symmetrical, with corner towers which have set-back tops with projecting keystones (called 'Egyptian diadems' at the opening). Doorcase frames like enormous bolection mouldings. Semicircular open arches flank the centre. Mullioned windows above. The baths interior has parabolic concrete arches, with a tier of smaller arches supporting a clerestory: a progressive design, influenced by the Royal Horticultural Hall in Westminster. Derelict 2019.

NEW CROSS HOSPITAL, Wolverhampton Road. This started as the Wolverhampton Union Workhouse of 1900–3 by the specialist *Arthur Marshall*. Towards the road the former OFFICES, with heavy rusticated windows and doorcase with segmental pediment. Huge late C20 extensions, many by *George:Trew:Dunn* (Maternity and Psychiatric Unit 1971, Geriatric Unit 1974); Postgraduate Medical Centre by *Mason, Richards & Partners*, 1971. More recent work of little architectural

---

*Banks's St Matthew (dem.) was criticized by *The Ecclesiologist* in 1849 as 'exceedingly bad', and Holy Trinity looks like his response.

interest, e.g. Accident and Emergency Department by *Keppie*, 2015.

ST STEPHEN'S C. OF E. SCHOOL, Woden Road. 1898 by *Fred Hunter Lynes*. Long gabled range, symmetrical with boys' and girls' sides around a central hall. The tricky detail is the big chimneys in the gable valleys, supported on little arches of flying flues. Jacobean-style cupolas, set on the ridge immediately behind, play hide-and-seek as you walk past.

HEATH TOWN ESTATE, Wednesfield Road. 1967–70 by the Borough Architect *Albert Chapman* (group architect *L.J. Simonds*, assistant *J.B. Beech*), with builders *Wates (Midlands) Ltd*, chief architect *A.S. Whale*. The best example of Brutalist housing in the conurbation, now much reduced by demolitions. High white towers, lower ranges – nine-storey flats and five- and seven-storey maisonettes with projecting concrete balconies – in plum brick. Elevated walkways run along the blocks.

MERRY HILL

A modest but real suburban centre at Five Ways, where Trysull Road and Coalway Road meet.

ST JOSEPH OF ARIMATHEA, Coalway Road. 1988–90 by *George Sidebotham* of *Twentyman Percy & Partners*. Brick, with tall gables. HALL of 1954, r.

ST MICHAEL (R.C.), Coalway Road. 1966–8 by *Desmond Williams & Associates*. The Liverpool Cathedral moment. A circular church in purple-brown brick, articulated by triplet brick piers enclosing full-height slit windows and prominent drainpipes. Each bay has an inward-facing roof-light above. Small pyramid-shaped central lantern. Low entrance block linked to a W tower of brick sides linked by concrete beams. Over the entrance a delicate bronze figure of St Michael by *Sean Compton*. Good interior, all brick too, and hardly altered. Circular roof-light surrounded by a ribbed ceiling with toothed ends, like a great flower. The side roof windows appear behind beams linking ceiling to walls, a nice effect. Original FITTINGS, including marble ALTAR and FONT, in a circular stepped basin. – Hanging CRUCIFIX by *Compton*.– REREDOS. Ascension, of cast metal, not quite abstract, by *Robert Brumby*. – STAINED GLASS by *Bronwen Gordon*, abstract patterns, working from red by the entrance to blue behind the altar.

Former dual-purpose CHURCH HALL, W, modest Romanesque by *G.B. Cox*, 1925–6.

WARSTONES JUNIOR AND INFANT SCHOOL, Warstones Road. By *Wallace Wood*, 1939–40. Flat-roofed blocks around a cut-off tower, a simpler version of Elston Hall School (p. 732).

At the Five Ways crossing, the MERRY HILL pub is by *W.A. Hutchings*, 1929–30, brick and half-timber. On Coalway Road opposite St Michael, ¼ m. E, a long line of houses of 1926–7, built by the Borough Council for sale. A standard *Wood* design with hipped-roofed centre, here with half-timbering, and a big central chimney.

OXLEY AND FORDHOUSES

C20 suburbs N of the city.

THE EPIPHANY, Lymer Road. 1959–60 by *Alan Young*. Plain brick box with a concrete frame.

ELSTON HALL PRIMARY SCHOOL, Stafford Road. 1938, by *Wallace Wood* and the Borough Engineer *H.B. Robinson*. Single-storey ranges formally planned round two quadrangles. Central tower with low pyramid roof. Westmorland slate roofs, laid in diminishing courses.

PENDEFORD HIGH SCHOOL (now Ormiston NEW Academy), Marsh Lane. Two schools by *Richard Twentyman*, 1958 and 1964, largely rebuilt by *Capita Symonds*, 2012 etc.

OXLEY HOUSE, Leverton Rise, off South Street. An unexpected stuccoed villa of *c.*1830 for Alexander Hordern, banker. The family link to Bushbury (p. 708), and hints of John Nash's manner, strongly suggest *James Morgan* as architect. Single-storey stone Ionic portico with end pilasters. Two central windows, not three, but smoothly handled. Minimal pediment. Projecting domed room on the S with pilasters and big acroteria. Large entrance hall; cantilevered staircase with decorative iron balusters. Now flats.

GOODYEAR TYRE FACTORY, Stafford Road. Of 1927–8. Demolished except for its CLOCK TOWER, with low pyramid roof and tall finial, now among housing (Mercury Drive etc.)

HOP POLE pub (former), Oxley Moor Road. By *Richard Twentyman*, 1937–8. It had his last surviving pub interior, destroyed *c.*2013. Traditional – gables, classical doorcases – but austerely handled.

OXLEY RAILWAY VIADUCT. 1847–9 by *Robert Stephenson* and *William Baker*, for the Shrewsbury & Birmingham Railway. Twelve tall blue-brick arches. A skew arch crosses the Birmingham Canal of 1768, with locks running down to the Staffordshire and Worcestershire Canal at Aldersley Junction.

AUTHERLEY JUNCTION, off Blaydon Road. Here the Birmingham and Liverpool Junction Canal (later Shropshire Union) of 1831–5, engineer *Thomas Telford*, leaves the Staffordshire and Worcestershire. Original work the dignified TOWPATH BRIDGE with an elliptical skew arch at the junction, the STOP LOCK and the TOLL HOUSE, with the usual canted front bay, but of uncommon U-plan with two rear wings. Further NW, two surviving ranges of a later STABLE BLOCK. Across the canal to the N, a weir, pond and little PUMPING HOUSE.

DOVECOTE, off Ryefield, behind the Dovecote pub. C18, restored. Octagonal, with pyramid roof.

PENN

Mentioned in Domesday as owned by William FitzAnsculph and, before the Conquest, by Godiva. Most of the ancient parish is in Staffordshire. Modern development began in the 1850s at the NE end in Penn Fields, and spread along Penn Road around 1900, as an extension to Wolverhampton. Interwar housing linked this to Upper Penn, round St Bartholomew's church, and this part was absorbed by Wolverhampton in 1933. The whole of the area inside the city was developed by the late C20. Penn Fields is described with Graiseley (p. 725).

ST BARTHOLOMEW, Church Hill and Vicarage Road. A *mixtum compositum*. The W tower was rebuilt by *William Baker*, 1764–5. Gothick, with pointed windows and ogee surrounds to the belfry openings, but classical alternating quoins. Typical Baker pinnacles (cf. Ellenhall and Seighford, both Staffs.). The brick is a casing over a sandstone core, perhaps medieval, visible in the ringing chamber. Tactful vestry on the N, dated 1826; large extension further N by *Arrol & Snell*, 2000, also in keeping, with fine brickwork and sandstone dressings. The W part of the N arcade is Perp, with octagonal piers and capitals with deep concave mouldings. The N wall also contains Perp work: see e.g. the lower part of the NW buttress. The large blocked openings here were C18 windows. The W part of the S aisle is of 1845 by *William Evans*, Gornal stone, with lancet windows. The arcade is a thin version of the Perp one opposite. The E parts of nave and aisles, and the chancel and S chapel are all by *Paley & Austin*, 1871–2. The vicar was E.G. Paley's brother. Early Dec, Bromsgrove stone inside and out. Arcades with octagonal piers, lancets in the aisles. E windows with cusped intersecting tracery, in the chancel with a sexfoiled circle at the top. They also follow what was here before. Chancel arch and chancel S arcade with circular shafts. No clerestory. Collar-beam roofs with lots of wind-braces. Nothing strains at originality but everything is spaciously conceived. NE vestry of 1902 by *J. Lavender*, SE vestry by *Wood, Goldstraw & Yorath*, 1958, tactful again.

FURNISHINGS. By *Paley & Austin*, 1872, the CHOIR STALLS, REREDOS (carvers *Bell & Almand*), ALTAR RAIL, partly surviving PARCLOSE SCREEN and E nave PEWS. – NAVE ALTAR and reordering by *Charles Brown* (*Hinton Brown Langstone*), 1979. – PULPIT. C17, with fluting on the base and foliage cornice. – FONT. Perp, octagonal, with panelled base and panelled short stem. – WEST GALLERY of 1751–2. The strapwork on the piers must be C19. – CHANCEL SCREEN by *B. Ingelow*, 1896, now in the S chapel. – LADY CHAPEL, S, with FURNISHINGS by *C.E. Ponting*, 1915, his only work in the area. SCREEN, delicate and refined. Thin moulded mullions with caps and bases, a Devon type. Dec tracery in the arches. The rear part of Ponting's ENGLISH ALTAR survives. – Medieval TILES preserved in the chancel. – STAINED GLASS. E window by *Preedy*, 1872, brightly coloured small scenes and tabernacle work. S chapel E, the former E window, of *c*.1860. S chapel S, two by *Hardmans*, 1902 and 1889. Others of 1864 and 1865. – MONUMENTS. Some nice tablets, e.g. Peter Payton †1771, William Pershouse †1789. – John, Esther and John Marsh, by *Flaxman*, 1802. High and slender tablet with a standing mourning woman beneath the profile medallion of the deceased. – Eleanor Bradney †1817, by *Joseph Stephens I* of Worcester. Kneeling woman with an anchor. – CHURCHYARD with nice rustic gravestones, including Elizabeth Russell †1700 (against the vestry wall) and Thomas Shepherd †1718, S side, both with angel heads. – CROSS near the W tower. Medieval base moved here in 1912, with shaft and cross added by *F.T. Beck*. This work uncovered the circular BASE and STEPS of its medieval predecessor, on the S side. – CHURCH ROOM of 1913 by *A. Eaton Painter*, extended 1933, W.

SPRINGDALE METHODIST CHURCH, Warstones Road. 1953 by *W. Cyril Moss* of *Crouch, Butler & Savage*. Late C20 additions.

PENN HALL (now Special School), Vicarage Road. The core is C17 or earlier, with steep-roofed ranges running E–W. Relatively unaltered N range, with E gable of stepped brickwork. W front added in 1748–54 by *William Baker* for Thomas Bradney. Dated 1748 at the SW corner. Seven bays, with tapering window keystones, doorcase with eared architrave and pediment, and ball finials. Downpipe hopper dated 1783. Smaller windows on the S side, perhaps earlier in origin. The present entrance, in a projecting bay beyond, introduces the work done by *Henry T. Hare* from 1902, for Thomas Francis Waterhouse, war hero and fraudster. Accomplished Neo-Georgian, just too rich to be genuine. Round-headed doorway under a big broken segmental pediment enclosing a lead sundial. Pediment above with cartouche.

Most of the INTERIORS are *Hare*'s. Entrance hall with panelling, beamed ceiling with plaster panels which have flowers in the corners, and a fireplace with plaster relief. A room to the S has a fireplace with a cornice and wide bolection moulding, flanked by shell niches above cupboards. The open-well staircase (now filled by a lift) is C18 but seems much remodelled by Hare. Rich plasterwork, perhaps C18, around the lantern. A room on the S side has reworked C17 panelling. Plaster frieze, its flowers (and hacking) probably Hare, but the caryatids in the corners probably C17 and apparently *in situ*. The original entrance corridor has a groin-vault, perhaps C18, but the panelled arches must be Hare's. The rooms flanking it are the important C18 survivals. The SE room has eared doorcases with Rococo carving of eagles and garlands in the friezes, beautifully undercut, and a fireplace with tapering pilasters and a Rococo garland. Egg-and-dart mouldings in doors and cornice. SW room with similar cornice and plainer doorcases. The fireplace is *Hare*'s: rich garlands, framed picture of the Battle of Dover by *A. Latham Gibbons*, and a cartouche.

WEST TERRACE by *Hare*, with curving seats and stone balls. SUMMERHOUSE, N, C18, probably by *Baker*. Doric doorway with lunette, blunt pediment. To the E a former BARN, with blank brick ogee arches, dated 1779, but largely rebuilt c.1984. STABLES beyond, perhaps C18. The school's buildings, to the N, are of 1976 etc. by *Albert Chapman*, Director of Architectural Services, low and friendly in brick and dark facing panels, with hipped roofs, and a pyramid with lantern.

UPPER PENN VILLAGE. The old settlement runs W from St Bartholomew's along Vicarage Road. PENNOVER, the cottage on the corner of THE AVENUE, may be C17, as it has chamfered ceiling beams. Opposite, a terrace of c.1900 probably by *T.A. Lowry*. Further E, the Hall. E of the church, the OLD STAG'S HEAD, probably C18, much rebuilt. Further E in Pennwood Lane, ALMSHOUSES dated 1761, a row of five with plain central pediment, terribly mutilated with render and uPVC.

PENN ROAD (A449). Going out from Wolverhampton, the ROEBUCK pub was designed by *A.T. & Bertram Butler* in 1939 but completed only in 1955–6. L-shaped, brick (now painted). Hipped-roofed centre broken by a big chimney, mansard-roofed wings. The former SWAN pub (now restaurant) is apparently C18 brick, under render and applied timber. Set back N, opposite Church Hill, THE WOODLANDS. Of 1899 by *Henry T. Hare*, for Neville Hanbury Mander. Refined Jacobean, influenced by Norman Shaw. The entrance front, facing NW, has an entrance gable with a terracotta date plaque between windows, and a porch suspended on iron brackets. Chamfered r. corner with stone low down, a hint of power. Twinned gables l., one with a big chimney. Big bay on the SW. The garden front, SE, is more peaceful: three gables, the l. above a round-arched loggia, then a tall chimney; central gable with projecting canted bay, r. gable plain. Panelled entrance hall with a fireplace with four-centred arch, Dutch-style tiles and cartouche. NW extension for a rest home. Original STABLES with a nice tapering cupola with big louvres; also GATEPIERS. PENN HOSPITAL, S side, is built around a five-bay late C18 house, formerly THE BEECHES. First-floor windows with moulded lintels, pedimented doorcase with panelled pilasters and upright leaf capitals. Early two-bay extension, l. The HOLLY BUSH pub, N side, is by *Richard Twentyman*, 1936, now nastily timber-clad. ⅓ m. W, the SPRING HILL on the corner of Warstones Road and Spring Hill Lane, 1937, also *Twentyman*, also now timber-clad.

IVY TERRACE, Wakeley Hill, off Church Hill. Unusual C18 cottage terrace with door-hoods of slate slabs on consoles, ribbon-moulded string, and plaque with the name picked out in stones.

TETTENHALL

Wolverhampton's most affluent residential area, separated from the rest of the city by the Smestow Brook valley to the SE. A ridge runs above the valley from Aldersley SW to beyond Wightwick. The old road to Whitchurch and Chester ran along what is now Meadow View Terrace, and up Old Hill. The village was a scatter of cottages around Lower Green by St Michael's church, and Upper Green on the hill. Its history is bound up with that of the collegiate church. From the C16 the college and most of its land belonged to the Wrottesley family. The village developed in the C18 along Lower Street. The Staffordshire and Worcestershire Canal was built along the valley by *James Brindley*, *Samuel Simcock* and *Thomas Dadford Sen.* in 1766–72. The big embankment over the valley and the deep cutting of The Rock, now the A41, are improvements of 1820–3.

Substantial development started c.1860, with e.g. Avenue House and Elmsdale Hall. The most important houses are those of the Mander paint-making family: Wightwick Manor and The Mount, and the fantasy of The Dippons. There was a Local Board from 1883 and an Urban District Council from 1894, absorbed by Wolverhampton in 1966.* The greatest Victorian loss is *George Bidlake*'s Woodthorne, vigorous Gothic of 1869, for H. H. Fowler, 1st Viscount Wolverhampton.

CHURCHES

ST MICHAEL AND ALL ANGELS, Church Road. The medieval collegiate church, recorded in Domesday, was dissolved in 1548. The building had an E.E. chancel and flanking chapels, and Dec N arcade. A S extension by *Edward Haycock*, 1825, was removed in a restoration designed by *G.E. Street*, 1877, and executed by his son *A.E. Street*, 1882–4. A severe fire in 1950 left only the W tower and S porch. The tower is C15, with a restored three-light Perp window which has typical West Midlands beast hoodstops. The porch is *Street*'s: E.E., with a quadripartite stone vault.

The body of the church is by *Bernard Miller*, 1952–5. There is no better example of the post-war revival of interest in Victorian architecture. From outside the plan looks traditional: wide nave, aisles and chancel, all in Hollington stone. What strikes you first is the cross-gables of the aisles, a High Victorian motif.

---

*Boundary changes have left the rural part in Staffordshire, including Wightwick Hall and Wrottesley Hall.

But the gables are filled with bold tracery of a radical Arts and Crafts kind, reminiscent of Lethaby or E. S. Prior, and the SE nave bell-turret brings a whiff of Charles Rennie Mackintosh. This inventive reworking produces a church both contemporary and reassuringly traditional. The leadwork, following Lethaby, is interesting, e.g. the N hoppers with historical dates.

The nave has pointed arcades of three wide bays. Very short piers, less than head height. Stylized foliage capitals. Collar-beam roof, with big braces to alternate trusses, and flat sections at the sides. The aisle roofs have big beams from arcades to wall. Hanging copper LAMPS like upturned chalices, PEWS with mullions, between Jacobean and early modern. The plan shows early Liturgical Movement influence: the apparent chancel is actually a Lady Chapel, and the focus is a liturgical centre of ALTAR, stone PULPIT and LECTERN at the E end of the nave. Three-sided RAILS with Gimson-esque cut-outs. STATUES of angels by *Alan Durst* against the trusses above the altar. Until 1985 there was a wall behind the altar linking pulpit and lectern, and the plan was exactly that of the suggested 'Late Medieval Aisled Church Rearranged' in Addleshaw and Etchells's influential *The Architectural Setting of Anglican Worship* (1948). The Lady Chapel has a SCREEN, ORGAN CASE and return STALLS with stylized linenfold and circle and diamond shapes, again a touch of C17 revival. – FONT. Brilliant swirling patterns of mosaic by *G. Mayer Marten*, 1955. – STAINED GLASS. E window by *George Cooper-Abbs*, 1956.

Large churchyard entered through a LYCHGATE of *c.*1890. – WAR MEMORIAL by *Walter Tower (Kempe & Co.)*, 1920, with floriated cross. – S of the tower, CHEST TOMB of John Wilkes †1767, with end pilasters. – C20 GRAVES to the SW, the most prominent the Bayliss family †1914 etc., a tapering pier with crenellated top.

CHRIST CHURCH, Church Road, Tettenhall Wood. 1865–6 by *Bateman & Corser*. High Victorian Dec, the only survivor of a spiky Birmingham manner associated with this firm and Yeoville Thomason. Rock-faced Codsall stone with Bath stone dressings. Gables round the apse and along the aisles. Stump of a SE tower. The tracery has lots of trefoils and cinquefoils, in circles and some spherical triangles. Roguish NW porch running straight into a traceried window. Spacious interior. It had iron arcades, but in 1897 *T.H. Fleeming* replaced them with C13-style stone columns. High collar-beam roof with arched braces. They run round the apse too. – Original PULPIT, FONT with red marble colonnettes, and PEWS. – STAINED GLASS. Apse by *Hardmans*, 1879–92. N aisle by *Kempe & Co.*, 1927, 1929. Also glowing designs by *A.J. Davies*: S aisle, two of 1930 and one (Healing the Sick) of 1934, Lady Chapel, 1930, and W, 1934. S aisle, late *T.W. Camm*, 1958. – WAR MEMORIAL, N aisle. Copper tablet by *William Morris & Co. (Westminster)*, 1920.

CHRIST THE KING, Pendeford Avenue, Aldersley. Mission church and hall by *Bernard Miller*, 1956. Low, with a clerestory marking the sanctuary. Cedar shingles on the ritual E wall. Unfortunate C21 ripple glass. In an external frame, BELL dated 1604. Folding doors separate the sanctuary. The FONT has corners tapering in and out to central baluster shapes, a touch of Miller's Neo-Victorian.

ST THOMAS OF CANTERBURY (R.C.), Wood Road. 1964–5 by *Jennings Homer & Lynch*. An impressively blocky Brutalist design in brown brick, articulated by a projecting stone panel, and a rendered band defining a cornice. Belfry-like tower, just a brick pier and panel linked by a top slab, enclosing a cross. The interior concentrates light on the altar by a hidden lantern and sawtooth roof. The (ritual) S wall has a long row of narrow lights, the N wall etched-glass STATIONS OF THE CROSS, effectively backlit. Lady Chapel at the NE. – Original FONT and ALTAR, reduced in size, a slab on stocky tapering legs.

TETTENHALL WOOD UNITED REFORMED CHURCH, Mount Road. 1872–3 by *Bidlake & Fleeming*. A sweet village chapel in rock-faced sandstone. Plate tracery, buttresses with long nosings, gable moulding over the doorway punching into the string above. Ritual SW tower with miniature belfry and spire. Collar-beam roof, W gallery.

OTHER MAJOR BUILDINGS

WIGHTWICK MANOR (National Trust), Bridgnorth Road. A *tour de force* of *Edward Ould*, of the Liverpool and Chester firm of *Grayson & Ould*; built for Theodore Mander, in two phases, 1887 and 1893. In both the principal feature is timber framing. But they are markedly different, reflecting a change in Late Victorian taste. The earlier part is in the Old English style of Shaw and Nesfield, though it also reflects the local half-timber revival in Chester and the work of Ould's teacher, John Douglas. Timber is mixed with tile-hanging and red Ruabon brick: quaint, but in a bright, hard way, the sources Gothic as well as Jacobean. The later part shows the change in taste towards a softer, gentler Domestic Revival. There is more and richer half-timbering, and a scholarly awareness which reflects Ould's study of ancient buildings. It could almost be mistaken for a C15 or C16 building (and visitors often think it is the older part). Edward Hubbard said that only at Hill Bark, Cheshire (1891) was Ould so pure.

The result is an extensive house of great variety. It is difficult to describe without yielding to the temptation of doing what the *Buildings of England* must not do, i.e. to discuss a collection, not the fitments and fixtures of a house. Theodore Mander died in 1900, and the house passed to his son Geoffrey. In 1935 (Sir) Geoffrey and Lady Mander decided that house and contents should be preserved as a period piece. It was acquired by the National Trust in 1937, for the collections rather than the building – the Trust at first proposed to cut down and render the tower. Listing in 1950 marked a change in attitudes. There was a campaign of repair and improvement in 1989–96, and the collections have been augmented by much else of the Pre-Raphaelite and Morris schools.*

From the s the two dates can at once be distinguished, l. 1887, r. and round the corner 1893. The older part has three projecting wings making an E-plan front. Low tower in Ruabon brick behind. The r. wing is cranked at an angle. Hidden steelwork where it meets the tower. Two-storey entrance porch at the NW corner, set at forty-five degrees against banded tile-hanging and tremendous bargeboards. Bressumer carved with the date, and an owl and bat. In the newer part the timber work, made by *Rattee & Kett* of Cambridge, is much more decorative, with diagonal and S-struts, and cambered beams in the gables. Base of local Gornal sandstone. The large gabled bay and high windows are inspired by Cheshire buildings like Churche's Mansion, Nantwich of 1577, but also by Ockwells Manor, Berkshire of *c.*1450. The E front has a projecting first-floor window based on the C16 Little Moreton Hall, Cheshire.

The interior also has variety and picturesqueness. Mark Girouard noticed that much of it reflects the early C17, while the exterior is inspired by the C16. The first part is all 1887. The ENTRANCE HALL has an irregular shape and in the Arts and Crafts way is also a living room. Fireplace in a N bay, with relieving arch, copper hood and unusual *De Morgan* tiles, dark green and laid herringbone fashion. *Kempe* stained glass of the Virtues, dated 1888. On the W, the DRAWING ROOM, with walnut panelling, Jacobean-style plaster ceiling and an Italian C16 alabaster fireplace. This has the finest *De Morgan* tiles, white and dark green, with animals and birds. In the bay window excellent *Kempe* stained glass of *c.*1875, brought from his house, Old Place, Lindfield. Chandelier by *W.A.S. Benson* of *Morris & Co*. A secret staircase runs up to what was Mrs Mander's boudoir. On the s side the LIBRARY, with oak-ribbed ceiling, fireplace with *Maw* tiles, and 1870s glass by *Madox Brown* and *Burne-Jones*, made by *Morris & Co.*, acquired 1947. Up steps from the Entrance Hall is the UPPER HALL, really a corridor, and originally the staircase hall. On the s, the MORNING ROOM. Fireplace again with *De Morgan* tiles. On the N the replacement STAIRCASE of 1893, with a fine plaster ceiling, perhaps by *Leonard Shuffrey*, centred on a sun's head. Then Theodore Mander's TURKISH BATH of 1888, restored in 1994.

At the end the 1893 wing starts. Along a screens passage and through two arches into the principal interior, the GREAT PARLOUR, really a re-created Great Hall, which goes through the two storeys. Arch-braced tie-beam roof on moulded wallposts, linked to the shallow-pitched panelled ceiling by longitudinal brackets. E gallery on big arched braces. Large inglenook

---

*The furnishings include *Morris* wallpapers in many rooms, some original; some brass chandeliers by *W.A.S. Benson*; and furniture brought in includes items from the Putney home of Swinburne and Theodore Watts-Dunton. Burne-Jones's 'Love Among the Ruins' is a major presence in the Great Parlour.

with a fireplace with gesso decoration of luxuriant roses and floral tiles. Full-height bay window with *Kempe* glass of 1893. A coloured plaster frieze also by Kempe runs all round, with the story of Orpheus and Eurydice. It is in a C16 manner, recalling the frieze at Hardwick Hall, Derbyshire (but includes a kangaroo). Beyond, the BILLIARD ROOM with a ceiling by *Shuffrey* with delicate rib patterns, and frieze with signs of the zodiac in cartouches. Inglenook with openwork pillars cut from single piece of oak, and *Morris* 'Daisy' tiles. Elevated fixed seating (to watch play) in the E bay. Then the DINING ROOM with another *Shuffrey* ceiling: pendants with little heads, foliage and dogs in the frieze. Full-height panelling and a built-in sideboard. N of the parlour the VISITORS' STAIRCASE, with humpy balusters and an unusual rushwork dado. The principal bedroom, the OAK ROOM of 1893, was restored in 1994, with a ribbed barrel-vaulted ceiling and panelled beams separating the former dressing room. A little WRITING ROOM behind a baluster screen. Panelled main corridor with another plaster ceiling. The NIGHT NURSERY has a frieze of 1908 painted by *Cecil Aldin*.

Tucked behind the house to the N, the C17 OLD MALTHOUSE, L-shaped, brick, much restored by *Ould*, c.1888. The windows are his, and the fireplace in the main first-floor room. Surviving box framing and queen-strut roof. Early C20 panelled DARKROOM. Immediately E, the remaining part of the OLD MANOR, a C17 recasting of late medieval and later fabric. The cross-wing is of c.1600, and the hall was rebuilt and extended c.1630, including the porch with the Wightwick arms. Again remodelled and extended by *Ould*, 1888, with Ruabon brick dressings and windows, and a studded entrance door. Mullion-and-transom window on the first floor, now inside. Very simple tie-beam and queenpost roof. Attic door made from late medieval woodwork. Ground-floor shop of 1989–96. To the NW, STABLES remodelled from farm buildings by *Ould*, with much tile-hanging. Tearoom of 2012 by *MBLA*. Re-erected DRINKING FOUNTAIN of 1861.

GARDENS. *Alfred Parsons* was consulted in 1899 but Theodore Mander's death stopped work. His widow, Flora, obtained designs from *Thomas H. Mawson* in 1904. Work was completed in 1910 with the lawns, balustrade and terrace S of the house. Geoffrey Mander continued work between the wars. The gardens extend E of Wightwick Bank, across a replacement BRIDGE by *J.E.M. Macgregor*, 1950, modelled on the Mathematical Bridge at Queens' College, Cambridge. – STONEWORK from the bombed House of Commons, a pair of crowns W of the entrance, and pieces E of the Old Manor.

THE MOUNT, Mount Road. Now a hotel. A house was bought by Charles Benjamin Mander in 1865. A watercolour of 1883 shows a central block with tall hipped roof and a NW wing, both with sash windows: probably C18. This building is still there, engulfed. Charles Tertius Mander bought the house from his father in 1890. His architect was *Edward Ould*, but the Jacobethan style here is very different from Wightwick Manor.

Theodore and Geoffrey Mander were Liberals and their house is a dream of John Ball; Charles Tertius was a Tory and The Mount is beefsteak and the Cockaigne Overture. His first phase, in 1891, using Ould but 'to his own ideas', added an entrance range at the N, with a spectacular stair hall, and a gabled SW wing out from the hipped-roofed block. The second phase, in 1908, when *Hastwell Grayson* and *Leonard Barnish* from *Grayson & Ould* were also involved, added a Great Hall at the NW, and regularized the SW garden front.

The approach is across a car park from the N, where everything is irregular, with late C20 extensions. Hipped-roofed block to the l., entrance block in front, and Great Hall all to the r. *Ould*'s work is all of red brick with Cotswold stone dressings. The entrance block has a hipped roof and an elongated star-shaped chimney, picturesquely combined with the square, parapeted stair hall. Full-height canted bay l. with a balancing oriel r. The hall has full-height mullion-and-transom windows and a square r. bay. Its SW front has a matching bay l., balanced by a canted bay r. Then plainer gables, the 1891 wing and a late C20 bow. Beyond is the end of the hipped-roofed block.

We enter into the panelled ENTRANCE HALL and some spatial games. A gallery runs round three sides. The staircase rises through an arcade on the fourth one and back round a landing below a big window. Above, an oriel window looks into the hall. It has alternate caryatids and Atlantes supporting a rich C17-style cornice and swan's-neck pediment. The gallery has a balustrade with posts which have finials of dogs sitting up, holding lamps in their paws. Little extra staircases to the room with the oriel. Octagonal lantern. A ground-floor passage with a delicate plasterwork vault leads to the GREAT HALL. This was both living hall and ballroom (with a sprung floor). A gallery runs round the NE and SE sides, accessed from the main staircase, and ends in an arcaded 'cabin' at the NW, above a fireplace with paired Ionic columns and an achievement of arms. Strapwork ceiling in swinging curves, with pendants, by *Leonard Shuffrey*. Heraldic GLASS by *Bryans & Webb* of Stourbridge. From the cabin a secret staircase – the only imitation of Wightwick Manor here – runs down l. of the fireplace. The detail is wonderfully refined; the two great Mander houses have in common scholarship and quality.

STABLES to the E by *Ould*, 1891, with shaped gables enclosing circular windows.

THE DIPPONS, Dippons Drive. The creation of the scholar and historian Gerald Mander between 1912 and his death in 1951: a delightful fantasy, like a miniature Portmeirion, now hidden among late C20 housing. His architect was *James A. Swan*. The house was rebuilt in 1914–15. Tudor Revival, in finely detailed brickwork, including the mullions and transoms of the full-height bay windows. Shell-hood doorcase, like a late C17 addition. The house spreads N, becoming more domestic. A 'Garden House' is recorded for 1922, 'Gateway and outbuildings' in 1927. A pair of pyramid-roofed brick and stone towers set diagonally are linked by an archway. Timber-framed wing behind to the l., with a cart entrance. Stables to the r., altered with black-and-white gables by *Arrol & Snell*; dated 1992, with the initials of Neil Avery, who rescued the buildings, starting in 1977. Beyond, an ogee-roofed tower, probably of *c*. 1938–9. A narrow lane runs along the W side, past a rear wing with another shell porch and a timber oriel window with plaster coving dated 1929.

TETTENHALL COLLEGE, Wood Road. An independent school founded in 1863 by Nonconformists. Early C19 LODGE and GATEPIERS, belonging to Tettenhall Towers (*see* below). Neo-Georgian administration block of 1954 by *Bertram Butler*; top storey 1974. Going E, on the N, converted STABLES, Late Georgian (after 1807) with severe pilasters and pediment. Pretty domed cupola. MAIN SCHOOL, further NE, 1865–7, is by *George Bidlake*. Three-storey range with wings, robust brick Gothic with lots of rogue detail. NW entrance front with a small angle porch and a big r. gable with a good four-light window. Slim central niche above a buttress, and quatrefoil with stubby colonnettes. The SE front has a sharp spirelet at the l. end and an oriel on a triangular pier penetrating a buttress below. The central tower has lost its top. First-floor chapel in the SW wing with collar-beam trusses; stained glass by *Fellows Chaplin*, 2013. Open-well staircase with cast-iron balusters. To the S, *Bidlake*'s contemporary SWIMMING BATH, with a row of lunette windows and attached house, and his GYMNASIUM, a rectangle of red brick with yellow bands and star shapes, with a clerestory of large pointed windows, divided by brackets supporting the hipped roof.

Attached at the N end, but now in separate ownership, the original school building. A house of *c*. 1750–60, in the same heavy mid-Georgian style as Stourhurst, Stourbridge (p. 551), associated with *William & David Hiorne*. Central full-height canted bay, the ground floor an open porch. Venetian windows either side. Solid keystones everywhere, bracket cornice and parapet.

TETTENHALL TOWERS, to the SW, was purchased by the school in 1944. It starts with a house of before 1763 for Thomas Pearson. Its NW entrance front, now stuccoed, has pedimented ends and recessed centre, a progressive composition. This was extended in the early C19, before 1807, with a porch enclosed by Greek Doric columns and return pilasters, and a S block with a fine full-height semicircular bay and parapet with squared zigzag ornament. Doric loggia to the NE, now infilled. A slightly later r. wing ends in an octagonal tower again with zigzag ornament. Early C19 corridor to a small central hall with good iron gallery rail. Stair on the N. At the far end free-standing Ionic columns screen a long room facing the garden. Another Ionic screen, with a palmette frieze, subdivides the room. In 1854 the house was bought by the ironmaster *Colonel Thomas Thorneycroft*, who hugely extended it NE in a cruder Greek Revival style with two towers, expanded versions of the early

C19 one. He was an inventor – the house had his own drains, central heating, a lift, and telephones between rooms – and probably his own architect. His THEATRE survives, with three-sided gallery. Detail is an unscholarly mixture, Greekish and Jacobean. In the gallery, l., a panelled seat and flanking niches, survivors of the spectacular full-height inglenook with fireplace and military trophies illustrated in *The Builder* in 1880.

PERAMBULATIONS

1. Tettenhall village

A long walk from Lower Green and St Michael's church to Upper Green and back. The start is the approach to the church from CHURCH ROAD, S. On the NW side by the lychgate, THE HOUSE BY THE CHURCH is late C18, with simplified Wyatt ground-floor windows, platband and Tuscan former porch. Rear wing recast in 1911 by *W.J.H. Weller*: typical entrance porch with timber piers and angled bay. Casement windows set flush. Entrance hall with simple panelling and fireplace. But the best part of the interior is earlier, plasterwork of *c.* 1905–6 by *C.R. Ashbee* and the *Guild of Handicraft*. The drawing room has a deep frieze in three layers, small Art Nouveau-ish upright flowers in irregular patterns, flanking larger panels of bunches of fruit with foliage. The dining room has decoration round niches, a peacock with radiating feathers filling the keystone of the largest one. – SUMMERHOUSE at the rear, late C19, with two-bay Dec traceried arches, perhaps reused.

On the SE side of the approach by Lower Green, THE GREEN HOUSE, also three bays, dated 1794. Doorcase with open pediment. SW down Church Road past colonial-looking Edwardian bungalows, to where THE ROCK, cut by the Wolverhampton Turnpike Trust in 1820–3, runs W up a deep dramatic cutting. On the N side AVENUE HOUSE LODGE, by *J.J. Bateman*, 1860–1. His typical framed windows with segmental lintels, and striking circular chimneys. In OLD HILL, SW from the crossing with Church Road, ROCK HOUSE is mid-C18, articulated by a projecting central bay and corner pilasters, and prominent platband. Good pedimented doorcase with Gibbs surround. ROCK COTTAGE is late C18, now stuccoed. IVY HOUSE opposite is probably early C18: tall, gabled, with clasping buttresses. Round-headed doorcase with flattened fluted half-columns, perhaps early C19, the Gothick windows later still. WOODFIELDS is also probably Georgian, though its front is Early Victorian. Doorcase with heavy consoles. Further up on the r., the former ROCK HOTEL (now the Two Greens), 1893, a brick mass with a balustraded tower. Tudor entrance extension by *G.E. Stevens*, 1956.

Ahead, UPPER STREET leads W to the village centre and UPPER GREEN, an open space running W and N across the A41. The village clings to its S side, again mostly C19, with terraces running s along High Street and wsw along Limes Road. In High Street the former POLICE STATION, 1971 by *Philip Whittle*. Nicely placed first-floor oriel. Turning r., past the FOUNTAIN dated 1890, the E side of the green has the best cottages: Nos. 16–18, set back, c18, the l. end a single-bay, three-storey house with casement windows. Nos. 19 and 20 *c.* 1800, No. 20 with canted bays and ogee-roofed porch. On the A41 corner the CLOCK TOWER of 1911 by *F. T. Beck*, not tall but substantial, square with attached Doric columns at the corners and a projecting cornice. Across the main road, an early C20 BUS SHELTER.

Across the A41 on the E side, picturesque brick and timber cottages of 1913–14 also by *Beck*. They run round E into CLIFTON ROAD, where Nos. 16–20 are the first of a puzzling group with platbands and lintels of c18 type but solid pilastered doorcases that look *c.* 1830–40. So the earlier-looking details are probably a continuation of old designs. A lane leads SE to AVENUE HOUSE, by *J. J. Bateman*, 1860–1, for William Bissell, merchant (altered). An odd design, with the l. part higher. Rusticated pilasters and architraves with panels underneath. Circular chimneys, as on its lodge down the hill (*see* above). Back on Clifton Road, Nos. 28–32, like Nos. 16–20. Nos. 34–36 also have earlier Georgian detail – eared windows, heavy attic – but again the doorcases and windows above with minimal pediments suggest *c.* 1830–40. No. 38, severely plain with a side entrance, probably 1840s.

Now back and NE down STOCKWELL ROAD. On the l., THE OLD FARMHOUSE is dated 1520. L-shaped, roughcast except the timber-framed r. gable with curved braces and what looks like an infilled jetty. Much late c19 recasting, including the stone-mullioned windows. Further on, detached houses of 1967–8 by *Desmond T. Crews & Partners*. We turn NW, with, behind a wall, villas with stone mullion-and-transom windows, Gothic doorcases and jettied gables of *c.* 1880, perhaps by *T. H. Fleeming*. At the end on the l., STOCKWELL HOUSE, of 1758, with a fancy Early Victorian front. Stucco, with elongated consoles to the windows, and pilasters ending in semicircular projections above the cornice. Stockwell Road turns E here. LAMBSEY CROFT on the S side is by *Nightingale & Marchment*, 1913, rendered, with a chimney atop the r. gable and a teasingly off-centre bay and timber porch below. On the N side STOCKWELL END COTTAGE, white-painted early c19 brick, hiding an older core, and STOCKWELL END HOUSE, at first sight Late Victorian. The central Wightwick-style gable and r. wing with corner turret are of 1892, but the roughcast l. wing is timber-framed and probably c16. Tie- and collar-beam roof with big wind-braces, box framing and thick close studding in the side wall. The 1892 work has a Jacobean revival staircase with a little internal oriel like The Mount (p. 740). The main living-room fireplace has brought-in Salomonic Ionic columns. Behind, an outbuilding, brick and some stone, originally detached and probably a kitchen. Fireplace with stone piers, queenpost roof. Down narrow Lothians Road, N, the drive to TYNINGHAME, a half-timbered monster of 1893–4 with a Wightwick-style angled porch. The angular stone bay and half-hipped r. gable suggest *John Weller II*.

Now back up Stockwell Road and SE into CHURCH HILL ROAD, with C19 and C20 houses and cottages. No. 18, white render with brick ground floor, is by *W. Curtis Green*, 1910. Subtly composed, the r. gable is slightly larger than the l., and with a chimney resting on its r. end. Extended l., probably in 1928. At the end ABBEYFIELD, the former vicarage, of 1888–9 by *T.H. Fleeming*. Three blocks, all with hipped roofs. Main rooms l. with big bays, the central hall block with big unequal windows advertising the staircase, and service rooms r. The centre has coving and a dormer. Was Fleeming influenced by Philip Webb? Opposite is CHURCH HILL DRIVE with No. 10, by *Douglas Billingsley* of *Mason, Richards & Partners* for himself, 1969, amid trees. White-painted brick and glazing, deep flat roof. Mostly single-storeyed but a taller projection at the W. Nos. 1–2, N, look exactly like Parkdale (p. 716) so must be early 1880s by *John Weller II*.

A path by Abbeyfield leads down past St Michael's and E out of the churchyard into CHURCH WALK. Of c. 1830–40 GOTHIC COTTAGE, r., with picturesque bargeboards, and a severe Late Classical pair on the l. At the bottom is LOWER STREET. On the SW corner, THE OLD FARMHOUSE is early or mid-C18, with tall proportions, platbands, coving and a narrow full-height central projection. Next door, THE BARN is probably C17: see the SW gable with large timber-framed panels. Converted 1983–4 by *Grant Latham Partnership* with catslide extensions. Going N, first a Victorian classical pair with heavy architraves and end pediments, then a terrace of c. 1850–60. Nos. 86–88 are probably mid-C18. Three tall storeys, plain giant pilasters, platbands. The l. addition has a Late Georgian Tuscan doorcase. LOWLANDS is an altered stuccoed villa of c. 1830. Projecting Greek Doric porch *in antis*.

In Lower Street S of the Old Farmhouse, THE SWAN pub is probably C18, altered and extended. Further S is the former ST MICHAEL'S NATIONAL SCHOOL, its pedimented front of 1827 recast and extended to the rear, 1858–9 (*Griffin & Weller*), 1904, and later. S of the A41 and down Meadow View, E, the former TETTENHALL STATION, on the GWR Kingswinford loop line. Opened 1925, closed as early as 1932. BOOKING HALL with canopy, GOODS SHED and OFFICE in the yard, all still to designs of c. 1900. Then, from the school, up LOWER GREEN to St Michael's, with the former MITRE inn, remodelled in Tudor Revival in 1924, probably by *W.A. Hutchings*.

2. Wood Road

The start is at the SW end of High Street, with Tettenhall College (p. 742), and St Thomas of Canterbury (p. 738) to its W. Behind the latter in Haywood Drive, MORE HOUSE, now the presbytery. Cross-wing of *c.* 1600, with box framing in the gable-ends. The main wing, l., was largely rebuilt by *Col. Thomas Thorneycroft* in the late C19. Timber framing survives inside, but Thorneycroft made a miniature hall with a balustraded gallery above the fireplace, with an assemblage of imported woodwork, some Continental, probably C17, including many small figure scenes. Beyond, GORSTY HAYES MANOR HOUSE. Early C19. Three-bay front with a long ground-floor canted bay with Gothick windows, and a concave-roofed porch with fluted Ionic columns. A long wing, r., mostly modern, retains some C17 stonework and a re-set datestone of 1683.

Further SW down Wood Road, WOODCOTE ROAD, houses by *Mason, Richards & Partners*, 1973 etc., on the site of Tettenhall Wood House of 1831 by *Thomas Rickman* (dem. 1970). From here, GRANGE ROAD runs N. THE GRANGE has an C18 front range with moulded first-floor lintels. C19 canted bays and pretty fretwork doorcase. The rear wall is C16 or C17, with box framing and some close studding. Narrow staircase bay behind. The wall to the N has more box framing and a cut-off truss. Behind the house, a brick and timber BARN, probably C17, nicely converted by *Keith Cattell* of *Mason, Richards & Partners*, 1970. Also *Rickman*'s dining-room bay window from Tettenhall Wood House, re-erected as a SUMMERHOUSE. Seven-sided, with crisp Dec tracery. Further N, LIMES ROAD takes us E back to Upper Green with a consistent and attractive brick late C19 townscape.

Further SW down Wood Road, the late C19 timbered LODGE of Tettenhall Wood House, much extended. Also ELMHURST, Tudor Gothic, probably 1840s, much altered, with a good Neo-Georgian SW range probably of *c.* 1932. Further SW, the late C19 stable range of HIGHGROVE.

3. Tettenhall Wood

C19 and occasionally earlier cottages sprinkled among affluent modern houses. The start is the cross-roads just N of Christ Church (p. 737), with the INSTITUTE, brick and half-timber, 1893. To the NW in School Road, the former INFANTS' SCHOOL, gabled brick Gothic with a massive chimney, probably of 1858 and by *Edward Banks*, who worked for the schools in 1837. The former JUNIOR SCHOOL, E side, is mostly by *Fleeming & Son*, 1902 and 1910.

SE from the cross-roads, CHURCH ROAD has a house of *c.* 1830–40 with shaped gables on the corner of Grove Lane. Further on, Georgian cottages, also in the fork of Ormes Lane. Down The Holloway, SE, the former LODGE of Compton Hill House, *Rundbogenstil* of *c.* 1850–60. Up ORMES LANE. On the r., remains of SOUTHBOURNE, by *Bidlake & Fleeming*, 1875: GATEPIERS with sculptural tops, and the former STABLE with fancy brickwork. BROMLEY HOUSE is dated 1850, a fine late classical design with central pediment and a miniature Osborne-style tower. Heavy porch of c.1870. Sophisticated garden front: recessed centre with triple-arched porch, flanking projections with end pilasters and square bays. Good staircase with decorative iron balusters. All this suggests *Edward Banks*.

SW from the cross-roads, MOUNT ROAD rises gently. Down Tor Lodge Drive, to the SE, APPLECROSS HOUSE, Early Victorian, with hipped roof and stepped-in canted bays with colonnettes at the angles; and TOR LODGE of c.1830, stuccoed, altered by *George Bidlake*, 1867, including a heavy bracketed porch. Back on Mount Road, set back, The Mount (p.740). Opposite, cottages with half-timbering and tile-hanging by *Ould*, 1907 (Nos.58–60). E of these, DIPPONS DRIVE runs NW to The Dippons. Down the lane l. of the house, DIPPONS COTTAGE, by *Kenneth Hutchinson Smith*, 1927. Gable with old timbers and tile-hanging to the r. The lane becomes a path and emerges on to MILL LANE, W. Just S, a tower WINDMILL of 1720, converted to a house by the 1880s. For the area SW of this, *see* Perambulation 4.

4. Wightwick

The start is on BRIDGNORTH ROAD, S of Wightwick Manor. On the cross-roads the MERMAID INN, low and roughcast, C18, altered for Theodore Mander by *Edward Ould* in 1899 (l. end 1926). Further E, cottages for Mander by *Ould*: Nos. 260–264, 1896, and the main group of 1892–3, Nos. 244–258, a row set back with central timber gable and tile-hanging, flanked by pairs with more exuberant timberwork. Up FIRSWAY, NW, is ROCKLANDS, a long bungalow by *Webb & Gray*, 1924. Further E again, VIEWLANDS LODGE, formerly to Elmsdale Hall (*see* below), sandstone Jacobean of c.1855–60. Returning to the Mermaid, W beyond the Manor grounds is NETHERTON HOUSE, dated 1747. Three bays. C20 French windows and porch.

WIGHTWICK BANK runs up N from the cross-roads (narrow, with dangerous traffic and no continuous footpaths), past the Manor and under the Mathematical Bridge (p. 740). On the W side, WIGHTWICK HOUSE. Georgian, stuccoed, with sashes. Round-headed doorway. The porch looks C20. S wing with C19 canted bay. On the corner of PERTON BROOK VALE, cottages by *Ould*, 1896, mostly heavily altered. On the E, ELMSDALE HALL, sandstone Jacobean, probably late 1850s, for (Sir) John Morris. Tower with French pavilion roof; entrance with term-like tapering pilasters. Hidden to the N, a house of 1958 by *Diamond, Hodgkinson & Partners* (*Frank Briggs*), a prototype of modular brick-and-panel construction for the contractors, *John McLean & Sons*. Opposite on the corner of Old Lane, WYCOTT is of 1922 by *W. J. H. Weller*, roughcast and brick, now painted. Further up, a road junction. PERTON

ROAD runs w with, on the s side, No. 21 by *Charles Mason* of *Mason, Richards & Partners* for himself, 1967. Buff brick, shallow-pitched roof, full-height stairs window with slender timber mullions. To the E in the fork between Mount Road and Mill Lane (*see* Perambulation 3), roughcast cottages by *Joseph Lavender*, 1908.

OTHER BUILDINGS

WATERWORKS, Regis Road, W. Industrial classicism of 1845 by the engineer *Henry J. Marten*. Four-storey red brick PUMPING STATION with round-headed relieving arches, and groups of round windows in the attic-like top storey. Contemporary MANAGER'S HOUSE, with a hipped roof and again relieving arches. Brutalist additions of 1967–74 by *John Weller & Silvester*.

WROTTESLEY ROAD, N of the waterworks. No. 74 incorporates a cottage, probably C16, with studding below box framing. W of it three houses by *Richard Twentyman*: Nos. 78 and 85, 1933 and 1939, both altered, and COUNTISBURY, opposite, 1936–7, more traditional in massing but also with a horizontal window band.

WERGS ROAD (A41), NW. No. 38, TETTENHALL COURT, is by *W.J.H. Weller*, 1913. Full-height timber gable enclosing the wide porch, another gable to the r. over a canted bay. To the l. a brick wing angles forward, with big mullion-and-transom windows and crenellations. Another timber gable over the stable courtyard entrance.

At WERGS, ¾ m. NW, the CROWN INN, C18, extended and altered. To the w, THE GRANGE. By *J. R. Veall*, 1863, the former farmhouse (THE COACH HOUSE) by the entrance, with bargeboards. Main house rebuilt by *W.T. Orton*, 1926, smooth Birmingham-style Arts and Crafts Tudor.

COMPTON

Where the Bridgnorth road crosses the Staffordshire and Worcestershire Canal. To the NE, a very early *Brindley* narrow LOCK, of c. 1768, the pattern for others across the West Midlands. NW of the canal, two pubs, both altered: the big gabled ODDFELLOWS turning the corner, of 1936–7 almost certainly by *A.T. & Bertram Butler*, and the SWAN, late C18. E of Compton Hall (*see* below), affluent C19 and C20 housing. At the far end of Ash Hill, S, down THE BURROW, a fantastical timber CLOCK TOWER dated 1883. Octagonal ground floor with pointed arches which have carved spandrels and inscriptions inside, square stage with studding, open belfry.

COMPTON HALL, Compton Road West. A striking Italianate villa of the 1840s, built for the ironmaster Thomas Elwell, and ascribed to *Edward Banks*. Stuccoed. Hipped roof. The N front has wide outer bays with prominent rusticated quoins and a narrow recessed centre with a porch, which has a panelled arch. Deep eaves with plain mutules. E front of three bays but longer, with two semicircular bays. The circular windows are an alteration, perhaps early C20. The plan has a long through corridor. Original staircase with decorative iron rail. Three rooms were re-fitted by *Morris & Co.* in 1894–6 for Laurence Hodson. Refined Jacobean-style fireplaces and panelling. The former DRAWING ROOM has tiles in the fireplace, probably by *William De Morgan*, to a vibrant blue and green *Morris* design, 'Tulip and Trellis', and a ceiling painted with swirling foliage and flowers, said to be by *J.H. Dearle*. More *De Morgan* tiles in the fireplace of the small room to the N. The DINING ROOM has a delicate strapwork ceiling.

ALDERSLEY

N of Tettenhall village, with Christ the King church (p. 737). Two pubs. The CLAREGATE in Codsall Road is of *c.* 1938, almost certainly by *A.T. & Bertram Butler*. Brick, now painted, with an entrance range set diagonally between big wings. Tudor chimneys. THE PILOT pub in Green Lane is by *Richard Twentyman*, 1937, brick (now rendered), L-shaped.

WEDNESFIELD

9500

The name means 'Woden's field'. Some versions of the *Anglo-Saxon Chronicle* place Edward the Elder's victory over the Northumbrians in 910 here. The village was part of the royal peculiar of Wolverhampton, and of the lock-making area, but its distinctive industry from at least the early C19 was trap-making of all kinds, including rat traps. An Urban District Council from 1896, absorbed into Wolverhampton in 1966.

The village centre, on the Wolverhampton to Lichfield road, is confined by the twisting contour route of the Wyrley and Essington Canal of 1792–5 – the 'curly Wyrley' – with access across rebuilt humpback bridges. A S by-pass, the bleak Alfred Squire Road, came in the early post-war period. The modern A4124 runs further S through late C20 industrial estates. Much municipal housing from the 1920s onwards, not of high quality.

ST THOMAS, Church Street. A large, rather plain brick classical church, its E end facing up the High Street. W tower of 1746–50, with top balustrade and alternating quoins. The rest of the C18 church rebuilt larger in 1842–3 by *T.H.Wyatt & David Brandon*, in a mid-C18 style. The fine tower doorcase with Gibbs surround and segmental pediment looks 1750 but is probably of 1843. The interior was rebuilt in 1903 by *Fred T. Beck*, after a fire in 1902. His are the present chancel and apse. His pedimented N and S chancel windows look perfect Early Victorian, as does the pilastered apse. Nave windows also Beck's, with tall un-Georgian proportions, though the 1-3-1 rectangular and round-headed arrangement follows Wyatt & Brandon. Beck's interior is solid and reassuring classical, unusual for the date. Galleries on Doric columns, Ionic columns rising above them to support the barrel-vaulted ceiling. At the E the fronts cut back in quadrant curves, a nice touch. – Beck's FITTINGS are remarkably complete: REREDOS with Ionic columns and segmental pediment; CHOIR STALLS and DESKS with a touch of Jacobean; PULPIT with attached Doric columns, standing on slim columns; PEWS; FONT with domed cover. – ROOD and curving BEAM by *Bridgemans*, 1918–19. – STAINED GLASS. Apse, of 1882 (it survived the fire). S aisle by *A.J. Davies*, 1949–50; N by *Bronwen Gordon*, 1971.

ST GREGORY, Blackhalve Lane. 1965–6 by *Clifford Tee & Gale*. A maroon brick box with a sawtooth roof and clerestory all round. Laminated timber ceiling. Lady Chapel, S, its plan two interlocking semicircles, entered through a curving full-height passage. – HALL by *Richard Twentyman*, 1954, NE.

COUNCIL OFFICES, Alfred Squire Road. 1955 by *Thomas Peacock*, Council Surveyor. Black Country conservatism: a single-storey Neo-Georgian block with raised centrepiece which looks *c.*1930.

POLICE STATION, Alfred Squire Road. A late work by *Richard Twentyman*, 1971. A depressing location but a fine building. Four storeys. Concrete frame, faced in brown handmade bricks. The quality shows in the perfectly calculated way the lower three storeys project from the block, and cut in at the l. side.

LIBRARY, Rookery Street and Well Lane. By *Wolverhampton City Council Architects (Ian P. Wood)*, 2010. Free-form, with a timber-clad tower and angular rendered shapes. Set well back, opening out the townscape just where tightness is needed.

WEDNESFIELD HIGH SCHOOL, Lichfield Road. Mostly by *Tweedale*, 2011–12.

BOARD SCHOOL (former), Neachells Lane. 1895 by *T.H. Fleeming*. Brick and *Dennis*'s terracotta from Ruabon. Gabled elevation.

EDWARD THE ELDER PRIMARY SCHOOL, Lichfield Road. By *G.C. Lowbridge*. Dated 1910, a standard Staffordshire County Council design.

PUBS. NW of the parish church the BOAT INN. Stucco decoration probably of the 1830s, the building perhaps *c.*1800. Original BREWHOUSE, l. E of the church in High Street the DOG AND PARTRIDGE, a low C16 or C17 range with a two-storey C18 brick cottage attached l. Inside, chamfered beams, a partly exposed timber partition, and a big restored fireplace. In Lichfield Road, N, the VINE INN, a reformed pub of 1937 by *Watkin & Maddox* of Burslem. Maroon-grey brick, including the mullioned windows, with a steep roof, slightly Dutch. It is octagonal, not rectangular: the sides cant out to full-height chimneystacks. Ceramic name plaque above the door. Wonderfully unaltered interior: public bar l., smoke room r., lobby and staircase behind, another smoke room. Original furnishings, brass room-name plates, and leaded glass.* w of the village on Rookery Street the former PYLE COCK, a traditional 'two-room drinker' (now a nursery). Good reformed pubs, all altered. On Lichfield Road the former ALBION (now The Lancaster) by *J. Percy Clark*, 1937; shaped gables. In Wood End Road the PHEASANT, cubic Neo-Georgian by *O.M.Weller*, 1935–6. On Cannock Road the former NEW PEAR TREE by *James A. Swan*, 1936, with symmetrical central block and chunky Tudor chimneys. In Amos Lane the RED LION, by *Richard Twentyman*, 1938, modernized Tudor, end gables with big round-arched doorways.

ASHMORE PARK

A large 1950s municipal estate, partly Wolverhampton overspill. Houses and shops by *Thomas Peacock*, U.D.C. Surveyor. On GRIFFITHS DRIVE three churches. ST ALBAN was planned by *N.F. Cachemaille-Day* and *A.S.B. Hill*, 1965, with an octagonal nave; but only a small hall by *Hill* was built, 1967. CORPUS CHRISTI (R.C.) is by *Atkins & Walters*, 1991. The BAPTIST CHURCH, a heavy box with angled lantern, is by *Downing, Smith, Kendrick Hood & Partner*, 1968. Two recent schools: COPPICE PERFORMING ARTS COLLEGE, Ecclestone Road, by *Tweedale*, 2011; OAK MEADOW PRIMARY SCHOOL, Ryan Avenue, by *Architype*, 2010.

A MOAT survives off Griffiths Drive, in an open space surrounded by shops.

WHITMORE REANS AND DUNSTALL

Building began after the sale of the Whitmore End House estate in 1850. The Wolverhampton Freehold Land Society laid out much of the land in streets and small plots allocated among its shareholders for 1s. 7d. a week. It was first called Newhampton (hence the road name). An 1864 map shows the area round Coleman, Hunter and Sweetman streets built up. They remained separated by fields from Wolverhampton until *c.*1900. One major factory, Courtaulds' Dunstall Mill works (1924–73).

ST ANDREW, St Andrew's Close. 1965–7 by *Richard Twentyman*, his last church, and his only one designed on Liturgical Movement principles. It replaced a famously Anglo-Catholic church of 1864–5 by *Edward Banks* with a chancel of 1892 by *F.T. Beck*, destroyed by fire. Unimpressive low brick exterior, with a vestibule dividing the hall from the church. This is marked by projecting tower-like piers, but its walls are windowless, to stop noise from a road which was never built. It is the interior

---

*Also in Lichfield Road, E side, THE HILLS, 1914, by *Frank S. Clark*.

which matters, a space of unexpected numinous power. A simple rectangle, with the congregation on three sides of the altar. Beamed ceiling, walls rendered with a slightly rough finish (each wall was plastered in one go, to get a surface without marks or joins). The lighting comes down mysteriously, Ronchamp-like, from lanterns in the towers, and especially a long N–S roof-light above the altar. – ALTAR, PULPIT, BENCHES etc. by *Twentyman*. – FONT by *Banks* from the old church. – STAINED GLASS. Also unexpected, a wonderful W window by *John Piper*, made by *Patrick Reyntiens*, 1967–8. Piper's biographer Frances Spalding calls it 'a great flood of blue in which sweeping black lines and small vortexes swim and float'. – A small hexagonal N chapel, also rendered, has PEWS by *Banks*.

CRANMER METHODIST CHURCH, Newhampton Road West. By *Ronald Baker, Humphreys & Goodchild*, 1991–2. Chunky traditional revival. Octagonal sanctuary with lantern and pyramid roof.

TABERNACLE BAPTIST CHURCH, Dunstall Road. 1931 by *J. Tomlinson*. Brick, very conservative.

CHURCH OF GOD OF PROPHECY, Gloucester Street. 1989 by the *Alan Cotterell Partnership*.

WULFRUNA'S WELL, Gorsebrook Road, opposite Viaduct Drive. A small stone memorial erected in 1901 on the supposed site of Wulfruna's spring.

NEWHAMPTON ARTS CENTRE, Newhampton Road East. The former Higher Grade School of 1894 by *T.H. Fleeming* (the 1921 date is an addition). Ruabon brick and terracotta. Tall, tightly composed with pilasters and string courses. Hall range l., with a tapering cupola. Flemish-style entrance with a concave pediment. Extension r. down Dunkley Street, 1925–6 by *Fleeming & Son*, very conservative. Behind, new arts centre building by *Wolverhampton M.B.C. Architects (Keith Hodgkins)*, 1997–9. Brick, with tapered-in buttresses and a split curved roof.

WOLVERHAMPTON RACECOURSE, Dunstall Park. Laid out in 1887. The present grandstand and hotel of 1995 etc. by *Alan Cotterell Partnership (John Bradbury)*.

WATERLOO TERRACE, Newhampton Road East, N side. Stucco with canted bays, *c.* 1860.

The centre of Whitmore Reans is ½ m. W, on Newhampton Road West. The AVION CENTRE is a good development of shops, flats and a library, by *McAlster, Jones & Associates*, 1972, round a square. Yellow brick, two storeys, pitched roofs. The flats have pierced brick screen walls. Covered walkways with concrete roofs and heavy piers. The library, detached to the NE, is hexagonal. Just W, the former St Andrew's VICARAGE, by *F.T. Beck*, 1888, severe, with a big canted bay. A tiny LYCHGATE marks a path to the church. In Riches Street the NEWHAMPTON pub, remodelled from C19 houses by *W.S. Clements*, 1923.

SOLIHULL METROPOLITAN BOROUGH

Solihull	753
Churches	754
Public buildings	758
Perambulation	758
Other buildings	761
North of the centre: Hobs Moat and Lyndon	764
Catherine-de-Barnes	765
Bickenhill	766
Castle Bromwich	768
Chelmsley Wood	774
Earlswood	775
Dickens Heath	777
Elmdon	778
Kingshurst	780
Marston Green	780
National Exhibition Centre	781
Olton	781
Shirley	784

SOLIHULL

Solihull appears in Domesday as Ulverlei. The present name dates from the C13, when it was held by the Oddingselles (or Oddingeseles) family. There was a market charter of 1242, but until the early C20 Solihull was a large Warwickshire village. The railway arrived in 1852. There was a scatter of Late Victorian villas, and larger houses of which Tudor Grange is the best survivor. Modern suburban development started in the Edwardian period; Ashleigh Road shows it at its finest. Solihull gave its name to a Rural District Council in 1894, an Urban District in 1934 and a Borough as late as 1954. In 1974, when other local towns lost their independence, it became a Metropolitan Borough, including Chelmsley Wood, Castle Bromwich and countryside to the E towards Coventry.* It is still growing as a commuter town, but its pleasant suburbs have limited architectural interest.

*The borough E and SE of the M42 is covered in *The Buildings of England: Warwickshire*.

CHURCHES

17 ST ALPHEGE, Church Hill Road. A large church of red sandstone with a crossing tower and spire. The finest architecture is the late C13 chancel and the attached N chapel of St Alphege with its undercroft and its airy upper storey. The chapel is probably associated with William de Oddingselles's chantry foundation of 1277. There was clearly a break during construction, as the lowest courses are in regular blocks, the rest in smaller stones. The windows of chancel and chapel – including internal ones between them – are all in tracery of the same type, pre-ogee, and with the charming detail of the cusps being doubled: two addorsed volutes, as it were. Exceptions both the E windows, which have cusped intersecting tracery. Along the chancel walls inside runs a string course which rises round the window arches and performs blank pointed trefoils where there is wall space. This results in an enjoyable rhythm, as the W pair of windows is more widely spaced than the E pair and the space between the two pairs is yet wider. In that space the doorways are placed – rather arbitrarily – to the undercroft and the upper part of St Alphege's Chapel. The UNDERCROFT (St Francis's Chapel) has a two-bay rib-vault with hollow-chamfered ribs, the upper part with windows S into the chancel as well as N. In the chancel is a steeply gabled PISCINA with large leaves below. St Alphege's Chapel has a simpler version, and also a steeply pitched roof of close-set trusses, partly original and asymmetrical.

Next the tower and transepts, a complex build. The earliest surviving fabric is the short stretch of nave S wall just W of the

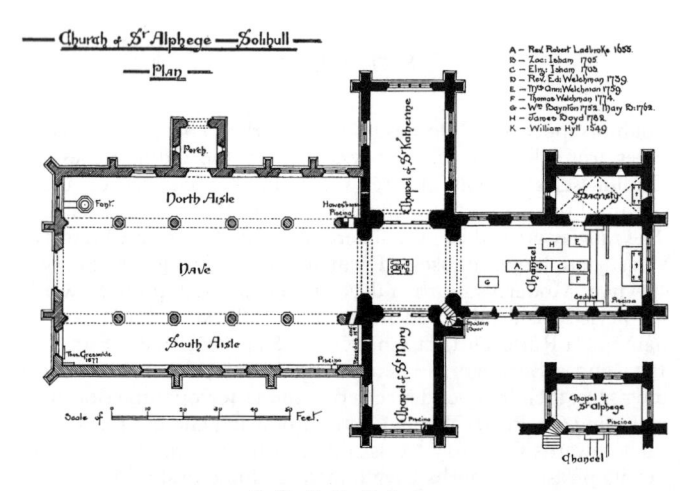

Solihull, St Alphege.
Plan, 1882

crossing, with an C18 opening and, above it, marks of a blocked Norman window, best seen from the S chapel. So there was an aisleless Norman church here. The lower part of the tower is C13, built in regular squared stones like the base courses of the chancel, and with cusped paired lancets. Perp belfry stage with paired twin bell-openings to each side. The spire fell in a gale in 1757 and was rebuilt, not as high, by *Joseph Pickford*, 1774–5, with raised bands and minimal Gothick quatrefoils. The transepts must come just after the chancel: late C13 or early C14. Their much-restored N and S windows have cusped intersecting tracery, and the N transept side windows complex cuspings. The joints between transept walls and the C13 tower side buttresses show in e.g. the N aisle E wall. The crossing arches are mid-C14 or even later, and rather coarse: capitals with convex and concave chamfers, multiplied mouldings on the bases. Arches with one plain and one hollow chamfer. So either the E and W arches were rebuilt to match the transepts, or more likely the whole crossing was rebuilt later. Marks of an earlier nave roof above the W arch. N aisle also C14, with two-light Dec windows. A part-arch survives in the nave N wall W of the crossing, perhaps to a small earlier chapel or vestry.

The nave and S aisle are late Perp. They were probably being roofed in 1533–5 when the parish accounts include 'Cariyng...howyng and Framyn' timber, and 'leyd' (lead). The arcades are of five bays and remarkably tall. Double-chamfered arches, octagonal piers. The W responds have another usual Perp section, with shafts between deep hollows. The W doorway outside also has deep hollow mouldings. The S aisle was rebuilt in 1751, which may explain the slightly unusual windows with paired quatrefoiled circles in each light, and the straight-headed five-light window with similar tracery at the E end, put in no doubt to light the pulpit. S aisle PISCINA with ogee arch. C16 nave roof with close-set trusses with arch-braced collars. Marks show it was originally ceiled, but it was opened out in 1856 by *G.E. Street*, who also scraped the interior. *John Oldrid Scott* carried out a major though careful restoration in 1879 (supervised by *Edward Holmes*), replacing the aisle roofs and rebuilding the W window and gable. *John Cotton* did more in 1887–8. St Francis's Chapel was restored in 1905–6 by *W.H. Bidlake*. The church has given much trouble statically, and the arcades indeed look dangerous enough. In 1947–8 *Leslie Temple Moore* added the big S aisle buttresses and the supporting half-arches inside, moving the eastern of the two-light windows. Moore also buttressed the W wall, 1951, and N aisle, 1953.

FURNISHINGS. Two restored SCREENS. Former N transept screen, moved to form the chancel reredos by *Charles Brown*, 1975. Another, reconfigured and heavily redone, screens a sacristy in the N transept. Both have one-light divisions and ogee tracery, but rounded central arches with C17-style drops, suggesting a history of alterations. – COMMUNION RAIL. A splendid piece, probably of 1681 when the church was re-pewed. Twisted balusters, pierced acanthus foliage and also pierced abstract panels of a mid- rather than a late C17 type. Re-pieced, with an extra length below the reredos; perhaps originally three-sided. – Chancel STALLS and PANELLING of 1847, reworked. – STATUES on the walls by *Alan Durst*, 1951. – The lower chapel retains its medieval ALTAR SLAB. – ROOD BEAM by *L. Temple Moore*, 1951 with figures by *Durst*. – English ALTAR, N transept, by *Temple Moore*, 1944, with painted panels. – ORGAN CASE, S transept. Early C18, said to be by *Thomas Swarbrick*; brought from St Martin in the Bull Ring, Birmingham in the early C19. Gothic tracery added. – PULPIT. Jacobean, with the familiar blank arches. – REREDOS, S aisle. Perp, of stone and quite a simple row of panelling. – REREDOS, N aisle. Of wood, with a pediment, early C18 style, by *Temple Moore*, 1944. The ALTAR here is a very richly carved coffer, like a *cassone*, probably of *c.*1600. Is it English? – FONT, W end. Octagonal, stem with attached columns, probably C13. – CANDELABRUM. Of brass, dated 1706. One tier of arms. – CHURCHWARDENS' STALLS, W end. Mixed classical-Gothic, with slim columns. By *Laurence King*, 1963. – GATE of wrought iron, N porch. By *Paris* of Warwick, dated 1746.

STAINED GLASS. E window signed by *Wailes*, 1845 (tracery lights and inscription 1867). Chancel N, two by *Lavers, Barraud & Westlake*, *c.*1872, †1867; S, another by them, 1872, and three by *Hardmans*, 1874, backgrounds removed. – St Alphege's Chapel. E window by *Bertram Lamplugh*, 1908–9, a beautiful Arts and Crafts piece. Calm figures with rich blue and red robes, complex foliage backgrounds with flowers and butterflies. The roundels in the tracery lights look C14. N, *Powells*, 1928; *Townsend & Howson*, 1936. W, central panel *Willement*, *c.*1848, plus medieval fragments. – Undercroft chapel. Two small lights of *c.*1905 (SS Alphege and Clare), two by *Harry Grylls* (*Burlison & Grylls*), 1938 (SS Thomas of Canterbury and Francis). – Nave and aisles, clockwise from S aisle E. Five-light window by *Kempe*, 1901, lovely landscape backgrounds; *Hardmans*, 1888; *William Pearce Ltd*, 1901; W, *Kempe*, 1880. Main W window by *Kempe*, a Tree of Jesse. A beautiful Annunciation in the tracery lights. N aisle: *Kempe*, 1880 (W); a good *Claude Price*, 1977; 1937, perhaps *Burlison & Grylls*; *Hardmans*, 1918; *Lawrence Lee*, 1961, a dramatic Martyrdom of St Thomas à Becket. Behind the pulpit, C18 glass from Hillfield Hall.

MONUMENTS. Chancel. Floor slabs, the finest to James Boyd †1782. – Slab with brass plate and coats of arms to Robert Ladbroke, rector, †1655. – Crossing N, brasses to William Hill †1549 and wives and children. – N transept. Holbech monument. Erected in 1726, with much genealogy; still added to. Large twin inscription tablets and on the cornice two ludicrously small busts. – Thomas Chattock †1844, by *W. Moysen*, tablet behind a Gothic arch. – Nave, many C18 tablets, e.g. Benjamin Palmer †1772 (S aisle) with portrait medallion; below, Greek tomb-chest to Frances Prince †1825, by *Seaborne*; Benjamin Palmer †1733, Ionic pilasters and broken segmental pediment. Also incised slabs to Richard and Thomas Greswold, 1537 and 1577, and a series of hatchments, mostly C17. – N aisle chapel, brass to William Hawes and wife, both †1610. They face each other, praying. Children behind, rhyming epitaph below. Stone surround with foliage in pilasters.

SHRINE, on the churchyard wall facing the war memorial, N: a crucifix under a canopy by *Elphege Pippet*, 1917. S of the churchyard is a fragment of a stone building (former rectory?), probably C14, with a four-centred-arched doorway, and a tall section of wall facing S. To the SW, the OLIVER BIRD HALL by *Laurence King & Charles Brown*, 1961–2. Brick and timber with triangular dormers. To the S, RECTORY, 1932–3 by *J.P. Osborne & Son*, Neo-Georgian.

ST AUGUSTINE (R.C.), Herbert Road. The old nave, alongside Herbert Road is *A.W.N. Pugin*'s earliest surviving church, of 1838–9, now much altered and extended. Red brick, its lancets later replaced by Perp-style windows: W (ritual) of 1904, the top of the original surviving above it; S, late C19. Porch said to be 1884 but dated 1897; bellcote 1897. Pugin's roof has the simplest arch-braced trusses. The C19 chancel (now Blessed Sacrament Chapel) is of 1878, probably by *G. Heveningham*, though *J.A. Hansom & Son* and the local architect *F.B. Endell* are other candidates. Perp, with a tall four-centred chancel arch. Perp E window of 1866, re-set. In 1977–9 a new church of brownish-red brick by *Brian Rush* was built at right angles to the old one, with a wide jagged opening. Side-lit through angled windows. In 2010 *Daniel Hurd* improved matters by rendering it inside. – FURNISHINGS. This was the church of the *Pippet* family of artist-craftsmen. – REREDOS, 1870, by *Joseph Pippet*. – PULPIT by *Dunstan Powell*, 1917. – TRIPTYCH. Flemish, C16, chancel N wall. Given by *Pugin* in 1839. – Wall and roof DECORATION by *Joseph Pippet*, 1892, renewed by *Hardmans*, 1930. – STATUES of 1892 etc. by *John Roddis* and *H.H. Martyn*, under canopies by *Joseph* and *Elphege Pippet*. – STAINED GLASS. Nearly all made by *Hardmans*. Old E window 1866, designer *John Hardman Powell*; chancel S, two of *c.*1900; nave S, 1900 (two), designer *Gabriel Pippet*, 1902, *Joseph Pippet*. W 1904, by *Elphege & Oswald Pippet*, made by *Harvey & Ashby*. Other late C19 *Hardman* windows in the new lobby, mostly designed by *Joseph Pippet*. – TABERNACLE and carved PANEL above the altar in the new church by *Stephen Foster*, 2010.

SOLIHULL METHODIST CHURCH, Blossomfield Road. A blocky cruciform design in golden-brown brick with a little Scandinavian cupola, by *McKewan & McKewan*, 1937. Restrained Art Deco detail. The leitmotif is a four-angled arch, in e.g. the front windows, and the roof inside. Passage aisles with low, panelled arcade piers. Unfortunate entrance canopy and front render, 2015 (*Hasker*). – STAINED GLASS. Ritual S transept, *Hardmans*, †1951; N transept, *Donald Brooke*, †1964.

CHRIST CHURCH UNITED REFORMED CHURCH, Warwick Road. 1965 by *George While* (*Bromilow, While & Smeeton*). The front is a curving brick wall and a glass entrance bay, l. Interior very asymmetrical, with laminated wood ceiling sloping away from the l. side, which has organ and choir gallery.

PUBLIC BUILDINGS

SOLIHULL SCHOOL, Warwick Road. Founded as the Free Grammar School in 1560; in Malvern House (p. 759) from 1615 to 1882. It inherited BRADFORD HOUSE, a three-bay villa traditionally dated 1799, but probably of *c.* 1830 and by *Bateman & Drury*: see the round-headed doorcase. Main building, SCHOOL HOUSE, by *J.A. Chatwin*, 1879–82, red brick, a mix of Perp and Queen Anne. Crenellated tower, set at the corner, with a recessed timber stage, all windows, and elongated spirelet. Rear extension of 2005–6 by *Corstorphine & Wright* (GEORGE HILL BUILDING) with sawtooth W front and tall atrium. To the NE, the former BIG SCHOOL (THOMPSON BUILDING) by *Buckland & Haywood*, 1931, massive Neo-Georgian. The quadrangle behind is also theirs, of 1932–53. Recent buildings include the bulky BUSHELL HALL of 2001–2 by *Nugent Vallis Brierley*, and more by the *Malcolm Payne Group*: DAVID TURNBULL MUSIC SCHOOL, 2009; COOPER BUILDING, 2015. The swooping-roofed ALAN LEE SPORTS PAVILION is by *Malcolm Edwards Associates*, 2002. – CHAPEL, some way E, in size and type like a church, by *C. Neville White*, 1958–60. Almost detached SW tower, big mullion-and-transom windows, and a N aisle with a colonnade of plain cylindrical columns. E wall MURAL of the Risen Christ by *Robert L. Hendra* and *Geoffrey F. Harper*, 1960, in an assertive style like Hugh Easton, their teacher.

SOLIHULL HOSPITAL, Lode Lane. The workhouse of 1837–8 by *James B. Harper* was demolished in the late C20. Present buildings mostly by *West Midlands Regional Health Authority Design Unit*, 1990–4.

For other public buildings *see* Perambulation.

PERAMBULATION

The start is THE SQUARE, immediately NW of St Alphege's church (p. 754). The WAR MEMORIAL is an anaemic Eleanor Cross by *W.H. Bidlake*, 1921, with reliefs of servicepeople. On the N side, the GEORGE HOTEL. The front block, probably C17, was replaced in 1991 by *ISH Partnership* with a complete fake, including acres of close studding. Genuine timber framing at the rear, also a formerly separate building, perhaps a barn, with square panelling and big posts. Rear extensions enclose a bowling green, here before 1790. The hotel now incorporates No. 1, W, three bays, brick, early to mid-C18, with a doubled platband and upper sashes with broad architraves. To the E just beyond the churchyard, where New Road turns N,

MALVERN HOUSE, the Grammar School until 1882. Almost certainly the 'Scholehouse' built in 1615. Central block and l. wing at least have timber framing, tie- and collar-beam trusses with queen-struts, and large panels, all looking late. Evidence of a former jetty on the E. Encased in brick probably in the 1750s, when much money was spent. C19 W and NE extensions. On the W side of The Square, Nos. 2–6, an impressive timber-framed range of *c.* 1500, partly refaced in C18 brick. Arcaded chimneystacks, probably C19.

HIGH STREET runs NW alongside. It starts promisingly, with the character of a small Warwickshire town such as Henley-in-Arden. On the NE side a mostly C18 group, e.g. the MASONS ARMS, with full-length top signboard. To the rear, a timber-framed wing with arch-braced tie-beam. Nos. 163–165, adjacent, are faced in C18 brick, but the three irregular gables and roof-lines suggest a longer history, and timber framing, as on the SW side at No. 144 (also No. 124). Nos. 138–142 here were the MALT SHOVEL INN, C17, with square panels and straight braces. Blocked courtyard entrance, r. Nos. 132–134 are an H-plan house, perhaps C16. Timber framing in the end gables, the rest rendered. Charming Gothick upper sashes.

The MANOR HOUSE (never manorial) was probably built by the Greswold family, who owned it until 1920; owned by a trust since 1945; repairs by *S.T. Walker & Partners*, 1977–8. Mostly late C16. Gables with lots of close studding: SE wing, small former porch, upper room with a coved-out and transomed six-light window. The chimney in line with the porch shows that there was originally a lobby-entry plan. The NW wing, with slightly simpler timbering, is earlier, perhaps *c.* 1490–1520. Both end gables are jettied above. All underbuilt in brick in the early C18, when the present entrance was made. Much-altered hall, with an early C20 fireplace from Touchwood Hall (*see* below), and probably C18 stairs. Good original moulded ceiling beams. The front room in the SE wing has fine early C18 fielded panelling with dado, wooden cornice and corner fireplace. Inserted shell-headed display cupboard from Touchwood Hall. The main roof trusses have tie- and collar-beams and crude wind-braces. At the NW they rest on the trusses of the earlier wing.

No. 124 next door looks C18, but has square timber panels inside. Nos. 116–120 are probably C16, jettied and close-studded, with diagonal braces. Date plaque, not original, 1571. By this point the street is losing its character. Mill Lane and Drury Lane to the NE, with many timber-framed buildings, the C18 Touchwood Hall and a school of 1893 by *W.H. Bidlake*, were all demolished for the MELL SQUARE development of 1964–7 by *R.A. Bullivant (Harry Weedon & Partners)*. Uninspired, except perhaps for the corners of Mill Lane, with brickwork and sawtooth glazed clerestories.* Opposite is the angular brick and glass entrance to the TOUCHWOOD

---

*Corner to Drury Lane, SE, glitzily rebuilt by *Corstorphine & Wright*, 2016.

CENTRE, 2001 by *Eric R. Kuhne & Associates*. Integrated into the townscape, it spreads behind the SW side of the High Street, with a similar entrance further NW and subterranean car parking at the rear. The malls have clerestory lighting and roofs in differing arrangements of folded curves. Two circular spaces where they meet, the NW one with huge Postmodern columns. Much pale buff brick and, as at the architects' Bluewater centre in Kent (1999), thematic reliefs of local scenes.

Behind Touchwood to the W, the LIBRARY AND ARTS COMPLEX ('The Core'), by *Stanley Sellers*, 1976. His usual russet-brown brick and Portland roach facings (cf. Homer Road, below). Aedicules to the SE front. Further SE, the COUNCIL BUILDINGS. The Civic Hall of 1959 by *E. Berry Webber* has gone. By *E. Berry Webber & Partners*, 1964–7, uninspired and badly planned, CHURCH HILL HOUSE, six-storeyed, of U-plan, and the CIVIC SUITE behind and below to the SE. Mildly Postmodern N extension (ORCHARD HOUSE) by *Solihull M.B.C. Architects Department*, 1988–9. A big half-timbered house of 1889, THE PRIORY, is incorporated to the E.

HOMER ROAD, to the SW, was rebuilt from the 1960s with large blocks, several by *Stanley Sellers*, with his favourite rough-faced brick and Portland roach facings. His is No. 51 (PARAGON), 1991, with chamfered framing, mansard and a little domed entrance. On the NE side, the POLICE STATION is by *Eric Davies*, Warwickshire County Architect (project architect *N. McKillop*), 1970, faced in angled concrete panels. *Sellers*'s MAGISTRATES' COURT, 1981, was demolished in 2018. No. 35, S side, is a cool glazed and canopied block by *Foggo Associates*, 2003. No. 31 is *Sellers*, 1990, heavier.

Back on the High Street, NE side just before Poplar Road. Arts and Crafts shops of 1906 by *Gateley & Parsons*, with buttresses and ball finials. POPLAR ROAD runs N, with Metroland timber-gabled shop ranges by *W.T. Orton*, 1931 etc. On the E side two buildings by *J.A. Chatwin*. The former PUBLIC HALL of 1876 is Venetian Gothic, red brick, seven bays, symmetrical, with a balcony over the big doorway. LLOYDS, 1877, is in the tough domestic style Chatwin used for the bank's smaller branches, here with timbered gables (cf. Deritend, p. 197). On the SW corner of Warwick Road the half-timbered former BARLEY MOW, by *Owen & Ward*, 1902. On the NE corner, No. 681 WARWICK ROAD is C18, the bays probably later. Early C19 extension, r. Under the render No. 685 is early C18: hipped roof, platband. Earlier timber-framed rear wing with square panels. The long range beyond, Nos. 691–699, was the PARISH WORKHOUSE of 1740–2, builder *Thomas Sandal*. Two storeys, segment-headed sashes, dormers. Mostly rebuilt and badly refaced by *Harry Weedon & Partners*, 1974; No. 697, warm orange brick, is in its original state. On the corner of Union Road, the former GOLDEN LION pub by *Batemans*, 1934–5, brick (now painted) with shaped gables.

OTHER BUILDINGS

Roughly clockwise from the E, with distances from St Alphege.

In Marsh Lane, ½ m. E, a LODGE by *J.A. Chatwin*, 1884, with timbered upper floor coved all round. For Chatwin's New Berry Hall, Tudor Gothic, for Joseph Gillott, 1870; demolished *c.* 1990. Further N, PINFOLD FARM (No. 93). C17. Box framing and big concave brackets. Ground floor much rebuilt in brick. The cross-wing gable extends into the angle with the main range. The N end, long a separate cottage, looks C18. Linked former BARN, S, with rustic kingpost trusses. Later brick walls.

FIELD FARM, Field Lane, 1½ m. NE. Two parallel E–W ranges, square-panelled, on sandstone bases. S range probably early C17, perhaps with a lobby-entry plan. Later C17 N range, the E end added first, perhaps as a kitchen: see the pattern of brackets. E ends refaced and the roof hipped, probably in the early C18, to make a polite front.

OLD BERRY HALL, Ravenshaw Lane, 1½ m. ENE. The home of the Waring family from 1505, perhaps earlier, until 1671. In a moat, of which three sides remain in water; C18 bridge on the S. An important C15 timber-framed house, now cut down. What remains is T-shaped, with a long E cross-wing. They represent the W wing and part of the main range of the original H-plan. Its original entrance front faces S. Main gable with two jetties and close studding. Smaller projection r. Ground floor underbuilt in brick all round. Porch of 1876, reusing C15 brackets carved with religious symbols and inscriptions. The W side shows the grandeur of the original house. All close-studded, unrelieved by braces or patterning, almost symmetrical, with narrow full-height projections near each end, perhaps for garderobes. The E end is cased in brick. A tie- and collar-beam truss in the end wall shows where it has been cut back. (In 1947 the interior had moulded C15 ceiling beams with carved bosses, a roof with cambered tie-beams and wind-braces, fireplaces with moulded and embattled bressumers, and C16 panelling in the W wing.)

RAVENSHAW HALL, Ravenshaw Lane, 2 m. E. An attractive C16 H-plan house, probably all originally close-studded. A little gabled projection on the E entrance front next to the S wing (cf. Shelly Farm, p. 763). The E part of this wing reconstructed in brick, probably early C18 (platband). Toothing shows the intention to alter the whole front. Much brick casing elsewhere. Original plank door, with a spyhole. One remaining three-light timber window (E front, N wing). The hall range has two bays of collar-beam trusses, cut through for access. – C16–C17 BARN to the S with square panels and curved braces. Tie- and collar-beam trusses with diagonal struts.

MALVERN HALL, ½ m. SE. The tree-lined approach from Warwick Road survives as BRUETON AVENUE, starting with some rendered Tudor houses and Neo-Georgian brick pairs by

W.N. Twist, 1925–7. Fine GATEPIERS with niches and statues, early C18 style but probably of 1811, the date on the gates.

The HOUSE has a complicated history. The cut-down central block remains from Humphrey Greswolde's house of 1702–4. In 1783 *John Soane* added five-bay wings for Henry Greswolde Lewis. Soane also stuccoed the original house, and removed detail – but by 1819–20, when John Constable painted it, Lewis was replacing 'architraves, coins, keystones, string courses'. Between 1899 and 1909 David Troman removed the top storey, replaced Soane's wings with the present smaller ones, and changed many details. He seems to have used local builders, *Deebank* and *Bragg Bros.* The result has much of the early C20: balustrades, pediment, bow windows. A Soane survivor is the curved Ionic porch, of Meriden stone, with a beautiful frieze of swags and bucrania. Entrance hall with a coved ceiling with good plasterwork, almost Rococo, so probably mid-C18. Soane opened it up through three arches to the staircase. Also his the austere balustrade, with iron stick balusters, flowers in diagonal struts, and curved ends with elegant slim newels. Good plasterwork above. A shallow bowed wall by Soane survives in a room l. of the entrance hall. The best Troman interior is in the l. wing, with a strapwork ceiling. School extension at an angle, NW, by *A.C. Bunch*, 1930, and more of the 1960s.

STABLES to the W of 1706, bricklayer *Henry Lynall*, carpenter *George Field*. The N range has a pedimented centre and three blank round-headed openings each side. Attached C19 cottage. Link block by *Glenn Howells Architects*, 2002. – C18 WALLED GARDEN, W, now enclosing the ARTS CENTRE of 2012 also by *Howells*.

The PARK W and S of the house survives as the public Malvern Park and Brueton Park. In trees near the present hall boundary, an C18 ICE HOUSE. Just a brick dome visible, with concrete capping and blocking. In Malvern Park, STATUE, The Horse Tamer by *Joseph Boehm*, 1874. A rearing horse held by a boy in working clothes. Also a heavy classical C19 LODGE, W.

BARN. No. 936 Warwick Road, ½ m. E, is the 'Barn à la Paestum' by *Soane*, 1798, for Henry Greswolde Lewis. Soane had been to Paestum, and measured and drawn the temples there, in 1779. The barn, now a house, is of brick and has four pairs of massive columns, a triglyph frieze and a roof with deep eaves. Central round-arched cart entrance. The details are all of interest. Each column has a ruthlessly simple abacus, just two courses of bricks, and special bricks forming the echinus. At the bottom of the columns are stone torus mouldings. Similar pilasters on the ends. At the rear the order returns to a single column at either side. It is not really *à la* Paestum – the columns are unfluted, the bases are incorrect, and the pairing of course is entirely un-Greek. What the building reflects rather is Soane's indebtedness to the most progressive Parisian style of the 1780s and 1790s.

Widney Manor Road runs S from the centre. MALVERN PARK FARM, ½ m. S, is C16, L-plan, with a show N front. First floor close-studded. Three big panelled dormers (altered). Ground floor underbuilt and rendered; ogee-arched porch, probably early C19. Lower E wing. Rear wing also square-panelled, and the angle inbuilt: probably also early C19: see the Tudor-style chimneys. LOVELACE HILL (No. 123), ½ m. further s, is by *C. E. Bateman*, 1908–9, the finest Arts and Crafts house in Solihull. An unusual design, single-storeyed with a deep roof and attic dormers, like a Carolean house with a floor missing. Held together by tall chimneys. The main front (with modern extension) faces the garden, sw. Rear stable court, its entrance with timber brackets. LOVELACE AVENUE is a private development immediately s. Its best early house, No. 24 by *E. F. Reynolds*, 1912, has been murdered by rendering and extensions. No. 38 is Arts and Crafts Tudor of around the same date. No. 79 is a lovely Frank Lloyd Wright-inspired house of 1955–9 by *Ross Harper* of *Yorke, Harper & Harvey*, for himself. Long bands of buff brick and dark timbering. Low-pitched roof with deep eaves, reflected in the canopy over the ground-floor windows.

s of the centre are large late C20 estates, Hillfield and, beyond, Monkspath, with rural survivors hidden down small roads. HILLFIELD HALL, off Fielding Lane, ¾ m. s, dated 1576 with the initials of William and Ursula Hawes, is very curious. Red brick, high and not wide. One bay each side, then two embattled octagonal towers, and a middle bay with a stepped gable – as if a yeoman farmer wanted a palace gateway. Main windows transomed, of two or three lights. The rest mostly of 1867 after a fire. Drastically restored in 1974; converted to houses 2005. HILLFIELD FARM, Libbard's Way, 1 m. s, is C18, three bays, three storeys, with a hipped roof. LIBBARD HOUSE, Stonebow Avenue, is similar but politer, with a minimal pediment and datestone 1800. Restored from dereliction after 1981. SHELLY FARM, Farmhouse Way, off Shelly Crescent, 1½ m. s (now a pub), retains a C16 or C17 hall range, with close studding. A N wing has gone, but a gabled projection next to it survives (cf. Ravenshaw Hall, p. 761). C18 brick s wing.

TUDOR GRANGE, Blossomfield Road, ½ m. w. A perfect example of the rich Birmingham industrialist's status house, opulent but architecturally pedestrian. 1887 by *T. H. Mansell*, for the jeweller Alfred Lovekin; extended 1901 by *Mansell & Mansell* for Alfred Bird, the custard manufacturer. Jacobean style. Shaped gables, lots of mullion-and-transom windows, and a stone porch with tapering pilasters. Single-storey E end of 1901. Loosely composed garden front with more shaped gables, and contrasting full-height bays, square and canted. Statues on the cornice, classical gods and goddesses, some added for Bird, by *Robert Bridgeman*. Stone terrace. Full-height panelled entrance hall with an open-well staircase. A lavishly fitted sequence of rooms – dining room, study, music room – faces SE. Ornate fireplaces, plasterwork ceilings and increasingly rich panelling, that in the music room with patterning and heads in strapwork on the pilasters. The drawing room, facing NW, has a sumptuous fireplace with three shell niches in the overmantel.

Beyond, the library of 1901, in the same style, with an arcade of two columns separating a passage at the far end. Plainer bedrooms. In the staircase window and the ground-floor rooms, much Flemish and German glass, some of good quality, mostly C17 – dates e.g. 1607, 1640, 1685. Linked STABLES to the W, also Jacobean, with a glazed central corridor. – LODGE, NE by *Mansell & Mansell*, 1901. (Large extensions approved for a care home by *PCPT*, 2020.)

Across Blossomfield Road from Tudor Grange is WHITE HOUSE WAY, the first part developed from 1963 with *James A. Roberts Associates* as architects. Detached houses and bungalows in open landscaping, with retained trees.

W and NW of the centre much early and mid-C20 housing, of solid quality but not architecturally memorable. ASHLEIGH ROAD encapsulates Edwardian Solihull. Developed by a Birmingham butcher, Joseph Wells, from 1903. He used the architect and surveyor *E.H. Wigley*, whose manner, with its liberal timbering, gives the road its character. Starting at the Warwick Road end, N, on the SE side, Nos. 1–17 are all by *Wigley*; Nos. 3 and 5, 1906, with twin-gabled garages. No. 21 is by *Ewen Harper*, 1906, quite different, with tile-hanging, polygonal bay and semicircular door-hood. Beyond The Crescent, Nos. 23–25 by *W. Alexander Harvey*, 1904, have escaped from Bournville: rendered central gabled bays and sweeping catslide roofs. In No. 27 *Wigley* confines timbering to a band between the windows. No. 29 is by *W.F. Edwards*, 1907. Nos. 31–33, 1908, is *Wigley*'s best design, suggesting he knew W.J.H. Weller's work: timbered inner gables and projecting brick outer ones. No. 37 is a lovely surprise, a restrained brick design by *J.B. Surman*, 1928, with hipped roofs and a broad central entrance projection. No. 39 is characteristic *Wigley* of 1905–6. Returning up the NW side, No. 36 is by *H. Peter Hing*, 1922. Nos. 22–30 are *Wigley*'s, dates 1904–10. Beyond Silhill Hall Road, No. 20 is *W. De Lacy Aherne*, 1904, with typical arcaded porch. More *Wigley* at Nos. 12–18 and 2–8; No. 14, of 1905–6, splendiferous, old-fashioned, with gabled bay jettied over tile-hanging and an oriel. No. 10 is by *Hipkiss & Stephens*, 1906–7, rendered.

In Streetsbrook Road, No. 433, with simple brickwork, is by *E.F. Reynolds* for himself, 1909.

In Lode Lane, N from the town centre, No. 48, THE GROVE, brick with timbering, *c.* 1890, almost certainly by *Alfred Reading*. N of the by-pass, THE HERMITAGE, dated 1863, picturesque Gothic probably by *J.A. Chatwin*.

NORTH OF THE CENTRE: HOBS MOAT AND LYNDON

1930s and post-war housing. Solihull's one very large factory is here.

ST MARY, Hobs Meadow, Hobs Moat. 1966–7 by *Laurence King*. Octagonal, with a lantern and spirelet, and a small heptagonal N chapel. The lantern is supported on slim columns. A similar column divides entrance and worship areas, and the FONT is built round it. Long bench PEWS surround a typical 1960s ALTAR on concrete piers, but the PULPIT is placed behind and above it, an unusual liturgical arrangement. – HALL, W, by *Leslie Temple Moore*, 1955. Long, massive and barn-like. Timber aisle posts, scissor-truss roof with long passing braces. Impressive architecture on a budget. – VICARAGE, W, also by *Temple Moore*.

LYNDON METHODIST CHURCH, Melton Avenue. 1958–9 by *Jackson & Edmonds*. A more modest version of their Digbeth-in-the-Field church (p. 297), with the same steep-pitched roof and triangular dormers. Laminated timber trusses inside, ceiled off at collar-beam level.

HOBS MOAT, immediately S of St Mary's church, is an impressive, nearly square moated site, now hidden in a small wood. Wide and deep ditch, with a bank on each side. Perhaps the manor house of the Oddingselles (*see* p. 753). Excavations from 1985 showed that the present inner bank had been built over an earlier low bank and ditch. Also found were remains of a small timber building and the stone base of another, both probably C13.

OLTON HALL pub (now OLTON TAVERN), Lode Lane. By *Batemans*, 1939. With big dormers and (now painted) gable.

JAGUAR LAND ROVER, Lode Lane. Originally a wartime 'shadow factory' of 1939–40. Car production began in 1948, particularly for Land Rover, who took over entirely in 1982. The North Works and shorter South Works run W–E. Beyond the South Works, the very long East Works of *c.* 1985. Recent work includes extensions to the North Works by *Hasker*, 2012; an oval reception building by the main entrance, linked to offices behind, by *Anglo Holt*, 2012; and a new gatehouse and extension to the South Works by *Ridge*, 2017.

CATHERINE-DE-BARNES

A small settlement 2 m. E, where the Solihull to Hampton-in-Arden road crosses the Warwick and Birmingham Canal. Brick SCHOOL-CHAPEL by *J.A. Chatwin*, 1879–80, now village hall. Segment-headed windows, timbering in a gable, small bellcote. The half-timbered BOAT INN immediately E is by *Newton & Cheatle*, 1924. ¼ m. S down Henwood Lane is BOGAY HALL. The N wing is C16, with a fine display of close studding. Its E front was jettied (see the surviving bracket, N) but was underbuilt in brick, in turn replaced in 1981 with imitation timber framing, which runs all down the main range. Tudor-style chimneys, the N one dated 1883. The porch must be contemporary. Further S, the former ISOLATION HOSPITAL, by *W.H. Ward*, 1909. The last one in use in England, closed and converted to housing, Catherine's Close, in 1987 (chimneys lost, new windows, porches etc.). Administration and nurses' quarters with projecting wings with half-hipped gables and former central entrance. Single-storey ranges beyond. To the N, scarlet fever block with central gable. Beyond, w, smaller blocks for diphtheria and typhoid fever. Further s again, HENWOOD MILL. Recorded in 1228, the present building probably C18. House, r., probably early to mid-C19. Casements throughout. Breast-shot wheel *in situ*, and much of the machinery inside.

BICKENHILL

A village stranded on the urban w side of the M42 and surrounded by the A45, the National Exhibition Centre, the noise of the airport, and growing urban Solihull: yet it survives. The church tower and spire are a landmark. Farms cluster round, and ridge-and-furrow is still visible in surrounding fields. Recent houses are, alas, not always sensitive.

ST PETER, Church Lane. The history begins inside with the N arcade, no later than *c.* 1150. Sturdy round piers, massive square abaci, totally unmoulded arches. The capitals are primitive, with odd zigzag, perhaps an attempt at scallops, and leaf shapes in the corners, some with bead decoration. The bases are more sophisticated, almost classical, with a torus ring. Survivors of the Norman nave to which this arcade related are the replaced interior arch of its s doorway, and a small niche above the doorway outside. Both have billet mouldings. The aisle was rebuilt wider in the C14, in small blocks of red sandstone, with a two-light Dec N window. Tie- and collar-beam roof with raking queen-struts, perhaps C17; repaired by *A. S. Dixon*, 1916.

The Perp contribution starts with the tower and spire, in pale local sandstone. The tower has diagonal buttresses, but is sheer, without string courses. Big four-light W window, the outer lights divided by a cusped transom, the central pair with an arrangement like an ogee-headed window split by a mullion, with cuspings resting on it. Further up, an embattled transom. The outer mullions have buttresses and pinnacles (crassly restored). SE stair-vice with restored doorway. Repair dates with churchwardens' names or initials, 1632 on the stair, 1667 and 1692 nearby. Spire with three tiers of hoodmoulded lucarnes, the top 20 ft (6 metres) rebuilt in 1887 after a lightning strike. The tower arch (opened out in 1898 following advice from *W.H. Bidlake*) has canted piers with tiers of panelling which stop abruptly and a two-centred arch without capitals, suggesting a change of plan. N chapel also Perp, but in a distinctive manner with exaggerated details, associated with south-west Midlands work, but also found locally at e.g. Coleshill and Middleton. Well-cut red sandstone ashlar.

Very wide arch to the chancel. It has big headstops of a harpy, with a woman's head in a horned head-dress and a dragon's body, and a cockatrice. Three-light flat-headed N window.

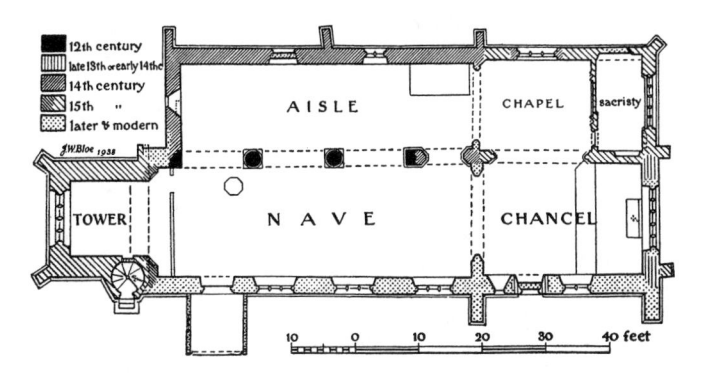

Solihull, Bickenhill, St Peter.
Plan, 1947

Original roof with arch-braced collars and wind-braces. Nail marks show it was ceiled. At the E end is a very interesting contemporary stone SCREEN, with a plain altar panel flanked by niches with delicately carved shafts, nodding ogee arches and huge crocketed finials. To the r. an almost triangular-headed doorway with big tilted king and queen headstops and more crockets. It leads to a small vestry or priest's room, oddly placed under the five-light E window. In its NE corner an original fireplace, the base of its chimney (capped in 1916) surviving on the E gable. Perp E vestries are found elsewhere, e.g. Shelton, Norfolk, but this arrangement is extremely unusual. At the W end of the aisle is a similar doorway with headstops and crockets. It led to another room, now gone, but the mark of its chimney visible on the gable.

The whole S side is of 1855–6 by *Joseph Nevill* of Coventry, quite attractive, in variegated sandstone, with flat-headed Dec windows. Timber-framed porch with close studding, following local traditions (e.g. Sheldon, p. 280). In the chancel Nevill kept the C13 S doorway, but the one- and two-light windows are all his, also part of the E wall. The five-light reticulated E window corresponds to what was there before. Chancel arch and wall probably also Nevill's. Smooth pale ashlar, with double chamfer. N chapel arch similar but simpler. N vestry extension, a brick box by *Crouch, Butler & Savage*, 1977–8.

FURNISHINGS. FONT. Perp, octagonal, with traceried top and stem. Angels in the lower panels of the bowl. Their wings have vertical folds and taper inside the panels, looking absolutely Art Deco. – PULPIT of *c.*1860, brought from Cold Norton, Essex. – COMMUNION RAIL of *c.*1700, with heavy but well-turned balusters, repaired and extended by *Dixon*, 1916. – CHOIR STALLS. 1869. – PEWS by *Nevill*, 1856. – Tower SCREEN by *Dixon*, 1916, unusual for him, with thorny tracery. – CHEST. A medieval dug-out, banded with iron. – STAINED GLASS. Nearly all *Hardmans*. E window 1869;

chancel SE 1870 (thinned out); nave S 1876 (bottom only remaining) and c.1870; N aisle 1898. N chapel, *Jones & Willis*, 1882. Chancel SW, medieval fragments including birds. Probably C14. – MONUMENT. N chapel. Fettiplace and Sarah Nott, tablet with obelisk. Erected by their son (†1775), which looks the likely date.

YEW TREE FARM, opposite the church. Late C18 or C19, with casement windows. W of the church, C19 farm buildings, now housing. A substantial timber-framed house was here in 1837; a small section of box framing remains, facing the church. CHURCH FARM of c.1850, with bargeboarded gables, has C16 or C17 fabric visible in the W wing: box framing, studding on the upper floor, and a tie- and collar-beam truss. On St Peter's Lane, CHURCH GARTH is the former vicarage, stucco, Regency, with shallow wings and recessed centre. Going S, GRANGE FARM, C19 and heavily rendered, may hide older fabric. Barn with box framing and big curved braces, probably C16.

CASTLE HILLS, ¾ m. W. Remote in the fields, yet with the continuous roar of the airport. L-shaped. N–S range of warm C18 brick, with big casement windows. Its irregularity and casual bonding show that it encases earlier fabric, probably the 'Mancion house' recorded in 1649. A cut-down group of star-shaped chimneys, C16 or early C17, on the entrance (E) side. The S wing, box-framed with close-studded upper floor at the rear, must be of a similar period. Big corner post, probably to support a dragon beam. (Seriously damaged by fire, 2020.) Barns to the N, derelict and part-demolished. Remains of a moat on the S. Dugdale states that a castle stood here.

CASTLE BROMWICH

Originally a hamlet in Aston parish, first mentioned in 1167. A CASTLE MOTTE of the C12 survives N of the present A452 (best seen from the churchyard). Excavations in 1970 disclosed prehistoric and Roman occupation of the site. The medieval castle bailey was entered though a timber gateway, and a timber building and possible ovens were found within. The village developed to the S, spreading E from the junction of the Birmingham and Chester roads; the Hall is to the W, the church to the NW. It is now sandwiched between the scarp and the A452 to the N, and Bradford Road to the S, with Shard End, now a post-war Birmingham council estate, beyond (p. 278). Precious fields to the W.

ST MARY AND ST MARGARET, Chester Road. The church represents more than meets the eye, but what meets the eye is more than enough to keep the mind engaged for a while. It is an Early Georgian church, the substantial W tower of 1724–6, the rest rebuilt, as recorded by inscriptions over the doors inside, between 1726 and 1731. Brick with dressings of local sandstone, very square with its consistent high parapets, in the provincial Baroque of e.g. Francis Smith, or the Trubshaws of Staffordshire – see e.g. the use of quoins of even length, or the way the parapet rises into a kind of segmental pediment above the W bays N and S. The nave is five bays long, the lower chancel two. The windows are segment-headed. Only the E window has a round arch. There is a surfeit of details, e.g. the W front of the tower with five motifs one on top of the other. The nave details are slightly different, with oblong panels above the windows, and under them an apron motif like a low fluted dome upside down. Inside, the first bays are singled out, as they are externally, and they are followed by five bays with Tuscan columns, not quite as high as one would expect, and segmental rusticated arches. That has absolutely nothing of the elegance of, say, Gibbs. The chancel has giant fluted pilasters. The ceilings are flat and very sparingly stuccoed only in the chancel and the W bay.

There is one reason for much of what was done, and it is an odd, unexpected reason. The previous church was a timber church of the C15 or early C16, with posts for arcade piers and a big open roof including a timber-framed clerestory (as at Needham Market, Suffolk). The structure of this earlier building is still there, with the roof ceiled off, and the posts encased by the Tuscan columns. Repairs by *C.E. Bateman* in 1890–1 revealed these facts. The roof is visible through a walkway from the tower. From the W the first truss is an addition, perhaps C18, with kingpost and square panels. Then comes the splendid

35

Solihull, Castle Bromwich, St Mary and St Margaret.
Reconstruction drawing by C.E. Bateman, 1893

eight-bay roof of the medieval church. The end trusses, originally exposed as gables, have tie-beams and two collar-beams, with close studding between. The intermediate trusses have upper and lower collars, and king- and raking struts between. The first two from the W have tie-beams below, suggesting a former gallery or built-in structure; the others have arched braces to the lower collar. Two tiers of chamfered wind-braces.

Who was responsible for the rebuilding? A contract existed of 1724 with the mason *Thomas Clear* alias *Smith* for a 'New Steeple'. *Joseph Clarke* appears frequently in receipts, but mostly as a supplier of stone. 'Clare' (probably *Clear*), *William Swift* and others were paid for work on the church in 1727–8. The 1724 contract also mentioned *Thomas White* of Worcester, 'carver', for deciding how much stone should be in the tower. The idea of White as an architect has been criticized by Howard Colvin and others. But the elliptical-arched aprons under the tower windows are similar to those under the ground-floor windows of Worcester Guildhall, where he certainly carved the trophy of arms; so perhaps he was involved in design here.

Remarkably complete C18 FURNISHINGS. *Joseph Westley* was paid for seating and wainscoting. – REREDOS. With pilasters and segmental pediment and the Lord's Prayer and the Creed in the 'predella'. The relief of the Ascension is by *Bateman*, 1902; it replaced COMMANDMENT BOARDS now on the N and S walls. – PULPIT. A beautiful three-decker, the pulpit itself round with a tester which has marquetry. The staircase rises on an ample curve. Some of the panels are of thin pierced foliage. The same applies to PARSON'S PEW and SQUIRE'S PEW.* – Family PEWS with curved fronts in the chancel. – Nave PEWS (doors removed 1899). – FONT. Nice gadrooned bowl. The heavy baluster stem with a shaft-ring, in different marbles, looks C19. – FONT COVER (now in tower) by *Bateman*, 1903, carved by *Bridgemans*; domed, with foliage panels. – WEST GALLERY with curved ends and fielded panels. It looks original but may be early C19, which its iron columns clearly are. – COMMUNION RAIL, 1744–5, a very fine wrought-iron piece including the royal arms. Also wrought-iron churchyard GATES. The Rev. W. E. Brooke referred to now lost Bridgeman papers in ascribing both to *Benjamin Taylor*. – In the churchyard across the road, the BATEMAN MEMORIAL. A tapering cross on a rocky base with names on copper discs, including J. J. Bateman †1903 and *C. E. Bateman* †1947, whose design it must be.

METHODIST CHURCH, School Lane. A small round-arched block with crusty brickwork by *J. Percival Bridgwater*, 1930, and its modest replacement by *K. Bradley Miller*, 1963–4.

CASTLE BROMWICH HALL. The hall lies immediately S of the church. It is still essentially the 'fair House of brick' built by Sir Edward Devereux, who came into full possession in 1599 and died in 1622. It was bought by Sir John Bridgeman (1631–1710)

---

*The horrible fixed projector screen is early C21.

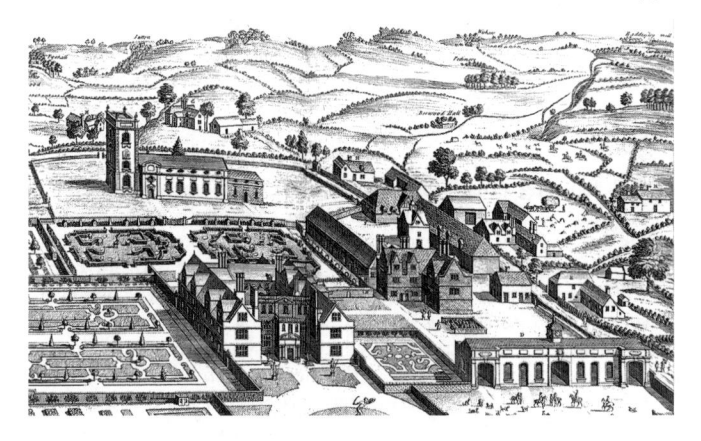

Solihull, Castle Bromwich Hall and church.
Engraving by E. Kirkall after Henry Beighton, 1726

in 1657 and altered after then, and between 1685 and 1703 by his cousin the architect *William Winde*. Correspondence shows that Sir John's wife, Mary, was deeply involved in the work. It has given us some of the best C17 plasterwork in the area, done by *Edward Goudge*, one of the finest of London's stuccoists. Between 1825 and 1849 *Rickman & Hutchinson*, later *Rickman & Hussey*, then *R.C. Hussey*, again extended and altered the house, for George Bridgeman, 2nd Earl of Bradford. Sold in 1947, used as offices until the late C20, the hall stood empty, with significant losses including paintings by *Laguerre*, until its conversion into a hotel from 2009.

The approach is from Birmingham Road, s, through a brick-walled forecourt with early C18 gatepiers topped by urns. An avenue runs s from the entrance for over ¼ m. into Shard End (q.v.). The early C17 house is square, of red brick laid in English bond, with mullion-and-transom windows, and a small internal courtyard (infilled, most recently in 2014). The s front has projecting wings. Their gabled top storeys may be very early additions, as the brick is lighter. The entrance range of the original house corresponds to a drawn plan in the hand of *John Smythson*, as identified by Mark Girouard. It had a single-storey porch of which the side walls remain. In the later C17 it was transformed into the memorable feature of the exterior, the 'frontispiece'. This is two storeys high and extends slightly beyond the porch side walls. Doorcase with coupled columns, the outer ones normal, the inner ones twisted, and a broken segmental pediment. The architrave has channelled rustication. The style is late 1650s or 1660s, with a French flavour; it closely resembles plates in Le Muet's *c.* 1650 edition of Vignola, as noted by Gordon Higgott. The upper floor continues the rustication and has a cross-window flanked by niches with slender, sculpturally indifferent allegorical figures carved in

1697 by *Sir William Wilson*. It is topped by a wrought-iron balustrade of 1690–1 by *Winde*. So the old porch was refronted, with the doorcase, for Sir John Bridgeman after 1657, and the upper floor was added then and altered for the statues; or possibly the upper floor was added later, to match. The top storey is by *Winde*, of 1697–8, with a central pedimented stone bay, and flanking cross-windows to match the earlier work. The prominent chimneys – the dominant vertical motif – against the inner faces of the wings were raised as part of this work: see their panelled top parts. The balustrade and urns look later still, probably of 1719, the date on the hoppers. They were rebuilt by *Hussey* in 1839. The W and N fronts have original large mullion-and-transom windows, symmetrically arranged on the W, nearly so on the N. The dormers above must be later, with larger bricks laid in English garden wall bond. NE kitchen wing by *Rickman & Hutchinson*, 1825, plain Tudor. The asymmetrically set turret with its arcaded top stage and ogee roof is by *Hussey*, 1848–9.

The entrance passage has the HALL on the l., presumably the original plan. It was remodelled by *Rickman & Hussey* – that is, *R.C. Hussey* – in 1838–9. The ornate stone fireplace with strapwork lintel is his; the elaborate arcaded overmantel looks genuine Jacobean, *ex situ*. Reused C17 panelling flanking it, and elsewhere. By *Hussey* also the screen between passage and hall, the arcaded frieze, the doorcases with steep broken pediments, and the ceiling with moulded ribs, plasterer *James Holmes*. Beyond is the spacious STAIRCASE, by *Winde*, of 1688. Twisted balusters on urn-like feet, closed string. Swept-up handrail and matching dado. The ceiling is by *Goudge*, with shields, and sprays of flowers, leaves and almost detached fruit. The DINING ROOM in the NW corner has another Goudge ceiling, flatter and more compactly organized, with a circle of foliage and corner panels. Full-height panelling and marble fireplace. Excellent again the plasterwork in the boudoir facing N. Up the stairs, the DRAWING ROOM is to the S. Big *Winde* doorcases with segmental pediments, and another marble fireplace. But the sumptuous tripartite ceiling, with the centre raised and coved, in absolutely convincing late C17 style, is by *Hussey*, of 1839. The plasterer was again *J. Holmes*, who called it 'highly enriched...with a profusion of flowers'. Beyond is the LONG GALLERY, nearly the length of the S front. Essentially original full-height panelling, i.e. early C17, but the simple dentil cornice is by *Winde*, 1698, and the doorcases must also be his. Ceiling with moulded ribs of 1842–3 by *Hussey*, plasterer *Holmes*. Finally N of the staircase is the most important bedroom, and beyond it another, now a bathroom. Both have *Goudge* ceilings.

Beyond the kitchen range is a separate L-shaped BAKEHOUSE block of the C17; further NE, a gabled PIGEON HOUSE of 1725 with a square cupola. The former STABLES are E of the house. Of *c.*1726 (Beighton's drawing of that year shows a slightly different design). Brick with sandstone quoins, pedimented centre, four bays either side, the outer ones arcaded.

The GARDENS lie N and W of the house (entry from Chester Road, NW of the church). The structure of an early C18 formal garden is preserved, with additions and alterations.* Mostly of four periods: early C18 work for the first Sir John Bridgeman; extensions by his son, also Sir John (†1747), 1720s onwards; restoration and completion of the gardens for George Bridgeman between 1819 and 1865, an early example of revived formal gardening; and restoration for the Castle Bromwich Hall Gardens Trust from 1982.

The early C18 parts are the Best Garden immediately W of the house, now lawned, and the North Garden between house and church, now laid in parterres with yew hedges around the walls. Designs by *Winde* exist for these. On the N side of the Best Garden a brick-built COLD BATH of 1733. To the W the gardens step downhill, work of the second Sir John from the 1720s, completed after his death by George Bridgeman. The walls are C18: N and S walls ending in piers surmounted by restored sphinx-like beasts. Poems to them are carved on the supporting plinths. A connecting W wall has a central *clairvoie*. On the N side the wall sets back enclosing a melon ground. A walk runs N–S below the Best Garden, and below that is the Upper Wilderness, probably laid out *c.*1860, now with modern planting. Beyond, an C18 lawn, the Archery Ground, runs N–S. Then two pavilions of *c.*1729 set in the walls, the GREEN HOUSE (N) and the SUMMER HOUSE or ORANGERY (S), linked by the Holly Walk. Much restored in the late C20, they have big pediments with cartouches and swags, rusticated quoins, and oval recesses with modern busts. The walk may be contemporary with the pavilions, but was renewed *c.*1820, and again in the late C20. W of the walk is the Lower Wilderness of *c.*1860, which includes a contemporary MAZE based on that at Hampton Court, replanted *c.*1990. Outside the walls on N, W and S is a slip or outer border, with ponds at the NW corner and on the W axis.

PERAMBULATION. RECTORY LANE runs E from the church. Nos. 1–3 are by *C.E. Bateman*, 1896, of C17 domestic ancestry but already the simplest Arts and Crafts. Warm brick, unmoulded mullioned windows. One chimney delicately corbelled out from the side of the gable. The RECTORY, beyond on the S side, also *Bateman*, 1907–8, is still Arts and Crafts but Neo-Early Georgian in keeping with the church, with parapeted centre and circular windows. To the S, from the cross-roads SE of the hall, the village runs E along Chester Road. Nos. 15–17, N side, were the Bridgeman Arms Inn until 1819. Probably early to mid-C18, with cross-windows on the first floor, and coved cornice. C19 porches. The Remembrance Club opposite appears early C19 under modern alterations, but the N wing may be older. On the N side again a group of cottages and

---

*Archaeological investigations by Christopher Currie and Martin Locock in 1989–91 found evidence of medieval walls near the house, and an early C17 formal layout there.

the former Post Office, incorporating a timber-framed gable. No. 61, 300 yds E, is an H-plan former farmhouse. Front gables probably early C18 (see their platbands), but the building looks older. C19 bargeboards. The rendered former CASTLE INN, NE side, is probably C18 or early C19. Opposite, set back, the VICTORY HALL (church centre), 1922, and CHURCH HALL of 1900 with decorative tympanum. THE GREEN opens to the S. On its W side, the former COACH AND HORSES pub by *Batemans*, 1936, originally thatched. Nos. 18–21, of *c.* 1895 probably by *Bateman & Bateman*, are a progressive design with plain rendering, semi-dormers and circular windows. The Green continues S as SCHOOL LANE (actually in Shard End), with some C18 or refaced C17 brick cottages (Nos. 32–38, with diagonal chimneys). Nos. 33–43 opposite (altered) belong with late C19 terraces on The Green, probably *Bateman & Bateman*.

BRADFORD ARMS, Chester Road, ¼ m. E of The Green. Two-bay wings, centre slightly recessed, hipped roof. Big cross-windows throughout. It looks late C17 or early C18; traditional date 1723. An inn from the mid C18, it looks like a small gentry house or substantial farm. Inside, a surprise: an imperial staircase, presumably original, with a heavy swept-up handrail but quite delicate balusters. Much extended in recent years for a hotel. Detached coachhouse and stable wings towards the road, formerly dated 1746.

CHELMSLEY WOOD

A Birmingham overspill estate E and NE of Marston Green, in size a New Town, with an original population of 55,000. A masterplan by *Jackson & Edmonds*, 1965, set down thirteen residential areas, each defined by a principal perimeter road and containing up to 1,200 houses. Housing nearly all by *J.A. Maudsley*, City Architect, 1966–73; mostly low-rise and brick-faced, with some timber boarding; also a few high blocks (some now demolished). A central linear park follows the Hatchford Brook and River Cole, with an artificial lake (Chief Landscape Architect *G.W. Hyden*). Main SHOPPING CENTRE at Pine Square of 1969–71 by *James J. Sharp*.* The new BLUEBELL CENTRE (library, council offices and supermarket), by *Barton Willmore*, 2010, gives it some focus. Front with two curving towers, tall atrium. POLICE STATION by *Eric Davies*, Warwickshire County Architect, 1971.

ST ANDREW, Pike Drive. A complex of church, with angled lantern (now Seventh Day Adventist), hall (with concrete staircase), vicarage and caretaker's house, all in dark red-blue brick, by *Crouch Butler Savage*, 1972.

ST ANNE (R.C.), Bosworth Drive. By *Cyril Horsley*, 1987–8, rising to an octagonal lantern.

---

*Imprisoned for corruption, along with Maudsley, in 1975.

The modest original SCHOOLS were by *Davies*. One survives as the BOSWORTH CENTRE, Bosworth Drive. Many recent replacements. BISHOP WILSON C. OF E. PRIMARY SCHOOL, Craig Croft, is by *Glancy Nicholls*, 2014, quadrant-curved, with glazed front, crisply done. GRACE ACADEMY, Chapelhouse Road, is by *BDP*, 2006. In Windward Way are SMITH'S WOOD ACADEMY by *BAM Design Ltd*, and FOREST OAK SPECIAL SCHOOL by *Solihull M.B.C. Building Design Group*, both 2005–6. Forest Oak's sixth-form centre is by *APEC*, 2013. SMITH'S WOOD PRIMARY (now Academy), Burton's Way, is by *ADP*, 2011; FORDBRIDGE PRIMARY, Crabtree Drive, is by *Baart Harries Newall (Paul Harries)*, 2014–15. JOHN HENRY NEWMAN CATHOLIC COLLEGE, Chelmsley Road, with a bulky drum, is by *Bond Bryan*, 2007. Behind it on Cooks Lane, CTC KINGSHURST ACADEMY, the first City Technology College, by *Ellis Williams Partnership*, 1988.

ALCOTT HALL, Berwicks Lane. Tall, compact brick C18 farmhouse. Two storeys and an attic, casement windows, platband. Converted to flats, with a modest extension, by *Nicol Thomas*, 2014–15.

EARLSWOOD

0570

The rural area S and W of Shirley, rich in timber-framed buildings. For the rest of the historic Tanworth parish, S of the M42, see *The Buildings of England: Warwickshire*.

ST PATRICK, Salter Street. The first plain brick church was of 1837–40 by *James Benjamin Harper* of Henley-in-Arden. The cross-gabled W tower was added in 1860–1 by *G.T. Robinson*, clearly a 'rogue' architect. Look at the buttressing of the porch, and the tower staircase on the N, supported on a curving part-arch and a stubby column. The entrance has a trumeau, with much foliage and a sculpted relief of the Ascension, with a bishop above. Stone-faced entrance lobby with a rib-vault. The original church was replaced in 1897–9 by *W.H. Bidlake*. His nave has triangular buttresses and his chancel is set high above an arcaded crypt (infilled, with low N extension, by *Richard Crook*, 2001–2).

The interior is Bidlake at his finest and most original. Buff brick, in contrast to the red outside. Massive triangular wall piers, windows in relieving arches which die into the piers. In this arrangement of planes there is hardly a wall surface as such. The chancel arch dies into piers in the same way. They are distinguished by statues in ogee-headed niches. This is all quite austere, but the tops of the nave piers have luscious corbels, of foliage and heads with streaming hair, supporting the big moulded ribs of the ceiling. The chancel is raised on eight steps and ends in a vaulted apse so small and low that it looks as if it were made to hold an Italian *presepe* or German

Krippe. – FITTINGS. An excellent ensemble by *Bidlake*, in rich late medieval style but with many original details; slightly disrupted (dais, moving of font) in 1999. Of 1899 the PULPIT, reached through an arch from the chancel; the PEWS; and the FONT with the symbols of the Evangelists. Of 1910 the REREDOS, with PAINTING of the Last Supper by *Fred Davis*; the CHOIR STALLS; and the chancel SCREEN with ogee arches and delicate tracery. Of 1913 the PARCLOSE SCREEN at the W, originally for a baptistery; the WEST GALLERY on timber vaulting; and the colouring of the roof. – Two PAINTINGS on canvas in the W niches by *Bernard Sleigh*, 1913: figures in wide landscapes. – STAINED GLASS. E window and two small lights in the apse by *Powells*, 1910. Nave S by *Pearce & Cutler*, 1920. In the bell-chamber two small windows by *Sleigh*, 1913. – SCHOOL, S. A cottage at the front, the rest a C19 and C20 mixture.

EARLSWOOD METHODIST CHURCH, Wood Lane. By *Crouch, Butler & Savage*, 1923. Very simple. Round-arched doorway.

EARLSWOOD LAKES. Three reservoirs, total area 66 acres, for the Stratford Canal, planned in 1813 by *William Whitmore* and constructed in 1821–3. The dam runs above the Wythall to Earlswood road. At the NW corner the former ENGINE HOUSE of 1823, three storeys with single-storey extensions. A feeder runs under the road by an original bridge, and NE to the canal.

OLD MOAT HOUSE, E off The Common. N part jettied on three sides, with close studding and braces on both floors. The modern date of 1480 over the door would fit. Moulded corner posts and a graceful surviving S-shaped bracket, NE. Evidence of a second jetty in the gable. Brick chimney inserted at its SW corner in the early C17. The clumping N buttress is C20. The ground-floor room has chamfered dragon beams and joists supporting the jetties. Splendid tie- and collar-beam roof truss, all chamfered and cusped, forming a two-centred pointed arch above the collar. It looks as if meant to be seen, but puzzlingly the attic floor appears original. The wing's S wall is close-studded, with a first-floor arched doorway, probably to a former hall range running E–W. In the later C17 this was replaced by a modest L-shaped building, now mostly refaced in brick, but box framing survives in the W gable. Complete moat, partly in water. To the E, a C17 BARN, with some surviving box framing. To the NW, a heavily restored box-framed cottage, perhaps originally a detached kitchen.*

Of other timber buildings, JERRING'S HALL, Tanworth Lane, has a long, much-restored range in two parts with close studding and some square panels. C18 N wing with simple Venetian windows above and below. COTTAGE FARM, Illshaw Heath Road, is square-panelled throughout, with a tie- and collar-beam truss in the gable. The original hearth was at the lower end of the hall, backing on to the cross-passage. BEDSWORTH

---

*James Lees-Milne visited the house in 1942 and met the Misses Smythe, who gave it to the National Trust. There was no telephone, running water, heating, light or bath, only 'an outdoor twin earth closet'.

FARM, Salter Street has an C18 brick W front with cross-windows, but a complex structure with three gables reveals itself on the E. Ground floor underbuilt in brick. Barns with queenpost trusses, in disrepair. CLAYBANK FARMHOUSE, Umberslade Road, has close studding to the ground floor and square panels above. FLOWER KNOTT COTTAGE, Dyers Lane, has timbering exposed on the l. side and the rear. Converted timber-framed BARNS survive at Little Cleobury Farm, Cleobury Lane, and Brookhouse, Salter Street.

SALTER STREET FARMHOUSE has a two-storey C17 brick range with clasping buttresses, probably a wing of a larger house. Single-storey link and timber-framed range behind. To the N a brick barn. Both are surrounded by an earlier moat. THE OLD FARMHOUSE, Lady Lane, has two brick gables and a third one set back, r. Also probably C17. WARING'S GREEN FARM is a handsome three-bay farmhouse with hipped roof, probably late C18, yet calling on earlier traditions in the central gabled projection, and double platband. Close studding inside at the rear. WINTERTON FARM, off Illshaw Heath Road, has the same pattern of a hipped-roofed C18 block and a timber-framed wing behind. MOUNT DAIRY FARM, Tanworth Lane, is a square C18 house, altered with unusual casements and a pedimented porch with unsophisticated cartouche and roses, probably early C20. BRAGGS FARM, Braggs Farm Lane, also C18, retains a semi-circular-headed porch. An unusual BARN and cartshed opposite with buttressed sides and weatherboarded ends.

Many brick cottages, C18 and early C19, e.g. the BULL'S HEAD and adjoining ROSE COTTAGE, Limekiln Lane. The BLUE BELL, Waring's Green is probably of shortly after 1796 as it adjoins the Stratford Canal and bridge. BIG CLEOBURY FARM, Cleobury Lane, is dated 1826. Tudor-style brick hoodmoulds. LODGE PADDOCKS, Warings Green Road, is a C19 farmhouse re-windowed and extended by *S.N. Cooke*, 1914.

DICKENS HEATH

A new village on farmland 1½ m. SW of Shirley. Planned by Solihull M.B.C. from 1989, based on a concept plan of 1992 by *John Simpson & Partners*, and developed by private builders from 1997; mostly complete by 2009. The most significant 'traditional revival' development in the West Midlands. Like Poundbury, the obvious inspiration, it combines high densities, a mixture in the centre of residential and commercial uses, and priority for pedestrians. The sources are the same: the English vernacular and classical traditions to *c.*1840, and the revived vernacular of the Arts and Crafts. The materials are mostly brick – red, yellow, grey – and render. But the quietness of the English vernacular tradition is absent. And it is not a 'poor man's Poundbury', because there is no social housing.

There are two set pieces, with a common masterplan by *Stephen George & Associates*. Landscaping by *Barry Chinn Landscape*

Architects. MARKET PLACE is of 2003–5. Big LIBRARY AND COMMUNITY CENTRE by *John Simpson Architects*, with pediment, big Doric frieze and Leon Krier-style open belfry. The hall entrance further l. has Tudor buttresses and finials. Courtyard with an 'early industrial' cliché, a stubby Doric colonnade with segmental arches. Going s between blocks by *George* l. and *Porphyrios Associates* r., the view is closed by another Porphyrios block, GRANGE HOUSE, with an arcade and a tower set forward, again with an open belfry. Beyond it a *Simpson* range with weighty pediments in relieving arches. Opposite, a block by *Liam O'Connor Architects* with double-height arches and big dormers. WATERSIDE, further s, was completed in 2006. It begins with the CUSTOMS HOUSE, by *George*, facing Rumbush Lane, with a pediment and lunette. Down an alley l. we come to formal lines of buildings flanking a pool. On the l. a brick range with square piers by *Liam O'Connor*, then a yellow-brick colonnaded block by *Simpson* with chunky two-storey iron balconies. On the r. plainer red brick ranges by *Glenn Howells* and *Porphyrios*. At the end, steps down to the Stratford Canal, with WATERS EDGE, blocks by *George* with square-pier colonnades l. and iron-beam arches r. The area between Market Place and Waterside was developed in 2014–17, again by *George*, but with alterations by developers.

N of the Market Place blocks of flats surround a generous playing field. The cottagey DICKENS HEATH PRIMARY SCHOOL, Three Acres Lane, is by *Solihull Council Building Design Group*, 2002, extended 2006.

ELMDON

The N half of the parish was taken for Birmingham Airport, the s is hemmed in by Solihull housing and Jaguar Land Rover. The remains of the old village are at the junction of the Coventry road (now A45) and Old Damson Lane.

ST NICHOLAS. All alone down a narrow lane and now surrounded by woods, the grounds of Elmdon Hall run wild. The medieval church, known from a drawing in the Aylesford Collection, had a little timber-framed tower. Present church by *John Standbridge*, 1781, for Abraham Spooner. Gothick, in greyish sandstone ashlar, three bays long, with a w tower and three-sided E apse. The windows have Y-tracery and deep concave moulded reveals. NW vestry of 1864. Overwhelming flat-roofed s extension of 1971–4 by *Philip Skelcher & Partners*. W doors with pointed tracery. The tower lobby has a plaster rib-vault. Door into the church again with tracery, but also Victorian iron gates. The nave is open to the extension behind big piers, and dominated by an arch-braced and panelled roof of 1881. The apse has an arch with mouldings like those of the windows, and another pretty rib-vault. – Original apse PANELLING, COMMUNION TABLE (restored 2000) and ALTAR RAILS; also WEST GALLERY on partly clustered columns. Two half-surviving BOX PEWS at the W; the rest removed in 1974 – STAINED GLASS. Apse by *Cox, Sons, Buckley & Co.*, 1904. Nave N side E, Netherlandish roundels against clear glass, one dated 1532, the others probably C17 (in the E window in 1848). N, *Hardmans*, 1865. Heraldic glass above, perhaps C18. – MONUMENTS. Flanking the apse, Abraham Spooner †1788, l., and his wife Anne †1783, alabaster tablets in elegantly Gothic surrounds, each with a classical draped urn in the centres. – Isaac and Barbara Spooner, †1816 and †1826, signed by (*Matthew*) *Seaborne* of Birmingham. Also elegant, Gothic, and with a classical vase. – Abraham Spooner Lillingston †1834, signed (*Solomon*) *Wilkes*. Gothic. – Jane, Countess of Rosse †1838. Classical tablet in Gothic frame; also *Wilkes*. – Many other minor tablets.

ELMDON HALL stood NW of the church. Its site is marked by a BEACON of 1992 (commemorating the formation of the Single European Market). Built between 1780 and 1795 for Abraham and Isaac Spooner; demolished 1956; similar in style to Moseley Hall (p. 323) and almost certainly by *Standbridge*.

Former RECTORY, now ELMDON GRANGE flats, 200 yds N. Built for the Rev. William Spooner in 1803, so perhaps by *Standbridge*. Three storeys, three wide bays, with just a rise in the parapet at the centre. Extension l. probably of 1823. Entrance on the r. side, altered in a heavier way, with a square pilastered bay. Stables at the rear.

WALLED GARDEN, hidden in the wood to the E. Late C18 or early C19, perhaps built by Abraham Spooner. Very large, covering 2¾ acres. Much of the brick wall remains, derelict. Segment-arched entrances. Towards the N end a circular brick reservoir. SW of the garden by Church Lane, a former fishpond.

The original buildings of BIRMINGHAM AIRPORT are on the A45, the entrance opposite Damson Parkway. The former EXCELSIOR HOTEL (now Holiday Inn) is of 1939–40, much extended. Down Terminal Road the original TERMINAL BUILDING by *Norman & Dawbarn*, 1937–9. Reinforced-concrete construction, to support the dramatic balanced cantilevers for covered loading on either side. Apart from the piers with massive finials, the front is quite functional. Spiral staircases at either end of the front balcony, alas without their tall lamps. Semicircular end facing the runways, with cantilevered balconies now partly infilled, and tapering-out hexagonal control tower. Internal concourse surrounded by a wide viewing gallery. Further back r. HANGAR NO. 2, also *Norman & Dawbarn*, 1940.

Just W of the A45 entrance on the S side, by the footbridge, ELMDON HALL LODGE. Single-storeyed, with a Greek Doric portico. Not on the tithe map of 1837; perhaps built by the Alston family, who bought the estate in 1840.

VILLAGE. A few cottages survive, also a farmhouse with four bargeboarded gables and a Gothic porch, *c.* 1840–50, hiding older fabric. Barn to its l., brick end to the road, but box-framed behind, C17 at least. Everything on the N side of the main road has gone for road widening.

KINGSHURST

A Birmingham municipal estate of 1953–9, just over the city boundary, by *A.G. Sheppard Fidler*, City Architect. The usual cottage terraces and some flats.

ST BARNABAS, Over Green Drive. By *Maurice A.H. Hobbiss*, 1955–7. Church and hall in a T-plan. A simplified version of the elder Hobbiss's manner. Low proportions, contrasted with a slim tower with round-headed belfry windows. Minimal Tudor windows, but the chancel distinguished by pointed Gothick ones. Arcades of unmoulded pointed arches, and a king- and queen-post roof with moulded tie-beams. The aisles have tie-beams too. Original font, clergy desk and altar rail.

ST ANTHONY OF PADUA (R.C.), Oakthorpe Drive. By *Remo & Mary Granelli* (*Rush Granelli & Partners*), 1966–7. Brutalism at its most immediately attractive. Set behind a forecourt, entered by a pylon-like archway from the street, it masses golden-brown brick cubes and a well-calculated rounded end, with roof structures of cut-off cones and a polygonal main lantern. Worship space with cedar-boarded ceiling, darkened by stained glass of 1981; similar, linked Lady Chapel. The rounded end marks the former baptistery. Forecourt damaged in 1993, alas, by a PRESBYTERY with double garage.

The PUBLIC BUILDINGS are by *John H.D. Madin* with *Sheppard Fidler*. Along Marston Drive a two-storey flat-roofed range of LIBRARY, YOUTH CENTRE etc., of 1960–5. SHOPPING CENTRE behind, through an archway, of 1958–9, nicely stepping uphill. (Under threat, 2021.)

Off Stonebridge Crescent, remains of a MOTTE-AND-BAILEY CASTLE. Original low motte, later heightened and surmounted by a timber tower and palisade. Kingshurst Hall, a seven-bay early C18 house with a hipped roof, demolished 1962, was built in the former bailey, just NE. Sandstone and brick revetment on the inner face of motte ditch, and brick BRIDGE over its NE arm.

MARSTON GREEN

A hamlet which became a C20 commuter village because of its station on the Birmingham to Coventry railway. Marston Hall, C16 and C17, was demolished *c.* 1980 for airport extensions.

St Leonard, Elmdon Road. 1937–8 by *Walter J. Knight*. Brick, Early Christian style, but incomplete: chancel shortened, tower not built. Tall clerestory; impressively proportioned interior. Good treatment of the aisles: arcades of circular brick piers, the plainest abaci, round arches, and transverse arches over the aisles. – STAINED GLASS. Aisles, by *Benjamin Warren*, 1954 etc. W window by *Margaret Traherne*, 1965, abstract, with bright orange, representing the flames of the Holy Spirit.
No. 5 Elmdon Road is timber-framed, probably C16, altered.

NATIONAL EXHIBITION CENTRE

A complex of exhibition halls, a concept familiar now, but unique in Britain when originally developed. Built by Birmingham City Council with the Birmingham Chamber of Commerce, the last of the city's great municipal projects, sold in 2015. The sadness is that it is so architecturally negligible. The original halls, by *Edward Mills & Partners*, 1973–6, face s and are grouped round entrance areas on two levels: 'a straight applying of industrialised building technique to a circulation diagram' (*Architectural Review*). Corrugated steel, now mostly painted red. Extended sw, also by *Mills*, with the ARENA, 1980, and FORUM, 1983. The Arena has an unobstructed interior supported by big external pylons. Large extensions to the N by *Seymour Harris Architects*, 1989–98, forming a U-shaped court facing E, with a birdcage-like glass atrium running all round. SE of the original buildings the artificial PENDIGO LAKE. Across it to the NE the METROPOLE HOTEL, dark brick, 'the Alcatraz style', by *Richard Seifert & Partners*, 1976. Facing the lake on the sw, RESORTS WORLD, a casino complex by *Benoy*, 2013–15. Monumental glass front with a central bow, but the entrance pushed round to the r.

BIRMINGHAM AIRPORT, to the W, is another architectural missed opportunity. Functional shed and concrete car parks by *Alfred A. Wood*, West Midlands County Planner and Architect, 1984. Extensions by *D5*, including a second terminal l. with sloping roof, 2000 and 2006, and a redesign bringing the two together, with a long serrated front canopy, 2010. A crop of hotels and offices around it, the best perhaps DIAMOND HOUSE of 1999. Across the runways a CONTROL TOWER by *CPMG*, 2011–13, shaped like an enormous taper-headed screw. For the former airport *see* Elmdon, p. 779.

OLTON

Olton ('old town') is probably the site of the oldest settlement in Solihull. The present suburb dates from the opening of the station on the Birmingham to Leamington railway in 1864.

St Margaret, Warwick Road. Chancel by *J. G. Bland* (*Bland & Cossins*) 1879–80; the rest, aisled nave, transepts and vestry, by *Benjamin Corser*, 1895–6. sw tower never built. Old-fashioned Dec in rock-faced sandstone. Ample interior; arcades with circular columns and double-chamfered arches. Plain sw HALL of 1971–2, sw. – Corser, who worshipped here, was responsible for much in the way of decoration and FITTINGS, including the attractive naturalistic flower capitals, PULPIT and low SCREEN of 1898, alabaster REREDOS of 1901, CHOIR STALLS, 1904, alabaster FONT, 1913, and COVER, 1920. The carvers for all these were *Bridgemans*. – STAINED GLASS. Chancel E and s windows by *Ward & Hughes*, 1895; N by *R.W. Winfield & Co.* (*T.W. Camm*), 1886/8; s chapel E *Hardmans*, 1959; N transept *Hardmans*, 1924; nave w *Hardmans*, 1920; aisles w, both *Clayton & Bell*, 1911.

Olton Friary (R.C.), St Bernard's Road. Begun as a diocesan seminary. A monastery since 1889, first Franciscan, now the Congregation of the Sacred Heart of Jesus of Betharram. A big L-shaped range by *Dunn & Hansom*, 1873, rich hard Gothic with vigorous detail: big buttresses, two-light windows divided by octagonal columns, dormers with bargeboards, and a conical turret with a splayed stone base. Complex brick cornice of Italian inspiration, but banded with blue bricks. The former refectory (now chapel) has a panelled ceiling with heavy moulded beams. Corridors articulated by pointed arches. Former classrooms with fireplaces with pointed arches and foliage in the spandrels. Dog-leg staircase with heavy fluted newel posts. On the first floor the former chapel, now library, entered through an elaborately carved doorway. It has a coved and panelled timber ceiling with moulded ribs. A corridor mostly of 1955 links to the church.

The CHURCH OF THE HOLY GHOST AND MARY IMMACULATE was added by *G. B. Cox* in 1926–9. Red brick with stone dressings, roof of Westmorland slates. Dec with a touch of French Gothic. Bulky and awkward exterior with alternate nave bays projecting for altars. SE transept for the friars, hidden from the congregation, with a slim tower cutting in from square to octagonal; belfry with traceried openings and spire. Narthex of 1970–1. A wide nave, without aisles to give a clear view of the altar (cf. Cox's Sacred Heart, Acocks Green, p. 301). The sides are articulated by full-height relieving arches, with open ones for the chapels. Boarded roof with moulded ribs. Lady Chapel with a two-bay N arcade. The stair beyond the SE transept has square newels with well-carved birds and beasts. – Many original *Cox* fittings. HIGH ALTAR 1932, PULPIT 1930, COMMUNION RAILS 1944, all with polished stones. – Lady Chapel ALTAR of 1939, with *opus sectile* panel and roundels. – Nave side altar with Franciscan saints, 1930. – STAINED GLASS in the Lady Chapel, almost certainly *Hardmans*.

Congregational Church (former), Kineton Green Road. 1900–1 by *J. P. Osborne*. Old-fashioned brick nave with cusped lancets, but the front has paired Perp windows, a porch with a two-bay arcade, and, the best thing, a Free Style tower with tapering buttresses and a pyramid roof supported on lines of long timber brackets.

PERAMBULATION. ST BERNARD'S ROAD, cut in 1869, runs s from St Margaret's church.* Later Victorian work at this end (also further s), earlier development beyond, with mostly Gothic designs. The E side has detached houses and pairs, the first (Nos. 4–10) all by *J. G. Dunn*, 1894. The w side has some grander single houses. No. 1, 1897, looks like *Dunn*; No. 3 with oversailing gable, by *Arthur Harrison*, 1897–8; Nos. 5 and 7, by *Essex, Nicol & Goodman*, with tile-hung gables, 1898 and 1900; No. 9, half-timbered, by *W. J. Davis*, 1898. Nos. 26–28, E side, with half-hipped porches, are by *J. P. Osborne*, 1890. Across the road, Nos. 15–19 by *Benjamin Corser*, with a repeated motif of triplet lancets. No. 21 is the earliest in the road, of 1872; Nos. 23–29 dour pairs of *c.* 1886. No. 42 opposite, 1884, is classical. Nos. 44 and 46, picturesque Gothic villas of 1880–1. Opposite, No. 31 of 1881, small and bargeboarded, was built for William Powell of the Proof House, so perhaps by *Bateman & Corser*. No. 35 is a lovely Voyseyesque rendered house of 1909 by *G. A. Cox* with differing end gables, an arty little dormer, and slate roof in diminishing courses (sadly re-windowed 2020). No. 41, a heavy mixture of Jacobean and tile-hanging, is by *Gateley & Parsons*, 1897. Nos. 51–53, plain brick relieved by mullion-and-transom staircase windows, by *John Harding & Son* of Salisbury, 1899. No. 55, with porch linked to bay, is by *Gateley & Parsons*, 1904. No. 57 is roadhouse Tudor by *W. T. Orton*, 1927–8. Nos. 59–61, plain but well detailed, by *A. Harrison*, 1896.

No. 74 opposite, THE SPINNEY, is by *Harry Bloomer*, 1911. Roughcast with casement windows, but not really Voysey-ish. Two big gables. Name panel with low-relief tree. The entrance hall has posts supporting a beamed ceiling, and a staircase with little cut-out diamonds in panels. Panelled dining room, the fireplace with octagonal columns. Above, a frieze painted on canvas by *Nora Yoxall & Elsie Whitford*, 1919–20: scenes from Robin Hood, in a simplified, almost childlike manner. No. 76, by *Harrison*, 1902, brick and render, has an eye-catching timbered staircase projection. Now a care home, with a tactful extension l. like a separate house, by *Robin Hurley*, 2007–8. No. 78 by *E. H. Wigley*, 1900, brick and tile-hung; No. 80 by *J. P. Osborne*, much-timbered; No. 82, brick, half-timber and render, by *Wood & Kendrick*, 1898. Returning to the w side, Nos. 69 and 73, set facing each other, are of *c.* 1880. Nos. 75–77, Voysey-ish, are by *Wigley*, 1911. No. 81 is *Bloomer & Gough*, 1931; Nos. 85–87, with odd patterned brickwork, by *Samuel Bridges* of Acocks Green, builder, 1908. Beyond, hidden in trees, is OLTON COURT, of 1895. The grandest house in the road, with a tower, but a pedestrian design, probably by *Bridges*, who added the l. wing,

---

*On the Warwick Road opposite St Margaret's, BANK HOUSE, Neo-Georgian by *Buckland & Haywood*, 1929 (side extensions 1999).

dated 1899. A convent school in the C20; converted to flats 2008 by *Lapworth Partnership*, with large extension. Beyond this, two modest Arts and Crafts houses, No. 103 by *W.J. Davis*, 1908, and No. 105 by *J.P. Osborne*, 1907–8. No. 107, also *Davis*, 1907, has a touch of Art Nouveau. Beyond the roundabout, WILLOW GRANGE is big, loose Queen Anne of *c.* 1890.

DOVEHOUSE LANE runs E from Warwick Road, ½ m. SE of St Margaret's. DOVEHOUSE FARM (No. 39), N side, is of *c.* 1500. Hall range parallel to the road faced in C18 brick, but the gable-end of the W cross-range has studding and a double jetty. The E end has an unusual truss with curved braces to the tie-beam, and raking struts above the collar. It may have been internal, to a former E wing. A square-panelled C17 barn joins on to the W wing. No. 77 is a half-butterfly semi-bungalow by *James A. Swan*, 1927. No. 70, opposite, coolly rendered, is by *Harvey & Wicks*, 1931, for *William Bloye*, who sculpted the small panel by the door.

SHIRLEY

A modest hamlet on the Stratford Road has become an unending C20 suburb. Its landmark, the former CEGB offices by *John H.D. Madin & Partners*, 1967, was demolished in 2017.

ST JAMES THE GREAT, Stratford Road. Nave and ritual W tower (actually E) by *Robert Ebbels*, 1830–2, rendered, with lancets and two-step buttresses. The tower has cut-out battlements but has lost its pinnacles. The triangular dormers go with *Edward Holmes*'s kingpost nave roof of 1862, which has twirly wrought-iron struts. Chancel and transepts by *John Cotton*, 1882–3, red brick, with some plate tracery. Big head corbels carved by *John Roddis*. The interior has suffered from being reoriented in 1969 and back again in 1993. – *Cotton*'s chancel STALLS survive. – REREDOS. Mosaic with praying angels, by *Powells*, 1886. – STAINED GLASS. Much by *Powells*: E window 1889 (central lights) and 1886; N 1892 and 1897; S 1897. All except the earliest probably by *George Parlby*. N transept N by *Camm & Co.*, 1901; E by *Camm Bros*, 1883. S transept perhaps *Hardmans*, †1911.

OUR LADY OF THE WAYSIDE, Stratford Road. 1965–7 by *Brian Rush* (*Rush Granelli & Partners*). A picturesque grouping in grey brick: church with a curving l. end and slit windows, linking entrance, and circular baptistery with stone fins, topped by a rocket-like fibreglass spire. A narthex leads to a weekday chapel and the main worship space: rather dark. It has a long brick altar wall and a bow-shaped roof, tilted, with open slats, to light the altar; also a ritual W gallery. Alcove-like Lady Chapel on the far side. – ALTAR, a block of Portland stone, by *Walter Ritchie*. Above it, an animated gilded Christ by *Elisabeth*

Frink. – Also by *Ritchie*, STATUE of Our Lady in the Lady Chapel and Crucifixion RELIEF in the narthex.

SHIRLEY BAPTIST CHURCH, Stratford Road. 1910 by *Ingall, Bridgewater & Co.* Tame Gothic with Bodleyesque late Dec tracery. It stands out in these surroundings.

The centre stretches down the STRATFORD ROAD for over a mile, with little worth mentioning. BARCLAYS BANK on the corner of Stanway Road is by *John H.D. Madin & Partners*, 1965–6, with crisp glazed elevations and a concrete-faced stair-tower. Opposite St James's church, the PLUME OF FEATHERS pub, an overgrown cottage mostly by *Atkinson's Brewery Building Dept*, 1923. Nos. 332–334, s of St James's, are probably early C19, much altered.

In SOLIHULL ROAD, running E from the centre, some C19 Gothic villas and Nos. 94–96, a lovely pair by *E.F. Reynolds*, 1910. The row of gables above a pent roof is indebted to Philip Webb.

TRW (formerly JOSEPH LUCAS RESEARCH CENTRE), Stratford Road, 1 m. s. 1963–5 by *Clifford Tee & Gale*. Long, symmetrical front in a shallow V, with a slightly concave centre. Curtain walling set behind two storeys of slim piers, between concrete floor-plates. Circular forebuilding (cf. the firm's Barrow Cadbury House, Selly Oak, p. 432). (Abstract concrete frieze in the entrance hall by *William Mitchell*.) Contemporary landscaping by *Sylvia Crowe*. Due for demolition 2020.

GOLDFINGER HOUSE (formerly Carr & Co.), Cranmore Boulevard, NE of the Stratford Road opposite. Hidden away in the business park on the SE side, offices and warehouse by *Ernö Goldfinger*, 1955–6. A crisp concrete-framed structure on pilotis. Its mullions and transoms create a complex pattern. The parapet has V-shaped cuts to remove water. Tower for lift shaft, tank and document store, concrete above glass. Open concrete spiral stair on the s. The foyer is glazed and recessed (enlarged 2007). Main staircase at the rear, with tubular handrails and metal grille panels in place of balusters. Lit by a wall of reeded glass blocks. Manager's office with original glass-and-veneer fitted cupboards.

SHIRLEY GOLF CLUB, Stratford Road, 1 m. further s. Founded by the Birmingham Jewish Golf Society, whose members had been refused entry to clubs elsewhere. Clubhouse by *John Madin*, 1956–9. Long, low, with a shallow butterfly roof, large windows, and a big slope-sided stone-faced chimney: California in Solihull. Many extensions, the entrance area by *Stanley Sellers*, 2003.

LIGHT HALL, off Dog Kennel Lane, 1 m. SSE. Mid-C18, three bays, tall, with giant pilasters, nice moulded brick cornice and hipped roof. Altered doorcase. C19 front bays.

THREE MAYPOLES pub (former), Tanworth Lane, 1 m. s. Mildly streamlined, *Moderne* with angled wings. By *W.S. Clements*, 1936–8.

GLOSSARY

Numbers and letters refer to the illustrations (by John Sambrook) on pp. 796–803.

ABACUS: flat slab forming the top of a capital (3a).

ACANTHUS: classical formalized leaf ornament (4b).

ACCUMULATOR TOWER: *see* Hydraulic power.

ACHIEVEMENT: a complete display of armorial bearings.

ACROTERION: plinth for a statue or ornament on the apex or ends of a pediment; more usually, both the plinth and what stands on it (4a).

AEDICULE (*lit.* little building): architectural surround, consisting usually of two columns or pilasters supporting a pediment.

AGGREGATE: *see* Concrete.

AISLE: subsidiary space alongside the body of a building, separated from it by columns, piers, or posts.

ALMONRY: a building from which alms are dispensed to the poor.

AMBULATORY (*lit.* walkway): aisle around the sanctuary (q.v.).

ANGLE ROLL: roll moulding in the angle between two planes (1a).

ANSE DE PANIER: *see* Arch.

ANTAE: simplified pilasters (4a), usually applied to the ends of the enclosing walls of a portico *in antis* (q.v.).

ANTEFIXAE: ornaments projecting at regular intervals above a Greek cornice, originally to conceal the ends of roof tiles (4a).

ANTHEMION: classical ornament like a honeysuckle flower (4b).

APRON: raised panel below a window or wall monument or tablet.

APSE: semicircular or polygonal end of an apartment, especially of a chancel or chapel. In classical architecture sometimes called an *exedra*.

ARABESQUE: non-figurative surface decoration consisting of flowing lines, foliage scrolls etc., based on geometrical patterns. Cf. Grotesque.

ARCADE: series of arches supported by piers or columns. *Blind arcade* or *arcading*: the same applied to the wall surface. *Wall arcade*: in medieval churches, a blind arcade forming a dado below windows. Also a covered shopping street.

ARCH: Shapes *see* 5c. *Basket arch* or *anse de panier* (basket handle): three-centred and depressed, or with a flat centre. *Nodding*: ogee arch curving forward from the wall face. *Parabolic*: shaped like a chain suspended from two level points, but inverted. Special purposes. *Chancel*: dividing chancel from nave or crossing. *Crossing*: spanning piers at a crossing (q.v.). *Relieving or discharging*: incorporated in a wall to relieve superimposed weight (5c). *Skew*: spanning responds not diametrically opposed. *Strainer*: inserted in an opening to resist inward pressure. *Transverse*: spanning a main axis (e.g. of a vaulted space). *See also* Jack arch, Triumphal arch.

ARCHITRAVE: formalized lintel, the lowest member of the classical entablature (3a). Also the moulded frame of a door or window (often borrowing the profile of a classical architrave). For *lugged* and *shouldered* architraves *see* 4b.

ARCUATED: dependent structurally on the arch principle. Cf. Trabeated.

ARK: chest or cupboard housing the

tables of Jewish law in a synagogue.

ARRIS: sharp edge where two surfaces meet at an angle (3a).

ASHLAR: masonry of large blocks wrought to even faces and square edges (6d).

ASTRAGAL: classical moulding of semicircular section (3f).

ASTYLAR: with no columns or similar vertical features.

ATLANTES: see Caryatids.

ATRIUM (plural: atria): inner court of a Roman or C20 house; in a multi-storey building, a toplit covered court rising through all storeys. Also an open court in front of a church.

ATTACHED COLUMN: see Engaged column.

ATTIC: small top storey within a roof. Also the storey above the main entablature of a classical façade.

AUMBRY: recess or cupboard to hold sacred vessels for the Mass.

BAILEY: see Motte-and-bailey.

BALANCE BEAM: see Canals.

BALDACCHINO: free-standing canopy, originally fabric, over an altar. Cf. Ciborium.

BALLFLOWER: globular flower of three petals enclosing a ball (1a). Typical of the Decorated style.

BALUSTER: pillar or pedestal of bellied form. *Balusters*: vertical supports of this or any other form, for a handrail or coping, the whole being called a *balustrade* (6c). *Blind balustrade*: the same applied to the wall surface.

BARBICAN: outwork defending the entrance to a castle.

BARGEBOARDS (corruption of 'vergeboards'): boards, often carved or fretted, fixed beneath the eaves of a gable to cover and protect the rafters.

BAROQUE: style originating in Rome c.1600 and current in England c.1680–1720, characterized by dramatic massing and silhouette and the use of the giant order.

BARROW: burial mound.

BARTIZAN: corbelled turret, square or round, frequently at an angle.

BASCULE: hinged part of a lifting (or bascule) bridge.

BASE: moulded foot of a column or pilaster. For *Attic* base see 3b.

BASEMENT: lowest, subordinate storey; hence the lowest part of a classical elevation, below the *piano nobile* (q.v.).

BASILICA: a Roman public hall; hence an aisled building with a clerestory.

BASTION: one of a series of defensive semicircular or polygonal projections from the main wall of a fortress or city.

BATTER: intentional inward inclination of a wall face.

BATTLEMENT: defensive parapet, composed of *merlons* (solid) and *crenels* (embrasures) through which archers could shoot; sometimes called *crenellation*. Also used decoratively.

BAY: division of an elevation or interior space as defined by regular vertical features such as arches, columns, windows etc.

BAY LEAF: classical ornament of overlapping bay leaves (3f).

BAY WINDOW: window of one or more storeys projecting from the face of a building. *Canted*: with a straight front and angled sides. *Bow window*: curved. *Oriel*: rests on corbels or brackets and starts above ground level; also the bay window at the dais end of a medieval great hall.

BEAD-AND-REEL: see Enrichments.

BEAKHEAD: Norman ornament with a row of beaked bird or beast heads usually biting into a roll moulding (1a).

BELFRY: chamber or stage in a tower where bells are hung.

BELL CAPITAL: see 1b.

BELLCOTE: small gabled or roofed housing for the bell(s).

BERM: level area separating a ditch from a bank on a hill-fort or barrow.

BILLET: Norman ornament of small half-cylindrical or rectangular blocks (1a).

BLIND: see Arcade, Baluster, Portico.

BLOCK CAPITAL: see 1a.

BLOCKED: columns, etc. interrupted by regular projecting

GLOSSARY

blocks (*blocking*), as on a Gibbs surround (4b).

BLOCKING COURSE: course of stones, or equivalent, on top of a cornice and crowning the wall.

BOLECTION MOULDING: covering the joint between two different planes (6b).

BOND: the pattern of long sides (*stretchers*) and short ends (*headers*) produced on the face of a wall by laying bricks in a particular way (6e).

BOSS: knob or projection, e.g. at the intersection of ribs in a vault (2c).

BOWTELL: a term in use by the C15 for a form of roll moulding, usually three-quarters of a circle in section (also called *edge roll*).

BOW WINDOW: *see* Bay window.

BOX FRAME: timber-framed construction in which vertical and horizontal wall members support the roof (7). Also concrete construction where the loads are taken on cross walls; also called *cross-wall construction*.

BRACE: subsidiary member of a structural frame, curved or straight. *Bracing* is often arranged decoratively e.g. quatrefoil, herringbone (7). *See also* Roofs.

BRATTISHING: ornamental crest, usually formed of leaves, Tudor flowers or miniature battlements.

BRESSUMER (*lit.* breast-beam): big horizontal beam supporting the wall above, especially in a jettied building (7).

BRICK: *see* Bond, Cogging, Engineering, Gauged, Tumbling.

BRIDGE: *Bowstring*: with arches rising above the roadway which is suspended from them. *Clapper*: one long stone forms the roadway. *Roving*: *see* Canal. *Suspension*: roadway suspended from cables or chains slung between towers or pylons. *Stay-suspension* or *stay-cantilever*: supported by diagonal stays from towers or pylons. *See also* Bascule.

BRISES-SOLEIL: projecting fins or canopies which deflect direct sunlight from windows.

BROACH: *see* Spire and 1c.

BUCRANIUM: ox skull used decoratively in classical friezes.

BULL-NOSED SILL: sill displaying a pronounced convex upper moulding.

BULLSEYE WINDOW: small oval window, set horizontally (cf. Oculus). Also called *œil de bœuf*.

BUTTRESS: vertical member projecting from a wall to stabilize it or to resist the lateral thrust of an arch, roof, or vault (1c, 2c). A *flying buttress* transmits the thrust to a heavy abutment by means of an arch or half-arch (1c).

CABLE OR ROPE MOULDING: originally Norman, like twisted strands of a rope.

CAMES: *see* Quarries.

CAMPANILE: free-standing bell-tower.

CANALS: *Flash lock*: removable weir or similar device through which boats pass on a flush of water. Predecessor of the *pound lock*: chamber with gates at each end allowing boats to float from one level to another. *Tidal gates*: single pair of lock gates allowing vessels to pass when the tide makes a level. *Balance beam*: beam projecting horizontally for opening and closing lock gates. *Roving bridge*: carrying a towing path from one bank to the other.

CANTILEVER: horizontal projection (e.g. step, canopy) supported by a downward force behind the fulcrum.

CAPITAL: head or crowning feature of a column or pilaster; for classical types *see* 3; for medieval types *see* 1b.

CARREL: compartment designed for individual work or study.

CARTOUCHE: classical tablet with ornate frame (4b).

CARYATIDS: female figures supporting an entablature; their male counterparts are *Atlantes* (*lit.* Atlas figures).

CASEMATE: vaulted chamber, with embrasures for defence, within a castle wall or projecting from it.

CASEMENT: side-hinged window.

CASTELLATED: with battlements (q.v.).

CAST IRON: hard and brittle, cast in a mould to the required shape.

Wrought iron is ductile, strong in tension, forged into decorative patterns or forged and rolled into e.g. bars, joists, boiler plates; *mild steel* is its modern equivalent, similar but stronger.

CATSLIDE: *See* 8a.

CAVETTO: concave classical moulding of quarter-round section (3f).

CELURE OR CEILURE: enriched area of roof above rood or altar.

CEMENT: *see* Concrete.

CENOTAPH (*lit.* empty tomb): funerary monument which is not a burying place.

CENTRING: wooden support for the building of an arch or vault, removed after completion.

CHAMFER (*lit.* corner-break): surface formed by cutting off a square edge or corner. For types of chamfers and *chamfer stops see* 6a. *See also* Double chamfer.

CHANCEL: part of the E end of a church set apart for the use of the officiating clergy.

CHANTRY CHAPEL: often attached to or within a church, endowed for the celebration of Masses principally for the soul of the founder.

CHEVET (*lit.* head): French term for chancel with ambulatory and radiating chapels.

CHEVRON: V-shape used in series or double series (later) on a Norman moulding (1a). Also (especially when on a single plane) called *zigzag*.

CHOIR: the part of a cathedral, monastic or collegiate church where services are sung.

CIBORIUM: a fixed canopy over an altar, usually vaulted and supported on four columns; cf. Baldacchino. Also a canopied shrine for the reserved sacrament.

CINQUEFOIL: *see* Foil.

CIST: stone-lined or slab-built grave.

CLADDING: external covering or skin applied to a structure, especially a framed one.

CLERESTORY: uppermost storey of the nave of a church, pierced by windows. Also high-level windows in secular buildings.

CLOSER: a brick cut to complete a bond (6e).

CLUSTER BLOCK: *see* Multi-storey.

COADE STONE: ceramic artificial stone made in Lambeth 1769–c.1840 by Eleanor Coade (†1821) and her associates.

COB: walling material of clay mixed with straw. Also called *pisé*.

COFFERING: arrangement of sunken panels (coffers), square or polygonal, decorating a ceiling, vault, or arch.

COGGING: a decorative course of bricks laid diagonally (6e). Cf. Dentilation.

COLLAR: *see* Roofs and 7.

COLLEGIATE CHURCH: endowed for the support of a college of priests.

COLONNADE: range of columns supporting an entablature. Cf. Arcade.

COLONNETTE: small medieval column or shaft.

COLOSSAL ORDER: *see* Giant order.

COLUMBARIUM: shelved, niched structure to house multiple burials.

COLUMN: a classical, upright structural member of round section with a shaft, a capital, and usually a base (3a, 4a).

COLUMN FIGURE: carved figure attached to a medieval column or shaft, usually flanking a doorway.

COMMUNION TABLE: unconsecrated table used in Protestant churches for the celebration of Holy Communion.

COMPOSITE: *see* Orders.

COMPOUND PIER: grouped shafts (q.v.), or a solid core surrounded by shafts.

CONCRETE: composition of *cement* (calcined lime and clay), *aggregate* (small stones or rock chippings), sand and water. It can be poured into *formwork* or *shuttering* (temporary frame of timber or metal) on site (*in-situ* concrete), or *pre-cast* as components before construction. *Reinforced*: incorporating steel rods to take the tensile force. *Pre-stressed*: with tensioned steel rods. Finishes include the impression of boards left by formwork (*board-marked* or *shuttered*), and texturing with steel brushes (*brushed*) or hammers (*hammer-dressed*). *See also* Shell.

CONSOLE: bracket of curved outline (4b).

COPING: protective course of masonry or brickwork capping a wall (6d).

CORBEL: projecting block supporting something above. *Corbel course*: continuous course of projecting stones or bricks fulfilling the same function. *Corbel table*: series of corbels to carry a parapet or a wall-plate or wall-post (7). *Corbelling*: brick or masonry courses built out beyond one another to support a chimney-stack, window, etc.

CORINTHIAN: see Orders and 3d.

CORNICE: flat-topped ledge with moulded underside, projecting along the top of a building or feature, especially as the highest member of the classical entablature (3a). Also the decorative moulding in the angle between wall and ceiling.

CORPS-DE-LOGIS: the main building(s) as distinct from the wings or pavilions.

COTTAGE ORNÉ: an artfully rustic small house associated with the Picturesque movement.

COUNTERCHANGING: of joists on a ceiling divided by beams into compartments, when placed in opposite directions in alternate squares.

COUR D'HONNEUR: formal entrance court before a house in the French manner, usually with flanking wings and a screen wall or gates.

COURSE: continuous layer of stones, etc. in a wall (6e).

COVE: a broad concave moulding, e.g. to mask the eaves of a roof. *Coved ceiling*: with a pronounced cove joining the walls to a flat central panel smaller than the whole area of the ceiling.

CRADLE ROOF: see Wagon roof.

CREDENCE: a shelf within or beside a piscina (q.v.), or a table for the sacramental elements and vessels.

CRENELLATION: parapet with crenels (*see* Battlement).

CRINKLE-CRANKLE WALL: garden wall undulating in a series of serpentine curves.

CROCKETS: leafy hooks. *Crocketing* decorates the edges of Gothic features, such as pinnacles, canopies, etc. *Crocket capital*: see 1b.

CROSSING: central space at the junction of the nave, chancel, and transepts. *Crossing tower*: above a crossing.

CROSS-WINDOW: with one mullion and one transom (qq.v.).

CROWN-POST: see Roofs and 7.

CROWSTEPS: squared stones set like steps, e.g. on a gable (8a).

CRUCKS (*lit*. crooked): pairs of inclined timbers (*blades*), usually curved, set at bay-lengths; they support the roof timbers and, in timber buildings, also support the walls (8b). *Base*: blades rise from ground level to a tie- or collar-beam which supports the roof timbers. *Full*: blades rise from ground level to the apex of the roof, serving as the main members of a roof truss. *Jointed*: blades formed from more than one timber; the lower member may act as a wall-post; it is usually elbowed at wall-plate level and jointed just above. *Middle*: blades rise from half-way up the walls to a tie- or collar-beam. *Raised*: blades rise from half-way up the walls to the apex. *Upper*: blades supported on a tie-beam and rising to the apex.

CRYPT: underground or half-underground area, usually below the E end of a church. *Ring crypt*: corridor crypt surrounding the apse of an early medieval church, often associated with chambers for relics. Cf. Undercroft.

CUPOLA (*lit*. dome): especially a small dome on a circular or polygonal base crowning a larger dome, roof, or turret.

CURSUS: a long avenue defined by two parallel earthen banks with ditches outside.

CURTAIN WALL: a connecting wall between the towers of a castle. Also a non-load-bearing external wall applied to a C20 framed structure.

CUSP: see Tracery and 2b.

CYCLOPEAN MASONRY: large irregular polygonal stones, smooth and finely jointed.

CYMA RECTA and CYMA REVERSA: classical mouldings with double curves (3f). Cf. Ogee.

DADO: the finishing (often with panelling) of the lower part of a wall in a classical interior; in origin a formalized continuous pedestal. *Dado rail*: the moulding along the top of the dado.
DAGGER: *see* Tracery and 2b.
DALLE-DE-VERRE (*lit.* glass-slab): a late C20 stained-glass technique, setting large, thick pieces of cast glass into a frame of reinforced concrete or epoxy resin.
DEC (DECORATED): English Gothic architecture c. 1290 to c. 1350. The name is derived from the type of window tracery (q.v.) used during the period.
DEMI- or HALF-COLUMNS: engaged columns (q.v.) half of whose circumference projects from the wall.
DENTIL: small square block used in series in classical cornices (3c). *Dentilation* is produced by the projection of alternating headers along cornices or stringcourses.
DIAPER: repetitive surface decoration of lozenges or squares flat or in relief. Achieved in brickwork with bricks of two colours.
DIOCLETIAN OR THERMAL WINDOW: semicircular with two mullions, as used in the Baths of Diocletian, Rome (4b).
DISTYLE: having two columns (4a).
DOGTOOTH: E.E. ornament, consisting of a series of small pyramids formed by four stylized canine teeth meeting at a point (1a).
DORIC: *see* Orders and 3a, 3b.
DORMER: window projecting from the slope of a roof (8a).
DOUBLE CHAMFER: a chamfer applied to each of two recessed arches (1a).
DOUBLE PILE: *see* Pile.
DRAGON BEAM: *see* Jetty.
DRESSINGS: the stone or brickwork worked to a finished face about an angle, opening, or other feature.
DRIPSTONE: moulded stone projecting from a wall to protect the lower parts from water. Cf. Hoodmould, Weathering.
DRUM: circular or polygonal stage supporting a dome or cupola. Also one of the stones forming the shaft of a column (3a).
DUTCH or FLEMISH GABLE: *see* 8a.

EASTER SEPULCHRE: tomb-chest used for Easter ceremonial, within or against the N wall of a chancel.
EAVES: overhanging edge of a roof; hence *eaves cornice* in this position.
ECHINUS: ovolo moulding (q.v.) below the abacus of a Greek Doric capital (3a).
EDGE RAIL: *see* Railways.
E.E. (EARLY ENGLISH): English Gothic architecture c. 1190–1250.
EGG-AND-DART: *see* Enrichments and 3f.
ELEVATION: any face of a building or side of a room. In a drawing, the same or any part of it, represented in two dimensions.
EMBATTLED: with battlements.
EMBRASURE: small splayed opening in a wall or battlement (q.v.).
ENCAUSTIC TILES: earthenware tiles fired with a pattern and glaze.
EN DELIT: stone cut against the bed.
ENFILADE: reception rooms in a formal series, usually with all doorways on axis.
ENGAGED or ATTACHED COLUMN: one that partly merges into a wall or pier.
ENGINEERING BRICKS: dense bricks, originally used mostly for railway viaducts etc.
ENRICHMENTS: the carved decoration of certain classical mouldings, e.g. the ovolo (qq.v.) with *egg-and-dart*, the cyma reversa with *waterleaf*, the astragal with *bead-and-reel* (3f).
ENTABLATURE: in classical architecture, collective name for the three horizontal members (architrave, frieze, and cornice) carried by a wall or a column (3a).
ENTASIS: very slight convex deviation from a straight line, used to prevent an optical illusion of concavity.
EPITAPH: inscription on a tomb.
EXEDRA: *see* Apse.

EXTRADOS: outer curved face of an arch or vault.
EYECATCHER: decorative building terminating a vista.

FASCIA: plain horizontal band, e.g. in an architrave (3c, 3d) or on a shopfront.
FENESTRATION: the arrangement of windows in a façade.
FERETORY: site of the chief shrine of a church, behind the high altar.
FESTOON: ornamental garland, suspended from both ends. Cf. Swag.
FIBREGLASS, or glass-reinforced polyester (GRP): synthetic resin reinforced with glass fibre. GRC: glass-reinforced concrete.
FIELD: see Panelling and 6b.
FILLET: a narrow flat band running down a medieval shaft or along a roll moulding (1a). It separates larger curved mouldings in classical cornices, fluting or bases (3c).
FLAMBOYANT: the latest phase of French Gothic architecture, with flowing tracery.
FLASH LOCK: see Canals.
FLÈCHE or SPIRELET (*lit.* arrow): slender spire on the centre of a roof.
FLEURON: medieval carved flower or leaf, often rectilinear (1a).
FLUSHWORK: knapped flint used with dressed stone to form patterns.
FLUTING: series of concave grooves (flutes), their common edges sharp (arris) or blunt (fillet) (3).
FOIL (*lit.* leaf): lobe formed by the cusping of a circular or other shape in tracery (2b). *Trefoil* (three), *quatrefoil* (four), *cinquefoil* (five), and *multifoil* express the number of lobes in a shape.
FOLIATE: decorated with leaves.
FORMWORK: see Concrete.
FRAMED BUILDING: where the structure is carried by a framework – e.g. of steel, reinforced concrete, timber – instead of by load-bearing walls.
FREESTONE: stone that is cut, or can be cut, in all directions.
FRESCO: *al fresco*: painting on wet plaster. *Fresco secco*: painting on dry plaster.
FRIEZE: the middle member of the classical entablature, sometimes ornamented (3a). *Pulvinated frieze* (*lit.* cushioned): of bold convex profile (3c). Also a horizontal band of ornament.
FRONTISPIECE: in C16 and C17 buildings the central feature of doorway and windows above linked in one composition.

GABLE: For types see 8a. *Gablet*: small gable. *Pedimental gable*: treated like a pediment.
GADROONING: classical ribbed ornament like inverted fluting that flows into a lobed edge.
GALILEE: chapel or vestibule usually at the W end of a church enclosing the main portal(s).
GALLERY: a long room or passage; an upper storey above the aisle of a church, looking through arches to the nave; a balcony or mezzanine overlooking the main interior space of a building; or an external walkway.
GALLETING: small stones set in a mortar course.
GAMBREL ROOF: see 8a.
GARDEROBE: medieval privy.
GARGOYLE: projecting water spout often carved into human or animal shape.
GAUGED or RUBBED BRICKWORK: soft brick sawn roughly, then rubbed to a precise (gauged) surface. Mostly used for door or window openings (5c).
GAZEBO (jocular Latin, 'I shall gaze'): ornamental lookout tower or raised summer house.
GEOMETRIC: English Gothic architecture *c.* 1250–1310. See also Tracery. For another meaning, see Stairs.
GIANT or COLOSSAL ORDER: classical order (q.v.) whose height is that of two or more storeys of the building to which it is applied.
GIBBS SURROUND: C18 treatment of an opening (4b), seen particularly in the work of James Gibbs (1682–1754).
GIRDER: a large beam. *Box*: of hollow-box section. *Bowed*: with its top rising in a curve. *Plate*: of I-section, made from iron or steel

plates. *Lattice*: with braced framework.

GLAZING BARS: wooden or sometimes metal bars separating and supporting window panes.

GRAFFITI: *see* Sgraffito.

GRANGE: farm owned and run by a religious order.

GRC: *see* Fibreglass.

GRISAILLE: monochrome painting on walls or glass.

GROIN: sharp edge at the meeting of two cells of a cross-vault; *see* Vault and 2c.

GROTESQUE (*lit.* grotto-esque): wall decoration adopted from Roman examples in the Renaissance. Its foliage scrolls incorporate figurative elements. Cf. Arabesque.

GROTTO: artificial cavern.

GRP: *see* Fibreglass.

GUILLOCHE: classical ornament of interlaced bands (4b).

GUNLOOP: opening for a firearm.

GUTTAE: stylized drops (3b).

HALF-TIMBERING: archaic term for timber-framing (q.v.). Sometimes used for non-structural decorative timberwork.

HALL CHURCH: medieval church with nave and aisles of approximately equal height.

HAMMERBEAM: *see* Roofs and 7.

HAMPER: in C20 architecture, a visually distinct topmost storey or storeys.

HEADER: *see* Bond and 6e.

HEADSTOP: stop (q.v.) carved with a head (5b).

HELM ROOF: *see* 1c.

HENGE: ritual earthwork.

HERM (*lit.* the god Hermes): male head or bust on a pedestal.

HERRINGBONE WORK: *see* 7ii. Cf. Pitched masonry.

HEXASTYLE: *see* Portico.

HILL-FORT: Iron Age earthwork enclosed by a ditch and bank system.

HIPPED ROOF: *see* 8a.

HOODMOULD: projecting moulding above an arch or lintel to throw off water (2b, 5b). When horizontal often called a *label*. For label stop *see* Stop.

HUSK GARLAND: festoon of stylized nutshells (4b).

HYDRAULIC POWER: use of water under high pressure to work machinery. *Accumulator tower*: houses a hydraulic accumulator which accommodates fluctuations in the flow through hydraulic mains.

HYPOCAUST (*lit.* underburning): Roman underfloor heating system.

IMPOST: horizontal moulding at the springing of an arch (5c).

IMPOST BLOCK: block between abacus and capital (1b).

IN ANTIS: *see* Antae, Portico and 4a.

INDENT: shape chiselled out of a stone to receive a brass.

INDUSTRIALIZED or SYSTEM BUILDING: system of manufactured units assembled on site.

INGLENOOK (*lit.* fire-corner): recess for a hearth with provision for seating.

INTERCOLUMNATION: interval between columns.

INTERLACE: decoration in relief simulating woven or entwined stems or bands.

INTRADOS: *see* Soffit.

IONIC: *see* Orders and 3c.

JACK ARCH: shallow segmental vault springing from beams, used for fireproof floors, bridge decks, etc.

JAMB (*lit.* leg): one of the vertical sides of an opening.

JETTY: in a timber-framed building, the projection of an upper storey beyond the storey below, made by the beams and joists of the lower storey oversailing the wall; on their outer ends is placed the sill of the walling for the storey above (7). Buildings can be jettied on several sides, in which case a *dragon beam* is set diagonally at the corner to carry the joists to either side.

JOGGLE: the joining of two stones to prevent them slipping by a notch in one and a projection in the other.

KEEL MOULDING: moulding used from the late C12, in section like the keel of a ship (1a).

KEEP: principal tower of a castle.

KENTISH CUSP: *see* Tracery and 2b.

KEY PATTERN: see 4b.
KEYSTONE: central stone in an arch or vault (4b, 5c).
KINGPOST: see Roofs and 7.
KNEELER: horizontal projecting stone at the base of each side of a gable to support the inclined coping stones (8a).

LABEL: see Hoodmould and 5b.
LABEL STOP: see Stop and 5b.
LACED BRICKWORK: vertical strips of brickwork, often in a contrasting colour, linking openings on different floors.
LACING COURSE: horizontal reinforcement in timber or brick to walls of flint, cobble, etc.
LADY CHAPEL: dedicated to the Virgin Mary (Our Lady).
LANCET: slender single-light, pointed-arched window (2a).
LANTERN: circular or polygonal windowed turret crowning a roof or a dome. Also the windowed stage of a crossing tower lighting the church interior.
LANTERN CROSS: churchyard cross with lantern-shaped top.
LAVATORIUM: in a religious house, a washing place adjacent to the refectory.
LEAN-TO: see Roofs.
LESENE (*lit.* a mean thing): pilaster without base or capital. Also called *pilaster strip*.
LIERNE: see Vault and 2c.
LIGHT: compartment of a window defined by the mullions.
LINENFOLD: Tudor panelling carved with simulations of folded linen. See also Parchemin.
LINTEL: horizontal beam or stone bridging an opening.
LOGGIA: gallery, usually arcaded or colonnaded; sometimes free-standing.
LONG-AND-SHORT WORK: quoins consisting of stones placed with the long side alternately upright and horizontal, especially in Saxon building.
LONGHOUSE: house and byre in the same range with internal access between them.
LOUVRE: roof opening, often protected by a raised timber structure, to allow the smoke from a central hearth to escape.
LOWSIDE WINDOW: set lower than the others in a chancel side wall, usually towards its W end.
LUCAM: projecting housing for hoist pulley on upper storey of warehouses, mills, etc., for raising goods to loading doors.
LUCARNE (*lit.* dormer): small gabled opening in a roof or spire.
LUGGED ARCHITRAVE: see 4b.
LUNETTE: semicircular window or blind panel.
LYCHGATE (*lit.* corpse-gate): roofed gateway entrance to a churchyard for the reception of a coffin.
LYNCHET: long terraced strip of soil on the downward side of prehistoric and medieval fields, accumulated because of continual ploughing along the contours.

MACHICOLATIONS (*lit.* mashing devices): series of openings between the corbels that support a projecting parapet through which missiles can be dropped. Used decoratively in post-medieval buildings.
MANOMETER or STANDPIPE TOWER: containing a column of water to regulate pressure in water mains.
MANSARD: see 8a.
MATHEMATICAL TILES: facing tiles with the appearance of brick, most often applied to timber-framed walls.
MAUSOLEUM: monumental building or chamber usually intended for the burial of members of one family.
MEGALITHIC TOMB: massive stone-built Neolithic burial chamber covered by an earth or stone mound.
MERLON: see Battlement.
METOPES: spaces between the triglyphs in a Doric frieze (3b).
MEZZANINE: low storey between two higher ones.
MILD STEEL: see Cast iron.
MISERICORD (*lit.* mercy): shelf on a carved bracket placed on the underside of a hinged choir stall seat to support an occupant when standing.

GLOSSARY

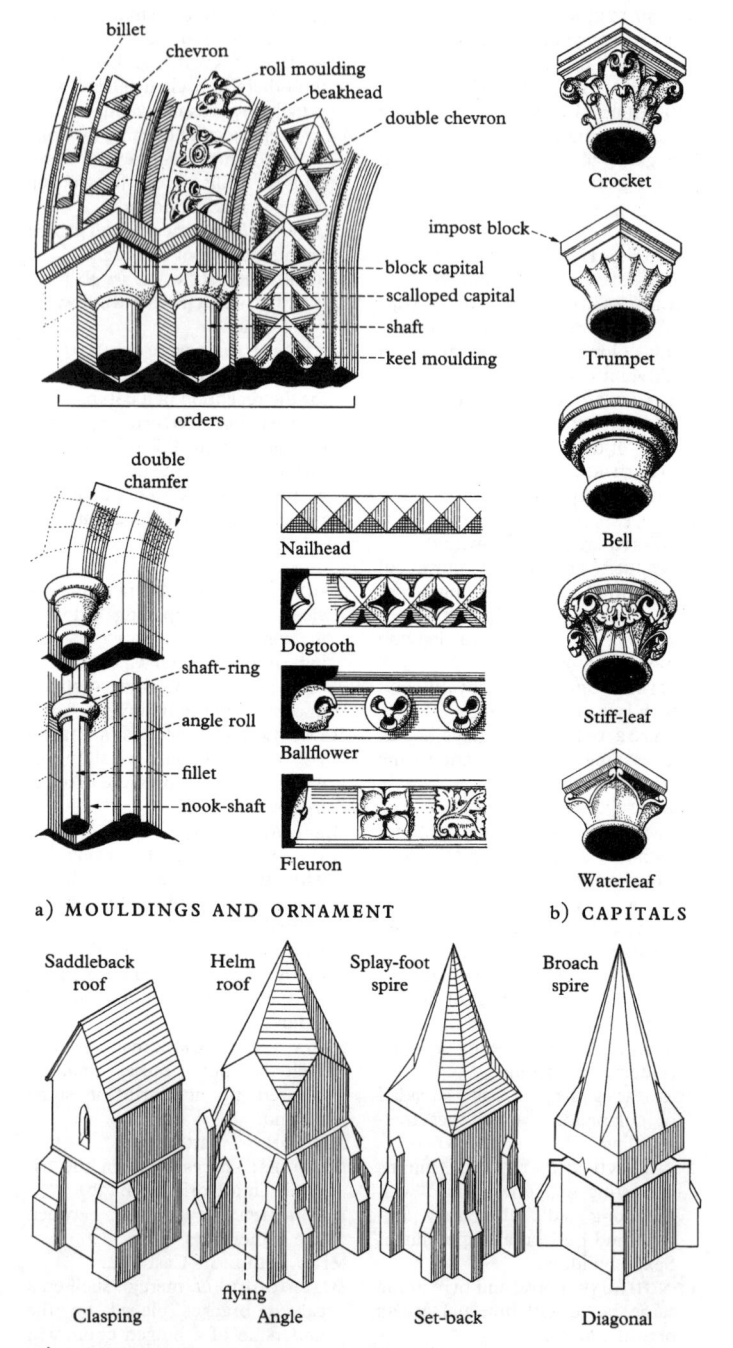

a) MOULDINGS AND ORNAMENT

- billet
- chevron
- roll moulding
- beakhead
- double chevron
- impost block
- block capital
- scalloped capital
- shaft
- keel moulding
- orders
- double chamfer
- shaft-ring
- angle roll
- fillet
- nook-shaft
- Nailhead
- Dogtooth
- Ballflower
- Fleuron

b) CAPITALS

- Crocket
- Trumpet
- Bell
- Stiff-leaf
- Waterleaf

c) BUTTRESSES, ROOFS AND SPIRES

- Saddleback roof
- Helm roof
- Splay-foot spire
- Broach spire
- Clasping
- flying
- Angle
- Set-back
- Diagonal

FIGURE 1: MEDIEVAL

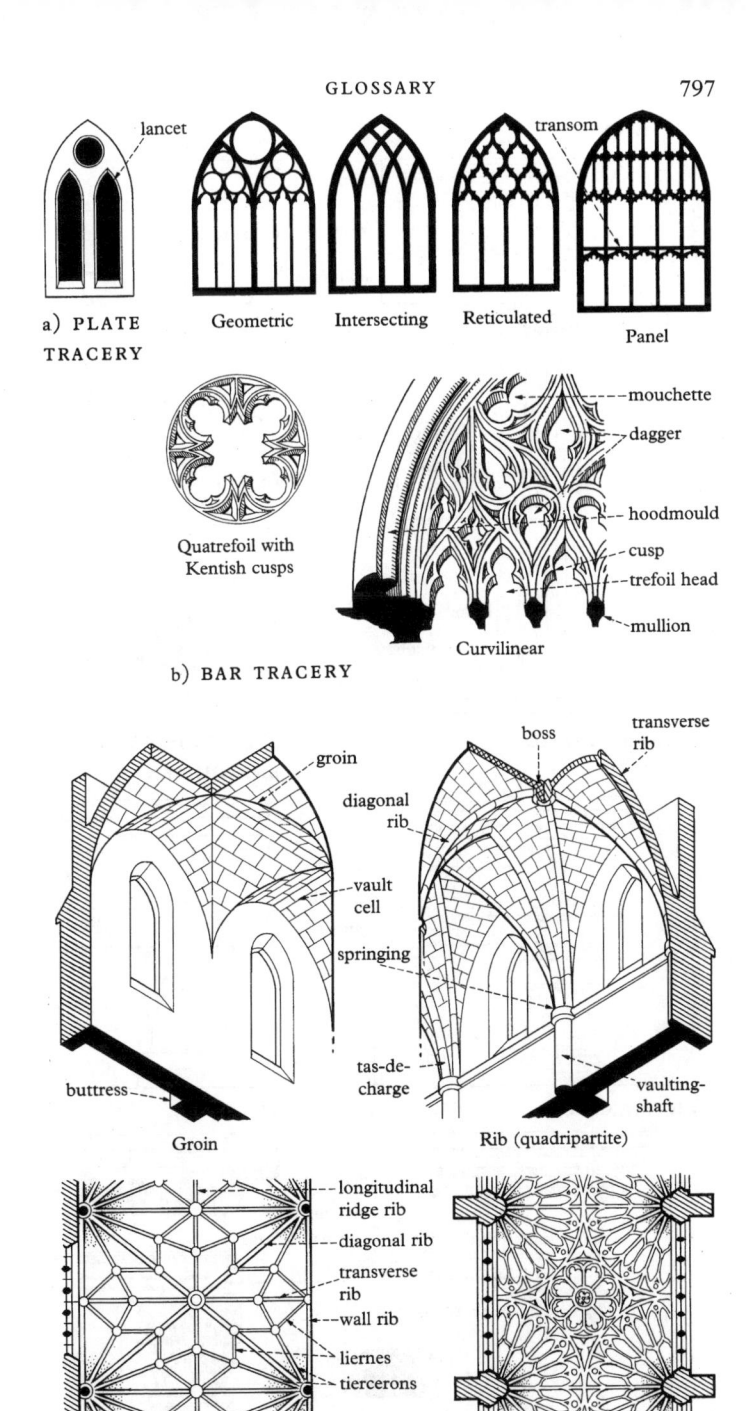

GLOSSARY

FIGURE 2: MEDIEVAL

a) PLATE TRACERY
- lancet
- Geometric
- Intersecting
- Reticulated (transom)
- Panel

b) BAR TRACERY
- Quatrefoil with Kentish cusps
- Curvilinear: mouchette, dagger, hoodmould, cusp, trefoil head, mullion

c) VAULTS
- Groin: groin, diagonal rib, vault cell, buttress
- Rib (quadripartite): boss, transverse rib, springing, tas-de-charge, vaulting-shaft
- Lierne: longitudinal ridge rib, diagonal rib, transverse rib, wall rib, liernes, tiercerons
- Fan

ORDERS

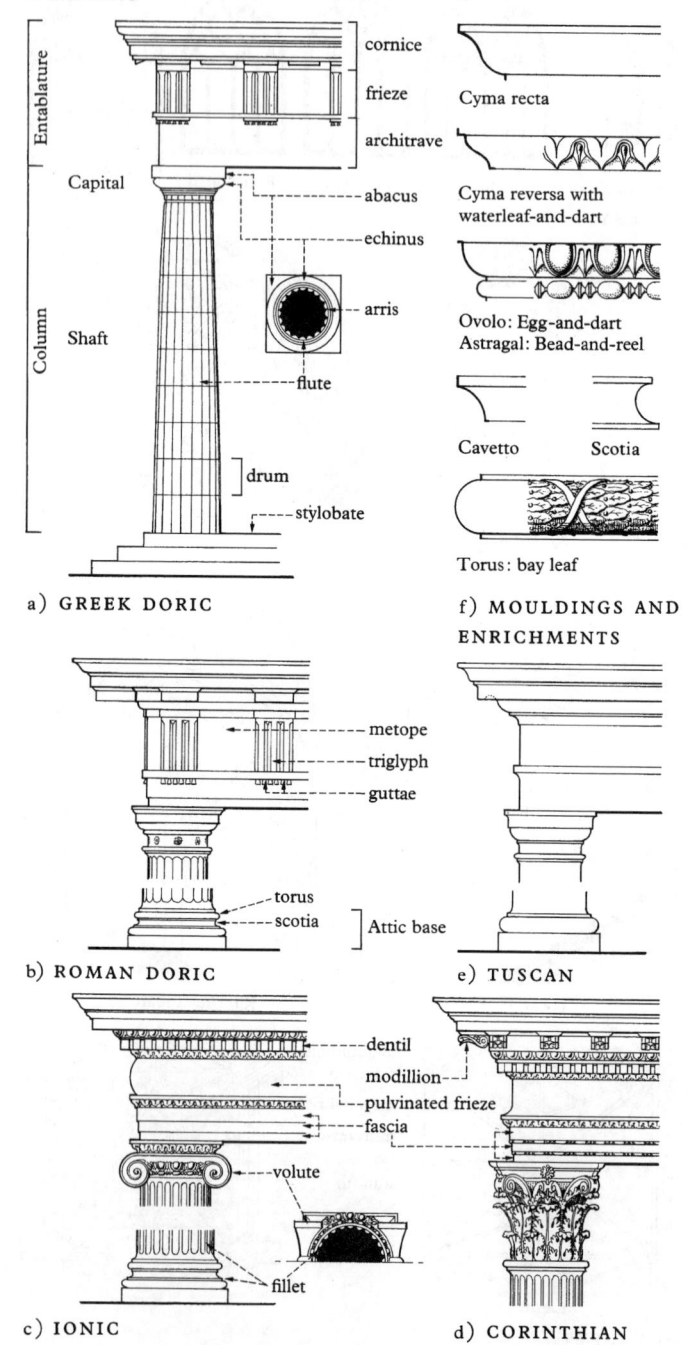

a) GREEK DORIC

- Entablature: cornice, frieze, architrave
- Capital: abacus, echinus
- Column / Shaft: arris, flute
- drum
- stylobate

b) ROMAN DORIC

- metope
- triglyph
- guttae
- torus
- scotia — Attic base

c) IONIC

- volute
- fillet

d) CORINTHIAN

- dentil
- modillion
- pulvinated frieze
- fascia

e) TUSCAN

f) MOULDINGS AND ENRICHMENTS

- Cyma recta
- Cyma reversa with waterleaf-and-dart
- Ovolo: Egg-and-dart
- Astragal: Bead-and-reel
- Cavetto
- Scotia
- Torus: bay leaf

FIGURE 3: CLASSICAL

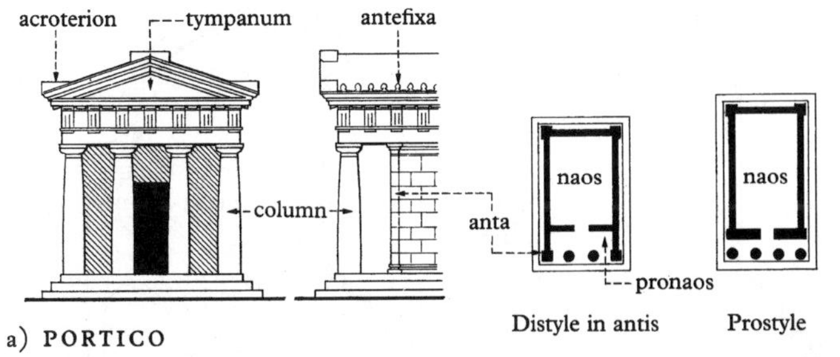
acroterion
tympanum
antefixa
column
anta
naos
naos
pronaos
Distyle in antis
Prostyle

a) PORTICO

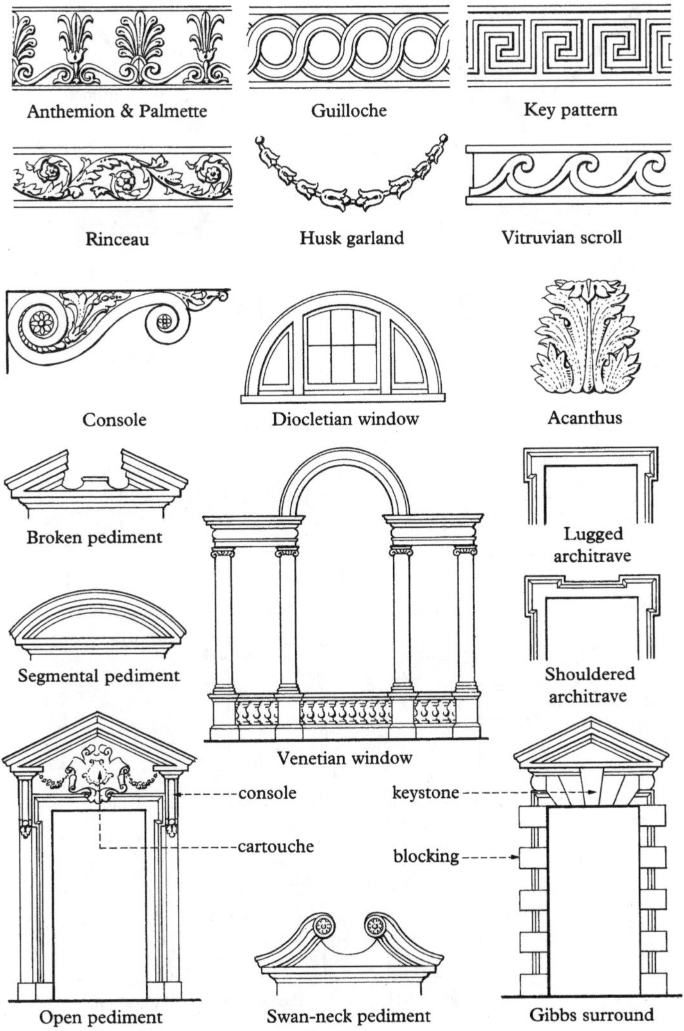
Anthemion & Palmette
Guilloche
Key pattern
Rinceau
Husk garland
Vitruvian scroll
Console
Diocletian window
Acanthus
Broken pediment
Lugged architrave
Segmental pediment
Shouldered architrave
Venetian window
console
cartouche
keystone
blocking
Open pediment
Swan-neck pediment
Gibbs surround

b) ORNAMENTS AND FEATURES

FIGURE 4: CLASSICAL

800 GLOSSARY

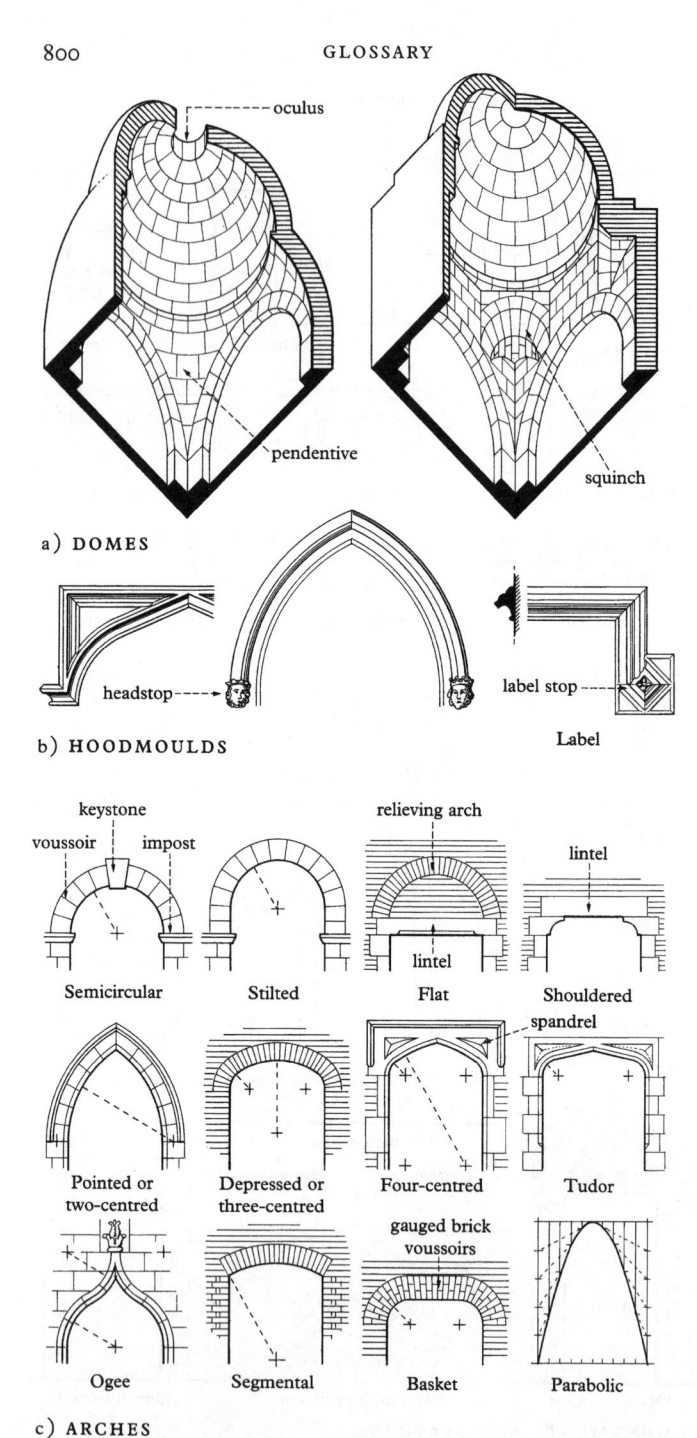

a) DOMES — oculus, pendentive, squinch

b) HOODMOULDS — headstop, label stop, Label

c) ARCHES

Semicircular — voussoir, keystone, impost
Stilted
Flat — relieving arch, lintel
Shouldered — lintel

Pointed or two-centred
Depressed or three-centred
Four-centred
Tudor — spandrel

Ogee
Segmental
Basket — gauged brick voussoirs
Parabolic

FIGURE 5: CONSTRUCTION

GLOSSARY 801

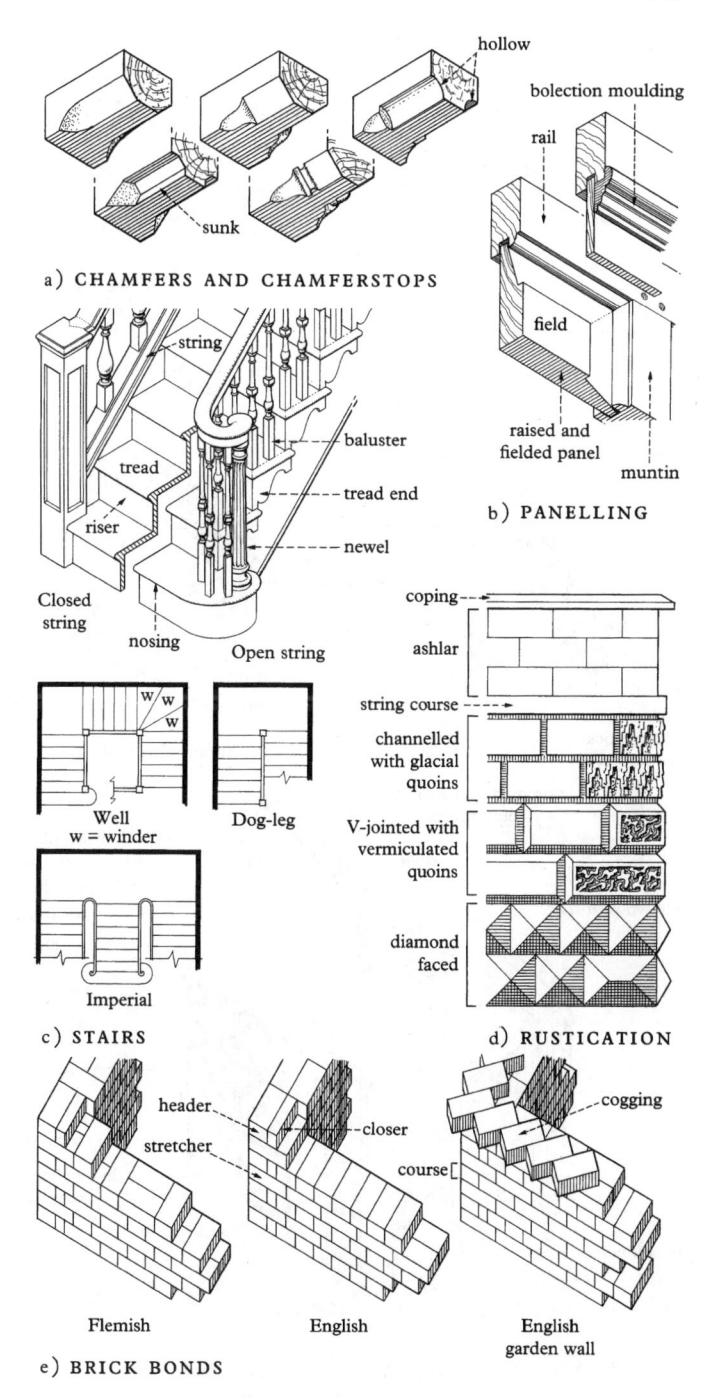

a) CHAMFERS AND CHAMFERSTOPS — hollow, sunk

b) PANELLING — bolection moulding, rail, field, raised and fielded panel, muntin

c) STAIRS — string, baluster, tread, tread end, riser, newel, Closed string, nosing, Open string; Well (w = winder), Dog-leg, Imperial

d) RUSTICATION — coping, ashlar, string course, channelled with glacial quoins, V-jointed with vermiculated quoins, diamond faced

e) BRICK BONDS — header, stretcher, closer, course, cogging; Flemish, English, English garden wall

FIGURE 6: CONSTRUCTION

802 GLOSSARY

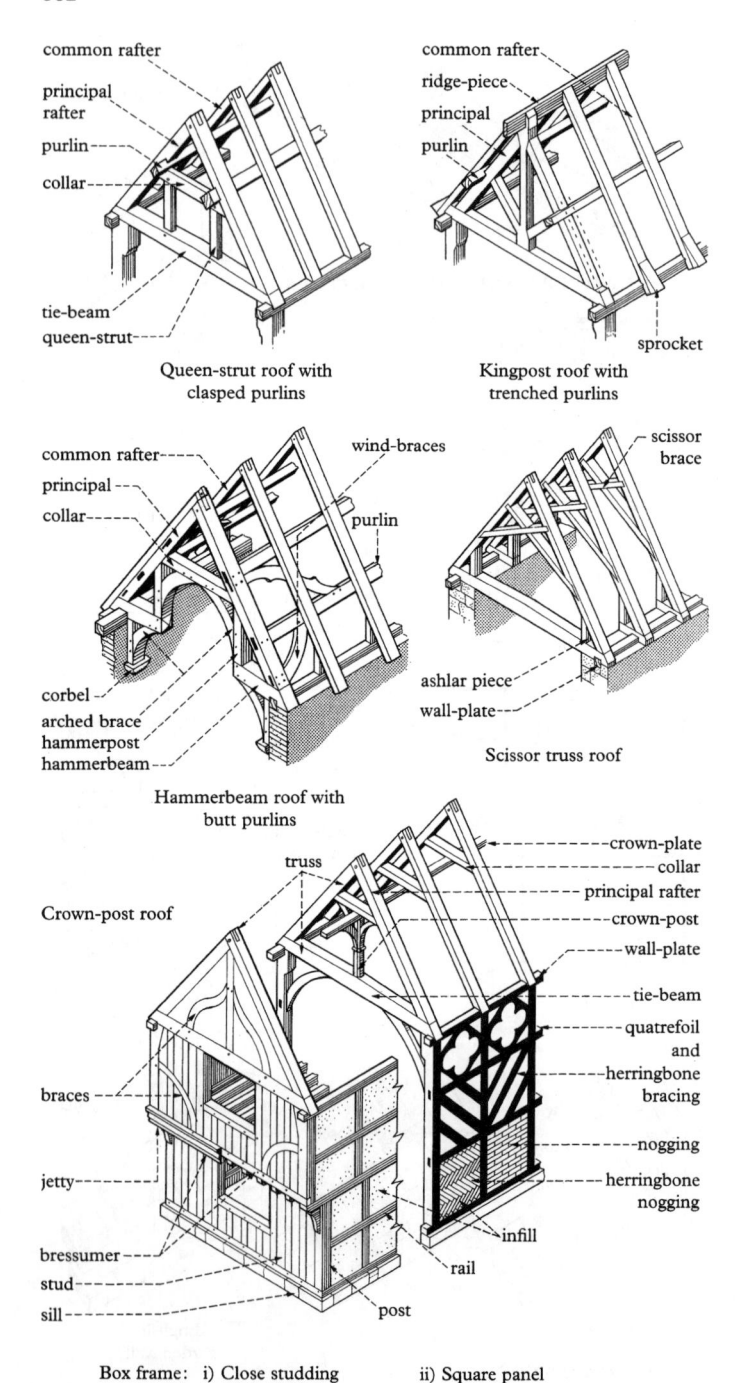

FIGURE 7: ROOFS AND TIMBER-FRAMING

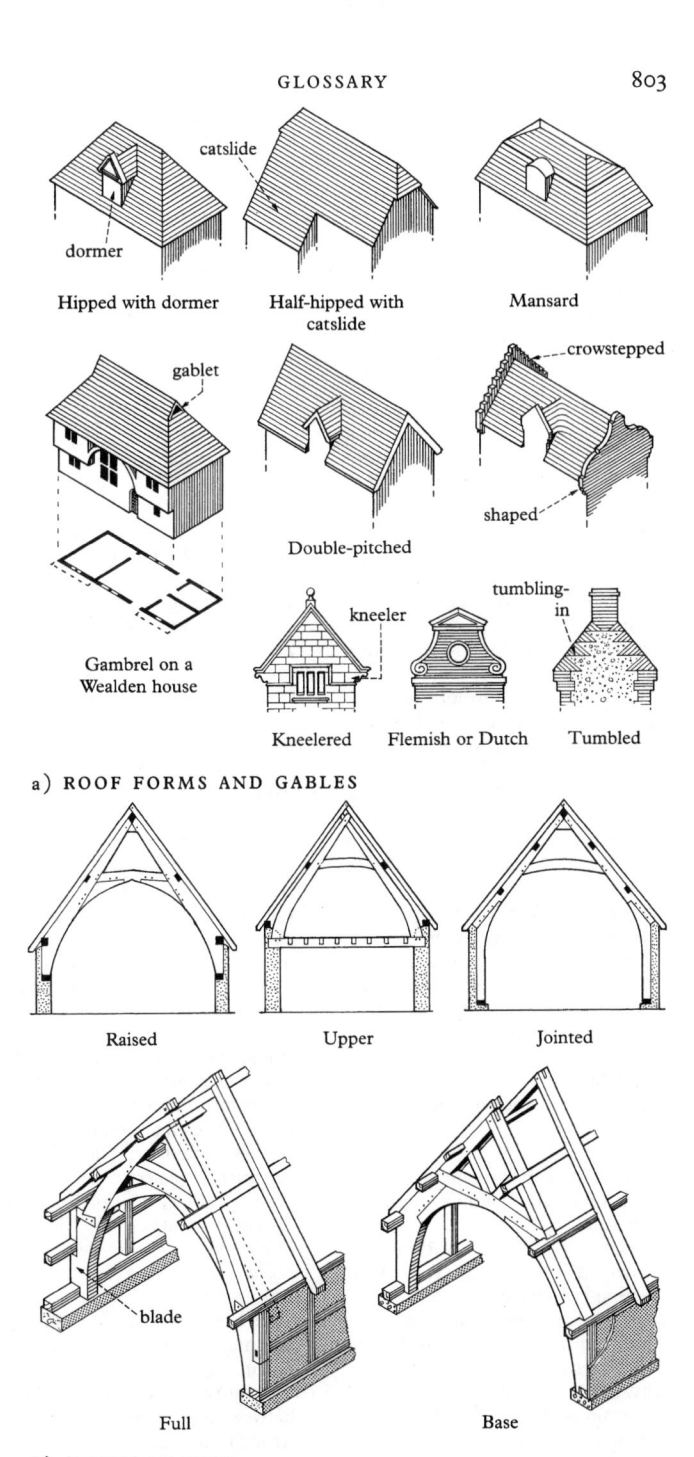

GLOSSARY 803

a) ROOF FORMS AND GABLES

Hipped with dormer (dormer, catslide)

Half-hipped with catslide

Mansard

Gambrel on a Wealden house (gablet)

Double-pitched

crowstepped / shaped

Kneelered (kneeler)

Flemish or Dutch

Tumbled (tumbling-in)

b) CRUCK FRAMES

Raised

Upper

Jointed

Full (blade)

Base

FIGURE 8: ROOFS AND TIMBER-FRAMING

MIXER-COURTS: forecourts to groups of houses shared by vehicles and pedestrians.

MODILLIONS: small consoles (q.v.) along the underside of a Corinthian or Composite cornice (3d). Often used along an eaves cornice.

MODULE: a predetermined standard size for co-ordinating the dimensions of components of a building.

MOTTE-AND-BAILEY: post-Roman and Norman defence consisting of an earthen mound (motte) topped by a wooden tower within a bailey, an enclosure defended by a ditch and palisade, and also, sometimes, by an internal bank.

MOUCHETTE: see Tracery and 2b.

MOULDING: shaped ornamental strip of continuous section; see e.g. Cavetto, Cyma, Ovolo, Roll.

MULLION: vertical member between window lights (2b).

MULTI-STOREY: five or more storeys. Multi-storey flats may form a *cluster block*, with individual blocks of flats grouped round a service core; a *point block*, with flats fanning out from a service core; or a *slab block*, with flats approached by corridors or galleries from service cores at intervals or towers at the ends (plan also used for offices, hotels etc.). *Tower block* is a generic term for any very high multi-storey building.

MUNTIN: see Panelling and 6b.

NAILHEAD: E.E. ornament consisting of small pyramids regularly repeated (1a).

NARTHEX: enclosed vestibule or covered porch at the main entrance to a church.

NAVE: the body of a church W of the crossing or chancel often flanked by aisles (q.v.).

NEWEL: central or corner post of a staircase (6c). Newel stair: see Stairs.

NIGHT STAIR: stair by which religious entered the transept of their church from their dormitory to celebrate night services.

NOGGING: see Timber-framing (7).

NOOK-SHAFT: shaft set in the angle of a wall or opening (1a).

NORMAN: see Romanesque.

NOSING: projection of the tread of a step (6c).

NUTMEG: medieval ornament with a chain of tiny triangles placed obliquely.

OCULUS: circular opening.

ŒIL DE BŒUF: see Bullseye window.

OGEE: double curve, bending first one way and then the other, as in an *ogee* or *ogival arch* (5c). Cf. Cyma recta and Cyma reversa.

OPUS SECTILE: decorative mosaic-like facing.

OPUS SIGNINUM: composition flooring of Roman origin.

ORATORY: a private chapel in a church or a house. Also a church of the Oratorian Order.

ORDER: one of a series of recessed arches and jambs forming a splayed medieval opening, e.g. a doorway or arcade arch (1a).

ORDERS: the formalized versions of the post-and-lintel system in classical architecture. The main orders are *Doric, Ionic*, and *Corinthian*. They are Greek in origin but occur in Roman versions. Tuscan is a simple version of Roman Doric. Though each order has its own conventions (3), there are many minor variations. The Composite capital combines Ionic volutes with Corinthian foliage. *Superimposed orders*: orders on successive levels, usually in the upward sequence of Tuscan, Doric, Ionic, Corinthian, Composite.

ORIEL: see Bay window.

OVERDOOR: painting or relief above an internal door. Also called a *sopraporta*.

OVERTHROW: decorative fixed arch between two gatepiers or above a wrought-iron gate.

OVOLO: wide convex moulding (3f).

PALIMPSEST: of a brass: where a metal plate has been reused by turning over the engraving on the back; of a wall painting: where one overlaps and partly obscures an earlier one.

PALLADIAN: following the examples and principles of Andrea Palladio (1508–80).

PALMETTE: classical ornament like a palm shoot (4b).

PANELLING: wooden lining to interior walls, made up of vertical members (*muntins*) and horizontals (*rails*) framing panels: also called *wainscot*. *Raised and fielded*: with the central area of the panel (*field*) raised up (6b).

PANTILE: roof tile of S section.

PARAPET: wall for protection at any sudden drop, e.g. at the wall-head of a castle where it protects the *parapet walk* or wall-walk. Also used to conceal a roof.

PARCLOSE: *see* Screen.

PARGETTING (*lit.* plastering): exterior plaster decoration, either in relief or incised.

PARLOUR: in a religious house, a room where the religious could talk to visitors; in a medieval house, the semi-private living room below the solar (q.v.).

PARTERRE: level space in a garden laid out with low, formal beds.

PATERA (*lit.* plate): round or oval ornament in shallow relief.

PAVILION: ornamental building for occasional use; or projecting subdivision of a larger building, often at an angle or terminating a wing.

PEBBLEDASHING: *see* Rendering.

PEDESTAL: a tall block carrying a classical order, statue, vase, etc.

PEDIMENT: a formalized gable derived from that of a classical temple; also used over doors, windows, etc. For variations *see* 4b.

PENDENTIVE: spandrel between adjacent arches, supporting a drum, dome or vault and consequently formed as part of a hemisphere (5a).

PENTHOUSE: subsidiary structure with a lean-to roof. Also a separately roofed structure on top of a C20 multi-storey block.

PERIPTERAL: *see* Peristyle.

PERISTYLE: a colonnade all round the exterior of a classical building, as in a temple which is then said to be *peripteral*.

PERP (PERPENDICULAR): English Gothic architecture c. 1335–50 to c. 1530. The name is derived from the upright tracery panels then used (*see* Tracery and 2a).

PERRON: external stair to a doorway, usually of double-curved plan.

PEW: loosely, seating for the laity outside the chancel; strictly, an enclosed seat. *Box pew*: with equal high sides and a door.

PIANO NOBILE: principal floor of a classical building above a ground floor or basement and with a lesser storey overhead.

PIAZZA: formal urban open space surrounded by buildings.

PIER: large masonry or brick support, often for an arch. *See also* Compound pier.

PILASTER: flat representation of a classical column in shallow relief. *Pilaster strip*: *see* Lesene.

PILE: row of rooms. *Double pile*: two rows thick.

PILLAR: free-standing upright member of any section, not conforming to one of the orders (q.v.).

PILLAR PISCINA: *see* Piscina.

PILOTIS: C20 French term for pillars or stilts that support a building above an open ground floor.

PISCINA: basin for washing Mass vessels, provided with a drain; set in or against the wall to the S of an altar or free-standing (*pillar piscina*).

PISÉ: *see* Cob.

PITCHED MASONRY: laid on the diagonal, often alternately with opposing courses (*pitched and counterpitched* or *herringbone*).

PLATBAND: flat horizontal moulding between storeys. Cf. stringcourse.

PLATE RAIL: *see* Railways.

PLATEWAY: *see* Railways.

PLINTH: projecting courses at the

foot of a wall or column, generally chamfered or moulded at the top.

PODIUM: a continuous raised platform supporting a building; or a large block of two or three storeys beneath a multi-storey block of smaller area.

POINT BLOCK: *see* Multi-storey.

POINTING: exposed mortar jointing of masonry or brickwork. Types include *flush*, *recessed* and *tuck* (with a narrow channel filled with finer, whiter mortar).

POPPYHEAD: carved ornament of leaves and flowers as a finial for a bench end or stall.

PORTAL FRAME: C20 frame comprising two uprights rigidly connected to a beam or pair of rafters.

PORTCULLIS: gate constructed to rise and fall in vertical grooves at the entry to a castle.

PORTICO: a porch with the roof and frequently a pediment supported by a row of columns (4a). A portico *in antis* has columns on the same plane as the front of the building. A *prostyle* porch has columns standing free. Porticoes are described by the number of front columns, e.g. tetrastyle (four), hexastyle (six). The space within the temple is the *naos*, that within the portico the *pronaos*. *Blind portico*: the front features of a portico applied to a wall.

PORTICUS (plural: porticūs): subsidiary cell opening from the main body of a pre-Conquest church.

POST: upright support in a structure (7).

POSTERN: small gateway at the back of a building or to the side of a larger entrance door or gate.

POUND LOCK: *see* Canals.

PRESBYTERY: the part of a church lying E of the choir where the main altar is placed; or a priest's residence.

PRINCIPAL: *see* Roofs and 7.

PRONAOS: *see* Portico and 4a.

PROSTYLE: *see* Portico and 4a.

PULPIT: raised and enclosed platform for the preaching of sermons. *Three-decker*: with reading desk below and clerk's desk below that. *Two-decker*: as above, minus the clerk's desk.

PULPITUM: stone screen in a major church dividing choir from nave.

PULVINATED: *see* Frieze and 3c.

PURLIN: *see* Roofs and 7.

PUTHOLES or PUTLOG HOLES: in the wall to receive putlogs, the horizontal timbers which support scaffolding boards; sometimes not filled after construction is complete.

PUTTO (plural: putti): small naked boy.

QUARRIES: square (or diamond) panes of glass supported by lead strips (*cames*); square floor slabs or tiles.

QUATREFOIL: *see* Foil and 2b.

QUEEN-STRUT: *see* Roofs and 7.

QUIRK: sharp groove to one side of a convex medieval moulding.

QUOINS: dressed stones at the angles of a building (6d).

RADBURN SYSTEM: vehicle and pedestrian segregation in residential developments, based on that used at Radburn, New Jersey, USA, by Wright and Stein, 1928–30.

RADIATING CHAPELS: projecting radially from an ambulatory or an apse (*see* Chevet).

RAFTER: *see* Roofs and 7.

RAGGLE: groove cut in masonry, especially to receive the edge of a roof-covering.

RAGULY: ragged (in heraldry). Also applied to funerary sculpture, e.g. *cross raguly*: with a notched outline.

RAIL: *see* Panelling and 6b; also 7.

RAILWAYS: *Edge rail*: on which flanged wheels can run. *Plate rail*: L-section rail for plain unflanged wheels. *Plateway*: early railway using plate rails.

RAISED AND FIELDED: *see* Panelling and 6b.

RAKE: slope or pitch.

RAMPART: defensive outer wall of stone or earth. *Rampart walk*: path along the inner face.

REBATE: rectangular section cut out of a masonry edge to receive a shutter, door, window, etc.

REBUS: a heraldic pun, e.g. a fiery cock for Cockburn.

REEDING: series of convex mouldings, the reverse of fluting (q.v.). Cf. Gadrooning.

RENDERING: the covering of outside walls with a uniform surface or skin for protection from the weather. *Limewashing*: thin layer of lime plaster. *Pebbledashing*: where aggregate is thrown at the wet plastered wall for a textured effect. *Roughcast*: plaster mixed with a coarse aggregate such as gravel. *Stucco*: fine lime plaster worked to a smooth surface. *Cement rendering*: a cheaper substitute for stucco, usually with a grainy texture.

REPOUSSÉ: relief designs in metalwork, formed by beating it from the back.

REREDORTER (*lit*. behind the dormitory): latrines in a medieval religious house.

REREDOS: painted and/or sculptured screen behind and above an altar. Cf. Retable.

RESPOND: half-pier or half-column bonded into a wall and carrying one end of an arch. It usually terminates an arcade.

RETABLE: painted or carved panel standing on or at the back of an altar, usually attached to it.

RETROCHOIR: in a major church, the area between the high altar and E chapel.

REVEAL: the plane of a jamb, between the wall and the frame of a door or window.

RIB-VAULT: *see* Vault and 2c.

RINCEAU: classical ornament of leafy scrolls (4b).

RISER: vertical face of a step (6c).

ROACH: a rough-textured form of Portland stone, with small cavities and fossil shells.

ROCK-FACED: masonry cleft to produce a rugged appearance.

ROCOCO: style current *c*. 1720 and *c*. 1760, characterized by a serpentine line and playful, scrolled decoration.

ROLL MOULDING: medieval moulding of part-circular section (1a).

ROMANESQUE: style current in the C11 and C12. In England often called Norman. *See also* Saxo-Norman.

ROOD: crucifix flanked by the Virgin and St John, usually over the entry into the chancel, on a beam (*rood beam*) or painted on the wall. The *rood screen* below often had a walkway (*rood loft*) along the top, reached by a *rood stair* in the side wall.

ROOFS: Shape. For the main external shapes (hipped, mansard, etc.) see 8a. *Helm* and *Saddleback*: *see* 1c. *Lean-to*: single sloping roof built against a vertical wall; lean-to is also applied to the part of the building beneath.
Construction. *See* 7.
Single-framed roof: with no main trusses. The rafters may be fixed to the wall-plate or ridge, or longitudinal timber may be absent altogether.
Double-framed roof: with longitudinal members, such as purlins, and usually divided into bays by principals and principal rafters.
Other types are named after their main structural components, e.g. *hammerbeam*, *crown-post* (*see* Elements below and 7).
Elements. *See* 7.
Ashlar piece: a short vertical timber connecting inner wall-plate or timber pad to a rafter.
Braces: subsidiary timbers set diagonally to strengthen the frame. *Arched braces*: curved pair forming an arch, connecting wall or post below with tie- or collar-beam above. *Passing braces*: long straight braces passing across other members of the truss. *Scissor braces*: pair crossing diagonally between pairs of rafters or principals. *Wind-braces*: short, usually curved braces connecting side purlins with principals; sometimes decorated with cusping.
Collar or *collar-beam*: horizontal transverse timber connecting a pair of rafter or cruck blades (q.v.), set between apex and the wall-plate.
Crown-post: a vertical timber set centrally on a tie-beam and supporting a collar purlin braced to it longitudinally. In an open truss

lateral braces may rise to the collar-beam; in a closed truss they may descend to the tie-beam.
Hammerbeams: horizontal brackets projecting at wall-plate level like an interrupted tie-beam; the inner ends carry *hammerposts*, vertical timbers which support a purlin and are braced to a collar-beam above.
Kingpost: vertical timber set centrally on a tie- or collar-beam, rising to the apex of the roof to support a ridge-piece (cf. Strut).
Plate: longitudinal timber set square to the ground. *Wall-plate*: plate along the top of a wall which receives the ends of the rafters; cf. Purlin.
Principals: pair of inclined lateral timbers of a truss. Usually they support side purlins and mark the main bay divisions.
Purlin: horizontal longitudinal timber. *Collar purlin* or *crown plate*: central timber which carries collar-beams and is supported by crown-posts. *Side purlins*: pairs of timbers placed some way up the slope of the roof, which carry common rafters. *Butt* or *tenoned purlins* are tenoned into either side of the principals. *Through purlins* pass through or past the principal; they include *clasped purlins*, which rest on queenposts or are carried in the angle between principals and collar, and *trenched purlins* trenched into the backs of principals.
Queen-strut: paired vertical, or near-vertical, timbers placed symmetrically on a tie-beam to support side purlins.
Rafters: inclined lateral timbers supporting the roof covering. *Common rafters*: regularly spaced uniform rafters placed along the length of a roof or between principals. *Principal rafters*: rafters which also act as principals.
Ridge, ridge-piece: horizontal longitudinal timber at the apex supporting the ends of the rafters.
Sprocket: short timber placed on the back and at the foot of a rafter to form projecting eaves.
Strut: vertical or oblique timber between two members of a truss, not directly supporting longitudinal timbers.
Tie-beam: main horizontal transverse timber which carries the feet of the principals at wall level.
Truss: rigid framework of timbers at bay intervals, carrying the longitudinal roof timbers which support the common rafters.
Closed truss: with the spaces between the timbers filled, to form an internal partition.
See also Cruck, Wagon roof.

ROPE MOULDING: *see* Cable moulding.

ROSE WINDOW: circular window with tracery radiating from the centre. Cf. Wheel window.

ROTUNDA: building or room circular in plan.

ROUGHCAST: *see* Rendering.

ROVING BRIDGE: *see* Canals.

RUBBED BRICKWORK: *see* Gauged brickwork.

RUBBLE: masonry whose stones are wholly or partly in a rough state. *Coursed*: coursed stones with rough faces. *Random*: uncoursed stones in a random pattern. *Snecked*: with courses broken by smaller stones (snecks).

RUSTICATION: *see* 6d. Exaggerated treatment of masonry to give an effect of strength. The joints are usually recessed by V-section chamfering or square-section channelling (*channelled rustication*). *Banded rustication* has only the horizontal joints emphasized. The faces may be flat, but can be *diamond-faced*, like shallow pyramids, *vermiculated*, with a stylized texture like worm-casts, and *glacial* (frost-work), like icicles or stalactites.

SACRISTY: room in a church for sacred vessels and vestments.

SADDLEBACK ROOF: *see* 1c.

SALTIRE CROSS: with diagonal limbs.

SANCTUARY: area around the main altar of a church. Cf. Presbytery.

SANGHA: residence of Buddhist monks or nuns.

SARCOPHAGUS: coffin of stone or other durable material.

SAXO-NORMAN: transitional Romanesque style combining Anglo-Saxon and Norman features, current c. 1060–1100.

SCAGLIOLA: composition imitating marble.

SCALLOPED CAPITAL: see 1a.

SCOTIA: a hollow classical moulding, especially between tori (q.v.) on a column base (3b, 3f).

SCREEN: in a medieval church, usually at the entry to the chancel; see Rood (screen) and Pulpitum. A *parclose screen* separates a chapel from the rest of the church.

SCREENS or SCREENS PASSAGE: screened-off entrance passage between great hall and service rooms.

SECTION: two-dimensional representation of a building, moulding, etc., revealed by cutting across it.

SEDILIA (singular: sedile): seats for the priests (usually three) on the S side of the chancel.

SET-OFF: see Weathering.

SETTS: squared stones, usually of granite, used for paving or flooring.

SGRAFFITO: decoration scratched, often in plaster, to reveal a pattern in another colour beneath. *Graffiti*: scratched drawing or writing.

SHAFT: vertical member of round or polygonal section (1a, 3a). *Shaft-ring*: at the junction of shafts set *en delit* (q.v.) or attached to a pier or wall (1a).

SHEILA-NA-GIG: female fertility figure, usually with legs apart.

SHELL: thin, self-supporting roofing membrane of timber or concrete.

SHOULDERED ARCHITRAVE: see 4b.

SHUTTERING: see Concrete.

SILL: horizontal member at the bottom of a window or door frame; or at the base of a timber-framed wall into which posts and studs are tenoned (7).

SLAB BLOCK: see Multi-storey.

SLATE-HANGING: covering of overlapping slates on a wall. *Tile-hanging* is similar.

SLYPE: covered way or passage leading E from the cloisters between transept and chapter house.

SNECKED: see Rubble.

SOFFIT (*lit.* ceiling): underside of an arch (also called *intrados*), lintel, etc. *Soffit roll*: medieval roll moulding on a soffit.

SOLAR: private upper chamber in a medieval house, accessible from the high end of the great hall.

SOPRAPORTA: see Overdoor.

SOUNDING-BOARD: see Tester.

SPANDRELS: roughly triangular spaces between an arch and its containing rectangle, or between adjacent arches (5c). Also non-structural panels under the windows in a curtain-walled building.

SPERE: a fixed structure screening the lower end of the great hall from the screens passage. *Spere-truss*: roof truss incorporated in the spere.

SPIRE: tall pyramidal or conical feature crowning a tower or turret. *Broach*: starting from a square base, then carried into an octagonal section by means of triangular faces; and *splayed-foot*: variation of the broach form, found principally in the south-east, in which the four cardinal faces are splayed out near their base, to cover the corners, while oblique (or intermediate) faces taper away to a point (1c). *Needle spire*: thin spire rising from the centre of a tower roof, well inside the parapet: when of timber and lead often called a *spike*.

SPIRELET: see Flèche.

SPLAY: of an opening when it is wider on one face of a wall than the other.

SPRING or SPRINGING: level at which an arch or vault rises from its supports. *Springers*: the first stones of an arch or vaulting rib above the spring (2c).

SQUINCH: arch or series of arches thrown across an interior angle of a square or rectangular structure to support a circular or polygonal superstructure, especially a dome or spire (5a).

SQUINT: an aperture in a wall or through a pier usually to allow a view of an altar.

STAIRS: see 6c. *Dog-leg stair*: parallel flights rising alternately in opposite directions, without an open well. *Flying stair*: cantilevered from the walls of a stairwell, without newels; sometimes called a *Geometric* stair when the inner edge describes a curve. *Newel stair*: ascending round a central supporting newel (q.v.); called a *spiral stair* or *vice* when in a circular shaft, a *winder* when in a rectangular compartment. (Winder also applies to the steps on the turn.) *Well stair*: with flights round a square open well framed by newel posts. See also Perron.

STALL: fixed seat in the choir or chancel for the clergy or choir (cf. Pew). Usually with arm rests, and often framed together.

STANCHION: upright structural member, of iron, steel or reinforced concrete.

STANDPIPE TOWER: see Manometer.

STEAM ENGINES: *Atmospheric*: worked by the vacuum created when low-pressure steam is condensed in the cylinder, as developed by Thomas Newcomen. *Beam engine*: with a large pivoted beam moved in an oscillating fashion by the piston. It may drive a flywheel or be *non-rotative*. *Watt* and *Cornish*: single-cylinder; *compound*: two cylinders; *triple expansion*: three cylinders.

STEEPLE: tower together with a spire, lantern, or belfry.

STIFF-LEAF: type of E.E. foliage decoration. *Stiff-leaf capital see* 1b.

STOP: plain or decorated terminal to mouldings or chamfers, or at the end of hoodmoulds and labels (*label stop*), or stringcourses (5b, 6a); see also Headstop.

STOUP: vessel for holy water, usually near a door.

STRAINER: see Arch.

STRAPWORK: late C16 and C17 decoration, like interlaced leather straps.

STRETCHER: see Bond and 6e.

STRING: see 6c. Sloping member holding the ends of the treads and risers of a staircase. *Closed string*: a broad string covering the ends of the treads and risers. *Open string*: cut into the shape of the treads and risers.

STRINGCOURSE: horizontal course or moulding projecting from the surface of a wall (6d).

STUCCO: see Rendering.

STUDS: subsidiary vertical timbers of a timber-framed wall or partition (7).

STUPA: Buddhist shrine, circular in plan.

STYLOBATE: top of the solid platform on which a colonnade stands (3a).

SUSPENSION BRIDGE: see Bridge.

SWAG: like a festoon (q.v.), but representing cloth.

SYSTEM BUILDING: see Industrialized building.

TABERNACLE: canopied structure to contain the reserved sacrament or a relic; or architectural frame for an image or statue.

TABLE TOMB: memorial slab raised on free-standing legs.

TAS-DE-CHARGE: the lower courses of a vault or arch which are laid horizontally (2c).

TERM: pedestal or pilaster tapering downward, usually with the upper part of a human figure growing out of it.

TERRACOTTA: moulded and fired clay ornament or cladding.

TESSELLATED PAVEMENT: mosaic flooring, particularly Roman, made of *tesserae*, i.e. cubes of glass, stone, or brick.

TESTER: flat canopy over a tomb or pulpit, where it is also called a *sounding-board*.

TESTER TOMB: tomb-chest with effigies beneath a tester, either free-standing (tester with four or more columns), or attached to a wall (*half-tester*) with columns on one side only.

TETRASTYLE: see Portico.

THERMAL WINDOW: see Diocletian window.

THREE-DECKER PULPIT: see Pulpit.

TIDAL GATES: see Canals.

TIE-BEAM: see Roofs and 7.

TIERCERON: see Vault and 2c.

TILE-HANGING: see Slate-hanging.

TIMBER-FRAMING: see 7. Method of construction where the structural frame is built of interlocking timbers. The spaces are filled with non-structural material, e.g. *infill* of wattle and daub, lath and plaster, brickwork (known as *nogging*), etc. and may be covered by plaster, weatherboarding (q.v.), or tiles.

TOMB-CHEST: chest-shaped tomb, usually of stone. Cf. Table tomb, Tester tomb.

TORUS (plural: tori): large convex moulding usually used on a column base (3b, 3f).

TOUCH: soft black marble quarried near Tournai.

TOURELLE: turret corbelled out from the wall.

TOWER BLOCK: see Multi-storey.

TRABEATED: depends structurally on the use of the post and lintel. Cf. Arcuated.

TRACERY: openwork pattern of masonry or timber in the upper part of an opening. *Blind tracery* is tracery applied to a solid wall.
Plate tracery, introduced c. 1200, is the earliest form, in which shapes are cut through solid masonry (2a).
Bar tracery was introduced into England c. 1250. The pattern is formed by intersecting moulded ribwork continued from the mullions. It was especially elaborate during the Decorated period (q.v.). Tracery shapes can include circles, *daggers* (elongated ogee-ended lozenges), *mouchettes* (like daggers but with curved sides) and upright rectangular *panels*. They often have *cusps*, projecting points defining lobes or *foils* (q.v.) within the main shape: *Kentish* or *split-cusps* are forked (2b).
Types of bar tracery (*see* 2b) include *geometric(al)*: c. 1250–1310, chiefly circles, often foiled; *Y-tracery*: c. 1300, with mullions branching into a Y-shape; *intersecting*: c. 1300, formed by interlocking mullions; *reticulated*: early C14, net-like pattern of ogee-ended lozenges; *curvilinear*: C14, with uninterrupted flowing curves; *panel*: Perp, with straight-sided panels, often cusped at the top and bottom.

TRANSEPT: transverse portion of a church.

TRANSITIONAL: generally used for the phase between Romanesque and Early English (c. 1175–c. 1200).

TRANSOM: horizontal member separating window lights (2b).

TREAD: horizontal part of a step. The *tread end* may be carved on a staircase (6c).

TREFOIL: see Foil.

TRIFORIUM: middle storey of a church treated as an arcaded wall passage or blind arcade, its height corresponding to that of the aisle roof.

TRIGLYPHS (*lit.* three-grooved tablets): stylized beam-ends in the Doric frieze, with metopes between (3b).

TRIUMPHAL ARCH: influential type of Imperial Roman monument.

TROPHY: sculptured or painted group of arms or armour.

TRUMEAU: central stone mullion supporting the tympanum of a wide doorway. *Trumeau figure*: carved figure attached to it (cf. Column figure).

TRUMPET CAPITAL: see 1b.

TRUSS: braced framework, spanning between supports. *See also* Roofs and 7.

TUMBLING or TUMBLING-IN: courses of brickwork laid at right-angles to a slope, e.g. of a gable, forming triangles by tapering into horizontal courses (8a).

TUSCAN: see Orders and 3e.

TWO-DECKER PULPIT: see Pulpit.

TYMPANUM: the surface between a lintel and the arch above it or within a pediment (4a).

UNDERCROFT: usually describes the vaulted room(s), beneath the main room(s) of a medieval house. Cf. Crypt.

VAULT: arched stone roof (sometimes imitated in timber or plaster). For types see 2c.
Tunnel or *barrel vault*: continuous semicircular or pointed arch, often of rubble masonry.

Groin-vault: tunnel vaults intersecting at right angles. *Groins* are the curved lines of the intersections.

Rib-vault: masonry framework of intersecting arches (ribs) supporting *vault cells*, used in Gothic architecture. *Wall rib* or *wall arch*: between wall and vault cell. *Transverse rib*: spans between two walls to divide a vault into bays. *Quadripartite* rib-vault: each bay has two pairs of diagonal ribs dividing the vault into four triangular cells. *Sexpartite* rib-vault: most often used over paired bays, has an extra pair of ribs springing from between the bays. More elaborate vaults may include *ridge ribs* along the crown of a vault or bisecting the bays; *tiercerons*: extra decorative ribs springing from the corners of a bay; and *liernes*: short decorative ribs in the crown of a vault, not linked to any springing point. A *stellar* or *star* vault has liernes in star formation.

Fan-vault: form of barrel vault used in the Perp period, made up of halved concave masonry cones decorated with blind tracery.

VAULTING SHAFT: shaft leading up to the spring or springing (q.v.) of a vault (2c).

VENETIAN or SERLIAN WINDOW: derived from Serlio (4b). The motif is used for other openings.

VERMICULATION: *see* Rustication and 6d.

VESICA: oval with pointed ends.

VICE: *see* Stair.

VILLA: originally a Roman country house or farm. The term was revived in England in the C18 under the influence of Palladio and used especially for smaller, compact country houses. In the later C19 it was debased to describe any suburban house.

VITRIFIED: bricks or tiles fired to a darkened glassy surface.

VITRUVIAN SCROLL: classical running ornament of curly waves (4b).

VOLUTES: spiral scrolls. They occur on Ionic capitals (3c). *Angle volute*: pair of volutes, turned outwards to meet at the corner of a capital.

VOUSSOIRS: wedge-shaped stones forming an arch (5c).

WAGON ROOF: with the appearance of the inside of a wagon tilt; often ceiled. Also called *cradle roof*.

WAINSCOT: *see* Panelling.

WALL MONUMENT: attached to the wall and often standing on the floor. *Wall tablets* are smaller with the inscription as the major element.

WALL-PLATE: *see* Roofs and 7.

WALL-WALK: *see* Parapet.

WARMING ROOM: room in a religious house where a fire burned for comfort.

WATERHOLDING BASE: early Gothic base with upper and lower mouldings separated by a deep hollow.

WATERLEAF: *see* Enrichments and 3f.

WATERLEAF CAPITAL: Late Romanesque and Transitional type of capital (1b).

WATER WHEELS: described by the way water is fed on to the wheel. *Breastshot*: mid-height, falling and passing beneath. *Overshot*: over the top. *Pitchback*: on the top but falling backwards. *Undershot*: turned by the momentum of the water passing beneath. In a *water turbine*, water is fed under pressure through a vaned wheel within a casing.

WEALDEN HOUSE: type of medieval timber-framed house with a central open hall flanked by bays of two storeys, roofed in line; the end bays are jettied to the front, but the eaves are continuous (8a).

WEATHERBOARDING: wall cladding of overlapping horizontal boards.

WEATHERING or SET-OFF: inclined, projecting surface to keep water away from the wall below.

WEEPERS: figures in niches along the sides of some medieval tombs. Also called mourners.

WHEEL WINDOW: circular, with radiating shafts like spokes. Cf. Rose window.

WROUGHT IRON: *see* Cast iron.

INDEX OF ARCHITECTS, ARTISTS, PATRONS AND RESIDENTS

Names of architects and artists working in the area covered by this volume are given in *italic*. Entries for partnerships and group practices are listed after entries for a single name.

Also indexed here are names/titles of families and individuals (not of bodies or commercial firms) recorded in this volume as having commissioned architectural work or owned, lived in, or visited properties in the area. The index includes monuments to members of such families and other individuals where they are of particular interest.

A 1 337
Abacus Architects 559
Abbey Hanson Rowe 216, 551
Abbott & Co. 524, 543, 623
Abercrombie, Sir Patrick 93
Acanthus Clews 244, 293
Acivico 267, 279, 282
Adams, Charles 463
Adams, Edward 631, 706
Adams, L. 507
Adams, Thomas 722
Adderley, Sir Charles, 1st Lord Norton 275
Adderley, Hubert, 6th Lord Norton 276, 294
Adderley, Fr James 275, 276
Adelphi Architects 498, 562n.
Adkins, George Caleb 588
Adkins, James 638
Adlam, Rev. Joseph 310
ADP 190, 267, 348, 375
  see also Architects Design Partnership
Adshead, P. 638
Aedas/Aedas Architects 140, 144, 164, 168, 171, 374, 582
Aedas AHR 269, 343
AFL 692
Agar-Ellis, Fr J.J. 284
Aherne, W. de Lacy 61, 179, 308, 319, 320, 327, 328, 329, 330, 331, 332, 333, 403, 456, 764
Ahrends Burton Koralek 432
Aikman, William 679
Al-Abbas Associates 288
Aladdin Co. 415
Albert, Prince 48, 129, 132, 684
Aldin, Cecil 740
Alexander & Henman 44, 251, 605, Pl. 81
Allcock, Sydney 179

Allen, John W. 72, 148–9, 161, 602, 613, 614, 615
Allen, Michael 549
Allford Hall Monaghan Morris 90, 289, 630
Allies & Morrison 87, 170
Allin, C.J. Fox 582
Allom, Sir Charles 126–7
Alrewych, Nicholas de 642
Alsop, Will 89, 607
Alsop Architects 607
Alston family 779
Anderson, Arthur G. 293
Anderson, W.E. Ellery 64, 284–5, 474, 579
Andrews, Claude E.A. 322
Andrews, F.B. 65, 78, 249, 294, 301, 307, 310, 357, 427, 444, 460, 584
Andrews & Hazzard 581
Andrews & Hickman 287, 302, 322
Andrews (F.B.) & Son 249
Anglo Holt 765
Anning Bell, Robert see Bell, Robert Anning
Ansell, Edward 462
Ansells' Brewery Architect's Dept 461
Anstruther-Gough-Calthorpe family 358
APEC/APEC Architects 122–3, 167, 173, 190, 304, 307, 308, 337, 409, 411, 520, 775
Arc-Hi-Structure 581
Archer, Andrew 111
Archer, Oswald 340, 681
Archer, Thomas 19, 105, 111, 114–15, 431, Pl. 33
Archial 234
Architects' Co-Partnership 284
Architects Design Partnership 370, 371, 372
  see also ADP

INDEX OF ARCHITECTS, ETC.

Architype 85, 701, 704, 711, 751
Arden family 465
Arderne, John 308
Ardin & Brookes & Partners 633
Arkell, Daniel 45, 181, 230, 238, 326, 428, 687
Armstrong, C.T. 677
Armstrong, John Ramsay 75, 78, 270, 310, 350, 352, 353, 355, 365, 426, 432
Armstrong, Walter Y. 136, 145n., 196, 344
Arnett, Patricia 606
ARP Associates 605
Arrol & Snell 91, 733, 742
Artec 168
Arup, Ove 479
Arup Associates 86, 369, 371
Asbury, Francis 658
Ash, John W. 687
Ashbee, C.R. 59, 63, 678n., 743
Ashcroft see Ashes
Ashes (or Ashcroft), William 111
Ashford, T.M. 84, 87, 334–5, 348, 390
Ashford, W.H. 278, 311, 428
Ashley & Newman 66, 85, 130, 189
Ashwell, Richard 237
Askew, Rev. Francis 237, 420
Associated Architects 84, 86, 88, 130, 131, 133, 135, 140, 160, 161, 171, 172, 177, 178, 179, 183, 184, 189, 191, 201, 205, 210, 232, 239, 277, 344, 352, 369, 371, 372, 374, 375, 390, 405, 415, 421, 428, 429, 535, 577, 612, 633, 639, 695, Pl. 134
Atkins 136
Atkins & Walters 751
Atkinson, George 370
Atkinson, Robert 75, 367, 370–1, Pl. 114
Atkinson's Brewery Building Dept 785
Atkinson's Brewery Surveyor's Department 718
Attwood, James 572
Attwood, Thomas 43, 48n., 106, 125, 140, 395, 404
Aukett Swanke 191
Aumonier, William 49, 132
Austin, Herbert 415
Austin Motor Co. 416
Austin-Smith:Lord 88, 90, 207, 683, 687, 688, 694
Avern, Ernest 304
Avery, Neil 742
Avery, Samuel 152
Axiom 719
Axis Design Collective 232, 414
Aye, U 414
AZMPL 136

Baart Harries Newall 90, 628, 652, 659, 775
Bache, Nicholas 679, Pl. 45
Backler, Joseph 25, 473

Bacon, Francis 579
Bacon, John Jun. 25, 396, 650
Bacon, Percy 664
Bacon, Robert 564
Bacon (Percy) Bros 496
Badham, R. 396
Bagot family 270
Bagot, Rev. Egerton Arden 270
Baguley, G.J. 678
Bailey, Brian 720
Bailey, F.E.F. 51, 618, 633, 634, 636, 637, 642, 646
Bailey, P.H. Ashby 65, 510
Bailey & McConnal 47, 72, 326, 516, 554, 571, 626, 631, 634, 635, 636, 637, 638, 645, 646
Baily, E.H. 25, 244, 321
Baily Garner 290
Bajaj, R.S. 250
Baker, Benjamin (architect) 41, 47, 72, 654, 663–4, 665, 666, 668
Baker, Benjamin (sculptor) 596
Baker, F.C. 150
Baker, J.P. 664, 667
Baker, Robert 496
Baker, T.W. 333
Baker, William 20–1, 24, 670, 677, 690, 732, 733, 734–5, Pl. 2
Baker Goodchild 647
Baker (Ronald), Humphries & Goodchild 92, 493, 719, 752
Baker (Frank) & Sons 627
Bakewell, Robert 115
Ball, Joseph Lancaster 41, 51, 59, 60, 61, 62, 63, 72, 74, 108, 139–40, 248, 251, 258, 260, 277, 285, 286, 338, 340, 351, 358, 364, 373, 379, 385, 388, 391, 394, 397, 400, 712, Pl. 12
see also Lethaby & Ball
Ball, Peter 116
Ball (J.L.) & Goddard 59, 251
Ballantine & Gardiner 321
Ballantine (James) & Son 440
Ballard, W.E. 239
Ballard, W.J. 183
Ballard & Mantel 207
BAM Design 775
Bankart, George 368, 373, 398, 399
Banks, Edward 35, 37, 38, 40, 48, 54, 664, 670, 684, 688, 691, 692, 709, 715, 716, 720, 727, 729–30, 746, 747, 748, 751–2, Pls. 70, 82
Banks, Thomas (brewer) 719
Banks, Thomas (sculptor) 25, 513
Bannington, E.E. 668
Bannister (Brian) & Associates 444
Bannister (Brian) Projects 250
Bantock, Baldwin 705–6
Barber, W.H. 156
Barfield, Samuel 134, 140, 339, 403n., 424–6, 629
Barkentin & Krall 491
Barker, George (developer) 260
Barker, George (engineer) 459–60

INDEX OF ARCHITECTS, ETC.

Barnes, Bishop Ernest 77, 116, 117, 291
Barnes, Richard J. 644
Barney, Joseph 678
Barnish, Leonard 741
Barnsley, Ernest 60, 364
Barnsley, G.R. 452
Barnsley, John 382
Barnsley Hewett & Mallinson 608
  see also BHM
Barnsley (John) & Sons 333, 380, 385
Baron Design 178
Barratt, J.N. 655
Barratt & Jones 461
Barratt, Shaw, Wheeler 642
Barratt, Shaw & Wheeler 312
Barrett, Oliver O'Connor 379
Barron (William) & Sons 591, 599
Barrowcliff & Allcock 67, 484
Barry, Sir Charles 36, 106, 116, 125, 132, 152, 374, 377, 383
Barton Fellows Ltd 374
Barton Willmore 774
Basevi, George 621
Bateman family 770
Bateman, C.E. 60, 61, 62, 63, 64, 66, 71, 77, 155, 158, 164, 171, 217, 259, 278, 286, 293n., 313, 314, 315, 318–19, 321, 328, 332, 382, 388, 392, 420, 429, 437, 438, 440, 441, 442, 443, 450, 453, 454, 457, 458, 459, 460, 474, 586, 595, 621, 624, 763, 769, 770, 773, Pls. 99, 118
Bateman, John Jones 39, 51, 53, 54, 55, 108, 144, 171, 308, 313, 318, 358, 378, 381, 385, 389, 402, 404, 430, 582, 589, 743, 744, 770
Bateman, Joseph 23, 52, 298, 338, 384, 461
Bateman, Simeon 547
Bateman, Thomas 23, 26, 384, 461
Bateman & Bateman 60, 71, 186, 202, 235, 236, 241, 318, 421, 447, 453, 462, 594, 774
Bateman (J.J.) & Benjamin Corser 37, 43, 44, 197, 200, 385, 386, 393, 394, 483, 737, 783
Bateman (Joseph) & George Drury 49, 53, 183, 186, 211, 216, 307, 313, 327, 383, 385, 386, 388, 393, 565n., 566, 612, 758
Bateman & Hunt 131
Batemans 45, 73, 80, 84, 209, 236, 264, 271, 284, 310, 313, 396, 401, 421–41, 423, 450, 465, 535, 584, 598, 658, 664, 760, 765, 774, Pl. 110
Bates, Ernest 43, 681
Bates, Harry 49, 131
Batson, Brendan 613
Bawden, Edward 124
Baxter, Joseph 338
Baylis, A.W. 410

BDG 201
BDP 85, 305, 369, 375, 384, 684, 775
  see also Building Design Partnership
Beach, T. Stanley 514, 521, 570n., 576
Beard (J. Stanley) & Bennett 335
Beck, Fred T. 56, 62, 63, 64, 69, 71, 501–2, 508, 510, 542, 556, 576, 579, 589, 622, 624, 642, 655, 661, 670, 671, 672, 676, 677, 678, 681, 685–6, 687, 691, 702, 703, 717, 718, 724, 725, 726, 727, 730, 734, 744, 749–50, 751, 752
Beckett, Henry 706
Beckley, Josiah 48, 495, 497, 498
Beddard, Jeremiah 557
Beddard, Joseph 544, 557
Beddard, William 557
Bedford, Eric 383
Beebee (decorator) 650
Beech, Arthur 725
Beech, J.B. 731
Bell, Daniel 513
Bell, Robert Anning 368
Bell & Almond 733
Bennett, Alderman T.E. 482n.
Bennett, J. & W. (sculptors) 244
Bennett & Son (sculptors) 396
Bennett (S.) & Son (builders) 491–2, 560
Bennett (T.P.) & Son (architects) 146
Benniman Design & Build 373
Bennison, Samuel 465
Benoy 88, 138, 169, 170, 781
Benoy (Gordon) & Partners 317
Benslyn, W.T. 75, 79, 81, 177, 405, 585, 612, Pl. 108
Benson, W.A.S. 739
Beresford Pite, Arthur see Pite, Arthur Beresford
Berman Guedes Stretton 371
Bermingham, Peter de 137
Best, Philip L. 507
Best & Lloyd 153
Bew, Dr 262
Bewlay, Ernest C. 62, 71, 79, 196, 389, 443, 516, 543, 617
  see also Cossins, Peacock & Bewlay; Peacock & Bewlay
BGS 95, 144
BHM/BHM Architects Ltd 85, 646
  see also Barnsley Hewett & Mallinson
Bickerdike Allen 371
Bicknell & Hamilton 90, 206
Biddle, G. 244
Bidlake, George 36, 38, 39, 43, 46, 47, 49, 51, 55, 59, 61, 252, 454, 501, 557, 558, 634, 635, 668, 671, 695, 696, 698, 701, 706, 712, 716, 718, 736, 742, 747
Bidlake, W.H. 60, 63, 64, 78, 108, 144, 162, 214, 218, 235n., 242, 245, 250, 251, 259, 286, 290, 296, 301, 305, 329, 332, 335–6, 338,

Bidlake, W.H. *cont.* 340, 350, 358, 373, 382–3, 393, 423, 438, 441, 458, 459, 461, 547, 624, 649–50, 755, 758, 759, 766, 775–6, Pls.64, 66, 98
Bidlake (George) & T.H. Fleeming 44, 47, 509, 593–4, 631, 635, 698, 721, 729, 738, 746
Bidlake (W.H.) & W.J. Knight 215, 441
Bidlake & Lovatt 40, 543
Billingsley, Douglas 83, 510, 745
Bindley, S.E. 614
Birch, C.B. 49, 488
Birch, Frank 79, 689, 721
Birch & Caulfield 637, 648
Bird, Francis 20, 297
Birkenhead, G.A. 204
Birmingham (de) family 123
Birmingham City Architect/Architect's Department 130, 169, 171, 177, 207, 233, 267, 306, 316, 317, 341
Birmingham City Council 117
Birmingham City Council Urban Design Department 85, 125, 191, 290
Birmingham City Engineer and Surveyor 152, 257, 261, 292, 334
Birmingham City Planning Department 288
Birmingham City Surveyor 234, 256, 291
Birmingham Department of Planning and Architecture 126, 408
Birmingham Design Services 268
Birmingham Guild 165, 208, 371, 398, 442, 555
Birmingham School of Architecture Live Projects Dept 264
Bissell, William 744
Blackall, Pippa 236
Blair, William 644
Blanchard (B.W.) & Partners 236
Bland, J.G. 56, 57, 177, 180, 265, 300–1, 309, 782, Pl.91
Bland (J.G.) & J.A. Cossins 51, 385, 782
BLB/BLB Architects 206, 694
Blomfield, Sir Arthur 335
Blomfield, Reginald 646
Bloomer, Clarence A. 72, 573, 574
Bloomer, Harry 783
Bloomer, William 72, 573
Bloomer & Gough 431, 783
Bloomer (Harry) Partnership 647
Bloomer (Harry) & Son 384
Bloomer Tweedale 716
Blore, Edward 38, 473
Blore, Robert II 710
Blount, Gilbert 39, 597
Blow, Detmar 62, 722, 724
Blow (Detmar) & Fernand Billerey 722, 723n.
Blower, S. 725
Bloxam, M.H. 123

Bloye, William 73, 93, 129, 152, 156, 157, 158–9, 163, 165, 169, 188, 227, 240n., 246, 256, 260, 264, 265, 267, 272, 279, 283, 284, 289, 297, 299, 342, 343, 346, 351, 353, 370, 372, 375, 382, 400, 401, 417, 423n., 427, 435, 441, 482, 484, 488, 575, 784, Pl.106
bluegreen 190
Blun, John 111
Blunt, J. 659
Blunt, James 454
BM3 240
Boden & Grove 475
Bodley, G.F. 419, 603
Boehm, Sir Joseph Edgar 762
Bohn, Peter 248, 262
Bond, Frederick Bligh 64, 65, 284–5, 597
Bond Bryan 189, 190, 401, 607, 608, 684, 698, 775
Bonham, Akram 66, 288
Bonham (Paul) & Associates 147, 347, 385, 443
Bonham Seager/Bonham Seager Associates 161, 180
Bonney, W.A. 501
Booker, Rev. Luke 473
Booth (sculptor, Nottingham) 473
Booth, Arthur 599
Boswell, George A. 423, 689
Boswell (J.V.) & Co. 423
Boswell & Tomlins 724
Bosworth, Charles W. 239, 240
Botham, J.R. 40, 57, 165, 196, 385
Botteley & Chaffer 605
Boulton (carving) 321, 537, 604, 625, 679
Boulton, Anne 254
Boulton, Matthew 25, 93, 169, 178, 242, 243, 251, 253–4
Boulton, Matthew Robinson (son) 254
Boulton, M.P.W. (grandson) 246, 255
Boulton, R.L. 221
Boulton (R.L.) & Sons/Boultons (carving) 49, 128, 277, 597, 603, 683
Boulton & Watt 577, 587
Bourne, Swaine 247, 322, 365, 407, 513, 581, 596, 655
Bourne, William 35, 36, 37, 38, 45, 55, 246, 472n., 474, 483, 486, 488, 489, 490, 508, 523, 530, 540, 570n., 575
Bourne (Swaine) & Son 513
Bournville Architects 203, 293
Bournville Trust Architectural Department 521
Bournville Village Trust Architects 270
Bournville Village Trust Architect's Department 420
Bournville Village Trust Architectural Services 351
see also BVT Architects
Bowden, George 578, 584, 585

INDEX OF ARCHITECTS, ETC. 817

Bowden (G.) & Son 581
Bowen, John 58, 307, 329
Bower, Benjamin 66, 76, 241, 402, 408, 417, 429
Bower, S.E. Dykes see Dykes Bower, S.E.
Bower Mattin 603, 605
Bowles Whittick Young 535
Bowyer (Bob) Associates 146
Boyd, Thomas 292
Boyd (Hugh) Associates 432
Boylan, Willie 720
BPN/BPN Architects 86, 182, 183, 184, 201, 305, 493, 613
    see also Bryant Priest Newman
Brabbs, Michael 411
Bradbury, John 687, 752
Braddock, Thomas & Peter H. 692
Bradford, George Bridgeman, 2nd Earl of 636, 771, 773
Bradford, Henry 200
Bradford, Stanley W. 628, 661
Bradley family 545, 551
Bradley, Gabriel 551
Bradley, George and Richard 474
Bradley, Horace G. 267, 302, 317, 404, 586
Bradley, John 551
Bradley, Richard 560
Bradley, William 524n.
Bradley (John) & Co. 495
Bradney, Thomas 734
Bragg Bros 762
Brakspear, Harold 513
Bramah, John Joseph 193
Branson, George 386
Brashier (Michael) Associates 317
Brassington, Mr 229, 434
Bray, Thomas 283
Brett, Lionel 686
Brettell, W.H. 573
Brevitt, A.P. 37, 38, 44, 47, 51, 52, 55, 502, 510, 542, 543, 544, 590, 598, 649, 651, 652, 654, 686, 687, 689, 693, 701
Bridge, William 502
Bridgeman 597, 625, 730
Bridgeman, George see Bradford, 2nd Earl of
Bridgeman, Sir John (d. 1710) and Lady (Mary) 20, 220, 770–1, 772, 773
Bridgeman, Sir John (d. 1747) 773
Bridgeman, John (sculptor, C20) 93, 303, 433, 655
Bridgeman, Robert 117, 580, 596, 763
Bridgeman (Robert) & Sons/Bridgemans 68, 150, 301, 363, 364, 396, 419, 443, 547, 548, 560, 595, 603, 623, 627, 650, 651, 655, 677, 703, 710, 750, 770, 782
Bridgens, Richard 24, 222, 224n., 245, Pl. 39
Bridges, Samuel 783

Bridgwater, Alan 262, 292, 401, 422, 483
Bridgwater, Derek 696
Bridgwater, J. Percival 301, 770
Briggs, Ella 82, 696, 701
Briggs, Frank 747
Briggs & Everall 606
Bright, John 48n.
Bright, Philip 383
Briley, John 382
Brindley, James 28, 414, 492, 577, 587, 588, 718, 736, 748
Brindley & Foster 361
Briscoe family 525
Bristow, M.H. 177
Bristow (J. Alan) & Partner 316
British Railways, London Midland Region 90, 136
Broad, Peter 291
Broadbank, S. 606
Broadbent, F. 293
Broadway Malyan 90, 195, 376, 415
Brock, J.C. 679
Brock, Thomas 156, Pl. 1
Brockholes, Thomas 679
Brocki, L. 604
Brocklehurst, A. 655
Brocklehurst (Arthur) & Co. 625, 642
Broderick, Laurence 138
Bromby, Gertrude 272
Bromilow, Francis E. 76, 410, 525
Bromilow, While & Smeeton 92, 176, 262, 289, 340, 403, 416, 422–3, 441, 442, 758
Bromley & Watkins 70, 229, 685
Bromsgrove Guild 194, 259, 266, 339, 361, 368, 555, 654
Bromwich, Fr Andrew 262
Brooke, D. 542
Brooke, Donald 301, 757
Brooke, Oswald D. 345
Brooks, William 24, 472, Pl. 40
Brophy (Frank) Associates 185, 558
Brophy Riaz 426
Browett, Eric 150
Brown, Charles (Brownhill Hayward Brown) 92, 263
Brown, Charles (Denys Hinton & Partners; Brown Matthews etc.) 91, 92, 124, 303, 581, 623, 626, 733, 755
Brown, Ford Madox 739
Brown, H. Marcus 79, 520, 688, 704, 718
Brown, John 620
Brown, John Thomas 578
Brown (H. Marcus) & Lewis 688
Brown Matthews 626
Brown (George) & Sons 498, 528
Browne Smith Baker 584
Brownhill, Peter 235, 263
Brownhill Hayward Brown 120, 235, 263, 438, 487, 637, 660, 698
Brownsword, J.J. 686
Bruce-Joy, Albert 48n.

Brumby, Robert 731
Bryans (plasterwork) 585
Bryans, Herbert 244
Bryans & Webb 741
Bryant, Chris 431
Bryant Priest Newman 84, 180, 197, 237, 239, 376, 401, 433, 479, 575, 607, 608
  see also BPN
Bryants 231
Bubb, J.G. 697
Buckland, Herbert Tudor 61, 67, 73n., 74, 217, 239, 263, 267, 271, 273, 278, 279, 289, 290, 293, 295, 306, 337, 341, 344, 382, 393, 404, 405, 423, 429
Buckland (H.T.) & William Haywood 58, 84, 267, 279, 355, 367, 371, 381, 415, 420, 758, 783n.
Buckland (H.T.) & Edward Haywood-Farmer 45, 60–1, 67, 71, 196, 218, 267, 335, 345, 370, 382, 387, 393, 447, 454
Bucknall Austin 234
Bucknall & Donnelly 645
Budd, Kenneth 93, 147, 197, 207
Budd, Oliver 197
Building Design Partnership 499
  see also BDP
Building Design Partnership/Leslie Jones Architects 88
Building Design Practice 87, 591
Building & Urban Design Associates 92, 215
Bull, Hubert 85, 189
Bullivant, R.A. 759
Bulloch, Archibald 630
Bullock, Edwin 259
Bunce, J.T. 387
Bunce, Kate 194, 362, 363
Bunce, Myra 194
Bunch, A.C. 74, 448, 762
Bunting, John 361
Bunton, Kenneth Gordon 281
Burchard, Christopher 370
Burdwood & Mitchell 81, 205
Burgess, H.O. 490, 520
Burke & Co. 602–3
Burley, Paul 313, 730
Burlison & Grylls 42, 244, 361, 548, 603, 621–2, 655, 756
Burnaby, Col. 48, 117
Burne-Jones, Sir Edward 116, 123, 248, 293, 301, 443, 739n., Pls. 75, 76
Burnett & Eprile 148
Burr, Arthur W. 519
Burrell Foley Fischer 171
Burritt, Elihu 30, 243
Burton (Montague) Architect's Department 342
Buss, A.E. 441, 622
Butcher, Matthew J. 186, 235, 267, 454, 455, 461

Butler, A.T. 69, 71, 72, 73, 75, 76, 81, 483, 485, 486, 487, 488, 489–90, 498, 501, 503, 505, 507, 514, 516, 517, 519, 520, 522, 525, 526, 531, 551, 552, 553, 554, 555, 556, 558, 561, 570, 571, 572, 573, 574, 592, 614, 640, 686, 692, 696, 700, 704, 708, Pl. 68
Butler, Bertram 742
Butler, Edmund 61, 437, 456
Butler, James 485, 692
Butler, William 172, 695
Butler, A.T. & Bertram 75, 81, 483, 488, 498, 499, 501, 521, 540, 555, 569, 693, 715, 720, 721, 735, 748, 749
Butler (Bertram) & Co. 690, 715, 726
Butler, Jackson & Edmonds 484
Butler (A.T.) & Partners 484, 572
Butler (Bertram) & Partners 196
Butler Wones 719
Butler Wones & Partners 537
Butterfield, William 36, 37, 38, 55, 378, 424
Butterworth, Harry 325
Button, Chester 74, 75, 578, 582, 583, 584, 586, Pl. 113
BVT Architects 352, 420, 432, 433
Bye, Albert 256, 338, 611
Bye (Albert), Simms & Gifford 79, 573

Cachemaille-Day, N.F. 91, 441, 751
Cadbury family 15, 349, 353
Cadbury, Barrow 202
Cadbury, George 60, 108, 210n., 348–50, 351, 353, 418, 420, 421, 429, 431–2
Cadbury, George Jun. 432
Cadbury, Richard 202, 323, 333, 349, 356
Cadbury Bros Architects' Department 356
Cadbury-Brown, H.T. 85, 374, 655
Caine, Osmund 441, 578
calderpeel 239, 282, 414, 420
Cale, G.H. Vernon 69, 633
Callear, R.P. 713
Calthorpe barons 393
Calthorpe, 1st Baron (d. 1798) 358, 360
Calthorpe, 3rd Baron (d. 1851) 36, 106, 358, 362, 384
Calthorpe, 4th Baron (d. 1868) 48
Calthorpe, 5th Baron (d. 1893) 376
Calthorpe, 6th Baron (d. 1910) 365
Camm, Florence 64, 246, 247, 266, 491, 501, 516, 540, 580, 651, 678, 725, Pl. 68
Camm, Robert 64, 246, 266, 491, 651, 678
Camm, Thomas William 42, 64, 92, 246, 247, 248, 249, 265, 266, 281,

475, 493, 500, 501, 506, 508, 513, 514, 516, 520, 522, 525, 527, 540, 541, 542, 550, 555, 560, 563, 572, 577, 578, 579, 580, 648, 651, 665, 678, 725, 737, 782
Camm, Walter 64, 246, 266, 281, 491, 501, 506, 514, 560, 651, 678
Camm Bros 345, 603, 784
Camm & Co. 230, 246, 249, 316, 363, 508, 524, 527, 556, 577, 579, 678, 784
Campbell, M. 187
Campbell, P. Colin 728
Capita 182
Capita Symonds 166, 732
Capronnier 396
Carding, J. 719
Carillion 166
Carillion TPS 705
Carnegie, Andrew 365
Caröe & Partners 703
Caröe & Passmore 672, 676
Carpenter, Andrew 370
Carpenter, R.C. 35, 106, 362
Carrick, Peter 91, 420
Carter, Abraham 545
Carter, J. Coates 474
Carter, Tony 591
Carters (tiles, Poole) 71, 585
Cartland family 318
Cartland, John Howard 318
Cartwright, Thomas I 20, 296, 676
Cartwright, Thomas (engineer) 410
Caruso St John 89, 629, Pl. 135
Casolini, Henry 642
Cassidy, John 73, 555
Casson, Sir Hugh 367
Casson (Sir Hugh) & Neville Conder 85, 367, 369, 373
Casson, Conder & Partners 370, 371
Catalyst Regeneration 288
Catesby, Robert 556
Catley, Thomas 215
Cattell, Keith 746
Catterson-Smith, Robert 286
Cazeley, William 387–8
Cemka Group 455
Cetti, Howard 485
Chadney, R.W.S. 397
Chadwick family 463
Chadwick, John (C18) 464
Chadwick, John de Heley Mavesyn (C19) 464
Challen, S.W. 184
Chamberlain, John Henry 37, 41, 46, 48, 55, 57, 58, 66, 107–8, 133–4, 140, 160, 166, 177, 182, 196, 215, 234, 278, 289, 328, 333–4, 337, 358, 378, 381, 382, 384, 386, 387, 388, 390, 397, 401, 403, 424, 430, 431, 578, 615, Pl. 85
Chamberlain, Joseph 46, 55, 107, 127–8, 140, 181, 333–4, 365, 368, 395

Chamberlain, Richard 390
Chamberlain, Walter 398
Chamberlin, John 706
Chambers, Sir William 220
Champneys, Basil 63, 108, 595
Chance, Sir James Timmins 582
Chance Bros 5, 42, 341, 542, 547, 566, 577, 580, 590, 603, 622, 665
Chaney, Walter 199
Chantrey, Sir Francis 25, 133, 244, 245, 549, Pl. 39
Chaplin, Graham 678
Chaplin, T. 117
Chapman, Albert 82, 85, 671, 684, 705, 713, 723, 729, 731, 735
Chapman, Frank W. 724
Chapman, John 476, 478
Chapman Taylor 148, 692
Charles I, King 711
Charles II, King 653, 677
Charles, E.J. 455
Charles, F.W.B. 94, 311, 711
Chatwin, Anthony 91, 114, 115–16, 122, 311, 328, 359, 360, 395, 396, 408, 419, 578, 580, 678
Chatwin, J.A. 32, 36, 38, 44, 49, 51, 52, 54, 56, 64, 108, 111, 122–3, 137, 143, 145n., 154, 161, 165, 176, 184, 197, 202, 214, 218–19, 227, 230, 232, 233, 235–6, 244, 246, 258, 264, 265, 266, 276, 291, 294, 296, 301, 310, 312, 315, 320–32, 326, 335, 345, 358, 359–60, 361, 363, 381, 383, 386, 388, 393, 395–6, 407, 413, 434, 442, 517, 533–4, 560, 579, 683, 685, 758, 760, 761, 764, 765, Pls. 63, 84
Chatwin, John 87, 170
Chatwin, Philip B. 63, 70, 77, 91, 108, 114, 116, 122, 152, 220, 246, 247, 252, 291, 301, 311, 320–1, 322, 360, 361, 362, 363, 380, 396, 408, 413, 420, 463, 472n., 527, 534n., 580, Pl. 88
Chatwin (J.A.) & Son 63, 70, 215, 217, 247, 252, 404–5, 451, 632
Chavasse, Joseph R. 720
Chavasse, W. 698
Cheadle, W.H. 544
Cheney, R.W. 394
Cherrington & Stainton 79, 178, 208, 292, 474, 488, 489, 521, 570n.
Cheshire, John 218, 280, 620
Chesterton, G.K. 274
Chesworth, Bob 543
Chettle, F.H. 698
Chetwoods Architects 324
Chinn (Barry) Landscape Architects 777–8
Chittenden, Thomas 709
Chrestien, John 282
Christian, Ewan 37, 55, 407, 620–1, 657, 672–6, 697
Christie (cinema organ-builder) 562

INDEX OF ARCHITECTS, ETC.

Christie, John 80, 201
Christophers, John 84, 307
Clanricarde, Hubert de Burgh-Canning, 2nd Marquess of 456
'Clare' 770
Clark, J. Percy 63, 81, 502, 503, 567, 590, 635, 668, 751
Clark, Robert Lindsey 584
Clarke, Derek 209, 273, 436
Clarke, E.F.C. 37, 597, 632
Clarke, Rev. Henry 419, 420
Clarke, James S. 405
Clarke, Joseph 770
Clarke, Michael 121
Clarke, Richard 41, 237
Clarke, Sir Samuel 21, 610
Clarke, Somers Jun. 37, 602–3
Clarke, T. Chatfeild 53, 389
Clarke Baker 561
Clarkson, John 716
Clarson, Arthur S. 67, 467
Clavering, J. Cecil 81, 263, 455, Pl. 112
Clayton & Bell 42, 194, 361, 523, 534, 537, 558, 622, 664, 782
Clear, Thomas (alias Smith) 770
Cleland & Hayward 79, 456, 460, 685, 691, 715
Clements, W.S. 137, 598, 685, 752, 785
Clewer, Selby 351
Clifford Tee & Gale 86, 187, 412, 432, 712, 750, 785
Close, H.F.B. 641
Clowes, Josiah 28, 308, 410
Clutton, Henry 363
Coade stone 488
Cockerell, C.R. 157, 358
Coda Group Architects 562
Cole (J.C.T.) & Partners 514, 527
Collett, Charles H. 189, 240, 290, 317, 586
Collier, L. 453
Collier, Tony 110
Collier (Tony) & Associates 722
Collier & Davies 239
Collier & Plucknett 129
Collins, H.A. 68, 612
Collins, J.M. 90
Collis, G.R. 362
Colmore family 159
Colmore, Charles 175
Colmore, William Barwick Cregoe 159
Colton, W.R. 129
Comber, R.J.H. 541
Comper, Sir Ninian 77–8, 508, 523
Compton, Sean 731
Conacher (organ-builder) 475
Conder, Neville 369, 374
 see also Casson & Conder
Conder Projects 564
Conner, Angela 189
Consarc 191
Constable, John 762

Convention Centre Partnership 168, 169
Cooke, Edward 718
Cooke, S.N. 70, 73, 75, 136, 137, 139, 140, 155, 157, 158, 163, 195, 205, 215, 236, 268, 273, 291, 314, 387, 391, 415, 420, 430, 433, 436, 566, 579, 777, Pl. 109
Cooke (S.N.) & Partners 79, 84, 92, 94, 139, 233, 234, 235, 268, 275, 447, 564, 567
Cooke (S.N.) & W.N. Twist 73, 165, 203, 634
Coombs, Ivan 527
Coonan, Rory 156
Cooper, Captain Frank 479
Cooper, Henry 631
Cooper, J. Brian 279
Cooper, Thomas 135
 see also Henman & Cooper
Cooper-Abbs, George 266, 502, 737
Copeland, William 195
Copnall, E. Bainbridge 372, 489
Coppinger (Siobhan) & Fiona Peever 140
Cordin, R.E. 636
Cornfield & Walsh 642
Cornwell, W.J. 575
Corser, Ben 206
Corser, Benjamin 108, 206, 782, 783
 see also Bateman & Corser
Corstorphine & Wright 161, 517, 758, 759n.
Coslett, George 484, 489, 532, 540
Cossins, Jethro A. 44, 47, 51, 56, 94, 108, 135, 187, 196, 199, 234, 359, 365n., 390, 448, 495–6, 651
Cossins (Jethro A.) & F. Barry Peacock 64, 66, 126, 135, 234, 304, 430
Cossins (J.A.), Peacock & Bewlay 45, 61, 67, 108, 129, 158, 177, 181, 202, 239, 274, 298, 325, 328, 351, 373, 386, 387, 388, 389, 411, 412, 427, 443, 457, 460, 461, 484, 495, 543, 571, 686
 see also Bland & Cossins
Cotterell (Alan) Partnership 544, 549, 692, 752
Cotterill, Jack 560
Cotton, George (C19) 298
Cotton, George T. (C20) 286
Cotton, Jack 151n.
Cotton, John 41, 505, 547, 570n., 625, 755, 784
Cotton, Ballard & Blow 136, 147, 148, 150, 153, 204, 384
Cotton & Bidlake 547
Cottrell & Vermeulen 315
Couch, Richard Oakley 533
Coudrey, T.W. 201
Coventry Churches Housing Association 83, 561
Cowan, D. 248, 514
Cowlishaw, C.G. 67, 592, 714

INDEX OF ARCHITECTS, ETC.

Cowper, E.A. 136
Cowper, Jonathan 343
Cox, Mr 217
Cox, David 353, 402
Cox, G.A. 162, 203, 294, 783
Cox, George Bernard 78, 92, 120, 220, 236, 241, 248, 260, 262, 263, 273, 274, 301, 314, 345, 364, 405, 411, 417, 426, 427, 443, 445, 543, 698, 731, 782
Cox, George Henry 47, 252, 548, 585, 648, Pl. 88
Cox, Thomas 54, 589, 603
Cox & Silk 208
Cox, Sons, Buckley & Co. 779
CPMG 267, 781
Crallan, H.P. 497
Crane, C. Howard 84, 415
Crane, Walter 49, 131
Cranston, James 36, 40, 46, 221, 646, 660, 662
Craven Dunnill 134, 240, 325, 600
Craze, Romilly 194, 433
Creighton, William 245
Cremin, Daniel 624
Cresswell (builder, Walsall) 661
Cresswell, J. (builder, Birmingham) 430
Creswick, Benjamin 63, 68, 70, 78, 107, 147–8, 234, 251, 339, 340, 352, 355, 356, 420
Crewe, Bertie 150, 209
Crews (Desmond T.) & Partners 83–4, 92, 524, 525, 534, 744
Crickmer, C.M. 62, 722, 724
Critchell, Martin 570
Crook, Richard 775
Cropper, Edward 185, 328
Crosbie, L. Stanley 584
Cross, F.W. 638
Crosskey, H.W. 106
Crouch, Joseph 61, 437, 456
Crouch (Joseph) & Edmund Butler 41, 61, 65, 67, 68, 69, 71, 147, 150, 179, 227, 233, 237, 249, 258, 259, 261, 265, 274, 303, 317, 329, 330, 343, 382, 444, 452, 455–6, 458, 462, 490, 726
Crouch Butler Savage 774
Crouch, Butler & Savage 66, 78, 162, 171, 181, 198, 237, 262, 293, 310, 348, 436, 444, 454, 460, 461, 548, 566, 598, 599, 625, 726, 734, 767, 776
Crouch Butler Savage Associates 634
Crowe, Sylvia 785
Crush, J. Arnold 80, 236, 567
Crutcher, Richard 20, 297, Pl. 36
Cruz, Sjölander da 84, 183, 430
Cubitt, James 39
Cullen, Mick 720
Cullen, Sean 720
Cullis, Stan 692
Culpin & Bowers 171

Culpin (Clifford) & Partners 88, 682, 691
Culwick, James 544
Cunningham, Laurie 613
Cunnington, John 233
Curtis, T.F. 443
Curzon, Henry 37, 513
Cutler, T.W. 448
Cutts, Joseph 605
Cutts, J.E.K. & J.P. 426, 514, 623
Cuzner, Bernard 441
CZWG 170

D5 187, 195, 308, 781
da Cruz, Sjölander see Cruz, Sjölander da
Dadford, Thomas Jun. 492, 494, 561, 562, Pl. 52
Dadford, Thomas Sen. 498, 718, 736
Dagley, C.L. 396
Dagley, W. 646
Dain, Sir Guy 428
Dale, R.W. 106, 124
Dallas & Lloyd 288
Dallow (John) & Sons 604
Daly, W. 597
Dancer, J. Kenneth 543
Danks Rawcliffe 373
Darby, Joe 93, 532
Dare (H.) & Son Ltd 76, 79, 312
darnton egs 577
Dartmouth, 1st Earl of 611
Dartmouth, 2nd Earl of 611
Daukes, S.W. 35, 603, 604
Davies, Archibald John 78, 266, 296, 322, 441, 514, 676, 678, 725, 737, 750
Davies, D.H. 82, 348
Davies, E.J. 257
Davies, Eric 760, 774–5
Davies, J.B. 64, 530, 560
Davies, Kenneth J. 136
Davies, Miles 170
Davies, Nigel 83, 380
Davies, Sidney 493, 541
Davies & Middleton 37, 38, 56, 473, 474–5, 487, 490, 508, 560n., 576, 590, 600, 645
Davis, C.E. 529
Davis, C.R. 492
Davis, Frank 333
Davis, Fred 64, 246, 259n., 423, 776
Davis, J.S. 51, 160, 184, 186, 392, 394
Davis, William (fl. 1709) 111
Davis, William (late C19) 184, 256, 258, 266, 321, 392, 421, 466
Davis, William John 185, 255, 324, 430, 452, 454, 456, 458, 460, 783, 784
Dawson, George 43, 48n., 106
Day, John 317
Day Architectural 205
Day (Ivor) & O'Brien 301
de Lacy Aherne, W. see Aherne, W. de Lacy

De Morgan see Morgan (De)
Deakin & Phipson 53, 381
Dean Walker Bateman 283
Dearle, J.H. 64–5, 534, 749
Deebank, Frederick Daniel 312
Deebank (builders) 762
Deeley, William 531
Delaney-Hall, David 152
Dempster, A.E. 70, 237, 427, 688
Dempster, W. 539
Dempster & Heaton 51, 65, 145, 146, 183, 215
Dennis (terracotta) 750
Dennison, F. 201
Derick, J.M. 35, 538, 540
Design Antenna 526
Deutsch, Otto 204
DeVall, George 456, 584
Devereux, Sir Edward 770
Devereux, Sir George 283
Devereux, Mitchell, Price & Davis 369
Devlin Plummer 236
Dewhurst Macfarlane 526
DGI International 90, 698
Diamond, Hodgkinson & Partners 747
Diamond Partnership 385
Diamond, Redfern & Partners 83, 86, 591, 684, 698, Pl. 129
Dicconson, Edward 679
Dickens, Charles 125
Dicker, Rev. C.W. 540
Dickinson, George 24, 291
Dix, A.J. 579, 624, 668
Dixon, Arthur S. 59, 60, 62, 63, 64, 71, 77, 116, 117, 162, 194, 284, 285, 294, 340, 351, 362, 373, 388, 393, 397–8, 491, 575, 678n., 766, Pl. 69
Dixon, Cornelius 254
Dixon, Humphrey 195
Dixon (John) & Associates 169
DJB (sculptor) 473
Dolman, J.E. 633
Dolphin, Robert 429
Doone Silver Kerr 88, 143
Dora, Sister (Dorothy Pattison) 49, 622, 628, 632
Doubleday, William 45, 57, 174, 180, 288, 420, 431, 686
Doubleday (William) & James R. Shaw 57, 183
Doulton (tiles and terracotta) 134, 443, 581, 597, 700
Dove, Tom E. 339
Dowell, N.C. 713
Dowling (D.P.) & Sons 248
Downing Smith Kendrick Hood 386–7
Downing, Smith, Kendrick Hood & Partner 751
Dowson, Philip 86, 369, 371
Doyle-Jones, Francis 454
Dredge, Frank 703

Drinkwater, H.G.W. 491, 530
dRMM 423
Dron & Wright 84, 182
Drury & Smith 508
Drysdale, George 78, 110, 276, 286, 567, Pl. 121
Duc, Louis-Joseph 363
Dudley, 1st Earl of 3, 28, 32, 33, 49, 58, 484, 488, 495, 524, 538–9, 542, 548
Dudley, 2nd Earl of 532, 704
Dudley, 3rd Earl of 447, 479, 557
Dudley, Dud 31, 471, 483
Dudley, John *see* Northumberland, Duke of
Dudley, Robert 526
Dudley M.B.C. Architects/Architect's Department 483, 533, 558
Dudley M.B.C. Borough Architect 483, 550
Dudley M.B.C. Construction & Design 502
Dudley M.B.C. Planning & Architecture Department 528
Dudley (M.B.C.) Property Consultancy 542
Dudley (Roger) & Sons 463
Dudley and Ward, Viscount 472
Dugdale, Sir William 219, 221, 438, 622
Duke & Simpson 385
Dunn, Alfred J. 209, 426
Dunn, J.G. 54, 69, 182, 183, 196, 249, 258, 259, 306, 333, 783
Dunn, Martin 520, 603, 604
Dunn & Broughall 605–6
Dunn (J.G.), Dallas & Lloyd 185
Dunn (A.M.) & E.J. Hansom 39, 396, 604, 605–6, 782
Dunn (J.G.) & F.W. Hipkiss 44, 221, 256, 259, 264, 629
Dunster, Peter 90
Dupuis, Mother Geneviève 426
Durose, Hamlet 40, 502, 503, 543, 566
Durrant, Graham 259
Durst, Alan 737, 756
Dussault, L.L. 255
Dutton, Clive 95
Dutton & Smith 579
Duvall, George 394
Duval Brownhill 91, 120, 284, 659, 662
Dyer Associates 186, 228, 630
Dyhouse, Garry 520
Dyke, Benjamin 459
Dykes Bower, S.E. 424, 596
Dyson (Michael) Associates 234

Eachus, S.H. 287, 502
Eachus Huckson Landscape Architects 632
Eagle Foundry 397

INDEX OF ARCHITECTS, ETC.

Earp, Thomas 579
Ebbels, Robert 34, 246, 508, 533, 590, 604, 672, 675, 714, 784
Ebner, J.F. 580
Eckstein, A. Conrad 704
Eden, F.C. 676
Edge, Charles 23, 41, 50, 53, 57, 94, 106, 125, 137, 139, 142, 151, 157, 180, 182, 185, 200, 258, 323, 324, 358, 361, 376–7, 381, 383, 389, 393, 421
Edge, Charles Allerton (son of Charles) 388, 392
Edge, Thomas (father of Charles) 142
Edge & Avery 49, 154–5, 377
Edmonds Gooding Miller Appleby 230
Edmunds, Mr (architect) 584
Edmunds, S. Doddimeade 636
Edmundson (R.B.) & Son 648
Edward VI, King 374
Edward VII, King 12, 68, 129, 365
Edward the Elder 749
Edwards (terracotta, Ruabon) 201
Edwards, Arthur 71, 149, 172, 185, 210, 228, 230, 255, 291, 319, 335, 405, 409, 428, 430, 454, 455
Edwards, Duncan 474, 484–5
Edwards, J.C. 131
Edwards, W.F. 73, 347, 520, 531, 570, 582, 764
Edwards, William 69, 686, 687, 693
Edwards (Malcolm) Associates 758
Edwards (John) & Partners 497
Edwards (Julie) & Ron Thompson 348
Eginton, Francis 25, 175, 219n., Pl. 37
Eginton, Harvey 43, 359–60, 482
Eglington, James 622
Eglington, John 54, 636–7
Eglington Sen. (sculptor) 220
Eld, Mr 378
Elizabeth I, Queen 477
Elkington, George Richards and Mary 424–5
Ellam, William 678
Ellerton, Peter 550
Elliott, A.W. 217
Elliott, Thomas (organ-builder) 473
Elliott & Whitfield 502
Ellis, Jonathan 51, 636
Ellis Williams Architects 507, 524, 655
Ellis Williams Partnership 85, 775
Elvins, Thomas 578
Elwell, Thomas 748
Emerson, Robert Jackson 490, 627, 628, 686, 688
Emery, Alfred 496
Endell, F.B. 757
England, George Pike 547
Engle (Bernard) & Partners 517, 692
Ensor, G.H.W. 581
Eprile, C.J. 148
Erridge, Arthur F. 560

Essex, Oliver 56, 58, 306, 326, 327, 330, 381, 692–3
Essex (O.) & John Goodman 79, 143, 150, 152, 153, 155, 156, 157, 182, 206, 252, 263, 394, 401, 454, 685
Essex Goodman Suggitt 577
Essex (O.), Goodman (J.) & J.A. Suggitt 147, 155, 160, 162
Essex (O.) & J.C. Nicol 57, 204, 299, 303, 329, 330, 333
Essex, Nicol & Goodman 69, 94, 148, 151, 163, 180, 188, 205, 303, 320, 326, 327, 328, 382, 391, 686, 783, Pl. 104
Este family 344
Ettwell, Elliott J. 52, 613
Evans, Mr (sculptor, Liverpool) 598
Evans, Daniel 472
Evans, Samuel 42, 246, 249, 266, 397, 474, 496, 502, 513, 530, 547, 560, 577, 578, 579, 580, 597, 598, 604, 654, 678, 726
Evans, Sebastian 42, 547, 603
Evans, Thomas 679, Pl. 45
Evans, William 733
Evans (C.) & Co. 597
Evans (Samuel) & Co. 551, 583, 589, 590, 603, 661, 725
Evans (Samuel) & Sons 496, 582, 730
Evers-Swindell, James 536
Evetts, L.C. 93, 322, 336
Eykyn, Roger 24, 175, 677, Pl. 37

Fairbairn, Ken 377
Fairbairn (William) & Sons 694n.
Fairhaven & Woods 680
Faizey, S.P. 633
Falconer, Peter 521
Falconer, Thomas 64, 285
Fallows, John 23, 43, 52, 53, 125, 157, 358, 379, 380, 381, 383, 384, 385, 387, 388, 389, 547, 625, 628, 640, Pl. 59
Fallows & Hart 183
Faraday, Michael 372
Farley, Reuben 610, 613
Farmer, Eric 92, 559n., 642
Farmer, H.E. 466
Farmer, W. 726
Farmer & Brindley 123, 315, 686
Farmer & Farmer 79, 556, 634, 653
Farrell (Terry) Partnership 87, 170
Farrington, Henry 54, 635
FAT 282
Faulkner, G. Repton 56, 319, 326, 331, 430
FaulknerBrowns Architects 88, 208
Feeney, John Frederick 130, 145, 151, 218, 219
Feeney, Patrick 92, 492, 508, 531, 679
Fehr, H.C. 66, 68, 627
Feibusch, Hans 93, 482
Feilden Clegg 372

INDEX OF ARCHITECTS, ETC.

Feilden Clegg Bradley 86, 189, 190, 191
Fell, Frank 276
Fellowes Prynne, E.A. see Prynne, E.A. Fellowes
Fellows Chaplin (glass-stainer) 742
Fenton, Don 402
Fereday, J.T. 498
Fernie (R.G.) & Partners 636
Ferrey, Benjamin 47, 277
Fiddian, F.W. 35, 53, 264–5, 358, 359, 362, 378, 379, 380, 381n., 382, 388, 389
Fidler, A.G. Sheppard 82, 85, 93n., 169, 231, 240, 252, 267, 268, 282, 284, 303, 311, 375, 406, 413, 414, 417, 428, 780
Field, George 762
Field, Steve 93, 483, 532, 613
Fillmore, Cecil E.M. 79, 80, 81, 209, 460, 514, 566, 602, 607, 613n., 614, 617
Fillmore (Cecil) & Partners 705, 720
Firmstone, Christopher 562
Fisher, Alfred 556
Fisher, F.R. 486
Fisher, Ken 411
FitzAnsculph, William 470, 475, 733
5plus 172
Flanagan, Terence 363
Flannery & de la Pole 607
Flaxman, John 25, 244, 734
Fleeming, T.H. 40, 45, 47, 49, 56, 62, 67, 69, 501–2, 508, 658, 685, 687, 695, 698, 712, 714, 728, 730, 737, 744, 745, 750, 752
Fleeming, W.H. 62
Fleeming & Son 620, 623, 681, 684, 713, 717, 727, 746, 752
Fleeming (T.H.) & Son 692
  see also *Bidlake & Fleeming*
Flewett, Thomas 41, 581
Florence, Mary Sargent 352
Florence, Professor Philip Sargent 87n., 431
Flower, Rob 291
Floyd, Oliver 257, 259, 317
Floyd (Oliver) & Salt 256, 317, 326
Foggo Associates 88, 760
Foley, J.H. 48, 129
Foley, Philip 534
Foley, Richard 31
Foley, Thomas 534–5
Folkes, H.E. 80, 486, 527, 529, 530, 532, 536, 545, 550, 552, 553, 554, 555, 558, 570n.
Folkes, J. Homery 76, 524, 530, 538, 545, 547, 550, 554, 555, 557
Folkes & Folkes 528, 545, 552
Ford, Alfred 278
Ford, E. Onslow 124
Ford, Emily 276
Ford, Rob 215
Foreign Office Architects 90, 136

Forster, John 638
Forster & Andrews 606
Forsyth, James 38, 473, 484
Forsyth, Moira 374
Forsyth, W. 549
Foster, Gordon H. 119, 263, 618, 624, 628, 631
Foster, James 32
Foster, John 125
Foster, Stephen 757
Foster, William Orme 557, 558
Foster & Partners 170
Foster, Ralphs & Mansell 635
Foulkes, William Tadman 180
Foulkes & Ryland 181
Fowler, C. Hodgson 419
Fowler, H.H. *see* Wolverhampton, 1st Viscount
Fowler, James 676
Fowler, John 59, 694
Fox, Henderson & Co. 136
Fraleys (sculptors) 221, 509
Frampton, E.R. 64, 660
Frampton, Sir George 219
Francis, Katie 339
Frankel, Rudolf 84, 208
Franklin, Joseph 59, 191
Franklin Cross 418, 429
Franklin Cross & Brookes 430
Franklin Cross & Nichols 238
Fraser, Gerald de Courcy 79, 139, 147, 689
Fraser (Ian), John Roberts & Partners 172
Freebody family 608
Freebody, William 609
Freeman, Owen 51, 72, 526, 527, 529, 552
Freer, Rev. T.L. 243
Freeth, William 565
Frink, Elisabeth 784–5
Frith, H.C. 501
Frith, John 34, 293
Frith, W.S. 49, 132
Frost Bevan 228
Furber, F.A. 541
Furnée, Bettina 156
Future Systems 88, 138

Gadd, George 349
Gaffin, Edward 697
Galbraith, Thomas 82, 500, 653
Gallagher, N.H.A. 691
Gallimore, Kenneth 704
Galton, Hubert 568
Galton, Samuel 568
Gammage, John 487, 490
Gammage & Dickinson 487
Gardiner, Starkie 132
Garman, Kathleen 629
Garratt, Job 492
Garratt & Simister 237
Gateley & Parsons 297, 760, 783
Geary, W.M. 495

INDEX OF ARCHITECTS, ETC.

Gelder, R. 611
George I, King 20, 111, 370
George (Stephen) & Associates 777, 778
George: Trew: Dunn 730
Georghiou, Costas 95, 672, 690
Gere, Charles M. 126, 266
Gething & Rolley 541
Gianese (mosaics, Venice) 340
Gibberd, Sir Frederick 85, 87, 146, 535, 536
Gibbings, W.W. 80, 242
Gibbons family 463
Gibbons, A. Latham 735
Gibbons, Arthur 497
Gibbons, F.H. 488
Gibbons, J.H. 347, 509, 590
Gibbs (glass-stainer) 422
Gibbs, Alexander 219, 422, 440
Gibbs, C.A. 422
Gibbs, James 20, 24, 220
Gibbs & Canning 124, 132, 221, 592
Gibbs & Co. 678
Gibson, Dan 714, 720n.
Gibson, James 175
Gibson, J.G.S. 65–6, 626, 627, 628, Pl. 86
Gibson, John 49, 157, 324
Giffard, Peter 679
Gifford, Andrew 662
Gilbert, Muriel 682
Giles & Gough 713
Gill, Fred J. 66, 72, 409, 578, 581, 582, 584, 585, 586, 623
Gillespie Yunnie 173
Gillott family 362n.
Gillott, Joseph 180, 393, 761
Glancy Nicholls/Glancy Nicholls Architects 88, 168, 171, 208, 292, 370, 373, 374, 380, 394, 775
Glasby, William 501
Glass, David 357n.
Glazzard Architects 177
Glazzard Associates 135, 161, 268
Glen, William 150
GMW/GMW Architects 151, 160
Goalen, Gerald 146
Goddard *see* Ball (J.L.) & Goddard
Goddard, H. 688, 719
Goddard & Co. 70, 140
Goddard & Gibbs 343, 441, 500, 622
Godiva 733
Godwin (tiles) 513, 564
Goldfinger, Ernö 84, 785
Goldie, Edward 65, 680
Goldsbrough, Francis 80, 421, Pl. 110
Gollins & Smeeton 379, Pl. 116
Goodman, J.C. 268
Goodman, John (architect) 194, 204, 328
  see also Essex, Nicol & Goodman
Goodman, John (builder, Harborne) 402, 403
Goodwin, Alan G. 173–4

Goodwin, Francis 24, 105, 175, 193, 513, 612, 620, 697, 699n., Pls. 41, 42
Goodwin (Alan) & Associates 173
Goold, Lewis W. 331
Gordon, Alex 633
Gordon, Bronwen 731, 750
Gore, Bishop Charles 63, 220, 272
Gormley, Antony 93, 156
Gotch & Partners 717
Gotch & Saunders 569, 599
Goudge, Edward 18, 771, 772
Gough family 267
Gough, G.S. 498
Gough, John 265
Gough, Piers 87, 170
Gough, Sir Richard 358, 360, 377
Gough, R.V. 329
Gough-Calthorpe family 357, 360
Gould Singleton 396, 571, 573
Gow, J. 117
Graebe, David 120
Grafton, Charles 388
Graham & Baldwin 504
Grandjean, Lee 206
Granelli, Mary 414
Granelli, Remo & Mary 82, 517, 780
Grant Associates 140
Grant Latham Partnership 745
Grants Estates 108, 356, 430
Graseley (de) family 727
Gray, C.C. 590
Gray, Charles G. 64, 595, 596, 679
Gray, David 76, 522, 524, 525
Gray, Tawny *see* Tawny Gray (Toin Adams)
Gray (C.C.) & Son 304
Grayson, Hastwell 741
Grayson & Ould 738, 741
Grazebrook, Commander 534
Grazebrook, Tom 62, 66, 75, 475, 492, 493, 494, 514, 528, 529, 530, 532, 535, 537, 538, 550, 551, 554, 558, 559, 560, 561
Greatorex, Albert D. 606
Green, Edward 521
Green, George 727
Green, Henry *see* Yorke, Henry
Green, Thomas 397
Green, W. Curtis 62, 745
Greening, Alfred T. 208, 402
Greenwood, Colin 572
Greenwood, Sydney 137
Greenwood, W. 565
Greenwood (Sydney) & T.J. Hirst 88
Greswold, Rev. Dr Henry 20, 296–7, Pl. 36
Greswold(e) family 296–7, 759
Grew, John A. 287
Grew (John A.) & Edwards 327, 430
Gribble, Charles Risdon 158
GRID 84, 188
Griffin, Edwin J. 258
Griffin, W.D. 36, 38, 654–5, 663–4, Pl. 9

826 INDEX OF ARCHITECTS, ETC.

Griffin & Weller 36, 596, 623, 725, 745
Griffith, Troyte 547
Griffiths, Joseph 535
Griffiths, Josiah 560
Griffiths, Robert 44, 48, 573, 592, 632
Griffiths, Stanley 78, 507, 531, 540, 541, 548, 571, 572, 574
Griffiths, T.D. 208
Griffiths, William 496, 497
Grimshaw (Nicholas) & Partners 89, 192, 193
Gropius, Walter 87, 151n., 153, 430, 431
Grosvenor, H. 40, 531
Grove, Edward 419
Grove, G.F. 519
Grubb, Edward 440
Grubb, Samuel 400
Grundy, Jonathan 588
Grylls, Harry 756
Guest, James 379
Guest, John or Thomas 542
Guest, Thomas 258, 266, 452, 542
Guest (Ian) & Associates 572
Guild of Handicraft 743
Gurmukhi Building Design 265
Gyde, E.L. 68n., 179, 460

Hackett, J.J. 72, 292
Hadderton, W. 614
Haden family 573
Haden-Best, George Haden 574
Hahn, Jean 421
Haigh, Fr Daniel 236–7
Haigh, Henry 237
Haines, H. Norman 347
Hakewill, Henry 611
Hale, Alfred 420
Hale, Edward 531
Hale, William 47, 52, 58, 66, 161, 197, 304, 305, 316, 317, 321, 325, 337, 382, 407, 408, 412, 414, 433, 434, Pl. 89
Hale (William) & Son 266, 304, 412
Halford, Henry 615
Hall, Henry 40, 665
Hall, L.M.B. 606
Hall, S. 247n.
Hall, Thomas 407, 408
Hall (Stanley) & Easton & Robertson 163
Halliday, John 25, 513–14
Halpern & Partners 421
Halpern Partnership 139, 171
Hamblin, A.H. 182, 466
Hamblin, Arthur 161, 401, 429
Hamilton, George E. 35, 502, 658, 715
Hamilton, Sir William and Lady 138n.
Hamilton & Medland 41, 181
Hamilton & Saunders 35, 589
Hammond, Arthur S. 405
Hancock, Tony 93, 147

Hand, H. Ireton 291
Handley, James 343
Hanley, C.E. 713
Hansom, Charles 38, 236–7, 679
Hansom, Joseph 125
Hansom (J.A.) & Son 757
Hansom (Joseph) & Edward Welch 42, 106, 125, 175, 232, 383n., Pl. 58
Harding (John) & Son 783
Hardman, Gerald J. 120, 121
Hardman, John 42, 121, 246, 247, 248, 360, 361, 445, 446, 542, 654, 655
Hardman, Sister Juliana 247
Hardman (John) & Co. 248, 294, 296, 578, 642
 see also Hardmans
Hardman, Powell & Co. 655
Hardman (John) Studios 233, 275, 277, 396, 492, 501, 502, 520, 679
 see also Hardmans
Hardmans 39, 42, 92, 121, 123, 204, 219, 230, 233, 237, 244, 247, 248, 265, 266, 274, 276, 277, 281, 285, 293–4, 296, 301, 321, 322, 345, 360–1, 363, 364, 396, 397, 407, 413, 419, 420, 422, 424, 426, 427, 447, 496, 508, 513, 523, 531, 540, 542, 543, 548, 596, 597, 623, 624, 625, 642, 644, 645–6, 659, 664, 679, 680, 702, 720, 734, 737, 756, 757, 767, 779, 782, 784, Pl. 74
 see also Hardman (John) & Co.
Hardwick, Philip Charles 59, 122, 192
Hardy, Adam 577, Pl. 134
Hardy, Thomas 482
Hare, Cecil G. 64, 273, 596, 644
Hare, Henry T. 45, 62, 66, 67, 519, 683, 700, 734–5
Hare, Nicholas 85, 305
Hare (Nicholas) Architects 190
Hares, John 710
Harley, John 54, 584
Harley, Roger H. 178, 179, 454
Harnald, W. 724
Harper (builder, Blackheath) 572
Harper, Ewen 56, 57, 181, 259, 287, 322, 326, 342, 364, 388, 431, 764
Harper, Geoffrey F. 758
Harper, G.J. 597
Harper, Harry 92, 270, 411, 508
Harper, Henry 249, 343
Harper, J. Alfred 331
Harper, James Benjamin 758, 775
Harper, Ross 83, 763
Harper (Ewen), Brother & Co. 15, 70, 74, 124, 143, 153, 178, 179, 188, 273n., 323–4, 457, 605
Harper, Ewen & J. Alfred 65, 67, 70, 71, 108, 123, 148, 155, 178, 186, 202, 237, 316, 320, 331, 342, 356, 411, 412, 453, 475, 520, 569, 570n., 581, 605, 661, 704, Pls. 71, 105

INDEX OF ARCHITECTS, ETC.

Harper (J. Alfred) & Son 147, 188, 269, 643
Harper & Sperring 570
Harpur family 661
Harpur, J. Lewis 497, 612
Harries, Paul 775
Harris, J. Seymour 84, 86, 143, 147, 232
Harris, John (plumber) 384
Harris, Renatus 678
Harris, William 26, 564
Harris (Seymour) Architects 781
Harris & Martin 158, 387
Harris, Martin & Harris 391, 490, 581, 584
Harris (J. Seymour) & Partners 146, 152, 172, 210, 517, 546–7, 552, 553, 615, Pl. 132
Harris (Seymour) Partnership 87, 88, 139, 144, 145, 146, 149, 151, 162, 205, 207, 290, 454, 544
Harrison, Arthur 44, 56, 60, 63, 66, 108, 137, 197, 202, 234, 277, 298, 311, 313, 316, 326, 331, 332, 339, 340, 342, 343, 346, 517, 578, 783
Harrison, D. 509
Harrison, E.G. 460
Harrison, F.W. 626, 647
Harrison, Joseph 647
Harrison Coton Harvey & Wicks 416
Harrison & Cox 108, 119, 200, 203, 220, 262, 348, 382, 443, 625
Harrison (E.G.) & Tracey 239
Harrison (Stockdale) & Sons 96
Harrod, C.F. Lawley 80, 200, 209
Hart & Co. 134
Hart & Son 151
Hart, Son & Peard 396
Hartill, E. 717
Hartland, Charles 544
Hartland, J.F. 307, 331
Harvey, H.W. 123
Harvey, Neil 420
Harvey, William Alexander 60, 65, 332, 350, 351, 352, 353–6, 357, 360, 410, 432, 612, 764, Pl. 100
Harvey & Ashby 130, 246, 321, 442, 443, 622, 757
Harvey (W.A.) & H.G. Wicks 74, 75, 76, 77, 108, 261, 279, 297, 314, 351, 352, 353, 377, 410, 412, 431, 432, 433, 434, 482, 488, 603, 655, 784, Pl. 90
Hasker 757, 765
Haskoll 136, 613
Hasleden, Ron 168
Hastilow, Noel 272, 307
Hathern Station Brick & Terracotta Co. 257
Hatton, Rod 85, 316
Haughton (Worcester) 597
Hawe, George 639
Hawes, J.C. 276

Hawes, William and Ursula 763
Hawkes, G.F. 68n., 179, 221, 460, 581
Hawkes, Harry Campbell 68, 78, 287, 317, 531
Hawkes, J.H. 186, 580
Hawkes, O.C. 315
Hawkes (O.C.) Ltd 541
Hawkes & McFarlane 312, 319
Hawkes (J.H.) & Son 183, 198, 263–4, 421, 531
Hawkins/Brown 189
Hawkins McGowan 325
Hawksley, Thomas 704
Haworth Tompkins 85, 277, 375
Hawtayne, W.C.C. 67, 448
Hay, G.S. 687
Haycock, Edward 736
Hayes, Louis 92, 233, 275, 564
Haylock, G.T. 188, 384, 391
Haywood, William 73–4, 80, 94, 169, 267, 367, 377, 402, 587
   see also Buckland & Haywood
Haywood-Farmer, Edward 61, 73n., 458
   see also Buckland & Haywood-Farmer
Headley, W.R. 206
Heal, Mr 347
Heal, Henry 347, 394
Healey, Everard 453, 460
Healey, Louis 625
Heatherley, A. 345
Heaton, Ralph 317, 373, 391, 395, 396, 404
Heaton, Butler & Bayne 42, 132, 215, 219, 230, 246, 266, 322, 361, 440, 502, 578, 676, 712
Heaton, Butler & Co. 361
Heaton (Ralph) & A.H. Dight 257
Helmle, J. 25, 542
Hemming, Samuel 49, 53, 155, 358, 388, 492
Hendra, Robert L. 597, 758
Hendriks, Henry 183
Henman, William 44, 45, 47, 65, 227, 239, 242, 251, 252, 365, 390, 393, 403, 582, 605, 606–7
Henman (William) & Thomas Cooper 45, 59, 69, 108, 135, 141, 144, 153, 163, 164, 382, 462
Henman (William) & Timmins 45, 390, 405, 607
Hennebique (system) 196
Hennessy, Hennessy & Co. 163
Henry III, King 515
Henry (Paul) Architects 265, 569
Hepworth, Dame Barbara 369, 689
Herbert, J.R. 39, 446
Herbert, Philip 267
Herickx, Gordon 370, 622
Heveningham, G. 757
Hewett, James 412
Hickling, R. 248

Hickman, Douglas 84, 86, 143, 144, 151, 153, 161, 244, 262, 289, 382, 385, Pl. 131
Hickman, Edward 536
Hickman & Smith 135
Hickton, J.H. 570n.
Hickton & Farmer 71, 72, 95, 491, 529, 618, 620, 625, 632, 633, 635, 636, 638, 639–40, 646, 647, 660, 701
Hickton, Farmer & Farmer 632, 646, 647
Hickton Madeley 83, 339, 382, 564
Hickton, Madeley & Partners 636
Hickton, Madeley & Salt 604
Higgins, Chris and Sue 411
Highbury Design 448
Highway, Isaac 35, 624, 651, 662
Hill, Alfred E. 41, 531
Hill, A.S.B. 751
Hill, D.R. 35, 43, 46, 216–17, 381, 441, 442
Hill, J. 347
Hill, Rowland 48n.
Hill, Thomas (C18) 494
Hill, Thomas (C19) 527
Hill, William 127
Hill & Egginton 265
Hill (Edwin) & Partners 154
Hiller, H.G. 534
Hilton, George 50, 485
Hilton & Caswell 543
Hinchliff (London) 534
Hind, Thomas 69, 687
Hing, H. Peter 76, 172, 228, 312, 314, 401, 648, 764
Hing (Peter) & Jones 87, 140, 146, 147, 154, 172, 173, 182, 242, 376–7
Hingley (Noah) & Sons 530
Hinton, Denys 371
Hinton, Moses 473
Hinton (Denys) & Associates 292, 589n.
Hinton Brown Langstone 189, 303, 502, 733
Hinton Brown, Madden & Langstone 602
Hinton (Denys) & Partners 124, 237, 297
Hiorne, David 742
Hiorne, William 24, 122, 190n., 438, 440, 742
Hiorne, William & David 20, 105n., 345, 377, 551n., 562
Hipkins, Stephen 528
Hipkiss & Stephens 181, 187, 326, 330, 632, 764
Hirst, Bertram V. 428
Hirst, T.J. 137
Hitch, Nathaniel 194, 644
Hitchman Stone Partnership 162
HKPA 89
Hobbiss family 277
Hobbiss, Holland W. 61, 75, 76, 77, 79, 80, 96, 108, 179, 214, 241, 256, 264, 265, 267, 271, 272, 273, 275–6, 277, 278, 283, 285, 289, 290, 293, 294, 302, 307, 315, 319, 335, 342, 343, 367, 369, 370, 372, 374–5, 381, 389, 391, 413, 418, 423n., 427, 455, 456, 457, 458, 486, 488, 489, 517, 575, 579, 580, 590, 703, Pls. 107, 119
Hobbiss, Maurice A.H. 179, 276, 307, 780
Hobbiss (Holland W.) & Partners 152, 210, 232, 272, 277, 307, 325, 370, 379, 390, 420
Hodder, Tony 475
Hodder Associates 651
Hodges, Roger 496
Hodgkins, Keith 752
Hodson, Charles J. 147, 209, 461
Hodson, Laurence 749
Hogg, T. Dunkley 76, 343, 410
HOK 168
HOK International 188
Holbache family 556
Holder, Sir John 335, 430
Holder Mathias 415
Holiday, Henry 285
Holland, William 296, 345, 442, 642, 664, 679
Holliday, J.R. 407
Holliday, Stephen J. 57, 206, 330, 606
Hollins (sculptor, fl. 1836) 297
Hollins, George 175
Hollins, Peter 38, 48, 111, 117, 175, 176, 244, 264, 293, 297, 321, 375, 473, 474, 492, 506, 534, 596, 603, 622, 649, 650, 697
Hollins, William 25, 26, 105, 117, 118, 171, 176, 199, 220, 243, 244, 245, 253–4, 260, 321, 360, 474, 505, 579, 596, 622, 670, 688
Hollins, Jones & Oldacre 398
Hollis, William 679
Holloway, D. 345
Holloway Foo 447
Holman, Edward 79, 158, Pl. 109
Holmes, Edward 36, 38, 44, 47, 49, 54, 108, 137, 150, 151, 153, 199, 227, 253, 319, 328, 329, 331, 408, 412, 424, 427, 428, 429, 447, 564, 573, 755, 784
Holmes, J. Brewin 41, 308, 328, 330, 331, 332
Holmes, James 772, Pl. 57
Holmes, Kenneth 416
Holmes (Kenneth) & Partners 569
Holt, G.W. 332
Holte, Sir Charles 20, 220
Holte, Sir Lister 220, 222
Holte, Sir Thomas (C17) 221, 224–5, 226
Holte, Sir Thomas (C18) 449n.
Holtom (E.G.) & F.W.B. Yorke 401
Holton & Connor 475, 489
Holyoak, Joe 201, 414

INDEX OF ARCHITECTS, ETC.

Homer, John 473
Homer, Ralph 541
Homer, W.E. 500, 531
Homfray, Mary 525
Hopcraft (W.) & Son 664, 718
Hope Bagenal 682
Hope (Henry) & Sons 376
Hopkins, A. 570
Hopkins, Albert 613
Hopkins, R. Jeffries 248
Hopkins, W.J. 37, 407, 520
Horder, P. Morley 275
Hordern family 709, 710
Hordern, Alexander 732
Hornblower, J.L. 538
Hornblower & Haylock 54, 201, 386
Horne, Edward 519
Horne (David) Associates 686
Horseley Co. 498, 694
Horseley Coal & Iron Co./Horseley Iron Co. 587, 659
Horsfall family 274, 466
Horsfall, James 274
Horsley, Cyril 92, 123, 231, 443, 774
Horsley Currall 443
Horsley, Currall & Associates 123, 231, 650
Horsley Huber & Associates 561
Horsman, Philip 658, 683, 685
Horsnaile, Christopher 20
Horton, John 26, 199
Horton, Samuel 596, 600n., 613, 625
Horton, William 35, 596, 597, 625, 654, 668
Horton & Scott 56, 596, 599
Houben, Francine 166
Howell, J.S. 187
Howell, Killick, Partridge & Amis 86, 217, 371, Pls. 128, 133
Howells, Glenn/Howells (Glenn) Architects 84, 86, 88, 138, 140, 171, 177, 178, 188, 191, 197, 230, 347, 369, 414, 429, 517, 687, 762, 778, Pl. 136
Howitt, T. Cecil 73, 158, 166, 168, 423
Howl, Philip 89, 317
Howl Associates 83, 692
Howland, Will 83, 85, 306, 394
Howrie, Jim 110
Huband, W.F. 315
Hubbard Ford & Partners 210
Hughes, Henry 642, 710
Hughes, J. 576
Hughes, R. 332
Hughes, Thomas 597
Hulme Upright 92, 704
Hulme & Upright 426
Hulme, Upright & Partners 597, 646
Hulme Upright Weedon 171
Humphries, Frank R. 493
Humphries, Sir Herbert H. 74, 188, 227, 240, 241, 267, 302, 314, 345, 412, 436
Humphries, Mark 160, 179, 180

Humphries, Slater & Co. 540
Hunstone, Advent 501, 645, 655, 664
Hunt, Percival J. 77, 262, 291
Hunt, Sidney 590
Hunt Thompson 231, 232
Hurd, Daniel 415, 757
Hurd (Daniel) Associates 232
Hurley, Robin 491, 496, 783
Hurley Robinson/Hurley Robinson Partnership 612, 666, 699
Hurn, J. Bruce 375
Huskisson, William 711
Huss, Richard 111
Hussey, R.C. 176, 276, 771, 772, Pl. 57
  see also Rickman & Hussey
Hutchings, John 67, 75, 497, 652, 684
Hutchings, W.A. 81, 667, 668, 694, 701, 704, 724, 732, 745
Hutchins, John 561
Hutton, William 31, 293
Hyden, G.W. 774

Ibbeson, Graham 613
IDP 190, 279, 280
Ind Coope & Allsopp Surveyor's Department 644
Ingall, George 41, 47, 55, 154, 199, 305, 306, 402, 444
Ingall, Bridgewater & Co. 785
Ingall Bridgewater & Porter 317
Ingall (George) & F.G. Hughes 47, 230, 305
Ingall (George) & Son 287, 302, 304, 342, 445
Inge, William 111, 153, 154
Ingelow, B. 734
Ingle, Edward 24, 593
Insall (Donald) Associates 305, 472
Insall (Donald) & Partners 95, 691
Inskip & Wilczynski 634
Institute for the Study of Worship and Religious Architecture 275
Inston (Peter) Design 464
Inston Sellers Hickinbotham 178
Ireland, Joseph 25, 604, 625, 679–80, Pl. 43
Ireson, J.R. 429
ISH Partnership 143, 162, 758
Ives, Roger 537

Jack, George 64, 195, Pl. 69
Jack, G.H. 229
Jackson (sculptor, Hagley) 505
Jackson, Herbert 93, 279, 528
Jackson, S.A. 529
Jackson, Thomas 24, 649
Jackson, W. 637
Jackson & Edmonds 77, 84, 92, 279, 280, 282, 297, 316, 324, 381, 461, 540, 765, 774, Pl. 117
Jackson (George) & Sons 132
Jacobs (architects) 682
Jaffray, Sir John 388

James, Bernard V. 203, 262, 625
James, G.E. 428
James, John 418
James, Joseph 36, 341, 580
James Totty Partnership 571
Jaray, Tess 169
Jarvis, Kim 413
JBKS 424
Jebb, G.R. 30, 586, 639
Jefferson Sheard 90, 553
Jeffries, Brian 92, 726
Jeffries & Shipley 79, 618, 625, 631, 632, 634, 635, 640, 643, 658, 667
Jellicoe, Geoffrey 94, 95, 622, 637
Jenkins, George 302
Jenkins, William 71, 188, 209, 228, 232, 235, 239, 278, 295, 306, 333, 404, 431, 434, 447, 449, 454, 536, 593
Jennens (A.E.) & Co. 76, 312
Jennens & Bettridge 442
Jennings, Henry 495, 497, 499, 500, 507, 571
Jennings, Sir Stephen see Jenyns, Sir Stephen
Jennings & Homer 79, 497, 507, 525, 563
Jennings Homer & Lynch 88, 262, 279, 286, 304, 316, 475, 495, 496, 497, 500, 502, 523, 524, 525, 531, 536, 539, 562n., 575, 644, 645, 646, 661, 698, 720, 738
Jenns Howl 286
Jenyns (Jennings), Sir Stephen 713
Jerde Partnership 234
Jesmond Group 688
Jesson family 440, 727
Johnson, Clare 535
Johnson, F.D. 290, 466
Johnson, Michael 186
Johnson, Moses 706, 725
Johnson, Thomas 26, 36, 404, 548, 564, 579, 650
Johnson, W. 726
Johnson (Richard) & Associates 172, 173
Johnson & Baxter 646, 665, 668
Johnson & Giles 508, 668, 693
Johnson, H. & R. 120
Johnson (Thomas) & Son 616
Jones, A. Douglas 110
Jones, David 414
Jones, George 23, 380
Jones, Graham 447
Jones, Jonah 413
Jones, K. 351
Jones, Leslie 454
Jones, Mark 505
Jones, Maurice 530
Jones, Stanley 609
Jones, W. Maurice 608
Jones, W.G. 565
Jones (Leslie) Architects 146, 499
Jones & Willis 246, 265, 343, 422, 442, 474, 475, 496, 508, 530, 531, 534, 558, 579, 597, 604, 622, 623, 641, 642, 648, 650, 659, 668, 698, 725, 768
Jordan, H.E. 209
Jordan, Robert Furneaux 390
Joseph, Samuel 472–3
Jouvenet, Jean 595
Joyce (Nick) Architects 308
Joynson, Charles William Davies 72, 75, 80, 593, 597, 598, 599, 639, 649, 650, 651–3, 699
Joynson Bros 55, 509, 599, 649, 651, 652

K4 95, 189, 304, 401, 461
Kaiser, Naseeruddin 250
Kaminsky, Bohdan 726
Katsoulis, Eirini 623
Kaye (Sidney), Eric Firmin & Partners 384
Keay, Ian 411
Kedward-Sheldon, F. 362
Keen, William 40, 571, 574, 576, 665
Kellet & Bentley 556
Kelly, Mick 720
Kelly (Ben) Design 607
Kelly & Surman 140, 189, 206, 381, 396
Kempe 246, 362, 363, 407, 419, 523, 580, 596, 727, 739–40, 756
Kempe, C.E. 64, 122
Kempe (C.E.) & Co. 321, 360, 727, 737
Kendrick, W.H. 610
Kenrick family 395
Kenrick, Archibald 397
Kenrick, J.A. 390
Kenrick, William 55, 403
Kenworthy, Edwin 255
Keppie (architects) 731
Kesby, W.D. 345
Kettle, Robert 439
Keyte, John 590
Kidson, Gordon 665
Kier, J.L. 479
Kincaid, James 338
Kinder (Arthur) & Son 58, 567
King, Harold C. 246, 492, 496, 508, 623
King, Laurence 756, 764
King, Simeon Theodore 207
King, W.C.H. 677
King (Laurence) & Charles Brown 757
King & Co. 598, 629
King, J. & W. 492
King (Thomas) & Sons 360, 474
Kings, Elizabeth 528
Kings, Raymond F. 236, 275, 624, 642
Kirby (Edmund) & Sons 604
Kirk, Dr 445
Knight, Walter J. 235n., 441, 781
see also Bidlake & Knight

INDEX OF ARCHITECTS, ETC.

Knowles, Sir Richard (Dick) 95
Kramer, Fritz 351
Kuhne (Eric R.) & Associates 88, 760
Kyte, Mr (fl. 1799) 494, Pl. 52

Laguerre, Louis 771
Lamplugh, Father 616
Lamplugh, Bertram 64, 285, 756, Pl. 77
Lanchester, F.W. 72, 333
Lanchester, H.V. 333
Lanchester & Lodge 375
Lanchester, Rickards & Lucas 333
Lane family 653
Lane, D.J. 517
Lane, Francis 498
Lane, Col. John 20, 676–7
Lane, Thomas (C16) 17, 676
Lane, Thomas (C18) 111
Lane & Cardus 596
Lane Lister 612
Langford & Williams 154
Langley, E. 461
Langley-Taylor (G.) & Partners 195
Lansbury, George 568n.
Lapworth/Lapworth Partnership 384, 392, 784
Latham, A. Gilbey 152, 258, 316
Latham (Derek) Architects 186
Latham (Derek) Associates 564
Lavender, H.E. 45, 618, 625, 626, 630, 632, 633, 634, 635, 637, 640, 644, 646, 662, 688
Lavender, Joseph 51, 71, 704, 712, 721, 726, 733, 748
Lavender, Joseph & H.E. 727
Lavender, Son & Close 77, 80, 624, 634, 640, 642
Lavender (Richard) & Richard Twentyman 77, 676, 724, 727, 730
Lavender, Twentyman & Percy 650, 653, 693
Lavers & Barraud 42, 219, 703
Lavers, Barraud & Westlake 42, 219, 293, 474, 501, 712, 756
Law, Paul 715
Law & Dunbar-Nasmith 205
Lawden, Joseph 485, 551
Lawlor, Patrick 217, Pl. 133
Lawrence & Wrightson 183
Lawson, John 433
Lawson, W. 433
Laxton, Samuel 51
le Sueur, Hubert *see* Sueur, Hubert le
Lea, Rev. George 214
Lea, James 173
Lea, John 634
Lea, William 519
Lea, James & Lister 45, 70, 81, 171, 193, 198, 200, 201, 206, 207, 208, 209, 228, 229, 237, 241, 257, 260, 302, 326, 329, 342, 409, 584, 585, Pl. 103

Lea (James & Lister) & Sons 189, 191, 203, 240, 278, 412, 552
Ledoyen, Arthur 110
Lee, John 309
Lee, Lawrence 93, 123, 276, 321, 756
Lee, R.G.W. 331
Lee, Stirling 117
Lee, Thomas 22, 24, 484, 501, 530, 542
Leech, Malcolm 85, 268, 278
Lees, John 726
Lees, Stephen 650
Lees-Milne, James 776n.
Leeson, Arthur Edgerton 74, 252, 373, 377, 453
Legg, G. 697
Leicester, B. 414
Leitch, Archibald 228
Leland, John 104, 406, 438, 449
Lemmon, A.E. 78, 220, 514, 616, Pl. 78
Lemmon, A.E. & P.E. 93, 502, 527
Lester, Lissa 375
Lethaby, W.R. 59–60, 63, 456, 458
Lethaby (W.R.) & J.L. Ball 68, 140–1, 458, Pl. 95
Level Seven Architects 140, 147, 152, 173, 499
Leveson, John 17, 676
Leveson, Admiral Sir Richard 17, 676
Levitt Bernstein 168
Levy (Ted), Benjamin & Partners 152
Lewin, G.H. 355
Lewis, Frank C. 71, 574
Lewis, Granville 394
Lewis, Henry Greswolde 762
Lewis, John T. 88, 483, 489, 510
Lewis, T. 506
Lewis & Percival 494
Lidbetter, Hubert 124, 432
Lifschutz Davidson 90, 367, 370
Lilley, Albert E.V. 726
Lindon-Morris, Julie 89, 618, 628
Lines, Samuel 154
Linthout, J. 221
Lion Foundry 588
Lion Ironworks 541
Lippi, Filippo 655
Lister, Paul 405
Littleton, Sir John 556
Livock, John 136
Lloyd, Edward John 30, 199
Lloyd, Frederick W. 66, 139, 153, 189, 191, 205
Lloyd, Herbert R. 61, 258
Lloyd, Kevin 684
Lloyd, Sampson II 337–8
Lloyd, Sampson III 337
Lloyd, T. Alwyn 76, 511, 545
Lloyd, W. Hawley 148, 337
Lloyd George, David 125
Lloyds Bank Premises Dept 699
LOC Associates 190

832   INDEX OF ARCHITECTS, ETC.

Lock (Max) & Partners 94, 437, 454
Locke, Joseph 59, 191, 192
Lodge, Oliver W.F. 362
Lodge, William and Ann 549
Lofthouse, W.G. 696, 700
Logan, Andrew 93, 490, 526
Lomax, Tom 93, 169, 632, 636
Long, Alfred 67, 73, 397, 493, 532, 541, 565, 566, 580, 600, 602, 607, 608, 615, 617, 640, Pl. 87
Lonsdale, H.W. 42, 132
Lord, R. 235
Loudon, J.C. 376–7
Lovatt, Henry 719
Lovegrove, H.W. Way 152, 237
Lovett, Henry 153
Lowbridge, G.C. 67, 74, 75, 483, 484, 497, 561, 651, 652, 668, 684, 699, 713, 750
Lowe, Mr 632
Lowndes, Mary 64, 215, 276, 440
Lowry, T.A. 687, 735
Loxton, Samuel 618, 633, 634, 636, 637, 639, 646, 647, 655, 680
Loxton Bros 598, 646, 659
Loxton & Newman 301
Lubetkin, Berthold 81, 479, Pl. 115
Lucas family 332
Lucas, Harry 332
Lucas, Joseph 332
Lugar, Robert 568, 657n.
Luttrell, Simon 456
Lyddyatt family 16
Lyddyatt, Edward 556
Lynall, Henry 762
Lynam, Charles 556
Lynch, Joseph T. 279, 524, 661
Lynes, Mr 202
Lynes, Fred Hunter 69, 71, 553, 688, 716, 717, 731
Lynn, S.F. 158
Lyons & Israel 74, 682
Lyons, Israel & Elsom 74, 696, 700
Lyons+Sleeman+Hoare 171, 608, 613
Lyttelton family 515
Lyttelton, John 515

McAlster, Peter 719
McAlster, Jones & Associates 88, 752
McAslan (John) & Partners 85, 591
Macaulay, F.W. 347
McAuley, Mother Catherine 247
McCarthy & Collings 78, 236
McConnal, H.H. 41, 618, 625, 627, 630, 638, 639
McDowall, Mary Creighton 352
Macfarlane (Walter) & Co. 591, 613, 721
McGowan, D.K. 178
Macgregor, J.E.M. 740
McGregor, Oliver 691
McKenna, John 93, 648
Mackenzie, Mr (organ case-designer) 127

McKeown, Professor Thomas 401
McKewan, Arthur 71, 75, 174, 184, 189, 196, 242, 249, 259, 263, 271, 301, 379, 434, 455
McKewan, Fillmore & McKewan 511, 696
McKewan & McKewan 249, 299, 757
McKillop, N. 760
McLean (David) Design 190
McLean (John) & Sons 747
McMichael, Gerald 65, 76, 315, 319, 331, 332, 406, 409, 569, 657
McMichael (Gerald) & A. Dennis Thacker 344
MacRea, Anthony 233
Maddox, F. Morrell 81, 503, 555
Madeley, C. Stanbury 625
Madeley, Graham S. 249
Madin, John H.D. 83, 84, 86, 88, 110, 139, 167, 172, 258, 333, 359, 374, 380, 381, 382, 383, 384, 385, 386, 387, 388, 389, 390, 410, 602, 608, 780, 785, Pl. 127
Madin (John) Design Group 84, 86, 89, 143, 144, 151, 153, 161, 166, 172, 205, 288, 375, 382, 384, 385, 403, 532, 613, Pl. 131
Madin (John H.D.) & Partners 86, 140n., 375, 378, 380, 384, 416, 588, 604, 693, 784, 785
Madox Brown, Ford see Brown, Ford Madox
Maguire & Co. 543
Maguire (Robert) & Keith Murray 91, 268, 579
Maile (G.) & Son 500, 531, 659, 662
Maile Studios 315
Make 88, 169, 210
Male, Dudley 419
Mallin & Co. 582
Mander family 736–41
Mander, Charles Benjamin 740
Mander, Charles Tertius 56, 740–1
Mander, Sir Geoffrey 706, 740, 741
Mander, Gerald 76, 741
Mander, Neville Hanbury 735
Mander, Theodore and Flora 56, 738–40, 747
Mangan, Wilfred 663
Manning, Joseph 726, Pl. 83
Manning (John) Partnership 277, 288
Mansell, Edward 196
Mansell, T.H. 54, 55, 391, 414, 430, 763
Mansell & Mansell 69, 70, 108, 152, 154, 160, 181, 198, 386, 763–4
Mantle, Paul A. 514
Manton, Charles 40, 665
Manzoni, Sir Herbert 48n., 74, 93–4, 95, 96, 109, 150, 177, 232
Mark, Fred 84, 403
Markwick, W.F. 626, 633
Marnham family 608
Marnham, Richard de 609

INDEX OF ARCHITECTS, ETC.

Marnock, R. Morrison 324
Marriner, Eric M. 236, 396
Marsh, Edward 39, 52, 487, 508, 509, 510
Marsh, Ernest 479
Marsh, H. George 169, Pl. 130
Marsh, J. 540
Marsh, J.B. 491
Marshall, Arthur 45, 65, 560, 680, 730, Pl. 73
Marshall, George 294
Marshall, H.J. 430
Marshall & Tweedy 423
Marshman & Warren 208
Marston, C.F. 437, 452, 453, 455
Marston, Job 309
Marston, John 704
Marston & Healey 61, 437, 453, 454, 460
Marten, G. Mayer 737
Marten, Henry J. 58, 704, 748
Martin, Frederick 47, 61, 69, 159, 216, 290, 337, 386, 391, 399, Pl. 93
Martin, Henry 66, 288
Martin, J. 713
Martin, W.H. 147, 265, 444, 537
Martin, William 46–7, 66, 133, 430
Martin & Chamberlain 4, 37, 38, 41, 44, 46–7, 49, 51, 53, 55, 58, 61, 67, 69, 94, 126, 133, 135, 139, 144, 145, 146, 159, 166, 167, 168, 171, 172, 173, 177, 195, 197, 201, 203, 210, 211, 215, 216, 217, 227, 234, 253, 288, 289, 290, 305, 334, 337, 339, 386, 389, 390, 397, 398, 402, 403, 417, 424, 429, 430, 486, 535n., 615, Pls. 85, 94
Martin & Martin 182, 278, 289, 382, 386, 391, 399, 405, 414
Martin & Martin & W.H. Ward 152, 216, 228, 325, 403, 424
Martin (Henry) & Son 391, 392, 584, 585
Martin, Ward & Keeling 273, 372
Martyn, H.H. 68, 132, 214, 286, 757
Martyn (H.H.) & Co. 483, 584, 636
Mary I, Queen 13, 439
Masey (carver) 676
Masly, P.E. 726
Mason, Charles 83, 748
Mason, E. 428
Mason, Josiah 240n.
Mason, Raymond 169
Mason Richards/Mason Richards Partnership 192, 374, 510, 544, 549, 646, 695
Mason, Richards & Partners 83, 690, 703, 730, 745, 746, 748
Mason & Richards & Partners 717, 721
Massie (Graham) & Partners 169
Masyn, William 12, 621
Mather, Andrew 521

Matthew (Robert), Johnson-Marshall & Partners 85, 189, 190, 630
  see also RMJM
Matthews, Robert F. 71, 230, 292, 342, 452, 455
Maudsley, J. Alan 82, 94, 264, 402, 413
Maule, H.P.G. 307
Maw & Co. (tiling) 71, 317, 536, 605, 606, 739
Mawson, E.P. 76, 90, 484
Mawson, Thomas H. 48, 720, 740
Maxfield, Paul 151
Mayer & Co. 315, 580, 655
Mayston, Arthur R. 66, 447
Mayston & Eddison 447
MBLA 740
Meacham, Isaac 506
Measures, Harry B. 201
Mecanoo 90, 166, 167, Pl. 137
Medland, Maberley & Medland 336
Meggatt, John 331
Meikle, Alan 394
Mellors, Paul 521
Melville (Rodney) & Partners 125, 227
Mendham, J. Bernard 433
Meredith, John W. 229
Meredith, J.T. 36, 47, 487, 514, 519, 570, 571, 572, 573
Meredith & Pritchard 67, 487, 506, 507, 574
Merritt, Anna Lea 621
Merryfield, Thomas 566
MESH Architectural Services 250
Meteyard, Sidney 77, 78, 194, 285, 411, 441, 443, 530, 531, 560
Metz Architects 484
Middleton, Ron 402
Mihailovic, Dusan 351
Mileham, C.N.H. 687
Miller, A.P. 721
Miller, Bernard 90, 696, 697, 698, 736, 737–8
Miller, J.A. 245
Miller, K. Bradley 770
Miller, Sanderson 20, 611, Pl. 47
Milligan, S.G.V. 428
Mills, David R. 527
Mills (Edward) & Partners 87, 781
Millward, Ezra 308
Milner, Edward 334
Milner, Bishop John 25, 39, 262–3, 447, 680
Milward, Edward 528
Milward, Thomas 528
Ministry of Public Building and Works 177, 210, 328, 691, 728
Ministry of Works Architects 719
Minns (S. Elden) & Partners 162
Minton (tiles etc.) 123, 193, 200, 229, 257, 473, 574, 654
Mistry, Dhruva 93, 156
Mitchell, Mary 82, 303, 374, 414

Mitchell, Stephen 85, 289, 348
Mitchell, William 93, 255, 785
Mitchell & Bridgwater 379, Pl. 116
Mitton, E. Stanley 330
MJP Architects 429
Moffat, James 196, 382
Moffat (James) & Sons 333
Molineux, Benjamin 691
Mollesley family *see* Moseley family
Monchaux, Paul de 170
Monckton, Mr 536
Monson, E.C.P. 273
Moody, Andrew 524, 730
Moorcroft, R.L. 683
Moore, A.W. 391
Moore, Charles E. 531, 540
Moore, Rev. H. 710
Moore, J.P. 497
Moore, Leslie Temple 755–6, 765
Moore, Rupert 422
Morgan (sculptor, Birmingham) 659
Morgan (De) (tiles) 739
Morgan, Gareth 422
Morgan, James 22, 677, 708–9, 732, Pl. 56
Morgan, Rev. M. 506
Morgan, R.B. 235
Morgan, William De 749
Morley (David) Architects 376
Morris, Ian 377
Morris, Sir John 747
Morris, Martin 527
Morris, T. 248, 444
Morris, William 739n., 740, 749
Morris (William) & Co. 65, 116, 123, 194, 293, 301, 443, 501, 534, 739, 749
Morris (William) & Co. (Westminster) 492, 730, 737
Morris, Smith & Partners 266
Morris & Whitehouse 248, 444
Morse, Dr Justinian 116
Morter, W.H. 324
Morton, D. & A. Home 295
Moseley (Mollesley) family 711
Moss, W. Cyril 78, 310, 444, 734
Mottershead, Fiona 262
Mountford, J. 164
Moysen, W. 756
Moysley, Edwarde 513
Multon (Leonard) & John Keeling 607
Multon (Leonard J.) & Partners 372, 423
Munro, Alexander 48, 140n.
Munro (James M.) & Son 148
Muntz, G.F. 577
Murdoch, William 25, 93, 169, 243, 587
Murray, Keith 268
  see also Maguire & Murray
Murray, K.L. 642, 665
Murray, W. Grant 606

Muthesius, Hermann 349, 354, 373, 454, 458
Myers, George 118, 120

Naddermier, Oscar 110
Naden, Henry 55, 56, 58, 205, 217, 263, 384, 393, 593, 600, 625
Naden, Thomas 38, 197, 228, 362–3, 394, 644
Nadin, R.A. Reay 437
Nadin, Thomas 560
Napier-Clavering, Claude 398, 399
Nash, John 21, 22, 358, 389, 654, 657n.
Naylor, Anthony J. 340
Naylor, J.R. 592
Nazir, Waheed 95
Neale, Peter 372
Neatby, W.J. 68, 155, 163, 214
Nelson, Horatio, Viscount 25, 138, Pl. 38
Nettlefold, J.S. 373, 399, 722
Neurath, Otto 82, 696
Nevill, Joseph 37, 767
Neville, William 401
Newall, Mark 628
Newcomen, Thomas 490, 589
Newey, C. Isaac 395, 404, 405
Newey, Isaac 347, 395
Newey, John 402
Newill, Mary 64, 259, 363
Newman, Cardinal John Henry 39, 262, 348, 363–4, 416–17
Newton, Ernest 59, 332, 431, 433, 460
Newton, Thomas W.F. 328
Newton (T.W.F.) & A.E. Cheatle 51, 69, 71, 108, 154, 155, 160, 161, 163, 164, 184, 206, 325, 379, 461, 640, 765
Nicholls, J.G. 605, 636
Nichols, G.B. 43, 581, 589n., 615, 625, 628, 636, 637
Nichols, J.R. 253, 331
Nichols & Morgan 43, 637
Nichols (G.B.) & Son 541
Nicholson (organ-builder) 249
Nicholson, A.K. 531
Nicholson, Sir Charles 64, 77, 467, 531, 620, 702
Nicholson & Lord 664
Nicholson (A.K.) Studio 664
Nicholsons (organ-builders) 680
Nicol, G. Salway 285, 303
Nicol, J. Coulson 303
  see also Essex & Nicol; Essex, Nicol & Goodman
Nicol & Nicol 63, 150, 151, 285, 301, 689
Nicol, Nicol & Thomas 239, 417, 690
Nicol & Nicol & Thomas 690
Nicol Thomas 87, 184, 197, 690, 775
Nicol Thomas Viner Barnwell 141, 291
Nicols, Edward 512
Nightingale, John 620

INDEX OF ARCHITECTS, ETC.

Nightingale Associates 343
Nightingale & Marchment 744
Nimptsch, Uli 376
Noble, C. Wycliffe 86, 432
Norgrove Studios 262, 535, 644
Norman & Dawbarn 89, 560, 683, 690, 704, 779
Norris, E. Bower 78, 92, 137, 278, 282, 340, 351, 413, 416, 420, 426, 435, 445, 590, 650, 655, 680, 721, 722
Norris, Edward Berks 443
Norrish & Stainton 84, 386, 408, 414
North & Partners 146
North, Robin & Wilsdon 152
Northumberland, John Dudley, Duke of 15, 476–7, 478
Norton, 1st Lord *see* Adderley, Sir Charles
Norton, 6th Lord *see* Adderley, Hubert
Norton, Charles 23, 602
Norton, Kenneth W. 497
Nost, John van the elder 20, 370
Nowell, Thomas & Jacob 416
Nugent Vallis Brierley 758
Nutt, John 321, 549
Nuttgens, J.E. 233

Oakden, Albert 497
Oakes, J. 396
O'Brien, Gerard 292
oconnell east 84, 694
O'Connor (glass-stainer) 42, 492, 540, 676, 710
O'Connor (Liam) Architects 710
Oddingselles (or Oddingeseles) family 753, 765
Oddingselles, William de 754
Office of Works 566
Offini, William de 611
Ogden, Derek 311
Oliver family 506
Oliver, Stephen 92, 226–7, 680
Oliver, W.J. 62, 723
One Creative Environments Ltd 337
online-architects 385
Orford, Charles Wyatt 207n., 362, 407, 410, 588, 712
Orton, Gavin 270
Orton, W.T. 58, 79, 158, 180, 197, 410, 415, 748, 760, 783
Osborn, F.B. 37, 38, 69, 108, 160, 215, 266, 274, 306, 338, 376–7, 381, 382, 391, 422
Osborn, Pemberton & White 162, 329
Osborn (F.B.) & Alfred Reading 56, 123, 136, 152, 171, 182, 207, 208, 298, 330, 331, 391, 566, 572
Osborne, E.C. 150
Osborne, F.J. 279, 304, 568–9
Osborne, J.P. 41, 61, 66, 84, 180, 182, 200, 231, 239, 242, 245, 249, 250, 251, 253, 258, 259, 293, 322, 327, 331–2, 394, 403, 412, 428, 433, 434, 456, 462, 532, 584, 782, 783

Osborne (F.) & Co. 590
Osborne (J.P.) & Son 74, 80, 163, 186, 208, 231, 233, 256, 258, 261, 262, 264, 267, 268, 281, 286, 299, 302, 346, 385, 416, 431, 466, 496, 569, 587, 757
Oswell, A.E. Lloyd 70, 578, 583, 585
Ould, Edward 56, 62, 670, 738, 740–1, 747, Pl. 97
Owen family 653n.
Owen, Sir Alfred (son of A.E. Owen) 463, 653n.
Owen, Alfred Ernest 463, 653
Owen, David 628
Owen, Sam 51, 261, 317, 325, 338
Owen & Ward 162, 196, 205, 228, 326, 327, 328, 332, 760
Owens, Richard 570n.

Pace, George 91, 123, 361
Paganel (de) family 470, 475
Paganel, Gervase 480
Page, Sir Arthur 722
Page, Sir Richard 722
Page/Park 68
Paget family 722, 723n.
Painter, A. Eaton 695, 704, 713, 717, 719, 728, 729, 734
Paley family 733
Paley & Austin 733
Palk, Rheece W. 163
Palmer, J.G. 597
Pancheri, Christopher 308
Pancheri, Robert 282, 361, 416
Pancheri & Hack 246, 321, 580
Panton Sargent 265
Paolozzi, Eduardo 372
Parbury, Kathleen 441
Pardoe, William 506
Pargeter, Mr 505
Pargiter, L.G. 383
Paris (ironwork, Warwick) 756
Parker, John 326
Parkes, Dorothy 578–9
Parkes, Frank 457
Parkinson, F.J. 475
Parlby, George 784
Parrett, Leslie 691
Parrott, Austin T. 82, 89, 90, 618, 628, 632, 646, 647
Parrott, Dr 164
Parrott, William 403
Parry, Eric 88, 140
Parry, Fr Pierce 262
Parry & Sons 409
Parsons, Alfred 740
Parsons, Owen 61, 62, 76, 328, 329, 330, 332, 333, 335, 392, 408, 411, 431, 457, 458, 459, 461, 717
Partington Associates 250
Patchett, James 196
Patel, Anuradha 93, 536
Patel Taylor 192
Patten, David 182, 607

836 INDEX OF ARCHITECTS, ETC.

Pattison, Dorothy *see* Dora, Sister
Paull (H.J.) & G.T. Robinson 647
Payne, E. Harding 66, 428
Payne, E.J. 117
Payne, Henry (glass-stainer) 64, 78, 194, 315, 321, 548, 570n.
Payne, Henry (painter) 126
Payne (Malcolm) Design Group 84, 335
Payne (Malcolm) Group 592, 758
Payne & Talbot 45, 135, 409
PB associates 548
PCKO 232
PCPT 135, 139, 392, 764
pd architects 612
Peacock, F. Barry 61, 70, 130, 386, 571, 686
Peacock, Thomas 750, 751
Peacock (F. Barry) & E.C. Bewlay 78, 80, 85, 130, 133, 137, 144, 184, 286, 325, 372, 379, 412, 430, 443, 455, 486, 616
 see also Cossins, Peacock & Bewlay
Peacock, Bewlay & Cooke 373
Peake (Anthony) Associates 87, 172
Pearce (glass-stainer) 176
Pearce, William 513, 569
Pearce & Co. 413
Pearce & Cutler 246, 266, 316, 321, 364, 365, 397, 527, 541, 542, 543, 776
Pearce (William) Ltd 443, 516, 550, 597, 604, 616, 756
Pearson, Frank 194
Pearson, John Loughborough 37, 38, 64, 194, 336, 420, 624, Pl.65
Pearson, Thomas 742
Pearson & Brown 549
Peart, Charles 474
Pedley, J.L. 303n.
Pedley, Joseph 111
Peel, Sir Robert 48, 275, 375
Peel, Victor S. 123, 236, 248, 396, 444, 728
Pegram, Henry 368
Penn, John 466
Penoyre & Prasad 90, 342, 591, 682
Pepler & Allen 722, 723, 724
Pepper, George E. 61, 70, 71, 80, 183, 184, 186, 258, 319, 320, 326, 328, 329, 330, 332, 452–3
Percivall & Ricketts 622
Percy, Geoffrey 704
Perkins, A.E. 345
Perks, Richard 111
Perks, Robert 680
Perrins, Bernard 421
Perrins, Thomas 530
Perritt, J. 579
Perry, Alfred Dickens 206, 560
Perry, Luke 583
Perry, Richard 168
Peter, Joseph 309

Petit, Rev. J.L. 710
Pevsner, Sir Nikolaus 431
Peyto, John de 280
Phillips, Elizabeth 111, 154
Phillips, Niall 89
Phillips, Trefor 402
Phillips (Niall) Architects 299, 683
Phillips (Michael) Associates 135
Phipps, C.J. 70, 687
Phipson, A.B. 51, 139, 146, 178, 199, 206, 392, 395, 401, 402, 405, 605
Phipson, W.A. 404
Phipson (A.B.) & Son 161
Phoenix, George 679
Phoenix (prefabs) 313
pHp architects 190
Picardi, Gennaro 639
Picardi Architects 639
Pick Everard 536
Pickford, Ernest 555
Pickford, Joseph 105n., 755, Pl.17
Piddock, John 563
Pietra Santa 277
Pigott Smith, John *see* Smith, John Pigott
Pilkington, Alfred J. 580
Pimley, Richard 111
Pincher, Edward 41, 47, 505, 532, 568, 602, 604, 605, 611, 613, 615, 652
Piper, John 93, 374, 752, Pl.125
Pippet family 757
Pippet, Elphege 277, 340, 757
Pippet, Gabriel 757
Pippet, Joseph A. 237, 496, 624, 757
Pippet, Elphege & Oswald 757
Pite, Arthur Beresford 75, 432
Pitt, J.H. 598
Pitt, William 659
Pittaway, J.K. 726
Planet Art 348
Plant, George H. 580, 614
Playne & Lacey 372
Plevins, Thomson 51, 53, 144, 150, 151, 159, 206, 209
Plevins & Norrington 209
Pollen, John Hungerford 39, 363–4, 416
Pollen, Patrick 248
Pollock, James and Thomas 194
Ponting, C.E. 644, 734
Poole, John 116, 138, 175, 246, 316, 347, 351, 440, 645
Poole (Henry) & Sons 709
Porphyrios Associates 87, 170, 778
Porter, Tom 82, 447, 448, 450, 463
Potter, Donald 623, 650, 703, 710
Potter, Joseph 47, 445–6, Pl.60
Potter, Joseph Jun. 43, 700
Potter (F.) & Associate 252
Powell, Alan 550
Powell, Dunstan J. 65, 322, 361, 364, 625, 757
Powell, Gerry 679, 720

Powell, James Crofts 564
Powell, John Hardman 121, 360, 447, 757
Powell, Sebastian Pugin 119
Powell, William 783
Powell Moya Partnership 135
Powell (James) & Sons/Powells 42, 281, 293, 422, 441, 442, 475, 513, 530, 547, 558, 560, 564, 603, 642, 645, 676, 710, 713, 756, 776, 784
Power, Fr John 276
Preedy, Frederick 37, 38, 315, 321, 322, 537, 734
Price, Mr 502
Price, Claude 93, 291, 293, 322, 442, 492, 578, 662, 756
Price, John 288
Price, P.J. 690
Price, Thomas G. 180, 181, 343, 452, 459
Pridmore (G.W.) & Son 510
Priest, Dave 630
Priestley, Dr Smith 164
Priestley, Joseph 48, 123, 140n.
Prince of Wales's Institute of Architecture 577, Pl.134
Pritchard, Thomas Farnolls 24, 658, 677n.
Pritchard & Pritchard 412
Property Services Agency 383
Property Services Agency, Midland Region Design Unit Architects 133
Proud, Thomas Frederick 57, 63, 182, 284, 303
Proud & Faulkner 331
Provis, A.W. 562
Provost, Allain 192
PRP 240
Prudential Assurance Architects' Department 152
Pryce, Thomas 635
Prynne, E.A. Fellowes 596
PSA Midland Region 89
PSA Projects 89, 684
Pudsey family 463
Pudsey, Henry 20, 440
Pugh, George 706
Pugh, Roy 539
Pugin, A.W.N. 35, 38–9, 41–2, 55, 106, 117–22, 152, 233, 247, 248, 341, 363, 374–5, 419, 445–7, 475, 680, 698, 757, Pls. 60, 62
Pugin, E.W. 38–9, 65, 119, 120, 233, 445, 447, 496, 548, 554, 597, 664n., 681, 703
Pugin, Peter Paul 121, 445
Pugin & Murray 247n.
Purcell family 647
Purdy, Martin 91, 275
Purvey May 256
Pye, William 190

Quad Projects 381

Quick, Harry 299

Radclyffe & Watson 385
Radford, Blantern 508
Radford Harper 270
Raffl (Paris) 625
Raggett, J.J. 231, 256, 270, 327
Raikes, Robert 709
Ralphs (Tim) Design Group 615
Ralphs & Mansell 641, 642, 659
Ramsell, Abraham 474
Randle, George 257
Randle, Walter W. 513
Randle, G.H. & W. 65, 491
Randle (George) & Son 582
Rao, Dr V.P.N. 577, Pl.134
Rastrick, John Urpeth 32, 559
Rathbone, David 372
Rathbone, D.T. 604
Rathbone & Taylor 372
Rattee & Kett 739
Rattison & Sons 235
Rawstorne, John 23, 152, 253n.
Raymond, G. 664
Rayner, George Henry 148
Reade Buray Associates 626, 665
Reading, Alfred 56, 57, 298, 326, 329, 330, 386, 764
 see also Osborn & Reading
Reardon, Michael 91, 116
Reardon (Michael) & Partners 114, 624
Redfern & Haigh 237
Redman, J.S. 493
Reed, W.G. (Bill) 83, 85, 89, 289, 348, 380, 394
Reedesign 666
Rees, Verner O. 367, 369
Rees (Verner), Laurence & Mitchell 85, 369
Reeves, Charles 44, 487, 550, 565
Regis, Cyrille 613
Reid, Budge 81, 489
Reid, J. Eadie 508
Reid (Geoffrey) Associates 234
Reilly, Sir Charles 82, 696
Renn & Thacker 376
Renton Howard Wood Levin 87, 168
 see also RHWL
Repton, Humphry 21, 324, 568, 657
Reynolds family 344, 403
Reynolds, Edwin F. 61, 63, 76, 77, 80, 108, 173, 184, 194, 230, 267, 269, 312, 313, 333, 344, 345, 362, 388, 396, 403, 409, 412, 435, 440–1, 457, 546, 567, 568, 578, 579, 582, 586, 602, 603, 649, 650, 763, 764, 785, Pl.120
 see also Wood & Kendrick & E.F. Reynolds, etc.
Reynolds, H.H. 332
Reynolds, John 403
Reynolds (Keith) Associates 165

838 INDEX OF ARCHITECTS, ETC.

Reyntiens, Patrick 752, Pl. 125
RGA Landscape Architects 315
RHWL 687
  see also Renton Howard Wood Levin
Rhys-Davies, Miall 82, 308, 374, 414, 517
Richard, Brother 515
Richard the mason 515
Richards (stained-glass designer) 597
Richards, Brent 526
Richards, F.W. 163
Richards, H. Ravenscroft 175
Richards, T. 503
Richards Tiles 277
Richardson, H. 250
Richardson, J. 176
Rickman, Thomas 24, 105, 118, 125, 165, 176, 320–1, 381n., 746
Rickman (Thomas) & R.C. Hussey 35, 422, 513, 771, 772
Rickman (Thomas) & Henry Hutchinson 22, 24, 49, 125, 150, 158, 203, 215, 235, 245, 376, 395, 396, 398, 771, 772
Rider, Norman T. 310
Ridge (architects) 765
Ridley family 727
Riland, John 437
Riland, Richard 450
Riley & Smith 70, 137, 150, 327
Rising, H. Whiteman 712
Ristich, Pedrag 351
Ritchie, Walter 784–5
rja 448
RMJM 376, 684
  see also Matthew (Robert), Johnson-Marshall & Partners
Robbins, P.B. 396
Robert of Beverley 478
Roberts, Mr 467
Roberts, C.A. Llewelyn 555
Roberts, D.J. 239
Roberts, Ernest 81, 267, 417, 497
Roberts, Gwyn 337
Roberts, James A. 86–7, 94, 138, 204, 207, 299, 608–10
Roberts, John Piddock 508
Roberts, William 523, 524
Roberts (James A.) Associates 153, 157, 454, 764
Roberts (James A.) & Partners 88, 689
Roberts Limbrick 341
Robinson, Mr 597
Robinson, G.H.T. 729
Robinson, G.J. 717
Robinson, G.T. 35, 36, 55, 438, 448, 647, 702, 775
Robinson, H. Fitzroy 85, 189
Robinson, H.B. 724, 730, 732
Robinson, Hurley 79, 81, 172, 239, 345, 404, 489

Robinson, Robert 30, 494, 560
Robinson, Thomas 41, 44, 51, 69, 72, 290, 493, 495, 496, 523, 528, 529, 530, 536, 541, 545, 549, 550, 552, 553, 554, 555, 558, 559n.
Robinson (Fitzroy) & Partners 87, 153, 159, 160
Robinson (Hurley) & Partners 87
Robinson (Hurley) & Son 162, 207, 301, 303
Robison, Marion 266
Robotham, David 169
Robothams 190, 375
Roches, Bishop Peter des 514
Roddis, John 38, 123, 128, 360, 605, 645, 666, 712, 757, 784
Roddis & Nourse 117, 232
Rogers, Harold S. 537
Rogers, Henry 729–30
Rogers, Richard 166
Rolfe Judd 166
Rollinson, Mark 495
Rollinson & Beckley 494, 495, 497, 498, 499, 507, Pl. 92
Romanoff, Maximilian 73, 169
Roper, G.F. 37, 702
Ross, William 391
Rosser, Clifford 607
Rotsey, Humphrey 408
Rotton, Ambrose and Bridget 201
Round, Abel 422, 566
Round, Charles 504
Round, Zachary 557
Rous, Herbert le 618
Rousseau, Jacques 224
Rouw, P. 117
Rowbotham, W.D. 59, 555
Rowe, A.B. 274, 302, 341
Rowe, A.V. 67, 74, 517, 521, 529, 550, 554, 567
Rowe, Henry 305, 428, 565
Rowe, Richard J. 698, 701
Rowles, S.C. 606
Rowse, Anthony 332
Royley, Robert 17, 676
Royleys (sculptors, Burton-on-Trent) 407
RPS Design 231, 252
RRA 414
Ruddock, S. 274
Ruhlmann, Tristan 310
Rupert, Prince 105
Rush, Brian 757, 784
Rush Davis 325, 631, 714
Rush Granelli & Partners 514, 780, 784
Rush (Brian A.) & Partners 396
Ruskin, John 107, 141, 148n., 333, 334, 352
Russell Hobbis 569–70
Rust, J. 680
Rutherford, John 68, 486

INDEX OF ARCHITECTS, ETC. 839

Rutherford, Rosemary 347, 542
Rutland, Edward 553
Ryan, Sally 629
Ryland family 324
Ryland, Louisa Anne 48, 133, 290, 324
Rysbrack, Michael 25, 220

Sacheverell family 15, 455, 463–5
Sacheverell, Sir George 465, 466
Sacheverell, George 20, 440
Sacheverell, Henry 463
Sadler, Mr 531
Sadler, Richard 452
St George's Guild 442
St John, Ambrose 417
St Paul's Associates 208
Salisbury, Frank O. 627
Salisbury, Henry James 680
Salvin, Anthony 11, 37, 641
Sandal, Thomas 20, 760
Sanders, T.W. 662, 663
Sandwell M.B.C. Architects/Architect's Department 591, 611, 613
Sandwell M.B.C. Building Services 572, 574
Sandwell M.B.C. Urban Design 584
Sandwell M.B.C. Urban Design & Building Services 89, 565
Sandy, H.T. 65, 301, 426, 427, 633
Sandy & Norris 292, 420
Sapcote & Sons 133
Sarum Partnership 444
Satchwell, Roland 81, 205, 528, 543, 585, 643
Satchwell & Roberts 274, 342
Saunders Boston 404
Saunders Partnership 299, 549, 571
Savage, C. 661
Savage, Thomas 160
Savills Commercial 573
Sawyer, Sir James 164
Scheemakers, Peter 374
Scoles, A.J.C. 248, 664
Scoles, J.J. 361
Scott, A. Irving 599, 600
Scott, Adrian Gilbert 92, 435
Scott, Sir Edward 656
Scott, E.M. 597
Scott, Sir Francis 656
Scott, Sir George Gilbert 513, 641, 656–7, 658
Scott, George Gilbert Jun. 37, 38, 60, 106, 128, 335–6, 364
Scott, Sir Giles Gilbert 233, 282, 297, 533–4, 535
Scott, Harold S. 259, 313, 372, 431, 587
Scott, J. 548
Scott, John Oldrid 513, 755
Scott, John S. 712
Scott, Sir Joseph 656, 657, 658
Scott, Richard Gilbert 92, 281–2, Pl.124
Scott, Robert Welbeloved 657
Scott, Warwick 288, 508, 542, 650
Scott, Brownrigg & Turner 163
Scott & Clark 65, 72, 75, 81, 499, 500, 501, 521, 522, 530, 532, 543, 551, 567, 568, 570, 576, 591, 593, 597, 598, 599, 605, 634, 653
Scott & Moffatt 641
Scott (H.S.) & Harry Weedon 258, 453
Seaborne, Matthew 25, 176, 220, 297, 757, 779
Seager (Robert) Design 95, 146, 687
Seale, Gilbert 627
Seale (G.) & Son 685
Searchfield, E.J. 498
Seeley, John 622
Seifert (Richard) & Partners 87, 169, 207, 781, Pl.130
Sellers, J.H. 453
Sellers, Stanley 87, 88, 89, 689, 760, 785
Sensi (Trastevere) 364
Sergison Bates 633
Shard End Panel 82, 278, Pl.126
Sharington, Sir William 476, 479
Sharp, James J. 774
Sharp, J.P. 327, 328, 335, 584
Sharp (J.P.) & Co. 47, 51, 55, 139, 146, 209, 317, 325, 327, 331, 333, 391, 401, 580, 584, 586
Sharp-Smith, Charles 718
Shaw, James R. 151, 293
Shaylor (contractor) 375
Shaylor, Graham 95
shedkm 242, 414, 633
Sheldon family 503
Sheldon, Edward 503
Shenstone, William 21, 514, 517–19
Shenton, Tony 540
Shepherd, C.K. 76, 431
Sheppard Robson 190, 216, 372, 375, 651, 684
Sheppard (Richard), Robson & Partners 85, 517, 521, 608, 646, 663
Sheppard (Lewis) & Son 575
Sheridan-Shedden, J.R. 82, 231, 232, 308
Shipley, H.W. 620
Shipley & Foster 618, 624, 631, 655
Shipway, Edwin 199
Short, Nathaniel 621
Shottery Guild 249
Shree Hindu Community Centre 343
Shrewsbury, 16th Earl of 120, 122, 445–6
Shrigley & Hunt 597, 697
Shuffrey, Leonard 739–40, 741
Shute, John 476
Shuttleworth, Ken 210

Siddalls, John 44, 648
Sidebotham, C.W. 501
Sidebotham, George 542, 556, 577, 710, 713, 725, 731
Sidell Gibson 87, 140, 142, 170, 172
Sidell Gibson Crouch Butler 252
Silcock, Arnold 75, 432
Silk, Christopher 332
Silver, Thomas 256, 257, 319
Simcock, Samuel 718, 736
Simcox, George 396, 398
Simcox, John 310, 312
Simister, H.W. 79, 288, 400, 409, 417, 420, 436
Simonds, L.J. 731
Simons Design 136
Simpson, A.A. 458
Simpson (Ian) Architects 83, 88, 183, 207
Simpson (John) Architects 778
Simpson (John) & Partners 777
Sinclair, Robert Cooper 695
Sinclair Architects 87, 152, 180, 383
Skeat, Francis 474, 540, 650
Skelcher (Philip) & Partners 209, 480, 778
Skelton, John 433
Skinner, Francis 479
Slater & Carpenter 11, 280
Sleigh, Bernard 776
Sloane, Mark 191
Smalbroke, Richard II 299
Smalman Smith, Francis see Smith, Francis Smalman
Smeaton, John 466, 577, 587
Smeeton, Reginald 176, 289
Smith, A. Freeman 317
Smith, Alexander 173
Smith, Alfred 297
Smith, Charles Surman 384
Smith, Francis (C18) 19, 297, 309, 377, 578–9, 679n., 722
Smith, Francis Smalman (C19) 40, 41, 45, 46, 507, 514, 527, 535, 536, 538, 545, 549, 551, 555, 558, 560
Smith, Gerald E.R. 604, 664
Smith, G.M. 235
Smith, H. 587
Smith, H.T.D. 729
Smith, John 560
Smith, John Greaves 91, 95, 494, 503, 603
Smith, John Pigott 106
Smith, Joshua Toulmin 197–8
Smith, Kenneth Hutchinson 76, 662, 706–7, 747, Pl. 6
Smith, Sidney F. 496
Smith, Solomon 22, 243, 462
Smith, T. Tayler 37, 702
Smith, Thomas 35, 46, 54, 55, 500, 514, 527, 536, 538, 541, 542, 545, 548, 550, 552, 553, 558, 624, Pl. 8

Smith, William the elder 18, 309, 437, 473, 611, 671, 713
Smith, William the younger (son of Francis Smith) 579
Smith (D.) & Son 376, 429
Smith (James) & Sons 391
Smithin, Sidney 421
Smythe, Misses 776n.
Smythson, John 771
Snow, A.L. 74, 241, 377
Soane, Sir John 21, 358, 762, Pl. 49
Solar Design 626
Solihull Council Building Design Group 778
Solihull M.B.C. Architects Department 760
Solihull M.B.C. Building Design Group 775
Solomon (Lewis), Kaye & Partners 171
Somers Clarke Jun. see Clarke, Somers Jun.
Somery (de) family 13, 435, 470, 478, 481, 482
Somery, John de 435, 476, 482
Somery, Roger de (d. 1272) 435, 476, 481
Somery, Roger de (son, d. 1291) 435, 476, 481
Sorby, T.C. 628
Southall, Joseph 129
Southall, L.J. 506
Sparks, Les 95
Spear, Francis 361
Speir & Beavan 62, 722, 723
Spence (Sir Basil), Glover & Ferguson 86, 190
Spence, T.R. 368
Spencer, Mr 261
Spon Lane Iron Foundry 260
Spooner family 779
Spooner, Abraham 240, 779
Spooner, Isaac 779
Spooner, Rev. William 779
Spreadbury, H. Vernon 315
Spriggs, Fred 281
Spurr, George 507
Spurrier, William 143
Squire, Richard 407, 523
Stagg, W. 642
Stallybrass, Basil 62, 722, 724
Standbridge, John 21–2, 323–4, 462, 778, 779
Stanford, Sir William 267
Stanger & Stanger 713
Stanley family 608
Stanley, A.G. 663
Stanley, S.A. 524
Stanley, Walter 609
Stanley-Morgan, Robert 275
Stanton, Edward 20, 220
Stanton (Edward) & Christopher Horsnaile 220

INDEX OF ARCHITECTS, ETC. 841

Stanton Williams 88, 89, 130, 170, 355
Stavely-Hill, H.S. 709
Steblina, Wasyl 726
Steele & Keay 286
Steffian Bradley Architects 630
Stensell, Alfred 645
Stephens, Charles 534–5
Stephens, Joseph I 734
Stephenson, Robert 59, 192, 732
Stephenson Studio 190
Steven, Bros & Co. 714
Stevens, Ernest 528, 541
Stevens, G.E. 743
Stevenson, William 600
Stieger, Jacqueline Gruber 123
Stilgoe, Henry E. 132, 196, 288, 405
Stillman, A.C.H. 651
Stjernstedt, Rosemary 370
Stockton & Son 580
Stockwell, Arthur 69, 206
Stokes, Richard 506
Stone Ecclesiastical 569
Stone, Toms & Partners 626
Stott, Sir Sidney 80, 242
Stourbridge Brick Co. 305
Stourbridge Stained Glass Works 505
Street, A.E. 736
Street, G.E. 37, 275n., 548, 650, 736, 755
Stretton (G.) & Sons 642
Stride, Lewis 38, 540
Stuart, J.C. 584
Stubington, Richard 78, 165, 363
Studholme, Robert 34, 265
Stuflesser, Ferdinand 435, 446
Sturge, Joseph 48, 210n., 384
Sueur, Hubert le 17, 676
Surman, J.B. 75, 76, 79, 81, 175, 202n., 256, 269, 274, 291, 293, 311, 339, 417, 458, 583, 612, 764, Pl. 108
Surman, Kelly & Surman 163
Surman (J.B.) & Partner 84, 423
Surman (J.B.) & Partners 230
Surridge, G. 348
Sutherland, Duke of 704
Sutton (de) family 470, 476
Sutton, John de, lord of Dudley 476, 481
Sutton & Wilkinson 543
Swaab, Roger 564
Swan, James A. 76, 77, 81, 245, 246, 273n., 297, 321, 422, 423, 430, 501, 502, 521, 622, 670, 672, 675–6, 678, 689, 698, 701, 741, 751, 784
Swan Architects 458
Swann, A.J. 73
Swarbrick, Thomas 116, 756
Swift, William 770
Swynnerton, Thomas 675

Symonds, Henry 247

Tadic, Dragomir 351
Talbot Brown & Fisher 382
Tandy, Fr William 427
Tangye, George and Sir Richard 128, 129, 133
Tanner, Douglas 391
Tanner, Sir Henry 68, 156, 592, 687
Tanner & Horsburgh 76, 391, 431, 453
Tapper, Walter 38, 655
Tappin, Stuart 479
Taunton, Donald 122, 321, 502
Tawny Gray (Toin Adams) 197
Taylor family 345
Taylor, Benjamin 770, Pl. 35
Taylor, Edward R. 133
Taylor, F.J. 326
Taylor, John 630
Taylor, John II 323–4
Taylor, Joseph 184
Taylor, Leonard J. 570, 573
Taylor, S.G. 394
Taylor, Thomas 636
TCN 210
Tecton 81, 477, 479–80, 489, Pl. 115
Tee (Clifford) & Gale see Clifford Tee & Gale
Telford, Thomas 28, 30, 387, 414, 577, 587, 588, 591, 593, 732, Pl. 53
Temple Cox Nicholls 150, 152, 155, 172, 245, 632
Temple Moore, Leslie see Moore, Leslie Temple
Teulon, S.S. 36, 37, 52, 106, 267, 358, 359n., 362, 377, 413
Theed, William 49, 714
Thomas, Mr (builder, Sparkbrook) 402
Thomas, Brian 93, 540, 650
Thomas, Christopher 262, 265, 567, 576, 579
Thomas, John 48, 384
Thomas, Percy 499
Thomas, Rachel 176
Thomas, T. Wynne 313
Thomas, William 35, 50, 233
Thomas & Kendall 125
Thomas (Percy) Partnership 87, 163, 168, 172, 492, 493, 499
Thomason, F.H. 179, 201
Thomason, (H.R.) Yeoville 40, 43–4, 45, 49, 51, 54, 57, 107, 108, 111, 124, 127–9, 130, 143, 144, 145, 151, 155, 158, 161, 185, 204, 210, 238, 296, 358, 378, 379, 381, 387, 392, 395, 396, 401, 438–40, 444, 447, 464, 516, 571, 583, 591, 699, Pls. 1, 61, 79
Thomason & Whitwell 185, 216, 229, 566
Thompson family 719

Thompson, Jabez 304
Thompson, J.C. 508, 523
Thompson, William 117, 474
Thomson, R. 245
Thorne Architecture 726
Thorneycroft, G.B. 48, 682, 715
Thorneycroft, Col. Thomas 742–3, 746
Thornton (sculptor, fl. 1869) 474
Thornton, Richard 376
Thornton, Roy 451
Thornton, Samuel 298
Thornycroft, Hamo 582
Thornycroft, Thomas 48, 682, 684
Thorp, J. ('herald painter') 309
Thorp, Jonathan 200
Thorpe, John 16, 221, 223–4, Pl. 29
3DReid 88, 148
Thurlow, E.H. 452
Thurlow, Lucas & James 155
Tibbalds Colbourne Karski Williams 95
Tibbetts, Leslie 536
Till, W.S. 48, 217, 290, 376
Timmins, S.D.W. 77, 717, 718, 728
Tin, Win 414
Tinworth, George 598
Titley, E.F. 45, 271, 332, 437, 444, 447, 449, 454, 457, 459, 460, 466
Titley & Jones 455, 459, 460
Tivey, T.W. 517
Toft, Albert 68, 73, 165, 166, 324, 627
Tolkien, J.R.R. 311
Tolkien, Tim 241
Toll End Works 576
Tolley, Bob 209, 436, 499
Tolmé, J.H. 405
Tomkins, H.C. 303
Tomlinson, Mr (bricklayer) 543
Tomlinson, J. 752
Tomlinson, James 487
Tompkins, Rev. J.C.W. 244
Tongue, Edward 642
Tower, Walter 737
Townsend, Robert 83, 401
Townsend & Howson 756
Townshend Associates 170
Townshend Landscape Architects 170
TPS Consult 234
Trabute, William 535
Traherne, Margaret 781
Travers, Martin 216, 285
Trehearne & Norman, Preston & Partners 160
Treleaven, M.V. 715
Trent, W.E. 486
Trent, W.E. & W.S. 600
Trentham, George 228
Tricht, Jehan Aert van 446n.
Trickett (E. Showell) & Son 276
Tripe, A.C. 94
Tripe & Wakeham 154
Troman, David 762
Trubshaw, James 270
Trunquet, Robert 439

Turley Associates 714
Turley (Robert) & Associates 154
Turner, O.A. 502
Turner Woolford Sharp 171, 178, 179
Turton family 610
Turton, William 410
Tutin, Richard 22, 26, 204, 699, Pl. 55
Twamley, William 466
Tweedale 631, 665, 677, 694, 712, 714, 750, 751
Twentyman, Richard 77, 79, 81, 82, 84, 87, 90, 91, 544, 623, 649, 650, 653, 670, 689, 690, 693, 703, 704, 705, 710, 713, 714, 720, 721, 732, 735, 748, 749, 750, 751–2, Pl. 123
see also Lavender & Twentyman
Twentyman & Percy 577
Twentyman Percy & Partners 542, 556, 604, 679, 702, 704, 709, 710, 712, 713, 721, 725, 731
Twist, W. Norman 79, 157, 181, 208, 250, 288, 306, 409, 412, 423, 762
Tye, Roderick 169
Tyler Parkes Partnership 633
Tylor, H. Bedford 60, 350, 353, 354–6
Type, Marcus O. 70, 71, 108, 163, 175, 178, 179, 187, 206, 304, 306, 325, 332, 333, 379
Tysatt, Father Tysan 542

U, Khin Zaw 414
Ullathorne, Fr John 39, 679
Ulm, Henry 12, 280, 296
Ulrik, Margot 707n.
Underhill, Baron C.S. 252, 283n.
Unite, George 183
Upright, Malcolm 704
Upton, Charles 292, 483
Urban Design 139, 278
Urban Design Team 267
Urry, Frederick 332

Valentine, John 462
van Nost, John the elder *see* Nost, John van the elder
Vasilyk, Roman 726
Vassalli, Francesco 691
Vaughan, John 483
Vaughan, Matthew 472
Vaughton, Sidney H. 179
Vaughton, Thomas 462
Veall, Ashton 542
Veall, J.R. 562, 623, 705, 715, 748
Velarde, F.X. 696
Verity (Frank) & Samuel Beverley 152
Vertegans, R.H. 254, 714
Vesey, John (Harman), Bishop of Exeter 6, 12, 13, 15, 16, 437, 438, 440, 449, 462, 463
Vicars, Albert 39, 195
Victoria, Queen 48, 127, 129, 131, 132, 156, 684

INDEX OF ARCHITECTS, ETC. 843

Villers, James 259
Villiers, C.P. 49, 714
Villiers-Wilkes, Emma 116
Voysey, C.F.A. 73n.
Vriendt, Albrecht Franz Lieven de 120
Vulliamy, Lewis 24, 26, 46, 495, 560, 561, 670, 688

Waals, Peter 582, 586
Wade, Andrew 266
Wade, George Edward 73, 541
Wadmore, J.F. 442
Wager, Frank 430
Wailes 42, 121, 530, 650, 676, 698, 756
Wainwright, Keith 281
Wainwright, W.J. 248
Waite, G.A. 665
Wakeford (Kenneth), Jerram & Harris 690
Walford, William 26, 688, 690
Walhouse, John 635
Walker, A.G. 73, 730
Walker, A.J. 717
Walker, Alfred Pickard 350, 355, 356
Walker, Arthur S. 659, 662
Walker, Gordon 248
Walker, S.T. 186, 388
Walker, William 513
Walker, W.R. 579
Walker, Burges & Cooper 30, 498, 533, 576
Walker (S.T.) & Duckham 95, 209, 484, 499
Walker (J.H.) Ltd 662
Walker (S.T.) & Partners 85, 91, 143, 167, 220, 252, 264, 273, 281, 297, 311, 313, 329, 348, 430, 436, 477, 759
Walker Troup 232, 589
Wall, A.B. 248, 543, 679
Wall, Jacqueline 178
Wallis, Gilbert & Partners 80, 228
Walsall M.B.C. Director of Architectural Services 652
Walsall M.B.C. Property Services 630
Walsh, Bishop Thomas 117, 119, 120
Walters, F.A. 364
Ward, A. 651
Ward, D. Henry 56, 57, 202, 316, 327, 329
Ward, Lloyd F. 403
Ward, W.H. 45, 51, 108, 135, 139, 145, 147, 148, 150n., 153, 171, 196, 246, 288, 765
Ward & Co. 660
Ward & Hughes 42, 176, 244, 246, 281, 315, 440, 443, 642, 644, 645, 678, 710, 782
Ward McHugh 615
Waring family 761
Warner & Dean 510
Warr, Bernard G. 172

Warre, Eleanor 644
Warren, Benjamin 249, 339, 575, 781
Warren, David 730
Warrington, William 42, 121, 446, 501, Pl. 60
Warwick, Earls of 437
Warwick, Roger de Newburgh, Earl of 449
Waterhouse, Alfred 127, 131
Waterhouse, Paul 70, 141
Waterhouse, Thomas Francis 734
Wates (builders) 528
Wates (Midlands) Ltd 731
Watkin & Maddox 81, 497, 555, 699, 750, Pl. 111
Watkins Gray Woodgate International 152
Watson, John D. 467
Watson & Coates 504
Watson & Johnson 80, 184, 199, 411
Watson, Johnson & Stokes 160
Watson, Stokes & Partners 643
Watt, James 24, 48, 93, 133, 140n., 169, 243, 245, 251, Pl. 39
Watt, James Junior 222, 224, 226, 245, 587
Watton, Harry 231
Waudby (John) & Son 678
Waygood (lift-builder) 129
WCEC Architects 517
Weale, William 25, 697
Webb, Aston 132
Webb, Christopher 322
Webb, E. Doran 65, 364, Pl. 67
Webb, Geoffrey 78, 246, 440, 474
Webb, G.F. 73, 76, 80, 483, 489, 493, 498, 505, 506, 526, 527, 538, 540, 554, 556, 560
Webb, John 22, 642
Webb, Joseph 562
Webb, Maurice 369
Webb, Thomas 494
Webb (Aston) & Ingress Bell 44, 67, 131, 132, 365–7, 368, 369, 372, 549, Pl. 80
Webb & Gray 76, 77, 81, 82, 472–3, 474, 475, 486, 488, 489, 495, 497, 500, 506, 507, 522, 524, 525, 526, 529, 539, 540, 548, 550, 555, 558, 561, 562n., 563, 571, 581, 747
Webb Gray & Partners 535
Webber, E. Berry 760
Webber (E. Berry) & Partners 760
webbgray 88, 613
Webster family 466
Webster, Gordon 710
Weedon, Harry 76, 80, 204, 242, 259, 263, 294, 383, 402, 415, 453, 455, 457, 458
Weedon Associates 267
Weedon (Harry) & Partners 81, 84, 183, 204, 415, 454, 489, 690, 759, 760

Weedon Partnership 144, 210, 380, 404, 454
Weeks, Noah 240
Weightman & Bullen 92, 120, 347, 380, 679
Weir's Glass 542
Weller, John I 718
Weller, John II 46, 55, 56, 592, 716–17, 719, 728, 745
Weller, O.M. 486, 499, 529, 540, 599n., 721, 729, 751
Weller, W.J.H. 62, 69, 538, 670, 691, 704, 708, 717, 719, 725, 728–9, 743, 747, 748, 764, Pl. 96
Weller & Proud 43, 605
Weller (John) & Silvester 748
Weller (John) & Sons 717
Wells, Joseph 764
Wells, Randall 62, 722–3
Wenyon, George H. 66, 72, 483, 589, 590, 592, 616, 617, Pl. 90
Wesley, John 692
West, Benjamin 25, 175, Pl. 37
West Hart Partnership 644
West Midlands Regional Health Authority Design Unit 758
Westlake, Nathaniel H.J. 42, 501
Westley, John 547
Westley, Joseph 770
Westley, William 19, 111, 451, 547, Pl. 34
Westmacott, Sir Richard 25, 117, 138, 220, Pl. 38
Weston, Howard C. 315
Whale, A.S. 731
Wheeler, Sir Charles 542, 677, 682
While, George 78, 90, 91, 416, 420, 422, 423, 441, 442–3, 444, 520, 758, Pl. 122
While, Thomas 513
Whinney, T.B. 70, 229, 450, 552, 652, 685
Whinney (T.B.) & Son 583
White, C. Neville 758
White, John 26, 495, 549
White, Thomas 19, 220, 770
White, Alderman William 210n.
White, Allom & Co. 126
White (K.C.) & Partners 219, 442
White & Sons 297
White (A.J.) & Styles 269, 451
Whitehouse, J.H. 352, 356
Whitehouse, Sidney Lunn 275, 287
Whitehouse, Thomas 26, 565
Whitford, Elsie 247n., 252
Whitgreave, G.T. 711
Whiting, B.J. 281
Whitling, H.J. 35, 442
Whitmore, William 30, 410, 776, Pl. 54
Whittall, W. & J. 568
Whittle, Philip 88, 483, 744
Whitwell, Cooper 239, 264

Whitwell, Thomas Stedman 23, 124, 143, 157
Whitwell (C.) & Son 67, 308, 428
Whitworth, Robert 28
Whorwood family 602, 603, 611
Wicks, H.G. 77, 279, 297, 314, 360, 603–4
   see also Harvey & Wicks
Wiggin, Sir Henry 402, 403
Wigginton, W. 581
Wigham 199
Wigley, Ernest H. 184, 196, 303, 330, 764, 783
Wilford, C. Edmund 76, 462
Wilkes, Job 625
Wilkes, Solomon 779
Wilkinson, Alfred 514
Wilkinson, Colonel J.H. 462
Wilkinson, John 701
Wilkinson, Thomas 327, 330
Willcock (builder) 591
Willcox & Raikes 266
Willement, Thomas 756
Willett, Rev. Frederick 602
Willett, William 72, 569, Pl. 72
Willetts, J.H. 575
William de Oddingselles see Oddingselles, William de
William de Offini see Offini, William de
Williams, A.V. 482n., 696
Williams, Bruce 93, 147
Williams, Charles 407
Williams, Douglas J. 181, 182
Williams, H.O. 268, 428
Williams, James 44, 132, 636
Williams, Laurence 336
Williams, Thomas F. 182
Williams (Desmond) & Associates 92, 316, 731
Williams & Boddy 302
Williams (Sir Owen) & Partners 235
Williams-Ellis, Clough 696
Williamson, Francis J. 48, 49, 128, 140n., 240n., 628, 632
Willis, B. 606
Willis, Henry 676
Willoughby, George H. 51, 688
Wills & Anderson 66, 570, 571
Willson, Ernest 269
Wilmot, S. Alex 76, 319, 350, 433
Wilmot, Thomas 650, 678
Wilson, C.L.N. 700
Wilson, Harry 256, 552, 689
Wilson, John W. 76, 437, 459, 460, 461
Wilson, Sir William 18, 19, 20, 115, 220, 297, 309, 440, 452, 456, 463, 772, Pl. 44
Wilson, William (engineer) 59, 694
Wilton, Joseph 220
Wimbourne, H. 632
Winde, William 18, 21, 771–3, Pl. 32

INDEX OF ARCHITECTS, ETC.

Winders, Frederick 236
Winfield (R.W.) & Co. 42, 527, 542, 560, 782
Wingfield, Jonathan 160
Winston, Charles 42, 710
Winteringham, Graham 90, 167, 281, 297, 313, 329
Winteringham, Toby 123
Wintle, Henry R. 184
Wippell, J. 502
Wippell (J.) & Co./Wippells 266, 560
Withers, J. 605
Withers, William 382, 391
Woden 749
Wolverhampton, H.H. Fowler, 1st Viscount 736
Wolverhampton City Council Architects 750
Wolverhampton City Council Property Services 720
Wolverhampton M.B.C. Architects 752
Wood, Alfred A. 187, 781
Wood, D. 351
Wood, Edgar 350, 351, 453
Wood, Francis 351
Wood, Ian P. 750
Wood, Joseph D. 71, 178, 230, 265, 290, 486, 715, 718, 720, Pl. 102
Wood, Spencer 80, 578, 586
Wood, Wallace 74, 75, 690, 707, 724–5, 730, 731, 732
Wood, William 465
Wood, Goldstraw & Yorath 91, 523, 648, 661, 664, 733
Wood & Kendrick 44, 45, 51, 68, 71, 74, 155, 181, 185, 188, 229, 231, 240, 252, 253, 255, 257, 290, 307, 317, 327, 342, 387, 404, 487, 501, 517, 531, 564, 565, 566, 580, 583, 584, 585, 586, 598, 600, 602, 603, 604, 606, 611, 612, 613, 614, 615, 616, 636, 638, 783
Wood & Kendrick & Edwin F. Reynolds 263, 435, 603, 639
Wood, Kendrick & Williams 336, 348, 440
Woodhams, Leonard 502, 597
Woodhouse, Henry 59, 694
Woodhouse & Willoughby 67, 484
Woodman, William the elder 20, 440
Woodward, Frederick 493, 529, 553, 555
Woodward, Geoffrey 489
Woodward, Tom 570
Wooldridge, H.E. 42, 603
Woolfall & Eccles 699
Woolner, Thomas 48, 129, 140
Woolworth (F.W.) Construction Dept 632
Wootton, Sam 647
Wootton, William 646

Worcester, R. 634
Wormal, George 71, 687
Wormald, John 315
Wornum, Grey 93
Wornum & Playne 369
Woropay, Vincent 133, 168
Worrall, A.W. 62, 75, 692, 719, 723, 724–5
Worseley, John 11, 674
Worthington, Katie 680
Worthington, Percy 549
Wotton, William 620
Wright, A. Macer 340
Wright, Billy 692
Wright, Christopher 75, 426
Wright, Harold N. 412
Wright, John Skirrow 48n.
Wright, Matvyn 91, 281
Wright, Thomas 264, 650
Wright, Walter 386, 488
Wright & Sons 506
WSM Architects 160
WSP 193
Wulfruna, Lady 670, 672, 677, 692, 696, 752
Wyatt, Mr 426
Wyatt, Benjamin 253
Wyatt, J. Drayton 38, 678, 697
Wyatt, James 21, 253–4, Pl. 51
Wyatt, John 449n.
Wyatt, Samuel 21, 175, 253–4, 426, 452, 588
Wyatt, William 26, 105, 242
Wyatt (T.H.) & David Brandon 35, 749–50
Wykes, William 139
Wynne, David 116, 117

Yabsley, Percy 309
Yarranton, Andrew 27–8, 492, 494
York, Josias Bull 401
Yorke, F.W.B. 76, 78, 81, 299, 312, 457, 568
Yorke, Henry (Henry Green) 273n.
Yorke, John 497
Yorke, Harper & Harvey 763
Yorke, Rosenberg & Mardall 85, 524, 528, 558, 565, 705
Young, Clement A. 256
Young, Rory 680
Young (Alan) & Partners 486, 498n., 562n.
Younger, Alan 93, 276, 542, 662, 710
Yoxall, Nora 247n., 251
Yoxall & Whitford 93, 440, 441
Yoxall (Nora) & Elsie Whitford 783

Zaera-Polo, Alejandro 136
Zaki, R. Amin 651
Zimbachs, Gunars 85, 316
Zunde, Joan 375

INDEX TO BIRMINGHAM

This index covers pp. 1–467; a separate index for the Black Country and Solihull (pp. 1–96 and 469–785) follows on pp. 870–84.

Birmingham entries are divided into *City centre* (pp. 104–64), *Inner areas* (pp. 164–211) and *Suburbs* (pp. 211–467). Sutton Coldfield is treated among the suburbs for ease of reference. Canals, railways, roads, tramways etc. are indexed under *Transport*. For more information, see the contents list on pp. 103–4 and the maps on pp. ii–iii, 112–13 and 212–13.

Principal references are in **bold** type; demolished buildings are shown in *italic*.

City centre 2, 9, **104–64**
  churches etc. **111–24**
    Augustinian priory 105
    Bishop's House (R.C.) *118n.*, *536*
    Carrs Lane United Reformed 92, **124**, 157
    Cathedral of St Chad (R.C.) 35, 39, 42, 92, 106, **117–22**, 536n., Pl. 62
    Cathedral of St Philip 3, 19, 25, 36, 48, 91, 105, **111–17**, 140, 143, 144, 152, 153, 154, 400, **431**, 473, Pls. 33, 75, 76
    Christ Church 117, 156, *336*
    Church of the Messiah 39
    Friends' Meeting House **124**, 139
    Masonic Hall (former) 137, **150**
    Methodist Central Hall (former) 65, **123–4**, Pl. 71
    New Meeting House (former) see St Michael (R.C.) below
    St Bartholomew see Inner areas (Eastside)
    St Chad (R.C.) see Cathedral of St Chad (R.C.) above
    St Martin in the Bull Ring 13, 36, 38, 91, 95, 105, 111, **122–3**, 138, 195, 756
    St Michael (R.C., former Unitarian New Meeting House) **123**, 190
    St Paul see Inner areas (Jewellery Quarter)
    St Peter, Dale End 105n., *215*
    St Peter (R.C.) *118n.*
    St Philip see Cathedral of St Philip above
    St Stephen see Inner areas (Jewellery Quarter)
    Salvation Army Citadel (former) **148**
  Newhall estate 105, 140, **159–64**, 174, 175
  public buildings 34, 73, 107, **125–36**
    Birmingham Chest Clinic (former) 74, **163**
    Birmingham Children's Hospital (former General Hospital) and Nurses' Home 45, **135**, **152**
    Birmingham Law Society (former Temperance hall) **155**, 204
    Birmingham and Midland Eye Hospital (former) 45, **135**, 161
    Birmingham and Midland Institute **130–1**, 164
    Central Library 89, 94, *166*
    Chamberlain Memorial Fountain 48, **140**
    Coroner's Court **133**
    Council House (with Museum and Art Gallery) 43–4, 48, 49, 107, **127–30**, 133, 156, Pl. 1
    Council House Extension 66, 89, **130**, 164
    County Court (former) 44, **132**
    Curzon Street Station see Inner areas (Eastside)
    Ear and Throat Hospital (former) 45, **135**, 160
    Gas Hall 89, **130**
    General Post Office 94, **156**
    Girls' Friendly Society Diocesan Lodge (former) **162**
    Guild of Handicraft (former) 60, 62, **162**
    Juvenile Court **133**, 152

Law Courts *see* Queen Elizabeth II Law Courts; Victoria Law Courts
Louisa Ryland House (former public buildings) 45, 47, **135–6**, 159, 164
Market Hall 94, *106*, *137*
Mason College see Suburbs (Edgbaston, University of Birmingham)
Medical Institute (former) **136**, 159
Moor Street Station 72, **136**, 196
Municipal School of Art *see* School of Art *below*
Museum and Art Gallery 43–4, **129–30**, Pl. 79
Nelson statue 25, **138**, Pl. 38
New Library **143**
New Street Station and signal box 51, 73, 90, **136**, 153, 192, **206**, 209, 577
Old Library 105
Odeon Cinema **152**
Parish Offices and Board of Guardians (former) 45, **135–6**, 159, 164
police station, Steelhouse Lane 74, **152**
Public Offices 105
Queen Elizabeth II Law Courts 88–9, **133**
Royal Birmingham Society of Artists (RBSA; former) **150**, **179**, 181
School of Art 46, 67, 107, 130–1, **133–5**, 159, 424, 629, Pl. 85
School Board Offices (former) 47, **135–6**, 159
Snow Hill Station **145**, 153
Stock Exchange (former) 79, **136**, 162
Theatre Royal 149, *150n.*
Town Hall 34, 42–3, *106*, **125–7**, 128, 140n., 156, Pl. 58
Victoria Law Courts 34, 42, 44, 49, 95, 124, **131–2**, 152, 365, 549, Pl. 80
Victoria (Queen) statue 48, **156**, Pl. 1
streets etc. (commercial centre) **137–64**
  Albert Street 60, **137**
  Alliance Assurance 70, **140**
  Aston Road 107
  Atlas Assurance 70, **141**
  Avebury House **163**
  Bank of England (now CBRE) 87, **153**
  Bennetts Hill 23, 79, *106*, **137**, **157–8**
  Beorma tower 95
  Big Top **148**
  Birmingham Banking Co. (former) 49, **158**
  Birmingham Daily Post and Mail (*building* and site) 86, 128, 139, 140n., **145**, **151**
  Birmingham Hospital Saturday Fund (former) **163**
  Birmingham Joint Stock Bank (now pub) 49, **154**
  Birmingham Office Co. (former) **163**
  Birmingham Town and District Banking Co. buildings 49–50, **144**
  Bishop's House 118n., *536*
  Blue Coat School 152, *400*
  Bull Ring 8, 109, 110, **137–9**, 150, Pl. 38
  Bull Ring Centre 88, 122, **137–8**
  Bull Street **139**, 146, 153
  Burlington Hotel (former Midland Hotel) 51, 52, **151**, 153
  Cannon House **147**
  Cannon Street 51, 69, *105*, **139**, 151, 153
  Carrs Lane 50, **124**, **139**, 157
  Cavendish House **158**
  Central Arcade (former) 51, 139, **145–6**
  Chamberlain House **160–1**
  Chamberlain Square 48, **139–40**
  Cherry Street *105*, 145, 146
  Church Street 69, 146, **161–2**, 163
  City Plaza **139**, 153
  Coleridge Chambers **148–9**
  Colmore Circus **140**
  Colmore Gate 87, **145**
  Colmore Row (New Hall Lane) 49–50, 51, 68, 79, 88, 104, 110, 137, **140–5**, 147, 152, 159
  Colonnade Building 150n.
  Commercial Union development 86, **146**
  Cornwall Court 87, **162**
  Cornwall Street 59, 62, 69, **162**, **163–4**
  Corporation Square shopping precinct 87, 139, **146**, 147
  Corporation Street 48, 51, 68, 69–70, 107, 108, 124, 137, **139**, **145–9**, 150, 210n.
  Crescent 23
  Crown Inn **147–8**
  Curzon Street 6, 70, **191–3**
  Daily Post building see Birmingham Daily Post and Mail above
  Daimler House **152**

City centre *cont.*
  streets etc. (commercial centre) *cont.*
    Dale End **149**
    Eagle Insurance (former) 68, **140–1**, Pl. 95
    Edmund Street 45, 69, **159–61**
    Embassy House **162**
    Exchange Building 153
    Fore Street 151
    Fountain Court **152**
    Fox and Grapes pub 19
    Gazette Buildings **147**, 150
    General Post Office 68, **156**
    Grand Hotel 52–3, 95, **144**, Pl. 94
    Great Charles Street **162–3**
    Great Western Arcade 51, **144–5**, **153**
    Great Western Hotel 52, 145n.
    Grosvenor House **150**
    Guildhall Buildings **153**
    High Street 105, 137, 138, **148–9**
    Horton's Estate 144
    House of Fraser (formerly Rackhams) **146**, 153
    Inge estate 22, 106, 137, 156
    Keep Brothers offices 162
    King Edward Building **148**
    King Edward House 79, **152**
    Lamb House 105
    Legal and General Assurance (former) 79, **158–9**, Pl. 109
    Lewis's (former) 79, 95, **147**
    Liberal Club 94
    Livery Street 145n., 161, **179**
    London & Lancashire Insurance Co. (former) 68, 70, **150**
    Lower Temple Street **149**, 153
    McLaren Tower **147**
    manor house 9, 137
    Maple House **147**
    markets 137, **139**
    Marks & Spencer **108**
    Marshall & Snelgrove (former) **151–2**
    Martineau Street 107, 146
    Midland Bank (former), New Street 49, 108, **151**
    Midland & City Arcades 51, 68, **155–6**
    Midland Educational Co., Corporation Street 51, 139, **146**
    Midland Hotel *see* Burlington Hotel *above*
    Midland Land and Investment Corporation **144**
    Minories 105, **147**
    Moat Lane 137
    National Provincial Bank (former) 49, **157–8**
    National Telephone Co. (former) **159–60**, 391, Pl. 93
    National Westminster Bank, Colmore Row 143
    Needless Alley 139, **153**
    Neville House 79, **157**
    Newhall estate 105, 140, **159–64**, 174, 175
    New Hall Lane *see* Colmore Row *above*
    Newhall Street 59, 68, 69, 70, **160**, 162, **163–4**
    New Oxford House **157**
    New Street 50, 68, 69, 86, 104, 107, 109, 137, 138, **149–52**, 153, 154, 374
    Norwich Union Fire Engine House *see* Trocadero *below*
    Ocean Insurance Corporation (former) 69, **154**
    Old Contemptibles pub (formerly the Albion) 52, **161**
    Old Joint Stock pub (former Birmingham Joint Stock Bank) 49, **154**
    Old Royal pub (originally the Red Lion) **161–2**
    Old Square 19, 93, 105, 124, 145, **147**, **225**, 451
    Pallasades Shopping Centre **136**
    Paradise Development 88, **140**
    Paradise Street 28, *131*, **152**, 375
    Park Street *19*, 138
    Parr's Bank (former) **158**
    Pavilions shopping centre (former) 88, **148**
    Phoenix Assurance Co. (former) 70, **143**
    Piccadilly Arcade (former cinema) **150–1**
    Post and Mail building see Birmingham Daily Post and Mail *above*
    Powell's Gun Shop 50, **139**
    Primark 88, **148**
    Prince's Corner **145**
    Priors Conygree Lane *see* Steelhouse Lane *below*
    Priory Queensway **147**
    Provost's House (former) **152**
    Queen's College Chambers **152**
    Queen's Corner **145**
    Rackhams (former) *see* House of Fraser *above*
    Rotunda 86–7, **138**
    Ruskin Chambers **148**
    St Paul's Square 22, 68n., 84, 88, 105, 159, 174, **178–9**, 460
    St Philip's Place **152**
    Scottish Union and National Insurance 69, **141–2**
    Selfridges 88, **138**, 148
    Shakespeare pub **149**
    Smart Bros 79, **155**
    Snow Hill 83, 86, **140**, 145

Steelhouse Lane (originally Priors Conygree Lane) 45, 74, 145, 148, **152**
Stephenson Place **152–3**
Stephenson Street **152–3**
Sun Building 79, **137**
Temple Row *19*, 105, 111, **153–4**, 451
Temple Row West 49, 69, **154**
Temple Street 23, 49, 79, 105, 111, **154–5**
Times Furnishing (former) **148**
Town Hall Chambers **150**
Trafalgar House **152**
Trocadero (former Norwich Union Fire Engine House) 49, **154–5**
TSB (former) 87, **153**
Union Chambers **153–4**
Union Club (former) **143**
Union Street 68, **155–6**
Unity Fire and General Insurance building (former) 49, **155**
Victoria House **146**
Victoria Square 73, 93, 94, 95, 106, 128, 140, 150, **156**, Pls. 1, 58
Warwick House (shop) 50
Waterloo Court 137, 142, **157**
Waterloo Street 23, 49, 79, 106, 137, 140, 154, **156–9**
Waterstones **148**
Wellington House 79, **143**
White House, The **151**
White Swan pub (former) **160**
Woolf (Thomas) furniture store (former) **147**
Woolworth Building **150**
Inner areas 104–10, **164–211**
Bordesley *see* Digbeth *below*
Brindleyplace *see* Broad Street *below*
Broad Street and Brindleyplace **164–74**
  churches etc. **165**
    Birmingham Progressive Synagogue **165**, 171
    Presbyterian Church of England (former) 40, **165**, 172
    St Luke (Gas Street Church) (former) **173**
    St Thomas *see* Smallbrook *below*
  major buildings **165–8**
    Baskerville House 74, **166**, 169
    Birmingham Municipal Bank (former) 74, 79, **168**
    Birmingham Repertory Theatre 70, 90, **167**
    Civic Centre schemes 73, 166, 167, 169
    Convention Centre *see* International Convention Centre *below*
    Hall of Memory 73, 78, **165–6**, **203**, Pl. 106
    Hyatt Hotel *see* International Convention Centre and Hyatt Hotel *below*
    Ikon Gallery (former Oozells Street School) 46, **168**
    International Convention Centre and Hyatt Hotel 87, 110, 165, **168**, 173
    Library of Birmingham 90, **166–7**, Pl. 137
    National Indoor Arena **168**
    Oozells Street School *see* Ikon Gallery *above*
    Register Office **168**, 172
    Symphony Hall 125, **168**
  streets etc. **168–74**
    ATV development **168–9**, Pl. 130
    Auchinleck House (former) **172**
    Berkley Street **172**
    Birmingham and District Bank (former) **171**
    Birmingham Gas Light and Coke Co. (former) **173**
    Bishopsgate Street **171**
    Brasshouse 105, **172**, 173
    Brewmaster's House and former malthouse 22, 105, **169**
    Brindleyplace development 87, 88, 95, 96, 110, 142, 165, **170**, 172, 188
    Broad Street 86, 88, 105, 142, 165, **169**, **171–2**
    Broadway office complex **172**
    Bulls Head (former City Tavern) **171**
    Butler's *brewery* and former tap **172–3**
    Canal House pub **173**
    CBSO Centre **172**
    Centenary Square 68, 93, 165, 168, **169**
    Centenary Way 110, **168–9**
    City Inn (former) **171**
    City Tavern (former) **171**
    Corporation Depot (former) **171**
    Crescent Theatre (1962) 90
    Crescent Theatre (1998) **170**
    Crown Inn (former) **172–3**
    Cumberland House **171**
    Figure of Eight bar **172**
    Gas Street 27, 87, **173–4**
    Gas Street Basin 28, **173–4**
    Granville pub (former) **172**
    Granville Street and Square **172**

Inner areas *cont.*
  Broad Street and Brindleyplace *cont.*
    streets etc. *cont.*
      Grosvenor Street West 171
      Hilton Garden Inn (former City Inn) 171
      ICC Energy Centre 169
      Islington 165
      Islington Glassworks owner's house (former) 105, 171
      James Brindley (now Canal House) pub 173–4
      Jury's Inn 172
      Kingston Buildings 169
      Lee Longlands (former shop) 79, 172
      Left Bank towers (Sheepcote Street) 88, 165, 171
      Lying-In Hospital (former) 171
      Novotel 172
      Oozells Square 170
      Park Regis 171–2
      Quayside Tower 172
      Retort House (former) 27, 173
      Sheepcote Street 171
      South Staffordshire Waterworks Co. offices (former) 171
      Symphony Court 171
      Transport House 171
      Travelodge 172
      Union Mill (former) 105, 171
      Water's Edge 169–70
      Worcester and Birmingham Canal Co. office (former) 173
  Deritend *see* Digbeth *below*
  Digbeth, Deritend, Bordesley and Highgate 57, 193–203
    churches etc. 193–5, 199
      Birmingham Central Mosque 195
      Friends' Hall and Institute (former) 202
      Holy Trinity (former) 24, 105, 193–4
      Muath Centre (former King Edward's Grammar Schools) 195
      St Alban (now St Alban and St Patrick) 37, 38, 42, 64, 78, 194, 336, Pl.65
      St Andrew, Bordesley *35, 106*
      St Anne (R.C.) 39, 195, 363, 364
      St Basil (former) 63, 64, 194–5, Pl.69
      St John, Deritend (c14 and c15) *193, 197n.*
      St Patrick, Frank Street *194n.*
      Unitarian chapel and Sunday School (former) 41, 57, 199
    streets, public buildings etc. 95, 110, 195–203
      Adderley Street 198–9
      Alcester Street 200, 201
      Allison Street 196
      almshouses (former), Warner Street *328*
      Anchor pub 200
      Ash & Lacy works (former) 196
      Banana Warehouse 57, 199
      Banbury Street 199
      Big Bulls Head pub 52, 197
      Birmingham Gun Barrel Proof House 26, 105, 199–200, 201
      Bond, The 199
      Bordesley (township) 198
      Bordesley Street 56, 196
      Bordesley Village 203
      Bradford Street 80, 200–1
      bus garage 198
      canal basin 29, 199
      Castle and Falcon pub (former) 196
      Cheapside 201
      cold store (former) 71, 196
      Conybere Street 202
      Darwin Street 202n.
      Deritend (settlement) 193, 197–200
      Devonshire House (former custard factory) 197
      Digbeth (formerly Well Street) 2, 95, 193, 195–7
      Digbeth Institute 197
      Englands shoe factory (former) 201
      Fazeley Street 41, 199
      Fellows Morton & Clayton 199
      fire station (former) 202
      Fisher & Ludlow buildings 80, 200, 201
      Floodgate Street mural 197
      Floodgate Street School (former) 67, 197
      Forge Tavern 198, 199
      Garrison Lane School (former) 203
      gas retort house (former) 199
      Gibb Street 88, 197
      Golden Lion inn 15, 105, 324
      Green Man sculpture 197
      guildhall (former) *see* Old Crown Inn *below*
      Harrison & Co. (former) 200–1
      Heath Mill 198
      Heath Mill Lane 198
      Hen and Chickens pub (former) 203
      Highgate Park 48, 201

Highgate Place **202**
High Street, Bordesley **198**
High Street, Deritend **197**, 324
Ladbroke House **196**
Lench's Trust Almshouses (former) 54, 56, **201**, **202**
Leopold Street 71, 84, **202**
Lion Warehouse 57, **196**
Lloyds Bank (former), High Street 49, **197**, 760
Market Tavern **201**
Medical Mission (former) **199**
Meriden Street **196**
Merry Maid pub **202**
Moor Street 193
mosaic mural 93, **197**
Moseley Arms pub 52, **201**
Moseley Road 23, 193, **201**, **202**
Moseley Street **201–2**
Old Bulls Head pub (former) **197**
Old Crown Inn (former guildhall) 14, 15, 46, 105, **197–8**, 280, 408
Old Wharf pub (former) **196**
Oxford Street 71, **196**
Park Villas **203**
Peacock pub (former) **202n.**
Pickford's warehouse (former) **199**
police stations 44, **196**, **201**
Rowton Hotel **201**
St Edmund's Boys Home (former) **198**
Samuel Heath & Sons (Cobden Works) 57, 71, 84, 106, **202**
South Birmingham College **197**
Sportsman (former pub) **203**
Spotted Dog (former pub) **196**
Stanhope Street **202**
Stratford House 15, **201–2**, 312
Ty-Phoo Tea factory (former) 80, **196**
Wagon and Horses pub (former) **198**
Watery Lane Middleway **203**
White Swan pub **200**
Wolverley House **196**
Eastside 110, **188–93**
Bishop Ryder Church 105n., 343
Aston University 85, 86, **188–90**, **191**, 218
Bartholomew Row 188, **190**
Belmont Works (former) **191**
Birmingham City University campus 86, **191**, 277
Birmingham Metropolitan College **190**
Black Horse pub **191**
Cardigan Street **191**
car park 188, **191**
Central Fire Station (former) 74, 95, **188–9**
Central Technical College 94
Curzon Building **191**
Curzon Street 6, 70, **191–3**
Curzon Street Station (former) and Lawley Street viaduct 39, 59, 188, **191–2**
Delicia Cinema (former) **189**
Eagle and Ball pub 52, **191**
Eastside City Park **191**, **192**
Emporium, The (student residential tower) 188, **190**
James Watt Queensway 188
Jennens Road **190**
Lawley Middleway **191**
Lawley Street **191–2**
Masshouse Circus development 110, *188*, **190**
Millennium Point 89, **192**
Moor Street **190**, 193
Ormiston Academy **190**
Parkside Building **191**, 192
Penn Street **191**
Royal Birmingham Conservatoire 86, **191**
Sacks of Potatoes pub **189**
St Bartholomew, Jennens Row 105n., 190n., **321**, 345
Think Tank museum **192**
University House (Birmingham City University) **190**
Viaduct Street 192
White Tower pub **191**
Woodcock Sports Centre and former First Class Bath 66, **189**
Woodman pub 70, **193**
Gough estate *see* Smallbrook *below*
Gun Quarter 57, 106, 118, **187–8**
Bath Street **187**
Bull pub **187**
Catholic School (former) 57, **187**
Corporation Street **188**
Gunmakers Arms 52, **187**
Halfords' cycle works (now council offices) **188**
infant welfare centre (former) 74, **188**
King Edward Inn (former) **188**
Lancaster Circus **188**
Little Shadwell Street **187**
Loveday Street 57, **187**
Price Street 57, 187
Princip Street 57, **188**
St Chad's Queensway 187
St Mary, Whittall Street 105n.
Shadwell Street 84, **187–8**
Steelhouse Lane 187
Welsh Congregational church **187**

Inner areas *cont.*
  Gun Quarter *cont.*
    Wesleyan chapel (former) 40, 57, **187**
    Whittall Street 187
  Highgate *see* Digbeth *above*
  Jewellery Quarter and Summer Lane 27, 57, 80, 106, **174–87**
    churches etc. **175–6**
      All Saints 105n.
      Cathedral of St Andrew (Greek Orthodox) *see* Catholic Apostolic Church *below*
      Catholic Apostolic Church (now Greek Orthodox Cathedral of St Andrew) 36, **176**
      Church of England cemetery and *chapel* **181**
      Congregational chapel (former Highbury Independent Chapel; now Ramgarhia Sikh Temple) 40, **176**
      Nonconformist Cemetery *41*, **185**
      Ramgarhia Sikh Temple *see* Congregational chapel *above*
      St George, Bridge Street West **176**
      St George, Great Hampton Row 24, 105n., **176**
      St Paul 6, 22, 24, 25, 26, 38, 105, 174, **175–6**, 573, Pl. 37
      St Stephen, New Town Row 35, 106, 423
    public buildings **176–7**
      Assay Offices 174, **177**, **178**
      Bhagwan Valmik Ashram *see* Icknield Street School *below*
      Birmingham City University Institute of Jewellery, Fashion and Textiles (former Municipal School for Jewellers and Silversmiths) 57, 174, **176–7**, 182
      Brearley/Teviot Children's Centre (former nursery school) 75, **177**, 186
      generating station (former) 67, **186**
      Icknield Street School (former) **177**
      Museum of the Jewellery Quarter **186**
      police station 74, **177**
      Post Office **185**
      Royal Birmingham Society of Artists **179**
      Telephone House **178**
      University College Birmingham (former College of Food and Domestic Arts) **177**
      University of Law (former Cannings factory) 80, **184**
    streets etc. **177–87**
      A.J. Pepper & Co. (former) **184**
      Alabaster & Wilson factory **180**
      Albion Street 84, **180–1**
      Anvic House **185**
      Aquinas House 57, **181–2**
      Argent Centre (former Wiley's pen works) 57, **180**, Pl. 91
      Baker & Finnemore factory **179**
      Barclays Bank, Frederick Street **181**
      Barker electroplating works (former) 71, **184**
      Barrel pub **186**
      Berndorf Metal Co. (former) **181**
      Bismillah Building (originally Barker electroplating works) 71, **184**
      BLOC hotel **183**
      Branston Street **185**, **186**
      Brook Street **179**
      Cannings factory (former) 80, **184**
      Caroline Street **183**
      C. Brandauer & Co. (former) **186**
      Century Buildings **187**
      Charlotte Street **178**, 179
      Church Inn **184**
      Clayton-Wright factory (former) **184**
      Constitution Hill 27, 51, 57, 71, 80, 174, **183–4**
      Cox Street **178**
      Crowngate House **185**
      Elliott button works (former) 57, 174, **182**
      fire station (former) **180**
      Fleet Street **178**
      Focus Foyer 83, **183**
      Frederick Street 57, 71, **181**
      Gem Buildings 68, **185**
      George & Dragon pub **180**
      George Street **180**
      G.J. Westwood & Son (former) **184**
      Golden Square **182**
      Gothic pub 52, **184**
      Gothic Works **179**
      Great Hampton Street 57, 71, 80, 174, 183, **184–5**
      Great Hampton Works **185**, **187**

INDEX TO BIRMINGHAM 853

Griffin House **179**
Hampton Street **183**
Harford Street 184
Harry Smith ironmongers (former) **185**
H.B. Sale factory (former) 57, **183**
Heaton House, 22, 106, **187**
Hen and Chickens pub **184**
Heritage Court **183**
Hockley Centre (Big Peg) 175, **182**
Hockley Hill 68, **185**
Hockley Street 184, **186**
Hylton Street **185**
japanning factory (former) 27, **184**
J. Ashford & Son (former) **184**
Jewellers Arms 52, **186**
Jewellery Business Centre **186**
Kenyon Street **183**
Key Hill 41, **185**
Key Hill Drive **185**
Legge Lane 174, **180**
Livery Street **179**
Lord Clifden pub **184**
Lucas factory (former) 108, 110, **184**
Ludgate Hill **179**
Manton's works (former) **180**
Mary Ann Street **178–9**
Newey Brothers works (former) 58, **186**
Newhall Square **178**
Newhall Street 71, **177–8, 179–80**
New Hall Works 57, **180**
New John Street 54, 174, **186**
Newman Brothers (former) **178**
Northampton Parade **182**
Northwood Street **183**
Old Snow Hill **183**, 186
Pelican Works **185**
Pickering & Mayall **183**
Plantagenet Buildings **186**
Post Office Tower (now BT) **177–8**
Quality Works **181, 184**
Queens Arms pub 71, **178**
Queens Chambers **183**
Regent Parade **183**
Regent Place 68, 69, **182–3**
Regent Street **182**
Rose Villa Tavern **181**
Royal Birmingham Society of Artists (former warehouse) **179**
St Nicolas's vicarage (former) **186**
St Paul's Square 22, 68n., 84, 88, 105, 159, 174, **178–9**, 460

Sovereign Court 87, **180**
Spencer Street **185, 186**
Squirrel Works 69, **183**, 185
Standard Works **182**
Stevens Terrace 84, **179**
Summer Hill Terrace 22, 106, **187**
Summer Lane 51, 58, 174, 175, **183**, 184, **186–7**
Sylvia Works (former) **184**
Taylor & Challen (former) 71, 80, **178, 184**, Pl. 105
Tenby Street North **182**
Thomas Fattorini **181**
Unity Works **182**
Victoria Works 57, **180**
Vittoria Street 84, 174, **182**
Vyse Street 174, **185–6**
Warstone Lane 41, **181–2**
Water Street **179**
White Horse Cellars **184**
YMCA (former) **183**
Smallbrook and the Gough estate **203–11**
  churches etc. **203–5**
    Athol Masonic Hall (formerly synagogue) 26, **204–5**, 210
    Bethel Presbyterian Church of Wales **204**, 209
    Christadelphian chapel (former) **204**
    Quaker Sunday (First Day) School 210n.
    St Catherine of Siena (R.C.) **203–4**
    St Jude 207n.
    St Thomas (former) 24, 105, 165, **203**
    Singers Hill Synagogue and Jewish School 40, **204**, 210, Pl. 61
  streets, public buildings etc. **205–11**
    Albany Hotel (former) **207**
    Albany House **208**
    Alexandra Theatre 81, **205**
    Arcadian shopping centre 88, **208**
    Australian Bar (former) **209**
    back-to-back houses **208–9**
    Beetham Tower 88, **207**
    Birmingham Athletic Institute (former) **206**
    Birmingham Hippodrome 81, **205**, 208
    Birmingham Royal Ballet **207**
    Black Lion pub (former) **207**
    Blucher Street 84, 86, **209–10**
    Borough Buildings **206**
    Bristol Street 71, 79, 203, **208**

Inner areas *cont.*
  Smallbrook and the Gough estate *cont.*
    streets, public buildings etc. *cont.*
      Bromsgrove Street 22, 71, 105, **208, 209**
      Cambridge Buildings **206**
      Centre City 87, **207**
      Commercial Street 88, **210**
      Craven Arms pub **210**
      Crown Inn **209**
      Cube, The 88, **210**
      Dudley Street **209**
      Electric Cinema 81, **209**
      Essex Street 208
      Futurist Cinema (former) 69, **206**
      Geoffrey Buildings **206**
      Grosvenor Casino **206**
      Heron car maker *see* Rosebery Buildings *below*
      Hill Street 203, **209**
      Holloway Circus 93, **207**, 208
      Holloway Head 207, **209**, 211
      Horse Fair 105, **207–8**
      Hurst Street 80, 203, 207, **208–9**, Pl. 5
      Inge Street 24, 95, 105, **208–9**, Pl. 5
      John Bright Street 45, 48, 71, 107, 205, **206**
      Koh-i-Noor restaurant **207**
      Lee Bank Business Centre **209**
      Lower Severn Street 206
      Mailbox, The (former sorting office) **210**
      Market Hotel (former) **209**
      Municipal Bank (former) **208**
      Navigation Street **206**
      New Street Station *see* City centre (public buildings)
      Norfolk House 87, **207**
      Old Fox pub **208**
      Old Rep Theatre 70, **205–6**
      Queen's Hospital (former) **211**
      Queen's Tavern (former) **207**
      Rose & Crown (former pub) 71, **209**
      Rosebery Buildings (former Heron car showrooms) 71, 108, **206**
      Scala House **207**
      Sentinels, The 87, **207**, 209
      Severn Street School (former) 46, **210**, 349
      Shaftesbury Coffee House and Temperance Hotel (former) **209**
      signal box 90, **206**
      Skin Hospital (former) 45, **206**
      Smallbrook (street) 209
      Smallbrook Queensway 86, 87, 88, 94, 203, **207**
      Smallbrook Street 203
      Station Street 203, **209**
      Suffolk Street Queensway **206, 207**, 210
      Thorp Street 208
      Trefoil House **210**
      Victoria pub **206**
      Village Inn **209**
      Warwickshire Rifle Volunteers' Drill Hall 208
      Wellington Hotel 71, **208**
      White Lion pub (former) **207**
      Wrentham Street 84, **208**
  Summer Lane *see* Jewellery Quarter *above*
  Suburbs (with Sutton Coldfield) 105–10, **211–467**
    Acocks Green **300–3**
      Acocks Green Baptist Church 65, 249, **301–2**
      Curtis Gardens Estate 82, 93, **303**
      public library 74, **302**
      Sacred Heart and Holy Souls (R.C.) and former school **301**, 782
      Shirley Road 61, **303**
    All Saints, Summerfield and Winson Green **211–18**
      churches etc. **214–15**
        Bishop Latimer Memorial Church (now Seventh Day Adventist) 63, 64, **214**
        Christ Church, Summerfield Crescent 36, **214–15**, 264
        Church of God of Prophecy 92, **215**
        St Patrick (R.C.) and presbytery, Dudley Road 65, **215**, 217
        St Peter (now New Testament Church of God), Summerfield 64, **215**, 217
      public buildings 211–14, **215–18**
        Birmingham City Hospital (former workhouse) 45, **216**
        Birmingham Prison, Winson Green Road (originally Borough Gaol) 43, 89, 211–14, **216–17**, Pl. 133
        Borough Asylum (later All Saints Hospital; now Prison Service offices) 43, 211–14, **217**
        Dudley Road Board School (former) *see* Summerfield Centre *below*

Handsworth New Road School (former) 67, **218**
public library 66, **216**
Summerfield Centre (former Dudley Road Board School) **215–16**
streets etc. **217–18**
  Handsworth New Road 60, **218**
  Summerfield Park 48, **217**
Alum Rock (or Little Bromwich) **272–3**
  Christ Church 77, **272**, Pl.119
  Community of St John the Divine (former Moat House) 64, **272–3**
Aston 106, **218–30**
  Aston Hall 3, 15–16, 105, 218, **221–7**, 245, Pls.29, 30
    Aston Park 48, 222, 224–5, **226–7**
  churches etc. **218–21**
    All Souls (now Church of God Universal), Witton 63, 78, **220**
    Christ Church Baptist Church (former) 40, **221**
    Sacred Heart of Jesus and St Margaret Mary (R.C.) 78, **220–1**
    St Peter and St Paul 12, 20, 25, 36, 38, **218–20**
  public buildings 218, **227–9**
    Aston Hall and Park *see* Aston Hall *above*
    Aston University *see* Inner areas (Eastside)
    Council House and library (former) **227**
    fire station (former) 74, **227**
    Higher Grade Board Schools (now Eden Boys Academy) 67, **227**
    Holte almshouses 218
    Prince Albert Primary School 47, **227**
    tramways depot (former) **228**
  streets and other buildings 108, 218, **228–30**
    A.E.I. *see* Associated Electrical Industries *below*
    Associated Electrical Industries (A.E.I., later G.E.C.) 80, **228**
    Aston Cross 218, **228–9**
    Aston Hotel (former) **228**
    Aston Villa football ground *see* Villa Park *below*
    Bartons Arms 70, **229–30**, 434, Pl.103
    Britannia pub (former) **229**
    Crocodile Works **230**
    Golden Cross pub (former) **228–9**
    Hen and Chickens pub (former) **229**
    Holte Hotel **228**
    Lichfield Road **228–9**
    Newtown **229–30**
    Swan and Mitre pub 70, **229**
    Villa Park football ground **228**, 265n.
    Whitehead Road 218
    Witton Lane 218, **228**
Balsall Heath **303–7**
  churches etc. **303–4**, 306
    Abbasi Islamic Centre **304**
    Balsall Heath Church Centre 91, **303**
    Muslim Students' House Masjid **304**
    St Barnabas **303–4**
    St John and St Martin (R.C.) **304**
    St Paul 303n.
    Sparkbrook Congregational Church **304**
  public and other buildings 303, **304–7**
    Anderton Park School 67, **305**
    Clifton Road Schools and School Board offices (former) 47, **305**
    John Bowen builder's yard (former) 58, **307**
    Joseph Chamberlain College 85, **305**
    Library and baths 66, **304–5**, Pl.89
    Moseley and Kings Heath Institute (former) **305**
    Nelson Mandela Primary School 85, **306**
    School of Art (former) **305**
    Tindal Street 84, **306–7**
    Zero Carbon House 84, **307**
Bartley Green **347–8**
  Bartley Green School and Design Centre 67, 85, **348**
  California **347**
  Heathy Farm Estate 82, **348**
  Hillcrest School (former Bartley Green Girls' Grammar School) 84, **348**
  housing estates 75, 82, **347**, **348**
  Methodist chapel (now California Christian Centre) **347**
  Newman University 86, 96, **347–8**, Pl.136
  St Michael 347
  St Michael and All Angels **347**
  Smarts brickworks 347
  Woodgate **347**
Billesley **307**
  Holy Cross 77, **307**

Suburbs *cont.*
  Birchfield **230–1**, 242
    Holy Trinity 36, 37, 42, **230**
  Bournville 7, 60, 291, 319, **348–57**, 431
    churches etc. **351–2**
      Friends' Meeting House 65, 350, **351–2**
      St Francis of Assisi (mission church, now church hall) 297, 350, **351**
    public buildings **352–3**
      baths **355**
      Bournville Almshouses **356**
      Day Continuation School (now Birmingham City University) 75, **352**
      Infants' School **352**
      Junior School **352**
      public hall (Woodlands Park Road) **357**
      Rowheath Pavilion **353**
      Ruskin Hall (now Birmingham City University; former village institute) **352**
      Women's Recreation Ground **356**
    streets, houses etc. 60, 108, 349–50, **353–7**
      Acacia Road **354**
      Beech Road **356**
      Bournbrook Hall 356
      Bournville Estate **349–50**
      Bournville Lane **355**, **356**
      Bournville Tenants' Estate 350, 356, **357**
      early houses 349, 355n.
      Elm Road **354**
      factory buildings **355–6**
      Green, The 350, **353**, 355
      Hawthorne Road **357**
      Holly Grove **354**
      Kingsley Road **357**
      Laburnum Road **354**
      Laurel Grove **356**
      Linden Road **354–5**, **356**
      Lloyds Bank **353**, 355
      Mary Vale Road 350, **356**
      Minworth Greaves 15, **353**
      Northfield Road **357**
      Oak Tree Lane **355**
      Old Farm Hotel **356**
      Raddlebarn Road 350, **353**
      St George's Court **355**
      Selly Manor 15, **353**
      Selly Oak Road **356**
      Sycamore Road 350, **353–4**, Pl. 100
      Thorn Road **355**
      Willow Road **354**
      Woodbrooke Road **355**
      Woodlands Park Road **357**

  Brandwood with Druids Heath **307–9**
    Bells Farm (Community Centre) 15, 299, **308–9**
    Brandwood End Cemetery 41, **308**
    Druids Heath Estate 82, **308**
    Kings Norton canal Tunnel **308**
    Monyhull Hall (and former Industrial School) 67, **308**
  California *see* Bartley Green *above*
  Castle Vale 82, 110, **231–2**, 466
  Druids Heath *see* Brandwood *above*
  Duddeston and Nechells **232–5**
    churches etc. **232–3**
      Presbyterian chapel (now Church of God of Prophecy) 41, **233**
      St Clement 36, **232–3**
      St Joseph (R.C.) 38, 39, **233**
      St Matthew 35, 106, **233**
      St Vincent (R.C.) 92, **233**
    streets, public buildings etc. 233, **234–5**
      Albion Vaults pub 52, **235**
      Bloomsbury Library (former) 66, 68, **234**
      Cromwell Junior and Infants School 47, **234**
      housing 75, 94, 232, **234**
      James Memorial Homes **232–3**
      Nechells Park Road **234**
      Nechells Primary School (now Academy) 46, **234**
      public baths (former) 66, 68, **234**
      railway buildings 59, **234–5**
      Vauxhall (district) 232
  Edgbaston 53, 106, **357–94**
    churches etc. **359–65**
      Church of the Redeemer 39
      Edgbaston Old Church *see* St Bartholomew *below*
      Friends' Meeting House 65, **365**
      Methodist church (former), Sandon Road 60, **364–5**
      Oratory of St Philip Neri (R.C.) 39, 65, **363–4**, Pl. 67
      St Augustine 38, 91, **360–1**, 393, Pl. 63
      St Bartholomew (Edgbaston Old Church) 17, 38, **359–60**, 378
      St George 38, 42, **361–2**, 378
      St Germain 63, 77, **362**
      St James (former) 36, 106, 358, **362–3**, 382
      St Margaret 590
      St Mary and St Ambrose 38, 42, 64, 78, **363**

public buildings 358, **365–77**
  Birmingham Chamber of Commerce 86, 93, **374**, 385
  Birmingham City University (City South campus) **375**
  Birmingham University *see* University of Birmingham *below*
  Birmingham Wildlife Conservation Park *see* Museum *below*
  Botanical Gardens 358, **376–7**
  Boy Scouts' War Memorial 73, 74, **377**
  Calthorpe Park 48, **376**
  Children's Hospital (former) **386**
  Edgbaston Hall (now golf clubhouse) 374, **377**
  Edgbaston Reservoir 28, 30, **387**, 414
  King Edward's School (boys) and King Edward VI High School (girls) 75, 105, 106, 358, **374–5**, 389, 489
  Lench's Trust Almshouses (former) 54, **386**
  Magdalen Asylum (former) **394**
  Metchley Roman Fort 7–8, **376**, 449
  Museum (now Birmingham Wildlife Conservation Park) 74, **377**
  Peel statue 48, **375**
  Queen Elizabeth Hospital **375–6**
  Queen's College (now Queen's Foundation) 75, 77, 367, **375**, 382
  Royal Institution for Deaf and Dumb Children (former) 358, **381**
  Sturge (Joseph) statue 48, **384**
  University of Birmingham *see below*
  Warwickshire County Cricket Ground 90, **376**
  waterworks and pumping station 58, **387**
  West Midlands Police Learning and Development Centre **375**
streets, houses etc. 110, 358–9, **377–94**
  Ampton Road 55, 108, 358, **378**, 389
  Apsley House 53, 383, **389**
  Arthur Road 358, **378–9**
  Balsall Heath Road 358
  Barnsley Road 60, 378, **379**
  Beech Mount **389**
  Berrow Court 55, **390**
  Bothy, The **383**
  Bristol Road 53, 83, 84, 358, 378, **379–80**
  Cala Drive 83, **380**
  Calthorpe Road 53, 86, 358, 378, **380–1**
  Carpenter Road 53, 55, 378, 380, **381**, 389
  Chad Road 53, 83, 378, **381**, 383, 388
  Chad Square **390**
  Chains, The **381**
  Charlotte Road 53, 378, **381**
  Church Road 84, 378, **381–2**
  Clarendon Road 54, 55, **393–4**
  Corinthians, The 53, **379**
  Edgbaston Hall 374, **377**, 379
  Edgbaston Park Road 60, 358, **372–3**
  Elvetham Road **382**
  Enfield Road **382**
  Estria Road 83, **380**
  Fairlawn **389**
  Farquhar Road 76, 358, 378, **382–3**
  Ferndale 55, **386**
  Fieldgate House **389**
  Five Ways 359, 378, 380, **384**
  Five Ways Tower and House **383**
  Francis Road **384**
  Frederick Road 86, 358, 378, **383**, Pl. 127
  Garth House 60, **373**, 393, Pl. 98
  George Road 23, 358, 378, **383–4**
  Goodknaves End **390**
  Gough Road 378, **381**
  Greenfield Crescent 378, **384**
  Guinea Gardens 377, **390**
  Hagley House **384**
  Hagley Road 22, 23, 51, 53, 56, 60, 86, 358, 378, **379**, **384–5**
  Harborne Road 55, 358, 378, **385–6**, 390
  Hermitage Road 61, 83, 378, **386**
  Highfield Road 53, 378, **386**
  Highland Lodge **389**
  High Point **388**
  Homestead, The 60, **392–3**
  House, The **389–90**
  Ivy Bush pub **385**
  Ladywood Middleway 54, **386**
  Lee Crescent 24, 378, **386**
  Leofric Court 83, **382**
  Lloyds Bank, Calthorpe Road 70, **380**
  Lyndon House **384**

Suburbs *cont.*
  Edgbaston *cont.*
    streets, houses etc. *cont.*
      Marriott Hotel 93n., **384**
      Masshouse **388**
      Metropolitan House 86, **384**
      Monument Road 378, **386–7**
      Monument, The (Perrott's Folly) 21, **387**, Pl. 48
      Neville House 86, **385**, Pl. 131
      Norfolk Road 53, 378, **387**
      Oak Grange 57, **386**
      Oakmount 57, **390**
      Pakenham Road **387**
      Park Grove 22, **387–8**
      Perrott's Folly *see* Monument, The *above*
      Plough and Harrow hotel 52, **384**
      Portland Road 54, **393**
      Priory Road 378, **387–8**
      Priory School 53, **389**
      Pritchatts Road 61, 74, 378, **388**
      Ravensbury 348, **390**
      Reservoir Road **387**
      Richmond Hill Road 83, 378, **388**
      Rotton Park estate 54, **385**, **393–4**
      Rotton Park Road 60, **394**
      Round House **392**
      Ryland Road 378, **388**
      St Augustine's Road 378, 385, **394**
      St Chad's Court **385**
      St George's Close **389**
      St James Road 378, **382**, 392
      Sandon Road **379**
      Selwyn Road 393
      Seven Gables **382–3**
      Sir Harry's Road 53, 358, 378, **388**
      Somerset Road 54, 358, **388**
      Spring Cottage **389**
      Spring Folly **389**
      Sun Street 358
      Tricorn House **384**
      Vicarage Road 53, 378, **388**
      Viceroy Close **379–80**, Pl. 116
      Wellington Road 53, 62, 358, 378, 379, 381, 383, **389**
      Westbourne Manor **390**
      Westbourne Road 56, 358, 378, **389–90**
      Westfield Road 55, 56, 61, 76, 378, **390–1**
      West Point 83, **386**
      Wheeleys Road 378, **391–2**
      Whetstone Close **382**
      White Swan pub 378, **390**
      Windsor Terrace **385**
      Wineyford Brown's Building **386**
      Winterbourne 60, **372–3**
      Woodbourne Road 60, 76, 378, 391, **392–3**
      Yateley Road 61, 335, **393**
      Yew Tree Road 53, 54, **393**
      York Road **394**
  University of Birmingham 67–8, 85, 358, **365–74**
    Ashley Building 86, **371**, Pl. 128
    Barber Institute 75, 367, **370–1**, Pl. 114
    Bramall Music Building 86, **369**
    Edgbaston Park Road buildings **372–3**
    Education Department 86, **371**
    Garth House 60, **373**, 393, Pl. 98
    Great Hall 365, **368**
    Guild of Students 75, 367, **369–70**
    libraries 367, **369**
    Mason College 47, 94, 365
    Mechanical and Civil Engineering departments 85, 93, **372**
    Metallurgy and Materials Building 86, **371**
    Muirhead Tower 86, 367, **369**
    Pritchatts Road lodges 74, 369, **371**
    St Francis' Hall 77, **370**
    Sport and Fitness building 90, **370**
    Staff House 86, **369**
    Strathcona Building 86, **371**, Pl. 128
    University Centre and Hepworth sculpture **369**
    Vale, The **373–4**
    Watson Building 85, **369**
    Winterbourne 60, **372–3**
  Erdington 6, **235–42**
    churches etc. **235–8**
      Erdington Congregational Church (now British Orthodox Church) 40, **237**
      Jewish cemetery **238**, 263
      St Barnabas 24, 36, 105, **235–6**
      St Margaret **236**
      St Margaret Mary (R.C.) 78, **236**
      St Thomas and St Edmund of Canterbury, Erdington Abbey (R.C.) and Highclare School 42, **236–7**, 240, Pl. 74
      Stockland Green Methodist Church 65, **237**
      Witton Cemetery (former Birmingham City Cemetery) 41, **237–8**, 263

public buildings 238–42
  Abbey Primary School 38, 237
  Aston Union Cottage Homes 238–9
  Brookvale Park 241
  canal buildings 241
  Erdington Skills Centre 86, 239
  Gravelly Hill Interchange ('Spaghetti Junction') 235, 241
  Highclare School *see* St Thomas and St Edmund of Canterbury (R.C.) *above*
  Highcroft Hospital (former Aston Union Workhouse) 44–5, 238–9
  Kingsbury School (former) 74, 239
  Osborne Primary School (former) 47, 239
  Plaza Cinema (former) 241
  public library 66, 239
  Salford Junction 241
  Slade Primary School 239
  tramway waiting room 240
streets, other buildings etc. 108, 235, 239–42
  Brookvale, The (former pub) 80, 241
  Burton's (former) 239
  Church House, The 239
  Conservative Club 239
  Cross Keys (former pub) 240
  Dunlop Rubber Co. *see* Fort Dunlop *below*
  Fort Dunlop 80, 108, 110, 242
  Gravelly Hill 235, 241
  Gravelly Lane 240
  Hazel's funeral parlour 239
  High Street 239–40
  Jerry's Lane 24, 241
  Josiah Mason's Orphanage 240n.
  Kingsmere 241
  Lad in the Lane (formerly Old Green Man) 14, 241
  Lyndhurst Estate 82–3, 240
  Mason Cottages 239–40
  Mason (Josiah) bust 240n.
  Navigation Inn (former) 80, 241
  Orphanage Road 239
  Red Lion pub 240
  Rookery House 240
  Slade Road 241
  Station Road 240
  Stockland pub (now Village Green) 241
  Summer Road 240
  White House, The 76, 241
  Witton Hall 242
  Wood End Lane 241
  Yenton, The (pub) 240
Four Oaks *see* Sutton Coldfield *below*
Frankley 83, 394
  Gannow Green Moat and fishpond 9, 394
Gannow Green *see* Frankley *above*
Hall Green 309–14
  churches etc. 309–10
    Ascension, The 19, 115, 309–10, 452
    Hall Green Baptist Church 78, 310
    Hall Green United Community Church (formerly Methodist) 78, 310
    Trinity United Reformed 78, 310
  streets and other buildings 109, 309, 311–14
    Baldwin, The (pub) 80, 313
    Bushmore Farm Estate 314
    Chalet, The 313
    Charles Lane Trust Almshouses 76, 311
    College Arms pub 313
    Fox Hollies Road 311, 312
    Gracewell 309, 311, 313
    Gracewell Cottages 311, 313
    Hamlet Road 312–13
    Hamlet, The (estate) 309, 312
    Petersfield Court 312
    prefabs 82, 313
    Robin Hood (now Toby Carvery pub) 313
    Sarehole 311, 313
    Sarehole Mill 26, 94, 311
    School Road 76, 79, 311–12
    Shaftmoor pub 80, 313
    South and City College 85, 311
    Stratford Road 76, 312–13
    Three Magpies pub (now 'The Maggies') 80, 312
    Wake Green Road 82, 313
    York, The (pub) 314
Hamstead *see* Perry Barr *below*
Handsworth 82, 106, 242–61
  churches etc. 243–51
    Archbishop Benson Church Hall (now United Church of God) 77, 245
    Asbury Memorial Methodist Church (now New Life Wesleyan) 41, 248
    Cannon Street Memorial Baptist Church 78, 249, 257
    Convent of the Sisters of Mercy (R.C.) 39, 247–8, 260

Suburbs *cont.*
  Handsworth *cont.*
    churches etc. *cont.*
      Elmwood United Reformed **249**
      Guru Nanak Niskham Sewak Jatha and Niskham Centre **250**, 256
      Hamstead Road Baptist Church (now Ikhewa Masjid) and Sunday Schools 41, 242, **249**, 322
      Handsworth Cemetery 63, 242, **250–1**, Pl. 66
      St Andrew 63, 64, 78, **245–6**
      St Augustine (R.C.) 78, **248**
      St Francis Institute **260**
      St Francis and Presbytery (R.C.) **248**, 260
      St James 34, **246**
      St Mary (and Watt Chapel) 10, 24–5, 25, 36, 38, 64, **243–5**, 258, 360, Pl. 39
      St Michael, St Michael's Road 36, **246–7**
      St Peter (now Church of God Seventh Day) 63, **247**
      Shri Guru Ravidass Bhawan **250**, 256
      Trinity Methodist Church **249**
    public buildings 82, **251–5**
      anti-aircraft battery (former) **261**
      Carnegie Infant Welfare Institute 74, **260**
      Council House (former) and library 44, **251**
      Handsworth Grammar School 47, **252**
      Handsworth Methodist College (now Hamstead Campus) 59, **250–2**, 375
      Handsworth New Road School (former) 67, **218**
      Handsworth Park **254–5**
      Hockley Circus/Hockley flyover 93, **255**
      King Edward VI School Handsworth **252**, Pl. 88
      Old Town Hall (former) **261**
      police station (former), Holyhead Road 74, **257**
      Soho House 21, 242, **253–4**, 255, Pl. 51
    streets, other buildings etc. 108, 109, 242, **255–61**
      Anchorage, The 61, **259**
      Barker Street **260**
      Butlers Road **261**
      Calthorpe Cottages **261**
      Chohan's **256**
      College Road **261**
      Community Roots Enterprise Centre **256**
      Cross Guns pub **256**
      Devonshire Road **258**
      Endwood Court 83, **258**
      Farcroft, The (pub) **261**
      Frighted Horse (former pub) **256**
      Gibson Road **258**
      Grove, The (pub) **261**
      Hamstead Hall Road **259**
      Hamstead Road 23, 54, 61, 242, **257**, **258**
      Handsworth New Road 60, **218**
      Handsworth Wood 1, 242, **258**
      Handsworth Wood Road 61, **258**, **259**
      Hawthorn House **259–60**
      Holyhead Road **257**
      Hunter's Lane **260**
      Hunters Road 247, **260**
      Ivy House Hotel (former) **256**
      Lansdowne Terrace **256**
      Lea Hall 21, **261**
      Limes, The **260**
      Mairs **256**
      Observatory pub 52, **260**
      Olde Toll Gate House, Ye (now Asian Resource Centre) 70, **257–8**
      Park Avenue **255**
      Park Farm Barn **261**
      Pump Tavern **256**
      Radnor Road 242, **258**
      Red Lion pub (former) 70, **257**
      Rhodes Almshouses **256**
      Roebuck Inn (former) **255**, 257
      Soho Avenue **255**
      Soho Co-operative Society (former HQ) **257**
      Soho Hill 80, 106, 242, **255–6**
      Soho House *see* public buildings *above*
      Soho Manufactory 26, 27, *105*, 242, *254*
      Soho Park 246, **255**
      Soho Road 242, **256**
      Somerset Road 56, **259**
      Supreme Works 80, **256**
      Villa Road **257–8**
      Wellington Terrace **260**
      Wood Lane **261**
      Wretham Road **260**
  Harborne **395–405**
    churches etc. **395–7**
      Masonic Hall (now Library) **404**
      Methodist church (currently Oasis Church) 41, **397**
      St Faith and St Laurence 77, **396**

St John the Baptist, High Street **396**
St John the Baptist, St John's Road *396*
St Mary (R.C.) and St Mary's Retreat (formerly Harborne Lodge) 22, 39, **396–7**, 398
St Peter 25, **395–6**
streets, other buildings etc. 395, **397–405**
　Albany Road **405**
　Albert Road **404**
　Bell Inn **404**
　Bishop's Croft 77, **397–8**
　Blue Coat School **400**
　Board Schools (former) 47, **401**
　Court Oak pub **405**
　Diocesan Offices (former) **403**
　Greenfield Road 55, **402**
　Green Man pub **401**, 405
　Grove Park **403–4**
　Grove, The 403–4
　Harborne Hall **398**
　Harborne Lodge *see* St Mary (R.C.) *above*
　Harborne Park Road **403**
　Harborne Railway 59, 395, **405**
　Harborne Road 395, **401**
　High Street 395, 400, **401**, **404**, **405**
　Hintlesham Avenue 83, 395, **401**
　Junction Inn 71, **404**
　Low Wood 61, **403**
　Manresa House **404**
　Metchley Abbey 22, **401–2**
　Metchley Grange Estate **402**
　Moor Pool Estate 291, **399–400**, 722
　New Inn 52, **402**
　Northfield Road **405**
　Old Church Road **404**
　Paganel Primary School 75, **405**
　Queen Alexandra College **405**
　Royalty Cinema (former) **404**
　St Mary's Road 61, 84, **402–3**
　St Peter's Road **404**
　Station Road **405**
　Stone House **399**, 436
　Tennal Grange **398–9**
　Tennal Industrial School (former) **405**
　Wiggin Cottages **402**
　York Street **401–2**
Hay Mills **273–4**
　Adelphi Cinema (former) **274**
　Coventry Road **273**
　Hay Hall *see* Tyseley *below*
　Pontifex factory 273n.
　Redhill Tavern (former) **274**
　St Cyprian 37, 38, 42, **274**
　Webster & Horsfall 58, 106, **274**, 466
Highters Heath **314**
　Immanuel 77, **314**
Hodge Hill **275**
　St Philip and St James 91, 275
　St Wilfrid (R.C.) 92, **275**
Kings Heath **314–19**
　churches etc. **315–16**
　　All Saints 6, 64, 78, **315**
　　Masonic Hall **319**
　　St Dunstan (R.C.) 92, **316**
　streets and other buildings 108, 314, **316–19**
　　Alcester House (now the Corks Club) **319**
　　Alcester Lanes End 54, 314, **319**
　　Appian Close **319**
　　Asda **317**
　　Cartland estate 314, **317–19**
　　Cross Guns (pub; now The Old Court) **317**
　　Gable House 60, **319**
　　Greenhill Road 61, **319**
　　Hare and Hounds pub **317**
　　Hedges Buildings **317**
　　High Street 51, 314, **316–17**
　　King Edward VI Camp Hill School **316**, 318
　　Kings Arms (now The Crown) **319**
　　Kings Heath House 53, **317–18**
　　Kings Heath Primary School 85, **316**
　　Kingsway Cinema (former) **317**
　　library and extension 89, **316–17**
　　Pavilion (former pub) **319**
　　Priory, The 318
　　Red Lion pub 71, 314, **318**
　　Scots Corner **317**
　　Stanley Road 60, **318**
　　Station Inn **316**
　　Vicarage Road 60, **317–19**
Kings Norton 8, **406–13**
　churches etc. **406–7**
　　Friends' Meeting House 92, **412**
　　Methodist church (now The Cotteridge Church) **411**
　　St Agnes 411
　　St John Fisher (R.C.) 92, **413**
　　St Nicolas 11, 12, 17, 37–8, **406–7**, Pl. 18
　public buildings **408**, **410**, **412**
　　canal structures 29, **308**, **410**, **411**, Pl. 54
　　Cotteridge schools 47, **432**
　　fire station, Cotteridge 74, **412**

Suburbs *cont.*
  Kings Norton *cont.*
    public buildings *cont.*
      Kings Norton Primary
        School 47, **408**
      Old Grammar School 14,
        407, **408**
      public library 66, **408**
      railway station **411**
      Wychall Primary School 84,
        408
    streets, houses etc. 406, **409–13**
      Beaks Hill Road 76, **410**
      Bull's Head pub **409**
      Camp Inn **412**
      Co-operative shop (former)
        79, **409**
      Cotteridge **411–12**
      Grange Hill Road 76, **410**
      Grant Arms pub 80, **412**
      Grassmoor Road 83, **410**
      Green, The 406, **409**
      Lifford Hall 18, **410–11**
      Longdales Road 8
      Middleton Hall Road **412**
      Pershore Road **412**
      Pool Farm 406
      Primrose Hill Farm 14, 406,
        411
      Rednal Road **409–10**
      Saracen's Head 9, 14, 198,
        280, 407, **408–9**
      Walkers Heath 7, **411**
      West Heath **412–13**
  Kingstanding 261–4
    churches and public buildings
      262–4
      Maryvale (formerly Oscott
        House) 25, 92, **262–3**
      Odeon Cinema (former) 81,
        263, Pl. 112
      Our Lady of the Assumption
        (R.C.) 92, **262**
      Perry Common Library 74,
        264
      St Luke 77, **262**
      Twickenham Primary School
        74, **263**
    streets, houses etc. 109, 261,
      264
      Banners Walk **264**
      College Arms pub **264**
      Deer's Leap pub **264**
      Greenwood Place **261**
      Hever Avenue **264**
      housing 75, **261, 264**
      Hurlingham Road 75, **261**
      Kings Road 261
      King's Standing round
        barrow 7, **261**
      Kingstanding Circle 261
      Kingstanding Road 261
      Old Oscott Hill 261
      Oscott House *see* churches
        and public buildings
        (Maryvale) *above*
      Pembury Croft **264**
      Rough Road 261
  Ladywood 110, **413–15**
    Birmingham Canal **414**
    Chamberlain Gardens Estate
      82, **414**
    Ledsam Street Works (former
      Belliss & Morcom) 84,
      414–15
    St John the Evangelist 36, 42,
      413–14
    St Margaret 276, 294
    St Mark 106
  Little Bromwich *see* Alum Rock
    above
  Longbridge and Rednal **415–18**
    Austin Motor Co. (former) and
      Austin Village 72, 84, 108,
      109, 110, **415–16**, 418
    Co-operative shop (former) 79,
      417
    Danilo Cinema (former) 81,
      417
    Hawkesley Farm Moat Estate
      82, **417**
    King George V (former pub)
      81, **417**
    library (former) 66, **417**
    Oratory House, Rednal 39,
      416–17
    Our Lady of Perpetual Succour
      (R.C.) 92, **416**
    St John the Baptist 90, **416**,
      422, 444, Pl. 122
  Lozells 106, **264–5**
    Aston Villa Methodist Church
      265
    St Paul and St Silas Church
      Centre 91, **264**
    St Silas (now Triumphant
      Church of God) 35–6, 38,
      42, **264–5**
  Mackadown *see* Sheldon *below*
  Mere Green *see* Sutton Coldfield
    below
  Metchley Abbey *see* Harborne
    above
  Metchley Roman Fort *see*
    Edgbaston *above*
  Minworth *see* Sutton Coldfield
    below
  Moseley **320–35**
    churches etc. **320–2**
      Hope Chapel **322**, 328
      Moseley Baptist Church
        (now Calvary Church of
        God in Christ) 41, 78, **322**
      St Agnes 64, 320, **321–2**
      St Anne 37, **322**
      St Mary 25, 38, 93, **320–1**

public buildings and parks 320, **325**
  Boer War Memorial 68, **324**
  Cannon Hill House (now National Institute of Conductive Education) 53, **324–5**
  Cannon Hill Park, Golden Lion and Midlands Art Centre 15, 48, 68, 105, **324**
  Highbury Park **334**
  King David School **325**, 328
  Lench's Close Almshouses **329**
  Uffculme School (with former Home for Aged Women) 67, **325**, **334**
streets, houses etc. 320, **323–35**, 358
  Alcester Road **325–6**, **327–8**
  Amesbury Road 61, **329**
  Anderton Park Road **330**
  Barclays Bank (former) 78, **325**
  Boscobel **326**
  Boundary Drive 84, **335**
  Brackley Dene **326**
  Britannic Assurance (former HQ) 87, **334–5**
  Bull's Head pub **325**
  Chantry Road 56–7, 320, 324, **326**
  Church Road **329**
  Colmore Crescent **332**
  Cotton Lane **330**, 331
  Court Hey **327**
  Dowell's Close **328**
  Dyott Road **333**
  Fighting Cocks pub **325**
  Gables Hotel **331**
  Golden Lion *see* public buildings *above*
  Goodby Road **335**
  Greystoke **335**
  Grove Avenue 57, 76, **330**, **331**
  Highbury 55, **333–4**, 390
  Hilver **332**
  Ideal Benefit Society (former) 79, **335**
  Mapledene **332**, **333**
  Moor Green House 335
  Moor Green Lane **334**, **335**
  Moseley Hall (now geriatric hospital) 21–2, **323–4**, **333**, 779
  Moseley village **325–8**
  Oxford Road 55, 61, 320, **331–2**, **333**
  Park Hill **327–8**
  Pitmaston 79, **335**, Pl. 107
  Prince of Wales pub **327**
  Queensbridge Road **333**
  Revesby **330**
  St Agnes Road 60, 61, **332**
  St Agnes vicarage **332**
  Salisbury Road 61, 324, **328–9**
  Trafalgar Hotel (former) **326**
  Uffculme **333**
  Village Inn (former Moseley Club) **328**
  Wake Green Road 56, 57, 320, **329–30**
  Waverley Court **330**
  Whitecroft **332**
Nechells *see* Duddeston *above*
Newtown *see* Aston *above*
Northfield 7, **418–22**
  churches etc. **418–20**
    Helier Chapel (former) 78, **420**
    Our Lady and St Brigid (R.C.) 78, **420**
    St David 91, **420**
    St Laurence 10, 11, 12, 42, **418–20**, Pl. 16
  streets, houses etc. 418, **421–2**
    Black Horse pub 80, **421–2**, Pl. 110
    Great Stone Inn 14, **421**
    library 66, **420**
    Manor House 418
    Royal Orthopaedic Hospital 45, **421**
Perry Barr 7, 8, 242, **265–7**
  Clifton Cinema (former) 81, **267**
  crematorium **266–7**
  Hamstead 265
  Hamstead Aqueduct 30
  Kynochs factory lodges 74, **267**
  Perry Hall **267**
  St John the Evangelist 34, **265–6**
  St Paul, Hamstead 78, **266**
  Towers, The 80, **267**
  Tucker Fasteners 96
Perry Beeches **268–9**
  Beeches, The (pub) 81, **269**
  Great Barr Schools (former) 75, **268**
  Perry Beeches Campus 85, **268–9**
  St Matthew 91, **268**
Pype Hayes **269–71**
  Bagot Arms pub **271**
  Berwood Bridge 29–30
  Pype Hayes Hall 16, **270–1**
  St Mary 7, **269–70**, 396, 650
  St Peter and St Paul (R.C.) 92, **270**
  United Reformed (former Congregational) Church 78, **270**

Suburbs *cont.*
  Quinton **422–3**, 520, **521**
    Christ Church 35, **422**
    Four Dwellings School (former) 84, **423**
    Hagley Road West **423**
    St Boniface 90, **422–3**
  Rednal *see* Longbridge *above*
  Ryknield Street *see* Sutton Coldfield *below*
  Salford *see* Erdington *above*
  Saltley 6, **275–8**
    Adderley Park 275
    Adderley Primary School 85, **278**
    Alum Rock Road **278**
    churches etc. **275–7**
      Our Lady of the Rosary and St Thérèse of Lisieux (R.C.) 78, 93, **276–7**
      St Mary and St John (now International Pentecostal Mission Church) **275–6**
      St Peter's College (former) 275, **277**
      St Saviour 64, **276**
    factory, Adderley Road 71, **278**
    Rockwood Academy (formerly Park View School) 85, **277–8**
    Saltley Academy *see* Small Heath *below*
    Saltley Gate **278**
  Sarehole *see* Hall Green *above*
  Selly Oak **423–33**
    churches etc. **424–7**
      College of the Ascension (now Al-Mahdi Institute) 75, **426**, 433
      convent and Selly Hall 21, 65, **426–7**
      Friends' Meeting House 78, **426**
      Harborne Healing Centre (formerly Our Lady and St Rose of Lima) **426**, 435n.
      Lodge Hill Cemetery **427**, 433
      St Edward (R.C.) 65, **426**
      St Mary 36, 37, 42, 108, **424–5**
      St Stephen 37, **424–6**
      Selly Park Baptist Church 41, **426**
      Weoley Hill Presbyterian Church (now United Reformed) 78, **426**
    public buildings 28, **427–8**
      College of the Ascension *see* churches *above*
      Dudley No. 2 Canal 28, **423**
      Jarratt Hall 84, **429**
      Kings Norton workhouse (former) *see* Selly Oak Hospital *below*
      pumping station and waterworks (former) 58, **429**
      Rendel Harris Memorial Library 75, **432**
      Selly Oak Colleges (now University of Birmingham) 75, 86, **432–3**, 785
      Selly Oak Hospital (former; originally Kings Norton Union workhouse) 44, 45, **427–8**
      Selly Oak Institute (former) **429**
      Selly Oak Library (former) 66, **428**
      Selly Oak Park 423
      Selly Oak Trust School 85, **428**
      student accommodation 84, 96, 424, **429**
      swimming baths (former) 66, **428**
      Technical Institute (former) **428**
      University of Birmingham buildings *see* Selly Oak Colleges *above*
      University of Birmingham School **428**, 433
    streets, houses etc. 108, 423–4, **428–33**
      Boscobel **431**
      Bournbrook 424, **428–9**
      Bournbrook Hotel (former) 52, **429**
      Bournbrook Road 62, **429**
      Bristol Road 423, **428–9**, **432–3**
      Fox Hill 76, **433**
      Harborne Lane 423
      Kensington Road 76, **431**
      Oakfield Road 55, 84, **429–30**, 431
      Oak Tree Lane 423
      Primrose Hill **432**
      Raddlebarn Road 350, 353
      St Wulstan's vicarage (former) 62, **429**
      Selly Manor (formerly in Raddlebarn Road) 353
      Selly Park Estate 18, **429–30**
      Selly Park Road **430–1**
      Selly Park Tavern 71, **430**
      Selly Wick Road 60, **430–1**
      Serpentine Road 57, **431**
      Southbourne Close **431**
      Station (former pub) **429**
      Third Avenue **430**
      Upland Road **431**
      Uplands, The 54, **431**
      Weoley Hill **433**
      Weoley Hill Estate 76, 350, **433**

Weoley Park Road 426, **433**, 435n.
Westley Richards factory 71, 429n.
Woodbrooke College 53, **432–3**
Shard End **278–80**, 771
  estate housing 82, **278–80**, Pl. 126
  Timberley Primary School (former) 84, **279**
Sheldon **280–4**
  churches etc. **280–2**
    Our Lady Help of Christians (R.C.) 92, **281–2**, Pl. 124
    St Giles 11, 12, 42, 296, 408, 786
    St Thomas 90, 91, **281**
    St Thomas More (R.C.) 92, **282**
  Kent's Moat **283–4**, 292
  Mackadown 280
  Sheldon Hall 15, **283**
Small Heath 106, **284–91**
  churches etc. **284–8**
    Green Lane Masjid *see* public buildings (public library) *below*
    Holy Family (R.C.) and Primary School **286**
    St Aidan (now All Saints) 63, 64, 91, **284–5**, 286
    St Benedict 63, **285**
    St Gregory the Great (now Bethel United Church of Jesus Christ) 63, 277, **285**, Pl. 12
    St Oswald of Worcester (former) 63, 285, **286–7**
    St Paul, Bordesley Green **286**
  public buildings 284, **288–90**
    Birmingham City Football Club **290**
    Dixon Road School (former) 46, **289**
    Heartlands Hospital (former Little Bromwich Hospital for Infectious Diseases) **288**
    Marlborough Infant School 67, **289**
    Oldknow Road School (now Ark Victoria Academy) 67, **289–90**
    Olive School Small Heath (former Waverley Technical Board School) **289**
    Princess of Wales Women's Unit **288**
    public library and swimming baths (now Green Lane Masjid) 66, **288**
    St Benedict's Primary School 67, **290**
    Small Heath Park 48, 284, **290**
    Small Heath School and Community Centre (now Wellbeing Centre) 85, **289**
    Starbank Junior School 74, **290**
  streets, houses etc. 284, **290–1**
    Brighton Arms (former pub) **290**
    co-operative housing **291**
    Coventry Road 284, **290**
    Finnemore Road **291**
    Ideal Village **291**
    Malt Shovel (former pub) **290**
    municipal flats (North, East and West Holme) 75, **291**
Sparkbrook **335–8**
  Angel Hotel (now Manjaros) 52, **338**
  Armourer Mills 58, **338**
  Braithwaite Road 54, **338**
  Christ Church and Sparkbrook Community Hub **336–7**
  Ladypool Primary School 47, **337**, 338
  Lloyd House (Farm) 20, 335, **337–8**
  St Agatha 63, 64, 93, 214, 245, **335–7**, Pl. 64
  St Agatha's vicarage (former) **338**
  Walford Road **338**
Sparkhill 295, **338–43**
  churches etc. **339–40**
    churches etc. by Harrison 339n.
    Congregational Church (former) 78, **340**
    English Martyrs (R.C.) 78, **340**
    St Christopher 63, **339**
    St John the Evangelist 37, 38, **339**, 342
    Salvation Army Hall (now Lighthouse Chapel) **340**, 342
    Sparkhill Methodist Church 92, **340**
  public buildings **340–2**
    library and community centre ('Yardley Town Hall') 44, **340–1**
    Moseley School (former Spring Hill Congregational College) **341–2**
  streets, houses etc. 108, **342–3**
    Antelope, The (former pub) **342**
    Burtons (former) **342**
    Lanchester Motor Co. (former) 72, **338**
    Mermaid (former pub) 338, **342**

Suburbs *cont.*
  Sparkhill *cont.*
    streets, houses etc. *cont.*
      Piccadilly Cinema (former) **342**
      St John's vicarage (former) **343**
      Showell Green Lane 61, 338, **343**
      Sportsman pub (now McDwyer's) **342–3**
      Springfield 339
      Stratford Road 338, **342**, **343**
      Waggon and Horses pub (former) **343**
      Warwick Road **342–3**
      Zinnia Centre **343**
  Springfield *see* Sparkhill *above*
  Stechford **291–2**
    All Saints 38, 93, **291**
    Cole Hall Farm 18, **292**
    Lea Hall Estate **292**
    railway buildings 291, **292**
    St Andrew (now Shilonite Gospel Church) 77, **291–2**
  Stirchley **433–4**
    British Oak pub 81, **434**
    parish church 433
    pillbox (former) 62, **434**
    public library 66, **434**
    Stirchley Community Primary School 47, 412, **434**
    Worthings (The) and Barn Close 75, **434**
  Summerfield *see* All Saints *above*
  Sutton Coldfield 1, 2, 110, **437–67**
    churches etc. **438–47**, **452**, **467**
      All Saints 194, **440–1**, 461
      Baptist church (former Town Primary School) **444**
      cemetery and crematorium **448**
      Emmanuel, Wylde Green 63, 78, 91, **441**
      Four Oaks (Wesleyan) Methodist Church 65, **444**
      Holy Trinity 12–13, 20, 24, 64, 91, 93, 437, **438–40**, 450, 595, Pl. 25
      Holy Trinity (R.C.) **443**, **452**
      Masonic Hall (former Town Hall) 43, **454**
      Methodist Church, South Parade 78, **444**
      Oscott College (R.C.) 39, 42, 47, **445–7**, Pl. 60
      Quaker Cottage (former Friends' meeting house) **467**
      St Chad 77, **441**, Pl. 118
      St Columba 91, **441**
      St George, Minworth 64, **467**
      St James, Hill 63, 64, **441–2**
      St John the Evangelist, Walmley 35, 165, **442**, 466
      St Michael, Boldmere 91, **442–3**
      St Peter, Maney 77, **443**, 455
      United Reformed church (formerly Congregational) 41, **444**
      Wylde Green United Reformed Church **445**
    Four Oaks *see* streets and houses *below*
    Minworth *see* streets and houses *below*
    public buildings 94, **447–67**
      almshouses (Sutton Coldfield Charitable Trust), Walmley **466**
      Bishop Vesey's Grammar School 74, **448**, 452
      canal 30, 466, **467**
      cemetery *see* churches *above*
      Cooper Memorial Home **455**
      Cottage Hospital *see* Sutton Coldfield Cottage Hospital *below*
      Council House and Town Hall 66, **447**, 454
      Hill School (former; now Old School House pub), Mere Green 26, **461**
      Junior School (former), Trinity Hill 67, **444**
      Magistrates' Court (former) 88, **452**
      Minworth Junior and Infants' School 67, **467**
      municipal electricity works (former) 67, **448**
      Oscott College *see* churches *above*
      railway station **449**, 454
      ring road 94, 437, **454**
      St Mary's College *see* churches (Oscott College) *above*
      sewage treatment works **466**
      Sutton Coldfield Cottage Hospital 45, **447**, 455
      Sutton Coldfield Grammar School for Girls 74, **448**
      Sutton Park 2, 8, 9, **449**, Pl. 3
      Technical School (former) **452–3**
      Town Hall (1858; now Masonic Hall) 43, **454**
      Town Hall (1905–6) *see* Council House and Town Hall *above*
      Vesey Gardens 438, **450**, 454
      War Memorial **454**
      workhouse 20, 454

Rykneild Street Roman road 8, **449**
streets and houses 13, 16, 18, 19, 437, **449–67**
  Albion House **450**
  Anchorage Road 61, **452–3**
  Ardencote **458**
  Ashfurlong Hall 13, 22, **462**
  Avoncroft 61, **456–7**
  Barker Road **460–1**
  Barley Mow (former pub) **461**
  Barn House **453**
  Beaconhurst **461**
  Beaconsfield Road **461**
  Beech Hill Road 76, 77, **461**, Pl. 117
  Birmingham Road **455–6**
  Boldmere **466**
  Bottle of Sack pub **455**
  Bracebridge Road 61, 62, **458**, **459**
  Briarwood **457**
  Bryn Teg **459**, Pl. 99
  Carhampton House 62, **457–8**
  Chester Road North **449**
  Church Hill **450**
  Coleshill Street 13, 16, 18, 19, 437, 450, **450**
  Collets Brook Farmhouse **462**
  Cottage Lane 30, **467**
  Cressington **457**
  Cull's House 16, 19, **451**
  Cup Inn (former) 71, **455**
  'Dam' 437
  Dene, The **459–60**
  Doe Bank House and former lodge **460**
  Driffold (road) 61, **455–6**
  Falcon Lodge Estate 82, **463**
  Four Oaks (village) **461**
  Four Oaks estate 437, **456–61**
  Four Oaks Hall **452**, **456**, **460**
  Four Oaks Road 61, **456**
  Fox Hill House and bottle kiln 22, 27, **462**
  Fox Inn **466**
  Gate House, The **461**
  Gate Inn **454**
  Gracechurch Centre **454**
  Grove, The 14, **463**
  Halloughton Road **461**
  Hartopp Road 60, 76, **457**, **458**, **459**
  Hawkesford (now Swanston Hall) **458**
  High Heath Cottage **450**
  High Street 6, 16, 19, 21, 437, **450–2**
  Highway, The **465**
  Hillwood Common Road 76, **462**
  Hindecliffe 61, **459**
  Hollington **457**
  Holmwood **459**
  Horse and Jockey pub **454**
  Hurst, The 59–60, **456**, 457
  Kenwood 76, **458**
  King Edward Square **454**
  King's Arms 80, **450**
  Ladywood Road, Four Oaks 60, *332*, *338*, **458–9**
  Langley Hall 9, **463**
  Langley Mill Farm 7, 8
  Leasowes, The 59, **460**
  Lichfield Road 68n., **452**, **460**, **461**
  Lloyds Bank, Birmingham Road **455**
  Lloyds Bank (former), High Street **451**
  Lower Parade 437, **454**
  Luttrell Road 62, 76, 96, **457**
  Maney Hill Road **455**
  Manor, The (and *medieval manor house*) **456**
  Manse, The **454**
  Mere Green 8, 26, **461**
  Midland Bank (former), High Street 70, **450**
  Mill Street 450, **454**
  Minworth (village) 15, 30, **466–7**
  Minworth Greaves 14, **467**
  Minworth Hall **467**
  Moat House 18, 309, **452**, Pl. 44
  Moor Hall **462**
  Mulroy Road **453**
  New Hall 13, 15, 16, 54, 455, **463–5**, 653n., Pl. 31
  New Hall Mill 10, 18, 26, **466**, Pl. 50
  Newhall Walk shopping centre **454**
  New Shipton Farm barn **466**
  Oakhurst **454**
  Oaklands Road 76, **460**
  Odeon (now Empire) cinema 81, **455**
  Old Barn, Wiggins Hill **467**
  Old Moor Hall Farm **462**
  Old Smithy, Maney 14, **455**
  Old Stone House **449–50**, 455, Pl. 24
  Parade 437, **454**
  Park House (former mill) 26, **449**
  Peddimore Hall 16, **465–6**
  Penns Hall **466**
  Pilkington Avenue **455**
  Rectory Park *437*
  Redcroft (later St Winnow; No. 22 Ladywood Road) 60, *332*, *338*, **458**

Suburbs *cont.*
  Sutton Coldfield *cont.*
    streets and houses *cont.*
      Reddicap Hill 6, 13, **463**
      Redlands 60, **457**
      Royal Hotel (former; now 'The Townhouse') 21, **452**
      Seven Gables 61, **456**
      Silverbirch **460**
      Sons of Rest **450**
      Station pub **454**
      Stone House **450**
      Streetly Lane **449**
      Sunnycroft **460**
      Sutton Park houses **449**
      Swanston Hall **458**
      Three Tuns 26, **451**
      Top o' the Hill **456**
      'Townhouse, The' 21, **452**
      Vesey cottages 6, 13, **449–50**, Pl.24
      Vesey Grange **450**
      Vesey House (Brick House) 16, **451**
      Vesey Manor 15, **455**
      Walmley village **466**
      Warren House Farm **450**
      Wellington Terrace **452**
      Wentworth Road **460**
      Westmoor **456**
      Wheatmoor Farm 22, **463**
      White Hart inn (former) 16, 21, **451**
      Wickham **457**
      Wiggins Hill 30, **467**
      Wiggins Hill Farm 16, **467**
      Withens **461**
      Woodgate 60, **458–9**
      Woodside 28, **458**
      Wylde Green **461**
      Wylde Green Road 450, **466**
      Wyndhurst **456**
      Yew Trees **457**
    Walmley *see* streets and houses *above*
    Wylde Green *see* streets and houses *above*
  Tyseley **343–5**
    Hay Hall 2, **344–5**
    railway buildings 72, 343, **344**
    Yardley Grammar School 343n.
  Walkers Heath *see* Kings Norton *above*
  Ward End **292–4**
    Fox and Goose pub **294**
    library 74, **293**
    St Margaret 34, 93, **292–3**
    St Margaret's Road cottages 61, **293**
    Ward End Hall 292
    Ward End House 53, **293–4**
    Ward End Primary School, Ingleton Road 75, **293**
  Washwood Heath Road **293**, **294**
  Wolseley Motors (*LDV*) 72, 292
  Washwood Heath **294–5**
    Metropolitan-Cammell factory (former) 294, **295**
    Washwood Heath Road **293**, **294**, **295**
  Weoley **435–6**
    Our Lady and St Rose of Lima (R.C.) 92, 426, **435**
    Shenley Fields Road 75, **436**
    Weoley Castle 9, 13, 399, **435–6**
    Weoley Castle Estate 75, 109, 435, **436**
  Weoley Hill *see* Selly Oak *above*
  Winson Green *see* All Saints *above*
  Witton *see* Aston *above*
  Woodgate *see* Bartley Green *above*
  Yardley **295–9**
    churches etc. **295–7**
      cemetery 297
      Digbeth-in-the-Field Congregational Church (now United Reformed) 92, **297**, 765
      St Edburgha 11, 12, 20, 25, **295–7**, Pl.36
    streets, houses, other buildings 23, 295, **298–9**
      Bierton School (former) 75, **297**
      Blakesley Hall 2, 15, **299**, Pl.27
      Cottagers' Institute (former) **298**
      Journey's End pub 81, **298**
      Old Yardley village 295, **298–9**
      South Yardley Library 74, **299**
      Swan Centre **299**
      Swan, The (pub) 299
      'Yardley Town Hall' *see* Sparkhill (library) *above*
      Yardley Trust School (former) **298**
  Yardley Wood 2, **345–6**
    Dog and Partridge pub (now Harvest Church) 81, **346**
    Our Lady of Lourdes (R.C.) 92, **345**
    Trittiford Mill 10
Transport, railways etc. **27–30**, 31, 72, 73, 90, 136
  Ashted Tunnel **191**
  Aston Turn **191**
  Birmingham Canal (Old and New Lines and branches) 28, **30**, 33, 165, **169**, 171, **173–4**
    Edgbaston Reservoir 30, **387**, 414
    Icknield Port Loop, Ladywood **414**

Birmingham to Derby railway 33, 275
Birmingham and Fazeley Canal **28, 29–30, 241**
  Minworth 30, 466, **467**
Birmingham & Gloucester Railway 33, 320
  Highgate Place overbridge 59, **202**
Birmingham and Warwick Junction Canal 29, **241**
Birmingham West Suburban Railway 424
Bordesley railway viaduct **198**
British Railways signal box 90, **206**
Camp Hill railway line 303
Curzon Street Station *see* Inner areas (Eastside)
'Curzon Street Tunnel' (railway bridges) **191**
Digbeth Branch Canal 28, 159, **189, 191**
Duddeston railway buildings 59, **234–5**
Dudley No. 2 Canal **28**
  Lapal Tunnel 28, **347**
  Selly Oak 28, **423**
GJR *see* Grand Junction Railway
Grand Junction Canal Co. buildings **199**
Grand Junction Railway 32, 59
  Curzon Street Station *see* Inner areas (Eastside)
  Duddeston Station and wagon repair shop 59, **234**
Gravelly Hill Interchange **235**, 241
Great Western Railway 33, 72, 136, 145*n.*, 300
  Digbeth viaduct and former goods depot **196**
  Tyseley station and locomotive works 72, 343, **344**
GWR *see* Great Western Railway *above*
Harborne Railway 59, 395, **405**
Hockley Flyover **255**
HS2 188, **193**
inner ring road and Queensways **94**, 109–10, 118, 147, 162, 168, 187, 188, 203, 207
Kings Norton canal structures 29, **308, 410, 411**, Pl. 54
L&BR *see* London & Birmingham Railway *below*
Lawley Street *see* London & Birmingham Railway *below*
LNWR *see* London & North Western Railway *below*

London & Birmingham Railway 32, 59, 192
  Curzon Street Station *see* Inner areas (Eastside)
  Eastside railway viaduct **191–2**
  Lawley Street railway viaducts and *station* 59, 136, **191–2**
  Stechford station and railway bridge 291, **292**
London & North Western Railway 30, 32–3
  Sutton Coldfield **449**, 454
  Windsor Street Goods Depot (former), Duddeston **234–5**
Metro tram line 156
Midland Railway 33, **411**
Moor Street Station 72, **136**, 196
New Street Station *see* City centre (public buildings)
Pershore turnpike **406**
Queensways *see* inner ring road *above*
Rykneild Street 8, **449**
Snow Hill Station **145**, 153
Soho Loop railway 254
Staffordshire and Worcestershire Canal, Digbeth branch *see* Digbeth Branch Canal *above*
Stratford-upon-Avon Canal 29, **410**
  Kings Norton 29, **308, 410**
Tame Valley Canal 29, 30, **241**
tramways 156, 240, 320
  Balsall Heath Depot (former) **306**
  Erdington waiting room (former) **240**
  Sparkbrook *Central Works* **338**
  Witton Lane Depot (former) **228**
turnpike roads **31**, 255, 265, 379, 406
Tyseley station and locomotive works 72, 343, **344**
Vauxhall Station 136
Walsall Road turnpike 265
Warwick and Birmingham Canal 29
  Bordesley 29, 30, **199**
Worcester and Birmingham Canal **28–9, 173–4, 410, 411**
  Kings Norton 29, **410, 411**, Pl. 54
  Selly Oak 29, **423**
  Stirchley pillbox **434**
  Wasthill Tunnel **410**
  Worcester Bar **173**
Wyrley and Essington Canal 28, 29

INDEX TO THE BLACK COUNTRY AND SOLIHULL

This index covers pp. 1–96 and 469–752; for Birmingham and Sutton Coldfield see the separate index above (pp. 846–69). For more information, see the contents lists on pp. 469–70, 563, 617 and 669, and the map on pp. ii–iii.

Canals, railways, roads, tramways etc. are indexed under *Transport*.

The following abbreviations are used in this index: (B) Birmingham; (D) Dudley; (Sa) Sandwell; (So) Solihull; (Wa) Walsall; (Wo) Wolverhampton.

Principal references are in **bold** type; demolished buildings are shown in *italic*.

Aldersley (Wo) *see* Tettenhall (Wo)
Aldridge (Wa) 1, 7, 618, **640–4**
  Manor House 22, **642**
  St Mary 11, 37, 91, **640–2**
  St Mary of the Angels (R.C.) 92, **642**
  Shutt Cross House 20, **643**
Amblecote (D) 3, 31, 75, **492–5**
  Bonded Warehouse 30, 95, 492, **494–5**, Pl. 52
  Brettell Lane 31, 32n., **493–4**
  Canal Basin and Canal Street **494**, 551
  Corbett Hospital 493
  Dennis Hall 20, 493, **494**
  High Street 492, **493–4**, 495
  Holy Trinity **492–3**
  Methodist church **493**
  Stourbridge Canal offices 30, **494**
  Sutton's Holloware offices (former) 80, **495**
  Vicarage Road 492, **493**
  White Horse (former pub) 52, **493–4**
Autherley (Wo) *see* Oxley and Fordhouses (Wo)

Baggeridge (D) *see* Gornal (D)
Bentley (Wa) *see* Darlaston (Wa)
Bickenhill (So) 1, **766–8**
  Castle Hills 16, **768**
  St Peter 10, 11, 12, 37, **766–8**, Pl. 20
Bilston (Wo) 4, 5, 31, 34, 672, **696–701**
  churches etc. **697–8**
    St Chad 90, **698**
    St Leonard 24, 25, 37, **697**, Pl. 42
    St Mary 24, **697–8**
  industries 5, 31, 32, 33, 696, 701
  public buildings **698–9**
    bus station 90, **698**
    Daisy Bank Centre (former school) 47, **701**
    drill hall (former) 67, **700**
    Girls' High School (former) 74, **699**, 713
    health centre (former) 74, **700**
    police station (former) 43, **700**
    Town Hall 44, **698**
    Wilkinson Primary School 85, **701**
  streets, houses etc. 94, **699–701**
    Barclays Bank 49, **699**
    Bradley 32n., **701**
    Great Western pub 52, **701**
    Greyhound and Punchbowl pub 16, 17, 81, **701**
    housing 82, 696, **701**
    Lawnside Green 82, **701**
    parsonage (former) 22, **699**, Pl. 55
    Pipe Hall 18, **699**
    Villiers Arms 81, **701**
Birchills (Wa) *see* Walsall (Wa)
Birmingham Airport (So) *see* Elmdon (So); National Exhibition Centre (So)
Black Country Living Museum (D) *see* Dudley (D)
Blackheath (Sa) *see* Halesowen (D); Rowley Regis (Sa)
Blakenall (Wa) 38, **644**
Blakenhall, Ettingshall and Parkfield (Wo) 32n., **702–5**
  All Saints 37, **702**
  Goldthorn Hill pumping station 58, **704**
  St Luke 36, 42, **702**

St Luke's C. of E. Primary School 85, **704**
St Martin 77, **703**
Sunbeam Motor Works 71, 670, **704**
Bloxwich (Wa) 28, 32n., 618, **645–7**
All Saints 37, 38, **645**
Bloxwich C. of E. Primary School 46, **646**
Turf Tavern **646–7**, Pl. 101
Walsall Academy 85, **646**
Wolverhampton Road 82, **646–7**
Bournville (B) *see* Birmingham index
Bradley (Wo) *see* Bilston (Wo)
Bradmore, Finchfield and Castlecroft (Wo) **705–8**
Spinney, The 62, **708**, Pl. 96
Uplands Junior School 85, **705**
Brierley Hill (D) 3, 32n., 33, **495–9**
churches etc. **495–7**
Congregational chapel (former) 41, **496**
St Mary (R.C.) 39, **496**
St Michael 24, 64, **495–6**
public buildings **497**, **498**
Civic Centre 88, **497**
Library and Technical Institute (now International Glass Centre) **497**
Market Hall 79, **497**
Town Hall (former) **497**
streets, houses etc. 48, **497–9**
Albion Street and warehouse **497–8**
Black Delph 28, 495, **498**
Chapel Street Estate **498**
Church Hill 48, **498**
Delph ('Black Delph') 28, 30, 32n., 495, **498–9**
Delph Mill **499**
Delph Road and bridge **499**
Dudley Canal buildings **498–9**
Dudley Road **497**, **499**
Harris & Pearson Brickworks Offices (former) **499**, Pl. 92
Merry Hill development 88, 495, **499**
Round Oak (former pub) **499**
Round Oak Iron and Steelworks 33, 495, **499**
Stevens & Williams Works (later Royal Brierley Crystal) 58, 495, **499**
Stourbridge Canal **499**
Tenth Lock (formerly Stores) **499**
Waterfront buildings, Merry Hill **499**
Brockmoor (D) **500**
Bottle and Glass pub 26, **491**
canal reservoirs **500**

Cookley works (later Richard Thomas & Baldwins) 80, *500*
Leys ironworks 500
St John 35, 42, **500**, Pl. 8
vicarage (former) 55, **500**
Bromley (D) *see* Kingswinford (D)
Brownhills (Wa) 28, 618, 640, **647–8**
Central Schools 47, **648**
Council Offices (former) 44, **648**
miner statue 93, **648**
St James and vicarage 35, 55, 91, **647–8**
Bushbury (Wo) **708–11**, 721
Bushbury Hall **711**
Bushbury Hill school 85, **711**
Moseley Hall 18–19, **711**
St Mary 11, 12, 37, 38, 42, **708–10**

Cakemore (D) *see* Halesowen (D)
Caldmore (Wa) *see* Walsall (Wa)
Castle Bromwich (So) 8, 753, **768–74**
Bradford Arms 18, **774**
castle 9, *768*
Castle Bromwich Hall 3, 15, 16, 18, 21, **770–3**, Pls. 32, 57
Green, The 60, **774**
St Mary and St Margaret *14*, 19, 26, **768–70**, 771, Pl. 35
Castlecroft (Wo) *see* Bradmore, Finchfield and Castlecroft (Wo)
Catherine-de-Barnes (So) *see* Solihull (So)
Chapel Ash, Tettenhall Road and West Park (Wo) **712–20**
churches etc. **712**
St Jude 36, 38, **712**
Trinity Methodist Church 718
public buildings **713–14**
City of Wolverhampton College 85, **713**
drill hall 67, **714**
Tettenhall Road 712, **715–18**
West Park and Villiers statue 48, 49, 712, **714**
Wolverhampton Girls' High School 62, **713**
Wolverhampton Grammar School 712, **713**
Wolverhampton and Midland Counties Eye Hospital (former) 45, **714**, **719**
streets, houses etc. **714–20**
Berrington Lodge 55, **716**
Bredon House 54, **718**
Combermere Arms 52, **715**
Compton Road 77, 712, **718**
Cottage, The 62, **717**
Crescent House 54, **717**
Deansgate (formerly Poplar Terrace) 54, **716**
Ely House 54, **715**
Halfacre 77, **720**

Chapel Ash, Tettenhall Road and West Park (Wo) *cont.*
  streets, houses etc. *cont.*
    Marston's Brewery **719–20**
    Montford House **716–17**
    Newbridge Avenue 62, **717**
    Newbridge Crescent 54, **717**
    Parkdale 55, **716**, 745
    Tettenhall Road 54, 55, 56, 77, **715–18**
Chelmsley Wood (So) 82, 753, 7 **74–5**
Clayhanger (Wa) *see* Brownhills (Wa)
Cocksheds (D) *see* Halesowen (D)
Compton (Wo) *see* Tettenhall (Wo)
Coopers Bank (D) *see* Gornal (D)
Coppice (D) *see* Coseley (D)
Coseley (D) 4, 32n., **500–4**
  churches etc. **502–4**
    Christ Church 4, 24, 42, 64, 72–3, **501**, 530, Pl.68
    Coppice Baptist Chapel **502**
    Ebenezer Baptist Chapel 40, **502**
    Hurst Hill Methodist Church 40, **502**
    Mount Tabor Methodist New Connexion Chapel (former) 40, **504**
    Old Meeting House (Unitarian) 40, **502–3**
    St Mary, Hurst Hill 4, 93, **501–2**
    Upper Ettingshall Methodist Church ('Sodom Chapel') 40, **503**
  public buildings, streets etc. **503–4**
    Christ Church Primary School **503**
    Coppice **501**
    Coseley tunnel, Birmingham Canal **504**
    Hurst Hill (Can Lane) **501**
    Pear Tree Lane 73, **503**
    Roseville **500–1**
    Sodom **501**, **503**
    Swan Village **504**
    Wallbrook **500–1**
    Woodcross **501**
    Woodsetton **504**
Cradley (D) **504–7**
  churches etc. **505–6**
    Baptist chapel 505
    Park Lane Chapel (Unitarian) 26, **505–6**
    Providence Methodist (New Connexion) Church **506**
    Trinity Wesleyan Methodist chapel 505
  public buildings **506–7**
    British School (now Cradley Baptist Church) 46, **506**
    Cradley C. of E. School and former teachers' houses 46, **507**
    High Town Ragged School 46, **506**
    infants' school (former) 67, **507**
    Twogates Ragged School (Independent Methodist) 46, **506**
  streets, houses etc. **506–7**
    Colley Gate 504, **506**
    Colley Lane (former High Street) 504, 505, **507**
    Jones & Lloyd 504
    Lyde Green **507**
    Netherend 504
    New British Iron Company, Corngreaves 33
    Rose and Crown pub 72, **507**
    Round of Beef (pub and shop) 52, **506**
    Windmill Hill 504, **506**
Cradley Heath (Sa) *see* Rowley Regis (Sa)

Darlaston (Wa) 4, 6, 31, 32n., 72, **648–54**
  churches etc. **649–51**
    All Saints (1850–1), Moxley 35, **654**
    All Saints (1871–2) 37, 650
    All Saints (1951–2) 90, 649, **650**, 653
    Emmanuel, Bentley 90, 649, **653–4**, Pl.123
    Kings Hill chapel 649
    Octagon Methodist Chapel 649
    St Andrew (former) **650**, **651**
    St Lawrence 24, 25, 37, 38, **649–50**
    Slater Street chapel 649
    Willenhall Cemetery 41, **654**
  public buildings 72, 649, **651–2**
    caretaker's house (*Kings Hill Board School*) 47, **652**
    Salisbury Primary School 67, **652**
    Town Hall 44, 72, **651**
  streets, houses etc. 72, **651–4**
    Atlas Works 80, **652**
    Bentley, 82, **653–4**
    Franchise Street 55, **652**
    Moxley 6, **654**
    Pardoe's Cottage 54, **651**
    Rubery Owen Offices and Institute (former) 649, **653**
Delph (D) *see* Brierley Hill (D)
Dickens Heath (So) *see* Earlswood (So)
Dock (D) *see* Wordsley (D)

INDEX TO BLACK COUNTRY AND SOLIHULL 873

Dudley (D) 1, 2, 3, 4, 31, 45–6, **470–563**
  churches etc. **472–5**, **491**
    Central Mosque (former St Edmund's Church School) 3, 4, 45, **489**
    Dixon's Green Methodist Church **475**, 489
    Dudley Priory 3, 4, 10, **480–1**
    Jehovah's Witnesses (former Odeon cinema) 81, **489**
    Old Meeting House (Unitarian) 26, **475**, 486
    Our Blessed Lady and St Thomas of Canterbury (R.C.) 38, 92, **475**
    Park Congregational Church 65, **475**
    St Augustine, Holly Hall 64, 65, **491**
    St Edmund ('Bottom Church') 19–20, 78, **473–4**, 488, 508, 552
    St Francis 77, **474**
    St James 3, 4, 5, 35, 37, 38, **474**
    St John the Evangelist 3, 4, 5, 35, 37, **474–5**
    St Luke **531**
    St Thomas ('Top Church') 6, 24, 25, **472–3**, 542, 543, 552, Pl. 40
    Wolverhampton Street Methodist Church **491**
    Woodside Primitive Methodist Church (now New Testament Church of God) **491–2**
    Woodside (Wesleyan) Methodist Church **491**
  Dudley Castle 1, 2, 3, 4, 7, 9, 13, 15, 470, 472, **475–80**, 489, 552, Pls. 23, 26
  public buildings 43, 45–6, **479–80**, **482–4**
    Apollo statue **488**
    Art Gallery 44, **483**
    Black Country Living Museum 5, 6, **490–1**
    Board of Guardians offices (former) 45, **487**
    Castle High School 67, **484**
    cemetery and Boer War memorial **490**
    Civic Centre (Town Hall, Municipal Buildings etc.) 74, 93, **482–3**, Pl. 90
    Claughton Centre (former Upper Standard School) 67, **484**
    County Court (former) 44, **487**
    Dudley (1st Earl of) statue 49, **488**
    Dudley Canal and Dudley Tunnel **491**
    Dudley College 75, **483**
    Dudley Evolve (Further Education College) **484**
    Dudley Golf Course 5
    Dudley Grammar School (now Castle High School) 67, **484**
    Dudley Training College 67, **490**
    Dudley Zoo 81–2, **479–80**, Pl. 115
    Garratt (Job) Monument **492**
    Hippodrome theatre (former) 81, **489**
    Library 66, **483**, Pl. 90
    Magistrates' Court 88, **483**
    Municipal Buildings *see* Civic Centre *above*
    New Park 10
    Odeon cinema (now Jehovah's Witnesses) 81, **489**
    Pegasus statue 93, **490**
    police station 43, **483**
    post office (former) 68, **486**
    Priory Hall and Park 4, 22, **484**
    St Edmund's Church School (now Central Mosque) 3, 4, 45, **489**
    St James's Church School 45–6, **490**
    St Thomas's School (former) 46, **486**
    Town Hall *see* Civic Centre *above*
    Woodside Library (former) 66, 491, **492**, 532
  streets, houses etc. 94, 472, **484–92**
    Barclays Bank 78, **486**
    Bean Car Factory offices (former) 71, **489**
    Bean Road **489**
    Birmingham Road 490, 491
    Castle Hill 7, **488–9**
    Castle Street **488**
    Co-op (former) **486**
    Coronation Gardens **488**
    Court House pub **488**
    Crown Inn (former) 71, **486**, 487, Pl. 102
    Dudley Arms Hotel 472
    Earl's lime kilns 5, **491**
    Ednam House 56, **487**
    Empire Tavern (former) **489**
    Finch House 3, 19, **486**
    Gladstone Liberal Club (former) **488**
    Green Man Entry 3, **488**
    Griffin pub **485**, 487n.
    Hartshill, Woodside and Holly Hall **491–2**
    Hen and Chickens (former pub) **488**
    High Street 50, 472, **485–6**
    Hobbs's Fish-and-chip Restaurant **490**

INDEX TO BLACK COUNTRY AND SOLIHULL

Dudley (D) *cont.*
streets, houses etc. *cont.*
King Charles House **488–9**
King and Queen (former pub) **486**
Lloyds Bank (former) 49, **486**
Low Town (hamlet) **492**
Market Place and fountain 94, 472, **484–5**, 488
Oakham Road 76, **489–90**
Priory Close **490**
Priory Estate 76, **490**
Priory Fields estate **487**
Priory House **488**
Priory Road **488**
Priory Street 19, 72, **486**, **487**, **488**
Railway Tavern (former) **489**
St James's Road **487**
Saracen's Head and Freemasons' Arms 52, **487**
Shakespeare, The (former beerhouse) 51–2, **487**
Station Hotel **489**
Stone Street 50, **485**, 487n.
Trebant 76, **487**
Wolverhampton Street 20, **486**
Woodside 28, **491–2**
Dudley Wood (D) *see* Netherton (D)
Dunstall (Wo) *see* Whitmore Reans and Dunstall (Wo)

Earlswood (So) 1, **775–8**
Dickens Heath **777–8**
Old Moat House 14, **76**
St Patrick 36, 63, **775–6**
Stratford Canal 29, 30, **776**
East Park, Moseley and Portobello (Wo) **720–1**
East Park 48, **720–1**
Mander Kidd office and warehouse 84, **721**
Edgbaston (B) *see* Birmingham index
Elmdon (So) **778–80**
Birmingham Airport buildings (former) **779**
Damson Parkway 7, 8
Elmdon Hall 21, **778**, 779
Tidbury Green 7
Ettingshall (Wo) *see* Blakenhall, Ettingshall and Parkfield (Wo)

Fallings Park and Low Hill (Wo) **721–5**
Fallings Park Garden Suburb 62, 503, **722–4**
Golden Lion pub 81, **724**
library 74, **724**
Low Hill 75, **724**
New Park Village 83, **723**

Old Fallings Hall (now Our Lady and St Chad Catholic Academy) 19, 711, 721, **722**
Old Fallings Lane 75, **725**
Our Lady of Perpetual Succour (R.C.) 78, **721**
Victoria Road **723**
Finchfield (Wo) *see* Bradmore, Finchfield and Castlecroft (Wo)
Fordhouses (Wo) *see* Oxley and Fordhouses (Wo)

Gornal (D) 4, 31, 32n., 33, **507–11**
churches etc. **508–10**
Five Ways Methodist (New Connexion) Chapel 40, **509**
Lake Street (Primitive) Methodist Church **509–10**
Ruiton Chapel 4, 39, **509**
St Peter 34–5, **508–9**
St Peter and the English Martyrs (R.C.) 92, **508**
Zoar Methodist (New Connexion) Chapel 65, **510**
public buildings, streets etc. **510–11**
Baggeridge Social Club 507, **510–11**
Coopers Bank 9, 490, **511**
Red Hall Schools 47, **510**
Ruiton 4, 507, **510**
Vale Street 83, **510**
Graiseley and Penn Fields (Wo) **725–9**, 733
Beckminster Methodist Church 78, **726**
Claremont House 54, **727**
Graiseley Old Hall 15, 16, **727**
Leylands 62, **729**
Longfield 62, **728**
Penn Road 54, 62, 725, **727**, **728–9**, 733
Royal School 64, **726–7**, Pl.83
St Chad 63, **725**
St Philip 36, **725–6**
United Reformed Church 92, **726**
Great Barr (Wa) 10, 602, **654–8**
Great Barr Hall 21, 22–3, 568, **656–7**, 658
Grove Vale Primary School 85, **655**
Q3 Academy 85, **655**
Red House 53, **657**
St Margaret 36, 38, **654–5**
vicarage (former) 55, **657**
war memorial, Barr Beacon 73, **658**
Great Bridge (Sa) *see* West Bromwich (Sa)
Greets Green (Sa) *see* West Bromwich (Sa)

Halesowen (D) 1, 2, 8, 31, 32n., 94, **511–22**
  churches etc. **511–17, 520–1**
    Blackheath Congregational Church 72, **520**
    Cocksheds (Primitive) Methodist Church 72, **520**
    Congregational chapel 511
    Halesowen Abbey 6, 10–11, 12, 511, **514–16**
    Primitive Methodist chapel, Blackheath 65
    Quinton Cemetery **521**
    St John the Baptist and cemetery chapel 10, 11, 12, 25, 38, 41, 64, **511–14**, 621, Pl. 15
    St Margaret **514**, 519
    St Paul, Blackheath 37, 91, **520**, 569
    Zion Methodist Chapel (former) 40, **517**
  public buildings **516–17, 519–21**
    canal buildings 28, **520**
    Hayley Green Isolation Hospital (former) 45, **519**
    Howley Grange Primary School 85, **521**
    Technical School (former) 74–5, **516–17**
  streets, houses etc. **516–22**
    Birmingham Municipal Bank (former) 79, **516**
    Bundle Hill 82, **517**
    Cornbow Centre 511, **517**
    Fairfield (pub) 81, **521**
    Grange, The (now Somers Sports and Social Club) 18, **519**
    Great Cornbow (street) 23, 511, **517**
    Greenhill House 2, 22, **521**
    Hasbury 6, **519**
    Hill and Cakemore **520–1**
    Lapal 28, **520**, **521–2**
    Leasowes, The (now Halesowen Golf Club) 21, **517–19**, 520
    Lloyds Bank (former) 49, **517**
    Lutley **522**
    New Hawne Colliery 58, **519–20**
    Old Hill 569, **572–4**
    Quinton 520, **521**
    see also Birmingham index
Hartshill (D) *see* Dudley (D)
Hayley Green (D) *see* Halesowen (D)
Heath Town (Wo) 32n., 76, 83, 721, **729–31**
  baths and library 74, **730**
  Holy Trinity and Almshouses 35, 38, 54, **729–30**, Pl. 82
  war memorial 73, **730**
  Wolverhampton Union Workhouse (now New Cross Hospital) 43, **730–1**
Hill and Cakemore (D) *see* Halesowen (D)
Holly Hall (D) *see* Dudley (D)
Hurst Hill (D) *see* Coseley (D)

Kingshurst (So) **780**
  bailey and *Kingshurst Hall* 9, **780**
  shopping and community centre 88, **780**
Kingswinford (D) 29, 31, 32n., **522–6**
  churches and public buildings **522–4**
    Crestwood School (former Brierley Hill Grammar School) 85, **524**
    Ketley Road bridge (now at Amblecote) **495**
    Kingswinford Methodist Church 92, **524**
    St Mary 10, 11, 37, 78, **522–4**, 589, Pl. 14
    Summerhill School 85, **524**
  streets, houses etc. 75, 522, **524–6**
    Bradley Hall 706
    Broadfield House 22, **526**
    Bromley Lane 73, **526**
    Buckingham Grove 84, **525**
    Manor House 20, **525**
    Moss Grove 76, 524, **525**
    shopping centre 88, **525**

Langley (Sa) *see* Oldbury (Sa)
Lapal (D) *see* Halesowen (D)
Little Bloxwich (Wa) *see* Bloxwich (Wa)
Low Hill (Wo) *see* Fallings Park and Low Hill (Wo)
Lutley (D) *see* Halesowen (D)
Lye and Wollescote (D) 76, **526–30**
  cemetery 41, **528**
  Christ Church 35, 42, 93, **527**
  Clifton cinema (former) 81, **528**
  Foxcote 7, **530**
  industries 31, 58, 526, **529–30**
  Lye Waste 526–7, **528–9**
  Monarch Works 80, **529**
  Rhodes Buildings 51, **529**
  St John, Dudley Wood 77, **531**
  Unitarian chapel (former) 40, **527–8**
  Wollescote Hall 16, **528**
Lyndon (So) *see* Solihull (So)

Marston Green (So) **780–1**
Merry Hill (Wo) **731–2**
  Merry Hill development *see* Brierley Hill (D)
  St Michael (R.C.) 92, **731**
  Warstones Junior and Infant School 75, **731**

Monkspath (So) *see* Solihull (So)
Moseley (Wo) *see* East Park, Moseley and Portobello (Wo)
Moxley (Wa) *see* Darlaston (Wa)
Mushroom Green (D) *see* Netherton (D)

National Exhibition Centre (So) 87, **781**
  Birmingham Airport **781**
Netherton (D) 4, **530–3**
  canal bridge **533**
  Dudley Wood 530
  Ebenezer Baptist Chapel 40, **531**
  Joe Darby Obelisk 93, **532**
  Library and Technical Institute 66, **532**
  Mushroom Green 94, **532–3**, 667
  Noah's Ark (Primitive) Methodist Chapel (former) 78, **531**
  Providence Methodist New Connexion Chapel 491
  St Andrew 4, 24, 64, **530–1**
  St John the Evangelist 77, **531**
Netherton Tunnel (Sa) *see* Rowley Regis (Sa)
New Invention (Wa) *see* Willenhall (Wa)
New Park Village (Wo) *see* Fallings Park and Low Hill (Wo)
Newtown (Wa) *see* Brownhills (Wa)

Oldbury (Sa) 1, 6, 7, 34, **564–9**
  churches etc. **564–8**
    Our Lady and St Hubert (R.C.) 78, **567–8**, Pl. 121
    St Hilda, Warley Woods 77, **567**
    Warley Institutional Church (now Salvation Army) 78, **568**
    Wesleyan Methodist church (now New Testament Church of God) 40, **564**
  public buildings **564–8**
    Bury Hill Park 73n.
    Causeway Green Primary School 85, **565**
    Court House (former) 26, **564–5**
    Jack Judge House (library etc.) 89, **565**
    Rood End Primary School 67, **566**
    Rounds Green School 67, **565**
    Sandwell Civic Centre 88, **564**
    Warley Woods (park) 21, **568**
  streets, houses etc. **565–9**
    Bell Inn 52, **567**
    Big House, The 19, **565**
    BIP works 84, **567**
    Bristnall Terrace 54, **567**
    British Cyanides (former) 80, **567**
    Junction Inn 6, 52, **565–6**, Pl. 11
    Langley **566–7**
    Langley Maltings (former Showells Brewery) 58, **567**
    Navigation pub 81, **567**
    Solvay (former Albright & Wilson) works 564, **566–7**
    Waggon and Horses pub 71, **565**
    Warley **567–9**
Old Hill (Sa) *see* Rowley Regis (Sa)
Oldswinford (D) **533–7**
  Hagley Road 54, **536**
  Oldswinford Castle 16, **535–6**
  Old Swinford Hospital 18, **534–5**, 551, 552
  rectory 18, **535**
  St Mary 38, 65, **533–4**
  Seven Stars pub 71, **536**
  Stourbridge College (former) 85, **536**
  Stourbridge Junction Station 72, 93, **536**
  Swinford Old Hall 19, **535**
  teachers' houses 46, **536**
Olton (So) **781–4**
  Dovehouse Farm 16, **784**
  Olton Friary (R.C.) 39, **782**
  St Margaret 42, **782**
Oxley and Fordhouses (Wo) **732–3**
  Autherley Junction 28, 30, 695, **732–3**
  Elston Hall Primary School 75, 731, **732**
  Oxley House 22, **732**, Pl. 56

Palfrey (Wa) *see* Walsall (Wa)
Parkfield (Wo) *see* Blakenhall, Ettingshall and Parkfield (Wo)
Pedmore (D) **537–8**
  Grove, The 62, **538**
  Pedmore Hall **537–8**
  St Peter 10, 37, 38, 547
  Wychbury hill-fort 7
Pelsall (Wa) 618, **658–9**
  canals **659**
  St Michael and All Angels 17, 35, 91, **658–9**
  Village Centre 89–90, **659**
Penn (Wo) **733–6**
  Penn Hall (now Special School) 20, 62, **734–5**
  Penn Road 733, **735**
  St Bartholomew and cross 25, 91, 710, **733–4**
  Upper Penn 733, **735**
Penn Fields (Wo) *see* Graiseley and Penn Fields (Wo)
Pensnett (D) 4, 31, 32, **538–40**
  Barrow Hill 5, **540**
  Old Vicarage 55, **540**
  St Mark 2, 4, 35, 38, 93, **538–40**
  war memorial 73, **540**

Pleck (Wa) *see* Walsall (Wa)
Portobello (Wo) *see* East Park, Moseley and Portobello (Wo)
Pouk Hill (Wa) *see* Walsall (Wa)

Quarry Bank (D) **540–2**
  chain shop 58
  Peace Memorial 73, **541**
Quinton (D) *see* Halesowen (D) *and* Birmingham index

Roseville (D) *see* Coseley (D)
Rowley (Sa) *see* Rowley Regis (Sa)
Rowley Regis (Sa) 2, 5, **569–77**
  churches etc. **569–73**, 575–7
    Cave Adullam Baptist Chapel, Blackheath 72, **569**, Pl. 72
    Ebenezer Strict Baptist Church 72, **573**
    Grainger's Lane Primitive Methodist church 65, 570n.
    Holy Trinity 36, **572–3**
    Macefield's Mission 72, **573**
    Methodist New Connexion (later *Kingsway International Christian Church*), Blackheath 65, **569**
    Providence Strict Baptist Chapel 40, **576**, 665
    St Giles 77, **565**
    St Michael, Tividale **600**
    St Paul, Blackheath *see* Halesowen (D)
  industries 31, 32n., 58, **570**, 574, 576
  public buildings **570–1**, 573–4
    Corngreaves Primary School 47, **571**
    library, Blackheath (former) 66, **570**
    library, Cradley Heath 66, 570, **571**
    Netherton Tunnel 30, 533, **576**
    Old Hill Primary School 47, **573**
    police station (former) 44, **573**, 592
    St Luke's Church School (former) **571**, 574
    Temple Meadow Primary School 67, **574**
    Workers' Institute, Cradley Heath 72, **490**, 572
  streets, houses etc. **569–77**
    Bell End **576**
    Blackheath (district) 520, **569–70**
    Britannia Inn 26, **576**
    Cobb's Engine House 58, **576**
    Cradley Heath 31, 32, 95, 530, **570–2**
    Four Ways pub 81, **576**
    Haden Hall 16, **573–4**
    Majestic cinema (former) 81, **571**
    Midland Bank (former) 70, **571**
    Old Hill (area) **572–4**
    oliver shop (former) **490**
    Rowley (village) **575–6**
    Rowley Regis Building Society (now Regis House) 79, **573**
    Sir Robert Peel pub 52, **576**
    Tividale (district) 490, **576–7**
    United Counties Bank (former) 49, **571**
    Vine pub 81, **569**
Ruiton (D) *see* Gornal (D)
Rushall (Wa) 7, 9, 618, **659–61**
  Chavasse Almshouses **661**
  Lichfield Road 18, **661**
  Rushall Hall and gatehouse 3, 13, **660–1**
  St Michael the Archangel 3–4, 12, 36, 64, **660**

Sandwell (Sa) 1, 95, **563–617**
  Old Portway Farm 5, **576**
  Rowley 2, 5, **575–6**
  St Giles 5, **575**
  Sandwell Academy *see* West Bromwich (Sa)
  Sandwell Park *see* West Bromwich (Sa)
Sedgley (D) 2, 4, 31, 32n., 82, **542–5**, 672
  All Saints 4, 10, 24, 25, 93, **542**
  Asda 88, **544**
  Beacon Hotel 52, **545**
  Brook Street *cottages* etc. **491**
  Clifton cinema 81, **543**
  Congregational church (now St Andrew, United Reformed and Methodist) 40, **543**
  Council House (former) 44, **544**
  Dormston House 22, **544**
  Grand Junction Hotel (former) **544**, Pl. 10
  Greenway 76, **545**
  Primitive Methodist church (former) 40, **543**
  St Chad and All Saints (R.C.) 25, **542–3**
  Sedgley Beacon Tower 4, **545**
  workhouse (former) 20, **544**
Shelfield (Wa) *see* Walsall Wood (Wa)
Shirley (So) **784–5**
  Goldfinger House (formerly Carr & Co.) 84, **785**
  Light Hall 19, **785**
  St James the Great 34, **784**
  Solihull Road 61, **785**
Short Heath (Wa) *see* Willenhall (Wa)
Shutt (or Shut) End (D) 29, 32, 33, 522

Smethwick (Sa) 72, **577–89**
  churches etc. **578–81**, **589**
    Akrill Memorial Methodist Church (former) **580**, 581, 584
    Baptist church, Regent Street 41, **581**
    Guru Nanak Gurdwara **581**, 583
    Holy Trinity 42, **579**
    Rolfe Street chapel **580**
    St Mark, Londonderry 91, **579**
    St Mary, Bearwood Road 36, **579–80**
    St Matthew, Windmill Lane 36, 42, **580**
    St Stephen, Lewisham Road **579**
    Smethwick Old Church 19, 577, **578–9**
  industries 33, **577**, **587–8**
    Chance Bros' glassworks 33, 42, 58, **588**
    Hawthorn House **588**
    Soho Foundry 58, 80, 577, **587–8**
  public buildings 577–8, **581–2**
    canals 28, 577, 578, **586–7**, 588
    Cape Schools 47, **585**, 648
    Council House 66, 72, **581–2**
    Crocketts Lane infants' school 47, **584**
    Engine Arm Aqueduct 30, **587**, Pl. 53
    Galton Bridge 30, **587**
    library (former Local Board offices) 43, **583**
    Magistrates' Courts 74, **584**
    Rolfe Street baths **490**
    School Board offices (former) 47, **584**
    Smethwick Baths 74, **586**, Pl. 113
    Smethwick New Pumping Station 30, **586–7**
    Thimblemill Library 74, **586**
  streets, houses etc. **582–9**
    Abbey, The (pub) 80, **586**
    Barleycorn (former pub) 80, **586**
    Bearwood **586**
    Blue Gates pub 80, **582**
    Grove Cinema (former) 81, **585**
    Henry Hope & Co. offices (former; now Hawthorn House) 84, **588**
    High Street **582–4**
    Hill Crest 578
    Lightwoods House 21, **588–9**
    Lloyds Bank branches 70, **583**, **585**
    Midland Bank (former) 70, **585**
    Rink Cinema (former) 81, **585**
    Rolfe Street **490**, *580*, 582
    St Paul's vicarage (former) 55, **589**
    South Road 54, **584**
    Thimblemill Road flats 75, **586**
    Thimblemill Road lodge (former) 61, **586**
    Waterloo Hotel 71, **585**
    Windmill Shopping Centre 578, **584**
Sodom (D) *see* Coseley (D)
Solihull (So) 1, 2, 9, **753–66**
  churches etc. **754–8**, **764–5**
    Lyndon Methodist Church 92, **765**
    St Alphege 10, 11, 12, 17, 64, **754–7**, Pls. 17, 77
    St Augustine (R.C.) **757**
  public buildings **758–60**
    isolation hospital (former), Catherine-de-Barnes 45, **765–6**
    Library and Arts Complex ('The Core') 89, **760**
    Public Hall (former) 44, **760**
    workhouses 20, *758*, **760**
  streets, houses etc. 753, **758–66**
    Ashleigh Road 76, 753, **764**
    Bradford House **758**
    Catherine-de-Barnes **765–6**
    Henwood Mill 26, **766**
    High Street **759**
    Hillfield Hall 756, **763**
    Hobs Moat **764–5**
    Homer Road 87, 88, **760**
    Lloyds Bank 49, **760**
    Lovelace Avenue 83, **763**
    Lyndon 92, **764–5**
    Malvern Hall 21, **761–2**
    Malvern House 758, **759**
    Masons Arms 26, **759**
    New Berry Hall 761
    Old Berry Hall **761**
    Olton Hall pub 80, **765**
    Poplar Road 79, **760**
    Ravenshaw Hall 16, **761**, 763
    Shelly Farm 761, **763**
    Square, The 18, **758**
    Sydenhams moat 9
    Touchwood Centre 88, **759–60**
    Touchwood Hall 759
    Tudor Grange 54, **763–4**
    Warwick Road barn 21, **762**, Pl. 49
Stourbridge (D) 1, 27, 31–2, 72, 511, **545–56**
  churches etc. **547–9**
    Friends' Meeting House 17, **549**
    Gigmill Methodist Church 78, **548**
    Methodist church, New Road 78, **548**, 726
    Our Lady and All Saints (R.C.) 39, 42, **548**

INDEX TO BLACK COUNTRY AND SOLIHULL 879

Presbyterian (Unitarian) chapel 25, 26, **548–9**
St John the Evangelist 37, **548**
St Michael 77, **548**
St Thomas 3, 19, 26, 42, **547–8**, Pl. 34
Stourbridge Cemetery *see* Wollaston (D)
public buildings **549–50**
  bus station 90, **553**
  County Court (former) 44, **550**
  King Edward VI College (formerly Stourbridge Grammar School) 46, **550**
  Longlands School 67
  Market Hall 26, 545, **549**
  Mary Stevens Park **555**
  ring road 94, 546
  Stourbridge College *see* Oldswinford (D)
  Stourbridge Union workhouse (former) 45, **560**
  Town Hall 44, 545, **549**
  viaduct, Birmingham Street **555–6**
  war memorial 73, **555**
streets, houses etc. **550–6**
  Bordeaux House 69, **553**
  Chequers, The (pub) 71, **553**
  Church Street Chambers 51, **553**
  Claremont **554**, 558
  Hagley Road 54, **553**
  Highfield House 55, **553**
  High Street 545*n*., **552–4**
  Lower High Street 20, 550, **551**
  Mitre pub 81, **551**
  Nickolls and Perks's shop 16–17, 545, **550**
  Old Bank 70, **552**
  Ryemarket Shopping Centre 88, 546–7, **552–3**, Pl. 132
  Stourcote **551**
  Stourhurst 20, **551**
  Talbot Hotel 16, **552**
Streetly (Wa) **661**
Sutton Coldfield (B) *see* Birmingham index
Swan Village (D) *see* Coseley (D)

Tettenhall (Wo) **736–49**
  Abbeyfield (former vicarage) 56, **745**
  Aldersley 28, **749**
  Avenue House 54, 736, **744**
  Avenue House Lodge **743**
  Bromley House 54, **746–7**
  Christ Church 37, **737**
  Church Hill Road 62, **745**
  Compton Hall 54, **748**
  Dippons, The 76, 670, 736, **741–2**, 747
  Elmsdale Hall 736, **747**

Mount, The 56, 62, 736, **740–1**, 744, 747
Netherton House 18, **747**
Perton Road 83, **747–8**
Rock House 19, **743**
St Michael and All Angels 90, **736–7**
station (former) **745**
Tettenhall College 47, **742**
Tettenhall Wood House **746**
Tynighame 56, **745**
waterworks 58, **748**
Wergs **748**
Wightwick Manor 16, 56, 62, 670, 706, 717, 736, **738–40**, 741, Pl. 97
Woodcote Road 83, **746**
Woodthorne 736
Tettenhall Road (Wo) *see* Chapel Ash, Tettenhall Road and West Park (Wo)
Tidbury Green (So) 7
Tipton (Sa) 28, 72, **589–93**
  churches etc. **589–90**, 592
    Boatmen's Mission Chapel (former) 30, **591**
    St John the Evangelist 5, 17, **589**
    St Mark, Ocker Hill 35, 63, **589–90**
    St Paul 34, **590**
  industries 32*n*., **490**, 589
  public buildings **590–3**
    canal buildings 28, 29, **591**
    drill hall (former) 67, **592**
    library (now Carnegie Centre) 66, **590–1**
    Neptune Health Park 90, **591**
    Park Lane Schools 600
    post office (former) 68, **592**
    RSA Academy 85, **591**
    St Martin's Primary School 46, **592**
    Toll End Library 589
    Victoria Park 48, **591**
  streets, houses etc. **591–3**
    bank by Thomason 49, **591**
    Dudley Port **592–3**
    Factory Junction 29, **591–2**
    Horseshoe Walk 83, **591**
    Park Lane West 56, **592**, **593**
    Tipton and Coseley Building Society 87, **591**
Tividale (Sa) *see* Rowley Regis (Sa)
Transport, railways etc.:
  Autherley Junction 28, 30, 695, **732–3**
  Bilston tramways depot (former) **700**
  Birmingham Canal (Old and New Lines and branches) **28**, 29, **30**, 33, 564, 616, 696
    Chillington (Wolverhampton) 30, **696**

Transport, railways etc. *cont.*
  Birmingham Canal (Old and New Lines and branches) *cont.*
    Coseley tunnel **504**
    Factory Junction, Tipton 29, **591–2**
    Netherton Tunnel 30, 533, **576**
    Oxley **732**
    Puppy Green Aqueduct, Tipton 30, **593**
    Smethwick 28, 30, 577, **586–7**, **588**
    Titford branch 564
    Walsall branch **616**
    West Bromwich **616**
    Wolverhampton 30, 670, **693–4**, **695**
  Birmingham and Liverpool Junction Canal (later Shropshire Union) 30, **732**
  Birmingham to Leamington railway 781
  Birmingham to Wolverhampton turnpike road **654**
  Black Country New Road 654
  Black Country Route 696
  Cannock Extension Canal, Pelsall **659**
  Chillington Canal Interchange Basin **696**
  Darlaston branch railway (former) **652**
  Dudley Canal (Nos. 1 and 2) **28**, 491
    Brierley Hill (No. 1 Canal) **498–9**
    Dudley (Dudley Tunnel and Castle Mill basin; No. 1 Canal) **491**
    Halesowen (No. 2 Canal) **520**
    Lapal Tunnel (No. 2 Canal) 28, **520**
    Netherton High Bridge (No. 2 Canal) **533**
  Grand Junction Railway 32, 616, 729
  Great Western Railway (GWR) 33
    Birmingham Street viaduct, Stourbridge **555–6**
    Kingswinford loop, Tettenhall **745**
    Stourbridge Junction station, Oldswinford 72, 93, **536**
    Wolverhampton 670, **693–4**, 696
  GWR *see* Great Western Railway *above*
  James Bridge Aqueduct, Darlaston **652**
  Kingswinford branch railway 538
  Kinver Light Railway **493**
  LNWR *see* London & North Western Railway *below*
  London & Birmingham Railway 32
  London & North Western Railway (LNWR) 32–3, **693–4**, **696**
  Lord Ward's Canal 491
  Midland Railway 33
  New Line *see* Birmingham Canal *above*
  Old Line *see* Birmingham Canal *above*
  Oxford, Worcester & Wolverhampton Railway 33
  Pensnett Railway 33, 34, 533, 538
    Brockmoor **500**
  Rushall Canal **616**
  Sedgley–Tividale turnpike toll house **490**
  Shrewsbury & Birmingham Railway 33
    Oxley railway viaduct **732**
    Wolverhampton offices, station and Queen's Building 670, 687, **688**
  Shropshire Union Canal **694**
  Shutt End Railway 32, 33, **522**
  South Staffordshire Railway 33
    Brownhills 647, **648**
  Staffordshire and Worcestershire Canal 28, 32, 718, 732, 736
    Tettenhall **736**, **748**
  Stourbridge Canal 28, 492
    Brierley Hill 495, **499**
    Fens branch (Brockmoor) 500
    Wordsley (Glasshouse Bridge and locks) 559, **560–2**, Pl. 4
  Stourbridge Extension Canal **29**, 538
    Brockmoor **500**
    Standhills branch 29, 495n.
  Stourbridge Railway 33, 570
  Stratford-upon-Avon Canal **29**, 30
    Amblecote 30, **494**
    Earlswood 29, 30, **776**
  Tame Valley Canal 29, 30
    West Bromwich **616**
  Town Arm Canal, Walsall 629
  turnpike roads 31, **490**, **654**, 666
  Walsall Canal 28, 29, **639**
  Walsall to Rugeley railway 645
  Walsall to Wolverhampton turnpike road 666
  Warwick and Birmingham Canal **30**, 765
  Wolverhampton railway stations 90, **683**
  Wyrley and Essington Canal 28, 668, 749
    Pelsall Junction and footbridge 28, **659**

Wallbrook (D) *see* Coseley (D)
Wallheath (D) 32n., **556–7**
  Holbeche House 16, 22, **556–7**
  Kingfisher (former lido) 82, **556**

Walsall (Wa) 1, 2, 3, 4, 5, **617–40**
  churches etc. **620–6**, *628*
    Hatherton Presbyterian Church (now United Reformed) 41, **625–6**
    Mellish Road Methodist Church 95, *620*
    St Andrew, Birchills **623**
    St Gabriel, Fulbrook 77, **623**
    St Mary and All Saints (former), Palfrey **623**, 679
    St Mary the Mount (R.C.) 25, **625**
    St Matthew and Memorial Gardens 11, 12, 24, 37, 42, 64, 94, **620–2**, 638, Pl. 41
    St Peter 35, **624–5**
  industries 32, 618, *629*, **630**
  public buildings **626–32**
    Arboretum 48, **632**
    Board of Guardians offices 45, **630**
    boatmen's rest 30, **639**
    bus station 90, **630**
    Butts School (former) 47, **635**
    canal structures 30, 629, **633**, **639**
    Civic Centre 88, **628**
    Council House and Town Hall 66, 68, **626–8**, Pl. 86
    Flint Art Gallery 89, **628**
    fountain, The Bridge 93, **632**
    Gala Baths 90, **632**
    Guildhall (former) 43, 95, 620, **628**
    Leather Museum **630**
    library, Goodall Street (1859) 43, **637**
    library, Lichfield Street (1906) 66, **628**
    New Art Gallery 89, 620, **629–30**, 633, Pl. 135
    police station 618
    Queen Mary's Grammar School 85, **630–1**
    St Matthew's Hall 43, **628**, Pl. 59
    Science and Art Institute (former) 44, 259, **629**
    Sister Dora Hospital nurses' home 45, **637**
    Sister Dora monument 49, 628, **632**
    Tantarra Street former Board School 47, **635**
    workhouse 43, **630**
  streets, houses etc. 53–4, **632–40**
    Albion Flour Mills (former) 58, **633**
    Arcade, The 51, **636**
    Birchills 30, **639**
    Birmingham Road 54, **637–8**
    Black Country Arms 26, **637**
    Borough Arms (former) 71, **635**
    Bradford Street 54, **636–7**
    Bridge, The (square) 93, 620, **632**, **636**
    Bridge Street 51, 79, 620, **634**
    Bridge Street garage 80, **634**
    Brookes leather factory 72, 618, **636**
    Caldmore **638–9**
    Digbeth 94, 95, 620, **637**
    Four Horse Shoes (former pub) 81, **640**
    George Street 54, **637**
    Green Lane 69, **633**
    Grove Terrace 54, **638**
    Hatherton Works 72, **635**
    High Street 620, **637–8**
    Imperial Buildings 51, **634**
    Imperial Cinema 72, **636**
    Leicester Buildings 79, **634**
    Leicester Street 618, **636**
    Lichfield Street 54, **635**
    Lloyds Bank, Park Street 70, **632**
    Old Still 16, *639*
    Palfrey **639**, 679
    Park Street 620, **632–3**
    Pleck **639–40**
    Ravenscraig Works 629
    Skip Lane house 77, **640**
    Staffordshire Bank 49, **634**
    Taylor's music shop (former) 51, **634**
    Victoria Terrace 54, **635**
    Walsall Observer offices (former) 79, **634**
    White Hart (former) 16, 550, **638–9**
Walsall Wood (Wa) **662–3**
  Castle Old Fort 7, **662**
  St John 91, 93, **662**
  schoolmaster's house 46, **662**
  Shelfield **663**
Warley (Sa) *see* Oldbury (Sa)
Warley Woods (Sa) *see* Oldbury (Sa)
Wednesbury (Sa) 2, 4, 5, 7, 28, 72, **593–600**
  churches etc. **593–7**
    Masonic Hall (former Congregational chapel) 5, **599**
    Primitive Methodist (now Baptist) church 65, **597**
    St Bartholomew 24, 26, 63, 64, **593–6**, 649
    St James 5, 35, **596–7**
    St John 5, *596*
    St Mary (R.C.) 39, 65, **597**
    St Paul 37, **597**
  industries 18, 31, 32n., 33, **593**
    Old Patent Tube Works 490
    Patent Shaft and Axletree Company 593, 633

Wednesbury *cont.*
public buildings **598–600**
Art Gallery 44, **598**
Brunswick Park 48, **599**
library 66, **598**
northern relief road 94, 593
pumping station 58, **600**
war memorial garden 73, **598**
streets, houses etc. **598–600**
Bridge Street 95
Cottage, The 54, **600**
Horse and Jockey pub 54, **600**
Market Place 19, **598**
Oakeswell Hall 599, *610n.*
Round House **600**
Spring Head 18, 56, **599**
Talbot Hotel (former; John Taylor Duce building) 51, **598**
Wharfedale Street 55, **599**
Wood Green Road 5, **600**
Wednesfield (Wo) 5, 32n., **749–51**
Red Lion pub 81, **751**
St Thomas 35, 64, **749–50**
Vine Inn 81, **750**, Pl. 111
Wergs (Wo) *see* Tettenhall (Wo)
West Bromwich (Sa) 1, 32n., 72, **600–17**
churches etc. **602–5**
All Saints (formerly St Clement) 37, 42, **602–3**
Christ Church 24, *612*
Good Shepherd with St John 602, **604**
Holy Trinity and vicarage 35, 54, 91, **603**
Methodist (Wesleyan) church, Beeches Road 41, **604–5**
Methodist (Wesleyan) church, Ryders Green 41, **605**
St Francis of Assisi 77, **603–4**
St Peter, Greets Green 36, 78, **616**, Pl. 78
Sandwell Priory 7, 8, 10, *611*
public buildings 72, **605–16**
Beacon of Light (sculpture) 93, **613**
canal structures **616**
Dartmouth Park **607–8**
Guardians' Board Room and Offices 45, **607**
King George V Primary School 67, **608**
library (former) 43, **605**
Lodge Primary School 67, **608**, Pl. 87
Menzies High School (now Phoenix Collegiate) 85, **608**
Post Office (former) 68, **612**
Public, The (now Central St Michael's Sixth Form) 89, **607**
Ryland Memorial School of Art (now Sandwell College, Fashion, Art and Design Building) 72, **606**
Sandwell Academy 85, **608**
Sandwell General Hospital (former West Bromwich Union Workhouse) 45, **606–7**
Town Hall 44, **605–6**, 612, Pl. 81
West Bromwich Institute (former) **606–7**
streets, houses etc. **608–17**
Barclays Bank (former), Great Bridge 78, **617**
Bratt Street 72, **613**
British Telecom (BT) building 88, **613**
Dudley & West Bromwich Bank (now Barclays Bank) 49, **612**
Free Press offices (former) 51, **612**
Great Bridge (area) 32n., **616–17**
Heath Terrace 23, **613**
High Street 600, **611–13**
Holy Trinity vicarage 54, **603**
J.B. & S. Lees (former) 80, **614–15**
Kenrick offices and warehouse 58, 602, **615–16**
Manor House 14, 21, 94, 600, **608–10**, Pl. 22
Oak House 15, **610–11**, Pl. 28
Sandwell Park 20, **611**, **615**
Sandwell Park Farm **611**, Pl. 47
shopping centres 88, **613**
Sow and Pigs pub 52, **614**
West Bromwich Building Society (former) 79, **612**, 613, Pl. 108
Wheatsheaf, The (pub) 52, **613**
West Park (Wo) *see* Chapel Ash, Tettenhall Road and West Park (Wo)
Whitmore Reans and Dunstall (Wo) **751–2**
Avion Centre 88, **752**
Cranmer Methodist Church 92, **752**
Newhampton Arts Centre (former Higher Grade School) 67, **752**
St Andrew 91, **751–2**, Pl. 125
Wightwick Manor (Wo) *see* Tettenhall (Wo)
Willenhall (Wa) 32, 34, 72, **663–8**, 672
churches etc. **663–5**, 668
Little London Baptist Chapel (former) 40, **665**
Methodist church (former), Froysell Street 40, **665**
Methodist church, Short Heath 41, **668**

Mount Calvary Baptist Chapel
  (former) 40, **665**
St Anne 5, **664**, Pl. 9
St Giles 36, 42, **663–4**
Trinity Methodist Church
  (former) 40, 42, **664–5**, 667,
  Pl. 70
Willenhall Cemetery *see*
  Darlaston (Wa)
Willenhall Lawn Cemetery **668**
public buildings **665–8**
  canal bridge **668**
  Central Schools (former) 47,
    665
  Council House (former) **665**
streets, houses etc. **666–8**
  Castle, The (former pub) 52,
    666
  Co-operative shop (former) 51,
    668
  County, The (pub) 81, **667**
  Duke of Cambridge pub 52,
    668
  Market Place 19, **666**
  New Invention **668**
  Short Heath **668**
Wollaston (D) **557–9**
  cottage terraces (Stourbridge
    Workmen's Dwellings Syndicate)
    62, **559**
  New Foundry (formerly Foster,
    Rastrick & Co.) 27, **559**
  New Inn 557
  Ridgewood High School 85, **558**
  St James and school 36, 46, **557–8**
  Stourbridge Cemetery 41, **558**
  Wollaston Hall 557
Wollescote (D) *see* Lye and
  Wollescote (D)
Wolverhampton (Wo) 1, 32n., 94,
  96, **669–96**
  churches etc. **672–81**
    Darlington Street Methodist
      Church 65, **680**
    *Queen Street Congregational
      Church* 39, 671
    St George (former) and
      vicarage **677**, 692
    St James, Horseley Fields 679
    St John 24, 38, 672, **677–8**, Pl. 2
    St Mary and St John (R.C.) 38,
      39, 42, **679**
    St Mary, Stafford Street **676**
    St Peter (Collegiate Church)
      10, 11, 12, 13, 17, 20, 37, 42,
      670, **672–7**, Pls. 19, 21
      Wolverhampton Cross 9, 10,
        670, **677**, 710, Pl. 13
    St Peter and St Paul (R.C.)
      and Giffard House 25, 39, 65,
      92, **679–80**, Pls. 7, 45
    St Stephen 63, **678–9**
    Saxon minster 670
  public buildings 26, 47, 670, **681–4**
    Albert (Prince) statue 48,
      684–5
    Art Gallery *see* Museum and
      Art Gallery *below*
    Board of Guardians offices
      (former) 45, **686**
    bridge (now at Black Country
      Living Museum) **491**
    bus station 90, 687, **688**
    canal buildings 28, **693–5**, 696
    Chillington Canal Interchange
      Basin 30, **696**
    Civic Centre 88, **682**
    Civic Hall 74, **682**
    County Court (former) 26,
      688
    Dispensary (former) 26, **688**
    Foyer building 83, **692**
    Grammar School (old) 671
    Grand Theatre 70, **687**
    Library 66, **683**
    Little's Lane Bridge 30, **695**
    Mechanics' Institute (former)
      26, **688**
    Museum and Art Gallery 44,
      49, 89, **683**, Pl. 84
    Old Library, Waterloo Road 670,
      691
    post office (former), Lichfield
      Street 68, **687–8**
    Pupil Teachers' Centre
      (former) 62, **692**
    Queen's Building (Shrewsbury
      & Birmingham Railway) 670,
      687, **688**
    Retail Market 671
    ring road 94, 671
    School of Art 86, **684**, Pl. 129
    School Board offices (former)
      47, **687**
    station and railway buildings
      90, **683**, 688, **693–4**
    Town Hall 43, 48, **681–2**
    University of Wolverhampton
      75, 86, **684**, 686
      School of Architecture and
        the Built Environment
        (formerly Springfield
        Brewery) 58, 86, **490**, **695**
    Victoria Hall (student
      accommodation) 84, 672
    Wolverhampton Combined
      Courts Centre 89, **683–4**
    Wolverhampton Wanderers
      football ground **691–2**
  streets and houses 54, 62, 76–7,
    95, 96, **491**, 670, **684–96**
    Albion Flour Mill 58, **694**
    Barclays Bank (former), Snow
      Hill 86, **693**
    Barclays Bank, Lich Gates 49,
      685

Wolverhampton *cont.*
  streets and houses *cont.*
    Beattie's 79, **689**
    Berry Street 51, **688**
    Bilston Street 670, 672
    Britannia (formerly Victoria) Hotel 52, **687**
    Broad Street 69, **687**
    Caribee Island 670
    Castlecroft Gardens 76, **707–8**, Pl. 6
    Chubb Lock Works (now Light House Media Centre) 95, **687**
    Clock Chambers 79, **690**
    Co-op (former), Lichfield Street **687**
    Co-op (former), Stafford Street 69, **687**
    Corn Hill 672, **694**
    Dale Street estate 82, **729**
    Darlington Street 69, 670, **690**, 691
    Dudley Street 671, 685, **689**
    Elephant and Castle pub **491**
    Express and Star offices 79, **688**
    Forder Carriage Works (former) 58, **692–3**
    George Street 23, **693**, Pl. 2
    Giffard Arms 81, **689**
    Giffard House (mass house) 25, **679–80**, Pls. 7, 45
    Gresham Chambers 69, **685–6**, 727
    Hatherton Arms 81, **696**
    Henn's 79, **689**
    High Green *see* Queen Square *below*
    i9 building **687**
    i10 building 88, **687**, **688**
    King Street 21, 672, **689**, Pl. 46
    Leaping Wolf pub 55, **696**
    Lichfield Street 48, 51, 69, 70, 670, 672, **685–6**, **687**
    Lloyds Bank, Queen Square 49, **685**
    Low Hill *see* Fallings Park and Low Hill (Wo)
    Mander Centre 88, 671, 672, **689**
    Metropolitan Bank (former) 70, **686**
    Molineux House 95, 670, 672, **691–2**
    National Provincial Bank (former), Queen Square 70, **685**
    New Market Square 87, **690**
    Old Hall 670
    Old Hall Street **692**
    Posada (bar) 71, **686**
    Prince Albert pub 71, **687**
    Prince's Square 48, 69, 670, 672, **686**, **688**
    Princess Street 79, **686**, **688**, **689**
    Queen Square (former High Green) 48, 70, 670, 671, **684–5**, 690, 691
    Queen Street 23, 26, 69, 70, **688**, 716
    Queen's Arcade 671
    Royal London Insurance 69, **686**, Pl. 104
    St James' Square 671
    School Street 671, **690**
    Sir Tatton Sykes (former pub) 52, **687**
    Snow Hill 23, **693**
    Springfield 672, 694, **695**
    Springfield Brewery 58, 86, **490**, **695**
    Sunbeam cycle factory (former) **695**, 704
    Sunbeam Motor Works *see* Blakenhall, Ettingshall and Parkfield (Wo)
    Tempest Street 83, **692**
    Union Mill Street 58, **694**
    Victoria Street **689**
    Vine Hotel (former) 52, **686**
    Waterloo Road 54, 55, **690–1**
    Wulfrun Centre 671, **692**
Woodcross (D) *see* Coseley (D)
Woodsetton (D) *see* Coseley (D)
Woodside (D) *see* Dudley (D)
Wordsley (D) 31, 32, **559–63**
  Dial Glassworks (Plowden & Thompson) 27, **563**
  Dock (area) 30, **562**
  flats 83, **561**
  Holy Trinity 24, 522, 559, **560**
  Methodist chapel (former) 492, **560**
  Red House Glass Cone (Museum) 27, **560–1**, Pl. 4
  school (former; Vulliamy) 46, **561**
  Stourbridge Canal area 30, 559, **560–2**, Pl. 4
  war memorial 73, **561**
  Wordsley Hospital (former; originally Stourbridge Union workhouse) 45, **560**
  Wordsley Manor 20, 561, **562**
Wychbury (D) *see* Pedmore (D)